D1597359

INTRODUCTION TO DERIVATIVES

Options, Futures, and Swaps

R. Stafford Johnson
Xavier University

Property of the ECE Dept.
Northeastern University
360 Huntington Ave
MS: 409/440DA
Boston, MA 02115

חבר

New York   Oxford
OXFORD UNIVERSITY PRESS
2009

Oxford University Press, Inc., publishes works that further Oxford University's
objective of excellence in research, scholarship, and education.

Oxford New York
Auckland Cape Town Dar es Salaam Hong Kong Karachi
Kuala Lumpur Madrid Melbourne Mexico City Nairobi
New Delhi Shanghai Taipei Toronto

With offices in
Argentina Austria Brazil Chile Czech Republic France Greece
Guatemala Hungary Italy Japan Poland Portugal Singapore
South Korea Switzerland Thailand Turkey Ukraine Vietnam

Copyright © 2009 by Oxford University Press, Inc.

Published by Oxford University Press, Inc.
198 Madison Avenue, New York, New York 10016
http://www.oup.com

Oxford is a registered trademark of Oxford University Press

All rights reserved. No part of this publication may be reproduced,
stored in a retrieval system, or transmitted, in any form or by any means,
electronic, mechanical, photocopying, recording, or otherwise,
without the prior permission of Oxford University Press.

Library of Congress Cataloging-in-Publication Data

Johnson, R. Stafford.
  Introduction to derivatives : options, futures, and swaps / R. Stafford Johnson.
    p. cm.
Includes bibliographical references and index.
ISBN 978-0-19-530165-6 (cloth : alk. paper)
1. Derivative securities. 2. Options (Finance) 3. Futures. 4. Swaps (Finance) I. Title.
HG6024.A3J6398 2008
332.64'5–dc22   2007032034

Printing number: 9 8 7 6 5 4 3 2 1

Printed in the United States of America
on acid-free paper

To Jan, Jamey, Matt, Wendi, and Scott

BRIEF CONTENTS

CONTENTS

EXHIBITS, FIGURES, AND TABLES

EXHIBITS

FIGURES

TABLES

PREFACE

Since the 1970s, many of the world economies have experienced relatively sharp swings in stock prices, interest rates, and exchange rates. This volatility, in turn, has increased the exposure of many debt, equity, and currency positions to market risk. Faced with this risk, many institutional investors, corporations, intermediaries, and financial mangers have increased their use of futures and option contracts as a hedge against such risk. Today, futures and options contracts on stocks, stock indexes, debt, and currencies, as well as such hybrid derivatives as swaps, interest rate options, caps, and floors, are used by banks and financial intermediaries to manage the maturity gaps between loans and deposits, by corporations and financial institutions to cap the rates on future loans or to reduce a currency position's exposure to exchange rate risk, and by portfolio managers, investment bankers, and security dealers in locking in the future purchase or selling price on their equity and fixed-income securities.

Today, understanding the dynamic and innovative investment environment requires that finance students and professionals understand the markets and uses for an increasing number of derivative securities. The purpose of this book is to provide finance students and professionals with an exposition on derivatives that will take them from the basic concepts, strategies and fundamentals to a more detailed understanding of the advanced strategies and pricing models. This synthesis of fundamental and advanced topics should provide students of finance with a better foundation in understanding the complexities and subtleties involved in the evaluation and selection of derivatives and derivative positions with detailed structures. The book is written for MBA, MS, and undergraduate finance students, as a training and instructional source for those involved in equity and debt management, and as a reference for CFA preparation for investment professionals. As a text, the book is designed for a one-semester course. Undergraduate students should have had an introductory course in investments, and MBA students should have had an introductory corporate finance course. Some basic statistics and mathematics are used. In addition, there are several chapters dealing with debt derivatives that require an understanding of bond fundamentals. The text includes three supplemental appendices on exponents and logarithms, statistics, and bond fundamentals to help students who need a review.

CONTENTS

The book is divided into five parts: Part I deals with the markets and strategies associated with options; Part II examines the pricing of options; Part III focuses on futures and futures option contracts; Part IV delineates the management of equity, currency, and debt positions with derivatives; Part V examines financial swaps; and Part VI focuses on embedded options and asset-backed securities.

In Chapter 1, we begin the analysis of derivatives by first examining the fundamental option strategies associated with calls and puts. With this foundation, we next discuss the functions and characteristics of the Chicago Board of Option Exchange and other exchanges. In Chapter 3, we expand our analysis of options by reviewing the fundamental strategies in more detail and by defining and describing other option strategies including those using currency, stock index, and debt options.

Part II consists of six chapters. In Chapter 4, we delineate the fundamental option pricing relationships. In Chapters 5, 6, and 7, we derive and examine the properties and applications of the Binomial Option Pricing Model for options on stocks, stocks paying dividends, indexes, currencies, and bonds. In Chapter 8, we describe the seminal Black–Scholes option pricing model, and in Chapter 9 we conclude the analysis of option pricing by examining how the Black–Scholes model can be used to define option strategies and by looking at exotic or non-generic options and how they can be priced using the option pricing models.

Part III covers futures and futures option contracts. Chapter 10 provides an overview of futures trading; Chapter 11 focuses on the pricing of futures contracts; and Chapter 12 examines the markets, uses, and pricing of options on futures contracts. In Part IV, the management of equity, currency, and debt positions are analyzed in four chapters. Chapters 13 and 14 examine the uses of stock index and currency derivatives. Chapters 15 and 16, in turn, examine the uses of interest rate futures and option contracts; Chapters 15 focuses on exchange-traded debt derivatives and Chapter 16 describes over-the-counter (OTC) debt derivatives and interest-rate products.

Part V covers financial swaps. Chapter 17 examines the markets and uses of generic interest rate swaps, and Chapter 18 looks at forward swaps, swaptions, cancelable swaps, extendable swaps, and other non-generic swaps. The pricing of interest rate swaps and their derivatives is examined in Chapter 19. Chapter 20 concludes the analysis of financial swaps by describing the markets, uses, and pricing of currency swaps and credit default swaps.

Part VI consists of two chapters covering embedded options and asset-backed securities and their derivatives. In Chapter 21, the option features of corporate securities are examined: warrants, rights, equity and debt as option positions, bonds with embedded call and put options, sinking fund agreements, and convertible clauses. In Chapter 22, asset-backed securities are examined, with particular emphasis on mortgage-backed securities. The chapter explains prepayment risk and its impact on a portfolio of mortgages and how mortgage-backed derivatives are constructed to address the problems of prepayment risk.

The breadth and depth of derivatives makes it very challenging for instructors to cover all of the subjects they would like in one semester. This book is no exception. To provide a comprehensive treatment, the book does cover most topics. Some chapters, though, represent extensions of concepts introduced and developed in earlier chapters. These chapters can be skipped without losing continuity. In my undergraduate classes, for example, I often skip chapters 4, 6, 7, 9, 19, and 22. The book starts with options, followed by futures and then swaps. Instructors who prefer to start with futures contracts can do so. Except for a minor reference to option pricing in Section 11.8, Chapter 10, "Futures and Forward Contracts," and Chapter 11, "Pricing Futures and Forward Contracts," are self-contained.

The material for this book draws from two other texts by the author: *Options and Futures* (West Publishing, 1995) and *Bond Evaluation, Selection, and Management* (Blackwell Publishing, 2004). In this book, there are a number new examples, cases, and problems. The text stresses concepts, model construction, and numerical examples. This is done to empower the reader to understand the tools with which answers can be found rather than just the answers. For example, in Chapters 5, a detailed derivation of the binomial option pricing model is presented, including mathematical derivations and examples. The emphasis on the derivation is done not for the sake of engendering a formula for pricing options but rather to emphasize the thought process and tools used in the study of options. A number of review questions, problems, and web exercises are provided at the end of each chapter to reinforce concepts. Solutions for many of these problems can be found in the CD included with the text. An Excel spreadsheets package is also included with the text. This package contains a number of programs for evaluating and pricing spot options, futures options, bonds, bonds with embedded options, and mortgage-backed securities. The programs can be used to solve a number of Excel problems in the text as well as check the answers to many of the problems and questions in this book.

End-of-chapter problems, problems done on Excel, and web exercises are designed not only to bring out the subject matter, but also to relate it to how it is done in practice or "as it is done on the street." Today, many practitioners manage securities and portfolio using a Bloomberg terminal. Bloomberg is a computer information and retrieval system providing access to financial and economic data, news, and analytics. Bloomberg terminals are common in most trading floors and are becoming more common in universities where they are used for research, teaching, and managing student investment funds. Bloomberg's derivative data and analytics system is quite extensive, including market information on exchange-traded and OTC options, futures and futures options, generic and non-generic swaps, and asset-backed securities. As an introduction to this system, the attached CD includes the file, "Guide to Bloomberg's Derivative Information and Programs," that provides an overview of the Bloomberg system, a listing of the types of derivatives that can be accessed from Bloomberg, and a description of some of the analytical functions that can be applied to derivatives. The file also includes Bloomberg exercises for each chapter in the text. These exercises are designed for students who have access to Bloomberg terminals either at their universities or possibly through internships they may have at financial companies and for practitioners who have access to such terminals at their jobs. Combining the chapter material with the Bloomberg chapter exercises should add depth to ones understanding of derivatives as well as an appreciation of the breadth of financial information and analytics provided by the Bloomberg system.

ACKNOWLEDGMENTS

Many people have contributed to this text. First, I thank my colleagues at Xavier University who have helped me in many different ways. I also thank the following reviewers for their thoughtful critiques: Gary Porter, John Carol University; Terry Nixon, Miami University; Reinhold Lamb, University of North Florida; Hugh Colaco, University of Connecticut; Richard Zuber, University of North Carolina at Charlotte; and Tom O'Brien, University of Connecticut.

My appreciation is extended to the staff at Oxford University Press, particularly Terry Vaughn, Executive Editor, Catherine Rae, Editorial Assistant, and Mary Araneo, Production Editor, who oversaw the book's development and were a continued source of encouragement. My appreciation is also extended to Shirlee James who helped in the preparation of the manuscript, Will Nealon for his assistance on developing the Excel programs, and the O'Connor family who helped support this effort through endowing the O'Connor Chair in Business Administration at Xavier University.

I also acknowledge some special people for their inspiration: Jerry Erhart, Dianne Erhart, James McDonald, Lillian Dansby, Jack Erhart, and JoAnn Erhart. Finally, I recognize the pioneers in the development of derivative theory and strategy: Fisher Black, Myron Scholes, John Cox, Stephen Ross, Mark Rubinstein, Richard Rendleman, Brit Bartter, Robert Merton, Frank Fabozzi, John Hull, Robert Kolb, Peter Ritchken, Hans Stoll, and others cited in the pages that follow. Without their contributions, this text could not have been written.

I encourage you to send your comments and suggestions to me: johnsons@xavier.edu.

R. Stafford Johnson
Xavier University

CHAPTER 1

OPTION CONCEPTS AND FUNDAMENTAL STRATEGIES

1.1   SHORT HISTORY OF THE DERIVATIVE MARKET

1.1.1   Futures Market

In the 1840s, Chicago emerged as a transportation and distribution center for agriculture products. Midwestern farmers transported and sold their products to wholesalers and merchants in Chicago who often would store and later transport the products by either rail or the Great Lakes to population centers in the East. Partly because of the seasonal nature of grains and other agriculture products and partly because of the lack of adequate storage facilities, farmers and merchants began to use *forward contracts* as a way of circumventing storage costs and pricing risk. These contracts were agreements in which two parties agreed to exchange commodities for cash at a future date but with the terms and the price agreed on in the present. For example, an Ohio farmer in June might agree to sell his expected wheat harvest to a Chicago grain dealer in September at an agreed-on price. This forward contract enabled both the farmer and the dealer to lock in a September wheat price in June. In 1848, the Chicago Board of Trade (CBT) was formed by a group of Chicago merchants to facilitate the trading of grain. This organization subsequently introduced the first standardized forward contract, called a "to-arrive" contract. Later, it established rules for trading the contracts and developed a system in which traders ensured their performance by depositing good-faith money to a third party. These actions made it possible for speculators as well as farmers and dealers who were hedging their positions to trade their forward contracts. By definition, *futures* are marketable forward contracts. Thus, the CBT evolved from a board offering forward contracts to the first organized exchange listing futures contracts—a futures exchange.

Since the 1840s, as new exchanges were formed in Chicago, New York, London, Singapore, and other large cities throughout the world, the types of futures contracts grew from grains and agricultural products to commodities and metals and finally to financial futures: futures on foreign currency, debt securities, and security indices. Because of their use as a hedging tool by financial managers and investment bankers, the introduction of financial futures in the early 1970s led to a dramatic growth in futures trading, with the user's list reading as a who's who of major investment houses, banks, and corporations.

The financial futures market formally began in 1972 when the Chicago Mercantile Exchange (CME) created the International Monetary Market (IMM) division to trade futures contracts on foreign currency. In 1976, the CME extended its listings to include a futures contract on a Treasury bill. The CBT introduced its first futures contract in October of 1975 with a contract on the Government National Mortgage Association (GNMA) pass through, and in 1977, they introduced the Treasury bond futures contract. The Kansas City Board of Trade was the first exchange to offer trading on a futures contract on a stock index when it introduced the Value Line Composite Index contract (VLCI) in 1983. This was followed by the introduction of the Standard and Poor's (S&P) 500 futures contract

1

by the CME and the New York Stock Exchange (NYSE) index futures contract by the New York Futures Exchange (NYFE).

Whereas the 1970s marked the advent of financial futures, the 1980s saw the globalization of futures markets with the openings of the London International Financial Futures Exchange, LIFFE (1982), Singapore International Monetary Market (1986), Toronto Futures Exchange (1984), New Zealand Futures Exchange (1985), and Tokyo Financial Futures Exchange (1985). Exhibit 1.1-1 lists the major exchanges trading futures and their Web sites. The increase in the number of futures exchanges internationally led to a number of trading innovations: electronic trading systems, 24-hour worldwide trading, and alliances between exchanges. The growth in the futures market also led to the need for more governmental oversight to ensure market efficiency and guard against abuses. In 1974, the Commodity Futures Trading Commission (CFTC) was created by Congress to monitor and regulate futures trading, and in 1982, the National Futures Association (NFA), an organization of futures market participants, was established to oversee futures trading. Finally, the growth in futures markets has led to the consolidation of exchanges. In 2006, the CME and the CBT approved a deal in which the CME acquired the CBT,

EXHIBIT 1.1-1   Major Futures and Options Exchanges

U.S. Exchanges

American Exchanges (AMEX)	www.amex.com
Chicago Board of Trade (CBT)	www.CBT.com
Chicago Board of Options Exchange (CBOE)	www.cboe.com
Chicago Mercantile Exchange (CME)	www.cme.com
Commodity Exchange (COMEX) (NY)	www.nymex.com
Kansas City Board of Trade (KCBT)	www.kcbt.com
Minneapolis Grain Exchange (MGE)	www.mgex.com
New York Mercantile Exchange (NYMEX)	www.nymex.com
Pacific Exchange (PXS)	www.pacificex.com
Philadelphia Exchange (PHLX)	www.phlx.com

Non-U.S. Markets

Amsterdam Exchanges (AEX)	www.euronext.com
Brussels Exchange (BXS)	www.euronext.com
Bolsa de Mercadorias y Futuros, Brazil (BM&F)	www.bmf.com.br
Deutsche Termin Borse, Germany (DTB)	www.exchange.de
Eurex (EUREX)	www.exexchange.com
International Petroleum Exchange, London (IPE)	www.ipe.uk.com
Hong Kong Futures Exchange (HKFE)	www.hkfe.com
London International Financial Futures and Options Exchange (LIFFE)	www.liffe.com
Marche a Terme International de France (MATIF)	www.matif.com
Marche des Options Negociables de Paris (MONEP)	www.monep.fr
MEFF Renta Fija And Variable, Spain (MEFF)	www.meff.es
New Zealand Futures and Options Exchange (NZFOE)	www.nzfoe.com
Osaka Securities Exchange (OSA)	www.ose.or.jp
Singapore International Monetary Exchange (SIMEX)	www.simex.com.sg
Stockholm Options Exchange (SOM)	www.omgroup.com
Sydney Futures Exchange (SFE)	www.sfe.com.au
Toronto Stock Exchange (TSE)	www.tse.com

Alliances

Eurex is an alliance of DTB, CBT, and exchanges in Switzerland and Finland.	www.eurexchange.com
GLOBEX is an alliance of CME, ME, MATIF, SIMEX and exchanges in Brazil and the Paris Bourse.	www.globexalliance.com
Euronext is an alliance of exchanges in Amsterdam, Brussels, and Paris.	

forming the CME Group, Inc. If approved, the new derivative exchange would have an average daily trading volume approaching 9 million contracts per day.

Formally, a forward contract is simply an agreement between two parties to trade a specific asset at a future date with the terms and price agreed on today. A futures contract, in turn, is a "marketable" forward contract, with marketability (the ease or speed in trading a security) provided through futures exchanges that not only list hundreds of contracts that can be traded but provide the mechanisms for facilitating trades. Futures and forward contracts are known as ***derivative securities***. A derivative security is one whose value depends on the values of another asset (e.g., the price of the underlying commodity or security). Another important derivative is an option. An option is a security that gives the holder the right, but not the obligation, to buy or sell a particular asset at a specified price on, or possibly before, a specific date.

1.1.2 Options Market

Like the futures market, the option market in the United States can be traced back to the 1840s when options on corn meal, flour, and other agriculture commodities were traded in New York. These option contracts gave the holders the right, but not the obligation, to purchase or to sell a commodity at a specific price on or possibly before a specified date. Like forward contracts, options made it possible for farmers or agriculture dealers to lock in a price for their goods at a future date. In contrast to commodity futures trading, though, the early market for commodity option trading was relatively thin. The market did grow marginally when options on stocks began trading on the over-the-counter (OTC) market in the early 1900s. This market began when a group of investment firms formed the Put and Call Brokers and Dealers Association. Through this association, an investor who wanted to buy an option could do so through a member of the association who either would find a seller through other members or would sell (write) the option himself.

The OTC option market was functional but suffered because it failed to provide an adequate secondary market. In 1973, the Chicago Board of Trade formed the Chicago Board of Option Exchange (CBOE). The CBOE was the first organized option exchange for the trading of options. Just as the CBT had served to increase the popularity of futures, the CBOE helped to increase the trading of options by making the contracts more marketable.

Since the creation of the CBOE, organized stock exchanges, such as the American Stock Exchange (AMEX), the Philadelphia Stock Exchange (PHLX), and the Pacific Stock Exchange (PSE), most of the organized futures exchanges, and many security exchanges outside the U.S. also began offering markets for the trading of options. As the number of exchanges offering options increased, so did the number of securities and instruments with options written on them. Today, option contracts exist not only on stocks but also on foreign currencies, security indices, futures contracts, and debt and interest rate-sensitive securities.

1.1.3 Overview

Futures and options contracts on stock, debt, and currency as well as such hybrid derivatives as swaps, interest rate options, caps, and floors are important securities for managing risk. Farmers, portfolio managers, multinational businesses, and financial institutions often buy and sell derivatives to hedge positions they have in the derivative's underlying asset against adverse price changes. Derivatives also are used for speculation. Many investors find buying or selling options or futures an attractive alternative to buying or selling the derivative's underlying security. Finally, many institutional investors, portfolio managers, and corporations use derivatives for ***financial engineering,*** combining their debt, equity, or currency positions with different derivatives to create a structured investment or debt position with certain desired risk-return features.

This book is an exposition on derivatives, describing the markets in which derivatives are traded; how they are used for speculating, hedging, and financial engineering; and how their prices are determined. Parts I and II deal with the markets, strategies, and pricing of options, whereas Part III focuses on futures and futures option contracts. With this foundation, Part IV of the book examines the management of equity, currency, and interest rate positions with derivatives. Part V focuses on the growing derivative market for interest rate, currency, and credit swaps, and Part VI examines embedded options and asset-backed securities. In this chapter, we begin our analysis of options by defining common option terms, discussing the fundamental stock option strategies, and identifying some of the important factors that determine the price of an option. This chapter will provide a foundation for the more detailed analysis of the markets, strategies, and pricing of stock options that will be examined in Parts I and II as well as the analysis of the non-stock options, which will be examined in some of the sections of Parts I and II and in greater detail in Part IV.

Web Information:

Chicago Mercantile Exchange: www.cme.com

Chicago Board of Trade: www.cbt.com

Commodity Futures Trading Commission: www.cftc.gov

National Futures Association: www.nfa.futures.org

Information on the CBOE: www.cboe.com

See Exhibit 1.1 for a listing of derivative exchanges and their Web sites

---

1.2   OPTION TERMINOLOGY

By definition, an option is a security that gives the holder the right to buy or sell a particular asset at a specified price on, or possibly before, a specific date. A call option would be created, for example, if on February 1, Ms. B paid $1,000 to Mr. A for a contract that gives Ms. B the right, but not the obligation, to buy "ABC Properties" from Mr. A for $20,000 on or before July 1. Similarly, a put option also would be created if Mr. A sold Ms. B a contract for the right, but not the obligation, to sell "ABC Properties" to Mr. A at a specific price on or before a certain date.

Depending on the parties and types of assets involved, options can take on many different forms. Certain features, however, are common to all options. First, with every option contract there is a right, but not the obligation, to either buy or sell. Specifically, by definition, a *call* is the right to buy a specific asset or security, whereas a *put* is the right to sell. Second, every option contract has a buyer and seller. The option buyer is referred to as the *holder*, and as having a *long* position in the option. The holder buys the right to *exercise* or evoke the terms of the option claim. The seller, often referred to as the option *writer*, has a *short* position and is responsible for fulfilling the obligations of the option if the holder exercises. Third, every option has an option price, exercise price, and exercise date. The price paid by the buyer to the writer for the option is referred to as the *option premium* (call premium and put premium). The *exercise price* or *strike price* is the price specified in the option contract at which the underlying asset can be purchased (call) or sold (put). Finally, the *exercise date* is the last day the holder can exercise. Associated with the exercise date are the definitions of European and American options. A *European option* is one that can be exercised only on the exercise date, whereas an *American option* can be exercised at any time on or before the exercise date. Thus, from our previous example, Mr. A is the writer, Ms. B is the holder, $1,000 is the option premium, $20,000 is the exercise or strike price, July 1 is the exercise date, and the option is American.

1.3 FUNDAMENTAL OPTION STRATEGIES

Many types of option strategies with esoteric names such as straddles, strips, spreads, combinations, and so forth exist. The building blocks for these strategies are six fundamental option strategies: call and put purchases, call and put writes, and call and put writes in which the seller covers her position. The features of these strategies can be seen by examining the relationship between the price of the underlying security and the possible profits or losses that would result if the option either is exercised or expires worthless.[1]

1.3.1 Call Purchase

To see the major characteristics of a call purchase, suppose an investor buys a call option on ABC stock with an exercise price (X) of $50 at a call premium (C) of $3. If the stock price reaches $60 and the holder exercises, a profit of $7 will be realized as the holder acquires the stock for $50 by exercising and then sells the stock in the market for $60: a $10 capital gain minus the $3 premium. If the holder exercises when the stock is trading at $53, he will break even: the $3 premium will be offset exactly by the $3 gain realized by acquiring the stock from the option at $50 and selling in the market at $53. Finally, if the price of the stock is at $50 or below, the holder will not find it profitable to exercise, and as a result, he will let the option expire, realizing a loss equal to the call premium of $3. Thus, the maximum loss from the call purchase is $3.

The investor's possible profit/loss and stock price combinations can be seen graphically in Figure 1.3-1 and the accompanying table. In the graph, the profits/losses are

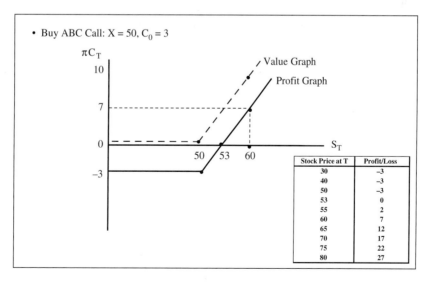

Stock Price at T	Profit/Loss
30	–3
40	–3
50	–3
53	0
55	2
60	7
65	12
70	17
75	22
80	27

FIGURE 1.3-1 Call Purchase

---

[1] As we will see later, most options are not exercised but instead are closed by holders selling their contracts and writers buying their contracts. As a starting point in developing a fundamental understanding of options, though, it is helpful to first examine what happens if the option is exercised.

shown on the vertical axis and the market prices of the stock at the time of the exercise and/or expiration (signified as T: S_T) are shown along the horizontal axis. This graph is known as a ***profit graph***. The line from the (50, −3) coordinate to the (60, 7) coordinate and beyond shows all the profits and losses per call associated with each stock price. That is, the (60, 7) coordinate shows the $7 call profit realized when the stock is at $60. The horizontal segment shows a loss of $3, equal to the premium paid when the option was purchased. Finally, the horizontal intercept shows the break-even price at $53. The break-even price can be found algebraically by solving for the stock price at the exercise date (S_T) in which the profit (π) from the position is zero. The profit from the call purchase position is:

$$\pi = (S_T - X) - C_0,$$

where C_0 is the initial (t = 0) cost of the call. Setting π equal to zero and solving for S_T yields the break-even price of S_T^*:

$$S_T^* = X + C_0 = \$50 + \$3 = \$53$$

The profit graph in Figure 1.3-1 highlights two important features of call purchases. First, the position provides an investor with unlimited profit potential; second, losses are limited to an amount equal to the call premium. These two features help explain why some ***speculators*** prefer buying a call rather than the underlying stock itself. Speculators are those who accept greater risk in return for greater expected returns. In this example, suppose that the price of ABC stock could range from $30 to $70 at expiration. If a speculator purchased the stock for $50, the profit from the stock would range from −$20 to +$20, or in percentage terms, from −40% to +40% (see Table 1.3-1). On the other hand, the return on the call option would range from +566% to −100%! Thus, the potential reward to the speculator from buying a call instead of the stock can be substantial—in this example, 566% compared to 40% for the stock—but the potential for loss also is large, −100% for the call versus −40% for the stock.

In addition to the profit graph, option positions also can be described graphically by ***value graphs***. A value graph shows the option's value or cash flow at expiration associated with each level of the stock price. The dotted line in Figure 1.3-1 displays the value graph for the call purchase. The graph shows that if $S_T \leq X$ ($S_T \leq \$50$), the call will have no value ($C_T = 0$), whereas if $S_T > X$ ($S_T > \$50$), the call will have a value of $C_T = S_T - X$.

1.3.2 Naked Call Write

The second fundamental strategy involves the sale of a call in which the seller does not own the underlying stock. Such a position is known as a ***naked call write***. To see the

TABLE 1.3-1   Rates of Return From Call and Stock Positions

Stock Price at Expiration S_T	Profit from Stock Purchased at $50 ($\pi_S$) $\pi_S = S_T - \$50$	Rate of Return from Stock (R_S) $R_S = \pi_S/\$50$	Profit From Call Purchased at $3 ($\pi_C$) $\pi_C = \text{Max}[S_T - \$50, 0] - \$3$	Rate of Return from Call (R_C) $R_C = \pi_C/\$3$
$70	$20	40%	$17	566%
$60	$10	20%	$7	233%
$50	$0	0%	−$3	−100%
$40	−$10	−20%	−$3	−100%
$30	−$20	−40%	−$3	−100%

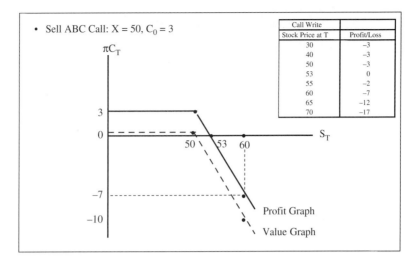

- Sell ABC Call: $X = 50$, $C_0 = 3$

Call Write	
Stock Price at T	Profit/Loss
30	−3
40	−3
50	−3
53	0
55	−2
60	−7
65	−12
70	−17

FIGURE 1.3-2 Naked Call Write

characteristics of this position, again assume the exercise price on the call option on ABC stock is \$50, and the call premium is \$3. The profits or losses associated with each stock price from selling the call are depicted in Figure 1.3-2 and its accompanying table. As shown, when the price of the stock is at \$60, the seller suffers a \$7 loss if the holder exercises the right to buy the stock from the writer at \$50. Because the writer does not own the stock, she would have to buy it in the market at its market price of \$60 and then turn it over to the holder at \$50. Thus, the call writer would realize a \$10 capital loss, minus the \$3 premium received for selling the call, for a net loss of \$7. When the stock is at \$53, the writer will realize a \$3 loss if the holder exercises. This loss will offset the \$3 premium received. Thus, the break-even price for the writer is \$53, the same as the holder's. This price also can be found algebraically by solving for the stock price in which the profit from the naked call write position is zero. That is:

$$\pi = (X - S_T) + C_0$$
$$0 = (X - S_T) + C_0$$
$$S_T^* = X + C_0$$
$$S_T^* = \$50 + \$3 = \$53$$

Finally, at a stock price of \$50 or less, the holder will not exercise, and the writer will profit by the amount of the premium, \$3.

As highlighted in the graph, the payoffs from a call write are just the opposite of the call purchase; that is, gains/losses for the buyer of a call are exactly equal to the losses/gains of the seller. Thus, in contrast to the call purchase, the naked call write position provides the investor with only a limited profit opportunity equal to the value of the premium, with unlimited loss possibilities. Although this limited profit and unlimited loss feature of a naked call write may seem unattractive, the motivation for an investor to write a call is the cash or credit received and the expectation that the option will not be exercised. As we discuss in Chapter 2, though, there are margin requirements on an option write position in which the writer is required to deposit cash or risk-free securities to secure the position.

The dotted line in Figure 1.3-2 shows the value graph for the naked call write. As shown in this graph, if the stock price is below the exercise price, the call value is $C_T = 0$.

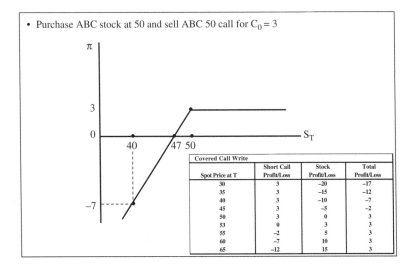

FIGURE 1.3-3 Covered Call Write

If $S_T = \$60$, the call writer will have to buy the stock for $60 and sell it (when the call is exercised) for $50. Thus, the cash flow is a $10 loss: $C_T = -(\$60 - \$50) = -\$10$.

1.3.3 Covered Call Write

One of the most popular option strategies is to write a call on a stock already owned. This strategy is known as a ***covered call write***. For example, an investor who bought ABC stock at $50 some time ago and who did not expect its price to appreciate in the near future, might sell a call on ABC stock with an exercise price of $50. As shown in Figure 1.3-3 and its accompanying table, if ABC stock is $50 or more, the covered call writer loses the stock when the holder exercises, leaving the writer with a profit of only $3. The benefit of the covered call write occurs when the stock price declines. For example, if ABC stock declined to $40, then the writer would suffer an actual (if the stock is sold) or paper loss of $10. The $3 premium received from selling the call, though, would reduce this loss to just $7. Similarly, if the stock is at $47, a $3 loss will be offset by the $3 premium received from the call sale.

1.3.4 Put Purchase

Because a put gives the holder the right to sell the stock, profit is realized when the stock price declines. With a decline, the put holder can buy the stock at a low price in the stock market and then sell it at the higher exercise price on the put contract. To see the features related to the put purchase position, assume the exercise price on an ABC put is again $50 and the put premium (P) is $3. If the stock price declines to $40, the put holder could purchase the stock at $40 and then use the put contract to sell the stock at the exercise price of $50. Thus, as shown by the profit graph in Figure 1.3-4 and its accompanying table, at $40 the put holder would realize a $7 profit (the $10 gain from buying the stock and exercising minus the $3 premium). The break-even price in this case would be $47:

$$\pi = (X - S_T) - P_0$$
$$0 = (X - S_T) - P_0$$

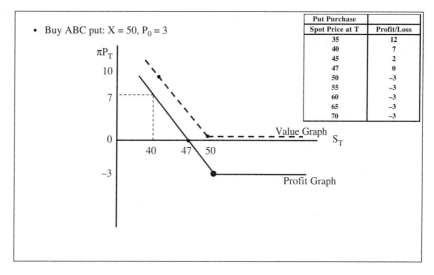

FIGURE 1.3-4 Put Purchase

$$S_T^* = X - P_0$$
$$S_T^* = \$50 - \$3 = \$47$$

Finally, if the stock is $50 or higher at expiration, it will not be rational for the put holder to exercise. As a result, a maximum loss equal to the $3 premium will occur when the stock is trading at $50 or more.

The put purchase position is also described in Figure 1.3-4 by its value graph (dotted line). As shown, if $S_T < X$, the value of the put is $P_T = X - S_T$; if $S_T \geq \$50$, the put is worthless: $P_T = 0$.

Thus, similar to a call purchase, a long put position provides the buyer with potentially large profit opportunities (not unlimited because the price of the stock cannot be less than zero) while limiting the losses to the amount of the premium. Unlike the call purchase strategy, the put purchase position requires the stock price to decline before profit is realized.

1.3.5 Naked Put Write

The exact opposite position to a put purchase (in terms of profit/loss and stock price relations) is the sale of a put, defined as the ***naked put write***. This position's profit and value graphs are shown in Figure 1.3-5. Here, if the stock price is at $50 or more, the holder will not exercise and the writer will profit by the amount of the premium, $3. In contrast, if the stock decreases, a loss is incurred. For example, if the holder exercises at $40, the put writer must buy the stock at $50. An actual $10 loss will occur if the writer elects to sell the stock, and a paper loss will occur if he holds on to it. This loss, minus the $3 premium, yields a loss of $7 when the market price is $40. As indicated in the graph, the break-even price in which the profit from the position is zero is $S_T^* = \$47$, the same as the put holder's:

$$\pi = (S_T - X) + P_0$$

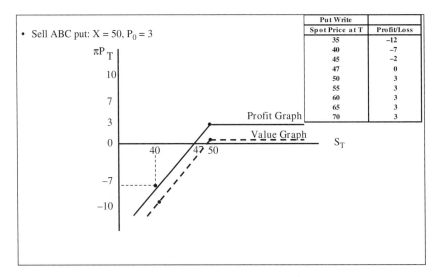

FIGURE 1.3-5 Naked Put Write

$$0 = (S_T - X) + P_0$$

$$S_T^* = X - P_0$$

$$S_T^* = \$50 - \$3 = \$47$$

1.3.6 Covered Put Write

The last fundamental option strategy is the covered put write. This strategy requires the seller of a put to cover her position. Because a put writer is required to buy the stock at the exercise price if the holder exercises, the only way she can cover the obligation is by selling the underlying stock short. Using our same numbers, suppose a writer of the ABC 50 put shorts ABC stock: borrows a share of ABC stock and then sells it in the market at $50. At expiration, if the stock price is less than the exercise price, and the put holder exercises, the covered put writer will buy the stock with the $50 proceeds obtained from the short sale and then return the share that was borrowed to cover the short sale obligation. The put writer's obligation is thus covered, and she profits by an amount equal to the premium as shown in Figure 1.3-6 and its accompanying table. In contrast, losses from covered put writes occur when the stock price rises above $53. When the stock price rises above $50, the put is worthless because the holder would not exercise, but losses would occur from covering the short sale. For example, if the writer had to cover the short sale when the stock was at $60, she would incur a $10 loss. This loss, minus the $3 premium the writer received, would equate to a net loss of $7. Finally, the break-even price for the covered put write in which profit is zero occurs at $53.

1.4 OTHER OPTION STRATEGIES

One of the important features of an option is that it can be combined with stock and other options to generate a number of different investment strategies. In this section, we introduce two well-known strategies: straddles and spreads. In Chapter 3, we examine these and other strategies in more detail.

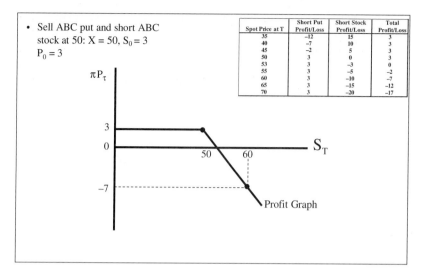

Spot Price at T	Short Put Profit/Loss	Short Stock Profit/Loss	Total Profit/Loss
35	–12	15	3
40	–7	10	3
45	–2	5	3
50	3	0	3
53	3	–3	0
55	3	–5	–2
60	3	–10	–7
65	3	–15	–12
70	3	–20	–17

- Sell ABC put and short ABC stock at 50: $X = 50$, $S_0 = 3$ $P_0 = 3$

FIGURE 1.3-6 Covered Put Write

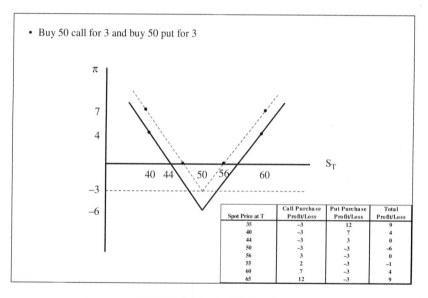

- Buy 50 call for 3 and buy 50 put for 3

Spot Price at T	Call Purchase Profit/Loss	Put Purchase Profit/Loss	Total Profit/Loss
35	–3	12	9
40	–3	7	4
44	–3	3	0
50	–3	–3	–6
56	3	–3	0
55	2	–3	–1
60	7	–3	4
65	12	–3	9

FIGURE 1.4-1 Straddle Purchase

1.4.1 Straddle

A **_straddle purchase_** is formed by buying both a call and put with the same terms—same underlying stock, exercise price, and expiration date. A straddle write, in contrast, is constructed by selling a call and a put with the same terms.

In Figure 1.4-1 and its accompanying table, the profit graphs are shown for call, put, and straddle purchases in which both the call and the put have exercise prices of $50 and premiums of $3.[2] The straddle purchase shown in the figure is geometrically generated by

---

[2] In most of examples in this chapter, calls and puts with the same terms are priced the same. In most cases, though, calls and puts with the same terms are not priced equally. The relation between call and put prices is discussed in Section 1.6.

vertically summing the profits on the call purchase position (dashed line) and put purchase position (dashed line) at each stock price. The resulting straddle purchase position is characterized by a "V"-shaped profit and stock price relation. Thus, the motivation for buying a straddle comes from the expectation of a large stock price movement in either direction. For example, at the stock price of $40, a $4 profit is earned: $10 profit on the put minus a $6 cost of the straddle purchase. Similarly, at $60, a $4 profit is attained: $10 profit on the call minus a $6 cost of the put. Losses on the straddle occur if the price of the underlying stock remains stable, with the maximum loss being equal to the costs of the straddle ($6) and occurring when the stock price is equal to the exercise price. Finally, the straddle is characterized by two break-even prices ($44 and $56).

In contrast to the straddle purchase, a ***straddle write*** yields an inverted "V"-shaped profit graph. The seller of a straddle is betting against large price movements. A maximum profit equal to the sum of the call and put premiums occurs when the stock price is equal to the exercise price; losses occur if the stock price moves significantly in either direction. A straddle write problem is included in the end-of-the-chapter problems.

1.4.2 Spread

A *spread* is the purchase of one option and the sale of another on the same underlying stock but with different terms: different exercise prices, different expirations, or both. Two of the most popular spread positions are the bull spread and the bear spread. A ***bull call spread*** is formed by buying a call with a certain exercise price and selling another call with a higher exercise price but with the same expiration date. A ***bear call spread*** is the reversal of the bull spread; it consists of buying a call with a certain exercise price and selling another with a lower exercise price. (The same spreads also can be formed with puts.)

In Figure 1.4-2 and its accompanying table, the profit graph for a bull call spread strategy is shown. The spread is formed with the purchase of a 50 call for $3 and the sale of a 55 call for $1 (same underlying stock and expirations). Geometrically, the profit and stock price relation for the spread shown in the figure is obtained by vertically summing

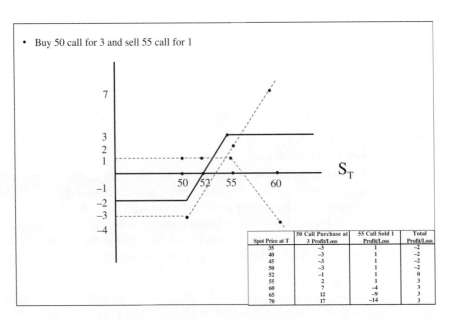

Spot Price at T	50 Call Purchase at 3 Profit/Loss	55 Call Sold 1 Profit/Loss	Total Profit/Loss
35	–3	1	–2
40	–3	1	–2
45	–3	1	–2
50	–3	1	–2
52	–1	1	0
55	2	1	3
60	7	–4	3
65	12	–9	3
70	17	–14	3

FIGURE 1.4-2 Bull Spread

the profits from the long 50 call position and the short 55 call position at each stock price. The bull spread is characterized by losses limited to $2 when the stock price is $50 or less, limited profits of $3 starting when the stock price hits $55, and a break-even price of $52.

A bear call spread results in the opposite profit and stock price relation as the bull spread: A limited profit occurs when the stock price is equal or less than the lower exercise price, and a limited loss occurs when the stock price is equal or greater than the higher exercise price. A bear spread problem also is included in the end-of-the-chapter problems.

1.5 OPTION PRICE RELATIONSHIPS

In our discussion of the fundamental option strategies, we treated the option premium as a given. The price of an option, though, is determined in the market and is a function of the time to expiration, the strike price, the price and the volatility of the underlying security, and the rate of return on a risk-free bond. The pricing of option contracts is explained in Part II of this book. However, at this point, we can identify some of the factors that determine the price of an option.

1.5.1 Call Price Relationships

The relationship between the price of a call and its expiration time, exercise price, and stock price can be seen by defining the call's intrinsic value and time value premium. By definition, the *intrinsic value* (IV) of a call at a time prior to expiration (let t signify any time *prior* to expiration) or at expiration (T again signifies expiration date) is the maximum (Max) of the difference between the price of the stock (S_t) and the exercise price or zero (because the option cannot have a negative value):

$$IV = Max[S_t - X, 0] \qquad (1.5\text{-}1)$$

Thus, if a call had an exercise price of $50 and the stock was trading at $60, then the intrinsic value of the call would be $10; if it were trading at $48, the IV would be zero. The intrinsic value can be used to define *in-the-money, on-the-money* and *out-of-the-money* calls. Specifically, an in-the-money call is one in which the price of the underlying stock exceeds the exercise price; as a result, its IV is positive. When the price of the stock is equal to the exercise price, the call's IV is zero, and the call is said to be on the money (or at the money). Finally, if the exercise price exceeds the stock price, the call would be out of the money and the IV would be zero:

Type	Condition	Example: X = 50
In-the-Money	$S_t > X \Rightarrow IV > 0$	$60 > 50 \Rightarrow IV = \$10$
On-the-Money	$S_t = X \Rightarrow IV = 0$	$50 = \$50 \Rightarrow IV = 0$
Out-of-the-Money	$S_t < X \Rightarrow IV = 0$	$40 < \$50 \Rightarrow IV = 0$

For an American call option, the IV defines a boundary condition in which the price of a call has to trade at a value at least equal to its IV:

$$C_t \geq Max[S_t - X, 0]$$

If this boundary condition does not hold ($C_t < Max[S_t - X, 0]$) an arbitrage opportunity exists. An *arbitrage* is any risk-free profit or free lunch situation. If $C_t < Max[S_t - X, 0]$), an arbitrageur could earn a riskless return by buying the call, exercising, and then selling the stock. For example, suppose an American call option on ABC stock with an exercise price of $50 was trading at $9 when the stock was trading at $60 (IV = Max($60 − $50, 0) = $10). In this situation we have an asset (the stock) selling at two different prices: One is $60, offered in the stock market; the other is $59 ($9 call premium plus $50 exercise price), available in the option market. In this case, an arbitrageur could realize a riskless profit of $1 (excluding commissions) per call by (1) buying the call at $9, (2) immediately exercising it (buying ABC stock at $50), and (3) selling the stock in the market for $60:

$S_t = 60, X = 50, C_t = 9$	
Position	**Cash Flow**
Buy ABC 50 Call for 9	−$9
Exercise ABC 50 Call: (Buy Stock for X = 50)	−$50
Sell Stock in Market for 60	+$60
Profit	+$1

Arbitrageurs seeking to profit from this opportunity would increase the demand for the ABC call, causing its price to go up until the call premium was at least $10 and the arbitrage opportunity disappeared. Thus, in equilibrium, the American call would have to trade at a price at least equal to its IV.

It is important to note that the exploitation of arbitrage opportunities by arbitrageurs ensures that the price of the option will change as the underlying stock price changes. For example, if the ABC stock were to increase from 60 to 70 to 80, then in the absence of arbitrage, the price of the ABC 50 call would have to increase to a price that is at least equal to 20 when the stock is at 70 and 30 when the stock is at 80. Thus, arbitrageurs ensure that the call option derives it value from the underlying stock. Finally, note that because the preceding arbitrage strategy governing the price of an American option requires an immediate exercise of the call, the resulting IV boundary condition does not hold for European options (the condition governing European options will be discussed in Chapter 4).

The other component of the value of an option is the ***time value premium*** (TVP). By definition, the TVP of a call is the difference between the price of the call and its IV:

$$\text{TVP} = C_t - \text{IV} \tag{1.5-2}$$

If the call premium were $12 when the price of the underlying stock on a 50 call was $60, the TVP would be $2. The TVP decreases as the time remaining to expiration decreases. Specifically, if the call is near expiration, we should expect the call to trade at a price close to its IV; if, however, 6 months remain to expiration, then the price of the call should be greater and the TVP positive; if 9 months remain, then the TVP should be even greater. In addition to the intuitive reasoning, an arbitrage argument also can be used to establish that the price of the call is greater with a greater time to expiration (this argument is presented in Chapter 4).

Combined, the IV and the TVP show that two factors influencing the price of a call are the underlying stock's price and the time to expiration. Specifically, expressing Equation 1.5-2 in terms of C_t:

$$C_t = \text{IV} + \text{TVP} \tag{1.5-3}$$

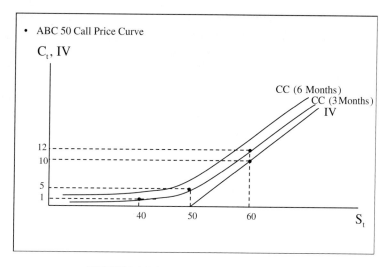

FIGURE 1.5-1 Call and Stock Price Relation

1.5.2   Call Price Curve

Graphically, the relationship between C_t and the TVP and IV, as defined in Equation 1.5-3, can be seen in Figure 1.5-1. In the figure, graphs plotting the call price and the IV (on the vertical axis) against the stock price (on the horizontal axis) are shown for a 50 call option. The IV line shows the linear relationship between the IV and the stock price. The line emanates from a horizontal intercept equal to the exercise price. When the price of the stock is equal or less than the exercise price of \$50, the IV is equal to zero; when the stock is priced at $S_t = \$55$, the IV is \$5; when $S_t = \$60$, the IV = \$10, and so on. The IV line, in turn, serves as a reference for the call price curves (CC). As we just noted, arbitrageurs ensure that the call price curve cannot go below the IV line. Furthermore, the IV line would be the call price curve if we are at expiration because the TVP = 0 and thus $C_T = $ IV. The call price curves (CC) in Figure 1.5-1 show the positive relationship between C_t and S_t. The vertical distance between a CC curve and the IV line, in turn, measures the TVP. Thus, the CC curve shown with 3 months to expiration has a call price of \$1 when the stock is below its exercise price at $S_t = \$40$: Its IV = 0 and TVP = \$1. When the stock is trading at its exercise price, the call is priced at \$5, the IV = 0, and the TVP = \$5; and when the stock is at \$60, the call is at \$12, the IV = \$10, and the TVP = \$2. The CC curve for the 6-month option is above the 3-month CC curve, reflecting the fact that the call premium increases as the time to expiration increases.

In summary, the graphs in Figure 1.5-1 show (1) that a direct relationship exists between the price of the call and the stock price as reflected by the positively sloped CC curves, (2) that the call will be priced above its IV as shown by the CC curves being above the IV line, and (3) the price of the call will be greater the longer the time to expiration as reflected by the distance between CC curves with different expiration periods. Finally, it should be noted that the slopes of the CC curves approach the slope of the IV line when the stock price is relatively high (known as a ***deep in-the-money call***), and the slope approaches zero (flat) when the price of the stock is relatively low (a ***deep out-of-the-money call***). These relationships, as well as how arbitrage ensures the other three relationships and similar ones for European options, are discussed in Chapter 4.

1.5.3 Variability

The call price curve illustrates the positive relation between a call price and the underlying security price and the time to expiration. An option's price also depends on the volatility of the underlying security.

Because a long call position is characterized by unlimited profits if the underlying security increases but limited losses if it decreases, a call holder would prefer more volatility rather than less. Specifically, greater variability suggests, on one hand, a chance that the security will increase substantially in price, causing the call to be more valuable. On the other hand, greater volatility also suggests a chance that the security price will decrease substantially. However, given that a call's losses are limited to just the premium when the security price is equal to the exercise price or less, the extent of the price decrease would be inconsequential to the call holder. Thus, the market will value a call option on a more volatile security greater than a call on one with lower variability.

The positive relationship between a call's premium and its underlying security's volatility is illustrated in Exhibit 1.5-1. The exhibit shows two call options: (1) a call option on Stock A with an exercise price of $X = 100$ and in which Stock A is trading at 100 and has a variability characterized by an equal chance it will either increase by 10% or decrease by 10% by the end of the period (assume theses are the only possibilities) and (2) a call option on Stock B with an exercise price of $X = 100$ and in which the stock is trading at 100 but has a greater variability than Stock A as characterized by an equal chance it will either increase or decrease by 20% by the end of the period. Given the variability of the underlying stocks, the IV of the call option on Stock B would be either 20 or 0 at the end of the period compared to possible values of only 10 and 0 for the call on Stock A. Because Stock B's call cannot perform worse than Stock A's call and can do better, it follows there would be a higher demand and therefore price for the call option on Stock B than the call on Stock A. Thus, given the limited loss characteristic of an option, the more volatile the underlying security, the more valuable the option, all other factors being equal.

EXHIBIT 1.5-1   Price and Variability Relation

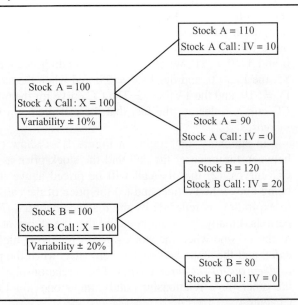

1.5.4 Put Price Relationships

Analogous to calls, the price of a put at a given point in time prior to expiration (P_t) also can be explained by reference to its IV and TVP. In the case of puts, the IV is defined as the maximum of the difference between the exercise price and the stock price or zero:

$$IV = Max[X - S_t, 0] \qquad (1.5\text{-}4)$$

Similar to calls, in-the-money, on-the-money, and out-of-the-money puts are defined as:

Type	Condition	Example: X = 50
In-the-Money:	$X > S_t \Rightarrow IV > 0$	$\$50 > \$40 \Rightarrow IV = \$10$
On-the-Money:	$X = S_t \Rightarrow IV = 0$	$\$50 = \$50 \Rightarrow IV = 0$
Out-of-the-Money	$X < S_t \Rightarrow IV = 0$	$\$40 < \$60 \Rightarrow IV = 0$

Like call options, the IV of an American put option defines a boundary condition in which the price of the put has to trade at a price at least equal to its IV: $P_t \geq Max[X - S_t, 0]$. If this condition does not hold, an arbitrageur could buy the put and the underlying stock and then exercise the put to earn a riskless profit. For example, suppose ABC stock is trading at 40 and an ABC 50 put were trading at 9, below its IV of 10. Arbitrageurs could realize a risk-free profit of $1 by (1) buying the put at 9, (2) buying the stock at 40, and (3) then selling the stock at X = 50 by exercising the put:

$S_t = 40, X = 50, P_t = 9$	
Position	**Cash Flow**
Buy ABC 50 Put for 9	−$9
Buy ABC Stock for 40 in the Market	−$40
Exercise ABC 50 Put:	
(Sell Stock on the put for X = 50)	+$50
Profit	+$1

As in the case of calls, arbitrageurs by pursuing this strategy would increase the demand for puts until the put price was equal to at least the $10 difference between the exercise and stock prices. Thus, in the absence of arbitrage, an American put would have to trade at a price at least equal to its IV.

Similar to call options, the TVP for the put is defined as:

$$TVP = P_t - IV \qquad (1.5\text{-}5)$$

Thus, the price of the put can be explained by the time to expiration and the stock price in terms of the put's TVP and IV:

$$P_t = IV + TVP \qquad (1.5\text{-}6)$$

1.5.5 Put Price Curve

Graphically, the put and stock price relationships are shown in Figure 1.5-2. The figure shows two negatively sloped put-price (PP) curves with different exercise periods and a negatively sloped IV line going from the horizontal intercept (where $S_t = X$) to the vertical

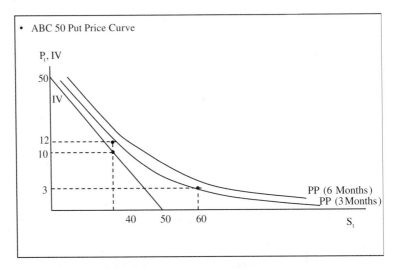

FIGURE 1.5-2 Put and Stock Price Relation

intercept where the IV is equal to the exercise price when the stock is trading at zero (i.e., $IV = X$ when $S_t = 0$). The graphs show the following:

1.   The price of the put increases as the price of the underlying stock decreases because the put's IV is greater the lower the stock price.

2.   The price of the put is above its IV with time remaining to expiration or else arbitrage opportunities would ultimately push the price up to equal the IV.

3.   The greater the time to expiration, the higher the TVP and thus the greater the put price.

4.   The slope of the PP curve approaches the slope of the IV line for relatively low stock prices (***deep in-the-money puts***) and approaches zero for relatively large stock prices (***deep out-of-the money puts***).

1.5.6   Variability

Like calls, the price of a put option depends not only on the underlying security price and time to expiration but also on the volatility of the underlying security. Because put losses are limited to the premium when the price of the underlying security is greater than or equal to the exercise price, put buyers, like call buyers, will value puts on securities with greater variability more than those with lower variability.

1.6   PUT–CALL PARITY

Consider a strategy of buying a share of stock for $50 and a put on the stock with exercise price of $50. The cash flow from this portfolio at expiration is shown in Table 1.6-1. As shown in Column 7, this stock and put portfolio has a minimum value of $50 (the exercise price) for $S_T < \$50$ and a value equal to the stock for $S_T \geq \$50$. Thus, an investor who purchased the stock some time ago could eliminate the downside risk of the stock by buying a put. In this case, the stock value has been "insured" not to fall below $50, the exercise price on the put. A combined stock and put position such as this is known as a ***"portfolio insurance"*** strategy. Portfolio insurance represents an example of how

TABLE 1.6-1   Cash Flows on Call, Put, Stock, and Bond Positions at Expiration

			Cash Flows at Expiration			
(1) S_T	(2) Long Call (X = 50)	(3) Bond	(4) Bond and Call Portfolio (3) + (4)	(5) Long Put X = 50	(6) Stock	(7) Stock and Put Portfolio (5) + (6)
$30	$0	$50	$50	$20	$30	$50
40	0	50	50	10	40	50
50	0	50	50	0	50	50
60	10	50	60	0	60	60
70	20	50	70	0	70	70

options can be used by hedgers. By definition, **hedgers** are those who take positions in certain securities (e.g., long put position) to reduce or possibly eliminate the risk germane to another position (e.g., stock position).

Given the values of the stock and put portfolio, consider now a portfolio consisting of a bond with a face value of $50 and a 50 call on the stock. As shown in Column 4 of Table 1.6-1, the values of this portfolio at time T are identical to the stock and put portfolio's values at each stock price. If the stock appreciates, the call becomes more valuable and the return on the bond is enhanced by the appreciation in the call price. On the other hand, if the stock falls below the exercise price, the call is worthless, and the portfolio simply is equal to the face value of the bond ($50). A bond and call portfolio such as this is referred to as a *fiduciary call*, and it can be used as a substitute for buying the stock and put.

The equality between the stock-put portfolio and the bond-call portfolio may be expressed algebraically as:

$$S_t + P_t = C_t + B_t \qquad (1.6\text{-}1)$$

This expression is commonly referred to as *put–call parity*. Because the two portfolios have exactly the same cash flows at expiration, their values at any time t must be identical or else arbitrage opportunities will exist. For example, if the bond-call combination is cheaper than the stock-put portfolio, an arbitrageur can earn a profit without taking risk and without investing any of her own money. To expedite the strategy, the arbitrageur would have to buy the cheap portfolio (bond and call) and sell the expensive one (stock and put). The put–call parity condition is governed by the **Law of One Price**. This law says that in the absence of arbitrage, any investments that yield identical cash flows most be equally priced.

Finally, note that if we solve Equation 1.6-1 for S_t, we obtain a new identity:

$$S_t = C_t + B_t - P_t \qquad (1.6\text{-}2)$$

where the "−" sign indicates a short position. This expression suggests that a portfolio consisting of long call, short put, and long bond positions should yield exactly the same cash flows at expiration as a long stock position. Thus, a synthetic stock position could be formed with such a portfolio. Several variations of the put–call parity equations may be used to create a synthetic long or short call, put, stock, or bond positions. Put–call parity and the formation of synthetic positions and their use are discussed in more detail in Chapter 4.

1.7   CONCLUSION

In this chapter, we have provided an overview of options by defining option terms, examining fundamental option strategies, and defining some of the basic determinants of the price of an option. The discussion, however, was general in nature. When investors speak of options, most of them refer specifically to options that can be purchased or sold on the option exchanges. In the next chapter, we examine those exchanges and the institutional aspects associated with trading options on them.

KEY TERMS

forward contracts	call purchase	time value premium
futures	profit graph	deep in-the-money call
derivative securities	speculator	deep out-of-the-money call
call	value graph	in-the-money put
put	naked call write	out-of-the-money put
long position	covered call write	deep in-the-money put
exercise	put purchase	deep out-of-the-money put
writer	naked put write	arbitrage
short position	covered put write	law of one price
option premium	straddle	portfolio insurance
exercise price	spread	hedger
strike price	intrinsic value	fiduciary call
exercise date	in-the-money call	put–call parity
European option	on-the-money call	
American option	out-of-the-money call	

SELECTED REFERENCES

Cox, J. C., and M. Rubinstein. *Option Markets*. Englewood Cliffs, NJ: Prentice-Hall, 1985.

Gombola, M. J., R. L. Roenfeldt, and P. L. Cooley. "Spreading Strategies in CBOE Options: Evidence on Market Performance." *The Journal of Financial Research* 1 (Winter 1978): 35–44.

McMillan, L. G. *Options as a Strategic Investment,* 2nd ed., New York: New York Institute of Finance, 1986.

Williams, J. C. "The Origin of Futures Markets." *Agriculture History* 56 (1982): 306–316.

PROBLEMS AND QUESTIONS

1. Show graphically the profit and stock price relationships at expiration for the following option positions. In each case, show the profit graph for each position at various stock prices and then aggregate the profits for the separate positions at each stock price to generate the profit graph for the total position.

   a. A straddle purchase formed with ABC call and put options, each with exercise prices of $60 and premiums of $5.

   b. A straddle write formed with ABC call and put options, each with exercise prices of $40 and premiums of $2.

   c. A covered call write formed by purchasing ABC stock at $48 and selling an ABC 50 call at $3.

   d. A synthetic long stock position formed by buying an ABC 50 call at $3 and selling an ABC 50 put at $3.

   e. A synthetic short stock position formed by selling an ABC 50 call at $3 and buying an ABC 50 put at $3.

   f. A put spread formed by buying an ABC 50 put at $1 and selling an ABC 55 put at $2.

   g. A stock insurance strategy formed by purchasing ABC stock at $50 and buying an ABC 50 put at $3.

2. Determine the break-even prices at expiration for the following:

   a. A covered call write formed by purchasing ABC stock at $45 and selling an ABC 50 call at $4.

   b. A covered put write formed by selling ABC stock short at $45 and selling an ABC 50 put at $6.

   c. A stock insurance strategy formed by purchasing ABC stock at $48 and buying an ABC 50 put at $4.

3. Suppose you bought a 6-month call option on ABC stock for $1.50. Suppose also the call option has an exercise price of $10, and the price of ABC stock is $11. What price would ABC stock have to sell for at the call's expiration for you to break even? At what price would the stock have to trade for at expiration for you to earn a 10% rate of return for the 6-month period?

4. Suppose you are bearish about ABC stock and buy a 6-month ABC 30 put option on the stock for $3 when ABC stock is trading at $29. What price would ABC stock have to sell for at the put's expiration for you to break even? At what price would the stock have to trade at expiration for you to earn a 10% rate of return for the 6-month period?

5. Construct a profit graph for a bull call spread formed with an ABC 50 call trading at $2 and an ABC 55 call trading at $6 (include stock prices at expiration of $40, $45, $50, $55, $60, and $65). What do you find significant about the position? How would the market react to this situation? What impact would its reactions have on the prices of the ABC 50 call and ABC 55 call?

6. Explain what arbitrageurs would do if the price of an American call on ABC stock with an exercise price of $70 were priced at $4 when the underlying price on ABC stock were trading at $75? What impact would their actions have in the option market on the call's price? Would arbitrageurs follow the same strategy if the call option were European? If not, why?

7. Explain what arbitrageurs would do if the price of an American put on ABC stock with an exercise price of $70 were priced at $9 when the underlying futures price on ABC stock were trading at $60. What impact would their actions have in the option market on the put's price?

8. Compare and contrast buying stock with a call purchase strategy.

9. Compare and contrast selling stock short with a put purchase strategy.

10. If the premium on an option increases, does that mean there is a greater demand for the option? Comment.

11. Let the exercise price be 40 for a put and a call; and assume there is a risk-free discount bond with face value of 40, the same maturity as the options, and trading at price of B.

a. Construct a table of expiration values (or cash flows) of a stock and put portfolio. Does it look like the cash flow for another position? Construct a table for that position. Comment on put–call parity.

b. Construct a table of expiration values that shows that a long bond and call positions and a short stock position are equivalent to the put.

c. Construct a table of expiration values that shows that a long stock and put positions and a short bond position (debt position) are equivalent to the call.

12. Explain intuitively why call and put options are more valuable the greater their underlying security's variability.

WEB EXERCISE

1. Determine the recent prices on exchange options by going to www.wsj.com/free and clicking on Market Data & Tools and Market Data Center (go to U.S. Stocks, Options, and Listed Option Quotes).

CHAPTER 2

THE OPTION MARKET

2.1 INTRODUCTION

In 1973, the Chicago Board of Trade formed the Chicago Board of Option Exchange (CBOE). As we noted in Chapter 1, the CBOE was the first organized exchange for the trading of options. Just as the CBT had served to increase the popularity of futures, the CBOE helped to increase the trading of options by making the contracts more marketable. Since the creation of the CBOE, organized stock exchanges, such as the New York Stock Exchange (NYSE), the American Stock Exchange (AMEX), and the Philadelphia Stock Exchange (PHLX), most of the organized futures exchanges and many security exchanges outside the United States also began offering markets for the trading of options. As the number of exchanges offering options increased, so did the number of securities and instruments with options written on them. Today, option contracts exist not only on stocks but also on foreign currencies, security indices, futures contracts, and debt and interest rate-sensitive securities (see Exhibit 1.1-1 for a listing of U.S. and non-U.S. derivative exchanges and their Web sites).

In addition to exchange-traded options, there is also a large over-the-counter (OTC) market in option contracts in the United States and a growing OTC market outside the United States. The OTC markets in and outside the United States consists primarily of dealers who make markets in the underlying spot security, investment banking firms, and commercial banks. The option contracts offered in the OTC market include foreign currencies, Treasury securities, interest rate-related securities, and special types of interest rate products such as interest rate calls and puts, caps, floors, and collars. These OTC options are primarily used by financial institutions and nonfinancial corporations to hedge their currency and interest rate positions.

In this chapter, the institutional aspects associated with trading options are examined in terms of the structure of the organized option exchanges, the standardization of option contracts and trading rules as established by the exchanges, and the functions and operations of option clearing corporations. In addition, we also examine in this chapter the transaction costs incurred by investors in buying and selling options and the different types of non-stock options available on both the organized exchanges and the OTC market.

2.2 OPTION EXCHANGES

The buying and selling of most securities in the United States and other countries with major financial markets is done through a network of brokers and dealers who operate through security exchanges. By definition, brokers are agents who, for a commission, bring security buyers and sellers together. Dealers, in turn, provide markets for investors to buy and sell securities by taking temporary positions in securities; they buy from investors who want to sell and sell to investors who want to buy. In contrast to brokers, dealers receive compensation in terms of the spread between the bid price at which they buy securities and the ask price at which they sell.

Whereas brokers and dealers serve the function of bringing buyers and sellers together, the exchanges, in turn, serve the function of linking brokers and dealers. The members of the exchanges consist almost exclusively of brokers and dealers who, as members, are the only ones who can trade securities on the exchange. In general, the primary objective of the exchange is to provide marketability to securities. An asset's marketability refers to the ease or speed with which it can be traded. The exchanges provide this not only by linking brokers and dealers but by standardizing the security contracts and establishing trading rules and procedures.

The option exchanges such as the CBOE and Philadelphia operate similar to the U.S. security exchanges in linking brokers and dealers. Like other organized exchanges, the organized option exchanges also provide marketability by standardizing options contracts and by establishing trading rules. Different from the stock exchanges (but similar to the futures exchanges), the option exchanges also provide marketability by using clearing corporations that guarantee and break up contracts after trades have been completed.

2.2.1 Structure

The option exchanges can be described in a number of ways. For one, an exchange such as the CBOE, Philadelphia, New York, and the like is a physical exchange, a building where brokers and dealers go to buy and sell securities on behalf of their investors/clients. On the trading floor of the CBOE are trading posts where exchange members and other brokers trade one of the options listed. Circling the floor of the CBOE are telephone and communication areas where brokers receive calls on orders from their retail brokerage firms across the country. With those orders, the brokers go to the trading post where the particular option is traded and execute the order. The mode of trading on derivative exchanges in the United States, London (LIFFE), Paris (MATIF), Sydney (SFE), Singapore (SIMEX), and other locations still takes place the way it did over 100 years ago on the CBT, with brokers and dealers going to a pit and using the *open-outcry* method to trade.

Although the open-outcry system is still used on the major exchanges, electronic trading systems are being used by the physical exchanges in the United States, London, Paris, and Sydney for after-hours trading. In addition to dual systems, since 1985, all new derivative exchanges have been organized as electronic exchanges. The German exchange (Deutsche Termin Boerse [DTB]) and the Stockholm Option Market (SOM), for example, were both set up as screen-based trading systems. Most of these electronic trading systems are order-driven systems in which customer orders (bid and ask prices and size) are collected and matched by a computerized matching system. This contrasts to a price-driven system such as the one used on the Swiss Options and Futures Exchange (SOFE) in which dealers provide bid and ask quotes and make markets.

The option exchanges also can be described as a corporate association consisting of member brokers. By exchange rules, only members can trade on the exchange. To obtain a membership, also referred to as a seat on the exchange, a company or individual must purchase it from an existing member who wants to sell. Members of the exchange can be classified in terms of their functions. Most brokerage firms with seats on the option exchanges function as floor brokers. *Floor brokers* execute buy and sell orders on behalf of their clients. Thus, an investor interested in buying or selling an option would set up an account with the member's investment-brokerage firm and buy or sell the option for a commission through the firm's floor broker. A second type of member is the floor trader. *Floor traders* buy and sell securities only for themselves and not for others. A third type of member, depending on the exchange, is a specialist or a market maker. Both *specialists* and *market makers* can be described as dealers who specialize in the trading of a specific option. Finally, some exchanges have ***Registered Option Traders*** (ROTs) as part of their membership. ROTs are members who can both buy and sell options for themselves and act as brokers but who cannot act as market makers or specialists.

2.2.2   Market Makers and Specialists

Security markets can be described as either being a "call market" or a "continuous market." A ***call market*** is designed so that investors who wish to trade in a particular security can do so only at that time when the exchange "calls" the security for trading. Once called, market clearing is accomplished via an auction; prices are quoted until a price is found in which the amount demanded is equal to the amount supplied. In contrast, a ***continuous market*** attempts to have constant trading in a security. To do so, time discrepancies caused by different times when some investors want to sell and others want to buy must be eliminated or at least minimized. Continuous markets, such as the NYSE and U.S. option exchanges, accomplish this by requiring specialists or market makers to take temporary positions in a security whenever there is a demand.

Trading on the Philadelphia exchange centers around specialists. Under the specialist system, the exchange's board assigns the options on a specific security to a specialist to deal. In this role, specialists, like dealers, act by buying options from sellers at low bid prices, hoping to sell to buyers at higher ask prices. Specialists quote a ***bid*** price (the maximum price they would be willing to pay) to investors interested in selling options and an ***ask*** price (the minimum price at which they would sell) to investors interested in buying. They hope to profit by the difference in the bid and ask prices, that is, the ***bid-ask spread***. In addition to dealing, the exchange also requires specialists to maintain the limit order book on the option they are assigned and to execute the orders.[1] A limit order is an investor's request to a floor broker to buy or sell a security at a given price or better. On the option exchanges, such orders are taken by floor brokers and left with the assigned specialist for execution. The specialist records the order in her limits book and then acts either as a broker by trying to trade the option at the client's specified price or as a dealer by buying (selling) the option for (from) her inventory.

The CBOE does not use specialists. Instead, they use market makers who act as dealers and ***Order Book Officials*** (OBOs) who keep the limit order book.[2] Like specialists, market makers are required by the exchange to trade in an assigned option if an investor cannot find someone with whom to trade. In turn, market makers who buy options at the bid price and then sell them at the ask price over a very short period of time are referred to as *scalpers*. In contrast, market makers who hold their position for a longer period of time are referred to as ***position traders***.

In terms of the rules of the exchange, the CBOE assigns more than one market maker to the options on a given stock. This contrasts to the specialist system in which typically only one specialist is assigned to a security. This rule serves to ensure a more competitive price. Also, the rules of the CBOE prohibit market makers from handling public (nonmember) orders in her assigned option, although a market maker can handle public orders in other options. Finally, exchange rules allow the exchange board to impose limits on the bid-ask spread. For example, the CBOE could impose limits of 1/4 of a point for options trading

---

[1] This latter responsibility often is used by the specialist to determine her bid and ask prices.

[2] The OBO is an employee of the exchange who keeps the limit order book. The OBO stands at the trading post of the option that has been assigned to him and unlike the specialist shows the order book to other members who are allowed to execute the order. Market makers, in turn, use the limit orders in the OBO's book to help them determine their own spreads.

less than \$0.50; 1/2 of a point for options trading between \$0.50 and \$10; 3/4 of a point for options trading between \$10 and \$20; and one point for options trading over \$20.

In summary, exchanges like the CBOE use market makers to ensure a continuous market for the options they list, employ OBOs to record limit orders, and assign more than one market maker to an option to provide some competition. In contrast, other exchanges use specialists who, like the market makers, maintain positions in a specific option to ensure a continuous market. Unlike the market-maker system, these exchanges assign only one specialist to an option, with that specialist being responsible for handling the limit book on the specific option.

2.2.3 Standardization

One of the important contributions provided by a security exchange is the standardization of security contracts. An exchange does this by establishing rules and procedures with respect to the securities that can be listed and the way in which they can be traded. By establishing such rules, the exchange enhances the marketability of an option by making it possible for investors to know exactly what is being offered and the terms of the transaction.

2.2.3.1 Listing

A corporation that wants an option on its stock listed on the CBOE or another exchange offering option trading must meet the exchange's initial listing requirements. Once listed, it also must adhere to its continuous listing requirements. The initial requirements of the CBOE relate to the company's ability to satisfy sufficient size and ownership distribution requisites. The listing requirements of non-stock options, such as bond and stock indices, foreign currency, and futures, include satisfying an approved proposal that specifies conditions such as the terms of the contract and if it's an index, how it is to be constructed. For U.S. exchanges, the proposal must be approved by both the option exchange and the Securities and Exchange Commission (SEC), the federal regulatory authority for stocks and options.

2.2.3.2 Exercise Dates

The expiration dates on options are set by the exchanges. The dates, in turn, are defined in terms of an expiration cycle. The cycles on a number of exchanges are either the *January cycle* with expiration months of January, April, July, and October, the *February cycle* with February, May, August, and November expiration months, or the *March cycle* with expiration months of March, June, September, and December. On the CBOE and many of the other U.S. option exchanges, the exercise time for many options is the Saturday after the third Friday of the expiration month. The last day on which the expiring option trades, though, is Friday (Saturday is used so brokers can complete the paperwork of notifying the exchanges that exercises are to take place). In a 3-month option cycle, only the options with the three nearest expiration months trade at any time. Thus, as an option expires, the exchange introduces a new option that, at its introduction, would have 9 months remaining before expiration; the remaining two options would accordingly have 3 and 6 months left to expiration. For example, in late March, as the March option in the March cycle expires, December options are introduced, giving investors options with three expiration months: June, September, and December. In addition, exchanges also offer longer term options known as *LEAPS* (long-term equity anticipation securities) on some stocks. These options have expiration up to 3 years, with the expiration month for many stocks being January.

2.2.3.3 Exercise Price

The exchange chooses the exercise prices for each option. Usually, at least three strike prices (sometimes as many as five) are associated with each option when an option cycle begins. For stock options, the exercise prices usually are set either $2.50, $5.00, or $10.00 apart depending on the price at which stock is trading. For example, if a stock is trading at $12.50, the exchange might offer options with exercise prices of $10.00, $12.50, and $15.00; if the stock is trading at $100, the exchange might offer options with exercise prices of $90, $95, $100, $105, and $110. Once an option with a specific exercise price has been introduced, it will remain listed until its expiration date. The exchange can, however, introduce new options with different exercise prices at any time. For example, if 1 month after introducing a January 50 option, the stock price increased dramatically from $45 to $70, the exchange could introduce a new January option with an exercise price of $75. Also, whereas an option, once listed, must remain so until expiration, the exchange can restrict trading on it. The exchange defines a restricted option as one in which holders or writers are not allowed to enter an order if the order represents an initial transaction. Usually, options are restricted when they are selling at a very low price, with little or no demand.

It should be noted that when a company declares a cash dividend, the exchange does not adjust the exercise price. This policy contrasts to the dividend adjustment policies used when options traded on the over-the-counter (OTC) market. Under the old OTC policy, if a company paid a cash dividend, the exercise price on the option was reduced by the amount of the dividend.

2.2.3.4 Contract Size

The standard size for a stock option contract is 100 calls. Thus a per share quote of an ABC July 50 call at $3 means that a call buyer actually would be purchasing 100 calls at $3 per call ($300 investment), giving her the right to buy 100 shares of stock at $50 per share (total exercise value of $5,000) on or before (if American) the third Friday of July.

In discussing the size of a stock option contract, one should note that the CBOE and other option exchanges automatically adjust options for stock splits and stock dividends. For example, if ABC stock is trading at $50, and there is a put option on it with an exercise price of $60, then a 2-for-1 stock split would result in an automatic adjustment in which the number of contracts doubles, and the exercise price is halved. Thus, the owner of one ABC 60 put contract (100 puts) would now have two ABC 30 puts (200 puts). Options also are adjusted automatically for stock dividends by changing the number of shares and the exercise price. For example, if the ABC Company declares a 2.5% stock dividend, then the 100 shares underlying an ABC 60 call option contract would be adjusted up to equal 102.5 shares, and the exercise price would be adjusted down by 2.5%. The exercise price then would equal $1/1.025 = .9756$ (rounded to the nearest eighth) of its initial value: $(.9756)(\$60) = \$58.537$. Contract sizes for non-stock options also are specified as multiples. For example, the quoted exercise price and premium on a S&P 100 index option contract must be multiplied by a 100 to determine the actual prices, and an investor buying one option on the euro is by contract actually purchasing 62,500 options, the standard contract size on this foreign currency option.

2.2.3.5 Limits

The CBOE and other option exchanges can impose two limits on option trading: exercise limits and position limits. These limits are intended to prevent an investor or groups of investors from having a dominant impact on a particular option. An *exercise limit* specifies the maximum number of option contracts that can be exercised in any period of five consecutive business days by any investor or investor group. An exercise limit is determined by the exchange for each stock and non-stock option. A *position limit* sets the maximum number of options an investor can buy and sell on one side of the market; the limit for each stock and non-stock option is the same as the exercise limit. A *side of the market* is either a bullish or bearish position. An investor who is bullish could profit by buying calls or selling puts, whereas an investor with a bearish position would hope to profit by buying puts and selling calls. A position limit of 30,000 contracts on ABC stock, for example, would limit a bullish investor to no more than 30,000 contracts involving the purchase of the ABC call and the sale of the ABC put. The exchange sets the limits for each stock with each stock's assigned limit being based on the option's trading volume and the number of shares it has outstanding. Options on the larger and more frequently traded stocks can have position limits as high as 75,000 contracts, whereas options on smaller and less frequently trade stocks can have limits as low as 13,500 contracts.

2.2.3.6 Flex Options

The CBOE also offers a *flex option*. These options allow the option trader to choose the expiration date, exercise price, and whether the option is American or European. Flex options are nonstandarized options that were introduced to compete with customized OTC options.

2.2.3.7 Option Quotation

Exhibit 2.2-1 shows part of the daily quotations for options on Dell Inc. with January and May expirations that were traded on January 4, 2007. The quotes were downloaded from the CBOE website (www.cboe.com). The middle column shows the exercise prices for both call and put options. The other columns show the volumes and premiums (closing, bid, and ask) for both call and put options. For example, Dell Inc. closed on January 4, 2007, at $26.24. The Dell call options with an exercise price of $25 expiring in May had a closing premium of $1.38, and the May Dell 25 put option closed at $0.20.

Two new option terms, option *class* and option *series*, can be noted in examining option price quotations. The term option class refers to all options on a given stock or security that are of a particular type, either call or put. Thus, all Dell calls in Exhibit 2.2-1 are one option class, and all the Dell puts represent another option class. The term option series refers to all of the options of a given class with the same exercise price and expiration. Thus, the Dell April 25 call is one series, and the Dell April 25 put is another.

2.2.4 Option Clearing Corporation

To make derivative contracts more marketable, derivative exchanges provide a clearinghouse (CH) or option clearing corporation (OCC), as it is referred to on the option exchange. In the case of options, the OCC intermediates each transaction that takes place on the exchange and guarantees that all option writers fulfill the terms of their options if they are assigned. In addition, the OCC also manages option exercises, receiving notices, and assigning corresponding positions to clearing members.

As an intermediary, the OCC functions by breaking up each option trade. After a buyer and seller complete an option trade, the OCC steps in and becomes the effective buyer to the option seller and the effective seller to the option buyer. At that point, there is no longer any relationship between the original buyer and seller. If the buyer of the option decides to exercise, he does so by notifying the OCC (through his broker on the exchange). The

EXHIBIT 2.2-1 Stock Option Quotes

DELL INC Closing Price: 26.24

Expiration **January–07**

Calls

Symbol	Last Trade	Change	Bid	Ask	Volume	Interest	Strike Price
DLYAC	11.2	−0.1	11.1	11.4	200	1,223.00	15
DLYAW	8.75	−1.65	8.7	8.9	2	1,172.00	17.5
DLYAD	5.7	0.02	6.2	6.4	1	20,357.00	20
DLQAX	3.8	0.85	3.7	3.9	78	35,336.00	22.5
DLQAE	1.38	0.53	1.4	1.45	3,608.00	104,985.00	25
DLQAY	0.1	0	0.1	0.15	901	68,413.00	27.5
DLQAF	0.05	0	0.05	0.05	5	52,373.00	30
DLQAZ	0.05	0	0.05	0.05	50	14,611.00	32.5

Puts

Symbol	Last Trade	Change	Bid	Ask	Volume	Interest
DLYMC	0.05	0	0.05	0.05	1	5,793.00
DLYMW	0.05	0	0.05	0.05	11	59,967.00
DLYMD	0.05	0	0.05	0.05	6	32,988.00
DLQMX	0.05		0.05	0.05	103	40,969.00
DLQME	0.2	−0.15	0.15	0.2	3,201.00	101,230.00
DLQMY	1.4	−0.8	1.3	1.4	1,312.00	24,590.00
DLQMF	4.09	−0.51	3.7	3.9	23	11,994.00
DLQMZ	7	−0.1	6.2	6.4	1	1,228.00

Expiation **May–07**

Calls

Symbol	Last Trade	Change	Bid	Ask	Volume	Interest	Strike Price
DLYAC	11.2	−0.1	11.1	11.4	200	1,223.00	15
DLYAW	8.75	−1.65	8.7	8.9	2	1,172.00	17.5
DLYAD	5.7	0.02	6.2	6.4	1	20,357.00	20
DLQAX	3.8	0.85	3.7	3.9	78	35,336.00	22.5
DLQAE	1.38	0.53	1.4	1.45	3,608.00	104,985.00	25
DLQAY	0.1	0	0.1	0.15	901	68,413.00	27.5
DLQAF	0.05	0	0.05	0.05	5	52,373.00	30
DLQAZ	0.05	0	0.05	0.05	50	14,611.00	32.5

Puts

Symbol	Last Trade	Change	Bid	Ask	Volume	Interest
DLYMC	0.05	0	0.05	0.05	1	5,793.00
DLYMW	0.05	0	0.05	0.05	11	59,967.00
DLYMD	0.05	0	0.05	0.05	6	32,988.00
DLQMX	0.05		0.05	0.05	103	40,969.00
DLQME	0.2	−0.15	0.15	0.2	3,201.00	101,230.00
DLQMY	1.4	−0.8	1.3	1.4	1,312.00	24,590.00
DLQMF	4.09	−0.51	3.7	3.9	23	11,994.00
DLQMZ	7	−0.1	6.2	6.4	1	1,228.00

Source: CBOE Web site: www.cboe.com, January 5, 2007.
To access quotes from the CBOE, go to CBOE.com, click on "Delayed Quotes Beta" (under "Quotes"), and then click on "Option Chains."

OCC (who is the holder's effective option seller) will randomly select one of the option sellers short on the exercised security and assign that writer the obligation of fulfilling the terms of the exercise request.

By breaking up each option contract, the OCC makes it possible for option investors to close their positions before expiration. If a buyer (seller) of an option later becomes a seller (buyer) of the same option, the OCC's computer will note the offsetting position in the option investor's account and will therefore cancel both entries. For example, suppose in January, Investor A buys an ABC March 50 call for 3 from Investor B. When the OCC breaks up the contract, it records Investor A's *right to exercise* with the OCC and Investor B's *responsibility* to sell ABC stock at 50 if a party long on the call contract decides to exercise, and the OCC subsequently assigns B the responsibility. The transaction between A and B would lead to the following entry in the clearing firm's records:

January Clearinghouse Records for March ABC 50 Call

1. Investor A has the *right* to exercise
2. Investor B has *responsibility*

Suppose that in February, the price of ABC stock is trading at 60, and the price of the March ABC 50 call is trading at 12. Seeing profit potential, suppose instead of exercising, Investor A decides to close her call position by selling a March 50 call at 12 to Investor C. After the OCC breaks up this contract, its records would have a new entry showing Investor A with the responsibility of selling ABC stock at X = \$50 if assigned. This entry, though, would cancel out Investor A's original entry, giving her the right to buy ABC stock at X = \$50:

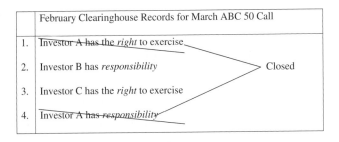

	February Clearinghouse Records for March ABC 50 Call	
1.	Investor A has the *right* to exercise	
2.	Investor B has *responsibility*	Closed
3.	Investor C has the *right* to exercise	
4.	Investor A has *responsibility*	

The OCC would accordingly close Investor A's position. Thus, Investor A bought the call for 3 and then closed her position by simply selling the call for 12. Her call sale, in turn, represents an offsetting position and is referred to as an ***offset*** or ***closing sale***.

If a writer also wanted to close his position at this date, he could do so by simply buying a March ABC 50 call. For example, suppose Investor B feared that ABC stock would continue to increase and therefore decided to close his short position by buying a March ABC 50 call at 12 from Investor D. After this transaction, the OCC would again step in, break up the contract, and enter Investor B's and D's positions on its records. The OCC's records would now show a new entry in which Investor B has the right to buy ABC at 50. This entry, in turn, would cancel Investor B's previous entry in which he had a responsibility to sell ABC at 50 if assigned. The offsetting positions (the right to buy and the obligation to sell) cancel each other, and the OCC computer system simply erases both entries.

	February Clearinghouse Records for March ABC 50 Call
1.	Investor B has *responsibility*
2.	Investor C has the *right* to exercise → Closed
3.	Investor B has the *right* to exercise
4.	Investor D has *responsibility*

Because Investor B's second transaction serves to close his opening position, it is referred to as a ***closing purchase***. In this case, Investor B loses 9 by closing: selling the call for 3 and buying it back for 12.

To recapitulate, by breaking up each transaction, the OCC provides marketability to options by making it easier for investors to close their positions. The OCC also enhances the marketability of option contracts by guaranteeing that the terms of a contract will be fulfilled if a holder exercises. To provide this insurance, the OCC has a claim on the securities and deposits that the option writer is required to maintain in an account with her brokerage firm as security. All covered option writers are required by the option exchanges to place their stock (for calls) or the cash or cash equivalents (for puts) in an escrow account of their brokerage firm, and all naked option writers are required to maintain cash or a cash equivalent in a deposit account with the brokerage firm equal to a certain percentage of the contract value. Margin requirements are discussed later in this chapter. If an option writer defaults on an assignment, the OCC can use its claim on the writer's security held in escrow or the margin deposit to obtain the cash or the security needed to honor the writer's responsibility. In addition to this claim, the OCC also maintains a special fund generated by its members to ensure sufficient capital to protect option buyers against assignment default. The OCC, by assuming the responsibility of guaranteeing the option writer's performance, eliminates the uncertainty option buyers might have concerning default and their need to examine the writer's credit worthiness. The elimination of such risk also helps to make options more marketable.

Operationally, the OCC functions through its members. Referred to as clearing firms, these members are typically investment firms who are members of the exchange. Each one maintains an account with the OCC, records and keeps track of the positions for each option buyer and seller the OCC places with it, maintains all margin positions, and contributes to the special fund used to guarantee assignment.

2.2.5 Summary

In summary, brokers and dealers combined with the option exchanges and the OCC create a network whereby investors in almost any part of the world can be linked to buy and sell options. It is a sophisticated system. However, for most investors, the procedure for buying and selling options, as with most securities, is quite simple. It usually takes a phone call or a computer account entry to a local broker or a local division of a national brokerage firm. In many cases, the investor is then assigned an account executive who usually sets up an account in which the investor can deposit cash when options and other securities are purchased or receive credits or proceeds when options are sold. Once the account is set up, then all an investor needs to do to buy or sell an option or any security is call or e-mail his account executive.

2.3 TYPES OF TRADES AND ORDERS

The OCC provides marketability by making it possible for option investors to close their positions instead of exercising. In general, there are four types of trades investors of exchange-traded options can make: opening, expiring, exercising, and closing transactions.

2.3.1 Opening Transactions

The opening transaction occurs when investors initially buy or sell an option. Investors would buy or sell an option through their broker, who, if he is a member of the exchange, would execute the order, or if not a member, would use one of his correspondent brokerage firms which is a member. In making an opening transaction, investors can instruct their broker to execute either:

1. A *market order* to buy or sell the option at the best price as soon as the order reaches the market.
2. A *market nonheld* or *not-held order* that gives the broker the right to use his own discretion in executing the order.
3. A *limit order* that specifies the maximum price the broker can pay when buying an option or the minimum he can accept when selling an option.
4. A *stop-loss order* that requires that the broker execute a market order once the option hits a specific price.
5. A *stop-limit order* that instructs the broker to execute a limit order when the option hits a specific price.
6. A *market-on-close order* that requires that the order be executed at or near the close of trading for the day.

In addition to instructing the broker as to the type of order, the investor also needs to tell her broker the number of options she wants to trade. For large orders in which the option investor wants multiple contracts, it is possible the market maker or specialist would fill only part of the order at a market price or possibly the entire order but at a lower price. Given this possibility, an investor also can instruct her broker to make the order either an *all-or-none order*, which tells the broker to execute the order in its entirety or not at all but allows for different prices; an *all-or-none, same-price order*, which instructs the broker to fill the entire order at the same price or not all; or an all-or-none order with a stipulation that the order is to be canceled if the entire order cannot be executed when it is initially introduced to the market.

2.3.2 Expiring Transactions

A second type of option trade involves allowing the option to expire; that is, doing nothing when the expiration date arrives. A holder of an option has the right to buy or sell the stock but has no obligation to do so. Thus, if an investor buys an "ABC 50 call," he would lose money if the option were exercised when the price of ABC stock was at $50 or below. Hence, an investor would allow the option to expire. Moreover, the value of the call would be zero when its exercise price is above the market value of the stock at expiration. In contrast, a put holder would not exercise when the stock price exceeds the exercise price. The put's value in this case would be zero at expiration, and the holder would allow the put to expire.

2.3.3   Exercising Transactions

The third type of trade available to the option holder is the exercise. Most options on the CBOE and other exchanges offering options can be exercised at any time during the exercise period. To exercise, a holder of a stock option first would notify her broker, who would in turn give the investor's instructions to the clearing firm of the OCC where the initial trade was cleared. The clearing firm then notifies the OCC who, after examining its records, randomly selects a clearing firm that has a short position in the option being exercised. On notification from the OCC, the assigned clearing firm then would randomly select one of the brokerage firms on its account with a short position in the option. Finally, the assigned brokerage firm would select one of its customers who is short in the stock option (either on a first-in/first-out basis or randomly). The assigned writer must then fulfill the terms of the option: selling the called stock at the exercise price or in the case of a put, buying the stock at the strike price. The holder who exercises a call then can keep the stock or notify his broker to sell it in the stock market; the holder who exercises a put would instruct his broker to purchase the stock in the market and then give an exercise order on the put.

It should be noted that option holders who exercise and writers who are assigned are charged a stock commission cost because their trades involve the purchase and sale of stock in terms of the option contract and possibly later in the stock market. Such costs can be relatively high. It also should be noted that most brokerage firms stipulate in their contracts with option investors that if investors are remiss in exercising or closing a profitable option by expiration, they will exercise (not close) the option for them. If the brokerage contract is silent on this point, however, and if at expiration the holder forgets or fails to exercise, the OCC automatically will exercise the option if it is profitable for it to do so.

2.3.4   Closing Transactions

The fourth type of trade available is a closing transaction or offsetting order. Instead of exercising, an option holder could close his position by selling the option in the market, and an option writer, instead of being assigned, could close by buying the option. In each case, the holder or writer would instruct his broker to execute one of the six types of orders noted previously in discussing opening transactions. If Investor A bought an ABC July 50 call at $3 when ABC stock was trading at $48 and wanted to close his transaction near expiration when the stock hit $60, he could do so by selling the call. If he sold, the call should trade at a price at least equal to the difference between the underlying stock price and the exercise price ($60 – $50). Thus, he should be able to sell the option for at least $10 per call and realize a profit on the contract of at least $700 (($10 - $3)100) or $7 per call. If there is some time to expiration, the holder will be able to sell the call with a time value premium (TVP). Similarly, if Investor B sold an ABC 50 call at $10 when the stock was trading at $58, and near expiration the stock went to $53, then she could close by buying the call at a price at least equal to $3 per call. If she does close her transaction by buying the call back at $3, then she will realize a profit on the contract of $700. Again, if there is some time to expiration, then the cost of buying back the call will exceed the IV because the call will include a TVP. To close put positions would, of course, be similar to calls except that the holder would hope to sell when the stock price moved down, and the writer would hope to buy back her put when the stock traded up.

In discussing closing transactions, it should be emphasized that it is usually advantageous for an option holder to sell the option instead of exercising because the selling price includes a TVP, whereas exercising does not. Also, exercising incurs higher commission costs than closing. For example, in our OCC case, Investor A sold her ABC 50 March call at 12 when the ABC stock was trading at 60; the $12 price was equal to an IV of 10 plus a TVP of 2. If Investor A had exercised her call instead of simply closing it, she would have purchased the stock for X = 50 when it is worth 60, realizing a value equal to the IV of 10. Thus, by exercising instead of selling the option, she lost the TVP. Thus, an option holder in most cases should close her position instead of exercising. There are, however, some exceptions to the general rule of closing instead of exercising. For example, if an American option on a security that was to pay a high dividend that exceeded the TVP on the option, then it would be advantageous to exercise.

Because many options are closed, the amount of trading and thus the marketability of a particular option can be determined by ascertaining the number of option contracts that are outstanding at a given point in time. The number of option contracts outstanding is referred to as **open interest**. Thus, in terms of closing transactions, open interest represents the number of closing transactions on an option that could be made before it expires. The exchange, in turn, keeps track of the amount of opening and closing transactions that occur. For example, an opening order to buy 5 calls would increase open interest by 5, and a closing order to sell 5 calls would lower open interest by 5. By following the open interest presented in several financial papers, investors can determine the amount of activity on an option. (Exhibit 2.2-1 shows the open interest on the options on Dell Inc.)

2.4 MARGINS, TRANSACTION COSTS, AND TAXES

2.4.1 Margins

With the right to buy or sell securities, call and put holders need some assurance that if they decide to exercise, the writer will be able to deliver the stock (if it's a call) or cash (if it's a put). As noted, the OCC provides this guarantee. Like option holders, the OCC also needs to know that any writer they assign to an exercised option can deliver. Accordingly, to provide assurance to the OCC, the option exchanges set margin requirements on short option positions, requirements that brokerage firms are allowed to increase. The requirements specify an initial amount of cash or risk-free securities a writer must deposit in an account with the broker (initial margin) and the value of the account that must be maintained (maintenance margin). The cash or risk-free securities deposited are used to secure the position; it does not represent borrowing. This is different than purchasing stock on margin. A stock margin purchase means that part of the purchase is financed by borrowing. In fact, all option purchases, whether they involve calls or puts, must be paid for in full; margin purchases are not allowed in option buying. The reason for the rule is that the risk associated with call or put purchases is equivalent to the risk of buying securities on margin.

2.4.1.1 Naked Short Positions

For a naked call write, the initial margin requirement is the maximum of either (1) the call premium plus 20% of the market value of the stock less an amount equal to the difference in the exercise value and the stock value if the call is out of the money or (2) the call premium plus 10% of the market value of the stock. Mathematically, for a written call on a stock the initial margin requirement (M_0) is:

$$M_0 = \{Max[C_0 + .20S_0 - Max[X - S_0, 0]], [C_0 + .10S_0]\} N,$$

where
N = number of calls.

If a writer sells an ABC 50 call contract for $3 when ABC is selling for $48, then the initial margin requirement would be $1,060:

$$M_0 = \{Max[[\$3 + .20(\$48) - Max[\$50 - \$48, 0]], [\$3 + .10(\$48)]]\}\$100$$

$$M_0 = \{Max[\$10.60, \$7.80]\}100$$

$$M_0 = \$1,060$$

The writer would therefore have to set up a margin account with her brokerage firm worth $1,060 in cash or risk-free securities. Because part of the cash comes from the $300 premium received from the option sale, the writer needs to deposit only $760 cash or risk-free securities in her margin account.

The margin requirements for a naked put are similar to that of the call. The only difference is that in calculating the first value, the exercise price is subtracted from the stock price if the put is out of the money. Thus, for a naked put on a stock the initial margin requirement is:

$$M_0 = \{Max[[(P_0 + .20S_0 - Max[S_0 - X, 0]], [P_0 + .10S_0]]\} N$$

If a writer sells an ABC 50 put contract for $4 when the stock is trading for $49, then the initial margin would be $1,380:

$$M_0 = \{Max[[\$4 + .20(\$49) - Max[\$49 - \$50, 0]], [\$4 + .10(\$49)]]\} 100$$

$$M_0 = \{Max[\$13.80, \$8.90]\} 100$$

$$M_0 = \$1,380$$

With the premium proceeds of $400, the writer would need to deposit $980 to satisfy the initial margin requirement.

The maintenance margin requirements on naked option write positions are the same as the initial margin requirements. In the previous naked call example, if the closing price on ABC stock later increased from $48 to $50 while the call price stayed at $3, the investor's margin at the new price would increase from $1,060 to $1,300:

$$M_0 = \{Max[[(\$3 + .20(\$50) - Max[\$50 - \$50, 0)]], [\$3 + .10(\$50)]]\} 100$$

$$M_0 = \{Max[\$13, \$8]\} 100$$

$$M_0 = \$1,300$$

The writer would therefore have to deposit an additional $240 in her margin account or close the option position by buying the ABC 50 call. In contrast, if the price decreased, the call writer's margin requirement would decrease, and the writer could withdraw some cash from her margin account. Similar situations would exist for the put writer: If the price of the underlying security decreased, additional cash would be needed to maintain the margin requirement; if the security increased in price, cash could be withdrawn.

2.4.1.2 Covered Short Positions

In a covered call write position, the writer does not need to maintain a margin account because she owns the underlying stock. The writer is required, however, to either keep the stock in escrow at the brokerage firm or if the stock is held at the writer's bank, have the bank (for a fee) issue an "Escrow Receipt," which is a letter of guarantee from the bank to the brokerage firm stating it will deliver the writer's stock should there be an assignment. If the option expires or if the writer closes the position, she can have access to the stock.

In setting up a covered call write position, the writer can purchase the stock on margin (i.e., borrow to finance part of the purchase). In this case, the margin requirements on the leveraged security are the same as the requirements for any margin purchase provided the call option the writer is selling has an exercise price below or equal to the security's price (i.e., the call is an out-of-the-money or on-the-money option). However, if the writer sells a call when the underlying stock price is above the exercise price (in-the-money call), she can borrow only an amount equal to 50% of the exercise price (not the stock's price) to finance the purchase of the stock. In both cases, the writer can include the proceeds from the option sale as part of her margin. By way of example, suppose a writer sells an ABC 45 call for \$7 when ABC stock is trading at \$50 and then covers the position by purchasing the stock on margin. Because the stock price exceeds the exercise, the maximum amount of funds the writer can borrow would be: $\$22.50 = (.5)(\$45)$. Because the call premium of \$7 can be used to satisfy the margin requirement, the writer would need to deposit in her margin account only \$20.50: $(\$50.00 - \$22.50) - \$7 = \$20.50$.

For a covered put position in which the writer has sold a put and the underlying stock short, the brokerage house generally requires the covered writer to maintain the usual margin requirements on a short sale. However, analogous to the above rule for a margined covered call, if the price of the stock is below the exercise price when the put is sold (i.e., the put is in the money), the writer then is required to deposit additional cash in her short margin account equal to the difference in the exercise and security price $(X - S)$.

2.4.1.3 *Spreads*

Recall from Chapter 1 that a spread is formed by buying a call (put) and selling another call (put) with different terms. With a spread, the short option position is considered covered by the long option. As a result, the margin requirements on the short position are not as large as a naked option write position. As a general rule, if the spread results in a debit, the spreader must deposit the net cost of the spread in her margin account; if the spread results in a credit, the spreader must deposit the difference between the exercise prices.

2.4.1.4 *Summary*

Given the number of margin rules that apply to both securities and options as well as the number of possible strategies that exist from combining different security and option positions, the calculations of margins for option positions can become quite complex. The calculations we have discussed provide a general approach to apply to many of the other option positions. Investors considering more complex option position (spreads, straddles, combinations, and the like), though, should consult their brokers on what their possible margin requirements could be.

2.4.2 Cost of Trading

Through the option exchanges, brokers, dealers, market makers, specialists, and the OCC have created a network whereby an investor can buy and sell options in a matter of minutes. The cost of maintaining this complex system is paid for by investors through the commission costs they pay to their brokers, the bid-ask spread investors pay to market makers or specialists when they set up and then later close their positions, and the fees charged by the clearing firms of the OCC that are usually included in the brokerage commission.

TABLE 2.4-1 Sample Commission Cost Schedule

Transaction Value	Commission Rate
Under $2,500	$20 + .02 (Transaction Value)
$2,500 − $9,999	$45 + .01 (Transaction Value)
$10,000 and Over	$120 + .0025 (Transaction Value)
Minimum Charge	$30 for the first plus $2.00 per contract thereafter
Maximum Charge	$30 per contract on the first 5 contracts plus $20 per contract thereafter

2.4.2.1 Commissions

In accordance with the Security Act Amendment of 1975, commissions on all security transactions are negotiable between the investor and the broker. For stocks involving a medium-size trade, the commission costs range from approximately 1% of the total stock value for discount brokerage firms, which provide basically trade execution, to 2% for full brokerage firms, which provide current quotes, research reports, account executives, and other ancillary services. For institutional investors who trade in larger volumes, the percentages are typically lower.

The commission cost for trading options historically has been higher than for stock trading. As an example, a hypothetical but representative stock option commission schedule applicable to an individual investor is shown in Table 2.4-1. If an investor buys or sells one ABC 50 call contract for $2.50, then from Table 2.4-1, his total premium, commission costs, and minimum commission cost would be

Premium = ($2.50)(100) = $250

Commission Cost = (.02)($250) + $20 = $25

Minimum Commission Cost = $30

Thus, in this case, the investor would be charged the minimum commission of $30. If the investor bought 10 ABC 50 contracts for $2.50 per contract, then his premium, commission costs, and minimum and maximum charges would be

Premium = ($2.50)(100)(10) = $2,500

Commission Cost = (.01)($2,500) + $45 = $70

Minimum Commission Cost = ($30)(1) + ($2.00)(9) = $48

Maximum Commission Cost = ($30)(5) + ($20)(5) = $250

In this case, he would pay the broker $70 in commission costs for executing the trade unless he could negotiate a better rate.

In the first case, the commission costs are equal to 12% of the option value, and in the second example, the commission is equal to 2.80%. To the extent that the schedule is representative of the fees charged by most brokerage firms, these commission costs are relatively high when compared to the 1% to 2% commissions associated with stock trading.

The option buyer pays a commission when he buys the option and when he sells the option. In the first preceding example, the total round trip cost of buying and selling an option would therefore be $60. Similarly, the option writer pays a commission when she sells and then later if she closes by buying the option. Usually, no brokerage fee is charged if the option expires.

If the option holder exercises, he is charged a commission for buying (calling) or selling (putting) the stock. Because the call (put) holder in exercising would eventually (initially) sell (buy) the stock, the total commission costs to exercise an option instead of closing it is relatively high. For example, suppose an investor bought an ABC 50 call contract for $3 when the stock was trading at $49 and then near the expiration date exercised the call when the stock was at $60, subsequently selling the stock in the market. The investor's before-commission cost profit would be $700 = ($10 − $3)100. If the broker charges the same commission rate of 1% for exercising as she does for stock trading, and if the broker charges the rates specified in Table 2.4-1 for trading options, then the investor's total commission costs would be $140:

Commissions for:	Commission Cost
Option Purchase	$30
Exercise: ($50)(100)(.01)	$50
Stock Sale: ($60)(100)(.01)	$60
Total	$140

On the other hand, if near expiration, the call holder sells the ABC 50 call for $10, the before-commission costs profit still would be $700, but the commission costs would be only $70 instead of $140: $30 for the purchase and $40 for the sale ((.02)($10)(100) + 20). Thus, as we earlier emphasized, because of the commission costs associated with exercising (as well as the time value premium), it usually is preferable to close an option instead of exercising.

For the same reason, an option writer always should want to avoid being assigned. Like an exercise, a call or put writer who is assigned must buy or sell the stock and as a result is charged a stock commission cost. Because the writer does not control this situation, it is important that she be cognizant of those circumstances when a call holder would exercise. Such circumstances are noted in subsequent chapters.

2.4.2.2 Fees

Part of the commission fees investors pay their brokers goes to cover the fees charged by the clearing firms of the OCC for handling, recording, and intermediating option transactions. These fees range from $0.50 to $1.00 per contract. The OCC also imposes fees on market makers or specialists and other members for clearing their transactions. The fees are lower than those charged commission brokers handling the public's transactions.

2.4.2.3 Bid-Ask Spread

The primary function of a market maker and specialist is to ensure a continuous market. To do this, they stand ready to buy and sell securities at their bid and ask prices. The bid–ask spread thus represents their compensation for providing liquidity. To the investor, though, the bid–ask spread represents another transaction cost involved in trading securities. For example, if a market maker's bid price is $4 and her ask price is $4.50, an option buyer who paid $4.50 for the option and then immediately sold it for $4.00 would be paying the market maker $0.50 for the services of providing a continuous market.

In summary, we reiterate that although the transaction costs of trading options may seem high, such costs are necessary to provide a continuous market that can link buyers and sellers across the world. Whether the trading costs are too high is difficult to determine. The fact that commissions are negotiable, and brokers are competitive suggests that brokerage fees probably are priced efficiently.

2.4.2.4 *Taxes*

An investor's dollar return from an option position takes the form of a capital gain or loss. For a noncorporate taxpayer, short-term capital gains are taxed at the same rate as ordinary income, whereas long-term gains are taxed at a lower rates than ordinary income. Capital losses, in turn, are deductible up to the amount of the capital gains plus ordinary income up to $3,000 and can be carried forward indefinitely. For option buyers, taxable gains and losses result when they sell their options to close, when they sell stock from an exercised call, when they exercise a put, and when their options expire. For option writers, gains and losses occur when writers buy back their options to close, when they sell securities on an assigned call option, when they sell the securities obtained from an exercised put option that they have been assigned, and when the option expires.

For example, suppose an investor buys an ABC 50 call contract for $3 and then near expiration sells the call for $10 when the stock is trading for $60. The call buyer would therefore have a capital gain of $7 to include in her net capital gain or loss position for calculating her tax liability. Alternatively, if the call buyer exercised the ABC 50 call, then she would be considered as having bought the stock for a purchase price equal to the exercise price plus the call premium $(X + C)$. If the investor subsequently sells the stock in the market at $60, then a capital gain is realized, and the investor is subject to a tax. It should be noted that for exercised stock options, taxes apply to the gains or losses when they are realized. Thus, if the investor held onto the exercised stock for 2 years and then sold it for $40, she would have a capital loss of $13($= $40 - 53) to apply to her tax calculations for the year in which the sale was realized. Finally, if the option expires at the end of the period, then the option holder would have a capital loss equal to the option premium, $3 in this example.

Similar tax considerations apply to a put holder. Capital gains or losses resulting from buying a put and then selling it and capital losses (equal to the premium) resulting when the put expires must be included with all asset gains and losses in determining the taxpayer's net capital gain or loss position. Unlike the long call position, if a put holder exercises, the gain or loss is realized at the time of the exercise because the put holder is selling. In this case, the selling price of the stock is the exercise price minus the put premium $(X-P)$. For example, if a put holder bought an ABC 50 put for 3, then later bought the stock at $40 and exercised the put, her capital gain would be: $($50 - $3) - $40 = 7.

For option writers, if they close their positions by buying back the option, then for tax purposes, there is a capital gain or loss equal to the difference in the selling price when the option was sold and the purchased price when it is later closed (the order of transaction is not important). For example, if a put writer sells an ABC 50 put for $3 and then later closes the position by buying back the ABC 50 put for $10 when the stock is trading at $40, then there would be a $7 loss the investor would need to include in her capital loss calculations. Call and put writers also are subject to a tax on the option premium when the option expires. In the case of an assignment for a call writer, a capital loss is realized at the time of the exercise. To the assigned call writer the loss is equal to the difference between exercise price minus the call premium $(X - C$; the sale price) and the price the writer pays for the securities in the market. When a put writer is assigned, the exercise price she pays the option buyer who is exercising minus the put premium she receives from the put sale represents the purchased price on the security. A capital loss or possibly a gain, though, is not realized for most put options until the assigned writer sells the stock, which could be years later.

In discussing taxes on options, several additional points should be noted. First, commission costs are tax deductible. In computing the capital gains or losses, the commission paid when buying an option is added to the purchase price; when selling an option, the commission is subtracted from the selling price.

Second, although stock options are subject to taxes or deductions only when the capital gain or loss is realized, the same treatment does not apply to index, debt, and foreign currency options. Specifically, in accordance with tax rules, all realized and unrealized capital gains resulting from many non-stock option positions must be included in the investor's calculations of her net capital gains or losses for the year in which they are initiated. Capital losses are deductible from non-stock option positions, though, in the year in which they are realized. For example, if an investor realized a profit of $1,000 in 2007 from buying and selling a call option on the euro and also had a call option on the Canadian dollar that she had paid $1,000 for during the year and that was worth $2,000 at the end of the year, the investor would be subject to taxes on the $1,000 realized gain on the euro option and also the $1,000 unrealized gain on the Canadian dollar option.

Third, the tax laws disallow the deduction of capital losses in the case of a wash sale in which the security is sold at a loss at the end of the year but is replaced shortly afterwards with basically the same security. Under the tax rules, the purchase of a call option 30 days before or after the option's underlying stock has been sold for tax purposes at a loss constitutes a wash sale, making the loss nondeductible. Although call purchases in conjunction with the underlying security's sale represent a wash sale, an investor can buy a put option to protect a capital gain in a given year while deferring tax payments until the subsequent year. For example, an investor who wanted to sell her stock in December to realize a gain but did not want to pay taxes for that year could delay taxes a year and protect her position by buying an on-the-money January put option on the stock.

Finally, it should be noted that tax laws are quite detailed and always changing. As such, current regulations always should be checked. The material given in this section, in turn, should be considered only as an overview aimed at giving the reader a perspective and not one of providing instructions for tax preparation.

2.5   NON-STOCK OPTIONS

Since the early 1980s, the financial markets have seen a proliferation of option securities. Innovations include different stock index options, various interest rate options, options on a number of currencies, and options on futures contracts.

2.5.1   Stock Index Options

Trading in stock index options began in March 1983 when the CBOE introduced an option on the Standard and Poor's 100 index (S&P 100). Because of its hedging uses by institutional investors, this option quickly became one of the most highly traded options. In late April 1983, the American Stock Exchange began offering trading on an option on the Major Market Index (MMI), an index similar to the Dow Jones Industrial Average (DJIA). The introduction of the AMEX's option soon was followed by the New York Stock Exchange's listing of the NYSE stock index option and the Philadelphia exchange's Value Line index option (index of 1700 stocks) and the National Over-the-Counter index option (index of 100 OTC stocks). Today, the most popular index options include options on the Dow Jones Industrial Average (DJX), Nasdaq (NDX), Russell 2000 (RUT), S&P 100 (OEX), and the S&P 500 (SPX). Exhibit 2.5-1 shows quotes for some of these index options taken from the CBOE Web site on January 5, 2007.

Theoretically, an index option can be thought of as an option to buy (call) or sell (put) a portfolio of stocks comprising the index in their correct proportions. Unlike stock options, index options have a ***cash settlement*** feature. When such an option is exercised, the assigned writer pays the exercising holder the difference between the exercise price and the spot index at the close of trading on the exercising day. Thus, an index option is

EXHIBIT 2.5-1 Stock Index Option Quotes

(SPX.X) S&P 500 INDEX — Close: 1,418.34

Expiration: March-07

	Calls							Strike Price	Puts						
	Symbol	Last Trade	Change	Bid	Ask	Volume	Interest		Symbol	Last Trade	Change	Bid	Ask	Volume	Interest
	JXAMB	0.25	−1.75	0.25	0.3	1,504.00	2,234.00	1,410.00	SXZAB	19.1	2.2	16.9	18.5	1,034.00	14,854.00
	SXZMB	6.2	−2.7	6.3	7.3	4,266.00	27,871.00	1,410.00	SXZAC	14.5	0.5	13.7	14.7	1,571.00	11,490.00
	SXZMC	8.8	−1.4	8	9	1,277.00	16,176.00	1,415.00	SXZAD	11.3	−0.2	10.6	11.8	4,302.00	33,612.00
	SXZMD	9.1	−3.8	9.9	10.9	6,058.00	14,031.00	1,420.00	JXAAE	0.25	−0.8	0.15	0.3	1,461.00	1,301.00
	JXAME	6.5	−6	5.7	6.7	461	349	1,425.00	SXZME	13	−2	11.8	13.4	15,529.00	37,695.00
	SXZAF	6.2	−0.5	5.8	6.5	3,739.00	21,928.00	1,430.00	SXZMF	15.4	−1.8	14.6	16.2	91	9,387.00
	SXZAG	4.4	−0.1	4	4.5	6,401.00	23,211.00	1,435.00	SXZMG	25	2.3	17.7	19.3	20	2,734.00

(NDX.X) NASDAQ–100 INDEX — Close: 1792.91

Expiration: March-07

	Calls							Strike Price	Puts						
	Symbol	Last Trade	Change	Bid	Ask	Volume	Interest		Symbol	Last Trade	Change	Bid	Ask	Volume	Interest
	NDYAV	23.4	12	24.6	24.8	536	3,547.00	1,795.00	NDYMV	21.2	−29.1	20.1	20.6	332	1,792.00
	NDYAP	21.8	12.3	21.9	22.1	2,476.00	10,314.00	1,800.00	NDYMP	22.8	−23.5	22.3	22.9	498	6,513.00
	NDYAW	16.2	9.8	17	17.5	1,852.00	2,301.00	1,810.00	NDYMW	28.9	−24.2	27.2	28	129	666
	NDYAG	11	6.4	11.1	11.5	2,742.00	10,441.00	1,825.00	NDYMG	37	−32.3	36.4	37.1	162	4,092.00
	NDYAX	9.9	6.2	9.6	10	643	6,028.00	1,830.00	NDYMX	41.7	−28.2	39.6	40.6	30	166

(OEX.X) S&P 100 INDEX — Close: 551

Expiration: March-07

	Calls							Strike Price	Puts						
	Symbol	Last Trade	Change	Bid	Ask	Volume	Interest		Symbol	Last Trade	Change	Bid	Ask	Volume	Interest
	XEOAK	7	−1	9.1	10	151	1,654.00	655	XEOMK	2.5	−0.9	2.1	2.75	113	1,540.00
	OEYAL	6.1	0.1	5.8	6.4	2,013.00	6,731.00	660	OEYML	4.3	−1	4.1	4.4	4,756.00	7,251.00
	OEYAM	3.3	0	3.2	3.5	3,512.00	5,638.00	665	OEYMM	6.6	−1.5	6.6	6.8	1,414.00	2,426.00

(DJX.X) 1/100 DOW JONES INDUSTRIAL AVERAGE INDEX — Close: 124.81

Expiration: March-07

	Calls							Strike Price	Puts						
	Symbol	Last Trade	Change	Bid	Ask	Volume	Interest		Symbol	Last Trade	Change	Bid	Ask	Volume	Interest
	DJWAS	2	−0.7	2.3	2.4	1	2,767.00	123	DJWMS	0.35	−0.2	0.3	0.4	36	8,822.00
	DJWAT	1.55	0	1.5	1.65	9,276.00	24,346.00	124	DJWMT	0.65	−0.05	0.55	0.6	2,777.00	8,548.00
	DJWAU	1.05	0.1	0.9	1	1,418.00	16,948.00	125	DJWMU	0.95	−0.15	0.9	0.95	339	5,074.00
	DJWAV	0.5	0	0.4	0.5	542	3,500.00	126	DJWMV	1.5	−0.3	1.4	1.5	118	2,869.00
	DJWAW	0.15	−0.1	0.15	0.25	99	8,176.00	127	DJWMW	2.45	−0.15	2.1	2.25	72	432
	DJWAX	0.05	−0.15	0.05	0.1	71	1,551.00	128	DJWMX	3.8	1.45	2.95	3.1	25	1,628.00

Source: CBOE Web site: www.cboe.com, January 5, 2007.
To access quotes from the CBOE, go to CBOE.com, click on "Delayed Quotes Beta" (under "Quotes"), and then click on "Option Chain."

viewed more correctly as an option giving the holder the right to purchase (call) or sell (put) cash at a specific exercise price. Specifically, for an index call option:

> **DEFINITION:** A call option on a stock index gives the holder the right to purchase an amount of cash equal to the closing spot index (S_t) on the exercising day at the call's exercise price. To settle, the exercising holder receives a cash settlement of $S_t - X$ from the assigned writer.

For example, a May 1200 S&P 500 call gives the holder the right to buy cash equal to the closing spot index on the exercising day for 1200 (as discussed following, there also is a multiplier). If the holder exercises when the spot index is 1300, he in effect is exercising the right to buy $1,300 of cash for $X = \$1,200$. With cash settlement, the assigned writer simply pays the holder $100.

The put option on a stock index, on the other hand, gives the holder the right to sell cash equal to the spot index value:

> **DEFINITION:** A put option on a stock index gives the holder the right to sell cash equal to the closing spot index on the exercising date at the put's exercise price. To settle, the exercising holder receives a cash settlement amount of $X - S_t$ from the assigned writer.

Thus, the holder of a May 1200 S&P 500 put who exercises the put when the spot index is at 1100 could view exercising as the equivalent to selling $1,100 cash to the assigned writer for $1,200. The writer would settle by paying the holder $X - S_t = \$100$.

The cash settlement feature of index options is one characteristic that differentiates them from stock options. Several other differentiating features of index options should be noted. First, the size of an index option is equal to a multiple of the index value. The S&P 100 and S&P 500 index options, for example, have contract multiples of $100. Thus, the actual exercise price on the preceding May 1200 put contract on the S&P 500 is $\$120,000 = (1200)(\$100)$. Second, the expiration features on many index options are similar to stock options, with most expiring on the third Friday of the expiration month. However, some index options, such as the S&P 100, have a shorter expiration cycle consisting of the current month, the next month, and third month from the present. The CBOE also offers longer maturity contracts on indexes that last up to 3 years as well as flex options on indices. Third, American index options have an *end-of-the-day exercise* feature. When an index option is exercised, the closing value of the spot index on the exercising day is used to determine the cash settlement. Because the spot index is computed continuously throughout the day, it is possible for a holder to exercise an in-the-money call early in the day only to have it closed at the end of the day out of the money (in such a case, the holder pays the writer the difference between X and S_t). Thus, an index option holder should wait until late in the day before giving his exercise notice. The assigned writer, in turn, is notified of the option assignment on the subsequent business day, at which time he is required to pay the difference in the exercise price and the closing index price. Fourth, a number of index options are European. Finally, the tax treatment on index option positions differs from stock options in that all realized and unrealized gains on index options that occur during the year are subject to taxes, and all realized and unrealized losses occurring during the year can offset an investor's capital gains.

2.5.2 Foreign Currency Options

In 1982, the Philadelphia Stock Exchange (PHLX) became the first organized exchange to offer trading in foreign currency options. Today, options on currencies traded on the PHLX include the Australian dollar, British pound, Canadian dollar, euro, Japanese yen, and Swiss franc. The contract sizes for many of PHLX's options are equal to half the size of the currency's futures listed on the Chicago Mercantile Exchange (CME). For example, the foreign currency call option contract on the British pound (BP) requires (on exercise) the purchase of 31,250 BP, whereas a long BP futures contract requires the purchase of 62,500 BP. If a foreign currency call (put) is exercised, the exercising holder is required to deliver dollars (foreign currency) to a bank designated by the OCC. The assigned writer is required to deliver the foreign currency (dollars) to the bank. Many of the currency options listed on the PHLX are both European and American. The quoted currency option prices found in financial publications and on Web sites (www.phlx.com) are in terms of the U.S. dollar prices for the purchase or sale of one unit of foreign currency. Many of the prices are quoted in cents (Japanese yen is in hundredths of a cent). Thus, the call option on the euro with an exercise price of 130 cents and exercise month of February (see Exhibit 2.5-2) would give the holder the right to buy 62,500 euros for $81,250 (= ($1.30/euro)(62,500 euros)). With the premium (ask price) on the 130 euro call at 1.41 cents, the cost of the euro contract is $881.25 (= ($0.0141/euro)(62,500 euros)).

Foreign currency options also are traded on a number of derivative exchanges outside the United States (see Exhibit 1.1-1). In addition to offering foreign currency futures, the CME and other futures exchanges also offers options on foreign currency futures.

2.5.3 Futures Options

Option contracts on stocks, debt securities, foreign currency, and indices are sometimes referred to as *spot options* or *options on actuals*. This reference is to distinguish them from *options on futures* contracts (also called options on futures, futures options, and commodity options). A futures option gives the holder the right to take a position in a futures contract. Specifically, a call option on a futures contract gives the holder the right to take a long position in the underlying futures contract (agreement to buy the underlying asset at a specific price on a specified date) when she exercises and requires the writer to take the corresponding short position in the futures (agreement to sell the underlying asset at the specified price on a specified date). Futures options are discussed along with futures contracts in Part III.

The current U.S. market for futures options began in 1982 when the Commodity Futures Trading Commission (CFTC) initiated a pilot program in which it allowed each futures exchange to offer one option on one of its futures contracts. In 1987, the CFTC gave the exchanges permanent authority to offer futures options. Currently, the most popular futures options are the options on the financial futures: S&P 500, T-bond, T-note, Eurodollar deposit, and the major foreign currencies. In addition to options on financial futures contracts, futures options also are available on gold, precious metals, agriculture commodities, and energy products.

2.5.4 Interest Rate Options

Many different types of interest rate options are available on the organized futures and options exchanges in Chicago, London, Singapore, and other major cities. Exchange-traded interest rate options include both futures options and spot options. On the U.S. exchanges, the most heavily traded options are the CME's and CBT's futures options on T-bonds, T-notes, and Eurodollar contracts. The CBOE, AMEX, and PHLX have offered

EXHIBIT 2.5-2 Foreign Currency Option Quotes

PHLX EURO	Close	1.3002								
Symbol	Last	Time	Net	Bid	Ask	Open	High	Low	Close	Vol
XEU	1.3002	13:00:54	−0.01	0	0	1.3088	1.3088	1.2992	1.3086	0

	Calls						Feb 2007		Puts					
Ticker	Last	Net	Bid	Ask	Vol	Open Interest	Strike	Ticker	Last	Net	Bid	Ask	Vol	Open Interest
.XEBBJ	4.97	0.00	1.9	2	0	0	129.0	.XEBNJ	0.56	0.00	0.64	0.74	0	8
.XEUBN	2.21	0.00	1.31	1.41	0	0	130.0	.XEUNN	1.04	+0.44	1.06	1.16	2	5
.XEBBR	0	0.00	0.84	0.94	0	0	131.0	.XEBNR	0.84	0.00	1.6	1.7	0	5
.XEUBV	1.62	0.00	0.54	0.64	0	8	132.0	.XEUNV	1.51	0.00	2.26	2.35	0	10
.XEBBC	0	0.00	0.38	0.43	0	0	133.0	.XEBNC	0	0.00	2.37	2.52	0	0
.XEUBG	0	0.00	0.25	0.3	0	0	134.0	.XEUNG	2.42	0.00	3.95	4.1	0	100
.XEBBK	0	0.00	0.17	0.22	0	0	135.0	.XEBNK	3.94	0.00	0.0	0	0	0

Source: Philadelphia Exchange Web site: www.PHLX.com, January 5, 2007.
To access quotes from the Philadelphia Exchange, go to PHLX.com, click on "Quotes & Trade Info."

options on actual Treasury securities and Eurodollar deposits. These spot options, however, proved to be less popular than futures options and have been delisted. A number of non-U.S. exchanges, though, do list options on actual debt securities, typically government securities. For example, many interest rate options listed on the European Options Exchange are spot options.

2.6   OTC OPTIONS

The Over-the-Counter Market (OTC) is an informal exchange for the trading of over 70,000 stocks and many corporate and municipal bonds, investment fund shares, mortgage-backed securities, shares in limited partnerships, and Treasury and federal agency securities. There are no membership or listing requirements for trading on the OTC; any security can be traded. The OTC can be described as a market of brokers and dealers linked to each other by a computer, telephone, and telex communications system. To trade, dealers must register with the Security Exchange Commission (SEC). As dealers, they can quote their own bid and asked prices on the securities they deal, and as brokers, they can execute a trade with a dealer providing a quote. The securities traded on the OTC market are those in which a dealer decides to take a position. Dealers on the OTC market range from regional brokerage houses making a market in a local corporation's stock or bond, to large financial companies making markets in Treasury securities, to investment bankers dealing in the securities they had previously underwritten, to dealers in federal agency securities and municipal bonds. The OTC market also includes dealers who offer forward contracts, interest rate derivative products, and options on currency and debt securities.

In the OTC option market, currency and interest rate option contracts are negotiable, with buyers and sellers entering directly into an agreement. Thus, the dealer's market provides option contracts that are tailor-made to meet the holder's or writer's specific needs. The market, though, does not have a clearinghouse to intermediate and guarantee the fulfillment of the terms of the option contract nor market makers or specialists to ensure continuous markets; OTC options, therefore, lack marketability. Because each OTC option has unique features, the secondary market is limited. Prior to expiration, holders of OTC options who want to close their position may be able to do so by selling their positions back to the original option writers or possibly to an OTC dealer who is making a market in the option. This type of closing is more likely to occur if the option writer is a dealer that can hedge option position and also if the option is relatively standard (e.g., OTC option on a T-bond). Because of this inherent lack of marketability, the premium on OTC options are higher than exchange-trade ones. For example, the bid–ask spread on an OTC T-bond is typically twice that of an exchange-traded T-bond futures option. Finally, because there is no option clearing corporation to guarantee the option writer, OTC options also have different credit structures than exchange-traded options. Depending on who the option writer is, the contract may require initial and maintenance margins to be established.

2.6.1   OTC Currency Options

The OTC currency market is a sophisticated dealer's market for currency. In this market, banks and investment houses provide tailor-made foreign currency option contracts for their customers, primarily multinational corporations. Compared to exchange-traded options, options in the OTC market are larger in contract size, often European, and are available on more currencies.

2.6.2   OTC Interest Rate Options[3]

Like OTC currency options, the OTC market for interest rate options is also large, consisting of debt and interest-sensitive securities and products. Currently, security regulations in the United States prohibit off-exchange trading in options on futures. All U.S. OTC options are therefore options on spot securities. The OTC markets in and outside the United States consist primarily of dealers who make markets in the underlying spot security, investment banking firms, and commercial banks. OTC options are primarily used by financial institutions and nonfinancial corporations to hedge their interest rate positions. The options contract offered in the OTC market include spot options on Treasury securities and special types of interest rate products such as interest rate calls and puts, caps, floors, and collars. These special instruments are examined in Chapter 16.

When options are structured on Treasury securities, terms such as the specific underlying security, its maturity and size, the option's expiration, and the delivery are all negotiated. For OTC Treasury options, the underlying security is often a recently auctioned Treasury (on-the-run bond), although some selected existing securities (off-the-run securities) are used. In such cases, OTC dealers often offer or will negotiate contracts giving the holder to right to purchase or sell a specific T-bond or T-note. For example, a dealer might offer a T-bond call option to a fixed income manager giving him the right to buy a specific T-bond maturing in year 2016 and paying a 6% coupon with a face value of $100,000. Because the option contract specifies a particular underlying bond, the maturity of the bond as well as its value will be changing during the option's expiration period. For example, a 1-year call option on the 15-year bond, if held to expiration, would be a call option to buy a 14-year bond. Note that in contrast, a spot T-bill option contract offered by a dealer on the OTC market usually calls for the delivery of a T-bill meeting the specified criteria (e.g., principal of $1 million and maturity of 91 days). With this clause, a T-bill option is referred to as a *fixed deliverable* bond, and unlike specific-security T-bond options, T-bill options can have expiration dates that exceed the T-bill's maturity.

Another feature of a spot T-bond or T-note option offered or contracted on the OTC market is that the underlying bond or note can pay coupon interest during the option period. As a result, if the option holder exercises on a non-coupon-paying date, the accrued interest on the underlying bond must be paid. For a T-bond or T-note option, this is done by including the accrued interest as part of the exercise price. Like futures options, the exercise prices on a spot T-bond or T-note option are quoted as an index equal to a proportion of a bond with a face value of $100 (e.g., 95). If the underlying bond or note has a face value of $100,000, then the exercise price would be

$$X = \left[\frac{\text{Index}}{100} \right] (\$100,000) + \text{Accrued Interest}$$

Finally, the prices of spot T-bond and T-note options are typically quoted in terms of points and 32nds of a point. Thus, the price of a call option on a $100,000 T-bond quoted at 1 5/32 is $1,156.25 = (1.15625/100)(\$100,000)$.

2.7   CONCLUSION

In this chapter, we've examined the characteristics of the option exchange market where many puts and calls are traded. We've also discussed the margin requirements, transactions

---

[3] This section assumes some knowledge of bonds and Treasury securities. For a primer on bond fundamentals, see supplemental Appendix C at the end of the text.

costs, and taxes involved in trading options, the different types of non-stock options, and the OTC option market. With this foundation, we are now ready to expand our treatment of options by looking at the many sophisticated positions that can be created with these derivatives.

Web Information:

Information on the CBOE: www.cboe.com.

For links to the Web sites of other exchanges, see Exhibit 1.1-1.
For general information and other links:
www.ace.uiuc.edu/ofor/resource.htm.
For market information and prices on futures options, go to
www.cme.com and www.cbt.com.
For information on NYSE stock exchanges, go to www.nyse.com.
For information on OTC market, go to
www.nasd.com and www.nasdaq.com.
For information on currency options and currency futures options go to
www.phlx.com and www.cme.com.

KEY TERMS

marketability	registered option trader	initial margin
open outcry	order book official	maintenance margin
continuous market	option clearing corporation	spot options
specialist	exercise limit	futures options
market maker	position limit	index options
option cycle	open interests	cash settlement
option class	opening transaction	OTC options
option series	expiring transaction	fixed deliverable bond
LEAPS	closing transaction	
flex options	offset	

SELECTED REFERENCES

Chance, D. M. *An Introduction to Options and Futures*, 4th ed., Orlando, FL: Dryden Press, 1998, Chapter 1.

Chicago Board Options Exchange. *Market Statistics 2005*, Chicago: Chicago Board Options Exchange, 2005.

Chicago Board Options Exchange. *Reference Manual*. Chicago: Chicago Board Options Exchange, 2005.

Chicago Board Options Exchange and Options Clearing Corporation. *Constitution and Rules*. Chicago: Commerce Clearing House, 2005.

Cox, J. C., and M. Rubinstein. *Options Markets*, Englewood Cliffs, NJ: Prentice-Hall, 1985, Chapters 1 and 3.

Hull, J. C. *Option, Futures, and Other Derivatives,* 5th ed., Upper Saddle River, NJ: Prentice Hall, 2003, Chapter 7.

PROBLEMS AND QUESTIONS

1. Explain the purpose and functions of the market maker and specialist on the option exchanges. What is the difference between them?

2. Explain the role and functions of the Option Clearing Corporation.

3. Suppose in February, Ms. X sold a June ABC 100 call contract to Mr. Z for $5 and then later closed her position by buying a June ABC 100 call for $7 from Mr. Y. Explain how the OCC would handle these contracts.

4. Explain the various types of option transactions.

5. Explain the adjustments in the option contracts the option exchanges would undertake for the following cases:

   a. An ABC 50 call contract with the ABC Company declaring a 3-for-2 stock split.

   b. An ABC 50 put with the ABC Company declaring a 5% stock dividend.

   c. An ABC 50 call with the ABC Company declaring a $10 cash dividend.

6. Explain how the organized exchanges have contributed to the growth of option trading.

7. Determine the initial margin requirements you would have if you were to sell a December ABC 60 call for $5 when ABC stock is trading at $58. How much cash would you have to deposit with your broker to satisfy your margin requirement? How much additional cash would you need to deposit if the maintenance margin requirement is the same as the initial, the price of ABC stock increased to $62, and the price of the 60 call option rose to $6?

8. What would your initial margin be if you sold a June ABC 40 put for $4 when the price of ABC stock was trading at $38? How much cash would you have to deposit with your broker? How much additional cash would you need to deposit if the maintenance margin requirement is the same as the initial, the price of ABC stock decreased to $36, and the price of the 40 put option increased to $6.50?

9. Using the commission schedule in Table 2.4-1, compute the commission costs on the following transactions:

   a. An ABC 80 call contract priced at $4 per call.

   b. Ten ABC 50 put contracts priced at $5 per put.

   c. Thirty XYZ 100 call contracts priced at $5 per call.

10. Explain why option holders should, in most cases, close their options instead of exercising. Under what condition would it be beneficial to exercise a call option early?

11. Explain how options offered by dealers on the OTC market differ from exchange-traded options.

12. Bullet Questions:

    a. What term is used to describe the number of option contracts outstanding?

    b. What exchange listed and then later delisted spot T-bill spot options?

    c. A September 1200 S&P 500 futures call option gives the holder the right to do what?

    d. A September 1200 S&P 500 futures put option gives the holder the right to do what?

WEB EXERCISES

1. Determine the recent prices on an exchange options on a stock by going to either www.cboe.com or www.wsj.com/free.

2. Determine the recent prices on currency option listed on the Philadelphia Exchange by going to www.phlx.com.

CHAPTER 3

OPTION STRATEGIES

3.1 INTRODUCTION

In Chapter 1, we defined the six fundamental option strategies and the straddle and spread in terms of their profit and stock price relationships near expiration. As we noted in Chapter 1, one of the important features of an option is that it can be combined with positions in the underlying security and other options to generate a number of different investment strategies. For example, a speculator who expected a stock to increase in the future but didn't want to assume the risk inherent in a stock or call purchase position could form a bull call spread. In contrast, a speculator who expected a stock to be stable over the near term could, in turn, try to profit by forming a straddle write (selling a call and a put). Thus, by combining different option positions, speculators can obtain positions that match their expectation and their desired risk-return preference. In this chapter, we extend the discussion of option strategies in Chapter 1 to a more detailed analysis of the fundamental strategies and introduce some new ones that can be used for either speculation or hedging.

3.2 CALL PURCHASE

The call purchase is one of the more popular option strategies. It often is viewed by investors as a leveraged alternative to purchasing stock. As we discussed in Chapter 1, compared to a long stock position, the purchase of a call yields higher expected returns, but like buying stock on margin, it also is more risky. For example, as shown in Figure 3.2-1, the stock purchased at $50 yields only a 20% rate of return (excluding any dividends) when its price reaches $60, whereas a 50 call option with a premium of $3 yields a rate of return of 233% (($10 – $3)/$3) when exercised or sold at its intrinsic value of $10 at expiration. In contrast, if the stock decreased to $40 (near expiration), then the loss on the stock would be 20% compared to a 100% loss on the call. Thus, like a leveraged stock purchase, a long call position yields a higher return-risk combination than a stock purchase.

In addition to providing investors with a short-run alternative to a long stock position, call purchases also can be used by investors as a way to purchase stock when they are temporarily illiquid. For example, suppose an investor has funds tied up in illiquid securities at a time when she wanted to buy the stock of a company that is expected to release unexpectedly good earnings information. The investor could acquire the stock first by buying a call option on it, then, after becoming liquid, exercising the option.

3.2.1 Follow-up Strategies

A call purchase position is used when the price of the stock is expected to increase. Expected stock increases could be based on fundamental factors such as an anticipated increase in a company's earnings, technical factors related to stock price movements, or market factors such as an expectation of national economic growth occurring in the future. Whatever the reason, once an investor has selected a call option on a stock, he must monitor the position

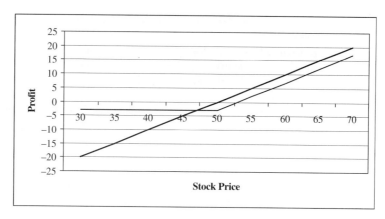

FIGURE 3.2-1 Call and Stock Purchase Profit Graphs

and determine what to do with the option if the price of the stock changes differently than he expected. Strategies used after setting up an initial option position are known as *follow-up actions*. These strategies, in turn, can be classified as either *aggressive follow-up strategies*, used when the price of the stock moves to a profitable position, and *defensive follow-up strategies*, employed when the stock price moves to an actual or potentially unprofitable position.

To see the types of aggressive strategies one can use, consider the case of an investor who, in October, buys an ABC December 60 call contract for $3 per call when the stock is trading at $58. Furthermore, suppose that shortly after buying the call, the price of ABC stock unexpectedly increases to $68, causing the 60 call to increase to $9. Faced with this positive development, the call investor has a number of alternatives open to her. First, the investor could *liquidate* by selling the 60 call for $9, realizing a profit of $600. If the investor strongly feels that the stock will continue to rise, then a second follow-up strategy simply is to *do nothing*. If the call purchaser wants to gain more than just $600—in case the stock continues to rise—but does not want to lose if the stock declines, she could follow up the call purchase strategy by creating a *spread*. As we discussed in Chapter 1, a call spread is formed by buying and selling a call option simultaneously on the same stock but with different terms. If, after the price of the stock reaches $68, the investor expected the price would continue to rise, then she might want to consider a *roll-up* follow-up strategy. As the name implies, a roll-up strategy requires moving to a higher exercise price. This can be accomplished in several ways. For example, our investor could sell the 60 call and use all of the $900 proceeds to buy December 70 calls. Finally, the call purchaser could set up a *combination* as a follow-up strategy. A combination purchase is defined as a long position in a call and a put on the same stock with different terms. For aggressive follow-up strategies, a combination could be formed by buying a put with a higher exercise price. See Exhibit 3.2-1 for a more detailed analysis of these aggressive follow-up strategies.

EXHIBIT 3.2-1 Aggressive Follow-Up Strategies for a Call Purchase

Consider the case of an investor who, in October, buys an ABC December 60 call contract for $3 per call when the stock is trading at $58. Furthermore, suppose that shortly after buying the call, the price of ABC stock unexpectedly increases to $68, causing the 60 call to increase to $9. Faced with this positive development, the call investor has a number of alternatives open to her.

1. First, the investor could **liquidate** by selling the 60 call for $9, realizing a profit of $600. The advantage of liquidating is certainty: The investor knows that even if the price of ABC stock declines,

she will still earn $600. The disadvantage of liquidating, of course, is the opportunity loss if the stock increases in price.

2. If the investor strongly feels that the stock will continue to rise, then a second follow-up strategy simply is to **do nothing**. As shown in column 3 in this exhibit's table, if the stock reaches $80 at expiration (T), then the investor would realize a profit of $1,700 by selling the call at a price equal to its intrinsic value of $20, $1,100 more than if she had liquidated. Of course, if the price of the stock decreases after reaching $68 and moves to $60 or less, then the investor loses the premium of $300 and will regret not liquidating the call back when the stock was at $68.

3. If the call purchaser wants to gain more than just $600—in case the stock continues to rise—but does not want to lose if the stock declines, she could follow up the call purchase strategy by creating a **spread**. A call spread is formed by buying and selling a call option simultaneously on the same stock but with different terms. In the case of aggressive follow-up strategies, a spread often is created by selling a call with a higher exercise price. In terms of our example, suppose the investor sells an ABC December 70 call for $3 when the stock is at $68. As shown in Column 4 of the table, at expiration, the investor would realize a limited profit of $1,000 if the price of ABC stock were $70 or above and would break even if the stock fell to $60 or less. Thus, the spread would yield the investor more profit than the liquidating strategy if the stock price were to increase and would lose less than the do-nothing strategy if the stock price were to fall.

4. If, after the price of the stock reaches $68, the expectation is that the price will continue to rise, then one might want to consider a roll-up follow-up strategy. As the name implies, a **roll-up strategy** requires moving to a higher exercise price. This can be accomplished in several ways. For example, our investor could sell the 60 call and use all of the $900 proceeds to buy 3 December 70 calls at $3. As shown in Column 5 of the table, this roll-up strategy would provide the investor with a relatively substantial gain near expiration if the stock were to increase in price but also would engender losses if the stock were to decline. To minimize the range in potential profits and losses, the investor alternatively could implement a roll-up strategy by selling the 60 call and then using only $600 of the $900 profit to buy two 70 calls. The profit and stock price relation for the initial call purchase with this follow-up strategy is shown in Column 6. As can be seen, the investor has the initial investment covered if the stock decreases and will gain if the price rises but not by as much as the first roll-up strategy.

(1) S_T	(2) Liquidate	(3) Do Nothing	(4) Spread	(5) Roll-up	(6) Roll-up	(7) Combination
$50	$600	−$300	$0	−$300	$0	$1400
55	600	−300	0	−300	0	900
60	600	−300	0	−300	0	400
63	600	0	300	−300	0	400
64	600	100	400	−300	0	400
65	600	200	500	−300	0	400
66	600	300	600	−300	0	400
67	600	400	700	−300	0	400
70	600	700	1000	−300	0	400
71	600	800	1000	0	200	500
75	600	1,200	1000	1200	1000	900
80	600	1,700	1000	2700	2000	1400
85	600	2,200	1000	4200	3000	1900

5. Finally, the call purchaser could set up a combination as a follow-up strategy. A combination purchase is defined as a long position in a call and a put on the same stock with different terms. For aggressive follow-up strategies, a combination could be formed by buying a put with a higher exercise price. The impact of this combination strategy is shown in Column 7 for the case in which our investor buys an ABC December 70 put for $3.

EXHIBIT 3.2-2   Defensive Follow-Up Strategies for a Call Purchase

Consider the case of an investor who, in October, buys an ABC December 60 call contract for $3 per call when the stock is trading at $58. Furthermore, suppose that shortly after buying the call, the price of ABC stock unexpectedly decreases to $55, causing the 60 call to decrease to $1.50. Faced with this negative development, the call investor has a number of alternatives open to her.

1. As shown in the table in this exhibit, if the holder **liquidated**, she would realize a loss of $150 compared to a $300 loss if she did nothing and the price of the stock stayed below the exercise price near expiration.

2. In contrast to the **do-nothing strategy**, liquidating does eliminate potential profit if the stock price reverses itself.

3. If the investor thinks, however, that the price decline is a signal of further price decreases, she could create a **spread** and possibly realize a profit (if the stock falls). As shown in Column 4, if the holder combined the long position in the 60 call with a short position in a 50 call trading for $7, the investor would earn a limited profit of $400 if the stock reached $50 or less. However, if after hitting $55, the stock increases to $60 or higher, the investor would lose $600.

(1) S_T	(2) Liquidate Sell $60 Call at $1.50	(3) Do Nothing	(4) Spread Keep 60 Call and sell 50 Call at $7	(5) Roll-Down Spread Sell 2 60 calls at $1.50 each and buy 55 call at $3
$40	−$150	$−300	$400	$−300
45	−150	−300	400	−300
50	−150	−300	400	−300
54	−150	−300	0	−300
55	−150	−300	−100	−300
58	−150	−300	−400	0
60	−150	−300	−600	200
63	−150	0	−600	200
65	−150	200	−600	200
70	−150	700	−600	200
75	−150	1,200	−600	200
80	−150	1,700	−600	200
85	−150	2,200	−600	200

4. Finally, if the holder felt that the stock would move back up but only modestly, she could create a **roll-down spread** by selling the 60 call plus another 60 call for $1.50 each and then using the $300 from the sale to buy a 55 call for $3. Thus, the investor would be long in a 55 call and short in a 60 call. As shown in Column 5, the investor would realize a limited profit of $200 if the stock increased to $60 or higher near expiration with this spread but would lose $300 if the stock stayed at $55 or decreased.

If, after purchasing a call, the price of the stock decreases, the investor then needs to consider defensive follow-up strategies. With some modifications, defensive follow-up strategies are similar to aggressive ones. The investor could either liquidate, hoping to minimize her losses by selling the call at a price reflecting a time value premium; do nothing, hoping that the price decrease is only temporary; or create a spread or roll-down to a lower exercise price, hoping to profit if the stock price changes moderately. See Exhibit 3.2-2 for examples of these different defensive follow-up strategies.

The aggressive and defensive follow-up strategies shown in Exhibits 3.2-1 and 3.2-2 are just some of the follow-ups an investor can use. Spreads or combinations using different expiration dates and/or expiration prices, liquidating only part of the initial strategy, investing more equity in a different call, or selling more than one call are examples of follow-up strategies an investor can employ. Whatever the strategy, though, it is important to remember that there is no optimum; rather, the correct follow-up depends ultimately on where the investor thinks the stock eventually will close and on how strongly she believes in that forecast.

3.2.2 Call Purchases in Conjunction With Other Positions

3.2.2.1 Simulated Put

Purchasing a call and selling the underlying stock short on a one-to-one basis yields the same type of profit and stock price relationship as a put purchase. This strategy is known as a *simulated put*.

In the table in Exhibit 3.2-3, the profit and stock price relation at expiration is shown for an investor who sold 100 shares of ABC stock short at $50 per share and purchased an ABC June 50 call contract at $3. The total profit and stock price relations at expiration are plotted in the table's accompanying figure. As can be seen, the simulated put strategy yields the same relationship as the purchase of a 50 put at $3.

Two strategies with the same profit and stock price relationships are referred to as *equivalent strategies*. Note, however, that although the put purchase and the simulated put formed with a long call and short stock position are equivalent in terms of their profit and stock price relations, they are not identical. Given the put–call parity relation discussed in Chapter 1, the equilibrium price of the 50 put is not likely to be $3 when the 50 call is priced at $3. Thus, the short sale and call purchase strategy do not yield an identical long 50 put position. To form an identical long put position with a put price consistent with put–call parity, a *synthetic put* requires not only buying the call and shorting the stock

EXHIBIT 3.2-3   Simulated Put—Short 100 Shares of Stock at 50 and the Purchase of One 50 Call Contract at 3

S_T	Call Profit (Max[$S_T - X, 0$] − C)	Profit on Short Stock (50 − S_T)	Total Profit
30	−300	2,000	1,700
40	−300	1,000	700
47	−300	300	0
50	−300	0	−300
60	700	−1,000	−300
70	1,700	−2,000	−300

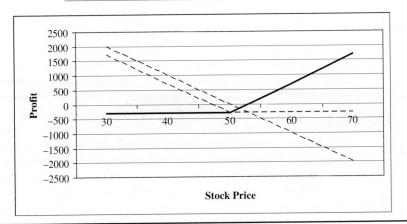

but also buying a bond with a face value equal to the exercise price. The equality between the put position and the short stock, long call, and long bond position can be expressed algebraically as

$$P_0 = C_0 - S_0 + B_0,$$

or as

$$\{+P\} = \{+C, +B, -S\},$$

where B_0 is price of the bond with a face value of X and where the + sign indicates a long position and the − sign a short position.

For short-run investments, the put purchase is a better strategy than a simulated or synthetic put. The simulated put requires the investor to post collateral on the stock shorted, to pay dividends to the share lender if they are declared, and to pay the higher commission costs. The simulated put, though, is worth keeping in mind as a hedge or follow-up strategy for a short sale. For example, an investor who went short in a stock as a long-run strategy might purchase a call to offset potential losses if the price of the stock increased due to an unexpected good earnings announcement. Such a strategy would represent an insurance strategy on a short stock position.

3.2.2.2   *Simulated Straddle*

The purchase of two calls for each share of stock shorted $\{+2C, -S\}$ yields a strategy equivalent to a straddle purchase. This strategy is defined as a ***simulated straddle***. To illustrate, suppose in our previous example the investor bought two 50 calls after going short in 100 shares of the stock at $50. As shown in the table and figure in Exhibit 3.2-4, the investor would obtain a "V"-shaped profit and stock price relation. He would have a limited maximum loss equal to $600 when the stock price equals $50, two break-even prices at $44 and $56, and virtually unlimited profit potential if the stock price increases or decreases past the respective upper and lower break-even prices.

Similar to the simulated put, a simulated straddle is less attractive as a short-run investment than its equivalent straddle strategy because of the higher commission costs, required dividend coverage on the short sale, and collateral associated with the short sale. However, like the preceding comparison of the put and simulated put, the simulated straddle is a strategy worth keeping in mind as a possible follow-up strategy for a short sale.

3.3   NAKED CALL WRITE

The second fundamental strategy we examined in Chapter 1 was the naked call write. Because of its limited profit and unlimited loss characteristic, this strategy is not very popular among option investors. However, it does have some attractive features. One such characteristic is that the option loses its time value premium as time passes. For example, if a writer sold a call, she could profit some time later if the price of the stock did not change. That is, the writer would be able to buy back the call at a lower price because of the lower time-value premium. Of course, if the stock increased in price, then the writer would lose if the increase in intrinsic value exceeded the decrease in the time value premium.

It should be remembered, however, that to establish a naked call write, an investor must post collateral in the form of cash or risk-free securities as a security in the event the call is exercised and she is assigned.

EXHIBIT 3.2-4 Simulated Straddle—Short 100 Shares of Stock at 50 and Purchase Two 50 Call Contracts at 3

S_T	Call Profit $2(\text{Max}[S_T - X, 0] - C)$	Short Security $(50 - S_T)$	Total Profit
30	−600	2000	1400
40	−600	1000	400
44	−600	600	0
50	−600	0	−600
56	600	−600	0
60	1400	−1000	400
70	3400	−2000	1400

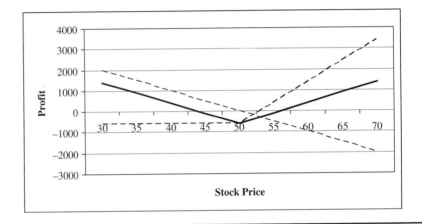

3.3.1 Follow-Up Strategies: Rolling Credit

Although a naked call write is less attractive than other strategies because of its limited profit and unlimited loss characteristic, one interesting but risky tactical or defensive follow-up strategy that could be used with a naked call write is the ***rolling-credit strategy***. Under this strategy, if the stock price increases, the naked call writer sells calls with a higher exercise price and then uses the proceeds (or credit) to close the initial short position by buying the call back. This strategy then is repeated every time the stock increases to a new, uncomfortable level. The hope, in turn, is that the stock eventually will stabilize or preferably decrease in price, and the writer will realize a profit approximately equal to the call sales.

For the rolling-credit strategy to work, three conditions must hold. First, the stock price eventually must stop rising. If the stock does not stop, then, with continuous follow-ups, the writer will realize losses when the stock exceeds the break-even price on the option position with the highest possible exercise price. Second, even if the stock eventually stops rising, a rolling-credit writer must have sufficient collateral (the collateral requirements increase exponentially as the stock price increases). Finally, the success of the rolling-credit strategy requires that the writer not be assigned. Because the writer has no control over assignment, he needs to select options that have a small chance of being exercised. A case in which early exercise is advantageous is discussed in Chapter 4. In summary, the rolling-credit strategy, on the surface, appears to be a simple strategy as well as an easy way of making money. However, for the strategy to work, the aforementioned conditions must hold. If they do not, then the rolling-credit writer can incur substantial losses, perhaps more than he initially had been prepared for.

If the stock price stays below the exercise price or decreases, the naked call writer may want to pursue an aggressive follow-up action. Such actions could include closing the present position and moving to a short position in a call with a lower exercise price, closing the short position and using the proceeds to buy a put if he is relatively more bearish, closing and buying a call with a low exercise price if he feels the stock has bottomed out, or simply liquidating the position.

As noted previously, there is no optimum follow-up strategy but rather a number of strategies available that an investor can use depending on what price he feels the stock eventually will reach.

3.4   COVERED CALL WRITE

The third fundamental option strategy examined in Chapter 1 was the covered call write, namely, long in the stock and short in the call $\{ +S, -C\}$. This strategy is quite popular among institutional investors who see it as a way of hedging a long stock position against an anticipated small stock price decrease or as a way of enhancing the return on a particular stock. For example, suppose an investor owned a stock that he did not expect to increase in the near term. By writing a call, the investor would be able to increase the total return if the stock price stays the same or decreases only slightly. If the stock increases significantly, though, the capital gains on the stock position would be offset by losses on the call.

As a short-run investment strategy, a covered call write has a lower return-risk trade-off than a long stock position. This may be seen by comparing columns 3 and 4 in Exhibit 3.4-1. Column 3 shows the profits for each stock price obtained from purchasing 100 shares of ABC stock at $50; column 4 shows the profits for a covered call position formed by purchasing 100 shares of ABC at $50 and selling an ABC 50 call contract at $5. As shown, if at expiration, the stock had declined from $50 to $40, the investor would realize a profit of $500 from the call premium, which would offset the $1,000 actual (if stock is sold) or paper loss from the stock. If the stock price stayed at $50 or increased beyond it, then the covered call writer would receive a profit of only $500. For example, if the stock were at $60 at expiration, the option would be trading at its intrinsic value of $10. To close the option position, the writer would have to pay $1,000 to buy the calls, which would negate the $1,000 actual or paper gain he would earn from the stock. Thus, the investor would be left with a profit equal to just the call premium of $500.

3.4.1   Types of Covered Call Writes

All covered writes require selling a call against the stock owned. This strategy, though, can be divided into two general types: an out-of-the-money covered call write and an in-the-money covered call write. The out-of-the-money write yields a higher return-risk trade-off than the in-the-money write. For example, suppose after buying 100 shares of ABC stock for $45 per share, an investor considered forming a covered call write either by selling an in-the-money ABC June 40 call trading at $8 or selling an out-of-the-money ABC June 50 call trading at $1. As shown in Exhibit 3.4-2, if the stock declined to $35 at expiration, then the investor would lose only $200 if she selected the in-the-money call compared to losing $900 if she had selected the out-of-the-money call. Similarly, at $40, the investor would receive a profit of $300 from the covered call write strategy with the 40 call compared to a loss of $400 from the 50 call. Thus, greater losses are associated with the out-of-the-money covered call write if the price of the underlying stock declines. In contrast, if ABC increased to $50 or higher, then the covered call write position formed

EXHIBIT 3.4-1   Covered Call Write—100 Shares of Stock Purchased at 50, 50 Call Contracts
Sold at 5

(1) S_T	(2) Profit on Short Call $(C - Max[S_T - X,0])$	(3) Profit on Long Stock $(S_T - 50)$	(4) Total Profit
30	500	−2,000	−1,500
40	500	−1,000	−500
50	500	0	500
55	0	500	500
60	−500	1,000	500
70	−1,500	2,000	500

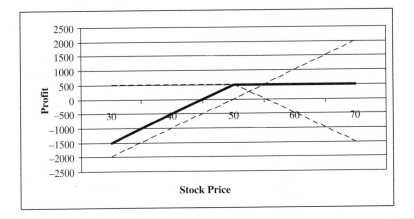

with the out-of-the-money 50 call would yield the investor a profit of $600, whereas the in-the-money 40 call would yield a profit of only $300. The out-of-the-money call therefore provides a higher return if the price of the stock increases. Finally, the break-even price for the in-the-money covered call write is less than the price for the out-of-the-money covered call write; that is, the 40 covered call has a break-even price of $37 compared to the 50 covered call's break-even price of $44. To recapitulate, the out-of-the-money covered call write is a higher return-risk strategy than the in-the-money one.

It should be noted that the investor is not limited to constructing covered call writes from the options available on the exchange. The investor could construct a covered call write using a portfolio of written calls with different exercise prices. For instance, in the preceding example, if a 45 call did not exist, then the investor could obtain the same profit-stock price relation available by selling fifty 40 calls and fifty 50 calls (half the standard contract size). This strategy would provide a moderate return-risk combination between those obtained with the 40 and the 50 calls.

3.4.2 Follow-up Strategies

As with all option positions, if the price of the underlying stock changes unexpectedly, then an investor may want to pursue a follow-up strategy. From our previous discussions of follow-up strategies, one should know that there are a number of possible actions one can take (creating a spread, combination, etc.). The proper action to pursue ultimately depends on the price one expects the stock to reach.

EXHIBIT 3.4-2   Types of Covered Call Writes

a. In-the-money covered call write: Stock purchased at 45 and 40 call sold at 8

S_T	Profit on Short Call $(C - \text{Max}[S_T - X, 0])$	Profit on Long Stock $(S_T - 45)$	Total Profit
35	800	−1,000	200
37	800	−800	0
40	800	−500	300
45	300	0	300
50	−200	500	300
55	−700	1,000	300
60	−1,200	1,500	300

b. Out-of-the-money covered call write: Stock purchased at 45 and 50 call sold at 1

S_T	Profit on Short Call $(C - \text{Max}[S_T - X, 0])$	Profit on Long Stock $(S_T - 45)$	Total Profit
35	100	−1,000	−900
40	100	−500	−400
44	100	−100	0
45	100	0	100
50	100	500	600
55	−400	1,000	600
60	−900	1,500	600

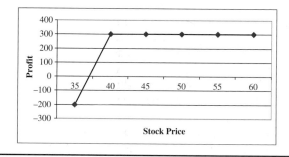
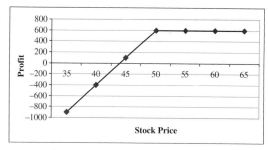

3.5   RATIO CALL WRITE

A ratio call write is a combination of a naked call write and a covered call write. It is constructed by selling calls against more shares of stock than one owns: for example, selling two calls for each share of stock purchased or owned {+S, −2C}. The table and figure in Exhibit 3.5-1 summarize the profit and stock price relations for a ratio call write formed by purchasing 100 shares of ABC stock for $60 per share and selling two June 60 calls at $5 per call. This ratio call write strategy generates an inverted "V" profit and stock price relation, with two break-even prices and a maximum profit occurring when the price of the stock equals the exercise price. Moreover, different ratio call write strategies (differing by their ratios) generate similar characteristics provided the ratio is greater than 1. As a result, an investor, by varying the ratio, can obtain a number of inverted V-type relations (not perfectly inverted V graphs), with each ratio call write differing in terms of its maximum profit, the magnitude of its gains and losses at each stock price, and its break-even prices. For example, as shown in Exhibit 3.5-2, if the ratio is changed from

EXHIBIT 3.5-1   2-to-1 Ratio Call Write—100 Shares of Stock Purchased at 60 and Two 60 Call Contracts Sold at 5 Each

S_T	Short Call Profit $2(C - \text{Max}[S_T - X,0])$	Profit on Long Stock ($S_T - 60$)	Total Profit
40	1,000	−2,000	−1,000
45	1,000	−1,500	−500
50	1,000	−1,000	0
55	1,000	−500	500
60	1,000	0	1,000
65	0	500	500
70	−1,000	1,000	0
75	−2,000	1,500	−500
80	−3,000	2,000	−1,000

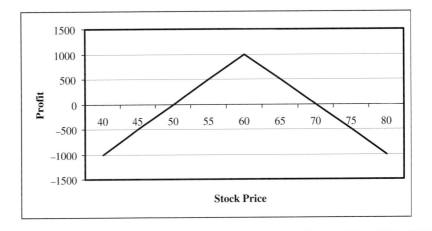

two written calls per share to three written calls per share, the break-even prices go from $50 and $70 to $45 and $67.50, respectively. The maximum profit increases from $1,000 to $1,500, and it occurs at $60 for both ratio call write strategies. Greater profits and losses at each stock price also are realized with three rather than two written calls.

In summary, the ratio call write is a useful strategy for investors who believe a certain stock will stabilize near a certain price. Thus, in the previous examples, both ratio call write strategies would be ideal for an investor who felt the stock would be at $60 near expiration. In addition, by varying the ratio, an investor can use a ratio call write strategy to determine the return/risk he wants to assume. A confident investor or one with more tolerance for risk, for example, might choose the 3 written calls per share strategy, obtaining a higher possible return but also greater risk, whereas an investor with less tolerance might choose a ratio such as 2 written calls per share, obtaining lower possible returns but also lower risks.

3.6 PUT PURCHASE

Just as the purchase of a call can be viewed as an alternative to a leveraged stock purchase, a put purchase can be thought of as a leveraged alternative to a short sale. As illustrated

EXHIBIT 3.5-2   Different Ratio Call Writes

3-to-1 Ratio Call Write

1 Stock Price S_T	2 Profit from Three 60 Call Contracts Sold for 5 Each	3 Profit from 100 Shares of Stock bought at 60	4 Total Profit 3 + 4
35	1,500	−2,500	−1,000
40	1,500	−2,000	−500
45	1,500	−1,500	0
50	1,500	−1,000	500
52.5	1,500	−750	750
55	1,500	−500	1,000
57.5	1,500	−250	1,250
60	1,500	0	1,500
62.5	750	250	1,000
65	0	500	500
67.5	−750	750	0
70	−1,500	1,000	−500
75	−3,000	1,500	−1,500
80	−4,500	2,000	−2,500
85	−6,000	2,500	−3,500
90	−7,500	3,000	−4,500

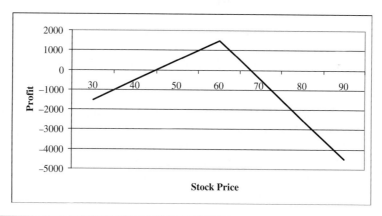

in Figure 3.6-1, a stock sold short at $50 will provide an investor with a $10 return and a rate, expressed as a proportion of a 50% margin, of 40% ($10/($50(.50)) when the stock declines to $40 and a 40% loss when it increases to $60. In contrast, the purchase of a 50 put at a premium of $5 yields a 100% rate of return (($10 − $5)/$5) when the stock is at $40, but a 100% loss if the stock is at $50 or higher. Thus, for short-run investments, investors who are bearish on a stock will find the purchase of a put represents a higher return-risk alternative to the short sale. In addition, the short sale carries with it an obligation to cover dividends, and total commission costs are higher for short sales than put purchases.

3.6.1   Put Selection

A put purchase strategy is used when the price of a stock is expected to decline. Such anticipated declines could be due to fundamental reasons governing the value of a stock,

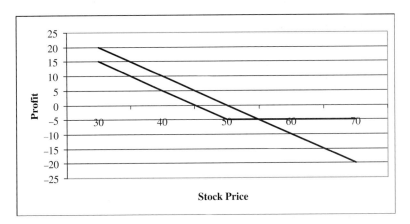

FIGURE 3.6-1 Profit Graphs for Put Purchase and Short Stock Position—Stock Shorted at 50 and 50 Put Purchased at 5

such as an expectation that a company's earnings will be lower than projected when next reported; or technical factors such as a belief that speculators may be selling the stock in the near term for profit-taking motives; or possibly market factors such as an expectation that the economy could be slowing or headed for a recession. Whatever the reason, bearish investors should keep two points in mind in selecting puts. First, an out-of-the-money put provides a higher return-risk investment than an in-the-money put. For example, suppose that ABC stock is at $59, an out-of-the-money ABC June 55 put is trading at $1, and an in-the-money ABC June 60 put is at $3. If the price of ABC decreases to $50 near expiration, then the 55 put could be sold at its intrinsic value of $5, yielding a rate of return of 400% (($5 − $1)/$1), whereas the 60 put could be sold at its intrinsic value of $10 to yield a rate of 233% (($10 − $3)/$3). In contrast, if ABC drops to only $55, then the out-of-the-money 55 put would be worthless, whereas the 60 put provides a profit of $2 (at $60 or higher, both puts yield 100% losses). Thus, an out-of-the-money put offers higher potential rewards but also higher risk than an in-the-money put. Second, it is important to be cognizant that in-the-money puts tend to lose their value faster than out-of-the-money puts when the price of the stock increases. This is because when the price of the underlying stock increases over time, the in-the-money put loses both its intrinsic value and its time value premium, whereas the out-of-the-money loses just its time premium.

3.6.2 Follow-Up Strategies

Once an investor has purchased a put, she needs to be able to identify the possible follow-up actions that can be pursued if the stock price changes are different from what she expects. Aggressive follow-up actions can be taken if the stock decreases more than expected, and defensive actions can be used if the stock increases in price.

If the stock price unexpectedly declines after purchasing a put, a put holder could liquidate, do nothing, roll down, create a put spread, or create a combination. These aggressive follow-up strategies are evaluated in Exhibit 3.6-1. If the price of the stock increases unexpectedly after an investor purchases a put, the investor needs to consider similar defensive actions. An example of implementing defensive strategies of liquidating, do nothing, or creating a spread are presented in Exhibit 3.6-2. As is always the case in follow-up strategies, the strategy to use depends on the price the investor expects to prevail and how confident she is in her expectation.

EXHIBIT 3.6-1 Aggressive Follow-Up Strategies for a Put Purchase

Suppose an investor, after buying an ABC June 60 put contract at $2 per put when the stock was at $62, sees the price of ABC decline to $55. Also, suppose at the stock price of $55, the ABC June 60 put contract is trading at $6, the ABC June 55 put contract is at $2, and the ABC June 55 call contract is trading at $3. The investor, in turn, could

1. **Liquidate** the 60 put to realize a profit of $400

2. **Do nothing**, thereby keeping the chances of increased profit at expiration still open but risking a loss if the stock price increases

3. **Roll down** by selling the 60 put for $600 and then using $400 to buy two 55 puts, thereby capturing her initial investment and keeping open the opportunity to profit if the stock declines further

4. **Spread,** by selling the June 55 put at $2 to match against the long position in the 60 put, thereby locking in a profit of $500 if the stock stays at $55 or decreases, ensuring a profit if the stock increases to just below $60, and providing a break-even position if the stock increases to $60 or higher

5. Create a **combination** by buying the June 55 call at $3 to match with the long 60 put, thereby providing profit if stock moves dramatically up or down or a break-even position if the stock stays within the $55–$60 range

These aggressive follow-up strategies are evaluated in the table in terms of their profit and stock price relations at expiration.

(1) S_T	(2) Do Nothing	(3) Liquidate by Selling 60 Put at $6	(4) Roll Down by Selling 60 Put and Buying Two 55 Puts at $2 Each	(5) Spread by Selling 55 Put at $2	(6) Combination Buy 55 call at $3
$40	$1,800	$400	$3,000	$500	$1,500
45	1,300	400	2,000	500	1,000
51	700	400	800	500	400
52	600	400	600	500	300
53	500	400	400	500	200
55	300	400	0	500	0
56	200	400	0	400	0
58	0	400	0	200	0
60	−200	400	0	0	0
64	−200	400	0	0	400
70	−200	400	0	0	1,000

3.6.3 Put Purchase in Conjunction With a Long Stock Position

3.6.3.1 Simulated Call

Purchasing a put while owning the underlying stock on a one-to-one basis ($\{+P, +S\}$) yields the same type of profit and stock price relation as a call purchase. In Exhibit 3.6-3, the profits at expiration for various stock prices are shown for a long put and stock position consisting of 100 shares of ABC stock purchased at $50 per share and an ABC 50 put contract purchased at $3. As can be seen in the table and the accompanying figure in the exhibit, the combined put and stock position yields the same relation as the purchase of a 50 call contract at $3. Note, however, that more often than not, calls and puts with identical terms are not likely to be equally priced. To form an identical long call position with a call price consistent with put–call parity, a *synthetic call* requires not only buying the put and stock but also shorting a bond with a face value equal to

EXHIBIT 3.6-2 Defensive Follow-Up Strategies for a Put Purchase

Suppose an investor, after buying an ABC June 60 put contract at $2 per put when the stock was at $62, sees the price ABC stock increase to $65, in turn causing the investor's ABC June 60 put to decrease to $1 and an ABC June 65 put to trade at $3. Under these circumstances, the investor could

1. **Liquidate** by selling the June 60 put for $1 (its time value premium), thereby losing only $100 instead of the initial $200 premium that would be lost if the stock equaled $60 or greater at expiration.

2. **Do nothing**, hoping that the price increase is only temporary.

3. Create a **spread** by selling the 65 put for $3, thereby profiting by $100 if the stock continues to increase but losing if it declines.

These defensive follow-up strategies are evaluated in the table in terms of their profit and stock price relations at expiration.

S_T	Do Nothing	Liquidate by Selling 60 Put at $1	Spread by Selling 65 Put at $3
$50	$800	−$100	−$400
55	300	−100	−400
58	0	−100	−400
60	−200	−100	−400
65	−200	−100	100
70	−200	−100	100
75	−200	−100	100

EXHIBIT 3.6-3 Long Stock and Put Position—Simulated Call and Stock Insurance

S_T	Put Profit 50 Put Contract Purchased at 3	Stock Profit 100 Shares of Stock Purchased at 50	Total Profit
30	1,700	−2,000	−300
40	700	−1,000	−300
50	−300	0	−300
53	−300	300	0
55	−300	500	200
60	−300	1,000	700

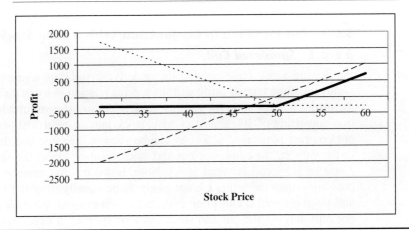

EXHIBIT 3.6-4   Value Graph and Table of Long Stock and Put Positions—Stock Insurance Cash Flows

S_T	50 Put Contact	100 Shares of Stock	Stock and Put Value
30	2,000	3,000	5,000
40	1,000	4,000	5,000
50	0	5,000	5,000
53	0	5,300	5,300
55	0	5,500	5,500
60	0	6,000	6,000

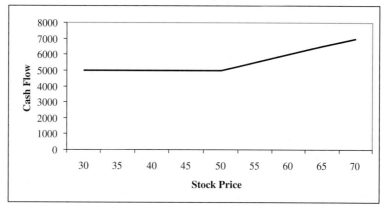

the exercise price (i.e., borrow an amount equal to the present value of exercise price: $PV(X) = B_0$):

$$C_0 = P_0 + S_0 - B_0,$$

or as

$$\{+C\} = \{+P, +S, -B\}$$

3.6.3.2 Portfolio Insurance

As we discussed in Chapter 1, the combined stock and put position is known as a ***portfolio insurance*** or ***stock insurance strategy***. The features of such a strategy are best seen by examining the position's cash flows and value graph, shown in the table and figure in Exhibit 3.6-4. As shown, the 50 put provides downside protection against the value of the stock position falling below $5,000. Thus, for the cost of the put premium, an investor can obtain insurance against decreases in the stock's price. Hedging a stock portfolio position with index put options and a currency position with currency puts are popular hedging strategies used by portfolio managers and currency traders and managers. Portfolio insurance using index and currency options are examined in more detail in Section 3.16.

3.7 NAKED PUT WRITE

The naked (or uncovered) put write strategy provides only limited profit potential if the stock price increases, with the chance of large losses if the stock price decreases. The position as defined in terms of its profit and stock price relationship near expiration is equivalent (although not identical) to the covered call write. Besides being equivalent to the covered call write, the naked put write strategy also is like the naked call write in that it provides an opportunity for investors to profit from the decrease over time in the option's time value premium. For example, an ABC June 60 put sold in March for $10 when ABC stock was trading at $55 would, with no change in the stock price, trade at $5 at expiration. Thus, a profit of $5 could be earned by the naked put writer from the decrease in the time value premium.

Also, similar to the naked call write, naked put write strategies with in-the-money puts provide higher return-risk combinations than those with out-of-the-money puts. For example, the June 60 put in the preceding example would provide profits of $1,000, $500, or 0 to the writer if the stock closed at $60, $55, or $50 at expiration, respectively, and losses of $500, $1,000, or $1,500 if the stock decreased to $45, $40 or $35, respectively. In contrast, an out-of-the-money June 50 put, sold for $3 when the stock was at 55, would provide only $300 profit if the stock traded at $50, $55, $60, or higher at expiration and would incur losses of $200 or $700 if the stock trades at $45 or $40, respectively. Thus, the more the put is in the money, the greater return-risk possibilities (at expiration) available from a naked put write position.

Finally, the defensive rolling credit follow-up strategy defined for the naked call write position (Section 3.3) can be applied to the naked put write strategy for cases in which the stock decreases in price. For example, if ABC decreased from $55 to $50, causing the June 60 put to go from $10 to $15, the writer of the June 60 put could roll down by selling ABC June 55 puts and then using the proceeds (or credit) to close the June 60. Like the rolling credit strategy for the uncovered call position, this strategy needs to be repeated each time the stock decreases to a new, uncomfortable level. In turn, the put writer will profit from this follow-up strategy provided the stock eventually stops decreasing, the option is not exercised, and the writer has sufficient collateral to cover each follow-up adjustment.

3.8 COVERED PUT WRITE

The covered put write strategy involves selling a put and the underlying stock short: $\{-P, -S\}$. It is equivalent (but not identical) to the naked call write, providing limited profit potential if the stock declines and unlimited loss possibilities if the price of the stock increases. The naked call write, though, has a smaller commission cost and lower collateral requirements than the covered put write. As a short-run strategy, the covered put write is not as good as the naked call write and as such, is seldom used as a strategy by option traders.

Analogous to a covered call write, a covered put write can be used as a hedging strategy for a short stock position or as a way of increasing returns for an investor who is short in the stock. For example, an investor who was short in ABC stock at 50 and was expecting a small increase in the price of the stock above 50 could offset some of the losses resulting from a stock price increase by selling a put option on ABC stock. The premium received from the put sale would then serve to partially offset losses on the short positions if the stock increased. If the stock decreased, though, then the short seller would find her profits from her short position offset by losses on her short put position.

3.9   RATIO PUT WRITE

The ratio put write is a combination of a covered put write and a naked put write. It is formed by selling puts against shares of stock shorted at a ratio different than 1-to-1, for example, selling two puts for each share of stock shorted: $\{-2P, -S\}$. In terms of its profit and stock price relationship near expiration, the ratio put write is equivalent to the ratio call write. Like the ratio call write, the ratio put position is characterized by an inverted "V"-shaped profit and stock relation (or a skewed "V"-shaped relation), two break-even prices, and a maximum profit occurring when the stock price is equal to the exercise price. Both strategies have relatively high commission costs because they both involve stock positions, and both are affected by dividends; the ratio call writer can receive dividends but suffers from a price decrease on an ex-dividend date, whereas the ratio put writer may have to pay dividends but gains by the price decrease on an ex-dividend date. The major difference between these equivalent strategies is that the ratio call write requires an investment to purchase the stock, whereas the ratio put write requires posting collateral to cover the short sale.

The ratio put write position can be reversed; puts and shares of stock can be purchased in a ratio different than 1-to-1, for example, $\{+2P, +S\}$. This strategy is known as a ***reverse hedge*** with puts. The strategy yields a "V"-shaped profit and stock price relation and is equivalent to the straddle purchase defined in Chapter 1 and the simulated straddle described in Section 3.2.

3.10   CALL SPREADS

As first defined in Chapter 1, a call spread is a strategy in which one simultaneously buys one call option and sells another on the same stock but with different terms. Because options on a given stock differ only in terms of their exercise prices and expiration dates, only three types of spreads exist. These are

1. The ***vertical*** (or ***money*** or ***price***) ***spread*** in which the options have the same expiration date but different exercise prices.
2. The ***horizontal*** (or ***time*** or ***calendar***) spread in which the options have the same exercise price but different expiration dates.
3. The ***diagonal spread***, which combines the vertical and horizontal spreads by having options with both different exercise prices and expiration dates.

3.10.1   Vertical (Money) Spreads

The most popular vertical or money spreads are the bull, bear, ratio, and butterfly spreads.

3.10.1.1   Bull and Bear Call Spreads

The bull money call spread is suited for investors who are bullish about a stock. As we discussed in Chapter 1, the strategy is to go long in a call with a given exercise price and go short in another call on the same stock with a higher exercise price. For example, suppose that when ABC stock is trading at $42, there is an ABC June 40 call trading at $3 ($C(X) = C(40) = \$3$) and an ABC June 45 call trading at $1 ($C(45) = \$1$). To form a bull spread, a spreader would buy the June 40 call and sell the June 45 call: $\{+C(40), -C(45)\}$. As shown in Exhibit 3.10-1, this bull money spread is characterized by (1) losses limited to $200 when the price of the stock hits $40 (the low exercise price) or less, (2) limited profits of $300 starting when the stock price reaches $45 (the high exercise price), and (3)

EXHIBIT 3.10-1   Bull Call Spread—Buy 40 Call at 3 and Sell 45 Call at 1

S_T	Long 40 Call $\text{Max}[S_T - 40, 0] - 3$	Short 45 Call Profit $1 - \text{Max}[S_T - 45, 0]$	Total Profit
30	−300	100	−200
35	−300	100	−200
40	−300	100	−200
42	−100	100	0
45	200	100	300
50	700	−400	300
55	1,200	−900	300

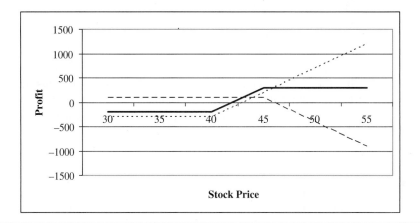

a break-even price of $42. This strategy is, in turn, suited for spreaders whose expectation is that the stock price will appreciate from $42 but not increase much beyond $45.

The bear money call spread is the exact opposite of the bull spread. It is formed by buying a call at a specific exercise price and selling a call on the same stock but with a lower strike price. In terms of the previous example, if the spreader bought the ABC June 45 call at $1 and sold the ABC June 40 at $3, {+C(45), −C(40)}, then as shown in Exhibit 3.10-2 and its accompanying figure, her profit would be limited to $200 if the stock price was $40 or less; her loss would be $300 if the price of the stock was $45 or higher; and the break-even price would be $42, the same as the bull spread. This bear spread would be suited for investors whose expectation is that the price of the stock would moderately fall to around $40.

3.10.1.2 Ratio Money Spread

The bull and bear spreads described previously are balanced spreads or 1-to-1 money spreads. A *ratio money spread*, in turn, is formed by taking long and short positions in options that have not only different exercise prices but ratios different than 1-to-1. The ratio money spread can be formed, for example, either by taking a long position in the low exercise call and a short position in the high one in different ratios or by going short in the low exercise call and long in the high one in different ratios. For a given ratio, these two spreads yield exactly opposite results.

Using the previous example, a ratio money spread could be formed by buying one ABC 40 call at $3 and selling two 45 calls at $1 each: {+C(40), −2C(45)}. As shown in

EXHIBIT 3.10-2   Bear Call Spread—Buy 45 Call at 1 and Sell 40 Call at 3

S_T	Long 45 Call $\text{Max}[S_T - 45, 0] - 1$	Short 40 Call Profit $3 - \text{Max}[S_T - 40, 0]$	Total Profit
30	−100	300	200
35	−100	300	200
40	−100	300	200
42	−100	100	0
45	−100	−200	−300
50	400	−700	−300
55	900	−1,200	−300

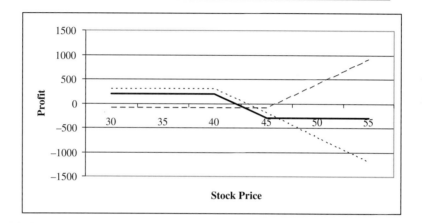

Exhibit 3.10-3b, this 1-to-2 ratio money spread is characterized by two break-even prices at $41 and $49, a maximum profit of $400 when the stock price reaches the exercise price of $45, limited losses of $100 if the stock declines, and unlimited losses if the stock increases. Hence, the motivation for this strategy is that the investor expects the stock price to increase to $45 and then stabilize around that value.

In general, the characteristics of the money spread can be varied by changing the spread's ratio. This can be seen by comparing the profit and stock price relations for the 1-to-1 bull spread shown in Exhibit 3.10-3a, with the 1-to-2 spread shown in Exhibit 3.10-3b, and with the 1-to-3 ratio spread shown in Exhibit 3.10-3c. The profit graphs of the three spreads are shown together in Figure 3.10-1.

3.10.1.3 Butterfly Money Spread

A fourth type of horizontal spread is the **butterfly spread** (also referred to as the **sandwich spread**). This spread is a combination of the bull and bear spreads. Specifically, a **long butterfly money call** spread is formed by buying one call at a low exercise price, selling two calls at a middle exercise price, and buying one call at a high exercise price. To see the profit and stock price relations that a long butterfly generates, suppose that when ABC's stock is selling for $50, the June 40 call on ABC is trading at $12, the June 50 is at $6, and the June 60 is at $3. As shown in Exhibit 3.10-4, buying one June 40, selling two June 50s, and buying one June 60 ({+C(40), −2C(50), +C(60)}) would generate an inverted "V" profit and stock price relation, with limited losses at high and low stock prices. The maximum profit occurs when the stock price equals the middle exercise price and the

EXHIBIT 3.10-3   Ratio Bull Call Spread

a. 1-to-1 Bull Spread

S_T	Long 40 Call $Max[S_T - 40, 0] - 3$	Short 45 Call Profit $1 - Max[S_T - 45, 0]$	Total Profit
30	−300	100	−200
35	−300	100	−200
40	−300	100	−200
42	−100	100	0
45	200	100	300
50	700	−400	300
55	1,200	−900	300

b. 1-to-2 Bull Spread

S_T	Long One 40 Call Contract $Max[S_T - 40, 0] - 3$	Short Two 45 Call Contracts $2(1 - Max[S_T - 45, 0])$	Total Profit
30	−300	200	−100
35	−300	200	−100
40	−300	200	−100
41	−200	200	0
42	−100	200	100
45	200	200	400
47	400	−200	200
49	600	−600	0
50	700	−800	−100
55	1,200	−1,800	−600

c. 1-to-3 Bull Spread

S_T	Long One 40 Call Contract $Max[S_T - 40, 0] - 3$	Short Three 45 Call Contracts $3(1 - Max[S_T - 45, 0])$	Total Profit
30	−300	300	0
35	−300	300	0
40	−300	300	0
41	−200	300	100
42	−100	300	200
45	200	300	500
47	400	−300	100
47.5	450	−450	0
48	500	−600	−100
49	600	−900	−300
50	700	−1,200	−500
55	1,200	−2,700	−1,500

limited losses start when the stock price is equal to the high ($60) and low ($40) exercise prices.

A *short butterfly money call spread* is the exact opposite of the long butterfly. It is formed by selling a low exercise call, buying two middle exercise calls, and selling a high exercise call. Exhibit 3.10-5 illustrates the profit and stock price relations for the short butterfly spread formed by selling the June 40 call, buying two June 50s, and selling the June 60: {−C(40), +2C(50), −C(60)}. As can be seen, the short butterfly yields a

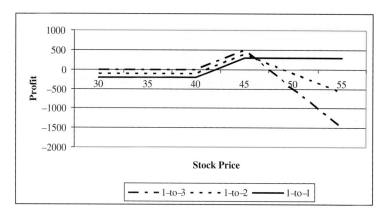

FIGURE 3.10-1 Ratio Bull Call Spreads

EXHIBIT 3.10-4 Long Butterfly Spread—Long 40 Call at 12, Short Two 50 Calls at 6, and Long 60 Call at 3

S_T	Profit 1 Long 40 Call at 12 $Max[S_T - 40, 0] - 12$	Profit 2 Short 50 Calls at 6 $2(6 - Max[S_T - 50, 0])$	Profit 1 Long 60 Call at 3 $Max[S_T - 60, 0] - 3$	Profit Total
30	−1,200	1,200	−300	−300
40	−1,200	1,200	−300	−300
43	−900	1,200	−300	0
45	−700	1,200	−300	200
50	−200	1,200	−300	700
55	300	200	−300	200
57	500	−200	−300	0
60	800	−800	−300	−300
70	1,800	−2,800	700	−300

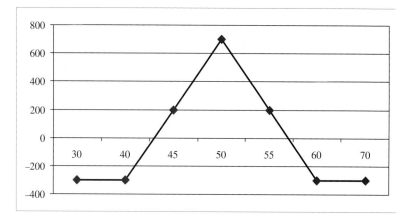

"V"-shaped profit and stock price relation, with limited profits at the high and low stock prices.

3.10.2 Horizontal (Time) Spreads

The horizontal (or time or calendar) spread is formed by simultaneously buying and selling options that are identical except for the time to expiration. For example, a horizontal spread

EXHIBIT 3.10-5   Short Butterfly Spread—Short 40 Call at 12, Long Two 50 Calls at 6, and Short 60 Call at 3

S_T	Profit One Short 40 Call at 12 $12 - \text{Max}[S_T - 40, 0]$	Profit 2 Long 50 Calls at 6 $2(\text{Max}[S_T - 50, 0] - 6)$	Profit 1 Short 60 Call at 3 $3 - \text{Max}[S_T - 60, 0]$	Profit Total
30	1,200	−1,200	300	300
40	1,200	−1,200	300	300
43	900	−1,200	300	0
45	700	−1,200	300	−200
50	200	−1,200	300	−700
55	−300	−200	300	−200
57	−500	200	300	0
60	−800	800	300	300
70	−1,800	2,800	−700	300

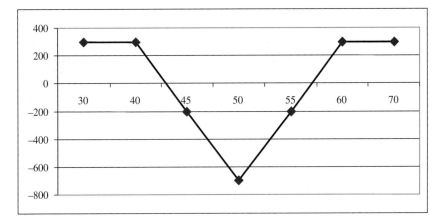

could be formed by selling an ABC June 40 call at $5 and buying a September 40 call at $9. A number of different types of time spreads exist. For example, a spreader may want to form a ratio time spread by going long in one long-term call and short in two short-term calls. An option investor also could form a butterfly time spread with three options with the same exercise prices but with different exercise dates.

Because horizontal as well as diagonal spreads have different exercise dates, it is impossible to know with certainty the value of the long-term option position at the expiration date of the short-term option position. As a result, time and diagonal spreads do not lend themselves to the same type of profit and stock price analysis associated with the strategies we have analyzed to this point. We can, however, estimate profit and stock price relations by using the option pricing model to estimate the price of the longer term option for each possible stock price at the expiration of the shorter term one. In Chapter 9, we discuss time and diagonal spreads.

3.11 PUT SPREADS

Horizontal, vertical, and diagonal put spreads are formed the same way as their corresponding call spreads, and they produce the same profit and stock price relation as their corresponding call spreads. For example, a call bear spread is formed by selling a call with a lower exercise price and buying one with a higher price, and a put bear spread is formed by going short in a low exercise put and long in a higher exercise one. Both strategies yield the same profit and stock price relation. Similarly, a calendar put spread is constructed like its corresponding call by buying (or selling) a short-term put and selling (buying) a longer term one.

In general, our preceding discussion on call spreads also applies to put spreads. It should be kept in mind that even though the put and call spreads are equivalent in terms of profit and stock price relation, differences do exist. For instance, with a bear put spread, the higher exercise price put will sell for more than the lower exercise one, leading to a debit position. The bear call spread, however, will have a higher premium associated with its lower exercise price option and a lower premium associated with its higher exercise call, thus leading to an initial credit position. In contrast, the bull put spread will yield a net credit position and the bull call a net debit one. Also, in comparing equivalent call and put spreads, it is important to note that the time value premium for puts may respond differently to stock price changes than do the time premiums for calls, thus leading to different uses of calendar put and calendar call spread strategies.

3.12 STRADDLE, STRIP, AND STRAP POSITIONS

The straddle is one of the more well-known option strategies. As defined earlier in Chapter 1, a straddle purchase is formed by buying both a put and a call with the same terms—same underlying stock, exercise price, and expiration date: {+C, +P}. A straddle write, in contrast, is formed by selling a call and a put with the same terms: {−C, −P}. For the straddle positions, the ratio of calls to puts is 1-to-1. Changing the ratio, in turn, yields either a strip or strap option strategy. Specifically, the *strip* is formed by having more puts than calls, and the *strap* is constructed with more calls than puts.

3.12.1 Straddle Purchase

The straddle purchase yields a "V"-shaped profit and stock price relation near expiration with two break-even prices and the maximum loss equal to the sum of the call and put premium that occurs when the stock is equal to the options' exercise price. In Exhibit 3.12-1, the profit and stock price relation is shown for a straddle purchase consisting of an ABC June 50 call purchased for $3 and an ABC June 50 put bought for $2.

The straddle purchase (or long straddle) is equivalent to the simulated straddle and the reverse hedge strategy. Because the simulated straddle and reverse hedge strategies involve stock positions, they have the disadvantage of higher commission costs compared to the straddle purchase. Thus, the straddle purchase is the preferable short-run strategy.

The straddle purchase, as with all strategies that are characterized by "V"-shaped profit and stock price relations, is well-suited for cases in which an investor expects substantial change in the price of the stock to occur but is not sure whether the change will be positive or negative. Although all long straddles are characterized by "V"-shaped profit graphs, different straddles on the same stock—differing in terms of their maximum loss, their break-even prices, and the rate of change in profits per change in stock prices (i.e., slopes)—can be generated by purchasing either an out-of-the-money call and in-the-money put, an out/in (call/put) straddle, or an in/out straddle.

Because many straddle strategies are based on anticipated events that could occur before the options' expiration date, they lend themselves to follow-up actions. As an example, suppose that when XYZ Oil Company's stock was trading at $50, an investor bought an XYZ 50 straddle, anticipating an OPEC crude oil production announcement in the near term. Then suppose that after the straddle was purchased, but before the options expired, OPEC announced a decrease in crude oil production, causing an increase in the price of XYZ stock and the prices on XYZ calls and a decrease in the prices of XYZ

EXHIBIT 3.12-1 Straddle Purchase—Long 50 Call at 3 and Long 50 Put at 2

S_T	Put Profit	Call Profit	Total Profit
30	1,700	−200	1,500
35	1,200	−200	1,000
40	700	−200	500
45	200	−200	0
50	−300	−200	−500
55	−300	300	0
60	−300	800	500
65	−300	1,300	1,000
70	−300	1,800	1,500

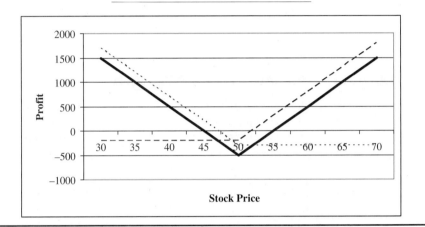

puts. Given this new situation, the investor could (1) liquidate if he felt the stock was at a maximum and would stay there, (2) sell the call and keep the put if he believed the market overreacted to the announcement and that therefore the stock would decline, (3) sell the put and hold the call if he believed the stock would increase even further, or (4) roll up the call (put) by liquidating the straddle and using the profit to buy XYZ calls (puts) with higher exercise prices. If the anticipated event does not occur, or if it does but its impact on the stock's price is less than expected, then the investor may want to consider liquidating, spreading one of the options (selling a put and/or a call with different exercise prices), or some other defensive action. As always, which follow-up strategy to choose depends on the investor's expectation after an event and his confidence in that expectation.

3.12.2 Straddle Write

The straddle write (or short straddle) yields an inverted "V"-shaped profit and stock price relation near expiration, with two break-even prices and a maximum profit equal to the sum of the call and put premiums occurring when the price of the stock is equal to the options' exercise price. The short straddle is equivalent to the ratio call write strategy discussed in Section 3.5. In Exhibit 3.12-2, the profit and stock price relation is shown for a straddle sale consisting of an ABC June 50 call sold for $3 and an ABC June 50 put sold for $2.

The straddle write and other equivalent strategies yielding inverted "V"-shaped profit graphs are ideal for cases in which one either expects little change to occur in the price of the stock or, given the stock's variability, is confident the price of the stock will fall within

EXHIBIT 3.12-2   Straddle Write—Short 50 Call at 3 and Short 50 Put at 2

S_T	Short Put Profit	Short Call Profit	Total Profit
30	−1,800	300	−1,500
35	−1,300	300	−1,000
40	−800	300	−500
45	−300	300	0
50	200	300	500
55	200	−200	0
60	200	−700	−500
65	200	−1,200	−1,000
70	200	−1,700	−1,500

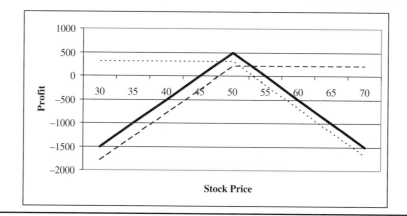

the range of the break-even prices. Thus, in contrast to the straddle purchaser, the straddle writer does not anticipate an event occurring in the near term that would affect the price of the underlying stock.

If an event does occur that increases or decreases the stock price, the writer may need to consider defensive follow-up action. For example, in our previous case in which the price of oil unexpectedly went up, a straddle writer who sold the straddle expecting no crude oil price changes could consider liquidating the short straddle, thus limiting his losses, possibly closing the call by buying it back, or closing the put position. A number of strategies, both defensive and aggressive, can be employed, including positions with different exercise prices and exercise dates.

3.12.3 Strips and Straps

Strips and straps are variations of the straddle. They are formed by adding an additional call position (strap) or an additional put position (strip) to a straddle. Specifically, the strip purchase (sale) consists of the long (short) straddle position plus the purchase (sale) of an extra put(s); the strap purchase (sale) consists of the long (short) straddle plus the additional purchase (sale) of a call(s). In Exhibit 3.12-3, the profit and stock price relations for long straddle, strip, and strap positions formed with an ABC 50 call trading at $3 and an ABC 50 put trading for $2 are shown. In Exhibit 3.12-4, the short positions for the strip, strap, and straddle formed with the same options are shown.

EXHIBIT 3.12-3   Straddle, Strip, and Strap Purchases—Long 50 Call at 3 and Long 50 Put at 2

S_T	Straddle 50 Call at 3, 50 Put at 2	Strip 50 Call at 3, Two 50 Puts at 2 Each	Strap Two 50 Calls at 3 Each, 50 Put at 2
30	1,500	3,300	1,200
35	1,000	2,300	700
40	500	1,300	200
42	300	900	0
45	0	300	−300
46	−100	100	−400
46.5	−150	0	−450
47	−200	−100	−500
48	−300	−300	−600
50	−500	−700	−800
54	−100	−300	0
55	0	−200	200
57	200	0	600
60	500	300	1,200
65	1,000	800	2,200
70	1,500	1,300	3,200

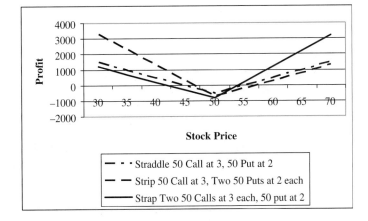

In comparing the three long positions, a number of differences should be noted. First, as we move from the straddle to the strip, the break-even prices move up from $45 and $55 to $46.50 and $57, respectively, and as we move from the straddle to the strap, the break-even prices move down to $42 and $54, respectively. Second, the range in break-even prices for the strip ($10.50) and the strap ($12) are greater than the range for the straddle position ($10). Third, the maximum losses are greater for the strip and strap than the straddle by an amount equal to the cost of the additional option. Finally, compared to the symmetrical returns on the straddle, the strip and strap positions provide asymmetrical payoffs. The strip's rate of increase in profit exceeds that of the straddle when the stock decreases from its maximum-loss price ($50) and equals the straddle's rate when the stock increases. Thus, a strip is particularly well-suited for cases in which (like a straddle) an investor expects a stock either to increase or decrease in response to an event but also expects that a stock decrease will be more likely than an increase. A strap, on the other

EXHIBIT 3.12-4   Straddle, Strip, and Strap Writes—Short 50 Call at 3 and Short 50 Put at 2

S_T	Straddle 50 Call at 3, 50 Put at 2	Strip 50 Call at 3, Two 50 Puts at 2 Each	Strap Two 50 Calls at 3 Each, 50 Put at 2
30	−1,500	−3,300	−1,200
35	−1,000	−2,300	−700
40	−500	−1,300	−200
42	−300	−900	0
45	0	−300	300
46	100	−100	400
46.5	150	0	450
47	200	100	500
48	300	300	600
50	500	700	800
54	100	300	0
55	0	200	−200
57	−200	0	−600
60	−500	−300	−1,200
65	−1,000	−800	−2,200
70	−1,500	−1,300	−3,200

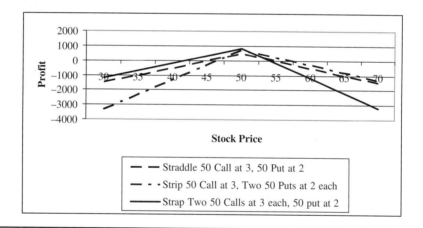

hand, has a greater rate of increase in profit than the straddle when the stock increases and the same rate when the stock decreases. Thus, this strap is more suited for those cases in which an investor thinks the probability of a stock increase is greater than the probability of a stock decrease.

Comparing the three short positions in Exhibit 3.12-4, the writer obtains wider ranges in the break-even prices and a greater maximum profit from selling a strip and strap than a straddle. A strip's losses, however, increase at a greater rate than a straddle write's losses when the stock price decreases from the maximum profit price and at the same rate when the stock increases. The opposite results occur in the case of the strap write. Finally, note that the characteristics of strips and straps can be changed by varying the ratios.

3.13   COMBINATIONS

A *combination* is a position formed with a call and a put on the same underlying stock but with different terms: that is, either different exercise prices (referred to as a money or a vertical combination), exercise dates (called a time, calendar, or horizontal combination), or both (diagonal combination). The most common combinations are the ones formed with different exercise prices—money combinations, often called *strangles*.

In Exhibit 3.13-1, the profit and stock price relations are shown for a long money combination (a long strangle) constructed with a 45 call purchased at $6 and a 40 put purchased at $1. With the price of the stock assumed to be at $48, the long combination consists of an in-the-money call and an out-of-the-money put, that is, a 45/40 (call/put), in/out combination. As shown, the combination position is characterized by a limited loss (equal to the combination cost ($700)) over a range of stock prices (equal to the range in exercises prices ($40 and $45)), and virtually unlimited profit potential if the stock increases or decreases. Short money combinations, of course, yield just the opposite—limited profit over a range of stock prices and potential losses if the price of the stock changes substantially in either direction. Like straddles, different combinations on the

EXHIBIT 3.12-1   Combination Purchase—Long 45 Call at 6 and Long 40 Put at 1

S_T	Put Profit 40 Put Purchased at 1	Call Profit 45 Call Purchased at 6	Total Profit
25	1,400	−600	800
30	900	−600	300
33	600	−600	0
35	400	−600	−200
39	0	−600	−600
40	−100	−600	−700
42	−100	−600	−700
45	−100	−600	−700
46	−100	−500	−600
50	−100	−100	−200
52	−100	100	0
55	−100	400	300
60	−100	900	800
63	−100	1,200	1,100

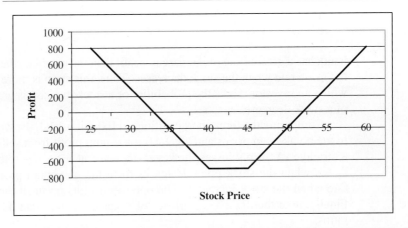

EXHIBIT 3.14-1 Long Condor

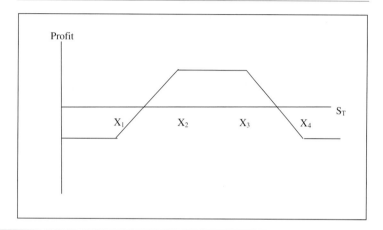

Call and Put Exercise Prices are X_1, X_2, X_3, X_4 Where $X_1 < X_2 < X_3 < X_4$

Calls:	Long X_1 and X_4; Short X_2 and X_3
Puts:	Long X_1 and X_4; Short X_2 and X_3
Calls and Puts:	Long X_1 Call, Short X_2 Call, Short X_3 Put, Long X_4 Put
Calls and Puts:	Long X_1 Put, Short X_2 Put, Short X_3 Call, Long X_4 Call

same stock can be formed with in-the-money and out-of-the-money calls and puts: out/in (call/put), in/out, out/out, and in/in combinations.

3.14 CONDORS

Condors are formed with four call and/or put options on the same stock but with different terms. They are a special type of butterfly spread involving bull and bear spreads with different exercise prices. Condors can be constructed in a number of ways. Exhibit 3.14-1 shows several ways in which a long condor can be formed with call and put options with four exercise prices: X_1, X_2, X_3, and X_4 in which $X_1 < X_2 < X_3 < X_4$. As shown in the figure in Exhibit 3.14-1, the long condor is similar to a short money combination, providing limited profit over a range of stock prices and possible losses if the stock price changes in either direction. Different from the combination, the losses on the long condor are limited. This limited loss feature, in turn, makes the condor less risky than the combination. A short condor position is formed by simply reversing the long condor's positions. The short condor, in turn, has the opposite characteristics of the long position (See Exhibit 3.14-2).

3.15 SIMULATED STOCK POSITIONS

From our discussions on option strategies, it should be clear that options can be used in different combinations to obtain virtually any profit and stock price relation. Given this, it should not be too surprising to find that options can be used to form synthetic securities such as long and short stock positions. A *simulated long position* may be formed by buying a call and selling a put with the same terms. Similarly, a *simulated short position*,

EXHIBIT 3.14-2   Short Condor

Call and Put Exercise Prices are X_1, X_2, X_3, X_4 Where $X_1 < X_2 < X_3 < X_4$

Calls:	Short X_1 and X_4; Long X_2 and X_3
Puts:	Short X_1 and X_4; Long X_2 and X_3
Calls and Puts:	Short X_1 Call, Long X_2 Call, Long X_3 Put, Short X_4 Put
Calls and Puts:	Short X_1 Put, Long X_2 Put, Long X_3 Call, Short X_4 Call

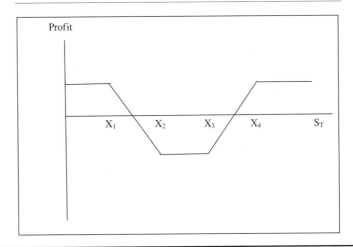

constructed by selling a call and buying a put with the same terms, is equivalent to the profit and stock price relation associated with selling the underlying stock short.

3.15.1   Simulated Long Position

In Exhibit 3.15-1, the profit and stock price relations are shown for a long stock position established by buying 100 shares of ABC stock at $50 per share and a simulated long position formed by buying an ABC June 50 call at $5 and selling an ABC June 50 put at $5. As can be seen, the relations in this example are exactly the same.

Several differences should be noted between the two equivalent positions shown in Exhibit 3.15-1. First, the costs of the positions are different. In the example, it would cost $5,000 to buy the stock, whereas the simulated long position would have a net cost equal to the difference in call premium minus the put (zero in the example) plus a margin requirement. Second, the long stock position could provide dividends that the simulated position does not. However, on an ex-dividend date, the prices of the stock, call, and put all will change. Third, the option position has a fixed life that ends at expiration, whereas an investor can hold the stock indefinitely. Finally, the call and put would more than likely not be equally priced (this would require a risk-free rate of zero). If they are not, then the simulated position would not be identical to the stock position. As we discussed in Chapter 1, to attain an identical position (a synthetic position) requires that a long bond position be included with the long call and short put positions.

3.15.2   Simulated Short Position

In Exhibit 3.15-2, the profit and stock price relations are shown for a short stock position set up by selling 100 shares of ABC stock short at $50 and a simulated short position

EXHIBIT 3.15-1 Simulated Long Stock Position

S_T	Profit From 50 Call Contract Bought at 5	Profit From 50 Put Contract Sold at 5	Profit From Simulated Long	Profit From Stock Bought at 50
40	−500	−500	−1,000	−1,000
45	−500	0	−500	−500
50	−500	500	0	0
55	0	500	500	500
60	500	500	1,000	1,000

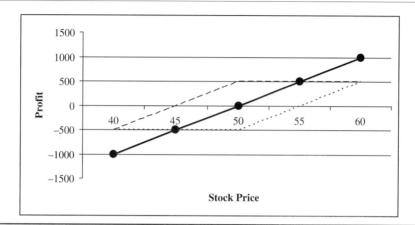

formed by selling an ABC June 50 call at $5 and buying an ABC June 50 put at $5. With the same premiums on the call and put, the actual and simulated short positions are the same. If the premiums differ, a bond also would be needed to form an identical short stock position (synthetic short position).

The differences in the short and simulated short positions are similar to the differences in the corresponding long positions. The simulated short position has different margin requirements and commission costs than the short stock position; the short stock position requires dividend coverage, whereas the simulated position does not, and the simulated short position has an expiration date, whereas the short stock position does not (although the holder is subject to covering the borrowed shares any time a share lender requests).

3.15.3 Splitting the Strikes

The preceding simulated long and short positions can be altered by setting up strategies similar to the ones previously but with different terms—exercise prices, dates, or both. When the differing term is the exercise price, the strategy is referred to as *splitting the strikes*.

In splitting the strike, an investor would go long in a call with a high exercise price and short in a put with a lower exercise price (usually both out of the money) if she were bullish and would do the opposite (write a call with a low exercise and buy a put with a high) if she were bearish. The profit and stock price relation for a bullish "splitting the strikes" position with ABC options is shown in Exhibit 3.15-3, and the bearish position is shown in Exhibit 3.15-4 in which it is assumed that an out-of-the-money ABC June 60 put is trading at $2 and an ABC out-of-the-money June 70 call is at $1 when ABC stock is trading at $63. As shown in the exhibits, the bullish and bearish positions provide a range

EXHIBIT 3.15-2   Simulated Short Stock Position

S_T	Profit From 50 Put Contract Purchased at 5	Profit From 50 Call Sold at 5	Profit From Simulated Short	Profit From Stock Shorted at 50
40	500	500	1,000	1,000
45	0	500	500	500
50	−500	500	0	0
55	−500	0	−500	−500
60	−500	−500	−1,000	−1,000

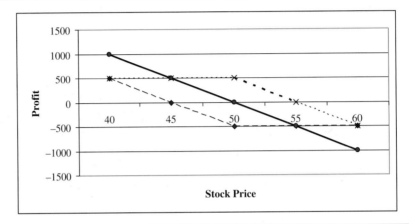

EXHIBIT 3.15-3   Splitting the Strike, Bullish Position

S_T	Call Profit Profit from 70 Put Sold at 1	Short Put Profit Profit from 60 Put Sold at 2	Total Profit
50	−100	−800	−900
55	−100	−300	−400
59	−100	100	0
60	−100	200	100
65	−100	200	100
70	−100	200	100
75	400	200	600
80	900	200	1,100

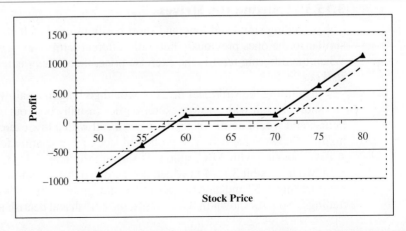

EXHIBIT 3.15-4 Splitting the Strike, Bearish Position

S_T	Put Profit Profit from 60 Put Bought at 2	Short Call Profit Profit from 70 Call Sold at 1	Total Profit
50	800	100	900
55	300	100	400
59	−100	100	0
60	−200	100	−100
65	−200	100	−100
70	−200	100	−100
75	−200	−400	−600
80	−200	−900	−1,100

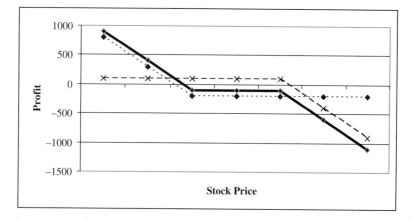

EXHIBIT 3.15-5 Selling Stock at T With a Short-Range Forward Contract: Long in Put With X_1 and Short in Call With X_2

Position	Cash Flows at Expiration		
	$S_T < X_1$	$X_1 \leq S_T \leq X_2$	$S_T > X_2$
Stock Sale	S_T	S_T	S_T
Short X_2 Call	0	0	$-(S_T - X_2)$
Long X_1 Put	$X_1 - S_T$	0	0
	X_1	S_T	X_2

of stock prices in which profits or losses are fixed and also smaller losses and profits at each stock price than their respective long and short stock positions.

Sometimes the exercise prices on the strike positions can be selected such that there is no cost: The premium on the short position defrays the cost of the long position. This position is sometimes referred to as a ***range forward contract*** or ***zero-cost collar***. A short-range forward contract consists of a long position in a put with a low exercise price, X_1, and a short position in a call with a higher exercise price, X_2. An investor holding the underlying

EXHIBIT 3.15-6   Purchasing Stock at T With a Long-Range Forward Contract: Short in Put With X_1 and Long in Call With X_2

	Cash Flows at Expiration		
Position	$S_T < X_1$	$X_1 \leq S_T \leq X_2$	$S_T > X_2$
Stock Purchase	$-S_T$	$-S_T$	$-S_T$
Long X_2 Call	0	0	$(S_T - X_2)$
Short X_1 Put	$-(X_1 - S_T)$	0	0
	$-X_1$	$-S_T$	$-X_2$

security and planning to sell it at time T could take a short-range forward contract to guarantee that the price of the stock could be sold at a price between the exercise prices at the option's maturity (see Exhibit 3.15-5). In contrast, a long-range forward contract consists of a short position in a put with a low exercise price, X_1, and a long position in a call with a higher exercise price, X_2. An investor planning to purchase the options' underlying security at time T could take a long-range forward contract to guarantee that the purchase price of the stock would be between the exercise prices at the option's maturity (see Exhibit 3.15-6). Note that when the exercise prices are the same, then the range forward position becomes a simulated long or short stock position that can be used to lock in the purchase or sale price at a specific price. This make the range forward contract a regular forward contract.

3.16   HEDGING STOCK PORTFOLIO, BOND, AND CURRENCY POSITIONS

As we noted in Chapter 1, the Chicago Board of Trade was establish to provide farmers, dealers, and businesses with a way of hedging against price risk by entering forward contracts to buy or sell a commodity at a future date at a price specified today. Although futures contracts enable businesses, farmers, and other economic entities to eliminate the costs of unfavorable price movements, they also eliminate the benefits realized from favorable price movements. However, one of the advantages of using options instead of futures contracts as a hedging tool is that the hedger, for the price of the option, can obtain protection against adverse price movements while still realizing benefits if the underlying asset moves in a favorable direction.

In later parts of this book, we devote considerable attention to examining how options, futures, and other derivative securities are used for hedging various positions: stock portfolios, commodities, debt positions, and currency positions. Some of the important uses of hedging with options, though, can be seen now by examining the purchase of index, currency, and OTC Treasury put options as a way of attaining downside protection on the future sale of a portfolio, currency, and bond and by examining the purchases of call options as a strategy for capping the costs of future purchases.

3.16.1   Hedging Portfolio Positions Using Index Options

In Section 3.6, we noted that one of important uses of stock index options is in providing portfolio insurance. This is a hedging strategy in which an equity portfolio manager protects the future value of her fund by buying index put options. The index put options, in turn, provide downside protection against a stock market decline while allowing the fund to grow if the market increases. To illustrate, consider the case of an equity fund manager who plans to sell a portion of a stock portfolio in September to meet an anticipated liquidity need. The portfolio the manager plans to sell is well diversified and highly correlated with the S&P 500, has a beta (ß) of 1.25, and currently is worth $V_0 = \$50M$. Suppose the market, as measured by the spot S&P 500, is currently at 1250 and that the manager expects a bullish market to prevail in the future, with the S&P 500 rising. As a result, the manager expects to benefit from selling her portfolio in September at a higher value. At the same time, though, suppose the manager is also concerned that the market could be lower in September and does not want to risk selling the portfolio in a market with the index lower than 1250. Suppose the CBOE has a September S&P 500 put option with an exercise price of 1250 and multiplier of 100 that is trading at 50. As a strategy to lock in a minimum value from the portfolio sale if the market decreases while obtaining a higher portfolio values if the market increases, suppose the manager decides to set up a portfolio insurance strategy by buying September 1250 S&P 500 puts. To form the portfolio insurance position, the manager would need to buy 500 September S&P 500 puts at a cost of $2.5M:

$$N_p = \beta \frac{V_0}{X}$$

$$N_p = 1.25 \frac{\$50,000,000}{(1250)(\$100)} = 500 \text{ puts}$$

$$\text{Cost} = (500)(\$100)(50) = \$2,500,000$$

Exhibit 3.16-1 shows for five possible spot index values ranging from 1000 to 1500, the manager's revenue from selling the portfolio at the September expiration date and closing her puts by selling them at their intrinsic values. Note, for each index value shown in Column 1, there is a corresponding portfolio value (shown in Column 4) that reflects the proportional change in the market and the portfolio beta of 1.25. For example, if the spot index were at 1000 at expiration, then the market as measured by the proportional change in the index would have decreased by 20% from its initial level of 1250 ($-.20 = (1000 - 1250)/1250$). Because the well-diversified portfolio has a beta of 1.25, it would have decreased by 25% ($\beta(\%\Delta \text{ S\&P500}) = 1.25(-.20) = -.25$), and the portfolio would, in turn, be worth only $37.5M, 75% of its initial value of $50M. Thus, if the market were at 1000, the corresponding portfolio value would be $37.5M($= (1 - \beta(\%\Delta S\&P500))V_0 = (1 - 1.25(.20))\$50M$). On the other hand, if the spot S&P 500 index were at 1500 at the September expiration, then the market would have increased by 20%($= (1,500 - 1,250)/1,250$), and the portfolio would have increased by 25% ($1.25(.20)$) to equal $62.5M($= 1.25(\$50M)$). Thus, when the market is at 1500, the portfolio's corresponding value is $62.5M. Given the corresponding portfolio values, Column 5 in Exhibit 3.16-1 shows the intrinsic values of the S&P 500 put corresponding to the spot index values, and Column 6 shows the corresponding cash flows that would be received by the portfolio manager from selling the 500 expiring September index puts at their intrinsic values. As shown in the exhibit, if the spot S&P 500 is less than 1250 at expiration, the manager would realize a positive cash flow from selling her index puts, with the put revenue increasing proportional to the proportional decreases in the portfolio values, providing, in turn, the requisite protection in value. On the other hand, if the S&P 500 spot index is equal or greater than 1250, the manager's put options would be worthless, but her revenue from selling the portfolio would be greater, the greater the index. Thus, if the market were 1250 or less at expiration, the value of the hedged portfolio (stock portfolio value plus put values) would be $50M; if the market were above 1250, the value of the hedged portfolio would increase as the market rises. Thus, for the $2.5M cost of the put options, the fund manager has attained a $50M floor for the value of the portfolio and benefiting with greater portfolio values if the market increases.

EXHIBIT 3.16-1   Stock Portfolio Hedged with S&P 500 Puts

Portfolio Hedged With S&P 500 Index Puts
Portfolio: Initial Value = $50M, β = 1.25
S&P 500 Put: X = 1250, Multiplier = 100, Premium = 50
Hedge: 500 Puts; Cost = (500)(50)($100) = $2.5M
Portfolio Value and Hedged Portfolio Value at the Expiration of the Option

1 S&P 500 Spot Index S_T	2 Proportional Change in the Market $g = (S_T - 1250)/1250$	3 Proportional Change in the Portfolio $\beta g = 1.25g$	4 Portfolio Value $V_T = (1+\beta g)$ $\$50M$	5 Put Value at T $P_T = IV = $ Max$[1250 - S_{T,}\ 0]$	6 Value of Put Investment $CF = 500$ $(\$100)\ P_T$	7 Hedged Portfolio Value Column 4 + Column 6
1000	−0.20	−0.250	$37,500,000	250	$12,500,000	$50,000,000
1125	−0.10	−0.125	$43,750,000	125	$6,250,000	$50,000,000
1250	0.00	0.000	$50,000,000	0	$0	$50,000,000
1375	0.10	0.125	$56,250,000	0	$0	$56,250,000
1500	0.20	0.250	$62,500,000	0	$0	$62,500,000

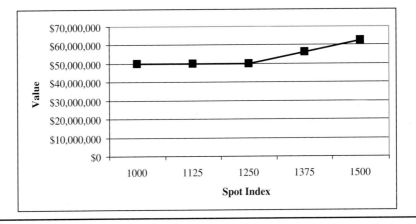

In addition to protecting the value of a portfolio, index options also can be used to hedge the costs of a future stock portfolio purchase. For example, suppose the preceding portfolio manager were anticipating a cash inflow of $50M in September, which she planned to invest in a well-diversified portfolio with a ß of 1.25 that was currently worth $50M when the current spot S&P 500 index was at 1250. Suppose there were a September S&P 500 call option trading at 50 and that the manager was fearful of a bull market pushing stock prices up, increasing the cost of buying the well-diversified portfolio. To hedge against this, the manager could lock in a minimum cost of the portfolio of $50M by purchasing 500 September 1250 S&P 500 index calls at a total cost of $2.5M:

$$N_C = \beta \frac{V_0}{X}$$

$$N_C = 1.25 \frac{\$50,000,000}{(1250)(\$100)} = 500 \text{ calls}$$

$$\text{Cost} = (500)\,(\$100)(50)\ =\ \$2,500,000$$

EXHIBIT 3.16-2   Stock Portfolio Purchase Hedged With S&P 500 Calls

Portfolio Hedged with S&P 500 Index Calls
Portfolio: Current Cost = $50M, β = 1.25
S&P 500 Call: X = 1250, Multiplier = 100, Premium = 50
Hedge: 500 Calls; Cost = (500)(50)($100) = $2.5M
Portfolio Cost and Hedged Portfolio Cost at the Expiration of the Option

1 S&P 500 Spot Index S_T	2 Proportional Change in the Market $g = (S_T - 1250)/1250$	3 Proportional Change in the Portfolio $\beta g = 1.25g$	4 Portfolio Cost $V_T = (1 + \beta_g)$ $50M	5 Call Value at T $C_T = IV =$ $Max[S_T - 1250,0]$	6 Value of Call Investment $CF = 500$ ($100) C_T	7 Hedged Portfolio Cost Column 4 − Column 6
1000	−0.20	−0.250	$37,500,000	0	$0	$37,500,000
1125	−0.10	−0.125	$43,750,000	0	$0	$43,750,000
1250	0.00	0.000	$50,000,000	0	$0	$50,000,000
1375	0.10	0.125	$56,250,000	125	$6,250,000	$50,000,000
1500	0.20	0.250	$62,500,000	250	$12,500,000	$50,000,000

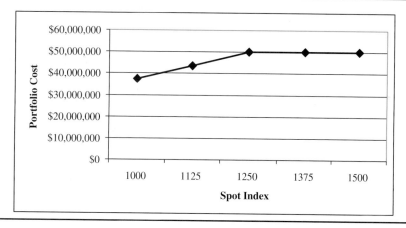

As shown in Exhibit 13.6-2, if the spot index is 1250 or higher at expiration, the corresponding cost of the portfolio would be higher; the higher portfolio costs, though, would be offset by profits from the index calls. For example, if the market were at 1500 in September, then the well-diversified portfolio with a β of 1.2 would cost $62.5M; the additional $12.5M cost of the portfolio would be offset, though, by the $12.5M cash flow obtained from the selling 500 September 1250 index calls at their intrinsic value of 250. Thus, as shown in the exhibit, for index values of 1250 or greater, the hedged costs of the portfolio would be $50M. On the other hand, if the index is less than 1250, the manager would be able to buy the well-diversified portfolio at a lower cost, with the losses on the index calls limited to just the premium. Thus, for the $2.5M costs of the index call option, the manager is able to cap the maximum cost of the portfolio at $50M while still benefiting with lower costs if the market declines.

3.16.2 Hedging Currency Positions With Currency Options

Until the introduction of currency options, exchange-rate risk usually was hedged with foreign currency forward or futures contracts. Hedging with these instruments allows foreign exchange participants to lock in the local currency values of their international revenues or expenses. However, with exchange-traded currency options and dealer's options, hedgers, for the cost of the options, can obtain not only protection against adverse exchange rate movements but (unlike forward and futures positions) gains if the exchange rate moves in a favorable direction.

To illustrate the use of currency options as a hedging tool for international debt and investment positions, consider the case of a U.S. investment fund with investments in Eurobonds that were to pay a principal in British pounds of £10M next September. For the costs of BP put options, the U.S. fund could protect its dollar revenues from possible exchange rate decreases when it converts while still benefiting if the exchange rate increases. For example, suppose a PHLX September BP put with an exercise price of $X = \$1.425/£$ is available at $P_0 = \$0.02/£$. Given a contract size of 31,250 British pounds, the U.S. fund would need to buy 320 put contracts ($n_p = £10,000,000/£31,250 = 320$) at a cost of $200,000 (Cost = $(320)(£31,250)(0.02/£)$) to establish a floor for the dollar value of its £10,000,000 receipt in September. Exhibit 3.16-3 shows the dollar cash flows the U.S. Fund would receive in September from converting its receipts of £10,000,000 to dollars at the spot exchange rate (E_T) and closing its 320 put contracts at a price equal to the put's intrinsic value (assume the September payment date and option expiration date are the same). As shown in Exhibit 3.16-3, if the exchange rate is less than $X = \$1.425/£$, the company would receive less than $14,250,000 when it converts its £10,000,000 to dollars; these lower revenues, however, would be offset by the cash flows from the put position. For example, at a spot exchange rate of $1.325/£, the company would receive only $13,250,000 from converting its £10,000,000 but would receive a cash flow of $1,000,000 from the puts ($1,000,000 = 320 Max[($1.425/£) − ($1.325/£), 0](£31,250)); this would result in a combined receipt of $14,250,000. As shown in the exhibit, if the exchange rate is $1.425/£ or less, the company would receive $14,250,000. On the other hand, if the exchange rate at expiration exceeds $1.425/£, the U.S. fund would realize a dollar gain when it converts the £10,000,000 at the higher spot exchange rate, whereas its losses on

EXHIBIT 3.16-3   Hedging £10,000,000 Cash Inflow With a British Pound Put Option

$X = \$1.425/£$, $P_0 = \$0.02/£$, Contract Size = £31,250
Number of Puts = 320, Total Cost of Puts = $(320)(31,250)(.02) = \$200,000$

1 Exchange Rate $E_T= \$/BP$	2 Dollar Revenue $E_T(10,000,000BP)$	3 Put Cash Flow	4 Hedged Revenue Col(2)+Col(3)
$1.200	$12,000,000	$2,250,000	$14,250,000
$1.250	$12,500,000	$1,750,000	$14,250,000
$1.275	$12,750,000	$1,500,000	$14,250,000
$1.300	$13,000,000	$1,250,000	$14,250,000
$1.325	$13,250,000	$1,000,000	$14,250,000
$1.350	$13,500,000	$750,000	$14,250,000
$1.375	$13,750,000	$500,000	$14,250,000
$1.400	$14,000,000	$250,000	$14,250,000
$1.425	$14,250,000	$0	$14,250,000
$1.450	$14,500,000	$0	$14,500,000
$1.475	$14,750,000	$0	$14,750,000
$1.500	$15,000,000	$0	$15,000,000
$1.525	$15,250,000	$0	$15,250,000

Put Cash Flow = $(320)(31250BP)(Max[\$1.425/BP − E_T, 0]$

EXHIBIT 3.16-4   Hedging £10,000,000 Cash Outflow With a British Pound Call Option

$X = \$1.425/£$, $C_0 = \$0.02/£$, Contract Size $= £31,250$
Number of Calls $= 320$, Total Cost of Calls $= (320)(31,250)(.02) = \$200,000$

1 Exchange Rate $E_T = \$/BP$	2 Dollar Cost $E_T(10,000,000BP)$	3 Call Cash Flow	4 Hedged Cost Col(2) − Col(3)
$1.200	$12,000,000	$0	$12,000,000
$1.250	$12,500,000	$0	$12,500,000
$1.275	$12,750,000	$0	$12,750,000
$1.300	$13,000,000	$0	$13,000,000
$1.325	$13,250,000	$0	$13,250,000
$1.350	$13,500,000	$0	$13,500,000
$1.375	$13,750,000	$0	$13,750,000
$1.400	$14,000,000	$0	$14,000,000
$1.425	$14,250,000	$0	$14,250,000
$1.450	$14,500,000	$250,000	$14,250,000
$1.475	$14,750,000	$500,000	$14,250,000
$1.500	$15,000,000	$750,000	$14,250,000
$1.525	$15,250,000	$1,000,000	$14,250,000

Call Cash Flow $= (320)(31250BP)(Max[E_T-\$1.425/BP,0]$

the put would be limited to the amount of the premium. Thus, by hedging with currency put options, the U.S. investment fund is able to obtain exchange rate risk protection in the event the exchange rate decreases whereas still retaining the potential for increased dollar revenues if the exchange rate rises.

Suppose that instead of receiving foreign currency, a U.S. company had a foreign liability requiring a foreign currency payment at some future date. To protect itself against possible increases in the exchange rate while still benefiting if the exchange rate decreases, the company could hedge the position by taking a long position in a currency call option. For example, suppose a U.S. company owed £10,000,000, with the payment to be made in September. To benefit from the lower exchange rates and still limit the dollar costs of purchasing £10,000,000 in the event the $/£ exchange rate rises, suppose the company bought 320 British pound call options with $X = \$1.425/£$ ($n_c = £10,000,000/£31,250 = 320$) at a cost of $0.02/£ (total cost $= \$200,000 = (320)(£31,250)(0.02/£)$). Exhibit 3.16-4 shows the costs of purchasing £10,000,000 at different exchange rates and the cash flows from selling 320 September British pound calls at expiration at a price equal to the call's intrinsic value. As shown in the exhibit, for cases in which the exchange rate is greater than $1.425/£, the company has dollar expenditures exceeding $14,250,000; the expenditures, though, are offset by the cash flows from the calls. On the other hand, when the exchange rate is less than $1.425/£, the dollar costs of purchasing £10,000,000 decreases as the exchange rate decreases, whereas the losses on the call options are limited to the option premium.

3.16.2.1   Hedging Future T-Bond Sales With an OTC T-Bond Put

Consider the case of a trust-fund manager who plans to sell ten $100,000 face value T-bonds from her fixed income portfolio in September to meet an anticipated liquidity need. The T-bonds the manager plans to sell pay a 6% interest and are currently priced at 94 (per $100 face value); and at their anticipated selling date in September, they will have exactly

EXHIBIT 3.16-5   Hedging a T-Bond Scale with an OTC T-Bond Put option

T-Bond: Maturity = 15, Coupon = 6%, Face Value = $100,000, number of T-Bonds to sell = 10
OTC T-Bond Put: Right to sell 10 T-Bonds at $940,000, cost of the option = $10,000

1 Spot T-Bond Price per $100 Face Value	2 Average Rate to Maturity	3 Revenue From Selling 10 T-Bonds by Exercising Put	4 Revenue From Selling the 10 T-Bonds on Spot Market if Put is Not Exercised	5 Cost of the Put	6 Hedged Revenue Col (3) + Col (4) − Col 5
90.0	0.0702	$940,000	$0	$10,000	$930,000
90.5	0.0696	$940,000	$0	$10,000	$930,000
91.0	0.0691	$940,000	$0	$10,000	$930,000
91.5	0.0686	$940,000	$0	$10,000	$930,000
92.0	0.0681	$940,000	$0	$10,000	$930,000
93.0	0.0670	$940,000	$0	$10,000	$930,000
93.5	0.0665	$940,000	$0	$10,000	$930,000
94.0	0.0660	$940,000	$0	$10,000	$930,000
94.5	0.0655	$0	$945,000	$10,000	$935,000
95.0	0.0650	$0	$950,000	$10,000	$940,000
95.5	0.0645	$0	$955,000	$10,000	$945,000
96.0	0.0639	$0	$960,000	$10,000	$950,000
96.5	0.0634	$0	$965,000	$10,000	$955,000
97.0	0.0629	$0	$970,000	$10,000	$960,000

15 years to maturity and no accrued interest. Suppose the manager expects long-term rates in September to be lower and therefore expects to benefit from higher T-bond prices when she sells her bonds, but she is also concerned that rates could increase and does not want to risk selling the bonds at prices lower than 94. As a strategy to lock in minimum revenue from the September bond sale if rates increase whereas obtaining higher revenues if rates decrease, the manager decides to buy spot T-bond puts from an OTC Treasury security dealer who is making a market in spot T-bond options. Suppose the manger pays a dealer $10,000 for a put option on ten 15-year, 6% T-bonds with an exercise price of 94 per $100 face value and expiration coinciding with the manager's September sales date. Exhibit 3.16-5 shows the manager's revenue from either selling the T-bonds on the put if T-bond prices are less than 94 or on the spot market if prices are equal to or greater than 94. As shown in the exhibit, if the price on a 15-year T-bond is less than 94 at expiration (or rates are approximately 6.60% or more), the manager would be able to realize a minimum net revenue of $930,000 by selling her T-bonds to the dealer on the put contract at X = $940,000 and paying the $10,000 cost for the put; if T-bond prices are greater than 94 (below approximately 6.60%), her put option would be worthless, but her revenue from selling the T-bond would be greater, the higher T-bond prices, whereas the loss on her put position would be limited to the $10,000 cost of the option. Thus, by buying the put option, the trust-fund manager has attained insurance against decreases in bond prices. Such a strategy represents a bond insurance strategy. In contrast, if the portfolio manager was planning to buy long-term bonds in the future and was worried about higher bond prices (lower rates), she could hedge the future investment by buying T-bond calls.

In summary, locking in bond positions, as well as currency and stock portfolios values with calls and puts, represents two important uses of options. As noted, in later parts of this book, we explore in more depth hedging currency, stock portfolio, debt, and commodities positions with options, futures, and other derivatives.

EXHIBIT 3.17-1 Summary of Different Option Positions

1. **Simulated Put**: Long in a call and short in a stock on a 1-to-1 basis.
2. **Simulated Straddle**: Long two calls for each share of stock shorted.
3. **Ratio Call Write**: Short in call and long in stock, with more calls than shares owned.
4. **Stock Insurance or Simulated Call**: Long in put and long in stock.
5. **Ratio Put Write**: Selling puts against shares of stock shorted at a ratio different than 1-to-1.
6. **Vertical or Money Spread**: Long and short in calls with different exercise prices (similar positions formed with puts).
7. **Horizontal or Time Spread**: Long and short in calls with different exercise dates (similar positions formed with puts).
8. **Diagonal Spread**: Long and short in calls with different exercise prices and dates (similar positions formed with puts).
9. **Bull Call Spread**: Long in call with low X and short in call with high X.
10. **Bull Put Spread**: Long in put with low X and short in put with high X.
11. **Bear Call Spread**: Long in call with high X and short in call with low X.
12. **Bear Put Spread**: Long in put with high X and short in put with low X.
13. **Ratio Money Spread**: Long and short positions in options with different exercise prices and/or times and also with ratios different than 1-to-1.
14. **Long Butterfly Spread**: Long in call with low X, short in 2 calls with middle X, and long in call with high X (similar position formed with puts).
15. **Short Butterfly Spread**: Short in call with low X, long in 2 calls with middle X, and short in call with high X (similar position formed with puts).
16. **Straddle Purchase**: Long call and put with similar terms.
17. **Strip Purchase**: Straddle purchase with additional puts (e.g., long call and long 2 puts).
18. **Strap Purchase**: Straddle purchase with additional calls (e.g., long 2 calls and long put).
19. **Straddle Sale**: Short call and put with similar terms.
20. **Strip Sale**: Straddle sale with additional puts (e.g., short 1 call and short 2 puts).
21. **Strap Sale**: Straddle sale with additional calls (e.g., short 2 calls and short 1 put).
22. **Long Vertical or Money Combination**: Long in call and put with different exercise prices (short positions formed by going short in call and put).
23. **Long Horizontal or Time Combination**: Long in call and put with different exercise dates (short positions formed by going short in call and put).
24. **Long Diagonal Combination**: Long in call and put with different exercise prices and dates (short positions formed by going short in call and put).
25. **Money Combination Purchase**: Long call and put with different exercise prices.
26. **Money Combination Sale**: Short call and put with different exercise prices.
27. **Condors**: Four call and/or put options on the same stock but with different terms.
28. **Simulated Long Stock Position**: Long in call and short in put with the same terms.
29. **Simulated Short Stock Position**: Long in put and short in call with the same terms.
30. **Splitting the Strikes**: Long in call and short in put with different exercise prices or dates (or long in put and short in call with different exercise prices or dates).

3.17 CONCLUSION

One important feature of an option is it can be combined with other options and the underlying security to produce a myriad of profit and stock price relations. In this chapter, we've examined how many of these strategies are formed and their characteristics. Exhibit 3.17-1 summarizes many of the strategies that were analyzed in this chapter. Because the value of an option at expiration is equal to its intrinsic value, our analysis of option strategies was done in terms of the position's profit and stock price relation at expiration. Option strategies also can be evaluated in terms of their profit and stock price relation prior to expiration and in terms of how the position changes in value in response to changes in such parameters as time to expiration and the variability of the underlying stock. These descriptions of option strategies are based on option pricing models. In the next five chapters, we examine how call and put options are priced; in Chapter 9, we return to our analysis of option strategies by evaluating the option strategies using the option pricing model.

KEY TERMS

follow-up strategies	reverse hedge	strip
simulated put	vertical spread	strap
equivalent strategies	horizontal spread	combination
simulated straddle	diagonal spread	condor
rolling credit	bull spread	simulated long position
ratio call write	bear spread	simulated short position
portfolio insurance	ratio money spread	spitting the strike
simulated call	butterfly money spread	range forward contract
ratio put write	put spread	

SELECTED REFERENCES

Bharadwahm, A., and J. B. Wiggins. "Box Spread and Put–Call Parity Tests for the S&P Index LEAPS Markets," *Journal of Derivatives* 8, (Summer 2001): 62–71.

Chance, D. M. *An Introduction to Options and Futures*, 4th ed., Orlando, FL: Dryden Press, 1998.

Chaput, J. S., and L. H. Ederington. "Option Spread and Combination Trading," *Journal of Derivatives* 10 4 (Summer 2003): 70–88.

Cox, J. C., and M. Rubinstein. *Option Markets*. Englewood Cliffs, NJ: Prentice-Hall, 1985.

Gombola, M. J., R. L. Roenfeldt, and P. L. Cooley. "Spreading Strategies in CBOE Options: Evidence on Market Performance." *The Journal of Financial Research* 1 (Winter 1978): 35–44.

Ervine, J., and A. Rudd. "Index Options: The Early Evidence." *Journal of Finance* 40 (July 1985): 743–756.

Faboozi, F., G. Gastineau, and S. Wunsch. "Introduction to Options on Stock Indexes and Stock Index Futures Contracts." In *Stock Index Futures*, edited by F. Faboozi and G. Kipnis. Homewood, IL: Dow Jones-Irwin, 1984.

Hull, J. C. *Option, Futures, and Other Derivatives,* 5th ed., Upper Saddle River, NJ: Prentice Hall, 2003, Chapter 9.

Leland, H. "Who Should Buy Portfolio Insurance?" *Journal of Finance* 35 (May 1980): 581–594.

Madura, J., and T. Veit. "Use of Currency Options in International Cash Management." *Journal of Cash Management* (January–February 1986): 42–48.

McMillan, L. G. *Options as a Strategic Investment*, 4th ed. Upper Saddle River, NJ: Prentice-Hall, 2001.

O'Brien, T. "The Mechanics of Portfolio Insurance?" *Journal of Portfolio Management* (Spring 1988): 40–47.

Pozen, R. "The Purchase of Protective Puts by Financial Institutions." *Financial Analysts Journal* 34 (July/August 1978): 47–60.

Rendleman, R., and R. McEnally. "Assessing the Costs of Portfolio Insurance." *Financial Analysts Journal* 43 (May–June 1987): 27–37.

PROBLEMS AND QUESTIONS

Note: A number of problems can be done in Excel either by writing a program or by using the "Basic Option Strategies" worksheet in the Excel spreadsheet called "Option Strategies." This spreadsheet is included with the "Excel Package" disc attached to the back cover of the text.

1. Evaluate the strategies in the following in terms of their profit and stock price relationships at expiration. In your evaluation, include a profit table that breaks down each strategy and identify the name of the strategy. Assume each stock position has 100 shares, and each option contract represents 100 options:

a. The short sale of ABC stock at $60 per share and the purchase of two ABC March 60 call contracts at $3 per call. Evaluate at expiration stock prices of 40, 45, 50, 54, 60, 66, 70, and 80.

b. The purchase of ABC stock at $75 per share and the sale of an ABC December 70 call contract at $8. Evaluate at expiration stock prices of 60, 65, 67, 70, 74, 75, 80, 85, and 90.

c. The purchase of 100 shares of ABC stock at $39 per share and the sale of two ABC October 40 call contracts at $6. Evaluate at expiration stock prices of 20, 27, 35, 40, 45, 53, and 60.

d. The purchase of an ABC September 50 call contract at $12 and the sale of an ABC September 60 call contract at $6. Evaluate at expiration stock prices of 40, 45, 50, 55, 56, 60, 65, and 70.

e. The purchase of one ABC July 50 call contract at $12, the sale of two July 60 call contracts at $6, and the purchase of one ABC July 70 call contract at $3. Evaluate at expiration stock prices of 40, 50, 53, 56, 60, 64, 67, 70, and 80.

f. The purchase of one ABC September 50 call contract at $12 and the sale of two ABC 60 September call contracts at $5. Evaluate at expiration stock prices of 40, 45, 50, 52, 55, 60, 65, 68, 70, and 75.

g. The purchase of ABC stock at $35 per share and the purchase of an ABC September 35 put contract for $3. Evaluate at expiration stock prices of 20, 25, 30, 35, 38, 40, 45, and 50.

h. The purchase of an ABC July 70 call contract at $3 and the purchase of an ABC July 70 put contract at $2. Evaluate at expiration stock prices of 50, 60, 65, 70, 75, 80, and 90.

i. The sale of an ABC June 65 call contract at $4 and the sale of an ABC June 65 put contract at $3. Evaluate at expiration stock prices of 50, 55, 58, 60, 65, 70, 72, 75, and 80.

j. The purchase of an ABC 40 call contract at $3 and the purchase of two ABC 40 put contracts at $2 each. Evaluate at expiration stock prices of 25, 30, 35, 36.5, 40, 45, 47, 50, and 55.

k. The sale of two 40 call contracts at $3 each and the sale of one 40 put contract at $2. Evaluate at expiration stock prices of 20, 25, 30, 32, 35, 40, 44, 45, and 50.

l. The purchase of an ABC 40 call contract at $3 and the purchase of an ABC 35 put contract at $3. Evaluate at expiration stock prices of 20, 25, 29, 30, 35, 40, 45, 46, 50, and 55.

m. The sale of an ABC 70 call contract at $4 and the sale of an ABC 60 put contract at $3. Evaluate at expiration stock prices of 40, 50, 53, 57, 60, 65, 70, 73, 77, 80, and 90.

n. The sale of an ABC 60 put contract at $2 and the purchase of an ABC 70 put contract at $7 when ABC stock is trading at 65. Evaluate at expiration stock prices of 50, 55, 60, 65, 70, 80, and 90.

o. The sale of an ABC 40 put contract at $3 and the purchase of an ABC 40 call contract at $3. Evaluate at expiration stock prices of 30, 35, 40, 45, and 50.

p. The purchase of an ABC 50 put contract at $2 and the sale of ABC 60 call contract at $1 when ABC stock is trading at 53. Evaluate at expiration stock prices of 40, 45, 49, 50, 55, 60, 65, and 70.

2. Evaluate the following index option positions in terms of their profit and spot index relations at expiration. In your evaluation, include a profit table and graph that breaks down each strategy.

   a. A long straddle formed with a 1200 S&P 500 call trading at 30 and a 1200 S&P 500 put trading at 20. Evaluate at spot index prices of 1000, 1050, 1100, 1150, 1200, 1250, 1300, 1350, and 1400.

   b. A simulated long index position formed by purchasing a 1200 S&P 500 call at 30 and selling a 1200 S&P 500 put at 30. Evaluate at spot index prices of 1000, 1050, 1100, 1150, 1200, 1250, 1300, 1350, and 1400.

3. Evaluate the following currency strategies in terms of their profit and exchange rate relations at expiration. In your evaluation, include a profit table and graph that breaks down each strategy.

   a. The purchase of a 150 (cents) British pound September call contract for 10 (cents) and the purchase of a 150 (cents) BP September put contract for 5. Evaluate at $/BP exchange rates at the option's September expiration of $1.30/BP, $1.35, $1.40, $1.45, $1.50, $1.55, $1.50, $1.65, and $1.70.

   b. The sale of a 150 (cents) British pound September call contract for 10 (cents) and the sale of a 150 (cents) BP September put contract for 5. Evaluate at $/BP exchange rates at the option's September expiration of $1.30/BP, $1.35, $1.40, $1.45, $1.50, $1.55, $1.50, $1.65, and $1.70.

4. Suppose shortly after Mr. Zapp purchased an ESD September 70 call contract at $3 per call, the price of ESD increased to $77, causing the price of his call to rise to $9 per call. Evaluate in terms of their profit and stock price relations the following follow-up actions Mr. Zapp could pursue:

   a. Liquidate

   b. Do nothing

   c. Spread by selling an ESD 80 call trading at $3 per call

   d. Roll up by selling the 70 call and using the profit to buy two ESD 80 calls at $3 per call

Evaluate the strategies at expiration stock prices of 60, 65, 70, 73, 75, 80, 81, 85, and 90.

5. Suppose shortly after you purchased an ABC September 50 call for $3, the price of the stock decreased to $46 per share on speculation of a future announcement of low quarterly earnings for the ABC Company. Suppose you believe the speculation is warranted and as a result believe the price of ABC stock will decline further. Explain how you could profit at expiration by changing your potentially unprofitable long call position to a potentially profitable spread position if the stock decreases. Assume there is an ABC September 40 call available at $8 and evaluate the spread at expiration stock prices of 35, 40, 45, 50, 55, and 60.

6. Suppose after selling an ABC June 50 call for $3 when the stock was at $50, the price of the stock increases to $55. Assume at the $55 stock price, the June 50 call is trading at $6, and there is an ABC June 55 call available that is trading at $2.50. Believing that ABC stock will stay at $55 at least until expiration, show how you could change your current unprofitable position to a potentially profitable one by implementing a rolling-credit strategy. How would your collateral requirements change? (Use margin formulas that are in Chapter 2.)

7. Compare and contrast the following strategies:

   a. Call purchase and leveraged stock purchase
   b. Put purchase and synthetic put
   c. In-the-money covered call write and out-of-the-money covered call write
   d. Ratio call writes with different ratios of short calls to shares of stock
   e. Bull spread and bear spread

8. Suppose after you purchased an ABC June 40 put at $2, the price of ABC stock dropped from $40 per share to $35 per share, causing the 40 put to increase to $6. Evaluate in terms of profit and stock price relations the following follow-up strategies:

   a. Liquidation
   b. Do nothing
   c. Spread by selling a 35 put contract at $2
   d. Roll down by selling the 40 put and purchasing two 35 puts at $2

   Evaluate at expiration stock prices of 20, 25, 30, 35, 38, 40, 45, and 50.

9. Compare and contrast the following positions:

   a. Put purchase and short sale
   b. Naked put write and covered call write
   c. Covered put write and naked call write
   d. Straddle, strip, and strap purchases

10. List a number of strategies that will yield an "Inverted V"-shaped profit and stock price relationship at expiration.

11. List a number of strategies that will yield a "V"-shaped profit and stock price relationship at expiration.

12. Construct a portfolio with calls with X = $80, $90, and $100 that will yield the following cash flows (CF) at expiration:

S_T	CF_T
$70	0
75	0
80	0
90	10
95	5
100	0
105	0
110	0

13. Set up a portfolio with calls with X = $40, $50, and $60 that will yield the following cash flows at expiration:

S_T	CF_T
$30	0
40	0
45	5
50	10
55	5
60	0
70	0

14. On May 10th, the XU Investment Trust determines it will have to liquidate part of its stock portfolio in September to finance the construction of the new $11M Business School Building. Fearful of a bear market, the Trust would like to hedge the portfolio sale. The portfolio they plan to sell is well diversified, has a ß of 1.10, and on May 10th is worth $11M. On May 10th, the S&P 500 spot index is at 1100 and a September S&P 500 put with an exercise price of 1100 (contract multiplier = $100) is trading at 30.

    a. How many S&P 500 put contracts would the trust need if it wanted to insure the portfolio with a portfolio insurance strategy?

    b. Evaluate the put-insurance strategy at spot index prices at expiration of 900, 1000, 1100, 1200, and 1300.

15. ABC International Investments has investments in British bonds. The bond portfolio pays approximately 625,000 BP in interest every 6 months, which the company converts to dollars. Recently the $/BP exchange rate has become more volatile. ABC expects, though, the $/BP exchange rate will increase from its current level of $E_0 = \$1.15/BP$. Explain how ABC could hedge its next interest payment of 625,000 BP to be paid at the end of March against exchange rate risk while still gaining if the spot $/BP exchange rate increases by buying March BP put with an exercise price of $1.15/BP for $0.05/BP (contract size = 31,250 BP). Assume the interest payment date and option expiration date are the same. Evaluate at $E_T = \$1.00/BP$, $1.05, $1.10, $1.15, $1.20, and $1.25.

16. The James Company, a U.S. corporation, has a debt obligation to a British bank for 937,500 BP. The present $/BP spot rate is $E_0 = \$1.10/BP$. The debt is to be paid at the end of June. The James Company believes that the U.S. dollar will strengthen against the pound (E_0 decrease) and would like to benefit by paying less in dollars for its debt. At the same time the company does not want to be subject to exchange-rate risk. Show how the company could meet its dual objectives by purchasing June BP call contracts with exercise price of $1.10 trading at $.04/BP (contract size = 31,250). Assume the payment date and June expiration date are the same. Evaluate at $E_T = \$0.95/BP$, $1.00, $1.05, $1.10, $1.15, $1.20, and $1.25.

17. A fixed-income fund manager plans to sell twenty $100,000 face value T-bonds from her government bond fund in March. The T-bonds she plans to sell pay 7% interest and are currently priced at 105. At the anticipated selling date, the bonds will have 15 years to maturity and no accrued interest. The manager believes that long-term rates could decrease but does not want to risk selling the bond at lower prices if rates increase. For $20,000, the manager can purchase an OTC T-bond option on her bonds from a dealer at an exercise price equal the current price and expiration coinciding with her March T-bond sales date.

   a. Describe the OTC option and its terms.

   b. Show in a table the manager's option-hedged revenue (do not include option cost) for possible spot T-bond prices at the March sale of 98, 99, 100, 101, 102, 103, 104, 105, 106, 107, 108, 109, and 110. Assume the manager will exercise her option if it is feasible (instead of closing) and that she will sell her bonds in the market if it not feasible.

18. Suppose the fixed-income fund manager in Question 17 were expecting a cash flow of $2,100,000 in March and planned to invest the cash flow in twenty 100,000 T-bonds. Suppose the T-bonds she plans to buy pay 7% interest, have 15 years to maturity, and are currently priced at 105. At the anticipated purchase date, assume such bonds will have no accrued interest. The manager believes that long-term rates could increase but does not want to risk buying the bonds at higher prices if rates decrease. For $20,000, the manager can purchase an OTC T-bond option on the 20 bonds from a dealer at an exercise price equal the current price and expiration coinciding with her March T-bonds purchase date.

   a. Describe the OTC option and its terms.

   b. Show in a table the manager's option-hedged cost (do not include option cost) for possible spot T-bond prices at the March purchase date of 98, 99, 100, 101, 102, 103, 104, 105, 106, 107, 108, 109, and 110. Assume the manager will exercise her option, if it is feasible (instead of closing), and that she will buy her bonds in the market if it not feasible.

WEB EXERCISES

1. Select several exchange call and put options and determine their recent prices by going to www.wsj.com/free and clicking "Market Data Center" ("U.S. Stocks" and "Listed Options Quotes"). Using your options, evaluate the following strategies with a profit table and graph (use Excel or the Excel program for "Option Strategies" included with the book): call purchase, put purchase, straddle purchase, straddle sale, synthetic long position, or synthetic short position.

2. Select one of the index options listed on the CBOE and determine its recent prices by going to www.cboe.com (in "Quotes," click "Delayed Quotes Beta," and then click "option Chains"). Using your index option, evaluate the following strategies with a profit table and graph (use Excel or the Excel program "Option Strategies"): call purchase, put purchase, straddle purchase, straddle sale, synthetic long position, and synthetic short position.

3. Select several currency options listed on the Philadelphia Exchange and determine their recent prices by going to www.phlx.com (click "Quotes & Trade Info."). Using your options, evaluate the following strategies with a profit table and graph (use Excel or the Excel program "Option Strategies"): call purchase, put purchase, straddle purchase, straddle sale, synthetic long position, and synthetic short position.

CHAPTER 4

FUNDAMENTAL OPTION PRICE RELATIONS

4.1 INTRODUCTION

In Chapter 1, we described how the price of an option is a function of the underlying stock's price and volatility and the option's time to expiration. An option's price also depends on other factors such as the risk-free return, whether the option is American or European, and whether the underlying security provides a return during the period such as a dividend or coupon interest. In this chapter, we begin our analysis of option pricing by examining how these factors determine the minimum and maximum prices of options; the price relationships between options with different exercise prices and times to expiration; and how dividends, interest rates, and volatility influence the price of an option. In our analysis, we examine each relationship separately. In Chapter 5, we will integrate many of the relationships by deriving the binomial option pricing model.

To facilitate our discussion, the symbols for the call premium (C) and put premium (P) is expressed (when it is helpful) in the following functional form: $C = C(X, T)$ or $P = P(X, T)$, where T is the time to expiration (which may be expressed as a proportion of the year: a 3-month option would expire in $T = .25$ of a year). Thus, $C(X, T) = C(50, 0.5) = \$15$ says that the price of a 6-month option with an exercise price of $50 is $15. Also, because some relations are applicable for European options, whereas others hold only for American options, an "e" or "a" superscript (C^a or C^e) is used when clarification is necessary. Similarly, when needed, the subscript "0" is used to indicate the current period, "T" to indicate the option's expiration period or date, and "t" to signify any time period between the present ($t = 0$) and expiration ($t = T$). Finally, we concentrate primarily on stock options; in Sections 4.12 and 4.13, though, we extend our discussion of boundary conditions to stock index and currency options.

4.2 MINIMUM AND MAXIMUM CALL PRICES

4.2.1 Maximum American and European Call Prices

Because a call option gives an investor the right to buy a specific stock, it would be irrational for the investor to pay more for the call than the underlying stock itself. Thus, whether the call is American or European, its maximum price, $MaxC_t$, is the market price of the stock:

> **RELATION:** The maximum price an investor would pay for a call is the underlying stock's price:
> $$MaxC_t = S_t$$

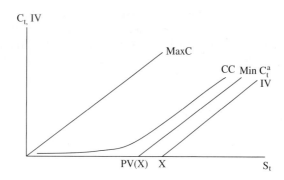

FIGURE 4.2-1 Call Option Boundary Condition

The maximum price defines the upper limit or bound of the call premium. Graphically, the upper limit is depicted in Figure 4.2-1 by the 45-degree line that shows the one-to-one relation between $MaxC_t$ and S_t.

4.2.2 Minimum Price of an American Call

As noted in Chapter 1, if a call option is American, then the call cannot trade at a price below its intrinsic value (IV). If it did, arbitrageurs could realize riskless returns by buying the call, exercising it, and selling the stock. For example, suppose a 40 American call is trading at 5 when the stock is trading at 50. Given these prices, an investor could buy the stock in the open market at a cost of 50 or alternatively buy the call and exercise it immediately at a cost of only 45 ($5 + 40 = 45$). Obviously, the investor would opt to acquire the stock indirectly through the option market. This action would lead to an increase in the demand for the call until the price of the call was equal to at least 10. In addition, with the call trading at 5, there also would be arbitrage opportunities from executing the aforementioned arbitrage strategy: Buy the call, and exercise it immediately at a cost of 45, then sell the stock for 50. In implementing this strategy, arbitrageurs would push the call premium up until it is at least equal to the intrinsic value of 10 and the arbitrage profit is zero:

RELATION: To preclude arbitrage, an American call will trade at a price that is *at least equal* to its intrinsic value:

$$C_t^a \geq Max[S_t - X, 0]$$

If this condition does not hold, then an arbitrage opportunity exists by buying the call, exercising immediately, and selling the stock.

The intrinsic value defines a boundary or limit that governs the price of an American call. This boundary condition is shown graphically in Figure 4.2-1 by the IV line. The IV, though, is not the minimum price of an American call on a nondividend paying stock. That is, if an American call trades at a price above its intrinsic value, satisfying the preceding boundary condition, riskless profit is still possible. For example, suppose in the preceding example, the 40 call was trading at 11 when the stock was at 50; the call had an expiration of 1 year; and there was a riskless zero coupon bond available in the market with a face value equal to the call's exercise price of 50, maturity of 1 year, and trading at discount rate of $R_f = 6\%$. In this case, an arbitrageur could receive a cash inflow of 1.26 by buying the call at 11, buying the bond at its present value (PV) for $PV(X) = PV(40) = 40/1.06 = 37.74$, and selling the stock short at 50 (i.e., $50 - 11 - 40/1.06 = 1.26$). At expiration, if the stock price is equal or greater than 40 ($S_T \geq X$), the arbitrageur could use the proceeds from the bond to exercise the call and then use the stock to cover the short position; the net cash flow in this case is zero. On the other hand, if the stock price is less than 40 ($S_T < X$), the call would be worthless. In this case, the arbitrageur would only need to use a portion of the 40 from the bond to buy the stock and cover the short position, realizing a cash inflow of $40 - S_T$. Thus, if the call is trading at 11, an arbitrageur receives an initial cash inflow of $S_0 - PV(X) - C_0^a = 50 - 37.74 - 11 = 1.26$, and at expiration receives additional cash if $S_T < 40$ and is able to cover the short position such that there are no losses if $S_T \geq 40$. Given this riskless opportunity, arbitrageurs would try to buy the call, in turn, pushing its price up until the initial cash flow (CF_0) is at least zero. This would occur when the price of the American call is equal to the difference in the stock price and the present value of the exercise price. That is

$$CF_0 = S_0 - PV(X) - C_0^a \leq 0$$

$$C_0^a \geq S_0 - PV(X)$$

$$C_0^a \geq Max[S_0 - PV(X), 0], \quad \text{to preclude negative prices}$$

Thus, in our example, the arbitrageurs would push the price of the American call to at least 12.26:

$$C_0^a \geq Max[S_0 - PV(X), 0]$$

$$C_0^a \geq \$50 - \frac{\$40}{1.06} = \$12.26$$

The boundary condition of $Max[S_t - PV(X), 0]$, in turn, defines the minimum price of an American call at any time t ($MinC_t^a$):

RELATION: In the absence of arbitrage, the minimum price of an American call is:

$$MinC_t^a = Max[S_t - PV(X), 0]$$

If the price of the American call is below this minimum, then an arbitrage opportunity exists by taking long positions in the call and a bond with a face value equal to the exercise price and a short position in the underlying stock.

The minimum price boundary condition is shown graphically in Figure 4.2-1 where $MinC_t^a = S_t - PV(X)$ is plotted against S_t.

4.2.3　Formal Proof of the Boundary Condition

The preceding boundary condition was established by showing that if the condition is violated, then an arbitrage opportunity exists that will provide an initial positive cash flow with no liabilities at expiration when the position is closed. As a rule, the arbitrage strategy underlying any boundary condition can be defined in terms of the violation of the condition, with the arbitrageur going long in the lower valued position and short in the higher valued one. Thus, in a case in which the minimum price condition for the American call is violated ($C_0^a < \text{Max}[S_0 - PV(X), 0]$), the arbitrage strategy, as we saw previously, should consist of a long position in the call and short position in ($S_0 - PV(X)$):

Boundary Condition	Boundary Condition Violation	Arbitrage Strategy $C_0^a < (S_0 - PV(X))$		
		Long	Short	Details
$C_0^a \geq S_0$ $-PV(X)$	$C_0^a < S_0$ $-PV(X)$	1. Long Call 2. Short ($S_0 - PV(X)$)	1. $\{+C_0^a\}$ 2. $\{-(S_0 - PV(X))\}$ $= \{-S_0, +PV(X)\}$	1. Buy Call 2. Buy Bond 3. Short Stock

This strategy would provide an initial positive cash flow of

$$CF_0 = S_0 - PV(X) - C_0^a > 0,$$

and as shown in Table 4.2-1, there would be no liabilities when the position is closed at expiration. That is, if $S_T \geq X$ at expiration, then the total cash flow is $(S_T - X) + X - S_T = 0$: $(S_T - X)$ received from the sale of the call, $+X$ from the principal received on the bond, and $-S_T$ cost to cover the short position. On the other hand, if $S_T < X$, the total cash flow is positive: The call is worthless, but the principal of X received on the bond exceeds the cost of S_T to close the short stock position. Given this riskless opportunity, the price condition is then established by arguing that if the market is efficient, then arbitrageurs, in seeking the opportunity, would drive the price of the call to a level where the initial cash

TABLE 4.2-1 Proof of Boundary Condition: $C_0^a \geq S_0 - PV(X)$

Boundary Condition	Boundary Condition Violation	Arbitrage Strategy $C_0^a < (S_0 - PV(X))$		
		Positions		Details
$C_0^a \geq S_0 - PV(X)$	$C_0^a < S_0 - PV(X)$	1. Long Call 2. Short ($S_0 - PV(X)$)	1. $\{+C_0^a\}$ 2. $\{-(S_0 - PV(X))\}$ $= \{-S_0, +PV(X)\}$	1. Buy Call 2. Buy Bond 3. Short Stock

Initial Positive Cash Flow of $CF_0 = S_0 - PV(X) - C_0^a > 0$,

No Liabilities at T:
Cash Flows at T from of a Long Call,
Long Bond, and Short Stock Portfolio

Strategy	Cash Flow at Expiration		
	$S_T < X$	$S_T = X$	$S_T > X$
Long Call	0	0	$(S_T - X)$
Long Bond	X	X	X
Short Stock	$-S_T$	$-S_T$	$-S_T$
	$(X - S_T) > 0$	0	0

NOTE: To preclude arbitrage, the current cash flow $-C_0 - PV(X) + S_0$ must be negative: $-C_0 - PV(X) + S_0 < 0$ or $C_0 > S_0 - PV(X)$.

flow is at least zero:

$$CF_0 = S_0 - PV(X) - C_0^a \leq 0$$

$$C_0^a \geq S_0 - PV(X)$$

$$C_0^a \geq Max[S_0 - PV(X), 0], \text{ to preclude negative prices}$$

The minimum price of an American call at any time t, is therefore

$$MinC_t^a = Max[S_t - PV(X), 0]$$

Thus, in terms of our example, the minimum price of the 40 call is: $12.26:

$$MinC_t^a = Max[S_t - PV(X), 0]$$

$$MinC_t^a = Max[50 - (\$40/1.06), 0]$$

$$MinC_t^a = \$12.26$$

(The methodology just described for establishing the boundary condition for the American call price is summarized in Row 2 of Exhibit 4.14-1 at the end of this chapter. The table describes the arbitrage strategies underlying many of the boundary conditions delineated in this chapter.)

4.2.4 Minimum Price of a European Call

In the preceding case, the minimum price for the American option was established by an arbitrage portfolio that required closing the positions in the call, bond, and stock at the call's expiration date. Because the call is closed at expiration, the distinction between American and European is not important in defining the minimum price. Thus, the minimum price of a European call option on a stock not paying a dividend can be determined by the same arbitrage argument used for the American option. Hence, the minimum price for a European call on a nondividend-paying stock is the same as that for an American:

RELATION: Minimum price on European call option:

$$MinC_t^e = Max[S_t - PV(X), 0]$$

It should be noted that because both the American and European calls (on a stock not paying a dividend during the life of the call) have exactly the same lower bounds, the right to early exercise, implicit in an American call, is worth nothing. Thus, the American call option should not be exercised early; it is worth more "alive" than "dead."

4.2.5 Boundary and Minimum Price Conditions for Calls on Dividend-Paying Stocks

In the preceding example, we established the minimum price of the call (whether it is American or European) to be 12.26. As noted, if the 40 call in our example were trading below 12.26, then an arbitrage profit could be realized by going long in the call, long in the bond, and short in the stock. Suppose the 40 call, though, were trading below its minimum at 10, but the stock was expected to go ex-dividend in 3 months, with the value of the dividend at that date expected to be worth $D = 3$. In this case, the arbitrage strategy

EXHIBIT 4.2-1 Boundary and Minimum Price Conditions for Call Options on Dividend-Paying Stocks

Boundary Condition on Call Option on Dividend-Paying Stock

> **RELATION** : **The price of an American or European call on a stock that is expected to go ex-dividend at t^* must be greater than $S_0 - PV(X, T) - PV(D, t^*)$:**

where: $C_t \geq \text{Max}[S_t - PV(X, T) - PV(D, t^*), 0]$

D = the value of the dividend at the ex-dividend date

$PV(X, T)$ = price of bond with face value of X and maturity at T

$PV(D, t^*)$ = price of bond with face value of D and maturity at t^*

t^* = ex-dividend date

Minimum Price on European Call: Relation

$$\text{MinC}_t^e = \text{Max}[S_t - PV(X, T) - PV(D, t^*), 0]$$

Minimum Price Condition on an American Call on a Dividend-Paying Stock

$$\text{MinC}_t^a = \text{Max}[S_t - X, S_t - PV(X, t^*), S_t - PV(D, t^*) - PV(X, T), 0]$$

For a formal derivation of these price conditions, see Appendix 4A.

---

governing the minimum call price, if implemented, would earn an initial cash flow of 2.26 $(50 - (40/1.06) - 10)$. At the end of 3 months, though, an arbitrageur would have an obligation to pay 3.00 to the share lender to cover the dividend payment on the short stock position. Because this dividend obligation exceeds the initial excess cash of 2.26, the strategy is no longer a free lunch.[1] The dividend payment in this example suggests that the boundary condition of $S_0 - PV(X)$ holds only for cases in which the underlying stock does not pay a dividend. In general, dividends have a negative impact on call values, with the minimum call price decreasing the greater the anticipated dividend payments. In addition, if the dividend is expected to be relatively high, an early exercise advantage for arbitrageurs may exist; if so, the minimum value of the American call will be greater than the European one. The boundary and the minimum price conditions governing American and European call options on dividend-paying stocks are defined in the Exhibit 4.2-1 and are formally derived in Appendix 4A at the end of this chapter.

4.3 OPTION PRICES WITH DIFFERENT EXERCISE PRICES

4.3.1 Price Relation of Calls with Different Exercise Prices

Suppose a July ABC 50 European call is trading at 3, whereas a July ABC 60 European call is at 4. On reflection, something is wrong. Intuitively, we should expect the

---

[1] Note: Because the price of the stock would fall on the ex-dividend date by approximately 3, the arbitrageur could offset her $3 dividend obligation on the short position by closing the short stock position by buying back the stock on the ex-dividend date at a price $3 less. By doing this, though, the arbitrageur would lose the short stock position required to hedge her other position and therefore lose her arbitrage position.

price of the call with the lower exercise price of 50 to be greater than the one with the higher exercise price of 60 because the former gives one the right to buy ABC stock at a lower price. To exploit this price imbalance, an arbitrageur could buy the 50 call and sell the 60 one (i.e., set up a bull spread). As shown in Exhibit 4.3-1, at expiration, arbitrageurs/spreaders would earn a profit regardless of the price of ABC stock. By exploiting this opportunity, though, they would increase the price of the 50 call and lower the price of 60 call until $C_0^e(50) > C_0^e(60)$, and the arbitrage opportunity disappears. Thus, arbitrageurs would ensure that the price of a lower exercise-priced call is greater than a higher priced one:

RELATION: Price condition for European calls with different exercise prices:

$$C_t^e(X_1) > C_t^e(X_2), \ \text{ for } X_2 > X_1$$

In addition to the intuitive reasoning, a more formal arbitrage argument also can be used to establish the condition: $C_0^e(X_1) > C_0^e(X_2)$. Specifically, if this condition is violated, $C_0^e(X_1) < C_0^e(X_2)$, then arbitrageurs will be able to earn riskless profit by forming a bull call spread by going long in the X_1 call and short in the X_2 call. This strategy would

EXHIBIT 4.3-1 Profit and Stock Price Relation for a Bull Spread—ABC 50 Call Purchased at 3 and ABC 60 Call Sold at 4

S_T	Profit on Long 50 Call: $Max[S_T-50,0]-3$	Profit on Short 60 Call: $4-Max[S_T-60,0]$	Total Profit
40	−300	400	100
45	−300	400	100
50	−300	400	100
55	200	400	600
60	700	400	1,100
65	1,200	−100	1,100
70	1,700	−600	1,100

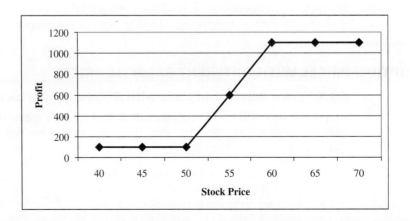

TABLE 4.3-1 Proof of Boundary Condition: $C_0^e(X_1) > C_0^e(X_2)$

Boundary Condition	Boundary Condition Violation	Arbitrage Strategy $C_0^e(X_1) < C_0^e(X_2)$	
		Positions	**Details**
$C_0^e(X_1) > C_0^e(X_2)$	$C_0^e(X_1) < C_0^e(X_2)$	1. Long in the X_1 Call	Buy X_1 Call
		2. Short in the X_2 Call	Sell X_2 Call

- **Initial positive cash flow of $CF_0 = C_0^e(X_2) - C_0^e(X_1) > 0$**
- **No liabilities at T when bull spread is closed**

	Cash Flow at Expiration		
Position	$S_T < X_1$	$X_1 \leq S_T \leq X_2$	$S_T > X_2$
Long X_1 Call	0	$S_T - X_1$	$S_T - X_1$
Short X_2 Call	0	0	$-(S_T - X_2)$
	0	$(S_T - X_1) > 0$	$(X_2 - X_1) > 0$

To preclude arbitrage, the initial cash flow must be negative.
Thus:

$$-C_0^e(X_1) + C_0^e(X_2) < 0 \text{ or } C_0^e(X_1) > C_0^e(X_2)$$

provide an initial positive cash flow of

$$CF_0 = C_0^e(X_2) - C_0^e(X_1) > 0$$

and as shown in Table 4.3-1, there would be no liabilities when the position is closed at expiration. That is, at expiration, there are three possible cases: $S_T < X_1, X_1 \leq S_T \leq X_2$, and $S_T > X_2$. If $X_1 \leq S_T \leq X_2$ or $S_T > X_2$, then the cash flows from the bull spread will be positive; if $S_T < X_1$, then the spread's cash flow will be zero. An arbitrage opportunity would therefore exist if there was no cost incurred in setting up the bull spread. To preclude this free lunch, the initial cash flows of the bull spread must therefore be negative:

$$CF_0 = -C_0^e(X_1) + C_0^e(X_2) < 0$$

or

$$C_0^e(X_1) > C_0^e(X_2), \text{ for } X_2 > X_1$$

In summary

RELATION: Given two European call options that are identical except for their exercise prices, the one with the lower exercise price (X_1) will be priced higher than the one with the higher exercise price (X_2); if not, then an arbitrage opportunity exists by forming a bull money spread.

The condition that $C_t^e(X_1) > C_t^e(X_2)$ also holds for an American option in which early exercise is possible. If it did not, then an arbitrageur/spreader again could take a long position in the call with the lower exercise price and a short position in the call with the higher exercise price. If he could hold the positions to expiration, then the same arbitrage profit discussed previously for the European calls could be earned. However, it is possible the spreader could be assigned on the short position. If this did occur, then the arbitrageur/spreader would have to buy the stock in the market at S_t and sell it to the option holder at X_2 for a loss on the short position of $X_2 - S_t$. However, the spreader can more than offset this loss by simply selling his lower exercise price call at $C_t^a(X_1) = S_t - X_1 + TVP$. Because $X_2 > X_1$, the cash flow from closing would exceed the cost of the assignment. Thus, if there were an early exercise at time t, the arbitrageur/spreader would still be able to earn a positive cash flow:

$$CF_t = C_t^a(X_1) - (S_t - X_2)$$
$$CF_t = (S_t - X_1 + TVP) - (S_t - X_2)$$
$$CF_t = X_2 - X_1 + TVP > 0$$

Hence, an American option like the European is governed by the condition that $C_0^a(X_1) > C_0^a(X_2)$.[2]

4.3.2   Price Limits on Calls With Different Exercise Prices

In addition to the condition that $C(X_1) > C(X_2)$, we also can establish with an arbitrage argument that the difference in the call premiums cannot be greater than the present value of the difference in the calls' exercise prices for European calls:

$$C_t^e(X_1) - C_t^e(X_2) < PV(X_2 - X_1)$$

and greater than the difference in the calls' exercise prices for American calls:

$$C_t^a(X_1) - C_t^a(X_2) < X_2 - X_1$$

For the case of the European calls, if the price-limit condition does not hold (i.e., $C^e(X_1) - C^e(X_2) > PV(X_2 - X_1)$, then an arbitrage opportunity would be available by going

1. Long in a bond with a face value of $X_2 - X_1$ and maturing at the option's expiration date: $\{+PV(X_2 - X_1)\}$
2. Short in the X_1 call: $\{-C(X_1)\}$
3. Long in the X_2 call: $\{+C(X_2)\}$

This strategy would yield an initial positive cash flow of $C_0^e(X_1) - C_0^e(X_2) - PV(X_2 - X_1)$, and as shown in Table 4.3-2, there would be no liabilities at expiration when the position is closed; that is, the cash flows would be either positive or zero but not negative when the position is closed. To preclude this free lunch, the initial cash flow must

---

[2] It should be noted that an exception to this rule can occur when there is a deep out-of-the-money option. With such an option, it is quite possible that the premiums for options with different exercise prices could be the same.

TABLE 4.3-2 Proof of Boundary Condition: $C_0^e(X_1) - C_0^e(X_2) < PV(X_2 - X_1)$

Boundary Condition	Boundary Condition Violation	Arbitrage Strategy $C_0^e(X_1) - C_0^e(X_2) > PV(X_2-X_1)$	
		Positions	Details
$C_0^e(X_1) - C_0^e(X_2)$ $< PV(X_2 - X_1)$	$C_0^e(X_1) - C_0^e(X_2)$ $> PV(X_2 - X_1)$	Short in $[C_0^e(X_1) - C_0^e(X_2)]$ Long in $PV(X_2 - X_1)$	1. Sell X_1 call 2. Buy X_2 call 3. Buy bond with face value of $X_2 - X_1$

- **This strategy yields an initial positive cash flow of $C_0^e(X_1) - C_0^e(X_2) - PV(X_2 - X_1)$**

- **At expiration there are no liabilities**

	Cash Flow at Expiration		
Position	$S_T < X_1$	$X_1 \leq S_T \leq X_2$	$S_T > X_2$
Short in X_1 Call	0	$-(S_T - X_1)$	$-(S_T - X_1)$
Long in X_2 Call	0	0	$(S_T - X_2)$
Long in Bond	$X_2 - X_1$	$X_2 - X_1$	$X_2 - X_1$
	$(X_2 - X_1) > 0$	$(X_2 - S_T) > 0$	0

To preclude arbitrage, the initial cash flow must therefore be negative:

$$C_t^e(X_1) - C_t^e(X_2) < PV(X_2 - X_1), \text{ for } X_2 > X_1$$

therefore be negative:

RELATION:

$$C_t^e(X_1) - C_t^e(X_2) < PV(X_2 - X_1), \text{ for } X_2 > X_1$$

In terms of the example used in the preceding section, if the options' expirations and the bond's maturity are 1 year, and the risk-free rate of return is 6%, then the difference in the prices of the ABC 50 European call and the ABC 60 European call should not be greater than $9.43:

$$C_t^e(50) - C_t^e(60) < PV(60 - 50) = \frac{10}{1.06} = 9.43$$

The preceding condition is applicable for European calls. Suppose an arbitrageur, though, is long in the bond and has a bear spread formed with American calls ($\{-C_0^a(X_1), +C_0^a(X_2)\}$), and both calls are exercised early at time t. The arbitrageur, in turn, would incur a negative cash flow of $X_2 - X_1$ at time t, which she can finance by borrowing $X_2 - X_1$ dollars at a rate R for the remainder of the period $(T-t)$. At expiration, closing the loan would cost $(X_2 - X_1)(1 + R)^{T-t}$. Because $(X_2 - X_1)(1 + R)^{T-t}$ is greater than the bond's cash flow of $(X_2 - X_1)$, the arbitrageur's strategy is no longer riskless. Thus, the price limit condition for European calls needs to be adjusted for American calls. This can be done by defining the price limit in terms of an arbitrage portfolio consisting of the bear spread and a riskless bond purchased for $X_2 - X_1$ instead of $PV(X_2 - X_1)$. This bond investment would have a face value of $(X_2 - X_1)(1 + R)^T$ at expiration, which would equal or exceed the maximum cost of covering the bear spread regardless of when the spread is exercised. Thus, for American call options the price limits condition would be

---

RELATION:

$$C_t^a(X_1) - C_t^a(X_2) < X_2 - X_1, \quad \text{for } X_2 > X_1$$

If this condition does not hold, then an arbitrage opportunity would exist by purchasing a riskless bond for $X_2 - X_1$ and forming a bear spread by selling the X_1 American call and buying the X_2 American call.

4.4   CALL PRICE AND TIME TO EXPIRATION RELATIONS

In Chapter 1, we noted that the greater a call's time to expiration, the greater its time value premium. The positive relation between a call's time to expiration and its price suggests that given two American call options on the same stock, with the same exercise prices, but with different expirations, the call with the greater expiration time (T_2) will be priced higher than the one with the smaller time (T_1). That is

$$C_t^a(T_2) > C_t^a(T_1), \quad \text{for } T_2 > T_1$$

Although this relationship is intuitive, an arbitrage argument involving a time spread can be used to establish the condition. Specifically, suppose that an ABC 50 call that expires in 6 months ($T_2 = .5$ per year) is selling for $C_0^a(.5) = \$5$, whereas an ABC 50 call expiring in 3 months ($T_1 = .25$) is selling at a higher price of $C_0^a(.25) = \$7$. An arbitrageur/spreader could realize a \$2 cash flow immediately by forming a time spread: buy the longer term call and sell the shorter term one:

Strategy	Cash Flow
Buy Longer Term Call: $C_0^a(.5)$	−\$5
Sell Shorter Term Call: $C_0^a(.25)$	\$7
Cash Flow	\$2

If the short-term ABC 50 call is ever exercised, whether at expiration or before, the arbitrageur can simply exercise the longer term option to meet the assignment; that is, she can buy the stock at $X = 50$ on the longer term option and then deliver it on the shorter-term call's assignment. Thus, once the arbitrage is set, there are no further liabilities. Given this riskless opportunity, arbitrageurs in the market would buy the longer term call, increasing its demand and price, and sell the shorter term call, depressing its price, until $C_t^a(.5) > C_t^a(.25)$, and the arbitrage opportunity disappears. Thus

---

RELATION: Given two American call options on the same stock, with the same exercise prices but with different expiration dates, the price of the longer term call will be greater than the price of a shorter term one. If this condition does not hold, then an

---

arbitrage profit can be realized by forming a time spread: buy the longer term call and sell the shorter term call. Such actions by arbitrageurs will ensure:

$$C_t^a(T_2) > C_t^a(T_1), \quad \text{for } T_2 > T_1$$

It should be noted that this particular strategy is not applicable to European options because the spreader cannot exercise her longer term call early to cover the expiring shorter term call.

4.5 CALL PRICE RELATIONS WITH STOCK PRICES, VOLATILITY, AND INTEREST RATES

In the last three sections, we've examined how arbitrageurs can ensure that certain price conditions are met. The actual price of the call will be within these price constraints. In this section, we examine three factors that have determining impacts on the price of the call: the price of the underlying stock, the variability in the price of the underlying stock, and interest rates.

4.5.1 Call Price and Stock Price Relation

The arbitrage conditions delineated in Section 4.2 ensure that a positive relationship exists between C_t and S_t. This call and stock price relation, however, is not a linear one. Specifically, if the price of the stock is very high relative to the exercise price (a "deep in-the-money call"), then the costs of acquiring the option will be relatively expensive (large intrinsic value), resulting in a low demand. As a result, at relatively high stock prices, arbitrageurs would ensure that the call price is at least equal to $S_t - PV(X)$ (or $S_t - PV(X, T) - PV(D, t^*)$ or $S_t - PV(X, t^*)$ for calls on dividend-paying stocks), but the time value premiums would be very small.

In contrast, when the price of the stock is substantially below its exercise price (a "deep out-of-the-money" call), investors would most likely have very little confidence in the option being profitable. As a result, the demand and price of the call would be extremely low, and the price of the call would be equal or approximately equal to zero. Moreover, with a low or zero demand for a deep out-of-money call, any incremental change in the stock price would have a negligible impact on the price of the call.

The relationships between the call and stock prices when the stock price is either very low or very high are seen graphically in Figure 4.2-1. As shown, at the low stock prices, the call option curve CC approaches the horizontal axis, suggesting that the call is (or almost is) worthless and that any marginal change in S_t has only a small impact on C_t. As the stock price increases, the call price curve begins to increase at an increasing rate, implying the TVP is increasing. This will continue until the stock is on or near the money; at that point, the TVP is at a maximum. Finally, as the stock increases further, the TVP starts to decrease; and at very high stock prices, the TVP is negligible, and the call option curve approaches the minimum boundary line.

4.5.2 Call Price and Volatility Relation

Most securities are governed by a negative relationship between the security's variability and its price. That is, assuming all other factors are constant, the greater a security's variability, the less demand for it and therefore the lower its price. The opposite relationship, however, exists for call options. Because a long call position is characterized by unlimited profits if the stock increases but limited losses if it decreases, a call holder would prefer more volatility rather than less. As we first discussed in Chapter 1, greater variability suggests, on one hand, a likelihood that the stock will increase substantially in price, causing the call to be more valuable. On the other hand, greater variability also suggests a chance of the stock decreasing substantially. However, given that a call's losses are limited to just the premium when the stock price is equal to the exercise price or less, the extent of the price decrease should be inconsequential to the call holder. Thus, the market will value a call option on a volatile stock more than a call on a stock with lower variability, all other factors being the same.

> **RELATION:** Given the limited loss characteristic of a call purchase position, a call option on a security with greater volatility (V_2) is more valuable than one with lower volatility (V_1), all other factors being equal:
>
> $$C_t(V_2) > C_t(V_1), \quad \text{for } V_2 > V_1$$

4.5.3   Call Price and Interest Rate Relation

A call option represents a deferred purchase of the underlying security. As a result, a direct, instead of inverse, relationship between call prices and interest rates may exist. To see this, consider the case of investors who are interested in purchasing XYZ stock for 100 and holding it for one period. If there is also available in the market an XYZ 100 call option, expiring at the end of the period and trading at 14, investors could buy either the stock at $S_0 = \$100$ or, alternatively, buy the XYZ call at 14 and invest the remainder of 86 in a risk-free bond maturing at the end of the period. Each investor's selection of the stock or call and bond will depend on her risk-return preference. If rates on the bond were to increase, though, the call and bond portfolio would yield a relatively higher return per risk at the call price of 14. The relatively more attractive rates on the bond and call, in turn, would serve to increase the demand for this portfolio, causing the price of the call to increase until a new equilibrium is attained. Thus, an increase in interest rates can lead to an increase in the price of a call. In summary

> **RELATION:** An increase in interest rates makes a bond and call portfolio relatively more attractive than a stock portfolio, causing, in turn, the demand and price of the call to increase. Alternatively, an interest rate decrease makes a bond and call portfolio less attractive, causing the price of the call to decrease. Thus, with other factors constant, a direct relationship exists between interest rates and call prices.

4.6   EARLY EXERCISE OF AN AMERICAN CALL

In Chapter 2, we noted that in most cases, a call holder should close his position by selling the call instead of exercising. That is, prior to expiration, the call holder who sells receives the intrinsic value and the time value premium as part of the selling price, whereas the call holder who exercises receives just the call's intrinsic value. An exception to this rule occurs, though, in the case in which the call's underlying stock is expected to go ex-dividend during the period, and the expected dividend exceeds the call's time value premium.

Most stock exchanges specify an ex-dividend date for a stock. Investors who purchase shares of the stock before the ex-dividend date are entitled to receive the dividend, cum-dividend, whereas those who buy on or after the ex-dividend date are not. On the ex-dividend date, the price of the stock should decrease by an amount approximately equal to the dividend because those who buy the stock at such time do not receive the dividend. Given the decrease in the price of the stock, a holder of an in-the-money call on that stock may find it profitable to exercise the call just before the stock goes ex-dividend.[3]

The formal argument for early exercise can be seen by considering a call holder's alternative cash flow positions on the ex-dividend date: one position resulting from exercising the call just prior to the date and the other position from not exercising. In the first case, if the holder exercises *just prior* to the ex-dividend date, then her cash flow *on* the ex-dividend date would be equal to the value of the stock on that date plus the value of the dividend (D) she is entitled to on the stock's date of record minus an amount X used by the holder to buy the stock on the call just prior to the ex-dividend date. If the stock is worth S_t just prior to the ex-dividend date, and we assume that the stock will decrease by an amount equal to the value of the dividend on the ex-divided date (D), then the price of the stock on ex-dividend date (S_x) would be: $S_x = S_t - D$. Thus, the holder's cash flow on the ex-dividend date (CF_{ex}) from exercising just before is equal to the call's intrinsic value just prior to the ex-dividend date: $S_t - X$. That is

$$CF_{ex} = S_X + D - X$$
$$CF_{ex} = (S_t - D) + D - X$$
$$CF_{ex} = S_t - X$$

Alternatively, if the call holder does not exercise, then her cash flow on the ex-dividend date would be equal to the price of the call on the date, C_{ex}, which would be equal to the call's intrinsic value plus its time value premium:

$$C_{ex} = IV + TVP$$
$$C_{ex} = (S_X - X) + TVP$$
$$C_{ex} = (S_t - D) - X + TVP$$

In comparing the two positions, a call holder should exercise if $CF_{ex} > C_{ex}$. This early exercise condition of $CF_{ex} > C_{ex}$ is met when D > TVP provided the call is in the

---

[3] For example, suppose investors expected ABC stock to sell for $54 at the end of the period and pay a $1 dividend. If investors, in turn, required a 10% expected rate of return for the period (E(R)) from buying the stock, then just prior to the ex-dividend date, they would pay $50 for ABC stock:

$$E(R) = (Div + (E(S) - S_0))/S_0 = (\$1 + (\$54 - \$50))/\$50 = .10$$

and at the ex-dividend date, they would pay $49.09:

$$E(R) = (Div + (E(S) - S_0))/S_0 = (0 + \$54 - \$49.09)/\$49.09 = .10$$

Thus, on the ex-dividend date, the price of the stock would have to fall by an amount approximately equal to the dividend to yield investors the same rate.

money on the ex-dividend date. That is

$$CF_{ex} > C_{ex}$$
$$S_t - X > S_t - D - X + TVP$$
$$D > TVP$$

In this case, the early exercise advantage exists because the dividend the holder is entitled to after exercising exceeds the TVP she is giving up.

If the size of the dividend is such that the call is out of the money on the ex-dividend date ($D > S_t - X$), then the holder should exercise early if $S_t - X > TVP$. That is, $CF_{ex} > C_{ex}$ when $S_t - X > TVP$:

$$CF_{ex} > C_{ex}$$
$$S_t - X > Max[S_t - D - X, 0] + TVP$$
$$S_t - X > TVP, \text{for the case of } D > S_t - X$$

This condition suggests that call options that would be likely candidates for early exercise would be those with low TVP's and/or high dividend payments.

4.7   MINIMUM AND MAXIMUM PUT PRICES

Similar to call options, put premiums also are governed by arbitrage conditions. As we will see, many of the conditions and relationships germane to puts are similar to the ones just examined for calls.

4.7.1   Maximum American and European Put Prices

Because a put increases in value as the stock decreases, its maximum price occurs when the stock price is equal to zero. For an American put with the stock price at zero, a put holder could sell the worthless stock for the exercise price. Thus, the maximum value of the American put would have to be the exercise price. For a European put with the price of the stock at zero, the holder would be able to sell the stock at X but not until expiration. Thus, the put would be worth the present value of the exercise price (assuming that the stock is zero and will remain there because the company is bankrupt). In summary, the maximum prices for American and European puts are

---

RELATION: Maximum price of American put:

$$MaxP_t^a = X$$

RELATION: Maximum price of European put:

$$MaxP_t^e = PV(X)$$

4.7.2   Minimum Price of an American Put

As discussed in Chapter 1, the minimum value of an American put (on a stock that pays no dividends) is the put's intrinsic value. This condition is governed by arbitrage.

For example, suppose an ABC 50 put is trading for 3 while the stock is at 45. One could achieve a riskless profit by buying the stock and the put for 48 and then selling the stock immediately at 50 by exercising the put. The net result of these transactions would be an arbitrage profit of 2. By executing this strategy, arbitrageurs would augment the demand for the put, causing its price to increase until the arbitrage profit disappears. The minimum put price where the arbitrage return is zero is the put's intrinsic value. Thus

---

RELATION: The minimum price of an American put on a stock that pays no dividends is the put's intrinsic value:

$$\text{MinP}_t^a = \text{IV} = \text{Max}[X - S_t, 0]$$

If this condition does not hold, then an arbitrage opportunity exists and may be exploited by buying the put and the underlying stock and then exercising the put immediately.

4.7.3 Minimum Price of a European Put

The minimum price of a European put on a stock that pays no dividends can be established by comparing an investment in a bond with a face value of X to an investment in a portfolio of the stock and put. In Table 4.7-1, the end-of-the-period cash flows are presented for the stock and put investment and an investment in a bond paying a face value of X and maturing at the expiration date on the put. As shown, if $S_T \leq X$, then the stock and put portfolio would yield the same cash flow as the bond (X); on the other hand, if $S_T > X$, the put would be worthless, but the stock would be worth more than the face value of the bond. Thus, because the put and stock portfolio yields the same cash flow at expiration as the bond investment in some cases ($S_T \leq X$) and a greater cash flow in others ($S_T > X$), it should be valued higher by investors. That is

$$P_t^e + S_t > PV(X)$$

TABLE 4.7-1 Comparison of Bond With Put and Stock Portfolio

	Cash Flows at Expiration		
Position	$S_T < X$	$S_T = X$	$S_T > X$
Investment 1:			
Bond Purchase	X	X	X
Investment 2:			
Put Purchase	$X - S_T$	0	0
+	+	+	+
Stock Purchase	S_T	S_T	S_T
	X	X	S_T
Investor Preference	**Indifferent**	**Indifferent**	**Investment 2**

Note: Investment 1 (long bond) provides the same cash flow (X) at expiration whether the stock goes up or down. Investment 2, {+P, +S}, provides a cash flow of X when $S_T \leq X$ and a greater flow of S_T if the stock price at expiration is greater than X. Hence, Investment 2 dominates 1 and should have a higher value at t = 0.

Solving the inequality for P_t^e and expressing it with a constraint that P_t^e cannot be negative defines the minimum price of a European put:

$$P_t^e > \text{Max}[PV(X) - S_t, 0]$$

$$\text{Min}P_t^e = \text{Max}[PV(X) - S_t, 0]$$

In addition to the intuitive reasoning, an arbitrage argument also can be used to establish the minimum price of a European put. Similar to the arbitrage strategy we presented earlier for determining the minimum price of a call, if a European put is below its minimum price ($P_t^e < PV(X) - S_t$), then arbitrageurs will be able to earn riskless profit by going long in the put, short in a risk-free bond with a face value of X and maturity of T, and long in the stock:

Boundary Condition	Boundary Condition Violation	Arbitrage Strategy $P_0^e < PV(X) - S_0$		
		Position	Position	Details
$P_0^e \geq PV(X) - S_0$	$P_0^e < PV(X) - S_0$	1. Long Put	1. $\{+P_0^a\}$	1. Buy Put
		2. Short $(PV(X) - S_0)$	2. $\{-(PV(X) - S_0)\}$	2. Short Bond
			$=\{-PV(X), +S_0\}$	3. Buy Stock

This strategy would provide an initial positive cash flow of

$$CF_0 = PV(X) - S_0 - P_0^e > 0,$$

and as shown in Table 4.7-2, there would be no liabilities when the position is closed at expiration. That is, if $S_T \leq X$ at expiration, the stock and put portfolio would yield a cash flow equal to X, which would just cover the short bond; and if $S_T > X$, the put would be worthless, but the stock's cash flow would exceed the proceeds needed to cover the bond, yielding a net cash flow of $S_T - X > 0$. This arbitrage opportunity would, in turn, force the price of the put to increase until it is at least equal to $PV(X) - S_t$. For example, suppose the price of an ABC 50 European put expiring in 1 year was 5 when the stock price was 45. If the risk-free rate is 6%, the minimum price of the European put would be 2.17 ($50/1.06 - 45$). If the put's market premium was 1.17, then an arbitrageur could realize a $1 cash flow at t = 0 by buying the stock-put portfolio for 46.17 ($45 + 1.17$) and shorting the bond for 47.17, and as shown in Table 4.7-2, there would be no liabilities when the position is closed at expiration. Thus

---

RELATION: The minimum price of European put (on a stock not paying dividends) is

$$\text{Min}P_t^e = \text{Max}[PV(X) - S_t, 0]$$

If this price condition does not hold, then an arbitrage opportunity exists by going long in the stock and put and short in a riskless pure discount bond with a face value of X and maturity of T.

It should be noted that because $PV(X) < X$, the minimum price of a European put is less than an American: $\text{Min}P_0^e < \text{Min}P_0^a$. In contrast, for call options on stocks that pay no dividends during the options' lives, the minimum prices of American and European calls are the same.

TABLE 4.7-2 Proof of Boundary Condition: $P_0^e \geq PV(X) - S_0$

Boundary Condition	Boundary Condition Violation	Arbitrage Strategy $P_0^e < PV(X) - S_0$		Details
		Positions		
$P_0^e \geq PV(X) - S_0$	$P_0^e < PV(X) - S_0$	1. Long Put	1. $\{+P_0^a\}$	1. Buy Put
		2. Short $(PV(X) - S_0)$	2. $\{-(PV(X) - S_0)\}$	2. Short Bond
			$= \{-PV(X), +S_0\}$	3. Buy Stock

- This strategy provides an initial positive cash flow of $CF_0 = PV(X) - S_0 - P_0^e > 0$
- There are no liabilities when the position is closed at expiration

	Expiration Cash Flow		
Position	$S_T < X$	$S_T = X$	$S_T > X$
Long Stock	S_T	S_T	S_T
Long Put	$X - S_T$	0	0
Short Bond	$-X$	$-X$	$-X$
	0	0	$(S_T - X) > 0$

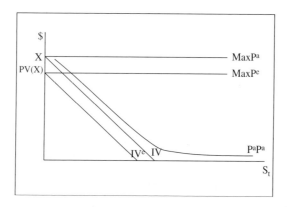

FIGURE 4.7-1 Put Option Boundary Condition

4.7.4 Boundary Conditions

The minimum and maximum put prices define the boundary conditions for this option. Graphically, these conditions are depicted in Figure 4.7-1 for European and American puts on a nondividend-paying stock. In the figure, the negatively sloped IV line with the vertical intercept of X defines the lower limit of an American put. Parallel to the IV line is the IV_e line with an intercept of PV(X). This line defines the lower price limit for a European put. Finally, the horizontal line at X and the one at PV(X) define the upper limits for the American and European puts, respectively. The actual price of an American or European put will fall somewhere within these boundary lines.

4.7.5 Minimum Price Conditions for Puts on Dividend-Paying Stocks

In Section 4.2, we noted that the boundary conditions governing European and American call options are impacted by the dividend on the underlying stock. Similarly, the minimum prices of American and European puts are affected by dividend payments. In general, the

EXHIBIT 4.7-1 Minimum Price Conditions for Put Options on Dividend-Paying Stock

Minimum Price of a European Put

If stock pays a dividend worth D at the ex-dividend date at time t*, the minimum price of a European put is

$$\text{MinP}_0^e = \text{Max}[\text{PV}(X,T) + \text{PV}(D,t^*) - S_0, 0]$$

If this condition does not hold, an arbitrage profit may be obtained by going long in the stock and the put and short in two discount bonds: the first with face value of \$D and maturity date t* and the second with face value of \$X and maturity date T.

Minimum Price of an American Put

$$\text{MinP}_0^a = \text{Max}[X - S_0, \text{PV}(X+D,t^*) - S_0, \text{PV}(X, T + \text{PV}(D,t^*)) - S_0, 0]$$

For a formal derivation of these price conditions, see Appendix 4B.

price of a put option is a positive function of dividends: As dividends increase, both American and European minimum put prices increase. This contrasts to the case of European and American call options, which are both inversely related to dividends. It should also be noted that the minimum price of an American put is greater than its European counterpart, regardless of whether the stock pays a low or a high dividend or no dividend at all. This also contrasts to the case of call options in which it is possible for American and European call values to be equal (i.e., no early exercise advantage) when dividends are relatively low. The impact of dividends on the minimum prices of American and European put options are defined in Exhibit 4.7-1 and are examined in detail in Appendix 4B at the end of the chapter.

4.8 PUT PRICES WITH DIFFERENT EXERCISE PRICES

4.8.1 Price Relation of Puts With Different Exercise Prices

In Section 4.3, we showed how an arbitrage strategy involving a bull call spread could be used to earn arbitrage returns if the price of the call with the lower exercise price exceeded the one with the higher exercise price. A similar arbitrage argument also can be used to establish the price relations between puts that are identical except for their exercise prices.

Intuitively, the put with the higher exercise price (X_2) should be priced greater than the one with the lower exercise price (X_1) because the former gives the put holder the right to sell the stock at a higher price. In addition to this reasoning, if the put with the higher exercise price is not priced higher, then in the case of European puts, arbitrageurs can earn riskless profit by forming a bear put spread—buying the higher exercise priced put for $P_0^e(X_2)$ and selling the lower exercise priced put for $P_0^e(X_1)$. For example, if an ABC July 50 European put is trading at 3 and an ABC July 60 European put is trading at 2 ($P_0^e(50) > P_0^e(60)$), then, as shown in Exhibit 4.8-1, an arbitrage return is earned at expiration by purchasing the 60 put and selling the 50 put. Given this arbitrage opportunity, arbitrageurs/spreaders will push the price of the 60 put up and the price of the 50 put down until $P_0^e(60) > P_0^e(50)$ and the arbitrage profit disappears.

EXHIBIT 4.8-1 Profit and Stock Price Relation for a Bear Spread—ABC 60 Put Purchased at 2 and ABC 50 Call Sold at 3

S_T	Profit on Long 60 Put Bought at 2	Profit on Short 50 Put Sold at 3	Total Profit
40	1,800	−700	1,100
45	1,300	−200	1,100
50	800	300	1,100
55	300	300	600
60	−200	300	100
65	−200	300	100
70	−200	300	100

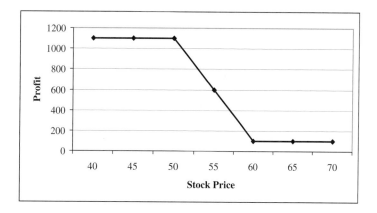

In addition to the intuitive reasoning, an arbitrage argument also can be used to establish the condition $P_0^e(X_2) > P_0^e(X_1)$. Specifically if this condition is violated ($P_0^e(X_2) < P_0^e(X_1)$), then arbitrageurs will be able to earn riskless profit by forming a bear put spread by going long in the X_2 put and short in the X_1 put. This strategy would provide an initial positive cash flow of

$$CF_0 = P_t^e(X_1) - P_t^e(X_2) > 0,$$

and as shown in Table 4.8-1, there would be no liabilities when the position is closed at expiration. That is, there are three possible cases at expiration: $S_T < X_1$, $X_1 \leq S_T \leq X_2$, and $S_T > X_2$. If $X_1 \leq S_T \leq X_2$ or $S_T > X_2$, then the cash flows from the bear spread will be positive; if $S_T < X_1$, then the spread's cash flows will be zero. An arbitrage opportunity would therefore exist if there was no cost incurred in setting up the bull spread. To preclude this free lunch, the initial cash flows of the bull spread must therefore be negative:

$$CF_t = -P_t^e(X_2) + P_t^e(X_1) < 0$$

or

$$P_t^e(X_2) > P_t^e(X_1), \text{ for } X_2 > X_1$$

TABLE 4.8-1   Proof of Boundary Condition: $P_0^e(X_2) > P_0^e(X_1)$

Boundary Condition	Boundary Condition Violation	Arbitrage Strategy $P_0^e(X_2) < P_0^e(X_1)$	
		Positions	**Details**
$P_0^e(X_2) > P_0^e(X_1)$	$P_0^e(X_2) < P_0^e(X_1)$	1. Long in the X_2 put	Buy X_2 put
		2. Short in the X_1 put	Sell X_1 put

- **This strategy would provide an initial positive cash flow of $CF_0 = P_t^e(X_1) - P_t^e(X_2) > 0$**
- **There are no liabilities when the position is closed at expiration**

	Cash Flows at Expiration		
Position	$S_T < X_1$	$X_1 \leq S_T \leq X_2$	$S_T > X_2$
Short X_1 Put	$-(X_1 - S_T)$	0	0
Long X_2 Put	$X_2 - S_T$	$X_2 - S_T$	0
	$X_2 - X_1 > 0$	$X_2 - S_T > 0$	0

To preclude arbitrage, the initial cash flow must be negative:

$CF_0 = -P_0^e(X_2) + P_0^e(X_1) < 0$ or $P_t^e(X_2) > P_t^e(X_1)$, for $X_2 > X_1$

Thus

> **RELATION:** Given two European puts that are identical except for their exercise prices, the put with the higher exercise price will be priced higher than the one with the lower exercise price. If this condition does not hold, then an arbitrage opportunity will exist by executing a bear put spread. Thus
>
> $$P_t^e(X_2) > P_t^e(X_1), \quad \text{for } X_2 > X_1$$

The condition that $P_t^e(X_2) > P_t^e(X_1)$ also holds for an American put. If the price on an American put with a lower exercise price exceeds a similar one with a higher strike price, then, as before, a riskless profit could be earned from the bear put spread. Prior to expiration, if the bear put spreader is assigned the put with the lower exercise price (the one she is short), then the spreader could buy the stock on the assignment at X_1 and use her long put position to sell the stock for X_2, realizing a positive cash flow of $X_2 - X_1$. Thus, even with early exercise, an arbitrage profit still can be realized from a bear put spread when $P_0^a(X_1) > P_0^a(X_2)$. Hence

> **RELATION:** Given two American puts that are identical except for their exercise prices, the put with the higher exercise price will be priced higher than the one with the lower exercise price. Thus
>
> $$P_t^a(X_2) > P_t^a(X_1), \quad \text{for } X_2 > X_1$$

4.8.2 Price Limits on Puts With Different Exercise Prices

For European puts, the price difference between two puts that are identical except for their exercise prices must be less than the difference in the present values of the two puts' exercise prices. That is

$$P_t^e(X_2) - P_t^e(X_1) < PV(X_2 - X_1)$$

If this condition does not hold ($P_0^e(X_2) - P_0^e(X_1) > PV(X_2 - X_1)$), then an arbitrage opportunity exists by going long in a riskless bond with a face value of $X_2 - X_1$ and maturity of T and by going short in the X_2 put and long in the X_1 put (i.e., construct a bull spread). This strategy would provide an initial positive cash flow of

$$CF_0 = P_0^e(X_2) - P_0^e(X_1) - PV(X_2 - X_1) > 0,$$

and as shown in Table 4.8-2, there would be no liabilities at expiration when the position is closed. To preclude this free lunch, the initial cash flow must be negative:

$$CF_0 = P_0^e(X_2) - P_0^e(X_1) - PV(X_2 - X_1) < 0$$
$$P_0^e(X_2) - P_0^e(X_1) < PV(X_2 - X_1)$$

RELATION:

$$P_0^e(X_2) - P_0^e(X_1) < PV(X_2 - X_1)$$

TABLE 4.8-2 Proof of Boundary Condition: $P_0^e(X_2) - P_0^e(X_1) < PV(X_2 - X_1)$

Boundary Condition	Boundary Condition Violation	Arbitrage Strategy $P_0^e(X_2) - P_0^e(X_1) > PV(X_2-X_1)$	
		Positions	Details
$P_0^e(X_2) - P_0^e(X_1) < PV(X_2 - X_1)$	$P_0^e(X_2) - P_0^e(X_1) > PV(X_2 - X_1)$	Short in $[P_0^e(X_2) - P_0^e(X_1)]$ Long in $PV(X_2 - X_1)$	1. Sell X_2 put 2. Buy X_1 put 3. Buy bond with face value of $X_2 - X_1$

- This strategy would provide an initial positive cash flow of $CF_0 = P_0^e(X_2) - P_0^e(X_1) - PV(X_2 - X_1) > 0$
- There are no liabilities at expiration when the position is closed

	Cash Flows at Expiration		
Position	$S_T < X_1$	$X_1 \le S_T \le X_2$	$S_T > X_2$
Long X_1 Put	$X_1 - S_T$	0	0
Short X_2 Put	$-(X_2 - S_T)$	$-(X_2 - S_T)$	0
Long Bond	$X_2 - X_1$	$X_2 - X_1$	$X_2 - X_1$
	0	$S_T - X_1 > 0$	$X_2 - X_1 > 0$

To preclude arbitrage, the initial cash flow must be negative:
$$CF_0 = P_0^e(X_2) - P_0^e(X_1) - PV(X_2 - X_1) < 0$$
$$P_0^e(X_2) - P_0^e(X_1) < PV(X_2 - X_1)$$

Thus, if the rate on a risk-free security is 10% annually, then the difference between the price of an ABC 60 and the price of an ABC 50 put, both expiring in 1 year, should not be greater than $9.09:

$$P_0^e(60) - P_0^e(50) < PV(60 - 50) = \frac{10}{1.10} = 9.09$$

If the put bull spread in the preceding arbitrage portfolio were formed with American puts that were exercised early at time t, then the arbitrageur would lose $X_2 - X_1$. If we assume the arbitrageur finances this short fall by borrowing $X_2 - X_1$ dollars at rate R for the remainder of the period, then at expiration, she would owe $(X_2 - X_1)(1 + R)^{T-t}$ on the debt: an amount that exceeds the face value on the bond. To ensure a free lunch, the arbitrageur would need to buy a bond that yields a cash flow at expiration that is at least equal to $(X_2 - X_1)(1 + R)^{T-t}$. This can be done by purchasing a riskless zero-coupon bond with a face value of $(X_2 - X_1)(1 + R)^T$ for the price of $X_2 - X_1$. Because $(X_2 - X_1)(1 + R)^T > (X_2 - X_1)(1 + R)^{T-t}$, the arbitrageur would thus have a bond that can generate a return at least as good as the put spread and often better. To avoid arbitrage, the American puts would have to be priced such that

> **RELATION:**
>
> $$P_0^a(X_2) - P_0^a(X_1) < X_2 - X_1$$

4.9 PUT PRICE AND TIME TO EXPIRATION RELATION

Similar to an American call, an American put with a greater time to expiration should be valued more than an identical put with a shorter time to expiration because the former has a better chance of being in the money. That is

$$P_t^a(T_2) > P_t^a(T_1), \quad for\ T_2 > T_1$$

If the longer term put is not priced higher, an arbitrage opportunity can be exploited by implementing a time spread. For example, suppose an ABC 50 put expiring in 6 months ($T_2 = .5$ per year) is trading at 5, whereas the ABC 50 put expiring in 3 months ($T_1 = .25$) is selling for 7: $P_0^a(50,.5) < P_0^a(50,.25)$. Given this situation, a $2 arbitrage opportunity can be realized by forming a time spread consisting of a short position in the higher priced, short-term put and a long position in the lower priced, long-term put. If the spreader is assigned on the short-term 50 put, whether at expiration or before, he can simply buy the ABC stock at 50 on the assignment and then sell the stock by exercising his longer term 50 put. Thus, if the longer term put is priced below the shorter term one, a spreader is sure of earning a riskless return. As spreaders exploit this opportunity, though, they will push the price of the longer term put up (as they try to buy it) and depress the price of the shorter term one (as they try to sell) until $P_0^a(T_2) > P_0^a(T_1)$. Thus

> **RELATION:** Given two American put options on the same stock, with the same exercise prices but different expiration dates, the price of the longer term put will be

greater than the shorter term one. If this condition does not hold, then an arbitrage opportunity can be realized from a time spread formed by going short in the longer term put and long in the shorter term one. Thus:

$$P_t^a(T_2) > P_t^a(T_1), \quad \text{for } T_2 > T_1$$

It should be noted that because a longer term European put cannot be exercised when a shorter term European put expires, the preceding arbitrage/spread strategy cannot be applied to ensure the preceding condition holds for European puts.

4.10 PUT PRICE RELATIONS WITH STOCK PRICES, VOLATILITY, AND INTEREST RATES

4.10.1 Put Price Relations With the Stock's Price and Volatility

The relationships described earlier between the price of a call and its underlying stock's price and variability similarly apply to puts. First, the negative relationship between a put premium and the price of the underlying stock is a nonlinear one: when a put is deep out of the money, its price changes very little in response to an incremental change in the price of the stock, and it will be equal (or almost equal) to zero; when a put is deep in the money, its price will have a very small TVP and will come closer to equaling the intrinsic value (or $PV(X) - S_t$ for European puts) as the stock price decreases. Second, because put losses are limited to the premium when the stock price is equal to or less than its exercise price at expiration, put holders will value puts on stocks with greater volatility more than those with lower volatility.

4.10.2 Put Price and Interest Rate Relation

In contrast to calls, put prices are inversely related to interest rates, assuming other factors are constant. The inverse relation can be seen by viewing a put as a security that defers the sale of a stock. That is, a stockholder has the alternative of selling her stock now and investing the cash proceeds in a risk-free security or holding the stock and buying a put to provide protection against a decline in the price of the stock. If interest rates increase, the first alternative of selling the stock and investing in a risk-free security becomes relatively more attractive than the second of using a put as a hedging tool. For example, suppose a holder of XYZ stock needs cash at the end of the year and is afraid that the price of XYZ could decrease from its current level of 100. His alternatives would be either to sell the stock for 100 and invest in a risk-free security for the remainder of the period or to hold the stock and hedge its value by buying an XYZ 100 put to ensure a minimum net cash flow of 100 (minus the cost of the put) from selling the stock and the put at expiration. The choice the stockholder makes depends on his risk-return preference (the stockholder loses the premium if XYZ stock decreases but gains if the stock increases vs. certainty from selling the stock and investing: $100(1 + \text{Rate})$). Whatever preference, more investors will opt for selling their stock and investing in a risk-free security than buying a put if interest rates rise. Accordingly, the demand and price of a put would decrease in light of an interest rate increase. Thus, the higher the interest rate, the lower the price of the put, all other factors being constant.

4.11 PUT AND CALL RELATIONSHIPS

4.11.1 Put–Call Parity for Options on a Stock Paying No Dividends

Up to now, we have examined separately how the limits on call and put prices are determined by arbitrage arguments involving positions in the underlying stock, bond, and option. As we might expect, because the prices of options on the same stock are derived from that stock's value, the put price and call price are also related to each other.

Recall from Chapter 1 that the relationship governing put and call prices is known as put–call parity. This relation can be defined in terms of an arbitrage portfolio consisting of either a *conversion*—a long position in the stock, a short position in a European call, and long position in a European put: $\{+S, +P, -C\}$—or a *reversal,* a short position in the stock, a long position in the European call, and short position in a European put (a reversal is the negative of a conversion): $\{-S, -P, +C\}$.

A conversion yields a certain cash flow at expiration equal to the exercise price. This is shown in Table 4.11-1. To preclude arbitrage, the riskless conversion portfolio must be worth the same as a risk-free pure discount bond with a face value of X, maturing at the end of the option's expiration period. Thus, in equilibrium

$$P_0^e - C_0^e + S_0 = PV(X)$$

Similarly, by reversing the previous strategy, we create a reversal. As shown in Table 4.11-2, a reversal results in a required fixed payment equal to X at expiration. To preclude arbitrage, a reversal should be equal to a short position in a bond $(-PV(X))$. Thus, the same put–call parity condition can be derived from a reversal position:

$$-P_0^e + C_0^e - S_0 = -PV(X)$$
$$P_0^e - C_0^e + S_0 = PV(X)$$

As we defined in Chapter 1, the preceding equation is referred to as the put–call parity model. If the put–call parity condition does not hold, then an arbitrage opportunity will exist. For example, suppose an ABC 50 call and put expiring in 1 year were trading for 5

TABLE 4.11-1 Conversion: $\{+S_0, +P_0^e, -C_0^e\}$

Position	Cash Flows at Expiration		
	$S_T < X$	$S_T = X$	$S_T > X$
Long Stock	S_T	S_T	S_T
Long Put	$X - S_T$	0	0
Short Call	0	0	$-(S_T - X)$
	X	X	X

TABLE 4.11-2 Reversal: $\{-S_0, -P_0^e, +C_0^e\}$

Position	Expiration Cash Flow		
	$S_T < X$	$S_T = X$	$S_T > X$
Short Stock	$-S_T$	$-S_T$	$-S_T$
Short Put	$-(X - S_T)$	0	0
Long Call	0	0	$(S_T - X)$
	$-X$	$-X$	$-X$

each, whereas the ABC stock was selling for 50. Furthermore, suppose the risk-free rate was 6% so that a 1-year pure discount bond with a face value of $X = 50$ was worth 47.17. In this case, the put–call parity equilibrium condition is violated.

$$P_0^e - C_0^e + S_0 > PV(X)$$

$$5 - 5 + 50 > \frac{50}{1.06} = 47.17$$

The actual bond is cheap (47.17) relative to the synthetic bond $\{+S, +P_0^e, -C_0^e\}(\$50)$, and the put–call parity condition is violated: $P_0^e - C_0^e + S_0 > PV(X)$. Arbitragers, in turn, could exploit this price imbalance by buying the bond and shorting the synthetic bond (short stock, short put, and long call). This strategy would yield an immediate cash flow of 2.83 ($P_0^e - C_0^e + S_0 - PV(X) = 5 - 5 + 50 - 47.17 = 2.83$), and as shown in Table 4.11-3, there would be no liabilities when the position is closed at expiration. That is, at expiration, the 50 cash flow from the bond would be exactly equal to the cash flow needed to cover the short synthetic position. In implementing this strategy, arbitrageurs, though, would alter the demands and supplies of calls and puts, causing their prices to change until the put–call parity equality condition is reached.

A similar argument may be used if the actual bond is expensive relative to the synthetic one. For example, suppose the ABC 50 call and put expiring in 1 year were trading for 5 each, whereas the ABC stock was selling for $45 instead of $50. Furthermore, suppose the risk-free rate was 6% so that a 1-year pure discount bond with a face value of $X = \$50$ was worth $47.17. In this case, the put–call parity equilibrium condition is again violated:

$$P_0^e - C_0^e + S_0 < PV(X)$$

$$5 - 5 + 45 < \frac{50}{1.06} = 47.17$$

TABLE 4.11-3 Proof of Put–Call Parity Condition: $P_0^e - C_0^e + S_0 = PV(X)$ Overpriced

Boundary Condition	Boundary Condition Violation	Arbitrage Strategy $P_0^e - C_0^e + S_0 > PV(X)$	
		Positions	Details
$P_0^e - C_0^e + S_0 = PV(X)$	$P_0^e - C_0^e + S_0 > PV(X)$	Short in $[P_0^e - C_0^e + S_0]$ Long in PV(X)	1. Sell Put 2. Buy Call 3. Short Stock 4. Buy bond with face value of X

- This strategy would yield an immediate cash flow of $P_0^e - C_0^e + S_0 - PV(X) > 0$
- There are no liabilities when the position is closed at expiration

Position	Expiration Cash Flow		
	$S_T < X$	$S_T = X$	$S_T > X$
Short Stock	$-S_T$	$-S_T$	$-S_T$
Short Put	$-(X - S_T)$	0	0
Long Call	0	0	$(S_T - X)$
Long Bond	X	X	X
	0	0	0

TABLE 4.11-4   Proof of Put–Call Parity Condition: $P_0^e - C_0^e + S_0 = PV(X)$ Underpriced

Boundary Condition	Boundary Condition Violation	Arbitrage Strategy $P_0^e - C_0^e + S_0 < PV(X)$	
		Positions	**Details**
$P_0^e - C_0^e + S_0 = PV(X)$	$P_0^e - C_0^e + S_0 < PV(X)$	Long in $[P_0^e - C_0^e + S_0]$ Short in PV(X)	1. Buy Put 2. Sell Call 3. Buy Stock 4. Short bond with face value of X

- **This strategy would yield an immediate cash flow of $PV(X) - P_0^e + C_0^e - S_0 > 0$**
- **There are no liabilities when the position is closed at expiration**

Position	Cash Flows at Expiration		
	$S_T < X$	$S_T = X$	$S_T > X$
Long Stock	S_T	S_T	S_T
Long Put	$X - S_T$	0	0
Short Call	0	0	$-(S_T - X)$
Short Bond	$-X$	$-X$	$-X$
	0	0	0

The actual bond is expensive (47.17) relative to the synthetic bond $\{+S, +P_0^e, -C_0^e\}(\$45)$. Arbitragers, in turn, could exploit this price imbalance by shorting the expensive real bond and buying the cheap synthetic one (buy put, sell call, and buy stock). This strategy would yield an immediate cash flow of 2.17 $(PV(X) - P_0^e + C_0^e - S_0 = 47.17 - 5 + 5 - 45 = 2.17)$, and as shown in Table 4.11-4, there would no liabilities when the position is closed at expiration. That is, at expiration, the $50 cash flow from the synthetic bond would be exactly equal to the cash flow needed to cover the short bond obligation. In implementing this strategy, arbitrageurs, though, would alter the demands and supplies of calls and puts, causing their prices to change until the put–call parity equality condition is reached.

4.11.2   The Price of a European Call and Put on a Stock Paying No Dividends

The put–call parity model can be used to determine the equilibrium price of a European put given the equilibrium price of a European call and the interest rate or the equilibrium price of a call given the equilibrium price of the put and the interest rate. That is, from the put–call parity equation

$$C_0^e = P_0^e + S_0 - PV(X)$$
$$P_0^e = C_0^e - S_0 + PV(X)$$

The right-hand side of the call equation shows the value of a portfolio consisting of long positions in the put and stock and a short position in the bond. This portfolio is referred to as a *synthetic call* because it replicates the cash flows from a European call. Similarly, the right-hand side of the put equation represents a portfolio consisting of long positions in the call and bond and a short position in the stock. Because this portfolio replicates the cash flows from a European put, it is referred to as a *synthetic put*.

TABLE 4.11-5 Conversion With Dividend-Paying Stock

Position	Expiration Cash Flow		
	$S_T < X$	$S_T = X$	$S_T > X$
Long Put	$X - S_T$	0	0
Short Call	0	0	$-(S_T -$
Long Stock	S_T	S_T	$X)$
Dividend	D_T	D_T	S_T
			D_T
	$X + D_T$	$X + D_T$	$X + D_T$

4.11.3 Put–Call Parity for European Options on a Stock With a Dividend

If there are ex-dividend dates during the period the option positions are held, then, as shown in Table 4.11-5, the conversion will yield a riskless cash flow equal to the exercise price plus the value of expected dividends at the options' expiration date (D_T). Because the conversion is riskless, its equilibrium value will be equal to the value of a risk-free bond with a face value equal to X plus the value of the dividend at the options' expiration date. That is

$$P_0^e - C_0^e + S_0 = PV(X + D_T)$$

4.11.4 Put–Call Parity Prices for American Calls and Puts

The put–call parity model depends on the relationships among the values of options, the price of the underlying stock, and the rate of return on a risk-free bond. The model holds strictly for European options and not for American.

4.11.5 Box Spread

In the put–call parity model, call and put premiums are related by real and synthetic stock positions. Another way of relating call and put prices is by a box spread.

A long box spread consists of a call bull money spread and a put bear money spread. As shown in Table 4.11-6, a long box spread with European options yields a certain return at expiration equal to the difference in the exercise prices. Because arbitrage ensures $C^e(X_1) > C^e(X_2)$ and $P^e(X_2) > P^e(X_1)$ for $X_2 > X_1$ (see Sections 4.3 and 4.8), a long box spread represents an investment expenditure in which

$$\text{Cost of Box Spread} = C_0^e(X_1) - C_0^e(X_2) + P_0^e(X_2) - P_0^e(X_1)$$

In contrast, a short box spread or reverse box spread is a combination of a call bear money spread and a put bull money spread. This spread generates a credit for the investor at the initiation of the strategy, and as shown in Table 4.11-7, requires a fixed payment at expiration equal to the difference in the exercise prices.

Because the return on a long box spread is riskless, we would expect the equilibrium price of the spread to be equal to the price on a risk-free pure discount bond with a face value of $X_2 - X_1$ and maturing at the same time as the options expire. That is

$$C_0^e(X_1) - C_0^e(X_2) + P_0^e(X_2) - P_0^e(X_1) = PV(X_2 - X_1)$$
$$C_0^e(X_1) - C_0^e(X_2) + P_0^e(X_2) - P_0^e(X_1) - PV(X_2 - X_1) = 0$$

TABLE 4.11-6 Long Box Spread: $\{+C(X_1), -C(X_2), -P(X_1), +P(X_2)\}$

Position	Cash Flows at Expiration		
	$S_T < X_1$	$X_1 \leq S_T \leq X_2$	$S_T > X_2$
Long X_1 Call	0	$S_T - X_1$	$S_T - X_1$
Short X_2 Call	0	0	$-(S_T - X_2)$
Short X_1 Put	$-(X_1 - S_T)$	0	0
Long X_2 Put	$X_2 - S_T$	$X_2 - S_T$	0
	$X_2 - X_1$	$X_2 - X_1$	$X_2 - X_1$

TABLE 4.11-7 Short Box Spread: $\{-C(X_1), +C(X_2), +P(X_1), -P(X_2)\}$

Position	Expiration Cash Flow		
	$S_T < X_1$	$X_1 \leq S_T \leq X_2$	$S_T > X_2$
Short X_1 Call	0	$-(S_T - X_1)$	$-(S_T - X_1)$
Long X_2 Call	0	0	$S_T - X_2$
Long X_1 Put	$X_1 - S_T$	0	0
Short X_2 Put	$-(X_2 - S_T)$	$-(X_2 - S_T)$	0
	$-(X_2 - X_1)$	$-(X_2 - X_1)$	$-(X_2 - X_1)$

Similarly, if we view a short box spread as a riskless loan, then with a fixed payment of $X_2 - X_1$ required on the short spread at expiration, the credit received from the spread should equal the proceeds from a loan requiring payment of $X_2 - X_1$ at maturity: $PV(X_2 - X_1)$. Thus

$$-C_0^e(X_1) + C_0^e(X_2) - P_0^e(X_2) + P_0^e(X_1) = -PV(X_2 - X_1)$$

If we assume borrowing and lending rates are the same, then in equilibrium, the short and long box spread condition yield the same equilibrium equation.

If the box spread equation does not hold, then arbitrage opportunities will exist. For example, if

$$C_0^e(X_1) - C_0^e(X_2) + P_0^e(X_2) - P_0^e(X_1) < PV(X_2 - X_1),$$

then an arbitrageur could borrow funds equal to $PV(X_2 - X_1)$ and buy the box spread, realizing a positive cash flow of $PV(X_2 - X_1) - [C_0^e(X_1) - C_0^e(X_2) + P_0^e(X_2) - P_0^e(X_1)]$. At expiration, the arbitrageur would have no liabilities (see Table 4.11-8): She would be able to pay her debt of $X_2 - X_1$ with the proceeds of $X_2 - X_1$ from the box spread. On the other hand, if

$$C_0^e(X_1) - C_0^e(X_2) + P_0^e(X_2) - P_0^e(X_1) > PV(X_2 - X_1),$$

then the arbitrageurs could earn riskless profit of $[C_0^e(X_1) - C_0^e(X_2) + P_0^e(X_2) - P_0^e(X_1)] - PV(X_2 - X_1)$ by forming a short box spread and buying the bond. At expiration, the arbitrageur would have no liabilities (see Table 4.11-9); that is, the principal of $X_2 - X_1$ on the bond would be used to cover the short box spread obligation of $X_2 - X_1$. The actions of arbitrageurs when the box spread equality condition is not zero will serve to change the demand and supply of the options until the spreads are priced equal to $PV(X_2 - X_1)$ and the arbitrage disappears.

TABLE 4.11-8 Proof of Box Spread Condition:
$C_0^e(X_1) - C_0^e(X_2) + P_0^e(X_2) - P_0^e(X_1) = PV(X_2 - X_1)$ Underpriced

Boundary Condition	Boundary Condition Violation	Arbitrage Strategy $C_0^e(X_1) - C_0^e(X_2) + P_0^e(X_2) - P_0^e(X_1) < PV(X_2 - X_1)$	
		Positions	**Details**
$C_0^e(X_1) - C_0^e(X_2)$ $+P_0^e(X_2) - P_0^e(X_1)$ $= PV(X_2 - X_1)$	$C_0^e(X_1) - C_0^e(X_2)$ $+P_0^e(X_2) - P_0^e(X_1)$ $< PV(X_2 - X_1)$	Long in $[C_0^e(X_1) - C_0^e(X_2) + P_0^e(X_2) - P_0^e(X_1)]$ Short in $PV(X_2 - X_1)$	1. Buy X_1 Call 2. Sell X_2 Call 3. Buy X_2 Put 4. Sell X_1 Put 5. Short bond with face value of $X_2 - X_1$

- **Strategy yields a positive cash flow of $PV(X_2 - X_1) - [C_0^e(X_1) - C_0^e(X_2) + P_0^e(X_2) - P_0^e(X_1)]$**
- **At expiration, there are no liabilities**

Position	$S_T < X_1$	$X_1 \leq S_T \leq X_2$	$S_T > X_2$
		Expiration Cash Flow	
Long X_1 Call	0	$S_T - X_1$	$S_T - X_1$
Short X_2 Call	0	0	$-(S_T - X_2)$
Short X_1 Put	$-(X_1 - S_T)$	0	0
Long X_2 Put	$X_2 - S_T$	$X_2 - S_T$	0
Short Bond	$-(X_2 - X_1)$	$-(X_2 - X_1)$	$-(X_2 - X_1)$
	0	0	0

As we did with the put–call parity model, the box spread equation can be solved in terms of any of the options' prices to define that option's equilibrium price. For example, solving for $C_0^e(X_1)$, we obtain

$$C_0^e(X_1) = C_0^e(X_2) - P_0^e(X_2) + P_0^e(X_1) + PV(X_2 - X_1)$$

This equation shows the equilibrium price of the X_1 call depends on the value of bond $(PV(X_2 - X_1))$, a simulated stock position formed with the higher exercise priced call and put $(C_0^e(X_2) - P_0^e(X_2))$, and the price of the lower exercise priced put $(P_0^e(X_1))$. If the equilibrium price for this option does not hold, then an arbitrage opportunity exists.

It should be noted that like the put–call parity relation, the box spread is defined in terms of the option values at expiration. As a result, the preceding equilibrium relations hold strictly for European and not for American options.

4.12 BOUNDARY CONDITIONS GOVERNING INDEX OPTIONS

In general, the arbitrage pricing relationships governing stock options can be extended to establish the boundary conditions and price relationships for index options. However, in extending stock option boundary condition to index options, three features unique to index options need special consideration: the cash settlement clause, the portfolio underlying the option, and the dividends from the stocks making up the index portfolio.

TABLE 4.11-9   Proof of Box Spread Condition: $C_0^e(X_1) - C_0^e(X_2) + P_0^e(X_2) - P_0^e(X_1) = PV(X_2 - X_1)$ Overpriced

| Boundary Condition | Boundary Condition Violation | Arbitrage Strategy $C_0^e(X_1) - C_0^e(X_2) + P_0^e(X_2) - P_0^e(X_1) > PV(X_2 - X_1)$ | |
		Positions	Details
$C_0^e(X_1) - C_0^e(X_2)$ $+P_0^e(X_2) - P_0^e(X_1)$ $= PV(X_2 - X_1)$	$C_0^e(X_1) - C_0^e(X_2)$ $+P_0^e(X_2) - P_0^e(X_1)$ $> PV(X_2 - X_1)$	Short in $[C_0^e(X_1) - C_0^e(X_2) + P_0^e(X_2) - P_0^e(X_1)]$ Long in $PV(X_2 - X_1)$	1. Sell X_1 Call 2. Buy X_2 Call 3. Sell X_2 Put 4. Buy X_1 Put 5. Long bond with face value of $X_2 - X_1$

- **Strategy yields an initial positive cash flow of $PV(X_2 - X_1) - [C_0^e(X_1) - C_0^e(X_2) + P_0^e(X_2) - P_0^e(X_1)]$**
- **At expiration, there are no liabilities**

| Position | Cash Flows at Expiration | | |
	$S_T < X_1$	$X_1 \leq S_T \leq X_2$	$S_T > X_2$
Short X_1 Call	0	$-(S_T - X_1)$	$-(S_T - X_1)$
Long X_2 Call	0	0	$-(S_T - X_2)$
Long X_1 Put	$X_1 - S_T$	0	0
Short X_2 Put	$-(X_2 - S_T)$	$-(X_2 - S_T)$	0
Long Bond	$X_2 - X_1$	$X_2 - X_1$	$X_2 - X_1$
	0	0	0

4.12.1   Cash Settlement

Many of the arbitrage strategies governing the price relationships for stock options involve taking an actual position in the underlying stock. Recall, for example, the arbitrage strategy used when an American call option on a stock was priced below its intrinsic value: The strategy required purchasing the call, exercising the option, and selling the stock. When an index option is exercised, the assigned writer pays the exercising holder cash equal to the difference between the closing day spot index price and the exercise price. Because of this cash settlement feature, the arbitrage strategy for index options priced below their intrinsic values does not require taking an actual position in the underlying security. For example, if a 1200 S&P 500 call were trading at 50 at the close of trading, and the closing spot index was at 1260, then an arbitrageur could buy the call contract for $5,000 (50 times the 100 multiplier) and then exercise to receive a $6,000 cash settlement from the assigned writer.

It should be noted that the end-of-the-day exercise rule associated with index options implies that the arbitrage strategy holds only for closing index prices. That is, arbitrageurs can be assured of an arbitrage profit if the price of an index option is below its intrinsic value as determined by the closing index price.

4.12.2   Spot Portfolio

Determining a boundary condition such as the put–call parity model for an index option requires defining arbitrage strategies involving positions in the underlying portfolio. To go long in the S&P 500 would require the simultaneous purchase of the index's 500 stocks in their correct proportions and the correct reinvestment of each stock's dividends for the option period. In practice, arbitrageurs can take positions in smaller proxy portfolios. A proxy portfolio could be formed with a small number of securities whose allocations in the portfolio are determined so as to maximize the correlation between the portfolio's returns and the spot indices'. A proxy portfolio also might be formed with a spider or a highly diversified mutual fund, such as an index fund, or as we discuss in Chapter 11, the portfolio could be replicated with a futures contract on the index.

Whether it is a mutual fund or a smaller sized, highly correlated portfolio, the proxy portfolio can be viewed as a position in the index. For example, if the spot S&P 500 were at 1250, then a highly diversified portfolio with a β of 1 and a current value $1.25 million could be thought to be equivalent to a hypothetical S&P 500 spot portfolio consisting of $N_0 = 1,000$ hypothetical shares of the index, with each share priced at $S_0 = \$1,250$:

$$V_0^P = N_0 S_0$$
$$V_0^P = (1,000)(\$1250) = \$1,250,000$$

The proxy portfolio, in turn, can be used to determine arbitrage strategies when the index option is mispriced. For example, suppose the S&P 500 spot index was currently at 1250, the risk-free rate was at 6%, and the price of a European 1250 S&P 500 index call expiring in 1 year was trading a 100. The put–call parity condition would require that the price of a European 1250 S&P 500 put expiring in 1 year be equal to 29.245283 (ignore dividends for this example):

$$P_0^e = C_0^e - S_0 + PV(X)$$
$$P_0^e = 100 - 1250 + \frac{1250}{1.06} = 29.245283$$

If the put were underpriced at 10, then an arbitrage could be formed by buying the put, selling the call, buying the index, and shorting the bond. This strategy would yield an initial cash flow of 19.245283 per index share, with no liabilities at expiration when the position is closed. This arbitrage also can be defined in terms of the $1.25 million proxy portfolio. Because the proxy portfolio is equivalent to 1,000 hypothetical shares of the index when the index is at 1250, an arbitrageur could

1. Buy 10 puts (index shares/100 multiplier = 1,000/100) at $P_0^e = 10$
2. Sell 10 calls (index shares/100 multiplier = 1,000/100) at $C_0^e = 100$
3. Borrow $1,179,245 = $1,250,000/1.06 (=PV(X) times hypothetical share)
4. Invest $1,250,000 in the proxy portfolio

As shown in Table 4.12-1, the arbitrageur would realize an initial cash flow of $19,245 (initial arbitrage cash flow per the index times the number of hypothetical index shares defining the proxy portfolio = $19.245(1,000) = \$19,245$). At expiration, the arbitrageur would sell her portfolio, close her option positions, and repay her $1,250,000 debt. She, in turn, would have no liabilities provided the proxy portfolio is perfectly correlated with the S&P 500. For example, if 1 year later the market increased by 10% ($g = \Delta S/S = .10$) such that the spot S&P 500 were at 1375(= 1250(1.10)), then the portfolio (if it were perfectly correlated) would be worth $1.375M(= $1.25M(1.10)), the cost of debt would be $1.25M(= $1,179,245(1.06)), the puts would be worthless, and it would cost $125,000 to close the short calls at their intrinsic value of 125: (10)(100) Max[$S_T - X, 0] = (10)(100)$Max[1375 - 1250, 0] = 125,000$. The net cash flow in this case would be zero. Thus, there would be no liability at a spot index of 1375. In contrast, if the

TABLE 4.12-1   Arbitrage Using Proxy Portfolio When the Put–Call Parity Condition for Index Option Is Violated

Spot S&P 500 Index $= S_0 = 1250$, Index Call: $C_0 = 100$,
Index Put: $P_0 = 10$, and Proxy Portfolio: Value $= \$1.25M$

$$P_0^e = C_0^e - S_0 + PV(X)$$

$$P_0^e = 100 - 1250 + \frac{1250}{1.06} = 29.245283$$

$$10 < 29.245283$$

Initial Position	Cash Flow	
Put Purchase: Buy 10 S&P 500 Puts at 10	Cash Outflow = (10)(10)(100)	$-\$10,000$
Call Sale: Sell 10 S&P 500 Calls at 100	Cash Inflow = (10)(100)(100)	$+\$100,000$
Purchase Proxy Portfolio: $1,250,000	Cash Outflow = $1,250,000	$-\$1,250,000$
Borrow PV(X): Borrow $1,250,000/1.06	Cash Inflow = $1,179,245	$+\$1,179,245$
		$+\$19,245$

	Market Increase $g = 10\%$ $S_T = 1250(1.10)$ $S_T = 1375$		Market decrease $g = -10\%$ $S_T = 1250(.90)$ $S_T = 1125$	
Closing Position				
Sell 10 Puts at IV	(0)(10)(100)	0	(125)(10)(100)	$125,000
Buy 10 calls at IV	(125)(10)(100)	$-\$125,000$	(0)(10)(100)	0
Sell Proxy Portfolio	$1,250,000(1.10)	$1,375,000	$1,250,000(.90)	$1,125,000
Repay Debt	$1,179,245(1.06)	$-\$1,250,000$	$1,179,245(1.06)	$-\$1,250,000$
		0		0

market decreased by 10% ($g = -.10$) 1 year later, then the spot S&P 500 would be at 1125($= 1250(.90)$). In this case, the proxy portfolio (if it were perfectly correlated) would be worth $1.125M($= \$1.25M(.90)$), the cost of debt still would be $1.25M($= \$1,179,245(1.06)$), the calls would be worthless, and the long puts would generate a cash flow of $125,000 when the arbitrageur sold them at their intrinsic value of 125: (10)(100) Max$[X - S_T, 0] = (10)(100)$Max$[1250 - 1125, 0] = 125,000$. The net cash flow would again be zero. Thus, there would be no liability at a spot index of 1125. In fact, for any spot index, there are no liabilities provided the proxy portfolio is perfectly correlated.

By earning an initial cash flow of $19,245, with no liabilities at expiration, arbitrageurs would try to set up this arbitrage strategy with the proxy portfolio and index options. By their action, though, they would decrease the call price and increase the put price until the initial cash flow were zero or equivalently where the put–call parity condition defining index options is met.

4.12.3   Dividend Adjustments

For a stock index option, the stocks comprising the index portfolio pay dividends. As a result, the boundary conditions for index options are similar to those for stocks that pay dividends. When a proxy portfolio is used to defined index option boundary conditions, then it is important that the dividends be incorporated. These dividends, in turn, represent part of the return earned on the proxy portfolio and should be highly correlated with the dividends underlying the index. Dividend payments that are expected to accrue on the proxy portfolio during the period (D_T) can be incorporated into the pricing of index options by expressing the total dividends as a proportion of the number of hypothetical index shares (N_0). For example, suppose in the previous example, the $1.25M proxy portfolio was expected to generate dividends worth $62,500 1 year later.[4] Because the proxy portfolio represents 1,000 hypothetical index shares, the equivalent dividend per index share would be $62.50(= $62,500/1,000$). With dividends, the appropriate put–call parity model for index options is

$$P_0^e - C_0^e + S_0 = PV(X + D_T)$$

In terms of our last example, the put–call parity condition would require that the price of a European 1250 S&P 500 put expiring in 1 year to be equal to 88.207547:

$$P_0^e = C_0^e - S_0 + PV(X + D_T)$$

$$P_0^e = 100 - 1250 + \frac{1250 + 62.50}{1.06} = 88.207547$$

As shown in Table 4.12-2, if the index put were underpriced at 10, then an arbitrage could be formed by buying 10 puts, selling 10 calls, borrowing $= \$1,238,207 = (\$1.25M + \$62,500)/1.06$ (or equivalently $PV(X + D_T)$ times hypothetical shares), and investing $1.25M in the proxy portfolio. By doing this, the arbitrageur would realize an initial cash flow of $78,207. At expiration, the arbitrageur would sell her portfolio, receive $62,500 in

TABLE 4.12-2 Arbitrage Using Proxy Portfolio When The Put–Call Parity Condition for Index Option With Dividends Is Violated

Spot S&P 500 Index $= S_0 = 1250$, Index Call: $C_0 = 100$,
Index Put: $P_0 = 10$, and Proxy Portfolio: Value $= \$1.25M$
with $D_T = \$62,500$
$P_0^e = C_0^e - S_0 + PV(X + D_T)$
$P_0^e = 100 - 1250 + \frac{1250+62.50}{1.06} = 88.207547$
$10 < 88.207547$

Initial Position	Cash Flow	
Put Purchase: Buy 10 S&P 500 Puts at 10	Cash Outflow=(10)(10)(100)	−$10,000
Call Sale: Sell 10 S&P 500 Calls at 100	Cash Inflow=(10)(100)(100)	+$100,000
Purchase Proxy Portfolio: $1,250,000	Cash outflow = $1,250,000	−$1,250,000
Borrow ($1,250,000 + $62,500)/1.06	Cash Inflow=$1,238,207	+$1,238,207
		+$78,207

Closing Position	Market Increase g = 10% S_T = 1250(1.10) S_T = 1375		Market decrease g = −10% S_T = 1250(.90) S_T = 1125	
Sell 10 Puts at IV	(0)(10)(100)	0	(125)(10)(100)	$125,000
Buy 10 calls at IV	(125)(10)(100)	−$125,000	(0)(10)(100)	0
Sell Proxy Portfolio	$1,250,000(1.10)	$1,375,000	$1,250,000(.90)	$1,125,000
Dividend Value	$62,500	$62,500	$62,500	$62,500
Repay Debt	$1,238,207(1.06)	−$1,312,500	$1,238,207(1.06)	−$1,312,500
		0		0

[4] Note that $62,500 is the value of dividends at T. This would include dividends received during the period and reinvested to time T.

dividends, close her option positions, and repay her $1,312,500 debt. She, in turn, would have no liabilities provided the proxy portfolio is perfectly correlated with the S&P 500 and she received dividends worth $62,500 (see Table 4.12-2). Such arbitrage actions, though, would decrease the call price and increase the put price until the initial cash flow were zero or equivalently where the put-call parity condition defining index option with dividends is met.

4.13 BOUNDARY CONDITIONS GOVERNING CURRENCY OPTIONS

Because foreign currency can be invested in interest-bearing foreign securities, the boundary conditions governing currency options are similar to stock and stock index options that pay dividends. In this section, we examine two currency option pricing relationships in which the foreign interest rate is a factor: the boundary conditions for the minimum prices of currency calls and puts and the foreign currency put–call parity model.

4.13.1 Minimum Values of Currency Options

The minimum price condition for a European or an American call option on a currency can be found by comparing two investments (for a U.S. resident):

1. The dollar purchase of $E_0(1 + R_F)^{-T}$ units of foreign currency (E_0 = dollar price of foreign currency (FC)): $E_0 = \$/FC$), with the foreign currency (FC) funds invested for the period T in a foreign risk-free security yielding a rate R_F.

2. The purchase of a European currency call option for C_0 and the purchase of a zero coupon bond maturing at the option's expiration date, with a face value (F) equal to the option's exercise price and yielding a U.S. risk-free rate of R_{US} for the period.

As shown in Table 4.13-1, at expiration, the values of each investment depend on the spot exchange rate, E_T. The first investment would be worth one FC at expiration and E_T dollars when converted to dollars; the second investment is equal to the exercise price if $E_T \leq X$ and worth E_T if $E_T > X$. Comparing the two, the second investment yields the same cash flows as the first in some cases and a better cash flow in others. A priori, we therefore would expect the market to value the second investment more than

TABLE 4.13-1   Minimum Value of a Currency Call

			Dollar Cash Flow at Expiration		
Investment		Current Dollar Investment	$E_T < X$	$E_T = X$	$E_T > X$
1	Investment in Foreign Security	$E_0(1 + R_F)^{-T}$	E_T	E_T	E_T
2	Call	C_0	0	0	$E_T - X$
	Bond	$X(1 + R_{US})^{-T}$	X	X	X
			X	X	E_T
	Preference:		Investment 2	Indifferent	Indifferent

Because Investment 2 yields the same cash flow as Investment 1 in some cases and better in other cases, it should be valued greater. Thus

$$C_0 + X(1 + R_{US})^{-T} > E_0(1 + R_F)^{-T} \text{ and } \text{Min} C_0 = \text{Max}[E_0(1 + R_F)^{-T} - X(1 + R_{US})^{-T}, 0]$$

the first. Hence

$$C_0 + X(1 + R_{US})^{-T} > E_0(1 + R_F)^{-T}$$

Expressing this inequality as an equality, with a constraint that C_0 cannot be negative, we obtain the minimum value of a currency call:

$$MinC_0 = Max[E_0(1 + R_F)^{-T} - X(1 + R_{US})^{-T}, 0]$$

If the market price of a currency call (C_0^m) is less than the minimum price, an arbitrage opportunity exists by taking a short position in the foreign security, borrowing $(1 + R_F)^{-T}$ FC and converting it to dollars at E_0, then using the dollars to buy the call and a U.S. risk-free security with a face value of X and maturity of T. As shown in Table 4.13-2, this strategy would yield an initial positive cash flow of $E_0(1 + R_F)^{-T} - (X(1 + R_{US})^{-T} - C_0^m)$ and no liabilities at expiration.

For American currency puts, the minimum price condition is defined by the put's intrinsic value. For European currency puts, the minimum price condition is

$$MinP_0^e = Max[X(1 + R_{US})^{-T} - E_0(1 + R_F)^{-T}, 0]$$

If the minimum price conditions are violated, then an arbitrage opportunity exists. In the case of the minimum put price condition, the arbitrage is formed by taking a position in the U.S. risk-free security and currency put and an opposite position in a foreign security.

As with stock options, a number of boundary conditions governing currency options exist. Several of the conditions and the arbitrage strategies underlying them are included as end-of-chapter problems.

TABLE 4.13-2   Arbitrage Strategy When $C_0^m < E_0(1 + R_F)^{-T} - X(1 + R_{US})^{-T}$

Strategy:
$$\{+C_0^m, -(E_0(1 + R_F)^{-T} - X(1 + R_{US})^{-T})\}$$

Strategy	Details	Current Cash Flow
Short $E_0(1 + R_F)^{-T}$	Borrow $(1 + R_F)^{-T}$ FC, convert to dollars at E_0 (owe 1FC at T)	$E_0(1 + R_F)^{-T}$
Long $X(1 + R_{US})^{-T}$	Buy U.S. zero-coupon bond with face value of X and maturity of T	$-X(1 + R_{US})^{-T}$
Long Call	Buy call	$-C_0^m$
Initial Cash Flow		$E_0(1 + R_F)^{-T} - X(1 + R_{US})^{-T} - C_0^m > 0$

Expiration

Position	Dollar Cash Flow at Expiration		
	$E_T < X$	$E_T = X$	$E_T > X$
Short Foreign Security: Dollar Costs of Repaying debt of 1FC: E_T	$-E_T$	$-E_T$	$-E_T$
Long Bond	X	X	X
Long Call	0	0	$E_T - X$
Cash Flow	$(X - E_T) > 0$	0	0

TABLE 4.13-3   Foreign Currency Conversion

Investment

1. Convert $E_0(1+R_F)^{-T}$ dollars to $(1+R_F)^{-T}$ units of foreign currency and invest in foreign risk-free security; the investment is worth one FC and E_T dollars at expiration.

2. Sell FC call and buy FC put

Position	Dollar Value of Conversion at Expiration		
	$E_T < X$	$E_T = X$	$E_T > X$
Dollar Value of Foreign Investment	E_T	E_T	E_T
Short Call	0	0	$-(E_T - X)$
Long Put	$X - E_T$	0	0
	X	X	X

4.13.2   Put–Call Parity Model

Recall that the put–call parity model for stock options was derived by determining the European call and put prices in which the arbitrage profit from a conversion (or reversal) strategy was zero. For European currency options, a conversion is formed by

1. Taking a long position in the foreign currency in which $E_0(1+R_F)^{-T}$ dollars are converted to foreign currency and invested in a foreign risk-free security at a rate of R_F

2. Forming a simulated short position in the foreign currency by taking a short position in a European currency call and a long position in a European currency put.

As shown in Table 4.13-3, at expiration, the foreign currency conversion yields a certain cash flow equal to the exercise price on the options. As a result, in equilibrium, the value of the conversion should be equal to the present value of a domestic (U.S.) riskless bond with a face value equal to X. Thus, the put–call parity relation for European currency options is

$$P_0^e - C_0^e + E_0(1+R_F)^{-T} = X(1+R_{US})^{-T}$$

$$P_0^e = C_0^e - E_0(1+R_F)^{-T} + X(1+R_{US})^{-T}$$

$$C_0^e = P_0^e + E_0(1+R_F)^{-T} - X(1+R_{US})^{-T}$$

4.14   CONCLUSION

Arbitrage involves buying and selling equivalent positions that are not equally priced. The exploitation of such opportunities by arbitrageurs serves to change the relative supplies and demands of the securities forming the positions until an equilibrium is attained in which the positions are equally valued. In this chapter, we have explored how arbitrage strategies involving positions with options, underlying stocks, and bonds govern the minimum and maximum option prices, the relative values of options with different exercise prices and times to expiration, and the relative values of puts and calls. These relations are summarized in Exhibit 4.14-1. In addition to examining arbitrage relationships, we have also analyzed the relationships

EXHIBIT 4.14-1 Summary of Boundary Conditions and Arbitrage Strategies Governing the Conditions

1 Condition	2 Violation	3 Arbitrage Strategy	
		Strategy	**Details**
1. $C_t^a > \text{Max}[S_t - X, 0]$	$C_t^a < (S_t - X)$	Long C_t^a Short $(S_t - X)$	(1) Buy Call (2) Buy Stock at X (exercise) (3) Sell Stock at S_t
2. $C_t > \text{Max}[S_t - PV(X), 0]$	$C_t < S_t - PV(X)$	Long C_t Short $(S_t - PV(X))$	(1) Buy Call (2) Buy Bond at PV(X) (3) Short Stock at S_t
3.a. Dividend Case $C_t^a > \text{Max}[S_t - PV(X,T) -$ $PV(D, t^*), 0]$ if $D \leq X - \dfrac{X}{(1+R)^{T-t^*}}$	$C_t < S_t - PV(X,T)$ $- PV(D, t^*)$	Long C_t Short $(S_t - PV(X,T)$ $-PV(D, t^*))$	(1) Buy Call (2) Buy Bond at PV(X,T) (3) Buy Bond at PV(D,t*) (4) Short Stock at S_t (5) Exercise at T
b. $C_t^a > \text{Max}[S_t - PV(D, t^*), 0]$ if $D > X - \dfrac{X}{(1+R)^{T-t^*}}$	$C_t < S_t - PV(D, t^*)$	Long C_t Short $(S_t - PV(D, t^*))$	(1) Buy Call (2) Short Stock at S_t (3) Buy Bond at PV(D,t*) (4) Exercise at t*
4. $C_t(X_1) > C_t(X_2)$	$C(X_1) < C(X_2)$	Long $C_t(X_1)$ Short $C_t(X_2)$	(1) Buy X_1 Call (2) Sell X_2 Call
5. $C_t^e(X_1) - C_t^e(X_2) <$ $PV(X_2 - X_1)$	$C_t^e(X_1) - C_t^e(X_2) >$ $PV(X_2 - X_1)$	Short $(C_t^e(X_1)$ $-C_t^e(X_2))$ Long $PV(X_2 - X_1)$	(1) Short X_1 Call (2) Long X_2 Call (3) Buy Bond at $PV(X_2 - X_1)$
6. $C_t^a(X_1) - C_t^a(X_2) < (X_2 - X_1)$	$C_t^a(X_1) - C_t^a(X_2) >$ $(X_2 - X_1)$	Short $(C_t^a(X_1)$ $-C_t^a(X_2))$ Long $(X_2 - X_1)$	(1) Short X_1 Call (2) Long X_2 Call (3) Buy Bond at $(X_2 - X_1)$
7. $C_t^a(T_2) > C_t^a(T_1)$	$C_t^a(T_2) < C_t^a(T_1)$	Long $C_t^a(T_2)$ Short $C_t^a(T_1)$	(1) Long T_2 Call (2) Short T_1 Call
8. $P_t^e > \text{Max}[PV(X) - S_t, 0]$	$P_t^e < (PV(X) - S_t)$	Long P_t^e Short $(PV(X) - S_t)$	(1) Long Put (2) Short Bond at PV(X) (3) Buy Stock at S_t
9. $P_t^e > \text{Max}[PV(X,T) +$ $PV(D, t^*) - S_t, 0]$	$P_t^e < (PV(X,T) +$ $PV(D, t^*)$ $-S_t)$	Long P_t^e Short $(PV(X,T)$ $+PV(D, t^*) - S_t)$	(1) Long Put (2) Sell bond at PV(X,T) (3) Sell bond at PV(D,t*) (4) Buy stock at S_t
10. $P_t^a > \text{Max}[X - S_t, 0]$	$P_t^a < (X - S_t)$	Long P_t^a Short $(X - S_t)$	(1) Long Put (2) Buy Stock at S_t (3) Sell Stock at X (exercise)
11. $P_t(X_2) > P_t(X_1)$	$P_t(X_2) < P_t(X_1)$	Long $P_t(X_2)$ Short $P_t(X_1)$	(1) Long X_2 Put (2) Short X_1 Put

continued

EXHIBIT 4.14-1   Continued

1	2	3	
Condition	**Violation**	**Arbitrage Strategy** Strategy	**Details**
12. $P_t^e(X_2) - P^e(X_1) < PV(X_2 - X_1)$	$P_t^e(X_2) - P_t^e(X_1) > PV(X_2 - X_1)$	Long $(P^e(X_2) - P^e(X_1))$ Short $PV(X_2 - X_1)$	(1) Long X_2 Put (2) Short X_1 Put (3) Short Bond at $PV(X_2 - X_1)$
13. $P_t^a(X_2) - P_t^a(X_1) < (X_2 - X_1)$	$P_t^a(X_2) - P_t^a(X_1) > (X_2 - X_1)$	Long $(P_t^a(X_2) - P_t^a(X_1))$ Short $(X_1 - X_2)$	(1) Long X_2 Put (2) Short X_1 Put (3) Short Bond at $PV(X_2 - X_1)$
14. $P_t^a(T_2) > P_t^a(T_1)$	$P_t^a(T_2) < P_t^a(T_1)$	Long $(P_t^a(T_2))$ Short $(P_t^a(T_1))$	(1) Long T_2 Put (2) Short T_1 Put
15. $P_t^e + S_t = C_t^e + PV(X)$	a. $P_t^e + S_t > C_t^e + PV(X)$ b. $P_t^e + S_t < C_t^e + PV(X)$	a. Short $(P_t^e + S_t)$ a. Long $(C_t^e + PV(X))$ b. Long $(P_t^e + S_t)$ b. Short $(C_t^e + PV(X))$	(1) Short Put (2) Short Stock (3) Long Call (4) Long Bond at $PV(X)$ (1) Long Put (2) Long Stock (3) Short Call (4) Short Bond at $PV(X)$
16. $C_t^e(X_1) - C_t^e(X_2)$ $+ P_t^e(X_2) - P_t^e(X_1)$ $- PV(X_2 - X_1) = 0$	a. $C_t^e(X_1) - C_t^e(X_2) + P_t^e(X_2)$ $- P_t^e(X_1) - PV(X_2 - X_1) < 0$ b. $C_t^e(X_1) - C_t^e(X_2) + P_t^e(X_2)$ $- P_t^e(X_1) - PV(X_2 - X_1) > 0$	a. Long $(C_t^e(X_1)$ $- C_t^e(X_2) + P_t^e(X_2) -$ $P_t^e(X_1) - PV(X_2 - X_1))$ b. Short $(C_t^e(X_1)$ $- C_t^e(X_2) + P_t^e(X_2)$ $- C_t^e(X_1) - PV(X_2 - X_1))$	(1) Long X_1 Call (2) Short X_2 Call (3) Long X_2 Put (4) Short X_1 Put (5) Short Bond at $PV(X_2 - X_1)$ (1) Short X_1 Call (2) Long X_2 Call (3) Short X_2 Put (4) Long X_1 Put (5) Long Bond at $PV(X_2 - X_1)$

between the price of the option and the underlying stock's price and volatility and the relationship between the option premium and interest rate. For the most part, our analysis in this chapter has examined each relationship separately. We are now ready to develop a model that will integrate many of the relationships—the Binomial Option Pricing Model.

KEY TERMS

maximum call price	maximum American put price	minimum European put price
minimum American call price	maximum European put price	conversion
minimum European call price	minimum American put price	reversal

synthetic call	box spread	foreign currency put–call parity
synthetic put	proxy portfolio	

SELECTED REFERENCES

Bhattacharya, M. "Transaction Data Tests of Efficiency of the Chicago Board Options Exchange." *Journal of Financial Economics* 12 (1983): 161–185.

Bodurtha, J., and G. Courtadon. "Efficiency Tests of the Foreign Currency Options Market." *Journal of Finance* 41 (March 1986): 151–162.

Cox, J. C., and M. Rubinstein. *Option Markets,* Englewood Cliffs, NJ: Prentice-Hall, 1985, 127–163.

Galai, D. "Empirical Tests of Boundary Conditions for CBOE Options." *Journal of Financial Economics* 6 (June–September 1978): 187–211.

Galai, D. "A Survey of Empirical Tests of Option Pricing Models." In *Option Pricing*, edited by M. Brenner, 45–80. Lexington, MA: Lexington Books, 1983.

Hull, J. C. *Option, Futures, and Other Derivatives,* 5th ed., Upper Saddle River, NJ: Prentice Hall, 2003, Chapter 8.

Johnson, L. "Foreign Currency Options, Ex Ante Exchange Rate Volatility, and Market Efficiency: an Empirical Test." *The Financial Review* (November 1986): 433–450.

Klemkosky, R., and B. Resnick. "Put Call Parity and Market Efficiency." *Journal of Finance* 34 (December 1979): 1141–1155.

Klemkosky, R., and B. Resnick. "An *Ex Ante* Analysis of Put–Call Parity." *Journal of Financial Economics* 8 (1980): 363–378.

Merton, R. "The Relationship Between Put and Call Option Prices: Comment." *The Journal of Finance* 28 (March 1973): 183–184.

Merton, R. "Theory of Rational Option Pricing." *Bell Journal of Economics* 4 (Spring 1973): 141–183.

Ronn, A. G., and E. I. Ronn. "The Box-Spread Arbitrage Conditions." *Review of Financial Studies*, 2, 1 (1989): 91–108.

Stoll, H. "The Relationship Between Put and Call Option Prices." *Journal of Finance* 24 (May 1969): 319–332.

Stoll, H. R. "The Relationship Between Put and Call Option Prices." *Journal of Finance* 31 (May 1969): 319–332.

PROBLEMS AND QUESTIONS

1. For each of the equilibrium and boundary conditions specified following, state when the condition is violated and the appropriate arbitrage strategy:

   a. $C_t^a \geq \text{Max}[S_t - X, 0]$

   b. $C_t^e \geq \text{Max}[S_t - PV(X), 0]$

   c. $P_t^a \geq \text{Max}[X - S_t, 0]$

   d. $P_t^e \geq \text{Max}[PV(X) - S_t, 0]$

   e. $C_t^e(X_1) > C_t^e(X_2)$

   f. $P_t^e(X_2) > P_t^e(X_1)$

   g. $C_t^e(X_1) - C_t^e(X_2) < PV(X_2 - X_1)$

   h. $P_t^e(X_2) - P_t^e(X_1) < PV(X_2 - X_1)$

   i. $C_t^a(T_2) > C_t^a(T_1)$

   j. $P_t^a(T_2) > P_t^a(T_1)$

k. $P_t^e + S_t = P_t^e + PV(X)$

l. $C_t^e(X_1) - C_t^e(X_2) + P_t^e(X_2) - P_t^e(X_1) = PV(X_2 - X_1)$

2. Prove the following conditions using an arbitrage argument. In your proof, show the initial positive cash flow when the condition is violated and prove that there are no liabilities at expiration or when the position is closed.

  a. $MinC_0 = Max[S_0 - PV(X), 0]$

  b. $MinP_0^a = Max[X - S_0, 0]$

  c. $MinP_0^e = Max[PV(X) - S_0, 0]$

  d. $C_0^e(X_1) - C_0^e(X_2) < PV(X_2 - X_1)$

3. Prove the following:

  a. End-of-Period Conversion Value $= X$

  b. End-of-Period Reversal Value $= -X$

  c. End-of-Period Long Box Spread Value $= X_2 - X_1$

  d. End-of-Period Short Box Spread Value $= -(X_2 - X_1)$

4. Assume the option's underlying stock pays a certain dividend worth \$D at the ex-dividend date (t*). Prove the following boundary conditions using an arbitrage argument:

  a. $C_0^e > Max[S_0 - PV(X, T) - PV(D, t^*), 0]$

  b. $P_0^a > Max[PV(X + D) - S_0, 0]$

5. Prove mathematically the following condition for the early exercise of a call by a call holder:

$$D > TVP$$

6. Explain what an arbitrageur would do in the following cases and how her arbitrage strategy would have no liabilities at expiration or when it is closed.

  a. The price of an ABC 40 call, expiring at the end of 6 months, is trading at \$1.05, ABC stock is at \$40, and the annual rate on a risk-free security is 6%.

  b. The price of an ABC European 40 call expiring at the end of 6 months is trading at \$0.75, ABC stock is trading at \$40 and is expected to pay \$0.25 dividend at the end of 3 months, and the annual risk-free rate is 6%.

  c. A September ABC 40 European call is trading at \$3, and a September ABC 50 European call is trading at \$4.

  d. A December ABC 40 European call is trading at \$6, and a December ABC 44 European call is selling at \$1, both options expire in 1 year, and the annual risk-free rate is 6%.

  e. A September ABC 40 American call is trading at \$6, and an October ABC 40 American call is trading at \$5.

  f. The price of an ABC 100 European put expiring at the end of 1 year is \$1, ABC stock is trading at \$92, and the annual risk-free rate is 6%.

  g. A March ABC 60 American put is trading at its intrinsic value, ABC stock is at \$56 and is expected to pay \$1 dividend at the end of 3 months (prior to the March expiration), and the annual risk-free rate is 5%.

    h. A December ABC 35 European put is selling at $1, and a December ABC 30 European put is selling for $3.

    i. A September ABC 45 European put is trading at $6 and a September ABC 40 European put is trading at $1, both puts expire in 1 year, and the annual risk-free rate is 6%.

    j. An ABC September 50 American put is trading at $6, and an ABC October 50 American put is trading at $5.

    k. ABC stock is selling at $50, an ABC October 50 European call is selling at $4, an ABC October 50 European put is selling at $5, and a pure discount bond with a face value of $50 and maturing at the options' expiration is trading at $49.

    l. ABC stock is selling at $60, an ABC October 60 European call is selling at $5, an ABC October 60 European put is selling at $3, and a pure discount bond with a face value of $60 and maturing at the options' expiration is trading at $59.

    m. An ABC September 50 European call is trading at $10, an ABC September 60 European call is at $8, an ABC September 50 European put is at $3, an ABC September 60 European put is at $1, and a pure discount bond with a face value of $10 is trading at $8.

7. Suppose just prior to going ex-dividend, LM stock is trading at $35 and is expected to go ex-dividend with a dividend expected to be worth $2.50 on the ex-dividend date. What advice would you recommend to a holder of an LM 30 American call option expiring in 2 weeks and trading with a TVP of $1?

8. Explain the condition and the likely circumstances in which an American call option might be exercised early.

9. Explain intuitively and with an example why call and put options are more valuable the greater their underlying stock's variability.

10. Explain the following option and stock price relations:

    a. Deep out-of-the-money call

    b. Deep in-the-money call

    c. Deep out-of-the-money put

    d. Deep in-the-money put

11. Suppose ABC stock is trading $30, an ABC 30 European call expiring in 1 year is trading at $3, and the annual risk-free rate is 6%. Using the put–call parity model, determine the equilibrium price of an ABC 30 European put expiring in 1 year.

12. Using the numbers in question 11, show with a profit table and graph how the synthetic put is the same as the actual 30 put when it is trading at its equilibrium price.

13. Suppose ABC stock is trading at $50, an ABC 50 European put expiring in 1 year is trading at $2, and the annual risk-free rate is 5%. Using the put–call parity model, determine the equilibrium price of an ABC 50 European call expiring in 1 year.

14. Using the numbers in question 13, show with a profit table how the synthetic call is the same as the actual 50 call when it is trading at the equilibrium price.

15. Using the put–call parity model, establish the conditions in which a European put would be trading below its IV.

16. Suppose a 40 American call with a 1-year life is trading at $5 when the stock is at $40, and the risk-free rate is 4%. Because $S_0 < C_0 + PV(X)$, it would seem that writing

a call, shorting a bond for $38.09 = 40/1.05$, and buying the stock for $40 would be an arbitrage portfolio because the net cash flow (at $t = 0$) is $3.09. Is it?

17. Determine the equilibrium price of a December S&P 500 call given the S&P 500 put is trading at 150. Assume the spot SP 500 index is at 1200, the risk-free rate is 6.5%, dividends per index share on the S&P 500 are worth a certain $25 at the December expiration, and 90 days to expiration ($T = .25$ per year).

18. PI Hedge Fund has formed a proxy portfolio that it is using to identify arbitrage opportunities using put–call parity relations. The proxy portfolio is highly correlated with the S&P 500 with a β of 1, is currently worth $25M, and is expected to pay dividends worth $1.25M at the end of 1 year. The current S&P 500 index is at 1250 and the risk-free rate is 6%.

   a. Define the PI Hedge Fund's proxy portfolio as an investment in hypothetical shares in the S&P 500. What is the dividend per index share?

   b. Determine the equilibrium price of a European 1250 S&P 500 index put expiring in 1 year given a European 1250 S&P 500 call expiring in 1 year is trading at 75.

   c. Describe the arbitrage strategy PI could employ if the S&P 500 put were trading at 50.

   d. Evaluate PI's arbitrage strategy from c at the index's expiration by first assuming the market increases by 10%, then assuming it decreases by 10%. Assume the portfolio is perfectly correlated with the market.

19. Prove the following boundary conditions hold for currency options by showing the arbitrage profits that could occur if the condition is violated and by showing that no liabilities exist at expiration or when the position is closed.

   a. $C_0 \geq E_0(1 + R_F)^{-T} - X(1 + R_{US})^{-T}$

   b. $C_0^a \geq E_0 - X$

   c. $P_0^e \geq X(1 + R_{US})^{-T} - E_0(1 + R_F)^{-T}$

   d. $P_0^a \geq X - E_0$

   e. $P_0^e + E_0(1 + R_F)^{-T} = C_0^e + X(1 + R_{US})^{-T}$

20. Prove that the cash flows at expiration from a reversal formed with currency options are equal to $-X$.

21. Using the put–call parity model, explain how one can form a synthetic long position in a foreign currency using European currency call and put options and a position in a U.S. risk-free bond. Show that your expiration values always are equal to $E_T(1+R_F)^T$.

22. Explain what an arbitrageur would do in the following circumstances:

   a. Dollar/Swiss Franc ($/SF) exchange rate is $0.51/SF, the Swiss risk-free rate is 4% (annual), the U.S. risk-free rate is 6%, and a SF call option with an exercise price of $0.50/SF and with a 3-month expiration ($T = .25$) is trading at $0.01/SF.

   b. $/SF exchange rate is $0.48/SF, the Swiss risk-free rate is 4% (annual), the U.S. risk-free rate is 6%, and a European SF put with an exercise price of $0.50/SF and with a 3-month expiration ($T = .25$) is trading at $0.01/SF.

   c. $/SF exchange rate is $0.52/SF, the Swiss risk-free rate is 4% (annual), the U.S. risk-free rate is 6%, a SF put with an exercise price of $0.50/SF and with an expiration of 3 months is trading at $0.0075, and a SF call with similar terms is trading at $0.04.

WEB EXERCISE

1. Select several exchange call and put options listed on the CBOE by going to www.wsj.com/free or www.cboe.com. Using your options, determine if they satisfy some of the boundary conditions specified in this chapter. Note: The stock options that you select are likely to pay a dividend that needs to be incorporated in the boundary conditions. To avoid the complications of dividend payments, you may want to look for options that expire in the near term. To get more information on a company go to: www.nasdaq.com, www.hoovers.com, or www.pinksheets.com.

APPENDIX 4A   BOUNDARY AND MINIMUM PRICE CONDITIONS FOR CALLS ON DIVIDEND-PAYING STOCKS

Boundary Condition

In the example in Section 4.2, we established that the minimum price of the 40 call expiring in 1 year (whether it is American or European) to be $12.26 given the stock was trading at 50 and the risk-free rate was 6%. As we noted, if the 40 call in that example were trading below $12.26, then an arbitrage profit could be realized by going long in the call, long in the bond, and short in the stock. Suppose the 40 call, though, were trading below its minimum at $10, but the stock was expected to go ex-dividend in 3 months, with the value of the dividend at that date expected to be $3.00. In this case, the arbitrage strategy governing the minimum call price, if implemented, would earn an initial cash flow of $2.26 ($50 − ($40/1.06) − $10). At the end of 3 months, though, an arbitrageur would have an obligation to pay $3.00 to the share lender to cover the dividend payment on the short stock position. Because this dividend obligation exceeds the initial excess cash flow of $2.26, the strategy is no longer a free lunch. The dividend payment in this example suggests that the boundary condition of $S_0 − PV(X)$ holds only for cases in which the underlying stock does not pay a dividend. A boundary condition (not the minimum price condition) for call options (American and European) on a dividend-paying stock can be established by simply adding to the arbitrage strategy a long position in a zero coupon bond with a maturity equal to the time to the ex-dividend date (t^*) and with a face value equal to the value of the dividend on that date (D). At the ex-dividend date, this bond would pay the arbitrageur $D, which she would use to cover her dividend obligation on the short stock position. As previously discussed, the stock, call, and other bond positions would yield either a zero or positive cash flow at expiration. To preclude arbitrage in this dividend-paying case, the initial cash flow of the position must be negative. That is

$$S_t − PV(X, T) − PV(D, t^*) − C_t < 0$$

where :
$PV(X, T)$ = price of bond with face value of X and maturity at T
$PV(D, t^*)$ = price of bond with face value of D and maturity
                at t^* (ex − dividend date)

Thus, in this example, the price of the call (American or European) on the dividend-paying stock must be at least equal to $9.31:

$$C_t \geq Max[S_t − PV(X, T) − PV(D, t^*), 0]$$

$$C_t \geq Max[50 − \frac{40}{1.06} − \frac{3}{(1.06)^{.25}}, 0]$$

$$C_t \geq 9.31$$

In summary:

> **RELATION:** The price of an American or European call on a stock that is expected to go ex-dividend at t*, with the value of the dividend at that date equal to D, must be greater than $S_0 - PV(X, T) - PV(D, t^*)$. If this condition does not hold, an arbitrage profit may be obtained by (1) shorting the stock, (2) buying the call, (3) buying a bond with $D face value and t* maturity, and (4) buying another bond with $X face value and T maturity.

Minimum Price on a European Call

Because a European call cannot be exercised early, the preceding boundary condition also defines the minimum price condition of a European call on a dividend-paying stock. Thus

> **RELATION:**
>
> $$\text{Min}C_t^e = \text{Max}[S_t - PV(X, T) - PV(D, t^*), 0]$$

Minimum Price on an American Call

$3-Dividend Case

If the call in the preceding example is American and is priced at the minimum European value of $9.31, then an arbitrage profit of $0.69 can be attained by buying the call, exercising immediately, and selling the stock. In the absence of arbitrage, the price of the American call would therefore have to be at least equal to its IV of $10, a condition we established earlier. Thus, in this example, the $3 dividend makes the American call, with its early exercise right, more valuable than the comparable European call. In this case, the early exercise feature makes it possible for arbitrageurs to close their arbitrage portfolios before they have to make dividend payments to their share lenders.

Suppose, though, the American call is trading at $10.25 (above its IV). At $10.25, an arbitrageur would still be able to realize another free lunch by

1. Shorting the stock
2. Buying the American call
3. Buying a 3-month bond with a face value of $X = \$40$
4. Exercising the call just before the ex-dividend date

Just before the ex-dividend date (at the end of 3 months), if the call is in or on the money ($S_t \geq 40$), the arbitrageur would be able to use the $40 from the bond to exercise the call and then use the stock received from the exercise to cover the short position, realizing a zero net cash flow. On the other hand, if the call is out of the money ($S_t < 40$), exercising the call would be worthless. In this case, the arbitrageur would be able to use some of the $40 bond principal to cover the short position, realizing a cash flow of $40 - S_t$ (plus the arbitrageur may be able to sell the out-of-money call with a time value premium). Thus, whether the call is in, on, or out of the money, this strategy has no liabilities just before the ex-dividend date. To preclude arbitrage, the price on the American call would have to be equal to at least $10.58—the price where the strategy's initial cash flow from shorting the stock, buying the call, and buying the bond is zero:

$$CF_0 = S_0 - PV(X, t^*) - C_0^a \geq 0$$

$$C_0^a \geq S_0 - PV(X, t^*)$$

$$C_0^a \geq Max[S_0 - PV(X, t^*), 0], \text{ to preclude negative prices}$$

$$C_0^a \geq Max[50 - \frac{40}{(1.06)^{.25}}, 0]$$

$$C_t^a \geq 10.58$$

The example suggests that for American calls on stocks with dividends, the time of the early exercise will ensure a specific minimum call value. In our example, immediate exercise ensures that the American call will be equal or greater than $10, exercising just before the ex-dividend date ensures that the call price will be equal or greater than $10.58, and exercising at expiration ensures that the call price will be equal or greater than $9.31. Because the second bound is the largest, it determines the American call's minimum price:

$$MinC_t^a = Max[S_t - X, S_t - PV(X, t^*), S_t - PV(D, t^*) - PV(X, T), 0]$$

$$MinC_t^a = Max[50 - 40, 50 - \frac{40}{(1.06)^{.25}}, 50 - \frac{3}{(1.06)^{.25}} - \frac{40}{(1.06)^1}, 0]$$

$$MinC_t^a = Max[10, 10.58, 9.31, 0]$$

$$MinC_t^a = 10.58$$

$1-Dividend Case

Now suppose that the stock paid only a $1 dividend instead of $3. If the call is European, its minimum price would be $11.28:

$$MinC_t^e = Max[S_t - PV(D, t^*) - PV(X, T), 0]$$

$$MinC_t^e = Max[50 - \frac{1}{(1.06)^{.25}} - \frac{40}{(1.06)^1}, 0]$$

$$MinC_t^e = Max[11.28, 0]$$

$$MinC_t^e = 11.28$$

For an American call, this $11.28 value is greater than the $10.58 value ensured from exercising just before the ex-dividend date. As a result, if the dividend is only $1, the minimum price of the American call would be $11.28, the same as the European:

$$MinC_t^a = Max[S_t - X, S_t - PV(X, t^*), S_t - PV(D, t^*) - PV(X, T), 0]$$

$$MinC_t^a = Max[50 - 40, 50 - \frac{40}{(1.06)^{.25}}, 50 - \frac{1}{(1.06)^{.25}} - \frac{40}{(1.06)^1}, 0]$$

$$MinC_t^a = Max[10, 10.58, 11.28, 0]$$

$$MinC_t^a = 11.28$$

In this case, the $1 dividend is not large enough to justify early exercise. As a result, the American and European calls have the same minimum values.

Threshold Dividend

The $1-dividend case shows that just the payment of a dividend is not enough to justify early exercise; rather, the dividend must be greater than a specific level for the American call to be more valuable than the European. The *threshold dividend* for determining whether early exercise is advantageous or not for the arbitrageur can be found algebraically by solving for the dividend (D^*) that makes the minimum American call value from exercising just prior to the ex-dividend date (t^*) equal to the minimum European value. As shown following, this dividend level is the one in which $D^* = X - (X/(1+R)^{T-t^*})$:

$$\text{MinC}_0^a = \text{MinC}_0^e$$

$$S_t - PV(X, t^*) = S_t - PV(X, T) - PV(D, t^*)$$

$$S_t - \frac{X}{(1+R)^{t^*}} = S_t - \frac{X}{(1+R)^T} - \frac{D}{(1+R)^{t^*}}$$

$$\frac{D}{(1+R)^{t^*}} = \frac{X}{(1+R)^{t^*}} - \frac{X}{(1+R)^T}$$

$$D = X - \frac{X}{(1+R)^T}(1+R)^{t^*}$$

$$D^* = X - \frac{X}{(1+R)^{T-t^*}}$$

In terms of our example, the threshold dividend would be $1.71:

$$D* = \$40 - \frac{\$40}{(1.06)^{1-.25}} = \$1.71,$$

and the minimum American and European call prices associated with that dividend would be $10.58:

$$\text{MinC}_t^a = \text{Max}[S_t - X, S_t - PV(X, t^*), S_t - PV(D, t^*) - PV(X, T), 0]$$

$$\text{MinC}_t^a = \text{Max}[50 - 40, 50 - \frac{40}{(1.06)^{.25}}, 50 - \frac{1.71}{(1.06)^{.25}} - \frac{40}{(1.06)^1}, 0]$$

$$\text{MinC}_t^a = \text{Max}[10, 10.58, 10.58, 0]$$

$$\text{MinC}_t^a = 10.58$$

and

$$\text{MinC}_t^e = \text{Max}[S_t - PV(D, t^*) - PV(X, T), 0]$$

$$\text{MinC}_t^e = \text{Max}[50 - \frac{1.71}{(1.06)^{.25}} - \frac{40}{(1.06)^1}, 0]$$

$$\text{MinC}_t^e = \text{Max}[10.58, 0]$$

$$\text{MinC}_t^e = 10.58$$

Thus, if the dividend is greater than $1.71, then the minimum value of the American call would be greater than the European call; if the dividend is equal or less than $1.71, then there would be no early exercise advantage to arbitrageurs, and the minimum values for the American and European calls would be the same.

Finally, note that $X - (X/(1+R)^{T-t^*}) = \$40 - (\$40/(1.06)^{.75}) = \$1.71$ is the present value of the interest foregone on a bond held to T. Thus, if the dividend is greater than the present value of the interest foregone, then the American call would be more valuable; if it is not, then the American and European values are the same.

Summary

To recapitulate, the preceding examples with different dividends illustrate several points.

1. Dividends have a negative impact on call values. In our examples, the minimum price for the European call decreased from $12.26 to $11.28 to $9.31 as we changed the dividend from zero to $1 to $3, and the price of the American call decreased from $12.26 to $11.28 to $10.58.

	No Dividend	$1 Dividend	1.71 Dividend	$3 Dividend
Minimum European Call Price	$12.26	$11.28	$10.58	$ 9.31
Minimum American Call Price	$12.26	$11.28	$10.58	$10.58

2. If the dividend is low, the early exercise advantage for arbitrageurs may not exist, and as a result, the American call would have the same minimum value as the European. In our example, this was the case when the dividend was $1.71 or less.

3. If the dividend is high, the early exercise advantage for arbitrageurs may exist; if so, the minimum value of the American call would be greater than the European one. This was the case in our example when the dividend was greater than $1.71.

PROBLEMS AND QUESTIONS

1. Suppose the current stock price of the ABC Corporation is $80, and the risk-free rate is 10% per year. Find the minimum price for an ABC 75 European call and an ABC 75 American call, both with expirations of 1 year, given the company is expected in 3 months to pay (a) no dividend, (b) a $4 dividend, and (c) a $10 dividend. Describe some of the relations you observed between the call prices and dividends.

2. Find the threshold dividend in Problem 1.

APPENDIX 4B   MINIMUM PRICE CONDITIONS FOR PUTS ON DIVIDEND-PAYING STOCKS

Minimum Price of a European Put

In Section 4.7, we established the minimum price condition of $PV(X) - S_t$ for a European put. Thus, the price of a 50 European put expiring in 1 year would have to be equal to $2.17 when the stock was at 45 and the risk-free rate was at 6%: $PV(X) - S_t = 50/106 - 45 = 2.17$. If the put were priced below 2.17, then an arbitrage opportunity would exist from buying the stock and put and shorting the bond. Suppose, though, that the stock was expected to go ex-dividend in 4 months ($t^* = 4/12$), with the dividend at that date expected to be worth $D = 3$. Because the arbitrageur is long in the stock, he would receive an additional cash flow of 3.00. Because the present value of the dividend is $PV(D, t^*) = \$3.00/(1.06)^{4/12} = \$2.94$, the minimum price of the European put should be worth $2.94 more than the minimum price of the put without the dividend; thus, the minimum price should be $5.11 = \$2.94 + \$2.17$. If the market price of the put were equal to its minimum European value without the dividend value of $2.17, an arbitrageur could realize a free lunch by buying the stock and put and by shorting (borrowing) both a bond with a face value of $X = 50$ and maturity of T and a bond with a face value of $D = 3.00$

and expiration of 4 months. This strategy would yield an initial cash flow of $2.94,

$$CF_0 = PV(X, T) + PV(D, t^*) - S_0 - P_0^e$$

$$CF_0 = \frac{50}{(1.06)} + \frac{3}{(1.06)^{4/12}} - 45 - 2.17 = 2.94$$

and there would be no liabilities when it is closed. That is, at the dividend-payment date, the arbitrageur would finance the $3.00 debt with the 3.00 dividend credit and at expiration would close the stock, bond, and put positions, obtaining (as shown in Table 4.7-2) either a zero or positive cash flow. To preclude this arbitrage, the European put would have to trade for at least $5.11. That is

$$CF_0 = PV(X, T) + PV(D, t^*) - S_0 - P_0^e$$

$$0 = PV(X, T) + PV(D, t^*) - S_0 - P_0^e$$

$$P_0^e = PV(X, T) + PV(D, t^*) - S_0$$

$$P_0^e = \frac{50}{(1.06)} + \frac{3}{(1.06)^{4/12}} - 45 - 2.17 = 5.11$$

Thus, in the presence of dividends, the minimum European put price is governed by the following relation:

RELATION: If the stock pays a dividend of $D at time t^*, the minimum price of a European put is

$$MinP_0^e = Max[PV(X, T) + PV(D, t^*) - S_0, 0]$$

If this condition does not hold, an arbitrage profit may be obtained by going long in the stock and the put and short in two discount bonds: the first with face value of $D and maturity date t^* and the second with face value of $X and maturity date T.

Minimum Price of an American Put

If the put in the preceding example is American and priced at $5.11, an arbitrageur could obtain a riskless profit (even though the put is above its IV) by buying the put and stock and shorting a bond with a face value equal in value to the exercise price plus dividend value and maturing at the ex-dividend date. Exploiting this, an arbitrageur would realize an initial cash flow of $1.87:

$$CF_0 = -S_0 - P_0^a + PV(X + D, t^*)$$

$$CF_0 = -45 - 5.11 + \frac{50 + 3}{(1.06)^{4/12}} = 1.87$$

At the ex-dividend date, the arbitrageur would finance the debt obligation of $53 with the 3 dividend value from the stock position and by selling the stock on the put for $50. To preclude this free lunch, the put would have to sell for at least $6.98:

$$P_0^a = Max[PV(X + D, t^*) - S_0, 0]$$

$$P_0^a = Max\left[\frac{50 + 3}{(1.06)^{4/12}} - 45, 0\right] = 6.98$$

As we saw earlier with the American call, the time of the early exercise ensures certain minimum put values. In this example, immediate exercise ensures that P_0^a will be equal or greater than 5 (IV), exercising at the dividend-payment date ensures P_0^a will be equal or greater than \$6.98, and exercising at expiration ensures P_0^a will be equal or greater than \$5.11 (the minimum European value). For American puts, the second bound is always greater than the third, and in this example, it is also larger than the first. Thus, the minimum put price is the second bound:

$$\text{MinP}_0^a = \text{Max}[X - S_0, PV(X + D, t^*) - S_0, PV(X, T + PV(D, t^*) - S_0, 0]$$

$$\text{MinP}_0^a = \text{Max}\left[50 - 45, \frac{50 + 3}{(1.06)^{4/12}} - 45, \frac{50}{1.06} + \frac{3}{1.06^{4/12}} - 45, 0\right]$$

$$\text{MinP}_0^a = \text{Max}[5.00, 6.98, 5.11, 0] = 6.98$$

Note, if the dividend were \$0.50 instead of \$3.00, the minimum price with immediate exercise would be \$5, the minimum price with exercising at the ex-dividend date would be \$4.53, and the minimum price with exercising at expiration would be \$2.66. Thus, the minimum price of the American put would be \$5.00:

$$\text{MinP}_0^a = \text{Max}[X - S_0, PV(X + D, t^*) - S_0, PV(X, T + PV(D, t^*) - S_0, 0]$$

$$\text{MinP}_0^a = \text{Max}\left[50 - 45, \frac{50.50}{(1.06)^{4/12}} - 45, \frac{50}{1.06} + \frac{0.50}{1.06^{4/12}} - 45, 0\right]$$

$$\text{MinP}_0^a = \text{Max}[5.00, 4.53, 2.66, 0] = 5.00$$

In summary, the minimum price condition for an American put paying a dividend is

---

RELATION: In the absence of arbitrage, the price of an American put on a dividend-paying stock is bound by the following condition:

$$\text{MinP}_0^a = \text{Max}[X - S_0, PV(X + D, t^*) - S_0, 0]$$

Note in examining the impact of dividends on the minimum put price, several points should be noted. First, the minimum price of the American put is greater than its European counterpart regardless of whether the stock pays a low or high dividend or no dividend at all. Second, because the American put's minimum price is always above the European's, the right to exercise is always positive. Finally, the price of the put options are a positive function of dividends: As dividends increase, both American and European minimum put prices increase.

PROBLEM

1. Suppose the current stock price of XAVR Corporation is \$50, and the annual risk-free rate is 10%. Find the minimum prices for the 60 European and 60 American put options, expiring in 1 year if in 3 months, the company is expected to pay (a) no dividends, (b) a \$4 dividend, and (c) a \$10 dividend. Describe the relations you observed between the put prices and dividends.

CHAPTER 5

THE BINOMIAL OPTION PRICING MODEL

5.1 INTRODUCTION

In the traditional supply and demand models in economics, the equilibrium price of a good is defined as that price in which the quantity demanded of the good equals the quantity supplied. If this condition is not met, then a surplus or shortage of the good will result, causing the good's price to change until the condition is satisfied. Like the supply and demand models of economics, the models for determining the equilibrium price of an option involve finding a unique value at which the option price naturally tends to be. The two most widely used models for determining the equilibrium price are the Black and Scholes (B–S) option pricing model (OPM) and the binomial option pricing model (BOPM). Black and Scholes derived their model in 1973 in a seminal paper in the *Journal of Political Economy*. The BOPM was derived by Cox, Ross, and Rubinstein (1979) and Rendleman and Bartter (1979).

The B–S OPM and the BOPM are similar in a number of ways. First, both models explain the equilibrium price of an option in terms of the same parameters—stock price (S), exercise price (X), time to expiration (T), the interest rate (R), and the underlying stock's variability (V)—and both are capable of explaining most of the boundary conditions and behavioral relationships described in the last chapter. Second, each model is limited to cases involving European options and in which there are no dividend payments made on the underlying stock. Adjustments are therefore required in each model when the right for early exercise exists and dividends are paid on the underlying stock. Finally, each determines the equilibrium price of an option in terms of arbitrage forces. Such arbitrage models are based on the law of one price. As we discussed in Chapter 1, this law states that two assets or portfolios with identical future cash flows must sell for the same price to avoid arbitrage opportunities. For example, if a call trades for $5, whereas a portfolio that exactly replicates the call's payoffs trades for $10, then we have an arbitrage opportunity. The price imbalance will create excess demand for the call and excess supply for the replicating portfolio, forcing their respective prices to converge to a single value. Both the B–S model and BOPM are based on valuing options in terms of replicating a portfolio, thereby using the law of one price to establish the equilibrium price.

The major difference in the models emanates from the assumption each makes concerning the underlying stock price's fluctuations over time, statistically referred to as its stochastic (or random) stock process. In the BOPM, the time to expiration is partitioned into a discrete or finite number of periods, each with the same length. In each period, the stock is assumed to follow a binomial process in which it either increases or decreases. The model then determines the equilibrium price of the option in which the cash flows from an arbitrage strategy consisting of positions in the stock, call, and a bond are zero for each discrete period. The B–S OPM, on the other hand, posits a continuous process in which the time intervals are partitioned into infinitely small periods or, equivalently, the number of periods to expiration is assumed to approach infinity. In this continuous model, the price of the option is determined by assuming that the same arbitrage strategy used in the BOPM is implemented and revised continuously. Thus, the BOPM should be viewed as a first approximation of the B–S OPM. As the lengths of the intervals in the BOPM are made smaller, the discrete process merges into the continuous one, and the BOPM and the B–S OPM converge.

In this and the following four chapters, we examine the two option pricing models. In this chapter, we derive the binomial model for call and put options and explain how it can be estimated. In Chapters 6 and 7, we explain how the binomial call and put models are adjusted when the underlying stock pays a dividend during the life of the option; and we extend the model to show how it is used to price index, currency, and debt options. In Chapter 8, we examine the B–S model, and in Chapter 9, we conclude our analysis of option pricing by describing some new option strategies based on the option pricing models.

In examining the BOPM in this chapter, we begin by first deriving the model for call and put options under the assumption there is only one period to expiration. With this background, the single-period model will then be extended to the more realistic multiple-period case. Because the BOPM is based on arbitrage relations, we also examine in this chapter the arbitrage strategies that market makers and other traders can pursue when the option's market price does not equal the BOPM value.

5.2 SINGLE-PERIOD BOPM

5.2.1 Valuing Call Options Through a Replicating Portfolio

In the BOPM, the equilibrium price of an option is based on the law of one price. For calls, this price is found by equating the price of the call to the value of a replicating portfolio, that is, a portfolio constructed so that its possible cash flows are equal to the call's possible payouts.

To construct a replicating portfolio, assume initially that options expire in one period, and at the end of the period, there are only two possible states. In this one-period, two-state economy, assume that at the end of the period, a stock, currently priced at $S_0 = \$100$, will be worth either $S_u = \$110$ if the upstate occurs or $S_d = \$95$ if the downstate occurs. Equivalently stated, assume that the stock will either increase to equal a proportion u times its initial price, where u is the relative stock price, S_u/S_0 (u = 1.1 in this case), or it will decrease to equal a proportion d times its initial value, S_d/S_0 (d =. 95 in this case).

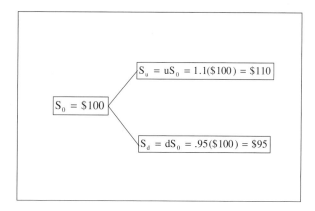

Next, consider a one-period European call option on the stock with an exercise price of $100. If the upstate occurs, the call will be worth its IV of $C_u = \$10$, and if the downstate occurs, the call will be worthless, $C_d = 0$. That is

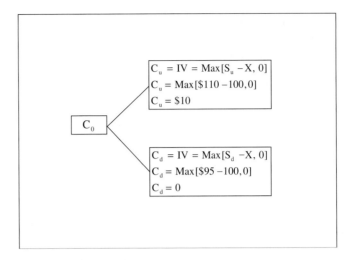

Third, assume there is a risk-free security to which funds can be lent (invested) or borrowed (sold short) for the period at a rate of R_f. To preclude arbitrage opportunities, assume $d < r_f < u$, where $r_f = (1 + R_f)$. That is, if $r_f > u$, there would be arbitrage profits by shorting the stock and buying the risk-free security; if $r_f < d$, there would be riskless profit by buying the stock and shorting the bond. To satisfy this condition, let us assume a period risk-free rate of 5% ($r_f = 1.05$) in our example. Finally, for simplicity, assume there are no taxes, margin requirements, commission costs, or dividends and that the stock and call are perfectly divisible.

With two securities (the stock and the risk-free security) and two states, a replicating portfolio whose outflows at the end of the period exactly match the call's can be formed by buying H_0 shares of stock at a price of S_0 partially financed by borrowing B_0 dollars at the risk-free rate (i.e., selling the risk-free security short). The current value of this portfolio, V_0, is

$$V_0 = H_0 S_0 - B_0 \tag{5.2-1}$$

(where the negative sign signifies borrowing) and, contingent on the future state, at the end of the period, the portfolio will have one of the following two possible values:

$$V_u = H_0 u S_0 - r_f B_0 \tag{5.2-2}$$

$$V_d = H_0 d S_0 - r_f B_0 \tag{5.2-3}$$

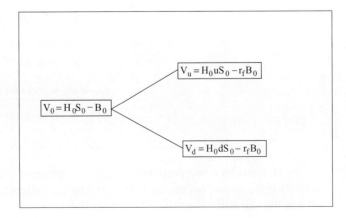

Given these two possible values, the replicating portfolio can be formed by finding the unknowns, H_0 and B_0, which make the two possible portfolio values, V_u and V_d, equal to the two possible call values, C_u and C_d in their respective states. Mathematically, this can be found by solving for the H_0 and B_0 values in which

$$H_0 u S_0 - r_f B_0 = C_u$$

$$H_0 d S_0 - r_f B_0 = C_d$$

The solutions are

$$H_0^* = \frac{C_u - C_d}{uS_0 - dS_0} \tag{5.2-4}$$

$$B_0^* = \frac{C_u(dS_0) - C_d(uS_0)}{r_f(uS_0 - dS_0)} \tag{5.2-5}$$

H_0^* in Equation (5.2-4) is the ratio of the range in possible call values to stock values, often referred to as the *hedge ratio* or *delta value*. In our example

$$H_0^* = \frac{C_u - C_d}{uS_0 - dS_0} = \frac{\$10 - 0}{\$110 - \$95} = .6667$$

$$B_0^* = \frac{C_u(dS_0) - C_d(uS_0)}{r_f(uS_0 - dS_0)} = \frac{(\$10)(\$95) - (0)(\$110)}{1.05[\$110 - \$95]} = \$60.32$$

Thus, to replicate the two possible call payouts, one would need to purchase .6667 shares of the stock at $100 per share, partially financed by borrowing $60.32. At the end of the period, this portfolio would replicate the two possible call payoffs of $10 or $0. That is

$$V_u = (0.6667)(\$110) - (1.05)(\$60.32) = \$10$$

$$V_d = (0.6667)(\$95) - (1.05)(\$60.32) = 0$$

Finally, by the law of one price, we can determine the equilibrium price of the call, C_0^*, by setting the current call value equal to the current value of the replicating portfolio. That is

$$C_0^* = H_0^* S_0 - B_0^* \tag{5.2-6}$$

For our example, the equilibrium call price is therefore $6.35:

$$C_0^* = (0.6667)(\$100) - (\$60.32) = \$6.35$$

5.2.2 Single-Period Arbitrage Call Strategy

In the economy we have just described, suppose the market price of the call, C_0^m, is not equal to C_0^*. Accordingly, an arbitrage portfolio consisting of a position in the call and an opposite position in the replicating portfolio can be formed to take advantage of this mispricing opportunity. For example, if the call price in our illustrative example were $7.35 instead of $6.35, arbitrageurs could sell the expensive call for $7.35 and go long in the replicating portfolio (buy .6667 shares of stock at $100 and borrow $60.32 in a risk-free security) to earn a positive cash flow of $1. As shown in Table 5.2-1, at expiration, the cash flows from the short call position and the long replicating portfolio position would cancel each other out at either stock price, and the initial profit of $1 would be worth $1.05. Thus, arbitrageurs would earn $1.05 with no cash outflows. As arbitrageurs try to sell calls at

TABLE 5.2-1   Overpriced Call Arbitrage Strategy, Single-Period Case

$S_0 = \$100, u = 1.1, d = .95, R_f = .05, X = \$100, C_0^* = \$6.35, H_0^* = .6667, B_0^* = \$60.32, C_0^m = \$7.35$

Initial Position	Cash Flow	Cash Flow
Sell Call	$C_0^m = \$7.35$	$7.35
Buy H_0^* Shares of Stock at \$100	$-H_0^*(S_0) = -(.6667)(\$100)$	−\$66.67
Borrow B_0^* Dollar	$B_0^* = \$60.32$	\$60.32
Initial Cash flow	$C_0^m - (H_0^* S_0 - B_0^*) = \$7.35 - \$6.35$	\$1.00

	Cash Flow at Expiration	
Closing Position	$S_u = \$110$ $C_u = \$10$	$S_d = \$95$ $C_d = 0$
Call: IV	−\$10.00	0
Stock: $(.6667)S_T$	\$73.34	\$63.34
Debt: $(\$60.32)(1.05)$	−\$63.34	−\$63.34
	0	0
Value of Initial Cash Flow = \$1(1.05)	\$1.05	\$1.05

$7.35, though, they will push the price of the call down until it is equal to $6.35. At that price the arbitrage opportunity is gone.

On the other hand, if the call is priced below $6.35, then the call is cheap relative to the replicating portfolio. In this case, arbitrage opportunities will exist by going long in the call and short in the replicating portfolio. For example, if $C_0^m = \$5.35$, then, as shown in Table 5.2-2, arbitrageurs could buy the call and take a short position in the replicating portfolio (sell .6667 shares of stock short at $100 and invest $60.32 in a risk-free security) to earn a positive cash flow (or credit) of $1. As shown in Table 5.2-2, at expiration, the cash flows from the long call position and the short replicating portfolio position would again cancel each other out at either stock price, and the initial profit of $1 would be worth $1.05. Thus, arbitrageurs would earn $1.05, with no cash outflows. As arbitrageurs try to buy calls at $5.35, though, they will push the price of the call up until it is equal to $6.35. At that price, the arbitrage opportunity is gone. Thus, in this binomial world, arbitrage forces ensure that the price of the call will be equal to the value of the replicating portfolio.

5.2.3   Rewriting the Equilibrium Call Price Equation

The equation for the equilibrium price of the call, (5.2-6), can be rewritten by substituting the values of H_0^* and B_0^* into (5.2-6) to obtain Equation (5.2-7):

$$C_0^* = H_0^* S_0 - B_0^*$$

$$C_0^* = \left[\frac{C_u - C_d}{(uS_0 - dS_0)} \right] S_0 - \left[\frac{C_u(dS_0) - C_d(uS_0)}{r_f(uS_0 - dS_0)} \right]$$

$$C_0^* = \frac{r_f S_0[C_u - C_d] - [C_u(d) - C_d(u)]S_0}{r_f S_0(u - d)}$$

TABLE 5.2-2 Underpriced Call Arbitrage Strategy, Single-Period Case

$S_0 = \$100, u = 1.1, d = .95, R_f = .05, X = \$100, C_0^* = \$6.35, H_0^* = .6667, B_0^* = \$60.32, C_0^m = \$7.35$

Initial Position	Cash Flow	Cash Flow
Buy Call	$-C_0^m = -\$5.35$	$-\$5.35$
Sell H_0^* Shares of Stock Short at $100	$H_0^*(S_0) = (.6667)(\$100)$	$\$66.67$
Invest B_0^* dollar	$-B_0^* = -\$60.32$	$-\$60.32$
Initial Cash flow	$(H_0^* S_0 - B_0^*) - C_0^m = \$6.35 - \$5.35$	$\$1.00$

	Cash Flow at Expiration	
Closing Position	$S_u = \$110$ $C_u = \$10$	$S_d = \$95$ $C_d = 0$
Call: IV	$\$10.00$	0
Stock: $-(.6667)S_T$	$-\$73.34$	$-\$63.34$
Investment: $(\$60.32)(1.05)$	$\$63.34$	$\$63.34$
	0	0
Value of Initial Cash Flow = $\$1(.05)$	$\$1.05$	$\$1.05$

$$C_0^* = \frac{1}{r_f}\left[\left(\frac{r_f - d}{u - d}\right)C_u + \left(\frac{u - r_f}{u - d}\right)C_d\right]$$

$$C_0^* = \frac{1}{r_f}[pC_u + (1 - p)C_d] \tag{5.2-7}$$

where:

$$p = \frac{r_f - d}{u - d}$$

$$1 - p = \frac{u - d}{u - d} - \frac{r_f - d}{u - d} = \frac{u - r_f}{u - d}$$

In terms of our illustrated example

$$C_0^* = \frac{1}{1.05}[(.6667)(\$10) + (.333)(0)] = \$6.35$$

where:

$$p = \frac{1.05 - .95}{1.1 - .95} = .6667$$

5.3 SINGLE-PERIOD BOPM FOR PUT OPTIONS

5.3.1 Valuing Put Options Through a Replicating Portfolio

Similar to the pricing of call option through a replicating portfolio, the equilibrium value of a European put also can be found by determining the value of a replicating put portfolio. To see this, consider again the one-period, two-state economy in which a stock can either increase to equal uS_0 or decrease to equal dS_0. A European put on the stock that expires at the end of the period would, therefore, be worth either P_u or P_d:

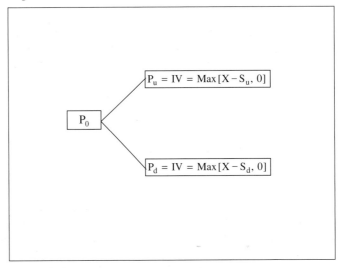

Given the two possible stock prices and put values, a replicating put portfolio can be formed by purchasing H_0^P shares of stock and investing I_0 dollars in a risk-free security (in which I_0 is the negative of borrowing B_o dollars). The current value of this portfolio, V_0, is

$$V_0 = H_0^P S_0 + I_0 \qquad (5.3\text{-}1)$$

and the portfolio's two possible values at expiration are

$$V_u = H_0^P u S_0 + r_f I_0 \qquad (5.3\text{-}2)$$

$$V_d = H_0^P d S_0 + r_f I_0 \qquad (5.3\text{-}3)$$

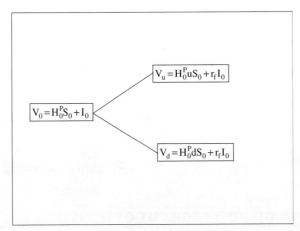

For this portfolio to have values at expiration that match those of the put, H_0^P and I_0 must be such that

$$H_0^P u S_0 + r_f I_0 = P_u \qquad (5.3\text{-}4)$$

$$H_0^P d S_0 + r_f I_0 = P_d$$

Thus, solving (5.3-4) simultaneously for H_0^{P*} and I_0^*, we obtain

$$H_0^{P*} = \frac{P_u - P_d}{uS_0 - dS_0} \tag{5.3-5}$$

$$I_0^* = \frac{-[P_u(dS_0) - P_d(uS_0)]}{r_f((uS_0 - dS_0)} \tag{5.3-6}$$

Note that because $P_d > P_u$, H_0^{P*} will be negative, and I_0^* will be positive except for the case in which $P_d = 0$. This implies that the replicating put portfolio is constructed with a short position in the stock (selling H_0^{P*} shares short) and a long position in the risk-free security (investing I_0^* dollars in a risk-free security). Thus, this strategy contrasts with the replicating call portfolio that is formed with a long position in the stock and borrowing funds. As an example, suppose in our single-period call example in which $u = 1.1, d = .95$, $S_0 = \$100$, and $r_f = 1.05$, there is a European put option on the stock with an exercise price of $\$100$. In our one-period, two-state model, the possible put values at expiration would be

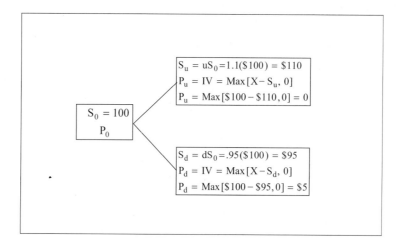

To replicate the possible values of the put, we would need to sell .33333 shares of the stock short ($H_0^{P*} = -.33333$) at $\$100$ per share and to invest $\$34.9206$ in the risk-free security. That is

$$H_0^{P*} = \frac{P_u - P_d}{uS_0 - dS_0} = \frac{0 - \$5}{\$110 - \$95} = -.33333$$

$$I_0^* = \frac{-[P_u(dS_0) - P_d(uS_0)]}{r_f(uS_0 - dS_0)} = \frac{-[0(\$95) - (\$5)(\$110)}{(1.05)(\$110 - \$95)} = \$34.9206$$

At the end of the period, this portfolio would have possible values that exactly match those of the put:

$$V_u = H_0^P uS_0 + r_f I_0 = (-.33333)(\$110) + (1.05)(\$34.9206) = 0$$

$$V_d = H_0^P dS_0 + r_f I_0 = (-.33333)(\$95) + (1.05)(\$34.9206) = \$5$$

Thus, by the law of one price, the equilibrium price of the put, P_0^*, would have to be equal to the value of the replicating put portfolio or arbitrage opportunities would exist. The equilibrium price of the put therefore is

$$P_0^* = H_0^{P^*} S_0 + I_0^* \tag{5.3-7}$$

And in terms of our example

$$P_0^* = H_0^{P^*} S_0 + I_0^*$$
$$P_0^* = (-.33333)(\$100) + \$34.9206 = \$1.59$$

5.3.2 Single-Period Arbitrage Strategy

If a put is not equal to its equilibrium value, then riskless profit can be earned from an arbitrage portfolio consisting of a position in the put and an opposite position in the replicating put portfolio. If the market price of the put, P_0^m, is above P_0^*, then arbitrageurs would take a short position in the put and a long position in the replicating portfolio. For example, if the market price of the put in our preceding example were $P_0^m = \$2.00$, then, as shown in Table 5.3-1, an initial cash flow of \$0.41 could be earned by selling the put, selling .33333 shares of the stock short, and investing \$34.9206 in a risk-free security. At expiration, the replicating portfolio would have possible values of either 0 or \$5 that would cover the possible put obligations, and the \$0.41 initial cash flow would be worth (\$0.41)(1.05) = \$0.43. In contrast, if the put is below P_0^*, then an initial positive cash flow could be earned by going long in the put and short in the replicating put portfolio. For example, as shown in Table 5.3-2, at $P_0^m = \$1.18$, a \$0.43 profit is earned by implementing this underpriced arbitrage strategy.

5.3.3 Rewriting the Equilibrium Put Price Equation

The equilibrium put value defined by Equation (5.3-7) can be defined alternatively in terms of Equation (5.3-8) following by substituting Equations (5.3-5) and (5.3-6) for $H_0^{P^*}$ and I_0^*

TABLE 5.3-1   Overpriced Put Arbitrage Strategy, Single-Period Case

$S_0 = \$100, u = 1.1, d = .95, R_f = .05, X = \$100, P_0^* = \$1.59, H_0^{P^*} = -.33333, I_0^* = \$34.92,$
$P_0^m = \$2.00$

Initial Position	Cash Flow	Cash Flow
Sell Put	$P_0^m = \$2.00$	\$2.00
Short $H_0^{P^*}$ Shares of Stock at \$100	$H_0^{P^*}(S_0) = (-.33333)(\$100)$	\$33.33
Invest I_0^* Dollar	$-I_0^* = \$34.92$	−\$34.92
Initial Cash flow	$P_0^m - (H_0^{P^*} S_0 + I_0^*) = \$2.00 - \$1.59$	\$0.41

	Cash Flow at Expiration	
Closing Position	$S_u = \$110$ $P_u = 0$	$S_d = \$95$ $P_d = 5$
Put: IV	0	−\$5.00
Stock: $(-.33333)S_T$	−\$36.67	−\$31.67
Investment: ($34.92)(1.05)	\$36.67	\$36.67
	0	0
Value of Initial Cash Flow = \$0.41(1.05)	\$0.43	\$0.43

TABLE 5.3-2 Underpriced Put Arbitrage Strategy, Single-Period Case

$S_0 = \$100, u = 1.1, d = .95, R_f = .05, X = \$100, P_0^* = \$1.59, H_0^{P^*} = -.33333, I_0^* = \$34.92,$
$P_0^m = \$1.18$

Initial Position	Cash Flow	Cash Flow
Buy Put	$P_0^m = \$1.18$	−$1.18
Buy $H_0^{P^*}$ Shares of Stock at $100	$H_0^{P^*}(S_0) = (.33333)(\$100)$	−$33.33
Borrow I_0^* Dollar	$I_0^* = \$34.92$	$34.92
Initial Cash flow	$(H_0^{P^*}S_0 + I_0^*) - P_0^m = \$1.59 - \$1.18$	$0.41

	Cash Flow at Expiration	
	$S_u = \$110$	$S_d = \$95$
Closing Position	$P_u = 0$	$P_d = 5$
Put: IV	0	$5.00
Stock: $(.33333)S_T$	$36.67	$31.67
Debt: $(\$34.92)(1.05)$	−$36.67	−$36.67
	0	0
Value of Initial Cash Flow = $0.41(1.05)	$0.43	$0.43

in Equation (5.3-7) and rearranging as follows:

$$P_0^* = H_0^{P^*}S_0 + I_0^*$$

$$P_0^* = \left[\frac{P_u - P_d}{(uS_0 - dS_0)}\right]S_0 + \left[\frac{-[P_u(dS_0) - P_d(uS_0)]}{r_f(uS_0 - dS_0)}\right]$$

$$P_0^* = \frac{r_f S_0[P_u - P_d] - S_0[P_u(d) - P_d(u)]}{r_f S_0(u - d)}$$

$$P_0^* = \frac{1}{r_f}\left[\left(\frac{u - r_f}{u - d}\right)P_d + \left(\frac{r_f - d}{u - d}\right)P_u\right]$$

$$P_0^* = \frac{1}{r_f}[pP_u + (1 - p)P_d] \tag{5.3-8}$$

where:

$$p = \frac{r_f - d}{u - d}$$

$$1 - p = \frac{u - d}{u - d} - \frac{r_f - d}{u - d} = \frac{u - r_f}{u - d}$$

In terms of our illustrated example

$$P_0^* = \frac{1}{1.05}[(.6667)(0) + (.333)(\$5)] = \$1.59$$

where:

$$p = \frac{1.05 - .95}{1.1 - .95} = .6667$$

5.3.4 Put-Call Parity Model

In Chapter 4, we delineated the put-call parity model. Recall that this model specifies the equilibrium relationship between the prices of call and put options on the same stock. In terms of the model, the equilibrium price of a European put is determined by the current value of a portfolio consisting of a long position in the call, a long position in a riskless bond with a face value equal to the exercise price, and a short position in the stock:

$$P_0^* = C_0^* + PV(X) - S_0 \tag{5.3-9}$$

Using this model, we can determine the same equilibrium put price that we obtained using the binomial put model by substituting the equilibrium call price as determined by the binomial call model. In terms of our examples, substituting the call value of \$6.35 (Section 5.2) into Equation (5.3-9), we obtain the same put values of \$1.59 that we did using the binomial put model. That is

$$P_0^* = C_0^* + PV(X) - S_0$$

$$P_0^* = \$6.35 + \frac{\$100}{1.05} - \$100 = \$1.59$$

5.4 THE MULTIPLE-PERIOD BOPM FOR CALLS

The BOPM defined previously is based on several simplifying assumptions. To obtain a more realistic model, we need to value options under the assumption there are multiple periods to expiration. In constructing a multiple-period model, we divide the time to expiration into a number of subperiods of smaller length. As the length of the time period becomes smaller, the assumption that stock price changes follow a binomial process of either increasing or decreasing in each period then becomes more plausible; and as the number of periods increase, the number of possible states at expiration is greater, again adding more realism to the model.

5.4.1 Two-Period BOPM

In deriving BOPM for multiple periods, we begin with the case in which we divide the expiration period into just two subperiods ($n = 2$). As before, we assume that the stock price at the end of each subperiod will equal a proportion u or d times its price at the beginning of the period. In addition, we also assume that both u and d and the risk-free borrowing and lending rate R_f are the same for each period.

To illustrate option pricing in a two-period case, we take our preceding one-period case in which $S_0 = \$100$, $R_f = .05$, $u = 1.1$, and $d = .95$ and break the expiration period into two periods in which $u = 1.0488$, $d = .9747$, and $R_f = .025$. The subperiod u and d values, in turn, reflect growth and decline rates in the stock price that are equal to approximately half of those reflected by u of 1.1 and d of .95 (how u and d can be estimated is discussed in Section 5.6). With two periods, there are now three possible stock prices at expiration. As shown in Figure 5.4-1, the stock can either increase two consecutive periods to equal $S_{uu} = u^2 S_0 = (1.0488)^2 \$100 = \$110$, decrease two periods to equal $S_{dd} = d^2 S_0 = (.9747)^2(\$100) = \$95$, or increase one period and decrease another to equal $S_{ud} = ud S_0 = (1.0488)(.9747)(\$100) = \$102.23$.

The method for pricing a call option on a stock with two periods to expiration is to start at expiration where we know the possible call values are equal to their IVs, next move from expiration to Period 1 and use the single-period BOPM to price the call at each

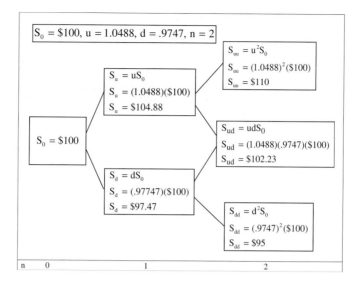

FIGURE 5.4-1 Two-Period Binomial Stock Prices

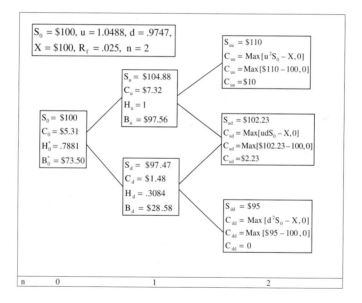

FIGURE 5.4-2 Two-Period Binomial European Call Prices

possible stock price (S_u and S_d), and then last move to the present and price the call using again the single-period model.

As shown in Figure 5.4-2, the three possible call prices at expiration are $C_{uu} = $ Max[$110 − $100, 0] = $10, $C_{ud} = $ Max[$102.23 − $100, 0] = $2.23, and $C_{dd} = $ Max[$95 − $100, 0] = 0. Moving to Period 1, the price of the call when the stock is $104.88 is $7.32, and the price when the stock is $97.47 is $1.48. That is, using the single-period BOPM, the call with one period to expiration would be priced at $C_u = $7.32 when the stock is at $S_u = \$104.88$:

$$C_u = \frac{1}{r_f}[pC_{uu} + (1 - p)C_{ud}] \tag{5.4-1}$$

$$C_u = \frac{1}{1.025}[.6788(\$10) + (.3212)(\$2.23)]$$

$$C_u = \$7.32$$

where:

$$p = \frac{r_f - d}{u - d} = \frac{1.025 - .9747}{1.0488 - .9747} = .6788$$

Or

$$C_u = H_u S_u - B_u$$

$$C_u = (1)(\$104.88) - \$97.56$$

$$C_u = \$7.32$$

where:

$$H_u = \frac{C_{uu} - C_{ud}}{u^2 S_0 - ud S_0} = \frac{\$10 - \$2.23}{\$110 - \$102.23} = 1$$

$$B_u = \frac{C_{uu}(ud S_0) - C_{ud}(u^2 S_0)}{r_f(u^2 S_0 - ud S_0)} = \frac{(\$10)(\$102.23) - (\$2.23)(\$110)}{1.025[\$110 - \$102.23]} = \$97.56$$

If the call is not priced at $7.32, an arbitrage portfolio could be formed with a position in the call (long if the call is underpriced and short if it is overpriced) and an opposite position in a replicating portfolio with $H_u = 1$ and B_u of $97.56.

When the stock is priced at $97.47, the call would have to be priced at $C_d = \$1.48$ or an arbitrage profit could be obtained by taking positions in the call and a replicating portfolio with $H_d = .3084$ and $B_d = \$28.586$:

$$C_d = \frac{1}{r_f}[pC_{ud} + (1 - p)C_{dd}] \tag{5.4-2}$$

$$C_d = \frac{1}{1.025}[.6788(\$2.23) + (.3212)(0)]$$

$$C_u = \$1.48$$

Or

$$C_d = H_d S_d - B_d$$

$$C_d = (.3084)(\$97.47) - \$28.58$$

$$C_d = \$1.48$$

where:

$$H_d = \frac{C_{ud} - C_{dd}}{ud S_0 - d^2 S_0} = \frac{\$2.23 - 0}{\$102.23 - \$95} = .3084$$

$$B_d = \frac{C_{ud}(d^2 S_0) - C_{dd}(ud S_0)}{r_f(ud S_0 - d^2 S_0)} = \frac{(\$2.23)(\$95) - (0)(\$102.23)}{1.025[\$102.23 - \$95]} = \$28.58$$

Finally, given the possible stock prices S_u and S_d and call values C_u and C_d for Period 1, we move to the present and again use the single-period BOPM to find the call's current value. In this example, the 100 call would be worth $C_0^* = \$5.31$. That is:

$$C_0^* = \frac{1}{r_f}[pC_u + (1-p)C_d] \qquad (5.4\text{-}3)$$

$$C_d = \frac{1}{1.025}[.6788(\$7.32) + (.3212)(\$1.48)]$$

$$C_u = \$5.31$$

Or

$$C_0^* = H_0^* S_0 - B_0^*$$

$$C_d = (.7881)(\$100) - \$73.50$$

$$C_d = \$5.31$$

where:

$$H_0^* = \frac{C_u - C_d}{uS_0 - dS_0} = \frac{\$7.32 - \$1.48}{\$104.88 - \$97.47} = .7881$$

$$B_0^* = \frac{C_u(dS_0) - C_d(uS_0)}{r_f(uS_0 - dS_0)} = \frac{(\$7.32)(\$97.47) - (\$1.48)(\$104.88)}{1.025[\$104.88 - \$97.47]} = \$73.50$$

If the call is not priced at $5.31, an arbitrage profit could be earned from an arbitrage portfolio with $H_0^* = .7881$ and $B_0^* = \$73.50$.

5.4.2 Equation for the Two-Period BOPM

Mathematically, the model for pricing a European call with two periods consists of three equations, (5.4-1), (5.4-2) and (5.4-3). This model can be simplified to one equation, by substituting (5.4-1) and (5.4-2) into (5.4-3) and rearranging so that

$$C_0^* = \frac{1}{r_f}[pC_u + (1-p)C_d]$$

$$C_0^* = \frac{1}{r_f}\left[p\left[\frac{pC_{uu} + (1-p)C_{ud}}{r_f}\right] + (1-p)\left[\frac{pC_{ud} + (1-p)C_{dd}}{r_f}\right]\right]$$

$$C_0^* = \frac{1}{r_f^2}\left[p^2 C_{uu} + 2p(1-p)C_{ud} + (1-p)^2 C_{dd}\right] \qquad (5.4\text{-}4)$$

5.4.3 n-Period BOPM

If the time interval to expiration (T) is subdivided into three subperiods (n = 3), the terminal stock prices can take one of four possibilities: $S_{uuu} = u^3 S_0$, $S_{uud} = u^2 d S_0$, $S_{udd} = u d^2 S_0$, and $S_{ddd} = d^3 S_0$. Using the binomial approach to value a call option, we again would start at expiration where we know the call's four possible IVs, then we would move to each preceding period and use the single-period BOPM to price the call at each possible stock price. An example of pricing a call with three periods is presented in Figure 5.4-3. In the example, our earlier single-period case is broken into three periods where u = 1.03228, d = .98305, and R_f = .016667.

In general, if the time interval is subdivided into n subperiods, the terminal stock prices can take on one of n + 1 possible values at expiration. Thus, for n periods, the model

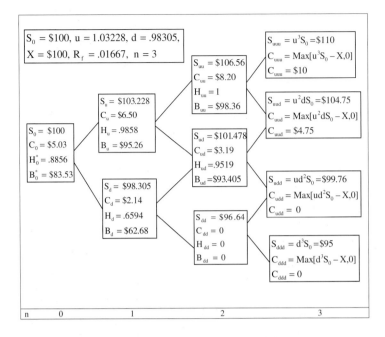

FIGURE 5.4-3 Three-Period Binomial European Call Prices

consists of the equation for p and all the call expressions associated with each possible stock price in every period, with each expression being similar to Equations (5.4-1) through (5.4-3). To obtain a general n-period equation for the equilibrium call price that is similar to (5.4-4), we again move from expiration to each preceding period, substituting the single-period BOPM equations associated with each call value and stock price in each period. This process results in the following n-period BOPM equation:

$$C_0^* = \frac{1}{r_f^n}\left[\sum_{j=0}^{n}\frac{n!}{(n-j)!j!}p^j(1-p)^{(n-j)}\left[\text{Max}[u^jd^{(n-j)})S_0 - X, 0)\right]\right] \qquad (5.4\text{-}5)$$

In Equation (5.4-5), the index j can be defined as the number of upward moves in the stock price in n periods, the term $u^j d^{(n-j)} S_0$ defines the possible stock prices at expiration, and the bracket expression $\text{Max}[u^j d^{(n-j)} S_0 - X, 0]$ defines the possible IVs. The term $n!/(n-j)!j!$ calculates the number of ways in which the stock can increase (j) in n periods. The expression is referred to as the "jth" binomial coefficient and is often denoted by the simpler notation of $\binom{n}{j}$ 1.[1] In our preceding two-period example (n = 2), three possible IVs exist:

$$\text{Max}\left[u^j d^{n-j} S_0 - X, 0\right]$$

$$j = 2 : \text{Max}\left[u^2 d^0 S_0 - X, 0\right] = C_{uu}$$

$$j = 1 : \text{Max}\left[u^1 d^1 S_0 - X, 0\right] = C_{ud}$$

$$j = 0 : \text{Max}\left[u^0 d^2 S_0 - X, 0\right] = C_{dd}$$

---

[1] In Equation (5.4-5), n! (read as n factorial) is the product of all the numbers from n to 1, and also 0! = 1.

We have $\binom{n}{j} = n!/(n-j)!j!$ for

$$j = 0 : \binom{2}{0} = \frac{2!}{2!0!} = 1$$

$$j = 1 : \binom{2}{1} = \frac{2!}{1!1!} = 2$$

$$j = 2 : \binom{2}{2} = \frac{2!}{0!2!} = 1$$

Thus, summing Equation (5.4-5) over $j = 0$ to $n = 2$ yields our two-period model (Equation (5.4-4)):

$$C_0^* = \frac{1}{r_f^2}\ \begin{aligned}&[1p^0(1-p)^2 \text{Max}[u^0d^2S_0 - X, 0] + 2p(1-p)\text{Max}[udS_0 - X, 0]\\ &+p^2(1-p)^0\text{Max}[u^2d^0S_0 - X, 0]]\end{aligned}$$

$$C_0^* = \frac{1}{r_f^2}\left[(1-p)^2 C_{dd} + 2p(1-p)C_{ud} + p^2 C_{uu}\right]$$

Extending Equation (5.4-5) to value the call options in the three-period example, we obtain

$$C_0^* = \frac{1}{r_f^3}\ \begin{aligned}&[1p^0(1-p)^3 \text{Max}[u^0d^3S_0 - X, 0] + 3p(1-p)^2\text{Max}[ud^2S_0 - X, 0]\\ &+3p^2(1-p)\text{Max}[u^2dS_0 - X, 0] + 1p^3(1-p)^0\text{Max}[u^3d^0S_0 - X, 0]]\end{aligned}$$

$$C_0^* = \frac{1}{r_f^3}\left[(1-p)^3 C_{ddd} + 3p(1-p)^2 C_{udd} + 3p^2(1-p)C_{udd} + p^3 C_{uuu}\right]$$

$$C_0^* = \frac{1}{1.016667^3}\ \begin{aligned}&[(.317144)^3(0) + 3(.682856)(.317144)^2(0)\\ &+3(.682856)^2(.317144)(\$4.75) + (.682856)^3(\$10)]\end{aligned}$$

$$C_0^* = \$5.03$$

where:

$$p = \frac{r_f - d}{u - d} = \frac{1.016667 - .98305}{1.03228 - .98305} = .682856$$

To summarize, the n-period BOPM, like the single-period model, is based on the assumptions that arbitrageurs will form riskless hedging strategies if the option is not priced correctly in terms of the model; that in each period, the stock will equal either a proportion u or d of its previous value; and that u, d, and R_f are the same for each period.

5.4.4 Multiple-Period Arbitrage Strategy

As in the single-period case, arbitrage opportunities exist if the initial market price, C_0^m, does not equal the BOPM value, C_0^*. Except for the last period (when the call's value equals its IV), there are no guarantees that the call option will be valued correctly at the end of each period. However, if the arbitrage portfolio is correctly adjusted each period, then the initial position eventually will be profitable. The arbitrage strategy and mechanics required to adjust the position each period depend on whether the call is initially overpriced and underpriced.

5.4.4.1 Overpriced Arbitrage Strategy

If the call is initially overpriced ($C_0^m > C_0^* = H_0^* S_0 - B_0^*$), then the overpriced arbitrage strategy can be set up by taking a short position in the call $\{-C_0^m\}$ and a long position in the replicating portfolio $\{+(H_0^* S_0 - B_0^*)\}$: buying H_0^* shares of stock at price S_0 and borrowing B_0^* dollars. To both ensure that the initial profit of at least $C_0^m - C_0^*$ is kept and to avoid losses, this strategy must be adjusted at the end of each subsequent Period t, if the option is overpriced for that period ($C_t^m > C_t^*$), by adjusting the replicating portfolio position for that period (H_t and B_t). This is done by buying or selling shares of stock necessary to obtain the hedge ratio (H_t) associated with that period and stock price (S_t). In adjusting, a *self-financing requirement* is needed to maintain the arbitrage position. This requirement prohibits any outside funds from being added or initial funds removed from the strategy. Thus, if additional shares are needed to obtain the new hedge (i.e., $H_t > H_{t-1}$), then to satisfy the self-financing requirement, funds equal to $(H_t - H_{t-1})S_t$ are borrowed at a rate R_f; if shares of stock need to be sold to move to the new hedge ($H_t < H_{t-1}$), then the proceeds from the sale $((H_t - H_{t-1})S_t)$ are used to pay off part of the debt. This adjustment of moving to a new hedge with a self-financing constraint will automatically move the debt level to its correct one: $B_t = (H_t - H_{t-1})S_t + r_f B_{t-1}$. Finally, readjustment needs to occur each period until that period is reached in which the option is underpriced or equal in value. Closing the position then will result in the optimal arbitrage return.

   Three points should be noted with respect to implementing this multiple-period strategy. First, at expiration, the option will have to equal its IV; thus, the option cannot be overpriced every period. Second, it is possible that arbitrageurs could realize a positive cash flow by closing the call when it is overpriced. Such closing would be suboptimal, however, because cash flows equal to at least the compounded value of $C_0^m - C_0^*$ can be earned by readjusting until that period is reached when the option is underpriced or equal in value. Finally, if the option is closed at expiration, the arbitrage profit will be equal to the future value of the initial price difference of $(C_0^m - C_0^*)r_f^n$. An example of the adjustment process for an initially overpriced call is presented in Appendix 5A.

5.4.4.2 Underpriced Arbitrage Strategy

If the call option is initially underpriced, then the exact opposite strategy and adjustment rules to the overpriced strategy apply. Specifically, if $C_0^m < C_0^* = H_0^* S_0 - B_0^*$, then an underpriced arbitrage strategy should be formed by taking a long position in the call, $\{+C_0^m\}$, and a short position in the replicating portfolio, $\{-(H_0^* S_0 - B_0^*)\} = \{-H_0^* S_0, +B_0^*\}$: sell H_0^* shares short and invest B_0^* dollars in a risk-free security. To ensure a minimum arbitrage profit of $C_0^* - C_0^m$, this strategy must be adjusted each period t that the call is underpriced ($C_t^m < C_t^*$) to obtain the correct replicating portfolio position with a hedge ratio of H_t and risk-free investment of B_t. If $H_t > H_{t-1}$; then to move to the new hedge, $H_t - H_{t-1}$ shares of stock must be sold short at price S_t, with the proceeds invested in the risk-free security at the rate R_f. On the other hand, if $H_t < H_{t-1}$, then $(H_t - H_{t-1})S_t$ funds must be borrowed at rate R_f and used to buy $(H_t - H_{t-1})$ shares of stock at price S_t to cover a portion of the short sale, with the investment being reduced by the amount of debt incurred. This readjustment must be done each period until that period is reached when the call is overpriced or equal in value. Closing the position then will yield an optimal arbitrage profit. An example of the adjustment process for an initially underpriced call is presented in Appendix 5A.

5.4.5 Pricing American Call Options on Nondividend-Paying Stock

In using a multiple-period BOPM to price an American call option, one needs to determine whether the right to exercise early adds value over and above the European value. The nodes in our two-period example in which this may happen are at t = 0 and t = 1. At S_u = $104.88 (Figure 5.4-2), if the call option were American and were exercised, the cash flow would only be $uS_0 - X$ = $4.88, whereas the BOPM price is C_u = $7.32. Hence, early exercise is not optimal. At S_d = $97.47, the call is out of the money; and at the current stock price (S_0 = $100), the exercise value is 0. The implication here is that for a nondividend-paying stock, the American call is worth the same as the European call in the BOPM framework: $C_0^{*a} = C_0^{*e}$. Alternatively stated, as long as there is some time until expiration and the interest rate is not zero, the European call will be worth more than the immediate exercise value.[2] Moreover, this implication would be consistent with our earlier point that American call options on stocks are worth more alive than dead, except for possible cases in which the underlying stock pays a dividend.

5.5 THE MULTIPLE-PERIOD BOPM FOR PUTS

5.5.1 Two-Period Case

The multiple-period put model is similar to the multiple-period call model just delineated. For a European put with two periods to expiration, we start at expiration where the three possible put values are equal to their IV: $P_{uu} = Max[X - u^2S_0, 0]$, $P_{ud} = [X - udS_0, 0]$, and $P_{dd} = Max[X - d^2S_0, 0]$. We then move to Period 1 and use the single-period binomial put model to determine the put values P_u and P_d when the stock is at uS_0 and dS_0, respectively. Finally, we move to the present to determine P_0^* given P_u and P_d. For example, to price a 100 European put on the stock in our two-period example where u = 1.0488, d = .9747, and R_f = .025, there are, as shown in Figure 5.5-1, three possible put values at expiration: P_{uu} = 0, P_{ud} = 0, and P_{dd} = $5. Moving to Period 1, the put value is P_d = $1.56 when the price of the stock is S_d = $97.47 and P_u = 0 when S_u = $104.88. That is, using the single-period put model

$$P_u = \frac{1}{r_f}[pP_{uu} + (1-p)P_{ud}] = H_u^P(uS_0) + I_u \tag{5.5-1}$$

$$P_u = \frac{1}{1.025}[(.6788)(0) + (.3212)(0)] = (0)(\$104.88) + 0$$

$$P_u = 0$$

where:

$$p = \frac{r_f - d}{u - d} = \frac{1.025 - .9747}{1.0488} = .6788$$

$$H_u^P = \frac{P_{uu} - P_{ud}}{u^2S_0 - udS_0} = \frac{0 - 0}{\$110 - \$102.23} = 0$$

$$I_u = \frac{-[P_{uu}(udS_0) - P_{ud}(u^2S_0)]}{r_f(u^2S_0 - udS_0)} = \frac{-[(0)(\$102.23) - (0)(\$110)]}{1.025[\$110 - \$102.23]} = 0$$

$$P_d = \frac{1}{r_f}[pP_{ud} + (1-p)P_{dd}] = H_d^P(dS_0) + I_d \tag{5.5-2}$$

---

[2] We noted this in Chapter 4 when we showed that the IV of an American call was not its minimum value and that the American and European calls both had the same minimum price condition of $Max[S_t - PV(X), 0]$.

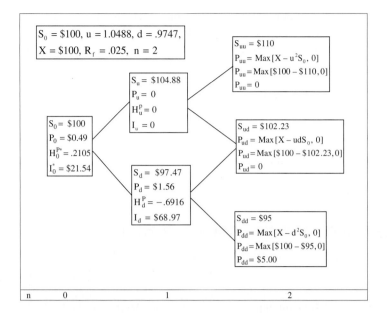

FIGURE 5.5-1 Two-Period Binomial European Put Prices

$$P_d = \frac{1}{1.025}[(.6788)(0) + (.3212)(\$5.00)] = (-.6916)(\$97.47) + \$68.97$$

$$P_d = \$1.56$$

where:

$$H_d^P = \frac{P_{ud} - P_{dd}}{udS_0 - d^2S_0} = \frac{0 - \$5.00}{\$102.23 - \$95} = -.6916$$

$$I_d = \frac{-[P_{ud}(d^2S_0) - P_{dd}(udS_0)]}{r_f(udS_0 - d^2S_0)} = \frac{-[(0)(\$95) - (\$5)(\$102.23)]}{1.025[\$102.23 - \$95]} = \$68.97$$

Finally, given $P_d = \$1.56$ and $P_u = 0$, the equilibrium price of the put using the single-period put model is $P_0^* = \$0.49$:

$$P_0^* = \frac{1}{r_f}[pP_u + (1-p)P_d] = H_0^{P^*}(S_0) + I_0^* \qquad (5.5\text{-}3)$$

$$P_0^* = \frac{1}{1.025}[(.6788)(0) + (.3212)(\$1.56)] = (-.2105)(\$100) + \$21.54$$

$$P_0^* = \$0.49$$

where:

$$H_0^{P^*} = \frac{P_u - P_d}{uS_0 - dS_0} = \frac{0 - \$1.56}{\$104.88 - \$97.47} = -.2105$$

$$I_0^* = \frac{-[P_u(dS_0) - P_d(uS_0)]}{r_f(uS_0 - dS_0)} = \frac{-[(0)(\$97.47) - (\$1.56)(\$104.88)]}{1.025[\$104.88 - \$97.47]} = \$21.54$$

5.5.2 Equation for the Multiple-Period Put Model

The two-period put model can be expressed in terms of one equation by substituting Equations (5.5-1) and (5.5-2) for P_u and P_d in Equation (5.5-3) and rearranging. Doing this yields

$$P_0^* = \frac{1}{r_f} [pP_u + (1 - p)P_d]$$

$$P_0^* = \frac{1}{r_f} \left[p \left[\frac{pP_{uu} + (1 - p)P_{ud}}{r_f} \right] + (1 - p) \left[\frac{pP_{ud} + (1 - p)P_{dd}}{r_f} \right] \right]$$

$$P_0^* = \frac{1}{r_f^2} \left[p^2 P_{uu} + 2p(1 - p)P_{ud} + p^2 P_{uu} \right] \tag{5.5-4}$$

Equation (5.5-4) takes on the same form as the binomial equation for calls. Like calls, for n periods, the equilibrium put price can be found by using the following n-period equation:

$$P_0^* = \frac{1}{r_f^n} \sum_{j=0}^{n} \frac{n!}{(n - j)!j!} (1 - p)^j p^{n-j} \text{Max}[X - u^j d^{(n-j)} S_0, 0] \tag{5.5-5}$$

5.5.3 Multiple-Period Arbitrage Strategies for Puts

The same overpriced and underpriced arbitrage strategies defined earlier for the single-period case can be used to set up the multiple-period arbitrage strategies for puts. For multiple periods, though, the arbitrage position (like those for calls) must be adjusted each period until profitable conditions exist to close. For example, for the case of an initially overpriced put ($P_0^m > P_0^* = H_0^{P^*} S_0 + I_0^*$), the arbitrage portfolio consisting of a short position in the put ($\{-P_0^m\}$) and a long position in the replicating put portfolio ($\{+(H_0^{P^*} S_0 + I_0^*)\}$) must be readjusted each subsequent period t if the put is overpriced by moving the position to the H_t^P required for that period and stock price. The overpriced strategy is then closed in the first period in which the put is underpriced or equal in value. Moreover, given a self-financing requirement, the adjustments needed to attain H_t^P will require either additional investments or borrowing, which will automatically result in the required I_t^* needed for the correct replicating portfolio for that period. An example using the two-period put model for an overpriced arbitrage portfolio with adjustments made in Period 1 is presented in Appendix 5A. The arbitrage strategy and adjustments for an initially underpriced put are just the opposite of the overpriced case.

5.5.4 Put–Call Parity Model: Multiple-Period Case

The same equilibrium put price also can be determined using the put–call parity model. In terms of our illustrative two-period example, the two-period binomial model's put value on the 100 put of $0.49 is obtained using the put–call parity model by substituting the two-period binomial call value of $5.31 (Section 5.4) into the model. Doing this yields

$$P_0^* = C_0^* + PV(X) - S_0$$

$$P_0^* = \$5.31 + \frac{\$100}{(1.025)^2} - \$100$$

$$P_0^* = \$0.49$$

5.5.5 Pricing American Put Options

In examining Figure 5.5-1, note that with one period to expiration, the value of the European put is $P_d = \$1.56$ when the stock is at $S_d = \$97.47$. If the put were American

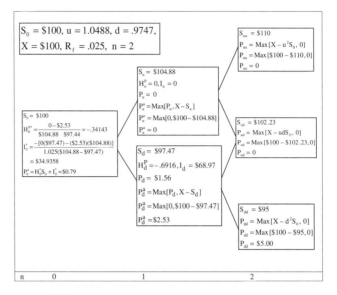

FIGURE 5.5-2 Two-Period BOPM for American Put

and priced at this European BOPM value, then a put holder would find it advantageous to exercise the put because it would provide him with a gain in wealth of $X - dS_0 = \$100 - \$97.47 = \$2.53$ compared to the put value of $1.56. Thus, the previous multiple-period BOPM for puts is only applicable for European puts.

The BOPM can be adjusted to value American puts, P_0^a, by simply specifying each put price at each node in terms of the following condition: $P^a = \text{Max}[P, X - S]$ in which P is the binomial value of the put as determined by using the single-period model with the two possible put prices determined for the next period. In Figure 5.5-2, the two-period BOPM for pricing an American put is shown for our illustrative case. With the advantage of early exercise, the price of an American put, P_0^{*a}, is $0.79 in this example, which, as we should expect, is greater than the BOPM's European put price of $0.49. This contrasts with call options in which there is no early exercise advantage and therefore no difference between European and American calls when the underlying stock pays no dividends. In the case of puts, an early exercise advantage can exit even when the underlying stock pays no dividends.

5.6   ESTIMATING THE BOPM[3]

The BOPM is defined in terms of the stock price, exercise price, number of periods to expiration, the risk-free rate, and the upward and downward parameters u and d. The first four parameters are observable. The u and d parameters, though, need to be estimated. The formulas for estimating u and d are obtained by solving mathematically for the u and d values that make the statistical characteristics (mean and variance) of the stock's logarithmic return equal to the characteristics' estimated values. As background to understanding this approach, we first examine the probability distribution that characterizes a binomial process.

---

[3] This section uses statistics and exponents. For a primer on these subjects, see Appendices A and B at the end of the book.

5.6.1 Probability Distribution Resulting from a Binomial Process

In the last section, we assumed a simple binomial approach in which in each period the stock price would either increase to equal a proportion u times its initial value or decrease to equal a proportion d times the initial value. At the end of n periods, this binomial process yields a distribution of n + 1 possible stock prices (e.g., for n = 3, there are four possible prices: $S_{uuu} = u^3 S_0$, $S_{uud} = u^2 dS_0$, $S_{udd} = ud^2 S_0$, and $S_{ddd} = d^3 S_0$). This distribution, though, is not normally distributed because stock prices cannot be negative. That is, the normal distribution extends from plus infinity to minus infinity. Because one tail of a distribution of stock prices must be equal to zero (no negative prices), it cannot be normally distributed. However, the binomial distribution of stock prices can be converted into a distribution of logarithmic returns: $g_n = \ln(S_n/S_0)$. This distribution can take on negative values and will be normally distributed if the probability of the stock increasing in one period (q) is 0.5.[4] Exhibit 5.6-1 shows the binomial distributions of stock prices for n = 1, 2, 3, and 4 periods and their corresponding logarithmic returns for the case in which u = 1.1, d = .95, S_0 = $100, and q = .5. As shown in the exhibit, when n = 1, there are two possible stock prices of $110 and $95, with respective logarithmic returns of .0953 and −.0513:

$$g_u = \ln\left(\frac{uS_0}{S_0}\right) = \ln u = \ln 1.1 = .0953$$

$$g_d = \ln\left(\frac{dS_0}{S_0}\right) = \ln d = \ln .95 = -.0513$$

EXHIBIT 5.6-1 Binomial Process of Stock Prices and Logarithmic Returns

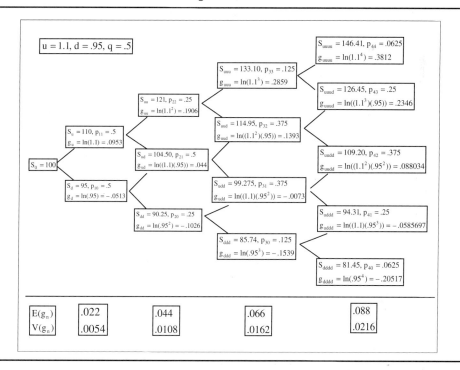

---

[4] A stock's logarithmic return is its continuously compounded rate of return. This rate is found by taking the natural logarithm (ln or Log_e) of the ratio of the end-of-period stock price (S_n) to its current value (S_0).

When n = 2, there are three possible stock prices of \$121, \$104.50, and \$90.25 with corresponding logarithmic returns of

$$g_{uu} = \ln\left(\frac{u^2 S_0}{S_0}\right) = \ln u^2 = \ln(1.1^2) = .1906$$

$$g_{ud} = \ln\left(\frac{udS_0}{S_0}\right) = \ln ud = \ln[(1.1)(.95)] = .044$$

$$g_{dd} = \ln\left(\frac{d^2 S_0}{S_0}\right) = \ln(d^2) = \ln(.95^2) = -.1026$$

When n = 3, there are four possible stock prices of \$133.10, \$114.95, \$99.275, and \$85.74, with logarithmic returns of $g_{uuu} = .2859$, $g_{uud} = .1393$, $g_{udd} = -.0073$, and $g_{ddd} = -.1539$.

The probability of attaining any one of these rates is equal to the probability of the stock price increasing j times in n periods, p_{nj}. That is, the probability of attaining stock price \$104.50 in Period 2 is equal to the probability of the stock price increasing one time (j = 1) in two periods (n = 2), p_{21}. In a binomial process, this probability can be found using the following formula:

$$p_{nj} = \frac{n!}{(n-j)!j!}q^j(1-q)^{n-j}$$

Thus after two periods, the probability of the stock price equaling \$121 is $p_{22} = .25$, \$104.50 is $p_{21} = .5$, and \$90.25 is $p_{20} = .25$. Using these probabilities, the expected value and the variance of the distribution of logarithmic returns after two periods would be equal to $E(g_2) = .044$ and $V(g_2) = .0108$:

$$E(g_n) = \sum_{i=0}^{n} p_{nj}g_{nj}$$

$$E(g_2) = \sum_{j=0}^{2} p_{2j}g_{2j}$$

$$E(g_2) = .25(-.1026) + .5(.0440) + .25(.1906)$$

$$E(g_2) = .044$$

$$V(g_n) = E\,[g_n - E(g_n)]^2 = \sum_{i=0}^{n} p_{nj}[g_{nj} - E(g_n)]^2$$

$$V(g_2) = \sum_{j=0}^{2} p_{2j}[g_{2j} - E(g_n)]^2$$

$$V(g_2) = .25[-.1026 - .044]^2 + .5[.044 - .044]^2 + 25[.1906 - .044]^2$$

$$V(g_2) = .0108$$

The means and variances for the four distributions are shown at the bottom of Exhibit 5.6-1. In examining each distribution's mean and variance, note that as the number of periods increases, the expected value and variance increase by a multiplicative factor such that $E(g_n) = nE(g_1)$ and $V(g_n) = nV(g_1)$. Also, note that the expected value and the variance are also equal to

$$E(g_n) = nE(g_1) = n[q \ln u + (1 - q) \ln d]$$

$$V(g_n) = nV(g_1) = nq(1 - q)[\ln(u/d)]^2$$

Thus, for n =2

$$E(g_2) = 2[.5 \ln(1.1) + (1 - .5) \ln(.95)] = .044$$

$$V(g_2) = 2(.5)(.5)[\ln(1.1/.95)]^2 = .0108$$

5.6.2 Solving for u and d

Given the features of a binomial distribution, the formulas for estimating u and d are found by solving for the u and d values that make the expected value and the variance of the binomial distribution of the logarithmic return of stock prices equal to their respective estimated parameter values under the assumption that q = .5 (or equivalently that the distribution is normal). If we let μ_e and V_e be the estimated mean and variance of the logarithmic return of stock prices for a period equal in length to the total period comprising the n periods, then our objective is to solve for the u and d values that simultaneously satisfy the following equations:

$$nE(g_1) = n[q \ln u + (1 - q) \ln d] = \mu_e$$

$$nV(g_1) = nq(1 - q)[\ln(u/d)]^2 = V_e$$

If q = .5, then the formula values for u and d that satisfy the two equations are

$$u = e^{\sqrt{V_e/n}+\mu_e/n} \tag{5.6-1}$$

$$d = e^{-\sqrt{V_e/n}+\mu_e/n} \tag{5.6-2}$$

The algebraic derivation of Equation (5.6-1) and 5.6-2) are presented in Exhibit 5.6-2.

EXHIBIT 5.6-2 Algebraic Derivation of u and d Formulas

The u and d formulas are found by solving the following two equation simultaneously for the unknowns:

$$nE(g_1) = n[q \ln u + (1 - q) \ln d] = \mu_e$$

$$nV(g_1) = nq(1 - q)[\ln(u/d)]^2 = V_e$$

This equation system, however, consists of two equations and three unknowns—u, d, and q—and cannot be solved without a third equation or information about one of the unknowns. If we assume, however, that the distribution of logarithmic returns is symmetrical, then we can set q = .5. Doing this yields the following two-equation system with two unknowns (u and d):

$$n[.5 \ln u + (1 - .5) \ln d] = \mu_e \tag{1}$$

$$n(.5)(1 - .5)[\ln(u/d)]^2 = V_e \tag{2}$$

continued

EXHIBIT 5.6-2   Continued

To solve Equations (1) and (2) simultaneously for u and d, first rewrite Equation (1) in terms of the ln d:

$$n[.5 \ln u + (1 - .5) \ln d] = \mu_e$$

$$.5[\ln u + \ln d] = \frac{\mu_e}{n}$$

$$\ln d = 2\left(\frac{\mu_e}{n}\right) - \ln u \tag{3}$$

Next, rewrite Equation (2) in terms of the ln u:

$$n(.5)(1 - .5)[\ln(u/d)]^2 = V_e$$

$$.5^2[\ln u - \ln d)]^2 = \frac{V_e}{n}$$

$$\sqrt{.5^2[\ln u - \ln d]^2} = \sqrt{\frac{V_e}{n}}$$

$$.5[\ln u - \ln d)] = \sqrt{\frac{V_e}{n}}$$

$$\ln u - \ln d = 2\sqrt{\frac{V_e}{n}}$$

$$\ln u = 2\sqrt{\frac{V_e}{n}} + \ln d \tag{4}$$

Substituting Equation (3) for ln d in (4), we obtain

$$\ln u = 2\sqrt{\frac{V_e}{n}} + 2\left(\frac{\mu_e}{V_e}\right) - \ln u$$

$$2 \ln u = 2\sqrt{\frac{V_e}{n}} + 2\left(\frac{\mu_e}{V_e}\right)$$

$$\ln u = \sqrt{\frac{V_e}{n}} + \left(\frac{\mu_e}{V_e}\right) \tag{5}$$

Similarly, substituting Equation (5) for ln u in Equation (3), we obtain

$$\ln d = 2\left(\frac{\mu_e}{n}\right) - \sqrt{\frac{V_e}{n}} - \frac{\mu_e}{n}$$

$$\ln d = -\sqrt{\frac{V_e}{n}} + \frac{\mu_e}{n} \tag{6}$$

Finally, expressing Equations (5) and (6) as exponents, we obtain the u and d values that simultaneously satisfy Equations (1) and (2) (Equations (5.6-1) and (5.6-2)):

$$u = e^{\sqrt{V_e/n} + \mu_e/n} \tag{5.6-1}$$

$$d = e^{-\sqrt{V_e/n} + \mu_e/n} \tag{5.6-2}$$

In terms of our example, if the *estimated* expected value and variance of the logarithmic return were $\mu_e = .044$ and $V_e = .0108$ for a period equal in length to n = 2, then using Equations (5.6-1) and (5.6-2), u would be 1.1 and d would be .95—the u and d with which we started the example:

$$u = e^{\sqrt{.0108/2}+.044/2} = 1.1$$

$$d = e^{-\sqrt{.0108/2}+.044/2} = .95$$

5.6.3   Annualized Mean and Variance

To facilitate the estimation of u and d for a number of options on the same stock but with different expirations, it is helpful to use an annualized mean and variance (μ_e^A and V_e^A). Annualized parameters are obtained by simply multiplying the estimated parameters of a given length by the number of periods of that length that make up a year. Thus, if quarterly data is used to estimate the mean and variance (μ_e^q and V_e^q), then we simply multiply those estimates by 4 to obtain the annualized parameters ($\mu_e^A = 4\mu_e^q$ and $V_e^A = 4V_e^q$). Thus, if the estimated quarterly mean and variance were .022 and .0054, then the annualized mean and variance would be .088 and .0216, respectively. Note that when the annualized mean and variance are used in the u and d formulas, then these annualized parameters must by multiplied by a proportion t, where t is defined as the time period being analyzed expressed as a proportion of a year:

$$u = e^{\sqrt{tV_e^A/n}+(t\mu_e^A/n)} \qquad\qquad (5.6\text{-}3)$$

$$d = e^{-\sqrt{tV_e^A/n}+(t\mu_e^A)/n} \qquad\qquad (5.6\text{-}4)$$

Typically, the time period being analyzed is the option expiration; thus, for an option expiring in a 6 months, t would be 0.5. In Equations (5.6-3) and (5.6-4), n is the number of subperiods of a specified length h that we want to divide the tree. Note that the length of the period, h, does not have to equal t. Thus, for an option expiring in 6 months (t = 0.5), if we want the length of our binomial periods to be monthly, then we would subdivide the tree into n = 6 subperiods each of length h = 1 month; if we want the length of the period to be weekly, then we subdivided the tree into n = 12 subperiods of length h = 1 week; and if we want the length to be daily, then we would subdivide the tree into n = 90 subperiods. As an example, suppose the annualized mean and variance of the logarithmic return of stock were $\mu_e^A = .044$ and $V_e^A = .0108$, and we wanted to evaluate an option on the stock expiring in 6 months (t = .5). If we want a single-period model, then n = 1 and the length of period in the binomial process would be 6 months (h equals t). In this case, u and d for a period of length h = 6 months would be 1.1 and .95:

$$u = e^{\sqrt{(.5)(.0108)/1}+(.5)(.044)/1} = 1.1$$

$$d = e^{-\sqrt{((.5)(.0108)/1}+(.5).(044)/1} = .95$$

If we want to make the binomial tree a two-period one, then n = 2, and the length of the period is h = 3 months. In this case, u and d for a period of length h = 3 months would be equal to 1.065 and .96:

$$u = e^{\sqrt{(.5)(.0108)/2}+(.5)(.044)/2} = 1.065$$

$$d = e^{-\sqrt{(.5)(.0108)/2}+(.5)(.044)/2} = .96$$

Finally, if we want to make the binomial tree a 90-period one, then n = 90, and the length of the period is h = day. In this case, u and d for a period of length 1 day would be to 1.008022 and .992527:

$$u = e^{\sqrt{(.5)(.0108)/90}+(.5)(.044)/90} = 1.008022$$

$$d = e^{-\sqrt{(.5)(.0108)/90}+(.5)(.044)/90} = .992527$$

It is also common to express the u and d equations in terms of the annualized standard deviation (σ^A) and to express the t/n term as Δt:

$$u = e^{\sigma^A\sqrt{\Delta t}+\mu_e^A \Delta t} \tag{5.6-5}$$

$$d = e^{-\sigma^A\sqrt{\Delta t}+\mu_e^A \Delta t} \tag{5.6-6}$$

$\Delta t \, (= t/n)$, in turn, is the length of the binomial period expressed as a proportion of a year. Note that the annualized standard deviation cannot be obtained simply by multiplying the quarterly standard deviation by 4. Rather, one must first multiply the quarterly variance by 4 and then take the square root of the resulting annualized variance.

5.6.4 u and d Formulas for Large n

In examining Equation (5.6-3) and (5.6-4), note that as the n term increases, the mean term in the exponent goes to zero quicker than the square root term. As a result, for large n (e.g., n = 30), the mean term's impact on u and d is negligible, and u and d can be estimated as

$$u = e^{\sqrt{(tV_e^A)/n}} = e^{\sigma^A\sqrt{\Delta t}} \tag{5.6-7}$$

$$d = e^{-\sqrt{(tV_e^A)/n}} = e^{-\sigma^A\sqrt{\Delta t}} = 1/u \tag{5.6-8}$$

Thus, as n becomes large, or equivalently, as the length of the period becomes smaller, the impact of the mean on u and d becomes smaller. This relation can be seen in Table 5.6-1 in which two sets of u and d values for various n values are shown for both the case in which $\mu_e = .022$ and $V_e = .0054$ and also the case in which $\mu_e = 0$ and $V_e = .0054$. As shown in the table, as n increases, the differences between the u and d values with the non-zero mean and those with the zero mean become smaller. Thus for the cases of large n, u and d can be estimated by simply using the variance. Note that for cases in which n is large or in which $\mu_e = 0$, u and d are inversely proportional.[5]

TABLE 5.6-1   u and d Values With Zero and Non-Zero Means

n	$\mu_e = .022$ $V_e = .0054$		$\mu_e = 0$ $V_e = .0054$		Difference	
	u	d	u	d	u	d
1	1.1	.95	1.0762	.9291	.0238	.0209
3	1.051	.9655	1.0433	.9584	.0077	.0071
10	1.02576	.9792	1.0235	.9770	.0023	.0022
30	1.01425	.9874	1.0135	.9867	.00075	.0007
60	1.0099	.9909	1.0095	.9906	.00040	.0003

[5] Note that the case of μ_e being insignificant for large n only holds if the underlying distribution of the logarithmic return is symmetrical.

5.6.5 Estimating μ_e^A and V_e^A Using Historical Data

To estimate u and d requires estimating the mean and variance: μ_e and V_e. The two most common ways of estimating these parameters are to calculate the stock's average mean and variance from a historical sample of stock prices or to determine the stock's implied parameter values. In Chapter 8, we discuss the latter approach. In computing averages, daily, weekly or perhaps quarterly historical stock price data can be used to calculate the mean and variance of the stock's historical logarithmic return. As an example, 13 historical quarterly closing prices on a nondividend-paying stock are shown in Exhibit 5.6-3. The 12 logarithmic returns are calculated by taking the natural log of the ratio of stock price in one period to the price in the previous period ($g_t = \ln(S_t/S_{t-1})$). From this data, the historical quarterly logarithmic mean return and variance are

$$\mu_e = \frac{\sum_{t=1}^{12} g_t}{12} = \frac{0}{12} = 0$$

$$V_e = \frac{\sum_{t=1}^{12} [g_t - \mu_e]^2}{11} = \frac{.046297}{11} = .004209$$

Multiplying the historical quarterly mean and variance by 4, we obtain an annualized mean and variance of 0 and .016836, respectively. Given the estimated annualized mean and variance, u and d can be estimated using Equations (5.6-3) and (5.6-4) once we determine the number of periods to subdivide the expiration period (or equivalently once we have decided the length of the period we want for our binomial period). For example, for a

EXHIBIT 5.6-3 Estimating μ_e and V_e With Historical Data

Quarter	Stock Price S_t	S_t/S_{t-1}	$g_t = \ln(S_t/S_{t-1})$	$(g_t - \mu_e)^2$
Y1.1	106	—	—	—
Y1.2	100	.9434	−.0583	.003395
Y1.3	94	.9400	−.0619	.003829
Y1.4	88	.9362	−.0659	.004350
Y2.1	94	1.0682	.0660	.004350
Y2.2	100	1.0638	.0619	.003829
Y2.3	106	1.0600	.0583	.003395
Y2.4	100	.9434	−.0583	.003395
Y3.1	94	.9400	−.0619	.003829
Y3.2	88	.9362	−.0660	.004350
Y3.3	94	1.0682	.0660	.004350
Y3.4	100	1.0638	.0619	.003829
Y4.1	106	1.0600	.0583	.003395
			0	.046297

$$\mu_e = 0 \qquad V_e^q = \frac{.046297}{11} = .004209$$

$$\mu_e^A = 4\mu_e^q = 4(0) = 0; \quad V_e^A = 4V_e^q = 4(.004209) = .016836; \quad t = .25$$

h = Length	n	$u = e^{\sqrt{tV_e^A/n}+(t\mu_e^A/n)}$	$d = e^{-\sqrt{tV_e^A/n}+(t\mu_e^A)/n}$
Month	3	1.0382	.9632
Week	12	1.0189	.9814
Day	90	1.00686	.9932

3-month option (t = .25), if we want to make the length of the period 1 month, then we set n equal to 3 to obtain a u of 1.0382 and a d of .9632. If we want a weekly period, then we set n = 12 to obtain u = 1.0189 and d = .9814. Finally, if we want a daily period, then we make n = 90 and obtain u and d values of 1.00686 and .9932 (see bottom of Exhibit 5.6-3).

5.6.6   Note on the Risk-Free Rate

In the BOPM, the risk-free rate used is the rate for the period. In calculating the risk-free rate, the rate on a Treasury or other risk-free security with a maturity equal to the option's expiration can be used. These rates are often quoted in terms of a simple annual rate (with no compounding). If a simple annual rate (R^A) is given, the period rate (R^P) needed for the BOPM is

$$R^P = (1 + R^A)^{\Delta t} - 1$$

Thus, given a 3-month option (t = .25), an annual risk-free rate of 6%, and the length of the period being evaluated of h = day or (n = 90 or Δ = t/n = .25/90 = .002778 per year), then the periodic (daily) risk-free rate would be .0162%:

$$R^P = (1.06)^{.002778} - 1 = .000162$$

Note that when the length of the period is relatively small, then the periodic rate can be determined by assuming continuous compounding. In this case, the periodic rate is

$$1 + R^P = r_f = e^{R^A \Delta t}$$

$$R^P = e^{R^A \Delta t} - 1$$

$$R^P = e^{(.06)(.002778)} - 1 = .000167$$

Because most rates are quoted on an annual basis, it is common to express the p term in the binomial equation in terms of the annualized risk-free rate and with continuous compounding:

$$p = \frac{r_f - d}{u - d} = \frac{e^{R^A \Delta t} - d}{u - d}$$

5.6.7   BOPM Excel Programs

To use the BOPM to estimate the equilibrium value of an option first requires that we estimate μ_e and V_e, determine the risk-free rate, and specify S_0, X, T, and n. Given these values, we can determine u, d, and r_f. Second, we calculate the possible IVs of the option. Third, we use the recursive multiple-period model to obtain the option price. Finally, if the option is American, at each node, we constrain the price of the option to be the maximum of it's binomial value or it IV (note: for call options on nondividend-paying stocks, there is no early exercise advantage, and thus the European and American call values are the same). This procedure for determining the price of an option is rather cumbersome, especially when a number of subperiods to expiration are used. The recursive procedure of the BOPM, though, easily lends itself to computer programming. An Excel option program that values American and European calls and puts is provided as part of the software that accompanies this book. The program is called "Binomial Option Pricing Model," and its features and uses are described in Appendix D, "Guide to Derivative Excel Programs." Several end-of-the-chapter problems are included that make use of this spreadsheet.

TABLE 5.6-2   Call and Put Values Generated From the Binomial Excel Programs

BOPM Values for Different n

$$\mu_e^A\ 0,\ V_e^A = .016836,\ R_f^A = .06,\ t = .25,\ S_0 = \$100,\ X = \$100$$

n	u	d	r_f	Call C_0^*
6	1.02684	.973862	1.0024308	$3.25
12	1.01890	.981446	1.0012146	$3.30
30	1.01191	988225	1.0004857	$3.34
100	1.00651	.993533	1.0001457	$3.35

n	European Put P_0^e	American Put P_0^a
6	$1.80	$2.00
12	$1.86	$2.03
30	$1.89	$2.04
100	$1.90	$2.04

5.6.8   Example

The BOPM values for a $100 call, $100 European put, and a $100 American put all expiring in one quarter on a nondividend-paying stock are shown for different n values in Table 5.6-2. The call and put values were generated using the "Binomial Option Pricing Model" Excel program. The u and d values were calculated using an estimated annualized mean of zero and annualized variance of 0.016836; the current price on the underlying stock was assumed to be $100, and the annual risk-free rate was 6%. As shown in the table, when the number of subperiods to expiration is n = 6, then u = 1.02684, d = .9739, r_f = 1.00243, and the equilibrium call price is $C_0^* = \$3.25$; the European put price is $P_0^e = \$1.80$, and the American put price is $P_0^a = \$2.00$. If the number of subperiods is divided into 12, then u = 1.01890, d = .981446, and r_f = 1.0012146; and the option prices are $C_0^* = \$3.30$, $P_0^e = \$1.86$, and $P_0^a = \$2.03$. Exhibit 5.6-4, in turn, shows the binomial tree of call prices and stock prices for the 12-period case, and Exhibit 5.6-5 shows the binomial tree of American and European put prices and stock prices for the six-period case. If the number of subperiods is divided into 30, then u = 1.01192, d = .988225, and r_f = 1.0004857; and the option prices are $C_0^* = \$3.34$, $P_0^e = \$1.89$, and $P_0^a = \$2.04$. If number of subperiods is divided into 100, then u = 1.00651, d = .9935, and r_f = 1.0001457; and $C_0^* = \$3.35$, $P_0^e = \$1.90$, and $P_0^a = \$2.04$. (Note: There is a small difference between the option values at n = 30 and n = 100.) In examining the American and European put values shown in Exhibit 5.6-5, note that in Periods 2, 3, 4, and 5 there is an early exercise advantage at the lower nodes that makes the American put value equal to its IV. This early exercise advantage, in turn, explains why the American put is valued greater than the European put.

5.7   FEATURES OF THE BOPM

In the BOPM, the equilibrium call price depends on the underlying stock price, exercise price, time to expiration, risk-free rate, and the stock's volatility (and mean for the case of small n). Mathematically, the impacts that changes in these variables have on the equilibrium call price can be seen in terms of the simulation presented in Exhibit 5.7-1. In the exhibit, combinations of the BOPM call values and stock prices are shown for different parameter values. Column (1) shows the call values given the parameter values used in the preceding example: X = 100, T = .25, R = .06, and annualized variance of 0.016836 ($\sigma^A = 0.12975$). For purposes of comparison, the other columns show the call and stock price relations generated with the same parameter values used in Column (1)

EXHIBIT 5.6-4   Call Values for 12-Period Binomial Tree

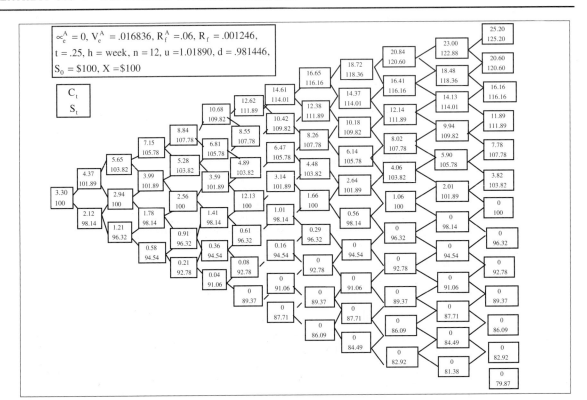

except for one variable: in Column (2), X = 95; in Column (3), T = .5; and in Column (4), σ^A = .2595.

In examining Exhibit 5.7-1, one should note several of the relationships that were explained either intuitively or with arbitrage arguments in Chapter 4. First, as shown in any of the columns, when the stock is relatively low, and the call is deep out of the money, the BOPM yields a very low call price but (as we should expect) one that is nonnegative. As the price of the stock increases by equal increments, the BOPM call prices increase at increasing rates up to a point, with the values never being below the difference between the stock price and the present value of the exercise price. Thus, over a range of stock prices, the BOPM yields a call and stock price relation that is nonlinear and satisfies the minimum and maximum boundary conditions. The nonlinear relationship also can be seen in the figure in Exhibit 5.7-1 where the BOPM call values and stock prices from Column 1 are plotted. As shown, the slope of this BOPM option price curve increases as the stock price increases, the curve does not yield negative values, and it is above the IV line and the minimum boundary S – PV(X) (not shown). The slope of the curve is referred to as the option's **delta.** Delta is equal to H^* in the BOPM. For a call, the delta ranges from 0 for deep-out-of-the-money calls to approximately 1 for deep-in-the-money ones. This can be seen in the figure that shows that the option curve is relatively flat for low stock prices and starts to become parallel to the minimum boundary line for high stock values. The nonlinear call and stock price relation also can be seen by the change in the slope of the BOPM option price curve as the stock price increases. In option literature, the change in slope (i.e., delta) per small change in the stock price defines the option's **gamma.**

EXHIBIT 5.6-5   Binomial Prices of American and European Puts for n = 6

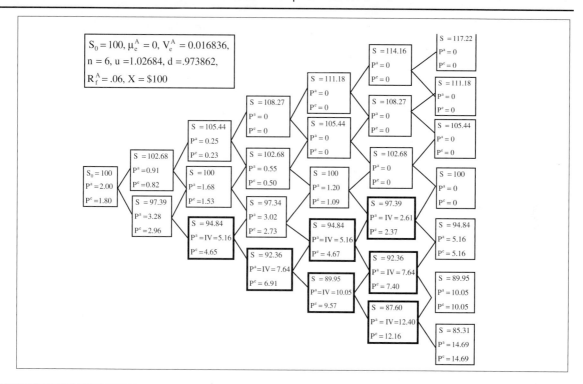

Second, by examining Columns (1) and (2), one should observe that for each stock price, higher call prices are associated with the call with the lower exercise price. Thus, as the exercise price decreases, the BOPM call price increases. Third, comparing Column (3) with Column (1) shows that the BOPM call price increases the greater the time to expiration. The changes in an option's prices with respect to a small change in the time to expiration (with other factors held constant) is defined as the option's *theta.* Fourth, a comparison of Columns (4) and (1) shows that the greater the stock's variability, the greater the call price. The change in the call price given a small change in the stock's variability is referred to as the option's **vega** (also called **kappa**).

Like the BOPM for calls, most of the relationships between the equilibrium price of a put and S, X, T, and σ that were examined both intuitively and with arbitrage arguments in Chapter 4 are captured in the BOPM put model. This can be seen in Exhibit 5.7-2 in which combinations of the BOPM European and American put prices and stock prices are shown for different parameters: X [Column (2)], T [Column (3)], and σ^A [Column (4)]. In examining any of the columns in the table, one first should observe the negative, nonlinear relationship between the BOPM put price and the stock price (i.e., the put has a negative delta and non-zero gamma). Next, comparing Column (2) with Column (1), one can observe that for each stock price, the lower the exercise price, the lower the BOPM put price. Finally, comparing Columns (3) and (4) with Column (1), one can see that, except for a deep out-of-the money put ($S_0 = 85$), the greater the time to expiration or the greater the stock's variability, the greater the put price. Thus, the BOPM put model captures many of the relationships described in Chapter 4.

It should be noted that the European binomial put model is unconstrained. That is, the model does not constrain the European put value to being equal to at least its IV. Thus,

EXHIBIT 5.7-1   BOPM Call Price and Stock Price Relation for Different Parameter Values

$S_0 = 100$, $\mu_e^A = 0$, $V_e^A = 0.016836$, $\sigma^A = .12975$, $n = 100$

	(1) X = 100 t = .25 $\sigma^A = .12975$ $R_f = .06$	(2) X = 95 t = .25 $\sigma^A = .12975$ $R_f = .06$	(3) X = 100 t = .5 $\sigma^A = .12975$ $R_f = .06$	(4) X = 100 t = .25 $\sigma^A = .2595$ $R_f = .06$
Stock Price	**Call Price**	**Call Price**	**Call Price**	**Call Price**
85	0.02	0.17	0.27	0.75
90	0.22	0.99	0.97	1.74
95	1.11	3.18	2.55	3.42
100	3.35	6.88	5.21	5.88
105	7.02	11.47	8.90	9.10
110	11.57	16.38	13.25	12.94
115	16.47	21.37	18.00	17.24

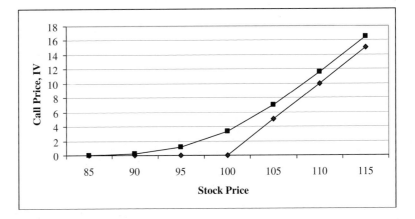

for an in-the-money put, the premium can be less than its IV, as shown in Column (1) of Exhibit 5.7-2 when the stock is at $85 and $90. The possibility that $P^e < IV$ reflects the fact that the BOPM model is limited to determining the price of a European put in which negative time value premiums are possible.

5.7.1 Risk-Neutral Probability Pricing

In addition to being consistent with many of the relationships we defined in Chapter 4, another interesting feature of the BOPM is that the option price conforms to a risk-neutral market. A risk-neutral market is defined as one in which investors will accept the same expected return (E(k)) from a risky investment as they would from a risk-free one. That is, $E(k) = R_f$, or equivalently the risk premium is zero: $RP = E(k) - R_f = 0$.

To see risk-neutral features of the option pricing model, consider how most securities are valued. The traditional finance approach to determining the value of a risky asset is to discount the asset's expected cash flows at a risk-adjusted rate (k). For this methodology to work, one needs to know (or at least be able to assume) a probability distribution for the cash flow and to know the risk-return preferences of investors. In our one-period, two-state economy described in Sections 5.2 and 5.3 (u = 1.1, d = .95, $S_0 = \$100$, X = $100, and

EXHIBIT 5.7-2 BOPM Put Price and Stock Price Relation for Different Parameter Values

Base Case: $S_0 = 100$, $\mu_e^A = 0$, $V_e^A = 0.016836$, $\sigma^A = .12975$, $n = 100$

		(1) $X = 100$ $t = .25$ $\sigma^A = .12975$ $R_f = .06$		(2) $X = 95$ $t = .25$ $\sigma^A = .12975$ $R_f = .06$		(3) $X = 100$ $t = .5$ $\sigma^A = .12975$ $R_f = .06$		(4) $X = 100$ $t = .25$ $\sigma^A = .2595$ $R_f = .06$	
		Put Price		**Put Price**		**Put Price**		**Put Price**	
Stock Price		**Eur**	**Amer**	**Eur**	**Amer**	**Eur**	**Amer**	**Eur**	**Amer**
85		13.58	15.00	8.80	10.00	12.39	15.00	14.30	15.06
90		8.77	10.00	4.61	5.13	8.10	10.00	10.29	10.73
95		4.67	5.18	1.81	1.94	4.68	5.48	6.97	7.21
100		1.90	2.04	0.50	0.53	2.34	2.64	4.43	4.56
105		0.58	0.60	0.10	0.10	1.02	1.12	2.65	2.72
110		0.13	0.13	0.01	0.01	0.38	0.41	1.50	1.53
115		0.02	0.02	0.001	0.001	0.12	0.13	0.79	0.81

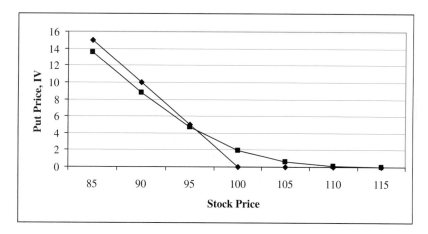

$r_f = 1.05$), the values of the call, put, and stock using this methodology would be

$$S_0 = \frac{E(S_T)}{(1+k)} = \frac{q(uS_0) + (1-q)(dS_0)}{1+k} = \frac{q(\$110) + ((1-q)\$95)}{1+k} \quad (5.7\text{-}1)$$

$$C_0 = \frac{E(C_T)}{(1+k)} = \frac{q(C_u) + (1-q)(C_d)}{1+k} = \frac{q(\$10) + (1-q)(0)}{1+k} \quad (5.7\text{-}2)$$

$$P_0 = \frac{E(P_T)}{(1+k)} = \frac{q(P_u) + (1-q)(P_d)}{1+k} = \frac{q(0) + (1-q)(\$5)}{1+k} \quad (5.7\text{-}3)$$

where q is the objective probability of the stock increasing in one period, and $(1-q)$ is the probability of it decreasing.

Unfortunately, determining the call and put values with this traditional approach is impossible given the number of unknowns (q and k). Suppose, though, we assume that we have a risk-neutral market in which investors will accept the same expected rate of return from a risky investment as they would from a risk-free one.[6] In a risk-neutral market, the prices of all assets (risky and risk-free) are priced without regard to risk and determined by discounting the expected future payouts at the risk-free rate. In our option pricing example, if we assume a risk-neutral market, then the price of our stock, call, and put would be

$$S_0 = \frac{E(S_T)}{(1+k)} = \frac{q(uS_0) + (1-q)(dS_0)}{r_f} = \frac{q(\$110) + ((1-q)\$95)}{1.05} \tag{5.7-4}$$

$$C_0 = \frac{E(C_T)}{(1+k)} = \frac{q(C_u) + (1-q)(C_d)}{r_f} = \frac{q(\$10) + (1-q)(0)}{1.05} \tag{5.7-5}$$

$$P_0 = \frac{E(P_T)}{(1+k)} = \frac{q(P_u) + (1-q)(P_d)}{r_f} = \frac{q(0) + (1-q)(\$5)}{1.05} \tag{5.7-6}$$

Given the current price of the stock ($S_0 = \$100$) and the period rate on the risk-free security ($R_f = 5\%$), we can now solve mathematically for the probabilities: q and $1-q$ (i.e., in a risk-neutral market, the market price of the stock determines the market's estimates of the probabilities of the stock increasing and decreasing). Solving Equation (5.7-4) for q, we obtain

$$\$100 = \frac{q(\$110) + (1-q)(\$95)}{(1.05)}$$

$$q = .6667$$

Or in parameter terms

$$S_0 = \frac{q(uS_0) + (1-q)(dS_0)}{r_f}$$

$$q = \frac{r_f - d}{u - d}$$

Note, q is the same as the p term in the BOPM call and put equations; p and $1-p$ are, in turn, referred to as ***risk-neutral probabilities***. Substituting the risk-neutral probabilities into the call and put Equations (5.7-5) and (5.7-6), we obtain

$$C_0^* = \frac{1}{r_f}[p\,C_u + (1-p)\,C_u] = \frac{1}{1.05}[.6667(\$10) + (.333)(0)] = \$6.35$$

$$P_0^* = \frac{1}{r_f}[p\,P_u + (1-p)\,P_d] = \frac{1}{1.05}[.6667(0) + (.333)(\$5)] = \$1.59$$

The present value of the expected stock price is also equal to its current value using the risk-neutral probabilities:

$$S_0 = PV[E(S_t)] = \frac{E(S_T)}{r_f}$$

$$S_0 = \frac{1}{r_f}[puS_0 + (1-p)dS_0]$$

$$S_0 = \frac{1}{1.05}\left[(.6667)(\$110) + (.3333)(\$95)\right] = \$100$$

---

[6] A priori, we would expect most investors would want a higher expected rate of return from the risky investment. Such a market is referred to as risk averse.

The option values exactly match those obtained by our replicating approach. Thus, the equilibrium prices of options can be obtained by assuming that the option values are determined as though they and other securities are trading in a risk-neutral market. Appendix 5B presents the risk-neutral probability argument for a multiple-period case.

The reason options can be valued as though they were trading in a risk-neutral market is that they are redundant securities. In financial theory, a redundant security is one in which the security's possible outflows can be replicated by another security or portfolio. This implies that the redundant security can be valued by its arbitrage relation with the replicating asset and not by investor preferences or the probabilities investors assign to possible future outcomes. As we saw in deriving the BOPM, because we can replicate an option's payouts with a portfolio of its stock and a bond, the option is a redundant security and therefore can be valued as though it were trading in a risk-neutral market.[7]

5.8 CONCLUSION

The BOPM is based on the law of one price in which the equilibrium price of an option is equal to the value of a replicating portfolio constructed so it has the same cash flow as the option. In this chapter, we have derived the binomial call and put models for the cases of single and multiple periods to expiration, and we have investigated the arbitrage arguments by examining the strategies one can use if the option is not priced in the market to equal its BOPM value.

As we discussed in Chapter 4, on the ex-dividend date, a dividend can cause the price of a call to decrease and that of a put to increase. This, in turn, can make the early exercise feature of both American calls and American puts more valuable. In the next chapter, we examine how to adjust the binomial model to value options on dividend-paying stocks and how to expand the model to price index options.

Web Information: Steven Ross

Stephen A. Ross is the Franco Modifliani Professor of Finance and Economics at the Massachusetts Institute of Technology (MIT) Sloan Scholl of Management. Ross received his doctorate of economics from Harvard University and has taught at the University of Pennsylvania, Yale School of Management, and MIT.

In addition to being the codiscoverer of the binomial model for pricing derivatives, Stephen Ross is also known as the inventor of the *Arbitrage Pricing Theory* and contributor to the creation of the *Cox–Ingersoll–Ross model* for interest rate dynamics. He is a cofounder of Roll & Ross Asset Management Corporation.

Biography

http://en.wikipedia.org/wiki/Stephen_Ross_(economist)

Major Works of Stephen A. Ross

http://cepa.newschool.edu/het/profiles/ross.htm

---

[7] In a financial theory, redundant securities are explained in terms of complete markets. A complete market is one in which all the possible state-contingent payouts are available to investors from a set of securities. Because a redundant security cannot add anything to the market, its value is determined solely by an arbitrage portfolio consisting of the redundant security and a portfolio of nonredundant securities constructed to have the same possible cash flows. For a discussion of complete markets, see Ritchken (1987).

KEY TERMS

binomial option pricing model	logarithmic return	gamma
replicating portfolio	annualized mean	theta
hedge ratio	annualized variance	vega (kappa)
self-financing requirement	delta	risk-neutral probabilities

SELECTED REFERENCES

Arditti, F., and K. John. "Spanning the State Space With Options." *Journal of Financial and Quantitative Analysis* 15 (March 1980): 1–9.

Arrow, K. "The Role of Securities in the Optimal Allocation of Risks Bearing." *Review of Economic Studies* (1964): 91–96.

Black, F., and M. Scholes. "The Pricing of Options and Corporate Liabilities." *Journal of Political Economy* 81 (May–June 1973): 637–659.

Boyle, P. "A Lattice Framework for Option Pricing With Two State Variables." *Journal of Financial and Quantitative Analysis* 23 (March 1988): 1–12.

Breenan, M. "The Pricing of Contingent Claims In Discrete Time Models." *Journal of Finance* 34 (March 1979): 53–68.

Cox, J. C., and S. Ross. "The Valuation of Options for Alternative Stochastic Processes." *Journal of Financial Economics* 3 (January–March 1976): 145–166.

Cox, J. C., S. Ross, and M. Rubinstein. "Option Pricing: A Simplified Approach." *Journal of Financial Economics* 7 (September 1979): 229–63.

Cox, J. C. and M. Rubinstein. *Option Markets*. Englewood Cliffs, NJ: Prentice-Hall, 1985: Chapter 5.

Hsia, C.-C. "On Binomial Option Pricing." *The Journal of Financial Research* 6 (Spring 1983): 41–50.

Hull, J. *Options, Futures, and Other Derivative Securities*. Englewood Cliffs, NJ: Prentice-Hall, 6th ed., 2006: Chapter 11.

Jarrow, R., and A. Rudd. *Option Pricing*. Homewood, IL: Irwin, 1983: Chapters 7–13.

John, K. "Efficient Funds in Financial Markets with Options: A New Irrelevance Proposition." *Journal of Finance* 37 (June 1981): 685–95.

John, K. "Market Resolution and Valuation in Incomplete Markets." *Journal of Financial and Quantitative Analysis* 19 (March 1984): 29–44.

Rendleman, R., and B. Bartter. "Two-State Option Pricing." *Journal of Finance* 34 (December 1979): 1093–110.

Ritchken, P. "Options: Theory, Strategy, and Applications." Glenview, IL: Scott, Foresman, 1987: Chapters 8–10.

Rubinstein, M. "The Valuation of Uncertain Income Streams and the Pricing of Options." *Bell Journal of Economics* 7 (Autumn 1976): 407–24.

Smith, C. W., Jr. "Option Pricing: A Review." *Journal of Financial Economics* 3 (January–March 1976): 3–51.

PROBLEMS AND QUESTIONS

1. Consider a one-period, two-state case in which XYZ stock is trading at $S_0 = \$35$, has u of 1.05 and d of 1/1.05, and the period risk-free rate is 2%.

   a. Using the BOPM, determine the equilibrium price of an XYZ 35 European call option expiring at the end of the period.

   b. Explain what an arbitrageur would do if the XYZ 35 European call were priced at $1.35. Show what the arbitrageur's cash flow would be at expiration when she closed. Show the cash flows at both possible stock prices at expiration.

    c. Explain what an arbitrageur would do if the XYZ 35 European call were priced at $1.10. Show at both possible stock prices what the arbitrageur's cash flow would be at expiration when she closed.

    d. Using the BOPM, determine the equilibrium price of an XYZ 35 European put option expiring at the end of the period.

    e. Explain what an arbitrageur would do if the XYZ 35 European put were priced at $0.75. Show what the arbitrageur's cash flow would be at both possible stock prices at expiration when she closed.

    f. Explain what an arbitrageur would do if the XYZ 35 European put were priced at $0.35. Show what the arbitrageur's cash flow would be at both possible stock prices at expiration when she closed.

2. Using the put–call parity model, determine the equilibrium price of the put option in Question 1 given the equilibrium call value as determined by the binomial model. Comment on the consistency of the binomial call and put models and the put–call parity model.

3. Assume two periods to expiration, $u = 1.05$, $d = 1/1.05$, $r_f = 1.02$, $S_0 = \$50$, no dividends, and $X = \$50$ on a European call expiring at the end of the second period. Find C_{uu}, C_{ud}, C_{dd}, C_d, C_u, C_0^*, H_u, H_d, H_0^*, B_u, B_d, and B_0^*.

4. Assume two periods to expiration, $u = 1.05$, $d = 1/1.05$, $r_f = 1.02$, $S_0 = \$50$, no dividends, and $X = \$50$ on a European put expiring at the end of the second period.

    a. Find P_{uu}, P_{ud}, P_{dd}, P_d, P_u, P_0^*, H_u^p, H_d^p, H_0^{p*}, I_u, I_d, and I_0^*.

    b. Determine the equilibrium price of a comparable call on the stock using the put–call parity model. Is the call price consistent with the binomial call price you determined in Question 3?

    c. If the put is American, what would its equilibrium price be?

5. Suppose XYZ stock is trading at $S_0 = \$101$, $u = 1.02$, $d = 1/1.02$, the period risk-free rate is 1%, and the stock pays no dividends.

    a. Using the n-period BOPM, determine the equilibrium price of an XYZ 100 European call expiring at the end of the third period ($n = 3$).

    b. Using the n-period BOPM, determine the equilibrium price of an XYZ 100 European put expiring at the end of the third period ($n = 3$).

6. Explain how subdividing the number of periods to expiration makes the BOPM more realistic.

7. Assume ABC stock follows a binomial process; is currently priced at $50; and has a u of 1.02, d of 1/1.02, and probability of its price increasing in one period of .5 ($q = .5$).

    a. Show with a binomial tree ABC's possible stock prices, logarithmic returns, and probabilities after one period, two periods, and three periods.

    b. What are the stock's expected logarithmic return and variance for each period?

    c. Define the properties of a binomial distribution.

    d. Verify that the u and d formulas yield the u and d values of 1.02 and 1/1.02 given the logarithmic return's mean and variance after three periods.

8. Describe the methodology used to derive the formulas for estimating u and d.

9. Suppose a stock has the following probability distribution of future prices after 4 months:

S_T	Probability of Occurrence
$66.23	.0625
63.32	.2500
60.54	.3750
57.88	.2500
55.34	.0625

a. Calculate the stock's expected logarithmic return and variance. Assume it is currently priced at $60.

b. Calculate the stock's annualized variance and mean.

c. What are the stock's u and d values for a period of length 1 month (n = 4), 1 week (n = 16), and 1 day (n = 120)?

d. Suppose the stock's mean is equal to zero. What are the stock's u and d values for the periods of lengths 1 month, week, and day? Comment on the importance of the mean in calculating u and d when n is large.

e. Using the "Binomial Option Pricing Model" Excel Program, determine the equilibrium price for an on-the-money 60 European call option on the stock expiring in 4 months for the periods of lengths 1 month, 1 week, and 1 day. Assume the annual risk-free rate is 6%.

f. Using the "Binomial Option Pricing Model" Excel Program, determine the equilibrium price for an on-the-money 60 European put on the stock expiring in 4 months for the periods of lengths 1 month, 1 week, and 1 day. Assume the annual risk-free rate is 6%.

g. Are the call and put prices you determined in e and f consistent with the put–call parity model?

10. Suppose the 60 put in Question 9f were American.

a. Given the mean and variance you calculated, determine the equilibrium prices for the American put using the "Binomial Option Pricing Model" Excel Program for periods of lengths 1 month, 1 week, and 1 day. Assume the stock price is $60, the put expires in 4 months, and the annual risk-free rate is 6%.

b. Do the binomial put prices for the American put differ from the European values you calculated in Question 9f? If so, why?

c. Show a binomial tree for the four-period case (length = 1 month). At each node, show the American put values, European values, and stock prices. At what nodes is there an early exercise advantage?

d. Would you expect American and European call prices to differ?

11. Suppose a stock has the following prices over the past 13 quarters:

Quarter	S_t
Y1.1	$55
Y1.2	50
Y1.3	47
Y1.4	44
Y2.1	47
Y2.2	50

Quarter	S_t
Y2.3	54
Y2.4	50
Y3.1	47
Y3.2	44
Y3.3	47
Y3.4	50
Y4.1	55

a. Calculate the stock's average logarithmic return and variance.

b. What is the stock's annualized mean and variance?

c. Calculate the stock's up and down parameters (u and d) for periods with the following lengths:

(1) 1 quarter

(2) 1 month

(3) 1 week (assume 12 weeks in a quarter)

(4) 1 day (assume 90 days in a quarter)

(5) Half day

(6) 1/8 of a day

d. Using the "Binomial Option Pricing Model" Excel Program, determine the equilibrium price for a 50 call on the stock expiring in 3 months for binomial periods of lengths 1 quarter, 1 month, and 1 day. Assume the stock is currently priced at $50, and the annual risk-free rate is 6%.

e. Using the "Binomial Option Pricing Model" Excel Program, determine the equilibrium price for a 50 European put on the stock expiring in 3 months for binomial periods of lengths 1 quarter, 1 month, and 1 day. Assume the stock is currently priced at $50, and the annual risk-free rate is 6%. Are the binomial put prices consistent with put–call parity?

12. Suppose the 60 put in Question 11e were American.

a. Using the "Binomial Option Pricing Model" Excel Program and the mean and variance you calculated in Question 11, determine the equilibrium prices for the American put for periods of lengths 1 month (n = 3) and 1 day (n = 90). Assume the stock price is $50, the put expires in 3 months, and the annual risk-free rate is 6%.

b. Do the binomial put prices for the American put differ from the European values you calculated in Question 11e? If so, why?

c. Show a binomial tree for the three-period case (length = 1 month). At each node, show the American put values, European values, and stock prices. At what nodes are there early exercise advantages?

13. Using the "Binomial Option Pricing Model" Excel Program and the mean and variance on the stock you calculated in Question 11

a. Determine the equilibrium prices for a 50 call with an expiration of 3 months (t = .25) and a binomial period of length 3 day (n = 90) given the following stock prices: $40, $42.50, $45, $47.50, $50, $52.50, $55, $57.50, and $60. Assume the annual risk-free rate is 6%.

b. On a graph, plot the call prices and IVs for each of the stock prices (you may want to do this in Excel).

c. Determine the equilibrium prices for a 55 call with an expiration of 3 months (t = .25) and a binomial period of length 1 day (n = 90) given the following stock prices: $40, $42.50, $45, $47.50, $50, $52.50, $55, $57.50, and $60. Assume the annual risk-free rate is 6%.

d. Determine the equilibrium prices for a 50 call with an expiration of 6 months (t = .5) and a binomial period of length 1 day (n = 90) given the following stock prices: $40, $42.50, $45, $47.50, $50, $52.50, $55, $57.50, and $60. Assume the annual risk-free rate is 6%.

e. Is the BOPM consistent with the pricing conditions governing different exercise prices and expirations? Comment on the features of the BOPM.

14. Assume a binomial, risk-neutral world in which $n = 1$, $S_0 = \$50.00$, $R_f = .02$, $u = 1.05$, and $d = .975$.

   a. What are the risk-neutral probabilities of the stock increasing in one period and decreasing in one period? Solve for the probabilities using the equation: $S_0 = PV(E(S_T))$.

   b. Using risk-neutral pricing, determine the equilibrium price of a call on stock with an exercise price of $50 and expiration at the end of the period.

   c. Using risk-neutral pricing, determine the equilibrium price of a put on the stock with an exercise price of $50 and expiration at the end of the period.

   d. Show that your answers in b and c are consistent with the BOPM's replicating approach.

15. Explain what is meant by risk-neutral pricing. What is the reason for pricing options using a risk-neutral pricing approach?

WEB EXERCISE

1. Estimate the price of call and put options on a stock.

   a. Select a CBOE option on a stock that is not expected to go ex-dividend during the option's expiration period. You may want to select an option with a short expiration period.

   b. In selecting your option, go to either www.cboe.com or www.wsj.com/free. For information on the stock, go to www.nasdaq.com, www.hoovers.com, or www.pinksheets.com. At those sites, you will find information on a company such as its profile, fundamentals, and price charts.

   c. After finding an option on a stock, estimate the stock's expected logarithmic return and variance using historical stock price information.

   d. Determine the risk-free rate by going to www.Bloombergs.com.

   e. Using the "Binomial Option Pricing Model" Excel Program, determine the price of the call and put on the stock.

   f. Compare your BOPM values to the actual market prices.

APPENDIX 5A   EXAMPLES OF MULTIPLE-PERIOD ARBITRAGE STRATEGIES

5A.1   Initially Overpriced Call

As an example of the adjustment process, consider the two-period case described in Section 5.4 (Figure 5.4-2) in which the market price of the call is initially $6 instead of the OPM price of $5.31. With the option overpriced, an arbitrageur would implement the overpriced arbitrage strategy by taking the following short position in the call and long position in the replicating portfolio

$\{-C_0^m\}, .\{+(H_0^* S_0 - B_0^*)\}$	
Initial Position	**Cash Flow**
Short Call	$6.00
Buy H_0^* Shares: $-.7881(\$100)$	-78.81
Borrow B_0^*	73.50
Cash Flow	$0.69

This portfolio would net the arbitrageur $0.69 $((C_0^m - C_0^*) = (\$6 - \$5.31))$ at the initiation of this strategy, which we assume the arbitrageur invests in a risk-free security. At the end of Period 1, the call should trade at $7.32 if the stock is trading at $S_u = \$104.88$. If the call is below this price (underpriced), the arbitrageur would earn an arbitrage return if she closes. For example, if the call is priced at $C_1^m = \$7$, the arbitrageur would earn $1.03 by closing the position. That is

$C_1^m < C_u$ **Close Position**	
Closing Position	**Cash Flows**
Call Purchase	$-\$7.00$
Stock Sale: $(.7881)(\$104.88)$	82.66
Debt Repayment: $-(\$73.50)(1.025)$	-75.34
Value of Initial Cash Flow: $(\$0.69)(1.025)$	0.71
Cash Flow	$1.03

In contrast, if the call in Period 1 is above $7.32, then closing the position would result in a loss or an arbitrage profit of less than the compounded value of $C_0^m - C_0^*$. For example, if the option is trading at $C_1^m = \$9$, closing the portfolio would result in a loss of $0.97. To avoid the loss, the arbitrageur would need to adjust the arbitrage portfolio. With the stock price at $104.88 and with one period to expiration, a portfolio of $H_u = 1$ share and a debt of $B_u = \$97.56$ is required to hedge the short call position. This adjustment, though, can be done by simply moving the hedge ratio from H_0 to H_u. In terms of the example, the arbitrageur would need to borrow $22.22 to buy $(H_u - H_0) = (1 - .7881)$ shares at $104.88 per share. This adjustment would move both her hedge ratio to $H_u = 1$ and debt to the required level of $B_u = \$97.56$: $B_u = \$73.50(1.025) + \$22.22 = \$97.56$. Next period, the arbitrageur would close the arbitrage portfolio at either stock price ($110 or \$102.23) and call values (\$10 or \$2.23) to earn a profit \$0.72 (equal to the future value of $C_0^m - C_0^*$: ($6.00 - \$5.31)(1.025)^2 = \$0.72$). That is

Closing Position at Expiration	$S_{uu} = \$110$ $C_{uu} = \$10$	$S_{ud} = \$102.23$ $C_{ud} = \$2.23$
Call Purchase (C_T^m)	−\$10.00	−\$2.23
Stock Sale ($H_u\ S_T$)	110.00	102.23
Debt Repayment ($B_u r_f = \$97.56(1.025)$)	−100.00	−\$100.00
Value of Initial Cash Flow $((C_0^m - C_0^*)r_f^2 = \$0.69(1.025^2)$)	\$0.72	0.72
Cash Flow	\$0.72	\$0.72

Thus, by readjusting when the option was overpriced in Period 1, the arbitrageur is able to realize a profit of \$0.72 instead of losing \$0.97 if she had closed then.

If the stock price in Period 1 was \$97.47, and the call was underpriced, closing would result in a profit. For example, if the call was trading at \$1.30 instead of \$1.48, closing would yield a profit of \$0.89. That is

$C_1^m < C_d$ Close	
Closing Position	**Cash Flows**
Call Purchase	−\$1.30
Stock Sale: (.7881)(\$97.47)	76.82
Debt Repayment: −(\$73.50)(1.025)	−75.34
Value of Initial Cash Flow: (\$0.69)(1.025)	0.71
Cash Flow	\$0.89

However, if the call was overpriced, closing would result in a loss or a less than optimal return. If $C_1^m = \$2.30$, for instance, closing would result in a loss of \$0.11. To avert this, the arbitrageur would need to readjust by moving to the correct H_d and B_d values. With $C_1^m = \$2.30$, this can be done by selling $H_0^* - H_d = (.7881 - .3084) = .4797$ shares at \$97.47 per share, then using the funds to repay \$46.75 of the debt. This adjustment will give the arbitrageur the required replicating portfolio position with $H_d = .3084$ and $B_d = (\$73.50)(1.025) - \$46.75 = \$28.586$ (some rounding errors do exist). At expiration, closing this arbitrage position will yield an arbitrage profit of \$0.72 regardless of whether the price is \$102.23 or \$95.00:

Closing Position at Expiration	$S_{ud} = \$102.23$ $C_{ud} = \$2.23$	$S_{dd} = \$95$ $C_{dd} = 0$
Call Purchase (C_T^m)	−\$2.23	0
Stock Sale ($H_d\ S_T = .3084\ S_T$)	31.53	29.30
Debt Repayment ($B_d r_f = \$28.586(1.025)$)	−29.30	−29.30
Value of Initial Cash Flow $((C_0^m - C_0^*)r_f^2 = \$0.69(1.025^2))$	0.72	0.72
Cash Flow	\$0.72	\$0.72

5A.2   Initially Underpriced Call

Using the two-period example (Figure 5.4-2), suppose the call is initially trading at a market price of \$5 instead of the BOPM value of \$5.31. Given this situation, an arbitrageur could (1) buy one call at $C_0^m = \$5$, (2) borrow .7881 shares of stock and sell them in the market at \$100 per share, and (3) invest $B_0^* = \$73.50$ in a risk-free security at 2.5% for the period. This portfolio would net the arbitrageur a positive cash flow of $C_0^m - C_0^* = \$0.31$, which she can invest in a risk-free security for the period. That is

$\{C_0^m\}, \{-(H_0^* S_0 - B_0^*)\}$	
Initial Position	**Cash Flow**
Long Call	−\$5.00
Short H_0^* Shares: (.7881)(\$100)	78.81
Invest B_0^* Dollars	−73.50
Cash Flows	\$0.31

If the call in Period 1 is $C_1^m = \$8$ when $S_u = \$104.88$ (overpriced), closing the position would yield a positive cash flow of \$1.00:

$C_1^m < C_u$ **Close**	
Closing Position	**Cash Flows**
Call Sale	\$8.00
Stock Purchase: −(.7881)(\$104.88)	−82.66
Value of B_0^* Investment: (\$73.50)(1.025)	75.34
Value of Initial Cash Flow: (\$ 0.31)(1.025)	0.32
Cash Flow	\$1.00

On the other hand, if the call is trading at $C_1^m = \$6$ (underpriced), then closing the position would result in a loss of \$1.00. To avoid this, the arbitrageur would need to readjust her portfolio by moving to a short position of $H_u = 1$ share of stock and a risk-free investment of $B_u = \$97.56$. The arbitrageur would accomplish this by selling .2119 shares short $((H_u - H_0) = (1 - .7881) = .2119)$ at \$104.88 per share and then investing the proceeds of \$22.22 in a risk-free security to obtain $B_u = \$97.56 = \$73.50(1.025) + \$22.22$. At expiration, the arbitrageur would then receive \$0.33 regardless of the stock's price. That is

	Expiration Cash Flow	
Closing Position	$S_{uu} = \$110$ $C_{uu} = \$10$	$S_{ud} = \$102.23$ $C_{ud} = \$2.23$
Call Sale (C_T^m)	\$10.00	\$2.23
Stock Purchase ($H_u S_T = 1 S_T$)	−110.00	−102.23
Value of B_u Investment ($B_u r_f = \$97.56(1.025)$)	100.00	100.00
Value of Initial Cash Flow $((C_0^* - C_0^m) r_f^2 = (\$5.31 - 5.00)(1.025)^2)$	\$0.33	0.33
Cash Flow	\$0.33	\$0.33

If the call is underpriced when the stock is at $S_d = \$97.47$ (e.g., if $C_1^m = \$1$ instead of $C_d = \$1.48$), then readjustment would require being short $H_d = .3084$ shares and an investment of $B_d = \$28.58$. In this case, an arbitrageur would need to borrow \$46.75 to buy .4797 shares $(.7881 - .3084)$ at \$97.47 per share, returning the shares to the share lender; this would result in moving the arbitrageur's portfolio to one with $H_d = .3084$ shares short and a risk-free investment of $B_d = \$73.50(1.025) - \$46.75 = \$28.586$. By closing the next period (expiration), the arbitrageur would then earn \$0.33 profit:

Closing Position	Expiration Cash Flow	
	$S_{ud} = \$102.23$ $C_{ud} = \$2.23$	$S_{dd} = \$95$ $C_{dd} = 0$
Call Sale	\$2.23	\$0
Stock Purchase $(H_d S_t = (.3084)S_T)$	−31.53	−29.30
Value of B_d Investment $(\$28.586)(1.025)$	\$29.30	29.30
Value of Initial Cash Flow $(\$5.31 - 5.00)(1.025)^2$	0.33	0.33
Cash Flow	\$0.33	\$0.33

Thus, as is the case of the initially overpriced option, an arbitrageur would find a riskless profit could be earned by readjusting her initially underpriced arbitrage portfolio each period until that period is reached where the option is over or equal in value and the arbitrage portfolio can be profitably closed.

5A.3   Initially Overpriced Put

Exhibit 5A-1 presents an example of an arbitrage strategy for an initially overpriced put based on the put example shown in Figure 5.5-1.

Problems and Questions

The following problems are based on Questions 3 and 4 (End-of-Chapter Problems and Questions).

1. Define the arbitrage strategy you would employ if the current market price of the call in Question 3 (End-of-Chapter Problems and Questions) were \$2.60. Assume any positive cash flow is invested in a risk-free security.

   a. What would your cash flow from your arbitrage be in Period 1 if you closed your initial strategy when the stock was priced at S_u and the call was selling at $C_t^m = \$3.75$? How would you readjust your initial strategy to avoid a loss? Show what your cash flow would be when you closed at the end of the second period (assume the stock will follow the binomial process and will be either $u^2 S_0$ or $ud\, S_0$).

   b. What would your cash flow from your arbitrage investment be in Period 1 if you closed your initial strategy when the stock was priced at S_d and the call was selling at $C_t^m = \$0.50$? How would you readjust your initial strategy to avoid the loss? Show what your cash flow would be when you closed at the end of the second period (assume the stock will follow the binomial process and will be either $ud S_0$ or $d^2 S_0$).

EXHIBIT 5.A-1   Arbitrage Strategy for an Overpriced Put: Two-Period Case (Based on Put Example in Figure 5.5-1)

Current Period

$$S_0 = \$100, \; R_f = .025, \; H_0^{P^*} = -.2105, \; I_0^* = \$21.54, \; P_0^* = \$0.49$$
$$P_0^m = \$0.60$$

Strategy: $\{-P_0^m\}$ and $\{+(H_0^{P^*}S_0 + I_0^*)\}$

Position	Cash Flow
Put Sale	$0.60
Short $H_0^{P^*}$ Shares at S_0	21.05
Investment of I_0^* in Riskless Security	−21.54
Initial Cash Flow	$0.11

Period 1: Closing Initial Position

$$S_d = \$97.47, \; R_f = .025, \; H_d^P = -.6916, \; I_d = \$68.97, \; P_d = \$1.56$$
$$\text{Possible Prices: } P_1^m = \$1.50 \text{ and } P_1^m = \$1.70$$

Closing Position	$P_1^m = \$1.50$	$P_1^m = \$1.70$
Put Purchase	−$1.50	−$1.70
Stock Purchase $(H_0^P S_d)$	−20.52	−20.52
Investment $(I_0^* r_f)$	22.08	22.08
Value of Initial Cash Flow (0.11r_f$)	0.11275	0.11275
Cash Flow	$0.17	−$ 0.027

Period 1: Readjusting when $P_1^m = \$1.70$

Readjustment Strategy:
1. Sell $(H_d^P - H_0^{P^*})$ shares short at S_d: $(.6916 - .2105)(\$97.47) = \$46.89$
2. Invest short sale Proceeds of $46.89 in risk-free security
New Position:
$H_d^P = -.6916$
$I_d = \$21.54(1.025) + \$46.89 = \$68.97$

Period 2: Closing Position Readjusted in Period 1

$$S_T: S_{ud} = \$102.23 \text{ or } S_{dd} = \$95; \; P_T: P_{ud} = 0 \text{ or } P_{dd} = \$5$$

Closing Position	$S_{ud} = \$102.23$	$S_{dd} = \$95$
Put Purchase	$0	−$5.00
Stock Purchase $(H_d^P S_T)$	−70.70	−65.70
Investment $(I_d r_f)$	70.70	70.70
Value of Initial Cash Flow (0.11r_f^2$)	0.1156	0.1156
Cash Flow	$0.1156	$0.1156

2. Define the arbitrage strategy you would employ if the current market price of the call in Question 3 (End-of-Chapter Problems and Questions) were $2.20. Assume any positive cash flow is invested in a risk-free security.

   a. What would your cash flow from your arbitrage investment be in Period 1 if you closed your initial position when the stock was priced at S_u and the call were selling at $C_t^m = \$3.25$? How would you readjust your initial strategy to avoid the loss? Show what your cash flow would be when you closed at the end of the second period (assume the stock will follow the binomial process and will be either $u^2 S_0$ or $ud S_0$).

   b. What would your cash flow from your arbitrage investment be in Period 1 if you closed your initial position when the stock was priced at S_d and the call was selling at $C_t^m = 0$? Would you readjust your initial strategy?

3. Define the arbitrage strategy you would employ if the current market price of the put in Question 4a (End-of-Chapter Problems and Questions) were $0.55. Assume any positive cash flow is invested in a risk-free security.

   In Period 1, what would your cash flow from your arbitrage investment be if you closed your initial position when the stock was priced at S_d and the call was selling at $C_1^m = \$1.65$? How would you readjust your initial strategy to avoid a loss? Show what your cash flow would be when you closed at the end of the second period (assume the stock will follow the binomial process and be either $ud S_0$ or $d^2 S_0$).

4. Define the arbitrage strategy you would employ if the current market price of the put in Question 4a (End-of-Chapter Problems and Questions) were $0.30. Assume any positive cash flow is invested in the risk-free strategy.

   In Period 1, what would your cash flow from your arbitrage investment be if you closed your initial position when the stock was priced at S_d and the put were selling at $C_1^m = \$1.25$? How would you readjust your initial strategy to avoid any loss? Show what your cash flow would be when you closed at the end of the second period (assume the stock will follow the binomial process and will be either $d^2 S_0$ or $ud S_0$).

APPENDIX 5B   RISK-NEUTRAL PROBABILITY PRICING—MULTIPLE-PERIOD CASE

The call and put values obtained using the multiple-period BOPM replicating approach also can be found using a risk-neutral pricing approach. This approach values an option as the present value of the expected terminal value of the option with the probabilities being the risk-neutral probabilities and the discount rate being the risk-free rate.

In a multiple-period case, the expected terminal value of a call ($E(C_T)$) or put ($E(P_T)$) after n periods can be obtained once we know the probabilities of the option's IVs. In a binomial process, the probabilities of an option equaling one of its possible IVs is given by the probability of j upward moves in an n period, p_{nj}. The risk-neutral probability, p_{nj}, in turn, can be found using the following equation:

$$p_{nj} = \frac{n!}{(n-j)!j!} q^j (1-q)^{n-j}$$

where p is the risk-neutral probability of the stock increasing in one period and as we showed in the single-period case, is equal to $[r_f - d]/[u - d]$. In our two-period example in Sections 5.3 and 5.4 (u = 1.0488, d = .9747, r_f = 1.025, S_0 = $100, and X = $100), the risk-neutral probability of the stock increasing in one period is p = [1.025 − 0.9747]/[1.0488 −

.9747] = .6788. Thus, the probabilities of the number of upward moves in n periods being j = 2, 1, or 0 in our example are

$$j = 2 : p_{22} = [2!/(0!2!)](.6788)^2 = .46077$$

$$j = 1 : p_{21} = [2!/(1!1!)](.6788)(.3212) = .43606$$

$$j = 0 : p_{20} = [2!/(2!0!)](.3212)^2 = .10317$$

With the period risk-free rate of 2.5%, the value of the 100 European call and 100 European put are therefore

$$C_0^* = \frac{E(C_T)}{r_f^n} = \frac{P_{22}\,C_{uu} + P_{21}\,C_{ud} + P_{20}\,C_{dd}}{r_f^2}$$

$$C_0^* = \frac{(.46077)(\$10) + (.43606)(\$2.23) + (.10317)(0)}{(1.025)^2} = \$5.31$$

$$P_0^* = \frac{E(P_T)}{r_f^n} = \frac{P_{22}\,P_{uu} + P_{21}\,P_{ud} + P_{20}\,P_{dd}}{r_f^2}$$

$$P_0^* = \frac{(.46077)(0) + (.43606)(0) + (.10317)(\$5)}{(1.025)^2} = \$0.49$$

The call and put values are the same as those we obtained using the replicating approach. In general, the call and put values for n periods using risk-neutral pricing are

$$C_0^* = \frac{E(C_T)}{r_f^n} = \frac{1}{r_f^n}\sum_{j=0}^{n} P_{nj}\left[\text{Max}[u^j\,d^{(n-j)}\,S_o - X, 0]\right]$$

$$P_0^* = \frac{E(P_T)}{r_f^n} = \frac{1}{r_f^n}\sum_{j=0}^{n} P_{nj}\left[\text{Max}[X - u^j\,d^{(n-j)}\,S_o, 0]\right]$$

These equations are identical to the multiple-period binomial call price equation and put equation [Equations (5.4-5) and (5.5-5)] defined using the replicating approach.

CHAPTER 6

THE BINOMIAL PRICING OF OPTIONS ON DIVIDEND-PAYING STOCKS AND STOCK INDICES

6.1 INTRODUCTION

A future dividend payment affects the value of an option in two ways. First, on the ex-dividend date, the price of the stock usually falls by an amount approximately equal to the dividend. This, in turn, leads to a decrease in the price of a call and an increase in the price of a put. Second, as we discussed in Chapter 4, a dividend payment may lead to an early exercise of a call just prior to the ex-dividend date and possibly a put on the ex-dividend date. If early exercise is advantageous, then an American option would be more valuable than a European one. The binomial model that we derived in Chapter 5 assumed that the underlying stock did not pay a dividend. Although both the binomial and Black–Scholes option models are quite sophisticated and provide insights into option pricing, neither is of much use in practice until they are adjusted to incorporate dividends.

In this chapter, we continue our analysis of the BOPM by showing how to adjust the BOPM for European and American options on stocks paying dividends. We begin by first looking at the impact a future dividend payment has on call and put prices using the single-period model. We then look at two approaches to adjusting the multiple-period binomial model for dividends—the **known dividend-payment approach** and the **Merton continuous dividend-yield approach**. After defining these dividend-adjusted approaches for stock options, we then show how the binomial model is adjusted to price options on stock indices, an option that has dividend-like features. In Chapter 7, we complete our analysis of the binomial option pricing model by showing how it is used to price currency and debt options.

6.2 PRICING OPTIONS ON DIVIDEND-PAYING STOCKS—SINGLE-PERIOD CASE

6.2.1 European Call Option

To see the implications dividends have on the BOPM, consider the case of a European call option on a dividend-paying stock with a single period to expiration. For this case, assume that the period starts on a non ex-dividend date and expires on the stock's ex-dividend date. For simplicity, also assume that the stock falls by an amount equal to the value of the dividend on the ex-dividend date (D_1). If we let uS_0 and dS_0 be the possible stock prices at the end of the period but just before the ex-dividend date, then the stock's possible prices on the ex-dividend date would be $S_u^x = uS_0 - D_1$ and $S_d^x = dS_0 - D_1$ (where x indicates ex-dividend date). Thus, if the stock in our single-period call example in Chapter 5 ($u = 1.1$, $d = .95$, $r_f = 1.05$, $S_0 = \$100$, $X = \$100$) was expected to pay a dividend worth $\$1$ on the ex-dividend date, then the possible stock prices would be $\$109$ and $\$94$. Because exchange-traded call options are not dividend protected, the price of the call would, in turn, be less on an ex-dividend date (as compared to a non-ex-dividend date) if the call is in the money. In this example, the two possible call prices (equal to their IVs) at the ex-dividend expiration date would be $9 and 0:

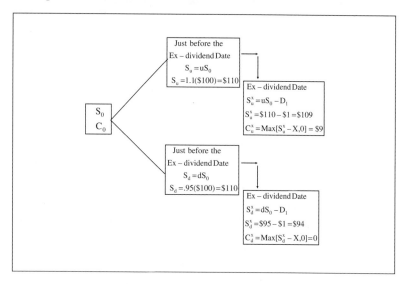

In adjusting the BOPM for dividends, note that if the price of the underlying stock is assumed to fall by an amount equal to the value of the dividend on the ex-dividend date, the dividends an arbitrageur with a replicating portfolio ($H_0 S_1 - B_0 D_1$) would earn (pay), $H_0 D_1$, from her long (short) position in the stock would be negated by the decrease in the price of the stock on the ex-dividend date. Thus, the arbitrageur's stock position in her replicating portfolio is defined by the stock prices just before the ex-dividend date (uS_0 and dS_0):

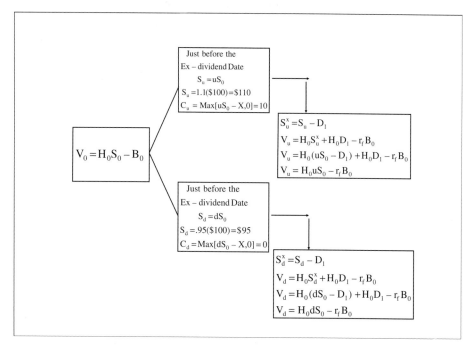

Given the possible call values and replicating portfolio values at expiration, the call's replicating portfolio is found by setting the two possible ex-dividend call prices equal to their respective replicating portfolio values and solving the two equations simultaneously for the H_0 and B_0:

$$H_0 u S_0 - r_f B_0 = C_u^x$$

$$H_0 d S_0 - r_f B_0 = C_d^x$$

$$H_0^* = \frac{C_u^x - C_d^x}{u S_0 - d S_0}$$

$$B_0^* = \frac{C_u^x(d S_0) - C_d^x(u S_0)}{r_f(u S_0 - d S_0)}$$

Thus, for the single-period BOPM, the only adjustment needed in forming the replicating portfolio (H_0^* and B_0^*) is to subtract the value of the dividend from the two nondividend-adjusted stock prices in computing the call's possible intrinsic values ($C_u^x = u S_0 - D_1$ and $C_d^x = d S_0 - D_1$). In terms of our example, the H_0^* and B_0^* values needed to form a replicating portfolio to match the possible call values of $C_u^x = \text{Max}[(\$110 - \$1) - \$100, 0] = \$9$ and $C_d^x = \text{Max}[(\$95 - \$1) - \$100, 0] = 0$ would be 0.6 and \$54.2857:

$$H_0^* = \frac{C_u^x - C_d^x}{u S_0 - d S_0} = \frac{\$9 - 0}{\$110 - \$95} = .6$$

$$B_0^* = \frac{C_u^x(d S_0) - C_d^x(u S_0)}{r_f(u S_0 - d S_0)} = \frac{(\$9)(\$95) - (0)(\$110)}{1.05[\$110 - \$95]} = \$54.2857$$

The equilibrium call price therefore would be

$$C_0^* = H_0^* S_0 - B_0^* = .6(\$100) - \$54.2857 = 5.71$$

$$C_0^* = \frac{1}{r_f}[p C_u^x + (1 - p)C_d^x] = \frac{1}{1.05}[(.6667)(\$9) + (.3333)(0)] = \$5.71$$

where

$$p = \frac{r_f - d}{u - d} = \frac{1.05 - .95}{1.1 - .95} = .6667$$

Thus, when the ex-dividend date coincides with expiration, the BOPM is adjusted simply by subtracting the dividends from the possible stock prices just before the ex-dividend date in computing the intrinsic values of the call (see Exhibit 6.2-1).

Note, if the market failed to incorporate the dividend in its call pricing, then an arbitrage opportunity would exist. For example, if the market priced the call with the BOPM but failed to include the \$1 dividend, then the market price of the call would be \$6.35 (see Section 5.2). At $C_0^m = \$6.35$, the call would be overpriced ($C_0^* = \$5.71$). To exploit this, arbitrageurs would go short in the call and long in the replicating portfolio: buy $H_0^* = 0.6$ shares of stock and borrow $B_0^* = \$54.2857$. This strategy would yield arbitrageurs an initial cash flow of \$0.64 with no liabilities at expiration:

$$\text{Cash Flow} = C_0^m - (H_0^* S_0 - B_0^*)$$

$$\text{Cash Flow} = \$6.35 - ((0.6)(\$100) - \$54.2857) = \$0.64.$$

EXHIBIT 6.2-1 BOPM Call Value and Replicating Portfolio: Single-Period Case With the Ex-Dividend Date the Same as the Expiration Date

uS_0 and dS_0 are possible stock prices just before ex-dividend date; D_1 = value of dividend on ex-dividend date; $uS_0 - D_1$ and $dS_0 - D_1$ are ex-dividend stock prices.
$u = 1.1, d = .95, S_0 = \$100, D_1 = \$1, r_f = 1.05,$ and $X = \$100$

$$V_u = H_0(uS_0 - D_1) + H_0 D_1 - r_f B_0$$
$$V_u = H_0 uS_0 - r_f B_0$$
$$C_u^x = IV^x = Max[(uS_0 - D_1 - X, 0]$$
$$C_u^x = Max[1.1(\$100) - \$1 - \$100, 0]$$
$$C_u^x = \$9$$

$$V_0 = H_0 S_0 - B_0$$
$$C_0^* = H_0^* S_0 - B_0^*$$
$$C_0^* = .6(\$100) - \$54.2857$$
$$C_0^* = \$5.71$$

$$V_d = H_0(dS_0 - D_1) + H_0 D_1 - r_f B_0$$
$$V_d = H_0 dS_0 - r_f B_0$$
$$C_d^x = IV^x = Max[(dS_0 - D_1 - X, 0]$$
$$C_d^x = Max[.95(\$100) - \$1 - \$100, 0]$$
$$C_d^x = 0$$

$$H_0^* = \frac{C_u^x - C_d^x}{uS_0 - dS_0} = \frac{\$9 - 0}{\$110 - \$95} = .6$$
$$B_0^* = \frac{C_u^x(dS_0) - C_d^x(uS_0)}{r_f((uS_0 - dS_0))} = \frac{(\$9)(\$95) - (0)(\$110)}{1.05[\$110 - \$95]} = \$54.2857$$

	Cash Flow at Expiration	
Closing Position	$S_u^x = \$110 - \$1 = \$109$ $C_u^x = \$9$	$S_d^x = \$95 - \$1 = \$94$ $C_d^x = 0$
Call ($C_T^m = IV$)	−$9.00	0
Stock ($H_0^* S_T = .6 S_T^x$)	$65.40	$56.40
Dividend ($H_0^* D = .6(\$1.00)$)	0.60	0.60
Debt ($B_0^* r_f = \$54.2857(1.05)$)	−57.00	−57.00
	0	0

Value of Initial Cash Flow = $0.64(1.05) = $0.67

In the absence of arbitrage, the price of the European call would therefore be $5.71. Thus, by lowering the price of the stock on the ex-dividend date, dividends decrease the value of the call by approximately 10%. A failure to incorporate the dividend could lead to large pricing errors.

6.2.2 American Call Option

In previous chapters, we've noted that for calls on nondividend-paying stocks, early exercise is never profitable, and therefore, the price of an American and European call will be the same. This is not the case, though, if the underlying stock pays a dividend during the life of the option. To see this, suppose that in the preceding example the call was American and as a result could be exercised the instant before going ex-dividend. Given this early exercise opportunity, the call holder would find it advantageous at the upper node to exercise the call the instant before expiration when the exercise value is $10 instead of holding the option to expiration on the ex-dividend date when the call value is only $9. No exercise advantage exists at the lower node when the stock price is at $95 just before expiration and $94 at expiration. The value of the American option in this case would be $6.35 compared to the $5.71 value for the European call that cannot be exercised until expiration:

$$C_0^{a*} = H_0^* S_0 - B_0^* = .6667(\$100) - \$60.32 = 6.35$$

$$H_0^* = \frac{Max[IV_u, C_u^x] - Max[IV_d, C_d^x]}{uS_0 - dS_0} = \frac{\$10 - 0}{\$110 - \$95} = .6667$$

$$B_0^* = \frac{(Max[IV_u, C_u^x])(dS_0) - (Max[IV_d, C_d^x])(uS_0)}{r_f(uS_0 - dS_0)}$$

$$B_0^* = \frac{(\$10)(\$95) - (0)(\$110)}{1.05[\$110 - \$95]} = \$60.32$$

$$C_0^{a*} = \frac{1}{r_f}[p(Max[IV_u, C_u^x]) + (1 - p)(Max[IV_d, C_d^x])]$$

$$C_0^{a*} = \frac{1}{1.05}[(.6667)(\$10) + (.3333)(0)] = \$6.35$$

$$C_0^{e*} = \frac{1}{r_f}[pC_u^x + (1 - p)C_d^x] = \frac{1}{1.05}[(.6667)(\$9) + (.3333)(0)] = \$5.71$$

Note that because of the early exercise advantage, the arbitrage position for the American option has a different replicating portfolio ($H_0^* = .6667$ and $B_0^* = \$60.32$) than the European call's replicating portfolio ($H_0^* = .6$ and $B_0^* = 54.2857$).

6.2.3 European Put Option

The dividend adjustments required for European put options are similar to those for calls. In the single-period case, if expiration is on the stock's ex-dividend date, the value of the dividend is subtracted from the stock price in determining the put's intrinsic value; and as with a call, no changes are necessary in the composition of the replicating put portfolio (see Exhibit 6.2-2).

As an example, consider a 100 European put option on the stock used in our illustrative one-period example ($u = 1.10$, $d = .95$, $r_f = 1.05$, and $S_0 = \$100$). If the stock is expected to go ex-dividend at expiration, with the dividend worth of $D_1 = \$1$ on that date, then the put's possible intrinsic values at expiration would be

$$P_u^x = Max[X - (uS_0 - D_1), 0] = Max[\$100 - (\$110 - 1), 0] = 0$$

$$P_d^x = Max[X - (dS_0 - D_1), 0] = Max[\$100 - (\$95 - 1), 0] = \$6$$

and the equilibrium put price would be

$$P_0^* = H_0^{P*} S_0 + I_0^* = (-.4)(\$100) + \$41.90 = 1.90$$

$$P_0^* = \frac{1}{r_f}[pP_u + (1 - p)P_d] = \frac{1}{1.05}[(.6667)(0) + (.3333)(\$6)] = \$1.90$$

EXHIBIT 6.2-2 BOPM Put Value and Replicating Portfolio: Single-Period Case With the Ex-Dividend Date the Same as the Expiration Date

---

uS_0 and dS_0 are possible stock prices just before ex-dividend date; $D_1 = $ value of dividend on ex-dividend date; $uS_0 - D_1$ and $dS_0 - D_1$ are ex-dividend stock prices.
$u = 1.1, d = .95, S_0 = \$100, D_1 = \$1, r_f = 1.05,$ and $X = \$100$

$$V_0 = H_0^P S_0 + I_0^*$$
$$P_0^* = H_0^{P*} S_0 + I_0^*$$
$$P_0^* = (-.4)(\$100) + \$41.90$$
$$P_0^* = \$1.90$$

$$V_u = H_0^P(uS_0 - D_1) + H_0^P D_1 + r_f I_0^*$$
$$V_u = H_0^P uS_0 + r_f I_0^*$$
$$P_u^x = IV^x = Max[X - (uS_0 - D_1), 0]$$
$$P_u^x = Max[\$100 - (1.1(\$100)) - \$1), 0]$$
$$P_u^x = 0$$

$$V_d = H_0^P(dS_0 - D_1) + H_0^P D_1 + r_f I_0^*$$
$$V_d = H_0^P dS_0 + r_f I_0^*$$
$$P_d^x = IV^x = Max[X - (dS_0 - D_1), 0]$$
$$P_d^x = Max[\$100 - (.95(\$100)) - \$1), 0]$$
$$P_d^x = \$6$$

$$H_0^P = \frac{P_u^x - P_d^x}{uS_0 - dS_0} = \frac{0 - \$6}{\$110 - \$95} = -.4$$

$$I_0^* = \frac{-[P_u^x(dS_0) - P_d^x(uS_0)]}{r_f(uS_0 - dS_0)} = \frac{-[(0)(\$95) - (\$6)(\$110)]}{1.05[\$110 - \$95]} = \$41.90$$

---

where

$$H_0^* = \frac{P_u^x - P_d^x}{uS_0 - dS_0} = \frac{0 - \$6}{\$110 - \$95} = -.4$$

$$I_0^* = \frac{-[P_u^x(dS_0) - P_d^x(uS_0)]}{r_f(uS_0 - dS_0)} = \frac{-[(0)(\$95) - (\$6)(\$110)]}{1.05[\$110 - \$95]} = \$41.90$$

Note that if the market were to price the put with the BOPM but fail to include the dividend, then the market price of the put would be $1.59 (see Section 5.3). At $P_0^m = \$1.59$, the put would be underpriced ($P_0^* = \$1.90$). To exploit this, arbitrageurs would go long in the put and short in the replicating put portfolio: buy .4 shares of stock and borrow $41.90. This strategy would yield arbitrageurs with an initial cash flow of $0.31 with no liabilities at expiration:

$$\text{Cash Flow} = -P_0^m + (H_0^{P*} S_0 + I_0^*)$$
$$\text{Cash Flow} = -\$1.59 + ((-.4)(\$100) + \$41.90) = \$0.31$$

Closing Position	Cash Flow at Expiration	
	$S_u^x = \$110 - \$1 = \$109$ $P_u^x = 0$	$S_d^x = \$95 - \$1 = \$94$ $P_d^x = \$6$
Put ($P_T^x = IV$)	$0.00	$6.00
Stock ($H_0^{P*}S_T^x = .4S_T$)	43.60	37.60
Dividend ($H_0^{P*}D = .4(\$1.00)$)	0.40	0.40
Debt ($I_0^*r_f = \$41.90(1.05)$)	−44.00	−44.00
	0	0

Value of Initial Cash Flow = $0.31(1.05) = $0.33

In the absence of arbitrage, the price of the put on this dividend-paying stock is $1.90, approximately 16% greater than a comparable put on a nondividend-paying stock. In general, by lowering the price of the stock on the ex-dividend date, a dividend increases the value of the put.

6.2.4   American Put Option

If the put option in the illustrative example had been American, then the exercise value just before the stock goes ex dividend would be $5 at the stock's lower node (zero at the upper node), and an instant later at expiration, its intrinsic value would be $6. Thus, unlike an American call, the early exercise advantage for an American put does not occur just before the ex-dividend date. In this single-period example, the put would be equal to $6 at expiration when the stock is trading at its ex-divided value of $94. If there were more periods to expiration, it is possible that the exercise value of $6 could exceed the binomial put value at the ex-dividend date. To reiterate, for an American put option on a dividend-paying stock, if there is an early exercise advantage, it will occur on the ex-dividend date; whereas for an American call option, the advantage will occur just before the ex-dividend date.

6.2.5   Put–Call Parity Model With Dividends

From Chapter 4, recall that when the underlying stock pays a dividend, the put–call parity model must be adjusted so that the value of a conversion ($\{+S_0, +P_0^e, -C_0^e\}$) will be equal to the present value of a portfolio consisting of a riskless pure discount bond with a face value equal to X plus the dividend value on the stock. That is

$$P_0^e - C_0^e + S_0 = PV(X + D)$$

In our single-period dividend examples, the price of the European call was $5.71, and the price of the European put was $1.90, using the dividend-adjusted binomial option model. The same put (call) price can also be found using the preceding dividend-adjusted, put–call parity model with the put (call) value determined from the binomial model. That is

$$P_0^e - C_0^e + S_0 = PV(X + D)$$
$$P_0^e = C_0^e - S_0 + PV(X + D)$$
$$P_0^e = C_0^e - S_0 + \frac{X + D}{r_f}$$
$$P_0^e = \$5.71 - \$100 + \frac{\$100 + \$1}{1.05} = \$1.90$$

6.3 PRICING OPTIONS ON DIVIDEND-PAYING STOCKS—MULTIPLE-PERIOD CASE

Suppose in our previous example, there were two periods to expiration. As before, suppose after one period, the stock would be at $110 and $95 the instant before the ex-dividend date and $109 and $94, respectively, on the ex-dividend date. In the next period, the stock will either rise or fall. Assuming the up and down parameters stay the same ($u = 1.1$ and $d = .95$), if the stock were at $109, then it could either increase to $119.90 or decrease to $103.55; if the stock were at $94, then its two possible prices would be $103.40 and $89.30 (see Figure 6.3-1). Note that in this dividend case, the tree does not recombine. Thus, as a result of one dividend payment in a two-period model, there are now four possible stock prices after two periods instead of three. Moreover, if there are multiple periods and multiple dividends, some periods when the stock trades ex-dividend and some when it trades cum dividend, and finally some periods when the stock goes from ex-dividend to cum dividend, then the number of possible nodes to evaluate can be quite large, making the binomial modeling of possible stock prices almost impossible.

To resolve this problem, there are two approaches to adjusting the binomial model for dividends. The first is sometimes referred to as the ***known dividend-payment approach***. This approach assumes the stock price reflects a future dividend payment, which is known with certainty, whereas all other factors affecting the stock prices are assumed to be uncertain. The second approach is to simply assume the stock pays a continuous dividend yield over the life of the option. This latter approach is based on the dividend-adjusted model developed by Robert Merton for the Black–Scholes model and accordingly is referred to here as the ***Merton continuous dividend-yield approach***. Because most stocks pay a fixed dollar dividend at specific dates, the Merton approach should be viewed as an approximation. Both models, though, treat dividends as if they were repayments of a portion of the share value of the stock. As such, dividends are thought of as a leakage of value of the stock, with the stock value dropping (as it does on the ex-dividend date) due to the leakage of the dividend. More formally, options on assets that generate a continuous dividend or interest payment, such as an index or currency option, are referred to as ***continuous-leakage*** options. If the underlying asset on the option engenders benefits

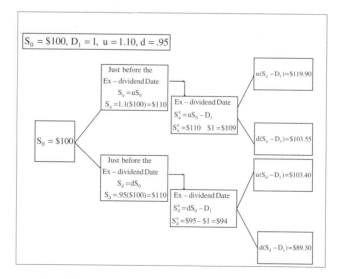

FIGURE 6.3-1 Multiple-Period Dividend Case

only discretely, such as an option on a stock making one dividend payment during the period, then the option is referred to as a ***discrete-leakage*** option. Finally, if the option's underlying asset generates no benefits, then it is called a ***zero-leakage*** option.

6.3.1   Known Dividend-Payment Approach

The known dividend-payment approach to valuing options consists of the following steps:

1. Calculate the current present value of all dividends to be paid during the life of the option: PV(D).

2. Subtract the present value of all dividends from the current price of the stock to obtain a dividend-adjusted stock price: $S_0^D = S_0 - PV(D)$.

3. Apply the up and down parameters to the dividend-adjusted stock price, S_0^D, to generate a binomial tree of stock prices.

4. After generating the tree, add to the stock prices at each node the present value of all future dividends to generate a dividend-adjusted binomial stock tree.

5. Given the dividend-adjusted binomial tree of stock prices, compute the option value by starting at expirations and applying the normal recursive method.

6. If the option is American, start one period before expiration and place a constraint that the American option price is the maximum of the binomial value or the exercise value, then roll the tree forward applying the same constraint.

The first 3 steps yield a binomial tree of stock prices that reflect the stock's approximate value after it pays a dividend. The fourth step of adding the value of the dividend back to the stock price allows the option's exercise values to be evaluated at different nodes to determine if early exercise is beneficial.

Example

As an example, suppose a stock is trading at $100, its annualized standard deviation is $\sigma^A = .3$, its mean is zero, and the stock will go ex-dividend (t*) in 120 days (t* = 120/365 = .328767 per year) with the value of the dividend worth $4 at that date. Suppose also that there are American call and put options on the stock, both with exercise prices of $100 and expirations of 180 days (T = 180 days or as a proportion of year: t = 180/365 = .493151), and that the simple annual risk-free rate is $R^A = 6\%$. To model the tree, we will use a five-period binomial tree (n = 5) and assume continuous compounding in calculating the periodic rates.

Steps:

1. The first step in valuing the options is to subtract the present value of the dividend from the current stock price to obtain the dividend-adjusted stock price. With continuous compounding, the present value of the dividend is $3.92, and the dividend-adjusted stock price is $96.08:

$$PV(D) = De^{-Rt^*}$$

$$PV(D) = \$4e^{-(.06)(120/365)} = \$3.92$$

$$S_0^D = S_0 - PV(D)$$

$$S_0^D = \$100 - \$3.92 = \$96.08$$

2. The second step is to generate a five-period binomial tree starting with the dividend-adjusted stock price. In this case, $u = 1.098797$, $d = 1/u = 0.910086$, and $p = .507916$:

$$u = e^{\sigma^A \sqrt{t/n}} = e^{.3\sqrt{(180/365)/5}} = 1.098797$$

$$d = e^{-\sigma^A \sqrt{t/n}} = e^{-.3\sqrt{(180/365)/5}} = .910086 = 1/u$$

$$p = \frac{r_f - d}{u - d} = \frac{e^{R^A(t/n)} - d}{u - d} = \frac{e^{(.06)((180/365)/5)} - .910086}{1.098797 - .910086} = .507916$$

The top boxes at each node in Exhibit 6.3-1 shows the stock prices (top line) for the five-period tree obtained from applying Step 2.

3. The third step is to add to the stock price at each node the present value of the dividend associated with that period. With the option expiring in 180 days, the length

EXHIBIT 6.3-1   Known Dividend-Payment Approach to Valuing American Options

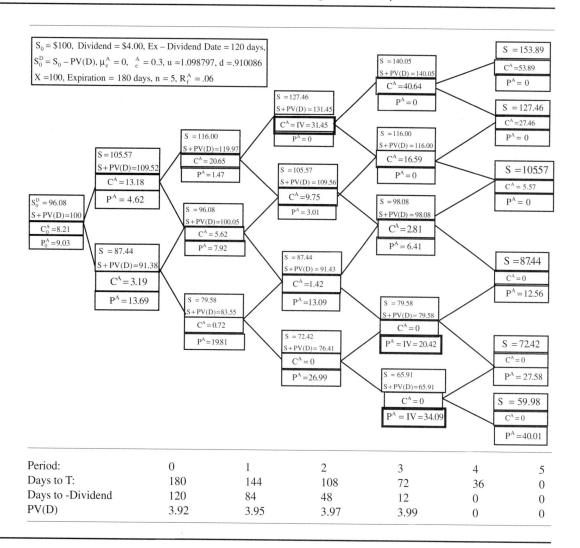

Period:	0	1	2	3	4	5
Days to T:	180	144	108	72	36	0
Days to -Dividend	120	84	48	12	0	0
PV(D)	3.92	3.95	3.97	3.99	0	0

of each period (or binomial step) in this example is $180/5 = 36$ days. Thus, 36 days will expire at the end of Period 1 ($j = 1$), 72 days at the end of Period 2 ($j = 2 : (j)T/n = (2)(180/5) = 72$), 108 days at the end of Period 3 ($j = 3 : (j)T/n = (3)(180/5) = 108$), and 144 days at the end of Period 4. With the ex-dividend date in 120 days, possible stock prices therefore have to be adjusted for Periods 1, 2, and 3 but not Periods 4 and 5. At Period 1, there would be 84 days to the ex-dividend date ($120 - 36$); at Period 2, there would be 48 days ($120 - 72$); and at Period 3, 12 days ($120 - 108$). The present values of the $4.00 dividend value at the end of Periods 1, 2, and 3 are, respectively, $3.95, $3.97, and 3.99:

$$n = 1 : PV(D_1) = De^{-Rt_1^*} = \$4e^{-(.06)(84/365)} = \$3.95$$

$$n = 2 : PV(D_2) = De^{-Rt_2^*} = \$4e^{-(.06)(48/365)} = \$3.97$$

$$n = 3 : PV(D_3) = De^{-Rt_3^*} = \$4e^{-(.06)(12/365)} = \$3.99$$

The second line in the top boxes at each node in Exhibit 6.3-1 shows the stock prices adjusted by adding the present value of the dividend to the nondividend-adjusted stock prices.

4. Given the binomial tree of dividend-adjusted stock prices, the call and put prices are obtained by using the normal recursive method defined in Chapter 5. Because the options are American, this step requires constraining the option price in Period 4 to be the maximum of its exercise value or binomial value. Given the prices determined in Period 4, we then roll the tree to the preceding periods, determining at each node the American price as the maximum of its binomial value or exercising value. The middle box at each node in Exhibit 6.3-1 shows the binomial call values, and the lower box shows the binomial put values.

As shown in Exhibit 6.3-1, the call option has an exercise value of $31.45 in period 3 when the stock is at $131.45, compared to a binomial value of $28.63:

$$C_{uuu} = Max\left[u^3S_0 - X, \frac{1}{r_f}[pC_{uuuu} + (1-p)C_{uuud}]\right]$$

$$C_{uuu} = Max\left[\$131.45 - \$100, \frac{1}{e^{(.06)((180/365)/5)}}[.507916(\$40.64) + (1-.507916)(\$16.59]\right]$$

$$C_{uuu} = Max\left[\$31.45, \$28.63\right] = \$31.45$$

Thus, an early exercise advantage exists for the call in Period 3 when the stock is at $131.45. As a result, the price of the American call would be equal to its exercise value of $31.45 at that node. Rolling that price and the other call prices forward, we end up with a price on the American call of $8.21.

In the case of the put option, it has an exercise value of $34.09 in Period 4 when the stock is at $65.91 compared to a binomial value of $33.50:

$$P_{dddd} = Max\left[X - d^4S_0, \frac{1}{r_f}[pP_{ddddu} + (1-p)P_{ddddd}]\right]$$

$$P_{dddd} = Max\left[\$100 - \$65.91, \frac{1}{e^{(.06)((180/365)/5)}}[.507916(\$27.58)\right.$$

$$\left. + (1 - .507916)(\$40.01]\right]$$

$$P_{dddd} = Max\left[\$34.09, \$33.50\right] = \$34.09$$

The put also has an early exercise advantage in Period 4 when the stock is priced at $79.58 (exercise value of $20.42 compared to binomial value of $19.83). Thus, the prices of the American put would be equal to their exercise values at these two nodes. Rolling those prices and the other put prices forward, we end up with a price on the American put of $9.03.

With a five-period tree, the European call and put values are $7.85 and $8.86, both lower than the American options. Thus, the known dividend-payment approach correctly prices American options greater than their European counterparts when an early exercise advantage exists. If the stock had not paid a dividend during the option period, then the values of both the American and European calls would be equal to $10.25. Thus, as we would hope, in the dividend-adjusted model, dividends have an inverse impact on the price of a call option; and in cases in which early exercise is beneficial, the dividend-adjusted model values an American call more than a European one. In the case of a put, if there was no dividend paid during the option period, then the price of the American put would be $7.54, whereas the European value would be $7.30. In examining the five-period tree for the American put in the nondividend case, one finds early exercise advantages at the two lowest nodes in Period 4 and one early exercise advantage at the lowest node in Period 3. Thus, even without dividends, an early exercise advantage exists with puts—a point we noted in Chapter 5.

The known dividend-payment approach for pricing options on stocks paying dividends is more accurate when we subdivided the tree into more periods. Part of the Excel package included with this book is the "Known Dividend-Payment Binomial Model" Excel program. This spreadsheet program calculates the prices for American and European call and put options for up to 200 subperiods. Using the program, the price of the American call is $8.25 and the price of the European put is $8.88 for n = 100.

6.3.2 Merton's Continuous Dividend-Yield Approach

Instead of using a known dividend to be paid at some future date, Merton's continuous dividend-yield approach assumes the dividend is paid out at a continuous rate. Because most stocks pay a dollar dividend quarterly, the application of Merton's approach to pricing an option on dividend-paying stock should be considered as an approximation. As we discuss later, though, Merton's model is more applicable to determining the price of options on currency and possibly stock indices.

Instead of accounting for a stock decrease on the ex-dividend date, the Merton approach assumes that the underlying stock pays a dividend at a continuous rate. To apply the binomial model to a stock paying a continuous dividend requires treating the stock as having a continuous leakage of value resulting from its continuous dividend payments. The binomial model can be adjusted for a continuous dividend payment by substituting the following continuous dividend-adjusted stock price for the current stock price in the binomial model:

$$S_0^D = S_0 e^{-\psi t}$$

where

ψ = annual dividend yield = annual dividend/stock price

In terms of our previous example, if the underlying stock were expected to generate an annual dividend yield of $\psi = .12$ (e.g., $12 annual dividend for a stock price of $100), then the dividend-adjusted stock price would be \$94.25:

$$S_0^D = S_0 e^{-\psi t}$$

$$S_0^D = \$100 e^{-(.12)((180/365))} = \$94.25$$

The most direct way to incorporate the dividend-adjusted stock price into the binomial model is to make use of risk-neutral pricing approach. Recall, in Chapter 5, we showed that one of the features of the option pricing model is that the option values obtained by the replication approach match those using risk-neutral pricing. As shown in Chapter 5, in equilibrium, the stock price under risk-neutral pricing is given as

$$S_0 = \frac{1}{r_f} [puS_0 + (1 - p)dS_0]$$

$$S_0 = \frac{1}{e^{R^A \Delta t}} [puS_0 + (1 - p)dS_0]$$

where

$$R^A = \text{the annual risk-free rate}$$

$$\Delta t = t/h = \text{the length of the binomial period}$$

Substituting the dividend-adjusted stock price for the current price, we obtain

$$S_0 = \frac{1}{r_f} [puS_0 + (1 - p)dS_0]$$

$$S_0 e^{-\psi \Delta t} = \frac{1}{e^{R^A \Delta t}} [puS_0 + (1 - p)dS_0]$$

$$S_0 e^{-\psi \Delta t} = e^{-R^A \Delta t} [puS_0 + (1 - p)S_0]$$

$$S_0 e^{(R^A - \psi)\Delta t} = [puS_0 + (1 - p)dS_0]$$

Solving the preceding equation for p yields a dividend-adjusted, risk-neutral probability reflecting a continuous dividend yield:

$$S_0 e^{(R^A - \psi)\Delta t} = [puS_0 + (1 - p)dS_0]$$

$$e^{(R^A - \psi)\Delta t} = pu + (1 - p)d$$

$$e^{(R^A - \psi)\Delta t} = p(u - d) + d$$

$$p = \frac{e^{(R^A - \psi)\Delta t} - d}{u - d} \qquad (6.3\text{-}1)$$

Equation (6.3-1) can be used to determine p in the equilibrium equations for call and put options:

$$C_0 = \frac{1}{e^{R^A \Delta t}} [pC_u + (1 - p)C_d]$$

$$P_0 = \frac{1}{e^{R^A \Delta t}} [pP_u + (1 - p)P_d]$$

Equation (6.3-1), in turn, shows that the dividend-adjusted, risk-neutrality probability treats the dividend yield as a negative interest rate in which the dividend yield represents a continuous leakage of value from the stock.

Example

To see the application of the Merton dividend-adjusted approach, suppose in our previous example ($S_0 = \$100, \sigma^A = .3, \mu^A = 0$, call and put options with X = \$100 and T = 180 days, n = 5, binomial period length of $\Delta t = t/n = (180/365)/5 = .098630$, and $R^A = 6\%$), the estimate annual dividend yield was 12%. The dividend-adjusted, risk-neutral probability would be .445197:

$$p = \frac{e^{(R^A - \psi)\Delta t} - d}{u - d}$$

$$p = \frac{e^{(.06 - .12)(.09863)} - .910086}{1.098797 - .910086} = .445197$$

where

$$u = e^{.3\sqrt{.09863}} = 1.098797$$
$$d = 1/u = .910086$$

Given the values for the p, u, and d parameters, the binomial option prices are determined using the normal recursive process of starting at expiration where the option's possible prices are set equal to their intrinsic values and then rolling the tree to the current period. Exhibit 6.3-2 shows the resulting binomial tree for the underlying stock, American and European calls, and American and European puts (both American and European puts are equal in value in this case). For this five-period case, the continuous dividend model prices the American and European calls less and the puts more than the known-dividend payment approach. The "Binomial Option Pricing Model" Excel program, included with this book, can be used to price American and European options using the Merton model for up to 200 subperiods. Using that program, the prices of the American call are $7.00 for n = 30 subperiods and $7.03 for n = 100; for the European call, the prices are $6.62 for n = 30 and $6.67 for n = 100; for the American and European puts, the prices are $9.45 for n = 30 and $9.50 for n = 100.

6.4 BINOMIAL PRICING OF STOCK INDEX OPTIONS

In general, the binomial model governing stock options can be extended to establish the price relationships for index options. However, in extending stock option pricing to index options, consideration has to be given to the stock portfolio or proxy portfolio defining the index and the dividends from the stocks making up the index portfolio.

6.4.1 Proxy Portfolio

As we discussed in Chapter 4, an index portfolio can be defined in terms of proxy portfolios that are highly correlated with the spot index or with a highly diversified index fund. Whether it is an index fund or a highly correlated portfolio, the proxy portfolio can be viewed as a position in the index. For example, if the spot S&P 500 were at 1250, a highly diversified index fund currently valued $1.25 million and with a beta of one could be thought of as the equivalent to a hypothetical spot portfolio consisting of $N_0 = 1,000$

EXHIBIT 6.3-2   Merton's Continuous Dividend-Yield Approach to Valuing Options

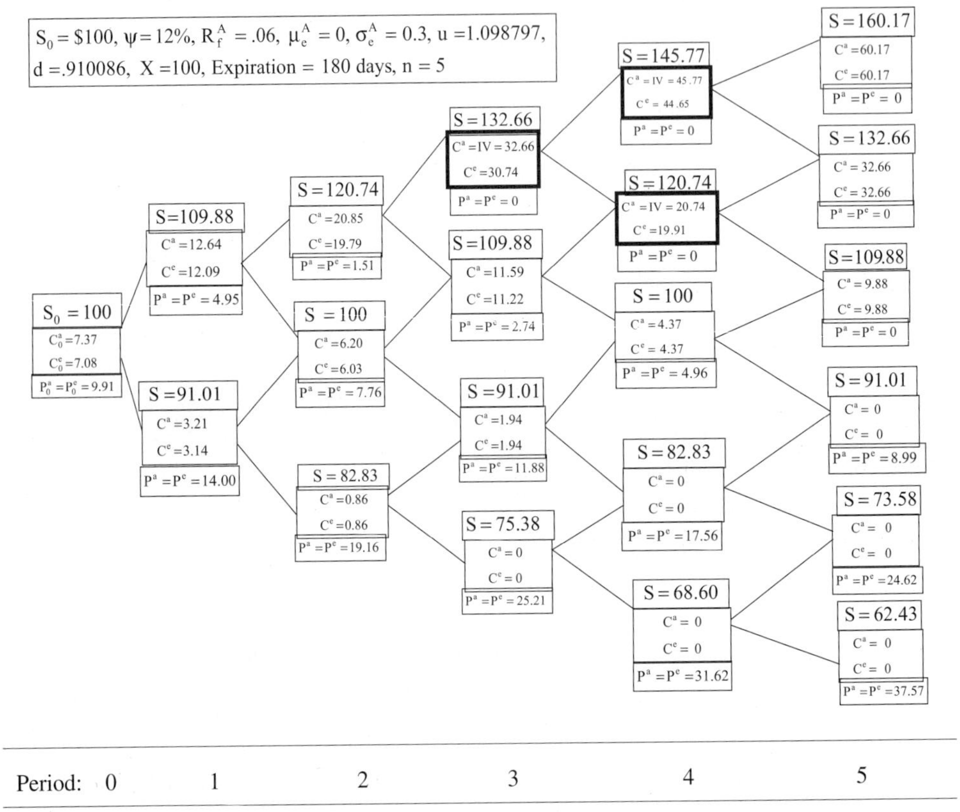

$S_0 = \$100$, $\psi = 12\%$, $R_f^A = .06$, $\mu_e^A = 0$, $\sigma_e^A = 0.3$, $u = 1.098797$, $d = .910086$, $X = 100$, Expiration = 180 days, $n = 5$

| Period: | 0 | 1 | 2 | 3 | 4 | 5 |

hypothetical shares of the index priced at $S_0 = \$1,250$ per index share. Such a portfolio, in turn, could be used to price index options and to determine the arbitrage strategies when the index option is mispriced.

To illustrate how a proxy portfolio can be used to determine the price of an index option, consider the pricing of an index call option using the single-period BOPM. In terms of the BOPM, the equilibrium price of the index call is equal to the value of a replicating portfolio consisting of H_0^* hypothetical shares of the spot index partially financed by borrowing B_0^* dollars. Suppose $u = 1.1$, $d = .95$, $R_f = .05$, and the current spot S&P 500 index is $S_0 = 1250$. For a one-period binomial model, the equilibrium price of a 1250 S&P 500 call option would be 79.40. In this case, the replicating portfolio would consist of $H_0^* = .6667$ hypothetical shares of the index, partially financed by borrowing $B_0^* = \$753.97$ (for simplicity, we are excluding the $100 multiple on the index options):

$$C_u = \text{Max}[uS_0 - X, 0] = \text{Max}[(1.1)(1250) - 1250, 0] = 125$$

$$C_d = \text{Max}[dS_0 - X, 0] = \text{Max}[.95(1250) - 1250, 0] = 0$$

$$H_0^* = \frac{C_u - C_d}{uS_0 - dS_0} = \frac{125 - 0}{1375 - 1187.50} = .6667$$

$$B_0^* = \frac{C_u(dS_0) - C_d(uS_0)}{r_f(uS_0 - dS_0)} = \frac{125(1187.50) - (0)(1375)}{1.05(1375 - 1187.50)} = 753.97$$

$$C_0^* = H_0^* S_0 - B_0^* = .6667(1250) - 753.97 = 79.40$$

$$p = \frac{r_f - d}{u - d} = \frac{1.05 - .95}{1.1 - .95} = .6667$$

$$C_0^* = \frac{1}{r_f}[pC_u + (1-p)C_d] = \frac{1}{1.05}[(.6667)(125) + (1 - .6667)(0)] = 79.40$$

If the market price of the index call did not equal 79.40, an arbitrage portfolio could be formed by taking a position in the call and an opposite position in the replicating portfolio. In terms of a proxy portfolio, the .6667 index shares priced at $S_0 = 1250$ would be equivalent to buying \$833.37 $((.6667)(1250))$ worth of a proxy index portfolio. Thus, the replicating portfolio consists of an \$833.37 investment in a proxy portfolio finance in part by borrowing $B_0^* = \$753.97$.

It should be kept in mind that for the more realistic multiple-period case, arbitrageurs would need to readjust their proxy portfolios each period.[1] With frequent revisions, arbitrageurs may find it advantageous to use a proxy portfolio consisting of only a few stocks or a mutual fund that is both highly correlated with the spot index and liquid. Also, because futures contracts are traded on indices, arbitrageurs alternatively could take positions in stock index futures instead of proxy spot portfolios. The relationship between options and futures is examined in Chapter 12.

6.4.2 Dividend Adjustments

Because many of the stocks comprising an index pay dividends, the dividends generated from the portfolio (not the individual stocks) need to be factored into the pricing of options on the index. Similar to options on individual stocks, when the portfolio's underlying stocks pay dividends, the option pricing model must be adjusted to account for the decrease in call prices or the increase in put prices that can occur on ex-dividend dates, and in the case of American call options, the models also need to be adjusted to account for the early exercise premium.

To see the impact dividends have on the price of an index option, suppose in the preceding single-period case, the stocks making up the index and the proxy portfolio all went ex-dividend at the end of the period. Like the single-period stock case, dividends will cause the stock index and proxy portfolio to fall on the ex-dividend date by the amount of the dividend. Suppose the dividend value on the ex-dividend date is expected to be equal to 1% of the current value of the index and proxy portfolio. For the index, the dividend would therefore be equal to $D_1 = 12.50$ per index share. At expiration, the two possible call values would be $C_u^x = \text{Max}[(1375 - 12.50) - 1250, 0] = 112.50$ and $C_d^x = \text{Max}[(1187.50 - 12.50 - 1250, 0] = 0$. As noted in the single-period stock option case, for the single-period BOPM, the only adjustment needed in forming the replicating portfolio is to subtract the value of the dividend from the two nondividend-adjusted index prices (uS_0 or dS_0) in computing the call's possible intrinsic values (C_u^x and C_d^x). In terms of our example, the H_0^* and B_0^* values needed to form a replicating portfolio to match the

---

[1] An alternative arbitrage portfolio could be formed by taking a position consisting of one share of the spot portfolio and a proportion of calls (instead of one call and a proportion of the spot portfolio). This portfolio would be easier to adjust each period.

possible call values of $C_u^x = 112.50$ and $C_d^x = 0$ would be 0.6 and \$678.57:

$$H_0^* = \frac{C_u^x - C_d^x}{uS_0 - dS_0} = \frac{112.50 - 0}{1375 - 1187.50} = .6$$

$$B_0^* = \frac{C_u^x(dS_0) - C_d^x(uS_0)}{r_f((uS_0 - dS_0))} = \frac{(112.50)(1187.50) - (0)(1375)}{1.05[1375 - 1187.50]} = 678.57$$

Using the replication approach, the equilibrium call price therefore would be 71.43:

$$C_0^* = H_0^*S_0 - B_0^* = .6(1250) - 678.57 = 71.43$$

$$C_0^* = \frac{1}{r_f}[pC_u^x + (1 - p)C_d^x] = \frac{1}{1.05}[(.6667)(112.50) + (.3333(0)] = 71.43$$

If the market price of the index option did not equal 71.43, then an arbitrage opportunity would exist by taking a position in the option and an opposite position in the replicating portfolio. In this case, a long position in the replicating portfolio would be equivalent to investing \$750 = $(H_0^*S_0^* = (.6)(1250))$ in a proxy index portfolio and borrowing $B_0^* = \$678.57$, with the proxy portfolio consisting of stocks expected to go ex-dividend at the end of the period and with the value of those dividends expected to be \$7.50(= (.01)(\$750); see Exhibit 6.4-1). For example, suppose the market priced the index call at \$79.40 (the BOPM value without the dividend). At $C_0^m = \$79.40$, the call would be overpriced ($C_0^* = \$71.43$). To exploit this, arbitrageurs would go short in the call at \$79.40 and long in the replicating portfolio: invest \$750 in the proxy portfolio and borrow $B_0^* = \$678.57$. This strategy would yield arbitrageurs an initial cash flow of \$7.97 with

EXHIBIT 6.4-1   Values of Call, Proxy Portfolio, and Replicating Portfolio-Single-Period Case

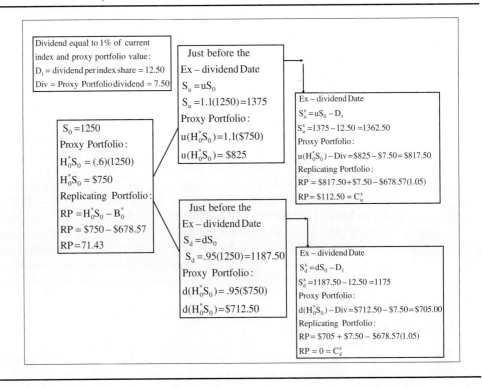

EXHIBIT 6.4-2   Cash Flow at Expiration

	Cash Flow at Expiration	
Closing Position	$S_u^x = 1375 - 12.50 = 1,362.50$ $C_u^x = 112.50$ **Proxy Portfolio:** $u(H_0^* S_0) - \text{Div} = (1.10)(750) - 7.50$ $= 825 - 7.50$ $= 817.50$	$S_d^x = 1,187.50 - 12.50 = 1175$ $C_d^x = 0$ **Proxy Portfolio:** $d(H_0^* S_0) - \text{Div} = (.95)(750) - 7.50$ $= 712.50 - 7.50$ $= 705.00$
Call ($C_T^m = IV$)	−112.50	0
Proxy Portfolio	817.50	705.00
Proxy Portfolio Dividend	7.50	7.50
Debt ($B_0^* r_f = 678.57(1.05)$)	−712.50	−712.50
	0	0

Value of Initial Cash Flow = 7.97(1.05) = 8.37

no liabilities at expiration (see Exhibit 6.4-2):

$$\text{Cash Flow} = C_0^m - (H_0^* S_0 - B_0^*)$$

$$\text{Cash Flow} = 79.40 - ((0.6)(1250) - 678.57) = 7.97$$

In the absence of arbitrage, the price of the European call would therefore be 71.43. Thus, by lowering the price of the stocks that comprise the index portfolio on their ex-dividend dates, dividends decrease the value of the index call. Just the opposite applies to put options.

The single-period binomial case helps to illustrate how arbitrage strategies using an option and a proxy portfolio determine the price of an index option. The practical application of the binomial model to the pricing of index options, though, requires a multiple-period model. As we noted in the case of stock options, in a multiple-period binomial model, the binomial tree fails to recombine when discrete dividend payments are included. This, in turn, causes the number of nodes to increase dramatically as the number of subperiods increase. Fortunately, both the known dividend-payment approach and the Merton continuous dividend-yield approach can be extended to the pricing of index options.

6.4.2.1 Merton Approach

For a stock index that includes many stocks, one could assume that the stocks comprising the index portfolio would pay dividends such that the index portfolio approaches paying dividends continuously during the period. If this were the case, then the Merton continuous dividend-yield approach would be well suited for pricing index options.

To see the application of the Merton model, suppose we want to price S&P 500 index call and put options each with X = 1250 and T = 180 days using a five-period binomial model. In pricing the options, suppose the following:

1. The current S&P 500 is at $S_0 = 1250$.
2. The index's estimated volatility and mean are $\sigma^A = .3$ and $\mu^A = 0$.

3. The annual continuous dividend yield generated from the stocks comprising the index portfolio is $\psi = .04$.

4. $R^A = 6\%$.

Using the Merton model, the dividend-adjusted, risk-neutral probability would be .486927:

$$p = \frac{e^{(R^A - \psi)\Delta t} - d}{u - d}$$

$$p = \frac{e^{(.06 - .04)(.09863)} - .910086}{1.098797 - .910086} = .486927$$

where

$$u = e^{.3\sqrt{.09863}} = 1.098797$$

$$d = 1/u = .910086$$

Exhibit 6.4-3 shows the resulting five-period binomial tree for the underlying index, American and European calls, and American and European puts. For this five-period case, the Merton model prices the American and European calls equally at 113.59. In contrast, the model prices the American put at 103.17 and the European put at 101.56. Unlike the call options, there are early exercise advantages with the put that occur at the two lower

EXHIBIT 6.4-3   Merton's Continuous Dividend-Yield Approach to Valuing Index Options

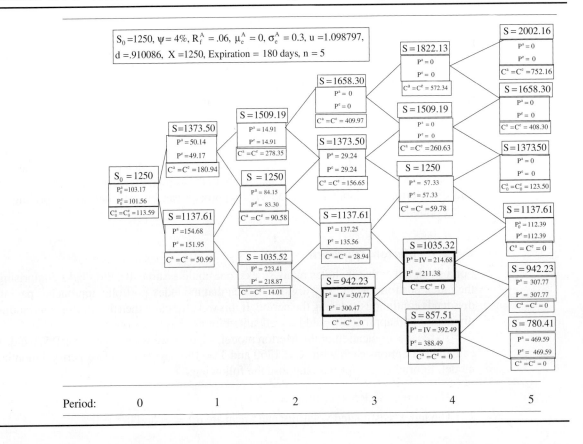

Period: 0   1   2   3   4   5

nodes in Period 4 and the lower node in Period 3. Using the "Binomial Option Pricing Model" Excel program, the prices of the American index call are 107.60 for n = 30 subperiods and 108.19 for n = 100; for the American index put, the prices are 97.26 for n = 30 and 97.68 for n = 100.

Note, in this example the dividend yield was less than the risk-free rate, and there was an early exercise advantage with the put but not the call. This is often the case if the dividend yield is less than the risk-free rate. In general, for the early exercise of an index call to be profitable, the dividend yield has to be relatively large (exceeding at least the risk-free rate). In contrast to index calls, the early exercise of an American put is advantageous if the dividend yield is less than the risk-free rate and the put is deep in the money. Thus, in periods in which dividend yields on stock indices are considerably less than the rates on risk-free securities, there is a greater chance that an American index put could be exercised early and an American index call would not. On one hand, in periods when dividend yields are greater than interest rates, the chance of early exercise is greater for American index calls than puts.

6.4.2.2 Known Dividend-Payment Approach

Even though stock indices such as the S&P 500 have many dividend-paying stocks, the dividend payments from those stocks often are paid discretely and at similar times, exhibiting distinctly seasonal patterns. As a result, the known dividend-payment approach may be more applicable to adjusting the index options for dividends than the Merton approach.

To apply the dividend payment approach, the dividends per index share need to be estimated for each payment period from the stocks making up the index or from the stocks comprising the proxy portfolio. For many indices, dividends per index share can be obtained from several financial information sources. If it is a proxy portfolio, dividend per index share can be determined once one has estimated the index portfolio's future dividends. For example, suppose a $12.5M highly correlated index fund were expected to pay dividends worth $100,000 in 30 days and $200,000 in 120 days. If the current S&P 500 was at 1250, then the proxy portfolio would be the equivalent of 10,000 index shares (= Portfolio Value/S_0 = $12,500,000/\$1250$) priced at $1250 per share, and the dividends per index share would be $10 in 30 days (dividends/index shares = $100,000/10,000 = $10) and $20 in 120 days ($200,000/$10,000 = $20).

Given the estimated dividends per index share, options on the index can be priced using the same approach defined in Section 6.3 for stock options. To see the application, suppose in our previous example ($S_0 = 1250, \sigma^A = .3$ and $\mu^A = 0$, call and put options with X = 1250 and T = 180 days, n = 5, length of the binomial period of $\Delta t = t/n = (180/365)/5 = .098630$, and $R^A = 6\%$), the index portfolio does pay a dividend per index share of $10 in 30 days and $20 in 120 days.

As we showed in the stock example, the first step in valuing the options is to subtract the present value of the dividends from the current index value to obtain a dividend-adjusted index price. In this case, the present value of the dividends is 29.56, and the dividend-adjusted index price is 1,220.44:

$$PV(D) = 10e^{-(.06)(30/365)} + 20e^{-(.06)(120/365)}$$

$$PV(D) = 9.95 + 19.61 = 29.56$$

$$S_0^D = S_0 - PV(D)$$

$$S_0^D = 1250 - 29.56 = 1220.44$$

The second step is to generate the binomial tree starting with the dividend-adjusted stock index. In this case, the parameter values for generating the tree are u = 1.098797, d = 1/u = 0.910086, and p = .507916:

$$u = e^{\sigma^A \sqrt{t/n}} = e^{.3\sqrt{(180/365)/5}} = 1.098797$$

$$d = e^{-\sigma^A \sqrt{t/n}} = e^{-.3\sqrt{(180/365)/5}} = .910086 = 1/u$$

$$p = \frac{r_f - d}{u - d} = \frac{e^{R^A(t/n)} - d}{u - d} = \frac{e^{(.06)((180/365)/5)} - .910086}{1.098797 - .910086} = .507916$$

The top boxes at each node in Exhibit 6.4-4 show the resulting index prices for the five-period tree.

The third step is to add to the index prices at each node the present value of the dividend associated with that period. With the call and put options expiring in 180 days, the length of each period in this example is 180/5 = 36 days. Thus, the nodes of the tree occur at 0, 36, 72, 108, 144, and 180 days from the present. The first dividend occurs in 30 days, so it only affects the node in the present. The second dividend occurs at 120 days; it affects nodes for the present and Periods 1, 2, and 3. The present values of dividends at

EXHIBIT 6.4-4   Known Dividend-Payment Approach to Valuing American Index Options

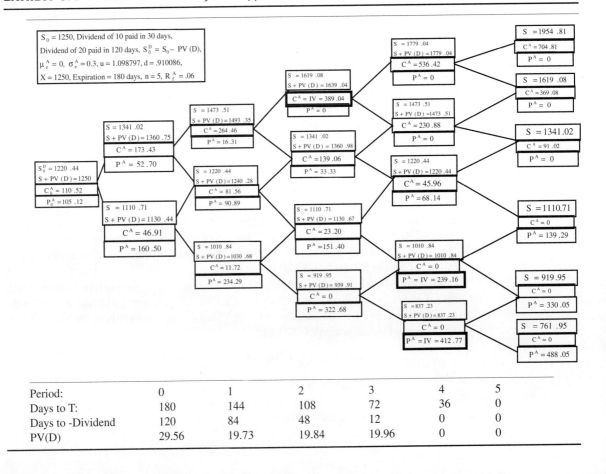

Period:	0	1	2	3	4	5
Days to T:	180	144	108	72	36	0
Days to -Dividend	120	84	48	12	0	0
PV(D)	29.56	19.73	19.84	19.96	0	0

the Periods 1, 2, and 3 are, respectively, 19.73, 19.84, and 19.96:

$$n = 1 : PV(D_1) = De^{-Rt_1^*} = \$20e^{-(.06)((120-36)/365)} = 19.73$$

$$n = 2 : PV(D_2) = De^{-Rt_2^*} = \$20e^{-(.06)((120-72)/365)} = 19.84$$

$$n = 3 : PV(D_3) = De^{-Rt_3^*} = \$20e^{-(.06)((120-108)/365)} = 19.96$$

The second line in the top boxes at each node in Exhibit 6.4-4 shows the index prices adjusted by adding the present value of the dividend to the nondividend-adjusted index prices. Finally, given the binomial tree of dividend-adjusted index prices, the call and put prices are obtained by using the normal recursive method. Because the options are American, the prices are determined at each node as the maximum of the binomial value or the exercising value. The middle boxes at each node in the exhibit shows the binomial call values, and the lower boxes show the binomial put values. Nodes in which there is an early exercise advantage are indicated with wider line boxes. As shown in the exhibit, the price of the American index call is 110.52, with an early exercise advantage occurring at the top node in Period 3. The price of the American put, in turn, is 105.12, with early exercise advantages occurring at the two lower nodes in Period 4. Using the "Known Dividend Payment Binomial Model" Excel program, the price of the American index call is 106.58 and the price of the American index put is 102.01 for n = 100.

6.5 CONCLUSION

A future dividend payment causes the price of the stock to fall on the ex-dividend date by an amount approximately equal to the dividend. This, in turn, leads to a decrease in the price of a call and an increase in the price of a put and may lead to an early exercise of a call just prior to the ex-dividend date and possibly a put on the ex-dividend date. In this chapter, we continued our analysis of the BOPM by showing how to adjust the BOPM for European and American options on stocks paying dividends using the known dividend-payment approach and the Merton continuous dividend-yield approach. Given the dividend-adjusted binomial model, we then showed how the binomial model is adjusted to price options on stock indices. In the next chapter, we conclude our analysis of the binomial model by showing how options on currency and bonds can be valued using the model.

Web Site: Robert C. Merton

Robert C. Merton is currently the John and Natty McArthur University Professor at the Harvard Business School. He received a PhD in Economics from Massachusetts Institute of Technology in 1970. Dr. Merton is past President of the American Finance Association and a member of the National Academy of Sciences. He received the Alfred Nobel Memorial Prize in the Economic Sciences in 1997.
http://www.google.com/search?q=Robert+Merton+Nobel&btng=Go

KEY TERMS

known dividend-payment approach

Merton continuous dividend-yield approach

continuous leakage

discrete leakage

zero leakage

SELECTED REFERENCES

Baily, W., and R. Stulz. "The Pricing of Stock Index Options in a General Equilibrium Model." *Journal of Financial and Quantitative Analysis* 24 (March 1989): 1–12.

Boyle, P. "A Lattice Framework for Option Pricing With Two State Variables." *Journal of Financial and Quantitative Analysis* 23 (March 1988): 1–12.

Chance, D. "Empirical Tests of the Pricing of Index Call Options." *Advances in Futures and Options Research* 1 (1986): 141–166.

Copeland, T. E., and J. F. Weston. F. *Financial Theory and Corporate Policy,* 2nd ed., Reading, MA: Addison-Wesley, 1983: Chapter 5.

Cox, J. C., and M. Rubinstein. *Option Markets.* Englewood Cliffs, NJ: Prentice-Hall, 1985: Chapter 5.

Cox, J. C., and S. A. Ross. "The Valuation of Options for Alternative Stochastic Processes." *Journal of Financial Economics* 3 (1976): 145–166.

Debreu, G. *The Theory of Value.* New York: Wiley, 1959.

Figlewski, S., and B. Gao. "The Adaptive Mesh Model: A New Approach to Efficient Option Pricing." *Journal of Financial Economics*, 53 (1999): 313–51.

Kolb, R. *Futures, Options, and Swaps.* Malden, MA: Blackwell Publishing, 2003: Chapter 16.

Li, A., P. Ritchken, and L. Sankarasubramanian. "Lattice Models for Pricing American Interest Rate Claims," *Journal of Finance*, 50 (June 1995): 719–37.

Merton, R. C., "Theory of Rational Option Pricing." *Bell Journal of Economics and Management Science* 4 (Spring 1973): 141–83.

Perrakis, S., and P. Ryan. "Option Pricing Bounds in Discrete Time." *Journal of Finance* 39 (June 1984): 519–25.

Rubinstein, M. "The Valuation of Uncertain Income Streams and the Pricing of Options." *Bell Journal of Economics* 7 (Autumn 1976): 407–24.

Rubinstein, M., and H. Leland. "Replicating Options With Positions in Stock and Cash." *Financial Analysts Journal* 37 (July–August 1981): 63–71.

PROBLEMS AND QUESTIONS

1. Consider a one-period, two-state case in which XYZ stock is trading at $S_0 = \$35$; is expected to go ex-dividend at the end of the period, with the company expected to pay a dividend worth $0.50 at the ex-dividend date; and the stock has nondividend-adjusted upward and downward parameter values of u of 1.05 and d of 1/1.05. Also assume the period risk-free rate is 2%.

   a. Using the BOPM, determine the equilibrium price of the XYZ 35 European call option.

   b. Using the BOPM, determine the equilibrium price of the XYZ 35 European put option.

   c. Using the put–call parity model, show that the put price is equal to BOPM's put value.

   d. What is the equilibrium price of the call option if it was American and therefore could be exercised just before the expiration date?

   e. Explain what an arbitrageur would do if the market priced the XYZ 35 European call equal to the BOPM's value but failed to factor in the $0.50 dividend. Show what the arbitrageur's cash flow would be at expiration when she closed. Does the arbitrage strategy also apply if the call were American?

   f. Explain what an arbitrageur would do if the market priced the XYZ 35 European put equal to the BOPM's value but failed to factor in the $0.50 dividend. Show what the arbitrageur's cash flow would be at expiration when she closed.

2. Suppose a XYZ stock is trading at $50, its annualized standard deviation is $\sigma^A = .4$, its mean is zero, and the stock will go ex-dividend in 100 days with the value of the dividend worth $2 at that date. Suppose also that there are American call and put options on the stock, both with exercise prices of $50 and expirations of 120 days, and that the simple annual risk-free rate is $R^A = 6\%$. Using a three-period binomial tree, determine the equilibrium prices of the options using the known dividend-payment approach. Using the "Known Dividend-Payment Binomial Model" Excel program, determine the equilibrium prices for the call and put options assuming they are European and American for the following number of subperiods: $n = 30$ and $n = 100$.

3. Suppose XYZ stock in Problem 2 has a continuous annual dividend yield of 10%. Determine the equilibrium prices of the American call and put options in Problem 2 using a three-period binomial tree and the Merton continuous dividend-yield approach. Using the "Binomial Option Pricing Model" Excel program, determine the prices of the options for the following number of subperiods: $n = 10, n = 30$, and $n = 100$.

4. Suppose the spot S&P 500 is currently at 1200, its annualized standard deviation is $\sigma^A = .25$, its mean is zero, and the stocks making up the index will pay dividends worth 1% of the current value 70 days from the present and another payment worth 1% in 160 days. Assume that 70 days and 160 days represent the ex-dividend dates for the index portfolio. Suppose also that there are American call and put options on the S&P 500, both with exercise prices of 1200 and expirations of 180 days, and that the simple annual risk-free rate is $R^A = 6\%$. Using a three-period binomial tree, determine the equilibrium prices of the index options using the known dividend-payment approach. Using the "Known Dividend-Payment Binomial Model" Excel program, determine the equilibrium prices for the call and put options assuming they are European and American for the following number of subperiods: $n = 30$ and $n = 100$.

5. Suppose the S&P 500 index in Problem 4 has a continuous annual dividend yield of 10%. Determine the equilibrium pricing of the American call and put option in Problem 4 using a three-period binomial tree and the Merton continuous dividend-yield approach. Using the "Binomial Option Pricing Model" Excel program, determine the prices of the options for the following number of subperiods: $n = 10, n = 30$, and $n = 100$.

6. The Cody Index Fund is an equity investment fund that is highly correlated with the S&P 500 index. Currently, the fund is worth $500M with the stocks in the portfolio expected to pay total dividends that will be worth 2.5% of the fund's current value in 30 days. The current S&P 500 index is at 1250. Define Cody's index portfolio as an investment in hypothetical shares in the S&P 500. What is the dividend per index share?

7. Assume the following:
   - Current spot S&P 500 index at 1250.
   - Annual risk-free rate $= 6\%$.
   - Dividend per index share equal to 1% of the current value in 30 days.
   - Ex-dividend date on the stocks in the portfolio paying dividends is expected to occur 30 days from the present.
   - Logarithmic return's annualized mean $= \mu^A = .10$.
   - Logarithmic return's annualized standard deviation $= \sigma^A = 0.25$.

Questions:

   a. Using the single-period BOPM, determine the price of a European S&P 500 index call with an exercise price of 1250 and expiring in 30 days.

   b. Define the index call's replicating portfolio in terms of a proxy portfolio.

   c. Show with a binomial tree the values of the spot index, proxy portfolio, and replicating portfolio. Include with your tree the values of the index and proxy portfolio the instant before expiration and on the ex-dividend date. Do the possible values of your replicating portfolio match the possible call values?

   d. Explain what an arbitrageur would do if the index call were priced at 45. Show what the arbitrageur's cash flow at expiration would be at the two possible index prices at expirations.

   e. Explain what an arbitrageur would do if the market priced the European 1250 index call equal to the BOPM's value but failed to factor in the dividend. Show what the arbitrageur's cash flow would be at expiration when she closed.

8. Suppose the call option in Question 7 were American and therefore could be exercised just before the ex-dividend date.

   a. Using the single-period BOPM, determine the equilibrium value of the option.

   b. Define the replicating portfolio underlying the American call option.

   c. Explain the arbitrage strategy that could be implemented if the American call were priced at 55.

9. Given the information in Problem 7:

   a. Use the single-period BOPM to determine the price of a European S&P 500 index put with an exercise price of 1250 and expiring in 30 days.

   b. Show with a binomial tree the values of the spot index, proxy portfolio, and replicating portfolio. Include with your tree the values of the index and proxy portfolio at both the instant before expiration and the ex-dividend date. Do the possible values of your replicating portfolio match the possible put values?

   c. Explain what an arbitrageur would do if the index put were priced at 55. Show in a table that the arbitrage portfolio has no liabilities at expiration given the two possible index prices at expirations.

10. Are the European call and put prices you determined in Problems 7 and 9 call consistent with put–call parity?

WEB EXERCISES

1. On February 16, 2007, there were 100 call and 100 put options on IBM each expiring on July 20. On February 16, IBM's stock closed at 98.99, its historical volatility was .1959 (annualized standard deviation of logarithmic return), and the short-term money market rate was 4.574%.

   a. The table following shows IBES projected dividend stream for IBM for ex-dividend dates from 5/8/07 to 2/9/12. Using the "Known Dividend-Payment Model" Excel program, determine the equilibrium prices for IBM call and put options as of February 16, 2007, for n = 100 subperiods.

Ex-Dividend Date	Projected Dividend	Ex-Dividend Date	Projected Dividend
5/8/07	.289	11/10/09	.327
8/8/07	.289	2/9/10	.327
11/8/07	.289	5/10/10	.344
2/7/08	.289	8/9/10	.344
5/8/08	.312	11/10/10	.344
10/10/08	.312	2/9/11	.344
11/10/08	.312	5/9/11	.361
2/9/09	.312	8/8/11	.361
5/8/09	.327	11/10/11	.361
8/10/09	.327	2/9/12	.361

b. On February 16, 2007, IBM's historical annual dividend yield was 2%. Using the "Binomial Option Pricing Model" Excel program, determine the price of IBM's call and put options using Merton's continuous dividend-yield binomial model.

c. Using IBM's projected dividend stream, price a currently traded call and put option on IBM stock using the "Known Dividend-Payment Model" Excel program. For information on currently traded IBM options, go to www.wsj.com/free.

d. Using IBM's historical dividend yield and volatility or your own estimates, price a currently traded call and put option on IBM using Merton's continuous dividend-yield binomial model. Use the "Binomial Option Pricing Model" Excel program. For information on currently traded IBM options, go to www.wsj.com/free.

2. On January 8, 2007, the S&P 500 call option with an exercise price of 1400 and expiration of June 16, 2007 (158 days), was trading at 66. On that date, the spot S&P 500 index closed at 1412.84, its historical volatility was .13644 (annualized standard deviation of logarithmic return), the index's dividend yield was 1.799%, and the short-term money market rate was 4.778%.

a. Using the "Binomial Option Pricing Model" Excel program, determine the price of the S&P 500 call option using Merton's continuous dividend-yield binomial model. How does the model value compare to the market price?

b. Using the S&P 500's historical dividend yield and volatility or your own estimates, price a currently traded S&P 500 call using Merton's continuous dividend-yield binomial model. Use the "Binomial Option Pricing Model" Excel program. For information on currently traded index options, go to www.wsj.com/free.

CHAPTER 7

THE BINOMIAL PRICING OF OPTIONS ON CURRENCIES AND BONDS

7.1 INTRODUCTION

In this chapter, we continue our analysis of the BOPM by showing how the model can be applied to pricing currency and debt options. The binomial pricing of currency options is very similar to the pricing of options on stocks and stock indices in which there is a continuous dividend yield. As such, Merton's continuous dividend-yield model can be used to price such options. The pricing of options on debt securities depends on interest rate movements. As such, the first step in pricing such options is to generate a binomial tree of interest rates. This tree can then be used to generate a binomial tree of the prices of the debt security from which the value of an option on the security can be determined. We begin by first looking at the how the binomial model is adjusted to price currency options.

7.2 BINOMIAL PRICING OF FOREIGN CURRENCY OPTIONS

Because foreign currency can be invested in interest-bearing foreign securities, the option pricing model for currency options needs to include the foreign interest rate. One way to adjust the binomial model for foreign interest rates is to use the Merton model. In applying the Merton model to currency options, the dollar value of the foreign currency (FC) takes the place of the stock price, and the foreign interest rate (R_F) is treated as the continuous dividend yield (ψ):

$$p = \frac{e^{(R_{US}-R_F)\,\Delta t} - d}{u - d}$$

In Section 6.3, we showed the derivation of the Merton model by solving for the risk-neutral probabilities that included a dividend-adjusted stock price. To see the intuition behind the FC BOPM, let us derive the FC BOPM using the alternative replication approach instead of risk-neutral probability approach.

7.2.1 Single-Period Foreign Currency BOPM

In terms of the BOPM, the equilibrium price of a European currency call option is equal to the value of a replicating portfolio formed by borrowing B_0^* dollars to finance partially the purchase of H_0^* units of foreign currency at an exchange rate E_0(dollar price of the FC, \$/FC), with the currency then invested in a foreign risk-free security for the period. To derive the currency option's replicating portfolio for a single period, assume

(1) The underlying exchange rate can either increase to equal a proportion u times its initial value or decrease to equal d times the initial value.

(2) The call option on the foreign currency is European and expires at the end of the period.

(3) The domestic (U.S.) risk-free security pays a rate of R_{US} for the period, with a terminal value of $r_{US} = (1 + R_{US})$, and the foreign risk-free security pays a rate R_F for the period, with a terminal value of $r_F = (1 + R_F)$.

The first two assumptions suggest the following exchange rate and currency option values:

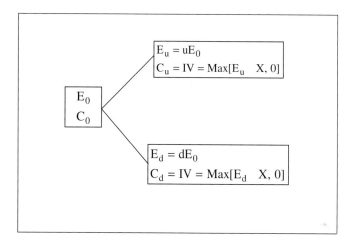

At the end of the period, the replicating portfolio would have a debt obligation of $r_{US} B_0$ dollars, and the foreign investment would be worth $H_0(r_F)$ units of FC, which would be converted to dollars at an exchange rate of either uE_0 or dE_0. Thus, at expiration, the replicating portfolio would have one of the following values:

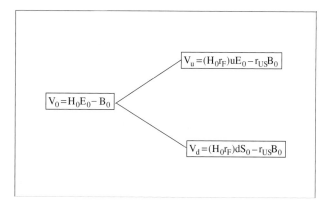

Solving for the H_0^* and B_0^* values in which

$$(H_0 r_F)uE_0 - r_{US} B_0 = C_u$$
$$(H_0 r_F)dE_0 - r_{US} B_0 = C_d$$

(7.2-1)

we obtain

$$H_0^* = \frac{C_u - C_d}{r_F(uE_0 - dE_0)} \qquad (7.2\text{-}2)$$

$$B_0^* = \frac{C_u(dE_0) - C_d(uE_0)}{r_{US}(uE_0 - dE_0)} \qquad (7.2\text{-}3)$$

The equilibrium currency call price is therefore

$$C_0^* = H_0^* E_0 - B_0^* \qquad (7.2\text{-}4)$$

or on substituting Equations (7.2-2) and (7.2-3) into (7.2-4) and rearranging

$$C_0^* = \frac{1}{r_f}[pC_u + (1-p)C_d]$$

where

$$p = \frac{r_{US} - r_F d}{r_F(u - d)}$$

or assuming continuous compounding

$$p = \frac{e^{R_{US}\Delta t} - (e^{R_F\Delta t})d}{e^{R_F\Delta t}(u - d)}$$

Note that if we multiply the right-side of the equation for p by $e^{-RF\Delta t}/e^{-RF\Delta t}$ and rearrange, we obtain the same risk-neutral probability as the Merton model:

$$p = \left(\frac{e^{-R_F\Delta t}}{e^{-R_F\Delta t}}\right) \frac{e^{R_{US}\Delta t} - (e^{R_F\Delta t})d}{e^{R_F\Delta t}(u - d)}$$

$$p = \frac{e^{(R_{US}-R_F)\Delta t} - d}{u - d}$$

Thus, as we should expect, the replication approach is equivalent to the Merton adjustment model.

The replication approach is based on an arbitrage argument. The standard arbitrage strategy used when the market price of the currency option does not equal the BOPM value involves taking opposite positions in the call and the replicating portfolio. For example, suppose u = 1.1, d = .95, R_{US} = .05, R_F = .03, and E_0 = \$1.50/FC. Using the preceding single-period currency BOPM, the equilibrium price of a \$1.50 FC call option expiring at the end of the period would be \$0.066 using the single-period model. As shown in Table 7.2-1, if the market price of the currency call were \$0.075, an arbitrageur could profit by selling the call and going long in the replicating portfolio: borrow B_0^* = \$0.9046, then buy H_0^* = .6472 FC at E_0 = \$1.50/FC, with the FC invested in the foreign risk-free security at R_F = .03. As shown in the table, the arbitrageur would have an initial cash flow \$0.009 and at expiration, would have no liabilities regardless of whether the exchange rate were $E_T = uE_0 = 1.1(\$1.50/FC) = \$1.65/FC$ or $E_T = dE_0 = .95(\$1.50/FC) = \$1.425/FC$.

In contrast, if the currency option were underpriced at \$0.05, an arbitrageur could buy the call and short the replicating portfolio: borrow H_0^* = .6472 FC at foreign rate of R_F = .03, convert at E_0 = \$1.50/FC to \$0.9708, and use the dollars to buy the call and a U.S. risk-free security paying R_{US} = .05. Table 7.2-2 shows that the arbitrageur would earn an initial cash flow of \$0.016, with no liabilities at expiration from implementing this strategy.

TABLE 7.2-1 Single-Period Overpriced Arbitrage Strategy

$u = 1.1, d = 0.95, R_{US} = .05, R_F = .03, E_0 = \$1.50/FC, X = \$1.50/FC,$

$C_u = Max[uE_0 - X,0] = \$0.15, C_d = Max[dE_0 - X,0] = 0,$

$H_0^* = [C_u - C_d]/[E_0 r_F(u - d)] = [\$0.15 - 0]/[\$1.50(1.03)(1.1 - .95] = .6472,$

$B_0^* = \dfrac{[C_u(dE_0) - C_d(uE_0)]}{r_{US} E_0(u - d)} = \dfrac{[\$0.15(.95)(\$1.50) - 0(1.1)(\$1.50)]}{(1.05)(\$1.50)(1.1 - .95)} = \$0.9046,$

$C_0^* = H_0^* E_0 - B_0^* = .6472(\$1.50) - \$0.9046 = \$0.066,$

$C_0^m = \$0.075$

Strategy	Cash Flow
Purchase H_0^* units of foreign currency at E_0 with the FC invested in foreign security: $H_0^* E_0 = .6472(\$1.50)$	−$0.9708
Borrow B_0^* dollar: $B_0^* = \$0.9046$	0.9046
Sell call: $C_0^m = \$.075$	0.075
Initial Cash Flow	$0.009

	End-of-the-Period Cash Flow	
Closing Position	$E_u = 1.1(\$1.50/FC)$ $E_u = \$1.65/FC$ $C_u = \$0.15$	$E_d = .95(\$1.50/FC)$ $E_d = \$1.425/FC$ $C_d = 0$
Convert $H_0^*(r_F)$ FC to dollars at E_T: E_T (.6472)(1.03)FC	$1.10	$0.95
Repay debt: $-r_{US}B_0^* =$ (1.05)(−$.9046)	−0.95	−0.95
Purchase call: C_T	−0.15	0
Cash Flow	0	0

Value of Initial Cash Flow = ($.009)(1.05) = $0.00945

7.2.2 Multiple-Period Foreign Currency BOPM

For multiple periods, the BOPM for currency options is derived using the same recursive methodology used to derive the BOPM for stock options. An example of a two-period model is shown in Exhibit 7.2-1 in which the previous $1.50 currency call is priced assuming the same parameter values used in the preceding single-period example. In the multiple-period model, the same arbitrage strategies and multiple-period readjustment rules described in Chapter 5 for mispriced stock options apply here for currency call options. Also, the BOPM for currency puts is the same as the BOPM for stock options described in Chapter 5 except for the inclusion of the foreign interest rate.

In describing the BOPM for currency options, two points should be kept in mind. First, the methodology for estimating u and d that was delineated in Chapter 5 also can be used to estimate the u and d values for the spot exchange rate by estimating the mean and variance of the exchange rate's logarithmic return ($\ln(E_t/E_{t-1})$). Second, the currency BOPM and its underlying arbitrage strategy can alternatively be defined in terms of foreign currency futures or forward contract positions instead of the spot exchange rate and foreign security positions. Managing an arbitrage strategy with futures, in turn, is much simpler than one involving spot positions. The BOPM derived in terms of currency futures is examined in Appendix 11B.

7.2.3 Example of Pricing FC Options

To see the application of the FC BOPM, suppose we want to price call and put options on the British pound (BP) each with X = $1.60/BP and T = 180 days using a five-period

TABLE 7.2-2   Single-Period Underpriced Arbitrage Strategy

$u = 1.1, d = 0.95, R_{US} = .05, R_F = .03, E_0 = \$1.50/FC, X = \$1.50/FC,$

$C_u = Max[uE_0 - X,0] = \$0.15, C_d = Max[dE_0 - X,0] = 0,$

$H_0^* = [C_u - C_d]/[E_0 r_F(u - d)] = [\$0.15 - 0]/ [\$1.50(1.03)(1.1 - .95)] = .6472,$

$B_0^* = \dfrac{[C_u(dE_0) - C_d(uE_0)]}{r_{US} E_0(u - d)} = \dfrac{(\$0.15)[(.95)(\$1.50)] - (0)[(1.1)(\$1.50)]}{(1.05)(\$1.50)(1.1 - .95)} = \$0.9046,$

$C_0^* = H_0^* E_0 - B_0^* = .6472(\$1.50) - \$0.9046 = \$0.066,$

$C_0^m = \$0.050$

Strategy	Cash Flow
Borrow H_0^* units of Foreign Currency and convert to dollars at E_0: $H_0^* E_0 = .6472(\$1.50)$	$0.9708
Invest B_0^* dollar in domestic risk-free security: $B_0^* = \$.9046$	−0.9046
Buy call: $C_0^m = \$.05$	−0.05
Initial Cash Flow	0.016

	End-of-the-Period Cash Flow	
Closing Position	$E_u = 1.1(\$1.50/FC)$ $E_u = \$1.65/FC$ $C_u = \$0.15$	$E_d = .95(\$1.50/FC)$ $E_d = \$1.425/FC$ $C_d = 0$
Repay foreign debt: $E_T(H_0^*(r_F)) = E_T$ $(.6472)(1.03)FC$	−$1.10	−$0.95
Investment return: $B_0^* r_{US} =$ $(1.05)(\$0.9046)$	0.95	0.95
Call sale: C_T	0.15	0
Cash Flow	0	0

Value of Initial Cash Flow = ($.016)(1.05) = $0.0168

binomial model. In pricing the options, suppose the following:

1. The spot \$/BP exchange rate is at $E_0 = \$1.60/BP$
2. The estimated volatility and mean are $\sigma^A = .3$ and $\mu^A = 0$
3. The annual U.S. risk-free rate is $R_{US} = .06$
4. The annual risk-free rate paid on BP is $R_F = .08$

The risk-neutral probability in this case would be .466021:

$$p = \frac{e^{(R_{US}-R_F)\,\Delta t} - d}{u - d}$$

$$p = \frac{e^{(.06-.08)((180/365)/5)} - .910086}{1.098797 - .910086} = .466021$$

where

$$u = e^{.3\sqrt{(180/165)/5}} = 1.098797$$

$$d = 1/u = .910086$$

Exhibit 7.2-2 shows the resulting five-period binomial tree for the spot exchange rate, American and European calls, and American and European puts. For this five-period case, the FC BOPM prices the American call at $0.1311, with early exercise advantages occurring at the top node in Period 3 and the top two nodes in Period 4. The price of the

EXHIBIT 7.2-1   Two-Period BOPM for Currency Call Option

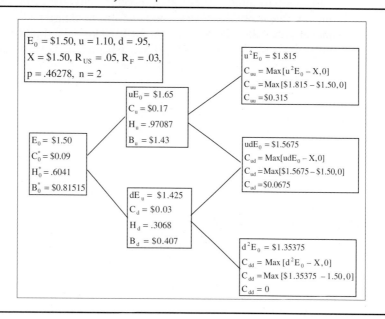

EXHIBIT 7.2-2   Five-Period BOPM for Currency Option

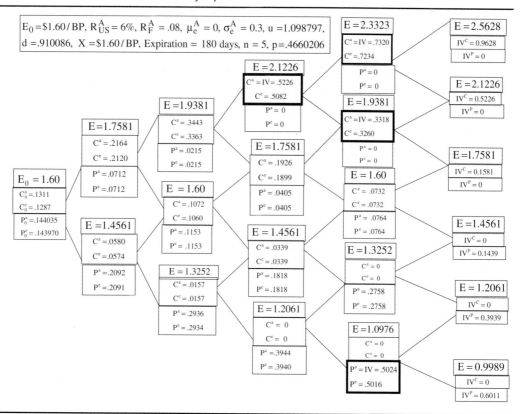

European call, in turn, is priced less at $0.1287. In general, early exercise of an American currency call option is more likely to occur if the call is in the money, $R_F > R_{US}$, the foreign interest rate is relatively large, and the time to expiration small. In contrast, the binomial model prices the American put at $0.144035, only slightly more than the European put value of $0.14397. The minor difference in price is due to a small early exercise advantage on the American put in Period 4 at the lowest node. For American currency puts, early exercise is more likely to occur if $R_{US} > R_F$, the foreign rate is relatively low, and the put is deep in the money.

Using the "Binomial Option Pricing Model" Excel program, the prices of the American BP call are $0.1237 for n = 30 subperiods and $0.1242 for n = 100; and for the European call, the prices are $0.1211 for n = 30 and $0.1219 for n = 100. For the American BP put, the prices are $0.1365 for n = 30 and $0.1372 for n = 100; and for the European put, the prices are $0.1364 for n = 30 and $0.1371 for n = 100.

7.3   PRICING OTC TREASURY-BOND OPTIONS[1]

Determining the value a call or put option on a bond requires estimating the value of the bond over time. One model that can be used to price bonds over time, as well as determine the values of call and put options on the bond, is the **binomial interest rate tree**. Patterned after the binomial option pricing model, this model assumes that **spot rates** follow a binomial process.

7.3.1   Spot Rates and Equilibrium Bond Prices

A spot rate is the rate on a zero-coupon bond. Given different spot rates on similar bonds with different maturities, the equilibrium price of a bond is the value obtained by discounting a bond's cash flows, CFs, by appropriate spot rates for that period (S_t). Theoretically, if the market does not price a bond with spot rates, arbitrageurs would be able to realize a risk-free return by buying the bond and stripping it into a number of zero-coupon bonds or by buying strip bonds and bundling them into a coupon bond to sell. Thus, in the absence of arbitrage, the **equilibrium price** of a bond is determined by discounting each of its CFs by their appropriate spot rates.

To illustrate this relationship, suppose there are three risk-free zero-coupon bonds, each with principals of $100 and trading at annualized spot rates of $S_1 = 7\%$, $S_2 = 8\%$, and $S_3 = 9\%$, respectively. If we discount the CF of a 3-year, 8% annual coupon bond paying a principal of $100 at maturity at these spot rates, its equilibrium price, B_0^*, would be $97.73:

$$B_0^* = \frac{C_1}{(1 + S_1)^1} + \frac{C_2}{(1 + S_2)^2} + \frac{C_3 + F}{(1 + S_3)^3}$$

$$B_0^* = \frac{\$8}{(1.07)^1} + \frac{\$8}{(1.08)^2} + \frac{\$108}{(1.09)^3} = \$97.73$$

Suppose this coupon bond were trading in the market at a price (B_0^M) of $95.03 to yield 10%:

$$B_0^M = \sum_{t=1}^{3} \frac{\$8}{(1.10)^t} + \frac{\$100}{(1.10)^3} = \$95.03$$

---

[1] This section requires some knowledge of fixed-income securities. See Supplemental Appendix C at the end of the text for an overview of fixed-income security analysis.

EXHIBIT 7.3-1 Equilibrium Bond Price: Arbitrage When Bond Is Undervalued

Market price of 3-year, 8% coupon bond = 95.03

Arbitrage:

Buy the bond for 95.03

Sell three stripped Zero-Coupon Bond (ZCB):

$$1-\text{year ZCB with } F = 8 : P_0 = \frac{8}{1.07} = 7.4766$$

$$2-\text{year ZCB with } F = 8 : P_0 = \frac{8}{(1.08)^2} = 6.8587$$

$$3-\text{year ZCB with } F = 108 : P_0 = \frac{108}{(1.09)^3} = 83.3958$$

Sale of stripped bonds = \$97.73

$\pi = 97.73 - 95.03 = 2.70$

At the price of \$95.03, an arbitrageur could buy the bond and then strip it into three risk-free zero-coupon bonds: 1-year, zero-coupon bond paying \$8 at maturity; a 1-year, zero-coupon bond paying \$8 at maturity; and a 1-year, zero-coupon bond paying \$108 at maturity. If the arbitrageur could sell the bonds at their appropriate spot rates, she would be able to realize a cash flow from the sale of 97.73 and a risk-free profit of \$2.70 (see Exhibit 7.3-1). Given this risk-free opportunity, this arbitrageur, as well as others, would implement this strategy of buying and stripping the bond until the price of the coupon bond was bid up to equal its equilibrium price of \$97.73.

On the other hand, if the 8% coupon bond were trading above its equilibrium price of \$97.73, then arbitrageurs could profit by reversing the preceding strategy. For example, if the coupon bond were trading at \$100, then arbitrageurs would be able to go into the market and buy proportions (assuming perfect divisibility) of the three risk-free, zero-coupon bonds (8% of Bond 1, 8% of Bond 2, and 108% of Bond 3) at a cost of \$97.73 and bundle them into one 3-year, 8% coupon bond to be sold at \$100. This strategy would, in turn, result in a risk-free profit of \$2.27. Thus, in the absence of arbitrage, the equilibrium price of a bond is the price obtained by discounting the bond's CFs by their appropriate spot rates.

7.3.2 Binomial Interest Rate Model

A binomial model of interest rates assumes a spot rate of a given maturity follows a binomial process in which in each period, it has either a higher or lower rate. To illustrate, suppose the current one-period spot rate (S) is 10%, the upward parameter u is 1.1, and the downward parameter d is .95. As shown in Exhibit 7.3-2, the two possible one-period rates after one period are 11% and 9.5%; the three possible one-period rates after two periods are 12.1%, 10.45%, and 9.025%; and the four possible rates after three periods are 13.31%, 11.495%, 9.927%, and 8.574%.

Given the possible one-period spot rates, suppose we wanted to value a bond that matures in three periods. Assume that the bond has no default risk or embedded option features and that it pays a 9% coupon each period and a \$100 principal at maturity. Because there is no default or call risk, the only risk an investor assumes in buying this bond is interest rate risk (changes in interest rate that change the value of the bond). In this case,

EXHIBIT 7.3-2   Binomial Tree of Spot Rates:

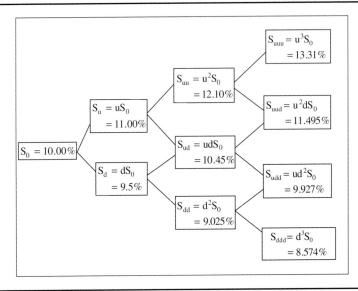

interest-rate risk exists in two periods: Period 3 when there are three possible spot rates, and Period 2 when there are two possible rates. To value the bond, we first determine the three possible values of the bond in Period 2 given the three possible spot rates and the bond's certain cash flow next period (maturity). As shown in Exhibit 7.3-3, the three possible values in Period 2 are $B_{uu} = 109/1.121 = 97.2346$, $B_{ud} = 109/1.1045 = 98.6872$, and $B_{dd} = 109/1.09025 = 99.9771$. Given these values, we next roll the tree to the first period and determine the two possible values there. Note that in this period, the values are equal to the present values of the expected cash flows in Period 2. If we assume there is an equal probability of the spot rate increasing or decreasing in one period (q = .5), then the two possible values in Period 1 would be 97.3612 and 98.9335:

$$B_u = \frac{.5[97.2346 + 9] + .5[98.6872 + 9]}{1.11} = 96.3612$$

$$B_d = \frac{.5[98.6872 + 9] + .5[99.9771 + 9]}{1.095} = 98.9335$$

Finally, using the bond values in Period 1, we roll the tree to the current period in which we determine the value of the bond to be 96.9521:

$$B_0 = \frac{.5[96.3612 + 9] + .5[98.9335 + 9]}{1.10} = 96.9521$$

7.3.3   Valuing T-Bond Options With a Binomial Tree

A T-bond underlying an OTC T-bond option is often a specified bond. As a result, the first step in valuing such an option is to determine the values of the specified T-bond at the various nodes on the binomial tree as we just did in the preceding case. As an example, consider an OTC option on a T-bond with a 6% annual coupon, face value of $100, and 3 years left to maturity. In valuing the bond, suppose we have a two-period binomial tree of risk-free spot rates, with the length of each period being year, the estimated upward and

EXHIBIT 7.3-3 Value of Three-Period Bond: u = 1.1, d =.95, S_0 = .10

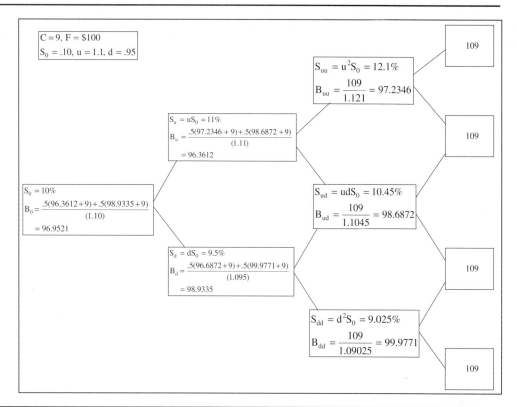

downward parameters being u = 1.2 and d = .8333, and the current spot rate being 6% (see Exhibit 7.3-4). To value the T-bond, we start at the bond's maturity (end of Period 3) when the bond's value is equal to the principal plus the coupon, 106. We next determine the three possible values in Period 2 given the three possible spot rates. As shown in the exhibit, the three possible values of the T-bond in Period 2 are 97.57 (= 106/1.084), 100 (= 106/1.06), and 101.760 (= 106/1.0416667). Given these values, we next roll the tree to the first period and determine the two possible values. The values in that period are equal to the present values of the T-bond's expected cash flows in Period 2; that is

$$B_u = \frac{.5[97.57 + 6] + .5[100 + 6]}{1.072} = 97.747$$

$$B_d = \frac{.5[100 + 6] + .5[101.760 + 6]}{1.05} = 101.79$$

Finally, using the bond values in Period 1, we roll the tree to the current period in which we determine the value of the T-bond to be 99.78:

$$B_0 = \frac{.5[97.747 + 6] + .5[101.79 + 6]}{1.06} = 99.78$$

Given the T-bond values in terms of the tree, the values of call and put options on the bond can be determined using the normal recursive process in which we start at expiration when the options are equal to their IVs and then roll the tree to the present. For example, suppose there is a European call on the T-bond, with the call having an exercise price of

EXHIBIT 7.3-4　Binomial Tree: Spot Rates and T-Bond Prices

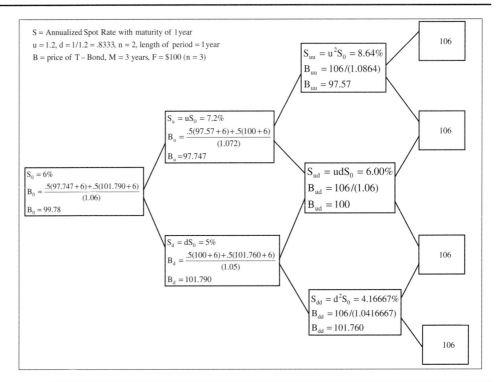

98 and expiration of 2 years. At the option's expiration, the underlying T-bond has three possible values: 97.57, 100, and 101.76. The 98 T-bond call's respective IVs are therefore 0, 2, and 3.76 (see Exhibit 7.3-5). Given these values, the call's possible values in Period 1 are .9328 (= (.5(0) + .5(2))/1.072) and 2.743 (= (.5(2) + .5(3.76))/1.05). Rolling these values to the current period, we obtain the price on the European T-bond call of 1.734 (= (.5(.9328) + .5(2.743))/1.06). If the call option were American, then its value at each node is the greater of the value of holding the call or the value from exercising. This valuation requires constraining the American price to be the maximum of the binomial value or its IV. In this example, if the T-bond option were American, then in Period 1, the option's price would be equal to its IV of 3.79 at the lower rate. Rolling this price and the upper rate's price of .9328 to the current period yields a price of 2.228.

A European put on the T-bond with similar terms as the call is valued using the same recursive process. In the case, given the bond's possible prices at expiration of 97.57, 100, and 101.76, the corresponding IVs of the put would be 0.43, 0, and 0, respectively. In Period 1, the put's two possible values would be .2006 (= (.5(.43) + .5(0))/1.072) and 0. Rolling these values to the current period yields a price on the European put of .0946 (= (.5(.2006) + .5(0))/1.06). Note, that if the put were American, then its possible prices in Period 1 would be .253 and 0, and it current price would be .119 (= (.5(.253) + .5(0))/1.06).

7.3.4　Estimating the Binomial Interest Rate Tree

7.3.4.1　Subdividing the Tree

As we have previously emphasized, the binomial model is more realistic when we subdivide the periods to maturity into a number of subperiods. To subdivide a binomial tree of

EXHIBIT 7.3-5   Binomial Tree: T-Bond Call Prices

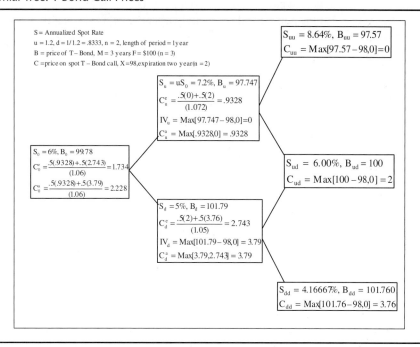

spot rates, let

> h = length of the period in years.
>
> n = number of periods of length h defining the maturity of the bond,
>
> where n = (maturity in years)/h.

Thus, a 3-year bond evaluated over quarterly periods (h = 1/4 of a year) would have a maturity of n = (3 years)/(1/4 years) = 12 periods and would require a binomial interest rates tree with n − 1 = 12 − 1 = 11 periods. If the spot rate and coupon are quoted on an annual basis, then the rates would have to be divided by 4, and the u and d parameters would have to reflect periods of length 1/4. To evaluate the bond over monthly periods (h = 1/12 of a year), the bond's maturity would be n = (3 years)/(1/12 years) = 36 periods and would require a 35-period binomial tree of spot rates, and the coupons (or accrued interests) and spot rates should reflect monthly periods.

7.3.4.2 Estimating the u and d Parameters

There are two general approaches to estimating binomial interest rate trees. The first (models derived by Rendleman and Bartter (1980) and Cox, Ingersoll, and Ross (1979)) is to estimate the u and d parameters based on the mean and variance of the spot rate's logarithmic return. Similar to estimating the u and d values for stock, indices, and currency, the estimating formula for u and d are obtained by solving for the u and d values that make the expected value and the variance of the binomial distribution of the logarithmic return of spot rates equal to their respective estimated parameter values:

$$u = e^{\sqrt{V_e/n} + \mu_e/n}$$

$$d = e^{-\sqrt{V_e/n} + \mu_e/n}$$

where μ_e and V_e = the estimated mean and variance of the logarithmic return of spot rates for a period equal in length to n periods.

If the annualized mean and variance are used, then they must be multiplied by h:

$$u = e^{\sqrt{hV_e^A} + h\mu_e^A}$$

$$d = e^{-\sqrt{hV_e^A} + h\mu_e^A}.$$

If the annualized mean and variance of the logarithmic return of 1-year spot rates were .044 and .0108, and we wanted to evaluate a 3-year bond with 6-month periods (h = 0.5), then we would use a six-period tree to value the bond (n = (3 years)/(1/2) = 6 periods), and u and d would be 1.1 and .95:

$$u = e^{\sqrt{(1/2).0108} + (1/2).044} = 1.1$$

$$d = e^{-\sqrt{(1/2).0108} + (1/2).044} = .95$$

If we make the length of the period monthly (h = 1/12), then we would value the 3-year bond with a 36-period tree, and u and d would be equal to 1.03424 and .9740:

$$u = e^{\sqrt{(1/12).0108} + (1/12).044} = 1.03424$$

$$d = e^{-\sqrt{(1/12).0108} + (1/12).044} = .9740$$

A binomial interest rates tree generated using the u and d estimation approach is constrained to have an end-of-the-period distribution with a mean and variance that matches the analyst's estimated mean and variance. The tree is not constrained, however, to yield a bond price that matches its equilibrium value. As a result, analysts using such models need to make additional assumptions about the risk premium to explain the bond's equilibrium price. In contrast, the second approach to generating a binomial interest rate tree (models derived by Black, Derman, and Toy (1990), Ho and Lee (1986), and Heath, Jarrow, and Morton (1992)) is to calibrate the binomial tree to the current spot yield curve. This *calibration model*, in turn, generates a binomial tree of spot rates that will price bonds equal to their equilibrium values.

7.3.4.3   Calibration Model

The calibration model generates a binomial tree by first finding spot rates that satisfy a variability condition between the upper and lower spot rates. Given the variability relation, the model then solves for the lower spot rate that satisfies a price condition in which the bond value obtained from the tree is consistent with the equilibrium bond price given current spot rates.

7.3.4.4   Variability Condition

The variability condition defines the relationship between the upper and lower spot rates. The condition is

$$S_u = S_d e^{2\sqrt{V_e/n}}$$

This variability condition is derived directly from the estimating formulas for u and d. That is, from the binomial process, we know

$$S_u = uS_0$$

$$S_d = dS_0$$

Therefore

$$\frac{S_u}{u} = S_0 = \frac{S_d}{d}$$

$$S_u = S_d \frac{u}{d}$$

Substituting the equations for u and d, we obtain

$$S_u = S_d \frac{e^{\sqrt{V_e/n} + \mu_e/n}}{e^{-\sqrt{V_e/n} + \mu_e/n}} = S_d e^{2\sqrt{V_e/n}}$$

or in terms of the annualized variance

$$S_u = S_d e^{2\sqrt{h V_e^A}}$$

Thus, given a lower rate of 9.5% and an annualized variance of .0054, the upper rate for a one-period binomial tree of length 1 year (h = 1) would be 11%:

$$S_u = 9.5\% e^{2\sqrt{.0054}} = .11$$

If the current 1-year spot rate were 10%, then these upper and lower rates would be consistent with the upward and downward parameters of u = 1.1 and d = .95. This variability condition would therefore result in a binomial tree identical to the one shown in Exhibit 7.3-2.

7.3.4.5 Price Condition

In addition to the variability relation between upper and lower spot rates, the calibration model also requires that the binomial tree be consistent with the current yield curve's spot rates. This is done by solving for a lower spot rate such that the tree has prices on bonds that are equal to the equilibrium bond prices. To see this, suppose the current market yield curve of spot rates has 1-, 2-, and 3-year spot rates of $S_1^m = 10\%$, $S_2^m = 10.12238\%$, and $S_3^m = 10.24488\%$, respectively, and that the estimated annualized variance is .0054. To satisfy the price condition, we first generate a one-period binomial interest rate tree that will price a 2-year, zero-coupon bond with a face value of $1 equal to its equilibrium price of $B_0^M = .8246$:

$$B_0^M = \frac{1}{(1 + S_2^m)^2} = \frac{1}{(1.1012238)^2} = .8246$$

Using an iterative (trial and error) approach, we find that a lower rate of $S_d = 9.5\%$ yields a binomial bond value that is equal to the equilibrium price of the 2-year bond of .8246 (see Exhibit 7.3-6). Thus, at $S_d = 9.5\%$, we have a binomial tree of 1-year spot rates of $S_u = 11\%$ and $S_d = 9.5\%$ that simultaneously satisfies our variability condition and price condition.[2]

---

[2] It should be noted that the lower rate of 9.5% represents a decline from the current rate of 10%, which is what we tend to expect in a binomial process. This is because we have calibrated the binomial tree to a relatively flat yield curve. If we had calibrated the tree to a positively sloped yield curve, then it is possible that both rates next period could be greater than the current rate.

EXHIBIT 7.3-6   Calibration of Binomial Tree to Two-Period, Zero-Coupon Bond With F = 1

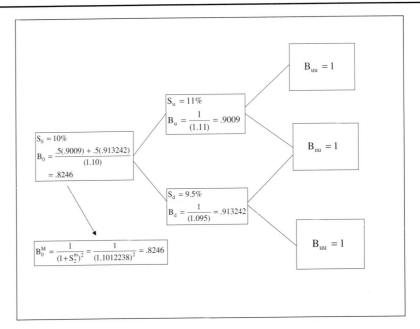

Given the 1-year spot rates after one period of 9.5% and 11%, we next move to the second period and determine the tree's three possible spot rates using a similar methodology. The variability condition follows the same form as the one period, that is

$$S_{ud} = S_{dd}e^{2\sqrt{hV_e^A}}$$

$$S_{uu} = S_{ud}e^{2\sqrt{hV_e^A}} = S_{dd}e^{4\sqrt{hV_e^A}}$$

Similarly, the price condition requires that the binomial value of a 3-year, zero-coupon bond be equal to the equilibrium price. Analogous to the one-period case, this condition is found by solving for the lower rate S_{dd} that, along with the preceding variability conditions and the rates for S_u and S_d obtained previously, yields a value for a 3-year, zero-coupon bond that is equal to the price on a 3-year, zero-coupon bond yielding 10.24488%. Using again an iterative approach, we find that a lower rate of $S_{dd} = 9.025\%$ yields a binomial value that is equal to the equilibrium price of the 3-year bond of .7463 (see Exhibit 7.3-7).

The two-period binomial tree is obtained by combining the upper and lower rates found for the first period with the three rates found for the second period (see Exhibit 7.3-8). This yields a tree that is consistent with the estimated variability condition and with the current term structure of spot rates. To grow the tree, we continue with this same process. For example, to obtain the four rates in Period 3, we solve for the S_{ddd} that along with the spot rates found previously for Periods 1 and 2 and the variability relations yields a value for a 4-year, zero-coupon bond that is equal to the equilibrium price.

Note that one of the features of using a calibrated tree to determine bond values is that the tree will yield prices that are equal to the bond's equilibrium price, that is, the price obtained by discounting cash flows by spot rates. For example, the value of a 3-year, 9%, option-free bond using the tree we just derived is 96.9521 (this is the illustrative example Exhibit 7.3-3). This value is also equal to the equilibrium bond price obtained

EXHIBIT 7.3-7   Calibration of Binomial Tree to Three-Period, Zero-Coupon Bond With F = 1

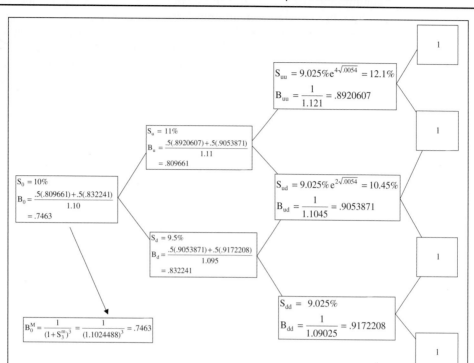

EXHIBIT 7.3-8   Calibrated Binomial Interest Rate Tree

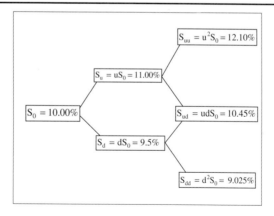

by discounting the bond's periodic cash flows at the spot rates of 10%, 10.12238%, and 10.24488%:

$$B_3^M = \frac{9}{1.10} + \frac{9}{(1.1012238)^2} + \frac{109}{(1.1024488)^3} = 96.9521$$

This feature should not be too surprising because we derived the tree by calibrating it to current spot rates. Nevertheless, one of the features of the calibrated tree is that it yields values on option-free bonds that are equal to the bond's equilibrium price. Recall, a bond's equilibrium price is an arbitrage-free price. That is, if the market does not price the bond at its equilibrium value, then arbitrageurs would be able to realize a riskless return either by buying the bond, stripping it into a number of zero discount bonds and selling them or by buying a portfolio of zero discount bonds, bundling them into a coupon bond, and selling it. Thus, one of the important features of the calibration model is that it yields prices on option-free bonds that are arbitrage free. Given this feature, the calibration model is a practical model for generating a binomial tree of spot rates for determining the value of options on bonds or, as we examine in Chapter 21, bonds with embedded options.

7.4   CONCLUSION

In this chapter, we examined how the binomial model is adjusted to price currency options. We then showed how options on bonds can be valued using a binomial tree of spot rates and how that tree can be estimated using the standard u and d estimation approach or the calibration model. In the next chapter, we turn our attention to the Black–Scholes OPM. As we see, this model is simpler to use (although more complicated to derive) and under certain assumptions, yields the same values as the BOPM.

KEY TERMS

spot rates	binomial interest rate tree
equilibrium bond price	calibration model

SELECTED REFERENCES

Biger, N., and J. Hull. "The Valuation of Currency Options." *Financial Management* (Spring 1983): 24–29.

Black, F., E. Derman, and W. Toy. "A One-Factor Model of Interest Rates and Its Application to Treasury Bond Options." *Financial Analysts Journal* (January/February 1990): 33–39.

Black, F., E. Derman, W. Toy, and J. C. Francis. "Using a One-Factor Model to Value Interest Rate-Sensitive Securities: With an Application to Treasury Bond Options." In *The Handbook of Interest Rate Risk Management,* edited by J. C. Francis and A. S. Wolf. New York: Irwin Professional Publishing, 1994.

Black, F., and P. Karasinski. "Bond and Option Pricing When Short Rates Are Lognormal." *Financial Analysts Journal* 47, no. 4 (1991): 52–59.

Bodurtha, J., and G. Courtadon. "Efficiency Tests of the Foreign Currency Options Market." *Journal of Finance* 41 (March 1986): 151–162.

Bodurtha, J., and G. Courtadon. "Tests of an American Option Pricing Model on the Foreign Currency Options Market." *Journal of Financial and Quantitative Analysis* 22 (June 1987): 153–167.

Borensztein, E., and M. Dooley. "Options of Foreign Exchange and Exchange Rate Expectations." *International Monetary Fund Staff Papers* 34 (December 1987): 643–680.

Boyle, P. "A Lattice Framework for Option Pricing With Two State Variables." *Journal of Financial and Quantitative Analysis* 23 (March 1988): 1–12.

Feiger, G., and B. Jacquillat. "Currency Option Bonds, Puts and Calls on Spot Exchange, and the Hedging of Contingent Foreign Earnings." *Journal of Finance* 5 (December 1979): 1129–1139.

Heath, D., R. Jarrow, and A. Morton. "Bond Pricing and the Term Structure of Interest Rates: A Discrete Time Approximation." *Journal of Financial and Quantitative Analysis* 25 (December 1990): 419–40.

Heath, D., R. Jarrow, and A. Morton. "Bond Pricing and the Term Structure of the Interest Rates: A New Methodology." *Econometrica* 60 (1992): 77–105.

Ho, T. S. Y., and S. B. Lee. "Term Structure Movements and Pricing Interest Rate Contingent Claims." *Journal of Finance* 41 (December 1986): 1011–29.

Ho, T. S., R. S. Stapleton, and M. G. Subrahmanyam. "The Valuation of American Options with Stochastic Interest Rates: A Generalization of the Geske–Johnson Technique." *Journal of Finance* 52 (June 1997): 827–40.

Johnson, L. "Foreign Currency Options, Ex Ante Exchange Rate Volatility, and Market Efficiency: an Empirical Test." *The Financial Review* (November 1986): 433–450.

Johnson, R. S., R. Zuber, and D. Loy. "An Investigation into Currency Options." *International Review of Economics and Business* (October–November 1986): 1077–1093.

Johnson, R. S. *Bond Evaluation, Selection, and Management.* Malden, MA: Blackwell Publishing, 2004: Chapters 9 and 10.

Kolb, R. *Futures, Options, and Swaps.* Malden, MA: Blackwell Publishing, 2003: Chapter 16.

Li, A., P. Ritchken, and L. Sankarasubramanian, "Lattice Models for Pricing American Interest Rate Claims," *Journal of Finance* 50 (June 1995): 719–37.

Longstaff, F. A., and E. S. Schwartz, "Interest Rate Volatility and the Term Structure." *Journal of Financial Economics* 5 (1977): 177–88.

Madura, J., and T. Veit. "Use of Currency Options in International Cash Management." *Journal of Cash Management* (January–February 1986): 42–48.

Merton, R. C., "Theory of Rational Option Pricing." *Bell Journal of Economics and Management Science* 4 (Spring 1973): 141–83.

Perrakis, S., and P. Ryan. "Option Pricing Bounds in Discrete Time." *Journal of Finance* 39 (June 1984): 519–25.

Rendleman, R J., Jr., and B. J. Bartter. "The Pricing of Options on Debt Securities." *Journal of Financial and Quantitative Analysis* XV (1980): 11–24.

Ritchken, P. "On Option Pricing Bounds." *Journal of Finance* 40 (September 1985): 1218–29.

Ritchken, P. "Options: Theory, Strategy, and Applications." Glenview, IL: Scott, Foresman, 1987: Chapters 8–10.

Rubinstein, M. "The Valuation of Uncertain Income Streams and the Pricing of Options." *Bell Journal of Economics* 7 (Autumn 1976): 407–24.

Rubinstein, M., and H. Leland. "Replicating Options With Positions in Stock and Cash." *Financial Analysts Journal* 37 (July–August 1981): 63–71.

Shastri, K., and K. Wethyavivorn. "The Valuation of Currency Options for Alternative Stochastic Processes." *Journal of Financial Research* 4 (December 1985): 455–468.

Taggart, R. A., *Quantitative Analysis for Investment Management,* 118–160. Upper Saddle River, NJ: Prentice Hall, 1996.

Tucker, A. "Empirical Tests of the Efficiency of the Currency Option Market." *Journal of Financial Research* (Winter 1985): 275–285.

PROBLEMS AND QUESTIONS

1. Assume the following:

   - U.S. risk-free rate (annual) = 6%
   - British risk-free rate (annual rate paid on British pounds) = .09
   - $/BP spot exchange rate = $1.50/BP
   - Annualized logarithmic return's mean (for $/BP exchange rate) = $\mu^A = 0$
   - Annualized logarithmic return's standard deviation = $\sigma^A = 0.25$

   Questions:

   a. Using the single-period BOPM, determine the price of a European BP call with an exercise price of 1.50 and expiring in 30 days.

   b. Explain what an arbitrageur would do if the BP call were priced at $0.07. Show what the arbitrageur's cash flow at expiration would be at the two possible spot exchange rates. Assume perfect divisibility.

    c. Determine the equilibrium price of the European call using a two-period BOPM. Show your call and exchange rate values in a two-period tree.

    d. What is the two-period BOPM value if the BP call were American?

2. Derive the single-period BOPM for a foreign currency (FC) put option.

3. Using the information on the BP in Question 1, determine the equilibrium price of a comparable European put using a two-period BOPM. Does the value of the put conform to the FC put–call parity condition (allow for some rounding differences)?

4. Using the information on the BP in Question 1, determine the equilibrium prices on American BP call and put options using the Merton model and a three-period binomial tree. Using the "Binomial Option Pricing Model" Excel program, determine the prices of the options for the following number of subperiods: n = 10, n =30, and n = 100.

5. Given the following spot rates on 1- to 4-year, zero-coupon bonds:

Year	Spot Rate
1	8.0%
2	8.5%
3	9.0%
4	9.5%

    a. What is the equilibrium price of a 4-year, 9% coupon bond paying a principal of $100 at maturity and coupons annually?

    b. If the market prices the 4-year bond such that it yields 10%, what is the bond's market price?

    c. What would arbitrageurs do given the prices you determined in (a) and (b)? What impact would their actions have on the market price?

    d. What would arbitrageurs do if the market price exceeded the equilibrium price? What impact would their actions have on the market price?

6. Comment on the arbitrage-free features of valuing a bond using a binomial interest rate tree generating by estimating u and d in terms of mean and variance.

7. Explain the methodology for estimating a binomial tree using the calibration model. Comment on the arbitrage-free features of this approach.

8. Given a variability of $\sigma = \sqrt{hV_e^A} = .10$ and current one- and two-period spot rates of $S_1^m = .07$ and $S_2^m = .0804$

    a. Generate a one-period binomial interest rate tree using the calibration model. (Hint: try $S_d = .08148$).

    b. Using the calibrated tree, determine the equilibrium price of a two-period, option-free, 10.5% coupon bond (F = 100).

    c. Does the binomial tree price the 10.5% option-free bond equal to the bond's equilibrium price? Comment on this feature of the calibration model.

9. Assume binomial process; current annualized spot rate on risk-free bond with maturity of 1 year of $S_0 = 5\%$; the size of the up and down parameters for a period equal in length to 1 year equal to u = 1.1 and d = 1/1.1; length of binomial period equal to 1 year; and probability of the spot rate increasing in one period of q = .5.

a. Generate a two-period binomial tree of spot rates.

b. Using the binomial tree, calculate the values at each node of a risk-free bond with a $100 face value, 5% annual coupon, and maturity of 3 years.

c. Using the binomial tree, determine the value of a European call option on the bond with an exercise price of 100 and expiration of 2 years.

d. Using the binomial tree, determine the value of an American call option on the bond with an exercise price of 100 and expiration of 2 years.

e. Using the binomial tree, determine the value of a European put option on the bond with an exercise price of 100 and expiration of 2 years.

f. Using the binomial tree, determine the value of an American put option on the bond with an exercise price of 100 and expiration of 2 years.

WEB EXERCISES

1. On February 19, 2007, there were British pound call and put options trading on the Philadelphia Exchange each with an exercise price of $1.95 and expiration of April (60 days). On February 19, the spot $/BP exchange rate was $1.9505, the BP volatility was .1229 (annualized standard deviation of logarithmic return), the two-month U.S. Treasury rate was 5.16%, and the two-month U.K. Treasury rate was 5.40%.

   a. Using the "Binomial Option Pricing Model" Excel program, determine the price of BP call option using Merton's continuous asset-yield binomial model. Use the "Binomial Option Pricing Model" Excel program.

   b. Using the BP volatility or your own estimates, price a currently traded BP call using Merton's continuous asset-yield binomial model. Use the "Binomial Option Pricing Model" Excel program. For information on currently traded currency option listed on the Philadelphia Exchange: www.phlx.com. Note: If there is no closing price, average the dealer's bid and ask prices.

   For information on exchange rates and interest rates in other countries go to www.fxstreet.com. For information on historical foreign exchange rates go to www.research.stlouisfed.org/fred2.

CHAPTER 8

THE BLACK–SCHOLES OPTION PRICING MODEL

8.1 INTRODUCTION

The realism of the BOPM is questionable when only a small number of periods to expiration exist. As we subdivide the expiration period—or equivalently, make the length of each period smaller—the number of possible stock prices at expiration increases, and the assumption of only two states in one period becomes more plausible. Thus, for the pricing of most options, the binomial model for large n is more realistic. Moreover, as we noted in Chapter 5, as n becomes large, the BOPM becomes the equation for the Black–Scholes (B–S) OPM. Thus, for large n, the equilibrium values of an option using the BOPM are approximately the same as those obtained using the OPM developed by Black and Scholes. In this chapter, we examine the B–S OPM.

8.2 THE BLACK–SCHOLES CALL OPTION MODEL

8.2.1 The Nature of the B–S OPM

The B–S OPM, not the binomial, was the first of the two OPMs. Like the binomial, the B–S model is applicable for both European options and cases in which the underlying stock does not pay dividends. Similarly, the B–S model is derived by assuming that no transaction costs and margin requirements are incurred, that securities are perfectly divisible, that funds can be borrowed or invested at a constant risk-free rate, and that the distribution of the stock's logarithmic return is normal. Last, the B–S OPM, like the binomial, determines the equilibrium value as the option price that is equal to the value of a replicating portfolio. Unfortunately, unlike the BOPM, the mathematics used in deriving the B–S OPM (stochastic calculus and a heat exchange equation) are complex; in fact, part of the contribution of the BOPM is that it is simpler to derive yet still yields the same solution as the B–S OPM for the case of large n. The B–S model, though, is relatively easy to use (the mathematical foundation of the B–S OPM is presented in Appendix 8A).

8.2.2 B–S OPM Formula

The B–S formula for determining the equilibrium call price is

$$C_0^* = S_0 N(d_1) - \left[\frac{X}{e^{RT}} \right] N(d_2) \tag{8.2-1}$$

$$d_1 = \frac{\ln(S_0/X) + (R + .5\sigma^2)T}{\sigma\sqrt{T}} \tag{8.2-2}$$

$$d_2 = d_1 - \sigma\sqrt{T} \tag{8.2-3}$$

where

T = time to expiration expressed as a proportion of the year.

R = continuously compounded annual risk-free rate of return.

σ = annualized standard deviation of the logarithmic return.

$N(d_1), N(d_2)$ = cumulative normal probabilities.

In Equation (8.2-1), X/e^{RT} is the present value of the exercise price (PV(X)) continuously compounded. R in the equation is the continuously compounded annual risk-free rate. This rate can be found by taking the natural logarithm of 1 plus the simple annual rate on a risk-free security with a maturity equal to the call's expiration date. Thus, if .06 is the simple annual rate, then the continuous compounded rate is $\ln(1 + .06) = .0583$. σ^2 in Equation (8.2-2) is the annualized variance of the logarithmic return that we defined in Chapter 5. The cumulative normal probabilities, $N(d_1)$ and $N(d_2)$, are the probabilities that deviations of less than d_1 and d_2, respectively, will occur in a standard normal distribution with a 0 mean and a standard deviation of 1. Cumulative normal probability tables can be found in many statistics and finance books. In pricing options with the B–S OPM, $N(d_1)$ and $N(d_2)$ should be carried out several decimal places. Because the probabilities provided in many tables are extrapolated, the following power function can be used instead of the table to obtain better estimations of $N(d_1)$ and $N(d_2)$:

$$n(d) = 1 - .5[1 + .196854(|d|) + .115194(|d|)^2 + .000344(|d|)^3$$
$$+ .019527(|d|)^4]^{-4} \qquad (8.2\text{-}4)$$

where

$|d|$ = absolute value of d.

If d is negative, then the n(d) value obtained from Equation (8.2-4) is subtract from 1; if d is positive, then the n(d) obtained from (8.2-4) is used:

$$N(d) = 1 - n(d), \quad \text{for } d < 0$$
$$N(d) = n(d), \quad \text{for } d > 0$$

Example

Suppose ABC stock is trading at \$45, has an estimated annualized standard deviation of $\sigma = .5$, and the continuously compounded annual risk-free rate is $R = 6\%$. Using the B–S OPM, the equilibrium price of an ABC 50 expiring in 3 months ($T = .25$) would be \$2.88:

$$C_0^* = S_0 N(d_1) - \left[\frac{X}{e^{RT}}\right] N(d_2)$$

$$C_0^* = (\$45)(.4066) - \left[\frac{\$50}{e^{(.06)(.25)}}\right](.3131) = \$2.88$$

where

$$d_1 = \frac{\ln(\$45/\$50) + [.06 + .5(.5)^2](.25)}{.5\sqrt{.25}} = -.2364$$

$$d_2 = -.2364 - .5\sqrt{.25} = -.4864$$

TABLE 8.2-1   BOPM Values for Different n

$$S_0 = \$45, X = \$50, T = .25, R = .06^+, \sigma = .5$$
$$\text{For BOPM: } u = e^{.5\sqrt{.25/n}}, d = 1/u$$

n	BOPM C*
2	$3.16
10	$2.94
16	$2.86
32	$2.87

B–S OPM Price = $2.88

$+$R is the continuously compounded annual rate used in the B–S model.
In the BOPM, the period rate obtained from the simple annual rate (R^A) is used:
R^A = simple annual rate = $e^R - 1 = e^{.06} - 1 = .061836$.

$$N(d_1) = N(-.2364) = 1 - [1 - .5[1 + .196854(.2364) + .115194(.2364)^2$$
$$+ .000344(.2364)^3 + .019527(.2364)^4]^{-4}]$$

$$N(d_1) = N(-.2364) = .4066$$

$$N(d_2) = N(-.4864) = 1 - [1 - .5[1 + .196854(.4864) + .115194(.4864)^2$$
$$+ .000344(.4864)^3 + .019527(.4864)^4]^{-4}]$$

$$N(d_2) = N(-.4864) = .3131$$

As noted previously, the B–S price differs from the BOPM price for small n but is approximately the same for large. This can be seen in Table 8.2-1 in which the B–S price of $2.88 is compared with the prices obtained using the binomial model for different values of n. As shown in the table, at n = 2, the BOPM's call value is $0.28 greater than the B–S's; at n = 10, the binomial price is $0.06 is greater than the B–S price; at n = 16, the difference is only $0.02; and at n = 32, only rounding errors exist. Thus, the example illustrates our earlier point that as n gets large, the BOPM converges to the B–S OPM.

8.2.3   Comparative Analysis

Like the BOPM, the B–S OPM's equilibrium call price depends on the underlying stock price, exercise price, time to expiration, risk-free rate, and the stock's volatility. Mathematically, the impacts that changes in these variables have on the equilibrium call price can be found by taking the partial derivatives of Equation (8.2-1) with respect to S, X, T, R, and σ. The impacts also can be seen in terms of the simulation presented in the table and graph in Exhibit 8.2-1. In the table, combinations of the B–S OPM values and stock prices are shown for different parameter values. The labeled Column 1 shows the call values given the parameter values used in the preceding example: X = 50, T = .25, R = .06, and σ = 0.5. For purposes of comparison, the other columns show the call and stock price relations generated with the same parameter values used in Column 1, except for one variable: in Column 2, X = 40; in Column 3, T = .5; in Column 4, σ = .75; and in Column 5, R = .08.

In examining Exhibit 8.2-1, first note the call and stock price relation. When the stock price is relatively low and the call is deep out of the money, the B–S OPM yields a very low call price. As the price of the stock increases by equal increments, the OPM call

EXHIBIT 8.2-1   B–S OPM Call Price and Stock Price Relation Given Different Parameter Values

Stock Price	1 X = 50, T = .25 $\sigma = .5, R = .06$ C_0^*	2 X = 40, T = .25 $\sigma = .5, R = .06$ C_0^*	3 X = 50, T = .5 $\sigma = .5, R = .06$ C_0^*	4 X = 50, T = .25 $\sigma = .75, R = .06$ C_0^*	5 X = 50, T = .25 $\sigma = .5, R = .08$ C_0^*
$30	$0.0841	$0.5967	$0.5453	$0.6292	$0.0890
35	0.4163	1.9065	1.3751	1.5028	0.4328
40	1.2408	4.2399	2.8365	2.9852	1.2826
45	2.8756	7.5682	4.9626	5.1006	2.9550
50	5.2999	11.5935	7.6637	7.7452	5.4210
55	8.5584	16.0952	10.9683	10.9782	8.7103
60	12.3857	20.8355	14.6539	14.5768	12.5702
65	16.6919	25.7002	18.7114	18.5269	16.8996
70	21.2865	30.6342	23.0555	22.7703	21.5083

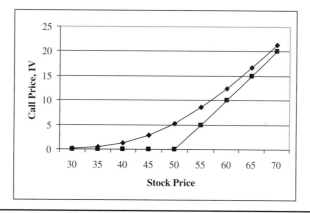

price increases at an increasing rate up to a point, with the values never being below the difference between the stock price and the present value of the exercise price. Thus, over a range of stock prices, the B–S OPM yields a call and stock price relation that is nonlinear and satisfies the minimum and maximum boundary conditions defined in Chapter 4. The nonlinear relationship also can be seen in the figure in Exhibit 8.2-1 where the B–S option call values and stock prices from Column 1 are plotted. Note that the slope of this B–S option price curve increases as the stock price increases, the curve does not yield negative values, and it is above the minimum boundary line and the IV line. As we noted with the BOPM in Chapter 5, the slope of the curve is referred to as the option's **delta**. Delta is equal to H* in the BOPM and to $N(d_1)$ in the B–S model. For a call, the delta ranges from 0 for a deep-out-of-the-money call to approximately 1 for a deep-in-the-money one. This can be seen in the figure in Exhibit 8.2-1 that shows that the option curve is relatively flat for low stock prices and starts to become parallel to the minimum boundary line for high stock values. The nonlinear call and stock price relation also can be seen by the change in the slope of the B–S option price curve as the stock price increases. In option literature, the change in slope (i.e., delta) per small change in the stock price defines the option's **gamma** (it is the second-order partial derivative of the call price with respect to changes in the stock price).

Second, in examining Columns 1 and 2, observe that for each stock price, there is a higher call price associated with the call with the lower exercise price. Thus, as the exercise price decreases, the B–S OPM call price increases. Third, in comparing Column 3 with Column 1, note that the B–S OPM call price increases, the greater the time to expiration. The change in an option's prices with respect to a small change in the time to expiration (with other factors held constant) is defined as the option's **theta**. Fourth, in comparing Columns 4 and 1, observe that the call price is greater, the greater the stock's variability. The change in the call price given a small change in the stock's variability is referred to as the option's **vega** (also called **kappa**). Last, in comparing Columns 1 and 5, note how the call price increases the greater the interest rate. The change in the call price given a small change in R is called the call's **rho**.

8.2.4 Black–Scholes OPM Excel Programs

An Excel option program that values call and put options using the B–S OPM is provided as part of the software that accompanies this book. The program, called "Black–Scholes Option Pricing Model" has eight spreadsheets. The "B–S OPM" worksheet calculates B–S call and put values given different stock prices, and the "B–S Greeks" worksheet calculates the delta, gamma, and theta values. Several end-of-the-chapter problems are included that make use of these Excel programs.

8.3 BLACK–SCHOLES ARBITRAGE PORTFOLIO

Like the BOPM, the B–S OPM's Equation (8.2-1) is equal to the value of its underlying replicating portfolio. That is

$$C_0^* = H_0^* S_0 - B_0^* \qquad (8.3\text{-}1)$$

where from the B–S model

$$H_0^* = N(d_1)$$

$$B_0^* = \left[\frac{X}{e^{RT}} \right] N(d_2)$$

Thus, the OPM call value of $2.88 in our previous example is equal to the value of a replicating portfolio consisting of 0.4066 shares of stock, partially financed by borrowing $15.42:

$$C_0^* = H_0^* S_0 - B_0^* = .4066(\$45) - \$15.42 = \$2.88$$

where

$$H_0^* = N(d_1) = .4066$$

$$B_0^* = \left[\frac{X}{e^{RT}} \right] N(d_2) = \left[\frac{\$50}{e^{(.06)(.25)}} \right] (.3131) = \$15.42$$

If the market price of the call does not equal the B–S value, then arbitrage opportunities will exist by taking a position in the call and an opposite position in the replicating portfolio. Like the multiple-period arbitrage strategies defined for the BOPM, arbitrageurs, after initiating the strategy, would need to close or readjust their arbitrage portfolios in each subsequent period using the same rules defined for overpriced and underpriced calls in Chapter 5.

In readjusting the arbitrage portfolio, two characteristics of the B–S model should be kept in mind. First, as we observed earlier, the slope of the option price curve changes as the stock price changes. In the B–S OPM, the slope of the curve is equal to $N(d_1)$. Thus, for arbitrageurs to maintain a riskless portfolio, they would need to readjust their hedge ratio by moving to the new $N(d_1)$ each time the stock price changes. Second, the hedge ratio also changes as the time to expiration changes. This characteristic suggests that even if the stock price does not change, arbitrageurs still need to readjust their hedge to keep the arbitrage portfolio riskless because $N(d_1)$ is constantly changing in response to the continuous decrease in the call's time to expiration. Moreover, in the continuous-time B–S model, the hedge ratio is changing continuously with the passage of time as well as with stock price changes; thus, to keep the portfolio riskless, arbitrageurs would need to readjust frequently and close as soon as profit opportunities appear.

In summary, arbitrage portfolios can be formed using the B–S OPM that are similar to the strategies defined for the BOPM. By the nature of the B–S model, such portfolios theoretically should be adjusted continuously (very frequently) to keep the portfolio riskless. In fact, because of the frequent adjustments that are necessary to earn an arbitrage return, some traders refer to such a strategy as "picking up nickels and dimes in front of a steam roller." A more detailed explanation of the arbitrage strategy underlying the B–S OPM along with an example illustrating the initiation and adjustment of the arbitrage portfolio is presented in Appendix 8B.

8.4 DIVIDEND ADJUSTMENTS FOR THE BLACK–SCHOLES CALL MODEL

As we discussed in Chapter 6, a dividend causes the price of a call to decrease on the ex-dividend date and can lead to an early exercise of the call if it is American. Because the B–S OPM values a European call without dividends, it needs to be adjusted for dividends and for American options. Two dividend adjustment models that use the B–S OPM are Fisher Black's *pseudo-American call model,* applicable to American calls when the stock pays a dividend and when ex-dividend dates are expected during the life of the option, and Merton's continuous dividend-yield approach. Black's pseudo model is analogous to the known dividend-payment approach define for the BOPM, and Merton's continuous dividend-yield payment model is simply an extension of Merton's continuous dividend-yield binomial model to the continuous-time B–S model.

8.4.1 Black's Pseudo-American Call Model

The Black's pseudo-American call model for pricing an American call option uses a dividend-adjusted stock price (S_0^D) in the OPM instead of the current stock price. When there is one dividend payment (D), the adjusted stock price is

$$S_0^D = S_0 - PV(D)$$

$$S_0^D = S_0 - \frac{D}{e^{Rt*}} \qquad (8.4\text{-}1)$$

where

$t^* = $ time to ex-dividend date expressed as a proportion of the year.

If more than one dividend payment is made during the option period, then the present value of each dividend is subtracted from the current stock price.

In the pseudo-American model, the call value computed with the dividend-adjusted stock price $C^*(S_0^D, T, X)$ is compared to the estimated call value obtained by assuming the call is exercised just prior to the ex-dividend date. This early-exercise call price (C^{ex}) is found using the time to the ex-dividend date (t^*) instead of expiration (T), the dividend-adjusted stock price (S_0^D) instead of S_0, and a dividend-adjusted exercise price (X–D) instead of X; that is, $C^{ex}(S_0^D, t^*, X–D)$. The dividend-adjusted exercise price is used instead of X to account for the advantage of early exercise that occurs just before the ex-dividend date. Finally, given the two estimated call prices, the larger of the two is selected as the estimate for the equilibrium call price:

$$C_0^a = Max[C^*(S_0^D, T, X), C^{ex}(S_0^D, t^*, X - D)]$$

Example

Consider again the B–S call pricing example in which the B–S price of the call was $2.88, given $S_0 = \$45$, $X = \$50$, $T = .25$, $\sigma = .5$ and $R = .06$. In this example, also assume that ABC stock is expected to go ex-dividend 2 months from the present ($t^* = 2/12 = .16667$), with the value of the dividend equal to $2.00. Using the pseudo-American model to estimate the value of the ABC 50 call, we first compute the adjusted stock price:

$$S_0^D = S_0 - \frac{D}{e^{Rt*}}$$

$$S_0^D = \$45 - \frac{\$2.00}{e^{(.06)(.16667)}} = \$43.02$$

Using $S_0^D = \$43.02$ in the B–S model instead of $S_0 = \$45$, we obtain a dividend-adjusted call price of $2.12, which is less than the B–S price of $2.88 obtained without the adjustment:

$$C_0^* = (\$43.02)(.33834) - \left[\frac{\$50}{e^{(.06)(.25)}}\right](.25246) = \$2.12$$

where

$$d_1 = \frac{\ln(\$43.02/\$50) + [.06 + (.5)(.5^2)].25}{.5\sqrt{.25}} = -.41644$$

$$d_2 = -.41643 - .5\sqrt{.25} = -.66643$$

$$N(d_1) = N(-.41643) = .33834$$

$$N(d_2) = N(-.66643) = .25246$$

Next, we estimate the call price assuming it will be exercised just prior to the ex-dividend date. In this example, the early-exercise call price is $1.86. This value is obtained by using $S_0^D = \$43.02$, X–D = \$50–\$2 = \$48, and $t^* = 2/12 = .16667$ for S_0, X, and T, respectively, in the B–S formula:

$$C_0^{ex} = (\$43.02)(.34973) - \left[\frac{\$48}{e^{(.06)(.16667)}}\right](.2775) = \$1.86.$$

where

$$d_1 = \frac{\ln(\$43.02/\$48) + [.06 + (.5)(.5^2)](.16667)}{.5(\sqrt{.16667})} = -.38556$$

$$d_2 = -.38556 - .5\sqrt{.16667} = -.58969$$

$$N(d_1) = N(-.38556) = .34973$$

$$N(d_2) = N(-.58969) = .2775$$

Finally, given the two prices, we select the larger of the two. Thus, in this example, the estimated call price is $2.12:

$$C_0^a = Max[C_0^*(S_0^D, T, X), C_0^{ex}(S_0^D, t^*, X - D)]$$

$$C_0^a = Max[C_0^*(\$43.02, .25, \$50), C_0^{ex}(\$43.02, .16667, \$48)]$$

$$C_0^a = Max[\$2.12, \$1.86]$$

$$C_0^a = \$2.12$$

Note that if the call option were European, then only the call value using the time to expiration is used ($2.12). The "Black–Scholes Option Pricing Model" Excel package includes a worksheet that prices options using Black's Pseudo-American Model.

8.4.2 Merton's Continuous Dividend-Adjustment Model

The other dividend-adjustment procedure is to use Merton's continuous dividend-adjustment model. In this model, the dividend-adjusted stock price, S_0^D, is substituted for the current stock price in the B–S formula:

$$S_0^D = S_0 e^{-\psi T}$$

where

ψ = annual dividend yield = annual dividend/stock price.

The Merton B–S model with a continuous dividend yield is defined as

$$C_0^* = S_0 e^{-\psi T} N(d_1) - X e^{-RT} N(d_2)$$

$$d_1 = \frac{\ln(S_0^D/X) + (R + .5\sigma^2)T}{\sigma\sqrt{T}} = \frac{\ln(S_0/X) + (R - \psi + .5\sigma^2)T}{\sigma\sqrt{T}}$$

$$d_2 = d_1 - \sigma\sqrt{T}$$

In terms of the preceding example, if the underlying stock is expected to generate an annual dividend yield of $\psi = .0889$ (e.g., $4 annual dividend per a stock price of $45), then the dividend-adjusted stock price would be $S_0^D = \$44.01$, and the continuous dividend-adjusted call price would be $2.48:

$$S_0^D = S_0 e^{-\psi T}$$

$$S_0^D = \$45 e^{-(.0889)((.25)} = \$44.01$$

$$C_0^* = (\$44.01)(.37236) - \left[\frac{\$50}{e^{(.06)(.25)}}\right](.28233) = \$2.48$$

where

$$d_1 = \frac{\ln(\$44.01/\$50) + [.06 + (.5)(.5^2)].25}{.5\sqrt{.25}} = -.32534$$

or

$$d_1 = \frac{\ln(\$45/\$50) + [.06 - .0889 + (.5)(.5^2)].25}{.5\sqrt{.25}} = -.32534$$

$$d_2 = -.32534 - (.5)(\sqrt{.25}) = -.57534$$

$$N(d_1) = N(-.32534) = .37236$$

$$N(d_2) = N(-.57534) = .28233$$

Comparing the two models, we see that each approach yields a different call value. Which one should be used depends on how dividends are paid. In the case of stock options in which dividends may be paid only once or twice during the option's life, the pseudo-American call model may be more applicable. However, in the case of a stock index option in which it can be argued that the volume of stocks comprising the index causes a flow of dividends, the continuous dividend-adjusted model may be more appropriate.

Note that in Chapter 6, we used the Merton dividend-adjusted binomial model to price American and European call options on a stock with a 12% annual dividend yield ($S_0 = \$100$, $\sigma^A = .3$, $\mu^A = 0$, $X = \$100$ and $T = 180$ days, $n = 5$, $R^A = 6\%$, and $\psi = 12\%$). For the case of $n = 100$ subperiods, the model priced the American call at $7.03 and the European at $6.67. Using the Merton B–S OPM (with $R = \ln((1.06) = .058269)$, we obtain the same price ($6.67) as the Merton dividend-adjusted binomial for the European call. (The Merton B–S model price can be calculated using the "B–S OPM" Excel worksheet and inputting the stock's dividend yield.) The Merton B–S OPM, though, does not price American options. Thus, one of the advantages of the discrete binomial model over the continuous B–S model is that one can stop at each node to determine if there is an early exercise advantage. This is not the case with Merton's continuous dividend-adjusted B–S model. In this example, the $0.06 price difference between the American and European binomial models implies a $0.06 early exercise value on the American call option. With Black's pseudo model, one is also able to stop at the ex-dividend date to determine if there is an early exercise advantage—the only time such an advantage would exist for a call.

8.5 B–S OPM FOR PUTS

8.5.1 B–S Put Model

The B–S OPM model for puts can be derived using the same methodology used to determine the B–S call value (see Appendix 8A). It also can be derived from the binomial model by letting n approach infinity. A simpler approach, though, is to make use of the put–call parity model. Specifically, assuming European options, the equilibrium put price in terms of the put–call parity model is

$$P_0^* = C_0^* - S_0 + PV(X)$$

$$P_0^* = C_0^* - S_0 + \frac{X}{e^{RT}} \tag{8.5-1}$$

where:

$$C_0^* = \text{call price determined by the B–S OPM.}$$

By substituting Equation (8.2-1) for C_0^*, the equilibrium put price can be specified alternatively as

$$P_0^* = -S_0(1 - N(d_1)) + \left[\frac{X}{e^{RT}}\right](1 - N(d_2)) \qquad (8.5\text{-}2)$$

Example

In Section 8.2, we calculated the B–S OPM for an ABC 50 call expiring in 3 months (T = .25) to be \$2.88 given a stock price of \$45, an annualized standard deviation of $\sigma = .5$, and a continuously compounded annual risk-free rate of R = 6%. The equilibrium price of a comparable put option on ABC using the B–S put model is \$7.13. That is

$$P_0^* = -S_0(1 - N(d_1)) + \left[\frac{X}{e^{RT}}\right](1 - N(d_2))$$

$$P_0^* = -\$45(.5934) + \left[\frac{\$50}{e^{(.06)(.25)}}\right](.6869)$$

$$P_0^* = \$7.13$$

where

$$1 - N(d_1) = N(-d_1) = 1 - .4066 = .5934$$

$$1 - N(d_2) = N(-d_2) = 1 - .3131 = .6869$$

8.5.2   Comparative Analysis

Like the B–S OPM for calls, most of the relationships between the equilibrium price of a put and S, T, σ, X, and R that were examined both intuitively and with arbitrage arguments in Chapter 4 are captured in the B–S put model. This can be seen by taking the partial derivatives of Equation (8.5-2) with respect to each of the explanatory variables and observing their signs. These relationships also can be seen in the table in Exhibit 8.5-1 in which combinations of the B–S put prices and stock prices are shown for different parameters: X (Column 2), T (Column 3), σ (Column 4), and R (Column 5). In examining any of the columns in the table, one first should observe the negative, nonlinear relationship between the B–S put price and the stock price (i.e., the put has a negative delta and non-zero gamma). Next, comparing Columns 2 and 5 with Column 1, one can observe that for each stock price, the lower the exercise price or the lower the interest rate the greater the B–S put price. Finally, comparing Columns 3 and 4 with Column 1, one can see that the greater the time to expiration or the greater the stock's variability, the greater the put price. Thus, the B–S put model captures many of the relationships described in Chapter 4.

It should be noted that the model is unconstrained. That is, the B–S put model does not constrain the put value to being equal to at least its intrinsic value. Thus, for an in-the-money put, the premium can be less than its IV, as shown in Column 1 when the stock is at \$30. The possibility that P* < IV reflects the fact that the B–S model is limited to determining the price of a European put in which negative time value premiums are possible.

EXHIBIT 8.5-1   B–S OPM Put Price and Stock Price Relation Given Different Parameter Values

	1 $X = 50, T = .25$ $\sigma = .5, R = .06$	2 $X = 40, T = .25$ $\sigma = .5, R = .06$	3 $X = 50, T = .5$ $\sigma = .5, R = .06$	4 $X = 50, T = .25$ $\sigma = .75, R = .06$	5 $X = 50, T = .25$ $\sigma = .5, R = .08$
Stock Price	P_0^*	P_0^*	P_0^*	P_0^*	P_0^*
$30	$19.3397	$10.0012	$19.0675	$19.8848	$19.0990
35	14.6719	6.3110	14.8973	15.7584	14.4428
40	10.4964	3.6444	11.3588	12.2408	10.2926
45	7.1312	1.9727	8.4848	9.3562	6.9650
50	4.5555	0.9979	6.1860	7.0008	4.4309
55	2.8140	0.4996	4.4905	5.2338	2.7203
60	1.6413	0.2400	3.1761	3.8324	1.5801
65	0.9475	0.1046	2.2337	2.7825	0.9095
70	0.5421	0.0387	1.5778	2.0259	0.5182

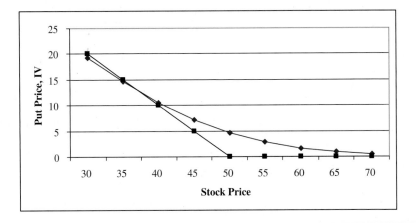

8.5.3   B–S Arbitrage Put Portfolio

The B–S put Equation (8.5-2) is equal to the value of the replicating put portfolio. That is

$$P_0^* = H_0^{P*}S_0 + I_0^*$$

where from the B–S model

$$H_0^{P*} = -(1 - N(d_1))$$

$$I_0^* = \left[\frac{X}{e^{RT}}\right](1 - N(d_2))$$

Thus, the put value of $7.13 in our previous example is equivalent to the value of a portfolio formed by selling .5934 shares of stock short at $45 per share and investing $33.83 in a risk-free security:

$$P_0^* = -(.5934)($45) + $33.83 = $7.13$$

where

$$H_0^{P*} = -(1 - N(d_1)) = -.5934$$

$$I_0^* = \left[\frac{X}{e^{RT}}\right](1 - N(d_2)) = \left[\frac{\$50}{e^{(.06)(.25)}}\right](.6869) = \$33.83$$

If the market price of the put exceeds the B–S put value, then an arbitrage opportunity exists by taking a short position in the put and a long position in the replicating put portfolio; if the market price is below the equilibrium value, then a riskless arbitrage portfolio can be constructed by going long in the put and short in the replicating portfolio. The overpriced and underpriced arbitrage put portfolios would need to be readjusted continuously (very frequently) until it is profitable to close. The same readjustment rules defined for BOPM's multiple-period arbitrage strategies, though, apply to the continuous B–S arbitrage case. The B–S arbitrage portfolio is described in more detail in Appendix 8B.

8.5.4 Dividend Adjustments for the B–S Put Model

As we discussed in Chapter 6, if a stock pays a dividend with the ex-dividend date occurring during the option period, then the price of the put would increase on the ex-dividend date as the price of the stock decreases by an amount approximately equal to the dividend. The value of a European put in which there is an ex-dividend date occurring during the period can be estimated by using either the first equation in the dividend-adjusted, pseudo-American model defined in Section 8.4 or Merton's continuous dividend-adjusted stock price model. For example, if ABC stock in our illustrative example had an ex-dividend date in 2 months, with the value of the dividend on that date equal to $2.00, then the dividend-adjusted stock price for a discrete dividend payment would be $43.02, and the dividend-adjusted put price would be $8.36:

$$P_0^* = -S_0^D(1 - N(d_1)) + \left[\frac{X}{e^{RT}}\right](1 - N(d_2))$$

$$P_0^* = -(.66166)(\$43.02) + \left[\frac{\$50}{e^{(.06)(.25)}}\right](.74754) = \$8.36$$

where

$$S_0^D = S_0 - \frac{D}{e^{Rt*}} = \$45 - \frac{\$2.00}{e^{(.06)(.16667)}} = \$43.02$$

$$1 - N(d_1) = 1 - .33834 = .66166$$

$$1 - N(d_2) = 1 - .25246 = .74754$$

The dividend-adjusted put price of $8.36 also can be obtained using the put–call parity model and the dividend-adjusted call price:

$$P_0^* = C_0^* - S_0^D + \frac{X}{e^{RT}}$$

$$P_0^* = \$2.12 - \$43.02 + \frac{\$50}{e^{(.06)(.25)}}$$

$$P_0^* = \$8.36$$

Alternatively, using the Merton B–S model in which the underlying stock is expected to generate an annual dividend yield of $\psi = .0889$, and the dividend-adjusted stock price is $S_0^D = \$44.01$, the continuous dividend-adjusted European put price is $7.73:

$$P_0^* = -(.627640(\$44.01) + \left[\frac{\$50}{e^{(.06)(.25)}}\right](.717670) = \$7.73$$

where

$$S_0^D = S_0 e^{-\psi T}$$

$$S_0^D = \$45 e^{-(.0889)((.25)} = \$44.01$$

$$d_1 = \frac{\ln(\$45/\$50) + [.06 - .0889 + (.5)(.5^2)].25}{.5\sqrt{.25}} = -.32534$$

$$d_2 = -.32534 - (.5)(\sqrt{.25}) = -.57534$$

$$1 - N(d_1) = 1 - N(-.32534) = 1 - .37236 = .627640$$

$$1 - N(d_2) = 1 - N(-.57534) = 1 - .28233 = .717670$$

The B–S put price also can be calculated using the put–call parity given the continuous dividend-adjusted call price of $2.48:

$$P_0^* = C_0^* - S_0^D + \frac{X}{e^{RT}}$$

$$P_0^* = \$2.48 - \$44.01 + \frac{\$50}{e^{(.06)(.25)}}$$

$$P_0^* = \$7.73$$

8.5.5   The Value of an American Put Given an Ex-Dividend Date

When an ex-dividend date occurs during the option period, the Black pseudo-American model defined for call options can be extended to estimate the value of an American put. Applied to puts, the pseudo-American put model selects the greater of either the European put value, as determined previously (with the dividend-adjusted stock price and time to expiration, T): $P^*(S_0^D, T, X)$, or the early-exercise put value obtained by assuming the put is exercised at or just after the ex-dividend date. As we did earlier for calls, in computing the early-exercise put price, the time to the ex-dividend date (t^*) is used instead of T, and the dividend-adjusted stock price (S_0^D) is used instead of S_0. However, for puts, the exercise price is used instead of the dividend-adjusted exercise price (X–D) that was used for calls. This is done to account for the fact that the early exercise advantage for puts occurs on or just after the ex-dividend date when the stock decreases and not just before as in the case of calls; thus, $P^{ex}(S_0^D, t^*, X)$. In terms of our previous example, if the put were American, then its value (P_0^a) would be the greater of either $8.36 or the early exercise value, P_0^{ex}. In this case, P_0^{ex} is $7.84:

$$P_0^{ex} = -(\$43.02)(.72110) + \left[\frac{\$50}{e^{(.06)(.16667)}}\right](.78510) = \$7.84.$$

where

$$d_1 = \frac{Ln(1225.58/1250) + [.058269 + .5(.3^2)](180/365)}{.5\sqrt{(180/365)}} = .1481$$

$$d_2 = (.1481) - (.5)\sqrt{(180/365)} = -.0626$$

$$N(d_1) = N(-.58554) = .27890$$

$$N(d_2) = N(-.78967) = .21490$$

$$1 - N(d_1) = .72110$$

$$1 - N(d_2) = .78510$$

The American put price is therefore $8.36:

$$P_0^a = Max[P_0^*(S_0^D, T, X), P_0^{ex}(S_0^D, t^*, X)]$$

$$P_0^a = Max[P_0^*(\$43.02, .25, \$50), P_0^{ex}(\$43.03, .16667, \$50)]$$

$$P_0^a = Max[\$8.36, \$7.84]$$

$$P_0^a = \$8.36$$

8.5.6 The Value of an American Put Without Dividends

The pseudo-American model estimates the value of an American put given an ex-dividend date. When dividends are not paid, and as a result, we do not have a specific reference date to apply the pseudo-American model, then determining the value of an American put becomes quite difficult. As we have pointed out before, this is not a problem with the B–S call model for stock options because the advantage of early exercise can occur only when an ex-dividend date exists; in such a case, a reference point in time for early exercise is known, and therefore the pseudo-American call model can be applied to determine the value of an American call. In the case of put options, if the price of the stock is such that the put is deep in the money, then it is possible for the price of the European put to be less than its IV. If the put were American, then at that stock price, it would have to be priced to equal at least its IV, or an arbitrage opportunity would exist by exercising the put early. Thus, the right of early exercise makes the price of an American put greater than a European, even if no dividends are to be paid during the life of the put.

In the BOPM, the equilibrium price of an American put or call was determined by constraining the price of the put or call to be the maximum of either its binomial value or its IV at each possible stock price. In the discrete BOPM in which limits can be placed on the number of possible stock prices (which still can be quite large), this approach is feasible. However, in the B–S model in which time is continuous, the BOPM approach of constraining each possible put or call price cannot be applied. As we showed in Chapters 5 and 6, the BOPM can be constrained to price American puts. In addition to the American BOPM, there are several other models, such as the Barone–Adesi and Whaley (BAW) Model, which have been developed to estimate the price of American options.

8.6 ESTIMATING THE B–S OPM

Like the BOPM, the B–S OPM is defined totally in terms of the stock price, exercise price, time to expiration, interest rate, and volatility. The first three variables are observable. The appropriate interest rate needs to be selected, and the stock's volatility needs to be estimated.

8.6.1 Interest Rates

In selecting the risk-free rate for the B–S OPM, practitioners often select the rate on a Treasury bill, commercial paper, or other money market security with a maturity equal to the option's expiration. These rates sometimes are quoted in terms of a simple annual rate, R^A. The rate used in the B–S OPM, though, is the continuous compounded annual rate, R. As we noted earlier, the continuous compounded rate is equal to the natural logarithm of 1 plus the simple annual rate:

$$R = \ln(1 + R^A)$$

Many financial papers and Web sites report the rates on Treasury bills and other money market securities as the dealer's quoted annual bid discount rate (B) and ask rate (A). Given bid and ask quotes, the price (P) of a bill expressed as a proportion of a $100 face value (F), and the continuous compounded annual rate (R) are

$$P = 100 - \left[\frac{B + A}{2}\right]\left[\frac{\text{Days to Maturity}}{360 \text{ Days}}\right]$$

$$R = \frac{\ln(100/P)}{\text{Days to Maturity}/360 \text{ Days}}$$

Thus, a T-bill expiring in one quarter (90 days/360 days = .25) and with a quoted bid yield of 4.8% and ask of 4.75% would have an estimated value equal to 98.80625 per $100 par value and a continuous compounded rate of 4.8037%:

$$P = 100 - \left[\frac{4.8\% + 4.75\%}{2}\right](.25)$$

$$P = 98.80625$$

$$R = \frac{\ln[100/98.80625]}{.25} = .048037$$

8.6.2 Volatility

The volatility of the underlying security is the only input that needs to be estimated in the B–S OPM. The B–S OPM price of an option is quite sensitive to variability. As a result, the applicability of the model depends on obtaining a good estimate of this parameter. Two methods often are used to estimate the variance of the logarithmic return: calculating the stock's historical variance and solving for the stock's implied variance. As noted in Chapter 5, a stock's historical variability is computed using a sample of historical stock prices.

The implied variance is that variance that equates the OPM's value to the option's market price. Unfortunately, one cannot simply set the B–S OPM's price equal to the option's market price, and then solve algebraically to find a unique solution for the variance. The implied variance can be found, though, by trial and error: substituting different variance values into the B–S model until that variance is found that yields an OPM value equal to the market price. One iterative algorithm that can be used to find the implied variance is known as the Newton–Raphson technique. This approach uses a search procedure to find the volatility. The technique was first suggested by Manaster and Koehler. The algorithm is described in supplemental Appendix D at the end of the book. The "Implied Volatility" Excel program included with the book's Excel package solves for the implied volatility using the Newton–Raphson algorithm.

The implied variance can also be approximated for an at-the-money option using the following formula:

$$\sigma^2 = \frac{.5(C_0 + P_0)\sqrt{2\pi/T}}{X(1 + R)^T}$$

Exercise Price	Time to Expiration	Market Call Price	Implied Standard Deviation
100.00	0.101370	2.15	0.1864
105.00	0.101370	0.65	0.1908
100.00	0.265753	3.90	0.1932
105.00	0.265753	1.95	0.1887

For example, if the risk-free rate is 6%, and an ABC 50 call and 50 put expiring in one quarter are trading at $2.86 and $2.12, respectively, when ABC stock is trading at $50, the stock's implied variance would be approximately .25:

$$\sigma^2 = \frac{.5(\$2.86 + \$2.12)\sqrt{2\pi/.25}}{\$50(1.06)^{.25}} = .25$$

Conceptually, the implied variance can be thought of as the market's consensus of the stock's volatility. That is, if we assume that the OPM is specified correctly except for the variance, then differences in estimated option prices would be due to the different investor's estimates of the variance. The option price that ultimately prevails in the market would then be the one associated with a variance that reflects the average of all investors' estimated variances. Theoretically, we should expect the implied variance for different options on the same stock to be the same. In practice, this does not occur. Table 8.6-1, for example, shows different implied standard deviations for four call options on IBM stock as of January 13, 2007. At that date, IBM was trading at $99.34 and had an estimated dividend yield of 2%, and the money market rate was 4.574%. The implied volatilities were obtained using The "Implied Volatility" Excel program. For options with different expiration dates but the same exercise price, differences in implied variances could be explained by investors believing that the stock's variance will change over time. For options that have different exercise prices only, the reasons for differences in implied variances are not as obvious. Whatever the reasons, though, when differences exist, one needs to determine which implied variance should be used.

One way to select an implied variance or standard deviation is to use the arithmetic average for the different implied variances on the stock. With arithmetic averaging, though, equal weight is given to all of the options. If the implied variance represents the market's

TABLE 8.6-1 Implied Volatility on IBM Stock January 13, 2007

IBM Options	Call Price
February 2007 100 Call	2.15
February 2007 105 Call	0.65
April 2007 100 Call	3.90
April 2007 105 Call	1.95
IBM Stock = 99.34	Money Market Rate = 4.574%
Dividend Yield = 2%	

consensus, then perhaps options with relatively low demands, such as deep in- and out-of-the-money ones, should not be given the same weight as other options. Another approach is to select the one implied variance that has the minimum pricing error. In this approach, each option's implied variance is used to compute the OPM values for each option. The absolute deviations of the calculated OPM values from the market price, expressed as a proportion of the OPM price ($|C_0^m - C_0^*|/C_0^*$) are computed next for each implied variance. The implied variance that yields the smallest average proportional deviation then is selected. A third and very popular approach is to generate a volatility smile (volatility and exercise price relation) for different expiration periods and select the volatility that is closet to the option under consideration.

8.6.3   Volatility Smiles and Term Structure

A common approach among option traders is to select the volatility based on the option's *volatility smile* and its *volatility term structure*. A volatility smile is a plot of the implied volatilities given different exercise prices. The volatility term structure, in turn, refers to the relation between an option's implied volatility and its time to expiration. Figure 8.6-1 shows a volatility smile for a stock. The smile shows that the stock's volatility decreases the higher the exercise price. Thus, the volatility used to price a lower exercise-priced option (deep in-the-money call or a deep out-of-the-money put) is greater than the volatility used to price a higher exercised-priced option (deep out-of-the-money call or a deep in-the-money put). The negatively sloped smile shown in the figure is typical for many stock options.[1] Volatility smiles can be used to generate an implied probability distribution for

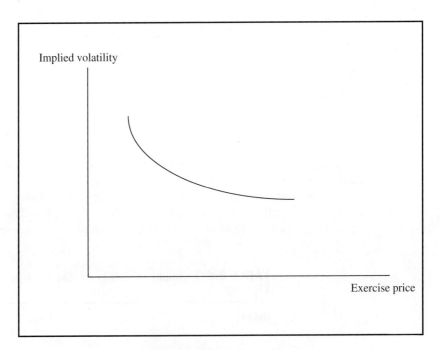

FIGURE 8.6-1 Volatility Smile

---

[1] See (in Selected References for this chapter) Rubinstein (1985, 1994) and Jackwerth and Rubinstein (1996). Note, not all volatility smiles are negatively sloped. Currency options, for example, tend to have U-shaped volatility smiles. See Hull and White (1998).

TABLE 8.6-2   Volatility Surface

	\$90	\$95	\$100	\$105
	Exercise Price			
1 month	20.2%	20.0%	19.6%	19.4%
3 month	20.0%	19.9%	19.7%	19.6%
6 month	19.8%	19.8%	19.8%	19.8%
9 month	19.6%	19.7%	19.9%	20.0%

the underlying stock's price or logarithmic return.[2] When a smile is relatively flat, then the implied distribution of the logarithmic returns approaches a normal distribution (or equivalently stated, the distribution of stock prices is lognormal). In this case, the smile is consistent with the Black–Scholes model's standard assumption of normality. When the smile is negatively sloped, though, the implied probability distribution of logarithmic returns tends to be skewed to the left. Accordingly, a negatively sloped smile is referred to as a *volatility skew*.

Volatility term structure shows the relation between a stock's implied volatility and the time to the option's expiration. When volatilities are relatively low, then they tend to increase the greater the option's maturity. In contrast, when volatilities are relatively high, they tend to decrease the greater the option's maturity. Combining a stock's volatility smile with an estimate of its volatility term structure in a table generates what is referred to as a *volatility surface*. Table 8.6-2 shows an example of a volatility surface that reflects a negatively sloped smile with (1) the volatility decreasing with greater times to expiration for the low-exercised options (the ones with the higher volatility) and (2) the volatility increasing with greater times to expiration for the higher exercised options (the ones with the lower volatility). Option traders use volatility surfaces to help them determine the appropriate volatilities to use when pricing an option with either the B–S OPM or the binomial model. One of the Web Exercises at the end of this chapter involves determining a stock's volatility smile and surface.

8.7   PRICING INDEX OPTIONS WITH THE B–S OPM

8.7.1   European Stock Index Options

If the dividend payments on the index portfolio approximate a continuous stream, then Merton's continuous dividend-adjusted B–S model can be used to determine the equilibrium price of a European index option. In this case, instead of the spot index (S_0), a dividend-adjusted spot index (S_0^D) is used in which

$$S_d = S_0 e^{-\psi T}$$

where

ψ = annual dividends per index share paid by all the stocks comprising the index (properly weighted) divided by the current index (or dividend per index share from a proxy portfolio).

To illustrate, consider the index pricing example from Chapter 6 in which we used the Merton dividend-adjusted binomial model to price European call and put options on

[2] See D. T. Breeden and R. H. Litzenberger (1978).

the S&P 500, each with X = 1250 and T = 180 days (180/365). In pricing the options, we assumed the following:

1. The current S&P 500 is at $S_0 = 1250$.
2. The index's estimated volatility and mean are $\sigma^A = .3$ and $\mu^A = 0$.
3. The annual continuous dividend yield generated from the stocks comprising the index portfolio is $\psi = .04$.
4. Simple annual rate $= R^A = 6\%$ (continuous compounded rate $= \ln(1.06) = .058269$).

Using Merton's dividend-adjusted B–S model, the equilibrium price of the call is 107.45, and the price of the put is 96.45:

$$S_0^D = S_0 e^{-\psi T}$$

$$S_0^D = 1250 e^{-(.04)((180/365))} = 1225.58$$

$$d_1 = \frac{\text{Ln}(1225.58/1250) + [.058269 + .5(.3^2)](180/365)}{.5\sqrt{(180/365)}} = .1481$$

$$d_2 = .1481 - (.5)\sqrt{(185/365)} = -.0626$$

$$N(d_1) = N(.1481) = .5587$$

$$N(d_2) = N(-.0626) = .4753$$

$$1 - N(d_1) = .4413$$

$$1 - N(d_2) = .5247$$

$$C_0^* = S_0^D N(d_1) - \left[\frac{X}{e^{RT}}\right] N(d_2)$$

$$C_0^* = (1225.58)(.5587) - \left[\frac{1250}{e^{(.058269)(180/365)}}\right](.4753) = 107.45$$

$$P_0^* = -S_0^D(1 - N(d_1)) + \left[\frac{X}{e^{RT}}\right](1 - N(d_2))$$

$$P_0^* = -(.4413)(1225.58) + \left[\frac{1250}{e^{(.058269)(180/365)}}\right](.5247) = 96.45$$

Or using the put–call parity model

$$P_0^* = C_0^* - S_0^D + \frac{X}{e^{RT}}$$

$$P_0^* = 107.45 - 1225.58 + \frac{1250}{e^{(.058269)(180/365)}}$$

$$P_0^* = 96.46$$

Alternatively, using the Merton's dividend-adjusted BOPM for n = 100, the European call price is 108.19 (only 0.69% more than the B–S Merton call price), and the European put price is 96.15 (only 0.32% less than the B–S Merton put value).

8.7.2 American Index Options

Although some index options are European, many are American. The pseudo-American OPM can be used to price American call options on dividend-paying stocks. For index options, this would require identifying ex-dividend dates for the stocks comprising the index. Using the pseudo model would be comparable to using the known dividend-payment binomial model explained in Chapter 6. The other alternative for pricing American index options is to use Merton's continuous dividend-adjusted BOPM constrained to price American options. In terms of the preceding example, the Merton-adjusted BOPM for an American call option prices the American index option at 108.19 (the same as the European in this example), and it prices the American put at 97.68—$1.23 more than the binomial European value.

8.8 PRICING CURRENCY OPTIONS WITH THE B–S OPM

As we noted in Chapter 7, a foreign currency option is similar to an option on a stock or stock index paying a continuous dividend. As such, the Merton continuous dividend-adjusted B–S model with the foreign interest rate substituted for the annual dividend yield can be used to price the European option. The application of the Merton model was first noted by Garman and Kohlhagen (G–K) who extended the continuous-time B–S OPM to the pricing of currency options. The Merton B–S OPM uses a foreign interest rate-adjusted exchange rate, E_0^D (analogous to the continuous dividend-adjusted stock price) as the price of the underlying asset in the B–S equation:

$$E_0^D = E_0 e^{-R_F T}$$

$$C_0^* = E_0^D N(d_1) - \left[\frac{X}{e^{R_{US} T}} \right] N(d_2)$$

$$P_0^* = -E_0^D (1 - N(d_1)) + \left[\frac{X}{e^{R_{US} T}} \right] (1 - N(d_2))$$

where

R_F = foreign risk-free rate.

R_{us} = domestic risk-free rate.

σ = annualized standard deviation of the spot exchange rate's logarithmic return.

To see the application of the FC BOPM, consider the example from Chapter 7 in which we priced call and put options on the British pound (BP) each with X = $1.60/BP and T = 180 days using a binomial model. In that example, we assumed the following:

1. The spot $/BP exchange rate = E_0 = $1.60/BP
2. The estimated volatility = σ^A = .3
3. The estimated mean = μ^A = 0
4. The annual U.S. risk-free rate = R_{US} = .06 (continuously compounded rate = .058269)
5. The annual risk-free rate paid on BP = R_F = .08

For n = 100, the Merton BOPM model priced the American BP call at $0.1219 and the American BP put at $0.1371. Using the Merton B–S model, the equilibrium price of the European BP call is $0.1210, which is only slightly less than the binomial price, and the price of the European put is $0.1376, which also is only slightly less than the binomial put value:

$$C_0^* = E_0^D N(d_1) - \left[\frac{X}{e^{RT}}\right] N(d_2)$$

$$C_0^* = (\$1.5381)(.5215) - \left[\frac{\$1.60}{e^{(.058269)(180/365)}}\right](.4381) = \$0.1210$$

$$P_0^* = -E_0^D(1 - N(d_1)) + \left[\frac{X}{e^{RT}}\right](1 - N(d_2))$$

$$P_0^* = -(\$1.5381)(.4785) + \left[\frac{\$1.60}{e^{(.058269)(180/365)}}\right](.5619) = \$0.1376$$

where:

$$E_0^D = E_0 e^{-R_F T}$$

$$E_0^D = \$1.60 e^{-(.08)((180/365))} = \$1.5381$$

$$d_1 = \frac{Ln(\$1.5381/\$1.60) + [.058269 + (.5)(.3^2)](180/365)}{.3\sqrt{(180/365)}} = .0545$$

$$d_2 = .0545 - .3\sqrt{(180/365)} = -.1562$$

$$N(d_1) = N(.0545) = .5215$$

$$N(d_2) = N(-.1562) = .4381$$

$$1 - N(d_1) = .4785$$

$$1 - N(d_2) = .5619$$

Although there are a number of exchange-listed currency options that are European, many are American. As such, Merton's continuous asset-adjusted BOPM for American options is more applicable to pricing American currency options than Merton's asset-adjusted B–S model. In terms of the previous example, the Merton asset-adjusted BOPM for an American call option prices the American BP call option at $0.1242 and the American BP put at $0.1372 for n = 100 subperiods.

8.9   PRICING BOND OPTIONS WITH THE B–S OPM

The value of an option on a bond can also be estimated using the B–S OPM. The B–S formula for determining the equilibrium price of a call or put option on a generic bond is

$$C_0^* = B_0 N(d_1) - X N(d_2) e^{-RT}$$

$$P_0^* = X(1 - N(d_2))e^{-RT} - B_0(1 - N(d_1))$$

$$d_1 = \frac{\ln(B_0/X) + (R + .5\sigma^2)T}{\sigma\sqrt{T}}$$

$$d_2 = d_1 - \sigma\sqrt{T}$$

where:

B_0 = price of the bond

σ^2 = annualized variance of the bond's logarithmic return = $V(\ln(B_n/B_0))$

As an example, suppose there is a 3-year bond with a 10% annual coupon selling at par (F = 100) and call and put options on the bond each with an exercise price of 100 and expiration of 1 year. Assuming the risk-free rate is 6%, and the variability on the underlying bond's logarithmic return is $\sigma = 0.10$, the call and put prices using the Black–Scholes model would be 7.45 and 1.63, respectively.

$$C_0^* = B_0 N(d_1) - X N(d_2) e^{-RT}$$

$$C_0^* = 100(.7423) - 100(.7091) e^{-(.06)(1)} = 7.45$$

$$P_0^* = X(1 - N(d_2)) e^{-RT} - B_0(1 - N(d_1))$$

$$P_0^* = 100(1 - .7091) e^{-(.06)(1)} - 100(1 - .7423) = 1.63$$

$$d_1 = \frac{\ln(100/100) + (.06 + .5(.10^2))1}{.10\sqrt{1}} = .6500$$

$$d_2 = .6500 - .10\sqrt{1} = .5500$$

$$N(d_1) = N(.6500) = .7423$$

$$N(d_2) = N(.5500) = .7091$$

It should be noted that there are two problems using the standard OPM to price bond options. First, recall the B–S OPM is based on the assumption of a constant variance. In the case of a bond, though, its variability tends to decrease as its maturity becomes shorter. Second, the OPM assumes that the interest rate is constant. For debt options, the volatility of the bond is due to a large extent to volatility of interest rates. Because of these problems, mispricing can result in determining the equilibrium price of a debt option with the B–S OPM. Thus, the use of the B–S OPM to value the call and put option on a bond should be viewed only as an approximation. The binomial interest rate tree described in Chapter 7, in turn, may be a more accurate model to use in pricing bond options than then B–S model.

8.10 OTHER OPTION PRICING MODELS

Several empirical studies have been conducted that compare the B–S OPM prices with observed market prices. These studies have found the B–S model tends to underprice in-the-money calls and overprice out-of-the money calls, with the degree of mispricing being greater the shorter the option's time to expiration. The studies have found, though, that the B–S model is good at pricing on-the-money calls with some time to expiration. Appendix 8C describes the methodologies and results of some of these empirical studies. The observed pricing biases associated with the B–S model can be explained in terms of violations of the assumptions underlying the model.

One of the underlying assumptions of the B–S model is that the variance is stable. Because the variance is the only parameter in the OPM that must be estimated, the applicability of the model depends, in part, on the variance being stable. Moreover, the equilibrium option price is quite sensitive to changes in the underlying stock's variability. As a result, if there is considerable disagreement in the market about the size of the stock's variance, or if the variance is in fact unstable—changing frequently over time and with different stock prices—then one prevailing option price will not exist, and the OPM will not be capable of determining the equilibrium price of an option. Other option models have been developed to account for cases in which the assumption of a constant variance over time and stock prices does not hold. Merton's mixed diffusion jump model, for example, accounts for the possibilities of infrequent jumps in stock prices; and Cox and Ross's constant elasticity of variance model accounts for cases in which the variance is inversely related to the stock price. The interested reader is encouraged to examine these models and others referenced at the end of this chapter.

Another underlying assumption of the B–S model is that the distribution of the underlying stock's logarithmic return is normal. Several empirical studies have provided evidence that the distributions of stock and stock index returns exhibit persistent skewness (e.g., Kon (1990), Aggarwal and Rao (1990), and Turner and Weigel (1992)). Studies by Stein and Stein (1991), Wiggins (1987), and Hestin (1993) have demonstrated that when skewness exists, the B–S model consistently misprices options. To address the pricing bias resulting from the assumption of normality, Jarrow and Rudd (1982) and Corrado and Tie Su (1996) have extended the B–S model to account for cases in which there is skewness in the underlying security's return distribution. Similarly, Câmara and Chung (2006) and Johnson, Pawlukiewicz, and Mehta (1997) have extended the binomial option pricing model to include skewness. Again, the interested reader is encouraged to examine these models and others referenced at the end of this chapter.

8.11 CONCLUSION

In this chapter, we defined the seminal B–S OPM and examined how the equilibrium price of an option can be estimated using the model. In general, empirical studies have provided support for the B–S model as a valid pricing model, especially for near-the-money options. The observed pricing errors could be the result of problems in estimating the variance or the presence of skewness in the distribution of logarithmic return. The overall consensus, though, is that the B–S OPM is a useful pricing model. In fact, aside from empirical studies, the strongest endorsement of the B–S OPM comes from its ubiquitous use. Today, the OPM may be the most widely accepted model in the field of finance. In the next chapter, we continue our analysis of the B–S OPM by examining some of its other uses and how it is used to price exotic options.

Web Information

Fisher Black received a Ph.D. in Applied Math from Harvard University in 1964. In 1971, he taught at the University of Chicago and later at the MIT Sloan School of Management. In 1985, he joined Goldman Sachs.

Biography

http://en.wikipedia.org/wiki/Fischer_Black
Major Works: http://cepa.newschool.edu/het/profiles/black.htm

Myron S. Scholes is Chairman of Platinum Grove Asset Management, an alternative investment fund, specializing in liquidity provision services to the global wholesale capital markets. Professor Scholes is the Frank E. Buck Professor of Finance Emeritus at the Stanford University Graduate School. Professor Scholes is widely known for his seminal work in options pricing, capital markets, tax policies, and the financial services industry. For option pricing work, he was awarded the Alfred Nobel Memorial Prize in Economic Sciences in 1997.

Biography

http://nobelprize.org-prizes/economics/laureates/1997/scholes-autobio.html

KEY TERMS

Delta

gamma

theta

vega (kappa)

rho

pseudo-American model

continuous dividend-adjusted B-S OPM

implied variance

volatility smile

volatility skew

volatility term structure

volatility surface

SELECTED REFERENCES

Aggarwal, R. and R. P. Rao. "Institutional Ownership and Distribution of Equity Returns." *The Financial Review* 25 (1990), 211–29.

Amin, K., and R. A. Jarrow. "Pricing Foreign Currency Options Under Stochastic Interest Rates." *Journal of International Money and Finance* 10 (1991): 310–29.

Ball, C., and W. Torous. "On Jumps in Common Stock Prices and Their Impact on Call Pricing." *Journal of Finance* 40 (1985): 155–173.

Baily, W., and R. Stulz. "The Pricing of Stock Index Options in a General Equilibrium Model." *Journal of Financial and Quantitative Analysis* 24 (March 1989): 1–12.

Barone-Adesi, G., and R. Whaley. "Efficient Analytic Approximation of American Option Values." *The Journal of Finance* 42 (June 1987): 301–320.

Beckers, S. "Standard Deviations Implied in Option Prices as Predictors of Future Stock Price Variability." *Journal of Banking and Finance* 5 (September 1981): 363–82.

Beckers, S. "The Constant Elasticity of Variance Model and Its Implications for Option Pricing." *Journal of Finance* 35 (June 1980): 661–73.

Beedles, W. L. "The Anomalous and Asymmetric Nature of Equity Returns: An Empirical Synthesis." *Journal of Financial Research* 7 (1984), 151–60.

Bhattacharya, M. "Empirical Properties of the Black–Scholes Formula Under Ideal Conditions." *Journal of Financial and Quantitative Analysis* 15 (December 1980): 1081–95.

Bhattacharya, M. "Transaction Data Tests of Efficiency of the Chicago Board Options Exchange." *Journal of Financial Economics* 12 (1983): 161–185.

Biger, N., and J. Hull. "The Valuation of Currency Options." *Financial Management* (Spring 1983): 24–29.

Black, F. "Fact and Fantasy in the Use of Options." *Financial Analysis Journal* 31 (July–August 1975): 36–41, 61–72.

Black, F. "How We Came Up with the Option Pricing Formula." *Journal of Portfolio Management* 15, 2 (1989): 4–8.

Black, F., and M. Scholes. "The Valuation of Option Contracts and a Test of Market Efficiency." *Journal of Finance* 27 (May 1972): 399–418.

Black, F., and M. Scholes. "The Pricing of Options and Corporate Liabilities." *Journal of Political Economy* 81 (May–June 1973): 637–659.

Bodurtha, J., and G. Courtadon. "Efficiency Tests of the Foreign Currency Options Market." *Journal of Finance* 41 (March 1986): 151–162.

Bodurtha, J., and G. Courtadon. "Tests of An American Option Pricing Model on the Foreign Currency Options Market." *Journal of Financial and Quantitative Analysis* 22 (June 1987): 153–167.

Boyle, P., and A. Ananthanarayanan. "The Impact of Variance Estimation in Option Valuation Models." *Journal of Financial Economics* 5 (December 1977): 375–88.

Breeden, D. T., and R. H. Litzenberger. "Prices of State-Contingent Claims in Option Prices," *Journal of Business* 51 (1978): 621–651.

Camara, A., and S. Chung. "Option Pricing for the Transformed-Binomial Class." *Journal of Futures Markets* (August 2006): 759–787.

Chance, D. "Empirical Tests of the Pricing of Index Call Options." *Advances in Futures and Options Research* 1 (1986): 141–166.

Cootner, P. H., ed. *The Random Character of Stock Market Prices*. Cambridge, MA: MIT Press, 1964.

Corrado, C. J., and Tie Su. "Skewness and Kurtosis in S&P 500 Index Returns Implied by Option Prices." *The Journal of Financial Research* 19 (1996): 175–192.

Copeland, T. E., and J. F. Weston. *Financial Theory and Corporate Policy.* Reading, MA: Addison-Wesley, 1984, 230–275.

Cox, J., and S. Ross. "The Valuation of Options for Alternative Stochastic Processes." *Journal of Financial Economics* 3 (January–March 1976): 145–166.

Cox, J., and M. Rubinstein. "A Survey of Alternative Option Pricing Models," in *Option Pricing,* edited by M. Brenner. Lexington, MA: Health, 1983.

Cox, J., S. Ross, and M. Rubinstein. "Option Pricing: A Simplified Approach." *Journal of Financial Economics* (September 1979): 229–263.

Derman, E., and I. Kani. "Riding on a Smile," *Risk* (February 1994): 32–39.

Ederington, L. H., and W. Guan. "Why Are Those Options Smiling." *Journal of Derivatives* 10, 2 (2002): 9–34.

Ervine, J., and A. Rudd. "Index Options: The Early Evidence." *Journal of Finance* 40 (July 1985): 743–756.

Galai, D. "A Survey of Empirical Tests of Option Pricing Models." In *Option Pricing*, edited by M. Brenner, 45–80. Lexington, MA: D.C. Health, 1983.

Galai, D. "A Convexity Test for Traded Options." *Quarterly Review of Economics and Business* 19 (Summer 1979): 83–90.

Garman, M., and W. Kohlhagen. "Foreign Currency Option Values." *Journal of International Money and Finance* 2 (December 1983): 231–237.

Geske, R. "A Note on an Analytic Formula for Unprotected American Call Options on Stocks With Known Dividends." *Journal of Financial Economics* 7 (December 1979): 375–380.

Geske, R. "Pricing of Options with Stochastic Dividend Yield." *Journal of Finance* 33 (May 1978): 618–25.

Geske, R., and H. Johnson. "The American Put Option Valued Analytically." *The Journal of Finance* 39 (December 1984): 1511–1524.

Geske, R., and R. Roll. "On Valuing American Call Options With the Black–Scholes Formula." *Journal of Finance* 39 (June 1984): 443–55.

Heston, S. L. "A Closed Form Solution for Options and Stochastic Volatility With Applications to Bond and Currency Options." *Review of Financial Studies* 6 (1993), 327–44.

Hull, J. C. *Options, Futures, and Other Derivatives.* Upper Saddle River, NJ: Prentice Hall, 2006: Chapter 16.

Hull, J. C., and A. White. "Value at Risk when Daily Changes in Market Variables Are Not Normally Distributed," *Journal of Derivatives* 5 (Spring 1998): 9–19.

Itô, K. "On Stochastic Differential Equations." Memiore, *American Mathematical Society* 4 (December 1951): 1–51.

Jackwerth, J. C., and M. Rubinstein. "Recovering Probability Distributions from Option Prices." *Journal of Finance* 51 (December 1996): 1611–1631.

Jarrow, R., and A. Rudd. "Approximate Option Valuation for Arbitrary Stochastic Processes." *Journal of Financial Economics* 10 (1982): 347–369.

Johnson, R. S., J. E. Pawlukiewicz, and J. Mehta. "Binomial Option Pricing With Skewed Asset Returns." *Review of Quantitative Finance and Accounting* 9 (1997): 89–101.

Kon, S. J. "Models of Stock Returns—A Comparison." *Journal of Finance* 39 (1984): 147–65.

Lantane, H., and R. Rendleman, Jr. "Standard Deviations of Stock Price Ratios Implied in Option Prices." *Journal of Finance* 31 (May 1976): 369–82.

MacBeth, J., and L. Merville. "An Empirical Examination of the Black-Scholes Call Option Pricing Model." *Journal of Finance* 34 (December 1979): 1173–86.

MacBeth, J., and L. Merville. "Tests of the Black–Scholes and Cox Call Option Valuation Models." *Journal of Finance* (May 1980): 285–300.

Manaster, S., and R. Rendleman, Jr. "Option Prices as Predictors of Equilibrium Stock Prices." *Journal of Finance* 37 (September 1982): 1043–58.

Melick W. R., and C. P. Thomas. "Recovering an Asset's Implied Probability Density Function From Option Prices: An Application to Crude Oil during the Gulf Crisis." *Journal of Financial and Quantitative Analysis* 32 (March 1997): 91–115.

Merton, R. "Option Pricing When Underlying Stock Returns Are Discontinuous." *Journal of Financial Economics* 3 (January–February 1976): 125–144.

Merton, R. C. "The Theory of Rational Option Pricing." *Bell Journal of Economics and Management Science* 4 (Spring 1973): 141–83.

Neftci, S. *Introduction to Mathematics of Financial Derivatives.* New York: Academic Press, 1996.

Rogalski, R. "Variances of Option Prices in Theory and Evidence." *Journal of Portfolio Management* 4 (Winter 1978): 43–51.

Roll, R. "An Analytic Valuation Formula for Unprotected American Call Options on Stocks with Known Dividends." *Journal of Financial Economics* 5 (November 1977): 251–258.

Rubinstein, M. "Implied Binomial Trees," *Journal of Finance* 49 (July 1994): 771–818.

Rubinstein, M. "Nonparametric Tests of Alternative Option Pricing Models Using All Reported Trades and Quotes on the 30 Most Active CBOE Option Classes From August 23,1976 through August 31, 1978." *Journal of Finance* 40 (June 1985): 455–480.

Rubinstein, M. "Nonparametric Tests of Alternative Option Pricing Models." Working Paper No. 117, University of California, Berkeley, Research Program in Finance, 1981.

Schmalensee, R., and R. Trippi. "Common Stock Volatility Expectations Implied by Option Premia." *Journal of Finance* 33 (March 1978): 129–47.

Shastri, K., and K. Wethyavivorn. "The Valuation of Currency Options for Alternative Stochastic Processes." *Journal of Financial Research* 4 (December 1985): 455–468.

Singleton, J. C., and J. Wingender. "Skewness Persistence in Common Stock Returns." *Journal of Financial and Quantitative Analysis* 21 (1986): 335–341.

Stapleton, R. C., and M. G. Subramanyam. "The Valuation of Options When Asset Returns Are Generated By a Binomial Process." *Journal of Finance* 39 (1984): 1525–1539.

Stein, E. M., and J. C. Stein. "Stock Price Distributions With Stochastic Volatility: An Analytical Approach." *Review of Financial Studies* 4 (1991): 727-752.

Sterk, W. "Comparative Performance of the Black–Scholes and Roll–Geske–Whaley Option Pricing Models." *Journal of Financial and Quantitative Analysis* 18 (September 1983): 345–54.

Trennepohl, G. "A Comparison of Listed Option Premiums and Black-Scholes Model Prices: 1973–1979." *Journal of Financial Research* 4 (Spring 1981): 11–20.

Trippi, R. "A Test of Option Market Efficiency Using a Random-Walk Valuation Model." *Journal of Economics and Business* 29 (Winter 1977): 93–98.

Turner, A. L., and E. J. Weigel. "Daily Stock Return Volatility: 1928–1989." *Management Science* 38 (1992): 1586–1609.

Whaley, R. "Valuation of American Call Options on Dividend Paying Stocks: Empirical Tests." *Journal of Financial Economics* 10 (March 1982): 29–58.

Whaley, R. "On the Valuation of American Call Options on Stocks With Known Dividends." *Journal of Financial Economics* 9 (June 1981): 207–212.

Wiggins, J. B. "Option Values under Stochastic Volatility: Theory and Empirical Estimates." *Journal of Financial Economics* 10 (1987), 351–72.

Xu, X., and S. J. Taylor. "The Term Structure of Volatility Implied by Foreign Exchange Options." *Journal of Financial and Quantitative Analysis* 29 (1994): 57–74.

PROBLEMS AND QUESTIONS

Note: Many of these problems can be done or answers checked using the B–S OPM Excel program that is included with the text.

1. Suppose ABC stock currently is trading at $60 per share, has an annualized standard deviation of .35, and will not pay any dividends over the next 3 months; also suppose that the continuously compounded annual risk-free rate is 6%.

   a. Using the Black–Scholes OPM, calculate the equilibrium price for a 3-month ABC 60 European call option.

b. Using the Black–Scholes OPM, calculate the equilibrium price for a 3-month ABC 60 European put option.

c. Show the Black–Scholes put price is the same price obtained using the put–call parity model.

d. Describe the arbitrage strategy one would pursue if the ABC 60 call were overpriced and if it were underpriced.

e. Describe the arbitrage strategy one would pursue if the ABC 60 put were overpriced and if it were underpriced.

f. What would be the new equilibrium prices of the ABC call and put if ABC stock increased to $60.50?

2. Suppose the ABC call in Problem 1 is priced at $4.91 when ABC stock is at $60.

a. Define the arbitrage strategy you would set up.

b. Show what would happen if you closed the position a short time later when the stock was at $60.50 and the price of the call was equal to its equilibrium value (assume the change in time is negligible).

3. Suppose the ABC put in Problem 1 is priced at $3.91 when ABC stock is at $60.

a. Define the arbitrage strategy you would set up.

b. Show what would happen if you closed the position a short time later when the stock was at $60.50 and the price of the call was equal to its equilibrium value (assume the change in time is negligible).

4. Suppose the ABC stock described in Problem 1 is expected to go ex-dividend in exactly 1 month, with the value of the dividend on that date expected to be $1.50. Using the Pseudo-American option model, calculate the equilibrium prices of the call and put options described in Problem 1.

5. Using the continuous-dividend-adjusted option model, calculate the dividend-adjusted stock price, dividend-adjusted call price, and dividend-adjusted put price for the ABC stock and options described in Problem 1. In your calculations, assume an annual dividend yield of 10%.

6. Given the following information, $S_0 = \$36$, $X = \$35$, $T = .5$, $R = .08$, and $\sigma = .25$.

a. Determine the equilibrium European call price using the B–S OPM.

b. Determine the equilibrium European put price using the B–S OPM or put–call parity model.

7. Discuss the applicability of the pseudo-American model for pricing American call options and American put options.

8. Suppose the spot S&P 500 is currently at 1200, its annualized standard deviation is $\sigma^A = .25$, and that the stocks making up the index will go ex-dividend in approximately 70 days. Suppose also that there is an American call option on the S&P 500 with an exercise price of 1200 and expiration of 100 days and that the continuously compounded annual risk-free rate is $R = 6\%$.

a. Using Black's pseudo-American model, determine the equilibrium price of the index call option given that stocks making up the index will pay dividends worth 1% of the current value 70 days from the present. Use the B–S Excel program.

b. Determine the equilibrium prices of the index call option given that stocks making up the index will pay dividends worth 2.5% of the current value 70 days from the present. Use the B–S Excel program.

c. What is the B–S OPM call price if you failed to include the dividend? Use the B–S Excel program.

d. Comment on your findings.

9. Suppose the following:

- Spot S&P 500 is currently at 1200
- Continuous annual dividend yield of $\psi = 10\%$
- Annualized standard deviation is $\sigma^A = .25$
- Continuously compounded annual risk-free rate is R = 6%.
- Simple annual risk-free rate = 6.1837%
- European call and put options on the S&P 500 index each with an exercise price of 1200 and expiration of 180 days

Questions:

a. Determine the equilibrium prices of the call and put options using Merton's dividend-adjusted B–S OPM. Use the B–S Excel program.

b. Determine both the American and European options prices using Merton's dividend-adjusted binomial model for n = 100 subperiods. Use the Excel program.

c. Compare prices using Merton's European binomial model with Merton's B–S model.

d. Compare the prices for Merton's American binomial with the European binomial. Is there any early exercise advantage?

10. Assume the following:

- U.S. continuously compounded risk-free rate (annual) = 6% (simple annual rate = .061837)
- British continuously compounded risk-free (rate paid on BP) = .09 (simple annual rate = .094175)
- $/BP spot exchange rate = $1.50/BP
- Annualized logarithmic return's standard deviation = $\sigma^A = 0.25$.
- European call and put options with X = $1.50 and expirations = 30 days.

Questions:

a. Determine the equilibrium prices on European BP call and put options using the Merton dividend-adjusted B–S model. Use the B-S Excel program.

b. Determine the prices of the options using Merton's dividend-adjusted Binomial model. Use the Excel program.

c. Determine the prices of the options assuming they were American using Merton's dividend-adjusted Binomial model. Use the Excel program.

d. Is there any early exercise advantage?

11. Discuss the assumptions of the B–S OPM and their applicability.

12. Compare and contrast the B–S OPM with the BOPM.

13. Given a T-bill with 180 days to maturity, a quoted annual bid yield of 7.5%, and an ask yield of 7.35%, calculate the following rates:

a. The continuously compounded risk-free rate.

b. The simple annual rate.

14. Explain the idea of the implied variance being the market's consensus of the correct variance.

15. Using the B–S OPM Excel program, calculate the call option price for each stock price shown following. Assume $R = 6\%$, $\sigma = .15$, $T = .25$ per year, $X = \$50$, and no dividends.

$$S_0 = 42, 44, 46, 48, 50, 52, 54, 56, 58, \text{ and } 60.$$

Show your results graphically.

Comment on the ability of the B–S OPM to capture the features of the call and stock price relations described in Chapter 4.

16. Using the B–S OPM Excel program, calculate the put option price for each stock price shown following. Assume $R = 6\%$, $\sigma = .15$, $T = .25$ per year, $X = \$50$, and no dividends.

$$S_0 = 42, 44, 46, 48, 50, 52, 54, 56, 58, \text{ and } 60.$$

Show your results graphically.

Comment on the ability of the B–S OPM to capture the feature that the put price is greater than its IV.

17. Using the B–S OPM Excel program, calculate the call option price for each annualized standard deviation shown following. Assume $R = 6\%$, $= S_0 = \$50$, $T = .25$, $X = \$50$, and no dividends.

$$\sigma = .13, .14, .15, \text{ and } .16.$$

Comment on the relationship.

18. Using the B–S OPM Excel program, calculate the call option price for each time to expiration value shown following (use 365-day year). Assume $= S_0 = \$50$, $\sigma = .15$, $R = 6\%$, $X = \$50$, and no dividends.

$$T = 90 \text{ days, } 120 \text{ days, and } 180 \text{ days.}$$

19. Given the following:

- An on-the-money ABC 50 call expiring in 90 days and priced at $3.50
- An ABC 50 put expiring in 90 days and priced at $2.50
- 90-day annualized risk-free rate of 6%
- No dividend payments on ABC stock

Determine the implied variance on ABC stock given that it is currently trading at $50. Check your answer using the "Implied Volatility" Excel program.

20. Using Merton's dividend-adjusted B–S OPM Excel program, determine the equilibrium BP call prices for each $/BP exchange rate shown following. Assume $R_F = .06$, $R_{US} = .045$, $X = \$1.50$, $\sigma = .275$, and $T = .25$.

$$E_0 = \$1.35/\text{BP}, 1.40, 1.45, 1.50, 1.55, 1.60, 1.65$$

Show your results graphically.

21. Using Merton's dividend-adjusted B–S OPM Excel program, determine the equilibrium BP put prices for each $/BP exchange rate shown following. Assume $R_F = .06$, $R_{US} = .045$, $X = \$1.50$, $\sigma = .275$, and $T = .25$.

$$E_0 = \$1.35/\text{BP}, 1.40, 1.45, 1.50, 1.55, 1.60, 1.65$$

Show your results graphically.

WEB EXERCISES

1. On February 16, 2007, there were 100 call and 100 put options on IBM each expiring on July 20. On February 16, IBM's stock closed at 98.99, its historical volatility was .1959 (annualized standard deviation of logarithmic return), IBM's historical annual dividend yield was 2%, and the short-term money market rate was 4.574%.

   a. Determine the price of IBM's call and put options using Merton's continuous dividend-yield B–S model (use the B–S OPM Excel program).

   b. Using IBM's historical dividend yield and volatility or your own estimates, price a currently traded IBM call and put using Merton's continuous dividend-yield B–S model. Use the B–S Excel program. For information on currently traded IBM options, go to www.wsj.com/free.

   c. Generate volatility smiles for two expirations for IBM using currently traded IBM options. Use the "Implied Volatility" Excel program. For information, go to www.wsj.com/free.

2. On January 8, 2007, the S&P 500 call option with an exercise price of 1400 and expiration of June 16, 2007 (158 days), was trading at 66. On that date, the spot S&P 500 index closed at 1412.84, its historical volatility was .13644 (annualized standard deviation of logarithmic return), index's dividend yield was 1.799%, and the short-term money market rate was 4.778%.

   a. Determine the price of S&P 500 call and put options using Merton's continuous dividend-yield B–S model (use the B–S OPM Excel program).

   b. Using the S&P 500's historical dividend yield and volatility or your own estimates, price a currently traded S&P 500 call and put using Merton's continuous dividend-yield B–S model. Use the B–S Excel program. For information on currently traded S&P 500 options, go to www.wsj.com/free.

   c. Generate volatility smiles for two expirations for the S&P 500 using currently traded options. Use the "Implied Volatility" Excel program. For information, go to www.wsj.com/free.

3. On February 19, 2007, there were British pound call and put options trading on the Philadelphia Exchange each with an exercise price of $1.95 and expiration of April (60 days). On February 19, the spot $/BP exchange rate was $1.9505, the BP volatility was .1229 (annualized standard deviation of logarithmic return), the 2-month U.S. Treasury rate was 5.16%, and the 2-month U.K. Treasury rate was 5.40%.

   a. Using the B–S OPM Excel program, determine the prices of BP options using Merton's continuous asset-yield B–S model.

   b. Using the BP volatility or your own estimates, price a currently traded BP call using Merton's continuous asset-yield binomial model. Use the Excel program. For information on currently traded currency option listed on the Philadelphia Exchange, go to www.phlx.com. Note: If there is no closing price, average the dealer's bid and ask prices.

   c. Generate volatility smiles for two expirations for the British pound using currently traded options. Use the "Implied Volatility" Excel program. For information, go to www.phlx.com.

   For information on exchange rates and interest rates in other countries, go to www.fxstreet.com. For information on historical foreign exchange rates, go to www.research.stlouisfed.org/fred2.

APPENDIX 8A   MATHEMATICAL FOUNDATION OF THE BLACK SCHOLE OPM[3]

The first step in deriving the B–S model is to construct a portfolio consisting of the stock and call that yields a return that is invariant to stock price changes per period of time. The value of the portfolio (V_h) is

$$V_h = n_S S + n_C C \qquad (8.A\text{--}1)$$

where

$$n_c = \text{number of calls}$$
$$n_s = \text{number of shares}$$

To make the portfolio invariant to small stock price changes requires finding the n_c and n_s values in which the derivative of Equation (8.A-1) with respect to S is zero: $\partial V_h/\partial S = 0$. To this end, we first take the partial derivative (8.A-1) with respect to S and set it equal to zero:

$$\frac{\partial V_h}{\partial S} = n_s \frac{\partial S}{\partial S} + n_c \frac{\partial C}{\partial S} = 0$$

$$n_s + n_c \frac{\partial C}{\partial S} = 0 \qquad (8.A\text{--}2)$$

Next, we constrain the portfolio to one written call by setting $n_C = -1$ in Equation (8.A-2); then we solve (8.A-2) for n_S to define the n_S value that makes $\partial V_h/\partial S = 0$:

$$n_s - 1\frac{\partial C}{\partial S} = 0$$

$$n_S = \frac{\partial C}{\partial S} \qquad (8.A\text{--}3)$$

Thus, the hedge portfolio is defined by Equation (8.A-1) with $n_c = -1$ and $n_s = \partial C/\partial S$. Because this portfolio is invariant to stock price changes, in equilibrium, it should yield a riskless rate of return per period of time. Thus, in equilibrium, the proportional change in the portfolio, dV_h/V_h, should equal the risk-free rate of return (R_f) per time (dt). Thus, our equilibrium condition is

$$\frac{dV_h}{V_h} = R_f dt. \qquad (8.A\text{--}4)$$

For example, if the annual risk-free rate (R_f) is 6%, and the length of the time period is a day, implying a daily risk-free rate (R_f) of $(1.06)^{(1/360)} - 1 = .000162$, then a hedged portfolio worth $100 should, in equilibrium, increase in value by $0.0162 per day (($.000162)($100) per day) or grow at a daily rate of .0162%.

The equilibrium change in the call price, dC, can be found by first taking the total derivative of Equation (8.A-1):

$$dV_h = n_s dS + n_e dC. \qquad (8.A\text{--}5)$$

---

[3] This appendix requires calculus.

Next, we substitute Equation (8.A-4) into (8.A5) to constrain the change in the portfolio value to equal its equilibrium change, and then we set $n_C = -1$ and $n_S = \partial C/\partial S$ to make the portfolio riskless. Doing this we obtain

$$R_f V_h dt = n_S dS + n_C dC$$

$$R_f[n_S S + n_C C]dt = n_S dS + n_C DC$$

$$R_f\left[\frac{\partial C}{\partial S}S - C\right]dt = \frac{\partial C}{\partial S}dS - dC. \qquad (8.A-6)$$

Last, we solve for (8.A-6) for dC:

$$dC = -R_f\frac{\partial C}{\partial S}S\,dt + R_f\,C\,dt + \frac{\partial C}{\partial S}dS \qquad (8.A-7)$$

Equation (8.A-7) defines the equilibrium change in the call price in terms of the rate of change in the value of a hedged portfolio set equal to the rate earned on a risk-free security.

Given Equation (8.A-7), the last step is to define the rate of change in the stock price per time and then translate that into the rate of change in the call price per time. Here, Black and Scholes assumed the change in the stock price through time follows a geometric *Weiner process*. When applied to stock prices, this process implies that the proportional change in stock prices (dS/S) grows along the path of its expected logarithmic return, known as a drift component, with the actual price being above or below the path at any time and with the extent of the deviation determined by the stock's variability. Thus, the proportional change in the stock price per time depends on the mean and variance of the stock's logarithmic return and, in a geometric Weiner process, is defined as

$$\frac{dS}{S} = \sqrt{\mu}dt + \sigma\,dZ \qquad (8.A-8)$$

where

μ = mean logarithmic return
σ = standard deviation of the logarithmic return
Z = standard normally distributed random variable

Given the proportional change in the stock price, Black and Scholes next used a technique known as *Ito's lemma* to determine the rate of change in the call. Specifically, by Ito's lemma, if the stock price change follows a Weiner process, and the call price is a function of the stock price and time ($C = f(S,t)$), then the total differential of the call function is given as

$$dC = \frac{\partial C}{\partial S}dS + \frac{\partial C}{\partial t}dt + \frac{1}{2}\frac{\partial^2 C}{\partial S^2}\sigma^2 S^2 dt \qquad (8.A-9)$$

Equation (8.A-9) defines the process by which the call price changes. Substituting (8.A-9) for dC in (8.A-7) and then solving for $\partial C/\partial t$, we obtain the equilibrium change in the call price per time that makes the hedge portfolio grow at the risk-free rate. That is

$$\frac{\partial C}{\partial S}dS + \frac{\partial C}{\partial t}dt + \frac{1}{2}\frac{\partial^2 C}{\partial S^2}\sigma^2 S^2 dt = \frac{\partial C}{\partial S}dS - R_f S\frac{\partial C}{\partial S}dt + R_f C\,dt$$

Dividing through by dt and solving for $\partial C/\partial t$, we obtain

$$\frac{\partial C}{\partial t} = -R_f S\frac{\partial C}{\partial S}dt - \frac{1}{2}\frac{\partial^2 C}{\partial S^2}\sigma^2 S^2 + R_f C \qquad (8.A-10)$$

Equation (8.A-10) is a differential equation. It can be solved subject to a boundary condition that the price of the call equals its IV at expiration. Black and Scholes solved Equation (8.A-10) for C with that constraint using the heat exchange equation from physics to obtain the B–S OPM Equation (8.2-1).

APPENDIX 8B BLACK–SCHOLES ARBITRAGE/HEDGING PORTFOLIO*

B–S Hedged Portfolio for Calls

In the B–S model, an arbitrage portfolio can be constructed by finding the proportion of shares of stock (n_s) per written call (n_c) that makes the value of a hedged portfolio (V_h) invariant to small changes in the stock price (this type of derivation also is done in Appendix 8A to obtain the B–S equation). The value of the hedged portfolio is

$$V_h = n_S S + n_C C \tag{8.B–1}$$

where

$$n_s = \text{number of shares of stock}$$
$$n_c = \text{number of calls}$$

Mathematically, the hedged portfolio is found by setting $n_C = -1$ in Equation (8.B-1) to constrain the portfolio to consist of one written call and then solving for the n_s value that makes the partial derivative of Equation (8.B-1) with respect to changes in S equal to zero: $\partial V_h/\partial S = 0$. Specifically, the partial derivative of Equation (8.B-1) with respect to S is

$$\frac{\partial V_h}{\partial S} = n_s \frac{\partial S}{\partial S} + n_c \frac{\partial C}{\partial S} = 0 \tag{8.B–2}$$

TABLE 8.B-1 Arbitrage Strategy Using the Black–Scholes OPM: $C_0^m = \$3.00$, $S_0 = \$45$, $X = \$50$, $C_0^* = \$2.88$

Initial Position	Cash Flow
Long $N(d_1)$ Shares of Stock: $-(.4066)(\$45)$	$-\$18.30$
Short One Call: $(1)(\$3.00)$	3.00
Borrow $N(d_1)S_0 - C_0^m$ funds: $(.4066)(\$45) - \$3.00$	15.30
Cash Flow	0

Closing Position when $C_t^m = C_t^*$:
$S_t = \$46$, $T = .25$ (approximately), and $C_t^m = C_t^* = \$3.30$

Position	Cash Flow
Stock Sale: $(.4066)(\$46)$	$\$18.70$
Call Purchase: $(-1)(\$3.30)$	-3.30
Debt Repayment: $-(\$15.30)(1.000026)^+$	-15.30
Cash Flow	$\$0.10$

$^+$The rate of .000026 represents the approximate hourly rate given a 6% annual rate.

*This appendix requires calculus.

Setting $n_C = -1$ and $\partial V_h/\partial S = 0$, then solving for n_S yields the number of shares needed to purchase per written call that makes the hedged portfolio invariant to small stock price changes:

$$0 = (-1)\frac{\partial C}{\partial S} + n_S$$

$$n_S = \frac{\partial C}{\partial S} \qquad (8.B\text{--}3)$$

In the B–S model, $\partial C/\partial S$ is equal to $N(d_1)$. Thus, in the B–S model, a hedged portfolio can be formed by selling a call ($n_c = -1$) and buying $N(d_1)$ shares of stock ($n_s = \partial C/\partial S = N(d_1)$) or a multiple of this strategy. For example, in our B–S pricing example (Section 8.2), $N(d_1)$ is .4066 when ABC stock is trading at \$45, and the OPM price for the ABC 50 call is \$2.88. To form a hedged portfolio, therefore, would require selling the ABC 50 call and buying $N(d_1) = .4066$ shares of stock. If we assume the market price of the call equals the B–S OPM price, then a \$1 increase (decrease) in the price of the stock would lead to a \$0.4066 increase (decrease) in the value of the stock position; however, this increase (decrease) would be offset by a \$0.4066 decrease (increase) in the short call position as the call increased (decreased) in price by $\partial C/\partial S = N(d_1) = .4066$. Thus, the value of the portfolio would not change in response to a relatively small change in the price of the stock, although it would change with the passage of time.

B–S Arbitrage Strategy

If the market price of the call is not equal to the B–S equilibrium price, then an arbitrage return could be earned from the arbitrage/hedging portfolio. For example, if the ABC 50 call were trading at \$3.00 instead of the OPM value of \$2.88, arbitrageurs could form an arbitrage portfolio by buying .4066 shares of ABC stock at \$45 per share, selling the ABC 50 call for \$3.00, and borrowing \$15.30 ((.4066)(\$45)–\$3.00) at the continuously compounded annualized rate of 6%. As shown in Table 8.B-1, if ABC stock increases from \$45 to \$46 an hour after the strategy is initiated, and as a result, the market price of the ABC 50 call increases from \$3.00 to the B–S OPM price of \$3.30, then arbitrageurs could realize a return of \$0.10 by closing their positions. If the ABC call is overpriced ($C_0^m > C_0^*$), however, then to avoid potential losses or a suboptimal return, arbitrageurs would need to readjust their hedge. In this example, the $N(d_1)$ associated with the stock price of \$46 (with $T = .25$ approximately) is .4412. Thus, arbitrageurs would need to borrow \$1.59 to buy an additional .0346 shares at \$46 per share to move to the new hedge of .4412 shares of stock. They, in turn, would continue to readjust until that period is reached when the call is equal or below its OPM value. In contrast, if the call is underpriced initially, $C_0^m < C_0^*$, then the arbitrage strategy and the readjustment rules are the opposite of the initially overpriced one.

B–S Arbitrage Portfolio for Puts

Like the call portfolio, the arbitrage put portfolio is constructed by finding the proportion of shares of stock (n_S) per puts purchased (n_P) that makes the change in the value of a hedged portfolio consisting of the stock and put invariant to changes in the stock price. That is, given the current value of the hedge put portfolio as

$$V_P = n_S S + n_P P = 0 \qquad (8.B\text{--}4)$$

where

n_p = number of puts.
n_s = number of shares of stock.

The proportion is found by setting $n_P = 1$ to constrain the portfolio to one put purchase and then solving for the n_S that makes the partial derivative of Equation (8.B-4) with respect to S equal to zero ($\partial V_p/\partial S = 0$):

$$\frac{\partial V_P}{\partial S} = n_S \frac{\partial S}{\partial S} + n_P \frac{\partial P}{\partial S} \qquad (8.B\text{--}5)$$

$$0 = (1)\frac{\partial P}{\partial S} + n_S$$

$$n_S = -\frac{\partial P}{\partial S}$$

In the B–S put model, $\partial P/\partial S = -(1 - N(d_1))$. Thus, to form a hedged portfolio that does not change in response to small stock price changes, a hedged ratio of $n_s/n_p = (-\partial P/\partial S)/1 = (1 - N(d_1))/1$ is required. In our put example (Section 8.5), $1 - N(d_1) = .5934$. If the put is equal to the B–S put price, then a portfolio consisting of one put and .5934 shares of stock would be immunized against a small stock price change per a given time period. For example, if the stock decreased (increased) by \$1, then the stock position would decrease (increase) by \$0.5934; this change, though, would be offset by a .5934 increase (decrease) in the value of the put, leaving the value of the hedged portfolio unchanged.

Arbitrage Put Portfolio

Given the hedge ratio, if the put is underpriced, then the arbitrage portfolio can be formed by buying one put and $(1 - N(d_1))$ shares of stock at S_0, totally financed by borrowing. If the put is overpriced, then the strategy consists of selling one put and $(1 - N(d_1))$ shares of stock short and investing the proceeds in a risk-free security. These strategies then are readjusted each period until it is profitable to close using the multiple period readjustment rules defined in Chapter 5 for the BOPM for puts.

APPENDIX 8C   EMPIRICAL TESTS OF THE B–S OPM

Two types of empirical tests have been applied to the B–S OPM. The first type is an efficient market one. In this test, researchers try to determine whether or not excess returns can be earned by employing the arbitrage trading strategies that underlie the OPM. The second test involves comparing the OPM prices with observed prices while trying to control for some of the biases that can be associated with such tests.

Efficient Market Tests

In the preceding chapters, we examined how arbitrageurs could force the market price of the option to equal the OPM value. If arbitrageurs act as we have described, then not only would the market price of the option equal its equilibrium value, but no opportunities would exist for abnormal returns to be earned from the arbitrage strategies delineated in the previous chapters. In academic literature, a market in which a security's market price is equal to its investment or true value is said to be efficient. Thus, an efficient option market would exist if professional investors, market makers, and other investors pursue arbitrage trading strategies (or behave as if they do) and, by so doing, ensure that the market price is equal to the OPM value.

In conducting empirical tests of the OPM, researchers need to consider whether the market truly is efficient. Significant differences between actual call prices (C_t^m) and OPM prices (C_t^*) do not necessarily invalidate the B–S model because such disparities also could be explained by an inefficient market in which traders do not seek or are not aware of abnormal return opportunities. Thus, in testing the validity of OPM, researchers face the problem that two hypotheses are being tested simultaneously: (1) the model is valid, and (2) the market is efficient. Given this problem, the standard procedure is to conduct an efficient market test in which the OPM is used to identify mispriced options and to define arbitrage trading rules. If no abnormal returns are observed from applying the strategies, then one could infer that the market is efficient, and the OPM is correct. If abnormal returns are observed, then an inefficient market could exist, and the OPM could be used to construct profitable trading strategies.

One of the first efficient market studies was conducted by Black and Scholes (1972). Using option price data from the over-the-counter (OTC) market, they simulated trading strategies using their model on approximately 550 options traded between 1966 and 1969. In their simulation, if the market price of a call were below its B–S OPM value, Black and Scholes assumed the call was purchased and hedged by selling $N(d_1)$ shares of stock short. On the other hand, if the call were overpriced relative to the B–S's values, then they assumed the call was sold and hedged by purchasing $N(d_1)$ shares. Black and Scholes also posited that the initial positions were adjusted daily by buying and selling shares necessary to maintain $N(d_1)$. From the simulations, they found opportunities for abnormal returns existed on a before-commission cost basis. However, when transaction costs were included, they found the abnormal returns disappeared. Thus, the results of their study suggested that the differences in observed and model values perhaps were significant statistically but not economically.

Galai, in a 1979 study, found results similar to Black and Scholes's. In his study, he replicated the Black–Scholes simulation tests using data on options traded on the CBOE during a 7-month period in 1973. Galai, in turn, found excess returns from the hedging strategies on a before-transaction cost basis but found they disappeared once such costs were included. Hence, the Galai study, like the Black and Scholes, suggested that applying arbitrage trading strategies based on the B–S model would not generate excess returns for nonmembers.

Galai also conducted an ex-ante test in which the trading strategies were defined in terms of closing prices on day t but were not executed until the next day, using closing prices for day t + 1. In contrast to the result from the first tests—ex-post tests—in which strategies were defined and executed with the same closing prices on day t, Galai found lower returns from the ex-ante tests. This finding suggested that option prices tend to adjust toward their theoretical values.

Price Comparisons

The second method for testing the OPM is to compare the prices obtained from the OPM to observed market prices. This was the approach used by MacBeth and Merville (1979). They compared the B–S prices, computed using implied variances, with daily closing prices on six corporations for the year 1975. They found that the B–S model tended to underprice in-the-money calls and overprice out-of-the money calls, with the degree of mispricing being greater the shorter the option's time to expiration. MacBeth and Merville did find, though, that the B–S model was good at pricing on-the-money calls with some time to expiration.

In a more recent study comparing observed and B–S model prices, Rubinstein (1981) also found that in-the-money options were mispriced. Rubinstein also compared the market prices with values obtained from other option models and found the B–S model yielded consistently better results than the other models. (Some of the other models tested were

Cox and Ross's constant elasticity of variance model (1976) and Merton's diffusion-jump model.)

Estimating Errors

Even with a model as highly detailed as the OPM, we should not expect empirical tests to show a strict conformity between theoretical and observed values. Two types of errors can result from conducting empirical tests: measurement errors and stochastic errors.

In such early empirical studies of the OPM as Galai's, measurement errors often resulted from the use of closing prices. When closing price data (such as found in the *Wall Street Journal*) are used, a timing problem, commonly referred to as a **non-simultaneity problem**, can exist. For example, suppose the reported closing prices on a call and its underlying stock were $7 and $100, respectively. Using these prices, a researcher estimating an OPM value of $6.35 could conclude that the option is overpriced. However, it could be that the $7 call price was the price on a last trade of the day that occurred some time before the last trade on the stock. The researcher should not assume that the market price of the call necessarily would have been the reported $7 when the stock closed trading at $100; thus, an inference that the call is mispriced or the OPM invalid cannot be deduced without some reservation.

If market activity in the stock and option market is heavy (to the extent that non-simultaneity problems discussed previously are minimal), researchers still have another problem using closing prices: They often do not know whether the prices reported are bid or ask prices or in between. For example, suppose the bid–ask spread is 1/2 point, and the reported closing price is $6. If the closing price was based on a bid price, the bid–ask spread would be 6–6 1/2, and if it was based on an ask, the spread would be 5 1/2–6. Thus, a researcher using a closing price of $6 could have an error of 8.333% ($0.5/$0.6) above or below the reported $6 closing price. Thus, any empirical research using closing prices that showed abnormal returns would have to be discounted to account for the bid–ask spread differential before conclusions regarding market inefficiencies could be drawn.

In the Rubinstein study and other more current empirical studies on the OPM, the non-simultaneity and bid–ask problems were minimized by the researchers using CBOE-recorded data. This database provided traded prices, quotes, and volume data to the nearest second. These studies, as do the Black and Scholes and Galai studies, though, suffer from measurement errors that have resulted from using estimates of the underlying stock's volatility in determining the OPM value. In fact, Geske and Roll (1984) argued that most errors in estimating the OPM are due primarily to incorrect estimates of the variance.

The second type of error is a stochastic one. This error can result from the exclusion of important explanatory variables and/or an incorrect mathematical specification of the model. In the Black and Scholes and Galai studies, one omission was the treatment of dividends. Not surprisingly, Whaley (1982) and Sterk (1983) have found less measurement error associated with the B–S OPM with dividend adjustments than without such corrections. Thus, for the Galai study, the nontreatment of dividends on options on dividend-paying stocks probably did lead to errors. The Black and Scholes study, however, was not subject to such errors because they used OTC options that were dividend protected: that is, if the stock price went ex-dividend, then the exercise price of the OTC call was lowered by the amount of the dividend.

Stochastic errors resulting from model misspecifications were examined in a 1980 study by Bhattacharya. Bhattacharya calculated the rates of return resulting from theoretical hedged portfolios formed using the B–S OPM and also B–S prices instead of market prices. That is, the portfolio values were calculated from observed stock prices, interest rates, and estimated variances but used the B–S model's call values instead of market prices. Bhattacharya found that with the exception of near-the-money calls with short periods to expiration, no significant mispricing by the B–S OPM existed, thus supporting the theoretical soundness of the B–S OPM.

Finally, stochastic errors could be due to assuming that the variance is constant. MacBeth and Merville (1980) provided evidence showing that the variance tends to change as the stock price changes. If this is the case, then an option pricing model such as Merton's diffusion-jump model or Cox and Ross's constant elasticity of substitution model could yield better results than the B–S OPM. Similarly, stochastic errors could also be the result of the model's assumption that the option's underlying security's logarithmic return is normally distributed. As noted in Section 8.10, several empirical studies have provided evidence that the distributions of stock and stock index returns exhibit persistent skewness.

QUESTIONS

1. Explain the following studies:
    a. Black–Scholes (1972)
    b. Galai (1977)
    c. MacBeth and Merville (1979)
2. Explain some of the problems researchers have in testing the validity of the OPM.

CHAPTER 9

APPLICATIONS OF THE OPTION PRICING MODEL, THE GREEKS, AND EXOTIC OPTIONS

9.1 INTRODUCTION

In this chapter, we continue our analysis of the B–S OPM by examining the applicability of the model in estimating an option's expected return, risk, beta, and Greek values (delta, gamma, and theta) and in defining different option strategies in terms of an option position's Greek values. We then introduce nongeneric options, known as *exotic options,* and show how the OPM can be used to price these derivatives.

9.2 APPLICATIONS OF THE OPM

Two practical applications of the OPM are its use in evaluating option positions with different holding periods and in defining an option's expected rate of return and risk.

9.2.1 Option Positions With Different Holding Periods

In Chapter 3, we examined a number of option strategies in terms of their profit and stock price relations. These strategies, though, were evaluated at expiration in terms of the option's IV. With the OPM, we now can examine these strategies in terms of their profit and stock price relations prior to expiration. The tables in Exhibit 9.2-1 show the stock price and profit relations for the long call, put, and straddle positions. The relations are defined for three points in time—t_1, t_2, and T. T is the time to expiration, and t_1 and t_2 are the times to dates prior to expiration in which t_1's date is earlier than t_2's. In determining the profits at t_1 and t_2, the B–S OPM is used to estimate the price of the options for each stock price, with the times to expiration being $T - t_1$ and $T - t_2$ when the positions are closed. The call and put options evaluated in the tables are based on the following:

- Exercise prices of $50 and expirations of 3 months (T = .25 per year)
- The options' underlying stock is initially priced at $S_0 = \$50$, has a volatility of $\sigma = .5$, and no dividends
- The annual (continuously compounded) risk-free rate is 5%
- The current price of the call is equal to the B–S price of $5.24
- The current price of the put is equal to the B–S price of $4.62
- The holding periods evaluated are 1 month ($t_1 = .08333$), 2 months ($t_2 = .16667$), and 3 months (T = .25)

In examining the call and put purchase strategies (Tables A and B in Exhibit 9.2-1), one should note that the profit is greater at each stock price the shorter the holding period. This

EXHIBIT 9.2-1 Option Strategies With Different Holding Periods—Table A: Call Purchase

$$S_0 = \$50, \sigma = .5, R_f = .05, T = .25, X = \$50, C_0^* = \$5.24$$

	Holding Period					
	1 Month (t_1)		2 Months (t_2)		3 Months (T)	
S_t	C^*	Profit	C^*	Profit	C^*	Profit
$40	$0.68	−$4.56	$0.19	−$5.05	0	−$5.24
45	1.98	−3.26	0.97	−4.27	0	−5.24
50	4.24	−1.00	2.96	−2.28	0	−5.24
55	7.49	2.25	6.30	1.06	5	−0.24
60	11.45	6.21	10.58	5.34	10	4.76

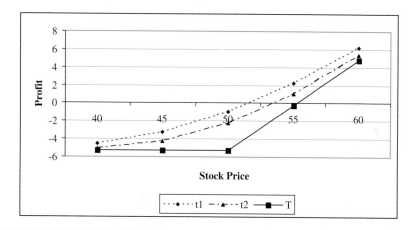

relationship reflects the fact that the earlier a call or put is sold, the greater its time value premium. One should be careful, though, in quickly concluding that short holding periods for long positions in calls and puts are superior to longer ones. Specifically, although a shorter holding period does provide a greater time premium than a longer one, the shorter period also means that the range in possible stock prices is more limited than the price range for a longer time period. Thus, the shorter the holding period, the less time is available for the stock to move to a profitable position. In contrast, the naked call and put write positions yield greater profits per stock price the longer the holding period. This is because the option's time value premium is smaller the closer the option is to expiration. As a result, the cost of closing the short position is less per stock price.

One strategy we were not able to analyze in Chapter 3 was the time (calendar or horizontal) spread. With the OPM, we now can evaluate this spread by using this model to determine both the prices and profits from a longer term option at the expiration of a shorter term one and the prices of both options when the holding period is shorter than the expiration of the shorter term option.

A horizontal spread evaluated using the OPM is shown in Exhibit 9.2-2. The table in the exhibit shows the profit and stock price relation for the case of a spreader who forms a calendar spread consisting of a short position in a July ABC 50 call and a long position in an October ABC 50 call. The spread is evaluated at the expiration of the July call in which the October call is assumed to be closed at a price equal to the B–S

EXHIBIT 9.2-1   Option Strategies With Different Holding Periods—Table B: Put Purchase

$$S_0 = \$50, \sigma = .5, R_f = .05, T = .25, X = \$50, P_0^* = \$4.62$$

	Holding Period					
	1 Month (t_1)		2 Months (t_2)		3 Months (T)	
S_t	P^*	Profit	P^*	Profit	P^*	Profit
$40	$10.26	$5.64	$9.98	$5.36	$10	$5.38
45	6.56	1.94	5.76	1.14	5	0.38
50	3.82	−0.80	2.75	−1.87	0	−4.62
55	2.08	−2.54	1.09	−3.53	0	−4.62
60	1.04	−3.58	0.37	−4.25	0	−4.62

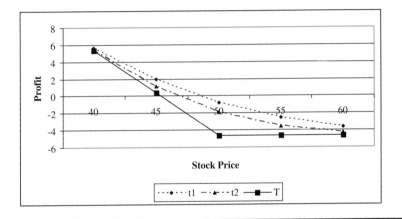

OPM value. Because the longer term call is more valuable than the shorter term one, the 50 July/October spread involves a cost. In the example in the table, it is assumed that ABC stock is priced at $50, has no dividends, and has a volatility of $\sigma = .5$ and that the investor buys the spread 3 months prior to the July expiration at a cost of $2.36 and that the risk-free rate is 6%. The $2.36 price is based on the B–S OPM in which the July 50 call, expiring in 3 months (T = .25), is $5.30, and the October 50 call, expiring in 6 months (T = .5), is $7.66. As shown in the exhibit, the calendar spread produces the greatest profit when the stock is stable. This is because the longer term call sells at a higher time value premium when it is on or near the money. If the investor expected the stock to move dramatically up or down, then the calendar spread should be reversed, with the spreader taking a long position in the near-term call and a short position in the longer term one.

Note that options strategies can be evaluated prior to expiration by using the "Option Strategies" Excel spreadsheet. Included with the spreadsheet is the worksheet Timed Option Strategies. This worksheet calculates profits at expiration and for an evaluation period prior to expiration; the program uses the Merton B–S OPM to calculate call and put prices for each inputted stock price. The spreadsheet also includes the worksheet Calendar Option Strategies. This worksheet determines profits for two selected evaluation periods using the Merton B–S OPM to calculate call and put prices for each inputted stock price.

EXHIBIT 9.2-1   Option Strategies With Different Holding Periods—Table C: Straddle Purchase

$$S_0 = \$50, \sigma = .5, R_f = .05, T = .25, X = \$50, C_0^* = 5.24, P_0^* = \$4.62$$

	Holding Period								
	1 Month (t_1)			2 Months (t_2)			3 Months (T)		
S_t	C^*	P^*	Profit	C^*	P^*	Profit	C^*	P^*	Profit
$40	$0.68	$10.26	$1.08	$0.19	$9.98	$0.31	0	$10	$0.14
45	1.98	6.56	−1.32	0.97	5.76	−3.14	0	5	−4.86
50	4.24	3.82	−1.80	2.96	2.75	−4.16	0	0	−9.86
55	7.49	2.08	−0.29	6.30	1.09	−2.46	5	0	−4.86
60	11.45	1.04	2.63	10.58	0.37	1.09	19	0	0.14

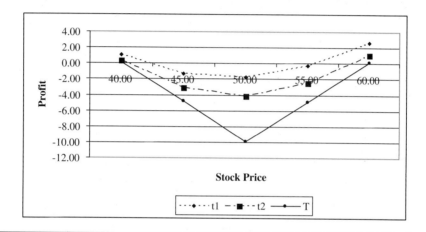

The program can be used to evaluate time spreads. For more information, see supplemental Appendix D.

9.2.2   Option Return-Risk Characteristics

Investors often evaluate and select securities and portfolios in terms of their expected return and risk characteristics. To evaluate and select options, investors need to be able to define these securities in terms of these characteristics. To this end, the OPM can be used to derive the equations for an option's expected rate of return and risk.

For a call option, the OPM prices the option by determining the value of the call's replicating portfolio. Recall that the replicating call portfolio consists of the purchase of H_0^* shares of stock, partially financed by borrowing B_0^* dollars. For a no-dividend case, the equilibrium expected rate of return on the call, $E(R_C)$, is equal to the expected rate of return on the replicating call portfolio, $E(Z_C)$. This rate is

$$E(R_C) = E(Z_C) = w_S E(R_S) + w_R R_f \qquad (9.2\text{-}1)$$

where

w_C = proportion of investment funds allocated to the stock

W_R = proportion of investment funds allocated to the risk-free security

EXHIBIT 9.2-2   Calendar Spread—Profit and Stock Price Relation—Evaluated at July Expiration

Short July Call : $T = .25, \sigma = .50, X = \$50, R_f = .06, C^* = \$5.30$
Long October Call : $T = .5, \sigma = .5, X = \$50, R_f = .06, C^* = \$7.66$

S_t	Profit From Short July 50 Call	October Call Price C_t^*	Profit From Long October 50 Call	Total Profit
$30	$530	$0.0841	−$757.59	−$227.59
35	530	0.4163	−724.37	−194.37
40	530	1.2408	−641.92	−111.92
45	530	2.8756	−478.44	51.56
50	530	5.2999	−236.01	293.99
55	30	8.5584	89.84	119.84
60	−470	12.3857	472.57	2.57
65	−970	16.6919	903.19	−66.87
70	−1,470	21.2865	1,362.65	−107.35

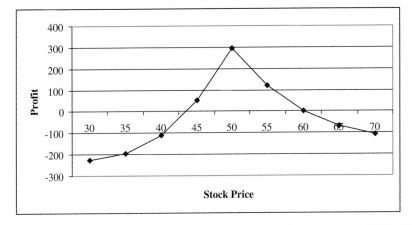

$E(R_S)$ = expected rate of return of the stock

$1 = w_R + w_S$

The total investment in the replicating call portfolios is $H_0^* S_0 - B_0^*$, which in equilibrium is equal to the call value (C_0^*); the investment in the stock is $H_0^* S_0$; and the risk-free investment is $-B_0^*$ (i.e., negative investment or borrowing). Thus, Equation (9.2-1) can be written as

$$E(R_C) = E(Z_C) = \left[\frac{H_0^* S_0}{C_0^*}\right] E(R_s) + \left[\frac{-B_0^*}{C_0^*}\right] R_f \qquad (9.2\text{-}2)$$

The risk of a portfolio consisting of risky and risk-free securities can be defined in terms of the portfolio's standard deviation or beta. The standard deviation and beta for the call or, equivalently, the replicating portfolio are

$$\sigma(R_C) = \sigma(Z_C) = w_s \sigma(R_s) = \left[\frac{H_0^* S_0}{C_0^*}\right] \sigma(R_s) \qquad (9.2\text{-}3)$$

$$\beta_C = \beta_Z = w_s \beta_S = \left[\frac{H_0^* S_0}{C_0^*}\right] \beta_S \qquad (9.2\text{-}4)$$

in which β_S = beta of the stock.

Equation (9.2-2) and Equations (9.2-3) or (9.2-4) can be used to define the expected rate of return and risk of a call option. In the equations, the OPM is needed to determine H_0^* (equal to $N(d_1)$ in the B–S model), C_0^*, and B_0^* ($[X/e^{(RT)}]N(d_2)$ in the B–S model).

For a put, the equilibrium expected rate of return ($E(R_p)$) is equal to the expected rate of return of a replicating put portfolio formed by selling H_0^{p*} shares of stock short and investing I_0^* in a risk-free security. The total investment in the replicating put portfolio is $H_0^{p*} S_0 + I_0^*$ (with $H_0^{p*} < 0$), which, in equilibrium, is equal to P_0^*. Thus, a put's expected rate of return, standard deviation, and beta can be defined as

$$E(R_p) = E(Z_p) = W_s E(R_s) + W_r R_f$$

$$E(R_P) = E(Z_P) = \left[\frac{H_0^{P*} S_0}{P_0^*}\right] E(R_S) + \left[\frac{I_0^*}{P_0^*}\right] R_f \tag{9.2-5}$$

$$\sigma(R_P) = \sigma(Z_P) = \sqrt{w_s^2 \sigma(R_S)^2} = \sqrt{\left[\frac{H_0^{P*} S_0}{C_0^*}\right]^2 \sigma(R_S)^2} \tag{9.2-6}$$

$$\beta_P = \beta_Z = w_S \beta_S = \left[\frac{H_0^{P*} S_0}{P_0^*}\right] \beta_S \tag{9.2-7}$$

In the B–S put model, $H_0^{p*} = -(1 - N(d_1))$, and $I_0^* = [X/e^{(RT)}](1 - N(d_2))$. It should be noted that with $H_0^{p*} < 0$, the put has a negative beta. The negative sign reflects the inverse relationship between the rate of return on a put and the market rate of return.

To illustrate, consider the example of the 50 call with $T = .25$ per year described in Section 8.2 and the 50 put with $T = .25$ described in Section 8.5. Using the B–S model, the price, hedge ratio, and B_0^* for the call were found in Chapter 8 to be $C^* = \$2.88$, $H_0^* = N(d_1) = 0.4066$, and $B_0^* = \$15.42$ given $S_0 = \$45$ and $R_f = .06$. Similarly, the price, hedge ratio, and I_0^* for the put were found to be $P_0^* = \$7.13$, $H_0^{p*} = -(1 - N(d_1)) = -.5934$, and $I_0^* = \$33.83$, respectively. If the underlying stock has an expected rate of return of $E(R_S) = .10$, standard deviation of $\sigma(R_s) = 0.5$, and a beta of $\beta = 1.5$, then the 50 call and 50 put would have the following return-risk characteristics:

Call:

$$E(R_c) = \left[\frac{H_0^* S_0}{C_0^*}\right] E(R_s) + \left[\frac{-B_0^*}{C_0^*}\right] R_f$$

$$E(R_c) = \left[\frac{.4066(\$45)}{\$2.88}\right](.10) + \left[\frac{-\$15.42}{\$2.88}\right](.06) = .314$$

$$\sigma(R_c) = \left[\frac{H_0^* S_0}{C_0^*}\right] \sigma(R_s) = 6.353(.5) = 3.1765$$

$$\beta_c = \left[\frac{H_0^* S_0}{C_0^*}\right] \beta_s = 6.353(1.5) = 9.5295$$

Put:

$$E(R_p) = \left[\frac{H_0^{p*} S_0}{P_0^*}\right] E(R_s) + \frac{I_0^*}{P_0^*} R_f$$

$$E(R_p) = \frac{-.5934(\$45)}{\$7.13}(.10) + \frac{\$33.83}{\$7.13}(.06) = -.0898$$

$$\sigma(R_p) = \sqrt{\left[\frac{H_0^{p*}S_0}{P_0^*}\right]^2}\,\sigma(R_s) = 3.745(.5) = 1.8725$$

$$\beta_p = w_s\,\beta_s = \left[\frac{H_0^{p*}S_0}{P_0^*}\right]\beta_s = -3.745(1.5) = -5.6175$$

Compared to the stock, the call and put yield higher expected returns and risks, with the put's negative expected return implying that the price of the stock must decline for a long position in the put to be profitable. The higher return-risk characteristics should not be surprising given that a call is equivalent to a leveraged stock position, and a put is equivalent to a leveraged short sale.[1]

It is important to note that the preceding measures for an option's return and risk hold only for a small time period and for small stock price changes. The equations for the expected return and risk using the B–S OPM are defined more appropriately as *instantaneous* expected rates of return, standard deviations, and betas.

9.3   GREEKS: DELTA, GAMMA, AND THETA[2]

In addition to defining the profit relations of option positions prior to expiration and measuring the return-risk characteristics of an option, the OPM also can be used to measure an option's Greek values: delta, gamma, vega, and rho values. Recall from Chapters 5 and 8, the option's delta (Δ) measures the change in the option's price per small change in the stock price, with other factors constant; the option's gamma (Γ) defines the change in the option's delta per small change in the stock price; the option's theta (θ) measures the change in the option's price per small change in the time to expiration; and the option's vega (Λ) and rho measure price changes per small changes in variability and interest rates, respectively. The equations for determining the delta, gamma, theta, vega, and rho values using the B–S model are shown in Table 9.3-1 for a European call on a nondividend and dividend-paying stock and in Table 9.3-2 for a European put. These parameter values can also be obtained using the "Black–Scholes Option Pricing Model" Excel program (BS Greeks worksheet).

9.3.1   Delta

Delta is a measure of an option's price sensitivity to a small change in the price of the underlying stock. The delta (Δ) for a European call on a nondividend-paying stock is $N(d_1)$, and for a European put is $N(d_1) - 1$. As shown in Figure 9.3-1a, the delta for a call is positive, ranging in value from approximately 0 for deep-out-of-the-money calls to approximately 1 for deep in-the-money ones. In contrast, the delta for a put is negative, ranging from approximately 0 to –1 (Figure 9.3-1c). Deltas change in response to not only stock price changes but also the time to expiration. As shown in Figures 9.3-1b

---

[1] Note that the w_s term in the preceding equations is equal to the option's price elasticity with respect to a change in the stock's price (ε):

$$\varepsilon_C = \%\Delta C/\%\Delta S = (\Delta C/\Delta S)(S/C) = (H_0^*S_0)/C_0^* = w_s$$

$$\varepsilon_p = (\%\Delta P/\%\Delta S) = (\Delta P/\Delta S)(S/P) = (H_0^{p*}S_0/P_0^*) = w_s$$

[2] This section makes use of calculus.

TABLE 9.3-1 Derivatives of the B–S Model for European Call Options

	Call on Stock Paying No Dividends	Call on Stock Paying Annual Dividend Yield of ψ
Delta	$\Delta = \dfrac{\partial C}{\partial S} = N(d_1)$	$\Delta = e^{-\psi T} N(d_1)$
Gamma	$\Gamma = \dfrac{\partial \Delta}{\partial S} = \dfrac{N'(d_1)}{S_0 \, \sigma \sqrt{T}}$	$\Gamma = \dfrac{N'(d_1) \, e^{-\psi T}}{S_0 \, \sigma \sqrt{T}}$
Theta	$\theta = -\dfrac{\partial C}{\partial T} = -\dfrac{S_0 \, N'(d_1)\sigma}{2\sqrt{T}}$ $+ RXe^{-RT} N(d_2)$	$\theta = -\dfrac{S_0 \, N'(d_1)\sigma \, e^{-\psi T}}{2\sqrt{T}} - \psi \, S_0 \, N(-d_1) \, e^{-\psi T}$ l $+ RXe^{-RT} N(-d_2)$
Vega (Kappa)	$\Lambda = \dfrac{\partial C}{\partial \sigma} = S_0 \sqrt{T} \quad N'(d_1)$	$\Lambda = S_0 \sqrt{T} N'(d_1) \, e^{-\psi T}$
Rho	$\dfrac{\partial C}{\partial R} = XT N(d_2) \, e^{-RT}$ where: $N'(d) = \dfrac{1}{\sqrt{2\pi}} \, e^{-(d^2/2)}$	$\dfrac{\partial C}{\partial R} = XT N(d_2) \, e^{-RT}$

TABLE 9.3-2 Derivatives of the B–S Model for European Put Options

	Put on Stock Paying No Dividends	Put on Stock Paying Annual Dividend Yield of ψ
Delta	$\Delta = \dfrac{\partial P}{\partial S} = N(d_1) - 1$	$\Delta = e^{-\psi T}[N(d_1) - 1]$
Gamma	$\Gamma = \dfrac{\partial \Delta}{\partial S} = \dfrac{N'(d_1)}{S_0 \, \sigma \sqrt{T}}$	$\Gamma = \dfrac{N'(d_1) \, e^{-\psi T}}{S_0 \, \sigma \sqrt{T}}$
Theta	$\theta = -\dfrac{\partial P}{\partial T} = -\dfrac{S_0 \, N'(d_1)\sigma}{2\sqrt{T}}$ $+ RXe^{-RT} N(-d_2)$	$\theta = -\dfrac{S_0 \, N'(d_1)\sigma \, e^{-\psi T}}{2\sqrt{T}} - \psi \, S_0 \, N(-d_1) \, e^{-\psi T}$ $+ RXe^{-RT} N(-d_2)$
Vega (Kappa)	$\Lambda = \dfrac{\partial P}{\partial \sigma} = S_0 \sqrt{T} \quad N'(d_1)$	$\Lambda = S_0 \sqrt{T} \quad N'(d_1) \, e^{-\psi T}$
Rho	$\dfrac{\partial P}{\partial R} = X T N(-d_2) \, e^{-RT}$ where: $N'(d) = \dfrac{1}{\sqrt{2\pi}} \, e^{-(d^2/2)}$	$\dfrac{\partial P}{\partial R} = X T N(-d_2) \, e^{-RT}$

and 9.3-1d, as the time to expiration decreases, the delta of an in-the-money call or put increases, whereas an out-of-the-money call or put tends to decrease.

In addition to measuring a derivative's price sensitivity to a change in the stock price, an option's delta also can be used to measure the probability that the option will be in the money at expiration. Thus, the call with a $\Delta = N(d_1) = .40$ has an estimated 40% chance of its stock price exceeding the option's exercise price at expiration.

9.3.2 Theta

As noted, theta (θ) is the change in the price of an option with respect to changes in its time to expiration, with all other factors constant. It is a measure of the option's time decay. Because theta measures the time decay of an option, it is usually defined as the negative of the partial derivative of the option's price with respect to expiration $(\theta = -(\partial C/\partial T)$ or $\theta = -(\partial P/\partial T))$. Except for the case of a deep in-the-money European put, the thetas on options are negative.

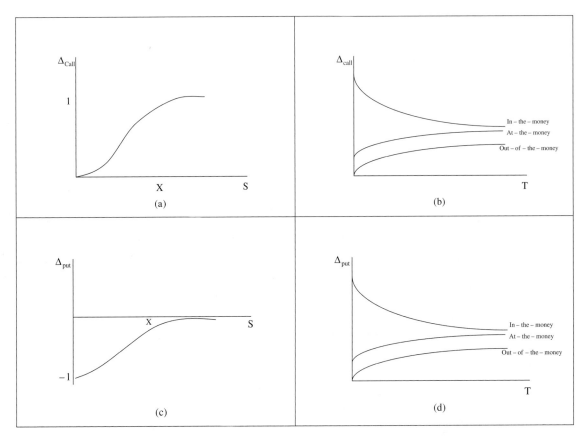

FIGURE 9.3-1 Delta Relations to Stock Price and Time to Expiration

Using our illustrative call and put examples (Sections 8.2 and 8.5) in which $S_0 = \$45$, $X = \$50$, $T = .25$, $\sigma = .5$, $R = .06$, $N(d_1) = N(-.2364) = .4066$, $N(d_2) = N(-.4846) = .3131$, and $N'(d_1) = (1/\sqrt{2\pi})e^{-(.23646^2/2)} = 0.3879$, the call would have a theta of -7.8024, and the put would have a theta of -6.698:

Call:

$$\theta = -\frac{S_0\,N'(d_1)\sigma}{2\sqrt{T}} - RXe^{-RT}N(d_2)$$

$$\theta = \frac{-(\$45)(.3879)(.5)}{2\sqrt{.25}} + (.06)(\$50)e^{-(.06)(.25)}(.3131) = -7.8024$$

Put:

$$\theta = -\frac{S_0\,N'(d_1)\sigma}{2\sqrt{T}} + RXe^{-RT}N(-d_2)$$

$$\theta = -\frac{(\$45)(.3879)(.5)}{2\sqrt{.25}} + (.06)(\$50)e^{-(.06)(.25)}(.6869) = -6.698$$

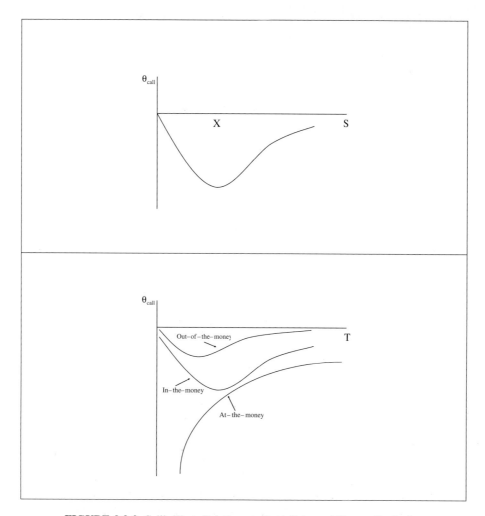

FIGURE 9.3-2 Call's Theta Relations to Stock Price and Time to Expiration

This means that if the option is held 1% of a year (approximately 2.5 trading days), and there were no changes in the stock's price, the call would decline in value by approximately $0.078, and the put would decrease by $0.06698.

Like delta, theta changes in response to changes in the stock price and time to expiration. These relationships are presented in Figure 9.3-2. As shown, a near-the-money option, with some time to expiration, has a relatively large theta or time decay.

9.3.3 Gamma

Gamma (Γ) measures the change in an option's delta for a small change in the stock price. It is the second derivative of the option price with respect to the stock price. In our illustrative example, the gamma for the call or put is .03448:

$$\Gamma = \frac{N'(d_1)}{S_0\,\sigma\,\sqrt{T}} = \frac{.3879}{(45)(.5)\sqrt{.25}} = .03448$$

Thus, a $1 increase in the stock price would increase the delta of the call or put by approximately 0.03448.

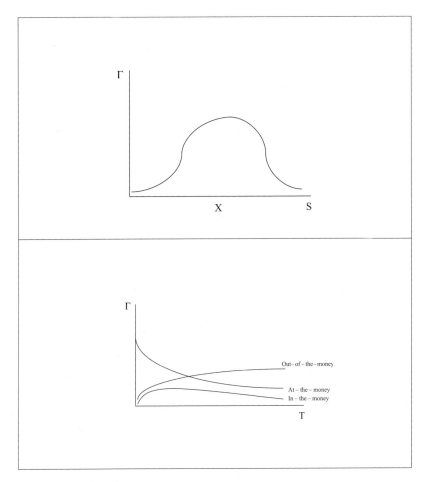

FIGURE 9.3-3 Gamma Relations to Stock Price and Time to Expiration

As shown in Figure 9.3-3, the gamma of a call or put varies with respect to the stock price and time to expiration.

9.3.4 Position Delta, Gamma, and Theta Values

The description of call and put options in terms of their delta, gamma, and theta values can be extended to option positions. For example, consider an investor who purchases n_1 calls at a price of C_1 per call and n_2 calls on another option on the same stock at a price of C_2 per call. The value of her portfolio (V) is

$$V = n_1 C_1 + n_2 C_2 \qquad (9.3\text{-}1)$$

The call prices are functions of S, T, σ, and R_f. Taking the partial derivative of Equation (9.3-1) with respect to S yields the position's delta, Δ_p:

$$\Delta_p = \frac{\partial V}{\partial S} = n_1 \left(\frac{\partial C_1}{\partial S} \right) + n_2 \left(\frac{\partial C_2}{\partial S} \right) \qquad (9.3\text{-}2)$$

$$\Delta_p = n_1 \Delta_1 + n_2 \Delta_2$$

where

$$\Delta_1 = \frac{\partial C_1}{\partial S} = H_1^* = N(d_1)_1$$

$$\Delta_2 = \frac{\partial C_2}{\partial S} = H_2^* = N(d_1)_2$$

The position delta measures the change in the position's value in response to a small change in the stock price, with other factors being constant. Moreover, by setting Equation (9.3-2) equal to zero and solving for n_1 in terms of n_2 (or vice versa), a ***neutral position delta*** can be constructed with a value invariant to small changes in the stock price. That is

$$0 = n_1 \Delta_1 + n_2 \Delta_2,$$

$$n_1 = -\left(\frac{\Delta_2}{\Delta_1}\right) n_2$$

$$n_1 = -\left[\frac{N(d_1)_2}{N(d_1)_1}\right] n_2 \qquad (9.3\text{-}3)$$

The position gamma (Γ_p) defines the change in the position's delta for a small change in the stock price, with other factors being constant. The gamma of the preceding call portfolio is found by taking the partial derivative of Equation (9.3-2) with respect to S to obtain

$$\Gamma_p = \frac{\partial \Delta_p}{\partial S} = n_1 \left(\frac{\partial \Delta_1}{\partial S}\right) + n_2 \left(\frac{\partial \Delta_2}{\partial S}\right) \qquad (9.3\text{-}4)$$

Knowing a portfolio's gamma and delta positions can be helpful in defining an investor's risk-return exposure. For example, suppose a delta-neutral portfolio is formed. If this portfolio has a positive gamma, then the portfolio will decline in value if there is little or no change in the stock price and increase in value if there is a large positive or negative change in the stock price. On the other hand, if the delta-neutral portfolio has a negative gamma, the portfolio value will increase if there is little or no change in the stock price and decrease in value if there is a large positive or negative change in the stock price. These relations are depicted in Figure 9.3-4 in which the relations between the change in the portfolio value, ΔV, and ΔS are shown for different position gammas given a delta-neutral portfolio. In addition, the graphs in Figure 9.3-4 also show that the responsiveness of ΔV to ΔS is greater the greater the absolute value of gamma.

Finally, the partial derivative of Equation (9.3-1) with respect to the time to expiration, T, gives us the call position's theta (Θ_p):

$$\Theta_p = \frac{\partial V}{\partial T} = n_1 \left(\frac{\partial C_1}{\partial T}\right) + n_2 \left(\frac{\partial C_2}{\partial T}\right) \qquad (9.3\text{-}5)$$

In general, the larger a position's theta, the greater its time value decay. Thus, taking a short position in an option portfolio with a large time value decay may be a profitable strategy, especially if the position also has a low delta and gamma value. If a position has a theta that is large in absolute value, then either its delta or gamma must be large. Thus, for a delta-neutral portfolio, if the portfolio's theta is large and negative, gamma tends to be large and positive; and if its theta is large and negative, its gamma tends to be large and positive.

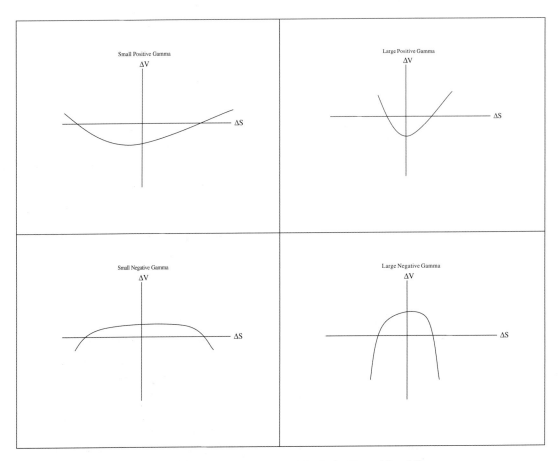

FIGURE 9.3-4 Relation Between ΔV and ΔS for Delta-Neutral Portfolio

9.3.5 Neutral Ratio Spread

A popular neutral delta strategy is the ***neutral ratio spread***. This spread position is formed with a time, money, or diagonal spread, with the proportion of short calls (or puts) to long calls being such that the portfolio is invariant to stock price changes (i.e., a position delta of zero). Equation (9.3-3) shows that a riskless ratio spread can be formed by purchasing (selling) one call ($n_2 = 1$) and selling (purchasing) $n_1 = -N(d_1)_2/N(d_1)_1$ of the other call or a multiple of this strategy (the negative sign in Equation (9.3-3) indicates opposite positions). For example, if the hedge ratio for a July 50 call is $N(d_1)_1 = .570$, and the hedge ratio for a July 60 call on the same stock is $N(d_1)_2 = .292$, then the ratio spread (also referred to as a ***delta spread***) needed to form a riskless position is

$$\frac{N(d_1)_2}{N(d_1)_1} = \frac{.292}{.570} = -.5123$$

A riskless ratio spread therefore could be constructed by purchasing one July 60 call and selling .5123 July 50 calls. If the stock increased by $1.00, the value of the long position in the July 60 call would increase by $0.292. This, however, would be offset by the decrease of $0.292 = (.5123)(.570)$ in the value of the short position in the October 50 call. Thus, a small change in the price of the stock would not change the value of this ratio spread.

The riskless ratio spread sometimes is used with the OPM to define arbitrage or quasi-arbitrage strategies: for example, a neutral ratio spread formed by buying an underpriced call and selling an overpriced or equal-in-value call on the same stock. Given that $N(d_1)$ changes as the stock price and time change, this ratio spread strategy would need to be readjusted each period to keep the spread riskless until it is profitable to close. Thus, the riskless ratio spread can be thought of as an alternative arbitrage strategy to the arbitrage portfolio defining the B–S OPM; in fact, given that the arbitrage strategy underlying the B–S model can require short sales and margin requirements, the ratio spread may in some cases be a better strategy to implement when the market and OPM prices are not equal. A problem dealing with forming an arbitrage with a ratio call write is included as one of the end-of-the-chapter problems.

9.4 EXOTIC OPTIONS

The stock, currency, and index options that we have examined so far in this text are all characterized by a set exercise price, expiration date, and specified underlying asset. Such options are commonly referred to as generic or plain vanilla options to distinguish then from other nonstandard options. Nonstandard options are often referred to as *exotic options*. Exotics are nongeneric products often created by financial engineers to meet specific hedging needs and return-risk objectives. They have been called the second generation of options. In contrast to the exchange-traded generic or plain vanilla options, exotic options are over-the-counter (OTC) derivatives that have more diverse properties. For example, a number of exotics exhibit path dependency in which the price of the option depends on previous or future prices of the underlying asset. For example, a barrier interest rate option that we discuss in Chapter 16 has a payoff that depends on whether an underlying security price or reference rate reaches a certain level. In addition to path-dependent options, there are exotic options characterized by different types of payoffs such as the entire asset or an exchange of one asset for another. There are also options on options, option to choose either a call or a put, and options on a basket of assets. In Parts IV and V of this book, we examine some of the uses of these nongeneric options. In this section, we conclude our analysis of option pricing by defining some of the more popular exotic options and showing how the OPM can be extended to pricing these derivatives.

9.4.1 Forward-Start Option

As the name suggests, a *forward-start option* is one that starts at a future date. The price of the option is paid at the present, but the option does not start until a specified future date. Furthermore, the exercise price on the option is specified to be the price of the underlying asset at the start of the option. Thus, the option will be at the money when it begins. *Executive call options* are typically structured as forward-start options in which the executive is to receive options on the company's stock at some future date or dates, with the exercise price set equal to the company's stock price at the time the options start.

The value of a forward-start option is equal to the value of a regular option valued in terms of the current price, an exercise price equal to the current price, and a time to expiration equal to the difference between the date the option expires (T) and the date the option begins (t_B): $T - t_B$. If the underlying asset generates a return from the time the option is valued (current date or valuation date), t_0, to the option's beginning date (t_B), such as a dividend yield on a stock or foreign interest-rate yield on a currency option, then the forward-start option is discounted by that rate for the period $t_B - t_0$. Thus, the value of a forward-start call (FSC) and forward-start put (FSP) are

$$FSC_0 = e^{-\psi(t_B-t_0)}C^*_{t_B}$$

$$FSP_0 = e^{-\psi(t_B-t_0)}P^*_{t_B}$$

where

ψ = annual yield on the asset

t_B = date the option starts

t_0 = current date or valuation date

$C^*_{t_B}$ = call price at the start of the option

$P^*_{t_B}$ = put price at the start of the option

The price of the option at date t_B can be estimated using the Black–Scholes–Merton continuous dividend-yield model in which ψ is the annual dividend yield on a stock or the foreign risk-free rate paid on currency, and S_0 is the current price of the underlying asset:

$$C^*_0 = S_0e^{-\psi(T-t_B)}N(d_1) - Xe^{-R(T-t_b)}N(d_2)$$

$$P^*_0 = -S_0e^{-\psi(T-t_B)}(1 - N(d_1)) + Xe^{-R(T-t_B)}(1 - N(d_2))$$

$$d_1 = \frac{\ln(S_0/S_0) + (R - \psi + .5\sigma^2)(T - t_B)}{\sigma\sqrt{T - t_B}}$$

$$d_2 = d_1 - \sigma\sqrt{T - t_B}$$

To illustrate, consider forward-start European call and put options on ABC stock each having an expiration of 1 year ($T = 1$) and starting in 6 months ($t_B = .5$). Suppose ABC stock is currently trading at \$50 and has an estimated annualized volatility of $\sigma = .5$ and an annualized dividend yield of $\psi = .05$. Also assume the continuously compounded annual risk-free rate is 6%. Using the Black–Scholes–Merton OPM, the continuous dividend-adjusted call and put prices at the start of the option are \$6.93 and \$6.69

$$d_1 = \frac{Ln(\$50/\$50) + [.06 - .05 + (.5)(.5^2)](1 - .5)}{.5\sqrt{1 - .5}} = .1909$$

$$d_2 = .1909 - (.5)(\sqrt{.5}) = -.1626$$

$$N(d_1) = N(.1909) = .5756$$

$$N(d_2) = N(-.1626) = .4356$$

$$C^*_0 = e^{-(.05)(1-.5)}(\$50)(.5756) - \$50e^{-(.06)(1-.5)}(.4356) = \$6.93$$

$$P^*_0 = -e^{-(.05)(1-.5)}\$50(1 - .5756) + \$50e^{-(.06)(1-.5)}(1 - .4356) = \$6.69$$

Given these option prices, the value of the forward-start call and put options would be \$6.76 and \$6.52.

$$FSC_0 = e^{-\psi(t_B-t_0)}C^*_{t_B} = e^{-(.05)(.5)}\$6.93 = \$6.76$$

$$FSP_0 = e^{-\psi(t_B-t_0)}P^*_{t_B} = e^{-(.05)(.5)}\$6.69 = \$6.52$$

9.4.2 Compound Options

A *compound option* is an option on an option. There are four types of compound options that can be formed from the generic call and put options:

- Call on call
- Put on call
- Call on put
- Put on put

The holder of a compound option has two exercise prices and exercise dates. In the case of a European call-on-call option, the holder of the compound option has the right to buy the call at an exercise price of X_1 at date T_1. The exercised call option, in turn, gives the holder the right to buy the underlying asset at an exercise price of X_2 at date T_2. If the holder exercises on that date, then he receives the underlying asset for a price of X_2. The holder of the call-on-call option will exercise the first option if the value of the option on that expiration date, C_{T1}, exceeds the first exercise price: $C_{T1} > X_1$.

The valuation of a compound option is similar to the valuation of American stock options in which there is a dividend payment. Recall, using the binomial model, we valued the American option by constraining the price of the call to be the maximum of its binomial value or its intrinsic value. In the case of a call-on-call option, picture a binomial tree where at the first expiration date T_1, there are different values of the second call given different underlying asset prices at that date. The possible values of first call at date T_1, C_{T1}^1, at each node, would then be equal to the maximum of the difference between the second call value, C_{T1}^2, minus the first exercise price or zero:

$$C_{T1}^1 = \text{Max}[C_{T1}^2 - X_1, 0]$$

Using a binomial framework, the possible values the first call at T_1 could then be rolled to the current period to determine the value of the compound option.

9.4.3 Chooser Options

A *chooser option* gives the holder the right to select either a call or a put option on an underlying asset at a specified expiration date, T_c: $\text{Max}[C_{T_c}, P_{T_c}]$. After selecting the option, the holder then has a generic call or put option. Chooser options are often referred to as "as-you-like options." Such options are particularly useful for hedging some future event such as the passage of an act or a legal decision that could have a significant economic effect.

Assuming the underlying call and put options have the same exercise price and expiration (T), then the value of the chooser option at the chooser date, t_c, will be the maximum of the call or put values:

$$V_C^{\text{Chooser}} = \text{Max}[C(S_c, T - t_c), \ P(S_c, T - t_c)]$$

If we substitute the put–call parity condition ($P = C - S - PV(X)$) for the put value, then the value of the chooser option can alternatively be expressed as

$$V_0^{\text{Chooser}} = \text{Max}[C(S_c, T - t_c), \ C(S_c, T - t_c) - S_c + PV(X)]$$
$$V_0^{\text{Chooser}} = C(S_c, T - t_c) + \text{Max}[S_c - PV(X), 0]$$

The current value of the chooser option can also be shown to be equal to the value a portfolio consisting of[3]

1. a call option priced in term of the current asset price and time to expiration of $T - t_0$ and

2. a put option priced with an exercise price of $Xe^{R(T-tc)}$, asset price of $S_0^{-\psi(T-tc)}$, and expiration of $t_c - t_0$:

$$V_0^{Chooser} = C(S_0, T - t_0, X) + P(S_0 e^{-\psi((T-t_c)}, Xe^{-R(T-t_c)}, t - t_c)$$

As an example, consider a chooser option given the following information:

- $S_0 = \$50$
- $X = \$50$
- $R = .06$
- $\psi = .05$
- $\sigma = .25$
- $T - t_0 = 1$ year
- $T - t_c = .5$ years

Using the Black–Scholes–Merton model to value the call and put options, the value of the chooser would be \$8.01:

$$V_0^{Chooser} = C(S_0, X, T - t_0) + P(S_0 e^{-\psi((T-t_c)}, Xe^{-R(T-t_c)}, t - t_c)$$

$$V_0^{Chooser} = C(\$50, \$50, 1\ year) + P(\$50 e^{-(.05)(.5)}, \$50 e^{-(.06)(.5)}, .5\ years)$$

$$V_0^{Chooser} = \$4.93 + \$3.08$$

$$V_0^{Chooser} = \$8.01$$

The table and graph in Exhibit 9.4-1 show the values of the chooser option given different stock prices. Not surprising, the shape of the graph reflects a straddle-like position.

9.4.4 Binary Options

Binary options have payoffs that are discontinuous, paying a certain amount or nothing if a certain condition is satisfied. Some of the more common binary options are **cash-or-nothing options, asset-or-nothing options**, and **supershares**.

9.4.4.1 Cash-Or-Nothing Options

A cash-or-nothing call pays a fixed amount of cash if the price of underlying asset at expiration exceeds a specified exercise price and nothing if it is equal or below:

$$S_T > X \Rightarrow receive\ Cash$$

$$S_T \leq X \Rightarrow receive\ 0$$

By contrast, a cash-or-nothing put pays a fixed amount of cash if the price of underlying asset at expiration is less than a specified exercise price, otherwise it pays nothing:

$$S_T < X \Rightarrow receive\ Cash$$

$$S_T \geq X \Rightarrow receive\ 0$$

---

[3] For a more detailed derivation of the pricing model for a chooser option, see Kolb (2003).

EXHIBIT 9.4-1 Chooser and Stock Price Relation

S_0	C*	P*	Chooser Value = C*+ P*
$30.00	$0.08	$18.55	$18.63
$35.00	$0.38	$13.86	$14.24
$40.00	$1.14	$9.46	$10.60
$45.00	$2.66	$5.75	$8.41
$50.00	$4.93	$3.09	$8.01
$55.00	$8.00	$1.48	$9.48
$60.00	$11.61	$0.64	$12.25
$65.00	$15.68	$0.26	$15.94
$70.00	$20.04	$0.09	$20.13

B-S-M Inputs:	Call	Put
	$X = 50, T = 1$ Year	$X = \$50e^{-(.06)(.5)}$
	$S = S_0$	$S = S_0e^{-(.05)(.5)}$
	Time = 1 year	Time = .5 years

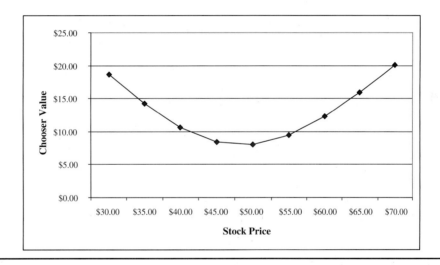

Note that different from generic options, there is no payment or receipt of the exercise price; it is only used to determine if the payoff of the cash is to be made.

The value of a cash-or-nothing call is equal to the present value of the expected cash payoff. In the case of a call, the probability of a payoff is equal to the probability of the asset price exceeding the exercise price. In the Black–Scholes–Merton model, this probability is equal to $N(d_2)$. Thus, the value of a cash-or-nothing call (CONC) expiring at date T is

$$V_0^{CONC} = PV(E(Cash))$$

$$V_0^{CONC} = (Cash)e^{-R(T-t_0)}N(d_2)$$

In the case of a cash-or-nothing put, the probability of a payoff is equal to the probability of the asset price being less than the exercise price. In the Black–Scholes–Merton model, this probability is equal to $1 - N(d_2)$. Thus, the value of a cash-or-nothing put (CONP) expiring at date T is

$$V_0^{CONP} = PV(E(Cash))$$

$$V_0^{CONP} = (Cash)\, e^{-R(T-t_0)}(1 - N(d_2))$$

As an example, consider cash-or-nothing call and put options given the following information:

- $S_0 = \$50$
- $X = \$55$
- Cash $= \$50$
- $R = .06$
- $\psi = .05$
- $\sigma = .25$
- $T - t_0 = 1$ year

Using the Black–Scholes–Merton model, the value of the cash-or-nothing call is $15.08, and the value of the cash-or-nothing put is $32.01:

$$d_1 = \frac{\ln(S_0/X) + (R - \psi + .5\,\sigma^2)(T - t_0)}{\sigma\sqrt{T - t_0}}$$

$$d_1 = \frac{\ln(\$50/\$55) + [.06 - .05 + (.5)(.25)]1}{.5\sqrt{1}} = -.2162$$

$$d_2 = d_1 - \sigma\sqrt{T - t_0}$$

$$d_2 = -.2162 - (.25)\sqrt{1} = -.4662$$

$$N(d_2) = N(-.4662) = .3203$$

$$V_0^{CONC} = (Cash)e^{-R(T-t_0)}N(d_2) = \$50e^{-(.06)(1)}(.3203) = \$15.08$$

$$V_0^{CONP} = (Cash)e^{-R(T-t_0)}(1 - N(d_2)) = \$50e^{-(.06)(1)}(1 - .3203) = \$32.01$$

Exhibit 9.4-2 shows the values of these options for different stock prices. As shown, the value of the cash-or-nothing call increases with greater stock prices, whereas the value of the cash-or-nothing put decreases.

9.4.4.2   Asset-Or-Nothing Options

An asset-or-nothing option is similar to the cash-or-nothing option except that the payoff is the asset instead of the fixed cash amount. Specifically, the holder of an asset-or-nothing call receives the asset if the price of underlying asset at expiration exceeds a specified exercise price and nothing if it is equal or below. By contrast, the holder of an asset-or-nothing put receives the asset if the price of underlying asset at expiration is less than a specified exercise price, otherwise it receives nothing.

The value of an asset-or-nothing call (put) is equal to the present value of the asset discounted at the yield, ψ, times the probability of the asset price at expiration (T) being greater (less) than the exercise price. Using $N(d_1)$ from the Black–Scholes–Merton to estimate the probabilities of $S_T > X$ and $S_T < X$, the values of an asset-or-nothing call (AONC) and a put (AONP) expiring at date T are

$$V_0^{AONC} = e^{-\psi(T-t_0)}S_0N(d_1)$$

$$V_0^{AONP} = e^{-\psi(T-t_0)}S_0(1 - N(d_1))$$

EXHIBIT 9.4-2 Cash-Or-Nothing (CON) Values and Stock Price Relation: X = $55, Cash = $50, R = .06, ψ = .05, σ = .25, and T − t_0 = 1 year

Stock Price	Value of CONC	Value of CONP
$30	$0.17	$28.08
$35	$0.95	$32.01
$40	$3.28	$34.39
$45	$7.95	$34.43
$50	$15.08	$32.01
$55	$24.16	$27.64
$60	$34.11	$22.39
$65	$44.09	$17.12
$70	$53.42	$12.50
$75	$61.86	$8.77
$80	$69.41	$5.93

CONC = CON call; CONP = CON put

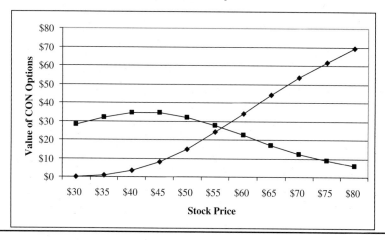

To illustrate, consider the following information on asset-or-nothing call and put options:

- $S_0 = \$50$
- $X = \$55$
- $R = .06$
- $\psi = .05$
- $\sigma = .25$
- $T - t_0 = 1$ year

Using the Black–Scholes–Merton model, the value of the asset-or-nothing call is $19.71, and the value of the asset-or-nothing put is $27.85:

$$d_1 = \frac{\ln(S_0/X) + (R - \psi + .5\sigma^2)(T - t_0)}{\sigma\sqrt{T - t_0}}$$

$$d_1 = \frac{\ln(\$50/\$55) + [.06 - .05 + (.5)(.25^2)]1}{.25\sqrt{1}} = -.2162$$

EXHIBIT 9.4-3   Asset-Or-Nothing Values and Stock Price Relation: X = \$55, S_0 = \$50, R = .06, ψ = .05, σ = .25, and T – t_0 = 1 year

Stock Price	Value of AONC	Value of AONP
\$30	\$0.34	\$28.20
\$35	\$1.67	\$31.63
\$40	\$5.10	\$32.95
\$45	\$11.20	\$31.60
\$50	\$19.71	\$27.85
\$55	\$29.58	\$22.74
\$60	\$39.74	\$17.33
\$65	\$49.31	\$12.52
\$70	\$57.96	\$8.63
\$75	\$65.64	\$5.70
\$80	\$72.45	\$3.64

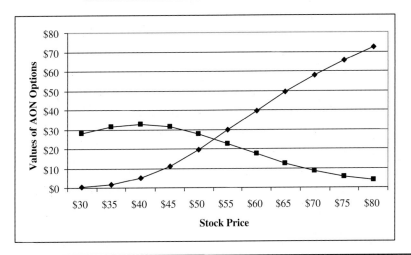

$$N(d_1) = N(-.2162) = .4145$$

$$V_0^{AONC} = e^{-\psi(T-t_0)}S_0 N(d_1) = e^{-(.05)(1)}\$50(.4145) = \$19.71$$

$$V_0^{AONP} = e^{-\psi(T-t_0)}S_0(1 - N(d_1)) = \$50e^{-(.05)(1)}(1 - .4145) = \$27.85$$

Exhibit 9.4-3 shows the values of asset-or-nothing options for different stock prices. Similar to the cash-or-nothing option, the value of the asset-or-nothing call increases with greater stock prices, whereas the value of the put decreases.

9.4.4.3 Supershares

A supershare is a financial claim that provides the holder a proportion on an underlying portfolio if the value of the underlying portfolio is between specified upper and lower portfolio values at some specified future date; if the portfolio value lies outside the bound, then the claim is worthless. If we let the upper and lower values defining the bound be X_U and X_L, S_T be the value of the portfolio at the expiration date, and the payoff be S_T/X_L, then the supershare claim can be defined in terms of the following condition:

$$\text{If } X_L \leq S_T \leq X_U \Rightarrow \text{Payoff} = \frac{S_T}{X_L}$$

$$\text{If } S_T \text{ is outside the bound, Payoff} = 0$$

A supershare is similar to a bull spread formed by buying an all-or-nothing call with an exercise price equal to the lower bound of the portfolio, X_L, and selling an all-or-nothing put with an exercise price equal to the upper bound, X_U:

$$V_0^{SS} = V_0^{AONC} - V_0^{AONP}$$

$$V_0^{SS} = \frac{e^{-\psi(T-t_0)}S_0}{X_L} [N(d_1^L) - N(d_1^U)]$$

where:

$$d_1^L = \frac{\ln(S_0/X_L) + (R - \psi + .5\sigma^2)(T-t_0)}{\sigma\sqrt{T-t_0}}$$
$$d_1^U = \frac{\ln(S_0/X_U) + (R - \psi + .5\sigma^2)(T-t_0)}{\sigma\sqrt{T-t_0}}$$

To illustrate, consider the following information on a supershare:

- $S_0 = \$50$
- $X_L = \$50$
- $X_U = \$55$
- $R = .06$
- $\psi = .05$
- $\sigma = .25$
- $T - t_0 = 1$ year

Using the Black–Scholes–Merton model, the value of the supershare is \$0.143445:

$$d_1^L = \frac{\ln(\$50/\$50) + [.06 - .05 + (.5)(.25^2)](1)}{.25\sqrt{1}} = .1650$$

$$N(d_1^L) = N(.1650) = .5653$$

$$d_1^U = \frac{\ln(\$50/\$55) + [.06 - .05 + (.5)(.25^2)](1)}{.25\sqrt{1}} = -.2162$$

$$N(d_1^U) = N(-.2162) = .4145$$

$$V_0^{SS} = \frac{e^{-\psi(T-t_0)}S_0}{X_L} [N(d_1^L) - N(d_1^U)]$$

$$V_0^{SS} = \frac{e^{-(.05)(1)}\$50}{\$50}[.5653 - .4145] = 0.143445$$

9.4.5 Path-Dependent Options

9.4.5.1 Lookback Options

Lookback options are options whose payoff or exercise price depends on the previous price of the option. For example, a lookback call option could be one in which the exercise price is the minimum price obtained over the option period, whereas a lookback put could be one in which the exercise price is equal to the maximum price obtained during the period. At expiration, the payoffs on the call and put would be

$$\text{Lookback Call Payoff at } T = \text{Max}[S_T - \text{Min}[S_{t0}, S_{t0+1}, S_{t0+2}, \cdots S_T], 0]$$

$$\text{Lookback Put Payoff at } T = \text{Max}[\text{Max}[S_{t0}, S_{t0+1}, S_{t0+2}, \cdots S_T] - S_T, 0]$$

Because a lookback call is defined by a minimum price, the holder has the right to buy the underlying asset at its lowest price for the period. Similarly, because a lookback put gives the holder the right to sell the asset at its maximum price over the period, it gives the holder a way of selling an asset at its highest possible price during a period.

It should be noted that because the exercise prices on lookback options are either the minimum (call) or maximum (put), they should always be exercised, and they should always be worth more than comparable generic options with set exercise prices.

9.4.5.2 Asian Options

Asian options are path-dependent options whose payoffs are determined by the average price of the underlying asset during all or part of the option's life.[4] The average price can be used to determine either the price of the asset or the exercise price.

The payoffs on average-asset-price Asian call and put options are

$$\text{Asian Call Payoff at } T = \text{Max}[S_{Ave} - X, 0]$$

$$\text{Asian Put Payoff at } T = \text{Max}[X - S_{Ave}, 0]$$

The payoffs on average-exercise-price Asian call and put options, in turn, are

$$\text{Asian Call Payoff at } T = \text{Max}[S_T - S_{Ave}, 0]$$

$$\text{Asian Put Payoff at } T = \text{Max}[S_{Ave} - S_T, 0]$$

Asian options are cheaper than comparable generic options. The options are useful for hedging an average price. For example, a portfolio manager who was planning to sell a portfolio at a future date could obtain downside protection equal to the average price of the portfolio by buying an Asian average-price index put option.

The average prices for most Asian options are calculated as arithmetic averages, although some are computed using a geometric average. There does not exist a close-form solution to the pricing of Asian option calculated using an arithmetic average; a solution can be found using the geometric average.[5]

9.4.5.3 Shout Option

A *shout option* is a European option giving the holder the right to "shout" or declare one time during the option's life a "price that the underlying asset hits." At the option's expiration, the holder receives the maximum of the IV defined by the shout price or the IV based on the terminal asset price. For example, consider a $100 ABC shout call in which the holder exercises her shout when ABC stock hits $110. If the price of ABC stock at expiration is less than $110, then the holder would receive a payoff of $10; if the stock

---

[4] The term "Asian Option" arises from the introduction of theses options by Bankers Trust who initially offered the options in their Tokyo office.

[5] For a more detailed discussion of the pricing of exotic option, including Asian and lookback options, see Kolb (2003), Chapter 18.

were greater than $110, then she would take the payoff equal to intrinsic value using the terminal stock price.

Shout options are similar to lookback options. They also can be valued using a binomial framework.

9.4.6 Barrier Options

Barrier options are options in which the payoff depends on whether an underlying security price or reference rate reaches a certain level. They can be classified as either knock-out or knock-in options: A *knock-out option* is one that ceases to exist once the specified barrier rate or price is reached; a *knock-in option* is one that comes into existence when the reference rate or price hits the barrier level. Both types of options can be formed with either a call or put, and the barrier level can be either above or below the current reference rate or price when the contract is established (down-and-out or up-and-out knock outs or up-and-in or down-and-in knock-in options). For example, a down-and-out, knock-out call is a call that ceases to exist once the reference price reaches the barrier level and the barrier level is below the reference price when the option was purchased. There are eight possible barrier options:

1. **Down-and-in call**: Call comes into existence if the stock price decreases to a lower barrier.

2. **Up-and-in call**: Call comes into existence if the stock price increases to an upper barrier.

3. **Down-and-in put**: Put comes into existence if the stock price decreases to a lower barrier.

4. **Up-and-in put**: Put comes into existence if the stock price increases to an upper barrier.

5. **Down-and-out call:** Call ceases to exist if the stock price decreases to a lower barrier.

6. **Up-and-out call**: Call ceases to exist if the stock price increases to an upper barrier.

7. **Down-and-out put**: Put ceases to exist if the stock price decreases to a lower barrier.

8. **Up-and-out put**: Put ceases to exist if the stock price increases to an upper barrier.

Barrier options sometimes pay a rebate when the barrier is hit. For example, a knock-in option could pay a rebate to the holder if the option expires without hitting its barrier; a knock-out option could pay a rebate when the option hits its barrier and the option ceases to exist.

Barrier options are cheaper than their plain vanilla counterparts. As such, they represent a less-expensive tool for hedging. For example, a portfolio manager considering a portfolio insurance strategy might consider buying a down-and-in put instead of a generic put. The barrier put, in turn, would be cheaper and yet might still provide the type of downside protection the manager is seeking.

9.4.7 Other Exotic Options

As one might expect, there are number of other exotic options. Some of the more popular are exchange options, rainbow options, basket options, Burmudan option, PRIMES and SCORES, and PERCS.

9.4.7.1 Exchange Option

An *exchange option* is an option to exchange one asset for another: for example, an option priced in U.S. dollars that gives the holder the right to exchange the Euro for British pounds at specific BP/Euro exchange, or an option to exchange shares of one stock for shares of another.

9.4.7.2 Rainbow Option

An extension of an exchange option is the ***rainbow option***. This option involves two or more assets, for example, a contract that allows one to choose between several assets. As we discuss in Chapter 10, the delivery procedures associated with T-bond and T-note futures contracts gives the holder the right to select from a number of bonds the one to deliver on the contract. This so-called wildcard option represents, in effect, a rainbow option. Another example of a rainbow option would be one that gives a bondholder the right to choose the currency in which the interest or principal is paid. Thus, the holder of the bond has in effect a call option giving her the right to choose the maximum value of two assets.

9.4.7.3 Basket Options

Related to options to select assets are ***basket options***. The payoff on these options depends on the value of a portfolio. The portfolio can be a portfolio of specific stocks, an index, or currencies. The supershare option that provides a payoff equal to a fraction of a portfolio is an example of a basket option. Similarly, the basket credit default swap that is examined in Chapter 20 is another example of a basket option. Options involving several assets can be valued using Monte Carlo simulation.[6]

9.4.7.4 Burmudan Option

A ***Burmudan option*** is an option that allows for early exercise only during part of the option's life. There may be, for example, an initial time period in which the option cannot be exercised. Often warrants issued by corporations have such early exercise restrictions (warrants are discussed in Chapter 21). Burmudan options can be valued using a binomial framework and constraining the appropriate nodes to be either the binomial value or the exercise value.

9.4.7.5 PRIMES and SCORES

In 1986, Americas Trust introduced the ***PRIME*** (Prescribed Right to Income and Maximum Equity) and the ***SCORE*** (Special Claims on Residual Equity). These securities traded for 5 years on the American Stock Exchange. Both securities entitled the holder to a claim on parts of the returns on an equity security. To create these securities, a trust unit was formed that was equal in value to a share of stock. Each trust unit was then divided into two units, a PRIME and a SCORE, and sold to investors. The holder of the PRIME would be entitled to any dividends paid on the stock and also at the expiration date of the PRIME, to the value of the stock (S_T) up to a specified value (X). That is

$$\text{Value of PRIME at } T = \text{Min}[S_T, X] + D_T$$

Thus, the PRIME was equivalent to a covered call position. The holder of the SCORE, on the other hand, would receive at expiration $S_T - X$ if $S_T > X$, and zero otherwise:

$$\text{Cash Flow on SCORE at } T = \text{Max}[S_T - X, 0].$$

---

[6] For a discussion on the pricing of basket options and exchange options, see Hull (2006), Chapter 22.

Thus, the SCORE represented a European call option on the stock underlying the trust unit.

At expiration, the sum of the PRIME (PR) and SCORE (SC) should be equal to the value of the stock. Thus, a priori one should expect the value of the PRIME and the SCORE to be equal to the value of the trust unit or its underlying stock: $PR_t + SC_t = S_t$. If not, arbitrage opportunities would exist. The American Stock Exchange initially provided trading for 24 trust units. They were replaced, though, by two similar securities: PERCS and LEAPS.

9.4.7.6   PERCS

Preferred Equity Redemption Cumulative Stocks, or simply **PERCS,** are similar to PRIMES except they are issued by a corporation instead of a trust, pay larger dividends, have a longer life (3 years), and are callable, with the premium declining over the period. When a PERC is called, it is exchanged for a common share at a call price. If it is not called, the holder is required to convert to common stock at expiration. If the stock price (S_t) is greater than the call price, the holder of the PERC receives less than S_t for a share (like a PRIME). A PERC is similar to a covered call write. In 1990, the CBOE began trading in Long-term Equity Anticipation Securities, or LEAPS (discussed in Chapter 2). LEAPS are similar to SCORES except that they are offered by the option exchange, instead of a trust, and they are American.

9.5   ADMONISHMENT: DERIVATIVE ABUSES

In discussing exotic options, it is important to be cognizant of some of the abuses that have occurred over the years as a result of the mismanagement of derivative positions. There are a number of cases in which companies incurred spectacular losses as a result of their traders taking speculative positions with derivatives. One classic case was the $2 billion loss in Orange County California in 1994 that occurred when the Robert Citron, the fund's trader, lost on speculative interest rate derivative positions. Some other cases of note include the following:

1. **Proctor and Gamble**: Proctor and Gamble (P&G) lost approximately $90M in 1994 by setting up an exotic derivative position with Bankers Trust. The derivative position involved a swap agreement (discussed in Chapter 17) based on changes in commercial paper (CP) rates. To profit, P&G needed CP rates to decrease. When this did not occur, the Company lost $90M. P&G subsequently sued Bankers Trust and settled out of court.

2. **Long-Term Capital Management**: Long-Term Capital Management was a hedge fund that lost approximately $4 billion in 1998. The fund set up positions in T-bond and long-term corporate bonds to profit from an expected narrowing of the default spread that instead widened following the defaults on Russian bonds. The Federal Reserve Bank of New York subsequently set up a $3.5 billion bailout of this hedge fund.

3. **Barings**: This British Bank loss approximately $1 billion when one of its traders took speculative positions instead of implementing mandated arbitrage positions. The losses eventually led to the collapse of this old British bank.

4. **Gibson Greeting**: The Gibson Greetings Company lost $20M in 1994 trading exotic interest rate options with Bankers Trust.

5. **Sumitomo Company**: The Sumitomo Company of Japan lost $2 billion in the 1990s from derivative positions.

In most of these cases, the companies had hired traders to manage their risk exposure to interest rates, exchange rates, and commodity and security prices. Over time, some of these traders (often under the illusion they could beat the market) took more speculative positions, causing a transformation of the company's treasury department into a de facto profit center and leading to substantial losses when the bets they made proved wrong. The cases, in turn, illustrate that although derivatives provide a powerful tool for managing asset and liability positions, they also require that those who are responsible for using them be prudent and knowledgeable.

Some Web Sites: Derivative Abuses

1. **Orange County California in 1994**
   http://www.erisk.com/Learning/CaseStudies/OrangeCounty.asp

2. **Proctor and Gamble:**
   http://www.erisk.com/Learning/CaseStudies/BankersTrust.asp
   http://www.businessweek.com/1995/42/b34461.htm

3. **Long-Term Capital Management**.
   http://www.erisk.com/Learning/CaseStudies/Long-TermCapitalManagemen.asp

4. **Barings:**
   http://www.erisk.com/Learning/CaseStudies/Barings.asp
   http://www.iht.com/articles/1995/02/27/head.php

5. **Gibson Greeting**:
   http://www.erisk.com/Learning/CaseStudies/BankersTrust.asp

---

9.6 CONCLUSION

In this chapter, we have examined how the B–S model can be used to define option positions prior to expiration as well as estimate expected return, risk, and Greek values of an option. We also introduced some new option strategies defined in terms the Greek values of an option or option position. Finally, we examined some of the newer derivatives that have been introduced over the last decade. Like generic options, these exotic options provide investors, portfolio managers, treasurers, and others with tools for speculating, hedging, and managing asset and liability positions. This completes our initial analysis of options and option pricing. In the next chapter, we look at another major derivative—futures contracts.

Web Information: Mark Rubinstein

Mark Rubinstein is a Professor of Finance at the Haas School of Business at the University of California at Berkeley. He is a graduate of Harvard University, Stanford University, and the University of California at Los Angeles. In addition to his seminal work on the binomial option pricing model, he is renowned for his work on exotic option valuation. In 1993, he served as President of the American Financial Association.

Biography and Research:
   http://www.haas.berkeley.edu/groups/finance/rubinste.html

KEY TERMS

efficient market tests	forward-start option	knock-in option
measurement errors	executive option	knock-out option
stochastic errors	compound option	down-and-in option
nonsimultaneity problem	chooser option	down-and-out option
option expected return	binary option	exchange option
option risk	cash-or-nothing option	rainbow option
option beta	asset-or-nothing option	basket option
position delta	supershares	Burmudan option
position gamma	path-dependent option	PRIMES
position theta	lookback option	SCORES
neutral position delta	Asian option	PERCS
neutral ratio spread	shout option	
delta spread	barrier option	

SELECTED REFERENCES

Aggarwal, R., and R. P. Rao. "Institutional Ownership and Distribution of Equity Returns." *The Financial Review* 25 (1990): 211–29.

Andersen, L. "A Simple Approach to the Pricing of Bermudan Swaption in the Multi-Factor LIBOR Market Model." *Applied Mathematical Finance* 7, no. 1 (2000): 1–32.

Arzac, E. R. "PERCs, DECs, and Other Mandatory Convertibles." *Journal of Applied Corporate Finance* 10 (1997): 54–63.

Bhattacharya, A. K. "Interest-Rate Caps and Floors and Compound Options." In *The Handbook of Fixed Income Securities*, 6th ed., edited by F. Fabozzi. New York: McGraw-Hill, 2001.

Chewlow, L., and C. Stricklan. *Exotic Options: The State of the Art.* London: Thomson Business Press, 1997.

Cornell, B. "Using the Option Pricing Model to Measure the Uncertainty Producing Effect of Major Announcements." *Financial Management* 7 (Spring 1978): 54–59.

Cox, J., and S. Ross. "The Valuation of Options for Alternative Stochastic Processes." *Journal of Financial Economics* 3 (January–March 1976): 145–166.

Dunbar, N. *Investing Money: The Story of Long-Term Capital Management and the Legends Behind It.* Chichester, England: Wiley, 2000.

Geske, R. "The Valuation of Compound Options." *Journal of Financial Economics* 7 (1979): 63–81.

Goldman, B., H. Sosin, and M. A. Gatto. "Path Dependent Options: Buy at the Low, Sell at the High." *Journal of Finance* 34 (December 1979): 1111–27.

Heston, S. "A Closed Form Solution for Options With Stochastic Volatility With Applications to Bond and Currency Options." *Review of Financial Studies* 6 (1993): 327–344.

Hull, J. C., and A. White. "How to Value Employee Stock Options." *Financial Analysts Journal* 60 (January/February 2004): 114–19.

Hull, J. *Options, Futures, and Other Derivatives.* Upper Saddle River, NJ: Prentice Hall, 2006, Chapter 22.

Jarrow, R., and A. Rudd. "Approximate Option Valuation for Arbitrary Stochastic Processes." *Journal of Financial Economics* 10 (1982): 347–69.

Johnson, H. "Options on the Maximum and Minimum of Several Assets." *Journal of Financial and Quantitative Analysis* 22 (September 1987): 277–83.

Jorion, P. *Big Bets Gone Bad: Derivatives and Bankruptcy in Orange County.* New York: Academic Press, 1995.

Jorion, P. "Risk Management Lessons From Long-Term Capital Management." *European Financial Management* 6 (September 2000): 277–300.

Kolb, R. *Futures, Options, and Swaps.* Malden, MA: Blackwell Publishing, 2003, Chapter 18.

Lowenstein, R. *When Genius Failed: The Rise and Fall of Long-Term Capital Management*. New York: Random House, 2000.

Margrabe, W. "The Value of an Option to Exchange One Asset for Another." *Journal of Finance* 33 (March 1978): 177–186.

Ritchken, P. "On Pricing Barrier Options." *Journal of Derivatives* 3, no. 2 (Winter 1995): 19–28.

Ritchken, P. *Options: Theory, Strategy, and Applications*, Glenview, IL: Scott, Foresman, 1987, Chapters 8–10.

Ritchken, P., L. Sankarasubramanian, and A. M. Vijh. "The Valuation of Path Dependent Contracts on the Average." *Management Science* 39 (1993): 1202–13.

Rubinstein, M. "On the Accounting Valuation of Employee Stock Options." *Journal of Derivatives* 3 (Fall 1995): 8–24.

Rubinstein, M. "One for Another." *Risk* (July/August 1991): 30–32.

Rubinstein, M. "Pay Now, Choose Later." *Risk* (February 1991): 44–47.

Rubinstein, M. "Somewhere Over the Rainbow." *Risk* (November 1991): 63–66.

Rubinstein, M., and E. Reiner. "Breaking Down the Barriers." *Risk* (September 1991): 28–35.

Rubinstein, M., and E. Reiner. "Unscrambling the Binary Code." *Risk* (October 1991): 75–83.

Smith, D. J. "Aggressive Corporate Finance: A Close Look at the Procter and Gamble-Bankers Trust Leveraged Swap." *Journal of Derivatives* 4, 4 (Summer 1997): 67–79.

Stein, E. M., and J. C. Stein. "Stock Price Distributions with Stochastic Volatility: An Analytical Approach." *Review of Financial Studies* 4 (1991): 727–52.

Sterk, W. "Tests of Two Models for Valuing Call Options on Stocks With Dividends." *Journal of Finance* 37 (December 1982): 1229–38.

Stulz, R. "Options on the Minimum or Maximum of Two Assets." *Journal of Financial Economics* 10 (1982): 161–185.

Taleb, N. N. *Dynamic Hedging: Managing Vanilla and Exotic Options*. New York: Wiley, 1996.

Zhang, P. G. *Barings Bankruptcy and Financial Derivatives*. Singapore: World Scientific, 1995.

Zhang, P. G., *Exotic Options: A Guide to Second Generation Options*, 2nd ed. Singapore: World Scientific, 1998.

PROBLEMS AND QUESTIONS

Note: Many of the calculations for B–S call and put prices and delta, gamma, and theta values can be done using the "Black–Scholes Option Pricing Model" and "Option Strategies" Excel programs.

1. Determine the profits from a time spread formed with a long position in an ABC 60 call expiring in 6 months (T = .5) and trading at $5.46 and short a position in an ABC 60 call expiring in 3 months (T = .25) and trading at $3.49. Assume the spread is closed at the expiration of the short-term call when ABC is trading at $65. Assume σ = .35, no dividends, and R = .05.

2. What would be your profit if you sold a 6-month 70 call at $5.79 and then closed it 3 months later (T = .25) when the stock was trading at 70? Assume ABC stock has σ = .25 and pays no dividends and R = .05.

3. Suppose ABC stock is trading at $50, its annualized standard deviation is 0.175, and the continuously compounded risk-free rate is 6% (annual).

   a. Calculate the B–S equilibrium call prices for an ABC 50 European call expiring in 90 days (T = .25) and an ABC 48 European call expiring in 90 days.

   b. Construct a neutral ratio spread with the 50 and 48 calls. What would your initial cash flow be if the calls were priced equal to their OPM values?

   c. What would happen to your neutral ratio hedge if the stock immediately increased by $1 and you closed your positions at call prices equal to their equilibrium values? What would happen if you closed your position after the stock decreased by $1?

d. Define the arbitrage strategy using the neutral delta strategy one could employ if the price of the ABC 48 call was equal to its equilibrium value, but the 50 call was underpriced at $2.05. Show the initial cash flow from closing the position shortly afterward at $S_t = \$51$ and $S_t = \$49$ and with the call values equal to the equilibrium values you used in 5c.

e. Describe the arbitrage strategy one could use if the 50 call were overpriced at $2.25.

4. Given the following information on the ABC stock in Problem 3—$S_0 = \$50$, $\sigma = .175$, $R = .06$, and $\beta_S = .35$—determine the following characteristics of an ABC 50 European call with an expiration of $T = .25$:

a. Equilibrium OPM call price (the same question as Problem 3a).

b. Expected rate of return of the call given $E(R_s) = .10$.

c. Standard deviation of the call (assume the stock has a variability of $\sigma = .175$).

d. Beta of the call.
Briefly comment on relative sizes of the expected returns, standard deviations, and β of the ABC call and stock.

5. Given the information on the ABC stock in Problem 3—$S_0 = \$50$, $\sigma = .175$, $R = .06$, $\beta_S = .35$, and $E(R_s) = .10$—determine the following characteristics of an ABC 50 European put with an expiration of $T = .25$:

a. Equilibrium OPM put price.

b. Expected rate of return of the put given $E(R_s) = -.10$.

c. Standard deviation of the put (assume the stock has a variability of $\sigma = .175$).

d. Beta of the put.

6. Suppose XYZ stock is trading at $100, its annualized standard deviation is $\sigma = .25$, it pays no dividends, and the continuous compounded risk-free rate is 6%.

a. Determine the B–S equilibrium call prices for an XYZ European 100 call expiring in 90 days ($T = .25$) and an XYZ European 105 call expiring in 90 days.

b. Determine the delta, theta, and gamma for the 100 call and 105 call.

c. Construct a neutral-delta hedged portfolio? What is the value of the portfolio? What is the position theta and gamma?

d. Given your neutral-delta hedged portfolio, what would you expect the change in the portfolio's value to be over a short period of time if there were no changes in the price of XYZ stock? What would you expect the change in value to be if there were a positive change or a negative change in the stock price?

e. What would be the portfolio's profit or loss if the price of XYZ stock increased to $105, and the 100 call and 105 call traded at their B–S values of $8.9597 and $6.0162, respectively?

f. What would be the portfolio's profit or loss if the price of the XYZ stock decreased to $95, and the 100 call and 105 call traded at their B–S values of $3.2890 and $1.8133, respectively? Are your results consistent with your answer in question d?

7. Assume: $S_0 = 50$, $\sigma = .5$, $X = 50$, zero dividends, $R = 5\%$, $T = .5$, and all call and put options are equal to their B–S values. Using the "Option Strategies" Excel program, evaluate the profit and stock price relations of a call purchase and a put purchase for holding periods of 1 month, 3 months, and expiration at $S_t = 30, 35, 40, 45, 50, 55,$

60, 65, and 70. Show your profit and stock price relation for each holding period in a table and graph.

8. Assume: $S_0 = 50, \sigma = .5, X = 50$, zero dividends, $R = 5\%, T = .5$, and all call and put options are equal to their B–S values. Using the "Option Strategies" Excel program, evaluate the profit and stock price relations of a straddle purchase and straddle sale for holding periods of 1 month, 3 months, and expiration at $S_t = 30, 35, 40, 45, 50, 55, 60, 65,$ and 70. Show your profit and stock price relation for each holding period in a table and graph.

9. Assume: $S_0 = 50, \sigma = .5, X = 50$, zero dividends, $R = 5\%, T = .5$, and all call and put options are equal to their B–S values. Using the "Option Strategies" Excel program, evaluate the profit and stock price relations of a covered call write for holding periods of 1 month, 3 months, and expiration at $S_t = 30, 35, 40, 45, 50, 55, 60, 65,$ and 70. Show your profit and stock price relation for each holding period in a table and graph.

10. Given the following information on forward-start call and put options

   - $S_0 = \$50$
   - $R = .06$
   - $\psi = .05$
   - $\sigma = .25$
   - $T - t_0 = 1$ year
   - $T - t_B = .5$ years,

   using the Black–Scholes–Merton model, determine the values of the forward-start call and put options.

11. Given the following information on a chooser option

   - $S_0 = \$100$
   - $X = \$100$
   - $R = .05$
   - $\psi = .04$
   - $\sigma = .20$
   - $T - t_0 = 1$ year
   - $T - t_c = .5$ years,

   using the Black–Scholes–Merton model, determine the value of the chooser option.

12. Given the following information on cash-or-nothing call and put options

   - $S_0 = \$100$
   - $X = \$105$
   - Cash $= \$100$
   - $R = .05$
   - $\psi = .04$
   - $\sigma = .20$
   - $T - t_0 = 1$ year,

using the Black–Scholes–Merton model, determine the values of the cash-or-nothing call and put options.

13. Given the following information on asset-or-nothing call and put options

   - $S_0 = \$100$
   - $X = \$105$
   - $R = .05$
   - $\psi = .04$
   - $\sigma = .20$
   - $T - t_0 = 1$ year,

   using the Black–Scholes–Merton model, determine the values of the asset-or-nothing call and put options.

14. Consider the following information for a supershare on a $100 portfolio ($S_0$):

   - $S_0 = \$100$
   - $X_L = \$100$
   - $X_U = \$110$
   - $R = .05$
   - $\psi = .04$
   - $\sigma = .20$
   - $T - t_0 = 1$ year
   - Supershare payoff $= S_T/X_L$

   Using the Black–Scholes–Merton model, determine the value of the supershare.

15. Explain the difference between a lookback call and a lookback put.

16. Explain the difference between an average-asset-price Asian option and an average-exercise-price Asian option.

17. Compared to generic options, what features of Asian options do option traders find attractive?

18. Explain with an example how a shout option works.

19. Define the different types of barrier options that can be created from generic call and put stock options.

20. Compared to generic options, what feature of barrier options do option traders find attractive?

21. Provide an example of the following exotic options:

   a. Forward-start option

   b. Compound option

   c. Rainbow option

22. Construct a cash flow table at expiration for a PRIME and SCORE on a unit of ABC stock with a termination price of $50. Assume ABC stock pays dividends worth $1.00 at expiration and evaluate at possible stock/unit prices at expiration of $40, $45, $50, $55, and $60. What are the PRIME and SCORE positions equivalent to?

WEB EXERCISES

1. On February 16, 2007, there were 100 call and 100 put options on IBM each expiring on July 20. On February 16, IBM's stock closed at 98.99, its historical volatility was .1959 (annualized standard deviation of logarithmic return), IBM's historical annual dividend yield was 2%, and the short-term money market rate was 4.574%.

   a. Using IBM's historical dividend yield and volatility, determine the option price, delta, gamma, and theta of IBM's call. Use Merton's continuous dividend yield B–S model (use BS Greeks Excel worksheet in "Black–Scholes Option Pricing Model" Excel program).

   b. Using IBM's historical dividend yield and volatility, determine the option price, delta, gamma, and theta of IBM's put. Use Merton's continuous dividend yield B–S model (use BS Greeks Excel worksheet in "Black–Scholes Option Pricing Model" Excel program).

   c. Using IBM's historical dividend yield and volatility or your own estimates, price a currently traded IBM call and put using Merton's continuous dividend-yield B–S model and determine the options' delta, gamma, and theta (use BS Greeks Excel worksheet in "Black–Scholes Option Pricing Model" Excel program). For information on currently traded IBM options, go to http://www.wsj.com/free.

   d. Using currently traded IBM options and using either IBM's historical dividend yield and volatility or your own estimates, evaluate the following strategies with a profit table and graph for several periods prior to expirations (use "Option Strategies" Excel programs): call purchase, put purchase, straddle purchase, straddle sale, and synthetic long or short positions.

2. On January 8, 2007, the S&P 500 call option with an exercise price of 1400 and expiration of June 16, 2007 (158 days), was trading at 66. On that date, the spot S&P 500 index closed at 1412.84, its historical volatility was .13644 (annualized standard deviation of logarithmic return), the index's dividend yield was 1.799%, and the short-term money market rate was 4.778%. Using IBM's historical dividend yield and volatility, determine the option price, delta, gamma, and theta of IBM's call. Use Merton's continuous dividend-yield B–S model (use BS Greeks Excel worksheet in "Black-Scholes Option Pricing Model" Excel program).

   a. Using the S&P 500's historical dividend yield and volatility, determine the option price, delta, gamma, and theta of the S&P 500 call. Use Merton's continuous dividend-yield B–S model (use BS Greeks Excel worksheet in "Black-Scholes Option Pricing Model" Excel program).

   b. Using the S&P 500's historical dividend yield and volatility, determine the option price, delta, gamma, and theta of the S&P 500 put. Use Merton's continuous dividend-yield B–S model (use BS Greeks Excel worksheet in "Black–Scholes Option Pricing Model" Excel program).

   c. Using the S&P 500's historical dividend yield and volatility or your own estimates, price a currently traded the S&P 500 call and put using Merton's continuous dividend-yield B–S model, and determine the options' delta, gamma, and theta (use BS Greeks Excel worksheet in "Black–Scholes Option Pricing Model" Excel program). For information on currently traded S&P 500 options, go to http://www.wsj.com/free.

   d. Using currently traded S&P 500 options and using either the S&P 500's historical dividend yield and volatility or your own estimates, evaluate the following strategies with a profit table and graph for several periods prior to expirations (use "Option Strategies" Excel programs): call purchase, put purchase, straddle purchase, straddle sale, and synthetic long or short positions.

CHAPTER 10

FUTURES AND FORWARD CONTRACTS

10.1 INTRODUCTION

The Chicago Board of Trade (CBT) was formed in 1848 by a group of Chicago merchants to facilitate the trading of grain. This organization subsequently introduced the first standardized forward contract (called a "to-arrive" contract) in which two parties agreed to exchange commodities for cash at a future date but with the terms and the price agreed on in the present. Later, the organization established rules for trading the contracts and developed a margin system in which traders ensured their performance by depositing good-faith money to a third party. These actions made it possible for speculators as well as farmers and dealers who were hedging their positions to trade their forward contracts. By definition, futures are marketable forward contracts. Thus, the CBT evolved from a board offering forward contracts to the first organized exchange listing futures contracts—a futures exchange.

Over time, new exchanges were formed in Chicago, New York, and other large cities throughout the world. The types of futures contracts also expanded from grains and agricultural products to commodities and metals and finally to financial futures such as futures on foreign currency (first offered by the Chicago Mercantile Exchange [CME]), Treasury bond futures contract (CBT), Treasury bill and Eurodollar futures (CME), and futures contracts on indices. Beginning in the 1970s, futures trading also became more global with the openings of the London International Financial Futures Exchange (1982), Singapore International Monetary Market (1986), Toronto Futures Exchange (1984), New Zealand Futures Exchange (1985), and Tokyo Financial Futures Exchange (1985).

Concomitant with the growth in future trading on organized exchanges has been the growth in futures contracts offered and traded on the over-the-counter (OTC) market. In this market, dealers offer and make markets in more tailor-made, forward contracts in currencies, indices, and various interest-rate products. Today, the total volume of forward contracts created on the OTC market exceeds the volume of exchange-traded futures contracts. The combined growth in the futures and forward contracts also created a need for more governmental oversight to ensure market efficiency and to guard against abuses. The Commodity Futures Trading Commission (CFTC), in turn, was created by Congress to monitor and regulate futures trading, and the National Futures Association (NFA), a private agency, was established to oversee futures trading.[1] The growth in futures markets also has led to the consolidation of exchanges. As noted in Chapter 1, the CME and the CBT in 2006 approved a deal in which the CME acquired the CBT, forming the CME

---

[1] An early justification for the need for government oversight was best demonstrated in the late 1980s when the FBI launched an investigation to see if a price-manipulation scheme known as "bucket trading" occurred on the CBT and CME. In a bucket trade, a commission broker with an order to execute tips off another broker (referred to as the "bagman") who proceeds to take a position in the futures. When conditions are favorable, the commission broker executes the order with the bagman.

Group, Inc. The combined derivative exchanges have an average daily trading volume approaching 9 million contracts per day.

10.1.1   Definition

Formally, a ***forward contract*** is an agreement between two parties to trade a specific asset at a future date with the terms and price agreed on today. A ***futures contract***, in turn, is a "marketable" forward contract, with marketability provided through futures exchanges that list hundreds of standardized contracts, establish trading rules, and provide for clearinghouses to guarantee and intermediate contracts. In contrast, forward contracts are provided by financial institutions and dealers; are less standardized and more tailor-made; are usually held to maturity; and unlike futures, they often do not require initial or maintenance margins. Both forward and futures contracts are similar to option contracts in that the underlying asset's price on the contract is determined in the present, with the delivery and payment occurring at a future date. The major difference between these derivative securities is that the holder of an option has the right, but not the responsibility, to execute the contract (i.e., it is a contingent-claim security), whereas the holder of a futures or forward contract has an obligation to fulfill the terms of the contract. In this chapter, we begin our analysis of futures and forward contracts by examining how futures positions are created and the role of the clearinghouse, the hedging and speculative uses of these contracts, the markets in which futures are traded, and the various types of futures and forward contracts that are offered by the exchanges and by dealers in the OTC market. In Chapter 11, we extend our analysis of futures and forward agreements by examining the pricing of such contracts. Finally, in Chapter 12, we return to options and examine options on futures contracts.

Web Information:

> Chicago Mercantile Exchange: www.cme.com
>
> Chicago Board of Trade: www.cbt.com
>
> See Exhibit 1.1 for a listing of derivative exchanges and their Web sites
>
> Commodity Futures Trading Commission: www.cftc.gov
>
> National Futures Association: www.nfa.futures.org

10.2   THE NATURE OF FUTURES TRADING AND THE ROLE OF THE CLEARINGHOUSE

10.2.1   Futures Positions

A speculator or hedger can take one of two positions on a futures (or forward contract) contract: a long position (or futures purchase) or a short position (futures sale). In a long futures position, one agrees to buy the contract's underlying asset at a specified price, with the payment and delivery to occur on the expiration date (also referred to as the delivery date); in a short position, one agrees to sell an asset at a specific price, with delivery and payment occurring at expiration.

To illustrate how positions are taken, suppose in June, Speculator A believes that the upcoming summer will be unusually dry in the Midwest, causing an increase in the price of wheat. With the hope of profiting from this expectation, suppose Speculator A decides to take a long position in a wheat futures contract and instructs her broker to buy one September wheat futures contract listed on the CBT (one contract is for 5,000 bushels).

To fulfill this order, suppose A's broker finds a broker representing Speculator B who believes that the summer wheat harvest will be above normal and therefore hopes to profit by taking a short position in the September wheat contract. After negotiating with each other, suppose the brokers agree to a price (f_0) of $2.40/bu on the September contract for their clients. In terms of futures positions, Speculator A would have a long position in which she agrees to buy 5,000 bushels of wheat at $2.40/bu from Speculator B at the delivery date in September, and Speculator B would have a short position in which he agrees to sell 5,000 bushels of wheat at $2.40/bu to A at the delivery date in September. That is

If both parties hold their contracts to delivery, their profits or losses would be determined by the price of wheat on the spot market (also called cash, physical, or actual market). For example, suppose the summer turns out to be dry, causing the spot price of wheat to trade at $2.50/bu at the grain elevators in the Midwest at or near the delivery date on the September wheat futures contract. Accordingly, Speculator A would be able to buy 5,000 bushels of wheat on her September futures contract at $2.40/bu from Speculator B, then sell the wheat for $2.50/bu on the spot market to earn a profit of $500 before commission and transportation costs are included. On the other hand, to deliver 5,000 bushels of wheat on the September contract, Speculator B would have to buy the wheat on the spot market for $2.50/bu, then sell it on the futures contract to Speculator A for $2.40/bu, resulting in a $500 loss (again, not including commission and transportation costs).

10.2.2 Clearinghouse

To provide contracts with marketability, futures exchanges use clearinghouses. Like the Option Clearing Corporation, the clearinghouses associated with futures exchanges guarantee each contract and act as intermediaries by breaking up each contract after the trade has taken place. Thus, in the preceding example, the clearinghouse (CH) would come in after Speculators A and B have reached an agreement on the price of September wheat, becoming the effective seller on A's long position and the effective buyer on B's short position:

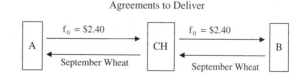

Once the clearinghouse has broken up the contracts, then A's and B's contracts would be with the clearinghouse. The clearinghouse, in turn, would record the following entries in its computer:

Clearinghouse Record:

---

1. Speculator A agrees to buy September wheat at $2.40/bu from the clearinghouse.
2. Speculator B agrees to sell September wheat at $2.40/bu to the clearinghouse.

As we earlier discussed with the Option Clearing Corporation, the intermediary role of the clearinghouse makes it easier for futures traders to close their positions before expiration. Returning to our example, suppose that the month of June is unexpectedly dry in the Midwest, leading a third speculator, Speculator C, to want to take a long position in the listed September wheat futures contract. Seeing a profit potential from the increased demand for long positions in the September contract, suppose Speculator A agrees to sell a September wheat futures contract to Speculator C for $2.45/bu. On doing this, Speculator A now would be short in the new September contract, with Speculator C having a long position, and there now would be two contracts on September wheat. Without the clearinghouse intermediating, the two contracts can be described as follows:

Agreements to Deliver

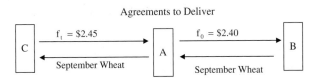

After the new contract between A and C has been established, the clearinghouse would step in and break it up. For Speculator A, the clearinghouse's record would now show the following:

Clearinghouse Records for Speculator A:

---

1. Speculator A agrees to *buy* September wheat from the clearinghouse for $2.40/bu.
2. Speculator A agrees to *sell* September wheat to the clearinghouse for $2.45/bu.

Thus

The clearinghouse accordingly would close Speculator A's positions by paying her $0.05/bu ($2.45/bu – $2.40/bu), a total of $250 on the contract ((5,000 bu)($0.05/bu)). Because Speculator A's short position effectively closes her position, it is variously referred to as a ***closing, reversing out,*** or ***offsetting position*** or simply as an ***offset.*** Thus, the clearinghouse, like the Option Clearing Corporation, makes it easier for futures contracts to be closed prior to expiration.

Commission costs and the costs of transporting commodities cause most futures traders to close their positions instead of taking delivery. As the delivery date approaches, the number of outstanding contracts (***open interest***) declines, with only a relatively few contracts still outstanding at delivery. Moreover, at expiration, the contract prices on futures contracts established on that date (f_T) should be equal (or approximately equal) to the prevailing spot price on the underlying asset (S_T). That is

At Expiration: $f_T = S_T$

If f_T does not equal S_T at expiration, an arbitrage opportunity would exist. Arbitrageurs could take a position in the futures contract and an opposite position in the spot market. For example, if the September wheat futures contract were available at $2.50 on the delivery date in September and the spot price for wheat were $2.55, arbitrageurs could go long in the September contract, take delivery by buying the wheat at $2.50 on the futures contract, then sell the wheat on the spot at $2.55 to earn a riskless profit of $0.05/bu. The arbitrageurs' efforts to take long positions, though, would drive the contract price up to $2.55. On the other hand, if f_T exceeds $2.55, then arbitrageurs would reverse their strategy, pushing f_T to $2.55/bu. Thus, at delivery, arbitrageurs will ensure that the prices on expiring contracts are equal to the spot price. As a result, closing a futures contract with an offsetting position at expiration will yield the same profits or losses as closing futures positions on the spot by purchasing (selling) the asset on the spot and selling (buying) it on the futures contract.

Returning to our example, suppose near the delivery date on the September contract, the spot price of wheat and the price on the expiring September futures contracts are $2.50/bu. To close his existing short contract, Speculator B would need to take a long position in the September contract, and to offset her existing contract, Speculator C would need to take a short position. Suppose Speculators B and C take their offsetting positions with each other on the expiring September wheat contract priced at $f_T = S_T = \$2.50/bu$. After the clearinghouse breaks up the new contract, Speculator B would owe the clearinghouse $0.10/bu, and Speculator C would receive $0.05/bu from the clearinghouse:

Clearinghouse Records for Speculator B:

1. Speculator B agrees to *sell* September wheat to the CH for $2.40/bu.
2. Speculator B agrees to *buy* September wheat from the CH at $2.50/bu.

Thus

And,

Clearinghouse Records for Speculator C:

1. Speculator C agrees to *buy* September wheat at $2.45/bu.
2. Speculator C agrees to *sell* September wheat for $2.50/bu.

Thus

To recapitulate, in this example, the contract prices on September wheat contracts went from $2.40/bu on the A and B contract, to $2.45/bu on the A and C contract, and then to $2.50/bu on the B and C contract at expiration. Speculators A and C each received $0.05/bu from the clearinghouse, whereas Speculator B paid $0.10/bu to the clearinghouse, the clearinghouse with a perfect hedge on each contract received nothing (other than clearinghouse fees attached to the commission charges), and no wheat was purchased or delivered.

10.3 FUTURES HEDGING

Futures markets and OTC forward contracts provide investors, businesses, and other economic entities a means for hedging their particular spot positions against adverse price movements. Two hedging positions exist: a long hedge and a short hedge. In a ***long hedge*** (or hedge purchase), a hedger takes a long position in a futures contract to protect against an increase in the price of the underlying asset or commodity. Long hedge positions are used, for example, by manufacturers to lock in their future costs of purchasing raw materials, by portfolio managers to fix the price they will pay for securities in the future, or by multinational corporations that want to lock in the dollar costs of buying foreign currency at some future date. In a ***short hedge***, one takes a short futures position to protect against a decrease in the price of the underlying asset. In contrast to long hedging, short hedge positions are used, for example, by farmers who want to lock in the price they will sell their crops for at harvest, by portfolio managers and investment bankers who are planning to sell securities in the future and want to minimize price risk, or by multinational corporations who have to convert future foreign currency cash flows into dollars and want to immunize the future exchange against adverse changes in exchange rates.

10.3.1 Long Hedge Example

To illustrate a long hedge position, consider the case of an oil refinery that, in December, anticipates purchasing 100,000 barrels of crude oil in February. Suppose the refinery wants to avoid the price risk associated with buying crude oil on the spot market in February.[2] In the absence of a forward contract or futures markets for crude oil, the only way the refining company could avoid price risk would be to buy the crude oil in December and store it until February. With crude oil futures contracts listed on the New York Mercantile Exchange, though, the refinery alternatively can minimize price risks by taking a long position in the February crude oil contract. With the standard size on crude oil futures of 1,000 barrels, the company would need to go long in 100 February crude oil contracts to hedge its February spot purchase. To this end, suppose the refinery purchases 100 February contracts at $50.00/barrel. At expiration, the company would probably find it advantageous (lower transportation costs) to purchase its 100,000 barrels of crude oil on the spot market at the spot price and then close its futures position by going short in the expiring February crude oil futures contract. Given that the spot and expiring futures prices must be equal (or approximately equal), the refinery will find that any additional costs of buying crude oil above the $50.00/barrel price on the spot market will be offset by a profit from its futures position; whereas on the other hand, any benefits from the costs of crude oil being less than the $50.00/barrel price would be negated by losses on the refinery's futures position. As a result, the refining company's costs of buying crude oil on the spot and closing its futures position would be $50.00/barrel, which is the initial February crude oil contract price they obtained in December.

The refining company's long hedge position is shown in Table 10.3-1. In the table body, the first row shows three possible spot prices at the February delivery date of $45.00,

---

[2] Oil companies often buy crude oil on contracts with producers that stipulate that the producer will deliver the crude oil at a specified price and on a specified date. These contracts represent forward contracts.

TABLE 10.3-1   Long Hedge Example

Initial Position: Long in February crude oil futures contracts at $50.00/barrel to hedge crude oil purchases in February.

At Delivery: Close February crude oil contract at $f_T = S_T$ and purchase crude oil on the spot market at S_T.

Positions	Costs per Barrel		
February Spot Price	$45.00	$50.00	$55.00
– Profit on Futures	(5.00)	0.00	5.00
Net Costs	$50.00	$50.00	$50.00

(Profit on Futures)/barrel = (Spot Price – $50.00)/barrel.

$50.00, and $55.00. The second row shows the profits and losses per barrel from the long futures position in which the offset position has a contract price (f_T) equal to the spot price (S_T). The last row shows the net costs per barrel of $50.00 resulting from purchasing the crude and closing the futures position. Thus, if the price of crude oil on the spot market were $45.00 at the February delivery date, the refinery would pay $45.00 per each barrel of crude oil and $5.00 per barrel to the clearinghouse to close its futures positions (i.e., the agreement to buy at $50.00 and the offsetting agreement to sell at $45.00 means the refining company must pay the clearinghouse $5.00); if the spot crude oil price were $55.00, the company would have to pay $55.00 per barrel for the crude oil but could finance part of that expenditure with the $5.00 per barrel it received from the clearinghouse from closing (i.e., agreement to buy at $50.00 and the offsetting agreement to sell at $55.00 means the clearinghouse will pay the refining company $5.00 per barrel).

10.3.2   Short Hedge Example

To illustrate how a short hedge works, consider the case of a wheat farmer who, in June, wants to lock in the price he will receive for his estimated 5,000 bushels of wheat expected to be harvested in September. If the farmer goes short in one September wheat futures contract (contract size is 5,000 bushels) priced at $2.40/bu in June, he would be able to receive $2.40/bu in revenue at the delivery date in September from selling the wheat on the spot market and closing the futures contract by going long in the expiring September contract trading at the spot price. This can be seen in Table 10.3-2. In the table body, the first row shows three possible spot prices of $2.00, $2.40, and $3.00; the second row shows the profits and losses from the futures position; and the third row shows the constant hedged revenue per bushel of $2.40 from aggregating both positions. If the farmer receives only $2.00 per bushel for his wheat, he realizes a $0.40 profit per bushel from his futures position (the agreement to sell September wheat for $2.40 is closed with an agreement to buy September wheat for $2.00, resulting in a $0.40 receipt from the clearinghouse). On the other hand, if the farmer is able to sell his wheat for $3.00 per bushel, he also will have to pay the clearinghouse $0.60 per bushel to close the futures position. Thus, regardless of the spot price, the farmer receives $2.40 per bushel.

10.3.3   Hedging Risk

The previous examples represent perfect hedging cases in which certain revenues or costs can be locked in at a future date. In practice, perfect hedges are the exception and not the

TABLE 10.3-2   Short Hedge Example

Initial Position: Short in a September wheat futures contract at $2.40/bu to hedge wheat sale in September.

At Delivery: Close wheat futures contract at $f_T = S_T$ and sell the harvested wheat on the spot market at S_T.

Positions	Revenue per Bushel		
Spot Wheat Price	$2.00	$2.40	$3.00
+ Profit from Futures	(0.40)	0.00	0.60
Revenue	$2.40	$2.40	$2.40

(Profit from Futures)/bu = ($2.40 − S_T)/bu.

rule. There are three types of hedging risks that preclude one from obtaining a zero-risk position: *quality risk, timing risk*, and *quantity risk*.

Quality risk exists when the commodity or asset being hedged is not identical to the one underlying the futures contract. The oil refinery in our previous example, for instance, may need to purchase a different grade or quality of crude oil than the one specified in the futures contract. In certain hedging cases, futures contracts written on a different underlying asset are used to hedge the spot asset. For example, a portfolio manager planning to buy corporate bonds in the future might hedge the acquisition by going long in T-bond futures. This type of hedge is known as a *cross-hedge*. Unlike *direct hedges* in which the future's underlying assets are the same as the assets being hedged, cross-hedging cannot eliminate risk but can minimize it.[3]

Timing risk occurs when the delivery date on the futures contract does not coincide with the date the hedged assets or liabilities need to be purchased or sold. For example, timing risk would exist in our first hedging example if the oil refining company needed crude oil the first of February instead of at the futures' expiration at the end of the month. If the spot asset or commodity is purchased or sold at a date t that differs from the expiration date on the futures contract, then the price on the futures (f_t) and the spot price (S_t) will not necessarily be equal. The difference between the futures and spot price is called the *basis* (B_t). The basis tends to narrow as expiration nears, converging to zero at expiration ($B_T = 0$). Prior to expiration, the basis can vary, with greater variability usually observed the longer the time is to expiration. Given this *basis risk*, the greater the time difference between buying or selling the hedged asset and the futures' expiration date, the less perfect the hedge.

To minimize timing risk or basis risk, hedgers often select futures contracts that mature before the hedged asset is to be bought or sold but as close as possible to that date. For very distant horizon dates, though, hedgers sometimes follow a strategy known as *rolling the hedge forward*. This hedging strategy involves taking a futures position and then at expiration, closing the position and taking a new one.

Finally, because of the standardization of futures contracts, futures hedging also is subject to quantity risk. Quantity risk would have been present in our second hedging example if the farmer had expected a harvest of 6,000 bushels instead of 5,000 bushels.

---

[3] Cross-hedging can occur when an entire group of assets or liabilities are hedged by one type of futures contract; this is referred to as macrohedging. Microhedging, on the other hand, occurs when each individual asset or liability is hedged separately.

With the contract size on the wheat futures contract being 5,000 bushels, 1,000 bushels of the farmer's harvest could not have been protected against price changes.

10.3.4 Hedging Models

The presence of quality, timing, and quantity risk means that pricing risk cannot be eliminated totally by hedging with futures contracts. As a result, the objective in hedging is to try to minimize risk. Several hedging models try to achieve this objective: price-sensitivity model, minimum variance model, naïve-hedge model, and utility-based hedging model. These models have as their common objective the determination of a **hedge ratio**: the optimal number of futures contracts (or option contracts) needed to hedge a position. In later chapters, we define and examine how some of these models can be used to hedge stock portfolios, debt securities, and foreign currency positions.

10.4 SPECULATING WITH FUTURES

Although futures are used quite extensively for hedging, they are also frequently used to speculate on expected price changes. A long futures position is taken when the price of the underlying asset is expected to rise, and a short position is taken when the price is expected to fall. Speculating on a change in the price of an asset or commodity by taking such outright or naked futures positions represents an alternative to buying or short selling the asset or commodity on the spot market. Because of the risk inherent in such **outright futures positions,** though, some speculators form spreads instead of taking a naked position. A futures spread is formed by taking long and short positions on different futures contracts simultaneously.

There are two general types of spreads: intracommodity and intercommodity. An **intracommodity spread** is formed with futures contracts on the same asset but with different expiration dates; an **intercommodity spread** is formed with two futures contracts with the same expiration but on different assets.

10.4.1 Intracommodity Spread

An intracommodity spread is often used to reduce the risk associated with a pure outright position. As we show later (Chapter 11), in examining futures price relations, more distant futures contracts (T_2) are more price sensitive to changes in the spot price, S, than near-term futures contracts (T_1):

$$\frac{\%\Delta f_{T_2}}{\%\Delta S} > \frac{\%\Delta f_{T_1}}{\%\Delta S}$$

Thus, a speculator who expects the price of a commodity or asset to increase in the future could form an intracommodity spread by going long in the asset's or commodity's longer term futures contract and short in a shorter term one. This type of intracommodity spread will be profitable if the expectation of the price increasing occurs. That is, the increase in the commodity or asset price will cause the price on the longer term futures contract to increase more than the shorter term one. As a result, a speculator's gains from his long position in the longer term futures will exceed his losses from his short position. If the spot price falls, though, losses will occur on the long position; these losses will be partially offset by profits realized from the short position on the shorter term contract. On the other hand, if a speculator believes the spot price will decrease but did not want to assume the risk inherent in an outright short position, he could form a spread with a short position in a longer term contract and a long position in the shorter term one. Note that in forming a spread, the speculator does not have to keep the ratio of long-to-short positions one-to-one, but instead could use any ratio (2-to-1, 3-to-2, etc.) to obtain the speculator's desired return-risk combination.

10.4.2 Intercommodity Spread

An intercommodity spread is formed with two futures contracts with the same expiration dates but on different commodities: for example, opposite positions on a June S&P 500 Index and a June Nasdaq 100 Index. In constructing intercommodity spreads, a spreader often makes use of the correlation between the underlying assets. For example, suppose the relation between gold and silver prices is such that when gold prices change by 10%, silver prices change in the same direction by 9%. A mildly bullish precious metals speculator who wanted a lower return-risk combination than implied by either metal could form an intercommodity spread by going long in a gold futures contract and short in a silver futures contract. If the spread is set up on a one-to-one basis, then for a 10% increase in gold prices and a corresponding 9% increase in silver prices, the spreader would realize a 1% gain; and for a decrease of the same percentages, the spreader would lose 1%.

Many different spreads, each with different return-risk combinations, can be formed by changing the ratio of long to short positions. Futures spreads formed with stock indices, debt, and foreign currency futures are discussed further in subsequent chapters.

10.5   THE MARKET AND CHARACTERISTICS OF FUTURES

10.5.1 Microstructure

Like other organized exchanges, futures exchanges are typically structured as membership organization with a fixed number of seats and with the seat being a precondition for direct trading on the exchange. On most futures exchanges, there are two major types of futures traders/members: commission brokers and locals. Commission brokers buy and sell for their customers. They carry out most of the trading on the exchanges, serving the important role of linking futures traders. *Locals,* on the other hand, trade from their own accounts, acting as speculators or arbitrageurs. They serve to make the market operate more efficiently. Some exchanges also permit members to engage in ***dual trading***. Under dual-trading rules, brokers are allowed to fill orders for customers as well as trade for their own accounts as long as the customers' orders are given priority.[4]

The mode of trading on futures exchanges in the United States, London (LIFFE), Sydney (SFE), Singapore (SIMEX), and other locations still takes place the way it did over 100 years ago on the CBT with brokers and dealers going to a pit and using the ***open outcry*** method to trade. In this system, orders are relayed to the floor by runners or by hand signals to a specified trading pit. The order is then offered in open outcry to all participants in the pit, with the trade being done with the first person to respond.[5]

---

[4] As a matter of security law, dual traders are not allowed to trade on their own accounts when they are about to trade for their clients. With advance knowledge of a client's position, a dual trader could profit by taking a favorable position before executing the client's order. This type of price manipulation is known as ***front running.***

[5] There are two rules governing an open outcry system. The first is that there can be only one best bid and best ask in the pit at a time. If the market on a particular commodity is at 12 bid and 14 offered, a trader may not start bidding at 11 or offering at 13. Anyone can match the best bid and ask. If someone offers to buy at 13, then all previous bidders must either match the new best bid or stay quiet. The second rule is that traders must trade with the party they recognize who meets their bid or offer. This rule results in different mannerisms (waves,

Although the open-outcry system is still extensively used on the major exchanges, electronic trading systems are being used by the physical exchanges in the United States, London, Paris, and Sydney for after-hours trading. The CME and CBT developed with Reuters (the electronic information service company) the ***GLOBEX*** trading system. This is a computerized order-matching system with an international network linking member traders. Similarly, SFE offers after-hours trading through their SYCOM system, and LIFFE offers such trading through their Automated Pit Trading (APT) system. In addition to dual systems, since 1985, all new derivative exchanges have been organized as electronic exchanges. The German exchange Deutsche Termin Boerse (DTB) and Stockholm Option Market (SOM), for example, were both set up as screen-based trading systems. Most of these electronic trading systems are order-driven systems in which customer orders (bid and ask prices and size) are collected and matched by a computerized matching system. This is in contrast to a price-driven system such as the one used on the Swiss Options and Futures Exchange (SOFE) in which dealers provide bid and ask quotes and make markets.

In addition to linking futures traders, the futures exchanges also make contracts more marketable by standardizing contracts, providing continuous trading, establishing delivery procedures, and providing 24-hour trading through exchange alliances.

10.5.2   Standardization

The futures exchanges provide standardization by specifying the grade or type of each asset and the size of the underlying asset (e.g., 5,000 bushels of wheat or a T-Bill with a face value of $1 million). Exchanges also specify how contract prices are quoted. For example, the contract prices on T-bill futures are quoted in terms of an index equal to 100 minus a discount yield, and a T-bond is quoted in terms of dollars and 1/32s of a T-bond with a face value of $100.

10.5.3   Continuous Trading

Many security exchanges use market makers or specialists to ensure a continuous market. On many futures exchanges, continuous trading also is provided but not with market makers or specialists assigned by the exchange to deal in a specific contract. Instead, futures exchanges such as the CBT, CME, and LIFFE provide continuous trading through locals who are willing to take temporary positions in one or more futures. These exchange members fall into one of three categories: ***scalpers,*** who offer to buy and sell simultaneously, holding their positions for only a few minutes and profiting from a bid-ask spread; ***day traders,*** who hold positions for less than a day; and ***position traders,*** who hold positions for as long as a week before they close. Collectively, these exchange members make it possible for the futures markets to provide continuous trading.

10.5.4   Price and Position Limits

Without market makers and specialists to provide an orderly market, futures exchanges impose ***price limits*** on many of their contracts as a tool to stopping possible destabilizing price trends from occurring. The exchanges specify the maximum price change that can occur from the previous day's settlement price. The price of a contract must be within its daily price limits unless the exchange intervenes and changes the limit. When the contract price hits its maximum or minimum limit, it is referred to as being limited up or limited

---

jumps, shouts, and the like) employed by traders to be recognized. On most exchanges, the open outcry system requires that every order be offered for execution. The SFE, SIMEX, and MATIF allow for cross-trading on large block trades in which the trade is prearranged off the exchange.

down. In addition to price limits, futures exchanges can also set *position limits* on many of their futures contracts. This is done as a safety measure both to ensure sufficient liquidity and to minimize the chances of a trader trying to corner a particular asset.

10.5.5 Delivery Procedures

Most futures contracts are closed prior to expiration. As a result, there are only a small number of contracts that are entered into that lead to actual delivery. Nevertheless, detailed delivery procedures are important to ensure that the contract price on the futures contract is determined by the spot price on the underlying asset and that the futures price converges to the spot price at expiration. The exchanges have various rules and procedures governing the deliveries of contracts and delivery dates. The date or period in which delivery can take place is determined by the exchange. When there is a delivery period, the party agreeing to sell has the right to determine when the asset will be delivered during that period. For financial futures, delivery is usually done by wire transfer.

Some futures contracts allow for the delivery of different assets at expiration. For example, on T-bond futures contracts, the delivered T-bond can be selected from a number of T-bonds, each differing in its maturity and/or coupon payments. In cases in which different assets can be delivered, the exchange uses a price adjustment procedure to convert the price of the deliverable asset to the price of the asset defined by the contract. Some futures have a cash-settlement delivery procedure like index options. Future contracts on stock indices and Eurodollar time deposits, for example, are settled in cash at delivery. In a cash-settled futures contract, a settlement price is defined that specifies how the position's closing value will be determined at delivery.

The dates when futures contracts can be delivered also varies. Many contracts call for delivery on or just after the delivery date. However, contracts such as T-bond futures can be delivered on any business day of the delivery month. In cases that have an extended delivery period, the exchange defines a delivery notification procedure that must be followed.

Finally, the lengths of futures contracts can vary. Many have the standard March, June, September, and December cycle. Agriculture commodities often have delivery dates set up to coincide with the underlying commodity's harvest season. Some futures contracts have delivery dates that extend out almost 2 years.

10.5.6 Alliances and 24-hour Trading

In addition to providing off-hour trading via electronic trading systems, 24-hour trading is also possible by using futures exchanges that offer trading on the same contract. For example, the CME, LIFFE, and SIMEX all offer identical contracts on 90-day Eurodollar deposits. This makes it possible to trade the contract in the United States, Europe, and the Far East. Moreover, these exchanges have alliance agreements making it possible for traders to open a position in one market and close it in another.

10.6 MARGINS REQUIREMENTS, TRANSACTION COSTS, AND TAXES

10.6.1 Margin Requirements

Because a futures contract is an agreement, it has no initial value. Futures traders, however, are required to post some security or good faith money with their brokers.[6] Depending on

---

[6] Technically, because the clearinghouse guarantees the futures contract, margins are required by the members of the clearinghouse; the clearinghouse members then require margins to be maintained by the brokerage firm on their client.

the brokerage firm, the customer's margin requirement can be satisfied either in the form of cash or cash equivalents (e.g., U.S. T-bills).

Like options, futures contracts have both initial and maintenance margin requirements. The ***initial*** (or ***performance***) ***margin*** is the amount of cash or cash equivalents that must be deposited by the investor on the day the futures position is established. The futures trader does this by setting up a commodity account with the broker and depositing the required cash or cash equivalents. The amount of the margin is determined by the margin requirement, defined as a proportion (m) of the contract value (usually 3%–5%). For example, if the initial margin requirement is 5%, then Speculators A and B in our first example would be required to deposit $600 in cash or cash equivalents in their commodity accounts as good faith money on their $2.40 September wheat futures contracts:

$$m[\text{Contract Value}] = .05[(\$2.40/\text{bu})(5{,}000\,\text{bu})] = \$600$$

At the end of each trading day, the futures trader's account is adjusted to reflect any gains or losses based on the settlement price on new contracts.[7] In our example, suppose the day after Speculators A and B established their respective long and short positions, the settlement price on the September wheat contact is $f_t = \$2.45/\text{bu}$. The value of A's and B's margin accounts would therefore be

$$\text{A: Account Value} = \$600 + (\$2.45/\text{bu} - \$2.40/\text{bu})(5{,}000\,\text{bu}) = \$850$$

$$\text{B: Account Value} = \$600 + (\$2.40/\text{bu} - \$2.45/\text{bu})(5{,}000\,\text{bu}) = \$350$$

With the higher futures price, A's long position has increase in value by $250, and B's short position has decreased by $250. When there is a decrease in the account value, the futures trader's broker has to exchange money through the clearing firm equal to the loss on the position to the broker and clearinghouse with the gain. This process is known as ***marking to market.*** Thus, in our case, B's broker and clearing firm would pass on $250 to A's broker and clearing firm.

To ensure that the balance in the trader's account does not become negative, the brokerage firm requires a ***maintenance margin*** (or ***variation margin***) be maintained by the futures traders.[8] The maintenance (or variation) margin is the amount of additional cash or cash equivalents that futures traders must deposit to keep the equity in their commodity account equal to a certain percentage (e.g., 75%) of the initial margin value. If the maintenance margin requirements were equal to 100% of the initial margin, then A and B would have to keep the equity values of their accounts equal to $600. If Speculator B did not deposit the required margin immediately, then he would receive a ***margin call*** from the broker instructing him to post the required amount of funds. If Speculator B did not comply with the margin call, the broker would close the position.

10.6.2 Points on Margin Requirements

Several points should be noted in describing margin requirements. First, the marking to market of futures contracts effectively settles the futures contract daily. Each day, the futures holder's gain or loss is added to or subtracted from the holder's account to bring the value of the position back to zero. Once marking to market has occurred, there are no outstanding balances. On the CME, clearing members' exchange payments in a day can

---

[7] On futures contracts, the settlement price is determined by the clearinghouse officials and is based on the average price of the last several trades of the day.

[8] Clearinghouse members are also required to maintain a margin account with the clearinghouse. This is known as a clearing margin.

range from $100M to over $2.5B. The purpose of this stringent settlement system is to reduce the chance of default.

Second, the minimum levels of initial and maintenance margins are set by the exchanges, with the brokerage firms allowed to increase the levels. Margins levels are determined by the variability of the underlying asset and can vary by the type of trader. The margins for hedgers are less than those for speculators.

Third, the maintenance margin requirement on futures requires constant management of one's account. With daily resettlement, futures traders who are undermargined have to decide each day whether to close their positions and incur losses or post additional collateral; similarly, those who are overmargined must decide each day whether or not they should close. One way for an investor to minimize the management of her futures position is to keep her account overmargined by depositing more cash or cash equivalents than initially required or by investing in one of a number of ***futures funds.*** A futures fund pools investors' monies and uses them to set up futures positions. Typically, a large percentage of the fund's money is invested in money market securities. Thus, the funds represent overmargined futures positions.

Finally, the margin requirements and clearinghouse mechanism that characterize futures exchanges also serve to differentiate them from customized forward contracts written by banks and investment companies. As noted previously, forward contacts are more tailor-made contracts with the underlying security, delivery date, and size negotiated between the parties; they usually do not require margins; they often are delivered at maturity instead of closed; and they are less marketable than futures contracts.

10.6.3 Transaction Costs

Maintaining margin accounts can be viewed as part of the cost of trading futures. In addition to margin requirements, transaction costs are also involved in establishing futures positions. Such costs include broker commissions, clearinghouse fees, and the bid-ask spread. On futures contracts, commission fees usually are charged on a per contract basis and for a round lot (i.e., the fee includes both opening and closing the position), and the fees are negotiable. The clearinghouse fee is relatively small and is collected along with the commission fee by the broker. The bid-ask spreads are set by locals and represent an indirect cost of trading futures.

10.6.4 Note on Taxes

In the United States, futures positions are treated as capital gains and losses for tax purposes. For speculators, a marked-to-market rule applies in which the profits on a futures position are taxed in the year the contract is established. That is, at the end of the year, all futures contracts are marked to the market to determine any unrealized gain or loss for tax purposes. For example, suppose in September, a futures speculator takes a long position on a March contract at a contract price of $1,000. If the position were still open at the end of the year, the speculator's taxes on the position would be based on the settlement price at year's end. If the contract were marked to market at $1,200 at the end of the year, then a $200 capital gain would need to be added to the speculator's net capital gains to determine her tax liability. If the speculator's position were later closed in March of the following year at a contract price of $1,100, then she would realize an actual capital gain of $100. For tax purposes, though, the speculator would report a loss equal to the difference in the settlement price at the end of the year ($1,200) and the position's closing price ($1,100): that is, a $100 loss. Both realized and unrealized capital losses, in turn, are deductibles that are subtracted from the investor's capital gains.

Note that the end-of-the-year, marked-to-market rule on futures applies only to spec-ulative positions and not to hedging positions.[9] Gains or losses from hedges are treated as ordinary income, with the time of the recognition occurring at the time of the gain or loss of income from the hedged item. Also note that when delivery on a futures contract takes place, taxes are applied when the asset actually is sold.

10.7 TYPES OF FUTURES AND FORWARD CONTRACTS

Various types of futures contracts are traded on the CBT, CME, LIFFE, and other exchanges. There are also a number of competing contracts offered by dealers on the OTC market. These contracts can be classified as a physical commodity, energy, stock index, foreign currency, or interest-earning asset.

10.7.1 Physical Commodities

Physical commodities include both agriculture and metallurgical commodities. Agricul-ture commodities consist of grains (e.g., wheat, corn, and oats), oil and meal (e.g., soybeans and sunflower), livestock (e.g., cattle, pork bellies, and live hogs), forest products (e.g., plywood), foodstuffs (e.g., orange juice and sugar), and textiles (e.g., cotton). Many of the agricultural commodities have different contracts for different grades and expiration months, with the expiration months on crops typically set up to conform to their harvest patterns. Metallurgical contracts include metal (e.g., gold, silver, platinum, and copper) and petroleum products (e.g., heating oil, crude oil, gasoline, and propane). Exhibit 10.7-1 shows the prices for various commodities as reported by the *Wall Street Journal* on their Web site (www.wsj.com/free) on March 5, 2007. The top of the exhibit shows the under-lying futures contract, the exchange where the contract is traded, the contract size, and the price.

Web Information:

Current prices on futures contracts on commodities listed on the various exchanges can be obtained by going to their Web sites; see Exhibit 1.1-1. For CBT, go to www.cbt.com.

10.7.2 Energy Contracts

The New York Mercantile Exchange (NYMEX) and the International Petroleum Exchange offer a number of futures contracts on crude oil, gasoline, and heating oil. Some of these contracts require a cash settlement, whereas others require physical delivery. The NYMEX and IPE also offer contracts on natural gas. One of the NYMEX contracts calls for the physical delivery of 10,000 million British thermal units (Btu) of natural gas to be made during the delivery month at a uniform rate. Finally, the NYMEX offer contracts on elec-tricity. A typical contract calls for receiving (delivering) a specified number of megawatt hours for a specified price at specified location during a particular month. The contracts can vary from a "5 × 8" contract in which power is received 5 days a week during the off-peak hours for a specified month to a "7 × 24" contract that calls for receiving power every day and hour during the month

---

[9] The marked-to-market tax rule was established in 1981. One of the reasons for the law was to stop the activities of future spreaders who would take long and short positions in similar futures contracts and then for tax purposes at the end of the year would close the position, thus showing a loss.

EXHIBIT 10.7-1 Commodity and Futures Quotes

Contract	Month	Last	Chg	Open	High	Low	Volume	Open Int	Exchange	Date	Time
Agriculture Futures											
COCOA	Mar '07	1795	−1	1720	1795	1719	5355	398	CEC	3/5/2007	10:27:08
COCOA	May '07	1767	−37	1796	1796	1763	1235	80705	CEC	3/5/2007	13:06:38
ORANGE JUICE	Mar '07	208.5	0.1	209	209.5	208	1453	580	CEC	3/2/2007	18:39:42
ORANGE JUICE	May '07	205.3	0.25	204.9	205.7	204	460	21682	CEC	3/2/2007	20:07:29
WHEAT	Mar '07	455'0	−4'4	460'6	460'6	455'0	867	3336	CBT	3/5/2007	3:01:45
WHEAT	May '07	464'4	−9'2	472'0	473'0	463'4	4600	206804	CBT	3/5/2007	11:59:59
CORN	Mar '07	402'4	−8'4	410'0	410'0	402'4	2268	18697	CBT	3/5/2007	11:36:34
CORN	May '07	413'2	−7'6	419'6	419'6	412'4	12160	532205	CBT	3/5/2007	11:59:56
WHEAT	Mar '07	455'0	−4'4	460'6	460'6	455'0	867	3336	CBT	3/5/2007	3:01:45
WHEAT	May '07	464'4	−9'2	472'0	473'0	463'4	4600	206804	CBT	3/5/2007	11:59:59
WHEAT	Jul '09	467'0	−3'0	467'0	472'0	467'0	2	1713	CBT	3/2/2007	20:05:03
FEEDER CATTLE	Mar '07	103.9	1.5	102.55	104.2	102.5	2593	7671	CME	3/2/2007	19:14:08
FEEDER CATTLE	Apr '07	105.5	1.53	104.2	105.8	104	2555	11232	CME	3/2/2007	19:14:08
FROZEN PORK BELLY	Mar '07	104	1.38	102.25	104.1	102.3	168	317	CME	3/2/2007	19:14:06
FROZEN PORK BELLY	May '07	106.2	1.58	105.25	106.7	104.7	128	891	CME	3/2/2007	19:14:06
LUMBER	Mar '07	249.4	0.6	249	250.4	247.5	207	1017	CME	3/2/2007	19:14:10
LUMBER	May '07	255.6	0.5	255	257	254.6	395	5173	CME	3/2/2007	19:14:10
Metal & Petroleum Futures											
GOLD	Mar '07	641.5	−20.8	641.5	641.5	641.5	1	6	COMX	3/2/2007	18:50:41
GOLD	Apr '07	639	−5.1	645.6	647	637.4	25635	233289	COMX	3/5/2007	13:25:55
SILVER	Mar '07	12.59	−0.26	12.86	12.89	12.55	56	1550	COMX	3/5/2007	13:06:03
SILVER	Apr '07	12.73	−0.18	12.935	12.94	12.7	8	145	COMX	3/5/2007	7:42:37
PLATINUM	Oct '07	1227	0	1226.8	1227	1227	15	30	NYME	3/2/2007	18:14:38
PLATINUM	Jan '08	1232	0	1231.8	1232	1232	2	2	NYME	3/2/2007	18:14:38
LIGHT CRUDE OIL	Dec '07	65.43	−0.88	65.8	65.8	65.27	639	146553	NYME	3/5/2007	13:30:59
LIGHT CRUDE OIL	Jan '08	66.55	−0.63	66.55	66.55	66.55	32	20593	NYME	3/2/2007	20:04:19
NATURAL GAS (DAY)	Jan '08	9.294	−0.01	9.36	9.36	9.27	91		NYME	3/2/2007	19:52:06
NATURAL GAS (DAY)	Feb '08	9.289	−0.01	9.36	9.36	9.28	22		NYME	3/2/2007	19:52:06

continued

EXHIBIT 10.7-1 Continued

Contract	Month	Last	Chg	Open	High	Low	Volume	Open Int	Exchange	Date	Time
Weather and Energy											
WEATHER HDD NEW YORK	Mar '07	665	10	670	675	665	200	930	CMG	3/2/2007	21:42:57
WEATHER HDD NEW YORK	Apr '07	360	0	360	360	360	0	0	CMG	3/2/2007	21:42:57
CLEARPORT: PJM SETTLE	Mar '07	65.28	2.36	65.28	65.28	65.28	388	1576	NYME	3/2/2007	22:03:01
CLEARPORT: PJM SETTLE	Apr '07	62.95	0.2	62.95	62.95	62.95	41	1682	NYME	3/2/2007	22:03:01

Source: *Wall Street Journal* (*WSJ*) Web site: www.wsj.com/free, March 5, 2007. To access quotes from the *WSJ,* go to www.wsj.com/free; click on "Market Data Center" and then "Commodity and Futures." Quotes in this table were downloaded into Excel from this *WSJ* site.

A somewhat related contract is a weather derivative. In 1999, the CME offered contracts on cumulative heating degree days (HDD) and cooling degree days (CDD). A day's HDD is a measure of the volume of energy needed for heating during a day, and a CDD is measure of the volume of energy required for cooling during a day. Each can be measured as

$$HDD = Max[65° - A, 0]$$
$$CDD = Max[A - 65°, 0]$$

where

A = average high and low temperature during a day.

The CME contracts are measured in terms of cumulative HDD or CDD for a specified month at a specified weather station (e.g., Atlanta, New York, or Cincinnati). These contracts call for a cash settlement.

In addition to exchange-traded energy and weather futures contracts, the exchanges also offer spot option and futures option contracts on energy and weather products. There is also an extensive OTC market for energy derivatives. For example, OTC dealers have offered for a number of years a long-term swap arrangement on crude oil in which one party agrees to exchange a fixed price on oil to another party who agrees to exchange a floating price (swap contracts are discussed in Chapters 17–20). Weather derivatives have been offered since the 1970s by OTC dealers.

10.7.3 Indices

There are a number of futures contracts available on various U.S. and non-U.S. derivative exchanges. Most of the contracts are on stock indices, but there are also some on commodities (e.g., DJ-AIG Commodity Index and the GSCI index), bond indexes (e.g., Municipal

EXHIBIT 10.7-2   Stock Index Futures Quotes

Contract	Month	Last	Chg	Open	High	Low	Volume	Open Int	Exchange	Date	Time
DOW JONES INDUS.	Sep '07	12303	0	12303	12303	12303	0	7	CBT	3/2/2007	22:02:44
DOW JONES INDUS.	Dec '07	12398	−144	12398	12398	12398	0	3	CBTE	3/2/2007	22:02:44
S&P 500	Mar '07	1378.9	−6.9	1387	1387.4	1371	13063	541067	CME	3/5/2007	14:13:13
S&P 500	Jun '07	1398.1	−19.3	1411.5	1417.5	1397.5	30417	94987	CME	3/2/2007	21:22:47
RUSSELL 2000 (DAY)	Mar '07	773.8	−16.6	788	789.25	773.25	864		CME	3/2/2007	21:22:49
RUSSELL 2000 (DAY)	Jun '07	780.8	−16.6	795	795.5	782.4	162		CME	3/2/2007	21:22:49
NASDAQ 100	Mar '07	1715	−11.25	1728.5	1728.5	1704.75	3719	55405	CME	3/5/2007	14:12:32
NASDAQ 100	Jun '07	1746.75	−32	1762	1775	1745.5	78	912	CME	3/2/2007	21:22:51

Source: *Wall Street Journal* (*WSJ*)Web site: www.wsj.com/free, March 5, 2007. To access quotes from the *WSJ*, go to www.wsj.com/free; click on "Market Data Center" and then "Commodity and Futures." Quotes in this table were downloaded into Excel from this *WSJ* site.

Bond Index) and currencies (e.g., the U.S. dollar index).[10] Exhibit 10.7-2 shows the prices for various indices as reported from *Wall Street Journal's* Web site (www.wsj.com/free) on March 5, 2007, and Exhibit 10.7-3 describes these and other indices and the futures contracts on them. Since their introduction in the early 1980s, the volume of index futures trading has grown exponentially. These index futures have many of the same characteristics as index options. For instance, like index options, the sizes of index futures contracts are equal to a multiple of the index value; and like index options, index futures are cash-settled contracts.

Web Information:

Current prices on futures contracts on indices listed on the various exchanges can be obtained by going to their Web sites; see Exhibit 1.1-1.

10.7.4 Stocks

Several non-U.S. exchanges offer futures trading on individual stocks including U.S. stocks. Until 2000, U.S. security laws prohibited such trading in the United States. This law, though, was changed in 2000, resulting in proposals for such trading.

---

[10] Stock index futures are sometimes referred to as "Pin-Stripe Pork Bellies."

EXHIBIT 10.7-3 Type of Stock Index Futures

1. **S&P 500 Index**: The index is based on a portfolio of 500 different stocks (400 industrials, 40 utilities, 20 transportation, and 40 financials). The index accounts for 80% of the market's capitalization of NYSE-listed stocks. CME trades two contracts on the S&P 500: one is $250 times the index; the other is $50 times the index (Mini S&P 500 contract).
2. **S&P MidCap 400 Index**: This index is based on a portfolio of 400 stocks with lower market capitalization. The CME offers a contract on the index with a $500 multiplier.
3. **Dow Jones Industrial Average**: The index is based on a portfolio of 30 blue-chip stocks. The CBT offers two contracts on the index: one with a $10 multiplier and another with a $5 multiplier (mini DJ industrial).
4. **Nasdaq 100 Index**: The index is based on 100 stocks using the National Association of Security Dealers Automatic Quotation Service. CME trades two contracts: one with a $100 multiplier and another with a $20 multiplier.
5. **NYSE Composite Index**: The index consist of all stocks traded on the NYSE. The New York Futures Exchange offers a contract with a $50 multiplier.
6. **Russell 2000 Index**: The index is based on the price of 2,000 small capitalization stocks in the U.S. The CME offers an index with a $500 multiplier.
7. **Russell 1000 Index**: The index is based on the price of 1,000 of the largest capitalization stocks in the United States. The NYFE offers an index with a $500 multiplier.
8. **U.S. Dollar Index**: This is a trade weighted index of six currencies: euro, yen, British pound, Canadian dollar, Swedish krona, and Swiss franc. The FINEX offers a contract on the index with a $1,000 multiplier.
9. **Nikkei 225 Stock Average**: This index is based on 225 of the largest stocks making up the Tokyo Stock Exchange. The CME offers a contract on the index with a $5 multiplier.
10. **Share Price Index**: This index is based on broad group of Australian stocks. The Sydney Futures Exchange (SFE) offers a future contract on this index with a multiplier of 25 Australian dollars.
11. **CAC-40**: This index is based on the 40 largest stocks trading in France. The French futures exchange (*Marche a Terme International de France* or MATIF) offers a contract on this index with a multiplier of 5 euros.
12. **Xetra DAX Index**: This index is based on 30 stocks trading in Germany. EUREX offers a contract on the index with a multiplier of 25 euros.
13. **FTSE 100 Index**: This index is based on 100 major U.K. stocks trading on the London Stock Exchange. The London International Financial Futures Exchange (LIFFE) offers a contract on the index with a multiplier of 10 British pounds.
14. **DJ Euro Stoxx 50 Index**: This index consists of 50 blue-chip European stocks. EUREX offers a contract on this index with a multiplier of 10 euros.
15. **CSCI**: This is a commodity index. The CME offers a contract on this index with a $250 multiplier.
16. **TRAKRS Long-Short Tech Index**: This index consists of technology stocks and short financial instruments representing the technology sector. The CME offers a contract on this index with a $1 multiplier.

10.7.5 Foreign Currency Futures and Forward Contracts

10.7.5.1 Currency Futures

Foreign currency futures contracts were introduced in May of 1972 by the International Monetary Market (IMM) of the CME. Today, the CME is the largest foreign currency futures exchange, followed by the London International Financial Futures Exchange (LIFFE). Currency futures also are traded on a number of other exchanges including the Philadelphia Exchange, the Singapore International Monetary Market, and the Sydney Futures Exchange. Exhibit 10.7-4 shows the prices for several currency futures as reported from *Wall Street Journal's* Web site (www.wsj.com/free) on March 5, 2007. The contracts on the CME call for the delivery (or purchase) of a specified amount of foreign currency at the delivery date. The contract prices are quoted in terms of dollars per unit of foreign currency. For example, a June futures contract on the Swiss franc with a settlement price of $0.8251 calls for the delivery (or purchase) of 125,000 Swiss francs (SF) at a price of $0.8251/SF (total contract price of $103,137.50).

10.7.5.2 Interbank Forward Market

Forward contracts on foreign currencies are provided in the Interbank Foreign Exchange Market. This OTC market is considerably larger than the currency futures market,

EXHIBIT 10.7-4   Foreign Currency Futures Quotes

Contract	Month	Last	Chg	Open	High	Low	Volume	Open Int	Exchange	Date	Time
BRITISH POUND	Mar '07	1.9208	−0.0226	1.9444	1.9449	1.9184	55995	152473	CME	3/5/2007	14:25:32
BRITISH POUND	Jun '07	1.9201	−0.0225	1.9434	1.944	1.9177	2511	6039	CME	3/5/2007	14:23:01
EURO	Mar '07	1.3086	−0.0113	1.3212	1.3219	1.3079	122779	206660	CME	3/5/2007	14:26:46
EURO	Jun '07	1.3132	−0.0113	1.3259	1.3264	1.3127	3470	6990	CME	3/5/2007	14:26:02
JAPANESE YEN	Mar '07	0.867	0.0088	0.8587	0.8701	0.8587	95836	256019	CME	3/5/2007	14:27:38
JAPANESE YEN	Jun '07	0.8768	0.0088	0.8692	0.8799	0.8692	1939	29401	CME	3/5/2007	14:27:36
SWISS FRANC	Mar '07	0.8194	−0.0034	0.8233	0.8268	0.8178	32443	86426	CME	3/5/2007	14:28:33
SWISS FRANC	Jun '07	0.8251	−0.004	0.8323	0.8331	0.824	581	2828	CME	3/5/2007	14:24:10
CANADIAN DOLLAR	Mar '07	0.8476	−0.0026	0.8503	0.8509	0.846	18480	133534	CME	3/5/2007	14:29:19
CANADIAN DOLLAR	Jun '07	0.8502	−0.0022	0.8538	0.8544	0.8483	582	10990	CME	3/5/2007	14:21:54
MEXICAN PESO	Mar '07	0.08905	−0.00007	.5089	0.08915	0.08877	52790	71626	CME	3/5/2007	14:30:30
MEXICAN PESO	Apr '07	0.088975	−0.00045	0.088975	0.088975	0.088975		0	CME	3/2/2007	22:03:28
AUSTRALIAN DOLLAR	Mar '07	0.7721	−0.0098	0.7817	0.7822	0.7715	26345	129172	CME	3/5/2007	14:31:32
AUSTRALIAN DOLLAR	Jun '07	0.7701	−0.0099	0.7798	0.7798	0.7698	645	3663	CME	3/5/2007	14:31:09
RUSSIAN RUBLE	Mar '07	0.03809	−0.00017	0.03805	0.03809	0.03805	9	6356	CME	3/5/2007	13:22:22
RUSSIAN RUBLE	Jun '07	0.03825	−0.00002	0.03825	0.03825	0.03825	211	3544	CME	3/2/2007	22:03:35

Source: *Wall Street Journal* (*WSJ*) Web site: www.wsj.com/free, March 5, 2007. To access quotes from the *WSJ*, go to www.wsj.com/free; click on "Market Data Center" and then "Commodity and Futures." Quotes in this table were downloaded into Excel from this *WSJ* site.

consisting primarily of major banks that provide forward contracts to their clients, which often are large multinational corporations and institutions. In the interbank market, banks provide tailor-made contracts to their customers. Typically, the minimum size of an interbank forward contract is $1 million, with expirations ranging from 1 to 12 months, although longer term maturities can be arranged.

> **Web Information:**
>
> Current prices on futures contracts on currency futures listed on the CME can be obtained by going to www.cme.com and clicking on "Quotes" in "Market Data" and then clicking on "currency products."
> For information on forward exchange rates, go to www.fxstreet.com.

EXHIBIT 10.7-5   Select Interest Rate Futures Contracts

Contract	Exchange	Contract Size	Deliver Month	Delivery
Treasury Bond	CBT	T-bond with $100,000 face value (or multiple of that)	Mar/June/Sept/Dec	T-bonds with an invoice price that is equal to the futures settlement price times a conversion factor plus accrued interest.
5-Year Treasury Note	CBT	T-note with $100,000 face value (or multiple of that)	Mar/June/Sept/Dec	T-notes that have maturity of no more than 5 years and 3 months. Invoice price is equal to the futures settlement price times a conversion factor plus accrued interest.
Treasury Note	CBT	T-note with $100,000 face value (or multiple of that)	Mar/June/Sept/Dec	T-notes maturing at least 6 1/2 years, but no more than 10 years. Invoice price is equal to the futures settlement price times a conversion factor plus accrued interest.
3-Month Treasury Bill	CME	$1,000,000	Mar/June/Sept/Dec	Delivery can be made on three successive business days. The first delivery day is the first day on which a 13-week T-bill is issued.
3-Month Eurodollar	CME	$1,000,000	Mar/June/Sept/Dec	Cash Settlement
1-Month LIBOR	CME	$3,000,000	All calendar months	Cash Settlement; settlement price based on a survey of participants in London Interbank Eurodollar market.
Municipal Bond Index	CBT	$1,000 times the closing value of the *Bond Buyer*™ Municipal Bond Index (a price of 95 means a contract size of $95,000)	Mar/June/Sept/Dec	Cash Settlement; settlement price based on *Bond Buyer*™ Municipal Bond Index value at expiration.
3-Month Euroyen	SIMEX	100,000,000 yen	Mar/June/Sept/Dec	Cash Settlement
10-Year Japanese Government Bond Index	TSE	100,000,000 yen face value	Mar/June/Sept/Dec	Exchange-listed Japanese government bond having a maturity of 7 years or more but less than 11 years.
Long Gilt	LIFFE	50,000 British pound	Mar/June/Sept/Dec	Delivery may be any gilt with 15 to 25 years to maturity.
3-Month Sterling Interest Rate	LIFFE	500,000 British pound	Mar/June/Sept/Dec	Cash settlement; settlement price based on the 3-month sterling deposit rate being offered to prime banks.

10.7.6 Interest Rate Futures[11]

Exhibit 10.7-5 describes the features of various interest rates futures contracts traded on the CBT, CME, LIFFE, and other exchanges; and Exhibit 10.7-6 shows the price quotes on several interest rates futures listed on the CME and CBT as reported in the *Wall Street Journal* on their Web site (www.wsj.com/free) on March 5, 2007. One of the first financial futures contracts listed on the CME was the T-bill contract. Today, the three most popular interest rate futures contracts are T-bonds, T-notes, and Eurodollar deposits.

---

[11] This section assumes some knowledge of bonds fundamentals. For a primer, see Appendix C at the end of the book.

EXHIBIT 10.7-6   Interest Rate Futures Quotes

Contract	Month	Last	Chg	Open	High	Low	Volume	Open Int	Exc-hange	Date	Time
10 Yr Note	Mar '07	108'31.0	0'04.0	109'00.0	109'09.5	108'29.5	73444	201624	CBT	3/5/2007	14:41:25
10 Yr Note	Jun '07	109'00.5	0'04.5	109'00.5	109'11.5	108'30.5	656965	1972993	CBT	3/5/2007	14:41:48
5 Yr Note	Mar '07	106'02.0	0'02.5	106'06.0	106'09.5	106'01.5	12058	140663	CBT	3/5/2007	14:41:46
5 Yr Note	Jun '07	106'08.5	0'03.0	106'08.0	106'17.0	106'07.0	323516	1317140	CBT	3/5/2007	14:42:50
2 Yr Note	Mar '07	102'14.0	0'01.7	102'16.0	102'17.2	102'13.5	3544	61972	CBT	3/5/2007	14:42:29
2 Yr Note	Jun '07	102'20.7	0'01.7	102'21.2	102'25.0	102'20.2	129428	802288	CBT	3/5/2007	14:44:06
FED FUNDS 30 DAY	Mar '07	94.755	0	94.755	94.76	94.755	23	117241	CBT	3/2/2007	20:24:41
FED FUNDS 30 DAY	Apr '07	94.77	0.01	94.765	94.775	94.765	521	149018	CBT	3/2/2007	20:24:41
EURO DOL-LAR 3 MONTH	Mar '07	94.6825	0.01	94.675	94.7	94.675	88285	1307597	CME	3/5/2007	14:47:34
EURO DOL-LAR 3 MONTH	Apr '07	94.725	0.005	94.74	94.74	94.725	183	9342	CME	3/5/2007	14:39:16

Source: *Wall Street Journal* (*WSJ*) Web site: www.wsj.com/free, March 5, 2007. To access quotes from the *WSJ*, go to www.wsj.com/free; click on "Market Data Center" and then "Commodity and Futures." Quotes in this table were downloaded into Excel from this *WSJ* site.

10.7.6.1 *T-Bill Futures*

T-bill futures contracts call for the delivery (short position) or purchase (long position) of a T-bill with a maturity of 91days and a face value (F) of $1 million. Futures prices on T-bill contracts are quoted in terms of an index. This index, I, is equal to 100 minus the annual percentage discount rate, R_D, for a 90-day T-bill:

$$I = 100 - R_D(\%)$$

Given a quoted index value or discount yield, the actual contract price on the T-bill futures contract is

$$f_0 = \frac{100 - R_D\%(90/360)}{100}\$1,000,000 \qquad (10.7\text{-}1)$$

Note that the index is quoted on the basis of a 90-day T-bill with a 360-day year. This implies that a 1-point move in the index would equate to a $2,500 change in the futures price. The implied yield to maturity (YTM_f) on a T-bill that is delivered on the contract is often found using 365 days and the actual maturity on the delivered bill of 91 days. For example, a T-bill futures contract quoted at a settlement index value of 95.62 ($R_D = 4.38\%$) would have a futures contract price of \$989,050 and an implied YTM_f of 4.515%:

$$f_0 = \frac{100 - 4.38(90/360)}{100} \, \$1,000,000 = \$989,050$$

$$f_0 = \frac{F}{(1 + YTM_f)^{91/365}}$$

$$\$989,050 = \frac{\$1,000,000}{(1 = YTM_f)^{91/365}}$$

$$YTM_f = \left[\frac{F}{f_0}\right]^{365/91} - 1$$

$$YTM_f = \left[\frac{\$1,000,000}{\$989,050}\right]^{365/91} - 1 = .04515$$

10.7.6.2 *Eurodollar Futures Contract*

A Eurodollar deposit is a time deposit in a bank located or incorporated outside the United States. A Eurodollar interest rate is the rate that one large international bank is willing to lend to another large international bank. The average rate paid by a sample of London Euro banks is known as the London Interbank Offer Rate (LIBOR). The LIBOR is higher than the T-bill rate. The LIBOR, in turn, is frequently used as a benchmark rate on bank loans and deposits.

The CME's futures contract on the Eurodollar deposit calls for the delivery or purchase of a Eurodollar deposit with a face value of \$1 million and a maturity of 90 days. Like T-bill futures contracts, Eurodollar futures are quoted in terms of an index equal to 100 minus the annual discount rate, with the actual contract price found by using Equation (10.7-1). For example, given a settlement index value of 95.09 on a Eurodollar contract, the actual futures price would be \$987,725:

$$f_0 = \frac{100 - 4.91(90/360)}{100} \, \$1,000,000 = \$987,725$$

The major difference between the Eurodollar and T-bill contracts is that Eurodollar contracts have cash settlements at delivery, whereas T-bill contracts call for the actual delivery of the instrument. When a Eurodollar futures contract expires, the cash settlement is determined by the futures price and the settlement price. The settlement price or expiration futures index price is 100 minus the average 3-month LIBOR offered by a sample of designated Euro banks on the expiration date:

$$\text{Expiration Futures Price} = 100 - \text{LIBOR}$$

The cash-settlement feature of Eurodollar contracts has made these contracts more liquid and, in turn, more popular than T-bill contracts where physical delivery is required.

In addition to the CME's Eurodollar futures, there are also a number of other contracts traded on interest rates in other countries. For example, there are Euroyen contracts traded on the CME and the Singapore Exchange, Euroswiss contracts traded on the LIFFE, and Euribor contracts (3-month LIBOR contract for the euro) traded on the LIFFE and *Marche a Terme International de France* or MATIF.

10.7.6.3 *T-Bond Futures Contracts*

The most heavily traded long-term interest rate futures contract is the CBT's T-bond contract. The contract calls for the delivery or purchase of a T-bond with a maturity of at least 15 years. The CBT has a conversion factor to determine the actual price received by the seller. The futures contract is based on the delivery of a T-bond with a face value of $100,000. On a T-bond futures contract, delivery can occur at any time during the delivery month. To ensure liquidity, any T-bond with a maturity of 15 years is eligible for delivery, with a conversion factor used to determine the actual price of the deliverable bond. Because T-bonds futures contracts allow for the delivery to be from a number of T-bonds at any time during the delivery month, the CBT's delivery procedure on such contracts is more complicated than the procedures on other futures contracts. T-bond delivery procedures are discussed in the next section.

T-bond futures prices are quoted in dollars and 32nds for T-bonds with a face value of $100. Thus, if the quoted price on a T-bond futures were 106-14 (i.e., 106 14/32 or 106.437), the price would be $106,437 for a face value of $100,000. The actual price paid on the T-bond or revenue received by the seller in delivering the bond on the contract is equal to the quoted futures price times the conversion factor, CFA, on the delivered bond plus any accrued interest:

$$\text{Seller's Revenue} = (\text{Quoted Futures Price})(\text{CFA}) + \text{Accrued Interest}$$

Thus, at the time of delivery, if the delivered bond has a CFA of 1.3 and accrued interest of $2 per $100 face value, and the quoted futures price is 94-16, then the cash received by the seller of the bond and paid by the futures purchaser would be $124.85 per $100 face value:

$$\text{Seller's Revenue} = (94.5)(1.3) + 2 = 124.85$$

10.7.6.4 *T-Note Futures Contracts*

T-note contracts are similar to T-bond contracts except that they call for the delivery of any T-note with maturities between 6 1/2 and 10 years; the 5-year T-note contracts are also similar to T-bond and T-note contracts except that they require deliver of the most recently auctioned 5-year T-note. Both contracts, though, have delivery procedures similar to T-bond contracts.

10.8   T-BOND AND T-NOTE DELIVERY PROCEDURES

One of the unique features of T-bond and T-note futures contracts is their delivery procedure. In general, the complex procedure is designed to ensure there are a sufficient number of bonds backing the large volume of outstanding T-bond and T-note futures and futures options contracts.

10.8.1   Cheapest-to-Deliver Bond

As noted, the T-bond futures contract gives the party with the short position the right to deliver, at any time during the delivery month, any T-bond with a maturity of at least 15 years. When a particular bond is delivered, the price received by the seller is equal to the quoted futures price on the futures contract times a conversion factor (CFA) applicable to the delivered bond. The invoice price, in turn, is equal to that price plus any accrued interest on the delivered bond:

$$\text{Invoice Price} = (f_0)(\text{CFA}) + \text{Accrued Interest}$$

The CBT uses a conversion factor based on discounting the deliverable bond by a 6% YTM. The CBT's rules for calculating the CFA on the deliverable bond are as follows:

- The bond's maturity and time to the next coupon date are rounded down to the closest 3 months.
- After rounding, if the bond has an exact number of 6-month periods, then the first coupon is assumed to be paid in 6 months.
- After rounding, if the bond does not have an exact number of 6-month periods, then the first coupon is assumed to be paid in 3 months and the accrued interest is subtracted.

Using these rules, a 5.5% T-bond maturing in 18 years and 1 month would be (1) rounded down to 18 years, (2) the first coupon would be assumed to be paid in 6 months, and (3) the CFA would be determined using a discount rate of 6% and face value of $100. The CFA for the bond would be .945419:

$$V = \sum_{t=1}^{36} \frac{2.75}{(1.03)^t} + \frac{100}{(1.03)^{36}} = 94.5419$$

$$CFA = \frac{94.5419}{100} = .945419$$

If the bond matured in 18 years and 4 months, the bond would be assumed to have a maturity of 18 years and 3 months. The bond's CFA would be found by determining the value of the bond 3 months from the present, discounting that value to the current period, and subtracting the accrued interest ($(3/6)(2.75) = 1.375$):

$$V = \frac{94.5419}{(1.03)^{.5}} = 93.1549$$

$$CFA = \frac{93.1549 - 1.375}{100} = .917799$$

During the delivery month, there are a number of possible bonds that can be delivered. The party with the short position will select that bond that is cheapest to deliver. The CBT maintains tables with possible deliverable bonds. The tables show the bond's current quoted price and CFA. For example, suppose three possible bonds are

Bond	Quoted Price	CFA
1	110.75	1.15
2	97.50	1.05
3	125.75	1.35

If the current quoted futures price were 90-16 (90.5), the costs of buying and delivering each bond would be

Bond	Cost of bond minus revenue from selling bond on futures
1	$110.5 - (90.5)(1.15) = 6.425$
2	$97.5 - (90.5)(1.05) = 2.475$
3	$125.75 - (90.5)(1.35) = 3.575$

Thus, the cheapest bond to deliver would be Number 2. Over time and as rates change, the cheapest-to-deliver bond can change. In general, if rates exceed 6%, the CBT's conversion system favors bonds with higher maturities and lower coupons; if rates are less than 6%, the system tends to favor higher coupon bonds with shorter maturities.

10.8.2 Delivery Process

Under the CBT's procedures, a T-bond futures trader with a short position who wants to deliver the contract has the right to determine during the expiration month not only the eligible bond to deliver but also the day of the delivery. The delivery process encompasses the following three business days:

*   **Business Day 1**, *Position Day*: The short position holder notifies the clearinghouse that she will deliver.
*   **Business Day 2**, *Notice of Intention Day*: The clearinghouse assigns a long position holder the contract (typically the holder with the longest outstanding contract).
*   **Business Day 3**, *Delivery Day*: The short holder delivers an eligible T-bond to the assigned long position holder who pays the short holder an invoice price determined by the futures price and a conversion factor.[12]

Web Information:

Current prices on futures contracts on the Eurodollar and other futures can be obtained by going to www.cme.com. For T-bonds, T-notes, and other futures, go to www.cbt.com.

10.9 CONCLUSION

In this chapter, we've provided an overview of futures and forward contracts. These derivative securities are very similar to options. Like options, they can be used as speculative tools to profit from changes in asset prices and as hedging tools to minimize price risk. Also like options, futures contracts are traded on organized exchanges that have many of the same trading rules and procedures that option exchanges have. Finally, futures and forward contracts, like options, are derivative securities, and as such, their prices are determined by arbitrage forces.

The fundamental difference between the contracts is that options give the holders a right, whereas futures or forward contract holders have an obligation. As a result, potential profits and losses on pure speculative futures positions are virtually unlimited compared to limited profit and loss potentials on fundamental speculative option positions. Hedging strategies with futures, although capable of eliminating downside risk, can also impact the upside potential as compared to option hedging, which can provide minimum and maximum limits.

Given this background in futures and forward contracts, we now turn our focus to the pricing of futures contracts.

---

[12] Because a short holder can notify the clearinghouse of her intention to deliver a bond at the end of the position day (not necessarily at the end of the futures' trading day), an arbitrage opportunity can occur when the futures exchange's closing differs from the closing time on spot T-bond trading. This feature of the T-bond futures contract is known as the ***wild-card option.*** This option tends to lower the futures price.

KEY TERMS

forward contracts	rolling the hedge forward	margin call
futures	basis	futures fund
financial futures	basis risk	marked-to-market tax rule
Commodity Futures Trading Commission	quantity risk	commodity futures
	intracommodity spread	electricity derivative
GLOBEX	intercommodity spread	weather derivative
clearinghouse	dual trading	index futures
long futures position	front running	currency futures
short futures position	open outcry	T-bill futures
offset	local	Eurodollar futures
long hedge	scalper	T-bond futures
short hedge	day trader	T-notes futures
open interest	position trader	conversion factor
direct hedge	price limits	cheapest-to-deliver bond
cross hedge	initial margin	wild-card option
hedge ratio	maintenance margin	
timing risk	marking to market	

SELECTED REFERENCES

Aiditti, F., L. Cai, M. Cao, and R. McDonald. "Whether to Hedge." *Risk* Supplement on Weather Risk (1999): 9–12.

Arrow, K. "Futures Markets: Some Theoretical Perspectives." *Journal of Futures Markets* 1 (Summer 1981): 107–116.

Cao, M., and J. Wei. "Weather Derivatives: Valuation and the Market Price on Weather Derivatives." *Journal of Futures Markets* 21 (November 2004): 1065–1089.

Carlton, D. "Futures Markets: Their Purpose, Their History, Their Growth, Their Successes and Failures." *Journal of Futures Markets* 4 (1984): 237–271.

Chance, D. *An Introduction to Derivatives*, 4th ed. Orlando, FL: Dryden Press, 1997.

Chewlow, L., and C. Stricklan. *Energy Derivative: Pricing and Risk Management.* Lacima Group 2000.

Duffie, D. *Futures Markets.* Englewood Cliffs, NJ: Prentice-Hall, 1989, Chapter 7.

Easterbrook, F. "Monopoly, Manipulation and the Regulation of Futures Markets." *Journal of Business* 59 (1966): 103–127.

Edwards, F. "The Clearing Association in Futures Markets: Guarantor and Regulator." *Journal of Futures Markets* 3 (Winter 1983): 369–392.

Eydeland, A., and H. German. "Pricing Power Derivatives." *Risk* (October 1998): 71–73.

Fishe, R., and L. Goldberg. "The Effects of Margins on Trading in Futures Markets." *Journal of Futures Markets* 6 (Summer 1986): 261–271.

Froot, K. A. "The Market for Catastrophe Risk: A Clinical Examination." *Journal of Financial Economics* 60 (2001): 529–71.

Froot, K. A. *The Financing of Catastrophe Risk.* Chicago, IL: University of Chicago Press, 1999.

Geman, H. "CAT Calls." *Risk* (September 1994): 86–89.

Haley, C. W. "Forward Rate Agreements (FRA)." In *The Handbook of Interest Rate Risk Management*, edited by J. C. Francis and A. S. Wolf. New York: Irwin Professional Publishing, 1994.

Hull, J. *Options, Futures and Other Derivative Securities,* 6th ed. Englewood Cliffs, NJ: Prentice Hall, 2005, Chapter 23.

Hardy, C. *Risk and Risk Bearing.* Chicago: University of Chicago Press, 1940, 67–69.

Hardy, C., and L. Lyon. "The Theory of Hedging." *Journal of Political Economy* 31 (1923): 271–287.

Hartzmark, M. "The Effects of Changing Margin Levels on Futures Market Activity, the Composition of Traders in the Market, and Price Performance." *Journal of Business* 59 (1986): 147–180.

Haushalter, G. D. "Financing Policy, Basis Risk, and Corporate Hedging: Evidence from Oil and Gas Producers." *Journal of Finance* 55 (2000): 107–52.

Jarrow, R., and G. Oldfield. "Forward Contracts and Futures Contracts." *Journal of Financial Economics* 9 (1981): 373–382.

Kane, A., and A. Marcus. "Valuation and Optimal Exercise of the Wild Card Option in the Treasury Bond Futures Market." *Journal of Finance* 41 (March 1986): 195–207.

Kane, E. "Market Incompleteness and Divergence Between Forward and Futures Interest Rates." *Journal of Finance* (May 1980): 221–34.

Kane, A., and A. Marcus. "Valuation and Optimal Exercise of the Wild Card Option in the Treasury Bond Futures Market." *Journal of Finance* 41 (March 1986): 195–207.

Kolb, Robert. *Futures, Options, and Swaps,* 4th ed. Oxford, England: Blackwell Publishers.

Kaldor, N. "Speculation and Economic Stability." *Review of Economic Studies* 7 (1939–1940).

Kaufman, P. *Handbook of Futures Markets.* New York: Wiley, 1984, Chapters 1–6,10.

Petzel, T. E. "Structure of the Financial Futures Markets." In *The Handbook of Interest Rate Risk Management,* edited by J. C. Francis and A. S. Wolf. New York: Irwin Professional Publishing, 1994.

Silber, W. "Marketmaker Behavior in an Auction Market: An Analysis of Scalpers in Futures Markets." *Journal of Finance* 39 (September 1984): 937–953.

Stulz, R. M. "Optimal Hedging Policies." *Journal of Financial and Quantitative Analysis* 19 (June 1984): 127–40.

Telser, L. "Margins and Futures Contract." *Journal of Futures Markets* 1 (Fall 1981): 225–253.

PROBLEMS AND QUESTIONS

1. Explain the differences between forward contracts and option contracts.

2. Explain the differences between forward and futures contracts.

3. Define and explain the functions provided by futures exchanges.

4. Answer the following questions regarding the functions of the clearinghouse:

    a. Explain how the clearinghouse would record the following:
       1) Mr. A buys a September wheat futures contract from Ms. B for $3.00/bu on June 20.
       2) Mr. D buys a September wheat futures contract from Mr. E for $2.98 on June 25.
       3) Ms. B buys a September wheat futures from Mr. D for $2.97 on June 28.
       4) Mr. E buys a September wheat futures from Mr. A for $3.02 on July 3.

    b. Show the clearinghouse's payments and receipts needed to close each position.

5. Explain why the price on an expiring futures contract must be equal or approximately equal to the spot price on the contract's underlying asset.

6. What is the major economic justification of the futures market?

7. Mr. Woody is the chief financial officer for the Corso Company, a large metropolitan real estate developer. In January, Mr. Woody estimates that the company will need to purchase 30,000 square feet of plywood in June to meet its material needs on one of its office construction jobs.

    a. Suppose there is a June plywood contract trading at $f_0 = \$0.20$/sq. ft. (contract size is 5,000 sq. ft.). Explain how Mr. Woody could hedge the company's June plywood costs with a position in the June plywood contract.

b. Show in a table Mr. Woody's net costs at the futures' expiration date of buying plywood on the spot market at possible spot prices of 0.18/sq. ft., 0.20/sq. ft., 0.22/sq. ft., and 0.24/sq. ft. and closing the futures position. Assume no quality, quantity, and timing risk.

c. Define the three types of hedging risk and give an example of each in the context of problem b.

d. How much cash or risk-free securities would Mr. Woody have to deposit to satisfy an initial margin requirement of 5%?

8. In May, Mr. Jones planted a wheat crop that he expects to harvest in September. He anticipates the September harvest to be 10,000 bushels and would like to hedge the price he can get for his wheat by taking a position in a September wheat futures contract.

a. Explain how Mr. Jones could lock in the price he sells his wheat with a September wheat futures contract trading in May at $f_0 = \$4.20/bu$ (contract size of 5,000 bushels).

b. Show in a Table Mr. Jones's revenue at the futures' expiration date from closing the futures position and selling 10,000 bushels of wheat on the spot market at possible spot prices of $4.00/bu, $4.20/bu, and $4.40/bu. Assume no quality, quantity, or timing risk.

c. Give examples of the three types of hedging risk in the context of problem b.

d. How much cash or risk-free securities would Mr. Jones have to deposit to satisfy an initial margin requirement of 5%?

9. Ms. Smith is an orange juice distributor who, in January, signed a contract to deliver 60,000 pounds of frozen orange juice to Churchill Downs on Kentucky Derby Day (first Saturday in May). Ms. Smith plans to buy the orange juice from a local distributor in May. With a small profit margin, though, Ms. Smith is afraid she might incur a loss if orange juice prices increase.

a. Explain how Ms. Smith could lock in her orange juice costs with a May frozen orange juice futures contract trading in January at $f_0 = \$0.95/lb.$ (contract size of 15,000 pounds).

b. Show in a table Ms. Smith's net costs at the futures' expiration date from closing the futures position and buying 60,000 pounds of frozen orange juice on the spot market at possible spot prices of $0.90/lb, $0.95/lb and $1.00/lb. Assume no quality, quantity, or timing risk.

c. How much cash or risk-free securities would Ms. Smith have to deposit to satisfy an initial margin requirement of 5%?

10. Ms. Hunter is a money market manager. In July, she anticipates needing cash in September that she plans to obtain by selling 10 T-bills she currently holds, each T-bill having a face value of $1M. At the time of the anticipated September sale, the T-bills will have a maturity of 91 days. Suppose there is a September T-bill futures contract with the contract's underlying T-bill having a maturity of 91 days and a face value of $1M and trading a discount yield of $R_D = 10\%$ or $f_0 = ((100 - (10)(.25))/100)(\$1,000,000) = \$975,000$.

a. Assuming Ms. Hunter is fearful that short-term interest rates could increase and T-bill prices could therefore decrease, how could she lock in the selling price on her September T-bill sale?

b. Show in a table Ms. Hunter's net revenue at the futures' expiration date from closing the futures position and selling her 10 T-bills at possible discount yields of R_D = 9%, 10%, and 11%. Assume no quality, quantity, or timing risk.

11. Explain the similarities between a gambler who bets the Bulls over the Suns when the Las Vegas point spread line is the Bulls by 10 points and a speculator who goes long in September wheat futures at $4.20/bu.

12. What spread positions would you form in the following cases:

a. In July, you expect the spot price of wheat to increase, and September and October wheat futures contracts are available.

b. In April, you expect long-term interest rates to increase, and June and September T-bond futures contracts are available.

c. The estimated relationship between the price of copper (P_c) and the price of lead (P_L) is $\%\Delta P_c = .9(\%\Delta P_L)$. You expect a decrease in the price of metals, and futures contracts are available on both metals.

13. Define price limits and explain why they are used.

14. Suppose on March 1, you take a long position in a June crude oil futures contract at $60/barrel (contract size = 1,000 barrels).

a. How much cash or risk-free securities would you have to deposit to satisfy an initial margin requirement of 5%?

b. Calculate the values of your commodity account on the following days given the following settlement prices:

3/2	$60.50
3/3	60.75
3/4	60.25
3/5	59.50
3/8	59.00
3/9	60.00

c. If the maintenance margin requirement specifies keeping the value of the commodity account equal to 100% of the initial margin requirement each day, how much cash would you need to deposit in your commodity account each day?

15. Define the basis and its relationship to the time to expiration.

16. Calculate the actual futures prices and implied futures YTM for the following three T-bill futures contracts:

T-bill Futures Contract	IMM Index
March	93.764
June	93.3092
September	91.8607

17. Suppose you were long in a June T-bond futures contract at 92-16. What would you have to pay at the futures expiration for a delivered T-bond if the bond's conversion factor was 1.2 and the accrued interest on the deliverable bond was $1.50 per $100 face value?

18. Briefly comment on the following:

   a. The importance of the delivery procedure on futures contracts, even though most futures contracts are closed by offsetting positions

   b. The advantages and disadvantages of price limits

   c. The marked-to-market tax rule on speculative futures positions

   d. The benefits of futures funds

   e. The role of locals in ensuring a continuous futures markets

   f. The basis and its relationship to the time to expiration

   g. Rolling the hedge

19. Short-Answer Questions:

   1) What was the primary factor that contributed to the dramatic growth in the futures trading over the last 20 years?

   2) What is a hedge called in which the asset underlying the futures contract is not the same as the asset being hedged?

   3) A farmer who hedged his expected sale of 7,000 bushels in early September with CBT wheat futures contracts would be subject to what types of hedging risks?

   4) Who ensures that the price on an expiring futures contract is equal or approximately equal to its spot price?

   5) What is the number of futures contracts outstanding at a given point in time called?

   6) How does a futures market provide continuous trading without market makers or specialists?

   7) What is the trading referred to when exchange members trade for both their clients and themselves?

WEB EXERCISES

1. Determine the recent prices on futures contracts on foreign currency, Eurodollars, T-bills, and other financial futures listed on the Chicago Mercantile Exchange by going to www.cme.com.

2. Determine the recent prices on some commodity futures contracts listed on the Chicago Board of Trade by going to www.cbt.com.

CHAPTER 11

PRICING FUTURES AND FORWARD CONTRACTS

11.1 INTRODUCTION

As a derivative security, the price of a futures contract depends on the spot price of the underlying asset. Like options, the relation between futures and spot prices is governed by arbitrage. The arbitrage relation explaining this relationship is referred to as the **carrying-cost model**. This model determines the equilibrium futures or forward price in terms of the nets cost of buying the underlying asset and holding it for the period. If the futures or forward price does not equal the cost of carrying the underlying asset, then an arbitrage opportunity exists by taking a position in futures or forward contract and an opposite position in the underlying asset. Thus, in the absence of arbitrage, the futures price is equal to the cost of carrying the asset. In this chapter, we examine the carrying-cost model that determines the equilibrium futures and forward prices for contracts on a commodity, zero-coupon bond, stock index, and currency. After deriving that model, we examine the relationships between forward prices and expected spot prices and between futures and forward prices. We conclude the chapter by returning to options and examining the pricing relationship between futures and options.

11.2 BASIS

The underlying asset price on a futures or forward contract primarily depends on the spot price of the underlying asset. As we pointed out in the last chapter, the difference between the futures price (f) or forward price (F) and the spot price is called the basis (B_t):

$$\text{Basis} = B_t = f_t - S_t \qquad (11.2\text{-}2)$$

(The basis also can be expressed as $S_t - f_t$.) For most futures contracts, the futures price exceeds the spot price before expiration and approaches the spot price as expiration nears. Thus, the basis usually is positive and decreasing over time, equaling zero at expiration ($B_T = 0$). Futures and spot prices also tend to be highly correlated with each other, increasing and decreasing together; their correlation, though, is not perfect. As a result, the basis tends to be relatively stable along its declining trend, even when futures and spot prices vacillate.

11.3 CARRYING-COST MODEL

Theoretically, the relationship between the spot price and the futures or forward price can be explained by the **carrying-cost model** (or **cost-of-carry model**). As noted, in this model, arbitrageurs ensure that the equilibrium forward price is equal to the net costs of carrying the underlying asset to expiration. The model is used to explain what determines the equilibrium price on a forward contract. As we examine in Appendix 11A, though, if short-term interest rates are constant, futures and forward prices will be equal, and thus, the carrying-cost model can be extended to the pricing of futures contracts as well. The carrying cost pricing examples presented for futures contracts in this chapter assume short-term rates are constant.

In terms of the carrying-cost model, the price difference between futures and spot prices can be explained by the costs and benefits of carrying the underlying asset to expiration. For financial futures, the carrying costs include the financing costs of holding the underlying asset to expiration, and the benefits include coupon interest or dividends earned from holding the asset. For commodities, the carrying costs include not only financing costs but also storage and transportation costs.

11.3.1 Pricing a T-Bill Futures Contract

To illustrate the carrying-cost model, consider the pricing of a T-bill futures contract. With no coupon interest, the underlying T-bill does not generate any benefits during the holding period and the financing costs are the only carrying costs. In terms of the model, the equilibrium relationship between the futures and spot price on the T-bill is

$$f_0 = S_0(1 + R_f)^T \qquad (11.3\text{-}1)$$

where:

f_0 = contract price on the T-bill futures contract

T = time to expiration on the futures contract

S_0 = current spot price on a T-bill identical to the T-bill underlying the futures

(Maturity of 91 days and face value of $1M) except it has a maturity of 91+T

R_f = risk-free rate or repo rate

$S_0(1 + R_f)^T$ = financing costs of holding a spot T-bill

If we assume continuous compounding and an annual risk-free of R^A, then the equilibrium forward or futures price is

$$f_0 = S_0 e^{R^A T} \qquad (11.3\text{-}2)$$

In pricing a futures or forward contracts, the repo rate often is used as the interest rate. The repo rate is the loan rate on a repurchase agreement. A repurchase agreement is a transaction in which a security holder (or short seller) sells a security with the obligation of repurchasing it at a later date. To the holder, the repurchase agreement represents a secured loan in which she receives funds from the sale of the security, with the responsibility of purchasing the security later at a higher price. The repo rate, in turn, is the loan rate implied on this loan.

If Equation (11.3-1) does not hold, an arbitrage opportunity exists. The arbitrage strategy is referred to as a ***cash-and-carry arbitrage*** and involves taking opposite positions in the spot and futures contracts. For example, suppose in June the following:

- 161-day T-bill priced at $97.5844 per $100 face value to yield 5.7%
- September T-bill futures contract expiring in 70 days
- 70-day risk-free rate or repo rate of 6.38%

Using the carrying-cost model, the equilibrium price of a September T-bill futures contract is $f_0 = \$987,487$ or $\$98.74875$ per $\$100$ par value:

$$f_0 = S_0(1 + R_f)^T$$

$$f_0 = 97.5844(1.0638)^{70/365} = 98.74875$$

where:

$$S_0 = \frac{100}{(1.057)^{161/365}} = 97.5844$$

If the market price on the T-bill futures contract were not equal to 98.74875, then a cash-and-carry arbitrage opportunity would exist. For example, if the T-bill futures price is at $f_0^M = 99$, an arbitrageur could earn a risk-free profit of $\$2,512.50$ per $\$1M$ face value or $\$0.25125$ per $\$100$ face value $(99 - 98.74875)$ at the expiration date by executing the following strategy:

1. Borrow $\$97.5844$ at the repo (or borrowing) rate of 6.38% and then buy a 161-day spot T-bill for $S_0(161) = 97.5844$

2. Take a short position in a T-bill futures contract expiring in 70 days at the futures price of $f_0^M = 99$

At expiration, the arbitrageur would earn $\$0.25125$ per $\$100$ face value ($\$2,512.50$ per $\$1M$ par) when he

1. Sells the T-bill on the spot futures contract at 99 and

2. Repays the principal and interest on the loan of $97.5844(1.0638)^{70/365} = 98.74875$:

$$CF_T = f_0^M - f_0^*$$

$$CF_T = 99 - 97.5844(1.0638)^{70/365}$$

$$= 99 - 98.74875 = .25125$$

$$CF_T = \frac{.25125}{100}(\$1M) = \$2,512.50$$

In addition to the arbitrage opportunity, when the futures is overpriced at 99, a money market manager currently planning to invest for 70 days in a T-bill at 6.38% also could benefit with a greater return by creating a synthetic 70-day investment by buying a 161-day bill and then going short at 99 in the T-bill futures contract expiring in 70 days. For example, using the preceding numbers, if a money market manager were planning to invest 97.5844 for 70 days, she could buy a 161-day bill for that amount and go short in the futures at 99. Her return would be 7.8% compared to 6.38% from the 70-day spot T-bill:

$$R = \left[\frac{99}{97.5844}\right]^{365/70} - 1 = .078$$

Both the arbitrage and the investment strategies involve taking short positions in the T-bill futures. These actions would therefore serve to move the price on the futures down toward 98.74875.

If the market price on the T-bill futures contract is below the equilibrium value, then the cash-and-carry arbitrage strategy is reversed. In our example, suppose the futures were priced at 98. In this case, an arbitrageur would go long in the futures, agreeing to buy a 91-day T-bill 70 days later and would go short in the spot T-bill, borrowing the 161-day bill, selling it for 97.5844, and investing the proceeds at 6.38% for 70 days. Seventy days later (expiration), the arbitrageur would buy a 91-day T-bill on the futures for 98 (f_0^M), use the bill to close his short position, and collect 98.74875 (f_0^*) from his investment, realizing a cash flow of \$7,487.50 or \$0.74875 per \$100 par:

$$CF_T = f_0^* - f_0^M$$

$$CF_T = 97.5844(1.0638)^{70/365} - 98$$

$$= 98.74875 - 98 = .74875$$

$$CF_T = \frac{.78475}{100}(\$1M) = \$7,487.50$$

In addition to this cash-and carry arbitrage, if the futures price is below 98, a money manager currently holding 161-day T-bills also could obtain an arbitrage by selling the bills for 97.5844 and investing the proceeds at 6.38% for 70 days and then going long in the T-bill futures contract expiring in 70 days. Seventy days later, the manager would receive 98.74875 from the investment and would pay 98 on the futures to reacquire the bills for a cash flow of .74875 per \$100 par.

11.3.1.1 *Equivalent Spot and Synthetic T-Bill Rates*

As illustrated in the preceding example, a money market manager planning to invest funds in a T-bill for a given horizon period either can invest in the spot T-bill or can construct a synthetic T-bill by purchasing a longer term T-bill and then locking in its selling price by going short in a T-bill futures contract. That is, in the preceding example, the manager either could buy a 70-day spot T-bill yielding a 6.38% rate of return and trading at $S_0 = 98.821$

$$S_0 = \frac{100}{(1.0638)^{70/365}} = 98.821$$

or could create a long position in a synthetic 70-day T-bill by buying the 161-day T-bill trading at $S_0 = 97.5844$ and then locking in the selling price by going short in the T-bill futures contract expiring in 70 days. If the futures price in the market exceeds the equilibrium value as determined by the carrying-cost model ($f_0^M > f_0^*$), then the rate of return on the synthetic T-bill (R_{syn}) will exceed the rate on the spot; in this case, the manager should choose the synthetic T-bill. As we saw, at a futures price of 99, the manager earned a rate of return of 7.8% on the synthetic compared to only 6.38% from the spot. On the other hand, if the futures price is less than its equilibrium value ($f_0^M < f_0^*$), then R_{syn} will be less than the rate on the spot; in this case, the manager should purchase the spot T-bill.

In an efficient market, money managers will drive the futures price to its equilibrium value as determined by the carrying-cost model. When this condition is realized, R_{syn} will be equal to the rate on the spot, and the money manager would be indifferent to either investment. In our example, this occurs when the market price on the futures contract is equal to the equilibrium value of 98.74875. At that price, R_{syn} is equal to 6.38%:

$$R_{syn} = \left[\frac{98.74875}{97.5844}\right]^{365/70} - 1 = .0638$$

Thus, if the carrying-cost model holds, the rate earned from investing in a spot T-bill and the rate from investing in a synthetic will be equal.

11.3.1.2 *Implied and Actual Repo Rates*

The rate earned from the synthetic T-bill is commonly referred to as the *implied repo rate.* Formally, the implied repo rate is defined as the rate in which the arbitrage cash flow (CF_T) from implementing the cash and carry arbitrage strategy is zero:

$$CF_T = f_0 - S_0(1 + R_f)^T$$

$$0 = f_0 - S_0(1 + R_f)^T$$

$$R = \left[\frac{f_0}{S_0}\right]^{1/T} - 1$$

The actual repo rate is the one we used in solving for the equilibrium futures price in the carrying-cost model; in our example, this was the rate on the 70-day T-bill (6.38%). Thus, the equilibrium condition that the synthetic and spot T-bill will be equal can be stated equivalently as an equality between the actual and the implied repo rates.

11.3.2 **Pricing a Forward Contract on a Stock Portfolio**

If the underlying asset on a forward or futures contract generates a benefit during the period such as dividends, the benefit needs to be subtracted from the costs of carrying the asset in determining the equilibrium price of the forward or futures contract. That is

$$f_0 = S_0(1 + R_f)^T - D_T \tag{11.3-3}$$

where :
D_T = the value of the benefits at time T

As an example, suppose there is a stock portfolio currently worth $S_0 = \$150$ that will pay dividends worth \$1.50 at T ($D_T = \$1.50$) and a forward contract on the stock portfolio expiring in 3 months (T = .25). If the risk-free rate is 8%, the equilibrium price of the forward contract (F) would be \$151.41:

$$F_0 = \$150(1.08)^{.25} - \$1.50 = \$151.41$$

If the actual contract price did not equal F_0, an arbitrage opportunity could be realized by applying the same cash-and-carry arbitrage strategy described for the T-bill futures contract. For example, if the forward price is \$154, an arbitrageur could borrow \$150 at 8%, buy the portfolio with the loan proceeds, and enter a forward contract to sell the portfolio at \$154 at the end of 3 months. At the end of the period, the arbitrageur would receive \$154 from the sale of the portfolio on the forward contract and \$1.50 in dividends and would owe \$152.91 in principal and interest on the debt, netting a riskless cash flow of \$2.59. The arbitrageur would, of course, pursue this strategy until the forward price is \$154.41. If the contract price is below $F_0 = \$151.41$, the arbitrageur reverses the strategy: He sells the portfolio short and takes a long position in the forward contract. This strategy also would yield a riskless return until the forward price is \$151.41.

If the dividends paid on the stocks comprising the portfolio approximate a continuous payment stream, then the equilibrium price on the forward contract can be estimated using the annualized continuous dividend yield for the portfolio, ψ. Using ψ and assuming continuous compounded with a risk-free rate of R^A, the equilibrium equation for the forward contract is

$$F_0 = S_0 e^{(R^A - \psi)T} \tag{11.3-4}$$

In the preceding case, if the stock portfolio paid an annualized dividend yield of $\psi = 4\%([(4)(\$1.50)]/\$150)$, and the risk-free rate is $R^A = 8\%$, then the equilibrium price of the forward contract would be \$151.51:

$$F_0 = S_0 e^{(R^A - \psi)T}$$

$$F_0 = \$150 e^{(.08 - .04)(.25)} = \$151.51$$

11.3.3 Pricing an Index Futures Contract

Although there are no futures contracts listed on actual stock portfolios, the preceding case can be extended to the pricing of stock index futures in which the underlying asset is a proxy portfolio. Equation (11.3-4) is often used to price an index futures contract. For example, if the current S&P 500 spot index is at 1250, the risk-free rate is 6%, and the annualized dividend yield on stocks comprising the index is $\psi = 4\%$, then the equilibrium price on the index futures expiring in 3 months (T = .25) would be 1256.25:

$$f_0 = S_0 e^{(R^A - \psi)T}$$

$$f_0 = 1250 e^{(.06 - .04)(.25)} = 1256.26$$

Note that in this case, the S&P 500 futures price exceeds the spot. If, however, the dividend yield had exceeded the risk-free rate, then the opposite would have occurred, with the futures price being less that the spot. Like the stock portfolio case, the pricing of index futures is governed by an arbitrage strategy consisting of a position in the index futures contract and an opposite position in a proxy portfolio. This arbitrage strategy is known as ***index arbitrage*** and is examined in Chapter 14.

11.3.3.1 *Pricing Forward Exchange Rates*

In international finance, the carrying cost model governing the relationship between spot and forward exchange rates is referred to as the ***interest rate parity theorem*** (IRPT). In terms of IRPT, the forward price of a currency or forward exchange rate (F_0) is equal to the cost of carrying the spot currency (priced at the spot exchange rate of E_0) for the contract's expiration period.

In terms of a U.S. dollar position, carrying a foreign currency for the period (T) would require borrowing $E_0/(1 + R_F)^T$ dollars at the rate R_{US} (where R_F is the foreign risk-free rate), converting the dollars to $1/(1 + R_F)^T$ units of foreign currency (FC) at the spot exchange rate of E_0, and investing the currency in the foreign risk-free security yielding R_F. At the end of the period, this arbitrage would yield one unit of FC and a debt obligation of $[E_0/(1 + R_F)^T](1 + R_{US})^T$. In the absence of arbitrage, the forward price of purchasing one unit of currency at T should not be different from the net financing cost of carrying the currency. Thus, the equilibrium forward price or exchange rate is

$$F_0 = E_0 \frac{(1 + R_{US})^T}{(1 + R_F)^T} \tag{11.3-5}$$

or assuming continuous compounding

$$F_0 = E_0 e^{(R_{US}^A - R_F^A)T} \tag{11.3-6}$$

Equations (11.3-5) and (11.3-6) define IRPT. The equation, in turn, shows that the relation between the forward and the spot rates depends on the relative levels of domestic and foreign interest rates. If the interest rate parity condition does not hold, an arbitrage opportunity will exist. The arbitrage strategy to apply in such situations is known as ***covered*** *interest arbitrage* (CIA). Introduced by John Maynard Keynes, CIA involves taking long and short positions in the currency spot and forward markets as well as positions in the domestic and foreign money markets. To illustrate, suppose the annualized U.S. and foreign interest rates are $R_{US} = 4\%$ and $R_F = 6\%$, respectively, and the spot exchange rate is $E_0 = \$0.40/FC$. By IRPT, a 1-year forward contract would be equal to $\$0.39245283/FC$:

$$F_0 = [\$0.40/FC] \left(\frac{1.04}{1.06} \right) = \$0.39245283/FC$$

If the actual forward rate, F_0^M, exceeds $\$0.39245283/FC$, an arbitrage profit would exist by (1) borrowing dollars at R_{US}, (2) converting the dollar to FC at E_0, (3) investing the fund in a foreign risk-free rate at the rate R_F, and (4) and entering a short forward contract to sell the FC at the end of the period at F_0^M. For example, if $F_0^M = \$0.40/FC$, an arbitrageur could

1. Borrow $40,000 at $R_{US} = 4\%$ [creating a loan obligation at the end of the period of $\$41,600 = (\$40,000)(1.04)$].
2. Convert the dollars at the spot exchange rate of $E_0 = \$0.40/FC$ to 100,000 FC $(= (2.5FC/\$)(\$40,000))$.
3. Invest the 100,000 FC in the foreign risk-free security at $R_F = 6\%$ (creating a return of principal and interest of 106,000 FC 1 year later).
4. Enter a forward contract to sell 106,000 FC at the end of the year at $F_0^M = \$0.40/FC$.

One year later, the arbitrageur would receive $42,400 when she sells the 106,000 FC on the forward contract and would owe $41,600 on her debt obligation for an arbitrage return of $800. Such risk-free profit opportunities, in turn, would lead arbitrageurs to try to implement the CIA strategy. This would cause the price on the forward contract to fall until the riskless opportunity disappears. The zero arbitrage profit would occur when the interest rate parity condition is satisfied.

If the forward rate is below the equilibrium value, then the CIA is reversed. In this example, if $F_0^M = \$0.38/FC$, an arbitrageur could

1. Borrow 100,000 FC at $R_F = 6\%$ (creating a 106,000 FC debt)
2. Convert the 100,000 FC at the spot exchange rate to $40,000
3. Invest the $40,000 in the U.S. risk-free security at $R_{US} = 4\%$
4. Enter a forward contract to buy 106,000 FC at the end of the year at $F_0^M = \$0.38/FC$

At the end of the period, the arbitrageur's profit would be $1,320:

$$\$40,000(1.04) - (\$0.38/FC)(106,000) = \$1,320$$

As arbitrageurs attempt to implement this strategy, they will push up the price on the forward contract until the arbitrage profit is zero; this occurs when the interest rate parity condition is satisfied.

11.3.4 Equilibrium T-Bond Futures Price

Because of the uncertainty over the bond to be delivered and the time of the delivery created by the delivery procedure, the pricing of a T-bond futures contract is more complex than the pricing of T-bill, stock index, or currency futures. Like all futures, the price on a T-bond futures contract depends on the spot price on the underlying T-bond (S_0) and the risk-free rate. If we assume that we know the cheapest-to-deliver bond and the time of delivery, the equilibrium futures price is

$$f_0 = [S_0 - PV(C)](1 + R_f)^T$$

where :

S_0 = current spot price of the cheapest-to-deliver T-bond (clean price plus accrued interest)

$PV(C)$ = present value of coupons paid on the bond during the life of the futures contract.

Example

As an example, suppose the following:

- The cheapest-to-deliver T-bond underlying a futures contract pays a 10% coupon, has a CFA of 1.2, and is currently trading at 110 (clean price).
- The cheapest-to-deliver T-bond's last coupon date was 50 days ago, its next coupon is 132 days from now, and the coupon after that comes 182 days later.
- The yield on all maturities is 6% (i.e., flat yield curve).
- The T-bond futures estimated expiration is T = 270 days.

The current T-bond spot price is 111.37, and the present value of the $5 coupon received in 132 days is 4.8957:

$$S_0 = \text{Clean price} + \text{Accrued Interest}$$

$$S_0 = 110 + \left[\frac{50 \text{ days}}{50 \text{ days} + 132 \text{ days}} \right] (5) = 111.37$$

$$PV(C) = \frac{5}{(1.06)^{132/365}} = 4.8957$$

The equilibrium futures price based on the deliverable bond with the 10% coupon is therefore 111.16 per $100 face value:

$$f_0 = [S_0 - PV(C)](1 + R_f)^T$$

$$f_0 = [111.37 - 4.8957](1.06)^{270/365} = 111.16$$

The quoted price on a futures contract written on the 10% delivered bond would be stated net of accrued interest at the delivery date. The delivery date occurs 138 days after the last coupon payment (270 − 132). Thus, at delivery, there would be 138 days of accrued interest. Given the 182-day period between coupon payments, accrued interest would therefore be 3.791 (= (138/182)(5)). The quoted futures price on the delivered bond would be 107.369(= 111.16 − 3.791), and with a CFA of 1.2, the equilibrium quoted futures price would be 89.47:

$$\text{Quoted Futures Price on Bond} = 111.16 - (138/182)5 = 107.369$$

$$\text{Quoted Futures Price} = 107.369/1.2 = 89.47$$

11.3.5 Arbitrage

Like T-bill futures, cash-and-carry arbitrage opportunities will exist if the T-bond futures were not equal to 111.16 (or its quoted price of 89.47). For example, if futures were priced at $f^M = 113$, an arbitrageur could go short in the futures at 113 and then buy the underlying cheapest-to-deliver bond for 111.37, financed by borrowing 106.4743 ($= S_0 - PV(C) = 111.37 - 4.8957$) at 6% for 270 days and 4.8957 at 6% for 132 days. Then, 132 days later, the arbitrageur would receive a $5 coupon that he would use to pay off the 132-day loan of $5 (= 4.8957(1.06)^{132/365})$. At expiration, the arbitrageur would sell the bond on the futures contract at 113 and pay off his financing cost on the 270-day loan of 111.16 $(= 106.4743(1.06)^{270/365})$. This, in turn, would equate to an arbitrage profit of $f^M - f_0^* = 113 - 111.16 = \$1.84$ per $100 face value. This risk-free return would result in arbitrageurs pursuing this strategy of going short in the futures and long in the T-bond, causing the futures price to decrease to 111.16 when the arbitrage disappears. If the futures price were below 111.16, arbitrageurs would reverse the strategy, shorting the bond, investing the proceeds, and going long in the T-bond futures contract.

11.3.6 Pricing a Futures Contract on a Commodity

For most commodities contracts, there usually are no benefits realized from carrying the underlying asset. There are, though, storage and transportation costs. Accordingly, the carrying-cost model for a typical commodity futures contract is

$$f_0 = S_0(1 + R_f)^T + (K)(T) + TRC \tag{11.3-7}$$

where :

K = storage costs per unit of the commodity per period

TRC = transportation costs

As an example, suppose in June, the spot price of a bushel of wheat is $2.00, the annual storage costs is $0.30 per/bushel, the risk-free rate is 8%, and the costs of transporting wheat from the destination point specified on the futures contract to a local grain elevator, or vice versa, is $0.01/bu. By the cost-of-carry model, the equilibrium price of a futures contract on September wheat (expiration of T = .25) would be $2.124/bu:

$$f_0 = \$2.00/bu(1.08)^{.25} + (\$0.30/bu)(.25) + \$0.01/bu = \$2.124/bu$$

If the actual futures price is $2.16, an arbitrageur would

1. Take a short position in the futures contract: agree to sell a September bushel of wheat for $2.16
2. Borrow $2 at 8% interest
3. Use the loan proceeds to buy a bushel of wheat for $2.00 and then store it for 3 months

At expiration, the arbitrageur would

1. Transport the wheat from the grain elevator to the specified destination point on the futures contract for $0.01/bu
2. Pay the financing costs of $2.0388/bu and the storage costs of ($0.30/bu)(.25) = $0.075/bu
3. Sell the bushel of wheat on the futures contract at $2.16/bu.

From this cash-and-carry strategy, the arbitrageur would earn a riskless return of $0.036/bu.

If the futures price on a commodity is below the equilibrium price, the strategy would need to be reversed. This would entail taking a short position in the spot commodity and a long position in the futures contract. In our wheat example, such an opportunity might be available, for example, to a mill company maintaining an inventory of wheat. Instead of holding all of its wheat, the company might sell some of it on the spot market and invest the proceeds in a risk-free security for the period and then go long in a futures contract to buy the wheat back. For many commodities, though, this reverse strategy may not be practical. For those commodities in which the reverse cash-and-carry arbitrage strategy does not apply, the equilibrium condition for the futures contract needs to be specified as an inequality. That is

$$f_0 \leq S_0(1 + R_f)^T + (K)(T) + TRC \qquad (11.3\text{-}8)$$

11.3.7   Normal and Inverted Markets

For many assets, the costs of carrying the asset for a period of time exceed the benefits. As a result, the futures price on such assets exceeds the spot price prior to expiration, and the basis $(f_t - S_t)$ on such assets is positive. By definition, a market in which the futures price exceeds the spot price is referred to as a ***contango*** or ***normal market.*** In contrast, if the futures price is less then the spot price (a negative basis), the costs of carrying the asset is said to have a ***convenience yield*** in which the benefits from holding the asset exceed the costs. A market in which the basis is negative is referred to as ***backwardation*** or an ***inverted market.***

For commodity futures, an inverted market often exists for unstorable commodities (e.g., eggs) or can occur in certain situations in which the existing supplies of a commodity (e.g., wheat) are limited but future supplies (e.g., the next wheat harvest) are expected to be abundant. For financial futures, an inverted market could occur if large coupon or dividend payments are to be paid during the period. For example, if the dividend in the previous stock portfolio example had been $3.00 instead of $1.50, then F_0 would have been $149.91 instead of $151.41, and the futures market on the portfolio would have been inverted.

11.4   PRICE RELATIONSHIP BETWEEN FUTURES CONTRACTS WITH DIFFERENT EXPIRATIONS

The same arbitrage arguments governing the futures and spot price relation also can be extended to establish the equilibrium relationship between futures prices with different expirations. Specifically, given a distant futures contract expiring in T_2 and a nearby contract on the same asset expiring in T_1, the equilibrium relationship between the futures prices on the two contracts (f_{T2} and f_{T1}) is

$$f_{T2} = f_{T1}(1 + R_{T1})^{T_2 - T_1} - D_{T2} + (K)(T_2 - T_1) + TRC \qquad (11.4\text{-}1)$$

where

R_{T1} = risk-free rate or repo rate at time T_1. The rate can be locked in with a futures
      contract.

D_{T2} = value of benefits at time T_2 received from holding the asset for the period
      from T_1 to T_2.

If the market price of the futures contract with T_2 expiration (f_{T2}^m) exceeded the equilibrium price, an arbitrageur could profit by forming an intracommodity spread by

1.   Taking a long position in the T_1 futures contract

2.   Taking a short position in the T_2 futures contract

3. Entering a futures contract to borrow at time T_1, f_{T1} dollars at rate R_{T1} for the period from T_1 to T_2

At T_1 expiration, the arbitrageur would

1. Borrow f_{T1} dollars at a rate of R_{T1} on the futures contract
2. Buy the asset on the T_1 futures contract for f_{T1}
3. Transport and store the asset (if necessary) for the period at a costs of $K(T_2 - T_1) +$ TRC

At the T_2 expiration, the arbitrageur would

1. Sell the asset on the T_2 futures contract for f_{T2}
2. Receive the D_{T2} benefits that have accrued during the $T_2 - T_1$ period
3. Repay the loan of $f_{T1}(1 + R_{T1})^{T2-T1}$
4. Pay the transportation and storage costs of $K(T_2 - T_1) +$ TRC

The arbitrageur's actions would result in a riskless CF of

$$CF = f_{T2}^M - [f_{T1}(1 + R_{T1})^{T2-T1} - D_{T2} + (K)(T_2 - T_1) + TRC]$$

Such actions, in turn, would continue until the equilibrium condition [Equation (11.4-1)] is satisfied.

Example

To illustrate, consider the futures price relationship for March and June lumber contracts. Suppose the following conditions are present:

1. The futures price on the March lumber contract is $f_{T1} = \$0.24$/sq. ft.
2. The March futures interest rate on a 3-month loan is 8% (annual)
3. The storage costs for lumber is $0.06/sq. ft. per year
4. The carrying-costs benefits and the costs of transporting lumber are zero (assume there is a storage facility at the location point specified on the lumber futures contract).

If the time period between the expiration on the June lumber contract and the March contract is $T_2 - T_1 = .25$/year, then the equilibrium price on the June contract would be $0.26/sq. ft.:

$$f_{T2} = \$0.24(1.08)^{.25} + \$0.06(.25) = \$.26/\text{sq.ft.}$$

If the June lumber futures contract is $0.28, then an arbitrageur could earn a $0.02/sq. ft profit by

1. Entering a March futures contract to borrow $0.24 at $R_{T1} = 8\%$
2. Going long in the March lumber contract at $f_{T1} = \$0.24$/sq. ft.
3. Taking a short position on the June lumber contract at $f_{T2} = \$0.28$

In March, the arbitrageur would

1. Borrow $0.24 at 8% interest on the futures contract
2. Purchase the lumber for $0.24/sq. ft. on the March contract
3. Store the lumber at an annual rate of $0.06/sq. ft. for .25 of a year

At the June expiration the arbitrageur would realize a $0.02/sq. ft. profit by

1. Selling the lumber on the June contract for $0.28/sq. ft.
2. Repaying the loan of $0.245 = $0.24(1.08)$^{.25}$
3. Paying the storage costs of $0.015 (($0.06/sq. ft.)(.25))

If the June lumber contract is less than the equilibrium price, the preceding intra-commodity spread strategy would need to be reversed. This would require taking a short position in the March contract, a long position in the June contract, and entering a futures contract to invest f_{T1} funds at rate R_{T1} for 90 days. The implementation of this reverse strategy may or may not be practical. For financial futures, for example, this reverse strategy generally can be applied. However, for many commodity futures contracts, the reverse strategy does not hold. For such commodity futures, Equation (11.4-1), in turn, needs to be expressed as an inequality.

11.5   RELATION BETWEEN THE FUTURES PRICE AND THE EXPECTED SPOT PRICE

The carrying-cost model relates the equilibrium futures price to the current spot price. The futures price also is related to an unknown expected spot price. Several expectation theories have been advanced to explain the relationship between the futures and expected spot prices.

One of the first theories was broached by the famous British economists John Maynard Keynes and J. R. Hicks. They argued that if a spot market were dominated by hedgers who, on balance, wanted a short futures position, then for the market to clear (supply to equal demand), the price of the futures contract would have to be less than the expected price on the spot commodity at expiration ($E(S_T)$). According to Keynes and Hicks, the difference between $E(S_T)$ and f_0 represents a risk premium that speculators in the market require to take a long futures position. For example, if f_0 is equal or less than $E(S_T)$, there would be too few speculators to take long positions, and an excess demand of short over long positions would occur. This excess, though, would force the contract price down, inducing speculators to take a long position. Thus, if there are more short hedgers than long, then equilibrium would require a risk premium of $E(S_T) - f_0$. Keynes and Hicks called this market situation ***normal backwardation.***

The opposite case in which $f_0 > E(S_T)$ could occur if the market consisted of hedgers who, on balance, wanted to go long. In this case, the price of the futures contract would have to exceed $E(S_T)$ to induce speculators to take a short position. C. O. Hardy also argued for the case of $f_0 > E(S_T)$, even in a market of short hedgers. His argument, though, is based on investor's risk behavior. He maintained that because speculators were akin to gamblers, they were willing to pay for the opportunity to gamble (risk-loving behavior). Thus, a gambler's fee, referred to as a ***contango*** or ***forwardation,*** would result in a negative risk premium.

Finally, there is a risk-neutral pricing argument in which futures contracts, like options, represent redundant securities. In this argument, the futures price represents an unbiased estimate of the expected spot price ($f_0 = E(S_T)$) and with risk-neutral pricing, investors purchasing an asset for S_0 and expecting an asset value at T of $E(S_T) = f_0$ require an expected rate of return equal to the risk-free rate (R_f). Thus

$$S_0 = \frac{E(S_T)}{(1 + R_f)^T}$$

$$S_0 = \frac{f_0}{(1 + R_f)^T} \qquad (11.5\text{-}1)$$

Solving Equation (11.5-1) for f_0, in turn, yields the carrying-cost model:

$$f_0 = S_0(1 + R_f)^T$$

Whether a risk premium exists is an empirical question. One of the first empirical studies to test for the existence of a premium was done by Houthakker (1957) who found abnormal returns could be earned from taking positions in corn, wheat, and cotton for the period from 1937 to 1957. Telser, in a 1958 study, and Gray, in a 1960 study, though, did not find these abnormal returns. In a relatively more recent empirical study, Michael Hartzmark (1987) found futures prices to be unbiased estimates of expected spot prices. Thus, the studies by Hartzmark, Telser, and Gray have supported the validity of the carrying-cost model.

11.6 THE VALUES OF FUTURES AND FORWARD CONTRACTS

The carrying-cost model determines the forward or futures price. A separate question is whether there is any value to the futures or forward contract. As we earlier noted, the major difference between options and futures is that the former gives the holder the right but not the obligation to execute the terms of the contract, whereas the latter is an obligation. As a result, in an options contract, the right to exercise has value, and the contract therefore has value when it is introduced; a futures or forward contract, though, is simply an agreement that has no inherent value when it is introduced.

In the case of forward contracts, there is a value to an existing contract. After its introduction, the value of a forward contract at time t should be equal to the present value of the difference between its initial contract price (F_0) and the contract price on a new forward contract with the same expiration date and underlying asset (F_t). That is, the value of a long position on the initial forward contract at time t ($V_t^{F_0}$) is

$$V_t^{F_0} = \frac{F_t - F_0}{(1 + R_f)^t}$$

For example, if the forward contract price on September wheat is $2.50 ($F_t$) when there is 1 month to expiration (t $=$ 1/12 of a year), and the annual risk-free rate is 6%, then the value of a long position on a September wheat forward contract initiated earlier at $2.40 would be $0.0995. That is

$$V_t^{F_0} = \frac{F_t - F_0}{(1 + R_f)^t} = \frac{\$2.50 - \$2.40}{(1.06)^{1/12}} \$0.0995$$

With 1 month to delivery, the $0.0995 value of the earlier contract reflects the $0.10 riskless return that can be realized at the end of 1 month by the holder of the earlier contract from forming an intracommodity spread by taking a short position in the new contract. At the September expiration, the spreader would be able to buy the wheat at $2.40 and sell it at $2.50.

Like forward contracts, futures contracts also can have values after their inceptions but only until they are marked to market. Once a futures contract is marked to market, its value reverts to zero.

11.7 RELATION BETWEEN FUTURES AND FORWARD PRICES

The price relationships we've described thus far hold only for forward contracts that have no initial or maintenance margin requirements. Under the assumption that short-term interest rates are constant over time, though, it can be shown that the prices of futures and forward contracts on the same underlying asset are the same. Accordingly, if this assumption is reasonable, the previous pricing relationships that we've specified for forward contracts also can be used to price futures contracts; if the assumption is not reasonable, then the previous pricing models for forward contracts can be used only to approximate the price of a futures contract. The formal relationship between futures and forward prices is presented in Appendix 11A.

11.8 RELATION BETWEEN FUTURES AND OPTIONS

Up to now, we have examined futures and option contracts separately. As we might expect, when an asset has both an option and a futures contract, the put, call, futures, and spot prices all are related to each other. The relation between options and futures can be seen in terms of the put–call-futures parity model and by constructing the replicating portfolio underlying the OPM with futures contracts.

11.8.1 Put-Call-Futures Parity

The put–call-parity model that we examined in Chapters 1 and 4 determines the equilibrium relationship between put and call prices from a conversion (or reversal) strategy consisting of long positions in the underlying asset and a European put and a short position in a European call. Recall, in the case of a nondividend-paying stock, the value of the conversion at expiration equals the options' exercise price, regardless of the price on the underlying spot asset. As a result, in equilibrium, the value of the conversion is equal to the present value of a riskless zero-coupon bond with a face value equal to the exercise price.

The put–call-futures parity model is similar to the put–call parity model. As the name implies, though, the put–call-futures parity model is derived using a futures position on the option's underlying asset instead of a position in the spot or cash asset. The model's conversion strategy consists of a long position in a futures contract at price f_0 and a synthetic short futures position formed by buying a European put and selling a European call on the futures' underlying spot security, with the options having the same expiration date as the futures contract. As shown in Table 11.8-1, with the price of the expiring futures contract (f_T) equal to the spot price on the underlying asset (S_T) at expiration, the value of the conversion formed with a long position in a futures contract is $X - f_0$ at expiration, regardless of the spot price. Thus, the equilibrium value of the conversion with a futures

TABLE 11.8-1 Put–Call-Futures Parity Conversion: $\{+f_0, +P_0^e, -C_0^e\}$

Position	Investment	$S_T < X$	$S_T = X$	$S_T > X$
			Expiration Cash Flow	
Long Futures	0	$S_T - f_0$	$S_T - f_0$	$S_T - f_0$
Long Put	P_0^e	$X - S_T$	0	0
Short Call	$-C_0^e$	0	0	$-(S_T - X)$
	$P_0^e - C_0^e$	$X - f_0$	$X - f_0$	$X - f_0$

position is equal to the value of a riskless pure discount bond with a face value of $X - f_0$ and maturity of T. That is

$$P_0^e - C_0^e + V_0^F = (X - f_0)(1 + R)^{-T}$$
$$P_0^e - C_0^e = (X - f_0)(1 + R)^{-T} \qquad (11.8\text{-}1)$$

where the initial value of the futures contract (V_0^F) is zero. If the equilibrium condition [Equation (11.8-1)] for put–call-futures parity does not hold, then an arbitrage opportunity will exist by taking a position in the put and futures contracts and an opposite position in the call and a riskless bond with face value equal to $X - f_0$.

11.8.1.1 Equivalence Between Put–Call-Spot and Put–Call-Futures Parity Models

The put–call-futures parity model defines the equilibrium relationship between call, put, and futures prices. If the carrying-costs model holds in which $f_0 = S_0(1 + R)^T$, then the put–call-futures parity model and the put–call parity model defined for the underlying spot will be equivalent. The equivalence of the models can be shown algebraically simply by substituting $S_0(1 + R)^T$ for f_0 in Equation (11.8-1) to obtain the put–call parity equation defined in terms of the spot asset:

$$P_0^e - C_0^e = (X - f_0)(1 + R)^{-T}$$
$$P_0^e - C_0^e = (X - S_0(1 + R)^T)(1 + R)^{-T}$$
$$P_0^e - C_0^e = X(1 + R)^{-T} - S_0$$

Note for foreign currency positions, the put–call-spot parity and put–call-futures parity also includes the foreign interest rate. That is, the foreign currency put–call-futures model is:

$$P_0^e - C_0^e = (X - f_0)(1 + R_{US})^{-T} \qquad (11.8\text{-}2)$$

where :
f_0 = forward or futures exchange rate.

Recall that the interest rate parity condition is $f_0 = E_0(1 + R_{US})^T(1 + R_F)^{-T}$. Thus, substituting $E_0(1 + R_{US})^T(1 + R_F)^T$ for f_0 in Equation (11.8-2), we obtain the foreign currency put–call-parity condition derived earlier in Chapter 4. That is

$$P_0^e - C_0^e = (X - f_0)(1 + R_{US})^{-T}$$
$$P_0^e - C_0^e = \left[X - E_0\left[\frac{1 + R_{US}}{1 + R_F}\right]^T\right](1 + R_{US})^{-T}$$
$$P_0^e - C_0^e + E_0(1 + R_F)^{-T} = X(1 + R_{US})^{-T}$$

11.8.2   BOPM in Terms of Futures Positions

If a European option's underlying asset also has a futures contract, then like the preceding put–call parity relations, the OPM can be specified in terms of the futures position. Moreover, if the carrying-cost model holds, and the futures contract and the option contract expire at the same time, then the OPM specified in terms of futures will be equal to the OPM defined in terms of the underlying spot asset. Two BOPM pricing examples from Chapter 6 are presented in Appendix 11B.

11.9   CONCLUSION

Futures and forward contracts, like options, are derivative securities, and as such, their prices are determined by arbitrage forces. In this chapter, we've examined that arbitrage relation by presenting the carrying-cost model. We also examined the relationships between forward prices and expected spot prices, futures and forward prices, and futures and option prices. In subsequent chapters, we examine in more detail how the carrying cost model is applied to the pricing of index, debt, and currency futures and how that model can be used to identify arbitrage and investment strategies. In the next chapter, we introduce a new derivative—options on futures contracts.

Web Information: John Maynard Keynes

Biography: http://cepa.newschool.edu/het/profiles/keynes.htm

KEY TERMS

basis	index arbitrage	risk-neural market
carrying-cost model	contango or forwardation	risk-averse market
repo rate	normal market	risk-loving market
cash-and-carry arbitrage	convenience yield	put–call-futures parity
interest rate parity theorem	backwardation	binomial replicating portfolio in terms of futures
covered interest arbitrage	inverted yield	

SELECTED REFERENCES

Aliber, R. "The Interest Rate Parity Theorem: A Reinterpretation." *Journal of Political Economy* (December 1973): 1451–1459.

Agmon, T., and Y. Amihud. "The Forward Exchange Rate and the Prediction of the Future Spot Rate." *Journal of Banking and Finance* (September 1981): 425–437.

Arrow, K. "Futures Markets: Some Theoretical Perspectives." *Journal of Futures Markets* 1 (Summer 1981): 107–116.

Black, F. "The Pricing of Commodity Contracts." *Journal of Financial Economics* 3 (January–February 1976): 167–179.

Branson, W. "The Minimum Covered Interest Differential Needed for International Arbitrage Activity." *Journal of Political Economy* (December 1979): 1029–1034.

Chang, E. "Returns to Speculators and the Theory of Normal Backwardation." *The Journal of Finance* 40 (March 1985): 193–208.

Cornell, B. "Spot Rates, Forward Rates, and Exchange Market Efficiency." *Journal of Financial Economics* (August 1977): 55–65.

Cornell, B., and M. Reinganum. "Forward and Futures Prices: Evidence from the Foreign Exchange Markets." *Journal of Finance* 36 (December 1981): 1035–1045.

Cox, J., J. Ingersoll, and S. Ross. "The Relation Between Forward and Futures Prices." *Journal of Financial Economics* 9 (December 1981): 321–46.

Cox, J., J. Ingersoll, and S. Ross. "The Relation between Forward and Futures Prices." *Journal of Financial Economics* 10 (December 1981).

French, K. "A Comparison of Future and Forward Prices." *Journal of Financial Economics* 12 (November 1983): 311–342.

Gray, R. "The Search for a Risk Premium." *Journal of Political Economy* 69 (June 1961): 250–260.

Grainblatt, M., and N. Jegadeesh. "The Relative Price of Eurodollar Futures and Forward Contracts." *Journal of Finance* 51 (September 1996): 1499–1522.

Hardy, C. *Risk and Risk Bearing*, Chicago: University of Chicago Press, 1940, 67–69.

Hardy, C., and L. Lyon. "The Theory of Hedging." *Journal of Political Economy* 31 (1923): 271–287.

Hartzmark, M. "Return to Individual Traders: Aggregate Results." *Journal of Political Economy* 95 (1987): 1291–1306.

Hicks, J. *Value and Capital,* 2nd ed. Oxford, England: Clarendon, 1939.

Houthakker, H. "Can Speculators Forecast Prices?" *Review of Economics and Statistics* 39 (1957): 143–151.

Huang, R. "An Analysis of Intertemporal Pricing for Forward Foreign Exchange Contracts." *Journal of Finance* 44 (March 1989): 183–194.

Huang, R. "Some Alternative Tests of Forward Exchange Rates as Predictors of Future Spot Rates." *Journal of International Money and Finance* (August 1984): 153–178.

Kaldor, N. "Speculation and Economic Stability." *Review of Economic Studies* 7 (1939–1940).

Keynes, J. *A Treatise on Money*. London: Macmillan, 1930.

Kim, D. T. "Treasury Bond Futures Mechanics and Basis Valuation." In *The Handbook of Fixed Income Securities*, 6th ed., edited by F. Fabozzi. New York: McGraw-Hill, 2001.

Kohlhagen, S. "The Forward Rate as an Unbiased Predictor of the Future Spot Rate." *Columbia Journal of World Business* (Winter 1979): 77–85.

Kolb, R., G. Gay, and J. Jordan. "Futures Prices and Expected Future Spot Prices." *Review of Research in Futures Markets* 2 (1983): 110–123.

Kolers, T., and W. Simpson. "A Comparison of the Forecast Accuracy of the Futures and Forward Markets for Foreign Exchange." *Applied Economics* (July 1987): 961–967.

Papdia, F. "Forward Exchange Rates as Predictors of Future Spot Rates and the Efficiency of the Foreign Exchange Market." *Journal of Banking and Finance* (June 1981): 217–240.

Park, H., and A. Chen. "Differences Between Futures and Forward Prices: A Further Examination of the Marking-to-the-Market Effects." *Journal of Futures Markets* (Spring 1985): 77–85.

Pindyck. R. S. "Inventories and the Short-Run Dynamics of Commodity Prices." *Rand Journal of Economics* 25 (1994): 141–159.

Richard, S., and M. Sundaresan. "A Continuous-Time Model of Forward and Futures Prices in a Multigood Economy." *Journal of Financial Economics* 9 (December 1981): 347–72.

Routledge, B. R., D. J. Seppi, and C. S. Spatt. "Equilibrium Forward Curves for Commodities." *Journal of Finance* 55 (2000) 1297–1338.

Working, H. "The Theory of Price of Storage." *American Economic Review* (December 1949): 1262–80.

PROBLEMS AND QUESTIONS

1. Define the basis and its relationship to the time to expiration. Define normal and inverted markets.

2. Using the carrying-cost model, determine the equilibrium price of a forward contract on a 90-day pure discount bond (PDB) with a face value of $1M and expiring in 180 days. Assume the price on a similar 270-day spot PDB is $954,484, and the annual risk-free rate is 6%. Describe the cash-and-carry arbitrage that arbitrageurs could implement if the contract price is at $985,000 and at $980,000.

3. Given (1) 121-day spot T-Bill trading at 98.318 to yield 5.25%, (2) 30-day risk-free rate of 5.15%, and (3) a T-Bill futures contract with an expiration of T = 30 days.

   a. What is the equilibrium T-bill futures price and its implied futures YTM (annualized)?

   b. Explain what a money market manager planning to invest funds for 30 days should do if the price on the T-bill futures were trading at 98.8. What rate would the manager earn?

c. Explain the arbitrage a money market manager could execute if she were holding a 121-day T-bills and the T-bill futures were trading at 98.

4. In the table following, the IMM Index prices on three T-bill futures contracts with expirations of 91, 182, and 273 days are shown, along with the YTM on a spot 182-day T-bill.

T-Bill Contract	Days to Expiration	IMM Index
March	91	93.764
June	182	93.3092
September	273	91.8607

Spot 182-Day T-bill: YTM = .0625

a. Calculate the actual futures prices and the YTMs (annualized) on the futures.

b. Given the spot 182-day T-bill is trading at an annualized YTM of 6.25%, what is the implied 91-day repo rate?

c. If the carrying-cost model holds, what would be the price of a 91-day spot T-bill?

d. What would be the equilibrium price on the March contract if the actual 91-day annualized repo rate were 4.75%? What strategy would an arbitrageur pursue if the IMM index price were at 93.764?

5. Using the carrying-cost model, determine the equilibrium price of a forward contract on ABC stock expiring in 90 days. Assume the current stock price is $100, the stock will pay dividends worth $0.50 at expiration, and the risk-free rate is 6%. Describe the arbitrage strategy that arbitrageurs could implement if the contract price is at $102 and $98.

6. Using the carrying-cost model, determine the equilibrium price of a forward contract on a barrel of crude oil expiring in 90 days. Assume the current spot price of crude oil is $52/barrel, the risk-free rate is 6% (annual), storage costs are $2/barrel per year, and the total transportation cost from supplier to storage facility and to the destination point on the forward contract is $0.20/barrel. Describe the arbitrage strategy that arbitrageurs could implement if the contract price is at $55. What would the arbitrage strategy be if the contract price were below the equilibrium price?

7. Using the carrying-cost model, determine the equilibrium price of a forward contract on ABC stock expiring in 180 days. Assume the price on a forward contract on ABC stock that expires in 90 days is 96, the forward risk-free rate on 90-day investments or loans made 90 days from the present is 6% (annual), and the stock pays no dividends. Describe the arbitrage strategy that arbitrageurs could implement if the contract price is at $98 and at $96.50.

8. Currently, the spot $/BP exchange rate is $1.42857/BP, the U.S. risk-free rate is 6%, and the British risk-free rate is 6%.

a. What is the equilibrium 1-year forward exchange rate as determined by IRPT?

b. Explain what an arbitrageur would do if the 1-year forward rate were priced at $1.45/BP.

c. Explain what an arbitrageur would do if the 1-year forward rate were priced at $1.40/BP.

9. Determine the conversion factors for the following T-bonds:

a. 4.5% (annual) T-bond maturing in 16 years and 2 months

    b. 4.5% (annual) T-bond maturing in 16 years and 4 months

    c. 8.0% (annual) T-bond maturing in 17 years and 7 months

    d. 8.0% (annual) T-bond maturing in 17 years and 10 months

10. The table following shows the conversion factors and quoted prices for three T-bonds eligible for delivery on a T-bond futures contract. Determine the cheapest-to-deliver bond for a T-bond futures with a contract price of 91.

Bond	Quoted Price	CFA
1	98.50	1.05
2	115.75	1.15
3	125.50	1.35

11. Given the following information related to a T-bond futures contract expiring in 6 months:
    - The best estimate of the cheapest-to-deliver bond on the T-bond futures contract pays an 8% coupon, is currently priced at 108 (clean price), and has a conversion factor of 1.21; the bond's last coupon date was 30 days ago, and its next coupon is 152 days, with the coupon after that coming in the next 183 days.
    - The yield curve is flat at 5%.
    - The best estimate for the expiation on a T-bond futures contract is 180 days.

    Using the carrying-cost model, determine the equilibrium price on the T-bond futures contract.

12. Explain what a contango market and a backwardation market are in terms of the carrying-cost model.

13. Explain the relationship between the expected spot price on an asset ($E(S_T)$) and the futures prices for the following markets in which there are more short hedgers than long hedgers:

    a. Risk averse (Keynes–Hicks normal backwardation market)

    b. Risk loving (Hardy's gambler's market)

    c. Risk neutral

14. Suppose on June 1, the spot price on crude oil was $58 per barrel and the price of September crude oil futures was $59. If the market were risk neutral, what would investors expect the spot price of crude oil to be at the September futures expiration date? If the market were risk averse, would investors expect the September spot price to be greater or less than the futures price?

15. Suppose the forward price on a crude oil contract expiring in 1 year were $48 per barrel. What would this forward contract be worth 6 months later if at that time a new contract on crude oil with 6 months to expiration were priced at $50 and the risk-free rate were 8%? Explain your answer.

16. What would be the value of a forward contract initiated on June 1 to purchase crude oil for $50/barrel on September 1 if the same contract were available on July 1 but with a contract price of $55/barrel? Assume on July 1 there are exactly 2 months to expiration, the risk-free rate is 6%, and the forward contracts are not marked to market. What arbitrage strategy could the holder of the June contract employ if the contract price in July is not correctly priced?

17. Why is the value of a forward contract or futures contract at the time of its origination equal to zero?

18. Determine the equilibrium price of a 1100 index European put expiring in 6 months (T = .5) when a 1100 index European call expiring in 6 months is trading at 72.74, a futures contract on the index expiring in 6 months is trading at 1109, and the annual risk-free rate is 6%. Assume no dividends and no multipliers for the options and futures contracts.

19. Explain what an arbitrageur would do if the index put in Question 18 were trading at 70. Show that the arbitrageur's strategy incurs no liabilities at expiration.

20. Determine the equilibrium price of a stock index futures contract expiring in 3 months (T = .25 per year) when a 1250 stock index European call is trading at 50, a 1250 stock index European put is trading at 40.12, and the annual risk-free rate is 5%. Assume no dividends and multipliers.

21. Explain what an arbitrageur would do if the futures contract in Question 20 were trading at 1240. Show that the arbitrageur's strategy incurs no liabilities at expiration.

22. Determine the equilibrium price of a generic foreign currency (FC) European call option with X = $0.40/FC and with an expiration of 3 months (T = .25 per year) given the price of a 3-month FC European put with X = $0.40/FC is trading at $0.05/FC, the 3-month $/FC forward exchange rate is trading at $0.38/FC, and the annual U.S. risk-free rate is 6%.

23. Explain what arbitrageurs would do if the call in Question 22 were trading at $0.04/FC. Show the strategy is riskless.

24. P.T. Investment Company has constructed a proxy portfolio it uses for identifying arbitrage opportunities. The portfolio is currently worth $12M, is highly correlated with the SP 500, has a ß = 1, and is expected to generate dividends worth $120,000 at end the end of 90 days.

   a. If the spot SP 500 is at 1200, and the annual risk-free rate is at 6%, what would be the equilibrium price on a SP 500 futures contract expiring in 90 days using P.T. Investment Company's proxy portfolio?

   b. Describe the program trading arbitrage strategy the P.T. Investment Company could employ using its proxy portfolio if the SP 500 futures contract is trading at 1213. Show the cash flow that would result when the P.T. Investment Company closes its position at expiration after the spot SP 500 increases 10% and after it decreases 10% (assume perfect divisibility).

   c. Using the put–call parity model with dividends and P.T. Investment Company's proxy portfolio, determine the equilibrium price of an SP 500 European put with an exercise price of 1200, expiration of 90 days, and multiplier of 100 when a comparable SP 500 call (X = 1200, expiration = 90 days, multiplier = 100) is trading at 50, and the annual risk-free rate is 6%.

   d. Describe the arbitrage strategy the P.T. Investment Company could employ using its proxy portfolio if the price of the 1200 SP 500 put described in c was trading at 40 (assume perfect divisibility). Determine the initial cash flow, and show there are no liabilities at expiration given a 10% increase in the spot index and a 10% decrease.

   e. Show that if the carrying-costs model holds, the equilibrium price of the 1200 put is the same using either the put–call parity model or the put–call-futures parity model.

    f. Describe the arbitrage strategy the P.T. Investments Company could employ using futures contracts instead of its proxy portfolio if the price of the 1200 SP 500 put was trading at 40.

APPENDIX 11A FORMAL RELATION BETWEEN FUTURES AND FORWARD PRICES

If short-term interest rates are constant over time, prices of futures and forward contracts on the same underlying asset will be equal. Accordingly, if this assumption is reasonable, the carrying-cost pricing relationships that we've specified for forward contracts can be used to price futures contracts; if the assumption is not reasonable, then the previous pricing models for forward contracts can be used only to approximate the price of a futures contract.

    To see the relationship between futures and forward prices, assume that both futures and forward contracts exist on the same asset and that each contract has 2 days to expiration. If the price on the futures contract with 2 days to expiration (f_2) exceeds the price on the forward contract (F_0), an arbitrageur could profit by taking a long position in the forward contract and a short position in $(1 + R)^{-(1/365)}$ futures contracts. At the end of the day, the futures contract would be marked to market, and the arbitrageur could (1) close the $(1 + R)^{-(1/365)}$ futures position at the end-of-the-day settlement price of f_1, and (2) take a new short position in a futures contract with only one day to expiration and with a contract price of f_1. If there is a profit (π) from closing the first position $(\pi = (f_2 - f_1)(1 + R)^{-(1/365)} > 0)$, the arbitrageur would invest the excess to expiration (1 day), and if there is a loss, she would borrow funds to finance the shortfall. If the funds are invested (borrowed) at the same rate as the previous day's rate, then at expiration (1 day later), the arbitrageur's profit (loss) would be

$$\pi = (f_2 - f_1)(1 + R)^{-(1/365)}(1 + R)^{(1/365)}$$
$$\pi = f_2 - f_1$$

At expiration (the next day), the arbitrageur would purchase the underlying asset on the forward contract at F_0 and then sell the asset on the futures contract at f_1 for a profit or loss equal to $f_1 - F_0$. The arbitrageur's total profit at expiration (π_T) would therefore be

$$\pi_T = (f_2 - f_1) + (f_1 - F_0)$$
$$\pi_T = f_2 - F_0$$

    Thus, if interest rates are constant over time (both days), then the preceding strategy would yield the arbitrageur a riskless cash flow of $f_2 - F_0$. In theory, arbitrageurs would exploit this opportunity by going short in the futures contract and long in the forward contract, readjusting each day when the futures contract is marked to market until the arbitrage profit is zero. Arbitrageurs would do this until $f_t = F_0$. Hence, if short-term interest rates are constant over time, in equilibrium, futures and forward prices will be equal. (The reader is encouraged to investigate the opposite arbitrage strategy in which $f_2 < F_0$.)[1]

---

[1] Several empirical studies have examined the differences between futures and forward prices. The results, though, are mixed. Cornell and Reinganum (1981), for example, found no significant difference between futures and forward prices on currencies, whereas French (1983) found significant difference between futures and forward prices on silver.

PROBLEMS AND QUESTIONS

1. Suppose the price on a futures contract on ABC stock that is expiring in 2 days is $100, and the price on a forward contract on ABC stock that is expiring in 2 days is $97.

   a. Show how an arbitrageur could earn a certain $3 profit if short-term interest rate were constant. Assume the current and next day rates are 6% (annual).

   b. What would be the market impact on the prices as a result of the arbitrageur's actions?

   c. Comment on the conditions necessary for futures and forward prices to be equal.

APPENDIX 11B   BOPM IN TERMS OF FUTURES POSITIONS

If a European option's underlying asset also has a futures contract, then the OPM can be specified in terms of the futures position. Moreover, if the carrying-cost model holds, and the futures contract and the option contract expire at the same time, then the OPM specified in terms of futures will be equal to the OPM defined in terms of the underlying spot asset. To illustrate this relation, we revisit two pricing examples we presented in Chapters 6 and 7 using the single-period BOPM: the pricing of an S & P 500 call index option and the generic foreign currency call option.

Single-Period BOPM for Index Option in Terms of Index Futures

In Chapter 6, we showed how the equilibrium price of the index call is equal to the value of a replicating portfolio consisting of an investment in a proxy portfolio (consisting of H_0^* hypothetical shares of the spot index times the sport index) partially financed by borrowing B_0^* dollars. In the single-period BOPM example presented in Section 6.4 ($S_0 = 1250$, $u = 1.1$, $d = .95$, $n = 1$, $r_f = 1.05$, $D_1 = 12.50$), the equilibrium call price on a 1250 S&P 500 index call was equal to 71.43 ($B_0^* S_0 - B_0^* = .6(1250) - 678.57 = 71.43$). If the market price of the index option in that example did not equal 71.43, then an arbitrage opportunity would exist by taking a position in the option and an opposite position in the replicating portfolio. In such a case, a long position in the replicating portfolio would be equivalent to investing $750 = ($H_0^* S_0^* = (.6)(1250)$) in a proxy index portfolio and borrowing $B_0^* = \$678.57$, with the proxy portfolio consisting of stocks expected to go ex-dividend at the end of the period and with the value of those dividends expected to be $7.50(= (.01)(\$750)$; see Exhibit 6.4-1).

With futures contracts on the index, the price of an index option can alternatively be defined in terms of a replicating portfolio formed with the index futures. To illustrate, assume the S&P 500 futures contract expires at the end of the period and that the price on the futures contract is equal to its carrying cost value of 1300:

$$f_0 = S_0(1 + R)^T - D_T$$
$$f_0 = S_0 r_f - D_1$$
$$f_0 = 1250(1.05) - 12.50 = 1,300$$

As shown in Exhibit 11.B-1, the two possible values at expiration from a long position in the futures contract are 62.50 and -125 (ignore multiplier), and the possible call values are $C_u^x = Max[(1375 - 12.50) - 1250, 0] = 112.50$ and $C_d^x = Max[(1187.50 - 12.50) - 1250, 0] = 0$. The two possible call values can be replicated by forming a portfolio consisting of $H_0^f = .6$ long futures contracts at $f_0 = 1300$ and a debt of $B_0^* = -71.43$

EXHIBIT 11.B-1   Single-Period BOPM for Index Call and Futures

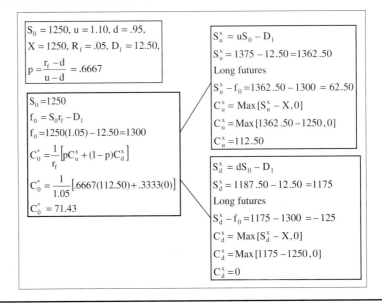

(where the negative sign means an investment of \$71.43). Formally, to construct this replicating portfolio with futures requires

$$H_0^f(uS_0 - D_1 - f_0) - B_0^* r_f = C_u^x \qquad (11B-1)$$

$$H_0^f(dS_0 - D_1 - f_0) - B_0^* r_f = C_d^x$$

The H_0^{f*} and B_0^* that satisfy Equation (11.B-1) are

$$H_0^{f*} = \frac{C_u^x - C_d^x}{S_0(u - d)} \qquad (11B-2)$$

$$B_0^* = \frac{C_u^x(dS_0 - D_1 - f_0) - C_d^x(uS_0 - D_1 - f_0)}{r_f S_0(u - d)} \qquad (11B-3)$$

In terms of the example

$$H_0^{f*} = \frac{112.50 - 0}{1,250(1.1 - .95)} = .6$$

$$B_0^* = \frac{(112.50)[(1187.50 - 12.50) - 1300] - (0)[(1375 - 12.50) - 1300]}{(1.05)(1250)(1.1 - .95)} = 71.43$$

Given the replicating portfolio, the equilibrium index call price is found by setting the index call price equal to the current value of the replicating portfolio. (In doing this, recall the futures contract does not have an initial value.) Thus, the equilibrium price on the index call is

$$C_0^* = H_0^{f*} V_0^f - B_0^*$$

$$C_0^* = H_0^{f*}(0) - B_0^*$$

$$C_0^* = -B_0^* \qquad (11B-4)$$

or on substituting Equation (11.B-3) for B_0^*

$$C_0^* = -B_0^* = -\frac{C_u^x(dS_0 - D_1 - f_0) - C_d^x(uS_0 - D_1 - f_0)}{r_f S_0(u - d)}$$

$$r_f C_0^* = C_u^x\left[\frac{f_0 - (dS_0 - D_1)}{S_0(u - d)}\right] + C_d^x\left[\frac{(uS_0 - D_1) - f_0}{S_0(u - d)}\right]$$

$$C_0^* = \frac{1}{r_f}[pC_u^x + (1 - p)C_d^x]$$ (11B-5)

where:

$$p = \frac{f_0 - (dS_0 - D_1)}{S_0(u - d)}$$

In terms of the example

$$C_0^* = -B_0^* = -(-71.43) = 71.43$$

or

$$C_0^* = \frac{1}{r_f}[pC_u^x + (1 - p)C_d^x]$$

$$C_0^* = \frac{1}{1.05}[.6667(112.50) + .3333(0)] = 71.43$$

where:

$$p = \frac{f_0 - (dS_0 - D_1)}{S_0(u - d)} = \frac{1300 - [(.95)1250 - 12.50]}{1250(1.1 - .95)} = .6667$$

Note that the equilibrium call price of 71.43 is the same price we obtained in Chapter 6 with the replicating portfolio specified in terms of a spot index position. The equality between the preceding BOPM with futures and the spot BOPM derived in Chapter 6 can be proved by substituting the carrying cost equation $(S_0 r_f - D_1)$ for f_0 in Equation (11.B-5). That is

$$p = \frac{S_0 r_f - D_1 - dS_0 - D_1}{S_0(u - d)}$$

$$p = \frac{S_0[r_f - d]}{S_0(u - d)}$$

$$p = \frac{r_f - d}{u - d}$$

Thus, if the carrying-cost model holds, and the futures contract expires at the same time as the call, then Equation (11.B-5) is the same equation we obtained earlier for the index call using the spot index.

BOPM Arbitrage Strategy Using Index Futures

In Section 6.4, we showed that when the market price of the index call did not equal 71.43, an arbitrage opportunity could be exploited by taking a position in the index call and opposite position in the replicating portfolio. The long position in the replicating portfolio, in turn, was formed by investing $H_0^* S_0 = (.6)(1250) = \$750$ in a proxy portfolio, with stocks in the portfolio going ex-dividend at the end of the period and with dividends

TABLE 11.B-1 Single-Period BOPM Arbitrage Strategy Using Futures: $C_0^m > C_0^*$

Position	Strategy
Short Call	Sell call at $C_0^m = 79.40$.
Futures	Take a Long Position in $H_0^{f*} = .6$ Index futures contracts at $f_0 = 1300$.
Investment	Invest $B_0^* = 71.43$ in a riskless security.
Investment	Invest excess of $C_0^m - C_0^* = 79.40 - 71.43 = 7.97$ in a riskless security.

	End-of-the-Period Cash Flow	
Position	$C_u^x = 112.50, S_u^x = f_T = 1362.50$	$C_d^x = 0, S_u^x = f_T = 1175$
Short Call	$= -112.50$	$= 0$
Futures	$.6(1362.50 - 1300) = 37.50$	$.6(1175 - 1300) = -75$
Investment	$71.43(1.05) = 75$	$71.43(1.05) = 75$
Investment	$(7.97)1.05 = 8.37$	$(7.97)1.05 = 8.37$
Cash Flow	8.37	8.37

worth 7.50 and by borrowing $B_0^* = \$678.57$. Instead of using a proxy portfolio, the replicating portfolio can alternatively be formed with index futures contracts. For example, if $C_0^m = 79.40$, then as shown in Table 11.B-1, an arbitrageur could earn a risk-free profit of 8.37 by

1. Selling the call at $C_0^m = 79.40$

2. Taking a long position in $H_0^{f*} = .6$ index futures contracts at $f_0 = 1300$

3. Investing 71.43 $(-B_0^*)$ plus 7.97 $(C_0^m - C_0^* = 79.40 - 71.43 = 7.97)$ in a risk-free security.

The arbitrage cash flow of 8.37 at expiration is the same arbitrage flow earned using the spot position and a proxy portfolio (see Section 6.4). Using futures or forward contracts instead of a spot position, though, simplifies the arbitrage strategy.

Single-Period Foreign Currency BOPM Priced in Terms of Currency Futures

As a second example of how to form a replicating portfolio in terms of futures contracts, consider the example we presented in Chapter 7 in which we priced a foreign currency call. In that example, we assumed the spot exchange rate was at $1.50/FC, the u and d parameter values were 1.1 and .95, respectively, the foreign risk-free rate for the period was 3%, and the periodic U.S. rate was 5%. Using the single-period BOPM, we determined the price on a $1.50 European call option on a foreign currency (FC) to be $C_0^* = \$0.0667/FC$. To price this same FC call option using a foreign currency future, assume there is a futures contract on the FC that expires at the end of the period and that the price on the futures contract is determined by the interest rate parity model. As shown in Exhibit 11.B-2, with $E_0 = \$1.50/FC$, $r_{US} = (1 + R_{US}) = 1.05$, and $r_F = (1 + R_F) = 1.03$, the current price on the futures contract (or the futures exchange rate) would be $f_0 = \$1.529126/FC$, and the two possible values at expiration from a long position in the futures contract would be

EXHIBIT 11.B-2 Single-Period BOPM With Currency Futures

$E_0 = \$1.50$, $u = 1.10$, $d = .95$,
$X = \$1.50$, $R_{US} = .05$, $R_F = .03$,
$p = \dfrac{r_{US} - r_F d}{r_F(u - d)} = .462783$

$E_0 = \$1.50$

$f_0 = E_0\left[\dfrac{r_{US}}{r_F}\right] = \$1.50\left[\dfrac{1.05}{1.03}\right] = \$1.529126$

$C_0^* = \dfrac{1}{r_{US}}\left[pC_u + (1-p)C_d\right]$

$C_0^* = \dfrac{1}{1.05}\left[.462783(\$0.15) + .53722(0)\right] = \$0.066$

$E_u = uE_0 = \$1.65$
Long futures
$E_u - f_0 = \$1.65 - \$1.529126 = \$0.121$
$C_u = Max[uE_0 - X, 0]$
$C_u = Max[\$1.65 - \$1.50, 0] = \$0.15$
$C_u = \$0.315$

$E_d = dE_0 = \$1.425$
Long futures
$E_d - f_0 = \$1.425 - \$1.529126 = -\$0.104$
$C_d = Max[dE_0 - X, 0]$
$C_d = Max[\$1.425 - \$1.50, 0]$
$C_d = 0$

$0.121 and $-$0.104. The possible call values of $C_u = Max[\$1.65 - \$1.50, 0] = \$0.15/FC$ and $C_d = Max[\$1.425 - \$1.50, 0] = 0$ can be replicated with a FC futures position and debt of B_0 dollars by forming a replicating portfolio consisting of $H_0^f = .6667$ long futures contracts at $f_0 = \$1.529126/FC$ and a debt of $B_0^* = -\$0.066$ (where the negative sign means an investment of 0.066). Specifically, to construct this replicating portfolio with futures requires

$$H_0^f(uE_0 - f_0) - B_0^* r_{US} = C_u \qquad (11B\text{-}6)$$
$$H_0^f(dE_0 - f_0) - B_0^* r_{US} = C_d$$

The H_0^{f*} and B_0^* that satisfy Equation (11.B-6) are

$$H_0^{f*} = \frac{C_u - C_d}{E_0(u - d)} \qquad (11B\text{-}7)$$

$$B_0^* = \frac{C_u(dE_0 - f_0) - C_d(uE_0 - f_0)}{r_{US}E_0(u - d)} \qquad (11B\text{-}8)$$

$$H_0^{f*} = \frac{\$0.15 - 0}{\$1.50(1.1 - .95)} = .6667$$

$$B_0^* = \frac{(\$0.15)[\$1.425 - \$1.529126] - (0)[\$1.65 - \$1.529126]}{(1.05)(\$1.50)(1.1 - .95)} = -\$0.066.$$

The equilibrium price on the FC call in terms of the replicating futures position is

$$C_0^* = H_0^{f*} V_0^f - B_0^*$$
$$C_0^* = H_0^{f*}(0) - B_0^*$$
$$C_0^* = -B_0^*$$
$$C_0^* = -(-\$0.066) = .066 \qquad (11B\text{-}9)$$

or

$$C_0^* = \frac{1}{r_{US}}[pC_u + (1-p)C_d] \tag{11B-10}$$

$$C_0^* = \frac{1}{1.05}\left[.46278(\$0.15) + .53722(0)\right] = \$0.66$$

where:

$$p = \frac{f_0 - dE_0}{E_0(u-d)} = \frac{r_{us} - r_f d}{r_F(u-d)}$$

$$p = \frac{\$1.529126 - (.95)(\$1.50)}{\$1.50(1.1 - .95)} = \frac{1.05 - (1.03)(.95)}{1.03(1.1 - .95)} = .46278$$

The equilibrium call price of $0.066 is the same price we obtained in Chapter 7 with the foreign currency BOPM specified in terms of a spot exchange rate position.

BOPM Arbitrage Strategy Using Currency Futures

In the preceding case, if the market price of the call is not equal to $0.066, then risk-free profit can be earned using an arbitrage strategy with a futures position instead of a spot. For example, if $C_0^m = \$0.075$, then as shown in Table 11.B-2, an arbitrageur could earn an arbitrage cash flow of $0.0094 at expiration by

1. Selling the call at $C_0^m = \$.075$
2. Taking a long position in $H_0^{f^*} = .6667$ currency futures contracts at $f_0 = \$1.529126$
3. Investing $0.066 $(-B_0^*)$ plus $0.009 $(C_0^m - C_0^* = \$0.075 - \$0.066 = \$0.009)$ in a risk-free security.

The arbitrage cash flow of $0.0094/FC is the same arbitrage flow earned using the spot FC position (see Section 7.2). Using futures or forward contracts instead of a spot

TABLE 11.B-2   Single-Period BOPM Arbitrage Strategy Using Futures: $C_0^m > C_0^*$

Position	Strategy
Short Call	Sell call at $C_0^m = \$.075$.
Futures	Take a Long Position in $H_0^{f^*} = .6667$ FC futures contracts at $f_0 = \$1.529126/FC$.
Investment	Invest $B_0^* = \$0.066$ in a riskless security.
Investment	Invest excess of $C_0^m - C_0^* = \$0.075 - \$0.066 = \$0.009$ in a riskless security.

End-of-the-Period Cash Flow

Position	$C_u = \$0.15, E_T = f_T = \$1.65/FC$	$C_d = 0, E_T = f_T = \$1.425/FC$
Short Call	$= -\$0.15$	$= 0$
Futures	$.6667(\$1.65 - \$1.529126) = \$0.0806$	$.6667(\$1.425 - \$1.529126) = -\$0.0694$
Investment	$\$0.066(1.05) = \$0.0693$	$\$0.066(1.05) = \$0.0693$
Investment	$(\$0.075 - \$0.066)1.05 = \$0.00945$	$(\$.075 - \$.066)1.05 = \$0.00945$
Cash Flow	$\$.0094$	$\$.0094$

position, though, simplifies the arbitrage strategy. Recall, with mispriced foreign currency options, the arbitrage strategy using the spot foreign currency market entails combining the option position with positions in the spot currency market and the spot domestic and foreign money markets. Thus, by using futures, arbitrageurs avoid having to use both of these markets.

PROBLEMS AND QUESTIONS

1. Given
    *   Spot exchange rate $= E_0 = \$0.40/FC$
    *   Period U.S. risk-free rate $= R_{US} = .02$
    *   Period FC risk-free rate $= R_F = .025$
    *   Proportional increase in spot exchange rate $= u = 1.05$
    *   Proportional decrease in spot exchange rate $= d = 1/1.05$
    *   Number of periods to expiration on European FC options contract $= n = 2$
    *   Number of periods to expiration on a FC futures contract $= n_f = 2$

    Questions:

    a. Assuming a two-period binomial framework, show with a binomial tree the equilibrium \$/FC futures exchange rate at each node using the Interest Rate Parity Theorem.

    b. Show the BOPM's equilibrium price as defined by a replicating portfolio formed with futures contracts at each node for a FC European call with an exercise price of \$0.40/FC.

2. Describe the replicating portfolio that includes FC futures contracts that an arbitrageur would use if the FC call in Question 1 were trading at \$0.01/FC. What would be the arbitrageur's cash flow in Period 1 if the spot \$/FC exchange rate were \$0.42/FC and the FC call were trading at \$0.03/FC (assume IRPT holds)? Explain the adjustments an arbitrageur would need to make to avoid a loss and the cash flow at expiration that would result after making the adjustments.

CHAPTER 12

OPTIONS ON FUTURES CONTRACTS

12.1 INTRODUCTION

Option contracts on stocks, debt securities, foreign currency, and indices are sometimes referred to as *spot options* or options on actuals. This reference is to distinguish them from *options on futures* contracts (also called *futures options* and *commodity options*). A futures option gives the holder the right to take a position in a futures contract. In this chapter, we examine this popular derivative security by examining the characteristics and market for this option, the speculative and hedging strategies formed with theses derivatives, and the pricing of futures options in terms of the BOPM and B–S model.

12.2 CHARACTERISTICS

A call option on a futures contract gives the holder the right to take a long position in the underlying futures contract when she exercises and requires the writer to take the corresponding short position in the futures. On exercise, the holder of a futures call option in effect takes a long position in the futures contract at the *current* futures price, and the writer takes the short position and pays the holder via the clearinghouse the difference between the current futures price and the exercise price. In contrast, a put option on a futures option entitles the holder to take a short futures position and the writer the long position. Thus, whenever the put holder exercises, he in effect takes a short futures position at the current futures price, and the writer takes the long position and pays the holder via the clearinghouse the difference between the exercise price and the current futures price. Like all option positions, the futures option buyer pays an option premium for the right to exercise, and the writer, in turn, receives a credit when he sells the option and is subject to initial and maintenance margin requirements on the option position.

In practice, when the holder of a futures call option exercises, the futures clearinghouse will establish for the exercising option holder a long futures position at the futures price equal to the exercise price and a short futures position for the assigned writer. Once this is done, margins on both positions will be required, and the position will be marked to market at the current settlement price on the futures. When the positions are marked to market, the exercising call holder's margin account on his long position will be equal to the difference between the futures price and the exercise price, $f_t - X$, whereas the assigned writer will have to deposit funds or near monies worth $f_t - X$ to satisfy her maintenance margin on her short futures position. Thus, when a futures call is exercised, the holder takes a long position at f_t with a margin account worth $f_t - X$; if he were to immediately close the futures, he would receive cash worth $f_t - X$ from the clearinghouse. The assigned writer, in turn, is assigned a short position at f_t and must deposit $f_t - X$ to meet her margin. If the futures option is a put, the same procedure applies except that holder takes a short position at f_t (when the exercised position is marked to market), with a margin account worth $X - f_t$, and the writer is assigned a long position at f_t and must deposit $X - f_t$ to meet her margin.

12.3 MARKET FOR FUTURES OPTIONS

The current U.S. market for futures options began in 1982 when the Commodity Futures Trading Commission (CFTC) initiated a pilot program in which it allowed each futures exchange to offer one option on one of its futures contracts. In 1987, the CFTC gave the exchanges permanent authority to offer futures options. Currently, the most popular futures options are the options on the financial futures: SP 500, T-bond (CBT), T-Note (CBT), Eurodollar deposit (CMM), and the major foreign currencies. In addition to options on financial futures contracts, futures options also are available on gold, precious metals, livestock, food and fiber, petroleum, and grains and oil.[1] Many of these contracts have expiration months, position limits, and contract specifications similar to their underlying futures contracts. Some futures options contracts, though, do not have the same expiration date as their underlying futures contract.

Web Information:

For market information and prices on futures options go to www.wsj.com/free, www.cme.com, and www.cbt.com.

12.3.1 Interest Rate Options

It should be noted that although many different types of interest rate options are available on both the OTC market and the organized futures and options exchanges in Chicago, London, Singapore, and other major cities, the most heavily traded interest rate options on the U.S. exchanges are the CME's and CBT's futures options on T-bonds, T-notes, and Eurodollar contracts. The CBOE, AMEX, and PHLX have offered options on actual Treasury securities and Eurodollar deposits. These spot options, however, proved to be less popular than futures options and have been delisted. A number of non-U.S. exchanges, though, do list options on actual debt securities, typically government securities. For example, many debt options listed on the European Options Exchange are spot options. In addition to exchange-traded options, there is also a large OTC market in debt and interest-sensitive securities and products in the United States and a growing OTC market outside the United States. Currently, security regulations in the United States prohibit off-exchange trading in options on futures. All U.S. OTC options are therefore options on actuals.

12.4 DIFFERENCES IN FUTURES AND SPOT OPTIONS

As we show, the pricing models for spot and futures options show that the two instruments are equivalent if the options and the futures contracts expire at the same time, the carrying-costs model holds, and the options are European. (In contrast, spot and futures

---

[1] Before 1936, the U.S. futures exchanges offered futures options for a number of years. In 1936, though, the instruments were banned when U.S. security regulations were tightened following the 1929 stock market crash. Futures options have been available on foreign exchanges for a number of years.

options will differ to the extent that these conditions do not hold.) There are, though, several factors that serve to differentiate the two contracts. First, because most futures contracts are relatively more liquid than their corresponding spot security, it is usually easier to form hedging or arbitrage strategies with futures options than with spot options. Second, futures options often are easier to exercise than their corresponding spot. For example, to exercise an option on a T-bond or foreign currency futures contract, one simply assumes the futures position; exercising a spot T-bond or a foreign currency option, though, requires an actual purchase or delivery. Finally, most futures options are traded on the same exchange as their underlying futures contract, whereas most spot options are traded on exchanges different from their underlying securities. This, in turn, makes it easier for futures options traders to implement arbitrage and hedging strategies than spot options traders.

12.5   FUNDAMENTAL FUTURES OPTIONS STRATEGIES

12.5.1   Stock Index Futures Options

Some of the characteristics of futures options can be seen by examining the profit relationships for the fundamental strategies formed with these options. Exhibit 12.5-1 shows the profit and futures price relationship at expiration for four fundamental option strategies using call and put options on the S&P 500 futures contract. Both the call and the put have an exercise price of 1250 times a $250 multiple and a premium of 10 times $250, and it is assumed the futures options expire at the same time as the futures contract.

Exhibit 12.5-1.a shows the profit and futures price relationship at expiration for the call purchase strategy. The numbers reflect a case in which the holder exercises the call at expiration, if profitable, when the spot price is equal to the price on the expiring futures contract. For example, at $S_T = f_T = 1270$, the holder of the 1250 futures calls would receive a cash flow of $5,000 and a profit of $2,500. That is, the holder, on exercising, would assume a long position in the expiring S&P 500 futures at 1270, which she subsequently would close by taking an offsetting short futures position at 1270, and the holder would receive $5,000 from the assigned writer $((f_T - X)\$250 = (1270 - 1250)\$250 = \$5,000)$.

EXHIBIT 12.5-1   Fundamental Futures Option Strategies

a. Long Position on S&P 500 Futures Call Option

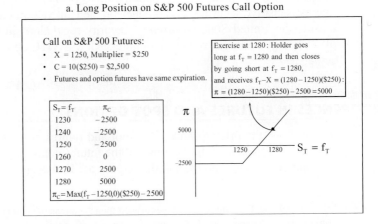

continued

EXHIBIT 12.5-1   Continued

b. Short Position on S&P 500 Futures Call Option

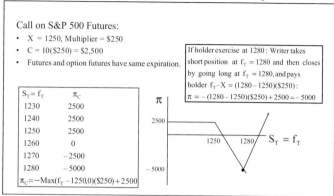

c. Long Position on S&P 500 Futures Put Option

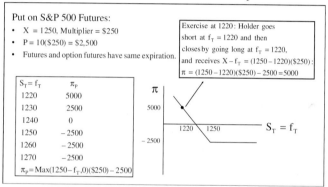

d. Short Position on S&P 500 Futures Put Option

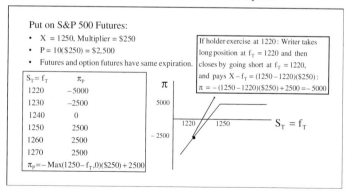

The opposite profit and futures price relation is attained for a naked call write position (Exhibit 12.5-1.b). In this case, if the index is at 1250 or less, the writer of a 1250 SP 500 futures call would earn the premium of \$2,500, and if $f_T > 250$, he, on assignment, would have to pay the difference between f_T and X and would have to assume a short position at f_T, which he would close with an offsetting long position.

Exhibits 12.5-1.c and 12.5-1.d show the long and short put positions. In the case of a put purchase, if the holder exercises when f_T is less than X, then she will receive $X - f_T$ and a short futures position that she can offset. For example, if $S_T = f_T = 1230$ at expiration, then the put holder, on exercising, would receive \$5,000 ((1250 – 1230)(\$250)) from the put writer for a net profit of \$2,500. Her short position then would be closed by taking a long position in the S&P 500 futures contract. The put writer's position, of course, would be the opposite.

12.5.2 Treasury-Bill Futures Options

Exhibit 12.5-2.a shows the profit and futures price relationship at expiration for a long call position on T-bill futures. The call has an exercise price equal to 90 (index) or $X = \$975,000$, is priced at \$1,250 (quote of 5 times a \$250 multiple: (5)(\$250) = \$1,250), and it is assumed the T-bill futures option expires at the same time as the underlying T-bill futures contract. The numbers shown in the exhibit reflect a case in which the holder exercises the call at expiration, if profitable, when the spot price is equal to the price on the expiring futures contract. For example, at $S_T = f_T = \$980,000$, the holder of the 90 T-bill futures call would receive a cash flow of \$5,000 for a profit of \$3,750 (= \$5,000 – \$1,250). That is, on exercising, the holder would assume a long position in the expiring T-bill futures priced at \$980,000 and a futures margin account worth \$5,000 ((f_T – X) = \$980,000 – \$975,000) = \$5,000). Given we are at expiration, the holder would therefore receive \$5,000 from the expired futures position, leaving her with a profit of \$3,750. The opposite profit and futures price relation is attained for a naked call write position. In this case, if the T-bill futures is at \$975,000 or less, the writer of the futures call would earn the premium of \$1,250, and if $f_T > \$975,000$, he, on the exercise by the holder, would assume a short position at f_T and would have to pay f_T – X to bring the margin on his expiring short position into balance.

Exhibit 12.5-2.b shows a long put position on the 90 T-bill futures purchased at \$1,250. In the case of a put purchase, if the holder exercises when f_T is less than X, then he will have a margin account worth $X - f_T$ on an expiring short futures position. For example, if $S_T = f_T = \$970,000$ at expiration, then the put holder, on exercising, would receive \$5,000 from the expiring short futures ($X - f_T = \$975,000 - \$970,000$), yielding a profit from her futures option of \$3,750. The put writer's position, of course, would be the opposite.

It should be noted that although the technicalities on exercising futures options are cumbersome, the profits from closing a futures option at expiration still are equal to the maximum of either zero or the difference in f_T – X (for calls) or $X - f_T$ (for puts) minus the option premium. Moreover, if the futures option and the underlying futures contract expire at the same time, as we assumed previously, then the expiring futures price will be equal to the spot price, $f_T = S_T$, and the futures option can be viewed simply as an option on the underlying spot security, with the option having a cash settlement clause.

12.5.3 Hedging With Futures Options

Hedging positions with futures locks in a future price and therefore eliminates not only the costs of unfavorable price movements but also the benefits from favorable movements. However, with futures or spot options, a hedger can obtain protection against adverse price movement while still realizing benefits if prices move favorably. To illustrate, consider again the crude oil and wheat hedging examples presented in Chapter 10.

EXHIBIT 12.5-2 Fundamental Futures Options Strategies-T-Bill Futures Options

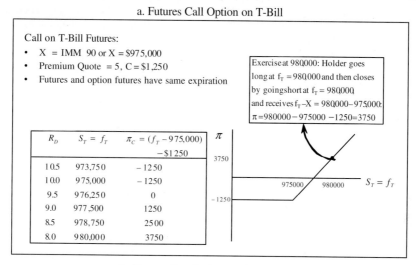

a. Futures Call Option on T-Bill

Call on T-Bill Futures:
- X = IMM 90 or X = \$975,000
- Premium Quote = 5, C = \$1,250
- Futures and option futures have same expiration

Exercise at 980000: Holder goes long at f_T = 980,000 and then closes by going short at f_T = 980,000 and receives $f_T - X$ = 980000 – 975,000: π = 980000 – 975000 – 1250 = 3750

R_D	$S_T = f_T$	$\pi_C = (f_T - 975,000)$ $- \$1250$
10.5	973,750	– 1250
10.0	975,000	– 1250
9.5	976,250	0
9.0	977,500	1250
8.5	978,750	2500
8.0	980,000	3750

b. Futures Put Option on T-Bill

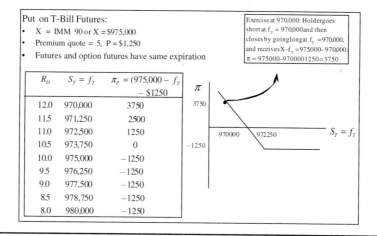

Put on T-Bill Futures:
- X = IMM 90 or X = \$975,000
- Premium quote = 5, P = \$1,250
- Futures and option futures have same expiration

Exercise at 970,000: Holder goes short at f_T = 970,000 and then closes by going long at f_T = 970,000, and receives $X - f_T$ = 975000 – 970,000: π = 975000 – 970000 1250 = 3750

R_D	$S_T = f_T$	$\pi_P = (975,000 - f_T)$ $- \$1250$
12.0	970,000	3750
11.5	971,250	2500
11.0	972,500	1250
10.5	973,750	0
10.0	975,000	– 1250
9.5	976,250	– 1250
9.0	977,500	– 1250
8.5	978,750	– 1250
8.0	980,000	– 1250

12.5.3.1 Long Hedge Example

In Chapter 10, we presented the case of an oil refinery that in December locked in the cost of purchasing 100,000 barrels of crude oil in February by a taking long position in 100 New York Mercantile Exchange (NYM)–listed February crude oil contracts (size = 1,000 barrels) at \$50/barrel. Suppose the company's treasury department, though, was confident that crude oil prices would be declining in the future but still wanted some protection if prices were to increase. For the costs of 100 NYM futures crude oil call options expiring in February, the company could obtain this objective of capping the costs of purchasing the crude oil in February while still benefiting if crude oil costs decrease. In this case, suppose there is a crude oil futures call that expires in February at the same time as the crude oil futures contract (the NYM actually offers a March contract and not a February one). Also, suppose that the option's exercise price is \$50, the contract size on the underlying crude oil futures contract is 1,000 barrels, and the cost of the option is \$2.00 per barrel. The refining company's futures call option hedge position is shown in Table 12.5-1. As shown

TABLE 12.5-1   Hedging a Crude Oil Purchase With a Call Option on a Crude Oil Futures

(1) $f_T = S_T$	(2) Cost of Crude Oil $S_T(100,000)$	(3) Cash Flow from Futures Call $(100)Max[f_T - \$50,0](1,000)$	(4) Hedged Costs Col (2) – Col (3)
\$35	\$3,500,000	0	\$3,500,000
40	\$4,000,000	0	\$4,000,000
45	\$4,500,000	0	\$4,500,000
50	\$5,000,000	0	\$5,000,000
55	\$5,500,000	\$500,000	\$5,000,000
60	\$6,000,000	\$1,000,000	\$5,000,000
65	\$6,500,000	\$1,500,000	\$5,000,000

Cost of the Futures Calls $= 100(\$2.00)(1,000) = \$200,000.$

TABLE 12.5-2   Hedging a Wheat Sale With a Put Option on a Wheat Futures

(1) $f_T = S_T$	(2) Revenue From Wheat Sale: $S_T(5,000)$	(3) Cash Flow From Futures Put $(1)Max[\$2.40 - f_T, 0](5,000)$	(4) Hedged Costs Col (2) – Col (3)
\$2.00	\$10,000	\$2,000	\$12,000
2.10	\$10,500	\$1,500	\$12,000
2.20	\$11,000	\$1,000	\$12,000
2.30	\$11,500	\$500	\$12,000
2.40	\$12,000	0	\$12,000
2.50	\$12,500	0	\$12,500
2.60	\$13,000	0	\$13,000
2.70	\$13,500	0	\$13,500

Cost of the Futures Puts $= (1)(\$0.10)(5,000) = \$500.$

in the table, for the \$200,000 cost of the options, the futures call option position serves to cap the refinery's cost of crude at \$5,000,000 while allowing them to realized lower costs if crude prices are less than \$50. For example, at \$40, the company would pay \$4,000,000 for the 100,000 barrels of crude, with its loss on the option limited to the \$200,000 costs of the futures calls. On the other hand, if crude oil prices are greater than \$50, the greater crude oil costs are offset by greater cash flows from the futures call options. For example, if crude prices were at \$60, the \$6,000,000 cost of 100,000 barrels would be offset by \$1,000,000 cash flow from the call options.

12.5.3.2   Short Hedge Example

In Chapter 10, we also presented the case of a wheat farmer who in June went short in one September wheat futures contract (contract size is 5,000 bushels) priced at \$2.40/bu in June to lock in the selling price on his estimated 5,000 bushels of wheat expected to be harvested in September. Suppose the farmer expected wheat prices to increase but wanted protections against an unexpected price decrease. Accordingly the farmer could obtain downside protection by purchasing a put option on a wheat futures contract. Table 12.5-2 shows this put insurance strategy in which the farmer purchases one September put option on a wheat futures contract with the option expiring at the same time as the futures, X = \$2.40, size = 5,000 bushels, and P = \$0.10. As shown, if wheat prices decrease, the farmer's lower revenues are offset by greater cash flows form the put. In contrast, if wheat prices increase, the farmer realizes greater revenues, and his losses are limited to the cost of the premium.

Note that there is no hedging risk in either of the hedging cases. With many futures options having expirations different from the expiration on the underlying futures contract, hedging with futures options often involves timing risk.

12.6 FUTURES OPTIONS PRICING RELATIONS

12.6.1 Arbitrage Relations

Many of the option price relations and the arbitrage strategies governing option prices that were delineated in Chapter 4 also apply to futures options. For example, the price on an American futures call option at time t must be at least equal to the call's intrinsic value as defined by the price on the futures contract at time t (f_t):

$$C_t^a = Max[f_t - X, 0]$$

If this condition does not hold, an arbitrageur could buy the call, exercise, and close the futures position. For example, if the 1250 call on the S&P 500 futures contract in the previous example were trading at 9 when the futures contract was trading at 1260, an arbitrageur could (1) buy the call at 9, (2) exercise the call to obtain $f_t - X = 1260 - 1250 = 10$ from the assigned writer plus a long position in the S&P 500 futures contract priced 1260, and (3) close the long futures position by taking an offsetting short position at 1260. Doing this, an arbitrageur would realize a riskless profit of $1 (or $250 per contract).

Some of the arbitrage strategies described in Chapter 4, such as the price relationships between spot options with different exercise prices and times to expirations, are similar for futures options. Differences between spot and futures options do exist, however. For example, the minimum price of a European futures call is obtained by comparing a long futures position to a long position in the futures option and an investment in a riskless bond with a face value of $f_0 - X$. This contrasts with a spot option in which the long position in the spot security is compared to a call option and a bond with face value equal to X.

12.6.2 Put–Call Parity Model for Futures Options

The put–call parity model for futures options can be derived from a conversion strategy consisting of a long position in a futures contract with a contract price of f_0 and a synthetic short futures position formed by purchasing a European put and selling a European call on the futures contract with an exercise price of X. As shown in Table 12.6-1, if the options and the futures contract expire at the same time, then the conversion would be worth $X - f_0$ at expiration, regardless of the price on the futures contract. Because the conversion yields a riskless return, in equilibrium, its value would be equal to the present value of a

TABLE 12.6-1 Put-Call-Futures Parity Conversion: $\{+f_0, +P_0^e, -C_0^e\}$

Position	Investment	$f_T < X$	$f_T = X$	$f_T > X$
		Expiration Cash Flow		
Long Futures	0	$f_T - f_0$	$f_T - f_0$	$f_T - f_0$
Long Put	P_0^e	$X - f_T$	0	0
Short Call	$-C_0^e$	0	0	$-(f_T - X)$
	$P_0^e - C_0^e$	$X - f_0$	$X - f_0$	$X - f_0$

riskless bond with a face value of $X - f_0$:

$$P_0^e - C_0^e = (X - f_0)(1 + R_f)^{-T} \qquad (12.6\text{-}1)$$

Note that Equation (12.6-1) is the same as the put–call-futures parity condition defined in Chapter 11 [Equation (11.8-1)]. Thus, the put–call parity defining the equilibrium relation for European futures options and the put–call-futures parity are the same provided the European spot options, European futures options, and futures contract expire at the same time. This equivalence should not be too surprising because the values of the futures contracts, spot options, and futures options all derive their values from the same underlying security. It also should be noted that if the carrying-cost model holds and the futures and options expire at the same time, then Equation (12.6-1) equals the equation for the put–call parity model for an equivalent European spot option.

12.7   SINGLE-PERIOD BOPM FOR FUTURES OPTIONS

If the carrying-costs model holds, and the option and futures contracts expire at the same time, then the price of a futures option also will be the same as the price of the spot option.[2] However, a number of futures options do not have the same expirations as their corresponding futures contracts, and as a result their equilibrium values will differ from those on the spot option. In this section, we examine a single-period BOPM for pricing futures options in which the expirations on the two derivatives differ.

The equilibrium price of a European call or put option on a generic futures contract is equal to the value of a replicating portfolio consisting of futures and debt (or investment) positions. To see this, assume a single period to expiration in which the possible values on the underlying spot asset are either uS_0 or dS_0. The relationship between the futures and spot price, as defined by the carrying-cost model, is

$$f_0 = S_0 r^{n_f} + K n_f + TRC - D_T \qquad (12.7\text{-}1)$$

where:

n_f = number of periods to expiration on the futures contract

$r = 1 +$ periodic risk-free rate

K = storage costs per period for holding the underlying asset

TRC = transportation cost of transporting the underlying asset from the storage

facility to the destination point on futures contract or vice versa at expiration

D_T = Value of benefits (e.g., dividends or coupon interest) on the underlying asset

assumed to be realized at expiration

Using the carrying-cost model, the two possible futures prices at the end of the period (f_u and f_d) are

---

[2] In Appendix 11B, we derived the BOPM in terms of futures contracts and showed that under certain conditions the BOPM defined by futures and the BOPM defined by spot positions are the same. This section draws from the article by Johnson, Zaben, and Gandard, *Journal of Financial Education* (forthcoming).

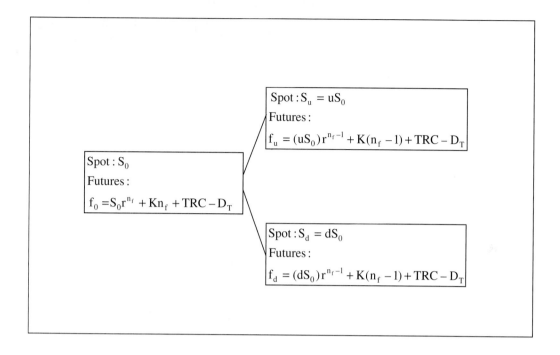

Given the possible prices on the futures contract, the equilibrium price on a European call or put option on the futures contract is found by constructing a replicating portfolio with cash flows that match the futures call option's possible values of C_u and C_d or the futures put option's possible values of P_u and P_d:

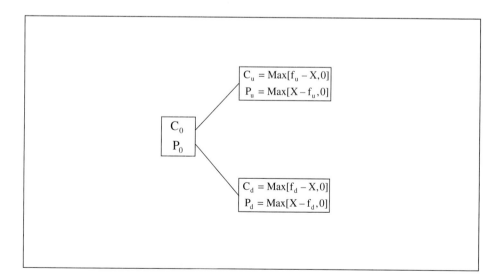

The replicating futures call portfolio (RP$_C$) is formed by taking a position in H_0^f futures contracts at f_0 and borrowing or investing B_0 dollars. Similarly, the replicating futures put portfolio (RP$_P$) is formed by taking a position in H_0^f futures contracts at f_0 and investing I_0 dollars. The possible values of the portfolios are

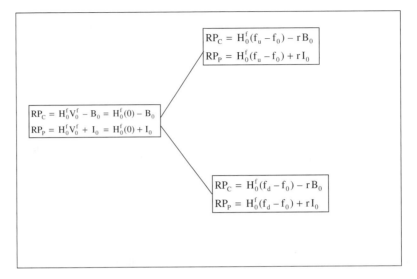

For the futures call, the equilibrium price is obtained by solving first for the H_0^{f*} and B_0^* that make the two possible replicating portfolio values at expiration equal to the possible call values and then setting the price of the call equal to the value of the replicating portfolio defined in terms of H_0^{f*} and B_0^*. That is

$$H_0^f(f_u - f_0) - B_0 r = C_u \qquad (12.7\text{-}2)$$

$$H_0^f(f_d - f_0) - B_0 r = C_d$$

$$H_0^{f*} = \frac{C_u - C_d}{f_u - f_d} \qquad (12.7\text{-}3)$$

$$B_0^* = \frac{C_u(f_d - f_0) - C_d(f_u - f_0)}{r(f_u - f_f)} \qquad (12.7\text{-}4)$$

$$C_0^* = H_0^{f*} V_0^f - B_0^*$$

$$C_0^* = H_0^{f*}(0) - B_0^*$$

$$C_0^* = -B_0^*$$

$$C_0^* = -B_0^* = -\frac{C_u(f_d - f_0) - C_d(f_u - f_0)}{r(f_u - f_d)} \qquad (12.7\text{-}5)$$

Note that the futures contract has no initial value ($V_0^f = 0$).

Given $f_d < f_0$, the bracket expression in Equation (12.7-5) is negative, implying B_0^* and therefore C_0^*, are positive and also implying H_0^{f*} is positive. Thus, if the futures call is overpriced, the arbitrage portfolio would require an investment of B_0^* dollars in a risk-free security and a long position in H_0^{f*} futures contracts.

For the futures put, the equilibrium price is obtain in a similar way by solving for the H_0^{f*} and I_0^* that make two possible replicating portfolio values at expiration equal to their two possible put values and then setting the price of the put equal to the value of the replicating portfolio defined in terms of H_0^{f*} and I_0^*:

$$H_0^f(f_u - f_0) + I_0 r = P_u \qquad (12.7\text{-}6)$$

$$H_0^f(f_d - f_0) + I_0 r = P_d$$

$$H_0^{f^*} = \frac{P_u - P_d}{f_u - f_d} \tag{12.7-7}$$

$$I_0^* = -\frac{[P_u(f_d - f_0) - P_d(f_u - f_0)]}{r(f_u - f_f)} \tag{12.7-8}$$

$$P_0^* = H_0^{f^*} V_0^f + I_0^*$$

$$P_0^* = H_0^{f^*}(0) + I_0^*$$

$$P_0^* = I_0^*$$

$$P_0^* = I_0^* = -\frac{P_u(f_d - f_0) - P_d(f_u - f_0)}{r(f_u - f_d)} \tag{12.7-9}$$

Given $f_d < f_0$, I_0^* and therefore P_0^* are positive, and $H_0^{f^*}$ is negative. Thus, the arbitrage portfolio for an overpriced put requires a short position in the futures contract and an investment in the risk-free security.

Both the equilibrium call price Equation (12.7-5) and put Equation (12.7-9) can alternatively be expressed in terms of risk-neutral probabilities (p) by substituting the carrying-cost equation for f_u, f_d, and f_0 (see Appendix 12A for the algebraic derivation). For financial futures, the resulting call and put equations are

$$C_0^* = \frac{1}{r}[pC_u + (1 - p)C_d] \tag{12.7-10}$$

$$P_0^* = \frac{1}{r}[pP_u + (1 - p)P_d]$$

where

$$p = \frac{r - d}{u - d}$$

$$C_u = Max[f_u - X, 0]$$

$$C_d = Max[f_d - X, 0]$$

$$P_u = Max[X - f_u, 0]$$

$$P_d = Max[X - f_d, 0]$$

12.7.1 Points on BOPM for Futures Options

Several points concerning the binomial pricing of futures options should be noted:

1. For call and put options on a currency futures contract, the equation for p includes the foreign interest rate ($r_F = (1 + R_F)$; see Appendix 12A for an algebraic derivation):

$$p = \frac{r_{US} - r_F d}{r_F[u - d]}$$

2. In the case of an index or currency option in which the stock index or currency is adjusted to reflect a continuous dividend yield or a continuous compounded foreign risk-free rate, the futures prices is

$$f_0 = S_0 e^{(R^A - \psi)n_f \Delta t}$$

where
ψ = Annual dividend yield or foreign risk-free rate

R^A = Annual risk-free rate (U.S. rate for currency option)

Δt = Length of binomial steps as a proportion of a year

n_f = number of periods to expiration

In this case, the equation for p includes the annual dividend or foreign risk-free yield. Defined in terms of annualized parameters, p is

$$p = \frac{e^{(R^A - \psi)\Delta t} - d}{u - d}$$

3. In the case of commodity futures options, the equilibrium option price Equation (12.7-10) includes a storage cost adjustment factor:

$$\frac{[C_u - C_d]K}{S_0 r^{n_f}} \quad \text{and} \quad \frac{[P_u - P_d]K}{S_0 r^{n_f}}$$

For call options, the adjustment is positive given $C_u > C_d$ (implying a storage cost); for puts, the adjustment is negative given $P_u < P_d$ (implying a negative storage cost or a short position in the commodity). In cases in which shorting the commodity is not applicable, the adjustment factor is not definable (see Appendix 12A for derivation).

12.7.2 BOPM Defined in Terms of the Futures Prices' Up and Down Parameters

The binomial model for options on financial futures is defined previously in terms of the up and down parameters for the underlying spot prices. It is more common, though, to defined the up and down parameters in terms of the futures prices, u^f and d^f. Specifically, if the carrying-cost model holds, then u^f and d^f are given as

$$u^f = \frac{f_u}{f_0} = \frac{uS_0 e^{(R^A - \psi)(n_f - 1)\Delta t}}{S_0 e^{(R^A - \psi)n_f \Delta t}} = \frac{u}{e^{(R^A - \psi)\Delta t}}$$

$$u = u^f e^{(R^A - \psi)\Delta t} \tag{12.7-11}$$

$$d^f = \frac{f_d}{f_0} = \frac{dS_0 e^{(R^A - \psi)(n_f - 1)\Delta t}}{S_0 e^{(R^A - \psi)n_f \Delta t}} = \frac{d}{e^{(R^A - \psi)\Delta t}}$$

$$d = d^f e^{(R^A - \psi)\Delta t} \tag{12.7-12}$$

The formulas for estimating the up and down parameters as defined in terms of futures price (u^f and d^f) are

$$u^f = e^{\sigma_f^A \sqrt{\Delta t} + \mu_f^A \Delta t} = e^{\sigma_S^A \sqrt{\Delta t} + (\mu_S^A - (R^A - \psi)\Delta t)} \tag{12.7-13}$$

$$d^f = e^{-\sigma_f^A \sqrt{\Delta t} + \mu_f^A \Delta t} = e^{-\sigma_S^A \sqrt{\Delta t} + (\mu_S^A - (R^A - \psi)\Delta t)} \tag{12.7-14}$$

where:

σ_f^A and μ_f^A = annualized volatility and mean on the futures price's logarithmic return

σ_S^A and μ_S^A = annualized volatility and mean on the spot price's logarithmic return.

The relationship between the volatility and mean on the futures price's logarithmic return and the spot's volatility and mean, in turn, is

$$\sigma_f^A = \sigma_S^A \tag{12.7-15}$$

$$\mu_f^A = \mu_S^A - (R^A - \psi) \tag{12.7-16}$$

The algebraic derivation of Equations (12.7-15) and (12.7-16) is presented in Appendix 12A.

Substituting Equations (12.7-11) and (12.7-12) into the equation for p, we obtain the equations for the futures call and put options defined in terms of the futures up and down parameters:

$$p = \frac{e^{(R^A - \psi)\Delta t} - d}{u - d}$$

$$p^f = \frac{e^{(R^A - \psi)\Delta t} - d^f e^{(R^A - \psi)\Delta t}}{u^f e^{(R^A - \psi)\Delta t} - d^f e^{(R^A - \psi)\Delta t}}$$

$$p^f = \frac{1 - d^f}{u^f - d^f}$$

and

$$C_0^* = \frac{1}{e^{R^A \Delta t}} [p^f C_u + (1 - p^f) C_d]$$

$$P_0^* = \frac{1}{e^{R^A \Delta t}} [p^f P_u + (1 - p^f) P_d]$$

The p^f term is the risk-neutral probability defined in terms of the up and down parameters for the futures price instead of the spot price. Note that if the carrying cost model holds, then p^f is equal to p.

Note that because u^f and d^f include the risk-free rate and the dividend yield, p^f is determined by both parameters, at least for discrete cases in which there are a small number of periods to expiration. For a multiple-period model that is defined by a large number of subperiods, the impact of the risk-free rate and dividend yield on the option price is small. Specifically, as the number of subperiods increases, or equivalently, as the length of the binomial period $\Delta t\ (= t/n)$ becomes smaller, the second term in the exponent of Equations (12.7-13) and (12.7-14)—a term that includes not only the mean but also the risk-free rate and dividend yield—goes to zero faster than the square root terms. As a result, for a large number of subperiods, the equations for u^f and d^f simplify to

$$u^f = e^{\sigma_S^A \sqrt{\Delta t}} = u$$

$$d^f = e^{-\sigma_S^A \sqrt{\Delta t}} = d$$

and therefore, all three terms—p^f, u^f, and d^f—are all absent of the risk-free rate and dividend yield. Thus, for the case of large n, the only input that needs to be estimated to determine the price of an option on a financial futures contract is the underlying futures' spot variability: σ_S.

In summary, for financial futures, the single-period binomial equations defining the equilibrium prices for call and put options on a futures contract are similar in form to the BOPM for the spot securities except for the C_u and C_d and P_u and P_d, which are defined in terms of the contract prices on the futures instead of the spot prices. If the futures contract and the futures option expire at the same time, then the possible prices on the futures contract at expiration will be equal to the possible spot prices ($f_u = S_u$ and $f_d = S_d$); in this case, C_u and C_d and P_u and P_d will be the same for the spot option and the futures option. Thus, if the futures contract and the option have the same expiration, the carrying-cost model holds, and the futures and spot options are both European, then futures and spot options will be equivalent.

12.7.3 Single-Period BOPM Example: Pricing a Call on a Stock Index Futures Given a Continuous Dividend Yield

In pricing the futures call on the S&P 500 futures, suppose the dividends on the underlying spot index approximate a continuous payment. In this case, we can price the option and futures using a continuous dividend-adjusted spot index. To see this, assume the following:

- The S&P 500 futures option expires in 90 days
- The S&P 500 futures contract expires at the end of 180 days
- The current spot index is $S_0 = 1250$
- The estimated annualized volatility and mean of the spot index's logarithmic return are $\sigma_S^A = .3$ and $\mu_S^A = 0$
- The annual risk-free rate is $R_f = .06$
- The futures price is determined by the carrying-cost model
- ψ = continuous annual dividend yield = 4%

If we price the futures call option using a single-period model, then the length of the binomial period in years is $\Delta t = 90/365$ and $u = 1.160637$, $d = .861596$, $r_f = e^{(.06)(90/365)}$, and $p = .479358$:

$$u = e^{\sigma^A \sqrt{\Delta t}} = e^{.3\sqrt{90/365}} = 1.160637$$

$$d = 1/u = .861596$$

$$p = \frac{e^{(R^A - \psi)\Delta t} - d}{u - d} = \frac{e^{(.06 - .04)(90/365)} - .861596}{1.160637 - .861596} = .479358$$

Using the carrying-cost model, the current futures price on the index expiring in 180 days is 1262.39, and as shown in Exhibit 12.7-1(a), the possible prices on the contract next period are $f_u = 1457.97$ and $f_d = 1082.32$, and the possible values of the futures call option expiring at the end of Period 1 are 207.97 and zero. Using the single-period BOPM, the equilibrium price of the call option on the index futures contract is 98.23:

$$C_0^* = -B_0^* = -\frac{C_u(f_d - f_0) - C_d(f_u - f_0)}{r_f(f_u - f_f)}$$

$$C_0^* = -\frac{(207.97)(1082.32 - 1262.39) - (0)(1457.97 - 1262.39)}{e^{(.06)(90/365)}(1457.97 - 1082.32)} = 98.23$$

or

$$C_0^* = \frac{1}{r_f}[pC_u + (1 - p)C_d]$$

$$C_0^* = \frac{1}{e^{(.06)(90/365)}}[(.479358)(207.97) + (.520642)(0)] = 98.23$$

As always, if the market price of the futures call option does not equal its equilibrium value, then an arbitrage opportunity will exist by taking a position in the call and an opposite position in the replicating portfolio.

Note that the index futures alternatively could be priced in terms of the up and down parameters of the futures prices [Equations (12.7-13), (12.7-14), (12.7-15), and (12.7-16)]. In this case, $u^f = 1.154928$, $d^f = .857357$, and $p^f = p = .479358$ (see Exhibit 12.7-1(b):

$$u^f = e^{\sigma_S^A \sqrt{\Delta t} + (\mu_S^A - (R^A - \psi)\Delta t)} = e^{.3\sqrt{90/365} + (0 - (.06 - .04))(90/365)} = 1.154927$$

$$d^f = e^{-\sigma_S^A \sqrt{\Delta t} + (\mu_S^A - (R^A - \psi)\Delta t)} = e^{-.3\sqrt{90/365} + (0 - (.06 - .04))(90/365)} = .857357$$

EXHIBIT 12.7-1   Binomial Pricing of Index Futures Call With Continuous-Dividend Yield

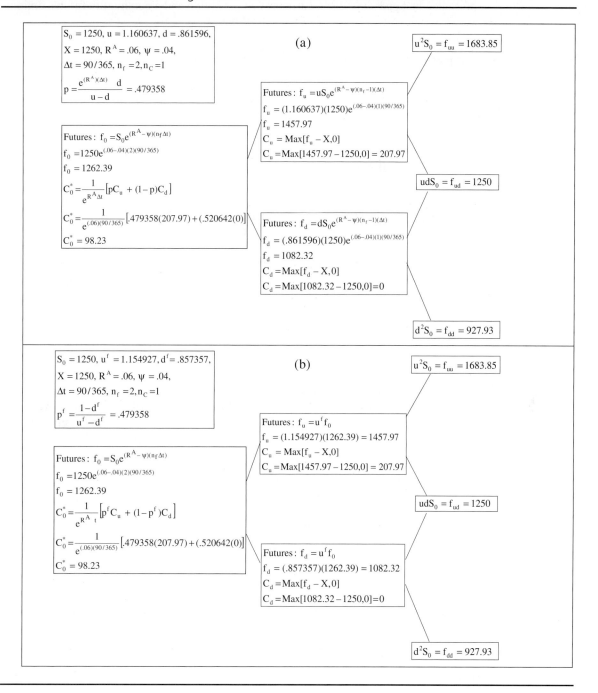

$$p^f = \frac{1 - d^f}{u^f - d^f} = \frac{1 - .857357}{1.154927 - .857357} = .479358$$

$$C_0^* = \frac{1}{r_f}[p^f C_u + (1 - p^f)C_d]$$

$$C_0^* = \frac{1}{e^{(.06)(90/365)}}[(.479358)(207.97) + (.52064)(0)] = 98.23$$

Two additional examples of pricing futures options using a single-period model are presented in Appendix 12B: a currency futures option and a commodity futures option.

12.8 MULTIPLE-PERIOD BOPM FOR FUTURES OPTIONS

The single-period binomial cases help to illustrate how arbitrage strategies using option and futures contracts determine the price of a futures option. The practical application of the binomial model to pricing futures options, though, requires a multiple-period model.

12.8.1 Pricing S&P 500 Index Futures Call and Put Options

To illustrate the application of the multiple-period binomial model to the pricing of futures options, consider the pricing of European and American call and put options on an S&P 500 index futures, each with $X = 1250$ and $T = 90$ days, using a three-period binomial model. In pricing the options, suppose the following:

- The current S&P 500 is at $S_0 = 1250$
- The spot index's estimated volatility and mean are $\sigma_S^A = .3$ and $\mu_S^A = 0$
- The annual continuous-dividend yield generated from the stocks comprising the index portfolio is $\psi = .04$
- $R^A = 6\%$
- The S&P 500 futures contract expires in 120 days

The length of the binomial period in years is $\Delta t = t/n = (90/365)/3 = 0.082192$, with the call and put option expiring in $(n_{Option})\Delta t = (3)(0.082192) = .246575$ years and the futures expiring in $n_f \Delta t = (4)(0.082192) = .328767$ years. Using the up and down parameters on the futures contract, the risk-neutral probability is $p^f = .488064$:

$$u^f = e^{\sigma_S^A \sqrt{\Delta t} + (\mu_S^A - (R^A - \psi)\Delta t} = e^{.3\sqrt{.082192} + (0 - (.06 - .04))(.082192)} = 1.088024$$

$$d^f = e^{-\sigma_S^A \sqrt{\Delta t} + (\mu_S^A - (R^A - \psi)\Delta t} = e^{-.3\sqrt{.082192} + (0 - (.06 - .04))(.082192)} = .91608$$

$$p^f = \frac{1 - d^f}{u^f - d^f} = \frac{1 - .91608}{1.088024 - .91608} = .488064$$

Exhibit 12.8-1 shows the resulting binomial tree for the underlying S&P 500 spot index, S&P 500 index futures, European and American futures call options, and European and American futures put options. For this three-period option case, the binomial model prices the European call at 83.73 and the American call at 84.01 and the European put at 75.61 and American put at 78.85. There is an early exercise advantage for the American call at the upper node in Period 2 and an early exercise advantage for the American futures put at the lower node in Period 2. As a result, both the American futures put and call options are price slightly higher than their European counterparts. Using the "Binomial Option Pricing Model" Excel program, the prices of the European and American S&P 500 futures calls are 77.04 and 77.30, respectively, for n = 30 subperiods; for the European and American futures put, the prices are 68.91 and 69.11, respectively, for n = 30 (see table at the bottom of Exhibit 12.8-1).

Exhibit 12.8-2 shows the binomial tree for an S&P 500 index futures expiring at the same time as the futures options (90 days) along with the prices on European and

EXHIBIT 12.8-1 Multiple-Period Binomial Pricing of Index Futures Call and Put Options

$X = 1250$, Option Expiration $= 90$ Days, and Futures Expiration $= 120$ Days

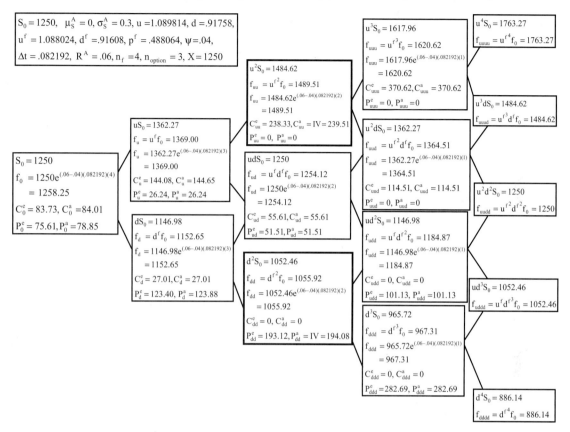

n	European Call	American Call	European Put	American Put
3	83.73	84.01	75.61	78.85
30	77.04	77.30	68.91	69.11

American futures call and put options and European and American spot index call and put options. The spot S&P 500 index options have the same exercise price of 1250 and expiration of 90 days as do the futures options. The table at the bottom of Exhibit 12.8-2 shows the binomial prices of the spot and futures options for 30 subperiods. As expected, in the case of European options, the futures and spot option prices are identical. This, in turn, confirms an earlier point that if the futures contract, the spot option contract, and the futures option contract all expire at the same time and the options are European, then the futures and spot options are identical. As such, the price on the futures option is equal to the price on the spot option. Price differences can be observed, however, between the American futures and American spot options. In the three-period case of the call options, the price of the American futures call is 89.89, whereas the price of the American spot call is 82.62, the same as the European spot option price. The price difference can be explained by the fact that the futures prices are higher than the spot

EXHIBIT 12.8-2 Multiple-Period Binomial Pricing of Index Futures and Spot Call and Put Options With Futures and Options Expiring at the Same Time

X = 1250, Option Expiration = 90 Days, and Futures Expiration = 90 Days

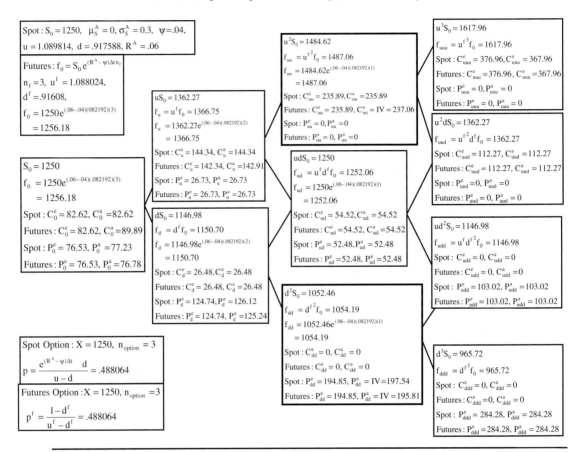

n	European Futures Call	American Futures Call	European Futures Put	American Futures Put
3	82.62	89.89	76.53	76.78
30	75.79	76.04	69.70	69.93

n	European Spot Call	American Spot Call	European Spot Put	American Spot Put
3	82.62	82.62	76.53	77.23
30	75.79	75.79	69.70	70.41

prices prior to maturity and also the presence of an early exercise advantage on the futures option that occurs at the upper node in Period 2. Similarly, an early exercise advantage also exists for the American futures put (lower node in Period 2) but not for the American spot put. The American future put price, though, is still less than the American spot because of the futures prices exceeding the spot prices prior to maturity. As a result, the price of the American futures put in this example is less than the price of the American spot put.

In general, if futures markets are normal, with futures prices greater than spot prices prior to maturity, then the futures prices will be consistently greater than the corresponding spot prices. As a result, an American futures call will, in turn, be worth more than its corresponding American spot call. Conversely, if the market is normal, then an American futures put will be priced less than the corresponding American spot put. As noted, this is the case in our example. Specially, with the risk-free rate of 6% exceeding the dividend yield of 4%, the futures market for the index is normal with the S&P 500 futures prices exceeding the corresponding spot prices at all nodes prior to maturity. Accordingly, the binomial model prices the American futures call (76.04 in the 30-period example) more than the American spot call (75.79) and the American futures put price (69.93) less than the American spot put (70.41). If the futures market were inverted, with the futures price consistently less than the spot price prior to maturity, then the opposite will occur: The American futures call will be less than the American spot call, and the American futures put will be priced more than the American spot put. An example of an inverted S&P 500 futures market is presented in Exhibit 12.8-3. The example is the same as the preceding case (Exhibit 12.8-2) except that the risk-free rate is assumed to be at 4% instead of 6%, and the dividend yield is assumed to be 6% instead of 4%. With the dividend yield exceeding the risk-free rate, the convenience yield on the futures exceeds the carrying cost, resulting in an equilibrium futures price (1,243.85) that is less than the spot (1250). As shown in the exhibit, the S&P 500 futures prices are less than the corresponding spot prices at all nodes prior to maturity. The binomial price of the American futures call (76.70 in the three-period example) is less than the American spot call (77.23), and the American futures put price (82.80 in the three-period case) exceeds the American spot put (82.62).

It should be noted that the difference between American futures options and American spot options holds for both cases in which the futures contract expires later than the option and when the futures and option expire at the same time.

12.8.2 Pricing Foreign Currency Futures Call and Put Options

As a second example of pricing futures options with a multiple-period binomial model, consider the pricing of call and put options on the British pound (BP) futures contract each with X = $1.60/BP and T = 90 days using a three-period binomial model. In pricing the options, suppose the following:

- The spot $/BP exchange rate is at $E_0 = \$1.60/BP$
- The estimated spot exchange rate's volatility and mean are $\sigma_S^A = .3$ and $\mu_S^A = 0$
- The annual U.S. risk-free rate is $R_{US} = .06$
- The annual risk-free rate paid on BP is $R_F = .04$
- Futures contract on the BP expires in 120 days
- Carrying-cost model holds
- Options on BP futures contract expire in 90 days

Like the S&P 500 example, the length of the binomial period in years is $\Delta t = t/n = (90/365)/3 = 0.082192$, with the call and put option expiring in $(n_{Option})\Delta t = (3)(0.082192) = .246575$ years and the BP futures expiring in $n_f \Delta t = (4)(0.082192) =$

EXHIBIT 12.8-3 Multiple-Period Binomial Pricing of Index Futures and Spot Options for an Inverted Futures Market

$$X = 1250, \text{ Option Expiration} = 90 \text{ Days, and Futures Expiration} = 90 \text{ Days}$$

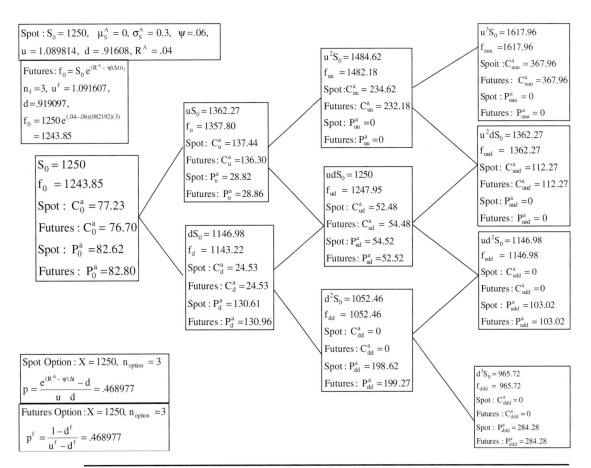

Spot : $S_0 = 1250$, $\mu_S^A = 0$, $\sigma_S^A = 0.3$, $\psi = .06$,
$u = 1.089814$, $d = .91608$, $R^A = .04$

Futures: $f_0 = S_0\, e^{(R^A - \psi)\Delta t\, n_f}$
$n_f = 3$, $u^f = 1.091607$,
$d = .919097$,
$f_0 = 1250\, e^{(.04-.06)(.082192)(3)}$
$\quad = 1243.85$

$S_0 = 1250$
$f_0 = 1243.85$
Spot : $C_0^a = 77.23$
Futures : $C_0^a = 76.70$
Spot : $P_0^a = 82.62$
Futures : $P_0^a = 82.80$

$uS_0 = 1362.27$
$f_u = 1357.80$
Spot: $C_u^a = 137.44$
Futures: $C_u^a = 136.30$
Spot: $P_u^a = 28.82$
Futures: $P_u^a = 28.86$

$dS_0 = 1146.98$
$f_d = 1143.22$
Spot : $C_d^a = 24.53$
Futures : $C_d^a = 24.53$
Spot : $P_d^a = 130.61$
Futures : $P_d^a = 130.96$

$u^2S_0 = 1484.62$
$f_{uu} = 1482.18$
Spot: $C_{uu}^a = 234.62$
Futures: $C_{uu}^a = 232.18$
Spot: $P_{uu}^a = 0$
Futures: $P_{uu}^a = 0$

$udS_0 = 1250$
$f_{ud} = 1247.95$
Spot: $C_{ud}^a = 52.48$
Futures: $C_{ud}^a = 54.48$
Spot: $P_{ud}^a = 54.52$
Futures: $P_{ud}^a = 52.52$

$d^2S_0 = 1052.46$
$f_{dd} = 1052.46$
Spot: $C_{dd}^a = 0$
Futures: $C_{dd}^a = 0$
Spot: $P_{dd}^a = 198.62$
Futures: $P_{dd}^a = 199.27$

$u^3S_0 = 1617.96$
$f_{uuu} = 1617.96$
Spoit :$C_{uuu}^a = 367.96$
Futures: $C_{uuu}^a = 367.96$
Spot : $P_{uuu}^a = 0$
Futures : $P_{uuu}^a = 0$

$u^2dS_0 = 1362.27$
$f_{uud} = 1362.27$
Spot: $C_{uud}^a = 112.27$
Futures: $C_{uud}^a = 112.27$
Spot: $P_{uud}^a = 0$
Futures: $P_{uud}^a = 0$

$ud^2S_0 = 1146.98$
$f_{udd} = 1146.98$
Spot : $C_{udd}^a = 0$
Futures : $C_{udd}^a = 0$
Spot : $P_{udd}^a = 103.02$
Futures : $P_{udd}^a = 103.02$

$d^3S_0 = 965.72$
$f_{ddd} = 965.72$
Spot : $C_{ddd}^a = 0$
Futures : $C_{ddd}^a = 0$
Spot : $P_{ddd}^a = 284.28$
Futures : $P_{ddd}^a = 284.28$

Spot Option : $X = 1250$, $n_{option} = 3$
$$p = \frac{e^{(R^A - \psi)\Delta t} - d}{u - d} = .468977$$

Futures Option : $X = 1250$, $n_{option} = 3$
$$p^f = \frac{1 - d^f}{u^f - d^f} = .468977$$

n	American Futures Call	American Spot Call	American Futures Put	American Spot Put
3	76.70	77.23	82.80	82.62
30	69.84	70.42	75.95	75.78

.328767 years. The up and down parameters on the futures contract are $u^f = 1.088024$ and $d^f = 0.91608$, and the risk-neutral probability is $p^f = .488064$:

$$u^f = e^{\sigma_S^A \sqrt{\Delta t} + (\mu_S^A - (R_{US} - R_F))\Delta t} = e^{.3\sqrt{.082192} + (0 - (.06 - .04))(.082192)} = 1.088024$$

$$d^f = e^{-\sigma_S^A \sqrt{\Delta t} + (\mu_S^A - (R_{US} - R_F))\Delta t} = e^{-.3\sqrt{.082192} + (0 - (.06 - .04))(.082192)} = .91608$$

$$p^f = \frac{1 - d^f}{u^f - d^f} = \frac{1 - .91608}{1.088024 - .91608} = .488064$$

EXHIBIT 12.8-4   Multiple-Period Binomial Pricing of British Pound Futures Call and Put Options

$X = \$1.60$, Option Expiration $= 90$ Days, and Futures Expiration $= 120$ Days

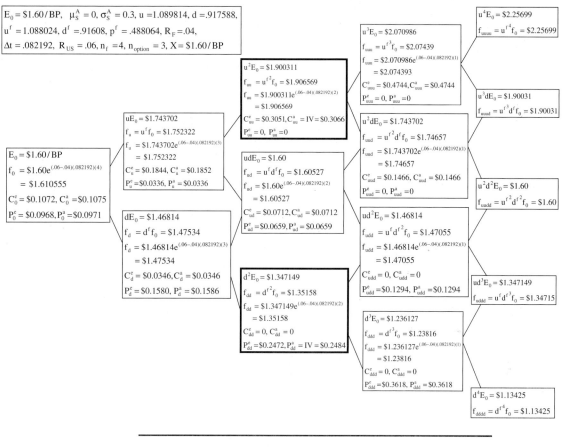

n	European Call	American Call	European Put	American Put
3	$0.1072	$0.1075	$0.0968	$0.0971
30	$0.0986	$0.09893	$0.0882	$0.0885

The binomial tree for the underlying spot $/BP exchange rate, BP futures contract, European and American futures calls, and European and American futures puts are shown in Exhibit 12.8-4; the table at the bottom of the exhibit shows the binomial prices on the futures options for 30 subperiods. In the three-period option case, the binomial model prices the European call at $0.1072 and the European put at $0.0968. As shown in the exhibit, there is an early exercise advantage for the American futures call at the upper node in Period 2, and an early exercise advantage for the American futures put at the lower node in Period 2. As a result, both the American futures put and call options are price slightly higher than their European counterparts. Using the "Binomial Option Pricing Model" Excel program, the prices of the European and American BP futures calls are $0.0986 and $0.09893, respectively, for n = 30 subperiods; for the European and American futures puts, the prices are $0.0882 and $0.0885, respectively, for n = 30.

12.9 VALUING INTEREST RATE FUTURES OPTIONS WITH A BINOMIAL INTEREST RATE TREE

In Chapter 7, we examined how the binomial interest rate model can be used to price spot options on bonds. The binomial interest rate tree can be used to price interest rate futures options such as those on T-bills and T-Bonds.

12.9.1   Valuing T-Bill Futures and Spot Options With a Binomial Tree

Exhibit 12.9-1 shows a two-period binomial tree for an annualized risk-free spot rate (S), and the corresponding prices on a T-bill (B) with a maturity of .25 years and face value of $100, and also a futures contract (f) on the T-bill, with the futures expiring at the end of Period 2. The length of each period is 6 months (6-month steps), the upward parameter on the spot rate (u) is 1.1 and the downward parameter (d) is $1/1.1 = 0.9091$, the probability of spot rate increasing in each period is .5, and the yield curve is assumed flat. As shown in the exhibit, given an initial spot rate of 5% (annual), the two possible spot rates after one period (6 months) are 5.5% and 4.54545%, and the three possible rates after two periods (1 year) are 6.05%, 5%, and 4.13223%. At the current spot rate of 5%, the price of the T-bill is $B_0 = 98.79 (= 100/(1.05)^{.25})$; in Period 1, the price is 98.67 when the spot rate is 5.5% $(= 100/(1.055)^{.25})$ and 98.895 when the rate is 4.54545% $(= 100/(1.0454545)^{.25})$.

EXHIBIT 12.9-1   Binomial Tree of Spot Rates, T-Bill Prices, and T-Bill Futures Prices

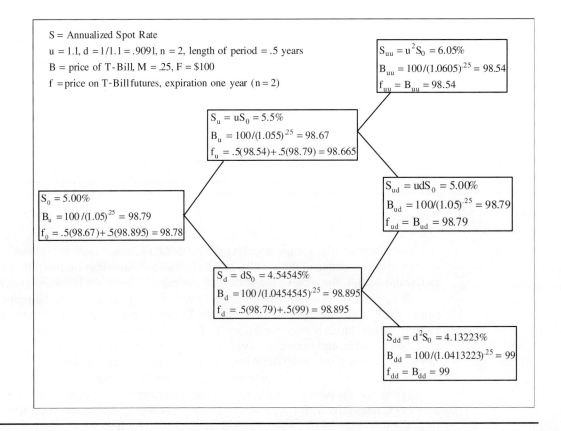

In Period 2, the T-bill prices are 98.54, 98.79, and 99 for spot rates of 6.05%, 5%, and 4.13223%, respectively.

The futures prices shown in Exhibit 12.9-1 are obtained by assuming a risk-neutral market. Recall that in Chapter 11, we showed that if the market is risk neutral, then the futures price is an unbiased estimator of the expected spot price: $f_t = E(S_T)$. The futures prices at each node in the exhibit are therefore equal to their expected prices next period. Given the spot T-bill prices in Period 2, the futures prices in Period 1 are 98.665($= E(B) = .5(98.54) + .5(98.79)$) and 98.895($= E(B) = .5(98.79) + .5(99)$). Given theses prices, the current futures price is $f_0 = 98.78(= E(f_1) = .5(98.665) + .5(98.895))$.

Given the binomial tree of spot rates, spot T-bill prices, and T-bill futures prices, we can determine the values of call and put options on spot and futures T-bills. For European options, we use the standard recursive methodology, starting at expiration when we price the possible option values equal to their IVs. Given the option's IVs at expiration, we then move to the preceding period and price the option to equal the present value of its expected cash flow for next period. Given these values, we then roll the tree to the next preceding period and again price the option to equal the present value of its expected cash flow. We continue this recursive process to the current period. If the option is American, then its early exercise advantage needs to be taken into account by determining at each node whether it is more valuable to hold the option or exercise. This is done by starting one period prior to the option's expiration and constraining the price of the American option to be the maximum of its binomial value (present value of next period's expected cash flow) or the IV (i.e., the value from exercising). Those values are then rolled to the next preceding period, and the American option values for that period are obtained by again constraining the option prices to be the maximum of the binomial value or the IV; this process continues to the current period.

12.9.1.1 Spot T-Bill Call

Suppose we want to value an OTC European call on a spot T-bill with an exercise price of 98.75 per \$100 face value and expiration of 1 year. To value the call option on the T-bill, we start at the option's expiration when we know the possible call values are equal to their IVs. In this case, at spot rates of 5% and 4.13223%, the call is in the money with IVs of .04 and .25, respectively; and at the spot rate of 6.05%, the call is out of the money and thus has an IV of zero (see Exhibit 12.9-2). Given the three possible option values at expiration, we next move to Period 1 and price the option at the two possible spot rates of 5.5% and 4.54545% to equal the present values of their expected cash flows next period. Assuming there is an equal probability of the spot rate increasing or decreasing in one period ($q = .5$), the two possible call values in Period 1 are .01947 and .1418:

$$C_u = \frac{.5(0) + .5(.04)}{(1.055)^{.5}} = .01947$$

$$C_d = \frac{.5(.04) + .5(.25)}{(1.0454545)^{.5}} = .1418$$

Rolling these call values to the current period and again determining the option's price as the present value of the expected cash flow, we obtain a price on the European T-bill call of .0787:

$$C_0 = \frac{.5(.01947) + .5(.1418)}{(1.05)^{.5}} = .0787$$

If the call option were American, its two possible prices in Period 1 are constrained to be the maximum of the binomial value (present value of next period's expected cash flows) or the IV (i.e., the value from exercising):

$$C_t^A = \text{Max}[C_t, IV]$$

In Period 1, the IV slightly exceeds the binomial value when the spot rate is 4.54545%. As a result, the American call price is equal to its IV of .145 (see Exhibit 15.9-2). Rolling this price and the upper rate's price of .01947 to the current period yields a price for the American T-bill call of .08. This price slightly exceeds the European value of .0787, reflecting the early exercise advantage of the American option.

12.9.1.2 T-Bill Futures Call

If the call option were on a European T-bill futures contract instead of a spot T-bill, with the futures and option having the same expiration, then the value of the futures option will be the same as the spot option. That is, at the expiration spot rates of 6.05%, 5%, and 4.13223%, the futures prices on the expiring contract would be equal to the spot prices (98.54, 98.79, and 99), and the corresponding IVs of the European futures call would be 0, .04, and .25—the same as the spot call's IV. Thus, when we roll these call values back to the present period, we end up with the price on the European futures call of .0787—the same as the European spot.

EXHIBIT 12.9-2   Binomial Tree of Spot Rates and T-Bill Call Prices

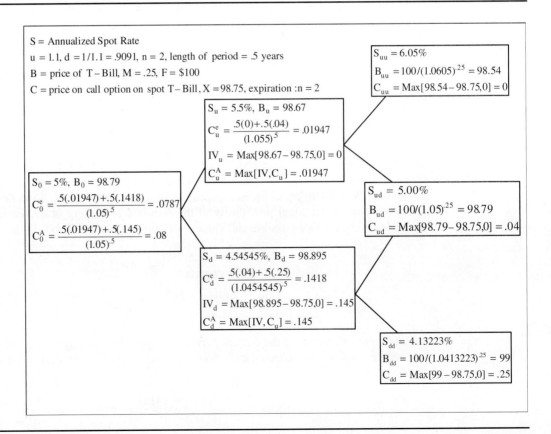

If the futures call option were American, then the option prices at each node need to be constrained to be the maximum of the binomial value or the futures option's IV. Because the IV of the futures call in Period 1 is zero when the spot rate is 5.5% (IV = Max[98.665 – 98.75, 0] = 0) and .145 when the rate is 4.54545% (IV = Max[98.895 – 97.75, 0] = .145), the corresponding prices of the American futures option would therefore be the same as the spot option: .01947 and .145. Rolling theses prices to the current period yields a price on the American T-bill futures call of .08—the same price as the American spot option.[3]

12.9.1.3   T-Bill Futures Put

In the case of a spot or futures T-bill put, their prices can be determined given the binomial tree of spot rates and their corresponding spot and futures prices. Exhibit 12.9-3 shows the binomial valuation of European T-bill futures put with an exercise price of 98.75 and expiration of 1 year (two periods). At the expiration spot rate of 6.05%, the put is in the money with an IV of .21, and at the spot rates of 5% and 4.13223%, the put is out of the money. In period 1, the two possible values for the European put are .1022 and 0. Because these values exceed or equal their IV's, they would also be the prices of the put

EXHIBIT 12.9-3   Binomial Tree of Spot Rates and T-Bill Futures Put Prices

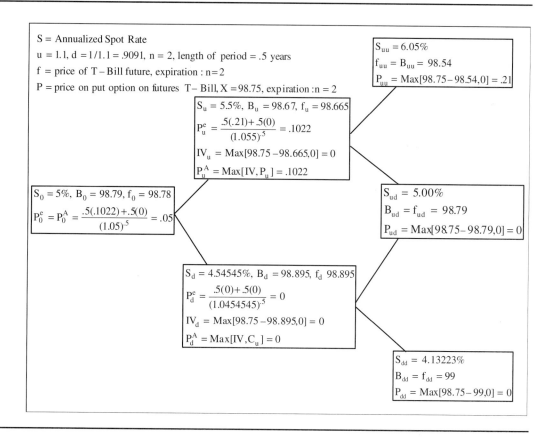

---

[3] It should be noted that if the futures option expired in one period, whereas the T-bill futures expired in two periods, then the value of the futures option would be .071.

if it were American. Rolling these values to the current period, we obtain the price for the futures put of .05.

It should be noted that the put price of .05 is consistent with the put–call futures parity relation:

$$P_0 - C_0 = \frac{X - f_0}{(1 + R_f)^T} = -\frac{f_0 - X}{(1 + R_f)^T}$$

$$P_0 = C_0 - \frac{f_0 - X}{(1 + R_f)^T}$$

$$P_0 = .0787 - \frac{98.78 - 98.75}{(1.05)^{.5}} = .05$$

12.9.2 Valuing T-Bond Futures Call Options

The T-bill underlying the spot or futures T-bill option is a fixed-deliverable bill; that is, the features of the bill (maturity of 91 days and principal of \$1M) do not change during the life of the option. In contrast, the T-bond underlying a T-bond spot or futures option is a specified T-bond (or the bond from an eligible group that is most likely to be delivered). Because of the specified bond clause on a T-bond or note option or futures option, the first step in valuing the option is to determine the values of the specified T-bond (or bond most likely to be delivered) at the various nodes on the binomial tree using the same methodology we used in Chapter 7 to value a coupon bond.

To illustrate, consider an earlier example presented in Chapter 7 in which we valued an OTC spot option on a T-bond with a 6% annual coupon, face value of \$100, and with 3years left to maturity. In that example, we valued the underlying T-bond using a two-period binomial tree of risk-free spot rates, with the length of each period being 1 year, the estimated upward and downward parameters being u = 1.2 and d = .8333, and the current spot rate being 6%. As shown in Exhibit 12.9-4, the value of the T-bond is 99.78. Exhibit 12.9-4 also shows the prices on a 2-year futures contract on the 3-year, 6% T-bond. The prices are generated by assuming a risk-neutral market. As shown, at the futures expiration (Period 2), the three possible futures prices are equal to their spot prices: 97.57, 100, and 101.76; in Period 1, the two futures prices are equal to their expected spot prices: $f_u = E(B_T) = .5(97.57) + .5(100) = 98.875$ and $f_d = E(B_T) = .5(100) + .5(101.76) = 100.88$; in the current period, the futures price is $f_0 = E(f_1) = .5(98.785) + .5(100.88) = 99.83$.

In Chapter 7, we valued European and American spot call options on the T-bond, with the calls having an exercise price of 98 and expiration of 2 years. Suppose the calls were options on the futures contract on the 3-year, 6% T-bond (or if that bond were the most likely to-be-delivered bond on the futures contract). As shown in Exhibit 12.9-5, the value of the European futures option is 1.734 (the same as the European spot option). The American futures call option, in turn, is 1.7985, which is less than the American spot option price of 2.228 (see Section 7.3).

12.10   BLACK MODEL FOR PRICING FUTURES OPTIONS

In 1976, Fisher Black extended the B–S OPM for spot options to the pricing of futures options. The Black futures model is defined as follows:

$$C_0^* = [f_0 N(d_1) - X N(d_2)] e^{-R_f T}$$

$$P_0^* = [X(1 - N(d_2)) - f_0(1 - N(d_1))] e^{-R_f T}$$

EXHIBIT 12.9-4   Binomial Tree: Spot Rates, T-Bond Prices, and T-Bond Futures Prices

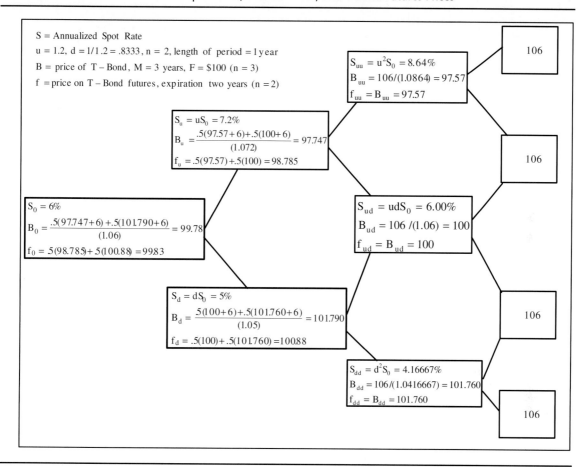

$$d_1 = \frac{\ln(f_0/X) + (\sigma_f^2/2)T}{\sigma_f\sqrt{T}}$$

$$d_2 = d_1 - \sigma_f\sqrt{T}$$

where:

$\sigma_f^2 =$ variance of the logarithmic return of futures prices $= V(\ln(f_n/f_0))$

$\sigma_f^2 = \sigma_S^2$ (volatility of spot prices)

$T =$ time to expiration expressed as a proportion of a year

$R_f =$ continuously compounded annual risk-free rate

The "Black–Scholes Option Pricing Model" Excel program includes the "Black Futures Call" and "Black Futures Put" worksheets for calculating the option prices using the Black model.

The Black futures model differs from the B–S OPM for spot securities by the exclusion of the risk-free rate in the equations for d_1 and d_2. The exclusion of the risk-free rate was also the case for the binomial model with a large number of subperiods. Like the BOPM

EXHIBIT 12.9-5   Binomial Tree: T-Bond Futures Call Prices

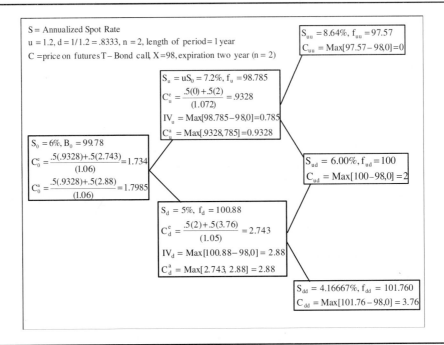

for futures options, if the carrying-cost model holds, and the underlying futures contract and the futures option expire at the same time, then the B–S OPM for European spot options and the Black model for European futures options will be the same. This can be proved by substituting $S_0 e^{-RT}$ for f_0 in the Black futures OPM to obtain the B–S OPM for the spot asset. It should also be noted that the Black model, like the B–S OPM, only prices European futures options. If the futures option is American, then an early exercise advantage may exist for both calls and puts. In such cases, the American binomial model presented in the last section can be used to estimate the option price.

12.10.1   Example: Pricing S&P 500 Futures Options

To illustrate the application of the Black model, consider the previous multiple-period binomial example in which we priced European call and put options on the S&P 500 index futures with $X = 1250$ and $T = 90$ days. In that example, we assumed the following:

- The current S&P 500 was at $S_0 = 1250$
- The spot index's estimated volatility $= \sigma^A = .3$
- The annual continuous-dividend yield generated from the stocks comprising the index portfolio was $\psi = .04$
- $R_f = 6\%$
- The S&P 500 futures contract expired in 120 days
- The price on the futures was equal to its carrying-cost value of 1285.25:

$$f_0 = S_0 e^{(R^A - \psi)T}$$

$$f_0 = 1250 e^{(.06 - .04)(120/365)}$$

$$f_0 = 1258.25$$

Using the Black futures option model, the price of the futures call option is 77.10, and the price of the futures put is 68.98:

$$C_0^* = [f_0 N(d_1) - X N(d_2)]e^{-R_f T}$$

$$C_0^* = [1258.25(.54699177) - 1250(.488003103)]e^{-(.06)(90/365)} = 77.10$$

$$P_0^* = [X(1 - N(d_2)) - f_0(1 - N(d_1))]e^{-R_f T}$$

$$P_0^* = [1250(1 - .4880) - 1258.25(1 - .5470)]e^{-(.06)(90/365)} = 68.98$$

$$d_1 = \frac{\ln(f_0/X) + (\sigma_f^2/2)T}{\sigma_f \sqrt{T}} = \frac{\ln(1258.25/1250) + (.09/2)(90/365)}{.3\sqrt{90/365}} = .11864345$$

$$d_2 = d_1 - \sigma_f \sqrt{T} = .11864345 - .3\sqrt{90/365} = -.03032551$$

$$N(d_1) = N(.11864345) = .54699177$$

$$N(d_2) = N(-.03032551) = .488013103$$

The Black OPM call price of 77.10 is $0.06 greater than the 30-period binomial value of 77.04, and the Black put value of 68.98 is 0.07 greater than the 30-period binomial value of 68.91. It should be noted that the call and put prices are also consistent with put–call futures parity:

$$P_0^* - C_0^* = PV(X - f_0)$$

$$P_0^* = (X - f_0)e^{-R_f T} + C_0^*$$

$$P_0^* = (1250 - 1258.25)e^{-(.06)(90/365)} + 77.10 = 68.98$$

Three additional examples of pricing futures options using the Black model are presented in Appendix 12C: options contracts on the British pound futures, crude oil futures, and T-bond futures.

12.11 CONCLUSION

In this chapter, we've examined the markets, fundamental strategies, and pricing of futures options. In today's security world, many securities can be traded on four different markets—spot, spot options, futures, and futures options. The pricing relationships we have examined in this chapter suggest that under certain conditions, some of these markets may indeed be redundant. Each of these markets, though, often provides different liquidity, delivery procedures, or comparative location advantages to particular investors and as such may be justified, at least for the foreseeable future.

KEY TERMS

Options on futures contracts	Put–call-futures parity model	Black futures option pricing model

SELECTED REFERENCES

Black, F. "The Pricing of Commodity Contracts." *Journal of Financial Economics* 3 (March 1976): 167–79.

Blomeyer, E., and J. Boyd. "Empirical Tests of Boundary Conditions for Options on Treasury Bond Futures." *The Journal of Futures Markets* 4 (1988): 185–198.

Brenner, M., G. Courtadon, and M. Subrahmanyam. "Options on the Spot and Options on Futures." *The Journal of Finance* 40 (December 1985): 1303–17.

Followill, R. "Relative Call Futures Option Pricing: An Examination of Market Efficiency." *The Review of Futures Markets* 6 (1987): 354–381.

Hilliard, J. E., and J. Reis. "Valuation of Commodity Futures and Options Under Stochastic Convenience Yields, Interest Rates, and Jump Diffusions in the Spot." *Journal of Financial and Quantitative Analysis* 33 (March 1998): 61–86.

Johnson, R. S., R. A. Zuben, and J. M. Gandard. "The Binomial Pricing of Options on Futures Contracts." *Journal of Financial Education* (forthcoming).

Miltersen, K. R., and E. S. Schwartz. "Pricing of Options on Commodity Futures With Stochastic Term Structures of Convenience Yields and Interest Rates." *Journal of Financial and Quantitative Analysis* 33 (March 1998): 33–59.

Ramaswany, K., and Sundaresan. "The Valuation of Options on Futures Contracts." *Journal of Finance* 60 (December 1985): 1319–40.

Shastri, K., and K. Tandon. "Options on Futures Contracts: A Comparison of European and American Pricing Models." *The Journal of Futures Markets* 6 (Winter 1986): 593–618.

Thorp, E. "Options on Commodity Forward Contracts." *Management Science* 29 (October 1985): 1232–42.

Whaley, R. "Valuation of American Futures Options: Theory and Tests." *The Journal of Finance* 41 (March 1986): 127–50.

Wolf, A. "Fundamentals of Commodity Options on Futures." *Journal of Futures Markets* 2 (1982): 391–408.

Wolf, A., and L. Pohlman. "Tests of the Black and Whaley Models for Gold and Silver Futures Options." *The Review of Futures Markets* 6 (1987): 328–47.

PROBLEMS AND QUESTIONS

1. Show graphically and in a table the profit and futures price relationships at expiration for the following positions on an S&P 500 futures options:

   a. A straddle purchase formed with the S&P 500 futures call and put options.

   b. A straddle write formed with S&P 500 futures call and put options.

   c. A simulated long futures position formed by buying an S&P 500 futures call and selling an S&P 500 futures put.

   d. A simulated short futures position formed by selling an S&P 500 futures call and selling an S&P 500 futures put.

   In each case, assume that the S&P 500 futures call and put options each have exercise prices of 1,200 and premiums of 50. Assume at the options' expiration, the futures index has 10 days left to expirations, the risk-free rate is 6% (annual), the S&P 500 dividend yield is 3% (annual), and the futures price is equal to the carrying-cost model's values of $f_0 = S_0 e^{(R_f - \Psi)T}$. Evaluate at spot index values at the futures expiration of 1,050, 1,100, 1,150, 1,200, 1,250, 1,300, and 1,350.

2. Explain what arbitrageurs would do if the price of an American S&P 500 futures call with an exercise price of 1100 were priced at 45 when the underlying futures price was trading at 1150. What impact would their actions have in the option market on the call's price?

3. Explain what arbitrageurs would do if the price of an American S&P 500 futures put with an exercise price of 1200 were priced at 45 when the underlying futures price was

trading at 1150. What impact would their actions have in the option market on the put's price?

4. Prove the following boundary conditions using an arbitrage argument. In your proof, show the initial positive cash flow when the condition is violated and prove there are no liabilities at expiration or when the positions are closed.

   a. European futures call option: $C_t \geq Max[PV(f_t - X), 0]$

   b. European futures put option: $P_t \geq Max[PV(X - f_t), 0]$

   c. Put–call futures parity for European futures options: $P_t - C_t = (X - f_t)/(1 + R_f)^T$

5. Bullet Questions:

   a. What right does a September $4.50 wheat futures call option gives the holder?

   b. What right does a September $4.50 wheat futures put option gives the holder?

   c. What is the conversion strategy underlying the put–call-futures parity model?

   d. What conditions are necessary to make the spot options and futures options equivalent?

   e. True or false: If the futures option contract and the underlying futures contract expire at the same time, then the futures options can be viewed as an option on the underlying spot security, with the option having a cash settlement clause.

6. Mr. Woody is the chief financial officer for the Corso Company, a large metropolitan real estate developer. In January, Mr. Woody estimates that the company will need to purchase 300,000 square feet of plywood in June to meet its material needs on one of its office construction jobs. Mr. Woody is confident that plywood prices will be decreasing in the future but does not want to assume the price risk if plywood prices were to increase. Suppose there is a June plywood futures call with $X = \$0.20/$sq. ft. (contract size is 5,000 square feet), selling at $C_0 = \$0.02$, and with the same June expiration as the underlying plywood futures contract. Explain how Mr. Woody could cap the company's June plywood costs with a position in the June plywood futures call. Evaluate the cap by showing a table of Mr. Woody's hedged costs at the plywood future option's expiration date by buying the plywood on the spot market at possible spot prices of 0.14/sq. ft., 0.16/sq. ft., 0.18/sq. ft., 0.20/sq. ft., 0.22/sq. ft., 0.24/sq. ft., 0.26/sq. ft., and 0.28/sq. ft. and closing the futures call options at their intrinsic values. Assume no quality, quantity, and timing risk.

7. In May, Mr. Jones planted a wheat crop that he expects to harvest in September. He anticipates the September harvest to be 100,000 bushels. Although he expects wheat prices to increase, he would still like downside protection against any unexpected decrease in wheat prices. Suppose there is a September wheat futures put contract available with $X = \$4.40/$bu (contract size of 5,000 bushels) expiring at the same time as the underlying September wheat futures and currently trading at $0.05. Explain how Mr. Jones could obtain downside protection by buying the put. Show in a Table Mr. Jones' hedged revenue at the futures' expiration date from closing the futures put at the intrinsic value and selling his 100,000 bushels of wheat on the spot market at possible spot prices of $3.60/bu, $3.80/bu, $4.00/bu, $4.20/bu, $4.40/bu, $4.60/bu, $4.80/bu, and $5.00/bu. Assume no quality, quantity, or timing risk.

8. Given the following:

   - The S&P 500 futures option expiring at the end of 60 days
   - The S&P 500 futures contract expiring at the end of 120 days
   - The current spot index is at $S_0 = 1200$
   - The estimated annualized volatility and mean of the spot index's logarithmic return are $\sigma^A = .25$ and $\mu^A = 0$
   - The annual risk-free rate is $R_f = 4\%$
   - The futures price is determined by the carrying-cost model: $f_0 = S_0 e^{(R_f - \psi)n_f \Delta t}$
   - ψ = continuous annual dividend yield = 6%

   Determine the following:

   a. Show the spot index and futures prices at each node for a two-period binomial tree with a length of each step equal to 60 days ($\Delta t = 60/365 = .164384$). In generating the tree, use the up and down parameters defining the spot index and those defining the
   futures.

   b. Explain the relationship between the spot and futures prices that you obtained in 8a.

   c. Using the BOPM, determine the equilibrium price for the 1200 index futures call expiring in 60 days (n = 1).

   d. Explain the arbitrage strategy you would employ if the price of the 1200 index futures call were priced at 60.

   e. Using the BOPM, determine the equilibrium price for the 1200 index futures put expiring in 60 days (n = 1).

   f. Explain the arbitrage strategy you would employ if the price of the 1200 index futures put were priced at 70.

   g. Show the equilibrium put and call prices conform to put–call futures parity.

9. Given the following futures and spot information (same information found in Problem 8):

   - S&P 500 futures and spot options each with an exercise price of 1200 and expiring at the end of 60 days
   - The S&P 500 futures contract expiring at the end of 120 days
   - The current price of the spot index is $S_0 = 1200$
   - The estimated annualized volatility and mean of the spot index's logarithmic return are $\sigma^A = .25$ and $\mu^A = 0$
   - The annual risk-free rate is $R_f = 4\%$
   - The futures price is determined by the carrying cost model: $f_0 = S_0 e^{(R_f - \psi)n_f \Delta t}$
   - ψ = continuous annual dividend yield = 6%

   Determine the following option prices using a 30-period binomial tree and the "Binomial Option Pricing Model Excel" program:

   a. American futures call

   b. European futures call

   c. American spot call

   d. European spot call

e. American futures put

f. European futures put

g. American spot put

h. European spot put

10. Based on your answers in Problem 9, explain the following relations:

a. The relationship between American and European futures options.

b. The relationship between American and European spot options.

c. The relationship between American futures and spot calls.

d. The relationship between American futures and spot puts.

11. Given the following futures and spot information (the same information in Problem 8):

- S&P 500 futures and spot options each with an exercise price of 1200 and expiring at the end of 60 days

- The S&P 500 futures contract expiring at the end of 120 days

- The current spot index is at $S_0 = 1200$

- The estimated annualized volatility and mean of the spot index's logarithmic return are $\sigma^A = .25$ and $\mu^A = 0$

- The annual risk-free rate is $R_f = 4\%$

- The futures price is determined by the carrying-cost model: $f_0 = S_0 e^{(R_f - \psi) n_f \Delta t}$

- ψ = continuous annual dividend yield = 6%

a. Show in a table and with a graph the Black futures option model's option prices and intrinsic values for different futures prices for a European futures call with X = 1200 and expiration of 60 days. Generate your table and graph using current spot index values of 1100, 1125, 1150, 1175, 1200, 1225, 1250, 1275, and 1300. Use "Black–Scholes Option Pricing Model" Excel program ("Black Futures Call" worksheet).

b. Show in a table and with a graph the Black futures option model's option prices and intrinsic values for different futures prices for a European futures put with X = 1200 and expiration of 60 days. Generate your table and graph using current spot index values of 1100, 1125, 1150, 1175, 1200, 1225, 1250, 1275, and 1300. Use "Black–Scholes Option Pricing Model" Excel program ("Black Futures Put" worksheet).

12. Given the following futures and spot information:

- S&P 500 futures and spot options each with an exercise price of 1200 and expiring at the end of 60 days

- The S&P 500 futures contract expiring at the end of 60 days

- The current spot index is at $S_0 = 1200$

- The estimated annualized volatility and mean of the spot index's logarithmic return are $\sigma^A = .25$ and $\mu^A = 0$

- The annual risk-free rate is $R_f = 6\%$

- The futures price is determined by the carrying-cost model: $f_0 = S_0 e^{(R_f - \psi) n_f \Delta t}$

- ψ = continuous annual dividend yield = 4%

Determine the following option prices for a 30-period binomial model using the "Binomial Option Pricing Model" Excel program:

a. American futures call

b. European futures call

c. American spot call

d. European spot call

e. American futures put

f. European futures put

g. American spot put

h. European spot put

13. Based on your answers in Problem 12, explain the following relation:

a. The relationship between the futures and spot prices.

b. The relationship between European futures and spot options.

c. The relationship between American futures and spot call options.

d. The relationship between American futures and spot put options.

14. Given the following futures and spot index information: (the same information in Problem 12):

- S&P 500 futures and spot options each with an exercise price of 1200 and expiring at the end of 60 days

- The S&P 500 futures contract expiring at the end of 60 days

- The current spot index is at $S_0 = 1200$

- The estimated annualized volatility and mean of the spot index's logarithmic return are $\sigma^A = .25$ and $\mu^A = 0$

- The annual risk-free rate is $R_f = 6\%$

- The futures price is determined by the carrying-cost model: $f_0 = S_0 e^{(R_f - \psi) n_f \Delta t}$

- ψ = continuous annual dividend yield = 4%

Determine the following futures option prices and spot option prices using the Black futures model and B–S OPM (use "Black–Scholes Option Pricing Model" Excel program).

a. European futures call

b. European spot call

c. European futures put

d. European spot call

Comment on the prices you obtain.

15. Assume the following:

- U.S. risk-free rate (annual) = 4%

- British risk-free (annual rate paid on British pounds) = 6%

- $/BP spot exchange rate = $1.50/BP

- Mean annualized logarithmic return (for spot $/BP exchange rate) = $\mu^A = 0$

- Annualized logarithmic return's standard deviation = $\sigma^A = 0.25$

- BP futures contract expiring in 120 days
- The BP futures price is determined by the interest-rate-parity condition: $f_0 = E_0 e^{(R_{US}-R_F)n_f \Delta t}$

Questions:

a. Using the single-period BOPM with the length of the period equal to 60 days, determine the price of a call on the BP futures contract with an exercise price of $1.50 and expiration of 60 days. (See Appendix 12B for an example of the single-period BOPM for foreign currency futures options.)

b. Explain what an arbitrageur would do if the BP futures call were priced at $0.09. Show what the arbitrageur's cash flow at expiration would be at the two possible spot exchange rates. Assume perfect divisibility.

c. Using put–call futures parity, determine the equilibrium price of a $1.50 BP futures put expiring in 30 days.

16. Given the following information (the same as Problem 15):

- U.S. risk-free rate (annual) = 4%
- British risk-free (annual rate paid on British pounds) = 6%
- $/BP spot exchange rate = $1.50/BP
- Mean annualized logarithmic return (for $/BP exchange rate) = $\mu^A = 0$
- Annualized logarithmic return's standard deviation = $\sigma^A = 0.25$
- BP futures contract expiring in 120 days
- The futures price is determined by the interest-rate-parity condition: $f_0 = E_0 e^{(R_{US}-R_F)n_f \Delta t}$

Determine the following:

a. The price of a European BP futures call with an exercise price of $1.50 and expiration of 60 days using the Black futures option model. Use "Black–Scholes Option Pricing Model" Excel program ("Black Futures Call" worksheet). (See Appendix 12C for an example.)

b. The price of a European BP futures call with an exercise price of $1.50 and expiration of 60 days using the "Binomial Option Pricing Model" Excel program for the case of n = 30 subperiods of length $\Delta t = 2/365$.

c. The price of a European BP futures put with an exercise price of $1.50 and expiration of 60 days using the Black futures option model. Use "Black–Scholes Option Pricing Model" Excel program ("Black Futures Put" worksheet).

d. The price of a European BP futures put with an exercise price of $1.50 and expiration of 60 days using the "Binomial Option Pricing Model" Excel program for the case of n = 30 subperiods of length $\Delta t = 2/365$.

17. Given the following futures and spot information:

- BP futures contract expiring in 60 days
- BP futures option contract expiring in 60 days
- BP spot option contract expiring in 60 days
- U.S. risk-free rate (annual) = 4%
- British risk-free (annual rate paid on British pounds) = 6%
- $/BP spot exchange rate = $1.50/BP

- Mean annualized logarithmic return (for $/BP exchange rate) $= \mu^A = 0$
- Annualized logarithmic return's standard deviation $= \sigma^A = 0.25$
- BP futures price determined by the interest-rate-parity condition: $f_0 = E_0 e^{(R_{US}-R_F)n_f \Delta t}$

Determine the following futures option prices and spot option prices using the Black futures model and B–S OPM. Use "Black–Scholes Option Pricing Model" Excel program. (See Appendix 12C for an example.)

a. European futures call

b. European spot call

c. European futures put

d. European spot call

Comment on the prices you obtain.

18. Given the following information:
    - $\sigma^A = 0.25$
    - $R_f = .06$
    - Price on crude oil futures $= \$55$
    - European call and put options on crude oil futures each with exercise price of $55 and expiration of 120 days

    Questions:

    a. Using the "Black–Scholes Option Pricing Model" Excel program, determine the equilibrium futures call and put prices.

    b. Using the "Binomial Option Pricing Model" Excel program, determine the price of the options using a 60-period tree of length 2 days.

19. Assume the following: binomial process; current annualized spot rate on risk-free bond with maturity of .25 years of $S_0 = 4\%$; up and down parameters for period equal in length to .5 years of $u = 1.1$, $d = 1/1.1$; length of binomial period .5 years (6-month steps); probability of the spot rate increase in one period of $q = .5$.

    a. Generate a three-period binomial interest-rate tree of spot rates.

    b. Using the binomial tree, calculate the values at each node of a T-bill with a $100 face value and maturity of .25 years.

    c. Using the binomial tree and assuming a risk-neutral world, calculate the values at each node of a futures contract on the previous T-bill with the expiration on the futures being at the end of third period (1.5 years).

20. Using the binomial tree from Question 19, determine the values of the following spot options on the T-bill described in Question 19:

    a. European call option with an exercise price of 99 and expiration of 1.5 years (the end of three periods).

    b. American call option with an exercise price of 99 and expiration of 1.5 years (the end of three periods).

    c. European put option with an exercise price of 99 and expiration of 1.5 years (the end of three periods).

    d. American put option with an exercise price of 99 and expiration of 1.5 years (the end of three periods).

21. Using the binomial tree generated from Question 19, determine the values of the following futures options on the T-bill futures described in 19:

    a. European call option with an exercise price of 99 and expiration of 1.5 years (the end of three periods).

    b. American call option with an exercise price of 99 and expiration of 1.5 years (the end of three periods).

    c. European put option with an exercise price of 99 and expiration of 1.5 years (the end of three periods).

    d. American put option with an exercise price of 99 and expiration of 1.5 years (the end of three periods).

22. Suppose a T-bill futures is priced at $f_0 = 99$ and has an annualized standard deviation of .00175 and that the continuously compounded annual risk-free rate is 4%:

    a. Using the Black futures option model, calculate the equilibrium price for a three-month T-bill futures call option with an exercise price of 98.95. Use "Black–Scholes Option Pricing Model" Excel program ("Black Futures Call" worksheet).

    b. Using the Black futures option model, calculate the equilibrium price for a three-month T-bill futures put option with an exercise price of 98.95. Use "Black–Scholes Option Pricing Model" Excel program ("Black Futures Put" worksheet).

    c. Show the Black futures model's put price is the same price obtained using the put–call futures parity model.

23. Suppose a T-bond futures expiring in 6 months is priced at $f_0 = \$95,000$ and has an annualized standard deviation of .10 and that the continuously compounded annual risk-free rate is 5%:

    a. Using the Black futures option model, calculate the equilibrium price for a 6-month T-bond futures call option with an exercise price of $100,000 (see Appendix 12C for an example).

    b. Using the Black futures option model, calculate the equilibrium price for a 6-month T-bond futures put option with an exercise price of $100,000 (see Appendix 12C for an example).

    c. Show the Black futures model put price is the same price obtained using the put–call-futures parity model.

WEB EXERCISES

1. Determine the recent prices on listed futures option contracts by going to www.wsj.com/free, www.cme.com, or www.cbt.com.

2. Estimate the prices on listed call and put options on interest rate futures contract (T-bond, 10-year Treasury, 5-year Treasury, or Eurodollar) using the binomial and Black futures option.

    a. In selecting your options, go to www.wsj.com/free.

    b. Estimate the futures volatility using the implied variance (use "Implied Volatility" Excel program).

    c. Estimate your option prices using the "Binomial Option Pricing Model" Excel program and Black–Scholes Option Pricing Model" Excel program (Black Futures Model worksheet).

    d. Compare your B–S Model and Binomial values to the actual market prices.

3. Estimate the prices on listed call and put options on currency futures contract using the binomial and Black futures option.

    a. In selecting your options, go to www.wsj.com/free.

    b. Estimate the futures volatility using the implied variance (use "Implied Volatility" Excel program).

    c. Estimate your option prices using the "Binomial Option Pricing Model" Excel program and Black–Scholes Option Pricing Model" Excel program (Black Futures Model worksheet).

    d. Compare your B–S Model and Binomial values to the actual market prices.

4. Estimate the prices on listed call and put options on an index futures contract using the binomial and Black futures option.

    a. In selecting your options, go to www.wsj.com/free.

    b. Estimate the futures volatility using the implied variance (use "Implied Volatility" Excel program).

    c. Estimate your option prices using the "Binomial Option Pricing Model" Excel program and Black–Scholes Option Pricing Model" Excel program (Black Futures Model worksheet).

    d. Compare your B–S Model and Binomial values to the actual market prices.

5. Estimate the prices on listed call and put options on a nonfinancial futures contract (agriculture, energy, livestock, or metal) using the binomial and Black futures option.

    a. In selecting your options, go to www.wsj.com/free.

    b. Estimate the futures volatility using the implied variance (use "Implied Volatility" Excel program).

    c. Estimate your option prices using the "Binomial Option Pricing Model" Excel program and Black–Scholes Option Pricing Model" Excel program (Black Futures Model worksheet).

    d. Compare your B–S Model and Binomial values to the actual market prices.

APPENDIX 12A   ALGEBRAIC DERIVATIONS

Derivation of Equation (12.7-10): $C_0^* = \frac{1}{r}\left[pC_u + (1-p)C_d\right]$ and $P_0^* = \frac{1}{r}\left[pP_u + (1-p)P_d\right]$

Given:

$$f_u - f_d = (uS_0 r^{n_f - 1} + K(n_f - 1) + TRC - D_T)$$

$$- (dS_0 r^{n_f - 1} + K(n_f - 1) + TRC - D_T) = S_0 r^{n_f}\left[\frac{u}{r} - \frac{d}{r}\right]$$

$$f_u - f_0 = (uS_0 r^{n_f - 1} + K(n_f - 1) + TRC - D_T)$$

$$- (S_0 r^{n_f} + K(n_f) + TRC - D_T) = S_0 r^{n_f} \left[\frac{u}{r} - 1 \right] - K$$

$$f_d - f_0 = (dS_0 r^{n_f - 1} + K(n_f - 1) + TRC - D_T)$$

$$- (S_0 r^{n_f} + K(n_f) + TRC - D_T) = S_0 r^{n_f} \left[\frac{d}{r} - 1 \right] - K$$

Substituting into Equation (12.7-5):

$$C_0^* = - \frac{C_u[S_0 r^{n_f} \left[\frac{d}{r} - 1 \right] - K] - C_d[S_0 r^{n_f} \left[\frac{u}{r} - 1 \right] - K]}{rS_0 r^{n_f} \left[\frac{u}{r} - \frac{d}{r} \right]}$$

$$= \frac{C_u S_0 r^{n_f} \left[1 - \frac{d}{r} \right] + C_d S_0 r^{n_f} \left[\frac{u}{r} - 1 \right] - C_u K + C_d K}{rS_0 r^{n_f} \left[\frac{u}{r} - \frac{d}{r} \right]}$$

$$= \frac{S_0 r^{n_f}[C_u \left[1 - \frac{d}{r} \right] + C_d \left[\frac{u}{r} - 1 \right] + [C_u - C_d]K}{S_0 r^{n_f}[u - d]}$$

$$= \frac{[C_u \left[1 - \frac{d}{r} \right] + C_d \left[\frac{u}{r} - 1 \right]}{[u - d]} + \frac{[C_u - C_d]K}{S_0 r^{n_f}[u - d]}$$

$$C_0^* = \frac{C_u \left[1 - \frac{d}{r} \right] + C_d \left[\frac{u}{r} - 1 \right]}{u - d} + \frac{[C_u - C_d]K}{S_0 r^{n_f}[u - d]}$$

$$= C_u \frac{\left[\frac{r}{r} - \frac{d}{r} \right]}{u - d} + C_d \frac{\left[\frac{u}{r} - \frac{r}{r} \right]}{u - d} + \frac{[C_u - C_d]K}{S_0 r^{n_f}[u - d]}$$

$$C_0^* = \frac{1}{r} \left[C_u \left[\frac{r - d}{u - d} \right] + C_d \left[\frac{u - r}{u - d} \right] \right] + \frac{[C_u - C_d]K}{S_0 r^{n_f}[u - d]}$$

$$C_0^* = \frac{1}{r} [pC_u + (1 - p)C_d] + \frac{[C_u - C_d]K}{S_0 r^{n_f}[u - d]}$$

where:

$$p = \frac{r - d}{u - d} \quad \text{and} \quad 1 - p = \frac{u - d}{u - d} - \frac{r - d}{u - d} = \frac{u - r}{u - d}$$

$$\frac{[C_u - C_d]K}{S_0 r^{n_f}} = \text{periodic storage cost adjustment factor}$$

For futures put option:

$$P_0^* = \frac{1}{r}[pP_u + (1-p)P_d] + \frac{[P_u - P_d]K}{S_0 r^{n_f}[u-d]}$$

$$C_0^* = \frac{1}{r}[pC_u + (1-p)C_d] \quad \text{and} \quad P_0^* = \frac{1}{r}[pP_u + (1-p)P_d]$$

Derivation of Risk-Neutral Probability (p) for Currency Futures Option

Given:

$$f_u - f_d = uE_0\left(\frac{r_{US}}{r_F}\right)^{n_f-1} - dE_0\left(\frac{r_{US}}{r_F}\right)^{n_f-1}$$

$$= E_0\frac{(r_{US}/r_F)^{n_f}}{(r_{US}/r_F)}[u-d] = \frac{f_0}{(r_{US}/r_F)}[u-d]$$

$$f_u - f_0 = uE_0\left(\frac{r_{US}}{r_F}\right)^{n_f-1} - E_0\left(\frac{r_{US}}{r_F}\right)^{n_f}$$

$$= E_0\left(\frac{r_{US}}{r_F}\right)^{n_f}\left(\frac{u}{(r_{US}/r_F)}-1\right) = f_0\left(\frac{u}{(r_{US}/r_F)}-1\right)$$

$$f_d - f_0 = dE_0\left(\frac{r_{US}}{r_F}\right)^{n_f-1} - E_0\left(\frac{r_{US}}{r_F}\right)^{n_f}$$

$$= E_0\left(\frac{r_{US}}{r_F}\right)^{n_f}\left(\frac{d}{(r_{US}/r_F)}-1\right) = f_0\left(\frac{d}{(r_{US}/r_F)}-1\right)$$

Substituting into equilibrium call equation:

$$C_0^* = -B_0^* = -\frac{C_u(f_d - f_0) - C_d(f_u - f_0)}{r_{US}(f_u - f_d)}$$

$$C_0^* = -\frac{C_u f_0\left[\frac{d}{(r_{US}/r_F)}-1\right] - C_d f_0\left[\frac{u}{(r_{US}/r_F)}-1\right]}{r_{US}\frac{f_0}{(r_{US}/r_F)}[u-d]}$$

$$= \frac{C_u\left[1 - \frac{d}{(r_{US}/r_F)}\right] + C_d\left[\frac{u}{(r_{US}/r_F)}-1\right]}{r_{US}\frac{r_F}{r_{US}}[u-d]}$$

$$C_0^* = C_u\left[\frac{1 - d\frac{r_F}{r_{US}}}{r_F(u-d]}\right] + C_d\left[\frac{u\frac{r_F}{r_{US}}-1}{r_F(u-d]}\right]$$

$$= C_u \left[\frac{\dfrac{r_{US}}{r_{US}} - d\dfrac{r_F}{r_{US}}}{r_F(u - d)} \right] + C_d \left[\frac{u\dfrac{r_F}{r_{US}} - \dfrac{r_{US}}{r_{US}}}{r_F(u - d)} \right]$$

$$C_0^* = \frac{1}{r_{US}} C_u \left[\frac{r_{US} - r_F d}{r_F[u - d]} \right] + C_d \left[\frac{r_F u - r_{US}}{r_F[u - d]} \right]$$

$$C_0^* = \frac{1}{r_{us}} [pC_u + (1 - p)C_d]$$

where:

$$p = \frac{r_{US} - r_F d}{r_F[u - d]}$$

$$1 - p = \frac{r_F[u - d]}{r_F[u - d]} - \frac{r_{US} - r_F d}{r_F[u - d]} = \frac{r_F u - r_{US}}{r_F[u - d]}$$

Algebraic Derivation of p^f, u^f, and d^f

$$u^f = \frac{u}{e^{(R^A - \psi)\Delta t}}$$

$$e^{\sigma_f^A \sqrt{\Delta t} + \mu_f^A \Delta t} = \frac{e^{\sigma_S^A \sqrt{\Delta t} + \mu_S^A \Delta t}}{e^{(R^A - \psi)\Delta t}}$$

$$\ln\left(e^{\sigma_f^A \sqrt{\Delta t} + \mu_f^A \Delta t} \right)$$

$$= \ln\left(\frac{e^{\sigma_S^A \sqrt{\Delta t} + \mu_s^A}}{e^{(R^A - \psi)\Delta t}} \right)$$

$$\sigma_f^A \sqrt{\Delta t} + \mu_f^A \Delta t = \sigma_S^A \sqrt{\Delta t} + \mu_S^A \Delta t - (R^A - \psi)\Delta t$$

$$\sigma_f^A = \frac{\sigma_S^A \sqrt{\Delta t} + \mu_S^A \Delta t - (R^A - \psi)\Delta t - \mu_f^A \Delta t}{\sqrt{\Delta t}} \quad (1)$$

$$d^f = \frac{d}{e^{(R^A - \psi)\Delta t}}$$

$$e^{-\sigma_f^A \sqrt{\Delta t} + \mu_f^A \Delta t} = \frac{e^{-\sigma_S^A \sqrt{\Delta t} + \mu_S^A \Delta t}}{e^{(R^A - \psi)\Delta t}}$$

$$\ln\left(e^{-\sigma_f^A \sqrt{\Delta t} + \mu_f^A \Delta t} \right)$$

$$= \ln\left(\frac{e^{-\sigma_S^A \sqrt{\Delta t} + \mu_s^A}}{e^{(R^A - \psi)\Delta t}} \right)$$

$$-\sigma_f^A \sqrt{\Delta t} + \mu_f^A \Delta t = -\sigma_S^A \sqrt{\Delta t} + \mu_S^A \Delta t - (R^A - \psi)\Delta t$$

$$\sigma_f^A = \frac{\sigma_S^A \sqrt{\Delta t} - \mu_S^A \Delta t + (R^A - \psi)\Delta t + \mu_f^A \Delta t}{\sqrt{\Delta t}} \quad (2)$$

Solving Equations (1) and (2) simultaneously for σ_S^A and μ_S^A:
Equation (1):

$$\sigma_f^A \sqrt{\Delta t} = \sigma_S^A \sqrt{\Delta t} + \mu_S^A \Delta t - (R^A - \psi)\Delta t - \mu_f^A \Delta t \qquad (3)$$

Equation (2) expressed in terms of $\mu_f^A \Delta t$:

$$\mu_f^A \Delta t = -\sigma_S^A \sqrt{\Delta t} + \mu_S^A \Delta t - (R^A - \psi)\Delta t + \sigma_f^A \sqrt{\Delta t} \qquad (4)$$

Substituting (4) into (3) and solving for σ_f^A:

$$\sigma_f^A \sqrt{\Delta t} = \sigma_S^A \sqrt{\Delta t} + \mu_S^A \Delta t - (R^A - \psi)\Delta t + \sigma_S^A \sqrt{\Delta t}$$
$$-\mu_S^A \Delta t + (R^A - \psi)\Delta t - \sigma_f^A \sqrt{\Delta t}$$
$$\sigma_f^A = \sigma_S^A \qquad (5)$$

Substituting σ_S^A for σ_f^A in Equation (4) and solving in terms of μ_f^A:

$$\mu_f^A \Delta t = -\sigma_S^A \sqrt{\Delta t} + \mu_S^A \Delta t - (R^A - \psi)\Delta t + \sigma_S^A \sqrt{\Delta t}$$

$$\mu_f^A = -[\mu_S^A - (R^A - \psi)]\Delta t$$

(6)

Given:

$$u = u^f e^{(R^A - \psi)\Delta t} \text{ and } d = d^f e^{(R^A - \psi)\Delta t}$$

Substituting into equation for p:

$$p = \frac{e^{(R^A - \psi)\Delta t} - d^f e^{(R^A - \psi)\Delta t}}{u^f e^{(R^A - \psi)\Delta t} - d^f e^{(R^A - \psi)\Delta t}} = \frac{1 - d^f}{u^f - d^f} = p^f$$

APPENDIX 12B   SINGLE-PERIOD BOPM PRICING EXAMPLES

Pricing Call and Put Options on a Currency Futures Contract

Consider European call and put options on a currency futures contract with an exercise price of X = \$1.50/FC. Assume the futures options expire at the end of the first period, whereas the currency futures contract expires at the end of two periods ($n_f = 2$). Also assume the spot exchange rate is currently at \$1.50/FC and has up and down parameters of u = 1.1 and d = .95, the periodic U.S. risk-free rate is 5%, and the periodic foreign rate is 3%, and the futures price is determined by the carrying-cost model.

Given these assumptions, the current price on the currency futures contract would be \$1.558818/FC, and as shown in Exhibit 12.B-1, the possible prices on the contract next period would be f_u = \$1.682039 and f_d = 1.45267, the possible values of the futures call option expiring at the end of the period would be \$0.182039 and zero (see Exhibit 12.B-1(a), and the possible values of the futures put option would be zero and \$0.04733 (see Exhibit 12.B-1(b). Using the single-period BOPM, the equilibrium price of the \$1.50 call option on the currency futures contract is \$0.080233 and the price on the put is \$0.024216:

Call:

$$C_0^* = -B_0^* = -\frac{C_u(f_d - f_0) - C_d(f_u - f_0)}{r_{US}(f_u - f_f)}$$

$$C_0^* = -\frac{(\$0.182039)(\$1.45267 - \$1.558818) - (0)(\$1.682039 - \$1.558818)}{1.05(\$1.682039 - \$1.45267)}$$

$$= \$0.080233$$

Or

$$C_0^* = \frac{1}{r}[pC_u + (1-p)C_d]$$

$$C_0^* = \frac{1}{1.05}\left[(.462783)(\$0.182039) + (.537217)(0)\right] = \$0.080233$$

where:

$$p = \frac{r_{US} - r_F d}{r_F[u - d]} = \frac{1.05 - (1.03)(.95)}{1.03[1.1 - .95]} = .462783$$

EXHIBIT 12.B-1   Binomial Pricing of Foreign Currency Futures Call and Put Options

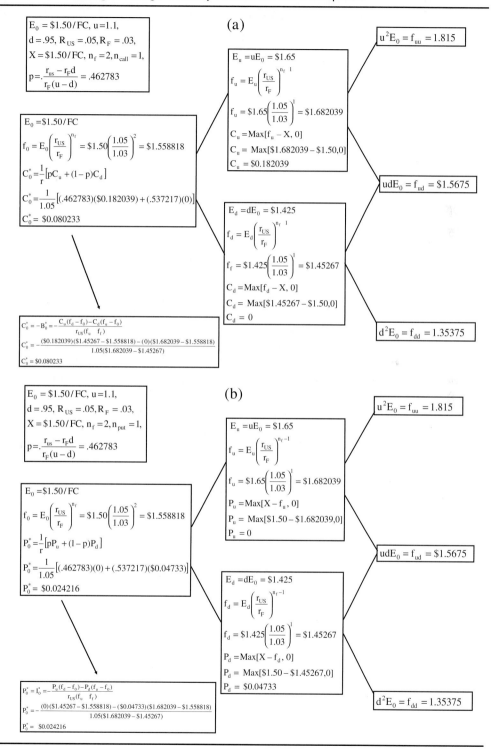

Put:

$$P_0^* = I_0^* = -\frac{P_u(f_d - f_0) - P_d(f_u - f_0)}{r_{US}(f_u - f_f)}$$

$$P_0^* = -\frac{(0)(\$1.45267 - \$1.558818) - (\$0.04733)(\$1.682039 - \$1.558818)}{1.05(\$1.682039 - \$1.45267)}$$

$$= \$0.024216$$

or

$$P_0^* = \frac{1}{r}\left[pP_u + (1-p)P_d\right]$$

$$P_0^* = \frac{1}{1.05}\left[(.462783)(0) + (.537217)(\$0.04733)\right] = \$0.024216$$

If the market price on a futures call option does not equal the equilibrium value, then an arbitrage opportunity will exist by taking a position in the option and an opposite position in the replicating portfolio. For example, if the market price of the $1.50 currency futures call were $C_0^m = \$0.10$ instead of $C_0^* = \$0.080233$, then as shown in Table 12.B-1, an arbitrage cash flow $0.020755 at expiration could be earned by selling the call for $0.10, going long in $H_0^{f*} = [C_u - C_d]/[f_u - f_d] = [\$0.182039 - 0]/[\$1.682039 - \$1.45267] = .793651$ currency futures contracts at $f_0 = \$1.558818$, and investing amounts of $B_0^* = \$0.080233$ and $C_0^m - C_0^* = \$0.10 - \$0.080233 = \$0.019767$ in a risk-free security. On the other hand, if the market price of the futures call is below $0.080233, then an underpriced BOPM arbitrage strategy is employed in which C_0^m dollars are borrowed at the risk-free rate and used to finance the purchase of the call, and a short position in H_0^{f*} futures contracts is taken at f_0.

In the case of the put, if the market price of the $1.50 currency futures put were $P_0^m = \$0.05$ instead of $P_0^* = \$0.024216$, then an arbitrage cash flow $0.027073 at expiration could be earned by selling the put for $0.05, going short in .206349 futures at

TABLE 12.B-1 Single-Period Arbitrage Strategy for Overpriced Foreign Currency Futures Call Option

$$f_0 = \$1.558818, n_f = 2$$
$$C_0^m = \$0.10, C_0^* = \$0.080233$$
$$u = 1.1, d = .95, r_{US} = 1.05, r_F = 1.03$$

Strategy:
Sell Call at $0.10
Long in $H_0^f = .793651$ Futures Contracts at $1.558818
Invest $B_0^* = \$0.080233$ in Risk-Free Security
Invest Excess of $C_0^m - C_0^* = \$0.10 - \$0.080233 = \$0.019767$ in Risk-free Security

	Cash Flow at Expiration	
Closing Position	$f_u = \$1.682039$ $C_u = \$0.182039$	$f_d = \$1.45267$ $C_d = 0$
Call Purchase: $-C_T$	−$0.182039	0
Closing Futures: .793651(f_T − $1.558818)	$0.097794	−$0.084245
Investment: $B_0^* r_{US} = \$0.080233(1.05)$	$0.084245	$0.084245
Investment: $(C_0^m - C_0^*) r_{US} = \$0.019767(1.05)$	$0.020755	$0.020755
	$0.020755	$0.020755

TABLE 12.B-2   Single-Period Arbitrage Strategy for Overpriced Foreign Currency Futures Put Option

$$f_0 = \$1.558818, \; n_f = 2$$
$$P_0^m = \$0.05, \; P_0^* = \$0.024216$$
$$u = 1.1, \; d = .95, \; r_{US} = 1.05, \; r_F = 1.03$$

Strategy:
Sell Put at $0.05
Short in $H_0^f = .206349$ Futures Contracts at $1.558818
Invest $I_0^* = \$0.024216$ in Risk-free Security
Invest Excess of $P_0^m - P_0^* = \$0.05 - \$0.024216 = \$0.025784$ in Risk-Free Security

	Cash Flow at Expiration	
Closing Position	$f_u = \$1.682039$ $P_u = 0$	$f_d = \$1.45267$ $P_d = \$0.04733$
Put Purchase: $-P_T$	0	$-\$0.04733$
Closing Futures: $.206349(\$1.558818 - f_T)$	$-\$0.025427$	$\$0.021904$
Investment: $B_0^* r_{US} = \$0.024216(1.05)$	$\$0.025427$	$\$0.025427$
Investment: $(P_0^m - P_0^*) \, r_{US} = \$0.025784(1.05)$	$\$0.027073$	$\$0.027073$
	$\$0.027073$	$\$0.027073$

contracts at $f_0 = \$1.558818 (H_0^{f^*} = [P_u - P_d]/[f_u - f_d] = [0 - \$0.04733]/[\$1.682039 - \$1.45267] = -0.206349)$ and investing amounts of $I_0^* = \$0.024216$ and $P_0^m - P_0^* = \$0.05 - \$0.024216 = \$0.025784$ in a risk-free security (see Table 12.B-2). On the other hand, if the market price of the futures call is below $0.024216, then an underpriced BOPM arbitrage strategy is employed in which P_0^m dollars are borrowed at the risk-free rate and used to finance the purchase of the put, and a long position in $H_0^{f^*}$ futures contracts is taken at f_0.

Pricing a Call on a Commodity Futures Contract

As a second example, consider a call option on a corn futures contract with an exercise price of X = $2.00/bushel. Assume the following:

- The corn futures option expires in 90 days
- The underlying corn futures contract expires at the end of 180 days
- The spot price on corn is $S_0 = \$2.00/bu$
- The estimated annualized volatility and mean of the spot corn price's logarithmic return are $\sigma^A = .3$ and $\mu^A = 0$
- The annual risk-free rate is $R_f = .06$
- The futures price is determined by the carrying-cost model.
- The annualized storage cost is $K^A = \$0.01/bu$
- Transportation cost of corn from storage facility to destination point on a futures contract is $0.01/bu

If we price the futures call option using a single-period model, then the length of the binomial period in years is $\Delta t = 90/365$, $u = 1.160637$, $d = .861596$, $r_f = e^{(.06)(90/365)}$,

EXHIBIT 12.B-2   Binomial Pricing of a Call Option on a Corn Futures Contract

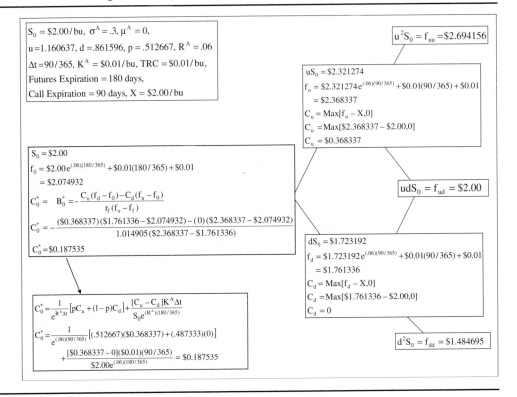

the storage cost for 90 days is K = \$0.002466, and p = .512667:

$$u = e^{\sigma^A \sqrt{\Delta t}} = e^{.3 \sqrt{90/365}} = 1.160637$$

$$d = 1/u = .861596$$

$$K = K^A \Delta t = (\$0.01/bu)(90/365) = \$0.002466/bu$$

$$p = \frac{r_f - d}{u - d} = \frac{e^{(.06)(90/365)} - .861596}{1.160637 - .861596} = .512667$$

Using the carrying-cost model, the current futures price on the corn contract expiring in 180 days is \$2.074932, and as shown in Exhibit 12.B-2, the possible prices on the contract next period are $f_u = \$2.368337$ and $f_d = 1.761336$, and the possible values of the futures call option expiring at the end of the period are \$0.368337 and zero. Using the single-period BOPM, the equilibrium price of the call option on the corn futures contract is \$0.187535:

$$C_0^* = -B_0^* = -\frac{C_u(f_d - f_0) - C_d(f_u - f_0)}{r_f(f_u - f_f)}$$

$$C_0^* = -\frac{(\$0.368337)(\$1.761336 - \$2.074932) - (0)(\$2.368337 - \$2.074932)}{1.014905(\$2.368337 - \$1.761336)}$$

$$= \$0.187535$$

TABLE 12.B-3   Single-Period Arbitrage Strategy for Overpriced Corn Futures Call Option

$$f_0 = \$2.074932, C_0^m = \$0.22, C_0^* = \$0.187535$$
$$u = 1.160637, d = .861596, R^A = .06, \Delta t = 90/365$$
$$\text{Future Expiration} = 180 \text{ days}, n_f = 2$$
$$\text{Call Option Expiration} = 90 \text{ days}, n_C = 1$$

Strategy:
Sell Call at $0.22
Long in $H_0^f = .606814$ Futures Contracts at $2.074932
Invest $B_0^* = \$0.187535$ in Risk-Free Security
Invest Excess of $C_0^m - C_0^* = \$0.22 - \$0.187535 = \$0.032465$ in Risk-Free Security

	Cash Flow at Expiration	
Closing Position	$f_u = \$2.368337$ $C_u = \$0.368337$	$f_d = \$1.761336$ $C_d = 0$
Call Purchase: $-C_T$	$-\$0.368337$	0
Closing Futures: $.606814(f_T - \$2.074932)$	$\$0.17804$	$-\$0.1903$
Investment: $B_0^* e^{RA(\Delta t)} = \$0.187535\, e^{(.06)(90/365)}$	$\$0.1903$	$\$0.1903$
Investment: $(C_0^m - C_0^*)e^{RA(\Delta t)} = \$0.032465 e^{(.06)(90/365)}$	$\$0.032949$	$\$0.032949$
	$\$0.032949$	$\$0.032949$

or

$$C_0^* = \frac{1}{r_f}[pC_u + (1-p)C_d] + \frac{[C_u - C_d]K\Delta t}{S_0 r^{n_f}}$$

$$C_0^* = \frac{1}{e^{(.06)(90/365)}}[(.512667)(\$0.368337) + (.487333)(0)]$$

$$+ \frac{[\$0.368337 - 0](\$0.002466)}{\$2.00 e^{(.06)(180/365)}}$$

$$= \$0.187535$$

where:

$$\frac{[C_u - C_d]K}{S_0 r^{n_f}} = \frac{[\$0.368337 - 0](\$0.002466)}{\$2.00 e^{(.06)(180/365)}} = \text{periodic storage adjustement cost factor}$$

If the market price on a futures call option does not equal the equilibrium value, then an arbitrage opportunity will exist by taking a position in the call and an opposite position in the replicating portfolio. For example, in the preceding case, if the market price of the $2.00 corn futures call were $C_0^m = \$0.22$ instead of $C_0^* = \$0.187535$, then as shown in Table 12.A-5, an arbitrage cash flow $0.032949 at expiration could be earned by selling the call for $0.22, going long in $H_0^{f*} = [C_u - C_d]/[f_u - f_d] = [\$0.368337 - 0]/[\$2.368337 - \$1.761336] = .606814$ corn futures contracts at $f_0 = \$2.074932$, and investing amounts of $B_0^* = \$0.187535$ and $C_0^m - C_0^* = \$0.22 - \$0.187535 = \$0.032465$ in a risk-free security. By contrast, if the market price of the futures call is below $0.187535, then an underpriced BOPM arbitrage strategy is employed in which C_0^m dollars are borrowed at the risk-free rate and used to finance the purchase of the call, and a short position in H_0^{f*} futures contracts is taken at f_0.

APPENDIX 12C   EXAMPLES OF PRICING FUTURES OPTIONS USING THE BLACK FUTURES OPTION MODEL

Pricing British Pound Futures Options

In Section 12.8, we priced call and put options on the British pound (BP) futures contract, each with X = \$1.60/BP and T = 90 days, using the binomial model. In that example, we assumed E_0 = \$1.60/BP, σ^A = .3, R_{US} = .06, R_F = .04, expiration on BP futures = 120 days, and expiration on BP futures option = 90 days. The price on the BP futures was

$$f_0 = E_0 e^{(R_{US} - R_F)T}$$

$$f_0 = \$1.60 e^{(.06 - .04)(120/365)}$$

$$f_0 = \$1.610555$$

Using the Black futures option model, the price of the BP futures call option is \$0.0986 and the price of the put is \$0.0882:

$$C_0^* = [f_0 N(d_1) - X N(d_2)]e^{-R_{US}T}$$

$$C_0^* = [\$1.610555(.54697524) - \$1.60(.48801454]e^{-(.06)(90/365)} = \$0.0986$$

$$P_0^* = [X(1 - N(d_2)) - f_0(1 - N(d_1))]e^{-R_f T}$$

$$P_0^* = [\$1.60(1 - .48801454) - \$1.610555(1 - .54697524)]e^{-(.06)(90/365)} = \$0.0882$$

$$d_1 = \frac{\ln(f_0/X) + (\sigma_f^2/2)T}{\sigma_f \sqrt{T}} = \frac{\ln(\$1.610555/\$1.60) + (.09/2)(90/365)}{.3\sqrt{90/365}} = .11860177$$

$$d_2 = d_1 - \sigma_f \sqrt{T} = .11860177 - .3\sqrt{90/365} = -.03036719$$

$$N(d_1) = N(.11860177) = .54697524$$

$$N(d_2) = N(-.03036719) = .48801454$$

The Black OPM call price of \$0.0986 is only \$0.0006 greater than the 30-period binomial value of \$0.0980, and the Black put value of \$0.0882 matches the 30-period binomial value. Also, as should be expected, the call and put prices are consistent with put–call futures parity:

$$P_0^* - C_0^* = PV(X - f_0)$$

$$P_0^* = (X - f_0)e^{-R_f T} + C_0^*$$

$$P_0^* = (\$1.60 - \$1.610555)e^{-(.06)(90/365)} + \$0.0986 = \$0.0882$$

Pricing Crude Oil Futures Options

As a second example, consider European call and put options on crude oil futures. Assume the time to expiration is 90 days, the current futures price is \$50, the exercise price is \$50, σ^A = .25, and R_f = .06. Using the Black model, both the call and put price are \$2.4184:

$$C_0^* = [f_0 N(d_1) - X N(d_2)]e^{-R_f T}$$

$$C_0^* = [\$50(.52454409) - \$50(.47545591]e^{-(.06)(90/365)} = \$2.4184$$

$$P_0^* = [X(1 - N(d_2)) - f_0(1 - N(d_1))]e^{-R_fT}$$

$$P_0^* = [\$50(1 - .47545591) - \$50(1 - .52454409)]e^{-(.06)(90/365)} = \$2.4184$$

$$d_1 = \frac{\ln(f_0/X) + (\sigma^2/2)T}{\sigma_f\sqrt{T}} = \frac{\ln(\$50/\$50) + (.25^2/2)(90/365)}{.25\sqrt{90/365}} = .06207040$$

$$d_2 = d_1 - \sigma_f\sqrt{T} = .06207040 - .25\sqrt{90/365} = -.06207040$$

$$N(d_1) = N(.06207040) = .52454409$$

$$N(d_2) = N(-.06207040) = .47545591$$

T-Bond Futures Put

Finally, consider 1-year put and call options on a T-bond futures contract, with each option having an exercise price of $100,000. Suppose the current futures price is $96,115, the futures volatility is $\sigma(\ln(f_n/f_0) = .10$, and the risk-free rate is .065. Using the Black futures option model, the price of the call option would be $2,139, and the price of the put would be $5,779:

$$C_0^* = [\$96,115(.36447) - \$100,000(.327485)]e^{-(.065)(1)} = \$2,139$$

$$P_0^* = [\$100,000(1 - .327485) - \$96,115(1 - .36447)]e^{-(.065)(1)} = \$5,779$$

where:

$$d_1 = \frac{\ln(96,115/100,000) + (.01/2)(1)}{.10\sqrt{1}} = -.34625$$

$$d_2 = -.34625 - .10\sqrt{1} = -.44625$$

$$N(-.34625) = .36447$$

$$N(-.44625) = .327485$$

Note that the call and future prices are also consistent with put–call futures parity:

$$P_0^* - C_0^* = PV(X - f_0)$$

$$P_0^* = (X - f_0)e^{-R_fT} + C_0^*$$

$$P_0^* = (\$100,000 - \$96,115)e^{-(.065)(1)} + \$2,139 = \$5,779$$

CHAPTER 13

MANAGING EQUITY POSITIONS WITH STOCK INDEX DERIVATIVES

13.1 INTRODUCTION

The annual volume of stock index futures, index options, and index futures options trading has grown dramatically over the last 20 years. The growth in the popularity of these derivatives can be attributed to their use as a stock portfolio management tool. In this chapter, we examine in more detail the speculative and hedging uses of these contracts as well as the arbitrage strategy known as program trading that is used when index derivative contracts are not priced correctly. We conclude the chapter by looking at dynamic portfolio insurance strategies that can be defined in terms of a binomial model using index futures and options.

13.2 SPECULATIVE STRATEGIES

As a speculative tool, stock index derivatives represent highly liquid alternatives to speculating on the overall stock market or on different types of stock indices (e.g., Russell 2000, Russell 1000, or Nasdaq 100). Index options and index futures options give speculators a tool for generating a number of different investment strategies. As we examined in Chapter 3, strategies such as outright call and put positions, straddles, strips, spreads, and combinations can be formed with spot and futures index options, making it possible for investors to speculate on expected bullish, bearish, or even stable market expectations with different return-risk exposures. In the case of stock index futures, bullish (bearish) speculators can take a long (short) position in an index futures contract.

In addition to outright positions, a speculator who wants to profit from directional changes in the market but who does not want to assume the degree of risk associated with an outright position can instead form intracommodity and intercommodity spreads with stock index futures. For example, a risk-averse spreader who is bullish on the stock market or a particular index could form an intracommodity spread by taking a short position in a nearer term index futures contract and a long position in a longer term one. Because longer term futures contracts are more price sensitive to spot market changes than shorter term ones, the spreader will find that for a subsequent increase in the market, the percentage gain in the long position on the distant contract will exceed the percentage loss on the short position on the nearby contract. In this case, the spreader will profit but not as much as she would with a pure speculative long position. On the other hand, if the market declines, the percentage losses on the long position will exceed the percentage gains from the short position. In this situation, the spreader will lose but not as much as she would have if she had an outright long position.

Instead of an intracommodity spread, a spreader alternatively could form an intercommodity spread by taking opposite positions in different index futures. For example, suppose the relation between the Russell 2000 index and the Russell 1000 index is such that when the Russell 2000 changes by 10%, the Russell 1000 changes by 9%. A risk-averse investor who is bearish on the market could set up an intercommodity spread by going short in the Russell 2000 contract and long in the Russell 1000 contract. Thus, similar to option spreads, index futures spreads allow investors to attain lower return-risk combinations than pure speculative positions. Moreover, by changing the ratios from one long to one short or by forming intercommodity spreads with different correlations, spreaders can attain a number of different return-risk combinations.

13.3   HEDGING WITH STOCK INDEX DERIVATIVES

One of the major uses of stock index derivatives is hedging stock portfolio positions. Several different types of hedging models can be applied to hedging portfolio positions. Depending on the underlying asset to be hedged, the most popular models are the ***Naive Hedging Model*** and the ***Price-Sensitivity Model***.

13.3.1   Naive Hedging Model

In most of the hedging cases we presented in this book, we assumed ideal conditions in which there was no quantity, quality, or timing risk extant. In such rare cases, a perfect hedge can be attained using a naive hedging model. In this model, the number of futures or option contracts (N) is found simply by dividing the current value of the spot position (V_0) by the price of the futures contract (f_0) or the exercise price on the option:

$$\text{Naive Hedge}: \ N = \frac{V_0}{f_0} \quad \text{or} \quad N = \frac{V_0}{X}$$

Thus, a portfolio manager who wants to lock in the future value of a $25 million portfolio highly correlated with the overall market when the futures price on the S&P 500 futures contract is 1000 ($250 multiplier) could do so by going short in N = 100 S&P 500 futures contracts:

$$N = \frac{V_0}{f_0} = \frac{\$25,000,000}{(1000)(\$250)} = 100 \text{ contracts}$$

Under ideal conditions, the combined value of the portfolio and the cash flows from the futures position would be worth $25 million at the futures delivery date.

In practice, we would expect some quality, quantity, and/or timing risks to exist in hedging a portfolio with index futures. For example, the $25 million portfolio may not be perfectly positively correlated with the S&P 500 spot index (quality risk). With less than perfect positive correlation, the percentage changes in the portfolio value would differ from those of the index. In such a case, a naive hedging model will not be able to provide a perfect hedge. Also, in most hedging applications, the time period for hedging the portfolio differs from the time period on the futures contract (timing risk), and the relative prices of the portfolio and futures contract usually do not yield a hedge ratio with a round number like 25 (quantity risk). For a manager wanting to hedge a stock portfolio with index futures in which such hedging risk exists, the price-sensitivity model may be more effective in reducing price risk than the naive hedging model.

13.3.2   Stock Index Price-Sensitivity Model

The price-sensitivity model determines the number of stock index futures contracts that will minimize the variability of the profits from a hedged portfolio consisting of the stock portfolio and stock index futures contracts. The model is derived in Appendix 13A at the end of this chapter. In this model, the number of futures contracts or hedge ratio (N_f) that will minimize the variability is

$$N_f = \beta \frac{V_0}{f_0}$$

where

$$V_0 = \text{current value of the stock portfolio}$$
$$f_0 = \text{price on the futures contract}$$
$$\beta = \text{beta of stock portfolio}$$

Thus, if a June S&P 500 futures contract is available at 1000, a portfolio manager wanting to hedge a $25 million portfolio with a beta of 1.5 would need 150 short contracts.[1]

$$N_f = \beta \frac{V_0}{f_0} = 1.5 \frac{\$25,000,000}{(1000)(\$250)} = 150 \text{ contracts}$$

The stock index price-sensitivity model easily can be extended to determining the optimum number of stock index option contracts needed to hedge a portfolio. When stock index options are used instead of futures to hedge a portfolio, the hedge ratio (N_p or N_c) is found by using the option's exercise price instead of the futures price (see Section 3.16 for an earlier example). That is

$$N = \frac{\beta V_0}{X}$$

13.3.3 Short Index Hedging Example

To illustrate the use of the price-sensitivity model, consider the case of a stock portfolio manager who in January feels that he may have to liquidate his stock portfolio in June. Because of this concern, suppose the manager decides to hedge the value of the stock portfolio by taking a short position in the June S&P 500 futures contract. Assume in this case that the portfolio is well diversified (no unsystematic risk); has a beta of 1.5; and in January, it is worth $25,000,000 when the S&P 500 spot index (S_0) is at 1250. Finally, suppose a June S&P 500 futures contract priced at 1250 is available. To hedge the portfolio using the price-sensitivity model, the manager would need to go short in 120 S&P 500 contracts:

$$N_f = \beta \frac{V_0}{f_0} = 1.5 \frac{\$25,000,000}{(1250)(\$250)} = 120 \text{ contracts}$$

As shown in Table 13.3-1, at the June expiration, the value of the futures-hedged portfolio would be $25,000,000, regardless of the market index level.

In this example, we have a perfect hedge. This is because we have assumed the portfolio is well diversified and the futures price and portfolio value are such that exactly

---

[1] A diversified portfolio with a beta greater than 1 can be thought of as a leveraged investment in the S&P 500. The number of hypothetical SP 500 shares would be equal to $n_f = \beta V_0 / S_0$ in which S_0 is the spot S&P 500 index, and the amount of debt used to finance the index stock would be the present value of $N_f S_0 - V_0$. Thus, if the spot S&P 500 index is at 1000, a $25 million dollar portfolio with $\beta = 1.5$ would be the equivalent to buying $N_f = 1.5(\$25M)/1000 = 37,500$ index shares at $1000 per share ($37.5M) and borrowing an amount equal to the present value of $12.50M ($37.5M − $25M).

TABLE 13.3-1 Value of the Hedged Stock Portfolio

(1) S&P 500 Spot Index at Expiration: $S_T = f_t$	(2) Proportional Change in Portfolio Value (βg): $\beta g = 1.5(S_T - 1250)/1250$	(3) Portfolio Value: $(1 + \beta g)\$25M$	(4) Futures Profit: $120(\$250)$ $(1250 - f_T)$	(5) Hedged Portfolio Value (3) + (4)
1000	−.30	$17,500,000	$7,500,000	$25,000,000
1125	−.15	21,250,000	3,750,000	25,000,000
1250	0	25,000,000	0	25,000,000
1375	.15	28,750,000	−3,750,000	25,000,000
1500	.30	32,500,000	−7,500,000	25,000,000

$$N_f = \frac{\beta V_0}{f_0} = \frac{-(1.5)(\$25,000,000)}{(\$250)(1250)} = 120 \text{ contracts}$$

120 contracts are needed. In most cases, we would not expect such conditions to exist. Also, if the carrying-cost model holds, we would not expect any difference to exist between locking in the June value of the portfolio with index futures and locking in the June portfolio value by selling the portfolio in January and investing the proceeds in a risk-free security for the period. Thus, if the portfolio manager actually knew he would be liquidating the portfolio in June, then selling 120 futures contracts in January and closing them in June along with liquidating the portfolio should be equivalent to selling the portfolio in January and investing the funds in risk-free security for the period. If this equivalence did not hold, an arbitrage opportunity would exist (the arbitrage strategy underlying the price of an index futures contract is discussed further in Section 13.7).

Suppose that instead of locking in a future portfolio value, the portfolio manager wanted portfolio insurance so that he had downside protection in case the market declined but still could profit if the market increased. In terms of the example, suppose there is a June 1250 S&P 500 spot put option trading at 50 that exists (recall the multiple on S&P 500 spot options is $100): $X = (1250)(\$100) = \$125,000$ and $P_0 = (\$100)(50) = \$5,000$. Using the price-sensitivity model, the manager could attain portfolio insurance by buying 300 put contracts for $1.5M:

$$N_p = \beta \frac{V_0}{X} = 1.5 \frac{\$25,000,000}{(1250)(\$100)} = 300 \text{ contracts}$$
$$\text{Cost} = (300)(\$100)(50) = \$1,500,000$$

As shown in Table 13.3-2, if the market is at 1250 or less at the June expiration, the value of the put-hedged portfolio would be worth $23,500,000 ($25,000,000 − $1,500,000). If the market is above 1250, the value of the hedged portfolio would rise as the market increases. Thus, for the costs of the puts, the portfolio manager can attain portfolio insurance: downside protection with the possibility of capital gains if the market rises.

13.3.4 Long Index Hedging Example

A portfolio manager who was planning to invest a future inflow of cash in a stock portfolio could lock in the purchase price of the portfolio by going long in a stock index futures contract. For example, suppose in January, the portfolio manager in the previous example was anticipating an inflow of cash in June and was planning to invest the cash in a stock portfolio with a beta of 1.5 and currently worth $25,000,000. If the June S&P 500 futures contract is at $f_0 = 1250$, the manager could hedge the purchase price by going long

TABLE 13.3-2 Value of Put-Hedged Stock Portfolio

(1) S&P 500 Spot Index at Expiration: S_T	(2) Proportional Change in Portfolio Value (βg): $\beta g = 1.5$ $(S_T - 1250)/1250$	(3) Portfolio Value: $(1 + \beta g)\$25M$	(4) Put Profit $\{300(\$100)$ $Max[1250 - S_T, 0]\}$ $- \$1.5M$	(5) Hedged Portfolio Value (3) + (4)
1000	−.30	$17,500,000	$6,000,000	$23,500,000
1125	−.15	21,250,000	2,250,000	23,500,000
1250	0	25,000,000	−1,500,000	23,500,000
1375	.15	28,750,000	−1,500,000	27,250,000
1500	.30	32,500,000	−1,500,000	31,000,000

$$N_p = \beta \frac{V_0}{X} = 1.5 \frac{\$25,000,000}{(1250)(\$100)} = 300 \text{ contracts}$$

$$\text{Cost} = (300)(\$100)(50) = \$1,500,000$$

TABLE 13.3-3 Future Portfolio Purchase Hedged With Index Futures and Hedged With Index Options

(1) S&P 500 Spot Index: S_T	(2) Proportional Change in Portfolio Value $\beta g = 1.5(S_T - 1250)/1250$	(3) Portfolio Costs $\$25M$ $(1 + \beta g)$	(4) Futures Profit $120(\$250)$ $(f_T - 1250)$	(5) Call Profit $\{300(\$100)$ $Max[S_T - 1250, 0]\}$ $- \$1.5M$	(6) Portfolio Costs With Futures (3) − (4)	(7) Portfolio Costs With Calls (3) − (5)
1000	−.30	$17,500,000	−$7,500,000	−$1,500,000	$25,000,000	$19,000,000
1125	−.15	21,250,000	−3,750,000	−1,500,000	25,000,000	22,750,000
1250	0	25,000,000	0	−1,500,000	25,000,000	26,500,000
1375	.15	28,750,000	3,750,000	2,250,000	25,000,000	26,500,000
1500	.30	32,500,000	7,500,000	6,000,000	25,000,000	26,500,000

$$N_f = \beta \frac{V_0}{f_0} = 1.5 \frac{\$25,000,000}{(1250)(\$250)} = 120 \text{ contracts}$$

$$N_c = \beta \frac{V_0}{X_0} = 1.5 \frac{\$25,000,000}{(1250)(\$150)} = 300 \text{ contracts}$$

$$\text{Cost} = (300)(\$100)(50) = \$1,500,000$$

in 120 contracts:

$$N_f = \beta \frac{V_0}{f_0} = 1.5 \frac{\$25,000,000}{(1250)(\$250)} = 120 \text{ contracts}$$

As shown in Table 13.3-3 (Column (6)), the long hedge position enables the manager to lock in cost of $25 million for purchasing the portfolio and closing the futures position.

In addition to an anticipatory hedge, the manager also could lock in a maximum portfolio cost (or the minimum number of shares purchased) with the possibility of lower costs (or more shares purchased) if the market declines by purchasing an index call option. Column (7) of Table 13.3-3 shows the costs of purchasing the portfolio and closing $N_c = 300$ June 1250 call options purchased at 50:

$$N_C = \beta \frac{V_0}{X} = 1.5 \frac{\$25,000,000}{(1250)(\$100)} = 300 \text{ contracts}$$

$$\text{Cost} = (300)(\$100)(50) = \$1,500,000$$

As shown in Table 13.3-1, if the index is at 1250 or higher, the costs of purchasing the portfolio and closing the call options are limited to $26,500,000 ($25,000,000 plus $1,500,000 cost of the calls), and if the index is less than 1250, the net costs decline as the index decreases.

13.4 MARKET TIMING

Instead of immunizing a portfolio's value against market or systematic risk, suppose a manager wanted to change her portfolio's exposure to the market. For example, a stock portfolio manager who is very confident of a bull market may want to give her portfolio more exposure to the market by increasing the portfolio's beta. Changing a portfolio's beta to profit from an expected change in the market is referred to as ***market timing.***

Without index derivative, the beta of a portfolio can be changed only by altering the portfolio's allocations of securities. With index futures, though, a manager can change the portfolio beta, β_0, to a new target beta, β_{TR}, simply by buying or selling futures contracts. The number of futures contracts needed to move the portfolio beta from β_0 to β_{TR} can be determined using the price-sensitivity model in which

$$N_f = \frac{V_0}{f_0}(\beta_{TR} - \beta_0)$$

where :
if $\beta_{TR} > \beta_0$, long in futures
if $\beta_{TR} < \beta_0$, short in futures

A portfolio's exposure to the market also can be changed by buying index call or put options. The number of options needed to change the beta is

$$N_f = \frac{V_0}{X}(\beta_{TR} - \beta_0)$$

where
if $\beta_{TR} > \beta_0$, long in index calls
if $\beta_{TR} < \beta_0$, long in index puts

13.4.1 Market-Timing Example

Consider the case of a stock portfolio manager who in September is confident the market will increase over the next 3 months and as a result wants to change her portfolio's beta from its current value of $\beta_0 = 1$ to $\beta_{TR} = 1.25$. Suppose the portfolio currently is worth $50 million, the spot S&P 500 index is at 1000, and the price on the December S&P 500 futures contract is 1000. To adjust the portfolio beta from 1 to 1.25, the manager would need to go long in $N_f = 50$ December S&P 500 index futures:

$$N_f = \frac{V_0}{f_0}(\beta_{TR} - \beta_0) = \frac{\$50,000,000}{(1000)(\$250)}(1.25 - 1) = 50$$

As shown in Table 13.4-1, if the market increases, the manager earns higher rates of return from the futures-adjusted portfolio than from the unadjusted portfolio. If the market declines, though, she incurs greater losses with the adjusted portfolio than with the unadjusted. For example, if the market increases by 10%, the portfolio increases from $50M to $55M (a 10% increase, reflecting a $\beta = 1$), and the long futures position generates an additional cash flow of $1.25M, increasing the portfolio value to $56.25M

TABLE 13.4-1   Market Timing

(1) S&P 500 Spot Index: $S_T = f_T$	(2) Proportional Change: $g =$ $(S_T - 185)/185$	(3) Futures Profit $(50)($250)$ $[f_T - 1000]$	(4) Portfolio Value $\$50M(1 + g)$	(5) Portfolio Value With Futures (3) + (4)
800	−.20	−$2,500,000	$40,000,000	$37,500,000
900	−.10	−1,250,000	45,000,000	43,750,000
1000	0	0	50,000,000	50,000,000
1100	.10	1,250,000	55,000,000	56,250,000
1200	.20	2,500,000	60,000,000	62,500,000

Portfolio Rates of Return and $\beta = \Delta$ Portfolio Rate$/\Delta g^+$

S&P 500 Spot Index: S_T	(6) Portfolio Rate: [Col(4)/$50M] − 1	(7) $\beta =$ Col(6)/Col(2)	(8) Futures-Enhanced Portfolio Rate: [Col (5)/$50M] − 1	(9) $\beta =$ Col (8)/Col(9)
800	−.20	1	−.25	1.25
900	−.10	1	−.125	1.25
1000	0	—	0	—
1100	.10	1	.125	1.25
1200	.20	1	.25	1.25

$$n_f = \frac{V_0}{f_0}(\beta_{TR} - \beta_0) = \frac{\$50,000,000}{(1000)(\$250)}(1.25 - 1) = 50$$

(a 12.5% increase, reflecting a $\beta = 1.25$). In contrast, if the market decreases by 10%, the portfolio decreases from $50M to $45M (a 10% decrease, reflecting a $\beta = 1$), and the long futures position loses $1.25 M, decreasing the portfolio value to $43.75M (a 12.5% decrease, reflecting a $\beta = 1.25$). Thus, the futures-enhanced portfolio is consistent with the characteristics of a portfolio with a β of 1.25.

The manager also could increase her portfolio's exposure by buying index calls. For example, if there is a December 1000 S&P 500 call option available, the manager could increase her market exposure by buying 125 calls:

$$N_C = \frac{V_0}{X}(\beta_{TR} - \beta_0) = \frac{\$50,000,000}{(1000)(\$150)}(1.25 - 1) = 125 \text{ calls}$$

13.5   SPECULATING ON UNSYSTEMATIC RISK

The price movements of an individual stock are affected by both systematic factors (market factors that affect all stocks) and unsystematic factors (factors unique to the securities of a particular industry or firm). Given this, suppose an investor is very confident that firm or industry factors in the future will lead to a stock price increase. However, suppose the investor also is bearish about the market, fearing that a general price decline in all securities would negate the anticipated positive impacts on the stock's price resulting from the specific firm or industry factors. The investor would therefore like to eliminate the stock's systematic factors, leaving his investment exposed only to the unsystematic factors. With index futures (and options), an investor can accomplish this by hedging away the systematic risk of the stock.

13.5.1 Speculating on Unsystematic Risk: Example

To illustrate how speculating on unsystematic risk works, consider the case of a bank trust department that in September identifies the ABC company as a good candidate for a takeover by a leveraged buyout firm. Based on this expectation, suppose the trust department is considering purchasing 50,000 shares of ABC stock but is hesitant because it is afraid the stock market could decline over the next 3 months (the time period they believe the takeover could happen). To hedge against the systematic risk, the trust department could go short in December index futures (or purchase December stock index put options). In this case, suppose ABC stock has a beta of 1.25 and is trading at $20 per share, the spot S&P 500 is at 1000, and the December S&P 500 futures contract is at 1000. The trust department could speculate on the stock's unsystematic risk while hedging the systematic risk by buying 50,000 shares of the ABC stock and going short in 5 December index futures contracts:

$$N_f = -\beta \frac{V_0}{f_0} = -(1.25)\frac{(50,000)(\$20)}{(1000)(\$250)} = 5 \text{ Short Contracts}$$

To see the possible impacts of using this strategy, consider the following three scenarios occurring in mid-December:

- **Scenario A:** The takeover of ABC and a bull market cause the price of ABC stock to increase by 15% to $23 and the spot S&P 500 to increase to 1050.

- **Scenario B:** The takeover of ABC and a bear market cause ABC stock to increase by 5% to $21 and the spot S&P 500 to decrease to 900.

- **Scenario C:** No takeover of ABC and a bear market cause ABC stock to decrease by 12% to $17.60 and the spot S&P 500 to decrease to 900.

Table 13.5-1 shows the values and rates of return for both the futures-hedged stock position and the unhedged stock position for each of the three cases.

As shown in Table 13.5-1, the highest returns are earned on the hedged stock if Scenario B occurs: The takeover takes place during a bear market. In this case, the trust department would gain both from speculating on the takeover and from the short futures position, earning a 17.5% rate of return. If the trust department did not hedge, then its rate

TABLE 13.5-1 Speculating on Unsystematic Risk

(1) Scenario	(2) Futures Profit $(5)(\$250)[1000 - f_T]$	(3) Stock Value Stock Price (50,000 Shares)	(4) Stock Value Hedged With Futures: (2) + (3)
A ABC Stock: $23 Bull Market: $S_T = f_T = 1050$	−$62,500	$1,150,000	$1,087,500
B ABC Stock: $21 Bear Market: $S_T = f_T = 900$	$125,000	$1,050,000	$1,175,000
C ABC Stock: $17.60 Bear Market: $S_T = f_T = 900$	$125,000	$880,000	$1,005,000

		Rates of Return:		
Scenario	Unhedged Rate $= \dfrac{\text{Col.(3)}}{(50,000)(\$20)} - 1$		Hedged Rate $= \dfrac{\text{Col.(4)}}{(50,000)(\$20)} - 1$	
A	15%		8.75%	
B	5%		17.5%	
C	−12%		0.5%	

of return would have been only 5%. Positive rates of return on the hedged stock position also are realized in Case A in which ABC stock rises during a bull market. Because the trust department has hedged away the systematic factors, the hedged returns are not as high as the unhedged position in this scenario. Finally, in Scenario C in which the takeover does not occur and the market declines, the hedged stock position is lower but not as much as the unhedged position. Thus, the best scenario for the trust department is case B in which both of the department's expectation occur—takeover and bear market.

13.6 STOCK INDEX FUTURES PRICING: CARRYING-COST MODEL

The equilibrium futures price on a stock index futures contract is determined by the carrying-cost model. As described in Chapter 11, the equilibrium index futures price is equal to the net costs of carrying a spot index portfolio or proxy portfolio to expiration (T). For the case of a discrete dividend payment on the portfolio worth D_T at expiration, the equilibrium price is

$$f_0^* = S_0(1 + R^A)^T - D_T \qquad (13.6\text{-}1)$$

where
S_0 = current spot index value
D_T = value of the stock index dividends at time T

For the continuous dividend case, the equilibrium futures price is

$$f_0^* = S_0 \, e^{(R^A - \psi)T} \qquad (13.6\text{-}2)$$

where
ψ = annual dividend yield

If the equilibrium condition does not hold, an arbitrage opportunity will exist by taking a position in the spot portfolio and an opposite one in the futures contract. For example, if the market price on the futures contract (f_0^m) exceeds the equilibrium price, an arbitrageur could earn a riskless profit of $f_0^m - f_0^*$ with an **index arbitrage** strategy in which she borrows S_0 dollars at the risk-free rate of R^A, buys the spot index portfolio (or proxy portfolio) for S_0, and locks in the selling price on the portfolio at time T by going short in the index futures at f_0^m.

The carrying-costs model for index futures also can be described as an investment in a riskless stock index portfolio paying a certain dividend or dividend yield. That is, an investor who purchases a spot index portfolio (at S_0) paying a certain dividend of D_T or dividend yield of ψ and then locks in the portfolio's selling price at time T by going short in an index futures contract at f_0 will earn a riskless one-period rate of return of

$$\text{Discrete: } R = \left[\frac{f_0 + D_T}{S_0} \right]^{1/T} - 1 \qquad (13.6\text{-}3)$$

$$\text{Continuous: } R = \frac{\ln \left[\dfrac{f_0^m}{S_0} \right]}{T} + \psi \qquad (13.6\text{-}4)$$

Because this investment is riskless, in equilibrium, the futures and spot prices should be such that the rate of return on the investment is equal to a riskless rate (if not, abnormal rates of return could be earned from this investment). Thus, setting the rate, R, in Equations

(13.6-3) and (13.6-4) equal to the risk-free rate, R^A, and then solving for f_0, we obtain the carrying-cost model, and solving for S_0 we obtain

$$\text{Discrete: } S_0 = \frac{f_0 + D_T}{(1 + R^A)^T} \tag{13.6-5}$$

$$\text{Continuous: } S_0 = f_0 e^{-(R^A - \psi)T} \tag{13.6-6}$$

Hence, if the carrying-cost model holds, then, in equilibrium, the rate of return from an investment in a spot portfolio with the selling price locked in with a futures contract is equal to the risk-free rate, and the spot portfolio price is equal to the present value of the futures price and the portfolio's dividends, with the discount rate being equal to the risk-free rate.

13.7 INDEX ARBITRAGE AND PROGRAM TRADING

13.7.1 Program Trading

Introduced to the financial vernacular in the 1980s, *program trading* refers to the use of computers in constructing and executing security portfolio positions. Program trading often involves using computer programs to (1) monitor real time data of stocks, futures, and option prices to identify any mispricing of stock portfolio values relative to the values of index futures or option positions; (2) define appropriate arbitrage strategies given mispriced portfolios vis-à-vis futures and option prices; and (3) execute orders so securities can be bought or sold quickly and simultaneously when arbitrage advantages exist.

A number of stock portfolio arbitrage and hedging strategies involve monitoring and periodic portfolio adjustments that can be classified as program trading. One group of these strategies is the index arbitrage strategies and the other is dynamic portfolio insurance strategies (discussed in Section 13.8).

13.7.2 Index Arbitrage

Index arbitrage strategies can be formed with stock index futures contracts and a portfolio consisting of either the stocks comprising the index in their proper allocation or a proxy portfolio. To illustrate an index arbitrage strategy, consider a proxy portfolio that is highly diversified, has a beta of 1, is valued at $25 million, and is expected to pay dividends worth $600,000 at the end of 6 months. If the spot S&P 500 index is at 1250, the portfolio can be viewed as a proxy portfolio consisting 20,000 hypothetical shares of the index, with each share priced at $1250 and paying a dividend of $30 per index share ($600,000/20,000).

Given this proxy portfolio, suppose the risk-free rate is 6% (annualized), and an S&P 500 futures contract exists that expires in 6 months (T = .5). In terms of the carrying-cost model, the equilibrium price on the futures contract using the proxy portfolio's dividend per share would be 1256.953768:

$$f_0^* = S_0(1 + R^A)^T - D_T$$

$$f_0^* = 1250(1.06)^{.5} - 30 = 1256.953768$$

If the actual futures price is above the equilibrium, for example, at $f_0^m = 1265$, an arbitrageur could earn a riskless profit of $8.046232 (= $1265 – 1256.953768) per index share, with an index arbitrage strategy formed by borrowing $1250 at 6%, buying an S&P 500 spot index share, and going short in the S&P 500 futures contract at 1265. As a program trading strategy using the proxy portfolio, the index arbitrage strategy would consist of borrowing

$25 million at 6%, purchasing the proxy portfolio, and going short in 80 (= 20,000/250) S&P 500 futures contracts (given the contracts $250 multiplier) expiring at the end of 6 months. As shown in Table 13.7-1, with the contract price on the expiring futures contract equal to the spot S&P 500 index at expiration, this strategy would yield a riskless profit of $160,925 (($1265 − 1256.953768)(20,000)) at expiration, regardless of the value of the index.

If the contract price on the futures contract is below 1256.953768, the preceding index arbitrage strategy is reversed. In this case, an arbitrageur would take a short position in the spot portfolio, long position in the risk-free security, and a long position in the futures contract. For example, if the index futures contract is at 1245, a portfolio manager with the $25 million proxy portfolio could sell it and invest the proceeds in the risk-free security for 6 months and then go long in 80 S&P 500 futures contracts. As shown in Table 13.7-2, at expiration, the manager could repurchase the same portfolio and close the futures position for a total cost of $24.9 million. The manager would have earned $739,075 during the period from the investment in the risk-free security; the $739,075, in turn, is $239,075 greater than the $600,000 in dividends foregone by selling the portfolio. By implementing this type of index arbitrage strategy, the manager would be able to earn an arbitrage profit of $239,075 ((1256.953768 − 1245)(20,000)), regardless of any changes in the market.

TABLE 13.7-1   Index Arbitrage When $f_0^m > f_0^*$

$f_0^* = 1256.953768$, $f_0^m = 1265$, $S_0 = 1250$
Strategy: Borrow $25 million at 6% interest for 6 months; purchase $25 million proxy portfolio; go short in 80 S&P 500 futures contracts expiring at the end of 6 months at 1265

Closing Position	Index Decreases: g = −.10 $S_T = f_T = 1125$	Index Increases: 1 g = .10 $S_T = f_T = 1375$
Debt: $25M(1.06)^{.5}$	−$25,739,075	−$25,739,075
Portfolio: $S_T(20,000) = \$25M(1 + g)$	22,500,000	27,500,000
Futures: $(80)(\$250)(1265 − f_T)$	2,800,000	−2,200,000
Dividends	600,000	600,000
Arbitrage Cash Flow	$160,925	$160,925

TABLE 13.7-2   Index Arbitrage When $f_0^m < f_0^*$

$f_0^* = 1256.953768$, $f_0^m = 1245$, $S_0 = 1250$
Strategy: Sell $25 million proxy portfolio; invest $25M in risk-free security at 6% interest for 6 months; go long in 80 S&P 500 futures contracts expiring at the end of 6 months at 1245.

Closing Positions	Index Decreases g = −.10 $S_T = f_T = 1125$	Index Increases g = .10 $S_T = f_T = 1375$
Portfolio Purchase: $−S_T(20,000) = −\$25M(1 + g)$	−$22,500,000	−$27,500,000
Futures: $(80)(\$250)(f_T − 1245)$	−2,400,000	2,600,000
Investment: $25M(1.06)^{.5}$	25,739,075	25,739,075
Dividends Foregone	−600,000	−600,000
Arbitrage Cash Flow	$239,075	$239,075

13.7.3 Stock Volatility and the Triple Witching Hour

Because the price of an expiring futures contract is equal to the spot index price at expiration, program traders who have implemented an index arbitrage strategy often will wait until the expiration day on the futures contract to close their positions. As a result, on or near the delivery day of the index futures contract, an abnormally large volume of trading often occurs on the exchanges as program traders, other arbitrageurs, and hedgers close their futures positions and liquidate or purchase large blocks of stock. This reversing of positions has often caused large swings to occur in stock prices, with the fluctuations being particularly dramatic on the *triple witching hour*—the last hour of trading on the day when index futures, stock index options, and options on stock index futures all expire.

Finance scholars have debated over the significance of the increased volatility on expiration days resulting from program trading. Some scholars argue that program traders often liquidate stocks during a bear market and purchase them during a bull market, thus causing the market prices of stocks to overshoot their equilibrium levels, leading to market inefficiency. Other scholars, though, maintain that index arbitrageurs actually move stock prices to their equilibrium levels, and any temporary increase in volatility that may occur on the expiration date should be viewed simply as part of the costs of ensuring an efficient market.[2]

13.8 DYNAMIC PORTFOLIO INSURANCE

Dynamic asset allocation is an active strategy of changing a bond and equity mix over time and in response to stock market changes to achieve a certain return distribution at the end of a period. For example, an investment fund's objective may be to have a return distribution on its portfolio at the end of 5 years that matches the market's return if the market increases but has a certain minimum return if the market declines. This type of dynamic asset allocation strategy represents essentially a long-run portfolio insurance strategy of trying to ensure a minimum portfolio value is attained while at the same time leaving the chance for gains in value to occur if certain states are realized. For a stock portfolio, the simplest strategy to ensure a minimum value is to buy put options on stock indices or to construct a fiduciary call. For institutional investors, though, this strategy may be difficult to implement if the time period that investors want for protection exceeds the put's expiration period. For longer horizon periods, portfolio managers alternatively can use a more dynamic strategy. For example, instead of using options, managers could form portfolios consisting of a stock portfolio and a risk-free security or risk-free bond portfolio and then use the binomial model framework to adjust the portfolio each period to attain end-of-the-period objectives. In this section, we examine dynamic portfolio insurance strategies using stock and risk-free bond portfolios.

13.8.1 A Dynamic Portfolio Insurance Strategy Using Index Puts

To illustrate the construction of a dynamic portfolio insurance strategy, first consider the case of a stock portfolio hedged with index put options using a binomial framework. In this case, assume a portfolio manager wants insurance for a diversified $25 million stock portfolio with a $\beta = 1$. In constructing the portfolio insurance strategy, suppose the manager divides the total period in which she wants insurance into two subperiods ($n = 2$) and estimates the proportional period increase and decrease for the spot index to be $u = 1.1$

---

[2] Stoll and Whaley in their 1987 study argued that price changes on the triple witching hour are no different than price changes that occur as a result of any block trade.

EXHIBIT 13.8-1   Dynamic Portfolio Insurance

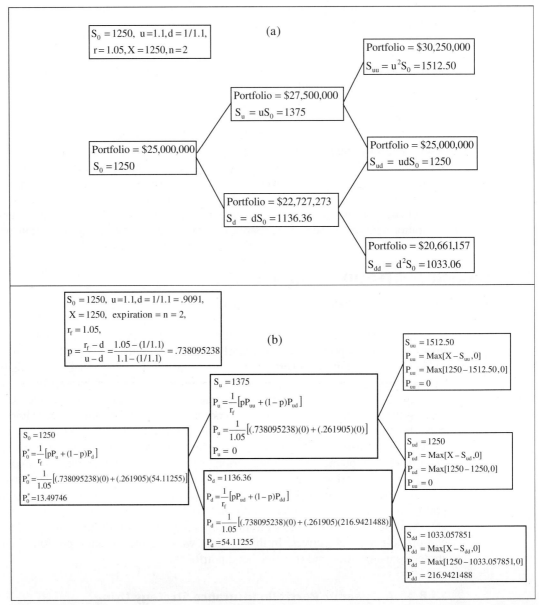

continued

and d = 1/1.1 = .9091. Also, assume the current spot index is at 1250, the portfolio pays no dividends during the period, and the rate on a risk-free bond is 5% per subperiod. Exhibit 13.8-1(a) shows the possible values of the portfolio and the spot index given the manager's estimated u and d values.

Given the three possible portfolio values at the end of Period 2, suppose the manager would like a minimum portfolio value of at least $25 million at the end of the period, with the possibility of a portfolio worth $30.25 million if the spot index reaches 1512.50. To achieve these dual objectives, suppose the manager decides to purchase European index

EXHIBIT 13.8-1   Continued

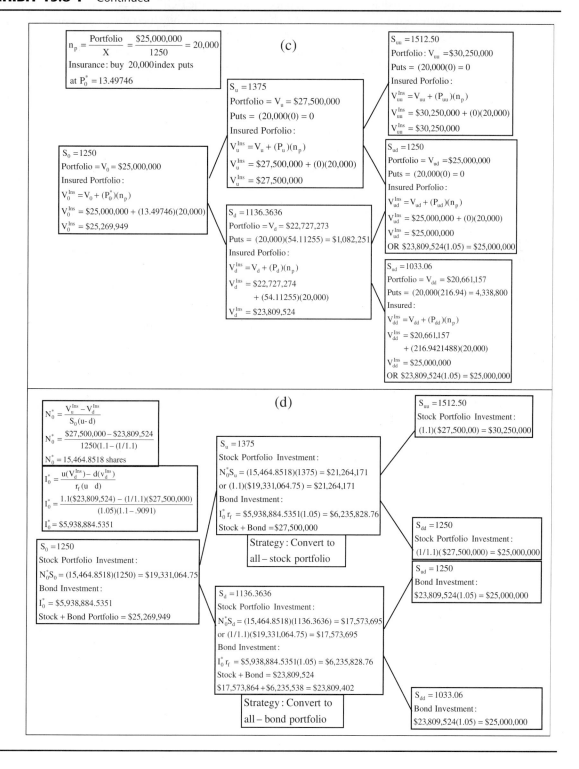

(c)

$$n_p = \frac{\text{Portfolio}}{X} = \frac{\$25,000,000}{1250} = 20,000$$

Insurance: buy 20,000 index puts

at $P_0^* = 13.49746$

$S_u = 1375$

Portfolio $= V_u = \$27,500,000$

Puts $= (20,000(0)) = 0$

Insured Porfolio:

$V_u^{Ins} = V_u + (P_u)(n_p)$

$V_u^{Ins} = \$27,500,000 + (0)(20,000)$

$V_u^{Ins} = \$27,500,000$

$S_0 = 1250$

Portfolio $= V_0 = \$25,000,000$

Insured Portfolio:

$V_0^{Ins} = V_0 + (P_0^*)(n_p)$

$V_0^{Ins} = \$25,000,000 + (13.49746)(20,000)$

$V_0^{Ins} = \$25,269,949$

$S_d = 1136.3636$

Portfolio $= V_d = \$22,727,273$

Puts $= (20,000)(54.11255) = \$1,082,251$

Insured Porfolio:

$V_d^{Ins} = V_d + (P_d)(n_p)$

$V_d^{Ins} = \$22,727,274$

$+ (54.11255)(20,000)$

$V_d^{Ins} = \$23,809,524$

$S_{uu} = 1512.50$

Portfolio: $V_{uu} = \$30,250,000$

Puts $= (20,000(0)) = 0$

Insured Porfolio:

$V_{uu}^{Ins} = V_{uu} + (P_{uu})(n_p)$

$V_{uu}^{Ins} = \$30,250,000 + (0)(20,000)$

$V_{uu}^{Ins} = \$30,250,000$

$S_{ud} = 1250$

Portfolio $= V_{ud} = \$25,000,000$

Puts $= (20,000(0)) = 0$

Insured Porfolio:

$V_{ud}^{Ins} = V_{ud} + (P_{ud})(n_p)$

$V_{ud}^{Ins} = \$25,000,000 + (0)(20,000)$

$V_{ud}^{Ins} = \$25,000,000$

OR $\$23,809,524(1.05) = \$25,000,000$

$S_{ud} = 1033.06$

Portfolio $= V_{dd} = \$20,661,157$

Puts $= (20,000(216.94) = 4,338,800$

Insured:

$V_{dd}^{Ins} = V_{dd} + (P_{dd})(n_p)$

$V_{dd}^{Ins} = \$20,661,157$

$+ (216.9421488)(20,000)$

$V_{dd}^{Ins} = \$25,000,000$

OR $\$23,809,524(1.05) = \$25,000,000$

(d)

$$N_0^* = \frac{V_u^{Ins} - V_d^{Ins}}{S_0(u-d)}$$

$$N_0^* = \frac{\$27,500,000 - \$23,809,524}{1250(1.1 - (1/1.1))}$$

$N_0^* = 15,464.8518$ shares

$$I_0^* = \frac{u(V_d^{Ins}) - d(v_d^{Ins})}{r_f(u-d)}$$

$$I_0^* = \frac{1.1(\$23,809,524) - (1/1.1)(\$27,500,000)}{(1.05)(1.1 - .9091)}$$

$I_0^* = \$5,938,884.5351$

$S_0 = 1250$

Stock Portfolio Investment:

$N_0^* S_0 = (15,464.8518)(1250) = \$19,331,064.75$

Bond Investment:

$I_0^* = \$5,938,884.5351$

Stock + Bond Portfolio $= \$25,269,949$

$S_u = 1375$

Stock Portfolio Investment:

$N_0^* S_u = (15,464.8518)(1375) = \$21,264,171$

or $(1.1)(\$19,331,064.75) = \$21,264,171$

Bond Investment:

$I_0^* r_f = \$5,938,884.5351(1.05) = \$6,235,828.76$

Stock + Bond $= \$27,500,000$

Strategy: Convert to

all – stock portfolio

$S_d = 1136.3636$

Stock Portfolio Investment:

$N_0^* S_d = (15,464.8518)(1136.3636) = \$17,573,695$

or $(1/1.1)(\$19,331,064.75) = \$17,573,695$

Bond Investment:

$I_0^* r_f = \$5,938,884.5351(1.05) = \$6,235,828.76$

Stock + Bond $= \$23,809,524$

$\$17,573,864 + \$6,235,538 = \$23,809,402$

Strategy: Convert to

all – bond portfolio

$S_{uu} = 1512.50$

Stock Portfolio Investment:

$(1.1)(\$27,500,00) = \$30,250,000$

$S_{dd} = 1250$

Stock Portfolio Investment:

$(1/1.1)(\$27,500,000) = \$25,000,000$

$S_{ud} = 1250$

Bond Investment:

$\$23,809,524(1.05) = \$25,000,000$

$S_{dd} = 1033.06$

Bond Investment:

$\$23,809,524(1.05) = \$25,000,000$

put options with a 1250 exercise price and expiring at the end of Period 2. Exhibit 13.8-1(b) shows the possible values of this put option using the BOPM for put options (for simplicity, we disregard the multiplier). As shown in the exhibit, the current binomial put value is 13.49746.

To ensure the $25 million portfolio, the manager would need to purchase $N_0 = \$25,000,000/1250 = 20,000$ stock index puts. The total cost of the put options would be $269,949 (= (20,000)(13.49746))$. As shown in Exhibit 13.8-1(c), if the spot index increases to 1375 at the end of Period 1, then the puts would be worthless, but the stock portfolio would be worth $27,500,000 and one period later, the stock portfolio would be worth either $30,250,000 or $25,000,000. On the other hand, if the index decreases to 1136.3636, the stock portfolio would be worth only $22,727,273, but the puts would be worth $1,082,251 (= (54.11255)(20,000))$, yielding an insured portfolio worth $23,809,524 as shown in Exhibit 13.8-1(c). The next period, the insured portfolio would be worth $25 million at either index value (1250 or 1033.06). Note that at the end of Period 1, the manager could have liquidated the portfolio and put options when the index was at 1036.3636 and invested the proceeds of $23,809,524 in a risk-free security at 5%. Doing this also would also yield $25,000,000 (= \$23,809,524(1.05))$ next period, regardless of the index values.

13.8.2 A Dynamic Portfolio Insurance Strategy Using Bonds

If the investment time period or the standardization of the put contracts makes it impossible to use index puts for insurance, the portfolio manger in our preceding case could obtain the same type of protection alternatively with a stock portfolio and an investment in a risk-free bond portfolio (I_0). To determine the correct stock portfolio and bond investment, we define the value of the manger's stock portfolio (V_0) in terms of hypothetical shares of the S&P 500 (N_0) times the spot index price. Because the $25M portfolio is well diversified with a $\beta = 1$, it can be viewed as an investment in $N_0 = \$25,000,000/1250 = 20,000$ hypothetical shares of the index, with each share worth $S_0 = \$1250$ per share:

$$V_0 = N_0 S_0 = (20,000)(1250) = \$25,000,000$$

Using the BOPM framework, at the end of the first period, this spot index portfolio would be worth either $27,500,000 or $22,727,273:

$$V_u = N_0(uS_0) = (20,000)(1375) = \$27,500,000$$
$$V_d = N_0(d(S_0) = (20,000)(1136.3636) = \$22,727,273$$

Given the dual objectives of attaining at the end of Period 2 a minimum $25,000,000 stock portfolio value if the market stays the same or declines and a $30,250,000 value if the market increases to 1512.50, the manager needs to construct an insured portfolio consisting of the stock portfolio and the risk-free bond (I_0) that at the end of Period 1 would be worth the two possible put-insured portfolio values of $V_u^{Ins} = \$27,500,000$ and $= V_d^{Ins} = \$23,809,524$:

$$\text{Index at } S_u = 1375: V_u^{Ins} = V_u + P_u n_p = \$27,500,000 + (0)(20,000)$$
$$= \$27,500,000$$
$$\text{Index at } S_d = 1136.3636: V_d^{Ins} = V_d + P_d n_p = \$22,727,273 + (54.11255)(20,000)$$
$$= \$23,809,524$$

This portfolio can be found by solving for the N_0^* and I_0^* in which

$$N_0(uS_0) + I_0r_f = V_u^{Ins}$$ (13.8-1)

$$N_0(dS_0) + I_0r_f = V_d^{Ins}$$

or in terms of the example

$$N_0(1375) + I_0(1.05) = \$27,500,000$$

$$N_0(1136.3636) + I_0(1.05) = \$23,809,524$$

Solving Equation (13.8-1) simultaneously for N_0^* and I_0^* yields

$$N_0^* = \frac{V_u^{Ins} - V_d^{Ins}}{S_0(u - d)} = \frac{\$27,500,000 - \$23,809,524}{1250(1.1 - (1/1.1))} = 15,464.8518 \text{ shares}$$

$$I_0^* = \frac{u(V_d^{Ins}) - d(v_d^{Ins})}{r_f(u - d)} = \frac{1.1(\$23,809,524) - (1/1.1)(\$27,500,000)}{(1.05)(1.1 - (1/1.1))}$$

$$= \$5,938,884.5351$$

Thus, to have the same type of portfolio insurance protection obtained with puts, the manager would need a stock portfolio that is the equivalent of an index portfolio consisting of $N_0^* = 15,464.8518$ index shares; this index portfolio, in turn, would be equivalent to investing $\$19,331,064.75$ $(= (15,464.8518)(\$1250))$ in a diversified portfolio. The manager also would need to invest $\$5,938,884.5351$ in a risk-free bond portfolio. The total stock-bond portfolio investment would be $\$25,269,949$, which is equal to the value of the original $\$25,000,000$ portfolio plus the cost of buying protective puts: $\$269,949$ $= (20,000)(\$13.49746)$: $V_0^{Ins} = \$25,269,949$. As shown in Exhibit 13.8-1(d), this stock-bond portfolio would be worth next period either $\$27,500,000$ if the index is at 1375 or $\$23,809,524$ if the index is 1136.3636:

$S_u = 1375$:

Stock + Bond Portfolio $= \$19,331,064.75(1.1) + \$5,938,884.5351(1.05)$

$$= \$27,500,000$$

$S_d = 1136.3636$:

Stock + Bond Portfolio $= \$19,331,064.75(1/1.1) + \$5,938,884.5351(1.05)$

$$= \$23,809,524$$

If the stock and bond portfolio is worth $\$27,500,000$, then the manager could convert the stock and bond portfolio to an all-stock portfolio that would be worth either $\$30,250,000$ or $\$25,000,000$ at the end of Period 2. If the portfolio is worth $\$23,809,524$, the manager then could convert the stock and bond portfolio to an all-bond portfolio, which would be worth $\$25,000,000$ $(= \$23,809,524(1.05))$ at the end of the next period regardless of whether the market increases or decreases. Thus, using a stock and bond portfolio with readjustments at the end of the first period, the manager can obtain the same portfolio protection provided by puts.

13.8.3 Constructing Stock-Bond Portfolios for n-Period Case

In the preceding two-period example, the stock and bond portfolio were converted to either an all-stock portfolio or an all-bond portfolio in Period 1. When there are more periods, the adjustments require more incremental changes in the stock and bond portfolios. In general, the construction of a dynamic stock and bond portfolio insurance portfolio using a binomial framework consists of the following steps:

1. Generate a binomial tree of spot index values (S) and corresponding portfolio values (V).

2. Generate a corresponding binomial tree for the values of a put option on the index (P) with the option expiring at the end of the investment period (this may be a hypothetical index put to match the investment period).

3. Determine the number of puts needed to insure the portfolio: $n_p = V_0/X$, with the cost of the insurance being determined by the binomial model's put value in the current period.

4. Generate a binomial tree for the values of put-insured portfolio: $V^{Ins} = V + n_p P$.

5. Generate a binomial tree for the number of hypothetical index shares (N*) and risk-free bond portfolio investment (I*) that make the stock and bond portfolio for the next period equal to the possible values of the put-insured portfolio (V^{Ins}). The tree of N* and I* values can be used to generate a binomial tree of stock and bond portfolio values that replicates the put-insured portfolio values.

6. Determine the stock and bond portfolio adjustments needed when moving from a node in one period to a node in the next period.

In general, when the stock index and portfolio increase, the stock and bond portfolio needs to increase its allocation to the stock portfolio and decrease the allocation to the bond portfolio. This can be done by selling some of the bond portfolio and investing the proceeds in the stock portfolio. By contrast, when the stock index and portfolio decrease, the stock and bond portfolio needs to increase its allocation to the bond portfolio and decrease the allocation to the stock portfolio. This can be done by selling some of the stock portfolio and investing the proceeds in the bond portfolio. Appendix 13B presents dynamic portfolio insurance examples for three periods and 10 periods.

13.9 DYNAMIC PORTFOLIO INSURANCE USING STOCK INDEX FUTURES

Dynamic portfolio insurance strategies can also be constructed and managed with stock index futures contracts.[3] These strategies require finding the number of futures contracts, referred to as the ***dynamic hedge ratio*** (N_f), which will replicate the put-insured stock portfolio. The model's derivation is presented in Appendix 13C at the end of this chapter. The dynamic hedge ratio, in turn, is

$$N_f = \left[\left[\frac{V_0^{Ins}}{S_0 + P_0} \right] [1 + (N(d_1) - 1))] - \frac{V_0^{Ins}}{S_0} \right] e^{-R^T} B - S \qquad (13.9\text{-}1)$$

$$N_f = \left[\left[\frac{V_0^{Ins}}{S_0 + P_0} \right] \left[1 + H_0^P \right] - \frac{V_0^{Ins}}{S_0} \right] (1 + R)^{-(n-1)} \quad \text{BOPM}$$

---

[3] The portfolio insurance strategy using index futures was first developed by Rubinstein (1985).

where

$$N_f < 0 \Rightarrow \text{short futures}$$

$$N_f > 0 \Rightarrow \text{Long futures}$$

The hedge ratio N_f can be estimated using either the continuous-time B–S OPM or the discrete BOPM. If the B–S model is used, $N(d_1) - 1$ is used to estimate the change in the put index price per small change in the spot index price, $\Delta P/\Delta S$, and the continuously compounded rate risk-free rate is used for R. If the BOPM is used, $\Delta P/\Delta S$ is equal to $H_0^p = (P_u - P_d)/S_0(u - d)$, and a discrete-period risk-free rate is used.

13.9.1 Dynamic Futures-Insured Portfolio: Two-Period Example

To see the equivalence between a put-insured portfolio and futures-insured one, consider the two-period portfolio insurance case (value of index portfolio = $V_0 = \$25,000,000$, spot index = $S_0 = 1250$ with $u = 1.1$ and $d = 1/1.1$, European put option on the index with $X = 1250$ and expiration of $n = 2$, and period risk-free rate = $R = 5\%$). Assume there is a futures contract on the index with a price determined by the carrying-cost model, and, for simplicity, assume there are no dividends and no multipliers on the futures or put option contracts. The period values of the spot index, put, and futures contract are shown in the top part of each node's block in Exhibit 13.9-1 along with the put hedge ratios ($H^p = [P_u - P_d]/S(u - d)$) and the dynamic hedge ratios, N_f (Equation (13.9-1)).

In our earlier example, the portfolio manager was able to attain a minimum portfolio value of $25,000,000 at the end of the period, with the possibility of the portfolio being worth $30,250,000 by purchasing 20,000 index puts. Instead of using index puts, the manager alternatively could attain the same insurance using index futures contracts. Assuming the prices on the futures contract are determined by the carrying-cost model, the manager, in seeking to form a futures-insured portfolio that replicates the put-insured ($V^{Ins} = V_0 + n_p(P_0^*)$), would first need to buy $25,269,949 worth of the diversified portfolio ($25,000,000 + (20,000)(13.497462)$ or if manager has a current $25,000,000 portfolio, buy an additional $269,949 more of the index portfolio). The additional $269,949 portfolio investment is equal to the costs of the puts; it thus represents the costs of the insurance. In addition to the portfolio, the manager also must go short in $N_{f0} = 4,524.863619$ index futures contracts at a price of 1378.125 ($f_0 = S_0(1 + R)^n = 1250(1.05)^2 = 1378.125$):

$$N_{f0} = \left[\left[\frac{V_0^{Ins}}{S_0 + P_0}\right]\left[1 + H_0^P\right] - \frac{V_0^{Ins}}{S_0}\right](1 + R)^{-(n-1)}$$

$$N_{f0} = \left[\left[\frac{\$25,269,949.25}{1250 + 13.497462}\right][1 - .22675737] - \frac{\$25,269,949.25}{1250}\right]\frac{1}{1.05}$$

$$N_{f0} = -4,524.863619$$

where

$$H_0^P = \frac{P_u - P_d}{S_0(u - d)} = \frac{0 - 54.112255}{1250(1.1 - (1/1.1))} = -.22675737$$

As shown in Exhibit 13.9-1, if the market decreases to 1136.3636 at the end of the first period, the combined portfolio and futures positions would be worth $23,809,523.81 (the

EXHIBIT 13.9-1   Dynamic Portfolio Insurance Strategy Using Index Futures

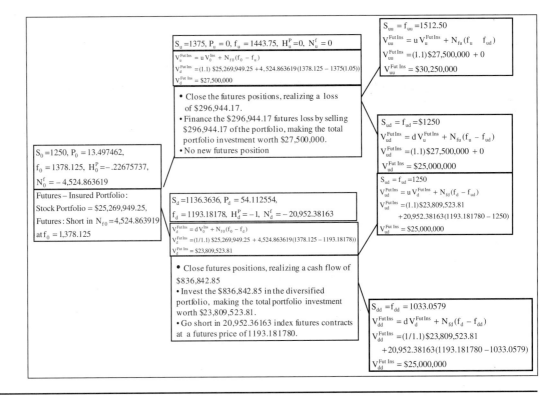

same as the put-insured portfolio):

$$V_d^{\text{Fut Ins}} = dV_0^{\text{Ins}} + N_{f0}(f_0 - f_d)$$

$$V_d^{\text{Fut Ins}} = (1/1.1)\,\$25,269,949.25 + 4,524.863619(1378.125 - 1136.3636(1.05))$$

$$V_d^{\text{Fut Ins}} = \$23,809,523.81$$

In this case, the manager could

1. Close the futures positions, realizing a cash flow of \$836,842.85 (= 4,524.863619 (1378.125 − 1136.3636(1.05)).

2. Invest the $836,842.85 in the diversified portfolio now worth $22,972,681 (= (1/1.1) ($25,269,949.25) = $22,992,681), making the total portfolio investment worth $23,809,523.81.

3. Go short in $N_{fd} = 20,952.36163$ index futures contracts at a futures price of 1193.181780 (= 1136.3636(1.05)):

$$N_{fd} = \left[\left[\frac{V_d^{Ins}}{S_d + P_d} \right] \left[1 + H_d^P \right] - \frac{V_d^{Ins}}{S_d} \right] (1+R)^{-(n-1)}$$

$$N_{fd} = \left[\left[\frac{\$23,809,523.81}{1136.3636 + 54.112554} \right] [1-1] - \frac{\$23,809,523.81}{1136.3636} \right] \frac{1}{(1.05)^0}$$

$$N_{fd} = -20,952.38163$$

With this adjustment, the manager would insure an investment value of $25,000,000 next period. That is

At $S_{ud} = 1250$

$$V_{ud}^{Fut\ Ins} = u\ V_d^{Fut\ Ins} + N_{fd}(f_d - f_{ud})$$

$$V_{ud}^{Fut\ Ins} = (1.1)\$23,809,523.81 + 20,952.38163(1193.181780 - 1250) = \$25,000,000$$

At $S_{dd} = 1033.0579$

$$V_{dd}^{Fut\ Ins} = d\ V_d^{Fut\ Ins} + N_{fd}(f_d - f_{dd})$$

$$V_{dd}^{Fut\ Ins} = (1/1.1)\$23,809,523.81 + 20,952.38163(1193.181780 - 1033.0579)$$

$$V_{dd}^{Fut\ Ins} = \$25,000,000$$

Note that the manager alternatively could liquidate the portfolio and close the futures position in Period 1, earning $23,809,523.81, and then invest the proceeds in a risk-free security at 5% to insure a $25,000,000 investment value at the end of the next period.

In contrast, if the market increases to 1375 at the end of the first period, then the combined stock portfolio and futures position would be worth $27,500,000:

$$V_u^{Fut\ Ins} = u\ V_0^{Ins} + N_{f0}(f_0 - f_u)$$

$$V_d^{Fut\ Ins} = (1.1)\ \$25,269,949.25 + 4,524.863619(1378.125 - 1375(1.05))$$

$$V_d^{Fut\ Ins} = \$27,500,000$$

In this case, the manager could

1. Close the futures positions, realizing a loss of $296,944.17 (= 4,524.863619(1378.125 − 1375(1.05))

2. Finance the $296,944.17 futures loss by selling $296,944.17 of the portfolio, making the total portfolio investment worth $27,500,000 (= (1.1)($25,269,949.25 − $296,944.17).

At $S_u = 1375$, the number of futures contracts needed for adjusting the portfolio is zero:

$$N_{fu} = \left[\left[\frac{V_u^{Ins}}{S_d + P_d} \right] \left[1 + H_u^P \right] - \frac{V_u^{Ins}}{S_u} \right] (1 + R)^{-(n-1)}$$

$$N_{fu} = \left[\left[\frac{\$27,500,000}{1375 + 0} \right] [1 - 0] - \frac{\$27,500,000}{1375} \right] \frac{1}{(1.05)^0}$$

$$N_{fu} = 0$$

Next period, the $27,500,000 all-stock portfolio would be worth either $30,250,000 or $25,000,000 at the end of the period—the same as the put-insured portfolio.

In practice, dynamic portfolio insurance strategies adjusted with index futures positions are constructed using a number of time periods and futures adjustments. In general, the management of a futures-adjusted dynamic portfolio insurance strategy requires (1) adjusting the stock portfolio over time by either investing futures profit in the stock portfolio or financing the losses on futures positions by selling some of the stock portfolio and (2) taking new futures positions. Like dynamic portfolio insurance strategies using put options and bond and stock portfolios, the objective of the stock and futures adjustments is to achieve an end-of-the-period portfolio distribution that attains higher values if the market increases and a minimum value if the market declines.

13.10   CONCLUSION

Since their introduction by the Kansas City Board of Exchange in the early 1980s, stock index futures, as well as spot and futures index options, have become a valuable tool in managing stock portfolio positions. Index derivatives provide a liquid way to speculate on the market by forming different types of intracommodity and intercommodity spreads and option positions. These derivative contracts also make it possible for stock portfolio managers to lock in future portfolio values or to obtain portfolio insurance. Managers also can use stock index derivatives to adjust the beta of a portfolio if they anticipate a bull or bear market, thus eliminating the need to change their portfolio allocations. They also can use index futures to eliminate a stock's systematic risk, enabling them to speculate on unsystematic factors. Finally, managers can use the BOPM for determining the investment rules needed to actively manage portfolios using futures positions or stock and bond portfolios to achieve end-of-the period distributions for an intermediate or long-term investment horizon that replicates portfolio insurance distributions.

Given the myriad of uses of index futures, it is not surprising that such instruments have grown since their introduction. Equally impressive as the growth in index futures, though, is the increased use of currency derivatives, in the management of currency positions. As we examine in the next chapter, these contracts, like index futures, can be used in a number of ways to manage foreign currency positions.

KEY TERMS

stock index price-sensitivity model	index arbitrage	dynamic asset allocation
market timing	program trading	dynamic portfolio insurance strategy
speculating on unsystematic risk	triple witching hour	dynamic hedge ratio

SELECTED REFERENCES

Asay, M., and C. Edeslburg. "Can a Dynamic Strategy Replicate the Returns of an Option?" *Journal of Futures Markets* 6 (Spring 1986): 63–70.

Clarke, R., and R. Arnott. "The Cost of Portfolio Insurance: Tradeoffs and Choices." *Financial Analysts Journal* 43 (November–December 1987): 35–47.

Etzioni, E. "Rebalance Disciplines for Portfolio Insurance." *Journal of Portfolio Management* 13 (Fall 1986): 59–62.

Figlewski, S. "Hedging Performance and Basis Risk in Stock Index Futures." *Journal of Finance* 39 (July 1984): 657–669.

Figlewski, S., and S. Kin. "Portfolio Management With Stock Index Futures." *Financial Analysts Journal* 38 (January–February 1982): 52–60.

Grant, D. "How to Optimize With Stock Index Futures." *Journal of Portfolio Management* 8 (Spring 1982): 32–36.

Gressis, N., G. Glahos, and G. Philippatos. "A CAPM-based Analysis of Stock Index Futures." *Journal of Portfolio Management* 10 (Spring 1984): 47–52.

Hill, J., and F. Jones. "Equity Trading, Program Trading, Portfolio Insurance, Computer Trading and All That." *Financial Analysts Journal* 44 (July–August 1988): 29–38.

Leland, H. "Who Should Buy Portfolio Insurance?" *Journal of Finance* 35 (May 1980): 581–594.

Modest, D., and M. Sundaresan. "The Relationship Between Spot and Futures Prices in Stock Index Futures Markets: Some Preliminary Evidence." *Journal of Futures Markets* 3 (1983): 15–41.

O'Brien, T. "The Mechanics of Portfolio Insurance." *The Journal of Portfolio Management* 14 (Spring 1985): 40–47.

Pozen, R. "The Purchase of Protective Puts by Financial Institutions." *Financial Analysts Journal* 34 (July/August 1978): 47–60.

Rendleman, R., Jr., and R. McEnally. "Assessing the Cost of Portfolio Insurance." *Financial Analysts Journal* 43 (May–June 1987): 27–37.

Rubinstein, M. "Portfolio Insurance and the Market Crash." *Financial Analysts Journal* 44 (January–February 1988): 38–47.

Rubinstein, M. "Alternative Paths to Portfolio Insurance." *Financial Analysts Journal* 41 (July–August 1985): 42–52.

Rubinstein, M., and H. Leland. "Replicating Options With Positions in Stock and Cash." *Financial Analysts Journal* 37 (July–August 1981): 63–71.

Santoni, G. "Has Program Trading Made Stock Prices More Volatile?" *Review* (Federal Reserve Bank of St. Louis) 69: 18–29.

Singleton, C., and R. Grieves. "Synthetic Puts and Portfolio Insurance Strategies." *Journal of Portfolio Management* 10 (Spring 1984): 63–69.

Smith, D. "The Arithmetic of Financial Engineering." *Journal of Applied Corporate Finance* 1 (1989): 49–58.

Stoll, H., and R. Whaley. "Expiration Day Effects of Index Options and Futures." Salomon Brothers Center for the Study of Financial Institutions, Monograph Series in Finance and Economics, Monograph 1986–3.

Stoll, H., and R. Whaley. "Program Trading and Expiration Day Effects." *Financial Analysts Journal* 43 (March–April 1987): 16–23.

PROBLEMS AND QUESTIONS

1. Define and evaluate a portfolio insurance strategy for a stock portfolio currently worth $10 million. Assume that an S&P 500 put option is available with an exercise price of 1250, expiration of 180 days, a 250 multiplier, and priced at 50. Also assume that the stock portfolio is perfectly positively correlated with the S&P 500 index and that the current spot S&P 500 index is at 1250. Evaluate the portfolio insurance strategy at possible spot index values at expiration of 1150, 1175, 1200, 1225, 1250, 1275, 1300, 1325, and 1350.

2. Mr. Fiore is a stock portfolio manager for the Investment Trust Company. On January 10, Mr. Fiore determines he will have to liquidate part of his stock portfolio in June. He would like to hedge the portfolio sale. The portfolio Mr. Fiore plans to sell is well diversified; has a β of 1.5; is expected to generate certain dividends worth $8,750,000 in June; and on January 10, the portfolio is worth $50,000,000. On January 10, the S&P 500 spot index is at 1000; a June S&P 500 futures contract is at 1000; and a June S&P 500 put with an exercise price of 1000 is trading at 35.

    a. Using the price-sensitivity model, determine how many S&P 500 put contracts Mr. Fiore would need if he wanted to insure the portfolio with a portfolio insurance strategy. Ignore the multiplier.

    b. Evaluate the put-insurance strategy at spot index prices at expiration of 900, 925, 950, 975, 1000, 1025, 1050, 1075, and 1100. Assume no quantity, quality, or timing risks, and ignore multipliers.

    c. Using the price-sensitivity model, determine how many S&P 500 futures contracts Mr. Fiore would need to hedge the sale of his $50 million portfolio in June.

    d. Show in a table the values of the portfolio, futures cash flows, and the hedged portfolio values on the June expiration date for possible spot index values of 900, 925, 950, 975, 1000, 1025, 1050, 1075, and 1100. Assume no quantity, quality, or timing risks, and ignore multipliers.

3. Ms. Piper is a stock portfolio manager for LM Investment Company. She is expecting a $20M inflow of cash from one of her investment clients on June 20th and is planning to invest the cash in a portfolio of stocks with a $\beta = 1$. Ms. Piper is concerned there will be a strong bull market and would like to hedge her June investment with a June S&P 500 futures contract trading at 1000. Currently, the S&P 500 spot index is at 1000, and there is exactly 1 month to the June expiration on the futures contracts.

    a. Describe Ms. Piper's June portfolio purchase as an investment in hypothetical shares of the S&P 500.

    b. Evaluate the June costs of Ms. Piper's portfolio as a purchase of hypothetical S&P 500 shares at spot index values of 900, 950, 1000, 1050, and 1100.

    c. How many futures contracts would Ms. Piper need to lock in her portfolio purchase such that it is equivalent to buying the portfolio at its current value?

    d. Evaluate the hedged portfolio cost at spot index prices at expiration of 900, 950, 1000, 1050, and 1100. Include $250 index futures multiplier.

4. Ms. Ellis manages a portfolio consisting of five stocks (A, B, C, D, and E). The table shows Ms. Ellis's stocks, shares, βs, and stock prices as of March 20.

(1) Stocks	(2) Shares	(3) 3/20 Price per Share	(4) β	(5) 9/20 Price per Share
A	20,000	$45	1.30	$39.15
B	10,000	50	.90	45.50
C	20,000	30	.75	27.75
D	5,000	15	1.20	13.20
E	15,000	35	1.40	35.00

    a. How many futures contracts would Ms. Ellis need to hedge the September 20th value of her portfolio if a September S&P 500 futures contract, expiring on September 20, were trading at $f_0 = 1000$ when the spot was at $S_0 = 1000$?

    b. Determine what would be the September values of Ms. Ellis's unhedged and futures-hedged portfolio if on September 20th, the market had decreased such that the spot S&P 500 were at 950 and the prices of her stocks were selling at the values indicated in Column 5 of the table. Assume no quality or timing risk.

5. Suppose Ms. Ellis, in Problem 4, believed there would be a bull market over the next 6 months (March 20 to September 20) and wanted to profit by increasing her portfolio β to 1.5. Explain how Ms. Ellis could increase her β to 1.5 using the September S&P 500 futures contract described in Problem 4. Compare Ms. Ellis's portfolio values on September 20th with and without the futures for possible proportional rates of change in the market from March 20 to September 20 of $-.15$, $-.10$, $-.05$, 0, .05, .10, and .15. Assume Ms. Ellis's possible portfolio values reflect her port-folio's beta.

6. On April 1, Mr. Colbert received information that General Pharmaceutical (GP) might be introducing a new acne drug next month. In response to the information, Mr. Colbert decided to buy 40,000 shares of GP priced at $P_g = \$35$/share and with a β of .8. Mr. Colbert, though, was concerned that the market could decline over the next month, negating any increase in GP stock.

   a. Explain how Mr. Colbert could construct a hedge with S&P 500 futures contracts expiring next month to reduce his exposure to systematic risk. Assume the current spot index and the futures contract are both 1120. Include 250 futures multiplier.

   b. Evaluate the value of the stock and the futures for the following scenarios occurring one month later:
      1. There is a bull market, and the new drug is introduced, causing $S_T = 1220$ and $P_g = \$50$.
      2. There is a bear market, and the new drug is introduced, causing $S_T = 1020$ and $P_g = \$40$.

   c. Compare the period rates of return for each scenario that would result with and without the futures position.

7. Determine the equilibrium price of a December S&P 500 futures contract available on September 20th. Assume the spot S&P 500 index is at 1212, the annual risk-free rate is 6.5%, dividends worth a certain $26.20 at the December expiration, and 90 days to expiration.

8. The PI Hedge Fund has formed a proxy portfolio that it is using to identify arbitrage opportunities using index arbitrage strategies. The proxy portfolio consists of five stocks. The stock prices, shares, dividend values at the end of the next 90 days, and βs are shown in the table. The current S&P 500 spot index is at 1250, and the annual risk-free rate is 6%.

Stock	Shares	Share Price	Share Dividends	β
A	20,000	$60	$0.75	0.90
B	10,000	70	0.50	0.95
C	20,000	50	0.70	1.1
D	10,000	60	0.60	1.05
E	20,000	40	0.60	1.032

   a. Define PI Hedge Fund's portfolio as an investment in hypothetical shares in the S&P 500. What is the dividend per index share to be paid in 90 days?

   b. Determine the equilibrium price of an S&P 500 futures contract expiring in T = 90 days using PI's proxy portfolio.

   c. Describe the index arbitrage strategy PI could employ if the S&P 500 futures were trading at 1260. Assume you can buy fractional contract shares, and include the 250 futures multiplier.

d. Evaluate the index arbitrage from c at the futures' expiration by first assuming the market increases by 10% and then assuming it decreases by 10%. Assume the portfolio is perfectly correlated with the market.

e. Describe the index arbitrage strategy PI could employ if the S&P 500 futures were trading at 1245 (assume perfect divisibility and no short sale restrictions).

f. Evaluate the index arbitrage from e at the futures' expiration by first assuming the market increased by 10% and then assuming it decreased by 10%. Assume the portfolio is perfectly correlated with the market.

9. Describe program trading.

10. What is the Triple Witching Hour?

11. Given the following:

   - S&P 500 put with $X = 1200$ and $n = 2$
   - S&P 500 call with $X = 1200$ and $n = 2$
   - S&P 500 spot index $= 1200$
   - $u = 1.075, d = 1/1.075$
   - Period risk-free rate of $R = 3\%$

   Questions:

   a. Assuming a BOPM process, construct a binomial tree showing the values of the spot index and index put at each node.

   b. Show the values at each node of a well-diversified stock portfolio currently worth $12 million and with a $\beta = 1$.

   c. How many put contracts would be needed to insure the stock portfolio (ignore multiplier)?

   d. Show the values at each node of a put-insured portfolio. Assume put prices are equal to their BOPM values.

12. Construct a dynamic stock portfolio and risk-free bond strategy that will replicate the put-insured portfolio in Problem 11. Show the portfolio's stock and bond composition at each node and the adjustments required.

13. Suppose there is an S&P 500 futures contract expiring at the end of two periods ($n = 2$). Construct a dynamic futures-adjusted portfolio with the futures contract that will replicate the put-insured portfolio in Problem 11. Show the values of the portfolio and futures contracts at each node and the adjustments required. Assume the futures prices are equal to their carrying cost values and that there are no dividends. Ignore the futures multiplier.

14. Short-Answer Questions:

   a. Anticipating an announcement in late June that the government will award GEM a contract to build jet engines, Ms. Webb would like to buy GEM stock, currently priced at $30 per share and with a beta of 1. Ms. Webb, though, is afraid a bear market could negate any price gain from the announcement. Given a June stock index futures contract, explain in general how Ms. Webb could minimize the exposure of a long position in GEM stock to systematic risk.

   b. What type of risk is an investor exposed to who buys stock in anticipation of an unexpected good earnings announcement and who is also short in a number of index futures contracts as determined by the price-sensitivity model?

  c. Define the arbitrage that could be realized when the contract price on an index futures contract is below its equilibrium level as determined by the carrying-cost model.

  d. How can a put-insured stock portfolio be replicated using index futures contracts?

  e. Define the spread strategy a speculator could implement if she is bullish on the stock market but does not want to assume the risk inherent in a long outright position.

  f. How is a dynamic portfolio-insured portfolio constructed?

WEB EXERCISES

1. Read more about CME index derivatives by going to www.cme.com ("CME Products" and "Equities").

2. Make a stock market forecast and then form an intracommodity spread with a listed index futures contract based on your forecast. For price quotes on futures, go to www.wsj.com/free (Market Data Center) or www.cme.com.

3. Using the current spot index, determine the carrying-cost value of a listed index futures contract. For current market quotes and information, go to www.cme.com and www.wsj.com/free.

4. Select and find information on a stock index mutual fund. Go to www.wsj.com/free (Market Data Center), select "Mutual Funds," and then go to "Fund Screener." Find the value of the index fund and the value of the current spot index that is correlated with the fund. Define the mutual fund as a proxy portfolio: number of index shares and index price.

5. Select an exchange-listed index futures call and put options and determine their recent prices by going to www.wsj.com/free and clicking "Market Data Center" ("Commodity and Futures"). Using your options, evaluate some of the following strategies with a profit table and graph (use Excel or the Excel program for "Option Strategies" included with the book): call purchase, put purchase, straddle purchase, straddle sale, synthetic long position, or synthetic short position.

6. Find links to other derivative sites by going to www.isda.org and clicking "Educational" and "Links."

APPENDIX 13A   DERIVATION OF THE STOCK PORTFOLIO PRICE-SENSITIVITY HEDGING MODEL

The price-sensitivity model for hedging a stock portfolio determines the number of stock index future contracts, n_f, that will minimize the variability of profits (π) on a portfolio consisting of a stock portfolio and the futures contract. The portfolio's profit is defined as

$$\tilde{\pi} = R_s S_0 + n_f (R_F f_0), \qquad (13.A\text{-}1)$$

where

$\quad R_S =$ uncertain rate of return on the stock portfolio.

$\quad S_0 =$ current value of the stock portfolio.

$\quad R_F =$ uncertain rate of return on the futures position.

The variance of π is

$$V(\pi) = E[\tilde{\pi} - E(\pi)]^2$$

$$V(\pi) = E[R_S\, S_0 + n_f\, R_F\, f_0 - S_0\, E(R_S) - n_f\, E(R_F)f_0)]^2$$

$$V(\pi) = S_0^2[R_S - E(R_S)]^2 + n_f^2\, f_0^2\, E[R_f - E(R_f)]^2$$

$$+\, 2\, S_0\, n_f\, f_0 E[R_S - E(R_S)][R_F - E(R_F)]$$

$$V(\pi) = S_0^2\, V(R_S) + n_f^2\, f_0^2\, V(R_F) + 2S_0 f_0 n_f\, \text{Cov}(R_S\, R_F) \qquad (13.A\text{-}2)$$

The first order condition for minimizing $V(\pi)$ is found by taking the derivative of (13A-2) with respect to n_f, setting the resulting equation equal to zero, and solving for n_f.[4] That is

$$\frac{dV(\pi)}{dn_f} = 2n_f\, f_0^2\, V(R_F) + 2S_0\, f_0\, \text{Cov}(R_S R_F) = 0 \qquad (13.A\text{-}3)$$

$$n_f = -\,\frac{S_0}{f_0}\, \frac{\text{Cov}(R_S R_F)}{V(R_F)} \qquad (13.A\text{-}4)$$

By definition, the stock portfolio's beta is

$$\beta = \frac{\text{Cov}(R_S R_M)}{V(R_M)}$$

where:

$V(R_m) = $ Variance of the rate of return on the spot market portfolio.

If we assume the rate of return on a stock index futures contract is highly correlated with the rate on the underlying spot index (R_m), then $\text{Cov}(R_S R_F)/V(R_F) = \text{Cov}(R_s, R_m)/V(R_m)$. Given this assumption, beta can be substituted for $\text{Cov}(R_S R_F)/V(R_M)$ in Equation (13A-4), and the optimum hedge can be expressed as

$$n_f^* = -\beta \frac{S_0}{f_0} \qquad (13.A\text{-}5)$$

Equation (13A-5) is the same as defined in Section 13.2.2.

APPENDIX 13B   EXAMPLES OF DYNAMIC PORTFOLIO INSURANCE STRATEGY USING BONDS

Three-Period Example

Suppose the portfolio manager in the two-period case presented in Section 13.8 ($S_0 = 1250, V_0 = \$25{,}000{,}000, u = 1.1, d = 1/1.1,$ and $R_f = .05$) wanted to construct a dynamic stock and bond portfolio for three periods instead of two.

Steps

1. **Generate a binomial tree of spot index and portfolio values**: Exhibit 13.B-1(a) shows the index and corresponding portfolio values. Note that in Period 3, there are

---

[4] The second order derivative of Equation (13A-2) with respect to n_f is positive, satisfying the second order condition. That is

$$d^2 V(\pi)/dn_f^2 = 2\, f_0^2\, V(R_F) > 0$$

four possible portfolio values ranging from an upper value of \$33,275,000 if the index increases three consecutive periods from 1250 to 1663.75 to a lower value of \$18,982,870 if the index decreases three straight periods to a level of 939.14.

2. **Generate a corresponding binomial tree of index put values**: Exhibits 13.B-1(b) shows the binomial values at each node for a European index put with $X = 1250$ and expiring at the end of three periods. The current value of index put is 19.7388.

3. **Determine the number of puts needed to insure the portfolio**: To insure the \$25,000,000 portfolio, the portfolio manager would need to buy $n_p = V_0/X = $ \$25,000,000/1250 = 20,000 index puts at a cost of \$394,776 $(= (20,000)(19.7388))$.

4. **Determine the values of the put-insured portfolio at each node of the binomial tree**: $V^{Ins} = V + n_pP$. The put-insured portfolio values at each node for the three periods are shown in Exhibit 13.B-1(c).

5. **Generate a binomial tree of N* and I***: Exhibit 13.B-1(d) shows the N* and I* values at each node for this three-period case (upper exhibit) and the corresponding stock and bond portfolio values (lower exhibit). The combined stock and bond portfolio values shown in Exhibit 13.8-2(d) are equivalent to the put-insured portfolio values shown in Exhibit 13.B-1(c) (allow for some rounding differences).

6. **Determine the stock and bond portfolio adjustments needed when moving from a node in one period to a node in the next period:** Exhibit 13.8-1(e) shows the requisites periodic stock and bond portfolio adjustments needed to keep the stock and bond portfolios equivalent to the put-insured portfolio. Exhibit 13.8-1(f) presents the stock and bond adjustments for each of the six possible paths that make up the three-period tree.

In general, when the stock index and portfolio increase, the stock and bond portfolio needs to increase its allocation to the stock portfolio and decrease the allocation to the bond portfolio. This can be done by selling some of the bond portfolio and investing the proceeds in the stock portfolio. For example, when the index increases from 1250 to 1375 in the first period, the stock and bond portfolio increases from \$25,394,676 (\$19,539,799 in stocks and \$5,854,877 in bonds) to \$27,641,401, with the stock portfolio worth \$21,493,780 $(= \$19,539,799(1.10))$ and the risk-free bond portfolio investment worth \$6,147,620 $(= \$5,854,877(1.05))$. To meet the two possible portfolio-insured values in Period 2 of \$30,250,000 and \$25,566,892.60, the \$27,641,401 stock and bond portfolio needs to consist of $S_uN_u = $ \$24,530,562.57 of the stock portfolio and $I_u = $ \$3,110,839.21 of the bond portfolio. To adjust the portfolio, the manager could sell \$3,036,781.64 of bonds $(I_0^* r_f - I_u = $ \$6,147,620.85 – \$3,110,839.20) and then use the proceeds to invest in the stock index portfolio, increasing the stock investment to the requisite amount of \$24,530,562 $(= \$21,493,780 + \$3,036,781.64)$:

> Adjustment:
>
> (1) Sell $I_0^* r_f - I_u$ of the bond portfolio:
> \$6,147,620.85 – \$3,110,839.21 = \$3,036,781.64
> (2) Invest \$3,036,781.64 in the stock portfolio.

> NewPortfolio:
>
> Stock = \$21,493,780 + \$3,036,781.64 = 24,530,562
> Bond = \$3,110,839.21
> Stock + Bond Portfolio = \$27,641,401

EXHIBIT 13.B-1   Dynamic Portfolio Insurance Three-Period Case

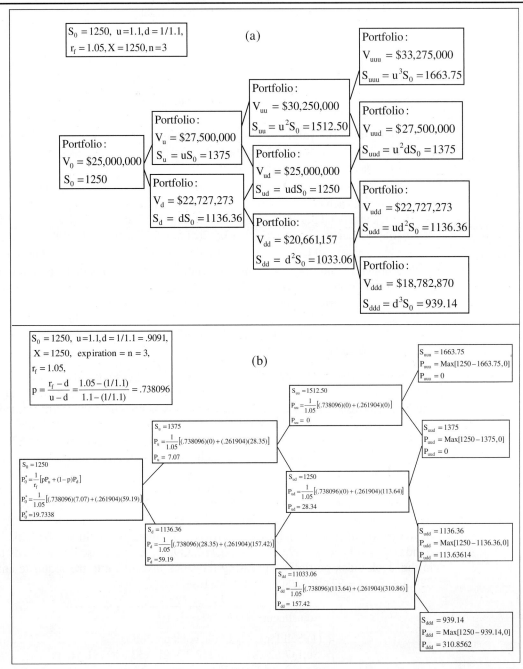

continued

EXHIBIT 13.B-1   Continued

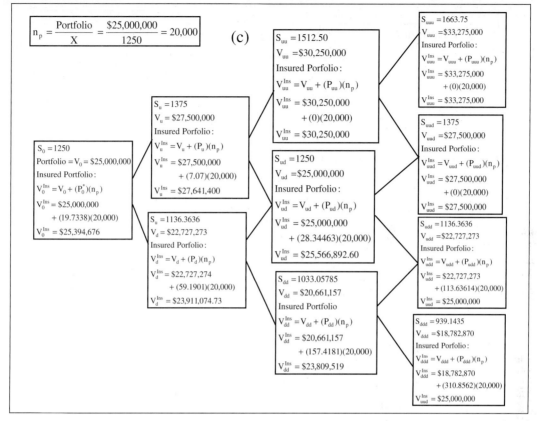

continued

EXHIBIT 13.B-1   Continued

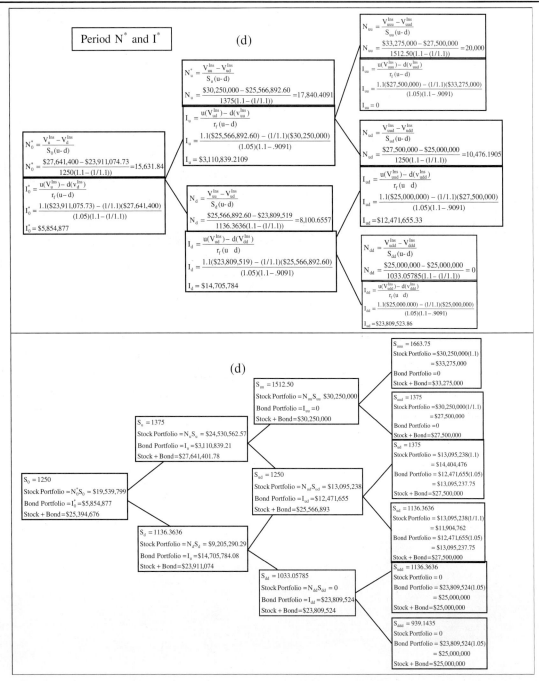

continued

EXHIBIT 13.B-1   Continued

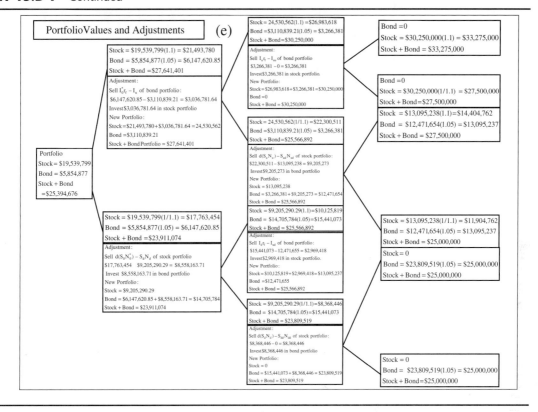

As shown in Exhibit 13.B-1(e), the adjusted stock and bond portfolio would be worth either $30,250,000 or $25,566,893—the portfolio-insured values corresponding to the upper and middle nodes in Period 2.

In contrast, when the index decreases from 1250 to 1136.3636 in the first period, the stock and bond portfolio decreases from $25,394,676 ($19,539,799 in stocks and $5,854,877 in bonds) to $23,911,074.73, with the stock portfolio worth $17,763,453.64 (= $19,539,799(1/1.10)) and the risk-free bond portfolio investment worth $6,147,620.85 (= $5,854,877(1.05). To meet the two possible portfolio-insured values in Period 2 of $25,566,892.60 and $23,809,524, the stock and bond portfolio needs to consist of $S_d N_d = \$9,205,290.29$ of stock and $I_d = \$14,705,784.08$ of bonds. To adjust the portfolio, the manager could sell $8,558,163.71 of the stock portfolio ($d(S_d N_0^*) - S_d N_d = \$17,763,454 - \$9,205,290.29$) and then use the proceeds to invest in the risk-free bond portfolio, increasing the bond investment to the requisite amount of $14,705,784 (= $$6,147,620.85 + $8,558,163.71):

Adjustment:

(1) Sell $d(S_0 N_0^*) - S_d N_d$ of the stock portfolio
$17,763,454 − $9,205,290.29 = $8,558,163.71

(2) Invest $8,558,163.71 in the bond portfolio

EXHIBIT 13.B-1 Stock and Bond Adjustments by Paths Three-Period Case

Path 1: d, d, d

	Stock	Stock	Stock	Bond	Bond	Bond	Stock + Bond
1	**2**	**3**	**4**	**5**	**6**	**7**	**8**
Period	Pre-Adjustment Value	Target Value	Adjustment in Stock	Pre-Adjustment value	Target Value	Adjustment in Bonds	Col (2) + col (5)
0	19,539,802.03	19,539,802.03		5,854,875.96	5,854,875.96		25,394,677.99
1	17,763,456.39	9,205,269.41	-8,558,186.98	6,147,619.76	14,705,806.74	8,558,186.98	23,911,076.15
2	8,368,426.74	0.00	-8,368,426.74	15,441,097.07	23,809,523.81	8,368,426.74	23,809,523.81
3	0			25,000,000.00			25,000,000.00

Path 2: u, d, d

	Stock	Stock	Stock	Bond	Bond	Bond	Stock + Bond
1	**2**	**3**	**4**	**5**	**6**	**7**	**8**
Period	Pre-Adjustment Value	Target Value	Adjustment in Stock	Pre-Adjustment value	Target Value	Adjustment in Bonds	Col (2) + col (5)
0	19,539,802.03	19,539,802.03		5,854,875.96	5,854,875.96		25,394,677.99
1	21,493,782.23	24,530,558.26	3,036,776.02	6,147,619.76	3,110,843.73	-3,036,776.02	27,641,401.99
2	22,300,507.50	13,095,238.10	-9,205,269.41	3,266,385.92	12,471,655.33	9,205,269.41	25,566,893.42
3	11,904,761.90			13,095,238.10			25,000,000.00

Path 3: d, u, d

	Stock	Stock	Stock	Bond	Bond	Bond	Stock + Bond
1	**2**	**3**	**4**	**5**	**6**	**7**	**8**
Period	Pre-Adjustment Value	Target Value	Adjustment in Stock	Pre-Adjustment value	Target Value	Adjustment in Bonds	Col (2) + col (5)
0	19,539,802.03	19,539,802.03		5,854,875.96	5,854,875.96		25,394,677.99
1	17,763,456.39	9,205,269.41	-8,558,186.98	6,147,619.76	14,705,806.74	8,558,186.98	23,911,076.15
2	10,125,796.35	13,095,238.10	2,969,441.74	15,441,097.07	12,471,655.33	-2,969,441.74	25,566,893.42
3	11,904,761.90			13,095,238.10			25,000,000.00

continued

EXHIBIT 13.B-1 Continued

Path 4: d, u, u

	Stock	Stock	Stock	Bond	Bond	Bond	Stock + Bond
1	**2**	**3**	**4**	**5**	**6**	**7**	**8**
Period	Pre-Adjustment Value	Target Value	Adjustment in Stock	Pre-Adjustment value	Target Value	Adjustment in Bonds	Col (2) + col (5)
0	19,539,802.03	19,539,802.03		5,854,875.96	5,854,875.96		25,394,677.99
1	17,763,456.39	9,205,269.41	-8,558,186.98	6,147,619.76	14,705,806.74	8,558,186.98	23,911,076.15
2	10,125,796.35	13,095,238.10	2,969,441.74	15,441,097.07	12,471,655.33	-2,969,441.74	25,566,893.42
3	14,404,761.90			13,095,238.10			27,500,000.00

Path 5: u, d, u

	Stock	Stock	Stock	Bond	Bond	Bond	Stock + Bond
1	**2**	**3**	**4**	**5**	**6**	**7**	**8**
Period	Pre-Adjustment Value	Target Value	Adjustment in Stock	Pre-Adjustment value	Target Value	Adjustment in Bonds	Col (2) + col (5)
0	19,539,802.03	19,539,802.03		5,854,875.96	5,854,875.96		25,394,677.99
1	21,493,782.23	24,530,558.26	3,036,776.02	6,147,619.76	3,110,843.73	-3,036,776.02	27,641,401.99
2	22,300,507.50	13,095,238.10	-9,205,269.41	3,266,385.92	12,471,655.33	9,205,269.41	25,566,893.42
3	14,404,761.90			13,095,238.10			27,500,000.00

Path 6: u, u, u

	Stock	Stock	Stock	Bond	Bond	Bond	Stock + Bond
1	**2**	**3**	**4**	**5**	**6**	**7**	**8**
Period	Pre-Adjustment Value	Target Value	Adjustment in Stock	Pre-Adjustment value	Target Value	Adjustment in Bonds	Col (2) + col (5)
0	19,539,802.03	19,539,802.03		5,854,875.96	5,854,875.96		25,394,677.99
1	21,493,782.23	24,530,558.26	3,036,776.02	6,147,619.76	3,110,843.73	-3,036,776.02	27,641,401.99
2	26,983,614.08	30,250,000.00	3,266,385.92	3,266,385.92	0.00	-3,266,385.92	30,250,000.00
3	33,275,000.00			0.00			33,275,000.00

> New Portfolio:
>
> Stock $= \$9,205,290.29$
> Bond $= \$6,147,620.85 + \$8,558,163.71 = \$14,705,784$
> Stock $+$ Bond $= \$23,911,074$

As shown in Exhibit 13.B-1(e), the adjusted stock and bond portfolio would be worth either $25,566,893 or $23,809,524—the portfolio-insured values corresponding to the middle and lower nodes in Period 2.

In period 2, the manager would again have to readjust the portfolio to obtain the required stock and bond positions needed to meet portfolio-insured values in Period 3. Note that in examining Exhibit 13.B-1(e), two of the four possible adjustments require moving to either an all-stock portfolio or all-bond portfolio. As shown in the exhibit, the four possible adjustments in Period 2 result next period in a distribution of possible portfolio values with a minimum value of $2,500,000 if the market is 1250 of lower and values greater than $25,000,000 if the market is 1250 or greater – the same distribution as the put-insured portfolio.

Ten-Period Example

In general, the management of a dynamic portfolio insurance strategy involves selling stock and investing in riskless securities after stock prices have fallen and buying stock and selling riskless securities after stock prices have increased. In practice, dynamic portfolio insurance strategies are constructed using a number of time periods. The rules for portfolio revising or rebalancing vary from strategies that adjust the portfolio frequently to those that rebalance only after the portfolio has changed by a certain percentage. A 10-period example is presented in Exhibit 13.B-2. The example shown in the exhibit involves setting up a dynamic stock and bond portfolio for a $25,000,000 index fund for a 5-year time period with planned adjustments to be made every 6 months. The exhibit shows the N* and I* values needed to construct a bond and stock portfolio that replicates a put-insured portfolio, the underlying stock portfolio and bond portfolio values comprising the portfolio. The dynamic portfolio is based on the following assumptions:

- The current S&P 500 is at $S_0 = 1250$.
- The index's estimated volatility and mean are $\sigma^A = .10$ and $\mu^A = 0$.
- The annual continuous dividend yield generated from the stocks comprising the index portfolio is assumed to be zero ($\psi = 0$) for simplicity.
- $R^A = 6\%$
- Put exercise price $= X = 1250$
- Put expiration $= 5$ years
- Number of binomial periods $= n = 10$
- Length of binomial period $= \Delta t = .5$ years
- Index portfolio value $= V_0 = \$25,000,000$ with $\beta = 1$

The u, d, and p values are

$$p = \frac{e^{R^A \Delta t} - d}{u - d}$$

$$p = \frac{e^{(.06)(.5)} - .931731}{1.073271 - .931751} = .697594$$

EXHIBIT 13.B-2 Dynamic Portfolio Insurance 10-Period Case

Current S&P 500 $= S_0 = 1250, \sigma^A = .10, \mu^A = 0, R^A = 6\%$
Put exercise price $= X = 1250$, Put expiration $= 5$ years, $n = 10$, $\Delta t = .5$ years
Portfolio value $= V_0 = \$25,000,000$, investment period $= 5$ years

					N^*					
9	8	7	6	5	4	3	2	1	0
20,000.0000	20,000.0000	20,000.0000	20,000.0000	19,999.9995	19,969.3805	19,858.1626	19,615.7718	19,204.8917	18,607.9004
20,000.0000	20,000.0000	20,000.0000	19,999.9981	19,888.0550	19,562.7630	18,971.9708	18,113.5754	17,022.2644	0.0000
20,000.0000	20,000.0000	19,999.9932	19,590.7290	18,698.7725	17,402.7999	15,833.6384	14,123.6928	0.0000	0.0000
20,000.0000	19,999.9752	18,503.7048	16,329.6955	13,960.6376	11,665.8742	9,581.9997	0.0000	0.0000	0.0000
19,999.9092	14,529.5425	10,555.4282	7,668.3120	5,570.8785	4,047.1342	0.0000	0.0000	0.0000	0.0000
0.0000	0.0000	0.0000	0.0000	0.0000	0.0000	0.0000	0.0000	0.0000	0.0000
0.0000	0.0000	0.0000	0.0000	0.0000	0.0000	0.0000	0.0000	0.0000	0.0000
0.0000	0.0000	0.0000	0.0000	0.0000	0.0000	0.0000	0.0000	0.0000	0.0000
0.0000	0.0000	0.0000	0.0000	0.0000	0.0000	0.0000	0.0000	0.0000	0.0000
0.0000	0.0000	0.0000	0.0000	0.0000	0.0000	0.0000	0.0000	0.0000	0.0000

continued

EXHIBIT 13.B-2 Continued

	I*									
	0	**1**	**2**	**3**	**4**	**5**	**6**	**7**	**8**	**9**
	1,887,284.37	1,143,844.83	587,059.15	230,349.59	52,896.45	0.94	3.21	10.93	37.24	126.84
	0.00	3,791,494.37	2,542,825.76	1,468,654.14	662,707.35	180,186.98	613,790.68	2,090,822.61	7,122,198.65	24,261,127.37
	0.00	0.00	7,052,358.94	5,275,627.19	3,474,845.12	1,842,009.66	4,859,453.09	11,732,524.77	23,544,092.04	24,261,127.37
	0.00	0.00	0.00	11,859,112.70	9,958,958.91	7,589,632.07	14,648,910.45	22,848,248.63	23,544,092.04	24,261,127.37
	0.00	0.00	0.00	0.00	17,434,380.89	16,424,731.48	22,172,970.80	22,848,248.63	23,544,092.04	24,261,127.37
	0.00	0.00	0.00	0.00	0.00	21,517,650.75	22,172,970.80	22,848,248.63	23,544,092.04	24,261,127.37
	0.00	0.00	0.00	0.00	0.00	0.00	0.00	0.00	0.00	
	0.00	0.00	0.00	0.00	0.00	0.00	0.00	0.00		
	0.00	0.00	0.00	0.00	0.00	0.00				

continued

EXHIBIT 13.B-2 Dynamic Portfolio Insurance: 10-Period Case—Stock and Bond Replicating Portfolio

10	9	8	7	6	5	4	3	2	1	0
50,703,035.04	47,241,596.06	44,016,465.60	41,011,511.17	38,211,701.58	35,603,031.88	33,174,563.26	30,918,962.60	28,831,579.47	26,908,911.48	25,147,159.89
44,016,459.54	41,011,505.51	38,211,696.31	35,603,026.93	33,172,448.59	30,914,991.15	28,830,896.98	26,921,233.20	25,184,791.94	23,616,708.70	0.00
38,211,691.04	35,603,022.02	33,172,443.88	30,907,799.01	28,822,244.40	26,928,065.59	25,228,338.94	23,716,489.31	22,378,731.10	0.00	0.00
33,172,439.31	30,907,794.31	28,797,755.56	26,915,174.47	25,271,564.04	23,849,076.08	22,618,219.32	21,547,194.59	0.00	0.00	0.00
28,797,750.10	26,831,765.26	25,284,116.80	24,026,044.29	22,970,202.34	22,057,284.36	21,246,968.20	0.00	0.00	0.00	0.00
25,000,000.00	24,261,127.37	23,544,092.04	22,848,248.63	22,172,970.80	21,517,650.75	0.00	0.00	0.00	0.00	0.00
25,000,000.00	24,261,127.37	23,544,092.04	22,848,248.63	22,172,970.80	0.00	0.00	0.00	0.00	0.00	0.00
25,000,000.00	24,261,127.37	23,544,092.04	22,848,248.63	0.00	0.00	0.00	0.00	0.00	0.00	0.00
25,000,000.00	24,261,127.37	23,544,092.04	0.00	0.00	0.00	0.00	0.00	0.00	0.00	0.00
25,000,000.00	24,261,127.37	0.00	0.00	0.00	0.00	0.00	0.00	0.00	0.00	0.00
25,000,000.00										

continued

459

EXHIBIT 13.B-2 Continued

Stock Portfolio	9	8	7	6	5	4	3	2	1	0
	47,241,596.06	44,016,465.60	41,011,511.17	38,211,701.58	35,603,030.93	33,121,666.82	30,688,613.01	28,244,520.32	25,765,066.65	23,259,875.52
	41,011,505.51	38,211,696.31	35,603,026.93	33,172,445.38	30,734,804.18	28,168,189.63	25,452,579.06	22,641,966.17	19,825,214.33	0.00
	35,603,022.02	33,172,443.88	30,907,788.08	28,208,453.72	25,086,055.94	21,753,493.82	18,440,862.12	15,326,372.16	0.00	0.00
	30,907,794.31	28,797,718.32	24,824,351.86	20,412,110.96	16,259,444.01	12,659,260.40	9,688,081.89	0.00	0.00	0.00
	26,831,638.42	18,161,918.14	12,293,519.52	8,321,291.89	5,632,552.88	3,812,587.32	0.00	0.00	0.00	0.00
	0.00	0.00	0.00	0.00	0.00	0.00	0.00	0.00	0.00	0.00
	0.00	0.00	0.00	0.00	0.00	0.00	0.00	0.00	0.00	0.00
	0.00	0.00	0.00	0.00	0.00	0.00	0.00	0.00	0.00	0.00
	0.00	0.00	0.00	0.00	0.00	0.00	0.00	0.00	0.00	0.00
	0.00	0.00	0.00	0.00	0.00	0.00	0.00	0.00	0.00	0.00

continued

EXHIBIT 13.B-2 Continued

Bond Portfolio	9	8	7	6	5	4	3	2	1	0
	0.00	0.00	0.00	0.00	0.94	52,896.45	230,349.59	587,059.15	1,143,844.83	1,887,284.37
	0.00	0.00	0.00	3.21	180,186.98	662,707.35	1,468,654.14	2,542,825.76	3,791,494.37	0.00
	0.00	0.00	10.93	613,790.68	1,842,009.66	3,474,845.12	5,275,627.19	7,052,358.94	0.00	0.00
	0.00	37.24	2,090,822.61	4,859,453.09	7,589,632.07	9,958,958.91	11,859,112.70	0.00	0.00	0.00
	126.84	7,122,198.65	11,732,524.77	14,648,910.45	16,424,731.48	17,434,380.89	0.00	0.00	0.00	0.00
	24,261,127.37	23,544,092.04	22,848,248.63	22,172,970.80	21,517,650.75	0.00	0.00	0.00	0.00	0.00
	24,261,127.37	23,544,092.04	22,848,248.63	22,172,970.80	0.00	0.00	0.00	0.00	0.00	0.00
	24,261,127.37	23,544,092.04	22,848,248.63	0.00	0.00	0.00	0.00	0.00	0.00	0.00
	24,261,127.37	23,544,092.04	0.00	0.00	0.00	0.00	0.00	0.00	0.00	0.00
	24,261,127.37	0.00	0.00	0.00	0.00	0.00	0.00	0.00	0.00	0.00

where
$$u = e^{.10\sqrt{.5}} = 1.073271$$
$$d = 1/u = .931731$$

Examining the stock portfolio and bond portfolio tables over the 5-year period shows the type of stock and bonds adjustment needed to achieve a distribution at the end of 5 years that would replicate a put-insured portfolio. Similar to the three-period case, when the index increases, more of the fund is allocated toward the stock portfolio, and when the market decreases, more is allocated toward the bond portfolio.

PROBLEMS AND QUESTIONS

1. Assume the following:

   - The current S&P 500 is at $S_0 = 1000$.
   - The index's estimated volatility and mean are $\sigma^A = .095310$ and $\mu^A = 0$.
   - The annual continuous-dividend yield generated from the stocks comprising the index portfolio is assumed to be zero ($\psi = 0$) for simplicity.
   - Period Rate $= R^A = 5\%$
   - Put exercise price $= X = 1000$
   - Put expiration $= 3$ years
   - No put multiplier
   - Number of binomial periods $= n = 3$
   - Length of binomial period $= \Delta t = 1$ year

   Answer the following:

   a. Construct a binomial tree showing the possible values of the spot index and index put at each node.
   b. Construct a binomial tree showing the values at each node of a well-diversified stock portfolio currently worth $30M and with a $\beta = 1$.
   c. How many index put contracts would be needed to insure the stock portfolio?
   d. Using the index put and the stock portfolio, construct a binomial tree showing the values at each node of a put-insured portfolio.

2. Construct a dynamic stock portfolio and risk-free bond strategy that will replicate the put-insured portfolio in Problem 1. Show the portfolio's bond and stock portfolio composition at each node and the adjustments required.

APPENDIX 13C   DERIVATION OF THE DYNAMIC HEDGE RATIO

The dynamic hedge ratio is defined as the number of futures contracts (n_f) that will replicate the put-insured stock index portfolio. The value of the put-insured stock index portfolio (V^{Ins}) consists of n shares of the stock index, priced at S per share, and n index put options priced at P, where the number of puts and index shares (n) are the same. That is

$$V^{Ins} = n(S + P) \qquad (13.C\text{-}1)$$

The change in the portfolio value for a small change in the stock index price is

$$\frac{\partial V^{Ins}}{\partial S} = n\frac{\partial S}{\partial S} + n\frac{\partial P}{\partial S}$$

$$\frac{\partial V^{Ins}}{\partial S} = n\left[1 + \frac{\partial P}{\partial S}\right] \tag{13.C-2}$$

From Equation (13C-1), n is equal to $V^{Ins}/(S + P)$. Substituting $V^{Ins}/(S + P)$ for n in (13C-2), we obtain

$$\frac{\partial V^{Ins}}{\partial S} = \frac{V^{Ins}}{S + P}\left[1 + \frac{\partial P}{\partial S}\right] \tag{13.C-3}$$

The futures-insured portfolio that will replicate the put-insured portfolio consists of n_s shares of the stock index and n_f futures contracts priced at f. The value of the futures-insured portfolio (V^{FutIns}) is

$$V^{Fut\,Ins} = n_s S + n_f\,f \tag{13.C-4}$$

For the futures-insured portfolio to provide the same portfolio protection as the put-insured portfolio, its current value must be equal to the put-insured portfolio's value. That is

$$V^{Ins} = V^{Fut\,Ins} = n_s S + n_f f = n_s S \tag{13.C-5}$$

where the initial value of the futures contract is zero. Because the futures contract has no initial value, Equation (13C-5) simplifies to

$$n_s = \frac{V^{Ins}}{S} \tag{13.C-6}$$

The derivative of (13C-4) with respect to S is

$$\frac{\partial V^{Fut\,Ins}}{\partial S} = n_s + n_f\,\frac{\partial f}{\partial S} \tag{13.C-7}$$

If we assume there are no dividends on the index portfolio, then

$$f = Se^{RT} \tag{13.C-8}$$

and

$$\frac{df}{dS} = e^{RT} \tag{13.C-9}$$

Substituting (13C-6) and (13C-9) into Equation (13C-7), we obtain

$$\frac{\partial V^{Fut\,Ins}}{\partial S} = \frac{V^{Ins}}{S} + n_f\,e^{RT} \tag{13.C-10}$$

For the futures-insured portfolio to replicate the put-insured portfolio, its value must change in response to the stock index price changes the same way the value of the put-insured portfolio's value does. That is, Equation (13C-3) must equal Equation (13C-10):

$$\frac{\partial V^{Ins}}{\partial S} = \frac{\partial V^{Fut\,Ins}}{\partial S}$$

$$\frac{V^{Ins}}{S + P}\left[1 + \frac{\partial P}{\partial S}\right] = \frac{V^{Ins}}{S} + n_f\,e^{RT} \tag{13.C-11}$$

Given the replicating condition defined by Equation (13C-11), the dynamic hedging ratio in which a futures-insured portfolio replicates the put-insured portfolio is found by solving Equation (13C-11) for n_f. Doing this yields

$$n_f = \left[\left[\frac{V^{Ins}}{S+P} \right] \left[1 + \frac{\partial P}{\partial S} \right] - \frac{V^{Ins}}{S} \right] e^{-RT} \qquad (13.C\text{-}12)$$

Equation (13C-12) for n_f is the same as Equation (13.9-1) for N_f.

CHAPTER 14

MANAGING FOREIGN CURRENCY POSITIONS WITH DERIVATIVES

14.1 INTRODUCTION

When corporations, institutional investors, and governments hold foreign assets or commodities or when such entities incur foreign debt positions or have to buy foreign goods and services, they are subject to exchange rate risk. As noted in Chapter 10, major banks provide exchange rate risk protection by offering forward contracts to financial and nonfinancial corporations to hedge their currency positions. In addition to contracts offered in this interbank forward market, hedging exchange rate risk is also done using foreign currency futures contracts listed on the Chicago Mercantile Exchange (CME) as well as a number of exchanges outside the United States. Large corporations usually hedge their currency positions in the interbank market, whereas smaller companies, many portfolio managers with foreign security investments, and individuals use the futures market.

Until the introduction of currency options, currency positions usually were hedged with foreign currency forward or futures contracts. Hedging with these instruments allowed foreign exchange participants to lock in the local currency values of their foreign currency positions. However, with currency options, hedgers, for the cost of the options, can obtain not only protection against adverse exchange rate movements but (unlike forward and futures positions) benefits if the exchange rates move in favorable directions. As we discussed in Chapter 2, the Philadelphia Stock Exchange (PHLX) was the first organized exchange to offer trading in foreign currency options. Today, such options are traded on a number of derivative exchanges outside the United States. In addition to spot currency options, the CME and other futures exchanges, as we noted in Chapter 12, also offer options on foreign currency futures. Finally, there is a sophisticated dealer's market that financial and nonfinancial corporations can use to manage their exchange rate positions. This interbank currency options market is part of the interbank foreign exchange market. In this dealer's market, banks provide tailor-made foreign currency option contracts for their customers, primarily multinational corporations. Compared to exchange-traded options, options in the interbank market are larger in contract size, often European, and are available on more currencies. Because these options are tailor-made to fit customer needs, though, there is not a significant secondary market for these options.

Since the introduction of the flexible exchange rate system in the early 1970s, the use of foreign currency derivatives has increased dramatically. In our discussion of derivatives in this book, we've examined how currency futures, options, and futures options are used for speculation and hedging and how the OPM and carrying-cost model are applied to the pricing of currency options and futures. In this chapter, we extend that analysis of currency derivatives by looking at some additional speculative and hedging uses of these contracts. We begin by reviewing the interest rate parity model and showing how it can be extended.

14.2   INTEREST RATE PARITY THEOREM

As we examined in Chapter 11, the carrying-cost model governing the relationship between spot and forward exchange rates is referred to as the ***interest rate parity theorem*** (IRPT). In terms of IRPT, the equilibrium forward price of a currency or forward exchange rate (F_0^*) is equal to the cost of carrying the spot currency (priced at the spot exchange rate of E_0) to the contract's expiration:

$$F_0^* = E_0 \frac{(1 + R_{US})^T}{(1 + R_F)^T} \qquad (14.2\text{-}1)$$

or in terms of continuously compounded U.S. and foreign annualized risk-free rates

$$F_0^* = E_0 e^{(R_{US}^A - R_F^A)T} \qquad (14.2\text{-}2)$$

If the interest rate parity condition does not hold, the ***covered interest arbitrage*** (CIA) strategy consisting of long and short positions in the currency's spot and forward contracts and positions in the domestic and foreign money markets can be used to exploit the price discrepancy between the market price and the IRPT price. Specifically, from a U.S. arbitrageur's position, if the actual forward rate, F_0^M, exceeds the equilibrium, then an arbitrage profit would exist by (1) borrowing dollars at R_{US}, (2) converting the dollar to foreign currency (FC) at E_0, (3) investing the funds in a foreign risk-free rate at the rate R_F, and (4) and entering a short forward contract to sell the FC at the end of the period at F_0^M. By contrast, if the forward rate is below the equilibrium value, then the CIA strategy is reversed. As arbitrageurs attempt to implement such strategies, they will drive the price on the currency forward or futures contract to their equilibrium levels (see Section 11.3 for an example).

14.2.1   Hedging Interbank Forward Contracts

Banks that provide forward contracts to their customers typically use the IRPT to hedge their contracts by taking a position in the spot market. For example, given $R_{US} = 4\%$, $R_F = 6\%$, and $E_0 = \$0.40/FC$, a bank could offer a 1-year forward contract at $F_0 = \$0.39245283/FC$ and then hedge the contract by using a CIA strategy. For example, if a bank's customer wanted to buy 10,000,000 FC 1 year from the present, then the bank could provide the customer with a forward contract in which the bank agrees to sell forward 10,000,000 FC to the customer at the end of 1 year for \$3,924,528. To hedge this short forward position, the bank, in turn, could

- Borrow \$3,773,585 (= (10,000,000 FC/1.04)(\$0.39245283))
- Convert the \$3,773,585 to 9,433,962 FC (= \$3,773,585(2.5FC/\$)
- Invest the 9,433,962 FC for 1 year at $R_F = 6\%$

One year later, the bank would have 10,000,000 FC (= 9,443,962(1.06)) and would owe \$3,924,528 (= \$3,773,585(1.04)), which would exactly offset the bank's forward position. On the other hand, if a bank's customer wanted to sell 10,000,000 FC 1 year from the present, then the bank could provide the customer with a forward contract in which it agrees to buy forward 10,000,000 FC to the customer at the end of 1 year for \$3,924,528. To hedge this long forward position, the bank would reverse the previous strategy: Borrow 9,433,962 FC at 6%, convert to \$3,773,585, and invest in a U.S. security at 4%. At the end of 1 year, the bank would have \$3,924,528 and would owe 10,000,000 FC, which would offset its long forward position.

In hedging their forward contracts, banks are in a position in which they can take care of any mispricing that occurs if the forward price does not satisfy the interest rate parity condition. By taking advantage of such opportunities, they would push the forward price to its equilibrium level.

14.2.2 Currency Futures Prices

As we discussed in Chapter 11, a sufficient condition for futures and forward prices to be equal is for short-term interest rates to be constant over time. In the case of currency futures and forward contracts, the requirement for equality is for both the foreign and domestic short-term rates to be constant. If this occurs, then the IRPT can be extended to determining the equilibrium futures exchange rate; if these rates are not stable, though, then the interest rate parity model would be only an estimate of the equilibrium futures price. Empirically, several studies comparing currency futures and forward exchange rates have found no significant differences between them.[1] Thus, even with market imperfections such as taxes and transaction costs, the IRPT appears to be a good description of what determines both the forward and futures exchange rates.

14.2.3 Investment Uses of Interest Rate Parity Theorem

In addition to determining the equilibrium currency futures or forward price, investors and borrowers can also use the IRPT to define the cutoff expected spot exchange rate for determining whether they should invest or borrow domestically or internationally. To illustrate, consider the preceding example in which $R_{US} = 4\%$, $R_F = 6\%$, $E_0 = \$0.40/FC$, and $f_0 = \$0.39245283/FC$. If an investor knew with certainty that the exchange rate 1 year later would be $f_0 = \$0.39245283/FC$, then she would be indifferent to an investment in a 1-year, U.S. risk-free security yielding 4% and a 1-year, foreign risk-free security yielding 6%. If the U.S. investor, though, were certain that the spot exchange 1 year later would exceed $\$0.39245283/FC$, then she would prefer to invest her dollars in the foreign security rather than the U.S. one. For example, if a U.S. investor knew the spot exchange rate 1 year later would be $E(E_T) = \$0.41/FC$, then she would prefer the foreign investment in which a rate of 8.65% could be earned instead of the U.S. security, which earns only 4%. To attain 8.65%, the investor would have to convert each of her investment dollars to $1/E_0 = 1/\$0.40/FC = 2.5\ FC$ and invest the 2.5 FC at $R_F = 6\%$. One year later, the investor would have 2.65 FC $(= 2.5FC(1.06))$, which she would be able to convert to $\$1.0865$ if the spot exchange rate were $\$0.41/FC$. Thus, the dollar investment in the foreign security would yield a dollar rate of 8.65%.

$$\text{Rate} = \frac{(\$0.41/FC)[2.5FC(1.06)]}{\$1} - 1 = .0865$$

On the other hand, if a U.S. investor knew with certainty that the exchange rate would be less than $\$0.39245283/FC$, then she would prefer the U.S. risk-free investment to the foreign one. For example, if $E(E_T) = \$0.39/FC$, then U.S. investor would earn only 3.35% from the foreign investment compared to 4% from the U.S. investment:

$$\text{Rate} = \frac{(\$0.39/FC)[2.5FC(1.06)]}{\$1} - 1 = .0335$$

The example suggests that in a world of certainty, the equilibrium forward rate as specified by the IRPT can be used to define the expected cutoff exchange rate, $E(E_T^c)$, needed to

---

[1] See Park and Chen (1985). A number of empirical studies that have investigated the validity of the IRPT also have been conducted. See Branson (1979) and Stokes and Newburger (1979).

determine if one should invest in a domestic or risk-free security:

$$E(E_T^c) = F_0 = E_0 \frac{(1 + R_{US})^T}{(1 + R_f)^T}$$

In the real world in which future spot exchange rates are unknown, the required cutoff rate depends on investors' attitudes toward risk. For example, if investors were risk neutral, then they would require no risk premium, and their required expected rate from the risky investment would be equal to the risk-free investment. In this case, the cutoff exchange rate for investors would be the equilibrium forward rate. However, if investors were risk averse, then the required expected rate from the risky investment would have to exceed the risk-free rate. This would require that investors' cutoff exchange rate exceed the forward rate. For example, if risk-averse U.S. investors required an annualized 2% risk premium (RP) to invest in a foreign security, then the expected cutoff exchange rate would be $0.40/FC:

$$E(E_T^c) = E_0 \frac{(1 + R_{US} + RP)^T}{(1 + R_f)^T}$$

$$E(E_T^c) = (\$0.40/FC) \frac{(1 + .04 + .02)^1}{(1.06)^1} = \$0.40/FC$$

Thus, if investors are risk averse, then $E(E_T)$ would have to be greater than F_0 for them to invest in the foreign security that is subject to exchange rate risk instead of the domestic investment.

14.3 CURRENCY SPECULATION

Currency options and futures give speculators a tool for generating a number of different investment strategies. As we examined in Chapter 3, strategies such as outright call and put positions, straddles, strips, spreads, and combinations can be formed with spot and futures currency options, making it possible for investors to speculate on exchange rate movements with different return-risk exposures. In the case of currency futures, speculators can take either outright positions or form intracommodity and intercommodity spreads with different currency futures.

14.3.1 Pure Speculative Positions With Futures

A speculator who is anticipating an increase in the spot exchange rate could profit by going long in a currency forward contract or futures; speculators who are forecasting a decrease in the exchange rate would, in turn, take short futures or forward contract positions. A long currency futures or forward position would be used by speculators who believe that the exchange rate ($/FC) will increase in the future, or equivalently stated, the dollar will depreciate. A dollar depreciation could occur when the U.S. economy is expected to grow, with the economic growth possibly accompanied by inflation. That is, when an economy is growing, the demand for imported goods and services often increases, and if inflation accompanies the economic growth, exports may decline. The increase in imports and decrease in exports would result in an excess demand for foreign currency that would cause the price of the foreign currency ($/FC exchange rate) to increase. In contrast, a short currency futures or forward position would be used by speculators who believe that the exchange rate ($/FC) will decrease in the future, or equivalently stated, for a U.S. investor, the dollar will appreciate. An exchange rate decrease could occur if an economic recession, possibly accompanied by lower prices, were expected. The recession would tend to cause a decrease in import demand, and the lower prices would tend to reduce imports and augment exports, both effects leading to an excess supply of foreign currency (or excess demand for dollars) that would serve to lower the \$/FC exchange rate.

It should be noted that the profitability from pure speculative positions in currency futures and forward contracts depends not only on correctly forecasting the direction of the change in the spot exchange rate but also on estimating the degree of the change. In terms of our illustrative example in which $R_{US} = 4\%$, $R_F = 6\%$, $T = 1$ year, $E_0 = \$0.40/FC$, and $F_0 = \$0.392/FC$, if the actual and equilibrium forward rates are equal, then the spot exchange rate would have to decrease by at least 2% for a speculator to profit from a short position in the forward contract. That is, a 2% decrease in the spot over 1 year would yield a spot exchange rate equal to the forward exchange rate: $E(E_T) = (1 - .02)(\$0.40/FC) = \$0.392/FC$. On the other hand, a speculator could profit from a long forward position provided the exchange rate did not decrease by more than 2%.

14.3.2 Speculating With Equivalent Money Market Positions

Note that speculating on the spot exchange rate using futures or forward contracts represents an alternative to using the money market. In our example, if a speculator expected the exchange rate to rise over the next year (or at least not decrease past \$0.392/FC), then instead of using the futures or forward market, he alternatively could borrow \$40,000, for example, convert the dollars to 100,000 units of FC, and invest FC in the foreign risk-free security at $R_F = 6\%$. If the spot exchange rate were greater than \$0.392/FC at the end of the year, then the speculator would earn a profit when he converted the FC back to dollars. For example, if $E_T = \$0.40/FC$, the speculator would realize an \$800 profit: 106,000 FC(\$0.40/FC) – \$40,000(1.04) = \$800. In contrast, if the speculator expected the spot exchange rate to decrease by more than 2% (such that the spot rate was less than \$0.392/FC), then instead of taking a short futures or forward position, he could borrow 100,000 FC, convert to \$40,000, and invest in the U.S. security at 4%. If the spot exchange rate decreased to $E_T = \$0.38$ by the end of the year, then the speculator would need only to pay \$40,280 to close his foreign loan obligation (\$0.38/FC(106,000FC)), leaving him with a profit of \$1,320 (= \$41,600 – \$40,380).

14.3.3 Speculating With Options

For the cost of an option, a currency speculator can alternatively buy a spot or futures currency call or put option. Figure 14.3-1 shows the profit and spot exchange rate relation at expiration for a long call position. The call option in this figure gives the holder the right to buy one unit of foreign currency (FC) at $X = \$1.50$, and it costs $C_0 = \$0.05/FC$. In contrast, if the exchange rate were expected to fall in the near future, a speculator could take a long currency put position. Figure 14.3-2 shows the profit and exchange rate relation at expiration for a put with $X = \$1.50/FC$ and costing $P_0 = \$0.05/FC$.

As is always the case with options, numerous profit and exchange rate relations can be obtain with different option positions: spreads, straddles, combinations, strips, and straps. Thus, a speculator who expected little change in the exchange rate could form a short straddle or combination with currency options to profit from such expectations. Similarly, positions defined by an option's or option position's delta, theta, and gamma can be applied to currency positions.

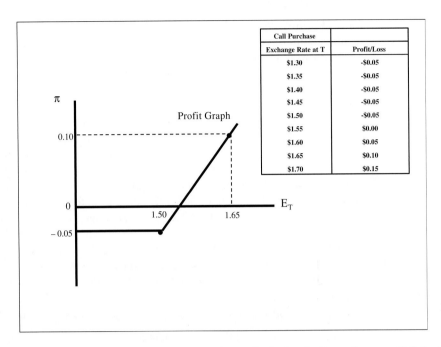

Call Purchase	
Exchange Rate at T	Profit/Loss
$1.30	-$0.05
$1.35	-$0.05
$1.40	-$0.05
$1.45	-$0.05
$1.50	-$0.05
$1.55	$0.00
$1.60	$0.05
$1.65	$0.10
$1.70	$0.15

FIGURE 14.3-1 Profit and Exchange Rate Relation at Expiration for Long Currency Call Position: $X = \$1.50/FC$, $C_0 = \$0.05/FC$

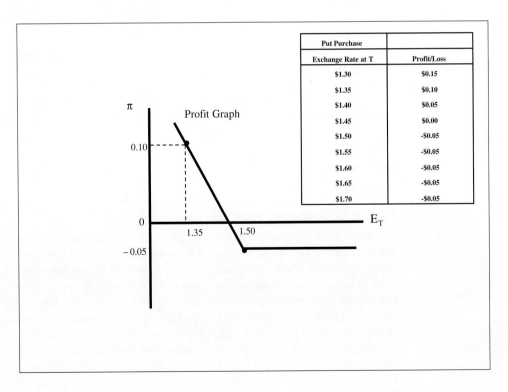

Put Purchase	
Exchange Rate at T	Profit/Loss
$1.30	$0.15
$1.35	$0.10
$1.40	$0.05
$1.45	$0.00
$1.50	-$0.05
$1.55	-$0.05
$1.60	-$0.05
$1.65	-$0.05
$1.70	-$0.05

FIGURE 14.3-2 Profit and Exchange Rate Relation at Expiration for Long Currency Put Position: $X = \$1.50/FC$, $P_0 = \$0.05/FC$

14.3.4 Currency Futures Spreads

Instead of assuming the risk inherent in an outright futures position, speculators instead can hedge some of their exchange rate risk by forming intercommodity or intracommodity currency spreads. A speculator could form an intercommodity spread by going long and short in different currency futures. For example, if a speculator expects the dollar price of both the Swiss franc and British pound to increase, she could form an intercommodity spread by going long in the currency with the greater exchange rate elasticity and short in the other currency. Similarly, a U.S. speculator who expects the dollar/euro exchange rate to change, for example, could form an intracommodity spread by taking a position in a shorter term euro currency futures contract and an opposite position in a longer term euro currency futures.

14.3.5 Cross-Exchange Rate Relations

Currency futures contracts on some exchanges are listed in terms of the one currency's price (e.g., U.S. dollar price of a currency). A speculator who trades on such an exchange and wants to speculate on an exchange rate not defined by that currency could do so by taking two futures positions, with the positions defined by the cross-exchange rate relationship.

The cross-exchange rate defines the relationship between different exchange rates. For example, if the spot BP/dollar (£/$) exchange rate is .66667£/$1 (or $1.50/£) and the euro/dollar (€/$) rate is .80€/$1 (or $1.25/€), then the equilibrium £/€ exchange rate would have to be 0.83333£/€:

$$0.66667£ = \$1 = 0.80€$$

$$0.66667£ = .80€$$

$$\frac{.66667}{.80}£ = 1€$$

$$0.83333£ = 1€$$

If the actual £/€ exchange rate is not 0.8333, then an arbitrage strategy, defined as **triangular arbitrage,** can be employed to earn riskless profit. For example, suppose the £/€ exchange rate is 0.86£/€ instead of 0.83333£/€. An arbitrageur with a position in dollars could earn a riskless return of $0.032 for each dollar invested by

1. Buying 0.80€ with $1
2. Converting the 0.80€ to 0.688£: (0.80€)(0.86 £/€) = 0.688£
3. Converting the .688£ to $1.032: (.688£)($1.50/£) = $1.032

By executing this triangular arbitrage strategy, the arbitrageur would be supplying the exchange market with € and would be demanding £, which would push the £/€ exchange rate toward 0.8333. On the other hand, if the £/€ exchange rate is at 0.80 (or 1.25 €/£), an arbitrageur could earn $0.04 by

1. Buying 0.66667£ for $1
2. Converting the 0.66667£ to 0.8333€: (0.66667£)(1.25€/£) = 0.8333€
3. Converting the 0.8333€ to $1.04: (0.8333 €)($1.25/€) = $1.04

These actions, in turn, would serve to push the £/€ exchange rate up toward 0.83333.

The triangular arbitrage strategy can, in turn, be used to define how currency futures priced in terms of dollars can be used to speculate on different exchange rates. For example, a speculator with a position in British pounds could speculate on a £/€ exchange rate decrease by going long in a BP futures contract and going short in a euro futures contract each priced in terms of dollars.

14.4   HEDGING WITH CURRENCY DERIVATIVES

In Chapter 3, we examined how foreign currency positions could be hedged with currency options. Recall that by going long in a currency call option, one can lock in the maximum dollar cost of a future cash outflow or liability denominated in a foreign currency while still maintaining the chance for lower dollar outlays if the exchange rate decreases. In contrast, by going long in a currency put, one can lock in the minimum dollar value of a future inflow or asset denominated in foreign currency while still maintaining the possibility of greater dollar inflows in case the exchange rate increases. With foreign currency futures and forward contracts, the domestic currency value of future cash flows or the future dollar value of assets and liabilities denominated in another currency can be locked in. Unlike option hedging, though, no exchange rate gains exist when futures or forward contracts are used.

14.4.1   Hedging Future Currency Cash Inflow

As noted, large multinational corporations usually hedge their currency positions in the interbank forward market or interbank dealer's option market, whereas smaller companies, some portfolio managers, and individuals often use the organized futures and option markets. In either case, the currency position usually is hedged with a naive hedging model in which the number of derivative contracts is equal to the value of the foreign currency position to be hedged.

To illustrate currency hedging, consider the option hedging example presented in Chapter 3 in which a U.S. investment fund was expecting a payment of £10M in principal on its Eurobonds next September. In that example, the U.S. fund obtained down-side exchange rate risk protection by purchasing 320 PHLX September BP put contracts (contract size = 31,250 BP) with an exercise price of X = $1.425/£ at $P_0 = $0.02/£:

$$n_p = £10,000,000/£31,250 = 320$$

$$\text{Cost} = (320)(£31,250)(0.02/£) = \$200,000$$

Exhibit 14.4-1 shows the dollar cash flows the U.S. fund would receive in September from converting its receipts of £10,000,000 to dollars at the spot exchange rate (E_T) and closing its 320 put contracts at a price equal to the put's intrinsic value (assume the September payment date and option expiration date are the same). As shown, if the exchange rate were less than X = $1.425/£, the company would have received less than $14,250,000 when it converted its £10,000,000 to dollars; these lower revenues, however, would have been offset by the cash flows from the put position. On the other hand, if the exchange rate at expiration exceeded $1.425/£, the U.S. fund would have realized a dollar gain when it converted the £10,000,000 at the higher spot exchange rate, with its losses on the put limited to the amount of the premium. Thus, by hedging with currency put options, the U.S. investment fund was able to obtain exchange rate risk protection in the event the exchange rate decreases while still retaining the potential for increased dollar revenues if the exchange rate rises.

Suppose the U.S fund is more certain of an exchange rate decrease and therefore does not believe the $200,000 put cost is worth the benefit of the upside potential. Instead of hedging with a BP put, the U.S. fund could hedge its September BP receipt with a BP

EXHIBIT 14.4-1 Hedging £10,000,000 Cash Inflow With British Pound Put Options and Futures

X = $1.425/£, P = .02, Contract Size = £31,250

Number of Puts = 320, Total Cost of Puts = (320)(31,250)(.02) = $200,000

CME BP Futures: f_0 = $1.425/£, Contract Size = £62,500, Number of Short Futures = 160

1	2	3	4	5	6
Exchange Rate E_T = $/BP	Dollar Revenue E_T(10,000,000BP)	Put Cash Flow	Put Hedged Revenue Col(2) + Col(3)	Futures Cash Flow	Futures Hedged Revenue Col(2) + Col(5)
$1.20	$12,000,000	$2,250,000	$14,250,000	$2,250,000	$14,250,000
$1.25	$12,500,000	$1,750,000	$14,250,000	$1,750,000	$14,250,000
$1.275	$12,750,000	$1,500,000	$14,250,000	$1,500,000	$14,250,000
$1.300	$13,000,000	$1,250,000	$14,250,000	$1,250,000	$14,250,000
$1.325	$13,250,000	$1,000,000	$14,250,000	$1,000,000	$14,250,000
$1.350	$13,500,000	$750,000	$14,250,000	$750,000	$14,250,000
$1.375	$13,750,000	$500,000	$14,250,000	$500,000	$14,250,000
$1.400	$14,000,000	$250,000	$14,250,000	$250,000	$14,250,000
$1.425	$14,250,000	$0	$14,250,000	$0	$14,250,000
$1.450	$14,500,000	$0	$14,500,000	–$250,000	$14,250,000
$1.475	$14,750,000	$0	$14,750,000	–$500,000	$14,250,000
$1.500	$15,000,000	$0	$15,000,000	–$750,000	$14,250,000
$1.525	$15,250,000	$0	$15,250,000	–$1,000,000	$14,250,000

Put Cash Flow = (320)(31,250BP)(Max[$1.425/BP − E_T, 0])

Futures Cash Flow = (160)(62,500)($1.425/BP − f_T)

futures contract. Suppose September BP futures on the CME are trading at $f_0 = \$1.425/£$. Because the contract size on the BP futures contract is 62,500£, the fund would need to go short in 160 BP contracts. Doing this, the company would in turn ensure itself of a $14,250,000 receipt at expiration when it converts its £10,000,000 to dollars at the spot $/£ exchange rate and closes its short futures contracts at futures prices equal to the spot exchange rate (see Columns (5) and (6) of Exhibit 14.4-1).

If an economic entity has a future debt obligation or payment that it is required to pay in foreign currency, then it can hedge the dollar cost by using either a currency call option or a long currency futures or forward contract. To illustrate this hedge, consider again the option hedging example presented in Chapter 3 in which a U.S. company owed £10,000,000, with the payment to be made in September. To benefit from possible lower exchange rates while still limiting the dollar costs of purchasing £10,000,000 in the event the $/£ exchange rate rises, the company bought 320 British pound call options with $X = \$1.425/£$ ($n_c = £10,000,000/£31,250 = 320$) at a cost of $0.02/£ (total cost = $200,000 = (320)(£31,250)(0.02/£). Exhibit 14.4-2 shows the company's costs of purchasing £10,000,000 at different exchange rates and the cash flows from selling 320 September British pound calls at expiration at a price equal to the call's intrinsic value. As shown in the exhibit, for cases in which the exchange rate was greater than $1.425/£, the company realized dollar expenditures exceeding $14,250,000; The expenditures, though, were offset by the cash flows from the calls. On the other hand, when the exchange rate was less than $1.425/£, the dollar costs of purchasing £10,000,000 decreased as the exchange rate decreased, whereas the losses on the call options were limited to the option premium.

If the company believed that $/£ exchange rate was more likely to increase and therefore did not believe the costs of the call options were worth the benefit of gaining from an unlikely exchange rate decrease, it could lock in the dollar cost of buying £10,000,000 by going long in September BP futures contract. Again, suppose September BP futures on the CME are trading at $f_0 = \$1.425/£$. To hedge it dollar cost, the company would need to go long in 160 BP contracts. Doing this, the company would in turn ensure itself of a $14,250,000 cost at expiration when it purchases the £10,000,000 at the spot $/£ exchange rate and closes its long futures contracts at futures prices equal to the spot exchange rate (see Columns (5) and (6) of Exhibit 14.4-2).

Note, in the preceding futures examples, the hedge involves a foreign currency conversion to or from dollars. If the hedge, though, does not involve the dollar, and the only currency futures and forward contracts available are those defined in dollars, then the cross-exchange rate relationship discussed needs to be used to set up the appropriate hedge. For example, suppose a German investor wanted to lock in the euro value of his future receipt of BP using dollar-denominated euro and British pound futures contracts. To do this, the investor would need to take positions in the $/€ and $/£ futures contracts and use the cross-exchange rate relationship to define each futures' position.

14.4.2   Hedging Currency Positions Using the Money Market

Instead of forward or futures contracts, financial and nonfinancial companies can also hedge their positions by using a money market position. For example, the previous company with the September £10,000,000 liability could lock in the dollar cost of the BP purchase by creating a BP asset worth £10,000,000 in September and a dollar liability in September. To see this, suppose the company can borrow dollars at 6% and invest BP at 6%, the spot exchange rate is $1.425/£, and the September payment date is 1 year from the present. To fix its dollar cost, the company would need to borrow $13,443,396.23 (= (£10,000,000)($1.425/£)/1.06)), convert to £9,433,962.26 (= ($13,443,396.23(£0.701754386/$)), and invest at 6%. One year later, the company

EXHIBIT 14.4-2 Hedging £10,000,000 Cash Outflow With a British Pound Call Option and Futures

X = $1.425/£, C = .02, Contract Size = £31,250
Number of calls = 320, Total Cost of Calls = (320)(31,250)(.02) = $200,000
CME BP Futures: f_0 = $1.425/£, Contract Size = £62,500, Number of Long Futures = 160

1	2	3	4	5	6
Exchange Rate	Dollar Cost	Call Cash Flow	Call Hedged Cost	Futures Cash Flow	Futures Hedged Cost
E_T = $/BP	E_T (10,000,000BP)		Col(2) − Col(3)		Col(2) − Col(5)
$1.200	$12,000,000	$0	$12,000,000	−$2,250,000	$14,250,000
$1.250	$12,500,000	$0	$12,500,000	−$1,750,000	$14,250,000
$1.275	$12,750,000	$0	$12,750,000	−$1,500,000	$14,250,000
$1.300	$13,000,000	$0	$13,000,000	−$1,250,000	$14,250,000
$1.325	$13,250,000	$0	$13,250,000	−$1,000,000	$14,250,000
$1.350	$13,500,000	$0	$13,500,000	−$750,000	$14,250,000
$1.375	$13,750,000	$0	$13,750,000	−$500,000	$14,250,000
$1.400	$14,000,000	$0	$14,000,000	−$250,000	$14,250,000
$1.425	$14,250,000	$0	$14,250,000	$0	$14,250,000
$1.450	$14,500,000	$250,000	$14,250,000	$250,000	$14,250,000
$1.475	$14,750,000	$500,000	$14,250,000	$500,000	$14,250,000
$1.500	$15,000,000	$750,000	$14,250,000	$750,000	$14,250,000
$1.525	$15,250,000	$1,000,000	$14,250,000	$1,000,000	$14,250,000

Call Cash Flow = (320)(31,250BP)(Max[E_T − $1.425/BP,0])
Futures Cash Flow = (160)(62,500)(f_T − $1.425/BP)

would have £10,000,000 (= £9,433,962.26(1.06)) from its BP investment that it could use to cover its £10,000,000 debt, and it would owe $14,250,000 (= $13,443,396.23(1.06))—the same dollar obligation it had by hedging with the long futures contracts. This will always be the case if the company can obtain the same interest rates that govern the interest rate parity condition.

By contrast, the company with the £10,000,000 September principal receipt, could hedge the dollar value by creating a £10,000,000 liability and a dollar asset. For example, suppose this company can invest dollars at 6% and borrow BP at 6%, the spot exchange rate is $1.425/£, and the September receipt date is 1 year from the present. To fix its dollar revenue, the company would need to borrow the £9,433,962.26 (= (£10,000,000)/1.06), convert to $13,443,396.22 (= ($1.425/£)£9,433,962.26), and invest at 6%. One year later, the company would owe £10,000,000 (= £9,433,962.26(1.06)) from its BP loan that it would pay with £10,000,000 principal receipt, and it would receive $14,250,000 (= $13,443,396.23(1.06)) from its dollar investment—the same dollar revenue it had by hedging with the short future contracts.

14.4.3 Hedging International Investments

Currency futures, forward, and option contracts often are used by portfolio managers to immunize their international portfolios against exchange rate risk. For example, suppose a U.S. institutional investment fund wanted to hedge the dollar value of their holdings of 10,000 shares of a French stock currently worth 100 euros per share. Suppose the $/€ spot and 3-month CME futures exchange rates were both $1.20/€ (or €0.8333/$), making the current dollar value of the stock worth $1,200,000 (= ($1.20/€)(10,000)(€100)). If the fund wanted to hedge the dollar value of their stock at the end of 3 months against exchange rate risk, they would need to go short in eight euro futures contracts (contract size is 125,000 euros):

$$n_f = \frac{\$1,200,000}{(\$1.20/\text{euro})(125,000 \text{ euros})} = 8 \text{ short euros futures contract}$$

If, at the end of 3 months, no change in the price of the French stock occurred, then the futures-hedged dollar value of the stock would be $1,200,000, irrespective of the spot $/€ exchange rate. If the $/€ decreased by 10% over the period from $1.20/€ to $1.08/€, then the dollar value of the stock also would decrease by 10% from $1,200,000 to $1,080,000; this $120,000 decrease in value, though, would be offset by a $120,000 profit from the futures position: 8(125,000 euros)[($1.20/€) − ($1.08/€)] = $120,000.

Hedging with currency futures or forward contracts allows international investors to focus on selecting stocks or portfolios without having to worry about short-run changes in the exchange rate. For instance, in the preceding example, if the price of the French stock increased by 5% from €100 to €105 at the same time the $/€ exchange rate decreased by 10% to $1.08/€, then an unhedged position would lose 5.5% in dollars:

$$\text{Rate} = \frac{(\$1.08/\text{euro})(105 \text{ euros})(10,000)}{\$1,200,000} - 1$$

$$\text{Rate} = -.055$$

If the position is hedged with eight euro futures contracts, though, the fund would receive a $120,000 futures profit, and their rate of return on the currency-hedged investment would be 4.5%:

$$\text{Rate} = \frac{(\$1.08/\text{euro})(105 \text{ euros})(10,000) + \$120,000}{\$1,200,000} - 1$$

$$\text{Rate} = .045$$

Thus, the futures hedge allows the investor to profit from good stock selection.

It should be noted that the rate of return in dollars earned from the currency-hedged stock in the preceding example is less than the 5% increase in the stock price. This is because a naive hedge protects only the initial value; dividends and stock appreciation are not hedged against exchange-rate risk. To also hedge stock price changes against exchange rate changes would require knowing the correlation between the exchange rate and the stock price.

14.5 CONCLUSION

The flexible exchange rate system that began in 1972 made it necessary for multinational corporations, international investors, and international organization to deal with the problems of exchange-rate risk. To this end, forward contracts on the interbank market, futures contracts on the exchanges, and currency options have provided these entities with a relatively effective exchange rate risk reduction tool. Another effective hedging tool for managing currency position are currency swaps. These derivatives are examined in Chapter 20.

KEY TERMS

interest rate parity	cross-exchange rate
covered interest arbitrage	triangular arbitrage

SELECTED REFERENCES

Aliber, R. "The Interest Rate Parity Theorem: A Reinterpretation." *Journal of Political Economy* (December 1973): 1451–1459.

Allayannis, G., and J. Weston. "The Use of Foreign Currency Derivatives and Firm Market Value." *Review of Financial Studies*, 14 (Spring 2001): 243–276.

Branson, W. "The Minimum Covered Interest Differential Needed for International Arbitrage Activity." *Journal of Political Economy* (December 1979): 1029–1034.

Brown, G. W. "Managing Foreign Exchange Risk With Derivatives." *Journal of Financial Economics*, 60 (2001): 401–448.

Cornell, B. "Spot Rates, Forward Rates, and Exchange Market Efficiency." *Journal of Financial Economics* (August 1977): 55–65.

Cornell, B., and M. Reinganum. "Forward and Futures Prices: Evidence from the Foreign Exchange Markets." *Journal of Finance* 36 (December 1981): 1035–1045.

Geczy, C., B. A. Minion, and C. Schrand. "Why Firms Use Currency Derivatives." *Journal of Finance*, 52, (1997): 1323–1354.

Ghon, R. S., and R. P. Chang. "Intra-day Arbitrage in Foreign Exchange and Eurocurrency Markets." *Journal of Finance*, 47 (1992): 363–380.

Grammatikos, T., and A. Saunders. "Stability and the Hedging Performance of Foreign Currency Futures." *Journal of Futures Markets* (Fall 1983): 295–305.

Hill, J., and T. Schneewis. "The Hedging Effectiveness of Foreign Currency Futures." *Journal of Financial Research* (Spring 1982): 95–104.

Huang, R. "An Analysis of Intertemporal Pricing for Forward Foreign Exchange Contracts." *Journal of Finance* 44 (March 1989): 183–194.

Huang, R. "Some Alternative Tests of Forward Exchange Rates as Predictors of Future Spot Rates." *Journal of International Money and Finance* (August 1984): 153–178.

Johnson, R., C. Hultman, and R. Zuber. "Currency Cocktails and Exchange Rate Stability." *Columbia Journal of World Business* 14 (Winter 1979): 117–126.

Kohlhagen, S. "The Forward Rate as an Unbiased Predictor of the Future Spot Rate." *Columbia Journal of World Business* (Winter 1979): 77–85.

Kolers, T., and W. Simpson. "A Comparison of the Forecast Accuracy of the Futures and Forward Markets for Foreign Exchange." *Applied Economics* (July 1987): 961–967.

Madura, J., and T. Veit. "Use of Currency Options in International Cash Management." *Journal of Cash Management* (January–February 1986): 42–48.

Madura, J., and E. Nosari. "Utilizing Currency Portfolios to Mitigate Exchange Rate Risk." *Columbia Journal of World Business* (Spring 1984): 96–99.

Panton, D., and M. Joy. "Empirical Evidence on International Monetary Market Currency Futures." *Journal of International Business Studies* (Fall 1978): 59–68.

Papdia, F. "Forward Exchange Rates as Predictors of Future Spot Rates and the Efficiency of the Foreign Exchange Market." *Journal of Banking and Finance* (June 1981): 217–240.

Park, H., and A. Chen. "Differences Between Futures and Forward Prices: A Further Examination of the Marking-to-the-Market Effects." *Journal of Futures Markets* (Spring 1985): 77–85.

Stokes, H., and H. Neuburger. "Interest Arbitrage, Forward Speculation and the Determination of the Forward Exchange Rate." *Columbia Journal of World Business* 4 (1979): 86–99.

Swanson, P., and S. Caples. "Hedging Foreign Exchange Risk Using Forward Exchange Markets: An Extension." *Journal of International Business Studies* (Spring 1987): 75–82.

PROBLEMS AND QUESTIONS

1. Explain the differences between the forward market and the futures market for foreign currency.

2. Suppose the spot dollar/Swiss franc exchange rate is $0.375/SF, the U.S. risk-free rate is 6% (annual), and the Swiss risk-free rate is 8%.

   a. Assuming the interest rate parity theorem holds, what should the equilibrium 90-day $/SF forward rate be?

   b. Suppose a U.S. bank provides one of its business customers with a forward contract in which the customer agrees to sell the bank 15 million Swiss francs at the end of 90 days at $F_0 = \$0.3732756/SF$. Assuming the bank can borrow and lend dollars and Swiss francs at the preceding risk-free rates, explain how the bank would hedge its forward position.

   c. Explain the type of forward contract the bank would provide the business customer and how it would hedge the contract if the business customer wanted to buy 15M SF at the end of 90 days.

3. Explain why a risk-neutral investor would be indifferent between a 90-day U.S. dollar investment in a risk-free security at 7% and a British pound investment at 5% if the investor expected the $/£ spot exchange rate at the end of 90 days to equal the forward rate as determined by the IRPT. In your explanation, assume the current spot exchange rate is $1.425/BP.

4. Suppose the U.S. investor in Question 3 were risk averse, instead of risk neutral, and wants a risk premium of 2% (annual) for assuming the exchange rate risk on the international investment.

a. Find the expected spot exchange rate that would make the risk-averse investor indifferent between the U.S. and British 90-day risk-free investments?

b. Demonstrate that the investor would earn that return if this expected exchange rate is realized.

5. Given the following euro and British pound spot exchange rates: .80€/$1 and £0.70/$1.

a. What is the equilibrium £/€?

b. Describe the triangular arbitrage strategy a U.S. arbitrageur would pursue if the BP price of a euro were .90£/€.

c. Describe the triangular arbitrage strategy a U.S. arbitrageur would pursue if the BP price of a euro were .85£/€.

6. Given the following:

$$E_0 = \$1.80/FC$$

$$F_0 = \$1.80(1 \text{ year forward contract})$$

$$R_{US} = 10\%(\text{annual})$$

$$R_F = 10\%(\text{annual})$$

a. Explain how you would speculate on the FC using the forward market if you expected the spot exchange rate to be $1.70/FC 1 year from now.

b. Explain how you would speculate on the FC using the money market if you expected the spot exchange rate to be $1.70/FC 1 year from now (assume you can borrow and lend at $R_{US} = R_F = 10\%$).

c. Explain how you would speculate on the FC using the forward market if you expected the spot exchange rate to be $1.90/FC 1 year from now.

d. Explain how you would speculate on the FC using the money market if you expected the spot exchange rate to be $1.90/FC 1 year from now (assume you can borrow and lend at $R_{US} = R_F = 10\%$).

7. Given the following:

- U.S. dollar/Canadian dollar ($/CD) exchange rate = $0.8333/CD or CD/$ = 1.20CD/$
- U.S. dollar/Australian dollar ($/AUD) exchange rate = $0.666/AUD or AUD/$ = 1.50 AUD/$
- R = 6% (annual) in the United States, Canada, and Australia.

a. Determine the equilibrium spot and 1-year forward CD/AUD exchange rates.

b. Explain how Canadian speculators could use CD/AUD forward contracts to profit if they expected the spot CD/AUD to decrease from 0.8CD/AUD to 0.75CD/AUD 1 year from now.

c. Explain how U.S. speculators would use the CME futures market if they also expected the CD/AUD spot exchange rate to decrease to 0.75CD/AUD 1 year from now and expected no change in $/AUD rate (assume futures and forward rates are the same).

8. B. P. Larken just signed a contract to play professional basketball in Mexico for the Mexican Stars. The team owner has agreed to pay his living expenses for the year and

an annual salary of 500,000 pesos, with half of the payment to be paid in December and the other half in March. B. P. Larken plans to play 1 year and then return to the United States. He would like to hedge the dollar value of his contract. Currently, the spot $/peso exchange rate is $0.16666/peso, the Mexican risk-free rate is 8% (annual), the U.S. risk-free rate is 6%, forward rates offered by U.S. and Mexican banks are governed by the IRPT, and the December payment date is .25 of a year away and the March date is .5.

a. Explain how Mr. Larken could hedge the dollar value of his salary using forward contracts.

b. Suppose Mr. Larken could not find a bank to provide him with a forward contract. Explain how he could alternatively hedge his salary against exchange rate risk by using the money market? Assume Mr. Larken can borrow pesos at 8% and can invest dollar at 6%.

9. The Parson's Company is a U.S. company with jewelry stores located across the United States. In January, the company signs a contract with Swiss Watch, Inc. to purchase 100,000 watches in March (T = .25 per year) at the cost of 30SF per watch, with the payments to be made at the time of the March delivery. Currently, U.S. and Swiss risk-free interest rates are both at 6% (annual), the $/SF spot exchange rate is $0.66667/SF, and the $/SF forward rates and the CME futures rate are governed by the IRPT.

a. Explain how the Parson Company could hedge its dollars costs of the watches against exchange rate risk using forward contracts.

b. Explain how the Parson Company could hedge its March payment by using the money market. Assume it can borrow and lend dollars and Swiss francs at 6%.

c. Explain how the Parson Company could hedge its March payment by taking a position in the CME's SF futures contract (contract size is 125,000 SF). Evaluate the hedge at possible spot exchange rates at the March expiration of $0.60/SF and $0.70/SF. Assume the watch payment occurs at the same time as the futures expiration.

d. Explain how the Parson Company could cap its March payment by purchasing a CME March SF futures call with an exercise price $0.66667/SF (contract size = 125,000 SF), trading at $0.05/SF, and with its March expiration matching the SF futures expiration. Evaluate the cap at possible spot exchange rates at the futures expiration of $0.60/SF, $0.625/SF, $0.65/SF, $0.675/SF, $0.70/SF, $0.725/SF, $0.750/SF, $0.775/SF, and $0.800/SF. Assume the watch payment occurs at the same time as the futures expiration.

10. Suppose ESPN (Disney) is expecting revenues of 6,250,000 BP next April (1 year from now: T = 1) from its United Kingdom Rugby sports productions division. Fearing that exchange rates could decrease when it converts its 6,250,000 BP, ESPN would like to hedge the dollar value of its revenue. Currently, the spot $/£ exchange rate is $1.50/£, the U.S. risk-free rate is 6%, the British risk-free rate is 6%, and the 1-year forward rate offered by U.S. and British banks is determined by the IRPT.

a. Explain how ESPN could hedge the dollar value of its revenue using a forward contract.

b. Explain how ESPN could alternatively hedge its revenue of 6,250,000 BP against exchange rate risk by using the money market. Assume ESPN can borrow British pounds and dollars at 6%.

c. Suppose BP futures contracts expiring in April (1 year from present) are trading on the CME at $1.50/£ (contract size = 62,500 BP). Show how ESPN could hedge its revenue against exchange rate risk by using the April contract. Assume that at the futures expiration, ESPN will close its futures position at an expiring futures price equal to the spot exchange rate and convert its BP revenue at the spot exchange rate. Evaluate the position by assuming possible spot $/£ exchange rate at expiration of $1.45/£ and $1.55/£.

d. Explain how ESPN could set a floor on the dollar value of its April revenue by purchasing a CME April BP futures put with an exercise price $1.50/£ (contract size = 62,500 BP) trading at $0.02/£. Assume the futures option's April expiration matches the BP futures expiration. Evaluate the floor at possible spot exchange rates at the futures expiration of $1.30/£, $1.35/£, $1.40/£, $1.45/£, $1.50/£, $1.55/£, $1.60/£, $1.65/£, and $1.70/£. Assume the 6,250,000BP revenue comes at the same time as the futures expiration.

11. Suppose ESPN (Disney) owes the United Kingdom Rugby Association 12,500,000 BP for the exclusive licensing right to produce Rugby matches on the European and U.S. cable systems. Suppose the licensing payment is due next May (1 year from now: T = 1). Fearing that exchange rates could increase when it buys the pounds, ESPN would like to hedge the dollar cost of buying the currency. Currently, the spot $/£ exchange rate is $1.50/BP, the U.S. risk-free rate is 6%, the British risk-free rate is 6%, and the 1-year forward rate offered by U.S. and British banks is determined by the IRPT.

a. Explain how ESPN could hedge the dollar cost of purchasing BP using a forward contract.

b. Explain how ESPN could alternatively hedge its 12,500,000 BP purchase against exchange rate risk by using the money market. Assume ESPN can borrow and lend BP at 6% and dollars at 6%.

12. A U.S. investor just bought one share of Heineken stock (listed on the Amsterdam Exchange) for 200 euros when the dollar/euro spot exchange rate was $1.20/€. The investor expects the stock to pay a dividend worth 5 euros and to appreciate by 10% 1 year from now.

a. Calculate the 1-year expected rate of return on the stock for an investment made in euros.

b. Assuming possible end-of-the-year exchange rates are $1.05/€, $1.10/€, $1.15/€, $1.20/€, and $1.25/€, calculate the possible 1-year expected rates of return on the stock in terms of a dollar investment.

c. If the U.S. risk-free rate were 7%, and the Netherlands' risk-free rate on euros were 5%, what would be the 1-year forward rate a bank could provide the investor if it provides forward contracts based on the IRPT?

d. What would be the investor's possible expected rates of return if she hedged the dollar price of the stock (€200) by going short in a forward contract as determined by the IRPT? Evaluate at possible exchange rate of $1.05/€, $1.10/€, $1.15/€, $1.20/€, and $1.25/€.

WEB EXERCISES

1. Read more about CME currency derivatives by going to www.cme.com ("CME Products" "Foreign Exchange").

2. Make an exchange rate forecast and then form an intracommodity spread with a listed index futures contract based on your forecast. For price quotes on futures, go to www.wsj.com/free (Market Data Center) or www.cme.com.

3. Determine the interest rate parity value of a listed currency futures contract. For current market quotes and information, go to www.cme.com and www.wsj.com/free.

4. Select exchange-listed currency futures call and put options and determine their recent prices by going to www.wsj.com/free and clicking "Market Data Center" ("Commodity and Futures") or www.cme.com. Using your options, evaluate some of the following strategies with a profit table and graph (use Excel or the Excel program for "Option Strategies" included with the book): call purchase, put purchase, straddle purchase, straddle sale, synthetic long position, or synthetic short position.

CHAPTER 15

MANAGING FIXED-INCOME POSITIONS WITH INTEREST-RATE DERIVATIVES

15.1 INTRODUCTION

In 1985, Merrill Lynch introduced the liquid yield option note (LYON). The LYON is a zero-coupon bond, convertible into the issuer's stock, callable (with the call price increasing over time), and putable (with the put price increasing over time). The LYON is a good example of how innovative the investment community can be in structuring debt instruments with option clauses. The innovation, as well as growth, in derivative products is, in part, the result of the relatively sharp swings in interest rates that have occurred in the United States, European Union, United Kingdom, Japan, and other industrial economies over the last 30 years. This volatility increased the exposure of many debt and fixed-income investment positions to interest rate risk. Faced with this risk, many corporate borrowers, money managers, intermediaries, and bond portfolio mangers increased their use of futures and option contracts on debt securities as a hedge against such risk. Today, futures and options contracts on debt securities as well as such hybrid derivatives as swaps, interest rate options, caps, and floors are used by banks and financial intermediaries to manage the maturity gaps between loans and deposits, by corporations and financial institutions to fix or cap the rates on future loans, and by fixed-income portfolio managers, money managers, investment bankers, and security dealers in locking in the future purchase or selling price on their fixed-income securities.

In this chapter, we continue our analysis of the use of derivative by examining how they are used in managing fixed-income positions. We begin by looking at how interest rate futures and options can be used for hedging future debt and bond investment positions against interest rate risk. We next look at how interest rate derivatives are used to create different speculative positions. We then conclude the chapter by examining how synthetic fixed-rate and floating-rate debt and investment positions are formed with interest rate derivatives. This chapter focuses on managing interest rate positions with exchange-traded futures options and futures. In Chapter 16, we extend the analysis of interest rate management to examining the uses of such OTC interest rate derivative products such as caps, floors, and collars that are offered by financial institutions.

15.2 HEDGING FIXED-INCOME POSITIONS

A fixed-income manager planning to invest a future inflow of cash in high-quality bonds could hedge the investment against possible higher bond prices and lower rates by going long in T-bond futures contracts. If long-term rates were to decrease, the higher costs of purchasing the bonds would then be offset by profits from his T-bond futures positions. On the other hand, if rates increased, the manager would benefit from lower bond prices, but he would also have to cover losses on his futures position. Similar long hedging positions using T-bill or Eurodollar futures could also be applied by money managers who were planning to invest future cash inflows in short-term securities and wanted to minimize their risk exposure to short-term interest rate changes. In such hedging cases, if rates were to increase, the manager would benefit from lower bond prices, but he would also have to cover losses on his futures position. Thus, hedging future fixed-income investments with futures locks in a future price and return and therefore eliminates not only the costs of unfavorable price movements but also the benefits from favorable movements. However, by hedging with either exchange-traded futures call options on Treasury or Eurodollar contracts or with an OTC spot call option on a debt security, a hedger can obtain protection against adverse price increases while still realizing lower costs if security prices decrease.

For cases in which bond or money market managers are planning to sell some of their securities in the future, hedging can be done by going short in a T-bond, T-bill, or Eurodollar futures contracts. If rates were higher at the time of the sale, the resulting lower bond prices and therefore revenue from the bond sale would be offset by profits from the futures positions (just the opposite would occur if rates were lower). The hedge also can be formed by purchasing an exchange-traded futures put options on Treasury or Eurodollar contracts or an OTC spot put option on a debt security. This hedge would provide downside protection if bond prices decrease whereas earning increasing revenues if security prices increase.

Short hedging positions with futures and put options can be used not only by holders of fixed-income securities planning to sell their instruments before maturity but also by bond issuers, borrowers and debt security underwriters. A company planning to issue bonds or borrow funds from a financial institution at some future date, for example, could hedge the debt position against possible interest rate increases by going short in debt futures contracts or cap the loan rate by buying an OTC put or exchange-traded futures put. Similarly, a bank that finances its short-term loan portfolio of 1-year loans by selling 90-day certificates of deposit (CDs) could manage the resulting maturity gap (maturity of the assets [1-year loans] not equal to the maturity of liabilities [90-day CDs]) by also taking short positions in Eurodollar futures or futures options. Finally, an underwriter or a dealer who is holding a debt security for a short-period of time could hedge the position against interest rate increases by going short in an appropriate futures contract or by purchasing a futures put option.

15.2.1 Naïve Hedging Model

The simplest model to apply to hedging a debt position is the ***naive hedging model***. For debt positions, a naive hedge can be formed by hedging each dollar of the face value of the spot position with one market-value dollar in the futures or option contract. For example, if a T-bond futures price is at 90, then $100/90 = 1.11$ futures contracts could be used to hedge each dollar of the face value of the bond. A naive hedge also can be formed by hedging each dollar of the market value of the spot position with one market-value dollar of the futures or futures option. Thus, if $98 were to be used to buy the aforementioned T-bond at some future date, then $98/90 = 1.089$ futures contracts could be purchased to hedge the position.

15.2.2 Long Hedge—Future 91-Day T-Bill Investment

15.2.2.1 *Hedging With a Long T-Bill Futures Contract*

Consider the case of a treasurer of a corporation who is expecting a $10 million cash inflow in June, which she is planning to invest in T-bills for 91 days. If the treasurer wants to lock in the yield on the T-bill investment, she could do so by going long in June T-bill futures contracts. For example, if the June T-bill contract were trading at the index price of 95, the treasurer could lock in a yield (YTM_f) of 5.1748% on a 91-day investment made at the futures' expiration date in June:

$$f_0(\text{June}) = \frac{100 - (5)(90/360)}{100}(\$1M) = \$987,500$$

$$YTM_f = \left[\frac{\$1M}{\$987,500}\right]^{365/91} - 1 = .051748$$

To obtain the 5.1748% yield, the treasurer would need to form a hedge in which she bought $n_f = 10.126582$ June T-bill futures contracts (assume perfect divisibility):

$$n_f = \frac{\text{Investment in June}}{f_0} = \frac{\$10,000,000}{\$987,500} = 10.126582 \text{ Long Contracts}$$

At the June expiration date, the treasurer would close the futures position at the price on the spot 91-day T-bills. If the cash flow from closing is positive, the treasurer would invest the excess cash in T-bills; if it is negative, the treasurer would cover the shortfall with some of the anticipated cash inflow earmarked for purchasing T-bills. For example, suppose at expiration the spot 91-day T-bill were trading at a YTM of 4.5%, or $S_T = \$1M/(1.045^{91/365}) = \$989,086$. In this case, the treasurer would realize a profit of $16,060.76 from closing the futures position:

$$\pi_f = [S_T - f_0]\, n_f$$

$$\pi_f = [\$989,086 - \$987,500]\, 10.126582$$

$$\pi_f = \$16,060.76$$

With the $16,060.76 profit on the futures, the $10 million inflow of cash (assumed to occur at expiration), and the spot price on the 91-day T-bill at $989,086, the treasurer would be able to purchase 10.126582 T-bills (M = 91 days and face value of $1 million):

$$\text{Number of 91-day T-bills} = \frac{\$10,000,000 + \$16,060.76}{\$989,086} = 10.126582$$

Then 91 days later, the treasurer would have $10,126,582, which equates to a rate of return from the $10 million inflow of 5.1748%—the rate that is implied on the futures contract:

$$\text{Rate} = \left[\frac{10.126582(\$1M)}{\$10M}\right]^{365/91} - 1 = .051748$$

On the other hand, if the spot T-bill rate were 5.5% at expiration, or $S_T = \$1M/(1.055)^{91/365} = \$986,740$, the treasurer would lose $7,696.20 from closing the futures position: $[\$986,740 - \$987,500]10.126582 = -\$7,696.20$. With the inflow of $10 million, the treasurer would need to use $7,696.20 to settle the futures position, leaving her only $9,992,303.80 to invest in T-bills. However, with the price of the T-bill lower in this case, the treasurer would again be able to buy 10.126582 T-bills ($9,992,303.80/\$986,740 = 10.126582$), and therefore realize a 5.1748% rate of return from the $10 million investment. Note that the hedge rate of 5.1748% occurs for any rate scenario.

15.2.2.2 *Hedging With a T-Bill Futures Call*

Suppose the treasurer expected higher short-term rates in June but was still concerned about the possibility of lower rates. To be able to gain from the higher rates and yet still hedge against lower rates, the treasurer could alternatively buy a June call option on a T-Bill futures contract. For example, suppose there is a June T-bill futures call with an exercise price of $987,500 (index $= 95, R_D = 5$) priced at $1,000 (quote $= 4; C = (4)(\$250) = \$1,000$), with the June expiration (on both the underlying futures and futures option) occurring at the same time the $10M cash inflow is to be received. To hedge the 91-day investment with this call, the treasurer would need to buy 10 calls at a cost of $10,000:

$$n_C = \frac{V_T}{X} = \frac{\$10M}{\$987,500} \cong 10 \text{ calls}$$

$$\text{Cost} = n_C C = (10)(\$1,000) = \$10,000$$

If T-bill rates were lower at the June expiration, then the treasurer would profit from the calls and could use the profit to defray part of the cost of the higher priced T-bills. As shown in Exhibit 15.2-1, if the spot discount rate on T-bills is 5% or less, the treasurer would be able to buy 10.12 spot T-bills (assume perfect divisibility) with the $10M cash inflow and profit from the futures calls, locking in a YTM for the next 91 days of approximately 4.75% on the $10M investment. On the other hand, if T-bill rates are higher, then the treasurer would benefit from lower spot prices, whereas her losses on the call would be limited to just the $10,000 costs of the calls. For spot discount rates above 5%, the treasurer would be able to buy more T-bills the higher the rates, resulting in higher yields as rates increase. Thus, for the cost of the call options, the treasurer is able to establish a floor by locking in a minimum YTM on the $10M June investment of approximately 4.75%, with the chance to earn a higher rate if short-term rates increase.

15.2.3 **Hedging a Future 182-Day T-Bill Investment**

Suppose in the preceding example, the treasurer was planning to invest the expected $10 million June cash inflow in T-bills for a period of 182 days instead of 91 days and again wanted to lock in the investment rate. Because the underlying T-bill on a futures contract has a maturity of 91 days, not 182, the treasurer would need to take two long futures positions: one position expiring at the end of 91 days (the June contract) and the other expiring at the end of 182 days (the September contract). By purchasing futures contracts with expirations in June and September, the treasurer would have the equivalent of one June T-bill futures contract on a T-bill with 182-day maturity.

The implied futures rate of return earned on a 182-day investment made in June, $YTM_f(\text{June}, 182)$, is equal to the geometric average of the implied futures rate on the contract expiring in June, $YTM_f(\text{June}, 91)$ and the implied futures rate on the contract expiring in September, $YTM_f(\text{Sept}, 91)$:

$$YTM_f(\text{June}, 182)$$
$$= \left[(1 + YTM_f(\text{June}, 91))^{91/365}(1 + YTM_f(\text{Sept}, 91))^{91/365} \right]^{365/182} - 1$$

In this example, if the index on the June T-bill contract is at 95, and the index on a September T-bill contract is at 94.8, then the implied futures rate on each contract's underlying T-bill would be 5.1748% and 5.38865%, respectively, and the implied futures rate on 182-day

EXHIBIT 15.2-1   Hedging a $10M Cash Flow in June With June T-bill Futures Calls

1	2	3	4	5	6
Spot Discount Rates R_D%	Spot Price = Futures Price at T	Call Profit/ Loss	Hedged Investment Funds: $10M +Col 3	Number of Bills: Col (4)/ Col(2)	YTM
3.75	$990,625	$21,250	$10,021,250	10.12	0.0474
4.00	$990,000	$15,000	$10,015,000	10.12	0.0474
4.25	$989,375	$8,750	$10,008,750	10.12	0.0474
4.50	$988,750	$2,500	$10,002,500	10.12	0.0475
4.75	$988,125	−$3,750	$9,996,250	10.12	0.0475
5.00	$987,500	−$10,000	$9,990,000	10.12	0.0475
5.25	$986,875	−$10,000	$9,990,000	10.12	0.0502
5.50	$986,250	−$10,000	$9,990,000	10.13	0.0529
5.75	$985,625	−$10,000	$9,990,000	10.14	0.0556
6.00	$985,000	−$10,000	$9,990,000	10.14	0.0582
6.25	$984,375	−$10,000	$9,990,000	10.15	0.0609

Profit $= 10[\text{Max}(f_T - \$987,500), 0] - \$10,000.$
YTM $= [(\text{Number of Bill})(\$1M)]/\$10M]^{365/91} - 1.$

investment made in June would be 5.28167%:

$$f_0(\text{June}) = \frac{100 - (5)(90/360)}{100}(\$1M) = \$987,500$$

$$\text{YTM}_f(\text{June}) = \left[\frac{\$1M}{\$987,500}\right]^{365/91} - 1 = .051748$$

$$f_0(\text{Sept}) = \frac{100 - (5.2)(90/360)}{100}(\$1M) = \$987,000$$

$$\text{YTM}_f(\text{Sept}) = \left[\frac{\$1M}{\$987,000}\right]^{365/91} - 1 = .0538865$$

$$\text{YTM}_f(\text{June}, 182) = \left[(1.051748)^{91/365}(1.0538865)^{91/365}\right]^{365/182} - 1 = .0528167$$

To actually lock in the 182-day rate for the $5 million investment, the treasurer would need to purchase 10.126582 June contracts and 10.131712 September contracts (again, assume perfect divisibility). That is, using a naive hedging model, the required hedging ratios would be

$$n_f(\text{June}) = \frac{\$10,000,000}{\$987,500} = 10.126582 \text{ Long Contracts}$$

$$n_f(\text{Sept}) = \frac{\$10,000,000}{\$987,000} = 10.131712 \text{ Long Contracts}$$

At the June expiration date, the treasurer would close both contracts and invest the cash inflows plus (or minus) the futures profit (costs) in 182-day T-bills. By doing this, the treasurer in effect would be creating a June futures contract on a T-bill with a maturity of 182-days. If the equilibrium pricing model governing futures (discussed in Chapter 11) holds, then the treasurer will earn a rate of return on the 182-day investment equal to 5.28%.

Note that if the treasurer wanted to hedge the 182-day investment with calls, then she would need to buy both June and September T-bill futures calls. At the June expiration, the manager would then close both positions and invest the $10M inflow plus (minus) the call profits (losses) in 182-day spot T-Bills.

15.2.4 Managing the Maturity Gap

15.2.4.1 Hedging With a Short Eurodollar Futures Contract

An important use of short hedges is in minimizing the interest rate risk that financial institutions are exposed to when the maturity of their assets does not equal the maturity of their liabilities—a *maturity gap*. As an example, consider the case of a small bank with a maturity gap problem in which its short-term loan portfolio has an average maturity greater than the maturity of the CDs that it is using to finance its loans. Specifically, suppose in June, the bank makes loans of $100M, all with maturities of 180 days. To finance the loans, though, suppose the bank's customers prefer 90-day CDs to 180-day CDs, and as a result, the bank sells $100M worth of 90-day CDs at a rate equal to the current LIBOR of 5%. Then 90 days later (in September), the bank would owe $101,210,311 = $100M(1.05)^{90/365}$; to finance this debt, the bank would have to sell $101,210,311 worth of 90-day CDs at the LIBOR at that time. In the absence of a hedge, the bank would be subject to interest rate risk. If short-term rates increase, the bank would have to pay higher interest on its planned September CD sale, lowering its interest spread; if rates decrease, the bank's spread would increase.

Suppose the bank is fearful of higher rates in September and decides to minimize its exposure to market risk by hedging its $101,210,311 CD sale in September with a September Eurodollar futures contract trading at an index value of 95. To hedge the liability, the bank would need to go short in 102.491454 September Eurodollar futures (assume perfect divisibility):

$$f_0(\text{Sept}) = \frac{100 - (5)(90/360)}{100}(\$1M) = \$987,500$$

$$n_f = \frac{\$101,210,311}{\$987,500} = 102.491454 \text{ Short Eurodollar Contracts}$$

At a futures price of $987,500, the bank would be able to lock in a rate on its September CDs of 5.23376%. With this rate and the 5% rate it pays on its first CDs, the bank would pay 5.117% on its CDs over the 180-day period:

$$YTM_f(\text{Sept}) = \left[\frac{\$1M}{\$987,500}\right]^{365/90} - 1 = .0523376$$

$$YTM_{180} = \left[(1.05)^{90/365}(1.0523376)^{90/365}\right]^{365/180} - 1 = .05117$$

That is, when the first CDs mature in September, the bank will issue new 90-day CDs at the prevailing LIBOR to finance the $101,210,311 first CD debt plus (minus) any loss (profit) from closing its September Eurodollar futures position. If the LIBOR in September has increased, the bank will have to pay a greater interest on the new CD, but it will realize a profit from its futures contracts, decreasing the amount of funds it needs to finance at the higher rate. On the other hand, if the LIBOR is lower, the bank will have lower interest payments on its new CDs, but it will also incur a loss on its futures position and therefore will have more funds that need to be financed at the lower rates. The impact that rates have on the amount of funds needed to be financed and the rate paid on them will exactly offset each other, leaving the bank with a fixed debt amount when the September CDs mature

EXHIBIT 15.2-2 Hedging Maturity Gap

(1) September LIBOR	R	.045	.055
(2) September spot and expiring futures price	$S_T = f_T = \$1M / (1 + R)^{90/365}$	$989,205	$986,885
(3) Profit on futures	$\pi_f = 102.491454$ $[\$987,500 - f_T]$	-$174,748	$63,032
(4) Debt on June CD	$\$100M(1.05)^{90/365}$	$101,210,311	$101,210,311
(5) Total funds to finance	Row (4) – Row (3)	$101,385,059	$101,147,279
(6) Debt at end of period	$[Row (5)](1 + R)^{90/365}$	102,491,433	102,491,462
(7) Rate paid for 180-day period	$[(Row (6)) / \$100,000,000]^{365/180}$ **(Allow for slight rounding differences)**	5.117%	5.117%

in December. This can be seen in Exhibit 15.2-2 where the bank's December liability (the liability at end of the180-day period) is shown to be approximately $102.4914M given September LIBOR scenarios of 4.5% and 5.5% (this will be true at any rate). Note, the debt at the end of 180 days of $102.4914M equates to a 180-day rate for the period of 5.117%:

$$R = \left[\frac{\$102.4914M}{\$100M} \right]^{365/180} - 1 = .05117$$

15.2.4.2 Hedging With a Eurodollar Futures Put

Instead of hedging its future CD sale with Eurodollar futures, the bank could alternatively buy put options on Eurodollar futures. By hedging with puts, the bank would be able to cap the maximum rate it pays on its September CD. For example, suppose the bank decides to hedge its September CD sale by buying September Eurodollar futures puts with expirations coinciding with the maturity of its September CD, exercise price of 95(X = $987,500), and a premium of 2 (multiplier = $250). With the September debt from the June CD of $101,210,311, the bank would need to buy 102.491454 September Eurodollar futures puts (assume perfect divisibility) at a total cost of $51,246 to cap the rate it pays on its September CD:

$$n_P = \frac{\$101,210,311}{\$987,500} = 102.491454 \text{ contracts}$$

$$\text{Cost} = (102.49154)(2)(\$250) = \$51,246$$

If the LIBOR at the September expiration is greater than 5%, the bank will have to pay a higher rate on its September CD, but it will profit from its Eurodollar futures put position, with the put profits being greater the higher the rate. The put profit would serve to reduce part of the $101,210,311 funds the bank would need to pay on its maturing June CD. This reduction would, in turn, offset the higher rate it would have to pay on its September CD. As shown in Exhibit 15.2-3, if the LIBOR is at a discount yield of 5% or higher, then the bank would be able to lock in a debt obligation 90 days later of $102.5434M (allow for slight rounding differences), for an effective 180-day rate of 5.2%. On the other hand, if the rate is less than 5%, then the bank would be able to finance its $101,261,557 debt (June CD of $101,210,311 and put cost of $51,246) at lower rates, whereas its losses on

EXHIBIT 15.2-3   Hedging Maturity Gap With Eurodollar Futures Puts

1	2	3	4	5	6	7
LIBOR %	Spot and Futures Price	Put Profit	Sept. Debt on June CD	Sept Funds Needed Col (4) − Col (3)	December Debt Obligation [Col (5)](1+ LIBOR)$^{(90/365)}$	June to Dec Hedged Rate [Col (6)/$100 M]$^{(365/180)}$ −1
3.50	$991,553	−$51,246	$101,210,311	$101,261,557	$102,124,166	0.044
3.75	$990,964	−$51,246	$101,210,311	$101,261,557	$102,184,935	0.045
4.00	$990,376	−$51,246	$101,210,311	$101,261,557	$102,245,594	0.046
4.25	$989,790	−$51,246	$101,210,311	$101,261,557	$102,306,143	0.047
4.50	$989,205	−$51,246	$101,210,311	$101,261,557	$102,366,583	0.049
4.75	$988,623	−$51,246	$101,210,311	$101,261,557	$102,426,914	0.050
5.00	$988,042	−$51,246	$101,210,311	$101,261,557	$102,487,136	0.051
5.25	$987,462	−$47,394	$101,210,311	$101,257,705	$102,543,351	0.052
5.50	$986,885	$11,794	$101,210,311	$101,198,517	$102,543,381	0.052
5.75	$986,309	$70,807	$101,210,311	$101,139,504	$102,543,411	0.052
6.00	$985,735	$129,647	$101,210,311	$101,080,664	$102,543,442	0.052
6.25	$985,163	$188,314	$101,210,311	$101,021,997	$102,543,472	0.052
6.50	$984,592	$246,809	$101,210,311	$100,963,502	$102,543,502	0.052

Spot and futures Price at T = $1M/(1 + LIBOR)$^{(90/365)}$

Put Profit = 102.491454(Max($987,500 − Col(2), 0)) − $51,246

Debt on June CD = $100M(1.05)$^{(90/365)}$

its futures puts would be limited to the premium of $51,246. As a result, for lower rates, the bank would realize a lower debt obligation 90 days later and therefore a lower rate paid over the 180-day period. Thus, for the cost of the puts, hedging the maturity gap with puts allows the bank to lock in a maximum rate on its debt obligation, with the possibility of paying lower rates if interest rates decrease.

15.3   CROSS HEDGING

15.3.1   Price-Sensitivity Model

The preceding examples represent perfect hedging cases in which certain revenues or costs can be locked in at a future date. Whether it is commodity, currency, equity position, or a fixed-income position, the presence of quality, timing, and quantity risks makes perfect hedges the exception and not the rule. In practice, hedging risk cannot be eliminated totally by hedging with futures contracts. As a result, the objective in hedging is to try to minimize risk. If the debt position to be hedged has a futures contract with the same underlying asset, such as in the previous hedging cases, then a naive hedge usually will be effective in reducing interest rate risk. Many debt positions, though, involve securities and interest rate positions in which a futures contract on the underlying security does not exist. In such cases, an effective cross hedge needs to be determined to minimize the price risk in the underlying spot position. Two commonly used models for cross hedging are the regression model and the price-sensitivity model. In the *regression model,* the estimated slope coefficient of the regression equation is used to determine the hedge ratio. The coefficient, in turn, is found by regressing the spot price on the bond to be hedged against the futures price.

The second hedging approach is to use the ***price-sensitivity model*** developed by Kolb and Chiang (1981) and Toevs and Jacobs (1986). This model has been shown to be relatively effective in reducing the variability of debt positions. The model determines the number of futures contracts that will make the value of a portfolio consisting of a fixed-income security and an interest rate futures contract invariant to small changes in interest rates (see Appendix 15A for a derivation of the model). The optimum number of futures contracts that achieves this objective is

$$n_f = \frac{Dur_S}{Dur_f} \frac{V_0}{f_0} \frac{(1 + YTM_f)^T}{(1 + YTM_S)^T} \qquad (15.3\text{-}1)$$

where:

Dur_S = duration of the bond being hedged

Dur_f = duration of the bond underlying the futures contract (for T-bond futures, this would be the cheapest-to-deliver bond)

V_0 = current value of bond to be hedged

YTM_S = yield to maturity on the bond being hedged

YTM_f = yield to maturity implied on the futures contract

For option hedging, the number of options (calls for hedging long positions and puts for short positions) using the price-sensitivity model is

$$n_{options} = \frac{Dur_S}{Dur_{option}} \frac{V_0}{X} \frac{(1 + YTM_{option})^T}{(1 + YTM_S)^T}$$

where:

Dur_{option} = duration of the bond underlying the option contract

15.3.2 Hedging a Commercial Paper Issue With a T-Bill Futures Contract

Suppose in June, the treasurer of the Hyland Manufacturing Company makes plans to sell CP in September to finance a $19.4M purchase of the company's raw materials needed for its fall production levels. To ensure funds totaling $19,427,268, the treasurer would like to issue CP in September with a face value of $20 million, maturity of 182 days, and paying the current CP rate of 6%. Fearing short-term interest rates could increase over the next 3 months, the treasurer would like to hedge the future CP issue by taking a short position in September T-bill futures contracts trading at an index value of 95. Using the price-sensitivity model, this could be accomplished with 40 September T-bill futures contracts:

$$n_f = \frac{Dur_S}{Dur_f} \frac{V_0}{f_0} \frac{(1 + YTM_f)^T}{(1 + YTM_S)^T}$$

$$n_f = \frac{182}{91} \frac{\$19,427,268}{\$987,500} \frac{1.05175^{91/365}}{1.06^{182/365}} \cong 40 \text{ short T-Bill futures}$$

where :

Dur_S = duration of CP = 182

Dur_f = duration of T-bill = 91

YTM_S = yield to maturity on CP = 6%

$$f_0(Sept) = \frac{100 - (5)(90/360)}{100}(\$1M) = \$987,500$$

$$YTM_f(Sept) = \left[\frac{\$1M}{\$987,500}\right]^{365/91} - 1 = .05175$$

EXHIBIT 15.3-1   Cross Hedge: Hedging CP Sale With T-Bill Futures

(1) Spot T-Bill Discount Yield R_D	(2) T-Bill Spot and Expiring Futures price $S_T = f_T$	(3) Futures Profit $\pi_f = 40$ [$987,500 - f_T$]	(4) Price of CP	(5) Hedged CP Revenue: Col (3) + Col (4)
4%	$990,000	-$100,000	$19,575,000	$19,475,000
5%	$987,500	0	$19,475,000	$19,475,000
6%	$985,000	$100,000	$19,375,000	$19,475,000

- CP is assumed to be sold at a discount yield that is 25 BP greater than the discount yield on T-bill.
- Hedged Rate on CP is 5.48%.

$$S_T = f_T = \frac{100 - R_D(90/360)}{100}(\$1M)$$

$$P_{CP} = \frac{100 - (R_D + .25)(180/360)}{100}(\$20M)$$

$$\text{Hedged Rate} = \left[\frac{\$20M}{\$19,475,000}\right]^{365/182} - 1 = .0548$$

To illustrate the impact of the hedge, suppose the 182-day CP issue is sold at the September futures' expiration at a price that reflects an annual discount yield (R_D) that is 0.25% higher than the spot T-bill discount yield. As shown in Exhibit 15.3-1, with 40 September T-bill futures contracts, the treasurer of the Hyland Company would be able to lock in $19,475,000 cash proceeds from selling the CP issue and closing the futures contracts. With $19,475,000 cash locked in, his hedged rate on the 182-day hedged CP issue would be 5.48%:

$$\text{Hedged Rate} = \left[\frac{\$20,000,000}{\$19,475,000}\right]^{365/182} - 1 = .0548$$

15.3.3   Hedging a Bond Portfolio With T-Bond Futures Puts

Suppose a bond portfolio manager is planning to liquidate part of his portfolio in September. The portfolio he plans to sell consist of a mix of A to AAA quality bonds with a weighted average maturity of 15.25 years, face value of $10M, weighted average yield of 8%, portfolio duration of 10, and current value of $10M. Suppose the manager would like to benefit from lower long-term rates that he expects to occur in the future but would also like to protect the portfolio sale against the possibility of a rate increase. To achieve this dual objective, the manager could buy an OTC spot or exchange-traded futures put on a T-bond. Suppose there is a September 95(X = $95,000) T-bond futures put option trading at $1,156 with the cheapest-to-deliver T-bond on the put's underlying futures being a bond with a current maturity of 15.25 years, duration of 9.818, and currently priced to yield 6.0%. Using the price-sensitivity model, the manager would need to buy 81 puts at a cost of $93,636 to hedge his bond portfolio:

$$n_p = \frac{Dur_S}{Dur_p} \frac{V_0}{X} \frac{(1 + YTM_p)^T}{(1 + YTM_S)^T}$$

$$n_p = \frac{10}{9.818} \frac{\$10M}{\$95,000} \frac{(1.06)^{15.25}}{(1.08)^{15.25}} \cong 81$$

$$Cost = (81)(\$1,156) = \$93,636$$

Suppose that in September, long-term rates were higher, causing the value of the bond portfolio to decrease from $10M to $9.1M and the price on September T-bond futures contracts to decrease from 95 to 86. In this case, the bond portfolio's $900,000 loss in value would be partially offset by a $635,364 profit on the T-bond futures puts: $\pi = 81(\$95,000 - \$86,000) - \$93,636 = \$635,364$. The manager's hedged portfolio value would therefore be $9,735,364; a loss of 2.6% in value (this loss includes the cost of the puts) compared to a 9% loss in value if the portfolio were not hedged. On the other hand, if rates in September were lower, causing the value of the bond portfolio to increase from $10M to $10.5M and the prices on the September T-bond futures contracts to increase from 95 to 100, then the puts would be out of the money and the loss would be limited to the $93,636 costs of the put options. In this case, the hedged portfolio value would be $10.406365M—a 4.06% gain in value compared to the 5% gain for an unhedged position. Exhibit 15.3-2 shows the put-hedged bond portfolio values for a number of pairs of T-bond futures and bond portfolio values. As shown, for increasing interest rates cases in which the pairs of the T-bond and bond portfolio values are less than 95 (the exercise price) and $10,000,000, respectively, the hedge portfolio losses are between 1% and 2.6%, whereas for decreasing interest rate cases in which the pairs of T-bond prices and bond values are greater than 95 and $10,000,000, respectively, the portfolio increases as the bond value increases.

EXHIBIT 15.3-2 Cross Hedge: Bond Portfolio Hedged With T-Bond Futures

1	2	3	4	5
T-Bond Prices	Bond Portfolio Values	Profit on T-Bond Futures Put	Hedged Bond Portfolio Value	Proportional Change in Value (Col 4/$10M−1)
86	$9,100,000	$635,364	$9,735,364	−0.0265
87	$9,200,000	$554,364	$9,754,364	−0.0246
88	$9,300,000	$473,364	$9,773,364	−0.0227
89	$9,400,000	$392,364	$9,792,364	−0.0208
90	$9,500,000	$311,364	$9,811,364	−0.0189
91	$9,600,000	$230,364	$9,830,364	−0.0170
92	$9,700,000	$149,364	$9,849,364	−0.0151
93	$9,800,000	$68,364	$9,868,364	−0.0132
94	$9,900,000	−$12,636	$9,887,364	−0.0113
95	$10,000,000	−$93,636	$9,906,364	−0.0094
96	$10,100,000	−$93,636	$10,006,364	0.0006
97	$10,200,000	−$93,636	$10,106,364	0.0106
98	$10,300,000	−$93,636	$10,206,364	0.0206
99	$10,400,000	−$93,636	$10,306,364	0.0306
100	$10,500,000	−$93,636	$10,406,364	0.0406

Note that if the manager were more certain that long-term rates would increase in the future, then he could minimize interest rate risk by alternatively going short in T-Bond futures and using the price-sensitivity model to determine the number of contracts he needed to effectively hedge his position.

15.4   SPECULATING WITH INTEREST RATE DERIVATIVES

Although interest rate derivatives are extensively used for hedging, they are also frequently used to speculate on expected interest rate changes. A long futures or call position can be taken when interest rates are expected to fall, and a short futures or put position can be taken when rates are expected to rise. In the case of futures, speculating on interest rate changes by taking an outright or naked futures position represents an alternative to buying or short selling a bond on the spot market. Because of the risk inherent in such outright futures positions, though, some speculators form intracommodity and intercommodity spreads instead of taking a naked position.

15.4.1   Intracommodity Spread

As we have previously noted, the prices on more distant futures contracts (T_2) are more price sensitive to changes in the spot price, S, than near-term futures (T_1):

$$\frac{\%\Delta f_{T_2}}{\%\Delta S} > \frac{\%\Delta f_{T_1}}{\%\Delta S}$$

Thus, a speculator who expects the interest rate on long-term bonds to decrease in the future could form an intracommodity spread by going long in a longer term T-bond futures contract and short in a shorter term one. This type of intracommodity spread will be profitable if the expectation of long-term rates decreasing occurs. That is, the increase in the T-bond price resulting from a decrease in long-term rates will cause the price on the longer term T-bond futures to increase more than the shorter term one. As a result, a speculator's gains from his long position in the longer term futures will exceed his losses from his short position. If rates rise, though, losses will occur on the long position; these losses will be offset partially by profits realized from the short position on the shorter term contract. On the other hand, if a bond speculator believes rates would increase but did not want to assume the risk inherent in an outright short position, he could form a spread with a short position in a longer term contract and a long position in the shorter term one. Recall, in forming a spread, the speculator does not have to keep the ratio of long-to-short positions one-to-one but instead could use any ratio (2-to-1, 3-to-2, etc.) to obtain his desired return-risk combination.

15.4.2   Intercommodity Spread

Intercommodity spreads consist of long and short positions on futures contracts with the same expirations but with different underlying assets. Such spreads can be used to form two active bond strategies: the *rate-anticipation swap* and the *quality swap*. These swap strategies can be set up as intercommodity spreads formed with different debt security futures.

Consider the case of a speculator who is forecasting a general decline in interest rates across all maturities (i.e., a downward parallel shift in the yield curve). Because bonds with greater maturities are more price sensitive to interest rate changes than those with shorter maturities, the speculator could set up a rate-anticipation swap by going long in a longer term bond with the position partially hedged by going short in a shorter term one. Instead of using spot securities, the speculator alternatively could form an intercommodity spread by going long in a T-bond futures contract that is partially hedged by a short position in a T-note (or T-bill) futures contract. On the other hand, if an investor were forecasting an increase in rates across all maturities, instead of forming a rate-anticipation swap with spot positions, she could go short in the T-bond futures contract and long in the T-note (or T-bill). Forming spreads with T-note and T-bond futures is sometimes referred to as the *notes over bonds (NOB) strategy.*

Another type of intercommodity spread is a quality swap formed with different futures contracts on bonds with different default risk characteristics, for example, a spread formed with futures contracts on a T-bond and a municipal bond index (MBI) or contracts on T-bills and Eurodollar deposits. Quality swaps formed with spot or futures are based on the ability to forecast a narrowing or a widening of the spread between the yields on the underlying bonds. For example, in an economic recession, the demand for lower default-risk bonds often increases relative to the demand for higher default-risk bonds. If this occurs, then the default risk spread (lower grade bond yield minus higher grade bond yield) would tend to widen. A speculator forecasting an economic recession could, in turn, profit from an anticipated widening in the risk premium by forming an intercommodity spread consisting of a long position in a T-bond futures contract and a short position in a MBI contract. Similarly, because Eurodollar deposits are not completely risk free, whereas T-bills are, a spreader forecasting riskier times (and therefore a widening of the spread between Eurodollar rates and T-bill rates) could go long in the T-bill futures contract and short in the Eurodollar futures contract. A spread with T-bills and Eurodollars contracts is referred to as a *TED spread.*

15.4.3 Speculating With Interest Rate Options

As we've emphasized often, one of the important features of options is that they can be combined with positions in the underlying security and other options to generate a number of different investment strategies. In the case of speculating on interest rates using options, a speculator who believes the Federal Reserve System will lower short-term interest rates in the near future to stimulate the economy could profit (if her expectation is correct) by taking a long position in a T-bill futures call. As a speculative strategy, this long call position can be viewed as an alternative to a long position in a T-bill futures contract. In contrast, if a speculator believes that short-term interest rates are going to increase in the near future, then she should take a long position in a T-bill futures put option. Similar positions could be taken in T-bond futures options by speculators who expect long-term rates to change. For example, a speculator convinced that the current economic growth will push long-term interest rates up over the next 3 months (and therefore the price on long-term bonds down) could try to profit from this expectation by buying a T-bond futures put, whereas a speculator who expected long-term rates to decrease could try to profit by buying a T-bond futures call.

Finally, between outright call and put positions, options can be combined in different ways to obtain various types of profit relations. A speculator who expected rates to increase in the future but didn't want to assume the risk inherent in a put purchase position could form a bear call spread. In contrast, a speculator who expected rates to be stable over the near term could, in turn, try to profit by forming a straddle write. Thus, by combining different option positions, speculators can obtain positions that match their expectation and their desired risk-return preference.

15.4.4 Managing Asset and Liability Positions

Interest rate derivatives can also be used by financial and nonfinancial corporations to alter the exposure of their balance sheets to interest rate changes. The change can be done for speculative purposes (increasing the firm's exposure to interest rate changes) or for hedging purposes (reducing exposure). As an example, consider the case of a bond fund that manages its bond portfolio against an aggregate bond index such as the Shearson-Lehman aggregate government-corporate index (this is an index consisting of approximately 5,000 investment-grade corporate, Treasury, and federal agency bonds). Suppose the fund expects interest rates to decrease in the coming year across all maturities. To outperform the index, suppose the fund would like to lengthen the duration of its bond fund relative to the index's duration. The fund could do this by swapping some of its shorter term Treasuries in its portfolio for longer term ones. Given that longer term (higher duration) bonds are more price sensitive to interest rate changes, the bond fund would find an interest rate decrease across all maturities would cause the value of its bond portfolio to increase proportionally more than the index if it made the swap. However, instead of increasing the duration of its bond portfolio by changing the fund's allocation from long-term to short-term Treasuries, the fund alternatively could take a long position in T-bond futures contracts. If rates, in turn, were to decrease across all maturities as expected, then the fund would realize not only an increase in the value of its bond portfolio but also a profit from its long futures position; on the other hand, if rates were to increase, then the fund would see not only a decrease in the value of its bond portfolio but also losses on it futures position. Thus, by adding futures to its fund, the fund would be changing its bond portfolio's exposure to interest rates by effectively increasing its duration.

Instead of increasing its balance sheet's exposure to interest rate changes, a company may choose to reduce it. For example, if the preceding bond fund expected interest rates to increase, it could reduce its bond portfolio's duration by taking a short position in an interest rate futures contract. This action would be similar to the bond portfolio hedging example discussed in Section 15.3.

In general, the fund's strategy of increasing or decreasing its exposure to interest rates with debt futures is analogous to the market-timing strategy discussed in Chapter 13 in which stock index futures were used to change a stock portfolio's beta in anticipation of a bull or bear market. Using derivatives to change the exposure of an asset or liability to interest rates, exchange rates, or other market parameters without changing the original composition of the assets and liabilities is referred to as ***off-balance sheet restructuring.***

It should be noted that companies need to guard against unplanned actions that might change their hedging positions to speculative ones. Many companies have traders hired to manage their risk exposure to interest rates. As time goes by, some traders (often under the illusion they can beat the market) take more speculative positions, often causing a transformation of the company's treasury department into a de facto profit center. As we noted in Chapter 9, there are a number of cases in which companies incurred spectacular losses as a result of their traders taking speculative positions with derivatives.

15.5   SYNTHEITC DEBT AND INVESTMENT POSITIONS

In the maturity-gap example, we assumed the bank's gap problem was created as a result of the bank's borrowers wanting 180-day loans and its depositor wanting 90-day CDs. Suppose the bank, though, does not have a maturity gap problem; that is, it can easily sell 180-day CDs to finance its 180-day loans and 90-day CDs to finance its 90-day loans. With no gap problem, the bank still may find that instead of financing with a 180-day spot CD, it would be cheaper if it financed its 180-day June loans with synthetic 180-day CDs formed by (1) selling 90-day June CDs, (2) rolling over the obligation 3 months later by selling 90-day September CDs, and (3) locking in the September CD rate now by taking a short position in the September Eurodollar futures contract. For example, in the maturity gap case, the bank was able to create a synthetic 180-day CD paying 5.117% given a September futures price at 95. If the actual 180-day CD exceeded 5.117%, then the bank would gain by financing its 180-day loans with 180-day synthetic CDs instead of by selling direct 180-day CDs.

In practice, exchange-traded interest rate futures contracts are usually priced so that such arbitrage opportunities for banks are rare. In Chapter 11, we examined the carrying-cost model as it applied to T-bill or Eurodollar futures contracts. If the equilibrium carrying-cost model governing Eurodollar futures prices holds, then the rate on the synthetic will be equal to the rate on the spot. Thus, the opportunity for the aforementioned bank to gain from a synthetic position is unlikely. There are some cases, though, in which the rate on debt and investment positions can be improved by creating synthetic positions with futures and other derivative securities such as swaps. These cases involve creating a synthetic fixed-rate loan by combining a floating-rate loan with short positions in Eurodollar contracts and creating a synthetic floating-rate loan by combining a fixed-rate loan with long positions in Eurodollar contracts. Similar synthetic fixed-rate and floating-rate investment positions can also be formed.

15.5.1 Synthetic Fixed-Rate Loan

A corporation wanting to finance its operations or its capital expenditures with fixed-rate debt has a choice of either a direct fixed-rate loan or a synthetic fixed-rate loan formed with a floating-rate loan and short positions in Eurodollar futures contracts whichever is cheaper. Consider the case of a corporation that can obtain a $10M fixed-rate loan from a bank at 9.5% or alternatively can obtain a 1-year, floating-rate loan from a bank. In the floating-rate loan agreement, suppose the loan starts on date 9/20 at a rate of 9.5% and then is reset on 12/20, 3/20, and 6/20 to equal the spot LIBOR (annual) plus 250 basis points divided by 4 : (LIBOR + .025)/4.

To create a synthetic fixed-rate loan from this floating-rate loan, the corporation could go short in a series of Eurodollar futures contracts—***Eurodollar strip.*** For this case, suppose the company goes short in a series of 10 contracts expiring at 12/20, 3/20, and 6/20 and trading at the following prices:

T	12/20	3/20	6/20
Index	93.5	93.75	94
f_0	$983,750	$984,375	$985,000

The locked-in rates obtained using Eurodollar futures contracts are equal to 100 minus the index plus the basis points on the loan:

$$\text{Locked-in rate} = [100 - \text{Index}] + BP/100$$

$$12/20 : R_{12/20} = [100 - 93.5] + 2.5 = 9\%$$

$$3/20 : R_{3/20} = [100 - 93.75] + 2.5 = 8.75\%$$

$$6/20 : R_{6/20} = [100 - 94] + 2.5 = 8.5\%$$

For example, suppose on date 12/20, the settlement LIBOR is 7%, yielding a settlement index price of 93 and a closing futures price of $982,500. At that rate, the corporation would realize a profit of $12,500(= (10)($1,250)) from its 10 short positions on the 12/20 futures contract:

$$f_T = \frac{100 - (100 - 93)(90/360)}{100}(\$1M) = \$982,500$$

Profit on 12/20 contract = (10)($983,750 − $982,500) = $12,500.

At the 12/20 date, though, the new interest that the corporation would have to pay for the next quarter would be set at $237,500:

$$12/20 \text{ Interest} = [(\text{LIBOR} + .025)/4](\$10\text{M})$$

$$12/20 \text{ Interest} = [(.07 + .025)/4](\$10\text{M})$$

$$12/20 \text{ Interest} = \$237,500$$

Subtracting the futures profit of $12,500 from the $237,500 interest payment (and ignoring the time value factor), the corporation's hedged interest payment for the next quarter is $225,000. On an annualized basis, this equates to a 9% interest on a $10M loan, the same rate as the locked-in rate:

$$\text{Hedged Rate} = \frac{4(\$225,000)}{\$10,000,000} = .09$$

On the other hand, if the 12/20 LIBOR were 6%, then the quarterly interest payment would be only $212,500(= ((.06 + .025)/4)(\$10\text{M})) = \$212,500). This gain to the corporation, though, would be offset by a $12,500 loss on the futures contract [i.e., at 6%, $f_T = \$985,000$, yielding a loss on the 12/20 contract of 10($983,750 − $985,000) = −$12,500]. As a result, the total quarterly debt of the company again would be $225,000($212,500 + $12,500). Ignoring the time value factor, the annualized hedged rate the company pays would again be 9%. Thus, the corporation's short position in the 12/20 Eurodollar futures contract at 93.5 enables it to lock in a quarterly debt obligation of $225,000 and a 9% annualized borrowing rate.

Given the other locked-in rates, the 1-year fixed rate for the corporation on its variable-rate loan hedged with the Eurodollar futures contracts would be 8.9369%:

$$\text{Synthetic fixed Rate} = \left[(1.095)^{.25}(1.09)^{.25}(1.0875)^{.25}(1.085)^{.25} \right]^{1} - 1 = .089369$$

Thus, the corporation would gain by financing with a synthetic fixed rate loan at 8.9369% instead of a direct fixed-rate loan at 9.5%.

15.5.2 Synthetic Floating-Rate Loan

A synthetic floating-rate loan is formed by borrowing at a fixed rate and taking a long position in a Eurodollar or T-bill futures contract. For example, suppose the corporation in the preceding example had a floating-rate asset and wanted a floating-rate loan instead of a fixed one. It could take the one offered by the bank of LIBOR plus 250 BP or it could form a synthetic floating-rate loan by borrowing at a fixed rate for 1 year and going long in a series of Eurodollar futures expiring at 12/20, 3/20, and 6/20. The synthetic loan will provide a lower rate than the direct floating-rate loan if the fixed rate is less than 9%. For example, suppose the corporation borrows at a fixed rate of 8.5% for 1 year with interest payments made quarterly at dates 12/20, 3/20, and 6/20 and then goes long in the series of Eurodollar futures to form a synthetic floating-rate loan. On date 12/20, if the settlement LIBOR were 7% (settlement index price of 93 and a closing futures price of $982,500), the corporation would lose $12,500(= (10)($982,500 − $983,750)) from its 10 long positions on the 12/20 futures contracts and would pay $212,500 on its fixed-rate loan ((.085/4)($10M) = $212,500). The company's effective annualize rate would be 9%([4($212,500 + $12,500)]/$10,000,000 = .09), which is .5% less than the rate paid on the floating-rate loan (LIBOR + 250BP = 7% + 2.5% = 9.5%). If the settlement LIBOR were 6%, though (settlement index price of 94 and a closing futures price of $985,000), the corporation would realize a profit of $12,500(= (10)($985,000 − $983,750)) from the 10 long positions on the 12/20 futures contracts and would pay \$212,500 on its fixed-rate loan. Its effective annualize rate would be 8%((4)(\$212,500 − \$12,500))/\$10,000,000 = .08), which again is .5% less than the rate on the floating-rate loan (LIBOR + 250BP = 6% +2.5% = 8.5%).

15.5.3   Synthetic Investments

Futures can also be used on the asset side to create synthetic fixed- and floating-rate investments. An investment company setting up a 3-year unit investment trust offering a fixed rate could invest funds either in 3-year fixed-rate securities or a synthetic one formed with a 3-year floating-rate note tied to the LIBOR and long positions in a series of Eurodollar futures whichever yields the higher rate. By contrast, an investor looking for a floating-rate security could alternatively consider a synthetic floating-rate investment consisting of a fixed-rate security and a short Eurodollar strip. Several problems at the end of this chapter deal with constructing these synthetic investments.

15.6   USING OPTIONS TO SET A CAP OR FLOOR ON A CASH FLOW

The preceding cases involved creating a fixed or floating rate on the cash flow of an asset or liability. When there is series of cash flows, such as a floating-rate loan or an investment in a floating-rate note, instead of constructing a synthetic position with a strip of futures contracts, a strip of interest rate options can alternatively be used. For example, a company with a 1-year floating-rate loan starting in September at a specified rate and then reset in December, March, and June to equal the spot LIBOR plus BP could obtain a maximum rate or cap on the loan by buying a series of Eurodollar futures puts expiring in December, March, and June. At each reset date, if the LIBOR exceeds the discount yield on the put, the higher LIBOR applied to the loan will be offset by a profit on the nearest expiring put, with the profit increasing the greater the LIBOR; if the LIBOR is equal to or less than the discount yield on the put, the lower LIBOR applied to the loan will only be offset by the limited cost of the put. Thus, a strip of Eurodollar futures puts used to hedge a floating-rate loan places a ceiling on the effective rate paid on the loan.

In the case of a floating-rate investment, such as a floating-rate note tied to the LIBOR or a bank's floating rate loan portfolio, a minimum rate or floor can be obtained by buying a series of Eurodollar futures calls, with each call having an expiration near the reset date on the investment. If rates decrease, the lower investment return will be offset by profits on the calls; if rates increase, the only offset will be the limited cost of the calls.

15.6.1   Setting a Cap on a Floating-Rate Loan With a Series of Eurodollar Puts

As an example of a cap, suppose Westwood Bank offers Roberts Department Store a \$15M floating-rate loan to finance its inventory over the next 2 years. The loan has a maturity of 2 years, starts on December 20th, and is reset the next seven quarters. Assume the initial quarterly rate on the loan is equal to 6%/4 (the current LIBOR plus 100 BP), and the other rates are set on the quarterly reset dates equal to one fourth of the annual LIBOR on those dates plus 100 basis points: (LIBOR% + 1%)/4. Suppose Roberts wants to cap the loan by purchasing a strip of CME Eurodollar futures puts consisting of the following

EXHIBIT 15.6-1   Capping a Floating-Rate Loan With Eurodollar Futures Puts

Loan starts on 12/12 at 6%(5% + 100BP); reset next seven quarters at LIBOR + 100 BP. Strip of seven Eurodollar futures puts each with $X = \$985,000$ and with expirations coinciding with loan reset dates. Expiring futures or settlement price: $f_T = S_T = \frac{\$1,000,000}{(1+\text{LIBOR})^{.25}}$

1	2	3	4	5	6	7	8	9
Date	LIBOR	Futures and Spot Price $S_T = f_T$	Put Cash Flow at Option's Expiration 15(Max[985000 − f_T,0]	Value of Put Cash Flow at Payment Date (Put CF at T) $(1 + \text{LIBOR})^{.25}$	Quarterly Interest at Payment Date .25[(LIBOR + .01)] ($15M)	Hedged Debt Col 6 − Col 5	Hedged Rate [(4)(Col 7)]/ $15M	Unhedged Rate LIBOR + 100BP
12/20	0.05							
3/20	0.05	$987,876.55	$0.00		$225,000.00	$225,000.00	0.060	0.060
6/20	0.06	$985,538.36	$0.00	$0.00	$225,000.00	$225,000.00	0.060	0.060
9/20	0.07	$983,227.59	$26,586.19	$0.00	$262,500.00	$262,500.00	0.070	0.070
12/20	0.08	$980,943.65	$60,845.22	$27,039.71	$300,000.00	$272,960.29	0.073	0.080
3/20	0.09	$978,686.00	$94,710.01	$62,027.23	$337,500.00	$275,472.77	0.073	0.090
6/20	0.10	$976,454.09	$128,188.65	$96,772.62	$375,000.00	$278,227.38	0.074	0.100
9/20	0.11	$974,247.40	$161,289.01	$131,279.76	$412,500.00	$281,220.24	0.075	0.110
12/20				$165,552.41	$450,000.00	$284,447.59	0.076	0.120

options:

T	3/20/T1	6/20/T1	9/20/T1	12/20/T1	3/20/T2	6/20/T2	9/20/T2
X	$985,000	$985,000	$985,000	$985,000	$985,000	$985,000	$985,000
P_0	2	2.1	2.2	2.3	2.35	2.4	2.45
Cost of 15 puts: 15($250)($P_0$)	$7,500	$7,875	$8,250	$8,625	$8,812.50	$9,000	$9,187.50

Given theses Eurodollar futures puts, Roberts could cap the floating-rate loan by buying a strip of 15 Eurodollar futures puts, with each put having an exercise price of $985,000(IMM index = X = 94). The total cost of the strip would be $59,250. Exhibit 15.6-1 shows the put-hedged rates on the loan and the unhedged rates for an increasing interest rate scenario in which the LIBOR increases (for illustration purposes, the increases are rather dramatic) from 5% on March 20 to11% seven quarters later. The numbers in the exhibit show Roberts quarterly interest payments, option cash flow, option values at the interest payment date, hedged interest payments (interest minus option cash flow), and hedged rate as a proportion of a $15M loan (option costs are not included) for each period, with the assumption that the options' expiration dates coincide with the reset dates. As shown, the put options allow Roberts to cap its loan between 7.3% and 7.6% (the rate differences are explain by assuming the option cash flow are reinvested to the interest payment date at different rates) when the LIBOR is greater than 6% while still benefiting Roberts with lower rates on its loan when the LIBOR is less than 6%.

15.6.2   Setting a Floor on a Floating-Rate Investment with a Series of Eurodollar Calls

As an example of a floor, suppose ABC Trust is planning to invest $15M in a Commerce Bank 2-year floating-rate note paying LIBOR plus 150 basis points. The investment starts on 12/20 at 5.5% (when the LIBOR = 4%) and is then reset the next seven quarters.

EXHIBIT 15.6-2   Setting a Floor on a Floating-Rate Investment With Eurodollar Futures Calls

Floating-Rate Note starts on 12/12 at 5.5% (4% + 150BP); reset next seven quarters at LIBOR + 150 BP. Strip of seven Eurodollar futures calls each with X = \$985,000 and expirations coinciding with the note's reset dates. Expiring futures or settlement price:
$$f_T = S_T = \frac{\$1,000,000}{(1+LIBOR)^{.25}}$$

1 Date	2 LIBOR	3 Futures and Spot Price $S_T = f_T$	4 Call Cash Flow at Option's Expiration 15(Max $[f_T - \$985,000,0]$	5 Value of Call Cash Flow at Payment Date (Call CF at T) $(1 + LIBOR)^{.25}$	6 Quarterly Interest Received .25[(LIBOR + .015)] (\$15M)	7 Hedged Interest Income Col 6 + Col 5	8 Hedged Rate [(4)(Col 7)]/ \$15M	9 Unhedged Rate LIBOR + 100BP
12/20	0.04							
3/20	0.04	\$990,242.74	\$78,641.04		\$206,250.00	\$206,250.00	0.055	0.055
6/20	0.05	\$987,876.55	\$43,148.21	\$79,415.92	\$206,250.00	\$285,665.92	0.076	0.055
9/20	0.06	\$985,538.36	\$8,075.43	\$43,677.74	\$243,750.00	\$287,427.74	0.077	0.065
12/20	0.07	\$983,227.59	\$0.00	\$8,193.92	\$281,250.00	\$289,443.92	0.077	0.075
3/20	0.08	\$980,943.65	\$0.00	\$0.00	\$318,750.00	\$318,750.00	0.085	0.085
6/20	0.09	\$978,686.00	\$0.00	\$0.00	\$356,250.00	\$356,250.00	0.095	0.095
9/20	0.10	\$976,454.09	\$0.00	\$0.00	\$393,750.00	\$393,750.00	0.105	0.105
12/20				\$0.00	\$431,250.00	\$431,250.00	0.115	0.115

Suppose ABC Trust would like to establish a floor on the rates it obtains on the floating-rate note with the following strip of CME Eurodollar futures call options:

T	3/20/T1	6/20/T1	9/20/T1	12/20/T1	3/20/T2	6/20/T2	9/20/T2
X	\$985,000	\$985,000	\$985,000	\$985,000	\$985,000	\$985,000	\$985,000
C_0	2	2.1	2.2	2.3	2.35	2.4	2.45
Cost of 15 Calls: 15(\$250)(C_0)	\$7,500	\$7,875	\$8,250	\$8,625	\$8,812.50	\$9,000	\$9,187.50

To set the floor on the floating note, ABC would need to buy 15 Eurodollar futures call strips with an exercise price of \$985,000 (IMM index = X = 95) at a total cost of \$59,250. Exhibit 15.6-2 shows the Trust's quarterly interest receipts, option cash flow, option values at the interest payment dates, hedged interest revenue (interest plus option cash flow), and hedged rate as a proportion of a \$15M investment (option costs excluded) for each period, with the assumption that the reset dates and option expiration dates coincide. The assumed LIBOR rates shown in the exhibit reflects an increasing interest rate scenario in which the LIBOR increases from 4% on March 20 to 10% seven quarters later. As shown, the call options allow ABC to attain a floor rate of approximately 7.6% on its investment when the LIBOR is 6% or less, with the benefit of higher yields when the LIBOR is greater than 6%.

15.7   CONCLUSION

Introduced during the volatile interest rate periods of the 1970s and 1980s, interest rate derivatives have become one of the most popular derivative contracts. In this chapter, we've examined the applications of exchange-traded futures and options. As we've seen, these derivatives can be used by (1) financial institutions to manage the maturity gap between their assets and liabilities; (2) financial and nonfinancial corporations to fix the rates on their floating-rate loans, to create synthetic fixed-rate or floating-rate debt and investment positions, or to set a cap on a floating-rate loan or a floor on a floating-rate note; and (3) fixed-income managers, money-market managers, and dealers to lock in the future purchase or selling price of their fixed-income securities. In the next chapter, we will continue the analysis of interest rate derivatives by examining the use of tailor-made OTC interest rate derivative products that are also widely used for fixed-income management.

KEY TERMS

maturity gap	rate-anticipation swap	TED strategy
regression model hedge	quality swap	off-balance sheet restructuring
price-sensitivity model	NOB Strategy	Eurodollar strip

SELECTED REFERENCES

Dehnad, K. "Characteristics of OTC Options." In *The Handbook of Interest Rate Risk Management,* edited by J. C. Francis and A. S. Wolf. New York: Irwin Professional Publishing, 1994.

Gartland, W. J., and C. Nicholas. Letica. "The Basics of Interest-Rate Options." In *The Handbook of Fixed Income Securities*, 6th ed., edited by F. Fabozzi. New York: McGraw-Hill, 2001.

Gay, G. D., R. W. Kolb, and R. Chiang. "Interest Rate Hedging: An Empirical Test of Alternative Strategies." *Journal of Financial Research* 6 (Fall 1983): 187–97.

Johnson, R. S. *Bond Evaluation, Selection, and Management.* Malden, MA: Blackwell Publishing, 2004, Chapters 12–15.

Klemkosky, R., and D. Lasser. "An Efficiency Analysis of the T-Bond Futures Market." *Journal of Futures Markets* 5 (1985): 607–620.

Kolb, R. W., and R. Chiang. "Improving Hedging Performance Using Interest Rate Futures." *Financial Management* 10 (Fall 1981): 72–79.

McCable, G., and C. Franckle. "The Effectiveness of Rolling the Hedge Forward in the Treasury Bill Futures Market." *Financial Management* 12 (Summer 1983): 21–29.

Rendleman, R., and C. Carabini. "The Efficiency of the Treasury Bill Futures Market." *Journal of Finance* 34 (September 1979): 895–914.

Rentzler, J. "Trading Treasury Bond Spreads Against Treasury Bill Futures—A Model and Empirical Test of the Turtle Trade." *Journal of Futures Market* 6 (1986): 41–61.

Resnick, B. "The Relationship Between Futures Prices for U.S. Treasury Bonds." *Review of Research in Futures Markets* 3 (1984): 88–104.

Resnick, B., and E. Hennigar. "The Relation Between Futures and Cash Prices for U.S. Treasury Bonds." *Review of Research in Futures Markets* 2 (1983): 282–299.

Senchak, A., and J. Easterwood. "Cross Hedging CD's with Treasury Bill Futures." *Journal of Futures Markets* 3 (1983): 429–438.

Siegel, D., and D. Siegel. *Futures Markets,* 203–342, 493–504. Chicago: Dryden Press, 1990.

Tamarkin, R. *The New Gatsbys: Fortunes and Misfortunes of Commodity Traders.* New York: Morrow, 1985.

Toevs, A., and D. Jacob. "Futures and Alternative Hedge Methodologies." *Journal of Portfolio Management* (Spring 1986): 60–70.

Viet, T., and W. Reiff. "Commercial Banks and Interest Rate Futures: A Hedging Survey." *Journal of Futures Markets* 3 (1983): 283–293.

Virnola, A., and C. Dale. "The Efficiency of the Treasury Bill Futures Market: An Analysis of Alternative Specifications." *Journal of Financial Research* 3 (1980): 169–188.

PROBLEMS AND QUESTIONS

1. In June, the Fort Washington Money Market Fund forecast a September cash inflow of $18M that it plans to invest for 91 days in T-bills. The fund is uncertain about future short-term interest rates and would like to lock in the rate on the September investment with T-bill futures contracts. Currently, September T-bill contracts are trading at 93 (IMM index).

a. What is the implied YTM on the September T-bill futures contract?

b. How many September contracts does Fort Washington need to lock in the implied futures YTM (assume perfect divisibility)?

c. Assuming the fund's $18M cash inflow comes at the same time as the September futures contract's expiration, show how the fund's futures-hedged T-bill purchase yields the same rate from a $18M investment as the implied YTM on the futures. Evaluate at spot T-bill rates at the futures' expiration of 6.5% and 8.5%.

2. Suppose Fort Washington Money Marker Fund in Question 1 expects interest rates to be higher in September when it plans to invest its $18M cash flow in 91-day T-bills but is worried that rates could decrease. Suppose there is a September T-bill futures call contract with an exercise price of 93 (IMM index), trading at 5, and expiring at the same time as the September T-Bill futures contract.

a. How many September T-bill futures calls options does Fort Washington need to lock in a minimum rate on its investments (do not assume perfect divisibility)? What is the cost?

b. Assuming the fund's $18M cash inflow comes at the same time as the September T-bill futures call contract expires, use the table following to determine the fund's option-hedged T-bill yield for possible spot discount rates at the option's expiration date of 6%, 6.25%, 6.5%, 7%, 7.5%, and 8%.

1	2	3	4	5	6
Spot Discount Rates	Spot Price = Futures Price	Call Profit/ Loss	Hedged Investment Funds	Number of Bills	YTM
6.00					
6.25					
6.50					
7.00					
7.50					
8.00					

3. First National Bank is planning to make a $10M short-term loan to Midwest Mining Company. In the loan contract, Midwest agrees to pay the principal and an interest of 12% (annual) at the end of 180 days. Because First National sells more 90-day CDs than 180-day CDs, it is planning to finance the loan by selling a 90-day CD now at the prevailing LIBOR of 8.25% and then 90 days later (mid-September) sell another 90-day CD at the prevailing LIBOR. The bank would like to minimize its exposure to interest rate risk on its future CD sale by taking a position in a September Eurodollar futures contract trading at 92 (IMM index).

a. How many September Eurodollar futures contracts would First National Bank need to effectively hedge its September CD sale against interest rate changes? Assume perfect divisibility.

b. Determine the total amount of funds the bank would need to raise on its CD sale 90 days later if the LIBOR is 7.5% and if it is 9% (assume futures are closed at the LIBOR). What would the bank's debt obligations be at the end of 180-day period? What is the bank's effective rate for the entire 180-day period?

4. Suppose First National Bank in Question 3 makes a $10M, 180-day loan to Midwest Mining Company, with the loan financed by selling a 90-day CD now at the prevailing LIBOR of 8.25% and then 90 days later (mid-September) selling another 90-day CD at the prevailing LIBOR. Suppose, though, the bank would like to minimize its exposure to interest rate risk on its future CD sale but would also like to benefit if CD rates decrease. Suppose there is a September Eurodollar futures put with an exercise price of 92 trading on the CME at 2.

   a. How many September Eurodollar futures puts would First National Bank need to effectively hedge its September CD sale against interest rate changes? Assume perfect divisibility.

   b. Assume that the Eurodollar futures are closed at the LIBOR, and the Eurodollar futures and futures options expire at the same time as the Bank's first CD. Using the table following, determine the total amount of funds the bank would need to raise on its September CD, the bank's debt obligations at the end of the 180-day period, and the bank's hedged rates for the entire 180-day period given the following LIBORs at the options' and first CD's maturity date of 7%, 7.5%, 8%, 8.5%, 9%, 9.5%, and 10%.

1	2	3	4	5	6	7
LIBOR	Spot and Futures Price	Put Profit	Debt on September- Issued CD	September Funds Needed	December Debt Obligation	Hedged Rate for 180 days
.07						
.075						
.08						
.085						
.09						
.10						

5. In January, the O'Brien Development Company closed a deal with local officials to develop a new office building. The project is expected to begin in June and take 272 days to complete. The cost of the development is expected to be $32M, with the Western Southern Insurance Company providing the permanent financing of the development once the construction is completed. O'Brien Development has obtained a 272-day construction loan from the Reinhart Financing Company. Reinhart Financing will disperse funds to O'Brien at the beginning of the project in June, with the interest rate on the loan being set equal to the prevailing CP rate on that date plus 50 BP. The loan will have a maturity of 272 days, with the principal and interest on the loan to be paid at maturity. Fearful that interest rates could increase between January and June, O'Brien would like to lock in its rate on the $32M construction loan by taking a position in June T-Bill futures contracts. Any profits from the futures O'Brien would use to defray the $32M constriction costs; and any losses, it would add to its $32M loan. Currently, 272-day CP is trading at YTM of 10% (annual) and June T-bill futures are trading at 91 (IMM index).

   a. Using the price-sensitivity model, explain how the O'Brien Development Company could immunize its construction loan against interest rate changes. Assume perfect divisibility.

   b. How much would O'Brien need to borrow at the June expiration if the CP rate was at 11% and the spot 91-day T-bill was trading at a discount yield of 10% (R_D)? What would O'Brien's futures-hedged interest rate on the 272-day, $32M loan be?

c. How much would O'Brien need to borrow at the June expiration if the CP rate was at 9% and the spot 91-day T-bill was trading at a discount yield of 8% (R_D)? What would O'Brien's futures-hedged interest rate on the 272-day, $32M loan be?

6. Mr. Devine is a fixed-income portfolio manager for Stacy Investments. Mr. Devine forecast a cash outflow of $10M in June and plans to sell his baseline bond portfolio. The fund currently is worth $10M, has an "A" quality rating, duration of 7 years, weighted average maturity of 15 years, annual coupon rate of 10.25%, and YTM of 10.25% (note that the fund is selling at its par value). Suppose Mr. Devine is afraid that long-term interest rates could increase and decides to hedge his June sale by taking a position in June T-bond futures contracts when the June T-bond contract is trading at 80-16 and the T-bond most likely to be delivered on the contract has a YTM of 9.5%, maturity of 15 years, and a duration of 9 years.

   a. Using the price-sensitivity model, explain how Mr. Devine could hedge his June bond portfolio sale against interest rate risk.

   b. Suppose long-term interest rates increase over the period such that at the June expiration, Mr. Devine's baseline portfolio (A rated, 10.25% coupon rate, 15-year maturity, and 7-year duration) is trading at 96 of par, and the price on the expiring June T-bond contract (f_T) is 76. Determine Mr. Devine's revenue from selling his baseline bond portfolio, his profit on the futures contracts, and his total revenue.

7. Suppose Mr. Devine plans to sell his baseline bond portfolio in June. The fund currently is worth its par value of $10M, has an "A" quality rating, weighted average maturity of 15 years, duration of 7 years, annual coupon rate of 7.5%, and YTM of 7.5%. Mr. Devine expects long-term rates will decrease but is also afraid that they could increase. Suppose that there is a 100 June T-bond futures put trading for 1-16, with the option's underlying June T-bond futures contract trading at 100 and the T-bond most likely to be delivered on the futures contract having a YTM of 5.5%, maturity of 15 years, duration of 9 years, and trading at par.

   a. Using the price-sensitivity model, explain how Mr. Devine could hedge his June bond portfolio sale against interest rate risk by buying the 100 June T-bond futures put options.

   b. Suppose long-term interest rates increase over the period such that at the June expiration Mr. Devine's baseline portfolio is trading at 96 of par, the price on the expiring June T-bond contract (f_T) is 94, and the price on the 100 T-bond futures put is trading at its intrinsic value. Determine Mr. Devine's revenue from selling his baseline bond portfolio, his profit on the 100 T-bond futures put contracts, and his total revenue.

   c. Suppose long-term interest rates decrease over the period such that at the June expiration, Mr. Devine's baseline portfolio is trading at 105 of par, the price on the expiring June T-bond contract (f_T) is 106, and the price on the 100 T-bond futures put is trading at its intrinsic value. Determine Mr. Devine's revenue from selling his baseline bond portfolio, his profit on the 100 T-bond futures put contracts, and his total revenue.

8. As an alternative to a 9-month, 10% fixed-rate loan for $10M, the Zuber Beverage Company is considering a synthetic fixed-rate loan formed with a $10M floating-rate loan from First National Bank and a Eurodollar strip. The floating-rate loan has a maturity of 270 days (.75 of a year), starts on December 20th, and the rate on the loan is set each quarter. The initial quarterly rate is equal to 9.5%/4 and the other rates are

set on 3/20 and 6/20 equal to one fourth of the annual LIBOR on those dates plus 100 basis points: (LIBOR % + 1%)/4. On December 20th, the Eurodollar futures contract expiring on 3/20 is trading at 91 (IMM index), and the contract expiring on 6/20 is trading at 92, and the time separating each contract is .25/year.

a. Explain how Zuber could use the strip to lock in a fixed rate. Calculate the rate the Zuber Company could lock in with a floating-rate loan and Eurodollar futures strip.

b. Calculate and show in a table the company's quarterly interest payments, futures profits, hedged interest payments (interest minus futures profit), and hedged rate for each period (12/20, 3/20, and 6/20) given the following rates: LIBOR = 10% on 3/20, and LIBOR = 9% on 6/20.

9. Given the following CME Eurodollar futures put options:
   • March Eurodollar futures put with exercise price of 91 (IMM index) selling at 2.
   • June Eurodollar futures put with exercise price of 91 (IMM index) selling at 2.1.

a. Explain how the Zuber Beverage Company in Question 8 could attain a cap on its floating-rate loan with these options. What is the cost of the put strip?

b. Show in the table following the company's quarterly interest payments, option cash flow, hedged interest payments (interest minus option cash flow), and hedged rate as a proportion of a $10M loan (do not include option cost) for each period (12/20, 3/20, and 6/20) given the following rates: LIBOR = 10% on 3/20, and LIBOR = 9% on 6/20. Assume the interest reset dates and option expiration dates coincide.

1	2	3	4	5	6	7	8	9
Date	LIBOR	Futures and Spot Price	Put Cash Flow at Option Expiration	Value of Put CF at Payment Date	Loan Interest on Payment Date	Hedged Debt	Hedged Rate	Unhedged Rate
12/20								
3/20								
6/20								

10. XSIF Trust is planning to invest $10M for 1 year. As an alternative to a 1-year fixed-rate note paying 8.5%, XSIF is considering a synthetic investment formed by investing in a Second National Bank 1-year floating-rate note (FRN) paying LIBOR plus 100 basis points and taking a position in a Eurodollar futures strip. The FRN starts on 12/20 at 9% (LIBOR = 8%) and is then reset the next three quarters on 3/20, 6/20, and 9/20. On December 20th, the Eurodollar futures contract expiring on 3/20 is trading at 91 (IMM index), the contract expiring on 6/20 is trading at 92, and the contract expiring on 9/20 is trading at 92.5; the time separating each contract is .25/year, and the reset dates on the floating-rate note and the expiration dates on the futures expiration are the same.

a. Explain how XSIF Trust could use a strip to lock in a fixed rate. Calculate the rate XSIF could lock in with a floating-rate note and Eurodollar futures strip.

b. Calculate and show in a table XSIF's quarterly interest receipts, futures profits, hedged interest return (interest plus futures profit), and hedged rate for each period (12/20, 3/20, 6/20, and 9/20) given the following rates: LIBOR = 9.5% on 3/20, LIBOR = 9% on 6/20, and LIBOR = 7% on 6/20.

11. Given the following CME Eurodollar futures call options:
    - March Eurodollar futures with exercise price of 93 (IMM index) selling at 2.
    - June Eurodollar futures with exercise price of 93 (IMM index) selling at 2.1.
    - September Eurodollar futures with exercise price of 93 (IMM index) selling at 2.2.

    a. Explain how XSIF Trust in Question 10 could attain a floor on its floating-rate note with the options. What is the cost of the options?

    b. Show in the table following XSIF's quarterly interest receipts, option cash flow, hedged interest revenue (interest plus option cash flow), and hedged rate as a proportion of a $10M investment (do not include option cost) for each period given the following rates: LIBOR = 7.5% on 12/20, 7% on 3/20, 6.5% on 6/20, and 6% on 9/20. Assume the interest reset dates and option expiration dates coincide.

1	2	3	4	5	6	7	8	9
Date	LIBOR	Futures and Spot Price	Call Cash Flow at Option Expiration	Value of CF at Payment Date	Interest Receipt on Payment Date	Hedged Income	Hedged Rate	Unhedged Rate
12/20								
3/20								
6/20								
9/20								

12. Explain the types of spreads bond speculators could use given the following cases:

    a. The yield curve is expected to shift down, with rates for bonds with differing maturities decreasing by roughly the same percentage.

    b. Although the economy is growing, leading economic indicators auger for an economic recession.

    c. Although the economy is in recession, leading economic indicators point to an economic expansion.

WEB EXERCISES

1. Read more about CME interest rate derivatives by going to www.cme.com ("CME Products" and "Interest Rates").

2. Make a forecast for future intermediate or long-term interest rates and then form an intracommodity spread with a listed T-bond or T-note futures contract based on your forecast. For price quotes on futures, go to www.wsj.com/free (Market Data Center).

3. Determine the carrying-cost value of a listed Eurodollar futures contract. For current market quotes and information, go to www.cme.com and www.wsj.com/free.

4. Select several exchange-listed interest rate futures call and put options and determine their recent prices by going to www.wsj.com/free and clicking "Market Data Center" ("Commodity and Futures"). Using your options, evaluate some of the following strategies with a profit table and graph (use Excel or the Excel program for "Option Strategies" included with the book): call purchase, put purchase, straddle purchase, straddle sale, synthetic long position, or synthetic short position.

APPENDIX 15A   DERIVATION OF THE KOLB–CHIANG PRICE-SENSITIVITY HEDGING MODEL

The Kolb–Chiang price-sensitivity model solves for the number of futures contracts (n_f) that makes the change in the value of a portfolio of a debt security and a debt futures contracts invariant to small changes in interest rates. The value of the portfolio is

$$V = B_0 + n_f f_0 \qquad (15.A\text{-}1)$$

where :
B_0 = current value of the debt security or portfolio

To measure the change in the portfolio value with respect to changes in interest rates, let R be the rate of return representing general interest rates in the economy (e.g., T-bond rate), YTM_s the discount rate on the debt instrument or debt portfolio, and YTM_f the discount rate implied by the futures contract. The change in the price of the bond resulting from a small change in R can be defined in terms of the impact of the change in R on YTM_s and the impact of the change in YTM_s on B_0. This relation can be defined by the chain rule in which

$$\frac{dB_0}{dR} = \frac{\partial B_0}{\partial YTM_S}\frac{\partial YTM_S}{\partial R} \qquad (15.A\text{-}2)$$

The change in f_0 resulting from a change in R can be similarly defined. That is

$$\frac{df_0}{dR} = \frac{\partial f_0}{\partial YTM_f}\frac{\partial YTM_f}{\partial R} \qquad (15.A\text{-}3)$$

Given $\partial B_0/\partial R$ and $\partial f_0/\partial R$, the optimum n_f can be found by taking the derivative of (15.A-1) with respect to R, setting the resulting equation equal to zero, and solving for n_f. That is

$$\frac{dV}{dR} = \frac{\partial B_0}{\partial YTM_S}\frac{\partial YTM_S}{\partial R} + n_f\left(\frac{\partial f_0}{\partial YTM_f}\right)\frac{\partial YTM_f}{\partial R} = 0 \qquad (15.A\text{-}4)$$

If we assume $\partial YTM_s/\partial R$ is approximately equal to $\partial/YTM_f/\partial R$, then the optimum n_f is

$$n_f^* = \frac{-\partial B_0/\partial YTM_S}{\partial f_0/\partial YTM_f} \qquad (15.A\text{-}5)$$

The duration of a security is equal to the percentage change in the security's price per percentage change in one plus the YTM. The durations for the bond and the futures, therefore, can be expressed as

$$DUR_S = \frac{\%\Delta B_0}{\%\Delta(1+YTM_S)} = \frac{\partial B_0/B_0}{\partial(1+YTM)/(1+YTM_S)} \qquad (15.A\text{-}6)$$

$$DUR_f = \frac{\%\Delta f_0}{\%\Delta(1+YTM_f)} = \frac{\partial f_0/f_0}{\partial(1+YTM_f)/(1+YTM_f)} \qquad (15.A\text{-}7)$$

Thus

$$\frac{\partial B_0}{B_0} = DUR_S\frac{\partial YTM_S}{1+YTM_S} \qquad (15.A\text{-}8)$$

$$\frac{\partial f_0}{f_0} = DUR_f\frac{\partial YTM_f}{1+YTM_f} \qquad (15.A\text{-}9)$$

Substituting (15.A-8) and (15.A-9) into (15.A-5), n_f^* can be written as

$$n_f^* = \frac{-DUR_S}{DUR_f} \frac{B_0}{f_0} \frac{(1 + YTM_f)}{(1 + YTM_S)} \qquad (15.A-10)$$

Equation (15.A-10) is the same as Equation (15.3-1).

CHAPTER 16

MANAGING FIXED-INCOME POSITIONS WITH OTC DERIVATIVES

16.1 INTRODUCTION

Today, there is a large OTC market in debt and interest-sensitive securities and products in the United States and a growing OTC market outside the United States. This market consists primarily of dealers, investment banking firms, and commercial banks. OTC derivatives are primarily used by financial institutions and nonfinancial corporations to manage their interest rate positions. The derivative contracts offered in the OTC market include spot options and forward contracts on Treasury securities; LIBOR-related securities such as forward rate agreements; and special types of interest rate products such as interest rate calls and puts, caps, floors, and collars. OTC interest rate derivatives products are typically private, customized contracts between two financial institutions or between a financial institution and one of its clients. Some of theses interest rate derivatives actually predate the establishment of interest rate futures markets. In this chapter, we continue that analysis of the management of fixed-income positions by examining the use of OTC interest rate derivatives. We begin by first looking at the types, features, and uses of the more popular OTC interest rate contracts: the forward rate agreements, interest rate calls, interest rate puts, caps, and floors. With this background, we then look at how caps and floors are used to manage interest rate positions. We conclude the chapter by showing how OTC interest rate options can be priced using the binomial interest rate tree and Black's futures option model.

16.2 TYPES OF OTC DERIVATIVES

16.2.1 Forward Rate Agreements

A *forward rate agreement,* FRA, is a contract requiring a cash payment or providing a cash receipt based on the difference between a realized spot rate such as the LIBOR and a prespecified rate.[1] For example, the contract could be based on a specified rate of $R_k = 6\%$ (annual), the 3-month LIBOR (annual) in 5 months, and a notional principal, NP (principal used only for calculation purposes) of $10M. In 5 months, the payoff would be

$$\text{Payoff} = (\$10M)\frac{[\text{LIBOR} - .06]\,(91/365)}{1 + \text{LIBOR}\,(91/365)}$$

If the LIBOR at the end of 5 months exceeds the specified rate of 6%, the buyer of the FRA (or long position holder) receives the payoff from the seller; if the LIBOR is less than 6%, the seller (or short position holder) receives the payoff from the buyer. Thus, if the

---

[1] The FRA evolved from *forward-forward* contracts in which international banks would enter an agreement for a future loan at a specified rate.

LIBOR were at 6.5%, the buyer would be entitled to a payoff of $12,267 from the seller; if the LIBOR were at 5.5%, the buyer would be required to pay the seller $12,297. Note that the terminology for FRAs is the opposite of futures. That is, in contrast to buyers and sellers of FRAs, in a Eurodollar or T-bill futures, the party with the long position hopes rates will decrease and prices will go up, whereas the short position holder hopes that rates will increase and prices will go down.

In general, a FRA that matures in T months and is written on an M-month LIBOR rate is referred to as a $T \times (T + M)$ agreement. Thus, in this example the FRA is a 5×8 agreement. At the maturity of the contract (T), the value of the contract, V_T, is

$$V_T = NP\frac{[LIBOR - R_k]\,(M/365)}{1 + LIBOR\,(M/365)}$$

FRAs originated in 1981 amongst large London Eurodollar banks that used these forward agreements to hedge their interest rate exposure. Today, FRAs are offered by banks and financial institutions in major financial centers and are often written for the bank's corporate customers. They are customized contracts designed to meet the needs of the corporation or financial institution. Most FRAs follow the guidelines established by the British Banker's Association. Settlement dates tend to be less than 1 year (e.g., 3, 6, or 9 months), although settlement dates going out as far as 4 years are available. The NP on a FRA can be as high as a billion and can be drawn in dollars, British pounds, and other currencies. FRAs are used by corporations and financial institutions to manage interest rate risk in the same way as financial futures are used. Different from financial futures, FRAs are contracts between two parties and therefore are subject to the credit risk of either party defaulting. This is not the case with futures contracts in which the clearinghouse and marked-to-market rules effectively eliminate credit risk. The customized FRAs are also less liquid than standardized futures contracts. The banks that write FRAs often takes a position in the futures market to hedge their position or a long and short position in spot money market securities to lock in a forward rate. As a result, in writing the FRA, the specified rate R_k is often set equal to the rate implied on a futures contract.

Example: Hedging the Rate on a Future CD Investment With a FRA

Suppose Cagle Manufacturing forecast a cash inflow of $10M in 2 months that it is considering investing in a Sun National Bank CD for 90 days. Sun National Bank's jumbo CD pays a rate equal to the LIBOR. Currently such rates are yielding 5.5%. Cagle is concerned that short-term interest rates could decrease in the next 2 months and would like to lock in a rate now. As an alternative to hedging its investment with Eurodollar futures, Sun National suggests that Cagle hedge with an FRA with the following terms:

- FRA would mature in 2 months (T) and would be written on a 90-day (3-month) LIBOR ($T \times (T + M)$) = 2×5 agreement.
- NP = $10M.
- Contract rate = R_k = 5.5%.
- Day count convention = 90/365.
- Cagle would take the short position on the FRA, receiving the payoff from Sun National if the LIBOR were less than R_k = 5.5%.
- Sun National would take the long position on the FRA, receiving the payoff from Cagle if the LIBOR were greater than R_k = 5.5%.

Exhibit 16.2-1 shows Cagle's FRA receipts or payments and cash flows from investing the $10M cash inflow plus or minus the FRA receipts or payments at possible LIBORs of

EXHIBIT 16.2-1 Hedging CD Investment With Forward Rate Agreement

LIBOR	Sun National Payoff	Cagle Payoff	Cagle CD Investment $10M + FRA Payoff	CF at CD Maturity CD Investment $(1+LIBOR (90/365))$	Hedged Rate [(CF at Maturity/ $10M) − 1](365/90)
0.0500	−$12,178.62	$12,178.62	$10,012,178.62	$10,135,616	0.0550
0.0525	−$6,085.60	$6,085.60	$10,006,085.60	$10,135,616	0.0550
0.0550	$0.00	$0.00	$10,000,000.00	$10,135,616	0.0550
0.0575	$6,078.21	−$6,078.21	$9,993,921.79	$10,135,616	0.0550
0.0600	$12,149.03	−$12,149.03	$9,987,850.97	$10,135,616	0.0550

$$\text{Payoff} = (\$10M)\frac{[LIBOR - .055]\,(90/365)}{1 + LIBOR(90/365)}$$

5%, 5.25%, 5.5%, 5.75%, and 6%. As shown, Cagle is able to earn a hedged rate of return of 5.5% from its $10M investment.

16.2.2 Interest Rate Call

An *interest rate call,* also called a *caplet,* gives the buyer a payoff on a specified payoff date if a designated interest rate, such as the LIBOR, rises above a certain exercise rate, R_x. On the payoff date, if the rate is less than R_x, the interest rate call expires worthless; if the rate exceeds R_x, the call pays off the difference between the actual rate and R_x times an NP, times the fraction of the year specified in the contract. For example, given an interest rate call with a designated rate of LIBOR, $R_x = 5\%$, NP = $1M, time period of 180 days, and day count convention of 180/360, the buyer would receive a $5,000 payoff on the payoff date if the LIBOR were 6%: (.06 − .05)(180/360)($1M) = $5,000.

Exhibit 16.2-2 shows the profit graph and table for an interest rate call with the following terms: exercise rate = 6%, reference rate = LIBOR, NP = $10M, time period as proportion of a year = .25, and the cost of the option = $12,500. As shown in the exhibit, if the LIBOR reaches 7.5% at expiration, the holder would realize a payoff of (.075 − .06)($10M)(.25) = $37,500 and a profit of $25,000; if the LIBOR is 6.5%, the holder would breakeven with the $12,500 payoff equal to the option's cost; if the LIBOR is 6% or less, there would be no payoff, and the holder would incur a loss equal to the call premium of $12,500.

Interest rate call options are often written by commercial banks in conjunction with future loans they plan to provide to their customers. The exercise rate on the option usually is set near the current spot rate, with that rate often being tied to the LIBOR. For example, a company planning to borrow from a bank at a future date at a rate equal to the LIBOR plus basis points (BP) could buy an interest rate call option from the bank with the call having an exercise rate equal to the current loan rate, expiration at the start of loan, and NP equal to the amount of the future loan. At expiration, the company would be entitled to a payoff if rates were higher than the exercise rate, offsetting the higher interest on the loan. On the other hand, if the rate is lower, there is no payoff, but the company does benefit from a lower interest rate on its loan. Thus, an interest rate call allows the company to cap its future interest rate. As a hedging tool, an interest rate call represents an alternative to purchasing a Eurodollar futures put option to cap a future loan rate.

EXHIBIT 16.2-2 Interest Rate Call Option

Exercise Rate = 6%, Reference Rate = LIBOR, NP = $10M, Period = .25 year, Option Cost = $12,500

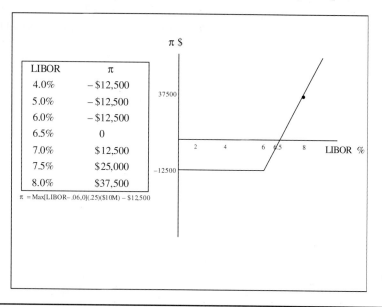

LIBOR	π
4.0%	− $12,500
5.0%	− $12,500
6.0%	− $12,500
6.5%	0
7.0%	$ 12,500
7.5%	$ 25,000
8.0%	$ 37,500

π = Max[LIBOR− .06,0](.25)($10M) − $12,500

Example: Hedging a Future Loan Rate With an OTC Interest Rate Call

As an example, suppose the Piper Manufacturing Company plans to finance one of its projects with a $20M, 90-day loan from North Bank, with the loan rate to be set equal to the LIBOR + 100 BP when the project commences 60 days from now. Furthermore, suppose that the company expects rates to decrease in the future but is concerned that they could increase. To obtain protection against higher rates, suppose the Piper Company buys an interest rate call option from North Bank for $40,000 with the following terms:

- Exercise rate = 7%.
- Reference rate = LIBOR.
- Time period applied to the payoff = 90/360.
- NP = $20M.
- Payoff made at the maturity date on the loan (90 days after option's expiration).
- Interest rate call's expiration = T = 60 days (time of the loan).
- Interest rate call premium of $20,000 to be paid at the option's expiration with a 7% interest: cost = $40,000(1 + (.07)(60/360)) = $40,467.

Exhibit 16.2-3 shows the company's cash flows from the call, interest paid on the loan, and effective interest costs that would result given different LIBORs at the starting date on the loan and the expiration date on the option. As shown in column 6 of the table, the company is able to lock in a maximum interest cost of 8.016% if the LIBOR is 7% or greater at expiration while still benefiting with lower rates if the LIBOR is less than 7%.

EXHIBIT 16.2-3   Hedging a Future $20M, 90-Day Loan With an OTC Interest Rate Call

Company's Loan: $20M at LIBOR + 100BP for 90 days (.25 per year)
Interest Rate Call Option: Exercise Rate = 7%, Reference Rate = LIBOR, NP = $20M, Time
Period = .25, Option Expiration = T = 60 days
Cost of Option = $40,000, payable at T plus 7% interest

1	2	3	4	5	6
LIBOR	**Interest Rate Call Payoff:** $20M[Max [LIBOR − .07,0](.25)	**Cost of the Option at T** $40,000(1 + .07(60/360))	**Interest Paid on Loan at its Maturity** (LIBOR + 100BP) (.25)($20,000,000)	**Cost at Maturity** Col (4) − Col (2)	**Annualized Hedged Rate** 4[Col (5)/ ($20M − Col (3))]
0.0550	$0	$40,467	$325,000	$325,000	0.06513
0.0575	$0	$40,467	$337,500	$337,500	0.06764
0.0600	$0	$40,467	$350,000	$350,000	0.07014
0.0625	$0	$40,467	$362,500	$362,500	0.07265
0.0650	$0	$40,467	$375,000	$375,000	0.07515
0.0675	$0	$40,467	$387,500	$387,500	0.07766
0.0700	$0	$40,467	$400,000	$400,000	0.08016
0.0725	$12,500	$40,467	$412,500	$400,000	0.08016
0.0750	$25,000	$40,467	$425,000	$400,000	0.08016
0.0775	$37,500	$40,467	$437,500	$400,000	0.08016
0.0800	$50,000	$40,467	$450,000	$400,000	0.08016
0.0825	$62,500	$40,467	$462,500	$400,000	0.08016
0.0850	$75,000	$40,467	$475,000	$400,000	0.08016

16.2.3   Interest Rate Put

An *interest rate put,* also called a *floorlet,* gives the buyer a payoff on a specified payoff date if a designated interest rate is below the exercise rate, R_x. On the payoff date, if the rate is more than R_x, the interest rate put expires worthless; if the rate is less than R_x, the put pays off the difference between R_x and the actual rate times an NP times the fraction of the year specified in the contract. For example, given an interest rate put with a designated rate of LIBOR, $R_x = 6\%$, NP = $1M, time period of 180 days, and day count of 180/360, the buyer would receive a $5,000 payoff on the payoff date if the LIBOR were 5%: $(.06 − .05)(180/360)(\$1M) = \$5,000$.

Exhibit 16.2-4 shows the profit graph and table for an interest rate put with the following terms: exercise rate = 6%, reference rate = LIBOR, NP = $10M, time period as proportion of a year = .25, and the cost of the option = $12,500. As shown in the exhibit, if the LIBOR were at 5% at expiration, the holder would realize a payoff of $(.06 − .05)(\$10M)(.25) = \$25,000$ and a profit of $12,500; if the LIBOR were 5.5%, the holder would break even with the $12,500 payoff equal to the option's cost; if the LIBOR were 6% or more, there would be no payoff, and the holder would incur a loss equal to the call premium of $12,500.

A financial or nonfinancial corporation that is planning to make an investment at some future date could hedge that investment against an interest rate decrease by purchasing a floorlet from a commercial bank, investment banking firm, or dealer. For example, suppose that instead of needing to borrow, the Piper Company was expecting a net cash inflow in the future from its operations and was planning to invest the funds in a bank CD paying the LIBOR. To hedge against any interest rate decreases, the company could purchase an

EXHIBIT 16.2-4   Interest Rate Put Option

Exercise Rate = 6%, Reference Rate = LIBOR, NP = $10M, Period = .25 year, Option Cost = $12,500

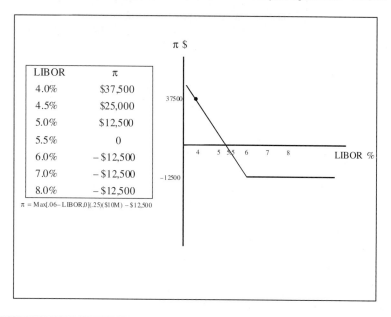

LIBOR	π
4.0%	$37,500
4.5%	$25,000
5.0%	$12,500
5.5%	0
6.0%	– $12,500
7.0%	– $12,500
8.0%	– $12,500

$\pi = \text{Max}[.06 - \text{LIBOR}, 0](.25)(\$10M) - \$12,500$

interest rate put (corresponding to the bank's CD it plans to buy) from the bank, with the put having an exercise rate equal to the current LIBOR, expiration coinciding with the date it expects its cash inflow, and an NP equal to the amount of funds it plans to invest. The interest rate put would provide a payoff for the company if the LIBOR were less than the exercise rate, giving the company a hedge against interest rate decreases. However, if the rate is higher, there is no payoff, but the company does benefit from a higher interest rate on its CD investment. Thus, an interest rate put allows the company to set a floor on it future interest earning. As a hedging tool, an interest rate put represents an alternative to purchasing a Eurodollar futures call option.

Example: Hedging a CD Rate With an OTC Interest Rate Put

Suppose the Hyland Manufacturing Company was expecting a net cash inflow of $20M in 60 days from its operations and was planning to invest the excess funds in a 90-day CD from Sun Bank paying the LIBOR. To hedge against any interest rate decreases occurring 60 days from now, suppose the company purchases an interest rate put from Sun Bank for $20,000, with the put having the following terms:

- Exercise rate = 7%.
- Reference rate = LIBOR.
- Time period applied to the payoff = 90/360.
- Day count convention = 30/360.
- NP = $20M.
- Payoff made at the maturity date on the CD (90 days from option's expiration).
- Interest rate put's expiration = T = 60 days (time of CD purchase).

EXHIBIT 16.2-5   Hedging a CD Investment With an Interest Rate Put Option

Company's Investment: $20M at LIBOR for 90 days (.25 per year)
Interest Rate Put Option: Exercise Rate = 7%, Reference Rate = LIBOR, NP = $20M, time period = .25,
option expiration = T = 60 days
Cost of Option = $20,000, payable at T plus 7% interest

1	2	3	4	5	6
LIBOR	Interest Rate Put Payoff: $20M[Max[.07 − LIBOR,0](.25)	Cost of the Option at T $20,000(1 + .07(60/360))	Interest Received on CD at its Maturity (LIBOR)(.25)($20,000,000)	Revenues at Maturity Col (2) + Col (4)	Annualized Hedged Rate 4[Col (5)/ ($20M + Col (3))]
0.0550	$75,000	$20,233	$275,000	$350,000	0.06993
0.0575	$62,500	$20,233	$287,500	$350,000	0.06993
0.0600	$50,000	$20,233	$300,000	$350,000	0.06993
0.0625	$37,500	$20,233	$312,500	$350,000	0.06993
0.0650	$25,000	$20,233	$325,000	$350,000	0.06993
0.0675	$12,500	$20,233	$337,500	$350,000	0.06993
0.0700	$0	$20,233	$350,000	$350,000	0.06993
0.0725	$0	$20,233	$362,500	$362,500	0.07243
0.0750	$0	$20,233	$375,000	$375,000	0.07492
0.0775	$0	$20,233	$387,500	$387,500	0.07742
0.0800	$0	$20,233	$400,000	$400,000	0.07992
0.0825	$0	$20,233	$412,500	$412,500	0.08242
0.0850	$0	$20,233	$425,000	$425,000	0.08491

- Interest rate put premium of $20,000 to be paid at the option's expiration with 7% interest: cost = $20,000(1 + (.07)(60/360)) = $20,233.

As shown in Exhibit 16.2-5, the purchase of the interest rate put makes it possible for the Hyland Company to earn a higher rate if the LIBOR is greater than 7% and to lock in a minimum rate of 6.993% if the LIBOR is 7% or less. For example, if 60 days later, the LIBOR is at 6.5%, then the company would receive a payoff (90 days later at the maturity of its CD) on the interest rate put of $25,000 = ($20M)[.07 − .065](90/360). The $25,000 payoff would offset the lower (than 7%) interest on the company's CD of $325,000 = ($20M)(.065)(90/360). At the maturity of the CD, the company would therefore receive CD interest and an interest rate put payoff equal to $350,000 (= $325,000 + $25,000). With the interest rate put's payoffs increasing the lower the LIBOR, the company would be able to hedge any lower CD interest and lock in a hedged dollar return of $350,000. Based on an investment of $20M plus the $20,233 costs of the put, the hedged return equates to an effective annualized yield of 6.993% = [(4)($350,000)]/[$20M + $20,233]. On the other hand, if the LIBOR exceeds 7%, the company benefits from the higher CD rates, whereas its losses are limited to the $20,233 costs of the puts.

16.2.4 Cap

A popular option offered by financial institutions in the OTC market is the *cap*. A plain-vanilla cap is a series of European interest rate call options—a portfolio of caplets. For example, a 7%, 2-year cap on a 3-month LIBOR, with an NP of $100M, provides, for the next 2 years, a payoff every 3 months of (LIBOR − .07)(.25)($100M) if the LIBOR on the reset date exceeds 7% and nothing if the LIBOR equals or is less than 7%. (Typically, the payment is not on the reset date but rather on the next reset date 3 months later.) Caps are often written by financial institutions in conjunction with a floating-rate loan and are used by buyers as a hedge against interest rate risk. For example, a company with a floating-rate loan tied to the LIBOR could lock in a maximum rate on the loan by buying a cap corresponding to its loan. At each reset date, the company would receive a payoff from the caplet if the LIBOR exceeded the cap rate, offsetting the higher interest paid on the floating-rate loan; on the other hand, if rates decrease, the company would pay a lower rate on its loan, whereas its losses on the caplet would be limited to the cost of the option. Thus, with a cap, the company would be able to lock in a maximum rate each quarter while still benefiting from lower interest costs if rates decrease.

16.2.5 Floor

A plain-vanilla *floor* is a series of European interest rate put options—a portfolio of floorlets. For example, a 7%, 2-year floor on a 3-month LIBOR, with an NP of $100M, provides, for the next 2 years, a payoff every 3 months of $(.07 - LIBOR)(.25)(\$100M)$ if the LIBOR on the reset date is less than 7% and nothing if the LIBOR equals or exceeds 7%. Floors are often purchased by investors as a tool to hedge their floating-rate investments against interest rate declines. Thus, with a floor, an investor with a floating-rate security is able to lock in a minimum rate each period while still benefiting with higher yields if rates increase.

16.3 HEDGING A SERIES OF CASH FLOWS—OTC CAPS AND FLOORS

In the last chapter, we examined how a strip of Eurodollar futures puts could be used to cap the rate paid on a floating-rate loan and how a strip of Eurodollar futures calls could be used to set a floor on a floating-rate investment. Using such exchange-traded options to establish interest rate floors and ceiling on floating rate assets and liabilities, though, is subject to hedging risk. As a result, many financial and nonfinancial companies looking for such interest rate insurance prefer to buy OTC caps or floors that can be customized to meet their specific needs.

Financial institutions typically provide caps and floors with terms that range from 1 to 5 years; have monthly, quarterly, or semiannual reset dates or frequencies; and use the LIBOR as the reference rate. The NP and the reset dates usually match the specific investment or loan (the better the fit, though, the more expensive the cap or floor), and the settlement dates usually come after the reset dates. In cases where a floating-rate loan (or investment) and cap (or floor) come from the same financial institution, the loan and cap (or investment and floor) are usually treated as a single instrument so that when there is a payoff, it occurs at an interest payment (receipt) date, lowering (increasing) the payment (receipt). The exercise rate is often set so that the cap or floor is initially out of the money, and the payments for these interest rate products are usually made up front, although some are amortized.

Example: A Floating Rate Loan Hedged With an OTC Cap

As an example, suppose the Webb Development Company borrows $100M from Commerce Bank to finance a 2-year construction project. Suppose the loan is for 2 years, starting on March 1 at a known rate of 8%, then resets every 3 months—6/1, 9/1, 12/1, and 3/1—at the prevailing LIBOR plus 150 BP. In entering this loan agreement, suppose the company is uncertain of future interest rates and therefore would like to lock in a maximum rate while still benefiting from lower rates if the LIBOR decreases. To achieve this, suppose the Webb Development Company buys a cap corresponding to its loan from Commerce Bank for $300,000, with the following terms:

- The cap consist of seven caplets with the first expiring on 6/1/Y1 and the others coinciding with the loan's reset dates.
- Exercise rate on each caplet = 8%.
- NP on each caplet = $100M.
- Reference rate = LIBOR.
- Time period to apply to payoff on each caplet = 90/360. (Typically the day count convention is defined by actual number of days between reset dates.)
- Payment date on each caplet is at the loan's interest payment date, 90 days after the reset date.
- The cost of the cap = $300,000; it is paid at beginning of the loan, 3/1/Y1.

On each reset date, the payoff on the corresponding caplet would be

$$\text{Payoff} = (\$100M)(\text{Max}[\text{LIBOR} - .08, 0])(90/360)$$

With the 8% exercise rate (sometimes called the ***cap rate***), the Webb Company would be able to lock in a maximum rate each quarter equal to the cap rate plus the basis points on the loan (9.5%) while still benefiting with lower interest costs if rates decrease. This can be seen in Exhibit 16.3-1 in which the quarterly interests on the loan, the cap payoffs, and the hedged and unhedged rates are shown for different assumed LIBORs at each reset

EXHIBIT 16.3-1   Hedging a Floating-Rate Loan With a Cap

Loan: Floating Rate Loan; Term = 2 years; Reset dates: 3/1, 6/1, 9/1, 12/1; Time frequency = .25; Rate = LIBOR + 150BP; Payment Date = 90 days after reset date.
Cap: Cost of cap = $300,000; Cap Rate = 8%; Reference Rate = LIBOR; Time frequency = .25; Caplets' Expiration: On loan reset dates, starting at 6/1/Y1; Payoff made 90 days after reset date.

1	2	3	4	5	6	7
Reset Date	Assumed LIBOR	Loan Interest on Payment Date (LIBOR + 150BP) (.25) ($100M)	Cap Payoff on Payment Date (Max[LIBOR− .08,0])(.25) ($100M)	Hedged Interest Payment Col. (3) − Col. (4)	Hedged Rate 4[Col (5)/ ($100M)	Unhedged Rate LIBOR + 150BP
3/1/Y1[n]	0.065					
6/1/Y1	0.070	$2,000,000	$0	$2,000,000	0.080	0.080
9/1/Y1	0.075	$2,125,000	$0	$2,125,000	0.085	0.085
12/1/Y1	0.080	$2,250,000	$0	$2,250,000	0.090	0.090
3/1/Y2	0.085	$2,375,000	$0	$2,375,000	0.095	0.095
6/1/Y2	0.090	$2,500,000	$125,000	$2,375,000	0.095	0.100
9/1/Y2	0.095	$2,625,000	$250,000	$2,375,000	0.095	0.105
12/1/Y2	0.100	$2,750,000	$375,000	$2,375,000	0.095	0.110
3/1/Y3		$2,875,000	$500,000	$2,375,000	0.095	0.115

[n] There is no cap on this date.

date on the loan. For the four reset dates from 3/1/Y2 to the end of the loan, the LIBOR exceeds 8%. In each of these cases, the higher interest on the loan is offset by the payoff on the cap, yielding a hedged rate on the loan of 9.5% (the 9.5% rate excludes the $300,000 cost of the cap). For the first two reset dates on the loan, 6/1/Y1 and 9/1/Y1, the LIBOR is less than the cap rate. At these rates, there is no payoff on the cap, but the rates on the loan are lower with the lower LIBORs.

Example: A Floating Rate Asset Hedged With an OTC Floor

As noted, floors are purchased to create a minimum rate on a floating-rate asset. As an example, suppose Commerce Bank in the preceding example wanted to establish a minimum rate or floor on the rates it was to receive on the 2-year floating-rate loan it made to the Web Development Company. To this end, suppose the bank purchased from another financial institution a floor for $200,000 with the following terms corresponding to its floating-rate asset:

- The floor consist of seven floorlets with the first expiring on 6/1/Y1 and the others coinciding with the reset dates on the bank's floating-rate loan to the Webb Company.
- Exercise rate on each floorlet = 8%.
- NP on each floorlet = $100M.
- Reference rate = LIBOR.
- Time period to apply to payoff on each floorlet = 90/360; payment date on each floorlet is at the loan's interest payment date, 90 days after the reset date.
- The cost of the floor = $200,000; it is paid at beginning of the loan, 3/1/Y1.

On each reset date, the payoff on the corresponding floorlet would be

$$\text{Payoff} = (\$100M)(\text{Max}[.08 - \text{LIBOR}, 0])(90/360)$$

With the 8% exercise rate, Commerce Bank would be able to lock in a minimum rate each quarter equal to the floor rate plus the basis points on the floating-rate asset (9.5%) while still benefiting with higher returns if rates increase. In Exhibit 16.3-2, Commerce Bank's quarterly interests received on its loan to Webb, its floor payoffs, and its hedged and unhedged yields on its loan asset are shown for different assumed LIBORs at each reset date. For the first two reset dates on the loan, 6/1/Y1 and 9/1/Y1, the LIBOR is less than the floor rate of 8%. At theses rates, there is a payoff on the floor that compensates the Commerce Bank for the lower interest it receives on the loan; this results in a hedged rate of return on the bank's loan asset of 9.5% (the cost of the floor excluded). For the five reset dates from 12/1/Y1 to the end of the loan, the LIBOR equals or exceeds the floor rate. At these rates, there is no payoff on the floor, but the rates the bank earns on its loan are greater given the greater LIBORs.

16.4 FINANCING CAPS AND FLOORS: COLLARS AND CORRIDORS

The purchaser of a cap or a floor is, in effect, paying a premium for insurance against adverse interest rate movements. The cost of that insurance can be reduced by forming a collar, corridor, or reverse collar.

EXHIBIT 16.3-2   Hedging a Floating-Rate Asset With a Floor

Asset: Floating rate loan made by bank; Term = 2 years; Reset dates: 3/1, 6/1, 9/1, 12/1; Time frequency = .25; Rate = LIBOR + 150BP; Payment Date = 90 days after reset date.
Floor: Cost of floor = $200,000; Floor Rate = 8%; Reference Rate = LIBOR; Time frequency = .25; Floorlets' expirations: On loan reset dates, starting at 6/1/Y1; Payoff made 90 days after reset date.

1	2	3	4	5	6	7
Reset Date	Assumed LIBOR	Interest Received on Payment Date (LIBOR + 150BP) (.25)($100M)	Floor Payoff on Payment Date (Max[.08 − LIBOR,0]) (.25)($100M)	Hedged Interest Income Col. (3) + Col. (4)	Hedged Rate 4[Col (5)/ $100M]	Unhedged Rate LIBOR + 150BP
3/1/Y1[n]	0.065					
6/1/Y1	0.070	$2,000,000	$0	$2,000,000	0.080	0.080
9/1/Y1	0.075	$2,125,000	$250,000	$2,375,000	0.095	0.085
12/1/Y1	0.080	$2,250,000	$125,000	$2,375,000	0.095	0.090
3/1/Y2	0.085	$2,375,000	$0	$2,375,000	0.095	0.095
6/1/Y2	0.090	$2,500,000	$0	$2,500,000	0.100	0.100
9/1/Y2	0.095	$2,625,000	$0	$2,625,000	0.105	0.105
12/1/Y2	0.100	$2,750,000	$0	$2,750,000	0.110	0.110
3/1/Y3		$2,875,000	$0	$2,875,000	0.115	0.115

[n] There is no floor on this date.

A *collar* is combination of a long position in a cap and a short position in a floor with different exercise rates. The sale of the floor is used to defray the cost of the cap. For example, the Webb Development Company in our previous case could reduce the cost of the cap it purchased to hedge its floating-rate rate loan by selling a floor. By forming a collar to hedge its floating-rate debt, the Webb Company, for a lower net hedging cost, would still have protection against a rate movement against the cap rate, but it would have to give up potential interest savings from rate decreases below the floor rate. For example, suppose the Webb Company decided to defray the $300,000 cost of its 8% cap by selling a 7% floor for $200,000, with the floor having similar terms to the cap (effective dates on floorlet = reset dates, reference rate = LIBOR, NP on floorlets = $100M, and time period for rates = .25). By using the collar instead of the cap, the Webb Company reduces its hedging cost from $300,000 to $100,000, and as shown in Exhibit 16.4-1, the company can still lock in a maximum rate on its loan of 9.5%. However, when the LIBOR is less than 7%, the company has to pay on the 7% floor, offsetting the lower interest costs it would pay on its loan. For example, when the LIBOR is at 6% on 6/1/Y1, Webb has to pay $250,000 90 days later on its short floor position, and when the LIBOR is at 6.5% on 9/1/Y1, the company has to pay $125,000; these payments, in turn, offset the benefits of the respective lower interest of 7.5% and 8% (LIBOR + 150) it pays on its floating-rate loan. Thus, for LIBORs less than 7%, the Webb Company has a floor in which it pays an effective rate of 8.5% (losing the benefits of lower interest payments on its loan), and for rates above 8%, it has a cap in which it pays an effective 9.5% on its loan.

In forming collars to finance capped floating rate loans, the borrower needs to determine the exercise rates on the caps and floors that best meet the cost of the hedge and his acceptable floor and cap rates. Specifically, if the exercise rate on the floor and cap are the same (e.g., 8% in our example), then the long cap and short floor will be equivalent to a forward contract. This low-cost (if not zero-cost) collar makes the floating-rate loan

EXHIBIT 16.4-1 Hedging a Floating-Rate Loan With a Collar

Loan: Floating Rate Loan; Term = 2 years; Reset dates: 3/1, 6/1, 9/1, 12/1; Time frequency = .25; Rate = LIBOR + 150BP; Payment Date = 90 days after reset date.
Cap Purchase: Cost of cap =$300,000; Cap Rate = 8%; Reference Rate = LIBOR; Time frequency = .25;
Caplets' Expiration: On loan reset dates, starting at 6/1/Y1; Payoff made 90 days after reset date.
Floor Sale: Sale of floor = $200,000; Floor rate = 7%; Reference rate = LIBOR; Time frequency = .25;
Floorlets' expiration: On loan reset dates, starting at 61/Y1; Payoff date = 90 days after reset date.

1	2	3	4	5	6	7	8
Reset Date	Assumed LIBOR	Loan Interest (LIBOR + 150BP)(.25) ($100M)	Cap Payoff Max[LIBOR− .08,0](.25) ($100M)	Floor Payment Max[.07− LIBOR,0] (.25)($100M)	Hedged Interest Payment Col. (3) − Col. (4) + Col (5)	Hedged Rate 4[Col (6)/ $100M]	Unhedged Rate LIBOR + 150BP
3/1/Y1[n]	0.050						
6/1/Y1	0.060	$1,625,000	$0	$0	$1,625,000	0.065	0.065
9/1/Y1	0.065	$1,875,000	$0	$250,000	$2,125,000	0.085	0.075
12/1/Y1	0.070	$2,000,000	$0	$125,000	$2,125,000	0.085	0.080
3/1/Y2	0.075	$2,125,000	$0	$0	$2,125,000	0.085	0.085
6/1/Y2	0.080	$2,250,000	$0	$0	$2,250,000	0.090	0.090
9/1/Y2	0.085	$2,375,000	$0	$0	$2,375,000	0.095	0.095
12/1/Y2	0.090	$2,500,000	$125,000	$0	$2,375,000	0.095	0.100
3/1/Y3		$2,625,000	$250,000	$0	$2,375,000	0.095	0.105

Loan interest, cap payoff, and floor payment made on payment date.
[n] There is no cap and floor on this date.

combined with a collar a synthetic fixed–rate loan. For floors, the lower the exercise rate, the lower its premium. As a result, by selling a floor with a lower floor rate (e.g., 7% or 6%), the borrower's net costs of forming a collar will increase, but the floor rate at which the borrower gives up interest savings will be lower. On the other hand, for caps, the higher the cap rate, the lower the premium. Thus, by buying a cap with a higher cap rate (e.g., 9% or 10%), the borrower's net costs of forming a collar will decrease, but the effective maximum rate on his loan will be higher.

An alternative financial structure to a collar is a corridor. A *corridor* is a long position in a cap and a short position in a similar cap with a higher exercise rate. The sale of the higher exercise-rate cap is used to partially offset the cost of purchasing the cap with the lower strike rate. For example, the Webb Company, instead of selling a 7% floor for $200,000 to partially finance the $300,000 cost of its 8% cap, could sell a 9% cap for say $200,000. If cap purchasers, however, believe there was a greater chance of rates increasing than decreasing, they would prefer the collar to the corridor as a tool for financing the cap. In practice, collars are more frequently used than corridors.

A *reverse collar* is combination of a long position in a floor and a short position in a cap with different exercise rates. The sale of the cap is used to defray the cost of the floor. For example, the Commerce Bank in our preceding floor example could reduce the $200,000 cost of the 8% floor it purchased to hedge the floating-rate loan it made to the Webb Company by selling a cap. By forming a reverse collar to hedge its floating-rate asset, the bank would still have protection against rates decreasing against the floor rate, but it would have to give up potential higher interest returns if rates increase above the cap rate. For example, suppose Commerce sold a 9% cap for $100,000, with the cap having similar terms to the floor. By using the reverse collar instead of the floor, the company

EXHIBIT 16.4-2   Hedging a Floating-Rate Asset With a Reverse Collar

Asset: Floating rate loan made by bank; Term = 2 years; Reset dates: 3/1, 6/1, 9/1, 12/1; Time frequency = .25; Rate = LIBOR + 150BP; Payment Date = 90 days after reset date.
Floor Purchase: Cost of floor = $200,000; Floor Rate = 8%; Reference Rate = LIBOR; Time frequency = .25.
Floorlets' expirations: On loan reset dates, starting at 6/1/Y1; Payoff made 90 days after reset date.
Cap Sale: revenue from cap = $100,000; Cap Rate = 9%; Reference Rate = LIBOR; Time frequency = .25.
Caplets' Expiration: On loan reset dates, starting at 6/1/Y1; Payoff made 90 days after reset date.

1	2	3	4	5	6	7	8
Reset Date	Assumed LIBOR	Interest Received (LIBOR + 150BP)(.25) ($100M)	Floor Payoff Max[.08 − LIBOR,0](.25) ($100M)	Cap Payment Max[LIBOR − .09,0](.25) ($100M)	Hedged Interest Income Col. (3) + Col. (4) − Col (5)	Hedged Rate 4[Col (6)/ $100M]	Unhedged Rate LIBOR + 150BP
3/1/Y1[n]	0.065						
6/1/Y1	0.070	$2,000,000	$0		$2,000,000	0.080	0.080
9/1/Y1	0.075	$2,125,000	$250,000	$0	$2,375,000	0.095	0.085
12/1/Y1	0.080	$2,250,000	$125,000	$0	$2,375,000	0.095	0.090
3/1/Y2	0.085	$2,375,000	$0	$0	$2,375,000	0.095	0.095
6/1/Y2	0.090	$2,500,000	$0	$0	$2,500,000	0.100	0.100
9/1/Y2	0.095	$2,625,000	$0	$0	$2,625,000	0.105	0.105
12/1/Y2	0.100	$2,750,000	$0	$125,000	$2,625,000	0.105	0.110
3/1/Y3		$2,875,000	$0	$250,000	$2,625,000	0.105	0.115

[n] There is no cap and floor on this date.

would reduce its hedging cost from $200,000 to $100,000, and as shown in Exhibit 16.4-2, would lock in an effective minimum rate on its asset of 9.5% and an effective maximum rate of 10.5%.

As with collars, in forming reverse collars to finance a floating-rate asset with a floor, the investor needs to determine the exercise rates on the caps and floors that best meet the cost of the hedge and the investor's acceptable floor and cap rates. Also, instead of financing a floor with a cap, an investor could form a ***reverse corridor*** by selling another floor with a lower exercise rate.

16.5   OTHER INTEREST RATE PRODUCTS

Caps and floors are one of the more popular interest rate products offered by the OTC derivative market. In addition to these derivatives, a number of other interest rate products have been created over the last decade to meet the many different interest rate hedging needs. Many of these products are variations of the generic OTC caps and floors—exotic options; two of these to note are barrier options and path-dependent options.

16.5.1   Barrier Options

Barrier options are exotic options in which the payoff depends on whether an underlying security price or reference rate reaches a certain level. As we noted in Chapter 9, barrier options can be classified as either knock-out or knock-in options: A ***knock-out option*** is one that ceases to exist once the specified barrier rate or price is reached; a ***knock-in option*** is one that comes into existence when the reference rate or price hits the barrier level. Both types of options can be formed with either a call or put, and the barrier level can be either above or below the current reference rate or price when the contract is established (down-and-out or up-and-out knock outs or up-and-in or down-and-in knock-in options). For example, a down-and-out, knock-out call is a call that ceases to exist once the reference price or rate reaches the barrier level, and the barrier level is below the reference rate or price when the option was purchased.

Barrier caps and floors with termination or creation feature are offered in the OTC market at a premium above comparable caps and floors without such features. Down-and-out caps and floors are options that cease to exist once rates hit a certain level, for example, a 2-year, 8% cap that ceases when the LIBOR hits 6.5% or a 2-year, 8% floor that ceases once the LIBOR hits 9%. By contrast, an up-and-in cap is one that becomes effective once rates hit a certain level: A 2-year, 8% cap that that becomes effective when the LIBOR hits 9% or a 2-year, 8% floor that becomes effective when rates hit 6.5%.

16.5.2   Path-Dependent Options

In the generic cap or floor, the underlying payoff on the caplet or floorlet depends only on the reference rate on the effective date. The payoff does not depend on previous rates; that is, it is independent of the path the LIBOR has taken. Some caps and floors, though, are structured so that their payoff is dependent on the path of the reference rate. An ***average cap***, for example, is one in which the payoff depends on the average reference rate for each caplet. If the average is above the exercise rate, then all the caplets will provide a payoff; if the average is equal or below, the whole cap expires out of the money. Consider a 1-year average cap with an exercise rate of 7% with four caplets. If the LIBOR settings turned out to be 7.5%, 7.75%, 7%, and 7.5%, for an average of 7.4375%, then the average cap would be in the money: $(.074375 - .07)(.25)(NP)$. If the rates, though, turned out to be 7%, 7.5%, 6.5, and 6%, for an average of 6.75%, then the cap would be out of the money.

Another type of path-dependent interest rate option is a ***cumulative cap (Q-cap).*** In a Q-cap, the cap seller pays the holder when the periodic interest on the accompanying floating-rate loan hits or exceeds a specified level. As an example, suppose the Webb Company in our earlier cap example decided to hedge its 2-year floating rate loan (paying LIBOR + 150BP) by buying a Q-Cap from Commerce Bank with the following terms:

- The cap consist of seven caplets with the first expiring on 6/1/Y1 and the others coinciding with the loan's reset dates.
- Exercise rates on each caplet = 8%.
- NP on each caplet = $100M.
- Reference rate = LIBOR.
- Time period to apply to payoff on each caplet = 90/360.
- For the period 3/1/Y1 to 12/1/Y1, the caplet will payoff when the cumulative interest starting from loan date 3/1/Y1 on the company's loan hits $6M.
- For the period 3/1/Y2 to 12/1/Y2, the caplet will payoff when the cumulative interest starting from date 3/1/Y2 on the company's loan hits $6M.
- Payment date on each caplet is at the loan's interest payment date, 90 days after the reset date.
- The cost of the cap = $250,000; it is paid at beginning of the loan, 3/1/Y1.

EXHIBIT 16.5-1   Hedging a Floating-Rate Loan With a Q-Cap

Loan: Floating Rate Loan; Term = 2 years; Reset dates: 3/1, 6/1, 9/1, 12/1; Time frequency = .25; Rate = LIBOR + 150BP; Payment Date = 90 days after reset date.
Q-Cap: Cost of Q-cap = $250,000; Cap Rate = 8%; Reference Rate = LIBOR; Time frequency = .25; Caplets' Expiration: On loan reset dates, starting at 6/1/Y1;
Payoff made 90 days after reset date; Cap become effective once cumulative interest reaches $6M; protection periods: Y1 and Y2.

1	2	3	4	5	6	7
Reset Date	Assumed LIBOR	Interest to be paid at next reset date (LIBOR + 150BP)(.25)($100M)	Cumulative Interest	Q-Cap Payment to be paid at next reset date	Hedged Interest Payment at payment date: Col (3) − Col (5)	Hedged Rate 4[Col (6)/ $100M]
3/1/Y1[n]	0.070	$2,125,000	$2,125,000	$0		
6/1/Y1	0.075	$2,250,000	$4,375,000	$0	$2,125,000	0.085
9/1/Y1	0.080	$2,375,000	$6,750,000	$0	$2,250,000	0.090
12/1/Y1	0.085	$2,500,000	$9,250,000	$125,000	$2,375,000	0.095
3/1/Y2	0.085	$2,500,000	$2,500,000	$0	$2,375,000	0.095
6/1/Y2	0.090	$2,625,000	$5,125,000	$0	$2,500,000	0.100
9/1/Y2	0.095	$2,750,000	$7,875,000	$375,000	$2,625,000	0.105
12/1/Y2	0.100	$2,875,000	$10,750,000	$500,000	$2,375,000	0.095
3/1/Y3					$2,375,000	0.095

[n] There is no cap on this date.

Comparison of Cap and Q-Cap

Loan: Floating Rate Loan; Term = 2 years; Reset dates: 3/1, 6/1, 9/1, 12/1; Time frequency = .25; Rate = LIBOR + 150BP; Payment Date = 90 days after reset date
Cap: Cost of cap = $300,000; Cap Rate = 8%; Reference Rate = LIBOR; Time frequency = .25; Caplets' Expiration: On loan reset dates, starting at 6/1/Y1; Payoff made 90 days after reset date.
Q-Cap: Cost of Q-cap = $250,000; Cap Rate = 8%; Reference Rate = LIBOR; Time frequency = .25; Caplets' Expiration: On loan reset dates, starting at 6/1/Y1;
Payoff made 90 days after reset date; Cap become effective once cumulative interest reaches $6M; protection periods: Y1 and Y2.

1	2	3	4	5	6	7	8
Reset Date	Assumed LIBOR	Loan Interest	Unhedged Loan Rate	Q-Cap Payment	Q-Cap Hedged Rate	Cap-Payments	Cap-Hedged Rate
3/1/Y1[n]	0.070	$2,125,000		$0			
6/1/Y1	0.075	$2,250,000	0.085	$0	0.085	$0	0.085
9/1/Y1	0.080	$2,375,000	0.090	$0	0.090	$0	0.090
12/1/Y1	0.085	$2,500,000	0.095	$125,000	0.095	$125,000	0.095
3/1/Y2	0.085	$2,500,000	0.100	$0	0.095	$125,000	0.095
6/1/Y2	0.090	$2,625,000	0.100	$0	0.100	$250,000	0.095
9/1/Y2	0.095	$2,750,000	0.105	$375,000	0.105	$375,000	0.095
12/1/Y2	0.100	$2,875,000	0.110	$500,000	0.095	$500,000	0.095
3/1/Y3			0.115		0.095		0.095

[n] There is no cap on this date.

Exhibit 16.5-1 shows the quarterly interest, cumulative interest, Q-cap payment, and effective interest for assumed LIBORs. In the Q-caps first protection period, 3/1/Y1 to 12/1/Y1, Commerce Bank will pay the Webb Company on its 8% caplet when the cumulative interest hits $6M. The cumulative interest hits the $6M limit on reset date 9/1/Y1, but on that date, the 9/1/Y1 caplet is not in the money. On the following reset date, though, the caplet is in the money at the LIBOR of 8.5%. Commerce would, in turn, have to pay

Webb $125,000 (90 days later) on the caplet, locking in a hedged rate on its loan of 9.5%. In the second protection period, 3/1/Y2 to 12/1/Y2, the assumed LIBOR rates are higher. The cumulative interest hits the $6M limit on reset date 9/1/Y2. Both the caplet on that date and the next reset date (12/1/Y2) are in the money. As a result, with the caplet payoffs, Webb is able to obtain a hedged rate of 9.5% for the last two payment periods on its loan.

When compared to a standard cap, the Q-cap provides protection for the 1-year protection periods, whereas the standard cap provides protection for each period. As shown in the lower table of Exhibit 16.5-1, a standard 8% cap provides more protection given the assumed increasing interest rate scenario than the Q-cap, capping the loan at 9.5% from date 12/1/Y1 to the end of the loan and providing payoffs on five of the seven caplets for a total of $1,375,000. In contrast, the Q-cap pays on only three of the seven caplets for a total of only $1,000,000. Because of its lower protection limits, the Q-cap costs less than the standard cap.

16.6 PRICING INTEREST RATE OPTIONS WITH A BINOMIAL INTEREST TREE

In Chapter 7, we examined how the binomial interest rate model can be used to price OTC bonds. We then extended the application in Chapter 12 to the valuation of T-bill and T-Bond futures options. The binomial interest rate model also can be used to price OTC interest rate calls and puts.

16.6.1 Valuing a Caplet and Floorlet With a Binomial Tree

The price of a caplet or floorlet can be valued using a binomial tree of the option's reference rate. Exhibit 16.6-1 shows a two-period binomial tree for an annualized risk-free spot rate (S) defining and interest rate call and put. The length of each period is 6 months (6-month steps), the upward parameter on the spot rate (u) is 1.1, the downward parameter (d) is $1/1.1 = 0.9091$, the probability of spot rate increasing in one period is .5, and the yield curve is assumed flat. As shown in the exhibit, given an initial spot rate of 5% (annual), the two possible spot rates after one period (6 months) are 5.5% and 4.54545%, and the three possible rates after two periods (1 year) are 6.05%, 5%, and 4.13223%.

Consider an interest rate call on the spot rate defined by our binomial tree, with an exercise rate of 5%, time period applied to the payoff of $\phi = .25$, and NP = 100. As shown in Exhibit 16.6-1, the interest rate call is in the money at expiration only at the spot rate of 6.05%. At this rate, the caplet's payoff is .2625 (= (.0605 − .05)(.25)(100)). In Period 1, the value of the caplet is .1278 (= [.5(.2625) + .5(0)]/(1.055)$^{.5}$) at spot rate 5.5% and 0 at spot rate 4.54545%. Rolling theses values to the current period, in turn, yields a price on the interest rate call of .06236 (= [.5(.1278) + .5(0)]/(1.05)$^{.5}$). In contrast, an interest rate put with similar features would be in the money at expiration at the spot rate of 4.13223%, with a payoff of .2169 (= (.05 − .0413223)(.25)(100) and out of the money at spot rates 5% and 6.05%. In Period 1, the floorlet's values would be .1061 (= [.5(0) + .5(.2169)]/(1.0454545)$^{.5}$) at spot rate 4.54545% and 0 at spot rate 5.5%. Rolling these values to the present period, we obtain a price on the floorlet of .05177 (= [.5(0) + .5(.1061)]/(1.05)$^{.5}$).

Because a cap is a series of caplets, its price is simply equal to the sum of the values of the individual caplets making up the cap. To price a cap, we can use a binomial tree to price each caplet and then aggregate the caplet values to obtain the value of the cap. Similarly, the value of a floor can be found by summing the values of the floorlets comprising the floor.

EXHIBIT 16.6-1   Binomial Tree: Caplet and Floorlet

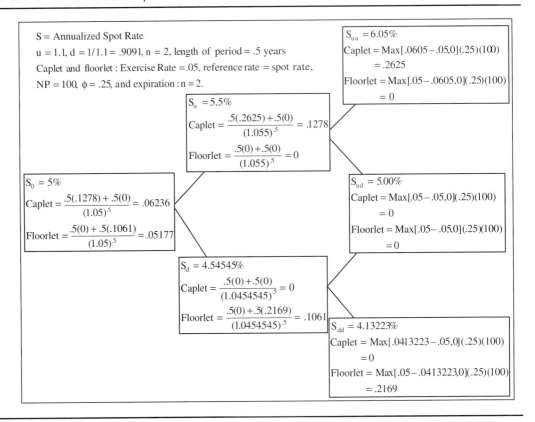

Note that in the preceding examples, the binomial trees' 6-month and 1-year steps were too simplistic. Ideally, binomial trees need to be subdivided into a number of periods. A spot option on the 2-year caplet or floorlet using monthly steps would translated into a 24-period tree with a distribution at expiration of 25 possible futures rates. In addition to subdividing the tree, the practical application of the tree also requires estimating the binomial tree's interest rates. In Chapter 7, we examined two general approaches to estimating binomial interest rate movements—estimating the u and d parameters based on the rate's mean and variability and using a calibration model in which the tree is calibrated to the current spot yield curve. Of the two approaches, the calibration model is the one used by most practitioners.

16.7 PRICING CAPLETS AND FLOORLETS WITH THE BLACK FUTURES OPTION MODEL

In Chapter 12, we defined the Black futures model for the pricing of futures options

$$C_0^* = [f_0 N(d_1) - X N(d_2)]e^{-R_f T}$$

$$P_0^* = [X(1 - N(d_2)) - f_0(1 - N(d_1))]e^{-R_f T}$$

$$d_1 = \frac{\ln(f_0/X) + (\sigma_f^2/2)T}{\sigma_f \sqrt{T}}$$

$$d_2 = d_1 - \sigma_f \sqrt{T}$$

where

σ_f^2 = variance of the logarithmic return of futures prices = $V(\ln(f_n/f_0))$

$\sigma_f^2 = \sigma_S^2$(volatility of spot prices) given the dividend yield and cost of carrying are functions of time

T = time to expiration expressed as a proportion of a year

R_f = annual risk-free rate

The Black futures option model also can be extended to pricing caplets and floorlets by

1. Substituting T* for T in the equation for C* (for a caplet) or P* (for a floorlet), where T* is the time to expiration on the option plus the time period applied to the interest rate payoff time period, ϕ: $T^* = T + \phi$
2. Using an annual continuous compounded risk-free rate for period T* instead of T
3. Using variability = σ = standard deviation of the LIBOR's logarithmic return
4. Multiplying the Black adjusted-futures option model by the NP times the time period: (NP) ϕ:

$$C_0^* = \phi(NP)[RN(d_1) - R_X\,N(d_2)]e^{-R_f T^*}$$

$$P_0^* = \phi(NP)[R_X(1 - N(d_2)) - R(1 - N(d_1))]e^{-R_f T^*}$$

$$d_1 = \frac{\ln(R/R_X) + (\sigma^2/2)T}{\sigma\sqrt{T}}$$

$$d_2 = d_1 - \sigma\sqrt{T}$$

Example: Pricing a Caplet

Consider a caplet with an exercise rate of X = 7%, NP = \$100,000, ϕ = .25, expiration = T = .25 year, and reference rate = LIBOR. If the current LIBOR were R = 6%, the estimated annualized standard deviation of the LIBOR's logarithmic return were .2, and the continuously compounded risk-free rate were 5.8629%, then using the Black model, the price of the caplet would be 4.34:

$$C_0^* = .25(\$100,000)[.06(.067845) - .07(.055596)]e^{-(.058629)(.5)} = 4.34$$

where:

$$d_1 = \frac{\ln(.06/.07) + (.04/2)(.25)}{.2\sqrt{.25}} = -1.49151$$

$$d_2 = d_1 - .2\sqrt{.25} = -1.59151$$

$$N(-1.49151) = .067845$$

$$N(-1.59151) = .055596$$

The "Black–Scholes Option Pricing Model" Excel program includes worksheets ("Black Caplet Model" and "Black Floorlet Model") for calculating caplets and floorlets using the Black futures model.

Example: Pricing a Cap

Suppose the caplet represented part of a contract that caps a 2-year floating-rate loan of $100,000 at 7% for a 3-month period. The cap consist of seven caplets, with expirations of $T = .25$ years, .5, .75, 1, 1.25, 1.5, and 1.75. The value of the cap is equal to the sum of the values of the caplets comprising the cap. If we assume a flat yield curve such that the continuous rate of 5.8629% applies and we use the same volatility of .2 for each caplet, then the value of the cap would be $254.38:

Expiration	Price of Caplet
0.25	4.34
0.50	15.29
0.75	26.74
1.00	37.63
1.25	47.73
1.50	57.04
1.75	65.61
	254.38

In practice, different volatilities for each caplet are used in valuing a cap or floor. The different volatilities are referred to as spot volatilities. They are often estimated by calculating the implied volatility on a comparable Eurodollar futures options.

16.8   CONCLUSION

In this chapter, we've examined how OTC interest rate options are used to manage different types of fixed-income investment and debt management positions and how the binomial interest rate tree and the Black futures model can be used to price such options. Like exchange-traded options, OTC options allow investors and borrowers to attain floor and cap limits on the rates they can earn on their investments or must pay on their loans while still allowing them to benefit if rates move in a favorable direction. In the next part of the book, we examine another popular derivative used extensively in managing interest rate, currency, and credit positions—financial swaps.

KEY TERMS

forward rate agreement	floor	knock-out option
caplet	corridor	knock-in option
floorlet	reverse collar	average cap
cap	reverse corridor	cumulative cap (q-cap)
cap rate	barrier options	

SELECTED REFERENCES

Abken, P. "Interest Rate Caps, Collars, and Floors." *Federal Reserve Bank of Atlanta Economic Review* 74(6) (1989): 224.

Abken, P. A. "Chapter 25: Introduction to Over-the-Counter (OTC) Options." In *The Handbook of Interest Rate Risk Management,* edited by J. C. Francis and A. S. Wolf. New York: Irwin Professional Publishing, 1994.

Bhattacharya, A. K. "Interest-Rate Caps and Floors and Compound Options." *The Handbook of Fixed Income Securities,* 6th ed., edited by F. Fabozzi. New York: McGraw-Hill, 2001.

Dehnad, K. "Characteristics of OTC Options." In *The Handbook of Interest Rate Risk Management,* edited by J. C. Francis and A. Simon Wolf. New York: Irwin Professional Publishing, 1994.

Goldman, B., H. Sosin, and M. A. Gatto. "Path Dependent Options: Buy at the Low, Sell at the High." *Journal of Finance* 34 (December 1979): 1111–27.

Ho, T. S., R. S. Stapleton, and M. G. Subrahmanyam. "The Valuation of American Options with Stochastic Interest Rates: A Generalization of the Geske-Johnson Technique." *Journal of Finance* 52 (June 1997): 827–40.

Hull, J., and A. White. "The Pricing of Options on Interest Rate Caps and Floors Using the Hull-White Model." *Journal of Financial Engineering* 2 (1993): 287–96.

Hull, J., and A. White. "Using Hull–White Interest Rate Trees." *Journal of Derivatives* (Spring 1996): 26–36.

Jamshidian, F. "An Exact Bond Option Pricing Formula." *Journal of Finance* 44 (March 1989): 205–9.

Johnson, R. S. *Bond Evaluation, Selection, and Management.* Malden, MA.: Blackwell Publishing, 2004, Chapters 12–15.

PROBLEMS AND QUESTIONS

1. Given a forward rate agreement (FRA) with the following terms:

   - Notional principal = $20M
   - Reference rate = LIBOR
   - Contract rate = R_k = .05 (annual)
   - Time period = 90 days
   - Day-count convention = actual/365

   Show in a table the payments and receipts for long and short positions on the FRA given possible spot LIBORs at the FRA's expiration of 4%, 4.5%, 5%, 5.5%, and 6%.

2. Explain the similarities and differences between an FRA tied to the LIBOR and a Eurodollar futures contract.

3. The Glasgo Manufacturing Company forecast a cash inflow of $20M in 2 months from the sale of one of its assets that it is considering investing in a 1st National Bank CD for 90 days. 1st National Bank's jumbo CD pays a rate equal to the LIBOR. Currently such rates are yielding 6%. Glasgo is concerned that short-term interest rates could decrease in the next 2 months and would like to lock in a rate now. As an alternative to hedging its investment with Eurodollar futures, 1st National suggests that Glasgo hedge with a forward rate agreement (FRA).

   a. Define the terms of the FRA that would effectively hedge Glasgo's futures CD investment.

   b. Show in a table the payoffs that Glasgo and 1st National would pay or receive at the maturity of the FRA given the following LIBORs: 5.5%, 5.75%, 6%, 6.25%, and 6.5%.

c. Show in a table Glasgo's cash flows from investing the $20M cash inflow plus or minus the FRA receipts or payments at possible LIBORs of 5.5%, 5.75%, 6%, 6.25%, and 6.5%. What is the hedged rate of return Glasgo would earn from its $20M investment?

4. Show graphically and in a table the profit and LIBOR relationships at expiration for the following positions on interest rate options:

a. An interest rate call purchase

b. An interest rate put purchase

c. An interest rate call sale

d. An interest rate put sale

In each case, assume that the interest rate call and put options each have exercise rates of 7%, the LIBOR as the reference rate, notional principals of $20M, time period of .25 per year, and premiums of $25,000. Evaluate at spot discount yields at expiration of 5%, 5.5%, 6.0%, 6.5%, 7%, 7.5%, 8%, 8.5%, and 9.0%.

5. The Fort Washington Money Market Fund expects interest rates to be higher in September when it plans to invest its $18M cash flow in a 90-day CD offered by Sun Bank paying the LIBOR. Suppose the fund decides to hedge the September investment by buying an interest rate put from Sun bank. The floorlet has the following terms:

- Exercise rate of 7%
- Payoff at the maturity of the CD
- Reference rate of LIBOR
- Time period of 90 days (.25)
- Notional principal of $18M
- Expiration at the time of the September cash flow investment
- Cost of floorlet is $100,000, payable at the expiration

Using the table following, determine the fund's hedged yield for possible spot LIBORs at the option's expiration date of 6%, 6.5%, 7%, 7.5%, and 8%:

1	2	3	4	5	6
LIBOR	Interest Rate Put	Cost of the Option at T	Interest Received on CD at its Maturity	Total Revenue at Maturity	Annualized Hedged Rate
6.00					
6.50					
7.00					
7.50					
8.00					

6. In January, the O'Brien Development Company closed a deal with local officials to develop a new office building. The project is expected to begin in June and take 270 days to complete. The cost of the development is expected to be $32M, with the Western Southern Insurance Company providing the permanent financing of the

development once the construction is completed. O'Brien Development has obtained a 270-day construction loan from the Reinhart Financial Company. Reinhart Financing will disperse funds to O'Brien at the beginning of the project in June, with the interest rate on the loan being set equal to the LIBOR plus 150 BP. The principal and interest on the loan are to be paid at maturity. Reinhart Financial is also willing to sell O'Brien an interest rate call with the following terms:

- Exercise rate of 10%
- Payoff at the maturity of the loan
- LIBOR reference rate
- Time period of 270 days or .75 per year
- Notional principal of $32M
- Expiration at the June start of the loan
- Cost of the caplet is $150,000

Using the table following, determine O'Brien's hedged loan rate for possible LIBORs at the June date of 8%, 9%, 10%, 11%, 11.5%, and 12%:

1	2	3	4	5	6
LIBOR	Interest Rate Call	Cost of the Option at T	Interest Paid on Loan at its Maturity	Total Cost at Maturity	Annualized Hedged Rate
8%					
9%					
10%					
11%					
11.5%					
12%					

7. Second National Bank is planning to make a $10M 180-day loan to the Tiger Golf Course Development Company. In the loan contract, Tiger agrees to pay the principal and an interest at the end of 180 days. Because Second National sells more 90-day CDs than 180-day CDs, it is planning to finance the loan by selling a 90-day CD now at the prevailing LIBOR of 8.25%, then 90 days later (mid-September) sell another 90-day CD at the prevailing LIBOR. The bank would like to minimize its exposure to interest rate risk on its future CD sale but would also like to benefit if CD rates decrease. Suppose a money-center bank is willing to sell Second National an interest rate call option tied to the LIBOR with a reference rate of 8.25% for $25,000, payable at the option's expiration.

a. Define the terms of the caplet such that they will match Second National Bank's September debt.

b. Assuming Second National Bank buys the caplet, show in the table following the total amount of funds it would need to raise on its September CD, the bank's debt obligations at the end of 180-day period in December, and the bank's caplet hedged rate for the entire 180-day period (assume 30/360-day count convention) for the following LIBORs at the option's and first CD's maturity date of 7%, 7.5%, 8%, 8.5%, 9%, 9.5%, and 10%:

1	2	3	4	5	6	7
LIBOR	Interest Rate Call Payoff	Cost of Caplet	Sept Debt on CD	Sept Funds Needed	Dec Debt Obligation	Hedged Rate for 180 days
.07						
.075						
.08						
.085						
.09						
.095						
.10						

8. Suppose Eastern Bank offers Gulf Refinery a $150M floating-rate loan to finance the purchase of its crude oil imports along with a cap. The floating-rate loan has a maturity of 1 year, starts on December 20th, and is reset the next three quarters. The initial quarterly rate is equal to 10%/4; the other rates are set on 3/20, 6/20, and 9/20 equal to one fourth of the annual LIBOR on those dates plus 100 basis points: (LIBOR % + 1%)/4. The cap Eastern Bank is offering Gulf has the following terms:

- Three caplets with expiration dates of 3/20, 6/20, and 9/20
- The cap rate on each caplet is 9.5%
- The time period for each caplet is .25 per year
- The payoffs for each caplet are at the interest payment dates
- The reference rate is the LIBOR
- Notional principal is $150M
- The cost of the cap is $500,000

Show in the table following the company's quarterly interest payments, caplet cash flows, hedged interest payments (interest minus caplet cash flow), and hedged rate as a proportion of a $150M loan (do not include cap cost) for each period (12/20, 3/20, 6/20, and 9/20) given the following rates: LIBOR = 10% on 3/20, LIBOR = 9.5% on 6/20, and LIBOR = 9% on 9/20:

1	2	3	4	5	6	7
Date	LIBOR	Cap Payoff on Payment Date	Loan Interest on Payment Date	Hedged Debt	Hedged Rate	Unhedged Rate
12/20/Y1						
3/20/Y1						
6/20/Y1						
9/20/Y1						
12/20/Y2						

9. XU Trust is planning to invest $15M in a Commerce Bank 1-year floating-rate note paying LIBOR plus 150 basis points. The investment starts on 3/20 at 9% (when the LIBOR = 7.5%) and is then reset the next three quarters on 6/20, 9/20, and 12/20. XU Trust would like to establish a floor on the rates it obtains on the note. A money-center

bank is offering XU a floor for $100,000 with the following terms corresponding to the floating-rate note:

- The floor consists of three floorlets coinciding with the reset dates on the note
- Exercise rate on the floorlets = 7%
- Notional principal = $15M
- Reference rate = LIBOR
- Time period on the payoffs is .25
- Payoff is paid on the payment date on the notes
- Cost of the floor is $100,000 and is paid on 3/20

Calculate and show in the table following XU Trust's quarterly interest receipts, floorlet cash flow, hedged interest revenue (interest plus floorlet cash flow), and hedged rate as a proportion of the $15M investment (do not include floor cost) given the LIBORs shown in the table:

1	2	3	4	5	6	7
Date	LIBOR	Interest on FRN on Payment Date	Floor Payoff on Payment Date	Hedged Interest Income	Hedged Rate	Unhedged Rate
3/20	.075					
6/20	.07					
9/20	.065					
12/20	.06					
3/20						

10. Suppose Commerce Bank sells XU Trust a 2-year $15M FRN paying the LIBOR plus 150 basis points. The note starts on 3/20 at 9% and is then reset the next seven quarters on dates 6/20, 9/20, and 12/20. Suppose a money-center bank offers Commerce Bank a cap for $200,000 with the following terms corresponding to its floating-rate liability:

- The cap consists of seven caplets coinciding with the reset dates on the note
- Exercise rate on the caplets = 7%
- Notional principal = $15M
- Reference rate = LIBOR
- Time period on the payoffs is .25
- Payoff is paid on the payment date on the notes
- Cost of the cap is $200,000 and is paid on 3/20

a. Show in a table Commerce Bank's quarterly interest payments, caplet cash flows, hedged interest cost (interest minus caplet cash flow), and hedged rate as a proportion of the $15M FRN loan (do not include cap cost) for each period given the following rates: LIBOR = 7.5% on 3/20, 8% on 6/20, 9% on 9/20, 8% on 12/20, 7% on 3/20, 6.5% on 6/20, 6% on 9/20, and 5.5% on 12/20.

b. To help defray part of the cost of the cap, suppose Commerce Bank decides to set up a collar by selling a floor to one of its customers with a floor rate of 6.5% for $150,000 with the following terms:

- The floor consists of seven floorlets coinciding with the reset dates on the note
- Exercise rate on the floorlets = 6.5%
- Notional principal = $15M

- Reference rate = LIBOR
- Time period on the payoffs is .25
- Payoff is paid on the payment date on the notes
- Cost of the floor is $150,000 and is paid on 3/20

Evaluate Commerce Bank's hedged interest costs from using the collar given the interest rate scenario in 10a.

c. Contrast Commerce Bank's cap hedge with its collar hedge.

d. Define another interest rate option position Commerce Bank might use to defray the costs of its cap-hedged floating-rate liability.

11. Suppose Commerce Bank in Question 10 decides to hedge its 2-year $15M FRN it sold to XU Trust (FRN Terms: Pays the LIBOR plus 150BP; starts on 3/20/y1 at 9%; reset the next seven quarters on dates 6/20, 9/20, and 12/20) by buying a Q-cap (or cumulative cap) from a money center bank for $150,000 with the following terms corresponding to its floating-rate liability:

- The cap consists of seven caplets coinciding with the reset dates on the note
- Exercise rate on the caplets = 7%
- Notional principal = $15M
- Reference rate = LIBOR
- Time period on the payoffs is .25
- For the period from 3/20/y1 to 12/20/y1, the caplet will pay when the cumulative interest starting from the loan date 3/20/y1 hits $700,000
- For the period from 3/20/y2 to 12/20/y2, the caplet will pay when the cumulative interest starting from the loan date 3/20/y2 hits $700,000
- Payoff is paid on the payment date on the notes
- Cost of the cap is $150,000 and is paid on 3/20/y1

a. Show in the table following Commerce Bank's quarterly interest payments, caplet cash flows from the Q-cap, hedged interest cost (interest minus caplet cash flow), and hedged rate as a proportion of the $15M FRN loan (do not include Q-cap cost) for each period given the following interest rate scenario: LIBOR = 7.5% on 3/20, 8% on 6/20, 9% on 9/20, 8% on 12/20, 7% on 3/20, 8% on 6/20, 9% on 9/20, and 10% on 12/20:

1	2	3	4	5	6	7	8
Date	LIBOR	Interest paid on FRN on Payment Date	Cumulative Interest	Q-Cap Payoff on Payment Date	Hedged Interest Payment	Hedged Rate	Unhedged Rate
3/20/Y1	.075		337,500				
6/20/Y1	.08	337,500	693,750				
9/20/Y1	.09	356,250		0			
12/20/Y1	.08			75,000			
3/20/Y2	.07		318,750				
6/20/Y2	.08	318,750	675,000				
9/20/Y2	.09	356,250					
12/20/Y2	.10						
3/20/Y3							

b. Given the preceding interest rate scenario, show in a table Commerce Bank's quarterly hedged interest costs if it were to hedge with the cap describe in Question 10.

c. Compare the bank's Q-cap-hedged rates and the cap-hedged rates. Should the Q-cap be priced higher or lower than the cap?

12. Suppose UK Trust plans to invest $15M in a 2-year FRN paying LIBOR. The FRN starts on 3/20 at 7.5% and is then reset the next seven quarters on 6/20, 9/20, and 12/20. UK Trust would like to establish a floor on the rates it obtains on the note. A money-center bank is offering UK a floor for $200,000 with the following terms corresponding to the floating-rate note:

- The floor consists of seven floorlets coinciding with the reset dates on the note
- Exercise rate on the floorlets = 7%
- Notional principal = $15M
- Reference rate = LIBOR
- Time period on the payoffs is .25
- Payoff is paid on the payment date on the notes
- Cost of the floor is $100,000 and is paid on 3/20

UK would like to finance the $200,000 cost of the floor by forming a reverse collar by selling a cap. The money-center bank is willing to buy a cap with an exercise rate of 8% from UK for $150,000 with similar terms to the floor.

a. Evaluate a reverse collar-hedged FRN investment UK could form with the cap and floor offered by the money-center bank given the following interest rate scenarios: LIBOR = 7.5% on 3/20, 7% on 6/20, 6.5% on 9/20, 6% on 12/20, 7% on 3/20, 8% on 6/20, 8.5% on 9/20, and 9% on 12/20. In your evaluation, include the quarterly interest receipts, cap and floor cash flows, hedged interest revenue, and hedged rate (do not include cost of the floor or revenue from selling the cap).

b. Define another interest rate option position UK Trust might use to defray the costs of its floor-hedged floating-rate investment.

13. Assume

- Binomial process
- Current annualized spot rate on risk-free bond with maturity of .25 years of $S_0 = 4\%$
- Up and down parameters for period equal in length to .5 years of u = 1.1 and d = 1/1.1
- Length of binomial period .5 years (six-month steps)
- Probability of the spot rate increase in one period of q = .5

Generate a three-period binomial tree of spot rates. Using the binomial tree, determine the values of an interest rate call option and interest rate put options, each with exercise rates of 4%, spot rates as reference rates, times periods of .25 years, and notional principal of 100.

WEB EXERCISE

1. Find links to interest rate derivative sites by going to www.isda.org and clicking "Educational" and "Links."

CHAPTER 17

INTEREST RATE SWAPS

17.1 INTRODUCTION[1]

In 1982, the Student Loan Marketing Association (Sallie Mae) issued a fixed-rate, intermediate-term bond through a private placement and swapped it for a floating-rate note issued by ITT. This exchange of the floating-rate loan for the fixed-rate one represented the first of what is referred to today as an ***interest rate swap.*** The swap provided ITT with fixed-rate funds that were 17 basis points below the rate they could obtain on a direct fixed-rate loan, and it provided Sallie Mae with cheaper intermediate-term, floating-rate funds—both parties therefore benefited from the swap.

Today, there exists an interest rate swap market consisting of financial and nonfinancial corporations who annually conduct trillions of dollars (as measured by contract value) in swap contract trades. Financial institutions and corporations use the market to hedge their liabilities and assets more efficiently—transforming their floating-rate liabilities and assets into fixed-rate ones or vice versa and creating synthetic fixed- or floating-rate liabilities and assets with better rates than the ones they can directly obtain. The strategy of swapping loans, though, is not new. In the 1970s, corporations began exchanging loans denominated in different currencies, creating a ***currency swap*** market. This market evolved from corporations who could obtain favorable borrowing terms in one currency but needed a loan in a different currency. To meet such needs, companies would go to swap dealers who would try to match their needs with other parties looking for the opposite positions.

Whether it is an exchange of currency-denominated loans or fixed and floating interest rate payments, a swap, by definition, is a legal arrangement between two parties to exchange specific payments. There are four types of financial swaps:

1. **Interest rate swaps**: The exchange of fixed-rate payments for floating-rate payments
2. **Currency swaps**: The exchange of liabilities in different currencies
3. **Cross-currency swaps**: The combination of an interest rate and currency swap
4. **Credit default swaps**: Exchange of premium payments for default protection

In this chapter, we examine the features, markets, and uses of standard interest rate swaps and in the next chapter we examine two interest rate swap derivatives—forward swaps and swaptions. The pricing of interest rate swaps and their derivatives is the subject of Chapter 19, and in Chapter 20, we examine the markets, uses, and pricing of currency and credit default swaps.

---

[1] Some of the material in this part of the book on swaps draws from Johnson, *Bond Evaluations, Selection, and Management,* 2004.

17.2 GENERIC INTEREST RATE SWAPS

17.2.1 Features

The simplest type of interest rate swap is called the ***plain vanilla swap*** or ***generic swap.*** In this agreement, one party provides fixed-rate interest payments to another party who provides floating-rate payments. The parties to the agreement are referred to as ***counterparties:*** The party who pays fixed interest and receives floating is called the ***fixed-rate payer;*** the other party (who pays floating and receives fixed) is the ***floating-rate payer.*** The fixed-rate payer is also called the floating-rate receiver and is often referred to as having bought the swap or having a long position; the floating-rate payer is also called the fixed-rate receiver and is referred to as having sold the swap and being short.

On a generic swap, principal payments are not exchanged. As a result, the interest payments are based on a notional principal (NP). The interest rate paid by the fixed payer often is specified in terms of the yield to maturity (YTM) on a T-note plus basis points (BP); the rate paid by the floating payer on a generic swap is the LIBOR. Swap payments on a generic swap are made semiannually, and the maturities typically range from 3 to 10 years. In the swap contract, a trade date, effective date, settlement date, and maturity date are specified. The ***trade date*** is the day the parties agree to commit to the swap; the ***effective date*** is the date when interest begins to accrue; the ***settlement*** or ***payment date*** is when interest payments are made (interest is paid in arrears 6 months after the effective date); and the ***maturity date*** is the last payment date. On the payment date, only the interest differential between the counterparties is paid. That is, generic swap payments are based on a ***net settlement basis:*** The counterparty owing the greater amount pays the difference between what is owed and what is received. Thus, if a fixed-rate payer owes $2M and a floating-rate payer owes $1.5M, then only a $0.5M payment by the fixed payer to the floating payer is made. All of the terms of the swap are specified in a legal agreement signed by both parties called the ***confirmation.*** The drafting of the confirmation often follows document forms suggested by the ***International Swap and Derivative Association (ISDA)*** in New York. This organization provides a number of master agreements delineating the terminology used in many swap agreements (e.g., what happens in the case of default, the business day convention, and the like).

Web Information:

For information on the International Swap and Derivative Association and size of the markets go to www.isda.org.

17.2.2 Interest Rate Swap: Example

Consider an interest rate swap with a maturity of 3 years, first effective date of 3/23/Y1, and a maturity date of 3/23/Y4. In this swap agreement, assume the fixed-rate payer agrees to pay the current YTM on a 3-year T-note of 6% plus 50 basis points, and the floating-rate payer agrees to pay the 6month LIBOR as determined on the effective dates with no basis points. Also assume the semiannual interest rates are determined by dividing the annual rates (LIBOR and 6.5%) by 2. Finally, assume the NP on the swap is $10M. (The calculations will be slightly off because they fail to include the actual day count convention; this is discussed in Section 17.3.)

Exhibit 17.2-1 shows the interest payments on each settlement date based on assumed LIBORs on the effective dates. In examining the table, several points should be noted. First, the payments are determined by the LIBOR prevailing 6 months prior to the payment date; thus, payers on swaps would know their obligations in advance of the payment date.

Second, when the LIBOR is below the fixed 6.5% rate, the fixed-rate payer pays the interest differential to the floating-rate payer; when it is above 6.5%, the fixed-rate payer receives the interest differential from the floating-rate payer. The net interest received by the fixed-rate payer is shown in Column 5 of the table, and the net interest received by the floating-rate payer is shown in Column 6.

As we discuss later, the fixed-rate payer's position is very similar to a short position in strip of Eurodollar futures contracts, with the futures price determined by the fixed rate. The fixed payer's cash flows also can be replicated by the fixed payer buying a $10M, 3-year, floating-rate note (FRN) paying the LIBOR and shorting (issuing) a 3-year $10M, 6.5% fixed-rate bond at par.

The floating-rate payer's position, on the other hand, is similar to a long position in a Eurodollar strip, and it can be replicated by shorting a 3-year, $10M FRN paying the LIBOR and purchasing a 3-year, $10M, 6.5% fixed-rate bond at par.

17.2.3 Synthetic Loans

One of the important uses of swaps is in creating a synthetic fixed- or floating-rate liability that yields a better rate than a conventional or direct one. To illustrate, suppose a corporation with an AAA credit rating wants a 3-year, $10M fixed-rate loan starting on March 23, Y1. Suppose one possibility available to the company is to borrow $10M from a bank at a fixed rate of 7% (assume semiannual payments) with a loan maturity of 3 years. Suppose, though, that the bank also is willing to provide the company with a 3-year floating-rate loan, with the rate set equal to the LIBOR on March 23rd and September 23rd each year for 3 years. If a swap agreement identical to the one described previously were available, then instead of a direct fixed-rate loan, the company alternatively could attain a fixed-rate loan by borrowing $10M on the floating-rate loan and then fix the interest rate by taking a fixed-rate payer's position on the swap:

Conventional Floating-Rate Loan	Pay Floating Rate
Swap: Fixed-Rate Payer Position	Pay Fixed Rate
Swap: Fixed-Rate Payer Position	Receive Floating Rate
Synthetic Fixed Rate	Pay Fixed Rate

EXHIBIT 17.2-1   Interest Rate Swap: 6.5%/Libor Swap With NP = $10M

1	2	3	4	5	6
Effective Dates	LIBOR	Floating-Rate Payer's Payment*	Fixed-Rate Payer's Payment**	Net Interest Received by Fixed-Rate Payer Column 3 − Column 4	Net Interest Received by Floating-Rate Payer Column 4 − Column 3
3/23/y1	0.055				
9/23/y1	0.060	$275,000	$325,000	−$50,000	$50,000
3/23/y2	0.065	$300,000	$325,000	−$25,000	$25,000
9/23/y2	0.070	$325,000	$325,000	$0	$0
3/23/y3	0.075	$350,000	$325,000	$25,000	−$25,000
9/23/y3	0.080	$375,000	$325,000	$50,000	−$50,000
3/23/y4		$400,000	$325,000	$75,000	−$75,000

*(LIBOR/2)($10,000,000)
**(.065/2)($10,000,000)

EXHIBIT 17.2-2 Synthetic Fixed-Rate Loan: Floating-Rate Loan Set at LIBOR and Fixed-Payer Position on 6.5%/LIBOR Swap

1	2	3	4	5	6
Effective Dates	LIBOR	Floating-Rate Interest Payment*	Net Interest Received by Fixed-Rate Payer	Net Interest Paid Column 3 − Column 4	Rate 2(Column 5)/10M
3/23/y1	0.055				
9/23/y1	0.060	$275,000	−$50,000	$325,000	0.065
3/23/y2	0.065	$300,000	−$25,000	$325,000	0.065
9/23/y2	0.070	$325,000	$0	$325,000	0.065
3/23/y3	0.075	$350,000	$25,000	$325,000	0.065
9/23/y3	0.080	$375,000	$50,000	$325,000	0.065
3/23/y4		$400,000	$75,000	$325,000	0.065

*(LIBOR/2)($10,000,000)

As shown in Exhibit 17.2-2, if the floating-rate loan is hedged with a swap, any change in the LIBOR would be offset by an opposite change in the net receipts on the swap position. In this example, the company (as shown in the exhibit) would end up paying a constant $325,000 every 6 months, which equates to an annualized borrowing rate of 6.5%: R = 2($325,000M)/$10M = .065. Thus, the corporation would be better off combining the swap position as a fixed-rate payer with the floating-rate loan to create a synthetic fixed-rate loan than simply taking the straight fixed-rate loan.

In contrast, a synthetic floating-rate loan can be formed by combining a floating-rate payer's position with a fixed-rate loan. This loan then can be used as an alternative to a floating-rate loan:

Conventional Fixed-Rate Loan	Pay Fixed Rate
Swap: Floating-Rate Payer Position	Pay Floating Rate
Swap: Floating-Rate Payer Position	Receive Fixed Rate
Synthetic Floating Rate	Pay Floating Rate

An example of a synthetic floating-rate loan is shown in Exhibit 17.2-3. The synthetic loan is formed with a 6% fixed-rate loan (semiannual payments) and the floating-rate payer's position in our illustrated swap. As shown in the exhibit, the synthetic floating-rate loan yields a 0.5% lower interest rate each period (annualized rate) than a floating-rate loan tied to the LIBOR.

Note that in both of the preceding examples, the borrower is able to attain a better borrowing rate with a synthetic loan using swaps than with a direct loan. When differences between the rates on actual and synthetic loans do exist, then swaps provide an apparent arbitrage use in which borrowers and investors can obtain better rates with synthetic positions formed with swap positions than they can from conventional loans.

EXHIBIT 17.2-3 Synthetic Floating-Rate Loan: 6% Fixed-Rate Loan and Floating-Payer Position on 6.5%/LIBOR Swap

1	2	3	4	5	6
		Net Interest Received by Floating-Rate Payer	Interest Paid on Fixed-Rate Loan*	Net Interest Paid	Rate 2(Column(5))/$10M
Effective Dates	LIBOR				
3/23/y1	0.055				
9/23/y1	0.060	$50,000	$300,000	$250,000	0.050
3/23/y2	0.065	$25,000	$300,000	$275,000	0.055
9/23/y2	0.070	$0	$300,000	$300,000	0.060
3/23/y3	0.075	−$25,000	$300,000	$325,000	0.065
9/23/y3	0.080	−$50,000	$300,000	$350,000	0.070
3/23/y4		−$75,000	$300,000	$375,000	0.075

*(.06/2)($10,000,000)

17.2.4 Similarities Between Swaps and Bond Positions and Eurodollar Futures Strips

17.2.4.1 Bond Positions

Swaps can be viewed as a combination of a fixed-rate bond and flexible-rate note (FRN). A fixed-rate payer position is equivalent to buying a FRN paying the LIBOR and shorting (issuing) a fixed-rate bond at the swap's fixed rate. From the previous example, the purchase of $10M worth of 3-year FRNs with the rate reset every 6 months at the LIBOR and the sale of $10M worth of 3-year, 6.5% fixed-rate bonds at par would yield the same cash flow as the fixed-rate payer's swap. On the other hand, a floating-rate payer's position is equivalent to shorting (or issuing) a FRN at the LIBOR and buying a fixed-rate bond at the swap's fixed rate. Thus, the purchase of $10M worth of 3-year, 6.5% fixed-rate bonds at par and the sale of $10M worth of FRNs paying the LIBOR would yield the same cash flow as the floating-rate payer's swap in the previous example.

17.2.4.2 Eurodollar Futures Strip

A plain vanilla swap can also be viewed as a series of Eurodollar futures contracts. To see the similarities, consider a short position in a Eurodollar strip in which the short holder agrees to sell 10 Eurodollar deposits, each with face values of $1M and maturities of 6 months, at the IMM-index price of 93.5 (or discount yield of $R_D = 6.5\%$), with the expirations on the strip being March 23rd and September 23rd for a period of $2\frac{1}{2}$ years.

With the index at 93.5, the contract price on one Eurodollar futures contract is $967,500:

$$f_0 = \left[\frac{100 - (6.5)(180/360)}{100} \right] (\$1,000,000) = \$967,500$$

Exhibit 17.2-4 shows the cash flows at the expiration dates from closing the 10 short Eurodollar contracts at the same assumed LIBOR used in the preceding swap example, with the Eurodollar settlement index being 100 − LIBOR. For example, with the LIBOR

EXHIBIT 17.2-4 Short Positions in Eurodollar Futures

1	2	3	4	5
			Cash Flow from Short Position	Cash Flow from Long Position
Closing Dates	LIBOR	f_T	$10[f_0 - f_T]$	$10[f_T - f_0]$
3/23/y1	0.055	$972,500	−$50,000	$50,000
9/23/y1	0.060	$970,000	−$25,000	$25,000
3/23/y2	0.065	$967,500	$0	$0
9/23/y2	0.070	$965,000	$25,000	−$25,000
3/23/y3	0.075	$962,500	$50,000	−$50,000
9/23/y3	0.080	$960,000	$75,000	−$75,000

$f_0 = 967,500$

$f_T = \left[\frac{100 - (\text{LIBOR}\%)}{100} (180/360) \right] (\$1,000,000)$

at 6% on 9/23/Y1, a $25,000 loss occurs from settling the 10 futures contracts. That is

$$f_T = \left[\frac{100 - (6)(180/360)}{100} \right] (\$1,000,000) = \$970,000$$

$$\text{Futures cash flow} = 10[f_0 - f_T] = 10[\$967,500 - \$970,000] = -\$25,000$$

Comparing the fixed-rate payer's net receipts shown in Column 5 of Exhibit 17.2-1 with the cash flows from the short positions on the Eurodollar strip shown in Exhibit 17.2-4, one can see that the two positions yield the same numbers. There are, however, some differences between the Eurodollar strip and the swap. First, a 6-month differential occurs between the swap payment and the futures payments. This time differential is a result of the interest payments on the swap being determined by the LIBOR at the beginning of the period, whereas the futures position's profit is based on the LIBOR at the end of its period. Second, we've assumed the futures contract is on a Eurodollar deposit with a maturity of 6 months instead of the more standard 3 months. In addition to these technical differences, other differences exist: Strips are guaranteed by a clearinghouse, whereas banks can act as guarantors for swaps; strip contracts are standardized, whereas swap agreements often are tailor-made.

17.3 SWAP MARKET

17.3.1 Structure

Corporations, financial institutions, and others who use swaps are linked by a group of brokers and dealers who collectively are referred to as *swap banks.* These swap banks consist primarily of commercial banks and investment bankers. As brokers, swap banks try to match parties with opposite needs (see Exhibit 17.3-1). Many of the first interest rate swaps were customized brokered deals between counterparties, with the parties often negotiating and transacting directly between themselves. As brokers, the swap bank's role in the contract is to bring the parties together and provide information; swap banks often maintain lists of companies and financial institutions that are potential parties to a swap. Once the swap agreement is closed, the swap broker usually has only a minor

EXHIBIT 17.3-1   Swap Market Structure

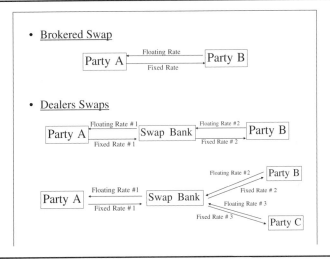

continuing role. With some ***brokered swaps,*** the swap bank guarantees one or both sides of the transaction. With many, though, the counterparties assume the credit risk and make their own assessment of the other party's default potential.

One of the problems with a brokered swap is that it requires each party to have knowledge of the other party's risk profile. Historically, this problem led to more swap banks taking positions as dealers instead of as brokers. With ***dealer swaps,*** the swap dealer often makes commitments to enter a swap as a counterparty before the other end party has been located. Each of the counterparties (or in this context, the end parties) contracts separately with the swap bank, who acts as a counterparty to each. The end parties, in turn, assume the credit risk of the financial institution instead of that of the other end party, whereas the swap dealer assumes the credit risk of both of the end parties.

In acting as dealers, swap banks often match a swap agreement with multiple end parties. For example, as illustrated in Exhibit 17.3-1, a $30M fixed-for-floating swap between a swap dealer and Party A might be matched with two $15M floating-for-fixed swaps. Ideally, a swap bank tries to maintain a perfect hedge. In practice, though, swap banks are prepared to enter a swap agreement without another counterparty. This practice is sometimes referred to as ***warehousing.*** In warehousing, swap banks will try to hedge their swap positions with opposite positions in T-notes and FRNs or using Eurodollar futures contracts. For example, a swap bank might hedge a $10M, 2-year floating-rate position by shorting $10M worth of 2-year T-notes and then use the proceeds to buy FRNs tied to the LIBOR. In general, most of the commitments a swap bank assumes are hedged through a portfolio of alternative positions—opposite swap positions, spot positions in T-notes and FRNs, or futures positions. This type of portfolio management by swap banks is referred to as ***running a dynamic book.***

17.3.2 Swap Market Price Quotes

By convention, the floating rate on a swap is quoted flat without basis point adjustments. The fixed rate on a generic swap, in turn, is quoted in terms of the yield to maturity (YTM) on an on-the-run T-bond or T-note; that is, the most recent note or bond issued with a maturity matching the swap. In a dealer swap, the swap dealer's compensation comes from a markup or bid-ask spread extended to the end parties. The spread is reflected on the

EXHIBIT 17.3-2 Swap Bank Quote

Swap Maturity	Treasury Yield (%)	Bid Swap Spread (BP)	Ask Swap Spread (BP)	Fixed Swap Rate Spread	Swap Rate
2 year	4.95	54	64	5.49%–5.59%	5.540%
3 year	5.12	72	76	5.84%–5.88%	5.860%
4 year	5.32	69	74	6.01%–6.06%	6.035%
5 year	5.74	70	76	6.44%–6.50%	6.470%

fixed-rate side. The swap dealer will provide a bid-ask quote to a potential party and will in some cases post the bid-ask quotes. The quotes are stated in terms of the bid rate the dealer will pay as a fixed payer in return for the LIBOR and the ask rate the dealer will receive as a floating-rate payer in return for paying the LIBOR. For example, a 70/75 swap spread implies the dealer will buy (take fixed-payer position) at 70 BP over the T-note yield and sell (take floating-payer position) at 75 BP over the T-note yield. Exhibit 17.3-2 shows some illustrative quotes being offered by a swap bank on four generic swaps. The quote on the 2-year swap indicates that the swap bank will take the fixed-rate payer's position at 5.49%/LIBOR (fixed rate = 4.95% + 54 BP) and the floating-rate payer's position at 5.59%/LIBOR (fixed rate = 4.95% + 64 BP). The average of the bid and ask rates is known as the *swap rate.*

It should be noted that the fixed and floating rates quoted on a swap are not directly comparable. That is, the T-note assumes a 365-day basis, whereas the LIBOR assumes 360 days. In addition, these rates also need to be prorated to the actual number of days that have elapsed between settlement dates to determine the actual payments. These adjustments can be accounted for by using the following formulas:

$$\text{Fixed-Rate Settlement Payment} = (\text{Fixed Rate})\left[\frac{\text{No. of Days}}{365}\right]\text{NP}$$

$$\text{Floating-Rate Settlement Payment} = (\text{LIBOR})\left[\frac{\text{No. of Days}}{360}\right]\text{NP}$$

To simplify the exposition, we ignore the day-count conventions in our other examples of generic swaps and simply divide annual rates by two (i.e., we will use a 180/360 day-count convention).

17.3.3 Opening Swap Positions

Suppose a corporate treasurer wants to fix the rate on the company's 5-year, $50M floating-rate liability by taking a fixed-rate payer's position on a 5-year swap with a NP of $50M. To obtain the swap position, suppose the treasurer calls a swap banker for a quote on a fixed-rate payer's position. After assessing the corporation's credit risk, suppose the swap dealer gives the treasurer a swap quote of 100 BP over the current 5-year T-note yield, and the corporate treasurer, in turn, accepts. Thus, the treasurer would agree to take the fixed-payer's position on the swap at 100 BP above the current 5-year T-note. Except for the rate, both parties would mutually agree to the terms of the swap. After agreeing to the terms, the actual rate paid by the fixed payer would typically be set once the swap banker hedges her swap position by taking, for example, a position in an on-the-run T-note. After confirming a quote on a 5-year T-note from her bond trader, the swap banker would then instruct the trader to sell (or short) $50M of 5-year T-notes with the proceeds invested in a 5-year FRN paying LIBOR. The yield on the T-note purchased plus the 100 BP would determine the actual rate on the swap. At a later date, the swap banker would most likely close the bond positions used to hedge the swap whenever she finds a floating-rate swap position to take on one or more swaps with similar terms.

Note that because swap banks can hedge opening swap positions with positions in an on-the-run T-note and FRN, the rates they in turn set on a swap contract is determined by the current T-note yields (with BP added to reflect credit risk). Thus, opening swap contracts are tied to T-note yields. This relation is also reinforced by an arbitrage strategy consisting of positions in a swap, T-note, and FRN.

17.3.4   Closing Swap Positions

Prior to maturity, swap positions can be closed by selling the swap to a swap dealer or another party. If the swap is closed in this way, the new counterparty either pays or receives an upfront fee to or from the existing counterparty in exchange for receiving the original counterparty's position. Alternatively, the swap holder could also hedge his position by taking an opposite position in a current swap or possibly by hedging the position for the remainder of the maturity period with a futures position. Thus, a fixed-rate payer who unexpectedly sees interest rates decreasing and as a result wants to change his position, could do so by selling the swap to a dealer, taking a floating-rate payer's position in a new swap contract, or by going long in an appropriate futures contract; this latter strategy might be advantageous if there is only a short period of time left on the swap.

If the fixed-payer swap holder decides to hedge his position by taking an opposite position on a new swap, the new swap position would require a payment of the LIBOR that would cancel out the receipt of the LIBOR on the first swap. The difference in the positions would therefore be equal to the difference in the higher fixed interest that is paid on the first swap and the lower fixed interest rate received on the offsetting swap. For example, suppose in our first illustrative swap example (Exhibit 17.2-1), a decline in interest rates occurs 2 years after the initiation of the swap, causing the fixed-rate payer to want to close his position. To this end, suppose the fixed-rate payer offsets his position by entering a new 1-year swap as a floating-rate payer in which he agrees to pay the LIBOR for a 6% fixed rate. The two positions would result in a fixed payment of $25,000 semiannually for 1 year (($.005/2$)NP). If interest rates decline over the next year, this offsetting position would turn out to be the correct strategy.

Offsetting Swap Positions

Original Swap: Fixed Payer's Position	Pay 6.5%	−6.5%
Original Swap: Fixed Payer's Position	Receive LIBOR	+LIBOR
Offsetting Swap: Floating Payer's Position	Pay LIBOR	−LIBOR
Offsetting Swap: Floating Payer's Position	Receive 6.0%	+6%
	Pay 0.5% (annual)	−0.5% (annual)

Instead of hedging the position, the fixed-rate payer is more likely to close his position by simply selling it to a swap dealer. In acquiring a fixed position at 6.5%, the swap dealer would have to take a floating-payer's position to hedge the acquired fixed position. If the fixed rate on a new 1-year swap were at 6%, the dealer would likewise lose $25,000 semiannually for 1 year on the two swap positions given an NP of $10M. Thus, the price the swap bank would charge the fixed payer for buying his swap would be at least equal to the present value of $25,000 for the next two semiannual periods. Given a discount rate of 6%, the swap bank would charge the fixed payer at least $47,837 for buying his swap; to the fixed holder, the swap has a negative value (SV) of $47,837:

$$SV_0^{Fix} = \frac{-\$25,000}{(1 + (.06/2))} + \frac{-\$25,000}{(1 + (.06/2))^2} = -\$47,837$$

In contrast, if rates had increased, the fixed payer would be able to sell the swap to a dealer at a premium. For example, if the fixed rate on a new swap were 7%, a swap dealer would realize a semiannual return of $25,000 for the next year by buying the 6.5%/LIBOR swap and hedging it with a floating position on a 1-year, 7%/LIBOR swap. Given a 7% discount rate, the dealer would pay the fixed payer a maximum of $47,492 for his 6.5%/LIBOR swap or the swap would have a positive value of $47,492:

$$SV_0^{Fix} = \frac{\$25,000}{(1 + (.07/2))} + \frac{\$25,000}{(1 + (.07/2))^2} = \$47,492$$

In general, the preceding case illustrates that the value of an existing swap depends on the rates on current swaps. Moreover, the fixed rate on current swaps depends on the yields on T-notes.

17.4 SWAP VALUATION

At origination, most plain vanilla swaps have an economic value of zero. This means that neither counterparty is required to pay the other in the agreement. An economic value of zero requires that the swap's underlying bond positions trade at par—*par value swap.* If this were not the case, then one of the counterparties would need to compensate the other. In this case, the economic value of the swap is not zero. Such a swap is referred to as an *off-market swap.*

Although most plain vanilla swaps are originally par value swaps with economic values of zero, as the preceding example illustrated, the economic values of existing swaps change over time as rates change; that is, existing swaps become off-market swaps as rates change. In our previous example, the fixed-payer's position on the 6.5%/LIBOR swap had a value of –$47,837 2 years later when the fixed-rate on new, 1-year, par value swaps was 6%; that is, the holder of the fixed position would have to pay the swap bank at least $47,837 to assume the swap. On the other hand, the fixed-payer's position on the 6.5%/LIBOR swap had a value of $47,492 when the fixed-rate on new 1-year par value swaps was 7%; that is, the holder of the fixed position would have received $47,492 from the swap bank.

Just the opposite values apply to the floating position. Continuing with our illustrative example, if the fixed rate on new 1-year par value swaps were at 6%, then a swap bank that assumed a floating position on a 6.5%/LIBOR swap and then hedged it with a fixed position on a current 1-year 6%/LIBOR swap would gain $25,000 semiannually over the next year. As a result, the swap bank would be willing to pay $47,837 for the floating position. Thus, the floating position on the 6.5% swap would have a value of $47,837:

Offsetting Swap Positions

Original Swap: Floating Payer's Position	Pay LIBOR	–LIBOR
Original Swap: Floating Payer's Position	Receive 6.5%	+6.5%
Offsetting Swap: Fixed Payer's Position	Pay 6%	–6%
Offsetting Swap: Fixed Payer's Position	Receive LIBOR	+LIBOR
	Receive 0.5% (annual)	0.5% (annual)

$$SV_0^{FL} = \frac{\$25,000}{(1 + (.06/2))} + \frac{\$25,000}{(1 + (.06/2))^2} = \$47,837$$

If the fixed rate on new 1-year par value swaps were at 7%, then a swap bank assuming the floating position on a 6.5%/LIBOR swap and hedging it with a fixed position on a current 1-year 6%/LIBOR swap would lose $25,000 semiannually over the next year. As a result, the swap bank would charge $47,492 for assuming the floating position. Thus, the floating position on the 6.5% swap would have a negative value of $47,492:

Offsetting Swap Positions

Original Swap: Floating Payer's Position	Pay LIBOR	–LIBOR
Original Swap: Floating Payer's Position	Receive 6.5%	+6.5%
Offsetting Swap: Fixed Payer's Position	Pay 7%	–7%
Offsetting Swap: Fixed Payer's Position	Receive LIBOR	+LIBOR
	Pay 0.5% (annual)	–0.5% (annual)

$$SV_0^{FL} = \frac{-\$25,000}{(1 + (.07/2))} + \frac{-\$25,000}{(1 + (.07/2))^2} = -\$47,492$$

In general, the value of an existing swap is equal to the value of replacing the swap—replacement swap—which depends on current T-note rates. Formally, the values of the fixed and floating swap positions are

$$SV^{fl} = \left[\sum_{t=1}^{M} \frac{K^S - K^P}{(1 + K^P)^t} \right] NP$$

$$SV^{fix} = \left[\sum_{t=1}^{M} \frac{K^P - K^S}{(1 + K^P)^t} \right] NP$$

where

K^S = Fixed rate on the existing swap.

K^P = Fixed rate on current par-value swap.

SV^{fix} = Swap value of the fixed position on the existing swap.

SV^{fl} = Swap value of the floating position on the existing swap.

Note that these values are obtained by discounting the net cash flows at the current YTM (K^P). As a result, this approach to valuing off-market swaps is often referred to as the **YTM approach.** However, recall from our discussion of bonds (Chapter 7) that the equilibrium price of a bond is obtained not by discounting all of the bond's cash flows by a common discount rate but rather by discounting each of the bond's cash flows by their appropriate spot rates—the rate on a zero-coupon bond. As we discussed in Chapter 7, valuing bonds by using spot rates instead of a common YTM ensures that there are no arbitrage opportunities from buying bonds and stripping them or buying zero-discount bonds and bundling them. The argument for pricing bonds in terms of spot rates also applies to the valuation of off-market swaps. Similar to bond valuation, the equilibrium value of a swap is obtained by discounting each of the swap's cash flows by their appropriate spot rates. The valuation of swaps using spot rates is referred to as the **zero-coupon approach.** The approach, in turn, requires generating a spot yield curve for swaps. Valuation using the zero-coupon approach is examined in Chapter 19.

17.5   COMPARATIVE ADVANTAGE AND THE HIDDEN OPTION

17.5.1   Comparative Advantage

Swaps are often used by financial and nonfinancial corporations to take advantage of apparent arbitrage opportunities resulting from capital-market inefficiencies. To see this, consider the case of the Star Chemical Company who wants to raise $150M with a 5-year loan to finance an expansion of one of its production plants. Based on its moderate credit ratings, suppose Star can borrow 5-year funds at a 10.5% fixed rate or at a floating rate equal to LIBOR + 75 BP. Given the choice of financing, Star prefers the fixed-rate loan. Suppose the treasurer of the Star Company contacts his investment banker for suggestions on how to finance the acquisition. The investment banker knows that the Moon Development Company is also looking for 5-year funding to finance its proposed $150M office park development. Given its high credit rating, suppose Moon can borrow the funds for 5 years at a fixed rate of 9.5% or at a floating rate equal to the LIBOR + 25 BP. Given the choice, Moon prefers a floating-rate loan. In summary, Star and Moon have the following fixed- and floating-rate loan opportunities:

Company	Fixed Rate	Floating Rate	Preference	Comparative Advantage
Star Company	10.5%	LIBOR + 75 BP	Fixed	Floating
Moon Company	9.5%	LIBOR + 25 BP	Floating	Fixed
Credit Spread	100 BP	50 BP		

In this case, the Moon Company has an absolute advantage in both the fixed and floating markets because of its higher quality rating. However, looking at the credit spreads of the borrowers in each market, the investment banker realizes that there is a **comparative advantage** for Moon in the fixed market and a comparative advantage for Star in the floating market. That is, Moon has a relative advantage in the fixed market in which it gets 100 BP less than Star; Star, in turn, has a relative advantage (or relatively less disadvantage) in the floating rate market in which it only pays 50 BP more than Moon. Thus, lenders in the fixed-rate market supposedly assess the difference between the two creditors to be worth 100 BP, whereas lenders in the floating-rate market assess the difference to be only 50 BP. Whenever a comparative advantage exists, arbitrage opportunities can be realized by each firm borrowing in the market in which it has a comparative advantage and then swapping loans or having an swap bank set up a swap.

For the swap to work, the two companies cannot just pass on their respective costs: Star swaps a floating rate at LIBOR + 75BP for a 10.5% fixed; Moon swaps a 9.5% fixed for a floating at LIBOR + 25BP. Typically, the companies divide the differences in credit spreads, with the most creditworthy company taking the most savings. In this case, suppose the investment banker arranges a 5-year, 9.5%/LIBOR generic swap with a NP of $150M in which Star takes the fixed-rate payer position and Moon takes the floating-rate payer position.

The Star Company would then issue a $150M FRN paying LIBOR + 75BP. This loan, combined with the fixed-rate position on the 9.5%/LIBOR swap would give Star a synthetic fixed rate loan paying 10.25%—.25% less than its direct fixed-rate loan:

Star Company's Synthetic Fixed-Rate Loan

Issue FRN	Pay LIBOR + 75BP	−LIBOR − .75%
Swap: Fixed-Rate Payer's Position	Pay 9.5%	−9.5%
Swap: Fixed-Rate Payer's Position	Receive LIBOR	+LIBOR
Synthetic Fixed Rate	Pay 9.5% + .75%	−10.25%
Direct Fixed Rate	Pay 10.5%	−10.5%

The Moon Company, on the other hand, would issue a $150M, 9.5% fixed-rate bond that when combined with its floating-rate position on the 9.5%/LIBOR swap, would give Moon a synthetic floating-rate loan paying LIBOR, which is 25 BP less than the rate paid on the direct floating-rate loan of LIBOR plus 25 BP:

Moon Company's Synthetic Floating-Rate Loan

Issue 9.5% fixed-rate bond	Pay 9.5%	−9.5%
Swap: Floating-Rate Payer's Position	Pay LIBOR	−LIBOR
Swap: Floating-Rate Payer's Position	Receive 9.5%	+9.5%
Synthetic Fixed Rate	Pay LIBOR	−LIBOR
Direct Fixed Rate	Pay LIBOR + 25BP	−LIBOR − .25%

Thus, the swap makes it possible for both companies to create synthetic loans with better rates than direct ones.

As a rule, for a swap to provide arbitrage opportunities, at least one of the counterparties must have a comparative advantage in one market. The total arbitrage gain available to each party depends on whether one party has an absolute advantage in both markets or each has an absolute advantage in one market. If one party has an absolute advantage in both markets (as in this case), then the arbitrage gain is the difference in the comparative advantages in each market: 50 BP = 100 BP − 50 BP. In this case, Star and Moon split the difference in the 50 BP gain. In contrast, if each party has an absolute advantage in one market, then the arbitrage gain is equal to the sum of the comparative advantages.

17.5.2 Hidden Option

The comparative advantage argument has often been cited as the explanation for the dramatic growth in the swap market. This argument, though, is often questioned on the grounds that the mere use of swaps should over time reduce the credit interest rate differentials in the fixed and flexible markets, taking away the advantages from forming synthetic positions. With observed credit spreads and continuing use of swaps to create synthetic positions, some scholars (e.g., Smith, Smithson, and Wakeman, 1986) have argued that the comparative advantage that is apparently extant is actually a hidden option embedded in the floating-rate debt position that proponents of the comparative advantage argument fail to include. They argue that the credit spreads that exit are due to the nature of the contracts available to firms in fixed and floating markets. In the floating market, the lender usually has the opportunity to review the floating rate each period and increase the spread over the LIBOR if the borrower's creditworthiness has deteriorated. This option, though, does not usually exist in the fixed market.

In the preceding example, the lower quality Star Company is able to get a synthetic fixed rate at 10.25% (.25% less than the direct loan). However, using the hidden option argument, this 10.25% rate is only realized if Star can maintain its creditworthiness and continue to borrow at a floating rate that is 75 BP above the LIBOR. If its credit ratings were to subsequently decline, and it had to pay 150 BP above the LIBOR, then its synthetic fixed rate would increase. Moreover, studies have shown that the likelihood of default increases faster over time for lower quality companies than it does for higher quality ones. In our example, this would mean that the Star Company's credit spread is more likely to rise than the Moon Company's spread and that its expected borrowing rate is greater than the 10.25% synthetic rate. As for the higher quality Moon Company, its lower synthetic floating rate of LIBOR does not take into account the additional return necessary to compensate the company for bearing the risk of a default by the Star Company. If it borrowed floating funds directly, the Moon Company would not be bearing this risk.

17.6 SWAPS APPLICATIONS

17.6.1 Arbitrage Applications—Synthetic Positions

In the preceding case, the differences in credit spreads in the fixed-rate and floating-rate debt markets or the hidden options on the floating debt position made it possible for both corporations to obtain different rates with synthetic positions than they could with direct loans. The example represents what is commonly referred to as an arbitrage use of swaps. In general, the presence of comparative advantage or a hidden option makes it possible to create not only synthetic loans with lower rates than direct but also synthetic investments with rates exceeding those from direct investments. To illustrate this, four cases showing how swaps can be used to create synthetic fixed-rate and floating-rate loans and investments are presented following.

17.6.1.1 Synthetic Fixed-Rate Loan

Suppose a company is planning on borrowing \$50M for 5 years at a fixed-rate. Given a swap market, suppose its alternatives are to issue a 5-year, 10%, fixed rate bond paying coupons on a semiannual basis or create a synthetic fixed-rate bond by issuing a 5-year FRN paying LIBOR plus 100 BP and taking a fixed-rate payer's position on a swap with an NP of \$50M. The synthetic fixed loan will be equivalent to the direct fixed-rate loan if it is formed with a swap that has a fixed rate equal to 9%; that is, the swap rate is equal to the fixed rate on the direct loan (10%) minus the BP (100 BP) on the FRN:

Synthetic Fixed-Rate Loan		
Issue FRN	Pay LIBOR + 1%	−LIBOR − 1%
Swap: Fixed-Rate Payer's Position	Pay 9% Fixed Rate	−9%
Swap: Fixed-Rate Payer's Position	Receive LIBOR	+LIBOR
Synthetic Rate	Pay 9% + 1%	−10%
Direct Loan Rate	Pay 10%	−10%

If the company can obtain a fixed rate on a swap that is less than 9%, then the company would find it cheaper to finance with the synthetic fixed-rate loan than the direct. For example, if the company could obtain an 8%/LIBOR swap, then the company would be able to create a synthetic 9% fixed-rate loan by issuing the FRN at LIBOR plus 100 BP and taking the fixed payer's position on the swap:

```
Synthetic Fixed-Rate Loan
FRN     Pay LIBOR +1%      = −LIBOR − 1%
Swap    Pay 8%  Fixed      = −8%
Swap    Receive LIBOR      = +LIBOR
        Pay 8%+1%          = −9%

Direct Loan Rate = 10%
```

17.6.1.2 Synthetic Floating-Rate Loan

Suppose a bank has just made a 5-year, $30M floating-rate loan that is reset every 6 months at the LIBOR plus 100BP. The bank could finance this floating-rate asset by either selling CDs every 6 months at the LIBOR or by creating a synthetic floating-rate loan by selling a 5-year fixed-rate note at 9% and taking a floating-rate payer's position on a 5-year swap with an NP of $30M. The synthetic floating-rate loan will be equivalent to the direct floating-rate loan paying LIBOR if the swap has a fixed rate that is equal to the 9% fixed rate on the note:

Synthetic Floating-Rate Loan		
Issue 9% Fixed-Rate Note	Pay 9% fixed Rate	−9%
Swap: Floating-Rate Payer's Position	Pay LIBOR	−LIBOR
Swap: Floating-Rate Payer's Position	Receive 9% Fixed Rate	+9%
Synthetic Rate	Pay LIBOR	−LIBOR
Direct Loan Rate	Pay LIBOR	−LIBOR

Thus, if the bank can obtain a fixed rate on the swap that is greater than 9%, say 9.5%, then it would find it cheaper to finance its floating-rate loan asset by issuing fixed-rate notes at 9% and taking the floating-rate payer's position on the swap. By doing this, the bank's effective interest payments are 50 BP less than LIBOR with a synthetic floating-rate loan formed by selling the 9% fixed-rate note and taking a floating-rate payer's position on a 5-year, 9.5%/LIBOR swap with NP of $30M:

```
Synthetic Floating-Rate Loan
Loan    Pay 9% fixed            = −9%
Swap    Pay LIBOR               = −LIBOR
Swap    Receive 9.5% Fixed Rate = +9.5%
        Pay LIBOR−.5%           = −(LIBOR−.5% )

Rate on Direct Floating-Rate Loan = LIBOR
```

17.6.1.3 Synthetic Fixed-Rate Investment

In the early days of the swap market, swaps were primarily used as a liability management tool. In the late 1980s, investors began to use swaps to try to increase the yield on their investments. A swap used with an asset is sometimes referred to as an **asset-based interest rate swap** or simply an asset swap. In terms of synthetic positions, asset-based swaps can be used to create either fixed-rate or floating-rate investment positions.

Consider the case of a fixed-income fund that is setting up a $100M investment trust consisting of 5-year, AAA quality, option-free, fixed-rate bonds. If the YTM on such bonds is 6%, then the investment company could form the trust by simply buying $100M worth of 6% coupon bonds at par. Alternatively, it could try to earn a higher return by creating a synthetic fixed-rate bond by buying 5-year, high quality FRNs currently paying the LIBOR plus 100 BP and taking a floating-rate payer's position on a 5-year swap with an NP of $100M. If the fixed rate on the swap is equal to 5% (the 6% rate on the bonds minus the 100 BP on the FRN), then the synthetic fixed-rate investment will yield the same return as the 6% fixed-rate bonds:

Synthetic Fixed-Rate Investment

Purchase FRN	Receive LIBOR + 1%	+LIBOR + 1%
Swap: Floating-Rate Payer's Position	Pay LIBOR	−LIBOR
Swap: Floating-Rate Payer's Position	Receive 5% Fixed Rate	+5%
Synthetic Rate	Receive 5% + 1%	+6%

Direct Investment Rate | Receive 6% | +6%

If the fixed rate on the swap is greater than 5%, then the synthetic fixed-rate loan will yield a higher return than the 6% bonds. For example, if the investment company could take a floating-payer's position on a 5.75%/LIBOR swap with maturity of 5 years, NP of $100M, and effective dates coinciding with the FRNs' dates, then the investment company would earn a fixed rate of 6.75%:

Synthetic Fixed-Rate Investment		
FRN	Receive LIBOR + 1%	= LIBOR +1%
Swap	Pay LIBOR	= −LIBOR
Swap	Receive 5.75% Fixed Rate	= +5.75%
	Receive 6.75% Fixed Rate	=6.75%
Rate on Fixed-Rate Bond = 6%		

17.6.1.4 Synthetic Floating-Rate Investment

This time consider an investment fund that is looking to invest $10M for 3 years in an FRN. Suppose the fund can either invest directly in a high-quality, 5-year FRN paying LIBOR plus 50 BP, or it can create a synthetic floating-rate investment by investing in a 5-year, 7% fixed-rate note selling at par and taking a fixed-rate payer's position. If the fixed rate on the swap is equal to 6.5% (the rate on the fixed-rate note minus the BP on the direct FRN investment), then the synthetic floating-rate investment will yield the same return as the FRN:

Synthetic Floating-Rate Investment

Purchase Fixed-Rate Note	Receive 7%	+7%
Swap: Fixed-Rate Payer's Position	Pay 6.5% Fixed Rate	−6.5%
Swap: Fixed-Rate Payer's Position	Receive LIBOR	+LIBOR
Synthetic Rate	Receive LIBOR + .5%	+LIBOR + .5%

Floating Investment Rate | Receive LIBOR + .5% | +LIBOR + .5%

If the fixed rate on the swap is less than 6.5%, then the synthetic floating-rate investment will yield a higher return than the FRN. For example, the fund could obtain a yield of LIBOR plus 100 BP from a synthetic floating-rate investment formed with an investment in the 5-year, 7% fixed-rate note and fixed-rate payer's position on a 6%/LIBOR swap:

Synthetic FRN		
Fixed-Rate Bond	Receive 7%	= +7%
Swap	Receive LIBOR	= +LIBOR
Swap	Pay 6% Fixed Rate	= −6%
	Receive LIBOR + 1%	= LIBOR + 1%
Rate on Direct FRN = LIBOR + .5%		

17.6.2 Hedging

Initially, interest rate swaps were used primarily in arbitrage strategies. Today, there is an increased use of swaps for hedging. Hedging with swaps is done primarily to minimize the market risk of positions currently exposed to interest rate changes. For example, suppose a company had previously financed its capital projects with intermediate-term FRNs tied to the LIBOR. Furthermore, suppose the company was expecting higher interest rates and wanted to fix the rate on its floating-rate debt. To this end, one alternative would be for the company to refund its floating-rate debt with fixed-rate obligations. This, though, would require the cost of issuing new debt (underwriting, registration, etc.) as well as the cost of calling the current FRNs or buying the notes in the market if they were not callable. Thus, refunding would be a relatively costly alternative. Another possibility would be for the company to hedge its floating-rate debt with a strip of short Eurodollar futures contracts. This alternative is relatively inexpensive, but there may be hedging risk. The third and perhaps obvious alternative would be to combine the company's FRNs with a fixed-rate payer's position on a swap, thereby creating a synthetic fixed-rate debt position. This alternative of hedging FRNs with swaps, in turn, is less expensive and more efficient than the first alternative of refinancing; plus, it can also effectively minimize hedging risk.

An opposite scenario to the preceding case would be a company that has intermediate to long-term fixed-rate debt that it wants to make floating either because of a change in its economic structure or because it expects rates will be decreasing. Given the costs of refunding fixed-rate debt with floating-rate debt and the hedging risk problems with futures, the most efficient way for the company to meet this objective would be to create synthetic floating-rate debt by combining its fixed-rate debt with a floating-rate payer's position on a swap.

17.6.3 Speculation

Because swaps are similar to Eurodollar futures contracts, they can be used like them to speculate on short-term interest rate movements. Specifically, as an alternative to a Eurodollar futures strip, speculators who expect short-term rates to increase in the future can take a fixed-rate payer's position; in contrast, speculators who expect short-term rates to decrease can take a floating-rate payer's position. Note, though, that there are differences in maturity, size, and marketability between futures and swaps that need to be taken into account when considering which one to use.

For financial and nonfinancial corporations, speculative positions often take the form of the company changing the exposure of its balance sheet to interest rate changes. For example, suppose a fixed-income bond fund with a portfolio measured against a bond index wanted to increase the duration of its portfolio relative to the index's duration based on an expectation of lower interest rates across all maturities. The fund could do this by selling its short-term Treasuries and buying longer term ones or by taking long positions in

Treasury futures. With swaps, the fund could also change its portfolio's duration by taking a floating-rate payer's position on a swap. If they did this and rates were to decrease as expected, then not only would the value of the company's bond portfolio increase, but the company would also profit from the swap; on the other hand, if rates were to increase, then the company would see decreases in the value of its bond portfolio as well as losses from its swap positions. By adding swaps, though, the fund has effectively increased its interest rate exposure by increasing its duration.

Instead of increasing its portfolio's duration, the fund may want to reduce or minimized the bond portfolio's interest rate exposure based on an expectation of higher interest rates. In this case, the fund could effectively shorten the duration of its bond fund by taking a fixed-rate payer's position on a swap. If rates were to later increase, then the decline in the value of the company's bond portfolio would be offset by the cash inflow realized from the fixed-payer's position on the swap.

17.7 CREDIT RISK

When compared to their equivalent fixed and floating bond positions, swaps have less credit risk. To see this, suppose one party to a swap defaults. Typically, the swap contract allows the nondefaulting party the right to give up to a 20-day notice that a particular date will be the termination date.[2] This notice gives the parties time to determine a settlement amount. The settlement amount depends on the value of an existing swap or equivalently on the terms of a replacement swap. For example, suppose the fixed payer on a 9.5%/LIBOR swap with NP of $10M runs into severe financial problems and defaults on the swap agreement when there are 3 years and six payments remaining and the LIBOR is now relatively low. Suppose the current 3-year swap calls for an exchange of 9% fixed for LIBOR. To replace the defaulted swap, the nondefaulting floating payer would have to take a new floating position on the 9%/LIBOR swap or sell it to a swap bank who would hedge the assumed swap with the floating position. As a result, she or the swap bank would be receiving only $450,000 each period instead of the $475,000 on the defaulted swap. Thus, the default represents a semiannual loss of $25,000 for 3 years. Using 9% as the discount rate, the present value of this loss would be $128,947:

$$PV = \sum_{t=1}^{6} \frac{\$25,000}{(1+(.09/2))^t} = \$128,947$$

Thus, given a replacement fixed swap rate of 9%, the actual credit risk exposure is $128,947. The replacement value of $128,947 is also the economic value of the original 9.5%/LIBOR swap.

Note that if the replacement fixed swap rate had been 10% instead of 9%, then the floating payer would have had a positive economic value of $126,892:

$$PV = \sum_{t=1}^{6} \frac{\$25,000}{(1+(.10/2))^t} = \$126,892$$

Under a higher interest rate scenario, the fixed payer experiencing the financial distress would not have defaulted on the swap, although he may be defaulting on other obligations.

---

[2] Swaps fall under contract law and not security law. The mechanism for default is governed by the swap contract, with many patterned after International Swap and Derivatives Association (ISDA) documents.

The increase in rates in this case has made the swap an asset to the fixed payer instead of a liability.

The example illustrates that two events are necessary for default loss on a swap: an actual default on the agreement and an adverse change in rates. Credit risk on a swap is therefore a function of the joint probability of financial distress and adverse interest rate movements.

In practice, credit risk is often managed by adjusting the negotiated fixed rate on a swap to include a credit risk spread between the parties: A less risky firm (which could be the swap bank acting as dealer) will pay a lower fixed rate or receive a higher fixed rate the riskier the counterparty. The credit rate adjustment also takes into account the probability of rates increasing and decreasing and its impact on the future economic value of the couterparty's swap position. In addition to rate adjustments, swap dealers can also manage credit risk by requiring collateral and maintenance margins.

It should be noted that historically, the default rate on swaps has been very small. This reflects the fact that swap agreements are made by financial institutions and relatively large companies with good credit ratings.

17.8   CONCLUSION

In this chapter, we have examined the market, uses, and valuations of generic interest rate swaps. Swaps provide investors and borrowers with a tool for more effectively managing their asset and liability positions. They have become a basic financial engineering tool to apply to a variety of financial problems. Over the years, the underlying structure of the generic swap has been modified in a number of ways to accommodate different uses. In the next chapter, we examine swap derivatives—forward swaps and swaptions—and show how they can be used to manage fixed-income positions. In Chapter 19, we examine the valuation of generic off-market swaps, forward swaps, and swaptions.

KEY TERMS

interest rate swap	settlement (or payment date)	swap rate
currency swap	maturity date	comparative advantage
plain vanilla swap (or generic swap)	net settlement basis	asset-based interest rate swap
counterparties	confirmation	par value swap
fixed-rate payer	International Swap and Derivative Association	off-market swap
floating-rate payer	dealer swaps	YTM approach
trade date	running a dynamic book	zero-coupon approach
effective date		

SELECTED REFERENCES

Bhattacharya, A. K., and F. J. Fabozzi. "Interest-Rate Swaps." In *The Handbook of Fixed Income Securities*, 6th ed., edited by F. Fabozzi, XX–XX. New York: McGraw-Hill, 2001.

Bicksler, J., and A. H. Chen. "An Economic Analysis of Interest Rate Swaps." *Journal of Finance* 41 (1986): 645–655.

Brown, K. C., and D. J. Smith. "Plain Vanilla Swaps: Market Structures, Applications, and Credit Risk." In *Interest Rate Swaps,* edited by C. R. Beidleman. Homewood, IL: Business One Irwin, 1991.

Cooper, I., and A. S. Mello. "The Default Risk of Swaps." *Journal of Finance* 48 (1991): 597–620.

Darby, M. R. Over-the-Counter Derivatives and Systemic Risk to the Global Financial System. National Bureau of Economic Research Working Paper Series 4801, 1994.

Goodman, L. S. "Capital Market Applications of Interest Rate Swaps." In *Interest Rate Swaps,* edited by C. R. Beidleman. Homewood, IL: Business One Irwin, 1991.

Haubrich, J. G. "Swaps and the Swaps Yield Curve," *Economic Commentary*, Federal Reserve Bank of Cleveland (December 2001): 1–4.

Iben, B. "Chapter 12: Interest Rate Swap Evaluation." In *Interest Rate Swaps,* edited by C. R. Beidleman. Homewood, IL: Business One Irwin, 1991.

Johnson, R. S. *Bond Evaluation, Selection, and Management*. Walden MA: Blackwell Publishing, 2004, Chapter 16.

Kawaller, I. B. "A Swap Alternative: Eurodollar Strips." In *Interest Rate Swaps,* edited by C. R. Beidleman. Homewood, IL: Business One Irwin, 1991.

Litzenberger, R. H., "Swaps: Plain and Fanciful." *Journal of Finance* 47 (1992): 831–50.

Marshall, J. F., and K. R. Kapner. *Understanding Swaps*. New York: Wiley, 1993.

Pergam, A. S. "Swaps: A Legal Perspective." In *The Handbook of Interest Rate Risk Management,* edited by J. C. Francis and A. S. Wolf. New York: Irwin Professional Publishing, 1994.

Smith, D. J. "Aggressive Corporate Finance: A Close Look at the Procter and Gamble-Bankers Trust Leveraged Swap." *Journal of Derivatives* 4 (Summer 1997): 67–79.

Smith, C. W., C. W. Smithson, and L. M. Wakeman. "The Evolving Market for Swaps." *Midland Corporate Finance Journal* 3 (1986): 20–32.

Smith, C. W., C. W. Smithson, and L. M. Wakeman. "The Market for Interest Rate Swaps." *Financial Management* 17 (1988): 34–44.

Sun, T., S. Sundaresan, and C. Wang. "Interest Rate Swaps: An Empirical Investigation." *Journal of Financial Economics* 36 (1993): 77–99.

Titman, S. "Interest Rate Swaps and Corporate Financing Choices." *Journal of Finance* 47 (1992): 1503–16.

Turnbull, S. M. "Swaps: A Zero Sum Game." *Financial Management* 16 (Spring 1987): 15–21.

Wall, L. D., and J. J. Pringle. "Alternative Explanations of Interest Rate Swaps: A Theoretical and Empirical Analysis." *Financial Management* 18 (Summer 1989): 59–73.

PROBLEMS AND QUESTIONS

1. Given the following interest-rate swap:
   - Fixed-rate payer pays half of the YTM on a T-note of 5.5%
   - Floating-rate payer pays the LIBOR
   - Notional principal is $10M
   - Effective dates are 3/1 and 9/1 for the next 3 years

   Questions:

   a. Determine the net receipts of the fixed-rate and floating-rate payers given the following LIBORs:
      - 3/1/y1   .045
      - 9/1/y1   .050
      - 3/1/y2   .055
      - 9/1/y2   .060
      - 3/1/y3   .065
      - 9/1/y3   .070

   b. Show in a table how a company with a 3-year, $10M floating-rate loan, with the rate set by the LIBOR on the dates coinciding with the swap, could make the loan a fixed-rate one by taking a position in the swap. What would be the fixed rate?

   c. Show in a table how a company with a 3-year, $10M fixed rate loan at 5.0% could make the loan a floating-rate one by taking a position in the swap.

2. Explain how the fixed payer and floating payer positions in Question 1 could be replicated with positions in fixed-rate and floating-rate bonds.

3. What positions in a Eurodollar futures strip would be similar to the fixed-payer and floating-payer positions in Question 1? Show in the table following the cash flows for each strip position given the LIBOR scenario in Question 1. Note that the interest payments on the swap are determined by the LIBOR at the beginning of the period, whereas the futures position's cash flows are based on the LIBOR at the end of its period.

Eurodollar Closing Dates	LIBOR	f_T	Cash Flow From Short Position	Cash Flow From Long Position
3/1/y1	.045			
9/1/y1	.050			
3/1/y2	.055			
9/1/y2	.060			
3/1/y3	.065			
9/1/y3	.070			

4. Explain some of the differences between a plain vanilla swap position and a Eurodollar strip.

5. Using a table showing payments and receipts, prove that the following positions are equivalent:
   a. Floating-rate loan plus fixed-rate payer's position is equivalent to a fixed-rate loan.
   b. Fixed-rate loan plus floating-rate payer's position is equivalent to a floating-rate loan.
   c. Floating-rate note investment plus floating-rate payer's position is equivalent to a fixed-rate investment.
   d. Fixed-rate bond investment plus fixed-rate payer's position is equivalent to a floating-rate investment.

6. What are the dealer's bid and ask quotes on a 3-year swap with a quoted 50/60 swap spread over a T-note with a yield of 5.5%?

7. The following table shows a swap bank's quotes on four generic swaps:

Swap	Swap Maturity	Treasury Yield	Bid Swap Spread (BP)	Ask Swap Spread (BP)	Fixed Swap Rate Spread	Swap Rate
1	2 years	5.00%	50	70		
2	3 years	5.10%	60	65		
3	4 years	5.20%	65	68		
4	5 years	5.30%	70	72		

   a. Complete the table by calculating the swap bank's fixed swap rate spreads and swap rates for the four swaps.

   b. Explain in more detail the positions the swap bank is willing to take on the first swap contract.

    c. Describe the swap arrangement for a swap bank customer who took a floating-rate payer's position with a notional principal of $50M on the third swap contract offered by the bank.

    d. Suppose two of the swap bank's customers take fixed-rate payer positions on the third contract offered by the bank, each with a notional principal of $25M. Show in a flow diagram the contracts between the swap bank and these customers and its customer in Question c.

8. Explain the alternative ways a swap holder could close her swap position instead of selling it to a swap bank.

9. If the fixed rate on a new par value, 2-year swap were at 5%, how much would a swap dealer pay or charge to assume an existing fixed-payer's position on a 6%/LIBOR generic swap with 2 years left to maturity and notional principal of $10M? How much would the dealer pay or charge if the fixed rate on a new par value 2-year swap were at 7%?

10. If the fixed rate on a new par value, 2-year swap were at 5%, how much would a swap dealer pay or charge for assuming an existing 6%/LIBOR floating-rate position on a generic swap with 2 years left to maturity and notional principal of $10M? How much would the dealer pay or charge if the fixed rate on a new par value 2-year swap were at 7%?

11. The Corsi Development Company is looking for 5-year funding to finance its proposed $350M shopping mall development. Based on its moderate credit ratings, Corsi can borrow 5-year funds at a 9.5% fixed rate or at a floating rate equal to LIBOR + 75 BP. Given the choice of financing, Corsi prefers the fixed-rate loan. The GP Consumer Products Company also wants to raise $350M with a 5-year loan to finance an expansion of one of its production facilities. Given its higher credit rating, suppose GP can borrow the funds for 5 years at a fixed rate of 8.5% or at a floating rate equal to the LIBOR + 25 BP. Given the choice, GP prefers a floating-rate loan. In summary, Corsi and GP have the following fixed and floating rate loan alternatives:

Company	Fixed Rate	Floating Rate
Corsi Company	9.5%	LIBOR + 75 BP
GP Company	8.5%	LIBOR + 25 BP

    a. Describe the GP Company's absolute advantage and each company's comparative advantage?

    b. What is the total possible interest rate reduction for both parties if each were to create a synthetic position with a swap?

    c. Explain how a swap bank could arrange a 5-year, 8.5%/LIBOR swap that would benefit both the Corsi and GP companies. What is the total interest rate reduction gain, and how is it split?

12. Suppose the Corsi and GP companies in Question 11 both have the same quality ratings with the following fixed- and floating-rate loan alternatives:

Company	Fixed Rate	Floating Rate
Corsi Company	9.50%	LIBOR + 50 BP
GP Company	9.25%	LIBOR + 75 BP

    a. Describe each company's absolute and comparative advantages.

    b. What is the total possible interest rate reduction for both parties if each were to create a synthetic position with a swap?

    c. Explain how a swap bank could arrange a 5-year swap in which Corsi and GP split the total interest rate reduction gain.

13. Explain the idea of comparative advantage in terms of Questions 11 and 12.

14. Explain the idea of hidden options in terms of Question 11.

15. Suppose a company wants to borrow $300M for 5 years at a fixed rate. Suppose the company can issue either a 5-year, 10%, fixed-rate bond paying coupons on a semiannual basis and a 5-year FRN paying LIBOR plus 100 BP.

    a. Explain how the company could create a synthetic 5-year, fixed-rate loan with a swap.

    b. What would the fixed rate on the swap have to be for the synthetic position to be equivalent to the direct loan position? Show the synthetic position in a table.

    c. Define the company's criterion for selecting the synthetic loan.

16. Suppose a financial institution wants to finance its 3-year, $300M, floating-rate loans by selling 3-year floating-rate notes. Suppose the institution can issue a 3-year, 6%, fixed rate note paying coupons on a semiannual basis and also a 3-year FRN paying LIBOR plus 100 BP.

    a. Explain how the institution could create a synthetic 3-year floating-rate note with a swap.

    b. What would the fixed rate on the swap have to be for the synthetic position to be equivalent to the floating-rate note? Show the synthetic position in a table.

    c. Define the institution's criterion for selecting the synthetic loan.

17. Suppose a financial institution wants to invest $300M in a 3-year fixed-rate note. Suppose the institution can invest in a 3-year, 6%, fixed-rate note paying coupons on a semiannual basis and selling at par and also in a 3-year FRN paying LIBOR plus 100 BP.

    a. Explain how the institution could create a synthetic 3-year fixed-rate note with a swap.

    b. What would the fixed rate on the swap have to be for the synthetic position to be equivalent to the fixed-rate note? Show the synthetic position in a table.

    c. Define the institution's criterion for selecting the synthetic investment.

18. Suppose a financial institution wants to invest $300M in a 3-year floating-rate note. Suppose the institution can invest either in a 3-year, 6%, fixed-rate note paying coupons on a semiannual basis and selling at par or in a 3-year FRN paying LIBOR plus 100 BP.

    a. Explain how the institution could create a synthetic 3-year floating-rate note with a swap.

    b. What would the fixed rate on the swap have to be for the synthetic position to be equivalent to the floating-rate note? Show the synthetic position in a table.

    c. Define the institution's criterion for selecting the synthetic investment.

19. Given a generic 5-year par value swap with a fixed rate of 5%, determine the values of the following off-market swap positions using the YTM approach:

    a. Fixed-rate position on a 5-year, 4%/LIBOR generic swap with NP = $100M

    b. Floating-rate position on a 5-year, 4%/LIBOR generic swap with NP = $100M

c. Fixed-rate position on a 5-year, 6%/LIBOR generic swap with NP = $100M

d. Floating-rate position on a 5-year, 6%/LIBOR generic swap with NP = $100M

20. Short-Answer Questions
1. Who generally assumes the credit risk in a brokered swap?
2. Who assumes the credit risk in a dealer's swap?
3. What is one of the problems with brokered swaps that contributed to the growth in the dealer-swap market?
4. What does the term warehousing mean?
5. What does the term running a dynamic book mean?
6. How do dealers typically quote the fixed rate and floating rate on a swap agreement they offer?
7. Describe the comparative advantage argument that is often advanced as the reason for the growth in the swap market.
8. What is the criticism that is often made against the comparative advantage argument?
9. What is the hidden option and how does it relate to a difference in credit spreads in the fixed and floating credit markets?
10. Explain how a company could take a swap position to replace its current floating-rate debt with a fixed-rate debt obligation.
11. Explain how a company could take a swap position to replace its current fixed-rate debt with a floating-rate debt obligation.
12. Explain how a company with investments in intermediate fixed-rate notes could take a swap position to create a floating-rate note. Why might a company want to do this?

WEB EXERCISES

1. Find out who the International Swap and Derivatives Association is by going to their Web site, www.isda.org and clicking on "About ISDA." At the site, also click on "Educational" to find a bibliography of swaps and derivatives articles and links to other derivative sites.

2. Examine the growth in the interest rate swap market by looking at the International Swap and Derivatives Association's Market Survey. Go to www.isda.org and click on "Survey and Market Statistics."

CHAPTER 18

SWAP DERIVATIVES: FORWARD SWAPS AND SWAPTIONS

18.1 INTRODUCTION

Since the mid-1980s there has been an active and growing swap market among financial and nonfinancial corporations. Concomitant with this growth has been the number of innovations introduced in swaps contracts over the years. Today, there are a number of nonstandard or nongeneric swaps used by financial and nonfinancial corporations to manage their varied cash flow and return-risk positions. Two of most widely used nongeneric swaps are the *forward swap* and options on swaps or *swaptions.* A forward swap is an agreement to enter into a swap that starts at a future date at an interest rate agreed on today. A swaption, in turn, is a right, but not an obligation, to take a position on a swap at a specific swap rate. In this chapter, we examine these two interest rate swap derivatives.

18.2 FORWARD SWAPS

Like futures contracts on debt securities, forward swaps provide borrowers and investors with a tool for locking in a future interest rate. As such, they can be used to manage interest rate risk for both debt and fixed-income positions.

18.2.1 Hedging a Future Loan With a Forward Swap

Financial and nonfinancial institutions that have future borrowing obligations can lock in a future rate by obtaining forward contracts on fixed-payer swap positions. For example, a company wishing to lock in a rate on a 5-year, fixed-rate $100M loan to start 2 years from today could enter a 2-year forward swap agreement to pay the fixed rate on a 5-year 9%/LIBOR swap. At the expiration date on the forward swap, the company could issue floating-rate debt at LIBOR that when combined with the fixed position on the swap would provide the company with a synthetic fixed rate loan paying 9% on the floating debt:

At the expiration date on the forward swap:

Instrument	Action	
Issue Flexible Rate Note	Pay	−LIBOR
Swap: Fixed-Rate Payer's Position	Pay Fixed Rate	−9%
Swap: Fixed-Rate Payer's Position	Receive LIBOR	+LIBOR
Synthetic Fixed Rate	Net Payment	9%

Alternatively, at the forward swap's expiration date, the company is more likely to sell the 5-year 9%/LIBOR swap underlying the forward swap contract and issue 5-year fixed-rate debt. If the rate on 5-year fixed-rate bonds were higher than 9%, for example, at 10%, then the company would be able offset the higher interest by selling its fixed position on the 9%/LIBOR swap to a swap dealer for an amount equal to the present value of a 5-year annuity equal to 1% (difference in rates: 10%–9%) times the NP. For example, at 10%, the value of the underlying 9%/LIBOR swap would be $3.8609M using the YTM swap valuation approach:

$$SV^{fix} = \left[\sum_{t=1}^{10} \frac{(.10/2) - (.09/2)}{(1 + (.10/2))^t}\right] \$100M = \$3.8609M$$

With the proceeds of $3.8609M from closing its swap, the company would only need to raise $96.1391M (= $100M − $3.8609M). The company, though, would have to issue $96.1391M worth of 5-year fixed-rate bonds at the higher 10% rate. This would result in semiannual interest payments of $4.8070M (= (.10/2)($96.1391)), and the interest rate based on the $100M funds needed would be approximately 9%.

In contrast, if the rate on 5-year fixed-rate loans were lower than 9%, say 8%, then the company would benefit from the lower fixed-rate loan but would lose an amount equal to the present value of a 5-year annuity equal to 1% (difference in rates: 8%–9%) times the NP when it closed the fixed position. Specifically, at 8%, the value of the underlying 9%/LIBOR swap is $4.055M using the YTM approach:

$$SV^{fix} = \left[\sum_{t=1}^{10} \frac{(.08/2) - (.09/2)}{(1 + (.08/2))^t}\right] \$100M = -\$4.055M$$

The company would therefore have to pay the swap bank $4.055M for assuming its fixed-payers position. With a payment of $4.055M, the company would need to raise a total of $104.055M from its bond issue. The company, though, would be able to issue $104.055M worth of 5-year fixed-rate bonds at the lower rate of 8%. Its semiannual interest payments would be $4.1622 (= (.08/2)($104.055)), and its rate based on the $100M funds needed would be approximately 9%.

18.2.2 Hedging a Future Investment

Instead of locking in the rate on a future liability, forward swaps can also be used on the asset side to fix the rate on a future investment. Consider the case of an institutional investor planning to invest an expected $10M cash inflow 1 year from now in a 3-year, high–quality, fixed-rate bond. The investor could lock in the future rate by entering a 1-year forward swap agreement to receive the fixed rate and pay the floating rate on a 3-year, 9%/LIBOR swap with an NP of $10M. At the expiration date on the forward swap, the investor could invest the $10M cash inflow in a 3-year FRN at LIBOR, which, when combined with the floating position on the swap, would provide the investor with a synthetic fixed-rate investment paying 9%:

At the expiration date on the forward swap:

Instrument	Action	
Buy Flexible Rate Note	Receive	LIBOR
Swap: Floating-Rate Payer's Position	Pay LIBOR	−LIBOR
Swap: Floating-Rate Payer's Position	Receive Fixed Rate	+9%
Synthetic Fixed Rate Investment	Net Receipt	9%

Instead of a synthetic fixed investment position, the investor is more likely to sell the 3-year 9%/LIBOR swap underlying the forward swap contract and invest in a 3-year fixed-rate note. If the rate on the 3-year fixed-rate note were lower than the 9% swap rate, then the investor would be able sell his floating position at a value equal to the present value of an annuity equal to the $10M NP times the difference between 9% and the rate on 3-year fixed-rate bonds; this gain would offset the lower return on the fixed-rate bond. For example, if at the forward swap's expiration date, the rate on 3-year, fixed-rate bonds were at 8%, and the fixed rate on a 3-year par value swap were at 8%, then the investment firm would be able to sell its floating-payer's position on the 3-year 9%/LIBOR swap underlying the forward swap contract to a swap bank for $262,107 (using the YTM approach with a discount rate of 8%):

$$SV^{fl} = \left[\sum_{t=1}^{6} \frac{(.09/2) - (.08/2)}{(1 + (.08/2))^t} \right] \$10,000,000 = \$262,107$$

The investment firm would therefore invest $10M plus the $262,107 proceeds from closing its swap in 3-year, fixed-rate bonds yielding 8%. The yield on an investment of $10M, though, would be approximately equal to 9%.

On the other hand, if the rate on 3-year fixed-rate securities were higher than 9%, the investment company would benefit from the higher investment rate but would lose when it closed its swap position. For example, if at the forward swap's expiration date, the rate on 3-year, fixed-rate bonds were at 10%, and the fixed rate on a 3-year par value swap were at 10%, then the investment firm would have to pay the swap bank $253,785 for assuming its floating-payers position on the 3-year 9%/LIBOR swap underlying the forward swap contract:

$$SV^{fl} = \left[\sum_{t=1}^{6} \frac{(.09/2) - (.10/2)}{(1 + (.10/2))^t} \right] \$10,000,000 = -\$253,785$$

The investment firm would therefore invest $9,746,215 ($10M minus the $253,785 costs incurred in closing its swap) in 3-year, fixed rate bonds yielding 10%. The yield on an investment of $10M, though, would be approximately equal to 9%.

18.2.3 Other Uses of Forward Swaps

The examples illustrate that forward swaps are like futures on debt securities. As such, they are used in many of the same ways as futures: locking in future interest rates, speculating on future interest rate changes, and altering a balance sheet's exposure to interest rate changes. Different from futures, though, forward swaps can be customized to fit a particular investment or borrowing need, and with the starting dates on forward swaps ranging anywhere from 1 month to several years, they can be applied to not only short-run but also long-run positions.

18.3 SWAPTIONS

One of the most innovative nongeneric swaps is the swap option or simply swaption. As the name suggests, a swaption is an option on a swap. The purchaser of a swaption buys the right to start an interest rate swap with a specific fixed rate or exercise rate and with a maturity at or during a specific time period in the future. If the holder exercises, she takes the swap position, with the swap seller obligated to take the opposite counterparty position. For swaptions, the underlying instrument is a forward swap, and the option premium is the up-front fee. The swaption can be either a right to be a payer or the right to be receiver of the fixed rate. A *receiver swaption* gives the holder the right to enter a particular swap agreement as the fixed-rate receiver (and floating-rate payer), whereas a *payer swaption* gives the holder the right to enter a particular swap as the fixed-rate payer (and floating-rate receiver). Finally, swaptions can be either European or American.

Swaptions are similar to interest rate options or options on debt securities. They are, however, more varied: They can range from options to begin a 1-year swap in 3 months to a 10-year option on an 8-year swap (sometimes referred to as a 10×8 swaption); the exercise periods can vary for American swaptions, and swaptions can be written on generic swaps or nongeneric. Like interest rate and debt options, swaptions can be used for speculating on interest rates, hedging debt and asset positions against market risk, and managing a balance sheet's exposure to interest rate changes. In addition, like swaps they also can be used in combination with other securities to create synthetic positions.

18.3.1 Speculation

Suppose a speculator expects the rates on high quality, 5-year fixed rate bonds to increase from their current 8% level. As an alternative to a short T-note futures or an interest rate call position, the speculator could buy a payer swaption. Suppose she elects to buy a 1-year European payer swaption on a 5-year, 8%/LIBOR swap with an NP of $10M for 50 BP times the NP; that is

- 1×5 payer swaption
- Exercise date = 1 year
- Exercise rate = 8%
- Underlying swap = 5-year, 8%/LIBOR with NP = $10M
- Swap position = fixed payer
- Option premium = 50 BP times NP

On the exercise date, if the fixed rate on a 5-year swap were greater than the exercise rate of 8%, then the speculator would exercise her right to pay the fixed rate below the market rate. To realize the gain, she could take her 8% fixed-rate payer's swap position obtained from exercising and sell it to another counterparty. For example, if current 5-year par value swaps were trading at 9%, and swaps were valued by the YTM approach, then she would be able to sell her 8% swap for $395,636:

$$\text{Value of Swap} = \left[\sum_{t=1}^{10} \frac{(.09/2) - (.08/2)}{(1 + (.09/2))^t} \right] (\$10M) = \$395,636$$

Alternatively, she could exercise and then enter into a reverse swap; for example, at the current swap rate of 8%, she could take the floating-payer's position on a 5-year, 8%/LIBOR swap. By doing this, she would receive an annuity equal to 1% of the NP for 5 years (or .5% semiannually for 10 periods), which has a current value of $395,636:

From Payer swaption:		
Swap: Fixed-Rate Payer's Position	Pay	8% per year for 5 years
Swap: Fixed-Rate Payer's Position	Receive	LIBOR

From Replacement Swap:		
Swap: Floating-Rate Payer's Position	Receive	9% per year for 5 years
Swap: Floating-Rate Payer's Position	Pay	LIBOR

Net Position	Receive	1% per year for 5 years

If the swap rate at the expiration date were less than 8%, then the payer swaption would have no value, and the speculator would simply let it expire, losing the premium she paid.

More formally, the value of the payer swaption at expiration is

$$\text{Value of Payer Swaption} = \left[\sum_{t=1}^{10} \frac{\text{Max}[(R/2) - (.08/2), 0]}{(1 + (R/2))^t}\right](\$10\text{M})$$

For rates, R, on par value 5-year swaps exceeding the exercise rate of 8%, the value of the payer swaption will be equal to the present value of the interest differential times the notional principal on the swap, and for rates less than 8%, the swap is worthless. Exhibit 18.3-1 shows graphically and in a table the values and profits at expiration obtained from closing the payer swaption on the 5-year 8%/LIBOR swap given different rates at expiration.

Instead of higher rates, suppose the speculator expects rates on 5-year high-quality bonds to be lower 1 year from now. In this case, her strategy would be to buy a receiver swaption. If she bought a receiver swaption similar in terms to the preceding payer swaption (a 1-year receiver option on a 5-year, 8%/LIBOR swap for $50,000), and the swap rate on a 5-year swap were less than 8% on the exercise date, then she would realize a gain from exercising and then either selling the floating-payer position or combining it with a fixed-payer's position on a replacement swap. For example, if the fixed rate on a 5-year par value swap were 7%, the investor would exercise her receiver swaption by taking the 8% floating-rate payer's swap and then sell the position to a swap bank or another party. With the current swap rate at 7%, she would be able to sell the 8% floating-payer's position for $415,830:

$$\text{Value of Swap} = \left[\sum_{t=1}^{10} \frac{(.08/2) - (.07/2)}{(1 + (.07/2))^t}\right](\$10\text{M}) = \$415,830$$

Alternatively, the swaption investor could exercise and then enter into a reverse swap. At the swap rate of 8%, she could take the fixed-payer's position on a 5-year, 8%/LIBOR swap. By doing this, the investor would receive an annuity equal to 1% of the NP for 5 years. The value of the annuity would be $415,830:

From Receiver Swaption:		
Swap: Floating-Rate Payer's Position	Pay	LIBOR
Swap: Floating-Rate Payer's Position	Receive	8% per year for 5 years

From Replacement Swap:		
Swap: Fixed-Rate Payer's Position	Receive	LIBOR
Swap: Fixed-Rate Payer's Position	Pay	7% per year for 5 years

Net Position	Receive	1% per year for 5 years

Thus, if rates were at 7%, then the investor would realize a profit of $365,830 (= $415,830 − $50,000) from the receiver swaption. If the swap rate were higher than 8% on the exercise

EXHIBIT 18.3-1   Value and Profit at Expiration From 8%/LIBOR Payer Swaption

Rates on 5-year Par Value Swaps at Expiration: R	Payer Swaption's Interest Differential Max((R − .08)/2,0)	Value of 8%/LIBOR Payer Swaption at Expiation: PV(Max[(R − .08)/2, 0]($10M))	Payer Swaption Cost	Profit from Payer Swaption
0.060	0.0000	$0	$50,000	−$50,000
0.065	0.0000	$0	$50,000	−$50,000
0.070	0.0000	$0	$50,000	−$50,000
0.075	0.0000	$0	$50,000	−$50,000
0.080	0.0000	$0	$50,000	−$50,000
0.085	0.0025	$200,272	$50,000	$150,272
0.090	0.0050	$395,636	$50,000	$345,636
0.095	0.0075	$586,226	$50,000	$536,226
0.100	0.0100	$772,173	$50,000	$722,173

$$\text{Value of Swap} = \left[\sum_{t=1}^{10} \frac{\text{Max}[(R/2) - (.08/2), 0]}{(1 + (R/2))^t} \right] (\$10M)$$

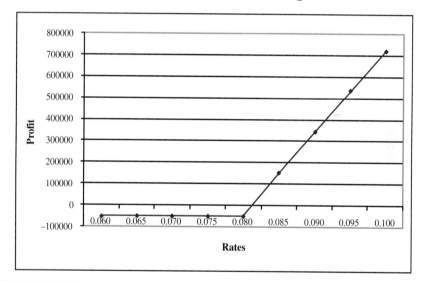

date, then the investor would allow the receiver swaption to expire, losing, in turn, her premium of $50,000.

Formally, the value of the 8%/LIBOR receiver swaption at expiration is

$$\text{Value of Receiver Swaption} = \left[\sum_{t=1}^{10} \frac{\text{Max}[(.08/2) - (R/2), 0]}{(1 + (R/2))^t} \right] (\$10M)$$

For rates, R, on par value 5-year swaps less than the exercise rate of 8%, the value of the receiver swaption will be equal to the present value of the interest differential times the NP on the swap; and for rates greater that 8%, the swap is worthless. Exhibit 18.3-2 shows graphically and in a table the values and profits at expiration obtained from

EXHIBIT 18.3-2   Value and Profit at Expiration From 8%/LIBOR Receiver Swaption

Rates on 5-year Par Value Swaps at Expiration R	Receiver Swaption's Interest Differential Max((.08 − R)/2,0)	Value of 8%/LIBOR Receiver Swaption at Expiation PV(Max[(.08 − R) /2, 0]($10M))	Receiver Swaption Cost	Profit from Receiver Swaption
0.060	0.0100	$853,020	$50,000	$803,020
0.065	0.0075	$631,680	$50,000	$581,680
0.070	0.0050	$415,830	$50,000	$365,830
0.075	0.0025	$205,320	$50,000	$155,320
0.080	0.0000	$0	$50,000	−$50,000
0.085	0.0000	$0	$50,000	−$50,000
0.090	0.0000	$0	$50,000	−$50,000
0.095	0.0000	$0	$50,000	−$50,000
0.100	0.0000	$0	$50,000	−$50,000

$$\text{Value of Swap} = \left[\sum_{t=1}^{10} \frac{\text{Max}[(.08/2) - (R/2), 0]}{(1 + (R/2))^t} \right] (\$10M)$$

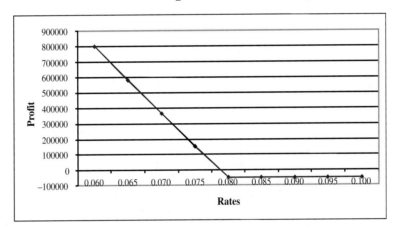

closing the receiver swaption on the 5-year 8%/LIBOR swap given different rates at expiration.

18.3.2 Hedging

18.3.2.1 Caps and Floors on Future Debt and Investment Positions

Like other option hedging tools, swaptions give investors and borrowers protection against adverse price or interest rate movements while allowing them to benefit if prices or rates move in their favor. Because receiver swaptions increase in value as rates decrease below the exercise rate, they can be used to establish floors on the rates of return obtained from future fixed-income investments. In contrast, because payer swaptions increase in value as rates increase above the exercise rate, they can be used for capping the rates paid on debt positions.

To illustrate how receiver swaption are used for establishing a floor, consider the case of a fixed-income investment fund that has a Treasury bond portfolio worth $30M in par value that is scheduled to mature in 2 years. Suppose the fund plans to reinvest the $30M in principal for another 3 years in Treasury notes that are currently trading to yield 6% but is worried that interest rate could be lower in 2 years. To establish a floor on its investment, suppose the fund purchased a 2-year receiver swaption on a 3-year, 6%/LIBOR, generic swap with a notional principal of $30M from First Bank for $100,000. Two years later, the swaption's value will be greater the lower the interest rate provided rates are less than 6%; this in turn offsets the lower investment rates and yields a fixed rate on the investment of approximately 6%. On the other hand, for rates higher than 6%, the swaption is worthless, whereas the investment's yield increases as rates increase. Thus, for the cost of $100,000, the receiver swaption provides the fund a floor with a rate of 6%.

In contrast to the use of swaptions to establish a floor on a future investment, suppose a firm had a future debt obligation whose rate it wants to cap. In this case, the firm could purchase a payer swaption. For example, suppose a company has a $60M, 9% fixed-rate bond obligation maturing in 3 years that it plans to refinance by issuing new 5-year fixed-rate bonds. Suppose the company is worried that interest rate could increase in 3 years and as a result wants to establish a cap on the rate it would pay on its future 5-year bond issue. To cap the rate, suppose the company purchases a 3-year payer swaption on a 5-year, 9%/LIBOR, generic swap with a notional principal of $60M from First Bank for $200,000. Two years later, the swaption's value will be greater the higher the interest rate provided rates exceed 9%; this, in turn, offsets the higher borrowing rates and yields a fixed rate on the bond issue of approximately 9%. On the other hand, for rates less than 9%, the swaption is worthless, whereas the debt's rate decreases as rates decrease. Thus, for the cost of $200,000, the payer swaption provides the fund a cap on its future debt with a rate of 9%.

18.3.2.2   Investor Hedging the Risk of an Embedded Call Option

The cap and floor hedging examples illustrate that swaptions are a particularly useful tool in hedging future investment and debt position against adverse interest rate changes. Swaptions can also be used to hedge against the impacts adverse interest rate changes have on investment and debt positions with embedded options. Consider the case of a fixed-income manager holding $10M worth of 10-year, high-quality, 8% fixed-rate bonds that are callable in 2 years at a call price equal to par. Suppose the manager expects a decrease in rates over the next 2 years, increasing the likelihood that his bonds will be called, and he will be forced to reinvest in a market with lower rates. To minimize his exposure to this call risk, suppose the manager buys a 2-year receiver swaption on an 8-year, 8%/LIBOR swap with an NP of $10M. If 2 years later, rates were to increase, then the bonds would not be called, and the swaption would have no value. In this case, the fixed income manager would lose the premium he paid for the receiver swaption. However, if 2 years later, rates on 8-year bonds were lower at say 6%, and the bonds were called at a call price equal to par, then the manager would be able to offset the loss from reinvesting the call proceed at a lower interest rate by the profits from exercising the receiver swaption.

18.3.2.3   Borrower Hedging the Risk of an Embedded Put Option

The contrasting case of a fixed-income manager hedging callable bonds would be the case of a financial manager who issued putable bonds some time ago and was now concerned that rates might increase in the future. If rates did increase, and bondholders exercised their option to sell the bonds back to the issuer at a specified price, the issuer may have to finance the purchase by issuing new bonds paying higher rates. To hedge against this scenario, the financial manager could buy a payer swaption with a strike rate equal to the coupon rate on the putable bonds. Later, if the current swap rate exceeded the strike rate, and the bonds were put back to the issuer, the manager could exercise his payer swaption to take the fixed-payer position at the strike rate and then sell the swap and use the proceeds to defray part of higher financing cost of buying the bonds on the put. On the other hand, if rates were to decrease, then the put option on the bond would not be exercised, and the payer swaption would have no value. In this case, the manager would lose the swaption premium.

18.3.2.4 *Arbitrage—Synthetic Positions*

Like other swaps, swaptions can be used to create synthetic bond or debt positions with supposedly better rates than conventional ones. Consider, for example, a company that wants to finance a $50M capital expenditure with 7-year, option-free, 9% fixed-rate debt. As we examined in Chapter 17, the company could issue 7-year, option-free, fixed-rate bonds or create a synthetic 7-year bond by issuing 7-year FRNs and taking a fixed-payer's position on a 7-year swap. With swaptions, as well as other nongeneric swaps, there are actually several other ways in which this synthetic fixed-rate bond could be created. For example, to obtain an option-free, fixed-rate bond, the company could issue a callable bond and then sell a receiver swaption with terms similar to the bond. This synthetic debt position will provide a lower rate than the rate on a direct loan if investors underprice the call option on callable debt.

18.4 CANCELABLE AND EXTENDABLE SWAPS

Generic swaps can have clauses giving the counterparty the right to extend the option or cancel the options. These swaps are known as cancelable and extendable swaps. Analogous to bonds with embedded call and put options, these swaps are equivalent to swaps with embedded payer swaptions and receiver swaptions.

18.4.1 Cancelable Swap

A *cancelable swap* is a generic swap in which one of the counterparties has the option to terminate one or more payments. Cancelable swaps can be callable or putable. A *callable cancelable swap* is one in which the fixed payer has the right to early termination. Thus, if rates decrease, the fixed-rate payer on the swap with this embedded call option to early termination can exercise her right to cancel the swap. A *putable cancelable swap*, on the other hand, is one in which the floating payer has the right to early cancellation. A floating-rate payer with this option may find it advantageous to exercise his early termination right when rates increase.

   If there is only one termination date, then a cancelable swap is equivalent to a standard swap plus a position in a European swaption. For example, a 5-year putable cancelable swap to receive 6% and pay LIBOR that is cancelable after 2 years is equivalent to a floating position in a 5-year, 6%/LIBOR, generic swap and a long position in a 2-year payer swaption on a 3-year 6%/LIBOR swap; that is, after 2 years, the payer swaption gives the holder the right to take a fixed-payer's position on a 3-year swap at 6% that offsets the floating position on the 6% generic swap. On the other hand, a 5-year callable swap to pay 6% and receive LIBOR that is cancelable after 2 years would be equivalent to a fixed position in a 5-year, 6%/LIBOR, generic swap and a long position in a 2-year receiver swaption on a 3-year 6%/LIBOR swap.

18.4.2 Extendable Swaps

An *extendable swap* is just the opposite of a cancelable swap: It is a swap that has an option to lengthen the terms of the original swap. The swap allows the holder to take advantage of current rates and extend the maturity of the swap. Like cancelable swaps, extendable swaps can be replicated with a generic swap and a swaption. The floating payer with an extendable option has the equivalent of a floating position on a generic swap and a receiver swaption. That is, a 3-year swap to receive 6% and pay LIBOR that is extendable at maturity to 2 more years would be equivalent to a floating position in a 3-year, 6%/LIBOR, generic swap and a long position in a 3-year receiver swaption on a 2-year 6%/LIBOR: In 3 years, the receiver swaption gives the holder the right to take a floating-payer's position on a 2-year swap at 6%, which in effect extends the maturity of the expiring floating position on the 6% generic swap. In contrast, the fixed payer with an extendable option has the equivalent of a fixed position on a generic swap and a payer swaption.

18.4.3 Synthetic Positions

Because cancelable and extendable swaps are equivalent to generic swaps with a swaption, they can be used like swaptions to create synthetic positions. For example, the synthetic fixed-rate debt position formed by issuing FRNs and taking a fixed-payer's position on a generic swap or by issuing callable bonds and selling a receiver swaption could also be created by (1) issuing callable bonds, (2) taking a fixed-payer's position on a generic swap, and (3) taking a floating-payer's position on a callable cancelable swap. In general, with swaptions, forward swaps, and extendable and cancelable swaps, there are a number of synthetic asset and liability permutations: callable and putable debt, callable and putable bonds, flexible rate securities, and flexible-rate debt. The interested reader may want to consider how some of those positions can be combined to create synthetic fixed-rate and floating-rate positions.

18.5 NONGENERIC SWAPS

Concomitant with this growth of swaps has been the number of innovations introduced in swaps contracts over the years. Today, there are a number of nonstandard or nongeneric swaps used by financial and nonfinancial corporations to manage their varied cash flow and return-risk positions. Nongeneric swaps usually differ in terms of their rates, principal, or effective dates. For example, instead of defining swaps in terms of the LIBOR, some swaps use the T-bill rate, prime lending rate, or the Federal Reserve's Commercial Paper Rate Index with different maturities. Similarly, the principals defining a swap can vary. An *amortizing swap,* for example, is a swap in which the NP is reduced over time based on a schedule, whereas a set-up swap (sometimes called an *accreting swap*) has its NP increasing over time. A variation of the amortizing swap is the *index-amortizing swap* (also called index-principal swap). In this swap, the NP is dependent on interest rates; for example, the lower the interest rate the greater the reduction in principal. There are also *zero-coupon swaps* in which one or both parties do not exchange payments until the maturity on the swap. Finally, there are a number of *non-U.S.-dollar interest rate swaps.* These swaps often differ in terms of their floating rate: London rate, Frankfort

EXHIBIT 18.5-1   Nongeneric Swaps

- *Non-LIBOR Swap*: Swaps with floating rates different than LIBOR. Example: T-bill rate, CP rate, or prime lending rate.
- *Delayed-Rate Set Swap:* This swap allows the fixed payer to wait before locking in a fixed swap rate—the opposite of a forward swap.
- *Zero-Coupon Swap*: Swap in which one or both parties do not exchange payments until maturity on the swap.
- *Prepaid Swap*: Swap in which the future payments due are discounted to the present and paid at the start.
- *Delayed-Reset Swap*: The effective date and payment date are the same. The cash flows at time T are determined by the floating rate at time T rather than the rate at time T-1.
- *Amortizing Swaps*: Swaps in which the NP decreases over time based on a set schedule.
- *Set-Up Swap or Accreting Swap*: Swaps in which the NP increases over time based on a set schedule.
- *Index-Amortizing Swap*: Swap in which the NP is dependent on interest rates.
- *Equity Swap*: Swap in which one party pays the return on a stock index and the other pays a fixed or floating rate.
- *Basis Swap*: Swaps in which both rates are floating; each party exchanges different floating payments. One party might exchange payments based on LIBOR and the other based on the Federal Reserve CP Index.
- *Total Return Swap*: Returns from one asset are swapped for the returns on another asset.
- *Non-U.S.-Dollar Interest Rate Swap*: Interest rate swap in a currency different than U.S. dollar with a floating rate often different than the LIBOR: Frankfort rate (FIBOR), Vienna (VIBOR), and the like.

(FIBOR), Copenhagen (CIBOR), Madrid (MIBOR), or Vienna (VIBOR). Exhibit 18.5-1 summarizes some of the common nongeneric swaps.

18.6   CONCLUSION

In this chapter, we have examined the markets and uses of swap derivatives: forward swaps, swaptions, cancelable swaps, and extendable swaps. Like exchange-traded options and futures, these swap derivatives provide investors and borrowers with tools for more effectively managing their asset and liability positions. Like generic swaps, swap derivatives have also become a basic financial engineering tool to apply to a variety of financial problems. For financial and nonfinancial corporations who buy and sell swaps and their derivatives, one of their important decisions is how to price these contracts. In the next chapter, we examine the valuation of generic off-market swaps, forward swaps, and swaptions.

KEY TERMS

forward swaps	cancelable swap	zero-coupon swaps
swaptions	extendable swap	non-U.S.-dollar interest rate swaps
receiver swaption	amortizing swap	
payer swaption	set-up swap (accreting swap)	index-amortizing swap

SELECTED REFERENCES

Bhattacharya, A. K., and F. J. Fabozzi. "Interest-Rate Swaps." In *The Handbook of Fixed Income Securities*, 6th ed. edited by F. Fabozzi. New York: McGraw-Hill, 2001.

Cucchissi, P. G., and R. M. Tuffli. "Swaptions Applications." In *Interest Rate Swaps*, edited by C. R. Beidleman. Homewood, IL: Business One Irwin, 1991.

Darby, M. R. Over-the-Counter Derivatives and Systemic Risk to the Global Financial System. National Bureau of Economic Research Working Paper Series 4801, 1994.

Johnson, R. S. *Bond Evaluation, Selection, and Management*. Walden MA: Blackwell Publishing, 2004, Chapter 16.

Pergam, A. S. "Swaps: A Legal Perspective." In *The Handbook of Interest Rate Risk Management*, edited by J. C. Francis and A. S. Wolf. New York: Irwin Professional Publishing, 1994.

PROBLEMS AND EXERCISES

1. Explain how a company planning to issue 4-year, fixed-rate bonds in 2 years could use a forward swap to lock in the fix rate it will pay on the bonds. Explain how the hedge works at the expiration of the forward contract.

2. The JEP Development Company is constructing a $300M office park development that it anticipates being completed in 2 years. At the project's completion, the company plans to refinance its short-term construction and development loans by borrowing $300M through the private placement of 10-year bonds. The JEP company has a BBB quality rating; its option-free, fixed-rate bonds trade 200 basis points above comparable Treasury bonds, and its floating-rate bonds trade at 150 basis points above the LIBOR. Currently, 10-year T-bonds are trading to yield 6%. With current rates relatively low, JEP is expecting interest rates to increase and would like to lock in a rate on the 10-year, fixed-rate bond 2 years from now. The company is considering locking in its rate by entering a forward swap with Star Bank. Star is willing to provide JEP a 2-year forward swap agreement on a 10-year, 7.25%/LIBOR swap.

   a. Explain the forward swap position that JEP would need to take to lock in the rate on its 10-year, fixed-rate bond to be issued 2 years from now.

   b. Given JEP hedges with a swap position, explain how it would obtain a fixed rate for 10 years at the forward swap's expiration date by issuing its floating rate notes at LIBOR plus 150BP. What is the fixed rate ABC would have to pay on its position?

3. Suppose the JEP Development Company in Question 2 hedges its planned $300M bond sale in 2 years by taking a position in the forward swap contract offered by Star Bank. Also suppose that at the forward swap's expiration date, 10-year T-bonds are trading at 7%, and the fixed rate on 10-year par value swaps that Star Bank would offer JEP is 150 BP above the T-bond yield.

   a. What would be the value of the swap underlying JEP's forward swap at the expiration date? Use the YTM valuation approach.

b. What would be the amount of funds JEP would need to refinance its $300M short-term loan obligation and close its swap position?

c. Given that ABC's fixed-rate bonds trade at 200 basis points above T-bond rates, what would be ABC's semiannual interest payments on the funds that it borrows?

d. What would be ABC's annualized rate based on $300M refinancing funds it needs?

4. Suppose the JEP Development Company in Question 2 hedges its planned $300M bond sale in 2 years by taking a position in the forward swap contract offered by Star Bank. Also suppose that at the forward swap's expiration date, 10-year T-bonds are trading at 5%, and the fixed rate on 10-year par value swaps that Star Bank would offer JEP is 50 BP above the T-bond yield.

a. What would be the value of the swap underlying JEP's forward swap at the expiration date? Use YTM valuation approach.

b. Given that JEP's fixed-rate bonds trade at 200 basis points above T-bond rates, what would be the amount of funds JEP would need to refinance its $300M short-term loan obligation and close its swap position?

c. What would be JEP's annualized rate based on $300M funds it needs for refinancing?

5. XSIF Investment Trust has bonds worth $20M in par value maturing in 1 year. To maintain the duration and quality ratings of its overall bond fund, the trust plans to reinvest the principal in 3-year, option-free bonds with a quality rating of "A." Such bonds are currently trading 200 basis points above comparable 3-year Treasury notes. XSIF Trust also could invest in 3-year, A-rated, floating-rate bonds. Such bonds are presently trading at 150 basis points above the LIBOR. Currently, 3-year T-notes are trading to yield 6%. XSIF is worried, though, that the Fed will lower interest rates in the next year to stimulate a sluggish economy. As a result, the trust would like to lock in a rate on its $20M investment. The Trust is considering locking in a rate by entering a forward swap agreement with Fort Washington Bank. To hedge its future investment, Fort Washington is willing to provide XSIF a 1-year forward swap agreement on a 3-year 6.5%/LIBOR swap.

a. Explain the forward swap position that XSIF would need to take to lock in the rate on a 3-year, fixed-rate bond investment to be made in 1 year.

b. Given XSIF's swap position, explain how it would obtain a fixed rate for 3 years at the forward swap's expiration date by investing in A-rated floating-rate notes at LIBOR plus 150BP. What is the fixed rate XSIF would earn from this hedged investment?

6. Suppose the XSIF Investment Trust in Question 5 hedges its planned $20M bond investment in 1 year by taking a position in the 1-year, 6.5%/LIBOR, forward swap contract offered by Fort Washington Bank. Also suppose that at the forward swap's expiration date the fixed rate on 3-year par value swaps that Fort Washington would offer JEP is 50 BP above the T-note yield.

a. What would be the values of the swap underlying XSIF's forward swap at the expiration date if 3-year T-notes are trading at 5% and 7%? Use the YTM valuation approach.

b. Determine XSIF's investments after its closes its swap position and its annualized rate based on the $20M investment at T-notes yields of 5% and 7%?

7. Suppose a speculative hedge fund anticipating higher rates in several years purchased a 2-year payer swaption on a 3-year, 6%/LIBOR, generic swap with semiannual payments and an NP of $20M for a price equal to 50BP times the NP. Explain what the fund would do at the swaption's expiration if the fixed rate on a 3-year par value swap were at 7% and at 5%. What would be the fund's profits or losses at those rates? Use YTM-approach in valuing the swap's position.

8. Show graphically and in a table the values and profits/losses at expiration that the hedge fund in Question 7 would obtain from closing its payer swaption on a 6%/LIBOR swap with a notional principal of $20M purchased at a price equal to 50 BP times the NP. Evaluate at fixed rates on 3-year par value swap at expiration of 4%, 4.5%, 5%, 5.5%, 6%, 6.5%, 7%, 7.5%, and 8%. Use YTM-approach in valuing the swap's position.

9. Suppose the speculative hedge fund in Question 7 was anticipating lower rates in several years and purchased a 2-year receiver swaption on a 3-year, 6%/LIBOR, generic swap with semiannual payments and NP of $20M for a price equal to 60 BP times the NP. Explain what the fund would do at the swaption's expiration if the fixed rate on 3-year par value swaps were at 7% and at 5%. What would be the fund's profits or losses at those rates? Use YTM-approach in valuing the swap's position.

10. Show graphically and in a table the values and profits/losses at expiration that the hedge fund in Question 9 would obtain from closing its receiver swaption on a 6%/LIBOR swap with an NP of $20M purchased at a price equal to 60 BP times the NP. Evaluate at fixed rates on 3-year par value swaps at expiration of 4%, 4.5%, 5%, 5.5%, 6%, 6.5%, 7%, 7.5%, and 8%. Use YTM-approach in valuing the swap's position.

11. The Washington Investment Fund has a Treasury bond portfolio worth $100M in par value that is scheduled to mature in 1 year. Washington plans to reinvest the $100M of principal for another 3 years in similar fixed-income bonds. Currently, such bonds are trading to yield 6%. Washington is worried that interest rate could be lower in 1 year and would like to establish a floor on the rate it would obtain for its futures 3-year investment. The fund is considering purchasing a 1-year receiver swaption on a 3-year, 6%/LIBOR, generic swap and NP of $100M from First American Bank for $500,000. Show in a table the values and profits/losses at expiration that Washington would obtain from closing the receiver swaption (use YTM approach to determine values) and the hedged rate (based on $100M investment) they would obtain from reinvesting for 3 years the $100M plus the proceeds from selling the swaption (do not include $500,000 cost). Determine the values, profits, and rates given possible fixed rates on a three-year par value swap at expiration of 4%, 4.5%, 5%, 5.5%, 6%, 6.5%, 7%, 7.5%, and 8%. Assume the rate on the par value swap and the 3-year T-note rate are the same and that the yield curve is flat.

12. The Ebersole Software Development Company has a $25M, 8% fixed-rate bond obligation maturing in 1 year. The company plans to finance the $25M principal liability by issuing new 5-year fixed-rate bonds. Currently, 5-year T-notes are trading to yield 6%, and Ebersole's bonds are trading at 200 basis points above the Treasury yields. Ebersole is worried that interest rates could increase in 1 year and would like to establish a cap on the rate it would pay on its future 5-year bond issue. Ebersole is considering purchasing a 1-year payer swaption on a 5-year, 8%/LIBOR, generic swap with NP of $25M from First South Bank for $250,000. Show in a table the values and profits/losses at expiration that Ebersole would obtain from closing the swaption

(use YTM approach to determine values) and the hedged rate (based on $25M debt) they would pay from issuing 5-year bonds to raise $25M minus the proceeds from selling the swaption (do not include $250,000 cost). Determine the values, profits, and rates at fixed rates on a 5-year par value swap at expiration of 6%, 6.5%, 7%, 7.5%, 8%, 8.5%, 9%, 9.5%, and 10%. Assume the rate on the par value swap and Ebersole's 5-year bond rate are the same and that the yield curve is flat.

13. The Zuber Bottling Manufacturing Company is considering financing the construction of its new $50M facility by selling 7-year, 10% fixed-rate, option-free bonds at par through a private placement. The company's investment banker has informed the company that it could also sell 7-year, 10.5% fixed-rate bonds at par with a call option giving the Zuber Company the right to buy back the bonds at par after 2 years. In addition, Zuber is also informed it can sell an FRN paying the LIBOR plus 25 BP. Zuber does not believe rates will decrease over the next 2 years and prefers the noncallable bonds. The Zuber Company, though, can take a long or short position with its investment banker on a 2-year receiver swaption on a 5-year, 10%/LIBOR swap selling at a price equal to 75 BP per year for 7 years.

    a. Explain how the Zuber Company could create a synthetic option-free bond with the callable bond and a position on the receiver swaption.

    b. What would be the effective rate Zuber would pay on its synthetic option-free bond if rates 2 years later were greater than 10%, the swaption holder does not exercise, and Zuber does not exercise the call option on its bonds?

    c. What actions would Zuber have to take to fixed its rate if rates 2 years later were less than 10% and the swaption holder exercises? What would be Zuber's effective rate for the remaining 5 years?

    d. Based on your analysis in b and c, what would be your financing recommendation to the Zuber Company: the synthetic option-free bond or the straight option-free bond?

14. Explain how a 10-year, 8%/LIBOR, putable swap cancelable after 5 years can be created with positions in a 10-year, 8%/LIBOR, generic swap and a 5-year payer swaption on a 5-year 8%/LIBOR swap.

15. Explain how a 10-year, 8%/LIBOR, callable swap cancelable after 5 years can be created with positions in a 10-year, 8%/LIBOR, generic swap and a 5-year receiver swaption on a 5-year 8%/LIBOR swap.

16. Given a borrower can issue floating rate notes, callable bonds, and putable bonds and can take positions in comparable generic swaps, callable and putable swaps, and call and payer swaptions, define five ways the borrower could form synthetic fixed-rate positions.

17. Define the following swaps and give an example of their use: amortizing, accreting, and index-amortizing swaps.

CHAPTER 19

SWAP VALUATION

19.1 INTRODUCTION[1]

The swap market consists of financial and nonfinancial corporations talking swap and swap derivative positions to create synthetic debt or investment positions and to structure debt or investments with caps and floors and other features that meet their particular return-risk preference. At the core of this market are the swap banks that create many of the swap positions. One of the most important decisions for a swap bank is determining the fixed rate on a new generic swap and forward swap. As we noted in Chapter 17, a generic interest rate swap can be replicated with a position in a T-note and an opposite position in a floating rate note (FRN). As a result, the fixed rate on the swap is typically set at the T-note rate with an adjustment for the counterparty's credit risk. Such a swap is known as a par value swap. The value of existing swaps similarly depends on what its swap rate is relative to the current rate on T-notes or equivalently the rate on current par value swaps. The rates set on new forward swaps, in turn, depend on future interest rates that can be locked in either with a futures contract or by taking long and short positions in bonds today. Given forward rates, the values of forward swap contracts and swaptions can be determined. In this chapter, we continue our analysis of swaps by examining how rates and values are determined on generic swaps, forward swaps, and swaptions.

19.2 SWAP VALUATION

19.2.1 Valuation of Off-Market Swaps

Although most plain vanilla swaps are originally par value swaps with economic values of zero, as we discussed in Chapter 17, their economic values change over time as rates change; that is, existing swaps become off-market swaps as rates change. For example, suppose a T-note with a maturity of 3 years and a coupon of 6% were priced at 102.75 of par to yield 5%:

$$B_0 = \sum_{t=1}^{6} \frac{6/2}{(1 + (.05/2))^t} + \frac{100}{(1 + (.05/2))^6} = 102.75$$

At the 5% discount rate, an existing 6%/LIBOR swap with 3 years to maturity and no credit risk would not have an economic value of zero, and as a result, some compensation or payment (depending on the position) would be required to close the position. For example, suppose the floating payer on the 6%/LIBOR swap wanted to close her position by transferring it to a new party who would take the floating-payer's position (the new

---

[1] This chapter assumes some knowledge of bond valuations and yields; for a primer, see Appendix C.

party perhaps being a swap bank). With rates at 5%, the perspective floating payer could hedge the cash flows for the 3-year 6%/LIBOR swap by forming a replicating position by shorting the 3-year, 6% bond for 102.75 per par and buying a 3-year FRN paying LIBOR for 100. The perspective party would pick up $2.75 by taking the floating position on the 6%/LIBOR swap and hedging it with the replicating position:

6%/LIBOR Floating-Rate Position			
Swap: Floating-Rate Payer's Position		Pay LIBOR	–LIBOR
Swap: Floating-Rate Payer's Position		Receive 6%	+6
Replication	**Initial Cash Flow**		
Short 6% Fixed Bond	Receive 102.75	Pay 6%	–6%
Buy FRN	Pay 100	Receive LIBOR	+ LIBOR
Net	Receive 2.75		
Net	**2.75**	**0**	**0**

The perspective party would therefore be willing to pay up to $2.75 per $100 par for the floating-payer's position on the 3-year, 6/LIBOR swap.

In contrast, suppose the fixed payer on the 6%/LIBOR swap wanted to close his position by transferring it to a new party (again the new party may be a swap bank). At a 5% yield, the perspective fixed payer could replicate the cash flows for the 3-year, 6%/LIBOR swap by buying a 3-year bond paying an annual coupon of 6% at 102.75 of par and shorting a 3-year FRN paying LIBOR for 100. The perspective party would lose $2.75 by taking the fixed-payer's position on a 6%/LIBOR swap and hedging it with the replicating position:

6%/LIBOR Fixed-Rate Position			
Swap: Fixed-Rate Payer's Position		Pay 6%	–6%
Swap: Fixed-Rate Payer's Position		Receive LIBOR	+LIBOR
Replication	**Initial Cash Flow**		
Buy 6% Fixed Bond	Pay 102.75	Receive 6%	+6%
Issue (or short) FRN	Receive 100	Pay LIBOR	–LIBOR
Net	Pay 2.75		
Net	**–2.75**	**0**	**0**

The perspective party would therefore require at least $2.75 in compensation from the current holder to take the fixed-payer's position on the 3-year, 6%/LIBOR swap.

In this example, the value of the 6%/LIBOR swap is a positive $2.75 for the floating-payer's position (i.e., the floating payer could sell her swap for $2.75 to the new party) and a negative $2.75 for the fixed-payer's position (i.e., the fixed payer would have to pay $2.75 to the new party to assume the swap). As we noted in Chapter 17, the value of an existing swap is equal to the value of replacing the swap—replacement swap. In this example, the current par value swap (with no credit risk) would be a 5%/LIBOR swap. Instead of a replicating portfolio, the fixed payer with the 6%/LIBOR swap could offset his position by taking a floating-payer's position on a current 3-year, 5%/LIBOR, par value swap. By doing this, he would be losing $0.50 semiannually per $100 par value for 3 years:

6%/LIBOR Fixed-Rate Position	Annual	Annual	Semiannual
Swap: Fixed-Rate Payer's Position	Pay 6%	–6%	Pay $3
Swap: Fixed-Rate Payer's Position	Receive LIBOR	+LIBOR	Receive LIBOR/2
Replacement: 5%/LIBOR Floating-Rate Position			
Swap: Floating-Rate Payer's Position	Pay LIBOR	–LIBOR	Pay LIBOR/2
Swap: Floating-Rate Payer's Position	Receive 5%	+5%	Receive $2.50
Net	**Pay 1%**	**–1%**	**Pay $0.50**

Thus, the replacement swap represents a loss of $0.50 per $100 par per period for six semiannual periods. Using 5% as the discount rate, the present value of this 6%/LIBOR fixed position is –$2.75:

$$PV = \sum_{t=1}^{6} \frac{-\$0.50}{(1 + (.05/2))^t} = -\$2.75$$

In contrast, the floating payer with the 6%/LIBOR swap could offset her position by taking a fixed-payer's position on a current 3-year, 5%/LIBOR, par value swap. By doing this, she would be gaining $0.50 per $100 par value semiannually for 3 years:

6%/LIBOR Floating-Rate Position	Annual	Annual	Semiannual
Swap: Floating-Rate Payer's Position	Pay LIBOR	–LIBOR	Pay LIBOR/2
Swap: Floating-Rate Payer's Position	Receive 6%	+6	Receive $3
Replacement: 5%/LIBOR Fixed-Rate Position			
Swap: Fixed-Rate Payer's Position	Pay 5%	–5%	Pay $2.50
Swap: Fixed-Rate Payer's Position	Receive LIBOR	+LIBOR	Receive LIBOR/2
Net	**Receive 1%**	**+1%**	**Receive $0.50**

Using 5% as the discount rate, the present value of the 6%/LIBOR floating position is $2.75:

$$PV = \sum_{t=1}^{6} \frac{-\$0.50}{(1 + (.05/2))^t} = -\$2.75$$

The underlying valuation concept germane to this example is that the current swap rate determines the value of an exiting swap or any off-market swap. Formally, the values of the fixed and floating swap positions are

$$SV^{fix} = \left[\sum_{t=1}^{M} \frac{K^P - K^S}{(1 + K^P)^t} \right] NP = \left[\sum_{t=1}^{6} \frac{(.05/2) - (.06/2)}{(1 + (.05/2))^t} \right] (100) = -2.75$$

$$SV^{fl} = \left[\sum_{t=1}^{M} \frac{K^S - K^P}{(1 + K^P)^t} \right] NP = \left[\sum_{t=1}^{6} \frac{(.06/2) - (.05/2)}{(1 + (.05/2))^t} \right] (100) = 2.75$$

where

$$K^S = \text{Fixed rate on the existing swap.}$$

$$K^P = \text{Fixed rate on current par value swap.}$$

$$SV^{fix} = \text{Swap value of the fixed position on the existing swap.}$$

$$SV^{fl} = \text{Swap value of the floating position on the existing swap.}$$

19.2.2   Equilibrium Value of a Swap—Zero-Coupon Approach

Note that the preceding swap values were obtained by discounting the net cash flows at the current yield to maturity, YTM (K^P or 6% on the 3-year bond). As we noted in Chapter 17, this approach to valuing off-market swaps is often referred to as the *YTM approach.* However, recall from our earlier discussion of bond valuation (Chapter 7) that the equilibrium price of a bond is obtained not by discounting all of the bond's cash flows by a common discount rate but rather by discounting each of the bond's cash flows by their appropriate spot rates—the rate on a zero-discount bond. Pricing bonds by using spot rates instead of a common YTM ensures that there are no arbitrage opportunities from buying bonds and stripping them or buying zero-discount bonds and bundling them. The argument for pricing bonds in terms of spot rates also applies to the valuation of off-market swaps. Similar to bond valuation, the equilibrium value of a swap is obtained by discounting each of the swap's cash flows by their appropriate spot rates. The valuation of swaps using spot rates is referred to as the *zero-coupon approach.* The approach, in turn, requires generating a spot yield curve for swaps.

19.2.3   Zero-Coupon Swap Yield Curve—Bootstrapping

Because there is not an active market for zero-discount swaps, implied zero-coupon swap rates need to be determined. One approach that can be used to estimate spot rates is a sequential process commonly referred to as *bootstrapping.* In the case of generating spot rates for bonds, this approach requires having at least one zero-coupon bond. Given this bond's rate, a coupon bond with the next highest maturity is used to obtain an implied spot rate; then another coupon bond with the next highest maturity is used to find the next spot rates and so on. Zero-coupon swap rates can also be estimated using a bootstrapping technique. For swaps, this requires applying the technique to a series of current generic swaps. For a yield curve defined by annual periods, the first step is to calculate the 1-year zero-coupon rate, $Z(1)$. Because current generic swaps are priced at par, the 1-year zero-coupon rate for a swap would be equal to the annual coupon rate on a 1-year generic swap, $C(1)$ (assume annual payment frequency instead of the normal semiannual). That is, for a par value of $1

$$1 = \frac{1 + C(1)}{1 + Z(1)}$$

$$Z(1) = C(1)$$

The 2-year swap, with an annual coupon rate of $C(2)$ and the 1-year zero coupon rate of $Z(1)$, can be used to calculated the 2-year zero discount rate, $Z(2)$:

$$1 = \frac{C(2)}{1 + Z(1)} + \frac{1 + C(2)}{(1 + Z(2))^2}$$

$$Z(2) = \left[\frac{1 + C(2)}{1 - [C(2)/(1 + Z(1))]}\right]^{1/2} - 1$$

The 3-year zero-coupon rate is found using the 3-year swap and the 1-year and 2-year zero-coupon rates. Other rates are determined in a similar manner. Using this recursive method, a zero coupon (or spot) yield curve for swaps can be generated from a series of generic swaps. These zero-coupon rates can then be used to discount the cash flows on a swap to determine its value.

Exhibit 19.2-1 shows a yield curve of zero-coupon rates generated from a series of current generic swap rates. The swap rates shown in Column 4 are the annual fixed rates paid on the swaps. Each rate is equal to the yield on a corresponding T-note plus the swap spread. The swap spread reflects the credit risk of the swap party and the maturity of the swap. The zero-coupon swap rates shown in Column 5 are generated from these swap rates using the bootstrapping approach.

Note that because swaps involve semiannual cash flows, the annualized zero spot rates at .5 intervals are usually interpolated. Thus, the rate at 1.5 years is $(.05 + .055138)/2 = .052569$; the rate at 2.5 years is $(.055138 + .060395)/2 = .0577665$. If the rate on a T-bill maturing in .5 years were 4%, then with the 100 BP credit spread the .5-year zero-coupon rate would be 5%. The zero coupon swap rates would be

Maturity in years	Zero Rate
.5	5%
1	5%
1.5	$(5\% + 5.5138\%)/2 = 5.2569\%$
2	5.5138%
2.5	$(5.5138\% + 6.0395\%)/2 = 5.77665$
3	6.0395%

19.2.3.1 Valuation

Given the zero-coupon rates, suppose there was a 6.5%/LIBOR off-market swap with a maturity of 2 years and NP of $10M. Given the 2-year par value swap (Exhibit 19.2-1) has a swap rate of 5.5%, the value of the fixed-payer's position on the 6.5% off-market swap using the zero-coupon approach would be –$187,473, and the value of the floating position would be $187,473:

$$SV^{fix} = \left[\frac{(.055/2)-(.065/2)}{(1+(.05/2))^1} + \frac{(.055/2)-(.065/2)}{(1+(.05/2))^2} + \frac{(.055/2)-(.065/2)}{(1+(.052569/2))^3} + \frac{(.055/2)-(.065/2)}{(1+(.055138/2))^4} \right] \$10,000,000 = -\$187,473$$

$$SV^{fl} = \left[\frac{(.065/2)-(.055/2)}{(1.+(.05/2))^1} + \frac{(.065/2)-(.055/2)}{(1+(.05/2))^2} + \frac{(.065/2)-(.055/2)}{(1+(.052569/2))^3} + \frac{(.065/2)-(.055/2)}{(1+(.055138/2))^4} \right] \$10,000,000 = \$187,473$$

Note with the current YTM on the 2-year bonds at 5.5%, the value of the 6.5%/LIBOR swap positions using the YTM approach would be –$186,971 (fixed) and $186.971 (floating):

$$SV^{fix} = \left[\frac{(.055/2)-(.065/2)}{(1+(.055/2))^1} + \frac{(.055/2)-(.065/2)}{(1+(.055/2))^2} + \frac{(.055/2)-(.065/2)}{(1+(.055/2))^3} + \frac{(.055/2)-(.065/2)}{(1+(.055/2))^4} \right] \$10,000,000 = -\$186,971$$

$$SV^{fl} = \left[\frac{(.065/2)-(.055/2)}{(1.+(.055/2))^1} + \frac{(.065/2)-(.055/2)}{(1+(.055/2))^2} + \frac{(.065/2)-(.055/2)}{(1+(.055/2))^3} + \frac{(.065/2)-(.055/2)}{(1+(.055/2))^4} \right] \$10,000,000 = \$186,971$$

EXHIBIT 19.2-1 Generic Swap Yield Curve for Zero-Coupon Rates

1 Maturity in Years	2 Yield on T-Note	3 Swap Spread BP	4 Swap Rate	5 Zero-Coupon Rate Z	6 Implied 1-Year Forward Rate
1	.040	100	.050	.050000	$RI_{10} = .05$
2	.045	100	.055	.055138	$RI_{11} = .0603$
3	.050	100	.060	.060395	$RI_{12} = .07099$
4	.055	100	.065	.0658547	$RI_{13} = .082402$

Zero Coupon Rates from Bootstrapping

$$Z(1) = .05$$

$$Z(2) = \frac{.055}{1 + .05} + \frac{1.055}{(1 + Z(2))^2}$$

$$Z(2) = \left[\frac{1.055}{1 - .052381}\right]^{1/2} - 1 = .055138$$

$$Z(3) : 1 = \frac{.06}{1.05} + \frac{.06}{(1.055138)^2} + \frac{1.06}{(1 + Z(3))^3}$$

$$Z(3) = \left[\frac{1.06}{1 - .111}\right]^{1/3} - 1 = .060395$$

One-Year Implied Forward Rates, RI_{1t}

$$RI_{10} = Z(1) = .05$$

$$RI_{11} : Z(2) = [(1 + Z(1)(1 + RI_{11}))]^{1/2} - 1$$

$$RI_{11} = \frac{(1 + Z(2))^2}{(1 + Z(1))} - 1 = \frac{(1.055138)^2}{1.05} - 1 = .0603$$

$$RI_{12} : Z(3) = [(1 + Z(1)(1 + RI_{11})(1 + RI_{12}))]^{1/3} - 1$$

$$RI_{12} = \frac{(1 + Z(3))^3}{(1 + Z(1))(1 + f_{11})} - 1 = \frac{(1.060395)^3}{(1.05)(1.0603)} - 1 = .07099$$

$$RI_{13} : Z(4) = [(1 + Z(1)(1 + RI_{11})(1 + RI_{12})(1 + RI_{13})]^{1/4} - 1$$

$$RI_{13} = \frac{(1 + Z(4))^4}{(1 + Z(1))(1 + f_{11})(1 + f_{12})} - 1 = \frac{(1.0658547)^4}{(1.05)(1.0603)(1.07099)} - 1 = .082402$$

Thus, if the fixed position were valued by the YTM approach at $186,971, then a swap dealer could realize an arbitrage by buying the 2-year swap at $186,971 and then selling (i.e., taking floating positions) four, off-market, 6.5%/LIBOR swaps with maturities of .5, 1, 1.5, and 2 years priced to yield their zero-coupon rates for a total of $187,473. As swap dealers try to exploit this arbitrage, they would drive the price of the swap to the $187,473. Thus, like bonds, the equilibrium price of a swap is obtained by discounting each of the net cash flows from an existing and current swap by their appropriate spot rates.

19.3 BREAK-EVEN SWAP RATE

A corollary to the zero-coupon approach to valuation is that in the absence of arbitrage, the fixed rate on the swap (the swap rate) is that rate, C*, that makes the present value of the swap's fixed-rate payments equal to the present value of the swap's floating payments, with *implied forward rates* being used to estimatethe future floating payments. The rate C* is referred to as the *break-even swap rate.* Break-even rates are used by swap dealers to help them determine the rates on new par value swaps. To see how these rates are determined, we first need to define an implied forward rate.

19.3.1 Implied Forward Rates

An implied forward rate, RI_{Mt}, is a future rate of return implied by the present interest rate structure. This rate can be attained by going long and short in current bonds. To see this, suppose the rate on a 1-year, zero coupon or pure discount bond is 10% (i.e., spot rate is $S_1 = 10\%$) and the rate on a similar 2-year pure discount bond is $S_2 = 9\%$. Knowing today's rates, we could solve for the implied rate (RI) on a 1-year bond (M = 1) purchased 1 year from now (t = 1) $RI_{Mt} = RI_{11}$ by solving the equation following for RI_{11}. That is

$$(1 + S_2)^2 = (1 + S_1)(1 + RI_{11})$$

$$S_2 = [(1 + S_1)(1 + RI_{11})]^{1/2} - 1$$

$$RI_{11} = \frac{(1 + S_2)^2}{(1 + S_1)} - 1$$

$$RI_{11} = \frac{(1.09)^2}{(1.10)} - 1 = .08$$

With 1-year and 2-year pure discount bonds presently trading at 9% and 10%, respectively, the rate implied on 1-year bonds to be bought 1 year from the present is 8%. This 8% rate, though, is simply an algebraic result. This rate actually can be attained, however, by implementing the following locking-in strategy:

1. Sell the 1-year pure discount bond short (or borrow an equivalent amount of funds at the 1-year pure discount bond (spot) rate).
2. Use the cash funds from the short sale (or loan) to buy a multiple of the 2-year pure discount bond.
3. Cover the short sale (or pay the loan principal and interest) at the end of the 1st year.
4. Collect on the maturing 2-year bond at the end of the second year.

In terms of the preceding example, the 8% implied forward rate is obtained by

1. Executing a short sale by borrowing the 1-year bond and selling it at its market price of $90.909 = $100/1.10 (or borrowing $90.909 at 10%).

2. With 2-year bonds trading at $84.168 = \$100/(1.09)^2$, buying $\$90.909/\$84.168 = 1.08$ issues of the 2-year bond.

3. At the end of the 1st year covering the short sale by paying the holder of the 1-year bond his principal of $100 (or repay loan).

4. At the end of the 2nd year receiving the principal on the maturing 2-year bond issues of $(1.08)(\$100) = \$108$.

With this locking-in strategy, the investor does not make a cash investment until the end of the 1st year when he covers the short sale; in the present, the investor simply initiates the strategy. Thus, the investment of $100 is made at the end of the 1st year. In turn, the return on the investment is the principal payment of $108 on the 1.08 holdings of the 2-year bonds that comes 1 year after the investment is made. Moreover, the rate of return on this 2-year investment is 8% (($108-$100)/$100). Hence, by using a locking-in strategy, an 8% rate of return on a 1-year investment to be made 1 year in the future is attained, with the rate being the same rate obtained by solving algebraically for R_{11}.

19.3.2 Forecasting Future Interest Rates With Implied Forward Rates

Often analysts forecast futures rates and future yield curves by simply calculating implied forward rates from current rates. Exhibit 19.3-1 shows spot rates on bonds with maturities ranging from 1 year to 5 years (Column 2). From these rates, expected spot rates (S_t) are generated for bonds 1 year from the present (Column 3) and 2 years from the present (Column 4). The expected spot rates shown are equal to their corresponding implied forward rates. For example, the expected rate on a 1-year bond 1 year from now ($E(S_{Mt}) = E(S_{11})$) is equal to the implied forward rate of $RI_{Mt} = RI_{11} = 11\%$. This rate is obtained by using the current 2-year and 1-year spot rates as we did in the preceding example:

$$S_2 = [(1 + S_1)(1 + RI_{11})]^{1/2} - 1$$

$$RI_{11} = \frac{(1 + S_2)^2}{(1 + S_1)} - 1$$

$$RI_{11} = \frac{(1.105)^2}{(1.10)} - 1 = .11$$

Similarly, the expected 2-year spot rate 1 year from now is equal to the implied forward rate on a 2-year bond purchased 1 year from now of $RI_{Mt} = RI_{21} = 11.5\%$. This rate is

EXHIBIT 19.3-1   Forecasting Yield Curves Using Implied Forward Rates

(1)	(2)	(3)	(4)
		Expected Spot Rates One Year From Present	**Expected Spot Rates Two Years from Present**
Maturity	**Spot Rates**		
1	10.0%	$RI_{11} = 11.0\%$	$RI_{12} = 12.0\%$
2	10.5%	$RI_{21} = 11.5\%$	$RI_{22} = 12.5\%$
3	11.0%	$RI_{31} = 12.0\%$	$RI_{32} = 13\%$
4	11.5%	$RI_{41} = 12.5\%$	
5	12.0%		

obtained using 3-year and 1-year spot rates:

$$(1 + S_3)^3 = (1 + S_1)(1 + RI_{11})(1 + RI_{12})$$

$$(1 + S_3)^3 = (1 + S_1)(1 + RI_{21})^2$$

$$RI_{21} = \left[\frac{(1 + S_3)^3}{(1 + S_1)}\right]^{1/2} - 1$$

$$RI_{21} = \left[\frac{(1.11)^3}{(1.10)}\right]^{1/2} - 1$$

$$RI_{21} = 11.5\%$$

The other expected spot rates for next year are found repeating this process.

A similar approach also can be used to forecast the yield curve 2 years, 3 years, and other years from the present. For example, the implied forward rate on a 1-year bond 2 years from the present is obtained using the current 3-year bond rate, the 1-year spot rate, and the implied forward rate RI_{11}:

$$(1 + S_3)^3 = (1 + S_1)(1 + RI_{11})(1 + RI_{12})$$

$$S_3 = [(1 + S_1)(1 + RI_{11})(1 + RI_{12})]^{1/3} - 1$$

$$RI_{12} = \frac{(1 + S_3)^3}{(1 + S_1)(1 + R_{11})} - 1$$

$$RI_{12} = \frac{(1.11)^3}{(1.10)(1.11)} - 1 = .12$$

All of these implied forward rates can be found using the following formula:

$$RI_{Mt} = \left[\frac{(1 + S_{M+t})^{M+t}}{(1 + S_t)^t}\right]^{1/M} - 1$$

It should be noted that if the carrying-cost model governing Treasury futures holds, then the rate implied by the futures contract, YTM_f, will also be equal to the implied forward rate, RI.

19.3.3 Implied Forward Swap Rates

Just as implied forward interest rates can be generated from current spot rates, implied forward rates on swaps can also be determined from current zero-coupon swap rates. Column 6 in Exhibit 19.2-1 shows the 1-year implied forward rates obtained from the zero-coupon rates (Column 5). For example, the 1-year implied forward swap rate (RI_{11}) of 6.03% is obtained given the 1-year and 2-year zero-coupon swap rates:

$$(1 + Z_2)^2 = (1 + Z(1))(1 + RI_{11})$$

$$Z(2) = [(1 + Z(1)(1 + RI_{11})]^{1/2} - 1$$

$$RI_{11} = \frac{(1 + Z(2))^2}{(1 + Z(1))} - 1$$

$$RI_{11} = \frac{(1.055138)^2}{1.05} - 1 = .0603$$

Similarly, the implied 1-year forward rate 2 years from the present (RI_{12}) of 7.099% is calculated from the current 3-year, zero-coupon, swap rate; 1-year, zero–coupon, swap rates; and the implied forward swap rate RI_{11}:

$$(1 + Z(3))^3 = (1 + Z(1))(1 + RI_{11})(1 + RI_{12})$$

$$Z(3) = [(1 + Z(1)(1 + RI_{11})(1 + RI_{12})]^{1/3} - 1$$

$$RI_{12} = \frac{(1 + Z(3))^3}{(1 + Z(1))(1 + RI_{11})} - 1$$

$$RI_{12} = \frac{(1.060395)^3}{(1.05)(1.0603)} - 1 = .07099$$

19.3.4   Break-Even Swap Rate

As noted, the break-even rate is the fixed rate on the swap (the swap rate), C*, that makes the present value of the swap's fixed-rate payments equal to the present value of the swap's floating payments, with implied one-period forward rates, RI_{1t}, being used to estimate the future floating payments. For an N-year swap with an NP of $1, this condition states that in equilibrium

$$\frac{C^*}{(1 + Z(1))} + \frac{C^*}{(1 + Z(2))^2} + \cdots + \frac{C^*}{(1 + Z(N))^N}$$

$$= \frac{Z(1)}{(1 + Z(1))} + \frac{RI_{11}}{(1 + Z(2))^2} + \cdots + \frac{RI_{1,N-1}}{(1 + Z(N))^N}$$

$$C^* = \frac{\dfrac{Z(1)}{(1 + Z(1))} + \dfrac{RI_{11}}{(1 + Z(2))^2} + \cdots + \dfrac{RI_{1,N-1}}{(1 + Z(N))^N}}{\dfrac{1}{(1 + Z(1))} + \dfrac{1}{(1 + Z(2))^2} + \cdots + \dfrac{1}{(1 + Z(N))^N}}$$

In terms of our example in Exhibit 19.2-1, by substituting the 1-year implied forward rates (Column 6) into the previous equation, we can obtain the break-even swap rates of 5% for the 1-year swap, 5.5% for the 2-year swap, and 6% for the 3-year swap. These break-even rates along with their calculations are shown in Exhibit 19.3-2.

The break-even swap rate C* is sometimes referred to as **_market rate._** Accordingly, if swap dealers were to set swap rates equal to the break-even rates, then there would be no arbitrage from forming opposite positions in fixed-rate and floating-rate bonds priced at their equilibrium values nor any arbitrage from taking opposite positions in a swap and a strip of swaps. The break-even swap rates that we just calculated in turn match the swap rates on the current swaps (column 4, Exhibit 19.2-1), implying that the all three are par value swaps with no arbitrage opportunities. As noted, break-even rates are used by swap dealers to help them determine the rates on new par value swaps as well as the compensation to receive or pay on new off-market swaps in which the swap rates are set different than the break-even rates.

19.4   BREAK-EVEN FORWARD SWAP RATES AND THE VALUATION OF A FORWARD SWAP

The value of a forward swap depends on whether the rate on the forward contract's underlying swap is different than its break-even forward swap rate. Like the break-even rate on a generic swap, the break-even rate on a forward swap, C_f^*, is that rate that

EXHIBIT 19.3-2 Break-Even Rates Generated From Information in Exhibit 19.2-1

1	2	2	3	4
Maturity in Years	Zero Coupon Rate Z	Implied 1-Year Forward Rate	Current Break-Even Rates C*	Break-Even Forward Rates one year forward
1	.05	.05	.05	.0603
2	.055138	.0603	.055	.06546
3	.060395	.07099	.06	
4	.0658547	.082402		

1 year $C^* = Z(1) = .05$

$$
2 \text{ year } C^* = \frac{\frac{Z(1)}{(1+Z(1))} + \frac{RI_{11}}{(1+Z(2))^2}}{\frac{1}{(1+Z(1))} + \frac{1}{(1+Z(2))^2}} = \frac{\frac{.05}{(1.05)} + \frac{.0603}{(1.055138)^2}}{\frac{1}{(1.05)} + \frac{1}{(1.055138)^2}} = .055
$$

$$
3 \text{ year } C^* = \frac{\frac{Z(1)}{(1+Z(1))} + \frac{RI_{11}}{(1+Z(2))^2} + \frac{RI_{12}}{(1+Z(3))^3}}{\frac{1}{(1+Z(1))} + \frac{1}{(1+Z(2))^2} + \frac{1}{(1+Z(3))^3}} = \frac{\frac{.05}{(1.05)} + \frac{.0603}{(1.055138)^2} + \frac{.07099}{(1.060395)^3}}{\frac{1}{(1.05)} + \frac{1}{(1.055138)^2} + \frac{1}{(1.060395)^3}} = .06
$$

1-year swap, one year forward

$$
\frac{C_f^*}{(1+Z(2))^2} = \frac{RI_{11}}{(1+Z(2))^2}
$$

$$
C_f^* = RI_{11} = .0603
$$

2 − year swap, 1 year forward

$$
\frac{C_f^*}{(1+Z(2))^2} + \frac{C_f^*}{(1+Z(3))^3} = \frac{RI_{11}}{(1+Z(2))^2} + \frac{RI_{12}}{(1+Z(3))^3}
$$

$$
C_f^* = \frac{\frac{RI_{11}}{(1+Z(2))^2} + \frac{RI_{12}}{(1+Z(3))^3}}{\frac{1}{(1+Z(2))^2} + \frac{1}{(1+Z(3))^3}} = \frac{\frac{.0603}{(1.055138)^2} + \frac{.07099}{(1.060395)^3}}{\frac{1}{(1.055138)^2} + \frac{1}{(1.060395)^3}} = .06546
$$

equates the present value of the fixed-rate flows to the present value of floating-rate flows corresponding to the period of the underlying swap.

To illustrate, consider a 2-year 6%/LIBOR swap, 1 year forward in which the applicable zero swap yield curve and corresponding implied forward rates are the ones shown in Exhibit 19.3-2. The break-even forward rate for this 2-year, 6%/LIBOR swap 1 year forward is found by solving for that coupon rate, C_f^*, that equates the present value of the forward swap's future fixed-rate payments of C_f^* in Years 2 and 3 to the present value of the implied 1-year forward rates 1 year and 2 years from the present of $RI_{11} = .0603$ and $RI_{12} = .07099$ (assume that the first effective date on the underlying swap starts at the expiration date of the forward swap). That is, C_f^* where

$$
\frac{C_f^*}{(1 + Z(2))^2} + \frac{C_f^*}{(1 + Z(3))^3} = \frac{RI_{11}}{(1 + Z(2))^2} + \frac{RI_{12}}{(1 + Z(3))^3}
$$

$$
C_f^* = \frac{\dfrac{RI_{11}}{(1 + Z(2))^2} + \dfrac{RI_{12}}{(1 + Z(3))^3}}{\dfrac{1}{(1 + Z(2))^2} + \dfrac{1}{(1 + Z(3))^3}}
$$

Substituting the implied forward rates and zero-coupon rates into the preceding equation, we obtain a 6.546% break-even forward rate for the 2-year, 6%/LIBOR swap

1 year forward:

$$C_f^* = \frac{\dfrac{RI_{11}}{(1+Z(2))^2} + \dfrac{RI_{12}}{(1+Z(3))^3}}{\dfrac{1}{(1+Z(2))^2} + \dfrac{1}{(1+Z(3))^3}} = \frac{\dfrac{.0603}{(1.055138)^2} + \dfrac{.07099}{(1.060395)^3}}{\dfrac{1}{(1.055138)^2} + \dfrac{1}{(1.060395)^3}} = .06546$$

Given the specified fixed rate on the forward swap is at 6% and not at its break-even rate of 6.546%, the fixed-payer's position on the underlying swap would have a value beginning in Year 1 equal to the annual rate differential of 0.546% times the swap's NP (= $10M) for 2 years: $(.00546)(\$10M) = \$54,600$. The present value of this cash flow is equal to $94,835. Thus, the current value of the 2-year, 6%/LIBOR swap 1 year forward is $94,835:

Forward Swap Rate $= 6\%$ Per Year

Break $-$ Even Swap Rate $= 6.546\%$ Per Year

Fixed Payer's Cash Flow $= (.06546 - .06)\$10,000,000 = \$54,600$ for

Years 2 and 3

$$\text{Present Value} = \frac{\$54,600}{(1.055138)^2} + \frac{\$54,600}{(1.060395)^3} = \$94,835$$

The floating-payer's position on the forward swap would be $-\$94,835$, implying the forward position holder would require compensation. Note that if the forward swap rate had been set equal to the 6.546% break-even rate, then the economic value of the forward swap would be zero.

19.5 THE VALUATION OF A SWAPTION

19.5.1 Intrinsic Value

As with other options, the value of a swaption can be broken down into its intrinsic value, IV, and its time value premium, TVP. In determining a swaption's IV, it is important to remember that the asset underlying the option is a forward contract. That is, a 3-year payer swaption on a 2-year, 7%/LIBOR swap is an option to take a fixed-payer's position on a 2-year swap 3 years forward. The asset underlying this payer swaption is therefore the fixed-payer's position on a 3-year forward contract with a forward swap rate of 7%. Thus, the first step in calculating a swaption's IV is to determine the break-even rate on the underlying forward contract C_f^*. For example, in our previous example, we found the break-even forward rate for a 2-year swap 1 year forward to be equal to $C_f^* = 6.546\%$.

Consider a 1-year payer swaption on a 2-year, 6%/LIBOR swap. The buyer of this payer swaption would be purchasing a 1-year option on a 2-year swap to receive the LIBOR and pay 6%. With the break-even forward rate equal to 6.546% and a strike rate of 6%, the payer swaption's intrinsic value is the 0.546% interest rate differential on the NP for 2 years beginning 1 year from the present. Using the zero-coupon swap rates from Exhibit 19.2-1, the IV of this payer swaption is $94,835:

Payer Swaption Exercise Rate $= C^X = 6\%$
Break-Even Forward Swap Rate $= C_f^* = 6.546\%$

$$\text{Intrinsic Value} = \text{Max}[C_f^* - C^X, 0]\left[\frac{1}{(1 + Z(2))^2} + \frac{1}{(1 + Z(3))^3}\right]NP$$

$$\text{Max}(.06546 - .06, 0)(\$10,000,000) = \$54,600$$

$$\text{Intrinsic Value} = \frac{\$54,600}{(1.05513)^2} + \frac{\$54,600}{(1.060395)^3} = \$94,835$$

Note, the IV of the payer swaption is directly related to the underlying break-even rate; that is, for break-even rates above the exercise rate, C^X (6%), the IV increases as the break-even rate increases; and for rates below C^X (6%), it is zero. Also note that if the strike rate were below the break-even rate, then the payer swaption would be in the money, and its IV would be positive; if it were equal, the option would be at the money and its IV would be zero; if the strike rate were above the forward rate, then the payer swaption would be out of the money with an IV of zero. In general, the IV of a payer swaption (IV_P) is

$$IV_p = \text{Max}[C_f^* - C^X, 0]\left[\sum_{t=1}^{M}\frac{1}{(1 + Z(T + t))^t}\right]NP$$

$$IV_p = \text{Max}[.06546 - .06, 0]\left[\frac{1}{(1.055138)^2} + \frac{1}{(1.060395)^3}\right](\$10M)$$

$$IV_p = \$94,835$$

where
$\quad\quad$ T = expiration on the swaption
$\quad\quad$ M = Maturity on the underlying swap

Just the opposite relations hold for receiver swaptions. The receiver swaption's IV (IV_C) is

$$IV_C = \text{Max}[C^X - C_f^*, 0]\left[\sum_{t=1}^{M}\frac{1}{(1 + Z(T + t))^t}\right]NP$$

Thus, the IV on a 1-year receiver swaption on a 2-year swap with a strike rate of 7% (the right to receive 7% and pay **LIBOR**) with an NP of $10M would be $78,855:

$$IV_C = \text{Max}[.07 - .06546, 0]\left[\frac{1}{(1.055138)^2} + \frac{1}{(1.060395)^3}\right](\$10M) = \$78,855$$

The receiver swaption, in turn, would be at the money with an IV of zero when its strike and forward rates are equal; out of the money with a zero IV when the forward rate is greater than the strike rate; and in the money when the forward rate is below the strike rate, increasing as the forward rate decreases.

19.5.2 Time Value Premium

Given there is some time to expiration, a swaption will trade at a value above its IV. Like other options, the swaption's TVP depends primarily on the volatility of the underlying forward rate, with the greater the volatility, the greater the swaption's TVP and value. The volatility of forward rates is often estimated using current swap rates or spot Treasury rates as a proxy for the implied futures rates.

19.5.3 Black Futures Option Model

Swaptions can be valued using a binomial interest rate framework similar to the one presented in Chapter 7. A simpler model for valuing swaptions, though, is the Black futures option model described in Chapter 12. For payer swaptions that give the holder the right to pay a fixed rate C^X and receive the LIBOR, the value of the cash flow received at each payment date t_i after the swaption's expiration T is

$$\frac{NP}{m}e^{-R_{fi}t_i}[C_f N(d_1) - C^X N(d_2)]$$

$$d_1 = \frac{\ln(C_f/C^X) + \sigma^2 T/2}{\sigma\sqrt{T}}$$

$$d_2 = d_1 - \sigma\sqrt{T}$$

where

$C^* = $ swaption exercise rate (annual)

$C_f = $ break-even forward rate underlying the swaption (annual)

$R_{fi} = $ continuously compound annual risk-free rate for period of t_i

$m = $ number of payments on a swap in a year

$\sigma^2 = $ volatility of the forward or swap rate $= Var(\ln(R_t^{Swap}/R_0^{Swap})$

$t_i = $ payment dates in years on the swap $= T + i/m$

$T = $ swaption's expiration in years

The value of the payer swaption, in turn, is the sum of the values of each cash flow. If the underlying swap lasts n years starting at the swaption expiration in T years, then the value of the swaption is

$$V_P = \sum_{i=1}^{mn} \frac{NP}{m}e^{-R_{fi}t_i}[C_f N(d_1) - C^X N(d_2)]$$

and its intrinsic value is

$$IV_P = \sum_{i=1}^{mn} \frac{NP}{m}e^{-R_{fi}t_i}[Max(C_f - C^X, 0)]$$

To illustrate, consider a 3-year payer swaption on a 2-year, 7%/LIBOR swap: $C^X = .07$, the forward rate $= C_f = .08$, $T = 3$, $m = 2$, $n = 2$, and $NP = \$10M$.[2] If we assume

---

[2] This example is based on the example presented in Johnson, *Bond Evaluations, Selection, and Management,* Chapter 16, 2004.

a flat yield curve for risk-free securities in which the continuously compounded rate is 6.74% and a volatility of the swap rate of $\sigma = .2$, then the value of the swaption (V_p) would be \$241,752:

$$V_P = [.08(.71202) - .07N(.583944)] \times$$
$$[\$10M/2][e^{-(.0674)(3.5)} + e^{-(.0674)(4)} + e^{-(.0674)(4.5)} + e^{-(.0674)(5)}]$$
$$= \$241,752$$

where

$$d_1 = \frac{\ln(.08/.07) + .2^2 3/2}{.2\sqrt{3}} = .558677$$

$$d_2 = d_1 - .2\sqrt{3} = .212267$$

$$N(d_1) = N(.558677) = .71202$$

$$N(d_2) = N(.212267) = .583944$$

The payer swaption's intrinsic value using the Black continuous model is \$150,292:

$$IV = [Max(.08 - .07, 0)][\$10M/2][e^{-(.0674)(3.5)} + e^{-(.0674)(4)}$$
$$+ e^{-(.0674)(4.5)} + e^{-(.0674)(5)}]$$
$$IV = \$150,292$$

As we would expect, the Black futures model yields payer swaption values that are directly related to the break-even forward rates. This can be seen in Exhibit 19.5-1, which shows a graph and table of the Black model values for the 3-year payer swaption on a 3-year, 7%/LIBOR swap given different break-even forward rates. As shown in the exhibit, for low forward rates in which the swaption is deep out of the money, the Black model yields very low payer swaption values. As the forward rates increase by equal increments, the payer swaption values increase at an increasing rate, up to a point, with the values never being below the IV. In addition, the Black model yields payer swaption values that are directly related to the time to expiration on the swaption, the maturity on the swap, and the underlying swap rate's volatility.

For a receiver swaption, the swaption gives the holder the right to receive the fixed rate and pay the LIBOR. The value of each cash flow is

$$\frac{NP}{m}e^{-R_{fi}t_i}[-C_f(1 - N(d_1)) + C^X(1 - N(d_2))]$$

and the value (V_C) and the intrinsic value of the receiver swaption (IV_C) are

$$V_C = \sum_{i=1}^{mn} \frac{NP}{m}e^{-R_{fi}t_i}[-C_f(1 - N(d_1)) + C^X(1 - N(d_2))]$$

$$IV_C = \sum_{i=1}^{mn} \frac{NP}{m}e^{-R_{fi}t_i}[Max(C^X - C_f, 0)]$$

EXHIBIT 19.5-1   Payer Swaptions Values Using Black Futures Model Given Different Forward Rates

3-year payer swaption on a 2-year 7%/LIBOR swap: $C^X = .07$, $T = 3$, $m = 2$, $n = 2$, $NP = \$10M$, $R_{fi} = 6.74\%$, $\sigma = .2$

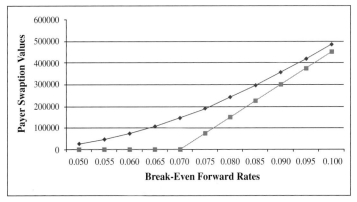

Break-Even Forward Rates	Payer Swaption Put Values	Payer Swaption Intrinsic Value
0.050	\$26,650	\$0
0.055	\$45,739	\$0
0.060	\$72,276	\$0
0.065	\$105,418	\$0
0.070	\$144,302	\$0
0.075	\$190,641	\$75,146
0.080	\$241,752	\$150,292
0.085	\$296,911	\$225,437
0.090	\$356,197	\$300,583
0.095	\$419,031	\$375,729
0.100	\$484,677	\$450,875

$$V_P = \sum_{i=1}^{mn} \frac{NP}{m} e^{-R_{fi}t_i}[C_f N(d_1) - C^X N(d_2)]$$

$$IV_P = \sum_{i=1}^{mn} \frac{NP}{m} e^{-R_{fi}t_i}[Max(C_f - C^X, 0)]$$

Using the Black futures model, the value of a 3-year receiver swaption on a 2-year, 7%/LIBOR swap would be \$91,461, and its intrinsic value would be zero:

$$V_C = [-.08(1 - N(.558677)) + .07(1 - N(.212267))] \times$$

$$[\$10M/2][e^{-(.0674)(3.5)} + e^{-(.0674)(4)} + e^{-(.0674)(4.5)} + e^{-(.0674)(5)}]$$

$$= \$91,461$$

$$IV_C = [Max(.07 - .08, 0)][\$10M/2][e^{-(.0674)(3.5)} + e^{-(.0674)(4)}$$

$$+ e^{-(.0674)(4.5)} + e^{-(.0674)(5)}] = 0$$

The Black futures model yields receiver swaption values that are inversely related to the break-even forward rates and directly related to the time to expiration on the swaption, the maturity on the swap, and the underlying swap rate's volatility. The inverse relation between the receiver swaption value and the forward rate is presented in Exhibit 19.5-2. The exhibit shows a graph and table of the Black model values for the 3-year receiver swaption on a 2-year, 7%/LIBOR swap given different break-even forward rates. As shown in the exhibit, for large forward rates in which the option is deep out of the money, the Black model yields very low receiver swaption values; and as the forward rates decrease by equal increments, the receiver swaption values increase at an increasing rate up to a point.

The "Black–Scholes Option Pricing Model" Excel program includes a worksheet ("Black Swaption Model") for calculating the values of payer and receiver swaptions using the Black futures option model.

EXHIBIT 19.5-2   Receiver Swaptions Values Using Black Futures Model Given Different Forward Rates

3-year receiver swaption on a 2-Year 7%/LIBOR swap: $C^X = .07$, $T = 3$, $M = 2$, $N = 2$, $NP = \$10M$, $R_{fi} = 6.74\%$, $\sigma = .2$

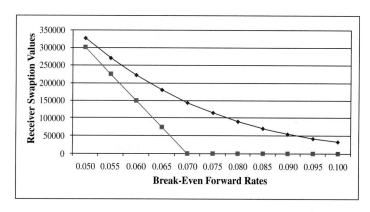

Break-Even Forward Rates	Swaption Value	Swaption Intrinsic Value
0.050	$327,233	$300,583
0.055	$271,176	$225,437
0.060	$222,568	$150,292
0.065	$180,563	$75,146
0.070	$144,302	$0
0.075	$115,495	$0
0.080	$91,461	$0
0.085	$71,473	$0
0.090	$55,614	$0
0.095	$43,302	$0
0.100	$33,802	$0

$$V_C = \sum_{i=1}^{mn} \frac{NP}{m} e^{-R_{fi}t_i} [-C_f(1 - N(d_1)) + C^X(1 - N(d_2))]$$

$$IV_C = \sum_{i=1}^{mn} \frac{NP}{m} e^{-R_{fi}t_i} [Max(C^X - C_f, 0)]$$

TABLE 19.5-1   Values at Expiration of a Payer Swaption and a Synthetic Payer Swaption Consisting of a Receiver Swaption and a Forward Swap Contract

Swap Rate on 2-year Generic Swap	6%	7%	8%
Long Payer swaption: Right to Pay 7%/Receive LIBOR	0	0	PV(8% − 7%)
Long Receiver swaption: Right to Receive 7%/pay LIBOR	PV(7% − 6%)	0	0
Forward Swap: Pay 7%/Receive LIBOR	PV(6% − 7%)	PV(7% − 7%)	PV(8% − 7%)
Net Value	0	0	PV(8% − 7%)

19.5.4   Put–Call-Futures Parity

Because the values of the forward swap, receiver swaption, and payer swaption ultimately depend on the underlying swap value at expiration, these derivative swaps are necessarily related. A put–call parity relation similar to the put–call-futures parity condition governing options and futures governs the relationship between them. In the case of swaptions, a payer swaption can be synthetically created with a similar receiver swaption and a forward swap contract as a fixed payer. This can be seen by observing that the possible values at expiration of the preceding 3-year payer swaption (payer on a 2-year swap with a strike rate of 7%) are identical to the values obtained from (1) a 3-year receiver swaption on a 2-year swap with an exercise rate of 7% and (2) a fixed position on a 2-year, 7%/LIBOR swap 3 years forward (see Table 19.5-1). Thus, by the law of one price, the value of a payer swaption is equal to the value of a similar receiver swaption plus the value of a similar long forward swap contract, F: $V_P = V_C + F$. The value of the forward contract, in turn, is equal to the difference between the payer and receiver swaption values: $F = V_P − V_C$.

In terms of our example, the receiver and payer swaption prices and the forward swaption price are consistent with the put–call-futures parity. That is, the value on the 2-year, 7%/LIBOR swap 3 years forward contract using continuous compounding and the 6.74% continuous compounded rate is $150,291:

$$F = [.08 − .07][\$10M/2][e^{-(.0674)(3.5)} + e^{-(.0674)(4)} + e^{-(.0674)(4.5)} + e^{-(.0674)(5)}]$$
$$= \$150,291$$

This value is equal to the difference in the Black futures model's payer and receiver swaptions values:

$$F = V_P − V_C = \$241,752 − \$91,461 = \$150,291$$

19.6   VALUATION OF CANCELABLE AND EXTENDABLE SWAPS

19.6.1   Valuing Cancelable Swaps

In Chapter 18, we defined a cancelable swap as a generic swap in which one of the counterparties has the option to terminate one or more payments. Recall that a callable cancelable swap is one in which the fixed payer has the right to early termination, whereas a putable cancelable swap is one in which the floating payer has the right to early cancellation. If there is only one termination date, then a cancelable swap is equivalent to a standard swap plus a position in a European swaption. For example, a 5-year putable cancelable swap to receive 7% and pay LIBOR that is cancelable after 3 years is equivalent to a floating position in a 5-year 7%/LIBOR generic swap and a long position in a three-year payer swaption on a two-year 7%/LIBOR swap; that is, after 3 years, the payer swaption gives the holder the right to take a fixed-payer's position on a 2-year swap at 7% that offsets the floating position on the 7% generic swap. On the other hand, a 5-year callable cancelable swap to pay 7% and receive LIBOR that is cancelable after 3 years would be equivalent to a fixed position in a 5-year, 7%/LIBOR, generic swap and a long position in a 3-year, receiver swaption on a 2-year, 7%/LIBOR swap.

The value of a cancelable swap is equal to the value of the generic swap plus the value of the underlying option (IV + TVP). If the preceding 5-year, 7%/LIBOR, generic swap is at par, then the value of a 5-year putable swap cancelable after 3 years would be equal to the value of a 3-year payer swaption on a 2-year, 7%/LIBOR swap. If the break-even forward rate on a 2-year swap 3 years forward were 8%, as was the case in our payer swaption example, then the value of cancelable swap with an NP of $10M would be equal to the payer swaption's value of $241,752 (using the Black futures model). The value of a 5-year callable swap cancelable after 3 years, in turn, would be equal to the value of a 3-year receiver swaption on a 2-year, 7%/LIBOR swap of $91,461 (using the Black futures model).

19.6.2 Valuing Extendable Swaps

Recall from Chapter 18 that an extendable swap is one that has an option to lengthen the terms of the original swap. Like cancelable swaps, extendable swaps can be replicated with a generic swap and a swaption. The floating payer with an extendable option has the equivalent of a floating position on a generic swap and a receiver swaption. That is, a 3-year swap to receive 7% and pay LIBOR that is extendable at maturity to 2 more years would be equivalent to a floating position in a 3-year, 7%/LIBOR, generic swap and a long position in a 3-year, receiver swaption on a 2-year 7%/LIBOR. If a 3-year, 7%/LIBOR, generic swap is at par, then the value of the extendable floating-payer swap would be equal to the value of a 3-year receiver swaption on a 2-year, 7%/LIBOR swap. If the break-even forward rate on a 2-year swap 3 years forward were 8%, as was the case in our swaption example, then the value of cancelable swap with an NP of $10M would be equal to the receiver swaption's value of $91,461 (using the Black futures model).

In contrast, the fixed payer with an extendable option has the equivalent of a fixed position on a generic swap and a payer swaption. The value of a 3-year swap to pay 7% and receive LIBOR that is extendable at maturity to 2 more years would therefore be equal to the value of the generic, 3-year, 7%/LIBOR swap and the value of a 3-year, payer swaption on a 2-year, 7%/LIBOR swap. If a 3-year, 7%/LIBOR, generic swap is at par, then the value of an extendable fixed-payer swap would be equal to the value of a 3-year payer swaption on a 2-year, 7%/LIBOR swap. If the break-even forward rate on a 2-year swap 3 years forward were again 8%, then the value of extendable swap with an NP of $10M would be equal to the payer swaption's value of $241,752.

19.7 CONCLUSION

In this chapter, we've examine how current and forward break-even swap rates are determined and how those rates determine the values of off-market swaps, forward swaps, and swaptions. As with all derivatives, the underlying economic principle governing the valuation of swaps and swap derivatives is the law of one price. In the case of swaps, this principle exists because a swap position can be replicated: A current swap can be replicated with fixed-rate and floating-rate bond positions; an off-market swap can be replicated with either a bond position or a par value swap. The ability of swap banks, in turn, to access other markets to hedge or offset their positions with bonds, swaps, and other derivative positions ultimately determines the swap rates and the values of swap and swap derivative positions.

In this and the last chapter, we examine the features, markets, uses, and pricing of the generic interest rate swaps, forward swaps, and swaptions. In the next chapter, we conclude our analysis of swaps by looking at two other popular financial swaps—the currency swap and the credit default swap.

KEY TERMS

replacement swap	bootstrapping	implied forward rate
YTM approach	break-even rate	forward swap rate
zero-coupon approach	market rate	

SELECTED REFERENCES

Brotherton-Ratcliffe, R., and B. Iben. "Yield Curve Applications of Swap Products." In *Advanced Strategies in Financial Risk Management*, edited by R. Schwartz and C. Smith. New York: New York Institute of Finance, 1993.

Brown, J. P. "Variations to Basic Swaps." In *Interest Rate Swaps,* edited by C. R. Beidleman. Homewood, IL: Business One Irwin, 1991.

Haubrich, J. G. "Swaps and the Swaps Yield Curve." *Economic Commentary*, Federal Reserve Bank of Cleveland (December 2001): 1–4.

Johnson, R. S. *Bond Evaluation, Selection, and Management.* Malden, MA: Blackwell Publishing Inc., 2004, Chapter 17.

Minton, B. A. "An Empirical Examination of the Basic Valuation Models for Interest Rate Swaps." *Journal of Financial Economics* 44 (1997): 251–77.

O'Brien, T. "A No-Arbitrage Term Structure Model and the Valuation of Interest Rate Swaps." In *The Handbook of Interest Rate Risk Management,* edited by J. C. Francis and A. S. Wolf. New York: Irwin Professional Publishing, 1994.

Smith, D. R. "Techniques for Deriving a Zero Coupon Curve for Pricing Interest Rate Swaps: A Simplified Approach." In *The Handbook of Interest Rate Risk Management,* edited by J. C. Francis and A. S. Wolf. New York: Irwin Professional Publishing, 1994.

Sun, T., S. Sundaresan, and C. Wang. "Interest Rate Swaps: An Empirical Investigation." *Journal of Financial Economics* 36 (1993): 77–99.

Turnbull, S. M. "Swaps: A Zero Sum Game." *Financial Management* 16 (Spring 1987): 15–21.

PROBLEMS AND QUESTIONS

1. Suppose a swap bank can go long and short in 4-year FRNs paying LIBOR and 4-year T-notes yielding 6%.

   a. Given these securities, define a 4-year generic par value swap the bank could offer its customers with AAA quality ratings. Exclude the basis points that the swap bank might add to its bid and ask prices and assume no credit risk.

   b. Explain how the swap bank determines basis points to add to the fixed rate on its fixed and floating positions.

   c. Suppose the swap bank provided one of its customers with a 6%/LIBOR fixed-rate position. Explain how the bank would hedge its position with the preceding securities if it did not have a customer taking an opposite swap position.

d. Suppose the swap bank provided one of its AAA-quality customers with a 4-year, 6%/LIBOR, floating-rate position. Explain how the bank would hedge its position with the preceding securities if it did not have a customer taking an opposite swap position.

2. Given the 6% yield on 4-year T-notes and LIBOR yields on FRN in Question 1, how much would the swap bank pay or charge to buy an *existing* floating-rate payer's position on a 4-year, 7%/LIBOR swap with an NP of $50M if it planned to hedge the purchase with positions in the T-note and FRN? Exclude the basis points that the swap bank might add to its bid and ask prices.

3. If the swap bank in Question 1 were offering 4-year, generic, 6%/LIBOR, par value swaps, how much would it pay or charge to buy a floating-rate payer's position on an *existing* 4-year, 7%/LIBOR swap with an NP of $50M if it planned to hedge the purchase with a position on its par value swaps? How much would it pay or charge for an existing fixed-payer's position on a 4-year, 7%/LIBOR with an NP of $50M? Exclude the basis points that the swap bank might add to its bid and ask prices.

4. Given the following spot rates on 1-year to 4-year zero-coupon bonds:

Year	Spot Rate
1	8.0%
2	8.5%
3	9.0%
4	9.5%

a. What is the equilibrium price of a 4-year, 9% coupon bond paying a principal of $100 at maturity and coupons annually?

b. If the market prices the 4-year bond such that it yields 10%, what is the bond's market price?

c. What would arbitrageurs do given the prices you determined in (a) and (b)? What impact would their actions have on the market price?

d. What would arbitrageurs do if the market price exceeded the equilibrium price? What impact would their actions have on the market price?

5. Given a 1-year pure discount bond (PDB) trading at 100 and promising to pay 106 at maturity and a 2-year 6% coupon bond with face value of 100, annual payments, and trading at 96.54:

a. Determine the 1-year and 2-year spot rates using the bootstrapping technique.

b. What is the equilibrium price of a comparable 2-year, 8% annual coupon bond (F = 100)?

6. Bond X is a 1-year PDB with face value of $1,000 trading at $945, and Bond Y is a 2-year PDB with a face value of $1,000 trading at $870:

a. Determine algebraically the implied forward rate RI_{11}.

b. Explain how the forward rate can be attained by a locking-in strategy.

7. Assume the following yield curve for zero-coupon bonds with a face value of 100:

Maturity	YTM
1 Year	7%
2 Years	8%
3 Years	8%
4 Years	7%
5 Years	6%

a. Using implied forward rates, estimate the yield curve 1 year from the present (implied rates on 1-year, 2-year, 3-year, and 4-year bonds).

b. Using implied forward rates, estimate the yield curve 2 years from the present (implied rates on 1-year, 2-year, and 3-year bonds).

8. The table following shows the swap rates for generic par value swaps with maturities from 1 to 5 years.

a. Using the bootstrapping approach, determine the zero-coupon swap rates with maturities of 1 to 5 years.

b. Using the zero-coupon approach, determine the values of fixed and floating positions on a 3-year, 5%/LIBOR, off-market swap with NP = $10M and with annual payments instead of the standard semiannual payments.

c. Using the YTM approach, determine the values of fixed and floating positions on a 3-year, 5%/LIBOR, off-market swap with NP = $10M and with annual payments instead of the standard semiannual payments.

d. Explain what a swap dealer/arbitrageur would do if the fixed-payer's position on the 3-year, 5%/LIBOR, off-market swap were priced using the YTM approach.

Maturity in Years	Swap Rate
1	.05
2	.053
3	.057
4	.0615
5	.0662

9. The table following shows swap rates for current par value swaps along with zero-coupon swap rates obtained using the bootstrapping approach (these are same rates found in Question 8).

Maturity in Years	Swap Rate	Zero Coupon Rate: Z(Maturity)
1	.05	.05
2	.053	.05308
3	.057	.05729
4	.0615	.062176
5	.0662	.0674697

a. Given the zero-coupon swap rates, determine the implied 1-year forward rates: RI_{11}, RI_{12}, RI_{13}, and RI_{14}.

b. Using the rates, determine the break-even rate for a 3-year, 5.7%/LIBOR swap. Assume the underlying swaps make payments annually, and payment dates are 1 year after effective dates.

   c. Using the rates, determine the break-even rate on a 2-year, 7%/LIBOR swap 3 years forward. Assume the underlying swaps make payments annually, and payment dates are 1 year after effective dates.

   d. What is the value of the fixed position on a 2-year, 7%/LIBOR swap 3 years forward with an NP = $10M?

10. The table following shows zero-coupon swap rates and implied 1-year forward rates. Using the zero-coupon valuation approach, determine the current value of a fixed payer's position on a forward swap position on a 3-year, 9%/LIBOR swap 3 years forward with an NP of $10M. Assume the underlying swap makes payments annually and not the standard semiannual length, that the first effective date on the underlying swap starts at the expiration of the forward swap, and that payment dates are 1 year after the effective dates.

Maturity in Years	Zero Coupon Rates: Z(Maturity)	Implied 1-Year Forward Rates: f_{1M}
1	5.0%	6.0%
2	5.5%	7.0%
3	6.0%	8.0%
4	6.5%	9.0%
5	7.0%	10.0%
6	7.5%	11.0%
7	8.0%	

11. The table following shows zero-coupon swap rates and implied 1-year forward rates (the same rates as those in Question 10).

Maturity in Years	Zero Coupon Rates: Z(Maturity)	Implied 1-Year Forward Rates: f_{1M}
1	5.0%	6.0%
2	5.5%	7.0%
3	6.0%	8.0%
4	6.5%	9.0%
5	7.0%	10.0%
6	7.5%	11.0%
7	8.0%	

Using these rates, determine the intrinsic values of the following swaptions:

   a. Three-year payer swaption on a 3-year, 7.94%/LIBOR swap with a notional principal of $10M.

   b. Three-year payer swaption on a 3-year, 11%/LIBOR swap with a notional principal of $10M.

   c. Three-year receiver swaption on a 3-year, 9.94%/LIBOR swap with a notional principal of $10M.

   d. Three-year receiver swaption on a 3-year, 7%/LIBOR swap with a notional principal of $10M.

Assume the underlying swaps makes payments annually and not the standard semi-annual length, that the first effective date on the underlying swap starts at the expiration of the forward swap, and that payment dates are 1 year after effective dates.

12. Use the Black futures option model to determine the value of a 3-year payer swaptions on a 3-year, 9%/LIBOR swaps with notional principal of $10M, break-even rate on

the underlying forward contract of .10, semiannual periods, continuous compounded risk-free rate of 6%, and a volatility of the swap rate of σ = .075. What is the value of a receiver swaption with similar terms? Do the swaption values conform to the put–call-futures parity condition?

13. Given a 2-year payer swaption on a 3-year, 7%/LIBOR swap with notional principal of $10M, semiannual periods, continuous compounded risk-free rate of 5%, and a volatility of the swap rate of σ = .10, use the Black futures option model to determine the values and intrinsic values of the swaption given the following break-even rates on the underlying forward contract: 5%, 5.5%, 6%, 6.5%, 7%, 7.5%, 8%, 8.5%, and 9%. Comment on the relation you observe.

14. Given a 2-year receiver swaption on a 3-year, 7%/LIBOR swap with notional principal of $10M, semiannual periods, continuous compounded risk-free rate of 5%, and a volatility of the swap rate of σ = .10, use the Black futures option model to determine the values and intrinsic values of the swaption given the following break-even rates on the underlying forward contract: 5%, 5.5%, 6%, 6.5%, 7%, 7.5%, 8%, 8.5%, and 9%. Plot the break-even forward rates, receiver swaption values, and receiver swaption intrinsic values. Comment on the relation you observe.

15. Determine the price of a 6-year, 9%/LIBOR, putable cancelable swap with notional principal of $10M cancelable after 3 years given (1) a current 6-year, 9%/LIBOR, generic swap is at par and (2) a 10% break-even rate on the underlying forward contract on a 3-year payer swaption on a 3-year, 9%/LIBOR swap. Assume the continuous compounded risk-free rate is 5%, and volatility of the swap rate is σ = .075.

16. What is the price of a 6-year, 9%/LIBOR, callable cancelable swap with notional principal of $10M cancelable after 3 years given (1) a current 6-year, 9%/LIBOR generic swap is at par, and (2) a 10% break-even rate on the underlying forward contract on a 3-year receiver swaption on a 3-year, 9%/LIBOR swap. Assume the continuous compounded risk-free rate is 5%, and volatility of the swap rate is σ = .075.

WEB EXERCISE

1. Examine links to swap data and pricing models by going to www.isda.org and clicking "Education."

CHAPTER 20

CURRENCY AND CREDIT SWAPS

20.1 INTRODUCTION

Since the mid-1970s there has been an active currency swap market amongst financial and nonfinancial corporations. Although there is some debate over the exact swap agreement marking the beginning of this market, many observers point to the World Bank and IBM swap in 1981 as the agreement that propelled the tremendous growth that has occurred in both currency and interest rate swap markets over the last two decades. Concomitant with this growth has been the number of innovations introduced in swaps contracts over the years. Today, there are a number of nongeneric swaps used by financial and nonfinancial corporations to manage their varied cash flow and return-risk problems. Over the last decade, one of the fastest growing swaps has been the credit default swap. This swap allows companies to trade credit risk and by so doing change the credit risk exposure of their debt and fixed-income assets. In this chapter, we conclude our analysis of swaps by examining currency swaps and credit default swaps.

20.2 CURRENCY SWAPS

In its simplest form, a currency swap involves an exchange of principal and interest in one currency for the interest and principal in another. For example, the Proctor and Gamble Company swaps a 9% loan in dollars to the British Petroleum Company for their 10% loan in sterling. The market for currency swaps comes primarily from corporations who can borrow in one currency at relatively favorable terms but need to borrow in another. For example, a U.S. multinational corporation that can obtain favorable borrowing terms for a dollar loan but really needs a loan in sterling to finance its operations in London might use a currency swap. To meet such a need, the company could go to a swap dealer who would try to match its needs with another party wanting the opposite position. For example, the dealer might match the U.S. corporation with a British multinational corporation with operations in the United States that it is financing with a sterling-denominated loan but would prefer instead a dollar-denominated loan. If the loans are approximately equivalent, then the dealer could arrange a swap agreement in which the companies simply exchange their principal and interest payments. If the loans are not equivalent, the swap dealer may have to bring in other parties who are looking to swap, or the dealer could take the opposite position and warehouse the swap.[1]

---

[1] Currency swaps evolved from back-to-back loans and parallel loans. In a back-to-back loan, companies exchange loans denominated in different currencies; in a parallel loan, one corporation loans to the subsidiary of a foreign multinational and vice versa. For example, a British parent company provides a loan to a British subsidiary of a U.S.-based multinational, whereas a U.S. parent company provides a dollar loan to an American subsidiary of a British company.

Example

As an example, suppose the British Auto Company plans to issue 5-year bonds worth £100M at 7.5% interest but actually needs an equivalent amount in dollars, $142.857M (current $/£ rate is $1.42875/£), to finance its new manufacturing facility in the United States. Also, suppose that the Barkley Shoe Company, a U.S. company, plans to issue $142.857M in bonds at 10%, with a maturity of 5 years, but it really needs £100M to set up its distribution center in London. To meet each other's needs, suppose that both companies go to a swap bank that sets up the following agreements:

Agreement 1:

1. The British Auto Company will issue 5-year, £100M bonds paying 7.5% interest. It will then deliver the £100M to the swap bank that will pass it on to the U.S. Barclay Company to finance the construction of its British distribution center.
2. The Barclay Company will issue 5-year, $142.857M bonds. The Barclay Company will then pass the $142.857M to the swap bank that will pass it on to the British Auto Company who will use the funds to finance the construction of its U.S. manufacturing facility.

The initial cash flows of the agreement are shown in Exhibit 20.2-1.a.

Agreement 2:

1. The British company, with its U.S. asset (assembly plant), will pay the 10% interest on $142.857M ($14.2857M) to the swap bank that will pass it on to the American company so it can pay its U.S. bondholders.
2. The American company, with its British asset (distribution center), will pay the 7.5% interest on £100M ((.075)(£100M) = £7.5M), to the swap bank that will pass it on to the British company so it can pay its British bondholders.

The yearly cash flows of interest are summarized in Exhibit 20.2-1.b.

Agreement 3:

1. At maturity, the British company will pay $142.857M to the swap bank that will pass it on to the American company so it can pay its U.S. bondholders.
2. At maturity, the American company will pay £100M to the swap bank that will pass it on to the British company so it can pay its British bondholders.

The cash flows of principals are shown in Exhibit 20.2-1.c.

20.2.1 Valuation

20.2.1.1 Equivalent Bond Positions

In the preceding swap agreement, the American company will receive $14.2857M each year for 5 years and a principal of $142.857M at maturity and will pay £7.5M each year for 5 years and £100M at maturity. To the American company, this swap agreement is the equivalent to a position in two bonds: A long position in a dollar-denominated, 5-year, 10% annual coupon bond with a principal of $142.857M and trading at par and a short position in a sterling-denominated, 5-year, 7.5% annual coupon bond with a principal of

£100M and trading at par. The dollar value of the American company's swap position in which dollars are received and sterling is paid is

$$SV = B_\$ - E_0 \, B_£$$

where

$$B_\$ = \text{Dollar-Denominated Bond Value}$$
$$B_£ = \text{Sterling-Denominated Bond Value}$$
$$E_0 = \text{Spot Exchange Rate} = \$/BP$$

The dollar value of the swap to the American Company in terms of equivalent bond positions is zero:

$$SV = \$142.857M - (\$1.428570/BP)(£100M) = 0$$

The British company's swap position in which it will receive sterling and pay dollars is just the opposite of the American's position. It is equivalent to a long position in a sterling-denominated bond and short position in a dollar-denominated bond. In this example, it likewise has a value of zero:

$$SV = E_0 \, B_£ - B_\$$$
$$SV = (\$1.42857/£)(£100M) - \$100M = 0$$

Similar to interest rate swaps, the currency swap's economic value of zero means that neither counterparty is required to pay the other. The zero value also implies that the underlying bond positions trade at par. Thus, the currency swap in this example is a par value swap. Note that the swap dealer in this example has a perfect hedge given his two opposite positions. If the dealer, though, had been warehousing swaps and provided a swap to just the American company, then it could have hedged its swap position of paying $14.2857M and receiving £7.5M by shorting the 7.5% sterling-denominated bond and buying the 10% U.S. dollar-denominated bond.

The economic values of the swap positions will change with changes in U.S. rates, R_{US}, British rates, $R_£$, and the spot exchange rate:

$$SV = f(R_{US}, R_£, E_0)$$

For example, suppose in our example that 1 year later rates on British pounds and the exchange rate were the same but rates on U.S. dollars were higher, with the YTM on the U.S. dollar-denominated bond at 10.5%. In this case, the value of a 4-year, 10%, dollar-denominated bond would be $140.617M; and the value of the 4-year, $14.2857 M–received/£7.5M–paid swap would be –$2.24M:

$$SV = \$140.617M - (\$1.42857/£)(£100M) = -\$2.24M$$

where

$$B_\$ = \sum_{t=1}^{4} \frac{\$14.2857M}{(1.105)^t} + \frac{\$142.857M}{(1.105)^4} = \$140.617M$$

$$B_{BP} = \sum_{t=1}^{4} \frac{7.5M \, BP}{(1.075)^t} + \frac{100M \, BP}{(1.075)^4} = 100M \, BP$$

EXHIBIT 20.2-1   Currency Swap

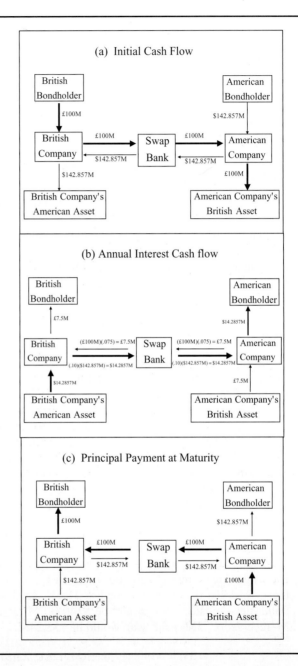

If the American company wanted to close its swap position by selling (or transferring) its remaining 4-year, $14.2857M received/£7.5M paid swap to a dealer, that dealer would require compensation of at least $2.24M. The dealer's fee of $2.24M would, in turn, defray his net hedging cost of selling a 4-year, 10%, dollar-denominated bond trading at 10.5% and buying a 4-year, 7.5%, sterling-denominated bond at par.

In general, the value of a dollar-received/foreign-currency-paid swap is inversely related to U.S. interest rates and the exchange rate and directly related to the foreign rate, whereas the value of a foreign–currency-received/dollar-paid swap, valued in dollars, is directly related to U.S. rates and the exchange rate and inversely related to the foreign rate.

20.2.1.2 Equivalent Forward Exchange Positions

Instead of viewing its swap as a bond position, the British company could alternatively view its interest agreement to pay $14.2857M for £7.5M each year for 5 years and its principal agreement to pay $142.857M for £100M at maturity as a series of long currency forward contracts in years 1, 2, 3, 4, and 5. In contrast, the American company could view its swap agreements to sell £7.5M each year for $10M and sell £100M at maturity for $142.857M as a series of short currency forward contracts. Exhibit 20.2-2 shows the annual cash flow exchanges for the two companies, with each of the exchanges representing a forward exchange contract.

In the absence of arbitrage, the value of the American company's swap of dollars received/British Pounds paid should be equal to (1) the sum the present values of $14.2857M received each year from the swap minus the dollar cost of buying £7.5M at the forward exchange rate and (2) the present value of the $142.857M received at Year 5 minus the dollar cost of buying £100M at the 5-year forward exchange rate. The equilibrium forward exchange rates, E_f, can be determined by using the interest rate parity relation:

$$E_f = E_0 \left(\frac{1 + R_{US}}{1 + R_{BP}} \right)^T$$

EXHIBIT 20.2-2   Swap Cash Flows to American and British Companies

American Company

Year	$ CF (Million)	£CF
0	–$142.857M	+£100M
1	+$14.2857M	–£7.5M
2	+$14.2857M	–£7.5M
3	+$14.2857M	–£7.5M
4	+$14.2857M	–£7.5M
5	+ ($142.857M + $14.2857M)	–(£100M + £7.5M)

British Company

Year	$ CF (Million)	£CF
0	+$142.857M	–£100M
1	–$14.2857M	+£7.5M
2	–$14.2857M	+£7.5M
3	–$14.2857M	+£7.5M
4	–$14.2857M	+£7.5M
5	–($142.857M + $14.2857M)	+(£100M + £7.5M)

Assuming a flat yield curve in the United States and Great Britain and using the 10% and 7.5% rates on the swap, the equilibrium forward rates for Years 1, 2, 3, 4, and 5 are

$$T = 1 : E_f = (\$1.42857/£)\left(\frac{1.10}{1.075}\right)^1 = \$1.46179256/£$$

$$T = 2 : E_f = (\$1.42857/£)\left(\frac{1.10}{1.075}\right)^2 = \$1.4957877/£$$

$$T = 3 : E_f = (\$1.42857/£)\left(\frac{1.10}{1.075}\right)^3 = \$1.5305735/£$$

$$T = 4 : E_f = (\$1.42857/£)\left(\frac{1.10}{1.075}\right)^4 = \$1.5661682/£$$

$$T = 5 : E_f = (\$1.42857/£)\left(\frac{1.10}{1.075}\right)^5 = \$1.60259074/£$$

In this example, the value of the American company's swap as a series of forward contracts is zero:

$$SV = \frac{\$14.2857M - (\$1.46179256/£)(£7.5)}{(1.10)^1} + \frac{\$14.2857M - (\$1.4957877/£)(£7.5)}{(1.10)^2}$$

$$+ \frac{\$14.2857M - (\$1.5305735/£)(£7.5)}{(1.10)^3} + \frac{\$14.2857M - (\$1.5661682/£)(£7.5)}{(1.10)^4}$$

$$+ \frac{\$14.2857M - (\$1.60259074/£)(£7.5)}{(1.10)^5} + \frac{\$142.857M - (\$1.60259074/£)(£100M)}{(1.10)^5}$$

$$SV = 0$$

Similarly, in the absence of arbitrage, the *dollar* value of the British company's swap of sterling received/dollars paid using forward exchange rate positions is equal to (1) the sum of present values from receiving £7.5M each year and converting it to dollars at the forward exchange rate minus the $14.2857M payments and (2) the present value of the £100M principal received times the 5-year forward exchange minus the $142.857M paid. Like the American company, given flat yield curves at 10% and 7.5%, the value of the British Company's swap is also zero.

In general, the value of a dollar-received/foreign–currency-paid swap as a series of forward contracts is

$$SV = \sum_{t=1}^{M} \frac{(\$Received) - E_{ft}(FC\,Paid)}{(1 + R_{US})^t}$$

and the dollar value of a FC received/$paid swap is

$$SV = \sum_{t=1}^{M} \frac{E_{ft}(FC\,Received) - (\$Paid)}{(1 + R_{US})^t}$$

Note that in the absence of arbitrage, the values of the swap positions as forward contracts are equal to their values as bond positions:

$$SV = \sum_{t=1}^{M} \frac{(\$Received) - E_{ft}(FC\,Paid)}{(1 + R_{US})^t} = B_\$ - E_0 B_{FC}$$

For example, if 1 year later rates were at 10.5%, then the value the U.S.-dollar-received/British–Pound-paid swap position as forward contracts is –$2.24M, the same value we obtained using the bond valuation approach:

$$T = 1 : E_f = (\$1.42857/\pounds)\left(\frac{1.105}{1.075}\right)^1 = \$1.46843707/\pounds$$

$$T = 2 : E_f = (\$1.42857/\pounds)\left(\frac{1.105}{1.075}\right)^2 = \$1.50941671/\pounds$$

$$T = 3 : E_f = (\$1.42857/\pounds)\left(\frac{1.105}{1.075}\right)^3 = \$1.55153997/\pounds$$

$$T = 4 : E_f = (\$1.42857/\pounds)\left(\frac{1.105}{1.075}\right)^4 = \$1.59483876/\pounds$$

$$SV = \frac{\$14.2857M - (\$1.46843707/\pounds)(\pounds7.5)}{(1.105)^1} + \frac{\$14.2857M - (\$1.50941671/\pounds)(\pounds7.5)}{(1.105)^2}$$

$$+ \frac{\$14.2857M - (\$1.55153997/\pounds)(\pounds7.5)}{(1.105)^3}$$

$$+ \frac{\$14.2857M - (\$1.59483876/\pounds)(\pounds7.5)}{(1.105)^4}$$

$$+ \frac{\$142.857M - (\$1.59483876/\pounds)(\pounds100M)}{(1.105)^4}$$

$$SV = -2.24M$$

20.2.2 Comparative Advantage

The currency swap in the preceding example represents an exchange of equivalent loans. Most currency swaps, though, are the result of financial and nonfinancial corporations exploiting a comparative advantage resulting from different rates in different currencies for different borrowers. Recall, in the case of interest rate swaps, we pointed out that observed differences in credit spreads could be the result of either comparative advantage or hidden options on floating-rate loans. In the case of currency swaps, though, the existence of such differences is more likely to be the result of actual comparative advantages.

To see the implications of comparative advantage with currency swaps, suppose the American and British companies in the preceding example both have access to each country's lending markets and that the American company is more creditworthy and as such, can obtain lower rates than the British company in both the U.S. and British markets. For example, suppose the American company can obtain 10% U.S. dollar-denominated loans in the U.S. market and 7.25% sterling-denominated loans in the British market, whereas the best the British company can obtain is 11% in the U.S. market and 7.5% in the British market:

With these rates, the American company has a comparative advantage in the U.S. market: It pays 1% less than the British company in the U.S. market compared to only .25% less in the British market. On the other hand, the British company has a comparative advantage in the British market: It pays .25% more than the U.S. company in Britain compared to 1% more in the United States. When such a comparative advantage exists,

Loan Rates for American and British Companies in Dollars and Pounds

Spot: $E_0 = \$/£ = \$1.42857/£$		
	Dollar Market (Rate on $)	**Pound Market (Rate on £)**
American Company	10%	7.25%
British Company	11%	7.5%

a swap bank is in a position to arrange a swap to benefit one or both companies. For example, suppose in this case, a swap bank sets up the following swap arrangement:

1. The American company borrows $142.857M at 10% and then agrees to swap it for £100M loan at 7%.
2. The British company borrows £100M at 7.5% and then agrees to swap it for $142.857M loan at 10.6%.

Exhibit 20.2-3 shows the annual cash flows of interest for the agreement (the cash flow at the outset and at maturity are the same as in previous examples shown in Exhibit 20.2-1). In this swap arrangement, the American company benefits by paying .25% less than it could obtain by borrowing British pounds directly in the British market, and the British company gains by paying 0.4% less than it could obtain directly from the U.S. market.

Note that the swap bank in this case will receive $15.142842M each year from the British company while only having to pay $14.2857M to the American company for a net dollar receipt of $0.857142M. On the other hand, the swap bank will receive only £7M from the American company while having to pay £7.5M to the British company for a net sterling payment of £0.5M:

Swap Bank's Dollar Position	**Swap Bank's £ Position**
Receives: (.106)($142.857M) = $15.142842M	Receives: (.07)(£100M) = £7M
Pays: (.10)($142.857M) = $14.2857M	Pays: (.075)(£100M) = £7.5M
Net $ Receipt: $15.142842M − $14.2857M = $0.857142M	Net £ Payment: £7.5M − £7M = £0.5M

Thus, the swap bank has a position equivalent to a series of long currency forward contracts in which it agrees to buy £0.5M for $0.857142M each year. The swap bank's implied forward rate on each of these contracts is $1.714284/£:

$$E_f = \frac{\$0.857142M}{£0.5M} = \frac{\$1.714284}{£}$$

The swap bank can hedge its position with currency forward contracts. If the forward rate is less than $1.714284/£, then the bank could gain from hedging the swap agreement with forward contracts to buy £0.5M each year for the next 5 years. For example, suppose the yield curves applicable for the swap bank are flat at 9.5% in U.S. dollars and 7% in pounds. Using the interest rate parity relation, the 1-, 2-, 3-, 4-, and 5-year forward exchange rates would be

$$E_f = E_0 \left(\frac{1 + R_{US}}{1 + R_{GB}}\right)^T$$

$$T = 1 : E_f = (\$1.42857/£)\left(\frac{1.095}{1.07}\right)^1 = \$1.4619478/£$$

EXHIBIT 20.2-3   Currency Swap: Comparative Advantage

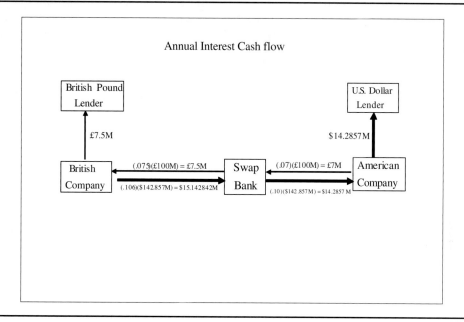

Annual Interest Cash flow

British Pound Lender

U.S. Dollar Lender

£7.5M

$14.2857M

British Company

$(.075)(£100M) = £7.5M$

Swap Bank

$(.07)(£100M) = £7M$

American Company

$(.106)(\$142.857M) = \$15.142842M$

$(.10)(\$142.857M) = \$14.2857M$

$$T = 2 : E_f = (\$1.42857/£)\left(\frac{1.095}{1.07}\right)^2 = \$1.4961055/£$$

$$T = 3 : E_f = (\$1.42857/£)\left(\frac{1.095}{1.07}\right)^3 = \$1.5310612/£$$

$$T = 4 : E_f = (\$1.42857/£)\left(\frac{1.095}{1.07}\right)^4 = \$1.5668336/£$$

$$T = 5 : E_f = (\$1.42857/£)\left(\frac{1.095}{1.07}\right)^5 = \$1.6034419/£$$

The swap bank could enter into forward contracts to buy £0.5M each year for the next 5 years at these forward rates. With all of the forward rates less than the implied forward rate $1.714284/£, the bank's dollar costs of buying £0.5M each year would be less than its $0.857142M annual inflow from the swap. By combining its swap position with forward contracts, the bank would be able to earn a total profit from the deal of $456,020 (see Exhibit 20.2-4).

Instead of forward contracts, the swap bank also could hedge its swap position by using a money market position. For example, on its first sterling liability of £0.5M due in 1 year, the bank would need to create a sterling asset worth £0.5M 1 year later (current value of £0.46728972M = £0.5M/1.07) and a dollar liability worth $0.857142M or less. The bank could do this by borrowing $0.66755608M (= ($1.42857/£)(£0.46728972M)) at 9.5%, converting it to £0.46728972M, and investing the sterling at 7% interest for the next year. One year later, the bank would have £0.5M (= £0.46728972M(1.07)) from the investment to cover its sterling swap liability and would have a dollar liability of $0.730974M (= $0.66755608M(1.095)), which is less than the $0.857142M dollar inflow from the

EXHIBIT 20.2-4 Swap Bank's Hedged Position

1	2	3	4	5	6
Year	$ CF (millions)	£ CF (millions)	Forward Exchange: $/£	$ Cost of Sterling (millions) Column (4) X Column (3)	Net $ Revenue (millions) Column (2) - Column (5)
1	$0.857142	−£0.50	1.4619478	$0.7309739	$0.12617
2	$0.857142	−£0.50	1.4961055	$0.7480528	$0.10909
3	$0.857142	−£0.50	1.5310612	$0.7655306	$0.09161
4	$0.857142	−£0.50	1.5668336	$0.7834168	$0.07373
5	$0.857142	−£0.50	1.6034419	$0.8017210	$0.05542
					$0.45602

swap. The bank would thus earn a profit of $0.12617M from the hedged cash flow—the same profit it would earn from hedging with the forward exchange contracts if the interest rate parity relation holds. By forming the same types of money market positions for each sterling liability, the bank could obtain the same total profit of $456,020 that it would have received from the forward-hedged positions.

In summary, the presence of comparative advantage creates a currency swap market in which swap banks look at the borrowing rates offered in different currencies to different borrowers and at the forward exchange rates and money market rates that they can obtain for hedging. Based on these different rates, they will arrange swaps that provide each borrower with rates better than the ones they can directly obtain and a profit for them that will compensate them for facilitating the deal and assuming the credit risk of each counterparty.

20.2.3 Nongeneric Currency Swaps

The generic currency swap has been modified to accommodate different uses. Of particular note is the *cross-currency swap* that is a combination of the currency swap and interest rate swap. This swap calls for an exchange of floating-rate payments in one currency for fixed-rate payments in another. There are also currency swaps with amortizing principals, cancelable and extendable currency swaps, forward currency swaps, and options on currency swaps.

20.3 CREDIT DEFAULT SWAPS

Default risk or credit risk is the risk that the borrower/issuer of a debt obligation will not meet all promises at the agreed-on times. A failure to meet any of the interest payments, the principal obligation, or other terms specified in the indenture (e.g., sinking fund arrangements, collateral requirements, or other protective covenants) places the borrower/issuer in default. In the United States, there have been a number of corporations that have defaulted and declared bankruptcy: Enron, Texaco, Federated Department Stores, Continental Airlines, Penn Central, Eastern Airlines, Southland Corporation, Pan Am, and Delta. For speculative-grade bonds with quality ratings below Baa and for loans for companies with the potential for financial distress, the possibility of default is one of the main risks that investors or creditors assume when they buy a bond or make a loan.

Traditionally, a bond portfolio manager or a financial institution with a portfolio of loans managed their portfolio's exposure to credit risk by the selection and allocation of credits (bonds or loans) in their portfolio. For example, a bond portfolio manager expecting recession and wanting to reduce her portfolio's exposure to credit risk would sell her lower quality bonds and buy higher quality ones. With the development of the credit default swap market, though, a bond manager or lender could change her credit risk by simply buying or selling swaps to change the credit risk profile on either an individual bond or loan or on a bond or loan portfolio.

20.3.1 Generic Credit Default Swap

Credit default swaps and other related credit swap derivatives are contracts in which the payoffs depend on the credit quality of a company. In a standard *credit default swap* (CDS), a counterparty, such as a bank, buys protection against default by a particular company from a counterparty (seller). The company is known as the reference entity, and a default by that company is known as a credit event. The buyer of the CDS makes periodic payments or a premium to the seller until the end of the life of the CDS or until the credit event occurs. If the credit event occurs, the buyer, depending on the contract, has either the right to sell a particular bond (or loan) issued by the company for its par value (physical delivery) or receive a cash settlement based on the difference between the par value and the defaulted bond's market price times an NP equal to the bond's total par value.

To illustrate, suppose two parties enter into a 5-year CDS with an NP of $200M. The buyer agrees to pay 95 BP annually for protection against default by the reference entity. If the reference entity does not default, the buyer does not receive a payoff and ends up paying $1,900,000 each year for 5 years. If a credit event does occur, the buyer will receive the default payment and pay a final accrual payment on the unpaid premium; for example, if the event occurs half way through the year, then the buyer pays the seller $950,000. If the swap contract calls for physical delivery, the buyer will sell the defaulted bonds for $200M. If there is a cash settlement, then an agent will poll dealers to determine a mid-market value. If that value were $30 per $100 face value, then the buyer would receive $140M minus the $950,000 accrued interest payment.

20.3.2 Terms

In the standard CDS, payments are usually made in arrears either on a quarter, semiannual, or annual basis. The par value of the bond or debt is the NP used for determining the payments of the buyer. In many CDS contracts, a number of bonds or credits can be delivered in the case of a default. A company like Motorola, for example, might have 10 bonds with similar maturities, coupons, and embedded option and protection features that a buyer of a CDS can select in the event of a default. In the event of a default, the payoff from the CDS is equal to the face value of the bond (or NP) minus the value of the bond just after the default. The value of the bond just after the default expressed as a percentage of the bond's face value is known as the *recovery rate* (RR). Thus, the payoff from the CDS is

$$\text{CDS Payoff} = (1 - \text{RR})\text{NP} - \text{Accrued Payment}$$

If that value on the $200M CDS were $30 per $100 face value, then the recovery rate would be 30%, and the payoff to the CDS buyer would be $140M $(= (1 - .30)\$200M)$ minus any accrued payment.

The payments on a CDS are quoted as an annual percentage of the NP. The payment is referred to as the *CDS spread*. Swap bankers function as both brokers and dealers in the

CDS market. As dealers, they will provide bid and ask quotes on a particular credit entry. For example, a swap bank might quote a 5-year CDS on a GM credit at 270 BP bid and 280 BP offer; that is, the swap bank will buy protection on GM for 2.7% of the underlying credit's principal per year for 5 years, and the swap bank will sell protection on GM for 2.8% of the principal.

20.3.3 Uses

CDSs are used primarily to manage the credit risk on debt and fixed-income positions. To see this, consider a bond fund manager who just purchased a 5-year BBB corporate bond at a price yielding 8% and wanted to eliminate the credit risk on the bond. To do this, suppose the manager bought a 5-year CDS on the bond. If the payments or spread on the CDS were equal to 2% of the bond's principal, then the purchase of the CDS would have the effect of making the 8% BBB bond a risk-free bond yielding approximately 6%. That is, if the bond does not default, then the bond fund manager will receive 6% from owning the bond and the CDS (8% yield on bond −2% payment on CDS). If the bond defaults, then the bond manager would receive 6% from the bond and CDS up to the time of the default and then would receive the face value on the bond from the CDS seller, which the manager can reinvest form the remainder of the 5-year period. Thus, the CDS allows the manager to reduce, or as in this case, eliminate, the credit risk on the bond.

In contrast, suppose a manager holding a portfolio of 5-year U.S. Treasury notes yielding 6% expected the economy to improve and therefore was willing to assume more credit risk in return for a higher return by buying BBB corporate bonds yielding 8%. As an alternative to selling his Treasuries and buying the corporate bonds, the manager could sell a CDS. If he were to sell a 5-year CDS on the preceding 5-year BBB bond to a swap bank for the 2% spread, then the manager would be adding 2% to the 6% yield on his Treasuries to obtain an effective yield of 8%. Thus with the CDS, the manager would be able to obtain an expected yield equivalent to the BBB bond yield and would also be assuming the same credit risk associated with that bond. As a second example, consider a commercial bank with a large loan to a corporation. Prior to the introduction of CDSs, the bank would typically have to hold on to the loan once it was created. During this period, its only strategy for minimizing its loan portfolio's exposure to credit risk was to create a diversified loan portfolio. With CDS, such a bank can now buy credit protection for the loan. In general, CDSs allow banks and other financial institutions to more actively manage the credit risk on their loan portfolio, buying CDSs on some loans and selling CDSs on others. Today, commercial banks are largest purchasers of CDSs, and insurance companies are the largest sellers.

20.3.4 The Equilibrium CDS Spread

In equilibrium, the payment or spread on a CDS should be approximately equal to the credit spread (also called quality or default risk premium) on the CDS's underlying bond or credit. A bond's default risk premium is equal to spread between the yield on the bond minus the yield on a U.S. Treasury security that is the same in all respects except for the default risk. In terms of the previous example, if the only risk on a 5-year BBB corporate bond yielding 8% were credit risk (i.e., there is no option risk associated with embedded call options and the like and no interest rate risk), and the risk-free rate on 5-year investments were 6%, then the BBB bond would be trading in the market with a 2% credit spread. If the spread on a 5-year CDS on a BBB quality bond or credit were 2%, then an investor could obtain a 5-year risk-free investment yielding 6% by either buying a 5-year Treasury or by buying the 5-year BBB corporate yielding 8% and purchasing the CDS on the underlying credit at a 2% spread.

If the spread on a CDS is not equal to the credit spread on the underlying bond, then an arbitrage opportunity would exist by taking positions in the bond, risk-free security, and the CDS. For example, suppose a swap bank were offering the preceding CDS for 1% instead of 2%. In this case, an investor looking for a 5-year, risk-free investment would find it advantageous to create the synthetic risk-free investment with the BBB bond and the CDS. That is, the investor could earn 1% more than the yield on the Treasury by buying the 5-year BBB corporate bond yielding 8% and purchasing the CDS on the underlying credit at a 1%. In addition to the investor gaining, an arbitrager could also realized a free lunch equivalent to a 5-year cash flow of 1% of the par value of bond by shorting the Treasury at 6% and then using the proceeds to buy the BBB corporate bond and the CDS. These actions by investors and arbitrageurs, in turn, would have the impact of pushing the spread on the CDS toward 2%—the underlying bond's credit risk spread.

On the other hand, if the swap bank were offering the CDS at a 3% spread, then an investor looking for a 5-year, risk-free investment would obviously prefer a 6% Treasury yielding 6% to a synthetic risk-free investment formed with the 5-year BBB corporate yielding 8% and a CDS on the credit requiring a payment of 3%. A more aggressive investor looking to invest in the higher yielding 5-year BBB bonds, though, could earn 1% more than the 8% on the BBB bond by creating a synthetic 5-year BBB bond by purchasing the 5-year Treasury at 6% and selling the CDS at 3%. Similarly, a bond portfolio manager holding 5-year BBB bonds yielding 8% could pick up an additional 1% yield with the same credit risk exposure by selling the bonds along with the CDS at 3% and then using the proceeds from the bond sale to buy the 5-year Treasuries yielding 6%. Finally, an arbitrager could realized a free lunch equivalent to a 5-year cash flow of 1% of the par value on the bond by shorting the BBB bond, selling the CDS, and then using proceeds to purchase 5-year Treasuries. With these positions, the arbitrageur would receive for each of the next 5 years 6% from her Treasury investment and 3% from her CDS while paying only 8% on her short BBB bond position. Furthermore, her holdings of Treasury securities would enable her to cover her obligation on the CDS if there was a default. That is, in the event of a default, she would be able to pay the CDS holder from the net proceed from selling her Treasuries and closing her short BBB bond by buying back the corporate bonds at their defaulted recovery price. Collectively, the actions of the investors, bond portfolio managers, and arbitrageur would have the effect of pushing the spread on CDSs from 3% to 2%.

In equilibrium, arbitrageurs and investors should ensure that the spreads on CDSs are approximately equal to spreads on the underlying bond or credit. This spread can be defined as the equilibrium spread or the ***arbitrage-free spread.*** The arbitrage-free spread, Z, on a bond or CDS can also be thought of as the bond investor's or CDS buyer's expected loss from the principal from default. To see this, consider a *portfolio* of 5-year BBB bonds trading at a 2% credit spread. The 2% premium that investors receive from the bond portfolio represents their compensation for an implied expected loss of 2% per year of the principal from the defaulted bonds. If the spread were 2%, and bond investors believed that the expected loss from default on such bonds would be only 1% per year of the principal, then the bond investors would want more BBB bonds, driving the price up and the yield down until the premium reflected a 1% spread. Similarly, if the spread were 2%, and bond investors believed the default loss on a portfolio of BBB bonds would be 3% per year, then the demand and price for such bonds would decrease, increasing the yield to reflect a credit spread of 3%. Thus, in an efficient market, the credit spread on bonds and the equilibrium spreads on CDSs represent the market's implied expectation of the expected loss per year from the principal from default. In the case of a CDS, the equilibrium spread can therefore be defined as the implied probability of default of principal on the contract.

20.3.5 CDS Valuation

The total value of a CDS's payments is equal to the sum of the present values of the periodic CDS spread (Z) times NP over the life of the CDS, discounted at the risk-free rate (R):

$$\text{PV(CDS Payments)} = \sum_{t=1}^{M} \frac{ZNP}{(1+R)^t}$$

In terms of the previous example, the present value of the payment on the 5-year CDS with an equilibrium spread of 2% and an NP of $1 would be $0.084247:

$$\text{PV(CDS Payments)} = \sum_{t=1}^{5} \frac{(.02)(\$1)}{(1.06)^t} = \$0.084247$$

The buyer (seller) of this 5-year CDS would therefore be willing to make (receive) payments over 5 years that have a present value $0.084247. Because the spread can also be viewed as an expected loss of principal, the present value of the payments is also equal to the expected default protection the buyer (seller) receives (pays). The value of the CDS protection, in turn, is equal to the present value of the expected payout in the case of default:

$$\text{PV(Expected Payout)} = \sum_{t=1}^{M} \frac{p_t\, NP(1-RR)}{(1+R)^t}$$

where

- p_t = probability of default in period t conditional on no earlier default.
- RR = recovery rate (as a proportion of the face value) on the bond at the time of default.
- NP = notional principal equal to the par value of the bond

Note that the probability of default, p_t, is defined as a conditional probability of no prior defaults. Thus the conditional probability of default in Year 4 is based on the probability that the bond will survive until Year 4. In contrast, an unconditional probability is the likelihood that the bond will default at a given time as seen from the present. Conditional default probabilities are referred to as **default intensities.** Over a period of time, these probabilities will change, increasing or decreasing depending on the quality of the credit. Instead of defining a CDS's expected payout in terms periodic probability density, p_t, the CDS's expected payout can alternatively be defined by the average conditional default probability, $\bar{p}$:

$$\text{PV(Expected Payout)} = \sum_{t=1}^{M} \frac{\bar{p}NP(1-RR)}{(1+R)^t} = \bar{p}NP(1-RR)\sum_{t=1}^{M} \frac{1}{(1+R)^t}$$

Given the equilibrium spread of .02 in our example and assuming a recovery rate of 30% if the underlying bond defaults, the implied probability density for our illustrative CDS would be .02857. This implied probability is obtained by solving for the $\bar{p}$ that makes the present value of the expected payout equal to present value of the payments of

$.084247:

$$PV(\text{Expected Payout}) = PV(\text{Payments})$$

$$\sum_{t=1}^{M} \frac{\bar{p}NP(1-RR)}{(1+R)^t} = \sum_{t=1}^{M} \frac{ZNP}{(1+R)^t}$$

$$\bar{p} = \frac{Z}{(1-RR)}$$

$$\bar{p} = \frac{.02}{(1-.30)} = .02857$$

$$PV(\text{Expected Payout}) = \sum_{t=1}^{M} \frac{\bar{p}NP(1-RR)}{(1+R)^t}$$

$$= \sum_{t=1}^{5} \frac{(.02857)(\$1)(1-.30)}{(1.06)^t} = \$0.084247$$

Note that if there were no recovery (RR = 0), then the implied probability would be equal to the spread Z, which as we noted earlier can be thought of as the probability of default of principal. The probability density implied by the market is referred to as the risk-neutral probability because it is based on an equilibrium spread that is arbitrage free.[2]

20.3.6 Alternative CDS Valuation Approach

Suppose in our illustrative example, the *estimated*-default intensity, sometimes referred to as the **real world probability,** on the 5-year BBB bond were .02 and not the implied probability of .02857. In this case, the present value of the CDS expected payout would be $0.058973 instead of $0.084247:

$$PV(\text{Expected Payout}) = \sum_{t=1}^{5} \frac{(.02)(\$1)(1-.30)}{(1.06)^t} = \$0.058973$$

Given the spread on the CDS is at 2%, and the present value of the payments are $0.084247, buyers of the CDS would have to pay more on the CDS than the value they receive on the expected payoff ($0.058973). If the real-world probability density of .02 is accurate, then buyers of the CDS would eventually push the spread down until it is equal to the value of the protection. For the payment on the CDS to match the expected protection, the spread would have to equal .014. This implied spread is found by solving for the Z that equates the present value of the payments to the present value of the expected payout given the

---

[2] The estimated recover rate, RR, is generally treated as a given. For generic CDSs, the value of the CDS is not as sensitive to RR as it is to Z. From 1982 to 2003, recovery rates on corporate bonds as a percentage of face value have ranged from 51.6% for senior secured debt to 24.5% for junior subordinated debt. The source is *Moody's*.

real-world probability of $\bar{p} = .02$ and the estimated recovery rate of RR $= .30$. That is

$$PV(\text{Payments}) = PV(\text{Expected Payout})$$

$$\sum_{t=1}^{M} \frac{ZNP}{(1+R)^t} = \sum_{t=1}^{M} \frac{\bar{p}NP(1-RR)}{(1+R)^t}$$

$$Z = \bar{p}(1-RR)$$

$$Z = (.02)(1-.30) = .014$$

$$PV(\text{Payments}) = \sum_{t=1}^{M} \frac{ZNP}{(1+R)^t} = \sum_{t=1}^{5} \frac{(.014)(\$1)}{(1.06)^t} = \$0.058973$$

We now have two alternative methods for pricing a CDS. On one hand, we can value the CDS swap given the credit spread in the market and then determine the present value of the payments; thus, in terms of our example, we would use the market spread of 2% and value the swap at $0.084247, with the implied probability density (or risk-neutral probability) being .02857. On the other hand, we can value the swap given estimated probabilities of default and then determine the present value of the expected payout; in terms of our example, we would use the estimated real-world probability of .02 and value the CDS at $.058973, with the implied credit spread being .014. The question becomes what valuation method should be used.

Although cogent arguments can be made for either case, many scholars argue for the use of valuing swaps with risk-neutral probabilities (or equivalently pricing swaps in terms of credit spreads on the underlying bonds) because it reflects an arbitrage-free price. Thus, they would price the 5-year CDS equal to the 2% spread with a total value of $0.084247. On the other hand, though, if one can estimate real-world probabilities on bonds and CDSs that are more accurate than the probabilities implied by the current credit spread, then eventually the bond and CDS market will price such claims so that the credit spread reflects the real-world probability. If this is the case, then in our example, one should price the 5-year CDS at $0.058973 given the estimated probability density of .02. The argument for pricing CDSs using real-world probabilities ultimately depends on the ability of practitioners to estimated default probabilities.

20.3.7 Estimating Default Rates and Valuing CDSs Based on Estimated Default Intensities

As just noted, the alternative to pricing a CDS in terms of its credit spreads is to determine the spread that will equate the present value of the payments to the present value of the expected payout based on estimates of the conditional probability. That is, given estimated periodic default intensities and the recovery rate (RR), the objective is to find the Z where

$$\sum_{t=1}^{M} \frac{ZNP}{(1+R)^t} = \sum_{t=1}^{M} \frac{p_t NP(1-RR)}{(1+R)^t}$$

There are several approaches for estimating conditional probabilities. The simplest and most direct one is to estimate the probabilities based on historical default rates.

20.3.7.1 Estimating Probability Intensities From Historical Default Rates

Table 20.3-1 shows three different probabilities for corporate bonds with quality ratings of Aaa, Baa, B, and Caa: cumulative default rates, unconditional probability rates, and conditional probability rates (probability intensities). The cumulative probabilities show the default chance through time. For example, the Baa corporate bonds have 0.20% chance

TABLE 20.3-1 Cumulative Default Rates, Probability Intensities, and CDS Values and Spreads

Average Cumulative Default Rates 1970–2003 (Moody's)

Year	1	2	3	4	5	PV(Expected Payoff) NP=$1 and RR = .3	CDS Spread Z
Aaa							
Cumulative Probability (%)	0.00	0.00	0.00	0.04	0.12		
Unconditional Probability (%)	0.00	0.00	0.00	0.04	0.08		
Conditional Probability p (%)	0.00	0.00	0.00	0.04	0.08		
Present Value of p at 6%	0	0	0	0.031684	0.059805	0.000640418	0.00015
Baa							
Cumulative Probability (%)	0.20	0.57	1.03	1.62	2.16		
Unconditional Probability (%)	0.20	0.37	0.46	0.59	0.54		
Conditional Probability p (%)	0.20	0.37	0.46	0.60	0.55		
Present Value of p at 6%	0.188679	0.329959	0.388439	0.472199	0.410164	0.012526079	0.002973646
B							
Cumulative Probability (%)	6.21	13.76	20.65	26.66	31.99		
Unconditional Probability (%)	6.21	7.55	6.89	6.01	5.33		
Conditional Probability p (%)	6.21	8.05	7.99	7.57	7.27		
Present Value of p at 6%	5.858491	7.164381	6.707997	5.999348	5.430715	0.218126524	0.051782449
Caa							
Cumulative Probability (%)	23.65	37.20	48.02	55.56	60.83		
Unconditional Probability (%)	23.65	13.55	10.82	7.54	5.27		
Conditional Probability p (%)	23.65	17.75	17.23	14.51	11.86		
Present Value of p at 6%	22.31132	15.79496	14.46605	11.48978	8.8615	0.510465268	0.121182611

$$PV(\text{Expected Payoff}) = \sum_{t=1}^{M} \frac{p_t \, NP(1-RR)}{(1+R)^t} \qquad Z = \frac{\sum_{t=1}^{M} \frac{p_t(1-RR)}{(1+R)^t}}{\sum_{t=1}^{M} \frac{1}{(1+R)^t}}$$

of defaulting after 1 year, 0.57% chance after 2 years, and 2.16% chance after 5 years. The cumulative probabilities shown in the table are the average historical cumulative default rates from 1970 to 2003 as complied by *Moody's*. The unconditional probabilities are the probabilities of default in a given year as viewed from time zero. The unconditional probability of a bond defaulting during year t is equal to the difference in the cumulative probability in year t minus the cumulative probability of default in year t-1. As shown in the table, the probability of a Caa bond default during Year 4 is equal to 7.54% (= 55.56% − 48.02%). Finally, the unconditional probability is the probability of default in a given year conditional on no prior defaults. This probability is equal to the unconditional probability of default in time t as a proportion of the bond's probability of survival at the beginning of the period. The probability of survival is equal to 100 minus the cumulative probability. For example, the probability that a Caa bond will survive until the end of Year 3 is 51.98% (100 minus its cumulative probability 48.02%), and the probability that the Caa bond will default during Year 4 conditional on no prior defaults is 14.51% (= 7.54%/51.98%). As noted earlier, conditional probabilities of default are known as default intensities. These probabilities, in turn, can be used to determine the expected payoff on a swap.

Using the unconditional probabilities generated from the historical cumulative default rates, the values and spreads for four CDSs with quality ratings of Aaa, Baa, B, and Caa are shown in Table 20.3-1. Each swap is assumed to have a maturity of 5 years, annual payments, NP of $1, and recovery rate of 30%. The values are obtained by determining the present values of the expected payoff, with the discount rate assumed to be 6% and with the possible defaults assumed to occur at the end of each year (implying there are no accrued payments). The spreads on the CDSs are the spreads that equate the present value of the payments to the present value of the expected payoff. For example, the present value of the expected payoff for the CDS with a B quality rating is .2181:

$$PV(\text{Expected Payoff}) = \sum_{t=1}^{M} \frac{p_t \, NP(1 - RR)}{(1 + R)^t}$$

$$PV(\text{Expected Payoff}) = (\$1)(1 - .3)$$

$$\left[\frac{.0621}{(1.06)} + \frac{.0805}{(1.06)^2} + \frac{.0799}{(1.06)^3} + \frac{.0757}{(1.06)^4} + \frac{.0727}{(1.06)^5} \right]$$

$$PV(\text{Expected Payoff}) = .2181$$

The spread on the B quality CDS that equates the present value of its payments to the expected payoff of $0.2181 is .05178:

$$\sum_{t=1}^{M} \frac{ZNP}{(1 + R)^t} = \sum_{t=1}^{M} \frac{p_t \, NP(1 - RR)}{(1 + R)^t}$$

$$Z \sum_{t=1}^{5} \frac{\$1}{(1.06)^t} = \$0.2181$$

$$Z = \frac{\$0.2181}{\sum_{t=1}^{5} \frac{\$1}{(1.06)^t}} = \frac{\$0.2181}{\$4.212364} = .05178$$

As shown in the table, the present values of the expected payoffs on the Caa quality CDS is $0.51046 and its spread is .12118. As expected, the greater the CDS values and spreads are, the greater the default risk.

20.3.7.2 Estimating Expected Default Rates—Implied Default Rates

The preceding default rates are based on historical frequencies. Past frequencies are often not the best predictors of futures probabilities. If the market is efficient such that prices of bonds reflect the market's expectation of future economic conditions, then the implied probabilities based on CDS's risk spread would represent an expected future default probability. We previously calculated the average implied probability by solving for $\bar{p}$ that equated the present value of the expected payoff to the present value of the payments based on the current bond's credit spread. Using this methodology, one could estimate the implied conditional probabilities for each year for a given quality rating using the CDS spread on 1-year to m-year swaps. This would result in a set of implied default probabilities that could be used to determine the spread on any m-year swap. As an example, the table following shows the spreads (Z) and the implied probability densities given an assumed recovery rate of 30% on five B-rated CDSs with maturities ranging from 1 to 5 years:

Maturity t	Spread	Implied Probability
1	0.0400	0.0571
2	0.0425	0.0607
3	0.0450	0.0643
4	0.0475	0.0679
5	0.0500	0.0714

The implied probability densities are equal to Z/(1 − RR). Given these probabilities, the value of a 5-year CDS based on its expected payoff would be $0.1883, and its spread would be .0447:

$$\text{PV(Expected Payoff)} = \sum_{t=1}^{M} \frac{p_t\,NP(1-RR)}{(1+R)^t}$$

$$\text{PV(Expected Payoff)} = (\$1)(1-.3)\left[\frac{.0571}{(1.06)} + \frac{.0607}{(1.06)^2} + \frac{.0643}{(1.06)^3}\right.$$
$$\left. + \frac{.0679}{(1.06)^4} + \frac{.0714}{(1.06)^5}\right]$$

$$\text{PV(Expected Payoff)} = \$0.1883$$

$$\sum_{t=1}^{M} \frac{ZNP}{(1+R)^t} = \sum_{t=1}^{M} \frac{p_t\,NP(1-RR)}{(1+R)^t}$$

$$Z\sum_{t=1}^{5} \frac{\$1}{(1.06)^t} = \$0.1883$$

$$Z = \frac{\$0.1883}{\sum_{t=1}^{5} \frac{\$1}{(1.06)^t}} = \frac{\$0.1883}{\$4.212364} = .0447$$

20.3.8   Summary of the Two Valuation Approaches

We previously noted that many scholars argue for valuing CDS in terms of credit spreads on the underlying bonds because it results in an arbitrage-free price. Pricing CDSs in terms of bond credits spreads also implies that the default probability for determining the expected payout by the seller is a probability implied by the credit spread of bonds traded in the market and not a real-world estimated probability. The alternative to pricing CDSs in terms of bond credit spreads is to determine the spread that will equate the present value of the payments to the present value of the expected payout based on estimates of the conditional probability. As we just discussed, default probabilities can be estimated using historical cumulative default rates and implied default rates. There are also a number of other more advanced estimating techniques that practitioners can use to determine default probabilities.[3] Several of these estimating approaches are referenced at the end of this chapter. Of particular note is the Gaussian Copula Model.

20.3.9   The Value of an Off-Market CDS Swap

Similar to a generic par value interest rate swap, a swap rate on a new CDS is generally set so that there is not an initial exchange of money. Over time and as economic conditions change the credit spreads on new CDSs, the value of an existing CDS will change. For example, suppose 1 year after a bond fund manager bought our illustrative 5-year CDS on BBB bond at the 2% spread, the economy became weaker, and credit spreads on 4-year BBB bonds and new CDSs on such bonds were 50 BP greater at 2.5% (assume for this discussion that CDS spreads are determine by bond credit spreads in the market). Suppose the bond fund manager sold her 2% CDS to a swap bank who hedged the CDS by selling a new 2.5% CDS on the 4-year BBB bond. With a buyer's position on the assumed 2% CDS and seller's position on the 2.5% CDS, the swap bank, in turn, would gain .5% of the NP for the next 4 years. Given a discount rate of 6%, the present value of this gain would be $0.017326. The swap banks would therefore pay the bond manager a maximum of $0.017326 for assuming the swap.

Offsetting Swap Positions

Buyer of 2% CDS Swap	Pay 2% of NP	Receive Default Protection
Seller of 2.5% CDS Swap	Receive 2.5%	Pay Default Protection

Receive .5% per year

$$ SV = \sum_{t=1}^{4} \frac{(\text{Current Spread} - \text{Existing Spread})(NP)}{(1 + R)^t} = \sum_{t=1}^{4} \frac{0.005(\$1)}{(1.06)^t} = \$0.017326 $$

With 4 years left on the current swap, the increase in credit spread in the market has increased the value of the buyer's position on the CDS swap by $0.17326 from $0.069302

---

[3] In the next chapter, we examine how the value of equity of a leveraged company could be estimated in terms of the value of its asset and debt using the B–S OPM. When the B–S OPM is applied to valuing equity, $1 - N(d_2)$ represents the risk-neutral probability that the company will default. Thus, another approach to estimating default probabilities is to determine $1 - N(d_2)$ on the credit entry's equity. It should be noted that the estimation of $1 - N(d_2)$ requires estimating the value of the firm's assets and its variability. Both of these parameters, though, are not directly observable. They can be estimated using Ito's lemma (see Appendix 8A).

to 0.086628:

$$\text{Existing CDS}: \text{PV(CDS Payments)} = \sum_{t=1}^{4} \frac{(.02)(\$1)}{(1.06)^t} = \$0.069302$$

$$\text{Current PV(CDS Payments)} = \sum_{t=1}^{4} \frac{(.025)(\$1)}{(1.06)^t} = \$0.086628$$

$$\text{Change in Value} = .017326$$

The increase in value on the buyer's position of the exiting swap reflects the fact that with poorer economic conditions, the 2% swap payments now provide greater default protection (i.e., the present value of the expect payout is greater).

For the initial seller, the increase in credit spreads causes a decrease in the value on the seller's positions. For example, suppose that an insurance company was the one who sold the 5-year CDS on the BBB bond at the 2% spread to the bond portfolio manager (via a swap bank) and that 1 year later the credit spread on new 4-year CDS on BBB bonds was again at 2.5%. If the insurance company were to sell its seller's position to a swap bank, the swap bank could hedge the assumed position by taking a buyer's position on a new 4-year, 2.5% CDS on the BBB bond. With the offsetting positions, the swap bank would lose .5% of the NP for the next 4 years. Given a discount rate of 6%, the present value of this loss would be $0.017326. The swap banks would therefore charge the insurance company at least $0.017326 for assuming the seller's position on the swap:

Offsetting Swap Positions

Seller of 2% CDS Swap	Receive 2% of NP	Pay Default Protection
Buyer of 2.5% CDS Swap	Pay 2.5%	Receive Default Protection

Pay .5% per year

$$\text{SV} = \sum_{t=1}^{4} \frac{(\text{Existing Spread} - \text{Current Spread})(\text{NP})}{(1+R)^t}$$

$$= \sum_{t=1}^{4} \frac{-0.005(\$1)}{(1.06)^t} = -\$0.017326$$

For the insurance company, the increase in the credit spread has decreased the value of their seller's position on the CDS swap by $0.17326. That is, for the increase in credit risk, the seller should be receiving 0.086628 instead of $0.069302. Alternatively stated, the poorer economic conditions reflected in the greater credit spreads have increased the probability of default on the BBB bonds and as a result has increased the present value of the seller's expected payoff. Specifically, with the credit spread increasing from 2% to 2.5%, the implied conditional default rate on the bond has increased from .02857 to .035714, increasing the present value of the seller's expected payout from $.069302 to $0.086628:

$$\text{Existing } \bar{p} = \frac{Z}{(1-RR)} = \frac{.02}{(1-.30)} = .02857$$

$$\text{Current}: \bar{p} = \frac{Z}{(1-RR)} = \frac{.025}{(1-.30)} = 0.035714$$

$$PV(\text{Expected Payout}) = \sum_{t=1}^{M} \frac{\bar{p}\,NP(1 - RR)}{(1 + R)^t}$$

$$\text{Existing}: PV(\text{Expected Payout}) = \sum_{t=1}^{4} \frac{(.02857)(\$1)(1 - .30)}{(1.06)^t} = \$0.069302$$

$$\text{Current}: PV(\text{Expected Payout}) = \sum_{t=1}^{4} \frac{(.035714)(\$1)(1 - .30)}{(1.06)^t} = \$0.086628$$

To summarize, an increase in the credit spread will increase the value of the buyer's position on an existing CDS and decrease the seller's position. Just the opposite occurs if economic conditions improve and credit spreads decrease.

20.3.10 Other Credit Derivatives

The market for CDSs has grown dramatically over the last decade. With that growth there has been an increase in the creation of other credit derivatives. The most noteworthy of these other credit derivatives are the binary swap, credit swap basket, CDS forward contracts, CDS option contracts, contingent swaps, and total return swaps.

20.3.10.1 Binary CDS

A *binary CDS* is identical to the generic CDS except that the payoff in the case of a default is a specified dollar amount. Often the fixed payoff is the principal on the underlying credit. When this is the case, then the only difference between the generic and binary swap is that the generic CDS adjusts the payoff by subtracting the recovery value, whereas the binary CDS does not. Without the recovery value, the value of a binary CDS is more sensitive to changes in credit spreads or default probabilities.

20.3.10.2 Basket CDS

In a *basket credit default swap,* there is a group of reference entities or credits instead of one, and there is usually a specified payoff whenever one of the reference entities defaults. Basket CDSs can vary by the type of agreement governing the payout. For example, an *add-up basket CDS* provides a payout when any reference credit in the basket defaults; a *first-to-default CDS* provides a payout only when the first entry defaults; a *second-to-default CDS* provides a payout when the second default occurs; and an *nth-to-default CDS* provides a payout when the nth credit entry defaults. Typically, after the relevant entry defaults, the swap is terminated.

20.3.10.3 CDS Forward Contracts

There is a dealers market for CDS forward and option contracts. Like any futures or forward contract, a CDS forward contract is a contract to take a buyer's position or a seller's position on a particular CDS at a specified spread at some future date. CDS forward contracts provide a tool for locking in the credit spread on future credit position.

20.3.10.4 CDS Option Contracts

A CDS option is an option to buy or sell a particular CDS at specified swap rate at a specified future time, for example, a 1-year option to buy a 5-year CDS on GM for 300 BP. At expiration, the holder of this option would exercise her right to take the buyer's position at 300 BP if current 5-year CDSs on GM were greater than 300BP; in contrast, she would allow the option to expire and take the current CDS on GM if it is offered at 300 BP or less.

20.3.10.5 Contingent CDSs

A *contingent CDS* provides a payout that is contingent on two or more events occurring. For example, the payoff might require both a credit default of the reference entity and an additional event such as a credit event with another entity or a change in a market variable.

20.3.10.6 Total Return Swaps

In a *total return swap,* there is an agreement to exchange the return on an asset (such as a bond, bond portfolio, stock, or stock portfolio) for some benchmark rate such as LIBOR plus BP. In the case of an exchange of the return on a bond or bond portfolio for LIBOR and BP, the return on the bond includes coupons and gains and losses on the bond. Such a swap allows parties to trade different risks, including credit risk.

A variation of the total return swap is the *equity swap*. In an equity swap, one party agrees to pay the return on an equity index, such as the S&P 500, and the other party agrees to pay a floating rate (LIBOR) or fixed rate. For example, on an S&P 500/LIBOR swap, the equity payer would agree to pay the 6-month rate of change on the S&P 500 (e.g., proportional change in the index between effective dates) times an NP in return for LIBOR times NP, and the debt payer would agree to pay the LIBOR in return for the S&P 500 return. Equity swaps are useful to fund managers who want to increase or decrease the equity or bond exposure of their portfolios as part of their overall asset allocation strategy.

20.3.11 CAT Bond

Somewhat related to credit risk is the catastrophic (CAT) risk that insurance companies face in providing protection against hurricanes, earthquakes, and other natural disasters. Insurance companies often hedge CAT risk through reinsurance. However, one CAT hedging product that insurance companies are increasingly using is the issuance of CAT bonds. A CAT bond pays the buyer a higher than normal interest rate. In return for the additional interest, the CAT bondholder agrees to provide protection for losses from a specified event up to a specified amount or when the losses exceed a specified amount. For example, an insurance company could issue a CAT bond with a principal of $200M against a hurricane cost exceeding $300M. The CAT bondholders would then lose some or all of their principal if the event occurs and the cost exceeds $300M.

20.4 CONCLUSION

In this chapter, we completed our analysis of swaps by examining the markets, uses, and valuation of currency and credit swaps. In general, swaps provide investors and borrowers with a tool for hedging asset and liability positions against interest rate, exchange rate, and credit spread fluctuations; an instrument for speculating on interest rates, exchange rates, and credit spread movements; and finally a tool for improving the returns received on fixed-income investments or paid on debt positions. In the next and final part of the book, we complete our odyssey of the world of derivatives by examining embedded options and the derivatives on portfolios of mortgages and other financial assets.

KEY TERMS

currency swaps	CDS spread	binary swap
cross-currency swap	arbitrage-free spread	basket credit swap
credit default swap	default intensity	CDS forward contract
recovery rate	real-world probability	CDS option contract

contingent CDS   equity swap

total return swap   CAT Bond

SELECTED REFERENCES

Alworth, J. "The Valuation of US Dollar Interest Rate Swaps." *BIS Economic Papers* 35 (January 1993): Basle, Switzerland.

Andersen, L., J. Sidenius, and S. Basu. "All Your Hedges in One Basket" *Risk* (November 2003).

Arak, M., L. Goodman, and A. Rones. "Credit Lines for New Instruments: Swaps, Over-the- Counter Options, Forwards and Floor-Ceiling Agreements." In *Proceedings of the Conference on Bank Structure and Competition*. Chicago: Federal Reserve Bank of Chicago, 1989.

Chance, D., and D. Rich. "The Pricing of Equity Swaps and Swaptions." *Journal of Derivatives* 5 (Summer 1998): 19–31.

Dattatreya, R. E., and K. Hotta. *Advanced Interest Rate and Currency Swaps: State-of-the Art Products Strategies and Risk Management Applications*. Chicago: Irwin, 1993.

Duffie, D., and K. Singleton. "Modeling Term Structures of Defaultable Bonds." *Review of Financial Studies* 12 (1999): 687–720.

Froot, K. A. "The Market for Catastrophic Risk: A Clinical Examination." *Journal of Financial Economis* 60 (2001): 529–571.

Froot, K. A. *The Financing of Catastrophic Risk*. Chicago: University of Chicago Press, 1999.

Hull, J. C. *Option, Futures, and Other Derivatives,* 6th ed. Upper Saddle River, NJ: Prentice Hall, 2005, Chapters 20–21.

Hull, J., M. Predescu, and A. White. "Relationship Between Credit Default Swap Spreads, Bond Yields, and Credit Rating Announcements." *Journal of Banking and Finance* 28 (November 2004): 2789–2811.

Hull, J. C., and A. White. "Valuation of a CDO and nth-to-Default Swap Without Monte Carlo Simulation." *Journal of Derivatives* 12 (Winter 2004): 8–23.

Hull, J. C., and A. White. "Valuing Credit Default Swaps I: No Counterparty Default Risk." *Journal of Derivatives* 8 (Fall 2000): 29–40.

Hull, J. C., and A. White. "Valuing Credit Default Swaps II: Modeling Default Correlations." *Journal of Derivatives* 8 (Spring 2001): 12–22.

Johnson, R. S. *Bond Evaluation, Selection, and Management*. Malden, MA: Blackwell Publishing, 2004, Chapter 17.

Kijima, M. "A Markov Chain Model for Valuing Credit Derivatives." *Journal of Derivatives* 6 (Fall 1998): 97–108.

Tavakoli, J. M. *Credit Derivatives: A Guide to Instruments and Applications*. New York: Wiley, 1998.

PROBLEMS AND QUESTIONS

1. Suppose the Canadian Beverage Company can issue 5-year, C$142.857M bonds paying 7.5% interest to finance the construction of its U.S. brewery but really needs an equivalent dollar loan, which at the current spot exchange rate of $0.70/C$ would be $100M. Also, suppose the American Development Company can issue 5-year, $100M bonds at 10% to finance the development of a hotel complex in Montreal but really needs a 5-year, C$142.875M loan.

   a. Explain how a swap bank could arrange a currency swap between the Canadian Beverage Company and the American Development Company after each company issues its bonds. Show the swap agreement's initial cash flow in a diagram.

   b. Explain how the swap bank would arrange for the annual interest payments. Assume the swap bank determines the interest swap exchange based on the rates each company pays on its bonds. Show the annual interest cash flows in a diagram.

c. Explain how the swap bank would arrange for the exchange of principal payments at maturity.

2. The American company in Question 1 has a swap position in which it has agreed to swap with the swap bank a 5-year, 10% loan of $100M for a 5-year, 7.5% loan of C$142.857M, whereas the Canadian company has a swap position in which it has agreed to swap with the swap bank a 5-year, 7.5% loan of C$142.857M for a 5-year, 10% loan of $100M.

   a. Define the American and Canadian companies' swap positions as equivalent bond positions in U.S. dollars and Canadian dollars.

   b. Define the American and Canadian companies' swap positions as equivalent forward exchange rate positions.

   c. What are the values of the American and Canadian companies' swap positions?

   d. What would be the values of the American Company' swap positions 1 year later if the spot exchange was $0.70/C$, rates on U.S. dollars were 10.5%, and rates on Canadian dollars were 7.5%? What would be the value of the Canadian Company's swap?

3. The following table shows the annual loan rates American and Canadian multinational companies can each obtain on a 5-year, $100M loan in U.S. dollars and an equivalent 5-year, C$142.857M loan in Canadian dollars.

Loan Rates for American and Canadian Companies in U.S. Dollars and Canadian Dollars

Spot: $E_0 = \$/C\$ = \$0.70/C\$$

	U.S Dollar Market (rate on $)	Canadian Dollar Market (rate on C$)
American Company	10%	7.25%
Canadian Company	11%	7.5%

   a. Suppose the U.S. multinational wants to borrow C$142.857M for 5 years to finance its Canadian operations, whereas the Canadian company wants to borrow $100M for 5 years to finance its U.S. operations. Explain how a swap bank could arrange a currency swap that would benefit the American Company by lowering the rate on its Canadian dollar loan by .25% and would benefit the Canadian Company by lowering its dollar loan by .4%. Describe the financial market conditions that allow the swap bank to provide such rates.

   b. Show the swap arrangements in terms of U.S. dollar and Canadian dollar interest payments and receipts in a diagram.

   c. Describe the swap bank's U.S. and Canadian dollar positions.

   d. Explain how the swap bank's position is equivalent to a series of long currency forward contracts at the rates shown in the table. What is the swap bank's implied forward exchange rate on the contracts?

   e. Assume that forward rates are governed by the interest rate parity theorem, that the swap bank can borrow and lend dollars at 9.5% and Canadian dollars at 7%, and that the yield curves for rates in both currencies are flat. Explain how the bank could hedge its swap position using currency forward contracts. What would be the swap bank's profit from its swap and forward positions?

4. The following table shows the annual loan rates American and Mexican companies can each obtain on a 5-year, $20M loan in the U.S. and/or equivalently on a 5-year 114.2857M peso loan in the Mexican market.

Loan Rates for American and Mexican Companies in U.S. and Mexico

Spot: E_0 = $/Peso = $0.175/peso

	American Market	Mexican Market
Risk-Free Rate	8%	6%
American Company	11%	8.5%
Mexican Company	12%	9.0%

a. Explain the comparative advantages that exist for the American and Mexican companies.

b. Suppose the U.S. Company wants to borrow 114.2857M pesos for 5 years to finance its Mexican operations, whereas the Mexican Company wants to borrow $20M for 5 years to finance its U.S. operations. Explain how a swap bank could arrange a currency swap that would benefit the American company by lowering its peso loan by .25% and would benefit the Mexican company by lowering its dollar loan by .1%. Show the initial cash flow, interest rate, and principal swap arrangements in a diagram.

c. Describe how the swap bank's position is similar to a series of peso forward contracts.

d. What would the bank's dollar position be if it hedged the swap position using the forward market at forward rates determined by IRPT and at the risk-free rates shown in the table? Assume a flat yield curve. Determine the swap bank's profit from its swap position and forward exchange rate position.

5. Short-Answer Questions:

1. What is the bond equivalent of a currency swap position in which the counterparty agrees to swap a 3-year, 10% loan of $14.6M for a 3-year, 7% loan of £10M?

2. What is the bond equivalent of a currency swap position in which the counterparty agrees to swap a 3-year, 7% loan of £10M for a 3-year, 10% loan of $14.6M?

3. What is the forward exchange rate equivalent of a currency swap position in which the counterparty agrees to swap a 3-year, 10% loan of $14.6M for a 3-year, 7% loan of £10M?

4. What is the forward exchange rate equivalent of a currency swap position in which the counterparty agrees to swap a 3-year, 7% loan of £10M for a 3-year, 10% loan of $14.6M?

5. What is the value of an existing currency swap position in which the counterparty agrees to swap a 2-year, 10% loan of $14.6M for a 2-year, 7% loan of £10M if the current dollar rate is 9%, sterling rate is 7.5%, and spot $/£ exchange rate is $1.45/£?

6. Describe comparative advantage in terms of American and British multinational companies who can each obtain loans in dollars and pounds at the following rates:

	Dollar Market (rate on $)	Pound Market (rate on £)
American Company	11%	8.25%
British Company	12%	8.5%

6. An American company agrees to exchange a 5-year, $10M, 9% fixed-rate loan to a swap bank for a 6%, 5-year, 25M euro loan and a German company agrees to exchange a 5-year, 25M, 6.5% fixed-rate euro loan to a swap bank for a 5-year, $10M, 9.5% loan.

   Questions:

   a. What would the American company exchange each year?

   b. What would the German company exchange each year?

   c. What would the swap bank's position be each year?

   d. How could the swap bank hedge its position?

7. Define a credit default swap and its terms. Explain how the swap works with an example.

8. Suppose a bond fund manager has a portfolio consisting of A to AAA quality bonds with an average maturity of 7 years and currently yielding 6%. Furthermore, suppose the manager expects the economy to be strong over the next year and would like to improve the yield on her portfolio by swapping 10% of her portfolio for lower quality B-rated bonds currently trading at a 3% credit spread. Explain how the manager could alternatively use a CDS on B-rated credit with a spread equal to that on B-rated bonds to achieve similar results.

9. Suppose the Vice President of Sun Bank is in the process of structuring a 5-year, $100M loan to the Jetgreen Company, a major airline carrier. Suppose the Vice President assesses Jetgreen's credit rating as B quality and believes that a credit spread of 5% is required on the loan. Explain the type of CDS the Vice President would need to buy to eliminate the credit risk on his pending loan to Jetgreen.

10. Given the following:

    • The yield on a 5-year, risk-free Treasury note = 5%

    • The yield on a 5-year, BB-quality bond = 8%, with the 3% spread reflecting only credit risk.

    • The credit spread on a 5-year CDS on the 5-year BB-quality bond of 2%

    a. Explain how a bond investor looking for a 5-year, risk-free investment could gain a 1% yield over the risk-free investment by using a CDS.

    b. Explain what an arbitrageur would do.

    c. Comment on the impact the actions by investors and arbitragers would have on determining the equilibrium spread on a CDS

11. Given the following:

    • The yield on a 5-year risk-free Treasury note = 5%

    • The yield on a 5-year BB-quality bond = 8%, with the 3% spread reflecting only credit risk.

    • The credit spread on a 5-year CDS on the 5-year BB-quality bond of 4%

    a. Explain how a bond investor looking to invest in the 5-year BB-rated bond could gain a 1% yield over that investment by using a CDS.

b. Explain what an arbitrageur would do.

c. Comment on the impact the actions by investors and arbitragers would have on determining the equilibrium spread on a CDS.

12. Explain how a 3% credit spread on 5-year, BB-quality bonds can be viewed as the expected loss from the principal resulting from default.

13. Given a discount rate of 5%, determine the present value of the payments on a 5-year CDS with a spread of 3% and a NP of $1. If the recovery rate on the underlying credit is 30%, what is the probability intensity implied by the spread?

14. Given an estimated 5-year average probability intensity of .0375 on a 5-year, BB-rated CDS, a recovery rate of 30%, and discount rate of 5%, determine the value and spread on CDS. Assume NP = $1.

15. Comment on the two alternative approaches to valuing a CDS.

16. The table following shows the historical cumulative probabilities for corporate bonds with quality ratings of AA and B:

Cumulative Probabilities (%)

Year	1	2	3	4	5
AA	0.10	0.40	1.10	1.50	1.75
B	6.00	13.00	20.00	28.00	36.00

a. Determine the unconditional and conditional default probabilities from the cumulative probabilities shown in the table.

b. Given your probability calculations, determine the values and spreads on a 5-year CDS with an AA-quality rating and a 5-year CDS with a B-quality rating. Assume each swap has an NP of $1 and a recovery rate of 30% and that the appropriate discount rate is 6%.

17. The table following shows the current spreads on 1- to 5-year CDSs each with a quality rating of B.

Maturity t	Spread
1	0.0490
2	0.0500
3	0.0510
4	0.0520
5	0.0530

a. Determine the implied probability intensities for Years 1 through 5. Assume recovery rate of 30%.

b. Given your probability calculations, determine the value and spread on a 5-year CDS with a B-quality rating. Assume each swap has an NP of $1 and a recovery rate of 30% and that the appropriate discount rate is 6%.

18. How much would a swap bank pay or require as compensation for assuming the buyer's position on an exiting 4-year, BBB-rated CDS with a spread of 2.5% if current 4-year, BBB-rated CDSs are trading at a spread of 2%? Assume the appropriate discount rate is 6%, NP is 1%, and the recovery rate is 30%. Explain why the value of the swap position changes.

19. How much would a swap bank pay or require as compensation for assuming the seller's position on an exiting 4-year, BBB-rate CDS with a spread of 2.5% if current 4-year, BBB-rated CDSs were trading at a spread of 2%? Assume the appropriate discount rate is 6%, NP is 1%, and the recovery rate is 30%. Explain why the value of the swap position changes.

20. Define the following swaps: binary swap, basket CDS, total return swap, and equity swaps.

WEB EXERCISES

1. Examine the growth in currency swaps and credit default swaps by looking at the International Swap and Derivatives Association's Market Survey. Go to www.isda.org and click on "Survey and Market Statistics."

2. Determine the recent spreads on credit derivative indexes by going to www.wsj.com/free and click "Bond, Rates, and Credit Markets" and "Credit Derivative."

CHAPTER 21

EMBEDDED OPTIONS

21.1 INTRODUCTION

Our examination of options has focused almost exclusively on exchange-traded and over-the-counter options. Many of the characteristics germane to exchange and OTC options, though, are embedded in the equity and debt securities of corporations. For example, the call and put features on corporate debt securities, the conversion clauses on convertible bonds, and the preemptive rights of existing stockholders are all option-like characteristics associated with corporate securities. In fact, the stock of a corporation with debt (a leveraged corporation) can be regarded as an option; that is, a company's stock in effect gives its shareholders the right to buy the firm from the company's creditors at an exercise price equal to the face value on the debt. If the company is successful, causing the value of the firm's assets to grow, then the shareholders will exercise their equity right and buy the company from the creditors at the exercise price equal to the debt's face value. If the value of the firm is less than the debt's face value, then the shareholders will choose not to exercise their option to reclaim the firm from the bondholders.

In this chapter, we examine the option features embedded in corporate securities. The analysis of the option characteristics of corporate securities, referred to as ***contingent claims analysis,*** was first examined in the seminal Black and Scholes option pricing article. We begin our analysis by looking at how a corporation's common stock and debt can be viewed as call options (in Appendix 21A, we analyze stock and debt as put options). This is followed by an analysis of the option features embedded in corporate bonds. Next, we examine warrants, rights, and convertible securities. We conclude the chapter by showing how the option pricing methodology can be used as a capital budgeting tool.

21.2 CORPORATE STOCK AND DEBT AS OPTIONS

21.2.1 Equity and Debt as Call Option Positions

The limited liability feature of common stock enables the stockholders of a leveraged corporation to view their equity position as a call option on the assets of the corporation, with the corporation's creditors being viewed as the writers of the call option and the owners of the firm. To illustrate, suppose a company has debt consisting only of a pure discount bond with a face value of F and maturing at time T. The stockholders of the company can view their equity position as a call option in which they can buy the company from the bondholders at an exercise price equal to the face value of the debt, with an expiration date equal to the bond's maturity. As shown in Figure 21.2-1(a), if the value of the assets of the firm (V^A) exceeds F at maturity, $V_T^A > F$, the shareholders of the company would exercise their option and purchase the company from the bondholders at the exercise price of F. If $V_T^A < F$ at maturity, then the shareholders would not (or could not) exercise. Thus,

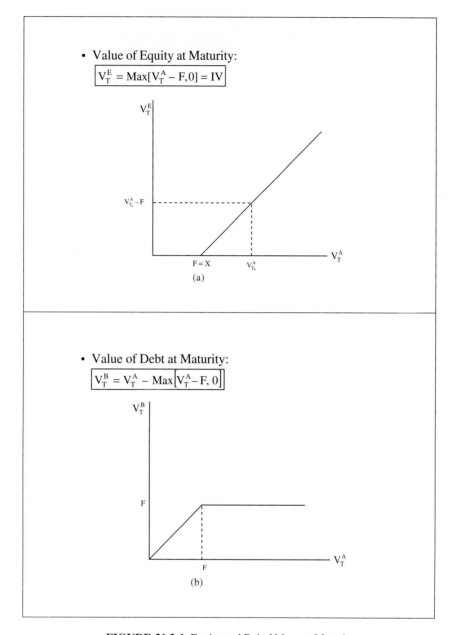

- Value of Equity at Maturity:

$$V_T^E = \text{Max}[V_T^A - F, 0] = IV$$

(a)

- Value of Debt at Maturity:

$$V_T^B = V_T^A - \text{Max}\left[V_T^A - F, 0\right]$$

(b)

FIGURE 21.2-1 Equity and Debt Values at Maturity

at expiration, the total value of equity of the company (V_T^E) would be

$$V_T^E = \text{Max}\left[V_T^A - F, 0\right] \qquad (21.2\text{-}1)$$

The bondholders' position, as noted, can be viewed as a covered call write position in which they (1) own the assets of the firm and (2) have a short position on a call option on the firm's assets. As shown in Figure 21.2-1(b), at expiration, if $V_T^A < F$, the call (or equity) position is worthless, and the bondholders retain their ownership of the company. If $V_T^A \geq F$, though, then the stockholders will buy the company from the bondholders at the exercise price of F. In this case, the value of the bond (V_T^B) is equal to F. Thus, the value of the bondholders' position at maturity is equal to the minimum of either F or V_T^A:

$$V_T^B = \text{Min}\left[V_T^A, F\right] \tag{21.2-2}$$

This minimum condition can be stated equivalently in terms of the following maximum condition:

$$V_T^B = V_T^A - \text{Max}\left[V_T^A - F, 0\right] \tag{21.2-3}$$

That is

	$\text{Min}\left[V_T^A, F\right]$	$V_T^A - \text{Max}\left[V_T^A - F, 0\right]$
If $V_T^A \geq F$	F	$V_T^A - \left[V_T^A - F\right] = F$
If $V_T^A < F$	V_T^A	$V_T^A - 0 = V_T^A$

Equation (21.2-3) shows the expiration value of the debt is equal to the value of the firm minus the intrinsic value of the call, which is equal to the expiration value of a covered call write position.

Prior to maturity, the value of the stock (V_t^E) would be equal to its intrinsic value plus a time value premium, and the value of the debt would be equal to the value of the firm minus the equity value. Figure 21.2-2 shows the values of equity and debt as functions of the value of the firm. In the figure, the IV line depicts the intrinsic value of the equity, the 45-degree line shows the maximum equity value, the curve in between shows the familiar call price curve representing the value of the equity, and the vertical distance between the 45-degree line (V_t^A) and the equity curve (V_t^E) shows the value of the debt.

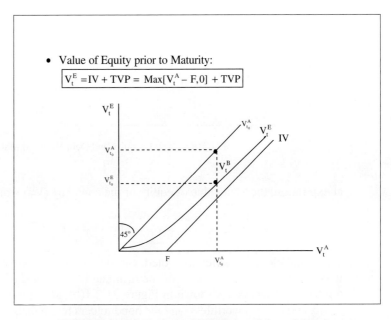

FIGURE 21.2-2 Equity and Debt Values Prior to Maturity

21.2.2 Valuing Equity as a Call Option With the B–S OPM

The value of equity can be estimated using the B–S OPM. Specifically

$$V_0^E = V_0^A N(d_1) - \left[\frac{F}{e^{RT}}\right] N(d_2) \tag{21.2-4}$$

$$d_1 = \frac{\ln(V_0^A/F) + (R + .5\,\sigma^2)T}{\sigma\sqrt{T}}$$

$$d_2 = d_1 - \sigma\sqrt{T}$$

As an example, suppose the ABC Company currently is worth $15 million, has a debt obligation consisting of a pure discount bond maturing in 2 years with a face value of $10 million, and has an asset variability of $\sigma = .5$. If the annual risk-free rate is 6%; the value of ABC stock, using the B–S OPM, would be $7.2 million; and the value of its debt would be $7.83 million. That is

$$d_1 = \frac{\ln(\$15M/\$10M) + [.06 + .5(.5)^2](2)}{.5\sqrt{2}} = 1.09667$$

$$d_2 = 1.09667 - .5\sqrt{2} = .38957$$

$$N(1.09667) = .86338$$

$$N(.38957) = .65175$$

$$V_0^E = (\$15M)(.86338) - \left[\frac{\$10M}{e^{(.06)(2)}}\right](.65175) = \$7.17M$$

$$V_0^B = V_0^A - V_0^E = \$15M - \$7.17M = \$7.83M$$

Note that the value of the stock is an increasing function of the variability of the firm's assets when we value equity as an option. This direct relation reflects the fact that equity provides an unlimited profit potential and limited loss (or limited liability) characteristic. Given the direct relationship between equity value and variability, it follows that if the objective of the company's managers is to maximize the wealth of its shareholders, then with other factors constant, managers in selecting among mutually exclusive investment projects should select the riskier one. If the market, in turn, values stock as a call option, then managers can augment the equity values of their company by selecting riskier investments (and finding creditors to help finance them).

21.2.3 Subordinated Debt

In the preceding section, we assumed that the corporation had only one class of debt. Consider now the case in which the company has the following two debt classes:

1. A pure discount bond with a priority or senior claim on the company's assets, a face value of F^S, and a current value of V_0^{BS}.
2. A pure discount bond with a claim on the company's assets that is subordinate to the senior bond's claim, a face value of F^J, and a current value of V_0^{BJ}.

For simplicity, assume that both bonds mature at the same time and that the company will not pay any dividends until the principals on the bonds have been paid. With the two debt obligations, the value of the firm is now defined as

$$V_0^A = V_0^E + V_0^{BS} + V_0^{BJ} \tag{21.2-5}$$

As before, the stockholders' position is equivalent to a long call option in which they have the right to buy the company from the bondholders. In this case, the exercise price is equal to the sum of F^S and F^J, and the value of the stockholders' position at maturity is

$$V_T^E = \text{Max}\left[V_T^A - (F^S + F^J), 0\right] \tag{21.2-6}$$

The senior bondholders' position is the same as described in the preceding section: They have a covered call position in which they own the asset and are short in a call option with an exercise price equal to F^S. At maturity, the value of their position is

$$V_T^{BS} = \text{Min}\left[V_T^A - F^S, 0\right] \tag{21.2-7}$$

$$V_T^{BS} = V_T^A - \text{Max}\left[V_T^A - F^S, 0\right]$$

The subordinated bondholders have a position that is equivalent to a portfolio with a long call position on the firm with an exercise price of F^S and a short call position on the firm with an exercise price of $F^S + F^J$. At expiration, the value of their position is

$$V_T^{BJ} = \text{Max}\left[V_T^A - F^S, 0\right] - \text{Max}\left[V_T^A - (F^S + F^J), 0\right] \tag{21.2-8}$$

This equivalence can be seen in Table 21.2-1. As shown in the table, if $V_T^A > (F^S + F^J)$ at maturity, the junior bondholders receive F^J; if $F^S < V_T^A < (F^S + F^J)$, the senior bondholders receive F^S, with $V_T^A - F^S$ left to the junior bondholders; finally, if $V_T^A < F^S$, the senior bondholders retain the company and the junior bondholders as well as the shareholders receive nothing. The three positions are summarized graphically in Figure 21.2-3.

21.3   OPTION FEATURES OF BONDS[1]

The default-risk characteristic of the bonds described previously represent an option-like feature inherent to the bond. Other embedded option characteristics of bonds also exist including coupon payments, the call rights of the issuer, the call rights in sinking funds clauses, and the put rights of the bondholders.

21.3.1   Coupon Bonds

In describing the preceding option characteristics of the stockholders' and creditors' positions, we assumed the debt claims were zero-coupon bonds. If the company's bonds pay

TABLE 21.2-1   Subordinate Debt Position at Maturity

Subordinate Debt Position

$$V_T^{BJ} = \text{Max}\left[V_T^A - F^S, 0\right] - \text{Max}\left[V_T^A - (F^S + F^J), 0\right]$$

If $V_T^A > (F^S + F^J)$	$V_T^{BJ} = V_T^A - F^S - \left[V_T^A - (F^S + F^J)\right] = F^J$
If $F^S < V_T^A < (F^S + F^J)$	$V_T^{BJ} = V_T^A - F^S - 0 = V_T^A - F^S$
If $V_T^A < F^S$	$V_T^{BJ} = 0$

[1] Some of the material in this section draws from R. S. Johnson, *Bond Evaluation, Selection, and Management* (2004), Chapter 9.

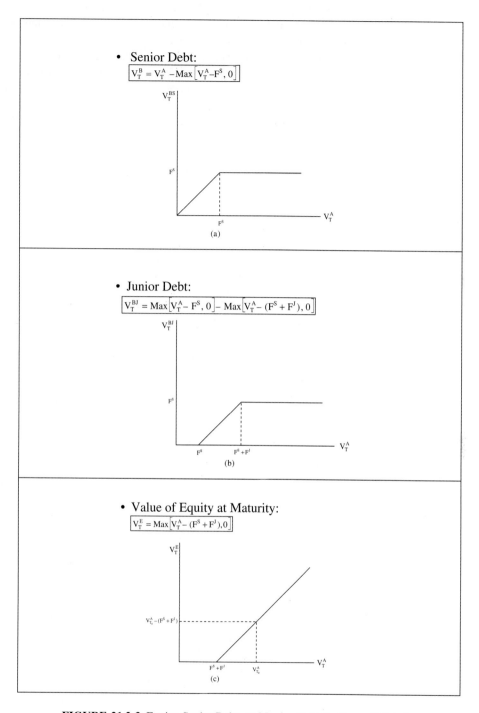

FIGURE 21.2-3 Equity, Senior Debt, and Junior Debt Positions at Maturity

coupons, then Equation (21.2-3) for valuing debt and Equation (21.2-1) for valuing equity only approximate the debt and equity values of the company. A more precise model is found by viewing the shareholders as having a long position and the bondholders a short position in a compound option: an option on an option. That is, for a coupon bond in which the principal is paid at maturity, the shareholders have the right to buy the company from the bondholders at an exercise price equal to the bond's face value ($X = F$) at expiration (T). In the period before expiration (T-1), the stockholders are responsible for paying the period coupon. This payment can be viewed by the stockholders as a call option, with an exercise price equal to the coupon payment, giving them the right to buy the call option with $X = F$ expiring at maturity—an option on an option. Similarly, the coupon payment two periods from maturity (T-2) also is a call option giving the stockholders the right to buy the call option on the option in period T-1 at an exercise price equal to the coupon payment. Thus, when the debt of the company consists of a coupon bond, the stockholders have a long position and the bondholders a short position on a compound call option.

21.3.2   Callable Bonds

Many bonds have call features that give the issuer the right to buy back the bond from the bondholders at a specified price. This feature is a benefit to the issuer. If interest rates decrease in the market, then the issuer can reduce his interest costs of financing assets by borrowing funds at a lower rate and using the proceeds to call the bond issue. When a bond issue is called, the bondholders sell their bonds back to the issuer, usually at a premium above the face value on the bond, the amount of the premium being specified in the bond indenture. Although the bondholders benefit from receiving the call premium, they also are in a situation in which they have to reinvest their funds in a market with lower interest rates.

Conceptually, when an investor buys a callable bond, she implicitly is selling a call option to the issuer, giving the issuer the right to buy the bond from the bondholder before maturity at a specified price. Theoretically, a callable bond can be priced as the sum of the value of an identical, but noncallable, bond minus the value of the call feature. The inclusion of option features in a bond contract also makes the evaluation of such bonds more difficult. A 10-year, 10% callable bond issued when interest rates are relatively high may be more like a 3-year bond given that a likely interest rate decrease would lead the issuer to buy the bond back. Determining the value of such a bond requires taking into account not only the value of the bond's cash flow but also the value of the call option embedded in the bond. One way to capture the impact of a bond's option features on its value is to use the binomial interest rate model. Such a model incorporates the random paths that interest rates follow over time. Moreover, by being discrete, the model allows one to examine each node to determine if the bond would be called.

21.3.2.1   Valuing a Three-Period Callable Bond With a Binomial Tree

In Chapter 7, we valued a three-period, 9% coupon bond with no default risk or option features using a two-period binomial interest rate tree with a current spot rate of $S_0 = 10\%$, $u = 1.1$, and $d = .95$. In valuing the bond, we first determined the three possible values of the bond in Period 2 given the three possible spot rates and the bond's certain cash flow next period (maturity). As shown in Exhibit 21.3-1, the three possible values in Period 2 are $B_{uu} = 109/1.121 = 97.2346$, $B_{ud} = 109/1.1045 = 98.6872$, and $B_{dd} = 109/1.09025 = 99.9771$. Given these values, we next roll the tree to the first period and determine the two possible values in that period, with the values being equal to the present values of the expected cash flows in Period 2 and with the probability of an increase in one period being $q = .5$:

$$B_u = \frac{.5[97.2346 + 9] + .5[98.6872 + 9]}{1.11} = 96.3612$$

$$B_d = \frac{.5[98.6872 + 9] + .5[99.9771 + 9]}{1.095} = 98.9335$$

EXHIBIT 21.3-1   Value of Three-Period Option-Free Bond

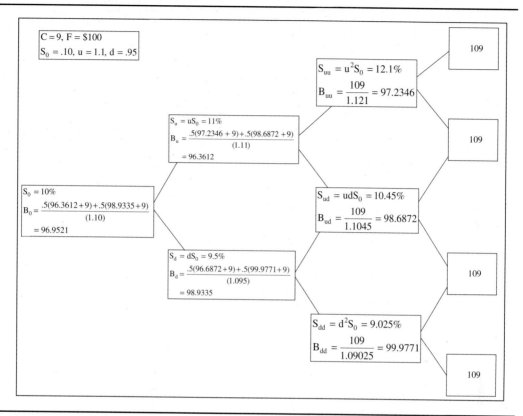

Finally, using the bond values in Period 1, we roll the tree to the current period in which we determine the value of the bond to be 96.9521:

$$B_0 = \frac{.5\,[96.3612 + 9] + .5\,[98.9335 + 9]}{1.10} = 96.9521$$

Now suppose that the three-period, 9% bond has a call feature that allows the issuer to buy back the bond at a call price (CP) of 98. Using the binomial tree approach, this call option can be incorporated into the valuation of the bond by determining at each node whether the issuer would exercise his right to call. The issuer will find it profitable to exercise whenever the call price is less than the bond price (assuming no transaction or holding costs). Thus, the value of the callable bond in each period is the minimum of its call price or its binomial value:

$$B_t^C = \text{Min}[B_t, CP]$$

To incorporate this constraint into the tree, we first compare each of the noncallable bond values with the call price in Period 2 (one period from maturity) and take the minimum of the two as the callable bond value. We next roll the callable bond values from Period 2 to Period 1 in which we determine the two bond values at each node as the present value of the expected cash flows; and then for each case, we select the minimum of the value we calculated or the call price. Finally, we roll those two callable bond values to the current period and determine the callable bond's price as the present value of Period 1's expected cash flows. The top figure in Exhibit 21.3-2 shows the binomial tree value of the three-period, 9% bond given a call feature with a CP = 98. Note, at the two lower nodes in Period

2, the bond would be called at 98, and therefore the callable bond price would be 98; at the top node, the bond price of 97.2346 would prevail. Rolling these prices to Period 1, the present values of the expected cash flows are 96.0516 at the 11% spot rate and 97.7169 at the 9.5% rate. Because neither of these values are less than the CP of 98, each represents the callable bond value at that node. Rolling these two values to the current period, we obtain a value of 96.2584 for the three-period callable bond. As we should expect, the bond's embedded call option lowers the value of the bond from 96.9521 to 96.2584.

Instead of using a price constraint at each node, the price of the callable bond can alternatively be found by determining the value of the call option at each node, V_t^C, and then subtracting that value from the noncallable bond value ($B_t^C = B_t^{NC} - V_t^C$). When there are three periods or more, we need to take into account that prior to maturity, the bond issuer has two choices: She can either exercise the option or she can hold it for another period. The exercising value, IV, is

$$IV = Max[B_t^{NC} - CP, 0]$$

whereas the value of holding, V_H, is the present value of the expected call value next period:

$$V_H = \frac{qV_u^C + (1-q)V_d^C}{1+S}$$

If V_H exceeds IV, the issuer will hold the option another period, and the value of the call in this case will be the holding value. In contrast, if IV is greater than V_H, then the issuer will exercise the call immediately, and the value of the option will be IV. Thus, the value of the call option is equal to the maximum of IV or V_H:

$$V^C = Max[IV, V_H]$$

The lower figure in Exhibit 21.3-2 shows this valuation approach applied to the three-period callable bond. Note that in Period 2, the value of holding is zero at all three nodes because next period is maturity when it is too late to call. The issuer, though, would find it profitable to exercise in two of the three cases where the call price is lower than the bond values. The three possible callable bond values in Period 2 are

$$B_{uu}^C = B_{uu}^{NC} - V_{uu}^C = 97.2346 - Max[97.2346 - 98, 0] = 97.2346$$

$$B_{ud}^C = B_{ud}^{NC} - V_{ud}^C = 98.6872 - Max[98.6872 - 98, 0] = 98$$

$$B_{dd}^C = B_{dd}^{NC} - V_{dd}^C = 99.9771 - Max[99.9771 - 98, 0] = 98$$

In Period 1, the noncallable bond price is greater than the call price at the lower node. In this case, the IV is 98.9335 − 98 = .9335. The value of holding the call, though, is 1.2166:

$$V_H = \frac{.5[Max[98.6872 - 98, 0]] + .5[Max[99.9771 - 98, 0]]}{1.095} = 1.2166$$

Thus, the issuer would find it more valuable to defer the exercise one period. As a result, the value of the call option is Max[IV, V_H] = Max[.8394, 1.2166] = 1.2166, and the value of the callable bond is 97.7169 (the same value we obtained using the price constraint approach):

$$B_d^C = B_d^{NC} - V_d^C = 98.9335 - 1.2166 = 97.7169$$

EXHIBIT 21.3-2   Value of Three-Period Callable Bond

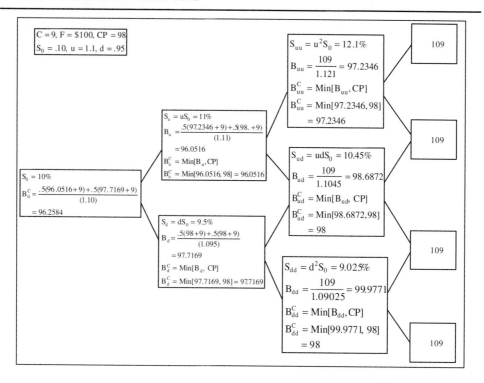

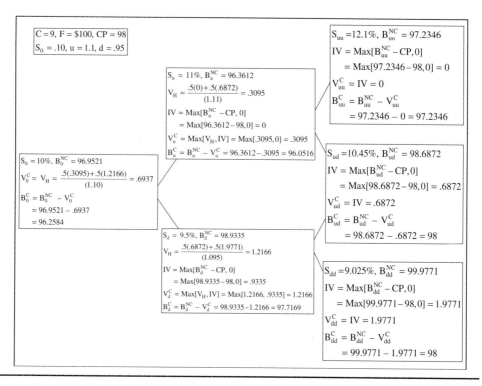

At the upper node in Period 1 in which the price of the noncallable is 96.3612, the exercise value is zero. The value of the call option in this case is equal to its holding value of .3095:

$$V_H = \frac{.5[\text{Max}[97.2346 - 98, 0]] + .5[\text{Max}[98.6872 - 98, 0]]}{1.11} = .3095$$

and the value of the callable bond is 96.0517 (the same value as the constraint one with some slight rounding):

$$B_u^C = B_u^{NC} - V_u^C = 96.3612 - .3095 = 96.0517$$

Finally, rolling the two possible option values of .3095 and 1.2166 in Period 1 to the current period, we obtain the current value of the option of .6937 and the same callable bond value of 96.2584 that we obtained using the first approach:

$$V_0^C = \frac{.5[.3095] + .5[1.2166]}{1.10} = .6937$$

$$B_0^C = B_0^{NC} - V_0^C = 96.9521 - .6937 = 96.2584$$

21.3.3 Putable Bond

In addition to call features, bonds can have other embedded options such as a put option, a stock convertibility clause, or a sinking fund arrangement in which the issuer has the option to buy some of the bonds back either at their market price or at a call price. The binomial tree can be easily extended to the valuation of bonds with these embedded option features.

A putable bond, or put bond, gives the holder the right to sell the bond back to the issuer at a specified exercise price (or put price), PP. In contrast to callable bonds, putable bonds benefit the holder: If the price of the bond decreases below the exercise price, then the bondholder can sell the bond back to the issuer at the exercise price. From the bondholder's perspective, a put option provides a hedge against a decrease in the bond price. If rates decrease in the market, then the bondholder benefits from the resulting higher bond prices; and if rates increase, then the bondholder can exercise, giving her downside protection. Given that the bondholder has the right to exercise, the price of a putable bond will be equal to the price of an otherwise identical nonputable bond plus the value of the put option (V_0^P):

$$B_0^P = B_0^{NP} + V_0^P$$

Because the bondholder will find it profitable to exercise whenever the put price exceeds the bond price, the value of a putable bond can be found using the binomial approach by comparing bond prices at each node with the put price and selecting the maximum of the two, $\text{Max}[B_t, PP]$. The same binomial value can also be found by determining the value of the put option at each node and then pricing the putable bond as the value of an otherwise identical nonputable bond plus the value of the put option. In using the second approach, the value of the put option will be the maximum of either its intrinsic value (or exercising value), $IV = \text{Max}[PP - B_t, 0]$, or its holding value (the present value of the expected put value next period). In most cases, though, the put's intrinsic value will be greater than its holding value.

To illustrate, suppose the three-period, 9%, option-free bond in our previous example had a put option giving the bondholder the right to sell the bond back to the issuer at an exercise price of PP = 97 in Periods 1 or 2. Using the two-period tree of one-period spot rates and the corresponding bond values for the option-free bond (Exhibit 21.3-1), we start, as we did with the callable bond, at Period 2 and investigate each of the nodes to determine if there is an advantage for the holder to exercise. In all three of the cases in Period 2, the bond price exceeds the exercise price (see Exhibit 21.3-3); thus, there are no exercise advantages in this period; and each of the possible prices of the putable bond are equal to their nonputable values, and the values of each of the put options are zero. In Period 1, though, it is profitable for the holder to exercise when the spot rate is 11%. At that node, the value of the nonputable bond is 96.3612 compared to PP = 97; thus the value of putable bond is its exercise price of 97:

$$B_u^P = Max[96.3612, 97] = 97$$

At the lower node in Period 1, it is not profitable to exercise. Thus at the lower node, the binomial bond price prevails. Rolling the two putable bond values in Period 1 to the present, we obtain a current value of the putable bond of 97.2425:

$$B_0^P = \frac{.5[97+9] + .5[98.9335 + 9]}{1.10} = 97.2425$$

The inclusion of the put option in this example causes the bond price to increase from 96.9521 to 97.2425, reflecting the value the put option has to the bondholder.

21.3.4 Sinking Fund Bonds

Many bonds have sinking fund clauses specified in their indenture requiring that the issuer make scheduled payments into a fund or buy up a certain proportion of the bond issue

EXHIBIT 21.3-3 Value of Putable Bond

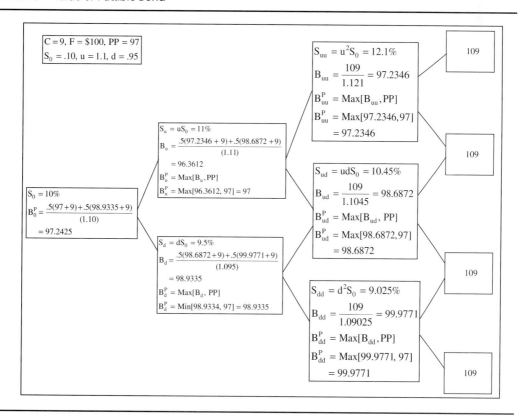

each period. Often when the sinking fund agreement specifies an orderly retirement of the issue, the issuer is given an option of either purchasing the bonds in the market or calling the bonds at a specified call price. This option makes the sinking fund valuable to the issuer. If interest rates are relatively high, then the issuer will be able to buy back the requisite amount of bonds at a relatively low market price; if rates are low and the bond price high, though, then the issuer will be able to buy back the bonds on the call option at the call price. Thus, a sinking fund bond with this type of call provision should trade at a lower price than an otherwise identical nonsinking fund bond.

Similar to callable bonds, a sinking fund bond can be valued using the binomial tree approach. To illustrate, suppose a company issues a $21M, three-period bond with a sinking fund obligation requiring that the issuer sink $7M of face value after the first period and $7M after the second, with the issuer having an option of either buying the bonds in the market or calling them at a call price of 98. Assume the same interest rate tree and bond values characterizing the three-period, 9%, noncallable described in Exhibit 21.3-1 apply to this bond without its sinking fund agreement. With the sinking fund, the issuer has two options: At the end of Period 1, the issuer can buy $7M worth of the bond either at 98 or at the bond's market price; and at the end of Period 2, the issuer has another option to buy $7M worth of the bond either at 98 or the market price. As shown in Exhibit 21.3-4, the value of the Period 1 option (in terms of $100 face value) is $V_0^{SF(1)} = .4243$, and the value of the Period 2 call option is $V_0^{SF(2)} = .6937$. Note that because the sinking fund arrangement requires an immediate exercise or bond purchase at the specified sinking fund dates, the possible values of the sinking fund's call features at those dates are equal to the intrinsic values. This differs from the valuation of a standard callable bond in which a holding value is also considered in determining the value of the call option.

Because each option represents 1/3 of the issue, the value of the bond's sinking fund option is

$$V_0^{SF} = (1/3)(.4243) + (1/3)(.6937) = .3727$$

and the value of the sinking fund bond is 96.5794 per $100 face value:

$$B_0^{SF} = B_0^{NSF} - V_0^{SF}$$
$$B_0^{SF} = 96.9521 - .3727 = 96.5794$$

Thus, the total value of the $21M face value issue is $20,281,674:

$$\text{Issue Value} = \frac{96.5794}{100}\$21,000,000 = \$20,281,674$$

Like a standard callable bond, a sinking fund provision with a call feature lowers the value of an otherwise identical nonsinking fund bond.

21.3.5 Pricing Callable and Putable Bonds With a Multiple-Period Tree

The binomial interest rate model for valuing callable and putable bonds is more realistic when we subdivide the periods to maturity into a number of subperiods. For example, suppose the three-period bond in our illustrative example were a 3-year bond. Instead of using a three-period binomial tree in which the length of each period is a year, suppose we evaluate the bond using a 36-period tree with the length of each period being 1 month. If we do this, we need to divide the 1-year spot rates and the annual coupon by 12, adjust the u and d parameters to reflect changes over a 1-month period instead of 1 year, and define

EXHIBIT 21.3-4   Value of Sinking Fund Call in Periods 1 and 2

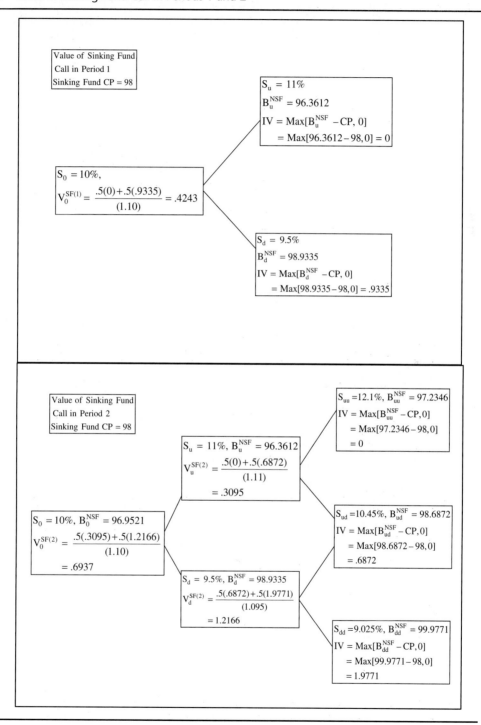

the binomial tree of spot rates for 35 periods, each with a length of 1 month. For example, if the annualized mean and variance of the logarithmic return of 1-year spot rates were .044 and .0108, then the u and d values for a 36-period tree of length 1 month (h = length of period in years = 1/12) would be equal to 1.03424 and .9740 (see Section 7.3 for an explanation of the u and d formulas for a binomial interest rate tree):

$$u = e^{\sqrt{hV_e^A} + h\mu_e^A} = e^{\sqrt{(1/12).0108} + (1/12).044} = 1.03424$$

$$d = e^{-\sqrt{hV_e^A} + h\mu_e^A} = e^{-\sqrt{(1/12).0108} + (1/12).044} = .9740$$

The monthly coupon accrued interest would be $0.75 ($9/12), and the monthly spot rate would be the annual spot rate divided by 12. Excel programs for generating multiple-period binomial interest rate trees (Binrate), valuing callable bonds (Binbondcall), and valuing putable bonds (Binbondput) are included with this text. The programs are in the folder "Binomial Interest Rate Excel Program." Using these programs to value the 3-year, 9% bond for this 36-period case and with an annualized mean and variance of .044 and .0108, we obtain an option-free bond price of 95.65, a callable bond price of 94.26 (CP = 98), and a putable bond price of 97.17 (PP = 97).

Recall that when using the u and d estimation approach, the tree is not constrained to yield a price for an option-free bond that matches its equilibrium value (i.e., the arbitrage-free price obtained by discounting the bond's cash flows by spot rates). As a result, analysts using such models need to make additional assumptions about the risk premium to explain the bond's equilibrium price. In contrast, the calibration model that was examined in Chapter 7 is constrained to obtain prices on option-free bonds that are equal to their equilibrium values.[2] Given this feature, the calibration model is usually more accurate than the u and d approach in pricing bonds with embedded call and put features.

21.3.6   Using the B–S OPM to Price Embedded Call and Put Options

In examining binomial interest rate models and their use in valuing bonds with embedded options, it should be noted that an approximate value of the embedded option features of a bond can also be estimated using the B–S OPM. The B–S formulas for determining the equilibrium price of an embedded call or put options are

$$V_0^C = B_0 N(d_1) - XN(d_2)e^{-R_f T}$$

$$V_0^P = X(1 - N(d_2))e^{-R_f T} - B_0(1 - N(d_1))$$

$$d_1 = \frac{\ln(B_0/X) + (R_f + .5\sigma^2)T}{\sigma\sqrt{T}}$$

$$d_2 = d_1 - \sigma\sqrt{T}$$

where
X = call price (CP) or put price (PP)
σ^2 = variance of the logarithmic return of bond prices = $V(\ln(B_n/B_0)$
T = maturity of the bond expressed as a proportion of a year

---

[2] In addition to satisfying an arbitrage-free condition on option-free bonds, the calibration model also values a bond's embedded options as arbitrage-free prices. For a discussion of this feature, see Johnson, Zuber, and Gandar (2002).

For example, suppose a 3-year, noncallable bond with a 10% annual coupon is selling at par (F = 100). A callable bond that is identical in all respects except for its call feature should sell at 100 minus the call price. In this case, suppose the call feature gives the issuer the right to buy the bond back at any time during the bond's life at an exercise price of 115. Assuming a risk-free rate of 6% and a variability of $\sigma = .10$ on the noncallable bond's logarithmic return, the call value using the Black–Scholes model would be 8.95:

$$V_0^C = B_0 N(d_1) - X N(d_2) e^{-R_f T}$$

$$V_0^C = 100(.62519) - 115(.55772) e^{-(.06)(3)} = 8.95$$

$$d_1 = \frac{\ln(100/115) + (.06 + .5(.10^2))3}{.10\sqrt{3}} = .31892$$

$$d_2 = .31892 - .10\sqrt{3} = .14571$$

$$N(d_1) = N(.31892) = .62519$$

$$N(d_2) = N(.14571) = .55772$$

Thus, the price of the callable bond is 91.05:

$$\text{Price of Callable Bond} = \text{Price of Noncallable Bond} - \text{Call Premium}$$

$$\text{Price of Callable Bond} = 100 - 8.95 = 91.05$$

As we noted in Chapter 7, the B–S OPM assumes interest rates are constant. For most bonds, though, the change in their value is due to interest rate changes. Thus, the use of the B–S OPM to value the call or a put option embedded in a bond should be viewed only as an approximation.

21.4 CONVERTIBLE SECURITIES

Warrants, rights, convertible bonds, and convertible preferred stock can be classified as convertible securities. These instruments give the holders the right to convert one security into another.

21.4.1 Warrants

A warrant is a call option giving the holder the right to buy a specified number of shares of another security at a specific price on or before a specific date. Most warrants are sold by corporations, usually giving the holder the right to buy a specified number of shares of the company's common stock any time on or before expiration, with expiration ranging between 3 to 5 years. As such, warrants represent a long-term American call option written by the corporation. Like exchange-traded call options, warrants are protected against stock splits and dividends but usually not cash dividends.

Corporations often issue warrants as a "sweetner" with other securities (e.g., subordinate bond or preferred stock). When they are issued with another security, they can be either nondetachable or detachable. If the holder of a nondetachable warrant wants to sell the warrant, she would have to sell the accompanying security with it or exercise the warrant. A detachable warrant, though, can be sold separately. Most outstanding warrants trade on the over-the-counter market, although a number of warrants are listed on the organized exchanges.

Most of the contractual characteristics (exercise price, expiration, etc.) of warrants are similar to those of call options on a stock. The fundamental difference between a call on a stock and a warrant on the same stock is that the writer of the warrant is the corporation, whereas the writer of a call option is an individual investor. This difference implies that when a warrant holder exercises, the corporation must issue new shares of stock. When the company, in turn, sells the shares on the warrant contract, it will receive cash from the warrant holders, which it can use to finance its capital projects; however, the company also will have its stock diluted. In contrast, when an exchange-traded call option on the stock is exercised, the writer sells his shares (if the writer is covered) or buys existing shares in the market (if naked) and sells them to the holder. Thus, exercising a call neither dilutes the company's stock nor increases its cash flows.

To illustrate the difference between warrants and call options, consider the case of the LM Corporation that owns a small crude oil well, currently worth $100,000. Assume the LM company is an all-equity company; has 100 shares of stock outstanding (n_0), with each share worth $1,000; and is owned by four shareholders, A, B, C, and D, each with 25 shares.[3]

To see the implications of a call option on the LM company, suppose that Shareholder D sells a call option to an Investor E, giving the investor the right to buy 25 shares of LM stock at X = $1,100 per share. After selling the call option, suppose the value of the oil well company increases from $100,000 to $120,000, initially raising the price of a share of LM stock from $1,000 to $1,200. If, after the increase in value, Investor E exercises her call option, Shareholder D simply would sell his 25 shares to E at $1,100 per share. For the LM corporation, the exercise of this call option would have no impact on the company's total number of shares of 100.

Now suppose that instead of Shareholder D selling a call option when the company is worth $100,000, the LM corporation sells a warrant to Investor E, giving E the right to buy $n_w = 25$ shares at $1,100 per share. Again suppose that the value of the company increases to $120,000, and E exercises her warrant. When E exercises, the LM corporation will have to print 25 new shares of stock and sell them to E. This, in turn, will dilute the company's equity shares. This dilution effect, though, will be offset partially by the receipt of $27,500 in cash from Investor E ((25 shares)($1,100 per share)). Thus, in this case, the exercise of the warrant affects the number of shares of the LM company and its value. Specifically, the new value of the LM company (V^{LM}) is $147,500 (value of the oil well [V^{oil}] plus the cash):

$$V^{LM} = V^{oil} + \text{Cash from the Exercised Warrant}$$

$$V^{LM} = \$120,000 + \$27,500 = \$147,500$$

and the LM company now has $n_0 + n_w = 125$ shares of stock, with the value of each share worth $1,180:

$$\frac{\text{Total Stock Value}}{\text{Total Shares}} = \frac{V^{LM}}{n_0 + n_w} = \frac{\$147,500}{125} = \$1,180$$

For Investor E, the dilution effect associated with the warrant causes the gain from exercising the warrant to be less than the gain from exercising the call. That is, E's return from exercising the call is $2,500: 25($1,200 − $1,100), whereas her return from exercising the warrant is only $2,000: 25($1,180 − 1,100). Formally, the difference between the two

---

[3] This example is based on a similar one presented by Westerfield, Ross, and Jaffey (1991).

options can be seen by comparing their intrinsic values (IV_C and IV_W):

$$IV_C = \text{Max}\left[\frac{V^{oil}}{n_0} - X, 0\right] \tag{21.4-1}$$

$$IV_W = \text{Max}\left[\frac{V^{oil} + Xn_w}{n_0 + n_w} - X, 0\right] \tag{21.4-2}$$

IV_W expressed in terms of IV_c is

$$IV_W = \left[\frac{n_0}{n_0 + n_w}\right] IV_C \tag{21.4-3}$$

The term $n_0/(n_0 + n_w)$ is a dilution factor. In the example, it is equal to $100/125 = .8$. Thus, Equation (21.4-3) shows that the intrinsic value of a warrant is equal to the intrinsic value of a call option on the same underlying stock times the dilution factor. Because warrants and call options on the same stock are perfectly correlated (they both derive their values from the same asset), the current warrant price (W_0), in turn, should be equal to the current call value times the dilution factor. That is

$$W_0 = \left[\frac{n_0}{n_0 + n_w}\right] C_0 \tag{21.4-4}$$

Accordingly, to price a warrant, we can use the OPM to value the warrant as a call and then multiply that value by the dilution factor to determine the value of the warrant.

21.4.2 Rights

Most state laws give the stockholders of a corporation the right to maintain their shares of ownership in the corporation. This **preemptive right** means that when a company issues new shares of stock, the existing shareholders must be given the first right of refusal. Corporations can accomplish this by issuing each stockholder a certificate, known as a **right** (or subscription warrant). From World War II through the 1960s, two thirds of all common stock issues were rights offerings. Beginning in the late 1960s, though, U.S. firms began to obtain shareholders' approval to eliminate preemptive rights. When a company does issue a right, the right entitles the existing shareholder to buy new issues of common stock at a specified price, known as the **subscription price,** for a specified period of time before the stock is sold to the general public. To maintain ownership proportionality, each share of stock receives one right, and to facilitate the new stock sale, the subscription price usually is set below the current stock price. After a company issues rights to its shareholders, the existing shares of stock sell cum rights (buyers of the stock are entitled to the right) to a specified ex-rights date, after which the stock sells without the right.

A right is similar to a warrant. Technically, it is a call option issued by the corporation giving the holder the right to buy stock at a specified price (subscription price) on or before a specific date. Like warrants, when a right is exercised, new shares are created, and the company has additional capital. Also, like warrants, rights can be sold in a secondary market. Rights differ from warrants in that their expiration periods are shorter (e.g., 1–3 months compared to 3–5 years for a warrant), and their exercise prices usually are set below their stock prices, whereas warrants usually have exercise prices above. Also, because of their short expiration periods, rights are usually not adjusted for stock splits and stock dividends.

To illustrate the characteristics of rights, consider the case of the ABC Corporation that is planning to raise $10 million in equity to finance the construction of a new plant.

The company currently is worth $100 million, has no debt, and has one million shares of stock outstanding (n_0), with each share trading at $100. Because of the preemptive rights of shareholders, ABC plans to finance its $10 million investment with a rights offering in which its existing shareholders will be given the opportunity to buy new shares of stock at a subscription price of $80, with each shareholder to receive one right for each share he owns.

The key question for the ABC Company is how many rights will be needed to purchase one new share of ABC stock at $80 per share. This can be found by first determining the number of shares that need to be sold to raise the desired capital. In this example, with its planned $10 million investment expenditure and a subscription price of $80, ABC would need to sell 125,000 new shares:

$$N_n = \text{Number of New Shares} = \frac{\text{Investment}}{\text{Subscription price}}$$

$$N_n = \frac{\$10,000,000}{\$80/\text{Share}} = 125,000 \text{ shares}$$

Because one right is given for each existing share, and ABC has one million existing shares, eight rights would be needed (N_R) to purchase one new share:

$$N_R = \frac{1,000,000}{125,000} = 8 \text{ rights}$$

Thus, shareholders would surrender eight rights and $80 to buy one new share. This rights offering, in turn, would provide ABC $10 million cash to finance its investment and would create 125,000 additional shares.

The intrinsic value of the right (IV_R) is equal to the difference between the market price of the stock (S_T) and the subscription price (X_S) divided by the number of rights needed to purchase one share:

$$IV_R = \frac{S_T - X_S}{N_R}$$

With 125,000 additional shares and $10 million cash inflow, the estimated price of ABC stock would be $97.78:

$$S_T = \frac{\text{Current Equity Value} + \text{Investment Value}}{\text{Old Shares} + \text{New Sahres}}$$

$$S_T = \frac{\$100,000,000 + \$10,000,000}{1,000,000 + 125,000} = \$97.78$$

With an $80 subscription price, eight rights would be worth $17.78 ($97.78 – $80), and one right would be worth $2.22:

$$IV_R = \frac{S_T - X_S}{N_R} = \frac{\$97.78 - \$80}{8} = \$2.22$$

21.4.3 Convertible Bonds

A *convertible bond* is similar to a bond with a nondetachable warrant. Like a regular bond, it pays interest and principal; and like a warrant, it can be exchanged for a specified number of shares of common stock.

Convertible bonds often are sold as subordinate issues by smaller, riskier companies. The conversion feature of the bond, in turn, serves as a "sweetner" to the debt issue. To investors, convertible bonds offer the potential for high rates of return if the corporation does well while still providing a downside protection with the bond. Convertible bonds usually sell at a lower yield than similar nonconvertible bonds and usually are callable.

21.4.4 Convertible Bond Terms

Consider the ABC Corporation's convertible bond that pays an annual coupon of 5%, a par value of $1,000, matures in 10 years, can be called at any time by the issuer at an exercise price (X_B) of $1,050, and can be converted by the holder at any time into 25 shares of ABC stock. The convertible features of the ABC bond can be described in terms of its conversion ratio, conversion price, conversion value, and straight debt value.

The *conversion ratio* (CR) is the number of shares of stock that can be acquired when the bond is tendered for conversion. The ABC convertible's conversion ratio is 25 shares of ABC stock for each bond. It should be noted that on some convertible bonds, the conversion ratio can change over time. Also, some convertible bonds allow conversion to be done either by tendering over the bond or paying a specified amount of cash (or some combination). For example, a convertible could stipulate that 25 shares of stock can be obtained in exchange for the bond or cash equal to a specific proportion of the company's stock value, whichever is smaller.

The *conversion price* (CP) is the bond's par value divided by the conversion ratio: $CP = F/CR$. The conversion price of the ABC convertible is $40. The conversion price is applicable only when the bond is trading at par. Many convertible bond contracts, though, specify changes in the conversion ratio over time by specifying changes in the conversion price instead of the conversion ratio.

The *conversion value* (CV) is the convertible bond's value as a stock. At a given point in time (t), the conversion value is equal to the product of the conversion ratio times the market price of the stock (P_t^S):$CV_t = (CR)P_t^S$. If the current price of ABC stock is $25, the conversion value of ABC's convertible bond is $625 = (25)($25)$.

The *straight debt value* (SDV) is the convertible bond's value as a nonconvertible bond. The SDV is found by discounting the convertible's cash flow by the yield on an identical but nonconvertible bond. Thus, in the case of the ABC convertible, if 10-year, 5% (coupon) callable bonds, with the same default risk as ABC, were trading to yield 10%, then the current SDV of the ABC convertible would be $692.77:

$$SDV_0 = \sum_{t=1}^{M} \frac{\text{Coupons}}{(1+R)^t} + \frac{F}{(1+R)^M}$$

$$SDV_0 = \sum_{t=1}^{10} \frac{\$50}{(1.10)^t} + \frac{\$1,000}{(1.10)^{10}} = \$692.77$$

21.4.5 Minimum and Maximum Convertible Bond Prices

Arbitrage forces ensure that the minimum price of a convertible bond (B_t^{CB}) is the greater of either its straight debt value or conversion value. Thus, the minimum price of a convertible bond is

$$\text{Min } B_t^{CB} = \text{Max}[CV_t, SDV_t]$$

If a convertible bond is priced less than its conversion value, arbitrageurs could buy it, convert to stock, then sell the stock in the market to earn an abnormal profit of $CV - B_t^{CB}$. Arbitrageurs seeking such opportunities would push the price of the convertible up until it is at least equal to its conversion value. Similarly, if a convertible is priced below its SDV, then one could profit by buying the convertible and selling it as a regular bond or by shorting a regular bond and buying the convertible. Thus, the minimum boundary condition for the ABC convertible bond is defined by the maximum of its CV or SDV.

In addition to a minimum price, if the convertible bond has a call feature, the exercise price at which the issuer can redeem the bonds (X_B) places a maximum limit on the price of the convertible. That is, for most issuers, it is advantageous for them to buy back the convertible bond once its price is equal to the exercise price. Buying back the bond, in turn, frees the company to sell new stock and debt at prices higher than the stock or straight debt values associated with the convertible. Thus, the maximum price of a convertible bond is its exercise price. The actual price of a convertible usually will sell at a premium above its minimum value but below the maximum.

21.4.6 Valuation of Convertibles Using Binomial Trees[4]

The valuation of a convertible bond with an embedded call is more difficult than the valuation of a bond with just one option feature. In the case of a callable convertible bond, one has to consider not only the uncertainty of future interest rates but also the uncertainty of future stock prices. A rate decrease, for example, may not only increase the convertible's SDV and the chance the bond could be called; if the rate decrease is also associated with an increase in the stock price, it may also increase the conversion value of the convertible and the chance of conversion. The valuation of convertibles therefore needs to take into account the random patterns of interest rates, stock prices, and the correlation between them.

To illustrate the valuation of convertibles, consider a three-period, 10% convertible bond with a face value $1,000 that can be converted to 10 shares of the underlying company's stock (CR = 10). To simplify the analysis, assume the bond has no call option and no default risk, that the current yield curve is flat at 5%, and that the yield curve will stay at 5% for the duration of the three periods (i.e., no market risk). In this simplified world, the only uncertainty is the future stock price. Suppose the convertible bond's underlying stock price follows a binomial process in which in each period, it has an equal chance it can either increase to equal u times its initial value or decrease to equal d times the initial value, where u = 1.1, d = 1/1.1 = .9091, and the current stock price is $P_0^S = 92$. The possible stock prices resulting from this binomial process are shown in Exhibit 21.4-1 along with the convertible bond's conversion values.

Because spot interest rates are assumed constant, the value of the convertible bond will only depend on the stock price. To value the convertible bond, we start at the maturity date of the bond. At that date, the bondholder will have a coupon worth 100 and will either convert the bond to stock or receive the principal of 1000. At the top stock price of 122.45, the convertible bondholder would exercise her option, converting the bond to 10 shares of stock. The value of the convertible bond, B^{CB}, at the top node in Period 3 would therefore be equal to its conversion value of 1,224.50 plus the $100 coupon:

$$B_{uuu}^{CB} = Max[CV_t, F] + C$$
$$B_{uuu}^{CB} = Max[1224.50, 1000] + 100$$
$$B_{uuu}^{CB} = 1324.50$$

Similarly, at the next stock price of 101.20, the bondholder would also find it profitable to convert; thus, the value of the convertible in this case would be its conversion value of 1012 plus the $100 coupon. At the lower two stock prices in Period 3 of 83.64 and 69.12,

[4] The example in this section is based on a similar one presented by Johnson, *Bond Evaluation, Selection, and Management* (2004), Chapter 9.

EXHIBIT 21.4-1   Value of Convertible Bond

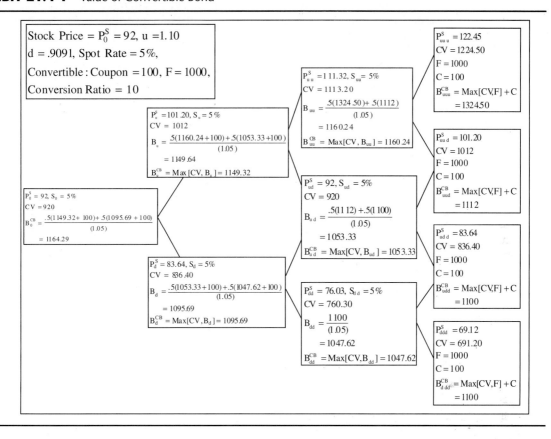

conversion is worthless; thus, the value of the convertible bond is equal to the principal plus the coupon: 1100.

In Period 2, at each node, the value of the convertible bond is equal to the maximum of either the present value of the bond's expected value at maturity or its conversion value. At all three stock prices, the present values of the bond's expected values next period are greater than the bond's conversion values, including at the highest stock price; that is, at $P_{uu}^S = 1113.20$, the CV is 1113.20 compared to the convertible bond value of 1160.24; thus the value of the convertible bond is 1160.24:

$$B_{uu} = \frac{.5[1324.50] + .5[1112]}{1.05} = 1160.24$$

$$B_{uu}^{CB} = Max[B_{uu}, CV] = [1160.24, 1113.20] = 1160.24$$

Thus, in all three cases, the values of holding the convertible bond option are greater than the conversion values. Similarly, the two possible bond values in Period 1 (generated by rolling the three convertible bond values in Period 2 to Period 1) also exceed their conversion values. Rolling the tree to the current period, we obtain a convertible bond value of 1164.29. As we would expect, this value exceeds both the convertible bond's current conversion value of 920 and its SDV of 1136.16 (assuming a 5% discount rate):

$$SDV = \frac{100}{(1.05)} + \frac{100}{(1.05)^2} + \frac{1100}{(1.05)^3} = 1136.16$$

As noted, the valuation of a convertible becomes more complex when the bond is callable. With callable convertible bonds, the issuer will find it profitable to call the convertible prior to maturity whenever the price of the convertible is greater than the call price. However, when the convertible bondholder is faced with a call, she usually has the choice of either tendering the bond at the call price or converting it to stock. Because the issuer will call whenever the call price exceeds the convertible bond price, he is in effect forcing the holder to convert. By doing this, the issuer takes away the bondholder's value of holding the convertible, forcing the convertible bond price to equal its conversion value.

To see this, suppose the convertible bond is callable in Periods 1 and 2 at a CP = 1100. At the top stock price of 1113.20 in Period 2, the conversion value is 1113.20 (see Exhibit 21.4-2). In this case, the issuer can force the bondholder to convert by calling the bond. The call option therefore reduces the value of the convertible from 1160.24 to 1113.20. At the other nodes in Period 2, neither conversion by the bondholders or calling by the issuer is economical; thus the bond values prevail. In Period 1, the call price of 1100 is below the bond value (1126.92) at the top node but above the conversion value (1012). In this case, the issuer would call the bond and the holder would take the call instead of converting. The value of the callable convertible bond in this case would be the call price of 1100. At the lower node, calling and converting are not economical, and thus the bond value of 1095.69 prevails. Rolling Period 1's upper and lower convertible bond values to the current period, we obtain a value for the callable convertible bond of 1140.80, which is less than the noncallable convertible bond value of 1164.29 and greater than the straight debt value of a noncallable bond of 1136.16.

EXHIBIT 21.4-2   Value of Convertible Bond With Call

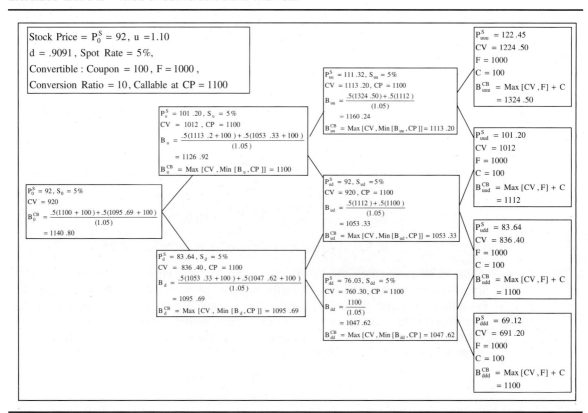

In the previous two cases, we assumed for simplicity that the yield curve remained constant at 5% for the period. As noted, the complexity of valuing convertibles is taking into account the uncertainty of two variables—stock prices and interest rates. A simple way to model such behavior is to use correlation or regression analysis to first estimate the relationship between a stock's price and the spot rate, and then either with a binomial model of spot rates identify the corresponding stock prices or with a binomial model of stock prices identify the corresponding spot rates. For example, suppose using regression analysis, we estimated the following relationship between the stock in our preceding example and the one-period spot rate:

$$S_t = .16 - .001P_t^S$$

Using this equation, the corresponding spot rates associated with the stock prices from the three-period tree would be

P_t^S	S_t
111.32	4.87%
101.20	5.90%
92.00	6.80%
83.64	7.64%
76.03	8.40%

Exhibit 21.4-3 shows the binomial tree of stock prices along with their corresponding spot rates. Given the rates and stock prices, the methodology for valuing the convertible bond is identical to our previous analysis. As in our previous case, at the top node in Period 2, the call price of 1100 is below the convertible bond value of 1161.68. In this case, the issuer will call the bond and the holder will find it more profitable to convert; that is, the conversion value of 1113.20 exceeds the call price of 1100. Thus, the convertible bond would be equal to the conversion value. In the other two cases in Period 2, the values of the convertibles are equal to the present values of their expected cash flows for the next period. In Period 1, the call price is less than the bond value (1108.96) and greater than the conversion value (1012) at the top node. In this case, the issuer would call, and the bondholder would find it better to accept the call instead of converting; thus, the convertible bond price at this node would be the call price of 1100. Rolling the tree to the current period with this value and the lower node value, we obtain a convertible bond value of 1097.99. This value is lower than the previous case in which we assumed a constant yield curve at 5%.

It should be noted that modeling a bond with multiple option features and influenced by the random patterns of more than one factor is more complex in practice than the simple model described previously. The preceding model is intended only to provide some insight into the dynamics involved in valuing a bond with embedded convertible and call options given different interest rate and stock price scenarios.

21.5 USING OPTIONS AS A CAPITAL BUDGETING TOOL

Many investment projects have option-like characteristics that traditional capital budgeting tools are unable to value. To see this, consider the case of East Side Developers (ESD), a development company that is thinking of purchasing and developing a 50-acre farm to eventually sell to area housing developers. Suppose the cost of the land is $0.5 million, and a number of developers other than ESD are interested in the property. Also, suppose

EXHIBIT 21.4-3   Value of Convertible Bond With Call and Different Spot Rates

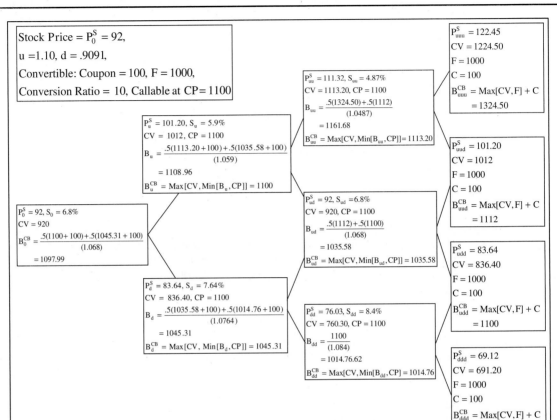

ESD estimates with a high degree of certainty the development expenditures for clearing, road construction, utility installation, and the like will be $2 million and will take 1 year to complete. Finally, suppose they project the expected revenue (after taxes) from selling the developed lots will be $3 million and will occur 1 year after their development.

Because of the uncertainty over the expected $3 million revenue from the lot sale, suppose ESD requires a rate of return on the project (cost of capital) of 20%. As a result, the net present value (NPV) of the project is a negative $0.0833M and should be rejected. That is

$$E(NPV) = -\$0.5M - \frac{\$2M}{1.20} + \frac{\$3M}{(1.20)^2} = -\$0.08333M$$

Suppose, however, that the risk of the project can be attributable directly to the uncertainty over whether a shopping mall will be developed near the proposed development location. Furthermore, suppose ESD knows that if the mall developers are able to secure an anchor tenant, they will be able to obtain their financing and the mall will be developed. If this occurs, ESD is certain it will be able to sell the lots for a total of $6 million; however, if the mall is not developed, they do not see any chance of selling the lots. Finally, suppose the information about the anchor tenant will not be known for another year, and ESD currently estimates there is a 50/50 chance that a tenant will be secured.

Given these contingencies, ESD alternatively can view the project as one in which it could pay $0.5 million for the land (continue to assume other developers are interested) and then wait 1 year before it decides on developing the lots, at which time they will know the status of mall. If the mall project is accepted, then ESD will be able to earn an almost certain revenue of $6M. Given the acceptance of the mall project, the NPV of ESD's project would be the present value of $6M, with the discount rate being the risk-free rate (or at least a lower discount rate than 20% because the project risk has been reduced) minus the $2M land development expenditures. If ESD uses a 10% discount rate, then the NPV of its project at Year 1 would be $3.454M, assuming the mall project is accepted. That is

$$NPV_1 = -\$2M + \frac{\$6M}{1.10} = \$3.454M$$

Thus, by waiting, the investment project now can be viewed as a call option costing $0.5 million (the purchase of the land), giving the developers the right to develop the project for an exercise price of $2 and a certain future return of $6M, with an expiration of 1 year. If the mall is developed, ESD will exercise its call realizing a gain in value of $3.454M; if the mall is not developed, the call is worthless and ESD will not exercise, losing its call premium of $0.5M. Given the 50/50 chance currently that the anchor tenant will be found, the expected NPV of the project is a positive $0.939167M.

$$NPV_0 = -\$0.5M + \frac{E(NPV_1)}{1.20}$$

$$NPV_0 = -\$0.5M + \frac{(.5)(\$3.454) + (.5)(0)}{1.20} = \$0.939167M$$

Thus, when viewed as an option, the project should be accepted.[5]

In summary, the example illustrates how investment projects can be viewed as options and how using an option perspective allows more flexibility to be incorporated into investment decisions than traditional capital budgeting approaches. The applications of options methodology to capital budgeting and other corporate finance decisions is known today as *real options*—a subject of growing interest in corporate finance.

21.6 CONCLUSION

In this chapter, we've examined the option features embedded in corporate securities. Our analysis of the contingent claims of corporations has included the option positions inherent in the equity and debt positions of leveraged corporations; the call and put option features embedded in corporate bonds; the option-conversion features of warrants, rights, and convertible securities; and the application of option methodology to capital budgeting.

Corporate securities, of course, are not the only securities with embedded option features. Some municipal bonds, for example, have embedded call and put option features. Of particular note are mortgage-backed and other asset-backed securities. A mortgage-backed security represents a claim on a portfolio of mortgages. Because most mortgages can be prepaid, there is a prepayment option and prepayment risk associated with the mortgage-backed securities. To address this prepayment risk, a number of derivative securities have

---

[5] Note, if the mall were not developed, but the developer could sell the undeveloped land for some amount, then the project could also be viewed as having put-like characteristics.

been created from the mortgage portfolios. Asset-backed securities and their derivatives are examined in Chapter 22.

KEY TERMS

contingent claims analysis	detachable warrant	conversion ratio
callable bond	dilution factor	conversion price
payable bond	rights	conversion value
sinking fund	preemptive right	straight debt value
warrant	subscription price	minimum convertible
nondetachable warrant	convertible bond	bond price

SELECTED REFERENCES

Arman, M., and N. Kulatilaka. *Real Options.* Boston, MA: Harvard Business School Press, 1999.

Baumol, W., B. Malkiel, and R. Quandt. "The Valuation of Convertible Securities." *Quarterly Journal of Economics* (1966).

Black, F., and M. Scholes. "The Pricing of Options and Corporate Liabilities." *Journal of Political Economy* 81 (1973): 637–659.

Brigham, E. "An Analysis of Convertible Debentures: Theory and Some Empirical Evidence." *Journal of Finance* (December 1985).

Constantinides, G. "Warrant Exercise and Bond Conversion in Competitive Markets." *Journal of Financial Economics* 13 (September 1984): 371–397.

Courtadon, G., and J. J. Merrick. "The Option Pricing Model and the Valuation of Corporate Securities." *Midland Corporate Finance Journal* (Fall 1983).

Galai, D., and M. Schneller. "Pricing Warrants and the Value of the Firm." *Journal of Finance* 33 (December 1978): 1333–1342.

Geske, R. "The Valuation of Compound Options." *Journal of Financial Economics* (March 1979).

Hsia, C. "Optimal Debt of a Firm: An Option Pricing Approach." *Journal of Financial Research* 4 (Fall 1981): 221–231.

Ingersoll, J. "A Contingent-Claims Valuation of Convertible Securities." *Journal of Financial Economics* (May 1977).

Johnson, R. S. *Bond Evaluation, Selection, and Management,* Malden, MA: Blackwell Publishing, 2004.

Johnson, R. S., R. Zuber, and J. Gandar. "Binomial Pricing of Fixed Income Securities for Increasing and Decreasing Interest Rate Case." *Applied Financial Economics* (2006): 1–18.

Johnson, R. S., R. Zuber, and J. Gandar. "Binomial Interest Rate Tree: A Synopsis of Uses and Estimation Approaches." *Journal of Financial Education* 27 (2001): 53-75

Lauterbach, B., and P. Schultz. "Pricing Warrants: An Empirical Study of the Black-Scholes Model and Its Alternatives." *Journal of Finance* 4 (September 1990): 1181–1210.

Mason, S., and R. Merton. "The Role of Contingent Claims Analysis in Corporate Finance." In *Recent Advances in Corporate Finance,* edited by E. Altman and M. Subrahmanyam. Homewood, IL: Dow Jones-Irwin, 1985.

Merton, R. C. "On the Pricing of Corporate Debt: The Risk Structure of Interest Rates." *Journal of Finance* 29 (1974): 4490–70.

Ross, S., R. Westerfield, and J. F. Jaffe. *Corporate Finance,* 634–648. Homewood, IL: Dow Jones-Irwin, 1991.

Schwartz, E. "The Valuation of Warrants: Implementing a New Approach." *Journal of Financial Economics* (January 1977).

Weil, R., J. Segall, and D. Green. "Premiums on Convertible Bonds." *Journal of Finance* (June 1968).

PROBLEMS AND QUESTIONS

1. Keening Land Developers is a real estate development company with a project in the Midwest currently valued at $20M. The Keening company financed the project by borrowing from the Southwest Savings and Loan. The loan called for a principal payment of $25 million at the end of 4 years (no coupon interest).

   a. Use the B–S OPM to determine the equity value of Keening Developers Midwest project. Assume $R = 6\%$ and the volatility of the project is $\sigma = .3$.

   b. What is the value of the creditors' position?

   c. Show graphically the following relations:

      1) The value of Keening's equity position at the loan's maturity as it relates to the value of its assets.

      2) The value of the creditors' position at the loan's maturity as it relates to the value of Keening's assets.

      3) The current equity and debt values as they relate to the value of the assets.

   d. Use the B–S OPM to determine the equity value of Keening Developers Midwest project and its debt value if the volatility was $\sigma = .5$.

   e. From an option perspective, comment on the relation between stock value and variability.

2. Given a current one-period spot rate of $S_0 = 5\%$, upward and downward parameters of $u = 1.1$ and $d = 1/1.1$, and the probability of spot rate increasing in one period of $q = .5$:

   a. Generate a two-period binomial tree of spot rates.

   b. Using a binomial tree approach, calculate the value of a three-period, option-free bond paying a 5% coupon per period and with a face value of 100.

   c. Using the binomial tree, calculate the value of the bond given it is callable with a call price $= CP = 100$.

   d. Using the tree, calculate the value of the bond given it is putable in Periods 1 and 2 with a put price $= PP = 100$.

3. Suppose a corporation issues a $9M, three-period, 5% coupon bond with a sinking fund obligation requiring the company to sink $3M in Period 1 and $3M in Period 2, with the company having the option to either buy the bonds in the market or call them at $CP = 100$. Using the same interest rate tree you generated in Question 2, calculate the value of the sinking fund bond.

4. ABC Thoroughbred Inc. is a small horse syndicate that owns one 3-year old racehorse named Box Spread. Based on Box Spread's racing record and potential breeding value, the estimated value of the horse and therefore ABC Thoroughbred Inc. is $1,000,000. ABC Thoroughbred Inc. has 10 shareholders, each with 100 shares (total shares $= n = 1,000$) and no debt. In addition, ABC also has a warrant that it sold to Mr. Lucky giving him the right to buy 100 shares of ABC for $1,300 per share.

   a. What would be the intrinsic value of Mr. Lucky's ABC warrant if Box Spread won the Kentucky Cup, a major stakes race, causing the value of the horse and ABC Inc. to increase to a value of $2,000,000?

   b. Instead of an ABC warrant, suppose one of the investors for ABC sold a call option to Mr. Lucky giving him the right to buy 100 shares of ABC stock at $1,300 per share. What would be the IV of the call if Box Spread won the Kentucky Cup?

c. Explain intuitively the difference between the call's IV and the warrant's IV.

d. Show the algebraic relationship between the values of a warrant and a call.

5. J.R. Inc. is a $50 million oil company. The company has one million shares outstanding and no debt. Expecting the price of oil to increase, J.R. Inc. is planning to raise $5 million through a rights offering to finance the purchase of an oil well. The company has decided to make the subscription price on a new share $25, and, to comply with the state's preemption right, the company will issue one right for each share.

a. Determine the number of rights that will be needed to buy one new share.

b. What is the intrinsic value of each right?

6. Given the following features of the XYZ convertible bond

- Coupon rate (annual) = 10%
- Face value = F = $1,000
- Maturity = 10 years
- Callable at $1,100
- YTM on a comparable, nonconvertible bond = 12%
- Conversion ratio = 10 shares
- Current stock price = S_0 = $90

Calculate the following:

a. XYZ's conversion price

b. XYZ's conversion value

c. XYZ's straight debt value

d. Minimum price of the convertible

e. The arbitrage strategy if the price of the convertible was $880

7. Given an ABC convertible bond with F = 1,000; maturity of three periods; CR = 10; current stock price of $100; and u = 1.1, d = .95, and q = .5 on the stock:

a. Calculate the value of the bond using a binomial tree of stock prices. Assume no call on the bond and a flat yield curve at 10% that is not expected to change.

b. Calculate the value of the bond using a binomial tree of stock prices. Assume the bond is callable at CP = 1200 and a flat yield curve at 10% that is not expected to change.

8. Excel problem: The following problems should be done using the Excel programs: Binbondcall.xls and Binbondput.xls (in "Binomial Interest Rate Excel Programs").

Given a binomial interest rate tree with the following features—S_0 = 6%, length of the tree = .5 years, and upward and downward parameters for .5 years of u = 1.0488 and d = .9747 and q = .5—determine the values of the following bonds:

a. The value of an option-free bond with maturity of 10 years, annual coupon of C = 6, semiannual payments, and F = 100.

b. The value of a callable bond with maturity of 10 years, annual coupon of C = 6, semiannual payments, F = 100, and call price of 100.

c. The value of a putable bond with maturity of 10 years, annual coupon of C = 6, semiannual payments, F = 100, and put price of 100.

d. The value of an option-free bond with maturity of 20 years, annual coupon of C = 6, semiannual payments, and F = 100.

e. The value of a callable bond with maturity of 20 years, annual coupon of C = 6, semiannual payments, F = 100, and call price of 100.

f. The value of a putable bond with maturity of 20 years, annual coupon of C = 6, semiannual payments, F = 100, and put price of 100.

9. Excel problem: The following problems should be done using the Excel programs: Binbondcall.xls and Binbondput.xls (in "Binomial Interest Rate Excel Programs").

Given the following:

- Current spot = 0.08
- Annualized mean for the spot rate's logarithmic return of .022
- Annualized variance for the spot rate's logarithmic return of .0054
- Binomial interest rate tree with monthly steps

Determine the values of the following:

a. 5-year, 8% option-free bond, with F = 100.

e. 5-year, 8% callable bond (F = 100) with call price = 100.

a. 5-year, 8% putable bond (F = 100) with put price = 100.

10. Given the following information on a callable bond:

- Coupon rate = 10% (annual), with payments made annually
- Face value = F = $1,000
- Maturity = 5 years
- Callable at $1,100
- Yields (YTM) on a similar noncallable bond = 10%
- Annualized standard deviation of the noncallable bond's logarithmic return = .15
- Continuously compound annual risk-free rate = 5%.

Questions:

a. What is the value of the noncallable bond?

b. Using the B–S OPM, what is the value of the callable bond's call feature to the issuer? Use "Black–Scholes Option Pricing Model" Excel program.

c. What is the value of the callable bond?

11. Given the following information on a putable bond:

- Coupon rate = 10% (annual), with payments made annually
- Face value = F = $1,000
- Maturity = 5 years
- Putable at $950
- Yield (YTM) on a similar nonputable bond = 10%
- Annualized standard deviation of the nonputable bond's logarithmic return = .15
- Continuously compound annual risk-free rate = 5%.

Questions:

a. What is the value of the nonputable bond?

b. Using the B–S OPM, what is the value of the putable bond's put feature to the holder? Use "Black–Scholes Option Pricing Model" Excel program.

c. What is the value of the putable bond?

12. Make up a capital budgeting case that is analyzed better with an option methodology than the traditional NPV approach.

WEB EXERCISES

1. Go to www.quicken.com/investments/mutualfunds/finder and find some of the top performing convertible bond funds (click "Convertibles").

APPENDIX 21A EQUITY AND DEBT AS PUT OPTIONS

In Section 21.2, we defined equity and debt in terms of their call positions. The stockholders' and bondholders' positions alternatively can be described in terms of put option positions. In this case, the stockholders' position of a leverage firm consists of (1) ownership of the firm, (2) a default-free debt obligation to the bondholders, and (3) a put option on the firm giving them the right to sell the company to the bondholders at an exercise price equal to the face value of the debt. At the bond's maturity, if $V_T^A < F$, the stockholders will sell the firm to the bondholders on their put option for F. Because the stockholders also owe the bondholders F on the default-free debt obligation, instead of receiving cash of F dollars, the stockholders will be paid by having the debt obligation canceled. In contrast, if $V_T^A > F$, the put is worthless. The stockholders, though, can pay their default-free debt obligation of F and retain ownership of the company. Thus, at expiration, the value of the equity position would be

$$V_T^E = V_T^A - F + \text{Max}\left[F - V_T^A, 0\right] = \text{Max}[V_T^A - F, 0] \qquad (21.A-1)$$

$$V_T^E = V_T^A - F + P_T = C_T$$

where

$$C_T = \text{Max}\left[V_T^A - F, 0\right]$$

$$P_T = \text{Max}[F - V_T^A, 0]$$

and the current value would be

$$V_0^E = V_0^A - \text{PV}(F) + P_0 = C_0 \qquad (21.A-2)$$

The creditors' position, on the other hand, consists of the long debt position in the default-free bond and a short put option position on the firm. If $V_T^A < F$ at maturity, the stockholders will sell the company on their put to the creditors who will pay for the company by canceling their debt obligation of F; if $V_T^A > F$, the creditors will receive F on their default-free bond from the shareholders. Thus, at maturity, the value of creditors' position is

$$V_T^B = \text{Min}\left[V_T^A, F\right] \qquad (21.A-3)$$

$$V_T^B = F - \text{Max}[F - V_T^A, 0]$$

$$V_T^B = F - P_T$$

and the current value is

$$V_0^B = PV(F) - P_0 \qquad (21.A\text{-}4)$$

21 A. 1 Valuing Equity as a Put Option With the B–S OPM

Equation (21.A-4) shows that the value of the risky bond is equal to the value of a default-free bond minus the value of the put option on the firm. Using the B–S OPM for puts, the value of the put is

$$P_0 = -V_0^A[1 - N(d_1)] + \left[\frac{F}{e^{RT}}\right][1 - N(d_2)] \qquad (21.A\text{-}5)$$

In terms of the example in Section 21.2, the value of the put option on the ABC Company using the OPM would be $1.07 million:

$$1 - N(d_1) = 1 - .86338 = .13662$$

$$1 - N(d_2) = 1 - .65175 = .34825$$

$$P_0 = -\$15M(.13662) + \left[\frac{\$10M}{e^{(.06)(2)}}\right](.34825) = \$1.039M$$

The value of the equity would therefore be $7.17M:

$$V_0^E = V_0^A - PV(F) + P_0$$

$$V_0^E = \$15M - \frac{\$10M}{e^{(.06)(2)}} + \$1.039M = \$7.17M$$

the same as obtained using the call option approach. Finally, the value of the risky debt of ABC is

$$V_0^B = PV(F) - P_0$$

$$V_0^B = \frac{\$10M}{e^{(.06)(2)}} - \$1.039M = \$7.83M$$

21 A. 2 Put–Call Parity Model

Viewing corporate securities as either call or put positions can be reconciled by the put–call parity model. For stock options, the model is defined as

$$S_0 + P_0 - C_0 = PV(X)$$

Extending the put-call parity model to the value of the firm we have:

| V_0^A | + | Value of the Put on the Asset | − | Value of the Call on the Asset | = | Value of the Default-Free Bond | (21.A-6) |

Solving Equation (21.A-6) for the call value shows the shareholders' call option as equivalent to owning the company, having a debt obligation on a default-free bond, and having a long position on a put:

Stockholders' Position:

| Value of Call on Asset | = | V_0^A | + | Value of the Put on the Asset | − | Value of the Default-Free Bond | (21.A-7) |

In terms of the example:

Value of the Call on the Asset $= \$15\text{ M} + \$1.039\text{M} - (\$10\text{Me}^{-(.06)(2)}) = \$7.17\text{M}$

Similarly, rearranging Equation (21.A-6), the creditors' position in terms of the call and put positions is

$$
\begin{array}{ccccc}
V_0^A & - & \begin{array}{c} \text{Value of the} \\ \text{Call on the} \\ \text{Asset} \end{array} & = & \begin{array}{c} \text{Value of the} \\ \text{Default-Free} \\ \text{Bond} \end{array} & - & \begin{array}{c} \text{Value of the} \\ \text{Put on the} \\ \text{Asset} \end{array}
\end{array}
\qquad (21.\text{A-8})
$$

In terms of the example

$$\$15\text{M} - \$7.17\text{M} = (\$10\text{Me}^{-(.06)(2)}) - \$1.039\text{M} = \$7.83\text{M}$$

Problems and Questions

The following questions refer to the Keening Company described in Problem 1 of the chapter "Problems and Questions."

1. Describe and calculate the current value of the equity position of the Keening Company using a put option in the valuation.

2. Describe and calculate the current value of the debt position of Southwest Savings and Loan.

3. What relationship governs the call and put valuation approaches?

CHAPTER 22

MORTGAGE- AND ASSET-BACKED SECURITIES AND THEIR DERIVATIVES

22.1 INTRODUCTION

The securitization of assets is one of the most innovative developments to occur in the security markets over the last two decades. *Securitization* refers to a process in which the financial assets of a corporation or financial institution are pooled into a package of securities backed by the assets. The process starts when an originator, who owns the assets, sells them to an issuer. The issuer then creates a security backed by the assets called an *asset-backed security* or *pass-through* that she sells to investors. This pass-through represents a derivative security, deriving its value from the underlying pool of assets. The most common types of asset-backed securities are those secured by mortgages, automobile loans, credit card receivables, and home equity loans. By far the largest type and the one in which the process of securitization has been most extensively applied is mortgages. Asset-backed securities formed with mortgages are called *mortgage-backed securities,* MBSs, or *mortgage pass-throughs.* These securities entitle the holder to the cash flow from a pool of mortgages. Typically, the issuer of an MBS buys a portfolio or pool of mortgages of a certain type from a mortgage originator such as a commercial bank, savings and loan, or mortgage banker. The issuer finances the purchase of the mortgage portfolio through the sale of the mortgage pass-throughs, which have a claim on the portfolio's cash flow. The mortgage originator usually agrees to continue to service the loans, passing the payments on to the MBS holders.

In this chapter, we examine asset-backed securities, with particular emphasis on mortgage-backed securities. Because most mortgages give the borrower the option to prepay, the mortgages or the claim on the mortgage portfolio (referred to as the collateral) is quite sensitive to interest rate changes. If interest rates are at a relatively high level and decrease, then prepayment increases, causing earlier cash flows of the mortgages to be larger; in contrast, if interest rates increase from a relatively low level, then prepayment decreases, reducing earlier cash flows. In an effort to attract institutional investors, mortgage-backed derivatives having different prepayment risk characteristics are formed from the mortgage portfolio. The most popular of these derivatives are collateralized mortgage obligations (CMOs) and stripped MBSs. Prepayment risk also makes the valuation of an MBS or its collateral more difficult. Because an MBS is sensitive to interest rates, one way to capture the impact of prepayment on the MBS's price is to construct a model that incorporates the random paths that interest rates follow over time. One such model is the binomial interest rate tree. Given the effects of prepayment on a MBS, we begin this chapter by first examining prepayment risk and its effect on a portfolio of mortgages. We next describe how mortgage-backed derivatives are constructed to address the problems of prepayment risk. Finally, we conclude the chapter by showing how MBSs can be evaluated.

22.2   PREPAYMENT

22.2.1   Prepayment Models

For the holder of a mortgage portfolio, prepayment creates an uncertainty concerning the portfolio's cash flows. For example, if a bank has a pool of mortgages with a weighted average mortgage rate of 7%, and mortgage rates, in turn, decrease in the market to 5%, then the bank's mortgage portfolio is likely to experience significant prepayment as borrowers refinance their loans. The option borrowers have to prepay makes it difficult for the lender to predict future cash flows or determine the value of the portfolio. A number of prepayment models have been developed to try to predict the cash flows from a portfolio of mortgages. Most of these models estimate the prepayment rate, referred to as the ***prepayment speed*** or simply ***speed,*** in terms of four factors: refinancing incentive, seasoning (the age of the mortgage), monthly factors, and prepayment burnout.

The refinancing incentive is the most important factor influencing prepayment. If mortgage rates decrease below the mortgage loan rate, borrowers have a strong incentive to refinance. This incentive increases during periods of falling interest rates, with the greatest increases occurring when borrowers determine that rates have bottomed out. The refinancing incentive can be measured by the difference between the mortgage portfolio's weighted average rate, referred to as the ***weighted average coupon rate,*** WAC, and the refinancing rate, R^{ref}. In general, the annualized prepayment speed, referred to as the ***conditional prepayment rate,*** CPR, is greater, the larger the positive difference between the WAC and R^{ref}.

A second factor determining prepayment is the age of the mortgage, referred to as ***seasoning.*** Prepayment tends to be greater during the early part of the loan, and then stabilizes after about 3 years. Figure 22.2-1 depicts a commonly referenced seasoning pattern known as the ***PSA model*** (Public Securities Association). In the standard PSA model, known as 100 PSA, the CPR starts at .2% for the 1st month and then increases at a constant rate of 0.2% per month to equal 6% at the 30th month; then after the 30th month, the CPR stays at a constant 6%. Thus for any month t, the CPR is

$$CPR = .06 \left(\frac{t}{30} \right), \text{ if } t \leq 30,$$

$$CPR = .06, \text{ if } t > 30$$

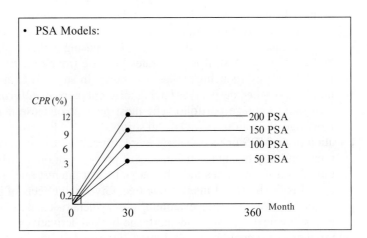

FIGURE 22.2-1 Public Securities Association (PSA) Prepayment Model

Note that the CPR is quoted on an annual basis. The monthly prepayment rate, referred to as the *single monthly mortality rate,* SMM, can be obtained given the annual CPR by using the following formula:

$$SMM = 1 - [1 - CPR]^{1/12}$$

The 100 PSA model is often used as a benchmark. The actual aging pattern will differ depending on the level of interest rates. Analysts often refer to the applicable pattern as being a certain percentage of the PSA. For example, if the pattern is described as being 200 PSA, then the prepayment speeds are twice the 100 PSA rates; and if the pattern is described as 50 PSA, then the CPRs are half of the 100 PSA rates (see Figure 22.2-1). Thus, a current mortgage pool described by a 100 PSA would have an annual prepayment rate of 2% after 10 months (or a monthly prepayment rate of SMM = .00168), and a premium pool described as a 150 PSA would have a 3% CPR (or SMM = .002535) after 10 months.

In addition to the effect of seasoning, mortgage prepayment rates can be influenced by the month of the year, with prepayment tending to be higher during the summer months. Prepayment may also be affected by what is referred to as a *burnout factor*—the tendency for premium mortgages to hit some maximum CPR and then level off. Finally, a pool of mortgages can be influenced by locational variations, the types of mortgages (e.g., single family or multiple family, residential or commercial, etc.), and the original terms of the mortgage (30 years or 15 years).

22.2.2 Estimating a Mortgage Pool's Cash Flow With Prepayment

The cash flow from a portfolio of mortgages consists of the interest payments, scheduled principal, and prepaid principal. The monthly payment of interest and scheduled principal on a mortgage, p, is found by solving for the p that makes the present value of all scheduled payments equal to the mortgage balance, F_0:

$$F_0 = \sum_{t=1}^{M} \frac{p}{(1 + (R^A/12))^t} = p\,PVIF_a = p\left[\frac{1 - 1/(1 + (R^A/12))^M}{R^A/12}\right]$$

$$p = \frac{F_0}{PVIF_a} = \frac{F_0}{\left[\frac{1 - 1/(1+(R^A/12))^M}{R^A/12}\right]}$$

where
F_0 = Face value of the loan
R^A = Annualized interest rate
p = Monthly payment
M = Maturity in months
$$PVIF_a = \sum_{t=1}^{M} \frac{1}{(1+(R^A/12))^t} = \left[\frac{1 - 1/(1+(R^A/12))^M}{R^A/12}\right]$$

Consider a bank that has a pool of current fixed rate mortgages that are worth $100 million, yield a WAC of 7%, and have a weighted average maturity of 360 months. For the 1st month, the portfolio would generate an aggregate mortgage payment of $665,302:

$$p = \frac{\$100,000,000}{\left[\frac{1 - 1/(1+(.07/12))^{360}}{.07/12}\right]} = \$665,302$$

From the \$665,302, \$583,333 would go toward interest, and \$81,969 would go toward the scheduled principal payment:

$$\text{Interest} = \left(\frac{R^A}{12}\right) F_0 = \left(\frac{.07}{12}\right) \$100,000,000 = \$583,333$$

$$\text{Scheduled Principal Payment} = p - \text{Interest} = \$665,302 - \$583,333 = \$81,969$$

The projected 1st month prepaid principal can be estimated with a prepayment model. Using the 100% PSA model, the monthly prepayment rate for the 1st month ($t = 1$) is equal to SMM = .0001668:

$$\text{CPR} = \left(\frac{1}{30}\right).06 = .002$$

$$\text{SMM} = 1 - [1 - .002]^{1/12} = .00016682$$

Given the prepayment rate, the projected prepaid principal in the 1st month is found by multiplying the balance at the beginning of the month minus the scheduled principal by the SMM. Doing this yields a projected prepaid principal of \$16,668 in the 1st month:

$$\text{prepaid principal} = \text{SMM}[F_0 - \text{Scheduled principal}]$$

$$\text{prepaid principal} = .00016682[\$100,000,000 - \$81,969] = \$16,668$$

Thus, for the 1st month, the mortgage portfolio would generate an estimated cash flow of \$681,971 and a balance at the beginning of the next month of \$99,901,363:

$$\text{CF} = \text{Interest} + \text{Scheduled principal} + \text{prepaid principal}$$

$$\text{CF} = \$583,333 + \$81,969 + 16,668 = \$681,971$$

$$\text{Beginning Balance for Month 2} = F_0 - \text{Scheduled principal} - \text{prepaid principal}$$

$$\text{Beginning Balance for Month 2} = \$100,000,000 - \$81,969 - \$16,668$$

$$= \$99,901,363$$

In the second month ($t = 2$), the projected payment would be \$665,192, with \$582,758 going to interest and \$82,434 to scheduled principal:

$$p = \frac{\$99,901,363}{\left[\frac{1-1/(1+(.07/12))^{359}}{.07/12}\right]} = \$665,192$$

$$\text{Interest} = \left(\frac{.07}{12}\right)(\$99,901,363) = \$582,758$$

$$\text{Scheduled principal} = \$665,192 - \$582,758 = \$82,434$$

Using the 100% PSA model, the estimated monthly prepayment rate is .000333946, yielding a projected prepaid principal in Month 2 of \$33,344:

$$\text{CPR} = \left(\frac{2}{30}\right).06 = .004$$

$$\text{SMM} = 1 - [1 - .004]^{1/12} = .000333946$$

$$\text{prepaid principal} = .000333946[\$99,901,363 - \$82,434] = \$33,334$$

Thus, for the 2nd month, the mortgage portfolio would generate an estimated cash flow of $698,526 and have a balance at the beginning of Month 3 of $99,785,595:

$$CF = \$582,758 + \$82,434 + \$33,334 = \$698,526$$

$$\text{Beginning Balance for Month 3} = \$99,901,363 - \$82,434 - \$33,334$$

$$= \$99,785,595$$

Exhibit 22.2-1 summarizes the mortgage portfolio's cash flow for the first 11 months and other selected months. This exhibit, as well as other exhibits in this chapter that show the cash flows from mortgages, mortgage-backed securities, and mortgage derivatives, are generated using the Excel programs included with this text: MBSCollateral. MBSSeqNIO, and MBSPac. These programs can be found in the folder "Mortgage-Backed Securities." In examining the exhibit, two points should be noted. First, starting in Month 30, the SMM remains constant at .00514301; this reflects the 100% PSA model's assumption of a constant CPR of 6% starting in Month 30. Second, the projected cash flows are based on a static analysis in which rates are assumed fixed over the time period. A more realistic model would incorporate interest rate changes and corresponding different prepayment speeds.

Web Information:

For more information on the mortgage industry, statistics, trends, and rates go to www.mbaa.org.

Mortgage rates in different geographical areas can be found by going to www.interest.com.

For historical mortgage rates, go to http://research.stlouisfed.org/fred2 and click on "Interest Rates."

22.3 MORTGAGE-BACKED SECURITIES

A mortgage originator with a pool of mortgages has options of holding the portfolio, selling it, or using it as collateral on securities to be issued. If the originator decides to sell the portfolio, there are three federal agencies—the Federal National Mortgage Association (FNMA), the Government National Mortgage Association (GNMA), and the Federal Home Loan Mortgage Corporation (FHLMC)—that buy certain types of mortgage loan portfolios (e.g., Federal Housing Administration [FMA]-insured mortgages or Veteran Administration [VA]-insured mortgages) and then pool them to create MBSs to sell to investors. Collectively, the MBSs created by these agencies are referred to as *agency pass-throughs.* Agency pass-throughs are guaranteed by the agencies, and the loans they purchase must be conforming loans, meaning they meet certain standards. In addition, there are also private entities that buy mortgages to create their own MBSs. These MBSs are referred to as *conventional pass-throughs.* When the mortgages are sold, the originator typically continues to service the loan for a service fee. Exhibit 22.3-1 describes types of agencies and conventional MBS and their features.

Web Information:

Agency information: www.fanniemae.com, www.ginniemae.gov, www.freddiemac.com

For general information on MBS go to www.ficc.com

EXHIBIT 22.2-1   Projected Cash Flows: Mortgage Portfolio = $100M, WAC = 7%, WAM = 360 Months, Prepayment: 100% PSA

Period	Balance	Interest	PVIF	p	Scheduled Principal	SMM	Prepaid Principal	CF
1	$100,000,000	$583,333	150.3076	$665,302	$81,969	0.00016682	$16,668	$681,971
2	$99,901,363	$582,758	150.1844	$665,192	$82,434	0.00033395	$33,334	$698,526
3	$99,785,595	$582,083	150.0604	$664,969	$82,887	0.00050138	$49,989	$714,958
4	$99,652,719	$581,308	149.9358	$664,636	$83,328	0.00066912	$66,624	$731,260
5	$99,502,766	$580,433	149.8104	$664,191	$83,758	0.00083718	$83,231	$747,423
6	$99,335,777	$579,459	149.6843	$663,635	$84,177	0.00100554	$99,802	$763,437
7	$99,151,798	$578,385	149.5575	$662,968	$84,582	0.00117422	$116,327	$779,295
8	$98,950,889	$577,214	149.4299	$662,189	$84,976	0.00134321	$132,798	$794,987
9	$98,733,116	$575,943	149.3016	$661,300	$85,357	0.00151252	$149,207	$810,507
10	$98,498,552	$574,575	149.1725	$660,300	$85,725	0.00168214	$165,544	$825,844
11	$98,247,283	$573,109	149.0427	$659,189	$86,080	0.00185208	$181,803	$840,992
29	$91,013,902	$530,914	146.5719	$620,951	$90,036	0.00496679	$451,600	$1,072,551
30	$90,472,266	$527,755	146.4269	$617,866	$90,112	0.00514301	$464,837	$1,082,703
31	$89,917,318	$524,518	146.2810	$614,689	$90,171	0.00514301	$461,982	$1,076,671
32	$89,365,165	$521,297	146.1344	$611,527	$90,231	0.00514301	$459,142	$1,070,670
33	$88,815,792	$518,092	145.9868	$608,382	$90,290	0.00514301	$456,316	$1,064,699
136	$44,753,413	$261,062	125.1129	$357,704	$96,643	0.00514301	$229,670	$587,375
137	$44,427,100	$259,158	124.8427	$355,864	$96,706	0.00514301	$227,992	$583,856
138	$44,102,402	$257,264	124.5710	$354,034	$96,770	0.00514301	$226,322	$580,356
139	$43,779,310	$255,379	124.2977	$352,213	$96,834	0.00514301	$224,660	$576,873
140	$43,457,817	$253,504	124.0227	$350,402	$96,898	0.00514301	$223,006	$573,408
141	$43,137,913	$251,638	123.7462	$348,600	$96,962	0.00514301	$221,360	$569,960
357	$451,214	$2,632	3.9423	$114,453	$111,821	0.00514301	$1,746	$116,199
358	$337,647	$1,970	2.9653	$113,865	$111,895	0.00514301	$1,161	$115,026

continued

EXHIBIT 22.2-1 Continued

Period	Balance	Interest	PVIF	p	Scheduled Principal	SMM	Prepaid Principal	CF
359	$224,591	$1,310	1.9826	$113,279	$111,969	0.00514301	$579	$113,858
360	$112,043	$654	0.9942	$112,697	$112,043	0.00514301	$0	$112,697

$$\text{Monthly Payments} = p = \frac{\text{Balance}}{\left[\frac{1-1/(1+(.07/12))^{\text{Remaing periods}}}{.07/12}\right]}$$

$\text{Interest} = (.07/12)(\text{Balance})$

$\text{Scheduled principal} = p - (.07/12)(\text{Balance})$

$\text{Prepaid principal} = \text{SMM}[\text{Beginning balance} - \text{Scheduled principal}]$

22.3.1 Features of Mortgage-Backed Securities

22.3.1.1 Cash Flows

Cash flows from MBSs are generated from the cash flows from the underlying pool of mortgages minus servicing and other fees. Typically, fees for constructing, managing, and servicing the underlying mortgages (also referred to as the mortgage collateral) and the MBSs are equal to the difference between the WAC associated with the mortgage pool and the MBS *pass-through (PT) rate.* Exhibit 22.3-2 shows the monthly cash flows for an MBS issue constructed from a mortgage pool with a current balance of $100M, a WAC of 7%, and a WAM of 350 months. The PT rate is 6.5%, and the speed is assumed to be 200% of the standard 100 PSA. The monthly fees implied on the MBS issue are equal to .04167% = (7% – 6.5%)/12 of the monthly balance.

The cash flows for the MBS issue shown in Exhibit 22.3-2 differ in several respects from the cash flows for the $100M mortgage pool shown in Exhibit 22.2-1. First, the MBS issue has a WAM of 350 months and an assumed prepayment speed equal to 200% of the standard PSA model compared to 360 months and an assumption of 100% PSA for the pool. As a result, the 1st month's CPR for the MBS issue reflects a 10-month seasoning in which t = 11 and a speed that is 200% greater than the 100 PSA. For the MBS issue, this yields a 1st month SMM of **.0037428** and a constant SMM of .0105962 starting in Month 20. Second, for the mortgage pool, a WAC of 7% is used to determine the mortgage payment, scheduled principal, and interest; on the MBS issue, though, the WAC of 7% is only used to determine the mortgage payment and scheduled principal, whereas the PT rate of 6.5% is used to determine the interest.

22.3.1.2 Price Quotes

Investors can acquire newly issued MBSs from agencies, originators, or dealers specializing in specific pass-throughs. There is also a secondary market consisting of dealers who operate in the OTC market as part of the *Mortgage-Backed Security Dealers Association.* These dealers form the core of the secondary market for the trading of existing pass-throughs.

Mortgage pass-throughs are normally sold in denominations ranging from $25,000 to $250,000, although some privately placed issues are sold with denominations as high as

EXHIBIT 22.3-1   Agency and Conventional Mortgage-Backed Securities

Government National Mortgage Association's Mortgage-Backed Securities

The Government National Mortgage Association's (GNMA) mortgage-backed securities or pass-throughs are formed with FHA- or VA-insured mortgages. They are put together by an originator (bank, thrift, or mortgage banker) who presents a block of FHA and VA mortgages to GNMA. If GNMA finds them in order, they will issue a guarantee and assign a pool number that identifies the MBS that is to be issued. The originator will transfer the mortgages to a trustee and then issue the pass-throughs, often selling them to investment bankers for distribution. The mortgages underlying GNMA's MBSs are very similar (e.g., single-family, 30-year maturity, and fixed rate), with the mortgage rates usually differing by no more than 50 basis points from the WAC. GNMA does offer programs in which the underlying mortgages are more diverse. Finally, because GNMA is a federal agency, its guarantee of timely interest and principal payments is backed by the full faith and credit of the U.S. government—the only MBS with this type of guarantee.

Federal Home Loan Mortgage Corporation's Mortgage-Backed Securities

The Federal Home Loan Mortgage Corporation (FHLMC or Freddie Mac) issues MBSs that they refer to as participation certificates (PCs). The FHLMC has a regular MBS (also called a cash PC), which is backed by a pool of either conventional, FHA, or VA mortgages that the FHLMC has purchased from mortgage originators. They also offer a pass-though formed through their Guarantor/Swap Program. In this program, mortgage originators can swap mortgages for a FMLMC pass-through. Unlike GNMA's MBSs, Freddie Mac's MBSs are formed with more heterogeneous mortgages. Like GNMA, the Federal Home Loan Mortgage Corporation backs the interest and principal payments of its securities, but the FHLMC's guarantee is not backed by the U.S. government.

Federal National Mortgage Association's Mortgage-Backed Securities

The Federal National Mortgage Association (FNMA or Fannie Mae) offers several types of pass-throughs, referred to as FNMA mortgage-backed securities. Like FHLMC's pass-throughs, FNMA's securities are backed by the agency but not by the government. Like the FHLMC, FNMA buys conventional, FHA, and VA mortgages and offers a SWAP program whereby mortgage loans can be swapped for FNMA-issued MBSs. Finally, like the FHLMC, FNMA's mortgages are more heterogeneous than GNMA's mortgages, with mortgage rates in some pools differing by as much as 200 basis points from the portfolio's average mortgage rate.

Conventional Pass-Throughs

Conventional pass-throughs are sold by commercial banks, savings and loans, other thrifts, and mortgage bankers. These nonagency pass-throughs, also called *private labels,* are often formed with nonconforming mortgages; that is, mortgages that fail to meet size limits and other requirements placed on agency pass-throughs. Larger issuers of conventional MBSs include Citicorp Housing, Countrywide, Prudential Home, Ryland/Saxon, and G.E. Capital Mortgage. These pass-throughs are often guaranteed against default through external credit enhancements such as the guarantee of a corporation, a bank letter of credit, or private insurance from such insurers as the Financial Guarantee Insurance Corporation (FGIC) or the Financial Security Assurance Company (FSA). Because of the default risk, conventional MBSs are rated by Moody's and Standard and Poor's, and unlike agency pass-throughs, they must be registered with the SEC when they are issued. Finally, most financial entities that issue private-labeled MBSs or derivatives of MBSs are legally set up so that they do not have to pay taxes on the interest and principal that passes through them to their MBS investors. The requirements that MBS issuers must meet to ensure tax-exempt status are specified in the Tax Reform Act of 1983 in the section on trusts referred to as *Real Estate Mortgage Investment Conduits, REMIC.* Private-labeled MBS issuers who comply with these provisions are sometimes referred to as REMICs.

EXHIBIT 22.3-2 Projected Cash Flows: Mortgage Portfolio = $100M, WAC = 7%, WAM = 350 Months, PT Rate = 6.5%. Prepayment: 200% PSA

Period	Balance	Interest	p	Scheduled Principal	SMM	Prepaid Principal	Principal	CF
1	$100,000,000	$541,667	$670,949	$87,616	0.0037428	$373,948	$461,563	$1,003,230
2	$99,538,437	$539,167	$668,438	$87,797	0.0040908	$406,832	$494,629	$1,033,796
3	$99,043,807	$536,487	$665,703	$87,948	0.0044402	$439,382	$527,329	$1,063,817
4	$98,516,478	$533,631	$662,747	$88,068	0.0047909	$471,562	$559,630	$1,093,261
5	$97,956,848	$530,600	$659,572	$88,157	0.0051430	$503,340	$591,497	$1,122,097
6	$97,365,351	$527,396	$656,180	$88,215	0.0054965	$534,683	$622,898	$1,150,294
7	$96,742,453	$524,022	$652,573	$88,242	0.0058514	$565,558	$653,800	$1,177,822
8	$96,088,653	$520,480	$648,755	$88,238	0.0062076	$595,934	$684,171	$1,204,652
9	$95,404,481	$516,774	$644,728	$88,202	0.0065653	$625,779	$713,980	$1,230,755
19	$87,030,479	$471,415	$593,773	$86,096	0.0102222	$888,767	$974,862	$1,446,277
20	$86,055,617	$466,135	$587,704	$85,713	0.0105962	$910,958	$996,670	$1,462,805
21	$85,058,946	$460,736	$581,476	$85,299	0.0105962	$900,401	$985,700	$1,446,436
22	$84,073,246	$455,397	$575,315	$84,887	0.0105962	$889,961	$974,848	$1,430,245
23	$83,098,398	$450,116	$569,219	$84,478	0.0105962	$879,636	$964,113	$1,414,230
349	$35,019	$190	$17,663	$17,458	0.0105962	$186	$17,645	$17,834
350	$17,374	$94	$17,476	$17,374	0.0105962	$0	$17,374	$17,468

Monthly Payments $= p = \dfrac{\text{Balance}}{\left[\dfrac{1-1/(1+(.07/12))^{\text{Remaing periods}}}{.07/12}\right]}$

Interest $= (.065/12)(\text{Balance})$

Scheduled principal $= p - (.07/12)(\text{Balance})$

Prepaid principal $=$ SMM[Beginning balance
$\qquad\qquad -$ Schedule dprincipal]

1st Month :

$\text{CPR} = 2\left(\frac{11}{30}\right).06 = .044$

$\text{SMM} = 1 - [1 - .044]^{1/12}$
$\qquad = .0037428$

$1 million. The prices of MBSs are quoted as a percentage of the underlying mortgages' balance. The mortgage balance at time t, F_t, is usually calculated by the servicing institution and is quoted as a proportion of the original balance, F_0. This proportion is referred to as the ***pool factor***, pf:

$$pf_t = \frac{F_t}{F_0}$$

For example, suppose a GNMA MBS, backed by a mortgage pool with an original par value of $100 million, is currently priced at 97-16 (the fractions on GNMA's MBSs are quoted like Treasury bonds and notes in terms of 32nds), with a pool factor of .90. An institutional investor who purchased $10 million of the MBS when it was first issued would now have securities valued at $8.775M that are backed by mortgages that are worth $9 million:

$$\text{Par value remaining} = (\$10M)(.90) = \$9M.$$

$$\text{Market value} = (\$9M)(.9750) = \$8.775M$$

The market value of $8.775M represents a clean price that does not include accrued interest. If the institutional investor were to sell the MBS, the accrued interest (ai) would need to be added to the flat price to determine the invoice price. The normal practice is to determine accrued interest based on the time period between the settlement date (SD; usually 2 days after the trade date) and the 1st day of the month, M_0. If the coupon rate on the GNMA MBS held by the institutional investor were 7% and the time period between SD and M_0 were 20 days, then the accrued interest would be $35,000:

$$ai_t = \frac{SD - M_0}{30} \frac{WAC}{12} F_t$$

$$ai_t = \left(\frac{20}{30}\right)\left(\frac{.07}{12}\right) \$9M = \$35,000$$

22.3.1.3 *Extension Risk and Average Life*

Like bonds and other fixed-income securities, the value of an MBS is determined by the MBS's future cash flow, maturity, liquidity, and risk. In contrast to other bonds, though, MBSs are also subject to prepayment risk. As discussed earlier, the mortgage borrower's option to prepay makes it difficult to estimate the cash flow from the MBS. The prepayment risk associated with MBSs is primarily a function of interest rates. If interest rates decrease, then the prices of MBSs, like the prices of all bonds, increase as a result of lower discount rates. However, the decrease in rates will also increase the prepayment speed, causing the earlier cash flow of the mortgages to be larger, which, depending on the level of rates and the maturity remaining, could also contribute to increasing the MBS's price. In contrast, if interest rates increase, then the prices of MBSs will decrease as a result of higher discount rates and possibly the smaller earlier cash flow resulting from lower prepayment speeds.

The effect of an interest rate increase in lowering the price of the bond by decreasing the value of its cash flow is known as ***extension risk.*** Extension risk can be described in terms of the relationship between interest rates and the MBS's ***average life.*** The average life of an MBS is the weighted average of the security's time periods, with the weights being the periodic principal payments (scheduled and prepaid principal) divided by the total principal:

$$\text{Average Life} = \frac{1}{12} \sum_{t=1}^{T} t \left(\frac{\text{principal received at } t}{\text{total principal}}\right)$$

For example, the average life for the MBS issue described in Exhibit 22.3-2 is 7.16 years:

$$\text{Average Life} = \frac{1}{12}\left(\frac{1(\$461,563) + 2(\$494,629) + \cdots + 350(\$17,374)}{\$100,000,000}\right) = 7.16 \text{ years}$$

The average life of an MBS depends on prepayment speed. For example, if the PSA speed of the $100M MBS issue were to increase from 200 to 250, the MBS's average life would decrease from 7.16 to 6.01, reflecting greater principal payments in the earlier years; in contrast, if the PSA speed were to decrease from 200 to 150, then the average life of the MBS would increase to 8.73. For MBSs, prepayment risk can be evaluated in terms of how responsive an MBS's average life is to changes in prepayment speeds:

$$\text{prepayment Risk} = \frac{\Delta \text{Average Life}}{\Delta \text{PSA}}$$

Thus, an MBS with an average life that did not change with PSA speeds, in turn, would have stable principal payments over time and would be absent of prepayment risk. Moreover, one of the more innovative developments in the security market industry over the last two decades has been the creation of derivative securities formed from MBSs that have different prepayment risk characteristics, including some that are formed that have average lives that do not change as prepayment speeds change. The most popular of these MBS derivatives are collateralized mortgage obligations.

22.4 MBS DERIVATIVES

22.4.1 Collateralized Mortgage Obligations

To address the problems of prepayment risk, many MBS issuers began to offer *collateralized mortgage obligations* (*CMOs*). These securities are formed by dividing the cash flow of an underlying pool of mortgages or an MBS issue into several classes, with each class having a different claim on the mortgage collateral and with each sold separately to different types of investors. The different classes making up a CMO are called *tranches* or bond classes. There are two general types of CMO tranches—sequential-pay tranches and planned amortization class tranches.

22.4.1.1 Sequential-Pay Tranches

A CMO with sequential-pay tranches, called a *sequential-pay CMO,* is divided into classes with different priority claims on the collateral's principal. The tranche with the first priority claim has its principal paid entirely before the next priority tranche, which has its principal paid before the third class, and so on. Interest payments on most CMO tranches are made until the tranche's principal is retired.

An example of a sequential-pay CMO is shown in Exhibit 22.4-1. This CMO consist of three tranches, A, B, and C, formed from the collateral making up the $100M MBS described in Exhibit 22.3-2. In terms of the priority disbursement rules, Tranche A receives all principal payment from the collateral until its principal of $40M is retired. After Tranche A's principal is retired, all principal payments from the collateral are then made to Tranche B until its principal of $30M is retired. Finally, tranche C receives the remaining principal that is equal to its par value of $30M. Although the principal is paid sequentially, each tranche does receive interest each period equal to its stated coupon rate (6.5%) times its outstanding balance at the beginning of each month.

Given the different possible prepayment speeds, the actual amount of principal paid each month and the time it will take to pay the principal on each tranche is uncertain. Exhibit 22.4-1 shows the cash flow patterns on the three tranches based on a 200% PSA prepayment assumption. As shown, the 1st month cash flow for Tranche A consist of a principal payment (scheduled and prepaid) of $461,563 and an interest payment of $216,667 [(.065/12)($40M) = $216,667]. Based on the assumption of a 200% PSA speed, it takes 50 months before A's principal of $40M is retired. During the first 50 months, the cash flows for Tranches B and C consist of just the interest on their balances, with no principal payments made to them. Starting in Month 50, Tranche B begins to receive the principal payment. Tranche B is paid off in Month 106, at which time principal payments begin to be paid to Tranche C. Finally, in Month 350, Tranche C's principal is retired.

EXHIBIT 22.4-1 Cash Flows From Sequential-Pay CMO Collateral: Balance = $100M, WAM = 350 Months, WAC = 7%, PT Rate = 6.5%, Prepayment: 200 PSA, Tranches: A: $40M, B = $30M, C = $30M

Month	Collateral Par = $100M Rate = 6.5%			Tranch A Par = $40M Rate = 6.5%			Tranche B Par = $30M Rate = 6.5%			Tranche C Par = $30M Rate = 6.5%		
	Balance	Interest	Principal	Balance	Interest	Principal	Balance	Principal	Interest	Balance	Principal	Interest
1	$100,000,000	$541,667	$461,563	$40,000,000	$216,667	$461,563	$30,000,000	0	$162,500	$30,000,000	0	$162,500
2	$99,538,437	$539,167	$494,629	$39,538,437	$214,167	$494,629	$30,000,000	0	$162,500	$30,000,000	0	$162,500
3	$99,043,807	$536,487	$527,329	$39,043,807	$211,487	$527,329	$30,000,000	0	$162,500	$30,000,000	0	$162,500
4	$98,516,478	$533,631	$559,630	$38,516,478	$208,631	$559,630	$30,000,000	0	$162,500	$30,000,000	0	$162,500
5	$97,956,848	$530,600	$591,497	$37,956,848	$205,600	$591,497	$30,000,000	0	$162,500	$30,000,000	0	$162,500
49	$61,202,531	$331,514	$722,223	$1,202,531	$6,514	$722,223	$30,000,000	0	$162,500	$30,000,000	0	$162,500
50	$60,480,308	$327,602	$714,215	$480,308	$2,602	$480,308	$30,000,000	$233,907	$162,500	$30,000,000	0	$162,500
51	$59,766,093	$323,733	$706,293	0	0	0	$29,766,093	$706,293	$161,233	$30,000,000	0	$162,500
52	$59,059,800	$319,907	$698,457	0	0	0	$29,059,800	$698,457	$157,407	$30,000,000	0	$162,500
53	$58,361,343	$316,124	$690,705	0	0	0	$28,361,343	$690,705	$153,624	$30,000,000	0	$162,500
54	$57,670,638	$312,383	$683,037	0	0	0	$27,670,638	$683,037	$149,883	$30,000,000	0	$162,500
55	$56,987,601	$308,683	$675,453	0	0	0	$26,987,601	$675,453	$146,183	$30,000,000	0	$162,500
56	$56,312,148	$305,024	$667,950	0	0	0	$26,312,148	$667,950	$142,524	$30,000,000	0	$162,500
57	$55,644,198	$301,406	$660,529	0	0	0	$25,644,198	$660,529	$138,906	$30,000,000	0	$162,500
58	$54,983,669	$297,828	$653,187	0	0	0	$24,983,669	$653,187	$135,328	$30,000,000	0	$162,500
59	$54,330,482	$294,290	$645,925	0	0	0	$24,330,482	$645,925	$131,790	$30,000,000	0	$162,500
101	$32,579,820	$176,474	$402,541	0	0	0	$2,579,820	$402,541	$13,974	$30,000,000	0	$162,500
102	$32,177,279	$174,294	$397,999	0	0	0	$2,177,279	$397,999	$11,794	$30,000,000	0	$162,500

103	$31,779,281	$172,138	0	0	$1,779,281	0	$393,506	$9,638	$30,000,000	0	$162,500
104	$31,385,774	$170,006	0	0	$1,385,774	0	$389,063	$7,506	$30,000,000	0	$162,500
105	$30,996,712	$167,899	0	0	$996,712	0	$384,668	$5,399	$30,000,000	0	$162,500
108	$29,855,704	$161,718	0	0	0	0	0	0	$29,855,704	$371,767	$161,718
109	$29,483,936	$159,705	0	0	0	0	0	0	$29,483,936	$367,561	$159,705
201	$8,527,772	$46,192	0	0	0	0	0	0	$8,527,772	$125,700	$46,192
202	$8,402,072	$45,511	0	0	0	0	0	0	$8,402,072	$124,198	$45,511
203	$8,277,874	$44,838	0	0	0	0	0	0	$8,277,874	$122,712	$44,838
204	$8,155,162	$44,174	0	0	0	0	0	0	$8,155,162	$121,243	$44,174
205	$8,033,919	$43,517	0	0	0	0	0	0	$8,033,919	$119,790	$43,517
349	$35,019	$190	0	0	0	0	0	0	$35,019	$17,645	$190
350	$17,374	$94	0	0	0	0	0	0	$17,374	$17,374	$94

Tranche	Maturity	Window	Average Life
A	50	49	2.17
B	106	57	6.30
C	350	244	14.60
Collateral	350	350	7.16

PSA	Collateral	Tranche A	Tranche B	Tranche C
100	10.98	3.59	10.74	21.08
150	8.74	2.68	7.98	17.57
200	7.16	2.17	6.30	14.66
250	6.01	1.84	5.20	12.39
300	5.16	1.61	4.44	10.63

Sequential-pay CMOs offer investors maturities, principal payment periods, and average lives different from those defined by the underlying mortgage collateral. For example, Tranche A in our example has a maturity of 50 months compared to the collateral's maturity of 350 months. Each tranche also has a larger cash flow during the periods when their principal is being retired. The period between the beginning and ending principal payment is referred to as the **principal pay-down window.** Tranche A has a window of 49 months, B's window is 57 months, and C's window is 244 months (see table at the bottom of Exhibit 22.4-1). CMOs with certain size windows and maturities often are attractive investments for investors who are using cash flow matching strategies. Moreover, issuers of CMOs are able to offer a number of CMO tranches with different maturities and windows by simply creating more tranches.

Finally, each of the tranches has an average life that is either shorter or longer than the collateral's average life of 7.16 years. With a 200% PSA model, Tranche A has an average life of 2.17 years, B has an average life of 6.30 years, and C has a life of 14.66 years. In general, a CMO tranche with a lower average life is less susceptible to prepayment risk. Such risk, though, is not eliminated. As noted earlier, if prepayment speed decreases, an MBS's average life will increase, resulting in lower than projected early cash flow and therefore lower returns. In the table at the bottom of Exhibit 22.4-1, the average lives for the collateral and the three tranches are shown for different PSA models. Note that the average life of each of the tranches still varies as prepayment speed changes.

22.4.1.2   Other Sequential-Pay-Structured CMOs

Many sequential-pay CMOs also have an **accrual bond class.** Such a tranche, also referred to as the **Z bond,** does not receive current interest but has it deferred. The Z bond's current interest is used to pay down the principal on the other tranches, increasing their speed and reducing their average life. CMO issuers often create **floating-rate** and **inverse floating-rate tranches** to attract investors who prefer variable rate securities. The monthly coupon rate on the floating-rate tranche is usually set equal to a reference rate such as the London Interbank Offer Rate, LIBOR, whereas the rate on the inverse floating-rate tranche is determined by a formula that is inversely related to the reference rate. Finally, many CMOs are structured with tranches that have different PT rates. When CMOs are formed this way, an additional tranche, known as a **notional interest-only (IO) class,** is often created. This tranche receives the excess interest on the other tranches' principals, with the excess rate being equal to the difference in the collateral's PT rate minus the tranches' PT rates.

22.4.1.3   Planned Amortization Class

Although providing investors with different maturities and average lives, sequential-pay-structured CMOs are still subject to prepayment risk. A CMO with a **planned amortization class, PAC,** though, is structured such that there is virtually no prepayment risk. In a PAC-structured CMO, the underlying mortgage collateral is divided into two general tranches: the PAC and the **support tranche** (also called the **support bond** or the **companion bond**). The two tranches are formed by generating two monthly principal payment schedules from the collateral; one schedule is based on assuming a relatively low PSA speed, whereas the other is obtained by assuming a relatively high PSA speed. The PAC bond is then set up so that it will receive a monthly principal payment schedule based on the minimum principal from the two principal payments. Thus, the PAC bond is designed to have no prepayment risk provided the actual prepayment falls within the minimum and maximum assumed PSA speeds. The support bond, on the other hand, receives the remaining principal balance and is therefore subject to prepayment risk.

To illustrate, suppose we form PAC and support bonds from the $100M collateral that we used to construct our sequential-pay tranches (underlying MBS = $100M, WAC = 7%, WAM = 350 months, and PT rate = 6.5%). To generate the minimum monthly principal payments for the PAC, assume a minimum speed of 100% PSA, referred to as the *lower collar,* and a maximum speed of 300% PSA, called the *upper collar.* Exhibit 22.4-2 shows the principal payments (scheduled and prepaid) for selected months at both collars. The fourth column in the exhibit shows the minimum of the two payments. For example, in the 1st month, the principal payment is $272,662 for the 100% PSA and $654,493 for the 300% PSA; thus, the principal payment for the PAC would be $272,662. In examining the exhibit, note that for the early months, the minimum principal payments come from the 100% PSA model, and in the later months, the minimum principal payments come from the 300% PSA model. Based on the 100 to 300 PSA range, a PAC bond can be formed that would promise to pay the principal based on the minimum principal payment schedule shown in Exhibit 22.4-2. The support bond would receive any excess monthly principal payment.

As noted, the objective in creating a PAC bond is to eliminate prepayment risk. In this example, the PAC bond has no risk as long as the actual prepayment speed is between 100 and 300. This can be seen by calculating the PAC's average life given different prepayment rates. The table at the bottom right of Exhibit 22.4-2 shows the average lives for the collateral, PAC bond, and support bond for various prepayment speeds ranging from 50% PSA to 350% PSA. As shown, the PAC bond has an average life of 6.60 years between 100% PSA and 300% PSA; its average life does change, though, when prepayments speeds are outside the 100 to 300 PSA range. In contrast, the support bond's average life changes as prepayment speed changes.

22.4.1.4 Other PAC-Structured CMOs

The PAC and support bond underlying a CMO can be divided into different classes. Often the PAC bond is divided into several sequential-pay tranches, with each PAC having a different priority in principal payments over the other. Each sequential-pay PAC, in turn, will have a constant average life if the prepayment speed is within the lower and upper collars. In addition, it is possible that some PACs will have ranges of stability that will increase beyond the actual collar range, expanding their effective collars.

In addition to a sequential structure, a PAC-structured CMO can also be formed with PAC classes having different collars; in fact, some PACs are formed with just one PSA rate. These PACs are referred to as *targeted amortization class (TAC) bonds.* Finally, different types of tranches can be formed out of the support bond class. These include sequential-pay, floating and inverse-floating rate, and accrual bond classes.

Given the different ways in which CMO tranches can be formed, as well as the different objectives of investors, perhaps it is not surprising to find PAC-structured CMOs with as many as 50 tranches. In the mid 1990s, the average number of tranches making up a CMO was 23.

22.4.2 Stripped Mortgage-Backed Securities

In the mid-1980s, FNMA introduced *stripped mortgage-backed securities.* Stripped MBSs generally consist of two classes: a *principal-only* (PO) class and an *interest-only* (IO) class. As the names imply, the PO class receives only the principal from the underlying mortgages, whereas the IO class receives just the interest.

In general, the return on a PO MBS is greater with greater prepayment speed. For example, a PO class formed with $100M of mortgages (principal) and priced at $85M would yield an immediate return of $15M if the mortgage borrowers prepaid immediately.

EXHIBIT 22.4-2 PAC and Support Bonds: PAC formed 100 and 300 PSA MODEL Collateral: Balance = $100M, WAM = 350 Months, WAC = 7%, PT Rate = 6.5%, Prepayment: 200 PSA

	PAC						Collateral					
Period	Low PSA Principal	High PSA Principal	Principal	Balance	Int	CF	Balance	Interest	Scheduled Principal	Prepaid Principal	Principal	CF
1	$272,662	$654,493	$272,662	$64,308,445	$348,337	$620,999	$100,000,000	$541,667	$87,616	$373,948	$461,563	$1,003,230
2	$289,468	$703,781	$289,468	$64,035,784	$346,860	$636,329	$99,538,437	$539,167	$87,797	$406,832	$494,629	$1,033,796
3	$306,164	$752,304	$306,164	$63,746,315	$345,293	$651,456	$99,043,807	$536,487	$87,948	$439,382	$527,329	$1,063,817
4	$322,738	$799,986	$322,738	$63,440,152	$343,634	$666,373	$98,516,478	$533,631	$88,068	$471,562	$559,630	$1,093,261
5	$339,184	$846,750	$339,184	$63,117,413	$341,886	$681,070	$97,956,848	$530,600	$88,157	$503,340	$591,497	$1,122,097
6	$355,493	$892,522	$355,493	$62,778,229	$340,049	$695,541	$97,365,351	$527,396	$88,215	$534,683	$622,898	$1,150,294
100	$377,997	$348,021	$348,021	$19,188,096	$103,936	$451,956	$32,986,953	$178,679	$58,212	$348,921	$407,133	$585,812
101	$376,117	$341,958	$341,958	$18,840,075	$102,050	$444,008	$32,579,820	$176,474	$57,931	$344,610	$402,541	$579,015
102	$374,246	$335,998	$335,998	$18,498,118	$100,198	$436,196	$32,177,279	$174,294	$57,651	$340,347	$397,999	$572,292
200	$230,868	$57,242	$57,242	$2,795,007	$15,140	$72,382	$8,654,992	$46,881	$35,890	$91,330	$127,220	$174,101
201	$229,749	$56,182	$56,182	$2,737,764	$14,830	$71,012	$8,527,772	$46,192	$35,716	$89,984	$125,700	$171,892
349	$114,556	$2,385	$2,385	$4,706	$25	$2,410	$35,019	$190	$17,458	$186	$17,645	$17,834
350	$114,042	$2,321	$2,321	$2,321	$13	$2,334	$17,374	$94	$17,374	$0	$17,374	$17,468

| Average Life | | | |
PSA	Collateral	PAC	Support
50	14.28	7.48	20.86
100	10.98	6.60	18.89
150	8.74	6.60	12.59
200	7.16	6.60	8.17
250	6.01	6.60	4.96
300	5.16	6.60	2.58
350	4.51	5.97	2.39

Period	Principal Col Pr-PAC Pr	Support Beginning Balance	Interest	CF
1	$188,902	$35,691,555	$193,329	$382,231
2	$205,161	$35,502,653	$192,306	$397,467
3	$221,166	$35,297,492	$191,195	$412,360
4	$236,891	$35,076,326	$189,997	$426,888
5	$252,313	$34,839,435	$188,714	$441,027
6	$267,406	$34,587,122	$187,347	$454,752
100	$59,112	$13,798,856	$74,744	$133,856
101	$60,583	$13,739,745	$74,424	$135,007
102	$62,001	$13,679,162	$74,095	$136,097
200	$69,977	$5,859,985	$31,742	$101,719
201	$69,518	$5,790,008	$31,363	$100,881
349	$15,260	$30,313	$164	$15,424
350	$15,053	$15,053	$82	$15,135

Because investors can reinvest the $15M, this early return will have a greater return per period than a $15M return that is spread out over a longer period. Because of prepayment, the price of a PO MBS tends to be more responsive to interest rate changes than an option-free bond. That is, if interest rates are decreasing, then like the price of most bonds, the price of a PO MBS will increase. In addition, the price of a PO MBS is also likely to increase further because of the expectation of greater earlier principal payments as a result of an increase in prepayment caused by the lower rates. In contrast, if rates are increasing, the price of a PO MBS will decrease as a result of both lower discount rates and lower returns from slower principal payments. Thus, like most bonds, the prices of PO MBSs are inversely related to interest rates; and like other MBSs with embedded principal prepayment options, their prices tend to be more responsive to interest rate changes.

Cash flows from an I0 MBS come from the interest paid on the mortgages portfolio's principal balance. In contrast to a PO MBS, the cash flows and the returns on an IO MBS will be greater the slower the prepayment rate. For example, if the mortgages underlying a $100M, 6.5% MBS with PO and IO classes were paid off in the 1st year, then the IO MBS holders would receive a one-time cash flow of $6.5M = (.065)($100M). If $50M of the mortgages were prepaid in the 1st year and the remaining $50M in the 2nd year, then the IO MBS investors would receive an annualized cash flow over 2 years totaling $9.75M = (.065)($100M) + (.065)($100M – $50M); if the mortgage principal is paid down $25M per year, then the cash flow over 4 years would total $16.25M (= (.065)($100M) + (.065)($100M – $25M) + (.065)($75M – $25M) + (.065)($50M – $25M)). Thus, IO MBSs are characterized by an inverse relationship between prepayment speed and returns: The slower the prepayment rate, the greater the total cash flow on an IO MBS. Interestingly, if this relationship dominates the price and discount rate relation, then the price of an IO MBS will vary directly with interest rates.

Note that issuers can form IO and PO classes not only with MBSs but also with CMOs. For example, one of the tranches of the PAC-structured CMOs or sequential-structured CMOs discussed in the preceding sections could be divided into an IO class and a PO class. Such tranches are referred to as **CMO strips.** CMOs can also be formed from PO MBSs. These CMOs are called **PO-collateralized CMOs.**

Web Information:

For information on the market for mortgage-backed securities go to
www.bondmarkets.com. For information on links to other sites click on "Links."

22.5 EVALUATING MORTGAGE-BACKED SECURITIES

Like all securities, MBSs can be evaluated in terms of their characteristics. With MBSs, such an evaluation is more complex because of the difficulty in estimating cash flows due to prepayment. Two common approaches used to evaluate MBS and CMO tranches are yield analysis and Monte Carlo simulation.

22.5.1 Yield Analysis

Yield analysis involves calculating the yields on MBSs or CMO tranches given different prices and prepayment speed assumptions or alternatively calculating the values on MBSs or tranches given different rates and speeds. For example, suppose an institutional investor is interested in buying an MBS issue described by the collateral in Exhibit 22.3-2. This

MBS issue has a par value of $100M, WAC = 7%, WAM = 350 months, and a PT rate of 6.5%. The value as well as average life, maturity, duration, and other characteristics of this security would depend on the rate that the investor requires on the MBS and the prepayment speed she estimates. If the investor's required return on the MBS is 8%, and her estimate of the PSA speed is 200, then she would value the MBS issue at $94,125,346. At that rate and speed, the MBS would have an average life of 7.16 years (see Exhibit 22.5-1). Whether a purchase of the MBS issue at $94,125,346 to yield 8% represents a good investment depends, in part, on rates for other securities with similar maturities, durations, and risk and in part on how good the prepayment rate assumption is. For example, if the investor felt that the prepayment rate should be 100% PSA, and her required rate with that level of prepayment is 8%, then she would price the MBS issue at $92,126,541 and the average life would be 10.98 years. In general, for many institutional investors, the decision on whether to invest in a particular MBS or tranche depends on the price the institution can command. For example, based on an expectation of a 100% PSA, our investor might conclude that a yield of 8% on the MBS would make it a good investment. In this case, the investor would be willing to offer no more than $92,126,541 for the MBS issue.

One common approach used in conducting a yield analysis is to generate a matrix of different values by varying the yields and prepayment speeds. Exhibit 22.5-1 shows the different values for our illustrative MBS given different yields and different prepayment speeds. Using this matrix, an investor could determine, for a given price and assumed speed, the estimated yield or determine, for a given speed and yield, the price. Using

EXHIBIT 22.5-1 Cash Flow Analysis: Mortgage Portfolio = $100M, WAC = 7%, WAM = 350 Months, PT Rate = 6.5

Rate/PSA	100	200	300
	Value	Value	Value
6%	$104,753,977	$103,452,785	$102,682,824
7%	$98,058,957	$98,570,418	$98,878,559
8%	$92,126,541	$94,125,346	$95,350,368
9%	$86,843,213	$90,063,744	$92,069,954
Average Life	10.98	7.16	5.16
	Vector	*Vector*	*Vector*
	Month Range: PSA	**Month Range: PSA**	**Month Range: PSA**
	1-50: 150	1-50: 150	1-50: 150
	51-100: 200	51-100: 200	51-100: 200
	101-150: 250	101-150: 250	101-150: 250
	151-200: 300	151-200: 300	151-200: 300
	210-250: 250	210-250: 250	210-250: 350
	251-300: 200	251-300: 200	251-300: 400
	301-350: 150	301-350: 150	301-350: 450
Rate	Value	Value	Value
6%	$103,634,342	$104,461,479	$103,461,479
7%	$98,493,449	$98,177,841	$98,497,098
8%	$93,803,103	$92,606,503	$93,815,874
9%	$89,510,779	$87,641,273	$89,529,186
Average Life	7.43	10.29	7.37

this approach, an investor can also evaluate for each price the average yield and standard deviation over a range of PSA speeds.

One of the limitations of the preceding yield analysis is the assumption that the PSA speed used to estimate the yield is constant during the life of the MBS; in fact, such an analysis is sometimes referred to as *static yield analysis.* In practice, prepayment speeds change over the life of an MBS as interest rates change in the market. To address this, a more dynamic yield analysis, known as *vector analysis,* can be used. In applying vector analysis, PSA speeds are assumed to change over time. In the preceding case, a matrix of values for different rates can be obtained for different PSA vectors formed by dividing the total period into a number of periods with different PSA speeds assumed for each period. A vector analysis example is also shown in Exhibit 22.5-1. Note that one way to generate different vectors of PSA speeds would be to use a binomial interest rate tree. Such an approach can also be applied in valuing MBSs using a Monte Carlo simulation approach.

22.5.2 Monte Carlo Simulation

Monte Carlo simulation involves generating a set of cash flows for an MBS or CMO tranche based on simulated future interest rate scenarios. From the cash flows, the value of the MBS can be determined given the assumed rates and an assumed speed. The simulation involves first generating a number of interest rate paths, next estimating the cash flow for each path based on a prepayment model that is dependent on the assumed interest rates, third determining the present values of each path's cash flows, and last calculating the average value and standard deviation of the distribution of values from the assumed paths. The average value is referred to as the theoretical value; it can be compared to the market price of the MBS or tranche to determine if it is overpriced or underpriced.

A binomial interest rate tree can be used in a Monte Carlo simulation to generate different interest rate paths. When a binomial tree is used, the simulation consists of the following steps:

1. *Step 1*: Using a binomial interest rate tree, generate interest rate paths for spot rates and refinancing rates.

2. *Step 2*: Estimate the cash flows for each interest rate path. The cash flows depend on the prepayment rates assumed. The second step requires defining a prepayment model in which the conditional prepayment rate is determined by the seasonality of the mortgages and by a refinancing incentive that ties the interest rate paths to the proportion of the mortgage collateral prepaid.

3. *Step 3*: Determining the present value of each path. In this step, the appropriate risk-adjusted spot rate for discounting each path's cash flows must be estimated. The risk-adjusted spot rate is equal to the riskless spot rate plus a risk premium. The estimated risk premium includes an option-adjusted spread and default risk premium. These premiums for one-period spot rates are estimated and added to spot rates at each node of the binomial tree. Given these rates, the period spot rate for discounting each cash flow can be obtained for each path by using the geometric mean.

4. *Step 4*: Determine the value of each path given the path's cash flow (Step 2) and interest rates (Step 3).

5. *Step 5*: Calculate the average value of the paths to obtain the theoretical value.

Typically, the trees are generated for monthly spot rates and for mortgage refinancing rates, with the length of each binomial period being 1 month and with the number of periods equaling the maturity of the MBS or tranche (e.g., 360 months). From these trees, thousands of interest rate paths can be generated. Given a large number of paths, a sample number of paths can be used to estimate the theoretical value. An illustrative example using a simple two-period tree is presented in Appendix 22A.

22.6 OTHER ASSET-BACK SECURITIES

MBSs represent the largest and most extensively developed asset-backed security. Since 1985, a number of other asset-backed securities have been developed. The three most common types are those backed by automobile loans, credit card receivables, and home equity loans. These asset-backed securities are structured as pass-throughs and many have tranches.

22.6.1 Automobile Loan-Backed Securities

Automobile loan-backed securities are often referred to as ***CARS*** (***certificates for automobile receivables***). The automobile loans underlying these securities are similar to mortgages in that borrowers make regular monthly payments that include interest and a scheduled principal. Also like mortgages, automobile loans are characterized by prepayment. For such loans, prepayment can occur as a result of car sales, trade-ins, repossessions and subsequent resales, wrecks, and refinancing when rates are low. Finally like MBSs, CARS are structured as PACS. CARS differ from MBSs in that they have much shorter lives, their prepayment rates are less influenced by interest rates than mortgage prepayment rates, and they are subject to greater default risk.

22.6.2 Credit-Card Receivable-Backed Securities

Credit-card receivable-backed securities are commonly referred to as ***CARDS*** (***certificates for amortizing revolving debts***). In contrast to MBSs and CARS, CARDS investors do not receive an amortized principal payment as part of their monthly cash flow. Instead, CARDS are often structured with two periods. In one period, known as the ***lockout period,*** all principal payments made on the receivables are retained and either reinvested in other receivables or invested in other securities. In the other period, known as the ***principal-amortization period,*** all current and accumulated principal payments are paid.

22.6.3 Home Equity Loan-Backed Securities

Home-equity loan-backed securities are referred to as ***HELS.*** They are similar to MBSs in that they pay a monthly cash flow consisting of interest, scheduled principal, and prepaid principal. In contrast to mortgages, the home equity loans securing HELS tend to have a shorter maturity and different factors influencing their prepayment rates.

Web Information:

For information on the market for asset-backed securities go to www.bondmarkets.com.

22.7 CONCLUSION

MBS and other asset-backed securities were introduced by financial institutions to attract the funds of institutional investors toward the financing of real estate and other commercial and consumer loans. Today, these securities have become one of the most popular financial assets held by institutional investors, competing with a number of different types of bonds for inclusion in the portfolios of institutional investors. Over time, these securities have been structured in different ways (as PACS, POs, IOs, etc.) to make them more attractive to different types of investors. More significantly, MBSs and other asset-backed instruments have revolutionized the way in which real estate, as well commercial and consumer assets, is financed.

Adding asset-backed securities and their derivatives to the list of derivatives already covered in this book highlights the fact that there are indeed a myriad of derivative securities and positions extant today. However, we still have not exhausted all the derivatives and possible positions, nor have we covered all the strategies, uses, markets, and derivative pricing models. What we hope we have done in this book, though, is develop a foundation for the understanding of derivatives. Moreover, to the extent that most assets derive their values from another asset, we hope we also have established a foundation and methodology for understanding finance through derivatives.

KEY TERMS

securitization

originator

asset-backed security

mortgage-backed securities

mortgage pass-throughs

prepayment risk

prepayment speed or
simply speed

weighted average
coupon rate

conditional prepayment
rate

seasoning

PSA model (Public
Securities Association).

single monthly mortality
rate

monthly factors

burnout factor

agency pass-throughs

conventional pass-throughs

real estate mortgage investment
conduits
REMIC

Mortgage-Backed
Security Dealers
Association

pool factor

extension risk

average life

collateralized mortgage
obligations

tranches

sequential-pay CMO

principal pay-down
window

accrual bond class

Z-bond

notional interest-only
(IO) class

planned amortization
class, PAC

support class or
companion bond

lower collar

upper collar

targeted amortization
class bonds

stripped mortgage-backed
securities

principal-only (PO) class

interest-only (IO) class

CMO strips

PO-collateralized CMOs

static yield analysis

vector analysis

theoretical value of
the MBS

CARS (certificates for automobile
receivables)

CARDS (certificates for
amortizing revolving debts)

lockout period

principal-amortization
period

SELECTED REFERENCES

Anderson, G. A., J. R. Barber, and C. H. Chang. "Prepayment Risk and the Duration of Default- Free Mortgage-Backed Securities." *Journal of Financial Research* 16 (1989): 1–9.

Bartlett, W. W. *Mortgage Backed Securities: Products, Analysis, Trading.* New York: New York Institute of Finance, 1989.

Bhattacharya, A., and H. Chin. "Synthetic Mortgage Backed Securities." *Journal of Portfolio Management* 18 (1992): 44–55.

Carron, A. S. "Understanding CMOs, REMICs and other Mortgage Derivatives." *Journal of Fixed-Income* 2 (1992): 25–43.

Cheyette, O. "Term Structure Dynamics and Mortgage Valuation." *Journal of Fixed Income* (March 1992): 28–41.

Dunn, K., and J. McConnell. "Valuation of GNMA Mortgage-Backed Securities." *Journal of Finance* 36 (1981): 599–616.

Fabozzi, F. J. *Bond Markets, Analysis and Strategies,* 3rd ed., 214-321. Upper Saddle River, NJ: Prentice-Hall, 1996.

Goldman, Sachs, and Company. *Understanding Securitized Investments and their Use in Portfolio Management.* Charlottesville, VA: Association of Investment Management and Research, 1990.

F. J. Fabozzi, ed. *The Handbook of Mortgage-Backed Securities.* Chicago: Probus, 1992.

Hayre, L., C. Mohebbi, and T. A. Zimmerman. "Mortgage Pass-Throughs." In *The Handbook of Fixed Income Securities*, 6th ed., edited by F. Fabozzi. New York: McGraw-Hill, 2001.

Hurst, R. R. "Securities Backed by Closed-End Home Equity Loans." In *The Handbook of Fixed Income Securities*, 6th ed., edited by F. Fabozzi. New York: McGraw-Hill, 2001.

Jacob, D., and A. Toevs. "An Analysis of the New Valuation, Duration and Convexity Models for Mortgage-Back Securities." In *The Handbook of Mortgage-Backed Securities,* rev. ed., edited by F. Fabozzi. Chicago: Probus, 1988.

Johnson, R. S. *Bond Evaluations, Selection, and Management.* Malden, MA: Blackwell Press, Chapter 11.

Lehman Brothers, Inc. "Collateralized Mortgage Obligations." In *The Handbook of Fixed Income Securities*, 6th ed., edited by F. Fabozzi. New York: McGraw-Hill, 2001.

McElravey, J. N. "Securities Backed by Credit Card Receivables." In *The Handbook of Fixed Income Securities*, 6th ed., edited by F. Fabozzi. New York: McGraw-Hill, 2001.

Morris, D. V. *Asset Securitization: Principles and Practices.* Executive Enterprise Publications, 1990.

Norton, J., and P. Spellman, eds. *Asset Securitization.* Cambridge, MA: Basil Blackwell, 1991.

Richard, S. F., and R. Roll. "Prepayments on Fixed Rate Mortgage Backed Securities." *Journal of Portfolio Management* 15 (1989): 73–83.

Roever, W. A., J. N. McElravey, and G. M. Schultz. "Securities Backed by Automobile Loans." In *The Handbook of Fixed Income Securities*, 6th ed., edited by F. Fabozzi. New York: McGraw-Hill, 2001.

Schwartz, B., and W. Torous. "Prepayment and the Valuation of Mortgage Pass-Through Securities." *Journal of Business* 15 (1992): 221–240.

PROBLEMS AND QUESTIONS

1. Suppose Commerce Bank sells mortgage-backed securities backed by its $50M portfolio of fixed-rate mortgages with the MBS having the following features:
   - Mortgage collateral = $50,000,000
   - Weighted average coupon rate (WAC) = 8%
   - Weighted average maturity (WAM) = 360 months
   - Estimated prepayment speed = 150 PSA
   - MBS pass-through rate = PT rate = 7%
   - Commerce will service the mortgage portfolio

Item	Month 1	Month 2
Balance	50,000,000	
Interest	291,667	
p	366,882	
Scheduled Principal		
CPR		
SMM		
Prepaid Principal		
Total Principal		
Cash Flow		

a. Show in the table the first 2 months of cash flows going to the MBS investors.

b. What compensation would ABC receive for servicing the mortgages?

2. Suppose the standard (100) prepayment profile for 10-year (120 month) conventional mortgages is one in which the CPR starts at zero and increases at a constant rate of .2% per month for 20 months to equal 4% at the 20th month; then after the 20 month, the CPR stays at a constant 4%.

a. Show graphically the 100% prepayment profile.

b. In the same graph, show the prepayment profile for speeds of 200%, 150%, and 50% of the standard.

c. Show in the table following the 1st month cash flow for an MBS portfolio of 10-year mortgages with the following features:

- Mortgage collateral = $50,000,000
- Weighted average coupon rate (WAC) = 9%
- Weighted average maturity (WAM) = 120 months
- Estimated prepayment speed = 200 PSA
- MBS pass-through rate = PT rate = 8.5%

Item	Month 1
Balance	
Interest	
p	
Scheduled Principal	
CPR	
SMM	
Prepaid Principal	
Total Principal	
Cash Flow	

3. Explain some of the factors that determine the prepayment speed on a mortgage portfolio.

4. Define agency pass-throughs and describe some of their features.

5. Define conventional pass-throughs and describe some of their features.

6. What is the market value (clean price) of a 6% MBS issue backed by a mortgage pool with an original par value of $100 million if its price is quoted at 103-16 with a pool factor of .90? What would be the invoice price an institutional investor holding $10M of par value of these bonds receive if she sold her holdings at 103-16 when there were 10 days between the settlement date on the sale and the 1st day of the next month?

7. Explain the relationship between extension risk, prepayment risk, and average life.

8. What was the primary motivation behind the creation of MBS derivatives in the 1980s?

9. Explain how the following CMOs are constructed and their features:

a. Sequential-pay tranche

b. Sequential-pay tranches with an accrual bond tranche

c. Floating-rate and inverse floating-rate tranches

d. Notional IO tranche

e. PAC and support bonds

f. Sequential-pay PAC

10. Explain the interest rate and value relation for a principal-only stripped MBS and an interest-only stripped MBS.

11. Given the following mortgage collateral and sequential-pay CMO:
   - Mortgage collateral = $200,000,000
   - Weighted average coupon rate (WAC) = 8%
   - Weighted average maturity (WAM) = 360 months
   - Estimated prepayment speed = 150 PSA
   - MBS pass-through rate = PT rate = 7.5%

   Sequential-Pay CMO
   - Tranche A receives all principal payment from the collateral until its principal of $100M is retired.
   - Tranche B receives its principal of $100M after A's principal is paid.
   - Tranches B receives interest each period equal to its stated coupon rate of 7.5% times its outstanding balance at the beginning of each month.

   Complete the table:

Month	Collateral Balance	Collateral Interest	Collateral Principal	A Balance	A Interest	A Principal	B Balance	B Interest	B Principal
1	200,000,000								

12. Given the following mortgage collateral and PAC:
   - Mortgage collateral = $200,000,000
   - Weighted average coupon rate (WAC) = 8%
   - Weighted average maturity (WAM) = 355 months
   - Estimated prepayment speed = 150 PSA
   - MBS pass-through rate = PT rate = 7.5%
   - PAC formed from the collateral with a lower collar of 100 and upper collar of 300
   - Support bond receiving the residual principal

   Complete the table:

Month	Collateral Balance	Collateral Interest	Collateral Principal	PAC Low PSA Principal	PAC High PSA Principal	PAC Minimum Principal	Support Principal
1	200,000,000						

13. What is yield analysis? Explain the difference between static yield analysis and vector analysis.

14. Explain the process involved in applying a Monte Carlo simulation using a binomial interest rate tree to valuing a mortgage portfolio or the collateral on an MBS.

15. Explain how the following asset-backed securities are constructed and their features:
    a. CARS
    b. CARDS
    c. HELS

16. Using the MBS collateral excel program (in "Mortgage-Backed Securities" folder), create an excel table for the following MBS:
    - Mortgage collateral = $50,000,000
    - WAC = 7%
    - PT rate = 6.5
    - WAM = 350
    - Seasoning = 10
    - PSA = 75%

Note that in your table, you may want to hide many of the rows and some of the columns. Do keep columns for Period, Balance, Interest, Scheduled Principal, Prepaid Principal, and Cash Flow.

17. Using the MBS collateral program (in "Mortgage-Backed Securities" folder), determine for the MBS in Question 16 the values and average lives for the following yield analysis matrix:

Discount Rate/PSA	50	100	150
5%	Value	Value	Value
6%			
7%			
8%			
Average Life			

18. Given the following mortgage collateral and PAC:
    - Mortgage collateral = $200,000,000
    - Weighted average coupon rate (WAC) = 7%
    - Weighted average maturity (WAM) = 355 months
    - Seasoning = 5 months
    - MBS pass-through rate = PT rate = 6.5%
    - PAC formed from the collateral with a lower collar of 100 and upper collar of 300
    - Support bond receiving the residual principal
    a. Using the MBSpac Excel program (in "Mortgage-Backed Securities" folder), determine the average life for collateral, PAC bond, and support bond given the PSA speeds shown in the table:

PSA	Collateral	PAC	Support
50	Average Life	Average Life	Average Lief
100			
150			
200			
250			
300			
350			

b. Comment on the PAC's average life given the different PSA speeds.

WEB EXERCISES

1. Learn more about agency MBS by going to their Web sites: www.fanniemae.com, www.ginniemae.gov, and www.freddiemac.com.

2. Learn more about the mortgage industry by going to the homepage of the Mortgage Bankers Association of America: www.mbaa.org.

3. Evaluate the quality ratings of MBS and CMO by going to www.moodys.com. At the site, click on "Structured Finance" and go to either "Commercial MBS," "Residential MBS," or "CDOs/Derivative" and then to "Watchlist" or "Ratings Action." Registration is required.

APPENDIX 22A   VALUING A MBS WITH A BINOMIAL INTEREST RATE: EXAMPLE USING A 2-PERIOD CASE

To illustrate how a binomial tree is used to value an MBS, consider a simple (but manageable) case of an MBS issue with a face value of $1,000,000, WAC = 8%, WAM = 10 years, PT rate = 8%, *annual* cash flows (instead of the standard monthly), and a balloon at the end of the *2nd* year.[1] For this simple case, assume the following:

- The current 1-year spot rate is $S_0 = 6\%$, and the current refinancing rate is $R_0^{ref} = 8\%$.

- The future spot and refinancing rates can both be described by a *two*-period binomial interest rate where u = 1.1, d = 1/1.1, the length of the period is 1 year, and q = .5.

- The following prepayment model applies:

$$CPR = 20\% \text{ if } (WAC - R^{ref}) > 0$$

$$CPR = 5\% \text{ if } (WAC - R^{ref}) \leq 0$$

- A risk-adjusted, 1-year spot rate is equal to the spot rate plus an option-adjusted spread of 2%: $S^{RA} = S + 2\%$.

Exhibit 22.A-1 shows the two-period binomial tree for the spot and refinancing rates along with the corresponding CPR speeds associated with each interest rate. With this two-period binomial process, there are four possible interest rate paths, as shown at the bottom of the exhibit.

---

[1] In a balloon mortgage, the borrower is given long-term financing, but at a specified future date, the mortgage rate and terms are renegotiated. The balloon payment is the original amount borrowed minus the principal amortized.

EXHIBIT 22.A-1   Binomial Tree of Spot Rates and Refinancing Rates: u = 1.1 and d = 1/1.1

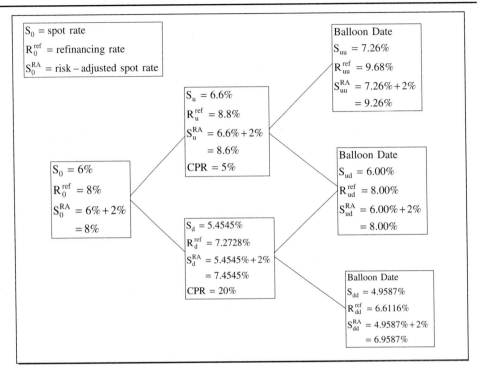

Period	Path 1	Path 2	Path 3	Path 4
0	6.0000%	6.0000%	6.0000%	6.0000%
1	5.4545%	5.4545%	6.6000%	6.6000%
2	4.9587% Balloon	6.0000% Balloon	6.0000% Balloon	7.2600% Balloon

Given the interest rate paths and corresponding prepayment rates, the first step is to estimate the cash flow for each interest rate path. With the balloon payment at the end of Year 2, the mortgage pool can be viewed as a 2-year asset with a principal payment made at the end of Year 2 that is equal to the original principal less the amount paid down. With the prepayment assumption, cash flows can be generated for the four interest rate paths. These cash flows are shown in Exhibit 22.A-2. Note that with the balloon payment in Period 2, Path 1 and Path 2 have the same cash flow, and Path 3 and Path 4 have the same cash flow.

Like any bond, an MBS or CMO tranche should be valued by discounting the cash flows by the appropriate risk-adjusted spot rates. For an MBS or CMO tranche, the risk-adjusted spot rate, z_t, is equal to the riskless spot rate, S_t, plus a risk premium. If the underlying mortgages are insured against default, then the risk premium would only reflect the additional return needed to compensate investors for the prepayment risk they are assuming. This premium is referred to as the option-adjusted spread (OAS). If we assume no default risk, then the risk-adjusted spot rate can be defined as

$$z_t = S_t + k_t$$

EXHIBIT 22.A-2   Cash Flow, Discount Rates, and Path Values

Period 1

Period 2

Path 1 and Path 2
$S_d = 5.4545\%, CPR = 20\%$

$$p = \$1,000,000 / \left[\frac{1-(1/1.08)^{10}}{.08} \right]$$

$= \$149,029$

Interest $= .08(\$1,000,000) = \$80,000$

Sch. Prin. $= [\$149,029 - \$80,000] = \$69,029$

Prepaid Prin. $= .20[\$1,000,000 - \$69,029]$
$= \$186,194$

$CF_1 = \$80,000 + \$69,029 + \$186,194 = \$335,223$

Path 1 and Path 2
Balloon Date
CF = Beginning Balance + Interest
Balance $= \$1,000,000 - (\$69,029 + \$186,194)$
$= \$744,777$
Interest $= .08(\$744,777) = \$59,582$
$CF_2 = \$744,777 + \$59,582 = \$804,359$

Path 3 and Path 4
$S_u = 6.5\%, CPR = 5\%$

$$p = \$1,000,000 / \left[\frac{1-(1/1.08)^{10}}{.08} \right]$$

$= \$149,029$

Interest $= .08(\$1,000,000) = \$80,000$

Sch. Prin. $= [\$149,029 - \$80,000] = \$69,029$

Prepaid Prin. $= .05[\$1,000,000 - \$69,029]$
$= \$46,549$

$CF_1 = \$80,000 + \$69,029 + \$46,549 = \$195,578$

Path 3 and Path 4
Balloon Date
CF = Beginning Balance + Interest
Balance $= \$1,000,000 - (\$69,029 + \$46,549)$
$= \$884,422$
Interest $= .08(\$884,422) = \$70,754$
$CF_2 = \$884,422 + \$70,754 = \$955,176$

Discount Rates:

Path 1 and Path 2 :
$Z_{10} = .08$
$Z_{20} = [(1.08)(1.07454)]^{1/2} - 1 = .0773$

Path 3and Path 4 :
$Z_{10} = .08$
$Z_{20} = [(1.08)(1.086)]^{1/2} - 1 = .083$

Path Values and Theoretical Value:

Path1 :
$$V_1 = \frac{\$335,223}{1.08} + \frac{\$804,359}{(1.0773)^2} = \$1,003,461$$

Path2 :
$$V_2 = \frac{\$335,223}{1.08} + \frac{\$804,359}{(1.0773)^2} = \$1,003,461$$

Path3 :
$$V_3 = \frac{\$195,578}{1.08} + \frac{\$955,176}{(1.083)^2} = \$995,470$$

Path4 :
$$V_4 = \frac{\$195,578}{1.08} + \frac{\$955,176}{(1.083)^2} = \$995,470$$

$$\text{AverageValue} = \frac{\$1,003,461+\$1,003,461+\$995,470+\$995,470}{4} = \$999,466$$

where k = OAS; and the value of each path can be defined as

$$V_i^{Path} = \sum_{m=1}^{T} \frac{CF_M}{(1+z_M)^M} = \frac{CF_1}{1+z_1} + \frac{CF_2}{(1+z_2)^2} + \frac{CF_3}{(1+z_3)^3} + \cdots + \frac{CF_T}{(1+z_T)^T}$$

where
i = ith path
z_M = spot rate on bond with M-year maturity.
T = maturity of the MBS.

For this example, it is assumed that the option-adjusted spread is 2% greater than the 1-year, riskless spot rates shown in Exhibit 22.A-1. From these current and future 1-year spot rates, the current 1-year and 2-year equilibrium spot rates can be obtained for each path by using the geometric mean. These rates are shown in Exhibit 22.A-2. Given these rates, the value of each path is then obtained by discounting their cash flow by their appropriate discount rates. Finally, given the values of each path, the theoretical value is obtained by calculating the average values of the four paths (see Exhibit 22.A-2).

$$\bar{V} = \frac{1}{N} \sum_{i=1}^{N} V_i^{path}$$

In this example, the theoretical value of the MBS issue is $999,466 as shown in Exhibit 22.A-2.

APPENDIX A

EXPONENTS AND LOGARITHMS

A.1 EXPONENTIAL FUNCTIONS

An exponential function is one whose independent variable is an exponent. For example

$$y = b^t$$

where:
y = dependent variable,
t = independent variable,
b = base (b > 1).

In calculus, many exponential functions use as their base the irrational number 2.71828, denoted by the symbol e:

$$e = 2.71828$$

An exponential function that uses e as its base is defined as a natural exponential function. For example

$$y = e^2$$

$$y = Ae^{Rt}$$

These functions also can be expressed as

$$y = \exp(t)$$

$$y = A \exp(Rt)$$

In calculus, natural exponential functions have the useful property of being their own derivative. In addition to this mathematical property, e also has a finance meaning. Specifically, e is equal to the future value (FV) of $1 compounded continuously for one period at a nominal interest rate (R) of 100%.

To see e as a future value, consider the future value of an investment of A dollars invested at an annual nominal rate of R for t years and compounded m times per year. That is

$$FV = A \left(1 + \frac{R}{m} \right)^{mt} \qquad \text{(A.1-1)}$$

If we let A = $1, t = 1 year, and R = 100%, then the FV would be

$$FV = \$1 \left(1 + \frac{1}{m} \right)^{m} \qquad \text{(A.1-2)}$$

If the investment is compounded one time (m = 1), then the value of the $1 at end of the year will be $2; if it is compounded twice (m = 2), the end-of-year value will be $2.25; if it is compounded 100 times (m = 100), then the value will be 2.7048138.

$$m = 1: \quad FV = \$1 \left(1 + \frac{1}{1}\right)^1 = \$2.00$$

$$m = 2: \quad FV = \$1 \left(1 + \frac{1}{2}\right)^2 = \$2.25$$

$$m = 100: \quad FV = \$1 \left(1 + \frac{1}{100}\right)^{100} = \$2.7048138$$

$$m = 1000: \quad FV = \$1 \left(1 + \frac{1}{1000}\right)^{1000} = \$2.716924$$

As m becomes large, the FV approaches the value of $2.71828. Thus, in the limit

$$FV = \lim_{m \to \infty} \left(1 + \frac{1}{m}\right)^m = 2.71828 \qquad (A.1\text{-}3)$$

If "A" dollars are invested instead of $1, and the investment is made for t years instead of 1 year, then given a 100% interest rate, the future value after t years would be

$$FV = Ae^t \qquad (A.1\text{-}4)$$

Finally, if the nominal interest rate is different than 100%, then the FV is

$$FV = Ae^{Rt} \qquad (A.1\text{-}5)$$

To prove Equation (A.1-5), rewrite Equation (A.1-1) as follows:

$$FV = A \left(1 + \frac{R}{m}\right)^{mt}$$

$$FV = A \left[\left(1 + \frac{R}{m}\right)^{m/R}\right]^{Rt} \qquad (A.1\text{-}6)$$

If we invert R/m in the inner term, we get

$$FV = A \left[\left(1 + \frac{1}{m/R}\right)^{m/R}\right]^{Rt} \qquad (A.1\text{-}7)$$

The inner term takes the same form as Equation (A.1-2). As shown earlier, this term, in turn, approaches e as m approaches infinity. Thus, for continuous compounding, the FV is

$$FV = Ae^{Rt}$$

Thus, a 2-year investment of $100 at a 10% annual nominal rate with continuous compounding would be worth $122.14 at the end of Year 2:

$$FV = \$100^{(.10)(2)} = \$122.14$$

A.2 LOGARITHMS

A logarithm (or log) is the power to which a base must be raised to equal a particular number. For example, given

$$5^2 = 25$$

the power (or log) to which the base 5 must be raised to equal 25 is 2. Thus, the log of 25 to the base 5 is 2:

$$\log_5 25 = 2$$

In general

$$y = b^t \quad \Leftrightarrow \quad \log_b y = t$$

Two numbers that are frequently used as the base are 10 and the number e. If the number 10 is used as the base, the logarithm is known as the common log. Some of the familiar common logs are

$$\log_{10} 1000 = 3 \quad (10^3 = 1000)$$

$$\log_{10} 100 = 2 \quad (10^2 = 100)$$

$$\log_{10} 10 = 1 \quad (10^1 = 10)$$

$$\log_{10} 1 = 0 \quad (10^0 = 1)$$

$$\log_{10} 0.1 = -1 \quad (10^{-1} = \frac{1}{10^1} = .10)$$

$$\log_{10} 0.01 = -2 \quad (10^{-2} = \frac{1}{10^2} = \frac{1}{100} = .01)$$

When e is the base, the log is defined as the natural logarithm (denoted $\log_e$ or ln). For the natural log, we have

$$y = e^t \quad \Leftrightarrow \quad \log_e y = \ln y = t$$

$$\ln e^t = t$$

Thus, given an expression such as $y = e^t$, the exponent t is automatically the natural log.

A.3 RULES OF LOGARITHMS

Like exponents, logarithms have a number of useful algebraic properties. The properties are stated following in terms of natural logs; the properties, though, do apply to any log regardless of its base.

Equality: If $X = Y$, then $\ln X = \ln Y$

Product Rule: $\ln(XY) = \ln X + \ln Y$

Quotient Rule: $\ln(X/Y) = \ln X - \ln Y$

Power Rule: $\ln(X^a) = a \ln X$

A.4 USES OF LOGARITHM

The preceding properties of logarithms make logarithms useful in solving a number of algebraic problems.

A.4.1 Solving for R

In finance, logs can be used to solve for R when there is continuous compounding. That is, from Equation (A.1-5)

$$FV = Ae^{Rt}$$

Using the preceding log properties, R can be found as follows:

$$Ae^{Rt} = FV$$

$$e^{Rt} = \frac{FV}{A}$$

$$\ln\left(e^{Rt}\right) = \ln\left(\frac{FV}{A}\right)$$

$$Rt = \ln\left(\frac{FV}{A}\right)$$

$$R = \frac{\ln(FV/A)}{t}$$

Thus, a $100 investment that pays $120 at the end of 2 years would yield a nominal annual rate of 9.12% given continuous compounding: $R = \ln(\$120/\$100)/2 = .0912$. Similarly, a pure discount bond selling for $980 and paying $1,000 at the end of 91 days would yield a nominal annual rate of 8.10% given continuous compounding:

$$R = \frac{\ln(\$1000/\$980)}{91/365} = .0810$$

A.4.2 Logarithmic Return

The expression for the rate of return on a security currently priced at S_0 and expected to be S_T at the end of one period (t = 1) can be found using Equation (A.1-5). That is

$$S_T = S_0 e^{Rt}$$

$$R = \ln\left(\frac{S_T}{S_0}\right)$$

When the rate of return on a security is expressed as the natural log of S_T/S_0, it is referred to as the security's logarithmic return. Thus, a security currently priced at $100 and expected to be $110 at the end of the period would have an expected logarithmic return of 9.53%: $R = \ln(\$110/100) = .0953$.

A.4.3 Time

Using a logarithm, one can solve for t in either the discrete or continuous compounding cases. That is

$$FV = A(1 + R)^t$$

$$A(1 + R)^t = FV$$

$$\ln\left[(1 + R)^t\right] = \ln\left(\frac{FV}{A}\right)$$

$$t\ln[1 + R] = \ln\left(\frac{FV}{A}\right)$$

$$t = \frac{\ln(FV/A)}{\ln(1 + R)}$$

$$Ae^{Rt} = FV$$

$$e^{Rt} = \frac{FV}{A}$$

$$\ln\left(e^{Rt}\right) = \ln\left(\frac{FV}{A}\right)$$

$$Rt = \ln\left(\frac{FV}{A}\right)$$

$$t = \frac{\ln(FV/A)}{R}$$

The equations can be used in problems in which one knows the interest or growth rate and wants to know how long it will take for an investment to grow to equal a certain terminal value. For example, given an annual interest rate of 10% (no annual compounding), an investment of $800 would take 2.34 years to grow to $1,000:

$$t = \frac{\ln(\$1000/\$800)}{\ln(1.10)} = 2.34 \text{ years}$$

SELECTED REFERENCE

Chiang, A. C. *Fundamental Methods of Mathematical Economics,* 267–302. New York: McGraw-Hill, 1976.

APPENDIX B

STATISTICAL CONCEPTS

In this appendix, we define some of the basic statistical concepts used in analyzing derivatives.

RANDOM VARIABLE: A random variable is a variable whose value is uncertain. Signified with a (tilde) over the symbol of the variable, a random variable is sometimes referred to as a stochastic variable. The opposite of a random variable is a deterministic or controlled variable, referred to as a nonstochastic variable.

PROBABILITY DISTRIBUTION: A probability distribution is a function that assigns probabilities to the possible values of a random variable. The function can be objective (such as using past frequencies or assuming the distribution takes a certain form) or subjective. Also, the distribution either can be continuous in which it takes on all possible values over the range of the distribution, with the probabilities being defined for a particular range, or discrete in which the distribution takes on only a few possible values, with probabilities assigned to each possible values. In Table B-1, a probability distribution is shown for next period's interest rates (random variable r). This discrete distribution is defined by five possible interest rate values (Column 1) and their respective probabilities (Column 2) and is shown graphically in Figure B-1.

The most common way to describe the probability distribution is in terms of its parameters: expected value or mean, variance, and skewness.

EXPECTED VALUE: The expected value of a random variable is the weighted average of the possible values of the random variable with the weights being the probabilities assigned to each possible value (P_i). The expected value or mean, along with the median and the mode, is a measure of the central tendency of the distribution. The expected value for random variable r is

$$E(\tilde{r}) = \sum_{i=1}^{T} P_i r_i = P_1 r_1 + P_2 r_2 + \cdots + P_T r_T$$
$$E(\tilde{r}) = (.1)(4\%) + (.2)(5\%) + (.4)(6\%) + (.2)(7\%) + (.1)(8\%) = 6\%$$

A random variable may be described in terms of an algebraic equation, for example

$$\tilde{r} = a + b\tilde{Y}$$

where a and b are coefficients and Y is the independent variable. To describe the expected value of r as $E(a + bY)$, one can make use of the following expected value operator rules:

1. Expected value of a constant (a) is equal to the constant:

$$\text{EV Rule 1: } E(a) = a.$$

TABLE B-1 Probability Distribution

(1) r_i	(2) P_i	(3) $P_i r_i$	(4) $[r_i - E(r)]$	(5) $[r_i - E(r)]^2$	(6) $P_i[r_i - E(r)]^2$	(7) $[r_i - E(r)]^3$	(8) $P_i[r_i - E(r)]^3$
4%	0.1	0.4	−2	4	0.4	−8	−0.8
5%	0.2	1.0	−1	1	0.2	−1	−0.2
6%	0.4	2.4	0	0	0.0	0	0.0
7%	0.2	1.4	1	1	0.2	1	0.2
8%	0.1	0.8	2	4	0.4	8	0.8
	1	$E(r) = 6\%$			$V(r) = 1.2$		$S_k(r) = 0$

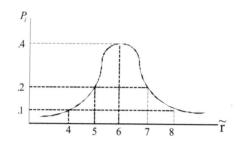

FIGURE B-1 Probability Distribution

2. Expected value of a constant times a random variable is equal to the constant times the expected value of the random variable:

$$\text{EV Rule 2: } E(b\tilde{X}) = bE(\tilde{X})$$

3. Expected value of a sum is equal to the sum of the expected values:

$$\text{EV Rule 3: } E(\tilde{X} + \tilde{Y}) = E(\tilde{X}) + E(\tilde{Y})$$

Applying the three rules to the equation $r = a + bY$, $E(r)$ can be expressed as

$$E(\tilde{r}) = a + bE(\tilde{Y})$$

VARIANCE: The variance of a random variable ($V(r)$) is the expected value of the squared deviation from the mean:

$$V(r) = E[\tilde{r} - E(r)]^2$$

The variance is defined as the second moment of the distribution. It is a measure of the distribution's dispersion, measuring the squared deviation most likely to occur. As an expected value, the variance is obtained by calculating the weighted average of each squared deviation, with the weights being the relative probabilities:

$$V(\tilde{r}) = \sum_{i=1}^{T} p_i[\tilde{r}_i - E(\tilde{r})]^2$$

$$V(\tilde{r}) = p_1[\tilde{r}_1 - E(\tilde{r})]^2 + p_2[\tilde{r}_i - E(\tilde{r})]^2 + \cdots + p_T[\tilde{r}_T - E(\tilde{r})]^2$$

The random variable described in Table B-1 has a variance of 1.2.

$$V(\tilde{r}) = (.1)[4\% - 6\%]^2 + (.2)[5\% - 6\%]^2 + (.4)[6\% - 6\%]^2$$
$$+ (.2)[7\% - 6\%]^2 + (.1)[8\% - 6\%]^2 = 1.2$$

STANDARD DEVIATION: The standard deviation, $\sigma(r)$, is the square root of the variance:

$$\sigma(\tilde{r}) = \sqrt{V(\tilde{r})}$$

The standard deviation provides a measure of dispersion that is on the same scale as the distribution's deviations. The standard deviation of the random variable in Table B-1 is 1.0954451; this indicates the distribution has an average deviation of plus or minus 1.0954451.

Note that the risk of a security is defined as the uncertainty that the actual return earned from investing in a security will deviate from the expected. By definition, the variance and standard deviation of a security's rate of return define the security's relative risk. That is, the greater a security's variance relative to another security, the greater that security's actual return can deviate from its expected, and thus, the greater the security's risk relative to the other security.

SKEWNESS: Skewness measures the degree of symmetry of the distribution. A distribution that is symmetric about its mean is one in which the probability of $r = E(r) + x$ is equal to the probability of $r = E(r) - x$ for all values of x. Skewness, $S_k(r)$, is defined as the third moment of the distribution and can be measured by calculating the expected value of the cubic deviation:

$$S_k(\tilde{r}) = \sum_{i=1}^{T} p_i[\tilde{r}_i - E(\tilde{r})]^3$$

$$S_k(\tilde{r}) = p_1[\tilde{r}_1 - E(\tilde{r})]^3 + p_2[\tilde{r}_i - E(\tilde{r})]^3 + \cdots + p_T[\tilde{r}_T - E(\tilde{r})]^3$$

The skewness of the distribution in Table B-1 is zero.

COVARIANCE: The covariance is a measure of the extent to which one random variable is above or below its mean at the same time or state that another random variable is above or below its mean. The covariance measures how two random variables move with each other. If two random variables, on average, are above their means at the same time and on average, are below at the same time, then the random variables would be positively correlated with each other and would have a positive covariance. In contrast, if one random variable, on average, is above its mean when another is below and vice versa, then the random variables would move inversely or negatively to each other and would have a negative covariance.

The covariance between two random variables, r_1 and r_2, is equal to the expected value of the product of the variables' deviations:

$$Cov(\tilde{r}_1\tilde{r}_2) = E[\tilde{r}_1 - E(\tilde{r}_1)][\tilde{r}_2 - E(\tilde{r}_2)]$$

$$Cov(\tilde{r}_1\tilde{r}_2) = \sum_{i=1}^{T} p_i[\tilde{r}_{1i} - E(\tilde{r}_1)][\tilde{r}_{2i} - E(\tilde{r}_2)]$$

TABLE B-2   Correlation Between Random Variables

State	P_i	r_{1i}	r_{2i}	$P_i r_{1i}$	$P_i r_{2i}$	$P_i[r_{1i} - E(r_1)]^2$	$P_i[r_{2i} - E(r_2)]^2$	$P_i[r_{1i} - E(r_1)]$ $[r_{2i} - E(r_2)]$
A	1/8	6%	24%	0.75	3.0	(1/8)(144)	(1/8)(64)	$(1/8)(-12)(8) = -12$
B	6/8	18%	16%	13.5	12.0	(6/8)(0)	(6/8)(0)	$(6/8)(0)(0) = 0$
C	1/8	30%	8%	3.75	1.0	(1/8)(144)	(1/8)(64)	$(1/8)(12)(-8) = -12$
				$E(r_1) = 18$	$E(r_2) = 6$	$V(r_1) = 36$ $\sigma(r_1) = 6$	$V(r_2) = 16$ $\sigma(r_2) = 4$	$Cov(r_1\,r_2) = -24$ $\rho_{12} = -1$

In Table B-2, the possible rates of return for Securities 1 and 2 are shown for three possible states (A, B, and C) along with the probabilities of occurrence of each state. As shown in the table, $E(r_1) = 18\%$, $V(r_1) = 36$, $E(r_2) = 16\%$, and $V(r_2) = 16$. In addition, the table also shows that in State A Security 1 yields a return below its mean, whereas Security 2 yields a return above its mean; in State B, both yield rates of return equal to their mean; in State C, Security 1 yields a return above its mean, whereas Security 2 yields a return below. Securities 1 and 2 therefore are negatively correlated and, as shown in Table B-2, have a negative covariance of -24.

CORRELATION COEFFICIENT: The correlation coefficient between two random variables r_1 and r_2 (ρ_{12}) is equal to the covariance between the variables divided by the product of each random variable's standard deviation:

$$\rho_{12} = \frac{Cov(r_1 r_2)}{\sigma(r_1)\,\sigma(r_2)}$$

The correlation coefficient has the mathematical property that its value must be within the range of minus and plus one:

$$-1 \leq \rho_{12} \leq 1$$

If two random variables have a correlation coefficient equal to one, they are said to be perfectly positively correlated; if their coefficient is equal to a minus one, they are said to be perfectly negatively correlated; if their correlation coefficient is equal to zero, they are said to be zero correlated and statistically independent. That is

If $\rho_{12} = -1 \Rightarrow$ Perfect Negative Corelation

If $\rho_{12} = 0 \Rightarrow$ Uncorrelated

If $\rho_{12} = 1 \Rightarrow$ Perfect Positive Correlation

PARAMETER ESTIMATES USING HISTORICAL AVERAGES: In most cases, we do not know the probabilities associated with the possible values of the random variable and must therefore estimate the parameter characteristics. The simplest way to estimate is to calculate the parameter's historical average value from a sample. For the rate of return on a security, this can be done by calculating the average rate of return per period or the holding period yield, HPY_t (stock HPY $= [(P_t - P_{t-1}) + \text{dividend}]/P_{t-1}$) over n historical periods:

$$\bar{r} = \frac{1}{n}\sum_{t=1}^{n} HPY_t$$

Similarly, the variance of a security can be estimated by averaging the security's squared deviations, and the covariance between two securities can be estimated by averaging the product of the securities' deviations. Note that in estimating variances and covariances, averages usually are found by dividing by n − 1 instead of n to obtain better unbiased estimates:

$$\hat{V}(r) = \frac{1}{n-1} \sum_{t=1}^{n} (HPY_t - \bar{r})^2$$

$$\hat{Cov}(r_1 r_2) = \frac{1}{n-1} \sum_{t=1}^{n} (HPY_{1t} - \bar{r}_1)(HPY_{2t} - \bar{r}_2)$$

An example of estimating parameters is shown in Table B-3 in which the average HPY, variances, and covariance are computed for a stock and a stock index (S_m).

TABLE B-3   Historical Averages and Regression Estimates

Time	S	Dividend	HPY	(HPY − Av.)	(HPY − Av.)^2
1	100	0			
2	105	0	0.050000	0.032324	0.0010448
3	110	1	0.057143	0.039467	0.0015576
4	115	0	0.045455	0.027779	0.0007716
5	110	1	−0.034783	−0.052459	0.0027519
6	105	0	−0.045455	−0.063131	0.0039855
7	100	1	−0.038095	−0.055771	0.0031104
8	105	0	0.050000	0.032324	0.0010448
9	110	1	0.057143	0.039467	0.0015576
			0.141408		0.0158244
			Av. = .017676		Var = .0022606
					Stan. Dev = .0475457

Time	S_m	R_m = HPY	(R_m − Av.)	(Rm − Av.)^2	(Rm − Av.)(HPY − Av.)
1	300				
2	315	0.050000	0.035583	0.001266	0.0011502
3	333	0.057143	0.042726	0.001825	0.0016863
4	346	0.039039	0.024622	0.000606	0.0006840
5	334	−0.034682	−0.049099	0.002411	0.0025757
6	319	−0.044910	−0.059327	0.003520	0.0037454
7	306	−0.040752	−0.055169	0.003044	0.0030769
8	320	0.045752	0.031335	0.000982	0.0010129
9	334	0.043750	0.029333	0.000860	0.0011577
		0.115339		0.014514	0.0150888
		Av. = 0.014417		Var =.0020735	Cov =.002156

$$\hat{\alpha} = \bar{r} - \hat{\beta}\bar{R}_m$$
$$= .017676 - 1.04\,(.014417) = .00268$$

$$\hat{\beta} = \frac{\hat{Cov}(r\,R_m)}{\hat{V}(R_m)} = \frac{.002156}{.002073} = 1.04$$

$$V(\varepsilon) = V(r) - \hat{\beta}^2 V(R_m)$$
$$= .0022606 - (1.04)^2 .002073 = .0000184$$

$$E(r) = \alpha + \beta E(R_m)$$
$$= .00268 + 1.04 E(R_m)$$

$$V(r) = \beta^2 V(R_m) + V(\varepsilon)$$
$$= (1.04)^2 V(R_m) + .0000184$$

LINEAR REGRESSION: Regression involves estimating the coefficients of an assumed algebraic equation. A linear regression model has only one explanatory variable; a multiple regression model has more than one independent variable. As an example, consider a linear regression model relating the rate of return on a security (dependent variable) to the market rate of return (R_m; independent variable) in which R_m is measured by the proportional change in a stock index. That is

$$\tilde{r}_j = \alpha + \beta \tilde{R}_{mj} + \varepsilon_j$$

where:
α = intercept.
β = slope = $\Delta r / \Delta R_m$
j = observation.
ε = error.

In the preceding equation, ε_j is referred to as the error term or stochastic disturbance term. Thus, the model assumes that for each observation j, errors in the relationship between r and R_m can exist, causing r to deviate from the algebraic relation defined by α and β. Because a priori the errors are not known, the regression model needs to provide assumptions concerning ε. The standard assumptions are:

$$E(\varepsilon_j) = 0$$

$$V(\varepsilon_j) \text{ does not change}$$

$$Cov(\varepsilon, R_m) = 0$$

Using the preceding assumptions and the expected value operator rules, the expected value and variance can be defined in terms of the regression model as follows:

$$E(r) = E[\alpha + \beta R_m + \varepsilon]$$

$$E(r) = \alpha + \beta E(R_m) + E(\varepsilon)$$

$$E(r) = \alpha + \beta E(R_m)$$

$$V(r) = E[r - E(r)]^2$$

$$V(r) = \beta^2 V(R_m) + V(\varepsilon)$$

The first term on the right for the equation $V(r)$ defines systematic risk: the amount of variation in r that can be attributed to the market (factors that affect all securities). The second term defines unsystematic risk: the amount of variation in r that can be attributed to factors unique to that security (industry and firm factors).

If two securities (1 and 2) both are related to R_m such as

$$r_1 = \alpha_1 + \beta_1 R_m + \varepsilon_1$$

$$r_2 = \alpha_2 + \beta_2 R_m + \varepsilon_2$$

(the j subscript is deleted) and ε_1 and ε_2 are independent ($Cov(\varepsilon_1, \varepsilon_2) = 0$), then the $Cov(r_1 r_2)$ simplifies to

$$Cov(r_1 r_2) = \beta_1 \beta_2 V(R_m)$$

The intercept and slope of the regression model can be estimated by the ordinary least squares estimation procedure. This techniques uses sample data for the dependent and independent variables (time series data or cross-sectional data) to find the estimates of α

and β that minimizes the sum of the squared errors. The estimates for α and β in which the errors are minimized are

$$\hat{\alpha} = \bar{r} - \hat{\beta}\bar{R}_m$$

$$\hat{\beta} = \frac{\hat{Cov}(rR_m)}{\hat{V}(R_m)}$$

where:
$\hat{Cov}(r, R_m), \hat{V}(R_m), \bar{r},$ and $\bar{R}_m$ are estimates (averages).

An estimate of unsystematic risk ($V\varepsilon$) can be found using the equation for $V(r)$. That is

$$\hat{V}(\varepsilon) = \hat{V}(r) - \hat{\beta}^2 V(\hat{R}_m)$$

where $V(r)$ and $V(R_m)$ can be estimated using the sample averages, and β can be estimated using the ordinary least squares estimating equation. In Table B-3, a regression model relating the rate of return on the security to the market rate as measured by the rate of change in the index is shown.

It should be noted that the coefficients between any variables can be estimated using a regression model. Whether the relationship is good or not depends on the quality of the regression model. All regression models, therefore, need to be accompanied by information about the quality of the regression results. Regression qualifiers include the coefficient of determination (R^2), t-tests, and F-tests.

APPENDIX C

BOND FUNDAMENTALS

C.1 INTRODUCTION[1]

In this appendix, we examine a number of features on bonds that are fundamental to an understanding of fixed-income securities. The features include bond value, rate of return, term structure, and bond risk.

C.2 BOND VALUATION

C.2.1 Pricing Bonds

An investor who has purchased a bond can expect to earn a possible return from the bonds' periodic coupon payments; from capital gains (or losses) when the bond is sold, called, or matures; and from interest earned from reinvesting coupon payments. Given the market price of the bond, the bond's yield is the interest rate that makes the present value of the bond's cash flow equal to the bond price. This yield takes into account these three sources of return. In Section C.3, we discuss how to solve for the bond's yield given its price. Alternatively, if we know the rate we require to buy the bond, then we can determine its value.

Like the value of any asset, the value of a bond is equal to the sum of the present values of its future cash flows:

$$V_0^b = \sum_{t=1}^{M} \frac{CF_t}{(1+R)^t} = \frac{CF_1}{(1+R)^1} + \frac{CF_2}{(1+R)^2} + \cdots + \frac{CF_M}{(1+R)^M} \qquad (C.2\text{-}1)$$

where V_0^b is the value or price of the bond, CF_t is the bond's expected cash flow in period t including both coupon income and repayment of principal, R is the discount rate, and M is the time to maturity on the bond. The discount rate is the required rate, that is, the rate investors require to buy the bond. This rate is typically estimated by determining the rate on a security with comparable characteristics.

Many bonds pay a fixed coupon interest each period, with the principal repaid at maturity. The coupon payment, C, is often quoted in terms of the bond's coupon rate, C^R. The coupon rate is the contractual rate the issuer agrees to pay on the bond. This rate is often expressed as a proportion of the bond's face value (or par) and is usually stated on an annual basis. Thus, a bond with a face value of $1,000 and a 10% coupon rate would pay an annual coupon of $100 each year for the life of the bond: $C = C^R F = (.10)($1,000) = 100.

---

[1] The material in this appendix draws from R. S. Johnson, *Bond Evaluation, Selection, and Management* (2004): Chapters 2–4.

The value of a bond paying a fixed coupon interest each year and the principal at maturity, in turn, would be

$$V_0^b = \sum_{t=1}^{M} \frac{C}{(1+R)^t} + \frac{F}{(1+R)^M} = \frac{C}{(1+R)^1} + \frac{C}{(1+R)^2} + \cdots$$

$$+ \frac{C}{(1+R)^M} + \frac{F}{(1+R)^M} \qquad \text{(C.2-2)}$$

With the coupon payment fixed each period, the C term in Equation (C.2-2) can be factored out and the bond value can be expressed as

$$V_0^b = C \sum_{t=1}^{M} \frac{1}{(1+R)^t} + \frac{F}{(1+R)^M}$$

The term $\Sigma 1/(1+R)^t$ is the present value of \$1 received each year for M years. It is defined as the present value interest factor (PVIF). The PVIF for different terms and discount rates can be found using PVIF tables found in many finance text books. It also can be calculated using the following formula:

$$\text{PVIF}(R, M) = \frac{1 - [1/(1+R)^M]}{R}$$

Thus, if investors require a 10% annual rate of return on a 10-year, high-quality, corporate bond paying a coupon equal to 9% of par each year and a principal of \$1,000 at maturity, then they would price the bond at \$938.55. That is

$$V_0^b = \sum_{t=1}^{M} \frac{C}{(1+R)^t} + \frac{F}{(1+R)^M}$$

$$V_0^b = \sum_{t=1}^{10} \frac{\$90}{(1.10)^t} + \frac{\$1000}{(1.10)^{10}}$$

$$V_0^b = \$90 \sum_{t=1}^{M} \frac{1}{(1.10)^t} + \frac{\$1000}{(1.10)^{10}}$$

$$V_0^b = \$90[\text{PVIF}(10\%, 10 \text{ yrs}] + \frac{\$1000}{(1.10)^{10}}$$

$$V_0^b = \$90 \left[\frac{1 - [1/1.10]^{10}}{.10} \right] + \frac{\$1000}{(1.10)^{10}}$$

$$V_0^b = \$938.55$$

C.2.2   Bond Price Relations

From the preceding example, several relationships should be noted. First, the value of the bond in the preceding example is not equal to its par value. This can be explained by the fact that the discount rate and coupon rate are different. Specifically, for investors in the previous case to obtain the 10% rate per year from a bond promising to pay an annual rate of $C^R = 9\%$ of par, they would have to buy the bond at a value, or price, below par: The bond would have to be purchased at a discount from its par, $V_0^b < F$.

In contrast, if the coupon rate is equal to the discount rate (i.e., R = 9%), then the bond's value would be equal to its par value, $V_0^b = F$. In this case, investors would be willing to pay $1,000 for this bond, with each investor receiving $90 each year in coupons. Finally, if the required rate is lower than the coupon rate, then investors would be willing to pay a premium over par for the bond, $V_0^b > F$. This might occur if bonds with comparable features were trading at rates below 9%. In this case, investors would be willing to pay a price above $1,000 for a bond with a coupon rate of 9%. Thus, the first relationship to note is that a bond's value (or price) will be equal, greater than, or less than its face value depending on whether the coupon rate is equal, less than, or greater than the required rate. That is

Bond-Price	**If $C^R = R \Rightarrow V^b = F$: Bond valued at par.**
Relation 1:	**If $C^R < R \Rightarrow V^b < F$: Bond valued at discount.**
	If $C^R > R \Rightarrow V^b > F$: Bond valued at premium.

The second bond relation to note follows from the first. Specifically, given known coupon and principal payments, the only way an investor can obtain a higher rate of return on a bond is for its price (value) to be lower. In contrast, the only way for a bond to yield a lower rate is for its price to be higher. Thus, an inverse relationship exists between the price of a bond and its rate of return. This, of course, is consistent with Equation (C.2-1) in which an increase in R increases the denominator and lowers V^b. Thus, the second bond relationship to note is that there is an inverse relationship between the price and rate of return on a bond. That is

Bond-Price	**If R $\uparrow \Rightarrow V^b \downarrow$**
Relation 2:	**If R $\downarrow \Rightarrow V^b \uparrow$**

The third bond relationship to note is the relation between a bond's price sensitivity to interest rate changes and its maturity. Specifically

Bond-Price	The greater the bond's maturity, the greater its price sensitivity
Relation 3:	to a given change in interest rates.

This relationship can be seen by comparing the price sensitivity to interest rate changes of the 10-year, 9% coupon bond in our previous example with a 1-year, 9% coupon bond. If the required rate is 10%, then the 10-year bond would trade at $938.55, whereas the 1-year bond would trade at $990.91 ($1,090/1.10). If the interest rate decreases to 9% for each bond (a 10% change in rates), both bonds would increase in price to $1,000. For the 10-year bond, the percentage increase in price would be 6.55% (($1,000 − $938.55)/$938.55), whereas the percentage increase for the 1-year bond would be only 0.9%. Thus, the 10-year bond is more price sensitive to the interest rate change than the 1-year bond.

Finally, consider two 10-year bonds, each priced at a discount rate of 10% and each paying a principal of $1,000 at maturity but with one bond having a coupon rate of 10%

and priced at $1,000 and the other having a coupon rate of 2% and priced at $508.43:

$$V_0^b = \sum_{t=1}^{10} \frac{\$100}{(1.10)^t} + \frac{\$1000}{(1.10)^{10}} = \$1000$$

$$V_0^b = \sum_{t=1}^{10} \frac{\$20}{(1.10)^t} + \frac{\$1000}{(1.10)^{10}} = \$508.43.$$

Now suppose that the rate required on each bond decreases to a new level of 9%. The price on the 10% coupon bond, in turn, would increase by 6.4% to equal $1,064.18, whereas the price on the 2% coupon bond would increase by 8.3% to $550.76:

$$V_0^b = \sum_{t=1}^{10} \frac{\$100}{(1.09)^t} + \frac{\$1000}{(1.10)^{10}} = \$1064.18$$

$$\text{proportional change} = \frac{\$1064.18 - \$1000}{\$1000} = .064$$

$$V_0^b = \sum_{t=1}^{10} \frac{\$20}{(1.090)^t} + \frac{\$1000}{(1.09)^{10}} = \$550.76$$

$$\text{proportional change} = \frac{\$550.76 - \$508.43}{\$508.43} = .083$$

In this case, the lower coupon bond's price is more responsive to given interest rate changes than the price of the higher coupon bond. Thus

Bond-Price Relation 4:	The lower a bond's coupon rate, the greater its price sensitivity to changes in discount rates.

C.2.3   Pricing Bonds With Different Cash Flows and Compounding Frequencies

Equation (C.2-2) can be used to value bonds that pay coupons on an annual basis and a principal at maturity. Bonds, of course, differ in the frequency in which they pay coupons each year, and many bonds have maturities less than 1 year. Also, when investors buy bonds, they often do so at noncoupon dates. Equation (C.2-2), therefore, needs to be adjusted to take these factors into account.

C.2.4   Semiannual Coupon Payments

Many bonds pay coupon interest semiannually. When bonds make semiannual payments, three adjustments to Equation (C.2-2) are necessary: (1) The number of periods is doubled, (2) the annual coupon rate is halved, (3) the annual discount rate is halved. Thus, if our illustrative 10-year, 9% coupon bond trading at a quoted annual rate of 10% paid interest semiannually instead of annually, it would be worth \$937.69. That is

$$V_0^b = \sum_{t=1}^{20} \frac{\$45}{(1.05)^t} + \frac{\$1000}{(1.05)^{20}} = \$937.69$$

$$V_0^b = \$45 \left[\frac{1 - [1/(1.05)]^{20}}{.05} \right] + \frac{\$1000}{(1.05)^{20}} = \$937.69$$

Note that the rule for valuing semiannual bonds is easily extended to valuing bonds paying interest even more frequently. For example, to determine the value of a bond paying interest four times a year, we would quadruple the periods and quarter the annual coupon payment and discount rate. In general, if we let n be equal to the number of payments per year (i.e., the compoundings per year), M be equal to the maturity in years, and, as before, R be the discount rate quoted on an annual basis, then we can express the general formula for valuing a bond as follows:

$$V_0^b = \sum_{t=1}^{Mn} \frac{C^A/n}{(1 + (R^A/n))^t} + \frac{F}{(1 + (R^A/n))^{Mn}}$$

C.2.5 Compounding Frequency

The 10% annual rate in the previous example is a simple annual rate: It is the rate with one annualized compounding. With one annualized compounding, we earn 10% every year, and \$100 would grow to equal \$110 after 1 year: \$100(1.10) = \$110. If the simple annual rate were expressed with semiannual compounding, then we would earn 5% every 6 months with the interest being reinvested; in this case, \$100 would grow to equal \$110.25 after 1 year: \$100(1.05)^2 = \$110.25. If the rate were expressed with monthly compounding, then we would earn .8333% (10%/12) every month with the interest being reinvested; in this case, \$100 would grow to equal \$110.47 after 1 year: \$100(1.008333)^{12} = \$110.47. If we extend the compounding frequency to daily, then we would earn .0274% (10%/365) daily, and with the reinvestment of interest, a \$100 investment would grow to equal \$110.52 after 1 year: \$100(1 + (.10/365))^{365} = \$110.52. Note that the rate of 10% is the simple annual rate, whereas the actual rate earned for the year is $(1 + (R^A/n))^n - 1$. This rate that includes the reinvestment of interest (or compounding) is known as the effective rate.

When the compounding becomes large, such as daily compounding, then we are approaching continuous compounding with the n term becoming very large. For cases in which there is continuous compounding, the future value (FV) for an investment of A dollars M years from now becomes

$$FV = Ae^{RM}$$

where e is the natural exponent (equal to the irrational number 2.71828). Thus, if the 10% simple rate were expressed with continuous compounding, then \$100 (A) would grow to equal \$110.52 after 1 year: $\$100e^{(.10)(1)} = \$110.52$ (allowing for some slight rounding differences, this is the value obtained with daily compounding). After 2 years, the \$100 investment would be worth \$122.14: $\$100e^{(.10)(2)} = \$122.14$.

Note that from the FV expression, the present value (A) of a future receipt (FV) is

$$A = PV = \frac{FV}{e^{RM}} = FVe^{-RM}$$

If R $=$ .10, a security paying \$100 2 years from now would be worth \$81.87, given continuous compounding: PV $=$ $100e^{-(.10)(2)} =$ \$81.87. Similarly, a security paying \$100 each year for 2 years would be currently worth \$172.36:

$$PV = \sum_{t=1}^{2} \$100e^{-(.10)(t)} = \$100e^{-(.10)(1)} + \$100e^{-(.10)(2)} = \$172.36$$

Thus, if we assume continuous compounding and a discount rate of 10%, then the value of our 10-year, 9% bond would be \$908.82:

$$V_0^b = \sum_{t=1}^{M} C^A e^{-Rt} + Fe^{-RM}$$

$$V_0^b = \sum_{t=1}^{10} \$90e^{-(.10)(t)} + \$1000e^{-(.10)(10)} = \$908.82$$

It should be noted that most practitioners use interest rates with annual or semiannual compounding. Most of our examples in this book, in turn, will follow that convention. However, continuous compounding is often used in mathematical derivations, and we make some use of it when it is helpful.

C.2.6 Valuing Bonds With Maturities Less than 1 Year

When a bond has a maturity less than 1 year, its value can be determined by discounting the bond's cash flows by the period rate. Many bonds with maturities less than a year are zero-coupon bonds (also called zeros and pure discount bonds); these bonds pay no coupons, and their returns are equal to the differences between their face values and their purchase prices. In valuing bonds with maturities less than 1 year, the convention is to discount by using an annualized rate instead of a period rate and to express the bond's maturity as a proportion of a year. Thus, on March 1, a zero-coupon bond promising to pay \$100 on September 1 (184 days) and trading at an annual discount rate of 8% would be worth \$96.19:

$$V_0^b = \frac{\$100}{(1.08)^{184/365}} = \$96.19$$

The \$96.19 bond value reflects a maturity using the actual number of days between March 1 and September 1 (184) and 365 days in the year. If we had instead assumed 30-day months and a 360-day year, then maturity expressed as a proportion of year would be .5, and the value of the bond would be $96.225(= \$100/(1.08)^{.5})$. The choice of time measurement used in valuing bonds is known as the day count convention. The day count convention is defined as the way in which the ratio of the number of days to maturity (or days between dates) to the number of days in the reference period (e.g., year) is calculated. The bond value of \$96.19 is based on a day count convention of actual days to maturity to actual days in the year (actual/actual), whereas the value of \$96.225 is based on a day count convention of 180 days to maturity (30 days times 6) to 360 days in the year (30/360). For short-term U.S. Treasury bills and other money market securities, the convention is to use actual number of days based on a 360-day year. In this book, the day count convention varies.

C.2.7   Valuing Bonds at Non-Coupon Dates

Equations (C.2-2) can be used to value bonds at dates in which the coupons are to be paid in exactly one period. However, most bonds purchased in the secondary market are not bought on coupon dates but rather at dates in between coupon dates. An investor who purchases a bond between coupon payments must compensate the seller for the coupon interest earned from the time of the last coupon payment to the settlement date of the bond. This amount is known as accrued interest. The formula for determining accrued interest is

$$\text{Accrued Interest} = \left[\frac{\text{Days from last coupon}}{\text{Days between last coupon and next coupon}} \right] [\text{Coupon Interest}]$$

In calculating the accrued interest, the ratio of days since the last coupon date to the days between coupon dates depends on the day count convention specified in the bond contract. For U.S. Treasury bonds, the convention is to use the actual number of days since the last coupon date and the actual number of days between coupon payments: an actual:actual ratio; for many corporate and municipal bonds, the practice is to use 30-day months and a 360-day year: 30:360 ratio.

The amount the buyer pays to the seller is the agreed-on price plus the accrued interest. This amount is often called the full price or dirty price. The price of a bond without accrued interest is called the clean price:

$$\text{Full Price} = \text{Clean Price} + \text{Accrued Interest}.$$

As an example, consider a 9% coupon bond with coupon payments made semiannually and with a principal of $1,000 paid at maturity. Suppose the bond is trading to yield a simple annual rate of $R = 10\%$ (or effective rate of 10.25%) and has a current maturity of 5.25 years. The clean price of the bond is found by first determining the value of the bond at the next coupon date. In this case, the value of the bond at the next coupon date would be $961.39:

$$V_0^b(5 \text{ years}) = \sum_{t=1}^{(5)(2)} \frac{\$90/2}{(1 + (.10/2))^t} + \frac{\$1000}{(1 + (.10/2))^{10}} = \$961.39$$

$$V_0^b(5 \text{ years}) = \$45 \left[\frac{1 - [1/(1.05)]^{10}}{.05} \right] + \frac{\$1000}{(1.05)^{10}} = \$961.39$$

Next, we add the $45 coupon payment scheduled to be received at that date to the $961.39 value:

$$\$961.39 + \$45 = \$1,006.39$$

The value of $1,006.39 represents the value of bond 3 months from the present. Discounting this value back 3 months and using a day count convention of 30/360 (3 months/6months) yields the bond's current value of $982.14:

$$V_0^b(5.25 \text{ years}) = \frac{\$1006.39}{(1.05)^{3/6}} = \frac{\$1006.39}{(1.1025)^{3/12}} = \$982.14$$

Finally, because the accrued interest of the bond at the next coupon payment goes to the seller, this amount is subtracted from the bond's value to obtain the clean price. Using again a 30/360 day count convention, the accrued interest is $22.50, and the clean price is $959.64:

$$\text{Accrued Interest} = \left[\frac{3\ \text{Months}}{6\ \text{Months}}\right](\$45) = \$22.50$$

$$\text{Clean Price} = \$982.14 - \$22.50 = \$959.64$$

Thus, the bond's full price (or dirty price) is $982.14, which is equal to its clean price of $959.64 plus the accrued interest of $22.50.

C.2.8 Price Quotes, Fractions, and Basis Points

Although many corporate bonds pay principals of $1,000, this is not the case for many noncorporate bonds and other fixed-income securities. As a result, many traders quote bond prices as a percentage of their par value. For example, if a bond is selling at par, it would be quoted at 100 (100% of par); thus, a bond with a face value of $10,000 and quoted at 80-1/8 would be selling at $(.80125)(\$10,000) = \$8,012.50$. When a bond's price is quoted as a percentage of its par, the quote is usually expressed in points and fractions of a point, with each point equal to $1. Thus, a quote of 97 points means that the bond is selling for $97 for each $100 of par. The fractions of points differ among bonds. Fractions are either in thirds, eighths, quarters, halves, or 64ths. On a $100 basis, a 1/2 point is $0.50 and a 1/32 point is $0.03125. A price quote of 97-4/32 (97-4) is 97.125 for a bond with a 100 face value. Bonds expressed in 64ths usually are denoted in the financial pages with a plus sign (+); for example, 100.2+ would indicate a price of 100 2/64.

It should also be noted that when the yield on a bond or other security changes over a short period, such as a day, the yield and subsequent price changes are usually quite small. As a result, fractions on yields are often quoted in terms of basis points (BP). A BP is equal to 1/100 of a percentage point. Thus, 6.5% may be quoted as 6% plus 50 BP or 650 BP, and an increase in yield from 6.5% to 6.55% would represent an increase of 5 BP.

C.3 THE YIELD TO MATURITY AND OTHER RATES OF RETURN MEASURES

The financial markets serve as conduits through which funds are distributed from borrowers to lenders. The allocation of funds is determined by the relative rates paid on bonds, loans, and other financial securities, with the differences in rates among claims being determined by risk, maturity, and other factors that serve to differentiate the claims. There are a number of different measures of the rates of return on bonds and loans. Some measures, for example, determine annual rates based on cash flows received over 365 days, whereas others use 360 days; some measures determine rates that include the compounding of cash flows, whereas some do not; and some measures include capital gains and losses, whereas others exclude price changes. The most common measures of rate are the yield to maturity, the annual realized return, and the geometric mean.

C.3.1 Yield to Maturity

The most widely used measure of a bond's rate of return is the yield to maturity (YTM). As noted earlier, the YTM, or simply the yield, is the rate that equates the purchase price of the bond, P_0^b, with the present value of its future cash flows. Mathematically, the YTM is found by solving the following equation for y (YTM):

$$P_0^b = \sum_{t=1}^{M} \frac{CF_t}{(1+y)^t}$$

The YTM is analogous to the internal rate of return used in capital budgeting. It is a measure of the rate at which the investment grows. From our first example, if the 10-year, 9% annual coupon bond were actually trading in the market for $938.55, then the YTM on the bond would be 10%. Unlike the current yield, the YTM incorporates all of the bonds cash flows (CFs). It also assumes the bond is held to maturity and that all CFs from the bond are reinvested to maturity at the calculated YTM.

C.3.1.1 Rates on Zero-Coupon Bonds: Spot Rates

Although no algebraic solution for the YTM exists when a bond pays coupons and principal that are not equal, a solution does exists in the case of a zero-coupon bond or pure discount bonds, PDBs, (we use both expressions) in which there is only one cash flow (F). That is

$$P_0^b = \frac{F}{(1+YTM_M)^M}$$

$$(1+YTM_M)^M = \frac{F}{P_0^b}$$

$$YTM_M = \left[\frac{F}{P_0^b}\right]^{1/M} - 1$$

where : M = maturity in years.

Thus, a pure discount bond with a par value of $1,000, a maturity of 3 years, and trading for $800 would have an annualized YTM of 7.72%:

$$YTM_3 = \left[\frac{\$1000}{\$800}\right]^{1/3} - 1 = .0772$$

Similarly, a pure discount bond paying $100 at the end of 182 days and trading at $96 would yield an annual rate using a 365-day year of 8.53%:

$$YTM = \left[\frac{\$100}{\$96}\right]^{365/182} - 1 = .0853$$

C.3.1.2 Rate on Pure Discount Bond With Continuous Compounding

Using the properties of logarithms (see Appendix A), the rate on a pure discount bond with continuous compounding is

$$P_0^b e^{Rt} = F$$

$$e^{Rt} = \frac{F}{P_0^b}$$

$$\ln(e^{Rt}) = \ln\left[\frac{F}{P_0^b}\right]$$

$$Rt = \ln\left[\frac{F}{P_0^b}\right]$$

$$R = \frac{\ln[F/P_0^b]}{t}$$

A pure discount bond selling for \$96 and paying \$100 at the end of 182 days would yield an annual rate of 8.1868% with continuous compounding:

$$R = \frac{\ln[\$100/\$96]}{182/365} = .081868$$

When the rate of return on a security is expressed as the natural log of the ratio of its end of the period value to its current value, the rate is referred to as the logarithmic return. Thus, a bond currently priced at \$96 and expected to be worth \$100 at the end of the period would have an expected logarithmic return of 4.082%: $R = \ln(\$100/96) = .04082$

It should be noted that the rate on a pure discount bond is called the spot rate. As we see next, spot rates are important in determining a bond's equilibrium price.

C.3.1.3   Spot Rates and Equilibrium Prices

We previously examined how bonds are valued by discounting their cash flows at a common discount rate. Given different spot rates on similar bonds with different maturities, the correct approach to valuing a bond, though, is to price it by discounting each of the bond's cash flows, CFs, by the appropriate spot rates for that period (S_t). Theoretically, if the market does not price a bond with spot rates, arbitrageurs would be able to realize a risk-free return by buying the bond and stripping it into a number of pure discount bonds or by buying strip bonds and bundling them into a coupon bond to sell. Thus, in the absence of arbitrage, the equilibrium price of a bond is determined by discounting each of its CFs by their appropriate spot rates.

To illustrate this relationship, suppose there are three risk-free pure discount bonds, each with principals of \$100 and trading at annualized spot rates of $S_1 = 7\%$, $S_2 = 8\%$, and $S_3 = 9\%$, respectively. If we discount the CF of a 3-year, 8% annual coupon bond paying a principal of \$100 at maturity at these spot rates, its equilibrium price, P_0^*, would be \$97.73:

$$P_0^* = \frac{C_1}{(1+S_1)^1} + \frac{C_2}{(1+S_2)^2} + \frac{C_3+F}{(1+S_3)^3}$$

$$P_0^* = \frac{\$8}{(1.07)^1} + \frac{\$8}{(1.08)^2} + \frac{\$108}{(1.09)^3} = \$97.73$$

Suppose this coupon bond were trading in the market at a price (P_0^M) of \$95.03 to yield 10%:

$$P_0^M = \sum_{t=1}^{3} \frac{\$8}{(1.10)^t} + \frac{\$100}{(1.10)^3} = \$95.03$$

At the price of \$95.03, an arbitrageur could buy the bond and then strip it into three risk-free pure discount bonds: a 1-year pure discount bond paying \$8 at maturity, a 1-year pure discount bond paying \$8 at maturity, and a 3-year pure discount bond paying \$108 at maturity. If the arbitrageur could sell the bonds at their appropriate spot rates, she would be able to realize a cash flow from the sale of 97.73 and a risk-free profit of $2.70. Given this risk-free opportunity, this arbitrageur, as well as others, would implement this strategy of buying and stripping the bond until the price of the coupon bond was bid up to equal its equilibrium price of $97.73.

On the other hand, if the 8% coupon bond were trading above its equilibrium price of $97.73, then arbitrageurs could profit by reversing the preceding strategy. For example, if the coupon bond were trading at $100, then arbitrageurs would be able to go into the market and buy proportions (assuming perfect divisibility) of the three risk-free, pure discount bonds (8% of Bond 1, 8% of Bond 2, and 108% of Bond 3) at a cost of $97.73 and bundle them into one 3-year, 8% coupon bond to be sold at $100. This strategy would result in a risk-free profit of $2.27.

C.3.2 Annual Realized Return

A useful extension of Equation for the PDB is the annual realized return, ARR (also called the average realized return and the total return). The ARR is the annual rate earned on a bond for the period from when the bond is bought to when it is converted to cash (which could be either maturity or a date prior to maturity if the bond is sold), with the assumption that all coupons paid on the bond are reinvested to that date. The ARR is computed by first determining the investor's horizon date, HD, defined as the date the investor needs cash; next finding the HD value, defined as the total funds the investor would have at his HD; and third solving for the ARR.

To illustrate, suppose an investor buys a 4-year, 10% annual coupon bond selling at its par value of $1,000. Assume the investor needs cash at the end of Year 3 (HD = 3), is certain he can reinvest the coupons during the period in securities yielding 10%, and expects to sell the bond at his HD at a rate of 10%. To determine the investor's ARR, we first need to find the HD value. This value is equal to the price the investor obtains from selling the bond and the value of the coupons at the HD. In this case, the investor, at his HD, will be able to sell a 1-year bond paying a $100 coupon and a $1,000 par at maturity for $1,000, given the assumed discount rate of 10%. That is

$$P_0^b = \frac{\$100 + \$1000}{(1.10)^1} = \$1000$$

Also at the HD, the $100 coupon paid at the end of the 1st year will be worth $121, given the assumption it can be reinvested at 10% for 2 years, $100(1.10)^2 = \$121$, and the $100 received at the end of Year 2 will, in turn, be worth $110 in cash at the HD, $100(1.10) = \$110$. Finally, at the HD, the investor would receive his third coupon of $100. Combined, the investor would have $1,331 in cash at the HD: HD value = $1,331 (see Exhibit C.3-1).

Given the HD value of $1,331, the ARR is found in the same way as the YTM for a pure discount bond. In this case, a $1,000 investment in a bond yielding $1,331 at the end of Year 3 yields an ARR of 10%:

$$P_0^b = \frac{\text{HD Value}}{(1 + \text{ARR})^{\text{HD}}}$$

$$(1 + \text{ARR})^{\text{HD}} = \frac{\text{HD Value}}{P_0^b}$$

EXHIBIT C.3-1   Annual Realized Return: ARR

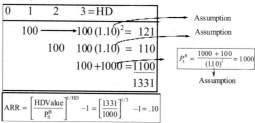

- Example: You buy 4-year, 10% annual coupon bond at par (F = 1000). <u>Assuming</u> you can reinvest CFs at 10%, your ARR would be 10%:

$$
\text{ARR} = \left[\frac{\text{HD Value}}{P_0^b} \right]^{1/\text{HD}} - 1
$$

$$
\text{ARR} = \left[\frac{\$1331}{\$1000} \right]^{1/3} - 1 = .10
$$

In this case, obtaining an ARR equal to the initial YTM should not be surprising because the coupons are assumed to be reinvested at the same rate as the initial YTM (10%), and the bond is also assumed to be sold at that rate as well (recall that the YTM measure implicitly assumes that all coupons are reinvested at the calculated YTM). If the coupons were expected to be reinvested at different rates or the bond sold at a different YTM, then an ARR equal to the initial YTM would not have been realized. Such differences, in turn, can be explained in terms of market risk

C.3.3   Geometric Mean

Another useful measure of the return on a bond is its geometric mean. Conceptually, the geometric mean can be viewed as an average of current and future rates. To see this, consider one of our previous examples in which we computed a YTM of 7.72% for a pure discount bond selling for $800 and paying $1,000 at the end of Year 3. The rate of 7.72% represents the annual rate at which $800 must grow to be worth $1,000 at the end of 3 years. If we do not restrict ourselves to the same rate in each year, there are other ways $800 could grow to equal $1,000 at the end of 3 years. For example, suppose 1-year bonds are currently trading at a 10% rate, a 1-year bond purchased 1 year from the present is expected to yield 8% ($R_{Mt} = R_{11} = 8\%$), and a 1-year bond to be purchased 2 years from the present is expected to be 5.219% ($R_{Mt} = R_{12} = 5.219\%$). With these rates, $800 would grow to $1,000 at the end of Year 3. Specifically, $800 after the 1st year would be $880 = $800(1.10); after the second, $950.40 = $800(1.10)(1.08); and after the third, $1,000 = $800(1.10)(1.08)(1.05219). Thus, an investment of $800 that yielded $1,000 at the end of 3 years could be thought of as an investment that yielded 10% the 1st year, 8% the 2nd year, and 5.219% the 3rd year. Moreover, 7.72% can be viewed not only as the annual rate in which $800 can grow to equal $1,000 but also as the average of three rates: 1-year bonds today ($R_{Mt} = R_{10}$), 1-year bonds available 1 year from the present ($R_{Mt} = R_{11}$), and 1-year bonds available 2 years from the present ($R_{Mt} = R_{12}$). That is

$$P_0^b(1 + YTM_M)^M = F = P_0^b[(1 + YTM_1)(1 + R_{11})(1 + R_{12})(1 + R_{13})\cdots(1 + R_{1,M-1})]$$

$$(1 + YTM_M)^M = \frac{F}{P_0^b} = [(1 + YTM_1)(1 + R_{11})(1 + R_{12})(1 + R_{13})\cdots(1 + R_{1,M-1})]$$

$$(1.0772)^3 = \frac{\$1000}{\$800} = [(1.10)(1.08)(1.05219)]$$

Mathematically, the expression for the average rate on an M-year bond in terms of today's and future 1-year rates can be found by solving the preceding equation for YTM_M. This yields

$$YTM_M = [(1 + YTM_1)(1 + R_{11})(1 + R_{12})(1 + R_{13})\cdots(1 + R_{1,M-1})]^{1/M} - 1$$

$$YTM_3 = [(1.10)(1.08)(1.05219)]^{1/3} - 1 = .0772$$

The preceding equation defines the rate of return on an M-year bond in terms of rates that are expected in the future. A more practical rate than an expected rate, though, is the implied forward rate.

C.3.3.1   Implied Forward Rate

An implied forward rate, f_{Mt}, is a future rate of return implied by the present interest rate structure. This rate can be attained by going long and short in current bonds. To see this, suppose the rate on a 1-year, pure discount bond is 10% (i.e., spot rate is $S_1 = 10\%$), and the rate on a similar 2-year pure discount bond is $S_2 = 9\%$. Knowing today's rates, we could solve for f_{11} in the equation following to determine the implied forward rate. That is

$$S_2 = [(1 + S_1)(1 + f_{11})]^{1/2} - 1$$

$$f_{11} = \frac{(1 + S_2)^2}{(1 + S_1)} - 1$$

$$f_{11} = \frac{(1.09)^2}{(1.10)} - 1 = .08$$

With 1-year and 2-year pure discount bonds presently trading at 9% and 10%, respectively, the rate implied on 1-year bonds to be bought 1 year from the present is 8%. This 8% rate, though, is simply an algebraic result. This rate actually can be attained, however, by implementing the following locking-in strategy:

(1) sell the 1-year pure discount bond short (or borrow an equivalent amount of funds at the 1-year pure discount bond (spot) rate);

(2) use the cash funds from the short sale (or loan) to buy a multiple of the 2-year pure discount bond;

(3) cover the short sale (or pay the loan principal and interest) at the end of the 1st year;

(4) collect on the maturing 2-year bond at the end of the 2nd year.

In terms of the previous example, the 8% implied forward rate is obtained by

(1) executing a short sale by borrowing the 1-year bond and selling it at its market price of $909.09 = \$1,000/1.10$ (or borrowing $909.09 at 10%);

(2) with 2-year bonds trading at $841.68 = $1,000/(1.09)^2$, buying $909.09/$841.68 = 1.08 issues of the 2-year bond;

(3) at the end of the 1st year, covering the short sale by paying the holder of the 1-year bond his principal of $1,000 (or repay loan);

(4) at the end of the 2nd year, receiving the principal on the maturing 2-year bond issues of $(1.08)($1,000) = $1,080$.

With this locking-in strategy the investor does not make a cash investment until the end of the 1st year when he covers the short sale; in the present, the investor simply initiates the strategy. Thus, the investment of $1,000 is made at the end of the 1st year. In turn, the return on the investment is the principal payment of $1,080 on the 1.08 holdings of the 2-year bonds that comes 1 year after the investment is made. Moreover, the rate of return on this 1-year investment is 8% $(($1,080 − $1,000)/$1,000)$. Hence, by using a locking-in strategy, an 8% rate of return on a 1-year investment to be made 1 year in the future is attained, with the rate being the same rate obtained by solving algebraically for f_{11}.

Given the concept of implied forward rates, the geometric mean now can be formally defined as the geometric average of the current 1-year spot rate and the implied forward rates. That is

$$YTM_M = [(1 + YTM_1)(1 + f_{11})(1 + f_{12})(1 + f_{13}) \cdots (1 + f_{1,M-1})]^{1/M} - 1$$

Two points regarding the geometric mean should be noted. First, the geometric mean is not limited to 1-year rates. That is, just as 7.72% can be thought of as an average of three 1-year rates of 10%, 8%, and 5.219%, an implied rate on a 2-year bond purchased at the end of 1 year, $f_{Mt} = f_{21}$, can be thought of as the average of 1-year implied rates purchased 1 and 2 years, respectively, from now. Thus

$$YTM_3 = [(1 + YTM_1)(1 + f_{11})(1 + f_{12})]^{1/3} - 1$$

$$YTM_3 = [(1 + YTM_1)(1 + f_{21})^2]^{1/3} - 1$$

$$YTM_3 = [(1 + YTM_2)^2(1 + f_{12})]^{1/3} - 1$$

Secondly, note that for bonds with maturities of less than 1 year, the same general formula for the geometric mean applies. For example, the annualized YTM on a pure discount bond maturing in 182 days (YTM_{182}) is equal to the geometric average of a current 91-day bond's annualized rate (YTM_{91}) and the annualized implied forward rate on a 91-day investment made 91 days from the present, $f_{91,91}$:

$$YTM_{182} = [(1 + YTM_{91})^{91/365}(1 + f_{91,91})^{91/365}]^{365/182} - 1$$

Thus, if a 182-day pure discount bond were trading at $P_0^b(182) = \$97$ (assume F of $100), and a comparable 91-day bond were at $P_0^b(91) = 98.35$, then the implied forward rate on a 91-day bond purchased 91 days later would be 5.7%. That is

$$YTM_{182} = \left[\frac{100}{97}\right]^{365/182} - 1 = .063$$

$$YTM_{91} = \left[\frac{100}{98.35}\right]^{365/91} - 1 = .069$$

$$f_{91,91} = \left[\frac{(1 + YTM_{182})^{182/365}}{(1 + YTM_{91})^{91/365}} \right]^{365/91} - 1$$

$$f_{91,91} = \left[\frac{(1.063)^{182/365}}{(1.069)^{91/365}} \right]^{365/91} - 1 = .057$$

C.4 TERM STRUCTURE OF INTEREST RATES

In the financial literature, the relationship between the yields on financial assets and their maturities is referred to as the term structure of interest rates. Term structure is often depicted graphically by a yield curve: a plot of YTM against maturities for bonds that are otherwise alike. Yield curves have tended to take on one of the three shapes shown in Figure C.4-1. They can be positively sloped with long-term rates being greater than shorter-term ones. Such yield curves are called normal or upward sloping curves. They are usually convex from below, with the YTM flattening out at higher maturities. Yield curves can also be negatively sloped, with short-term rates greater than long-term ones. These curves are known as inverted or downward sloping yield curves. Like normal curves, these curves also tend to be convex, with the yields flattening out at the higher maturities. Finally, yield curves can be relatively flat, with YTM being invariant to maturity. Occasionally a yield curve can take on a more complicated shape in which it can have both positively sloped and negatively sloped portions; these are often referred to as a humped yield curve. Four theories have evolved over the years to try to explain the shapes of yield curves: market segmentation theory (MST), preferred habitat theory (PHT), pure expectation theory (PET), and the liquidity premium theory (LPT).

C.4.1 Market Segmentation Theory

Market segmentation theory (MST) posits that investors and borrowers have strong maturity preferences that they try to attain when they invest in or issue fixed income securities. As a result of these preferences, the financial markets, according to MST, are segmented into a number of smaller markets, with supply and demand forces unique to each segment determining the equilibrium yields for each segment. Thus, according to MST, the major factors that determine the interest rate for a maturity segment are supply and demand conditions unique to the maturity segment. For example, the yield curve for high-quality

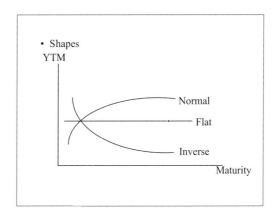

FIGURE C.4-1 Yield Curve Shapes

corporate bonds could be segmented into three markets: short-term, intermediate term, and long-term. The supply of short-term corporate bonds, such as commercial paper, would depend on business demand for short-term assets such as inventories, accounts receivables, and the like; whereas the demand for short-term corporate bonds would emanate from investors looking to invest their excess cash for short periods. The demand for short-term bonds by investors and the supply of such bonds by corporations would ultimately determine the rate on short-term corporate bonds. Similarly, the supplies of intermediate and long-term bonds would come from corporations trying to finance their intermediate and long-term assets (plant expansion, equipment purchases, acquisitions, etc.), whereas the demand for such bonds would come from investors, either directly or indirectly through institutions (e.g., pension funds, mutual funds, insurance companies, etc.) that have long-term liabilities. The supply and demand for intermediate funds would, in turn, determine the equilibrium rates on such bonds, whereas the supply and demand for long-term bonds would determine the equilibrium rates on long-term debt securities.

Important to MST is the idea of unique or independent markets. According to MST, the short-term bond market is unaffected by rates determined in the intermediate or long-term markets and vice versa. This independence assumption is based on the premise that investors and borrowers have a strong need to match the maturities of their assets and liabilities. For example, an oil company building a refinery with an estimated life of 20 years would prefer to finance that asset by selling a 20-year bond. If the company were to finance with a 10-year note, for example, it would be exposed to market risk in which it would have to raise new funds at an uncertain rate at the end of 10 years. Similarly, a life insurance company with an anticipated liability in 15 years would prefer to invest its premiums in 15-year bonds; a money market manager with excess funds for 90 days would prefer to hedge by investing in a money market security; and a corporation financing its accounts receivable would prefer to finance the receivables by selling short-term securities. Moreover, according to MST, the desire by investors and borrowers to avoid market risk leads to hedging practices that tend to segment the markets for bonds of different maturities.

C.4.2   Preferred Habitat Theory

MST assumes that investors and borrowers have preferred maturity segments or habitats determined by the maturities of their securities that they want to maintain. The preferred habitat theory (PHT) posits that investors and borrowers may stray away from desired maturity segments if there are relatively better rates to compensate them. Furthermore, PHT asserts that investors and borrowers will be induced to forego their perfect hedges and shift out of their preferred maturity segments when supply and demand conditions in different maturity markets do not match.

C.4.3   Pure Expectations Theory

Expectations theories try to explain the impact of investors' and borrowers' expectations on the term structure of interest rates. A popular model is the pure expectation theory (PET), also called the unbiased expectations theory (UET). Developed by Fredrick Lutz, PET is based on the premise that the interest rates on bonds of different maturities can be determined in equilibrium in which implied forward rates are equal to expected spot rates.

To illustrate PET, consider a market consisting of only two bonds: a risk-free, 1-year, zero-coupon bond and a risk-free, two-year, zero-coupon bond, both with principals of $1,000. Suppose that supply and demand conditions are such that both the 1-year and 2-year bonds are trading at an 8% YTM. Also suppose that the market expects the yield curve to shift up to 10% next year but as yet has not factored that expectation into its current investment decisions (see Exhibit C.4-1). Finally, assume the market is risk neutral such that investors do not require a risk premium for investing in risky securities (i.e., they will accept an expected rate on a risky investment that is equal to the risk-free rate). To see the impact of market expectations on the current structure of rates, consider the case of investors with horizon dates of 2 years. These investors can buy the 2-year bond with an annual rate of 8%, or they can buy the 1-year bond yielding 8%, then reinvest the principal and interest 1 year later in another 1-year bond expected to yield 10%. Given these alternatives, such investors would prefer the latter investment because it yields a higher expected average annual rate for the 2 years of 9%:

$$E(R) = [(1.08)(1.10)]^{1/2} - 1 = .09$$

Similarly, investors with 1-year horizon dates would also find it advantageous to buy a 1-year bond yielding 8% than a 2-year bond (priced at $857.34 = \$1,000/1.08^2$) that

EXHIBIT C.4-1   Pure Expectations Theory: Market Expectation of Higher Interest Rate

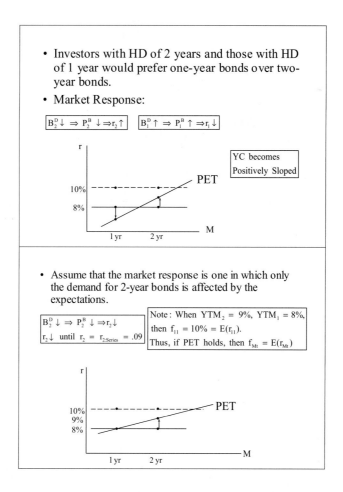

they would sell 1 year later to earn an expected rate of only 6%:

$$P_{Mt} = P_{2,0} = \frac{\$1,000}{(1.08)^2} = \$857.34$$

$$E(P_{11}) = \frac{\$1,000}{(1.10)^1} = \$909.09$$

$$E(R) = \frac{\$909.09 - \$857.34}{\$857.34} = .06$$

Thus, in a risk-neutral market with an expectation of higher rates next year, both investors with 1-year horizon dates and investors with 2-year horizon dates would purchase 1-year instead of 2-year bonds. If enough investors do this, an increase in the demand for 1-year bonds and a decrease in the demand for 2-year bonds would occur until the average annual rate on the 2-year bond is equal to the equivalent annual rate from the series of 1-year investments (or the 1-year bond's rate is equal to the rate expected on the 2-year bond held 1 year). In the example, if the price on a 2-year bond fell such that it traded at a YTM of 9%, and the rate on a 1-year bond stayed at 8%, then investors with 2-year horizon dates would be indifferent between a 2-year bond yielding a certain 9% and a series of 1-year bonds yielding 10% and 8%, for an expected rate of 9%. Investors with 1-year horizon dates would likewise be indifferent between a 1-year bond yielding 8% and a 2-year bond purchased at 9% and sold 1 year later at 10%, for an expected 1-year rate of 8%. Thus, in this case, the impact of the market's expectation of higher rates would be to push the longer term rates up. In this example, the equilibrium YTM on the 2-year bond is 9%, and the equilibrium YTM on the 1-year bond is 8%, yielding an implied forward rate of 10%, the same as the expected rate on a 1-year bond 1 year from now.

C.4.4 Liquidity Premium Theory

The liquidity premium theory (LPT), also referred to as the risk premium theory (RPT), posits that there is a liquidity premium for long-term bonds over short-term bonds. Recall how long-term bonds are more price sensitive to interest rate changes than short-term bonds. As a result, the prices of long-term securities tend to be more volatile and therefore more risky than short-term securities. According to LPT, if investors were risk averse, then they would require some additional return (liquidity premium) to hold long-term bonds instead of short-term ones.

C.5 BOND RISK

Investment risk is the uncertainty that the actual rate of return realized from an investment will differ from the expected rate. There are three types of risk associated with bonds and fixed income securities: default risk, call risk, and market risk.

C.5.1 Default Risk

Default risk (or credit risk) is the risk that the borrower/issuer will not meet all promises at the agreed-on times. A failure to meet any of the interest payments, the principal obligation, or other terms specified in the indenture (e.g., sinking fund arrangements, collateral requirements, or other protective covenants) places the borrower/issuer in default. If issuers default, they can file for bankruptcy, their bondholders/creditors can sue for bankruptcy, or both parties can work out an agreement. Many large institutional investors have their own credit analysis departments to evaluate bond issues to determine the abilities of companies to meet their contractual obligations. However, individual bond investors, as well as some institutional investors, usually do not make an independent evaluation of a bond's chance of default. Instead, they rely on bond rating companies. Currently, the major rating companies in the United States are Moody's Investment Services, Standard and Poor's, and Fitch Investors Service. These companies evaluate bonds by giving them a quality rating in the form of a letter grade. The grades start at "A" with three groups: Triple A bonds (Aaa for Moody's and AAA for Standard and Poor's) for the highest grade bonds, double A (Aa or AA) for bonds that are considered prime, and single A for those considered high quality. Grade A bonds are followed by "B" rated bonds, classified as either triple B (Baa or BBB) that have a medium grade, double B (Ba or BB), and single B. Finally, there are C-grade and lower grade bonds.

C.5.2   Call Risk

Call risk relates to the uncertainty that the issuer will call the bond. A call feature on a bond gives the issuer the right to buy back the bond before maturity at a stated price, known as the call price. The call price usually is set a certain percentage above the bond's par value, say 110 ($1,100 given a par value of $1,000); for some bonds, the call price may decrease over time (e.g., a 20-year bond's call price decreasing each year by 5%). Some callable bonds can be called at any time, whereas for others, the call is deferred for a certain period, giving the investor protection during the deferment period. Also, some bonds, as part of their sinking fund arrangements, are retired over the life of the bond, usually with the issuer having the choice of purchasing the bonds directly at market prices or calling the bonds at a specified call price.

A call provision is advantageous to the issuer. If interest rates in the market decline, an issuer can lower his interest costs by selling a new issue at a lower interest rate, then use the loan proceeds to call the outstanding issue. What is to the advantage of the issuer, though, is to the disadvantage of the investor. When a bond is called, the investor's realized rate of return is affected in two ways. First, because the call price is typically above the bond's face value, the actual rate of return the investor earns for the period from the purchase of the bond to its call generally is greater than the yield on the bond at the time it was purchased. However, if an investor originally bought the bond because its maturity matched her horizon date, then she will be faced with the disadvantage of reinvesting the call proceeds at lower market rates. Moreover, this second effect, known as reinvestment risk, often dominates the first effect, resulting in a rate of return over the investor's horizon period that is lower than the promised YTM when the bond was bought.

C.5.3   Market Risk

Market risk is the uncertainty that interest rates in the market will change, causing the actual rate of return earned on the bond to differ from the expected return. A change in interest rates has two effects on a bond's return. First, interest rate changes affect the price of a bond; this is referred to as price risk. If the investor's horizon date, HD, is different from the bond's maturity date, then the investor will be uncertain about the price he will receive from selling the bond (if HD < M) or the price he will have to pay for a new bond (if HD > M). Second, interest rate changes affect the return the investor expects from reinvesting the coupon—reinvestment risk. Thus, if an investor buys a coupon bond, he automatically is subject to market risk. One obvious way an investor can eliminate market risk is to purchase a pure discount bond with a maturity that is equal to the investor's horizon date. If such a bond does not exist (or does but does not yield an adequate rate), then an investor can minimize market risk by purchasing a bond with a duration equal to her horizon date. A bond's duration (D) can be defined as the weighted average of the bond's time periods, with the weights being each time period's relative present value of its cash flow:

$$D = \sum_{t=1}^{M} t \frac{PV(CF_t)}{P_0^b}$$

C.5.4 Duration

In addition to being the weighted average of a bond's time periods, duration is also an important measure of volatility. As a measure of volatility, duration is defined as the percentage change in a bond's price ($\%\Delta P = \Delta P/P_0$) given a small change in yield, dy. Mathematically, duration is obtained by taking the derivative of the equation for the price of a bond with respect to the yield and then dividing by the bond's price. Doing this yields

$$Duration = \frac{dP/P}{dy} = -\frac{1}{(1+y)} \left(\sum_{t=1}^{M} t \frac{PV(CF_t)}{P_0^B} \right)$$

where
dP/P_0 = percentage change in the bond's price.
dy = small change in yield.

The bracketed expression in the preceding equation is the weighted average of the time periods. Formally, the weighted average of the time periods is called Macaulay's duration, and the percentage change in the bond's price for a small change in yield is called the modified duration. Thus, the modified duration is equal to the negative of Macaulay's duration divided by $1 + y$:

$$Modified\ Duration = -\frac{1}{(1+y)} [Macaulay's\ Duration]$$

$$Macaulay's\ Duration = \left(\sum_{t=1}^{M} t \frac{PV(CF_t)}{P_0^B} \right)$$

SELECTED REFERENCES

Fabozzi, F. J. *Fixed Income Mathematics*. Chicago: Probus, 1988.
Fabozzi, F. J. *Bond Markets, Analysis and Strategies,* 3rd ed. Upper Saddle River, NJ: Prentice-Hall, 1996.
Johnson, R. S. *Bond Evaluation, Selection, and Management*. Malden, MA: Blackwell Publishing, 2004: Chapters 2–3.
Radcliffe, R. C. *Investment Concepts, Analysis, and Strategy*. Glenview, IL: Scott, Foresman and Company, 1982.
Rose, P. S. *Money and Capital Markets*. New York: McGraw-Hill/Irwin, 2003.

APPENDIX D

GUIDE TO DERIVATIVE EXCEL PROGRAMS

The Derivative Excel spreadsheets package included with the text contains a number of programs for evaluating and pricing spot options, futures options, bonds, bonds with embedded options, and mortgage-backed securities. The programs can be used to solve a number of Excel problems in the text as well as check the answers to many of the problems and questions in this book.

D.1 SPREADSHEET PROGRAMS

The disc includes programs in the following files and folders:

1. Option Strategies (file)
2. Binomial Option Pricing Model (file)
3. Known Dividend-Payment Binomial Model (file)
4. Black–Scholes Option Pricing Model (file)
5. Implied Volatility (file)
6. Binomial Interest Rates (folder)
7. Mortgage-Backed Securities (folder)
8. Bond Programs (file)

D.1.1 Option Strategies

The option strategies program consists of three worksheets that can be used to determine the profits at various asset prices for different option strategies. The user can construct her option strategies by selecting the positions that make up the strategy from a menu. The spreadsheet's three worksheets include

1. **Basic Option Strategies**: This worksheet determines profits at expiration based on the options' intrinsic values.
2. **Timed Option Strategies**: This worksheet determines profits at expiration and for an evaluation period prior to expiration. In calculating profits prior to expiration, the program uses the Merton B–S OPM to calculate call and put prices for each inputted stock price.
3. **Calendar Option Strategies**: This worksheet determines profits for two selected evaluation periods. The program uses the Merton B–S OPM to calculate call and put prices for each inputted stock price. The program can be used to evaluate calendar spreads.

- The "Basic Option Strategies" program can be used to work problems and Web exercises in Chapter 3 (Problems 1, 2, and 3; Web Exercises 1, 2, and 3) and Chapter 12 (Problem 1).

- "Timed Option Strategies" can be used to work problems in Chapter 9 (Problems 7, 8, and 9; Web Exercises 1 and 2).

D.1.2   Binomial Option Pricing Model

This program calculates European and American call and put prices for options on stocks, indexes, foreign currencies, and futures using the binomial option model. The program uses the recursive multiple-period model delineated in Chapters 5 through 7. The program also adjusts for dividends and foreign interest rates using the Merton Dividend-Adjustment Model.

In using the program, users are given an input box. In the box, the user first selects the type option:

1. Call or Put
2. American or European
3. Spot or Futures

Given the option, the user then enters

1. Underlying security (or futures) price
2. Exercise price
3. Number of periods to expiration (up to 200)
4. Annual risk-free rate and annual asset yield (annual dividend yield or foreign risk-free rate)

The user is then given choices:

1. Inputting the time to expiration as a proportion of a year or days to expiration, with the program calculating the time to expiration based on a 365-day year.
2. Inputting u and d parameters or inputting the annualized mean and annualized variance and then having the program calculate u and d.
3. Inputting the period risk-free rate or entering the annual riskless rate and having the program calculate the periodic rate.
4. Inputting continuous or discrete compounding. In calculating the periodic interest rate given an annual rate (R), the continuous compounding period rate is $R^P = e^{R(t/n)} - 1$ and the discrete compounding period rate is $R^P = (1 + R)^{(t/n)} - 1$).

The output of the program consists of a matrix of the option prices, starting at expirations and going to the current period. Once the calculation on a given option is made (e.g., American call), the user can then go back to the input box and select a different option on the underlying asset (e.g., American put). The user can also change the number of periods (given u and d are calculated from an inputted mean and variance). The program thus allows the user to quickly evaluate the option prices on an underlying security for a different number of subperiods and for four options: American call and put options and European call and put options.

Notes:

1. To apply the Merton Dividend-Adjustment Model, the annual dividend yield or foreign risk-free rate is inputted, the annual risk-free rate should be inputted instead of the periodic rate, and continuous compounding is selected instead of discrete.

2. To generate a matrix of stock prices, select call and American, and leave the exercise price box blank (hit delete for that box).

3. Options on futures contracts are limited to financial futures.

The binomial option pricing program can be used by students to do a number of the problems in the text:

1. Chapter 5: Problems 5, 10, 11, 12, 13

2. Chapter 6: Problems 3 and 5

3. Chapter 7: Problem 4

4. Chapter 8: Problems 9 and 10

5. Chapter 12: Problems 9, 12, and 16

The program also can be used to check their answers to many of the problems dealing with the binomial model.

D.1.3 Known Dividend-Payment Binomial Model

This program calculates European and American call and put prices for options on stocks using the known dividend-payment binomial model described in Chapter 6. The program uses the recursive multiple-period model. The user inputs the number of days for each ex-dividend date during the life of the option along with the stock's expected dividend per share. As described in Chapter 6, the program determines the value of an option as follows:

1. Calculates the current present value of all dividends to be paid during the life of the option: PV(D).

2. Subtracts the present value of all dividends from the current price of the stock to obtain a dividend-adjusted stock price: $S_0^D = S_0 - PV(D)$.

3. Applies the up and down parameters to the dividend-adjusted stock price, S_0^D, to generate a binomial tree of stock prices.

4. After generating the tree, adds to the stock prices at each node the present value of all future dividends to generate a dividend-adjusted binomial stock tree.

5. Given the dividend-adjusted binomial tree of stock prices, computes the option value by starting at expirations and applying the normal recursive method.

6. If the option is American, the program starts one period before expiration and places a constraint that the American option price has to be the maximum of the binomial value or the exercise value; it then rolls the tree forward applying the same constraint.

In using the program, users are given an input box and a dividend box. In the input box, the user selects

1. Call or Put

2. American or European

3. Underlying stock price

4. Exercise price

5. Number of periods to expiration (up to 200)

6. Annual risk-free rate

In the Dividend Box, the user inputs the number of days to each ex-dividend date and the estimated dividend.

The output of the program consists of a matrix of the option prices, starting at expirations and going to the current period. Once the calculation on a given option is made (e.g., American call), the user can then go back to the input box and select a different option on the underlying asset (e.g., American put). The user can also change the number of periods (given u and d are calculated from an inputted mean and variance). The program thus allows the user to quickly evaluate the option prices on an underlying security for a different number of subperiods and for four options: American call and put options and European call and put options.

The binomial option pricing program can be used by students to do Problems 2 and 4 and Web Exercise 1 in Chapter 6.

D.1.4   Black–Scholes Option Pricing Model

This program calculates call and put prices for options on stocks, indexes, foreign currency, and futures. The spreadsheet includes eight worksheets:

1. **B–S OPM**: This worksheet calculates the B–S and Merton OPM prices and the intrinsic values for call and put options. The program requires the user to input the asset price, exercise price, annualized variance, time to expiration, annualized risk-free rate, and security yield (annual dividend yield for options on stock and stock indexes and the foreign interest for a foreign currency option). When the security yield is inputted, the program calculates the option price based on the Merton model. A number of asset prices can be inputted, allowing the user to examine the option price and underlying security price relation.

2. **Black's Pseudo-American Model**: This worksheet calculates call and put prices using Black's Pseudo-American Model described in Chapter 8. The program requires the user to input the stock price, exercise price, annualized variance, time to expiration, annualized risk-free rate, time to the ex-dividend date, and dollar dividend value at the ex-dividend date. A number of asset prices can be inputted, allowing the user to examine the option price and underlying security price relation.

3. **B–S Greeks**: This worksheet calculates the delta, gamma, and theta values along with B–S and Merton OPM prices and the intrinsic values for call and put options. The program requires the user to input the asset price, exercise price, annualized variance, time to expiration, annualized risk-free rate, and security yield (annual dividend yield for options on stock and stock indexes and foreign interest for foreign currency option). When the security yield is inputted, the program calculates the option price and Greek values based on the Merton model. A number of asset prices can be inputted, allowing the user to examine the option price and Greek values for different underlying security prices.

4. **Black Futures Call**: This worksheet calculates the prices for futures call options using Black's futures options model. The program requires the user to input the current futures price, exercise price, annualized variance, time to the option's expiration, and annualized risk-free rate. A number of futures prices can be inputted, allowing the user to examine the call price and underlying futures price relation.

5. **Black Futures Put**: This worksheet calculates the prices for futures put options using Black's futures option pricing model. The program requires the user to input the current

futures price, exercise price, annualized variance, time to the option's expiration, and annualized risk-free rate. A number of futures prices can be inputted, allowing the user to examine the put price and underlying futures price relation.

6. **Black Caplet Model**: This worksheet calculates the prices and intrinsic values for interest rate call option (caplet) using Black's caplet model described in Chapter 16. The program requires the user to input the current reference rate (e.g., LIBOR), exercise rate, annualized variance, time on the loan, and notional principal. A number of reference rates can be inputted, allowing the user to examine the caplet price and underlying rate relation.

7. **Black Floorlet Model**: This worksheet calculates the prices and intrinsic values for interest rate put option (floorlet) using Black's floorlet model described in Chapter 16. The program requires the user to input the current reference rate (e.g., LIBOR), exercise rate, annualized variance, time on the loan, and notional principal. A number of reference rates can be inputted, allowing the user to examine the floorlet price and underlying rate relation.

8. **Black Swaption Program**: This program can be used to help calculate the values of receiver and payer swaptions using the Black Swaption program described in Chapter 19. The program calculates $[C_f N(d1) - C^X N(d2)]$ for payer swaptions and $[-C_f(1 - N(d1)) + C^X(1 - N(d2))]$ for receiver swaptions. To obtain the swaption values, these values need to be multiplied by

$$\sum_{i=1}^{mn} \frac{NP}{m} e^{-R_{fi} t_i}$$

Doing this yields the Black Swaption values. The Black–Scholes Option Pricing Excel programs can be used by students to do a number of the problems in the text:

Chapter	Problems	Program
8	1, 5, 6, 8, 9, 10,15, 16, 17, 18, 20, and 21	B–S OPM
8	4	Pseudo-American Option
9	6	B–S Greeks
9	3, 5, 6, 10, 11, 12, 13, and 14	B–S OPM
12	11, 14, 16,17, 18, and 23	Black Futures Call and Put
19	12, 13, 14, 15, and 16	Black Swaption
21	1, 10, and 11	B–S OPM

D.1.5 Implied Volatility

This program calculates an implied volatility using the Newton–Raphson search procedure. The technique was first suggested by Manaster and Koehler.

D.1.5.1 Algorthim

Inputs: Security price (S), annual security yield, exercise price (X), annual continuously compounded risk-free rate (R), time to expiration (T), and market price of the call (C^m).

Given the inputs, the program's first standard deviation estimate is

$$\sigma_1 = \sqrt{\left| \ln\left(\frac{S}{X}\right) + RT \right| \left(\frac{2}{T}\right)}$$

Given σ_1, the program then calculates the Black–Scholes–Merton call value, $C(\sigma_1)$. If this call price is not close to the market call price, C^m, then the next standard deviation estimate is

$$\sigma_2 = \sigma_1 - \frac{[C(\sigma_1) - C^m]e^{d_1^2/2}\sqrt{2\pi}}{S\sqrt{T}}$$

where d_1 is computed based on σ_1. Given σ_2, the program then calculates the Black–Scholes–Merton call value, $C(\sigma_2)$. If this call price is not close to the market call price, C^m, then the procedure is repeated with the next estimate:

$$\sigma_3 = \sigma_2 - \frac{[C(\sigma_2) - C^m]e^{d_1^2/2}\sqrt{2\pi}}{S\sqrt{T}}$$

The process is repeated until the model price is sufficiently close to the market price. In this Excel program, the process is repeated 10 times. The implied standard deviation is the one with the smallest absolute difference between $C(\sigma_1)$ and C^m.

D.1.6   Binomial Interest Rate Folder

The binomial interest rate folder includes three files that generate binomial interest rate trees and a binomial tree of option-free, callable and putable bond values:

1. **Binomial Rates**: This program calculates a binomial tree of spot rates. The user inputs current spot rate, length of the period, number of periods (up to 180), and either u and d parameters or the annualized mean and variance.

2. **Binbondcall**: This program calculates a binomial tree of option-free bond prices and callable bond prices. The user inputs current spot rate; length of the period; number of periods (up to 180); either u and d parameters or the annualized mean and variance; and the bond's coupon, face value, and call price.

3. **Binbondput**: This program calculates a binomial tree of option-free bond prices and putable bond prices. The user inputs current spot rate; length of the period; number of periods (up to 180); either u and d parameters or the annualized mean and variance; and the bond's coupon, face value, and put price.

The binomial option pricing program can be used by students to do problems 8 and 9 in Chapter 21.

D.1.7   Mortgage-Backed Securities Folder

The Mortgage-Backed Securities folder includes three files for determining the cash flows on mortgages, mortgage-backed securities, and mortgage-backed derivatives (sequential-pay and PAC tranches). For all three programs, the user inputs

1. The mortgage balance (e.g., $100M)
2. Maturity (e.g., 360 for a 30-year mortgage with monthly payments)
3. Payments per year (12 for standard mortgage)
4. Weighted average coupon on the mortgages (WAC)
5. Pass-through rate (PT rate) on the MBS
6. Discount rate for valuing the mortgages and mortgage derivatives

The programs can calculate prepaid principal based on the PSA model described in Chapter 22. That model assumes prepayment that starts at .2% for the 1st month and then increases at a constant rate of .2% to equal 6% at the 30th month and then stay at 6% thereafter. The model can be multiplied by a PSA speed to change the prepayment rate (e.g., PSA 150 or PSA = 50). In this model, the user needs to set "number of periods" at 30 and the "fixed CPR" at .06. The user can then adjust the PSA speed for the standard model by setting PSA (e.g., 100 for standard or 150). The user can adjust the prepayment profile by changing number of periods and fixed CPR.

Given the inputs, the mortgage Excel programs calculate cash flows for mortgages and mortgage derivatives:

1. **MBSCollateral:** This program calculates a number of cash flow items for mortgage collateral, mortgage-backed securities (MBS), and interest-only and principal-only mortgages derivatives. Cash flow items include periodic balance, interest, scheduled principal, prepaid principal, CPR, SMM, and total cash flow. The program also calculates the average life and value.

2. **MBSSeqNIO:** This program calculates cash flows on a sequential-pay collateralized mortgage obligation. The program is limited to just three sequential-pay tranches. The user can input different PT rates. When this is done, the program calculates the cash flow for a notional interest-only tranche. The output of the program consists of periodic interest, scheduled principal, prepaid principal, and total cash flow for each sequential-pay tranche, notional interest-only tranche, and collateral. The program also calculates the average life for the collateral and tranches.

3. **MBSPac**: This program calculates cash flows on an MBS PAC bond, support bond, and underlying mortgage collateral. To calculate the PAC cash flows, the user inputs the PSA speeds for the lower and upper collars. The output of the program consists of periodic interest, total principal (scheduled and prepaid), and total cash flow for the PAC, collateral, and support bond. The program also calculates the average life for each.

The mortgage-backed security programs can be used by students to do Problems 16, 17, and 18, in Chapter 22 and to check their answers to Problems 1, 2, 11, and 12 in that chapter.

D.1.8   Bond Programs

This Excel file includes five worksheets that can be used to evaluate bond and debt positions:

1. Bond valuation
2. Price yield
3. YTM
4. Annual realized return (total return)
5. Duration and convexity

GLOSSARY

Accreting swap   Swap in which the notional principal increases over time based on a set schedule.

Accrual bond class   A sequential-pay tranche whose interest is not paid but accrues until its principal payments are made.

Accrued interest   The interest on a bond or fixed income security that has accumulated since the last coupon date.

Agency pass-throughs   Mortgage-backed securities created by agencies: Federal National Mortgage Association, Government National Mortgage Association, and Federal Home Loan Mortgage Corporation.

American option   An option that can be exercised at any time on or before the exercise date.

Amortizing swap   Swap in which the notional principal is reduced over time based on a schedule.

Annualized mean   The mean obtained by multiplying a mean defined for a certain length of period (e.g., one week) by the number of periods of that length in a year (e.g., 52).

Annualized variance   The variance obtained by multiplying a variance defined for certain length of period (e.g., one week) by the number of periods of that length in a year (e.g., 52).

Anticipatory hedge   A hedging strategy of going long in a futures contract in order to lock in the future cost of a spot transaction.

Arbitrage   Transaction that provides a positive cash flow with no liabilities–a free lunch. An arbitrage opportunity exists when positions generating identical cash flows are not equally priced. In such cases, the arbitrage is formed by buying the lower-priced position and selling the higher-priced one.

Arbitrageur   An individual who engages in arbitrage.

Assignment   Procedure in which a brokerage firm or clearing firm selects one of its customers who is short in an option to fulfill the terms of the option after a holder has exercised.

Ask price   The price at which a dealer offers to sell a security.

Asset-based interest rate swap A swap used with an asset. In terms of synthetic positions, asset-based swaps can be used to create either fixed-rate or floating-rate investment positions.

Asset-or-nothing option An option that pays the value of the asset if the price of the underlying asset at expiration exceeds (call) or is less than (put) a specified exercise price; otherwise, it pays nothing.

Asian option Path-dependent option whose payoffs are determined by the average price of the underlying asset during all or part of the option's life.

Average cap Cap in which the payoff depends on the average reference rate for each caplet. For example, if the average is above the exercise rate, then all the caplets will provide a payoff; if the average is equal or below, the whole cap expires out of the money.

Average life The average amount of time the debt will be outstanding. It is equal to the weighted average of the time periods, with the weights being relative principal payments.

Backwardation A term used to describe a market in which the futures price is less than the spot price.

Barrier options Options in which the payoff depends on whether an underlying security price or reference rate reaches a certain level.

Basis The difference between futures and spot prices.

Basis points (BP) 1/100 of a percentage point. Fractions on bond yields are often quoted in terms of basis points.

Basis Risk *See* Timing risk.

Basket credit default swap A credit default swap based on a group of reference entities or credits instead of one. There is usually a specified payoff whenever one of the reference entities defaults.

Basket options An option whose payoff depends on the value of a portfolio.

Bear call money spread A vertical spread formed by purchasing a call at a certain exercise price and selling another call on the same security at a lower exercise price.

Bear put money spread A vertical spread formed by purchasing a put at a certain exercise price and selling another put on the same security at a lower exercise price.

Beta A measure of the responsiveness of a change in a security's rate of return to a change in the rate of return of the market.

Binary credit default spread A credit default swap in which the payoff in the case of a default is a specified dollar amount.

Binary option An option whose payoffs are discontinuous, paying a certain amount or nothing if a certain condition is satisfied.

Binomial option pricing model (BOPM) A model for determining the equilibrium value of an option by finding the option price that equals the value of a replicating portfolio. The model assumes a binomial world in which the option's underlying security price can either increase or decrease in a given period.

Binomial interest rate tree model Model that assumes that a spot rate follow a binomial process.

Black model   A model for pricing a futures option contract.

Black–Scholes model   A model for valuing European options.

Box spread   A combination of a call money spread and a put money spread. A long box spread consists of a call bull money spread and a put bear money spread; it yields a certain return at expiration equal to the difference in the exercise prices. A short box spread or reverse box spread is a combination of a call bear money spread and a put bull money spread; it generates a credit for the investor at the initiation of the strategy and requires a fixed payment at expiration equal to the difference in the exercise prices.

Bootstrapping   A sequential process used to estimate spot rates.

Break-even price   The price of the underlying security at the exercise date in which the profit from the option position is zero.

Break-even swap rate (also call the market rate)   The swap rate that equates the present value of the swap's fixed-rate payments to the present value of the swap's floating payments estimated using implied forward swap rates.

Bucket trading   A price-manipulation scheme in which a commission broker with an order to execute tips off another broker (referred to as the 'bagman') who proceeds to take a position in the security. When conditions are favorable, the commission broker executes the order with the bagman.

Bull call money spread   A vertical spread formed by purchasing a call at a certain exercise price and selling another call on the same security at a higher exercise price.

Bull put money spread   A vertical spread formed by purchasing a put at a certain exercise price and selling another put on the same security at a higher exercise price.

Burmuden option   An option that allows for early exercise only during part of the option's life.

Burnout factor   Term used to refer to the tendency for mortgages to hit some maximum prepayment rate and then level off.

Butterfly money call spread   A spread formed with three call options, each with different exercise prices. A long butterfly money spread is formed by buying one call at a low cxercise price, selling 2 calls at a middle exercise price, and buying one call at a high exercise price. A short butterfly spread is formed by selling one call at a low exercise price, buying 2 calls at a middle exercise price, and selling one call at a high exercise price.

Butterfly money put spread   A spread formed with three put options, each with different exercise prices. A long butterfly money spread is formed by buying one put at a low exercise price, selling 2 puts at a middle exercise price, and buying one put at a high exercise price. A short butterfly spread is formed by selling one put at a low exercise price, buying 2 puts at a middle exercise price, and selling one put at a high exercise price.

Calendar spread   *See* Horizontal spread.

Calibration model   Binomial model that generates a binomial interest rate tree by solving for the spot rates that satisfies a variability condition and a price condition that ensures that the binomial tree is consistent with the term structure of current spot rates.

Call An option that gives the holder the right to buy an asset or security at a specified price on or possibly before a specific date.

Call provision Provision in an indenture that gives the issuer the right to redeem some or all of the issue for a specific amount before maturity.

Call risk The risk that the issuer/borrower will buy back a bond, forcing the investor to reinvest in a market with lower interest rates.

Call spread A strategy in which one simultaneously buys a call and sells another call on the same stock but with different terms.

Callable bond A bond that gives the issuer the right to buy back the bond from the bondholders at a specified price before maturity.

Callable swap Swap in which the fixed payer has the right to early termination.

Cancelable swap Swap in which one of the counterparties has the option to terminate one or more payments. Cancelable swaps can be callable or putable: A callable cancelable swap is one in which the fixed payer has the right to early termination; a putable swap is one in which the floating payer has the right to early cancelation.

Cap A series of European interest rate calls that expire at or near the interest payment dates on a loan.

Caplet or Interest rate call See interest rate option.

Carrying-cost model (or cost-of-carry model) A model for determining the equilibrium price on a futures contract. In this model, the forward price equals the net costs of carrying the underlying asset to expiration.

CARDS (certificates for amortizing revolving debts) Term used to refer to credit-card receivable-backed securities.

CARS (certificates for automobile receivables) Term used to refer to automobile loan-backed securities.

Cash-and-carry arbitrage A riskless strategy formed by taking opposite positions in spot and forward contracts on a security. The strategy underlies the carrying-cost model.

Cash market See Spot market.

Cash-or-nothing option An option that pays a fixed amount of cash if the price of an underlying asset at expiration exceeds (call) or is less than (put) a specified exercise price; otherwise, it pays nothing.

Cash-settlement A feature on some futures and option contracts in which the contract is settled in cash at delivery instead of an exchange of cash for the underlying asset.

CAT bond A bond that pays the buyer a higher-than-normal interest rate. In return for the additional interest, the CAT bondholder agrees to provide protection for losses from a specified event up to a specified amount or when the losses exceed a specified amount.

Cheapest-to-deliver bond The least expensive bond (or note) among the Chicago Board of Trade's eligible bonds (or notes) a short holder of a Treasury bond (or note) futures contact can deliver.

Chooser option An option that gives the holder the right to select either a call or a put option on an underlying asset at a specified expiration date.

Clearinghouse   A corporation associated with a futures or options exchange that guarantees the performance of each contract and acts as intermediary by breaking up each contract after the trade has taken place.

Closing transactions   Term used to describe closing an option or futures position. It requires taking an opposite position: selling an option or futures contract to close an initial long position; buying an option or futures contract to close an initial short position.

Collar   Combination of a long position in a cap and a short position in a floor with different exercise rates. The sale of the floor is used to defray the cost of the cap.

Collateralized mortgage obligations (CMOs)   Derivative securities formed by dividing the cash flow of an underlying pool of mortgages or a mortgage-backed security issue into several classes, with each class having a different claim on the mortgage collateral and with each sold separately to different types of investors.

Combination purchase   A strategy formed by purchasing a call and a put on the same underlying security but with different terms: different exercise prices (money or vertical combination), dates (time, calendar, or horizontal combination), or both (diagonal combination).

Combination write   A strategy formed by selling a call and a put on the same underlying security but with different terms: different exercise prices (money or vertical combination), exercise dates (time, calendar, or horizontal combination), or both (diagonal combination).

Commodity Futures Trading Commission (CFTC)   The federal agency that oversees and regulates futures trading.

Compound option   An option on another option.

Conditional prepayment rate   Term used to define the annualized prepayment speed on a mortgage portfolio or mortgage-backed security.

Condor   A strategy consisting of four call and/or put options on the same security but with different terms.

Confirmation   The legal agreement governing a swap.

Contango   A term used to describe a market in which the futures price exceeds the spot price.

Contingent claims analysis   The analysis of the option characteristics embedded in corporate securities.

Continuous dividend adjustment model   The Black–Scholes OPM used when the underlying stock pays a dividend. The model uses a continuous dividend-adjusted stock price instead of the current stock price.

Continuous-leakage option   An option on an asset which generate a continuous flow of benefits (e.g., interests or dividends).

Contingent credit default swap   A credit default swap that provides a payout that is contingent on two or more events occurring

Continuously compounded return   The rate of return in which the value of the asset grows continuously. The rate is equal to the natural logarithm of one plus the simple (noncompounded) rate.

Convenience yield   A term used to describe when the benefits from holding an asset exceed the costs of holding the asset.

Conventional pass-throughs   Mortgage-backed securities created by private entities.

Conversion   A risk-free portfolio formed by going long in an underlying security, short in a European call, and long in a European put. The portfolio yields a certain cash flow equal to the exercise price at expiration regardless of the price of the underlying security.

Conversion ratio   The number of shares of stock that can be acquired when a convertible bond is tendered for conversion.

Conversion price   A convertible bond's par value divided by its conversion ratio.

Conversion value   A convertible bond's value as a stock. It is equal to the convertible bond's conversion ratio times the market price of the stock.

Convertible bond   A bond in which the holder can covert the bond to a specified number of shares of stock.

Cooling degree days (CDD)   A measure of the volume of energy needed for cooling during a day.

Cooperative linkage agreement   An agreement between exchanges in which a futures trader is allowed to open a position in one market and close it in another.

Corridor   Long position in a cap and a short position in a similar cap with a higher exercise rate.

Corpus   Term used to describe a principal-only security.

Counterparties   The parties to a swap agreement.

Covered call write   A position in which the writer of a call owns the underlying security.

Covered interest arbitrage   An arbitrage strategy consisting of long and short positions in currency spot and futures contracts and positions in domestic and foreign risk-free securities. The strategy is used by arbitrageurs when the interest-rate-parity condition does not hold.

Covered put write   A position in which seller of a put is short in the underlying security.

Credit default swap forward contract   Forward contract to take a buyer's position or a seller's position on a particular CDS at a specified spread at some future date.

Credit default swap option contract   Option to buy or sell a particular CDS at specified swap rate at a specified future time.

Credit default swap   Swap in which one counterparty buys protection against default by a particular company from another counterparty. The company is known as the reference entity and a default by that company is known as a credit event. The buyer of the swap makes periodic payments to the seller until the end of the life of the swap or until the credit event occurs.

Credit default swap spread   Payment made on a credit default swap.

Credit-sensitive bond   Bond with coupons that are tied to the issuer's credit ratings.

Cross-currency swap   A combination of an interest rate and currency swap

Cross-exchange rate   The exchange rate between two currencies that is implied by the relationship between three exchange rates.

Cross hedge   A futures hedge in which the futures' underlying asset is not the same as the asset being hedged.

Cumulative cap (Q-cap)   A cap in which the seller pays the holder when the periodic interest on a accompanying floating-rate loan hits a certain level.

Currency swap   A contract in which one party agrees to exchange a liability denominated in one currency to another party who agrees to exchange a liability denominated in a different currency.

Day count convention   The time measurement used in valuing bonds; it defines the convention used to define the time to maturity (actual days or 30-day months) and days in the year (360 days or 365 days).

Day trader   A trader who holds a position for a day.

Dealer   A trader who provides a market for investors to buy and sell a security by taking a temporary positions in the security.

Deep in-the-money call   A call in which the price of the underlying security is substantially above the call's exercise price.

Deep in-the-money put   A put in which the price of the underlying security is substantially below the put's exercise price.

Deep out-of-the-money call   A call in which the price of the underlying security is substantially below the call's exercise price.

Deep out-of-the-money put   A put in which the price of the underlying security is substantially above the put's exercise price.

Default intensities   Term used to define conditional default probabilities.

Delta   The change in an option price for a small change in the price of the underlying security

Derivative security   A security whose value depends on another security or asset.

Diagonal spread   A spread formed with options that have both different exercise prices and expiration dates.

Discrete-leakage option   An option on an asset that generates a discrete flow of benefits (e.g., interests or dividends).

Direct hedge   A futures hedge in which the futures' underlying assets is the same as the asset being hedged.

Dual trading   A security trading practice in which an exchange member trades for both her client and herself.

Duration   The average date that cash is received on a bond. It can be measured by calculating the weighted average of the bond's time periods, with the weights being the present value of each year's cash flows expressed as a proportion of the bond's price. It is also a measure of a bond's price sensitivity to interest rate changes.

Dynamic hedge ratio   The ratio that determines the number of stock index futures contracts that will replicate a put-insured stock portfolio.

Dynamic portfolio insurance   A strategy in which a stock portfolio is combined with bonds or futures and adjusted over time such that its possible future values replicates the values of a put-insured portfolio.

Early exercise   The exercise of an American option before its expiration.

Economic surplus   The difference between the market value of the assets and the present value of the liabilities.

Effective date   The date when interest begins to accrue.

Efficient market   A market in which the actual price of a security is equal to its intrinsic (true economic) value.

Embedded option   An option characteristic that is part of the features of a debt security. Features include call and put features on debt securities, the call provisions in a sinking fund, and the conversion clauses on convertible bonds.

End-of-the-day exercise feature   Feature of index options in which the closing value of the spot index on the exercising day is used to determine the cash settlement when the index option is exercised.

Equilibrium price of a bond   Price obtained by discounting the bond's cash flows by their appropriate spot rates.

Equity swap   Swap in which one party agrees to pay the return on an equity index, such as the S&P 500, and the other party agrees to pay a floating rate or fixed rate.

Equivalent strategies   Strategies that have the same profit and security price relationships.

Eurodollar deposit   A deposit in dollars in a bank located or incorporated outside the United States.

Eurodollar futures contract   A futures contract on a Eurodollar deposit. The contract has a cash-settlement feature.

European option   An option that can be exercised only on the exercise date.

Ex-dividend date   The date in which the ownership of stock is declared for purposes of determining who is entitled to dividends. Stock owners who purchase shares before this date are entitled to the dividend; investors who purchase shares of the stock on or after that date are not entitled to receive the dividend.

Exchange option   Option to exchange one asset for another.

Exchange rate   The number of units of one currency that can be exchanged for one unit of another. It is the price of foreign currency.

Exercise limit   The maximum number of option contracts that can be exercised on a specified number of consecutive business days by any investor or investor group. An exercise limit is determined by the exchange for each stock and non-stock option.

Exercise price   The price specified in the option contract at which the underlying asset or security can be purchased (call) or sold (put).

Expiration cycle   The standard expiration dates on an exchange-traded option or futures that are set by the exchanges.

Expiring transactions   Term used to describe doing nothing when the expiration date arrives.

Extendable swap   Swap that has an option to lengthen the terms of the original swap.

Fiduciary call   An investment in a risk-free bond and call option that yields a position equivalent to a portfolio insurance position.

Financial engineering   A term used to describe strategies of buying and selling derivatives and their underlying securities to create portfolios with certain desired features.

Financial swap   An agreement between two parties to exchange the cash flows from each party's liabilities.

Fixed-rate payer   The party in a financial swap that agrees to pay fixed interest and receive variable interest.

Flex option   Options that allow the option trader to choose the expiration date, exercise price, and whether the option is American or European. Flex options are nonstandarized options that were introduced to compete with customized OTC options.

Floating-rate payer   The payer in a financial swap that agrees to pay variable interest in return for fixed interest.

Floating-rate tranches   A sequential-pay tranche that pays a floating-rate.

Floor   A series of interest rate puts that expire at or near the effective dates on a loan. They are often used as a hedging tool by financial institutions.

Floorlet or interest rate put   See interest rate option.

Follow-up strategy   A strategy used after setting up an initial option position. The strategy can be classified as either an aggressive follow-up one, used when the price of the underlying security moves to a profitable position, and a defensive follow-up strategy, employed when the security price moves to an actual or potentially unprofitable position.

Foreign currency futures   A futures contract on a foreign currency.

Foreign currency option   An option on a foreign currency.

Forward contract   An agreement between two parties to trade a specific asset or security at a future date with the terms and price agreed upon today.

Forward rate agreement   A contract that requires a cash payment or provides a cash receipt based on the difference between a realized spot rate such as the LIBOR and a pre-specified rate.

Forward-start option   An option that starts at a future date.

Forward swaps   An agreement to enter into a swap that starts at a future date at an interest rate agreed upon today.

Futures contract   A marketable forward contract.

Futures fund   A fund that pools investors' monies and uses them to set up futures positions.

Futures hedge ratio   The optimal number of futures contracts needed to hedge a position.

Futures options (or Options on futures or commodity options)   An option contract that gives the holder the right to take a position in a futures contract on or before a specific date. A call option on a futures contract gives the holder the right to take a long position in the underlying futures contract when she exercises, and requires the writer to take the short position in the futures if he is assigned. A put option on a futures option entitles the holder to take a short futures position and the assigned writer the long position.

Futures spread   Futures position formed by simultaneously taking long and short positions in different futures contracts.

Gamma   The change in an option's delta with respect to a small change in the stock price.

Garman and Kohlhagen model   A model for pricing foreign currency options.

Generic swap   An interest rate swap in which fixed interest payments are exchanged for floating interest payments.

Geometric mean   The yield to maturity expresses as the geometric average of the current spot rate and implied forward rates.

GLOBEX   A computer trading system in which bids and asks are entered into a computer that matches them.

Heating degree days (HDD)   Measure of the volume of energy needed for heating during a day.

Hedge   A strategy in which an investor protects the future value of a position by taking a position in a futures contract, option, or other security.

Hedged funds   Special types of investment funds often structured so that they are largely unregulated. Minimum investment in such funds ranges from $100,000 to $20M, with the average investment being $1M. Many of the funds invest or set up investment strategies reflecting pricing aberrations.

Hedgable rates   See implied forward rates.

HELS   Term used to refer to home-equity loan-backed securities.

Horizontal spread   A spread formed with options that have the same exercise prices but different expiration dates.

IMM index   The quoted index price for futures on Treasury bill contracts and Eurodollar contracts traded on the International Monetary Market. The index is equal to 100 minus the annual percentage discount yield.

Implied forward rate   The rate in the future that is implied by current rates. The implied forward rate can be attained by a locking-in strategy consisting of a position in a short-term bond and an opposite position in a long-term one.

Implied futures rate   The rate implied on an interest rate futures contract.

Implied repo rate   The rate where the arbitrage profit from implementing a cash and carry arbitrage strategy with futures contracts is zero. This rate is also the one earned from an investment in a synthetic Treasury bill.

Implied variance   Variance that equates the OPM's price to the market price. Conceptually, it can be thought of as the market's consensus of the stock's volatility.

Implied volatility   *See* Implied variance.

Index arbitrage   An arbitrage strategy formed by taking a position in a spot index portfolio (or proxy portfolio) and an opposite one in a stock index futures contract. The strategy is implemented when the market price on the futures contract does not equal its equilibrium price as determined by the carrying-cost model.

Index-amortizing swap   (also called index-principal swap) Swap in which the notional principal is dependent on interest rates.

Initial margin The amount of cash or cash equivalents that must be deposited by the investor on the day a futures or options position is established.

Interbank market A spot and forward currency exchange market consisting primarily of major banks who act as currency dealers.

Intercommodity spread A spread formed with futures contracts with the same expiration dates but on different underlying assets.

Interest-only security Zero-discount bond that pays a principal received from the coupon interest from another security.

Interest rate option An option that gives the holder the right to a payoff if a specific interest rate is greater (call) or less (put) than the option's exercise rate.

Interest Rate Parity (IRPT) The carrying cost model that governs the relationship between spot and forward exchange rates.

Interest rate swap An agreement between to exchange interest payments on loans.

In-the-money option A call (put) option in which the price of the underlying asset is above (below) the exercise price.

Intracommodity spread A spread formed with futures contracts on the same underlying asset but with different expiration dates.

Intrinsic value of a call The maximum of zero or the difference between the call's underlying security price and its exercise price.

Intrinsic value of a put The maximum of zero or the difference between a put's exercise price and its underlying security's price.

Inverted market Market where the futures price is less than the spot price.

Kappa *See* Vega.

Knock-in option Option that comes into existence when the reference rate or price hits the barrier level.

Knock-out option Option that ceases to exist once the specified barrier rate or price is reached.

Kolb–Chiang Price-Sensitivity Model A price sensitivity model for hedging interest rate positions. The model determines the number of futures contracts that will make the value of a portfolio consisting of fixed-income security and an interest rate futures contract invariant to small changes in interest rates.

Known dividend-payment approach Option pricing model that assumes that the stock price reflects a future dividend payment, which is known with certainty, and all other factors affecting the stock prices, which are uncertain.

Law of one price An economic principle that two assets with the same future payouts will be priced the same.

LEAPS An acronym for Long-Term Equity Anticipation Securities. LEAPS are stock options with long-term expirations.

Liquidity The cash-like property of a security.

Locals Members of an exchange who trade from their own accounts, acting as speculators or arbitrageurs.

Logarithmic return The continuously compounded return. It is equal to the natural logarithm of the security price relatives.

London interbank bid rate (LIBID) The rate paid on funds purchased by large London Eurobanks in the interbank market.

London interbank offer rate (LIBOR) The rate on funds offered for sale by London Eurobanks. The average LIBOR among London Eurobanks is a rate commonly used to set the rate on bank loans, deposits, and floating-rate notes and loans. There are also similar rates for other currencies (e.g., Sterling LIBOR) and areas (e.g., Paris interbank offer rate, PIBOR, or the Singapore interbank offer rate, SIBOR).

Long futures hedge A long position in a futures contract taken in order to protect against an increase in the price of the underlying asset or commodity.

Long futures position A position in which one agrees to buy the futures' underlying asset at a specified price, with the payment and delivery to occur on the expiration date.

Lookback option Options whose payoff or exercise price depends on the previous price of the option.

LYON Zero-coupon bond that has the features of being convertible into the issuer's stock, callable, with the call price increasing over time, and putable, with the put price increasing over time.

Macaulay's duration Duration as measured as the weighted average of the time periods.

Maintenance margin The value of the commodity equity account that must be maintained.

Mark (or marking) to market Process of adjusting the equity in a commodity or margin account to reflect the daily changes in the market value of the account.

Mark-to-market tax rule Tax requirement in which the profits on a futures position is taxed in the year the contract is established. The rule requires that at the end of the year, all futures contracts be marked to the market to determine any unrealized gain or loss for tax purposes.

Market risk The risk that interest rates will change, changing the price of the bond and the return earned from reinvesting coupons.

Market maker A dealer on an exchange who specialize in the trading of a specific security.

Market timing A term used to describe the changing of a stock portfolio's exposure to the market by changing its beta. This can be done by changing the allocations of the stocks in the portfolio or by taking positions in index futures or option contracts.

Marketability An asset characteristic that defines the ease or speed with which the asset can be traded.

Merton continuous dividend yield approach Option pricing model that assumes the stock pays a continuous dividend yield over the life of the option.

Modified duration Duration measured as the percentage change in a bond's price given a small change in yield.

Money spread *See* Vertical spread.

Mortgage-backed securities Asset-backed securities formed with mortgages.

Mortgage-Backed Security Dealers Association Association of mortgage-backed securities dealers who operate in the over-the-counter market. These dealers form the core of the secondary market for the trading of existing pass-throughs.

Mortgage pass-throughs   See mortgage-backed securities.

Multiple listings   The listing of a security on more than one exchange.

Municipal bond index futures contract   A futures contract on the municipal bond index; an index based on the average value of 40 municipal bonds.

Naive hedging ratio   A hedge ratio in which one unit of a futures position hedges one unit of a spot position. The ratio is found by dividing the value of the spot position to be hedged by the price of the futures contract.

Naked call write   An option position in which an option trader sells a call but does not own the underlying stock.

Naked position   A term used to describe a long or short speculative futures position.

Naked put write   An option position in which an option trader sells a put but does not cover the put obligation by selling the underlying stock short.

National Association of Security Dealers Automatic Quotation System, NASDAQ   An information system in which current bid-asked quotes of dealers are offered; the system also sends brokers' quotes to dealers, enabling them to close trades.

National Futures Association (NFA)   An organization of firms that oversees futures trading.

Net settlement basis   Feature of a swap in which the counterparty owing the greater amount pays the difference between what is owed and what is received.

Neutral ratio spread (or Neutral delta strategy)   A spread position constructed such that its value is invariant to price changes in the options' underlying security. It is a spread with a position delta of zero.

NOB spread   A futures spread formed with Treasury note and Treasury bond futures contracts.

Normal market   Market in which the futures price exceeds the spot price.

Notional interest-only class   A tranche that receives the excess rate from other tranches' principals, with the excess rate being equal to the difference in the collateral rate minus the tranches' coupon rates.

Notional principal   The principal used to determined the amount of interest paid on a swap agreement. This principal is not exchanged.

Off-balance sheet restructuring   A method of changing a balance sheet's return-risk exposure by using derivatives such that the original composition of assets and liabilities is not changed.

Off-market swap   Swap that has a value. Many existing swaps are off-market swaps.

Official statement   Document similar to the prospectus for a stock or corporate bond, which details the return, risk, and other characteristics of a municipal issue and provides information on the issuer

Offsetting order   *See* Closing order.

On-the-run issues   Recently issued Treasury securities trading on the secondary market.

Open interest   The number of option or futures contracts that are outstanding at a given point in time.

Open outcry   Term used to describe the process of shouting bids and offers in an exchange trading area.

Open repo   An overnight repo that is automatically rolled over into another overnight repo until one party closes.

Opening transaction   The transaction in which an investor initially buys or sells an option or futures contract.

Option   A security that gives the holder the right to buy (call) or sell (put) an asset at a specified price on or possibly before a specific date.

Option class   Term used to describe all options on a given stock or security that are of a particular type, either call or put.

Option clearing corporation (OCC)   A firm whose primary function is to facilitate the marketability of option contracts. It does this by intermediating each option transaction which takes place on the exchange and by guaranteeing that all option writers fulfill the terms of their option contracts.

Option holder   The buyer of an option. The holder buys the right to exercise or evoke the terms of the option claim. An option buyer is said to have a long position in the option.

Options on actuals   See Spot options.

Option premium   The price of the option (call premium and put premium).

Option series   Term used to describe all of the options of a given class with the same exercise price and expiration.

Option writer   The seller of an option. The writer is responsible for fulfilling the obligations of the option if the holder exercises. The option writer is said to have a short position in the option.

Order book official   An employee of an exchange who keeps the limit order book.

Out-of-the-money   A call (put) option in which the price of the underlying security is below (above) the exercise price.

Outright position   *See* Naked position.

Over-the-counter market   An informal exchange for the trading of stocks, corporate and municipal bonds, investment fund shares, mortgage-backed securities, shares in limited partnerships, and Treasury and federal agency securities. There are no membership or listing requirements for trading on the OTC; any security can be traded.

Over-the-counter options   Options provided by dealers in the over-the-counter market. The option contracts are negotiable, with buyers and sellers entering directly into an agreement.

Par value swap   Swap that has a value of zero. An economic value of zero requires that the swap's underlying bond positions trade at par. Many plain vanilla swaps are originally par value swaps.

Pass-through rate   Rate paid to mortgage-backed security holders.

Pass-through securities   Securities formed by pooling a group of mortgages and other financial assets and then selling a security representing interest in the pool and entitling the holder to the income generated from the pool of assets.

Payer swaption   Swap that gives the holder the right to pay a specific fixed rate and receive the floating rate; that is, the right to take a fixed payer's position.

Performance margin   *See* Initial margin.

Pin-stripe pork bellies   Term used to describe stock index futures contracts.

Plain vanilla swap   *See* Generic swap.

Planned amortization class, PAC   A tranche formed by generating two monthly principal payment schedules from the collateral; one schedule is based on assuming a relatively low PSA speed, while the other is obtained by assuming a relatively high PSA speed. The PAC bond is then set up so that it will receive a monthly principal payment schedule based on the minimum principal from the two principal payments. The PAC bond is designed to have no prepayment risk provided the actual prepayment falls within the minimum and maximum assumed PSA speeds.

Position limit   The maximum number of option or futures contacts an investor can buy and sell on one side of the market. A side of the market is either a bullish or bearish position.

Position trader   A futures dealer who holds a position for a period longer than a day.

Preemptive right   The right of the stockholders of a corporation to maintain their shares of ownership in the corporation when new stock is issued.

Prepayment risk   The risk that a loan will be paid off early and the lender or bond holder will have to invest or create new loans in a market with a lower rate.

Prepayment speed or speed   Term used to define the estimated prepayment rate on a portfolio of mortgages or a mortgage-backed security.

Price limits   The maximum and minimum prices that a futures contract can trade.

Price-sensitivity model   A model that determines the optimum number of stock index futures contracts needed to hedge a stock portfolio.

PRIME   A security that pays the holder the dividend from a stock and cash equal to the value of the stock up to a specified value.

Principal-only security   Zero-discount bond that pays a principal received from another security.

Principal pay-down window   Term used to describe the period between the beginning and ending principal payment.

Private labels   See Conventional pass-throughs.

Program trading   Term used to describe the use of computers in constructing and executing security portfolio positions. Program trading often involves using computer programs to monitor real time data of stocks, futures, and option prices, to identify any mispricing of values of a stock portfolio relative to the values of index futures or option positions, and to define and execute appropriate arbitrage strategies when portfolios, futures, and option positions are mispriced.

Protective put   The purchase of a put to obtain protection against possible decreases in the value of a long position in the put's underlying security

Proxy portfolio   A portfolio constructed such that there is a high correlation between its returns and the returns of another portfolio or index.

PSA models The prepayment models of the Public Securities Association. In the standard PSA model for 30-year mortgage, known as 100 PSA, the CPR starts at .2% for the first month and then increases at a constant rate of .2% per month to equal 6% at the 30th month; then after the 30th month the CPR stays at a constant 6%.

Pseudo-American option model Black–Scholes OPM used when the underlying stock pays a dividend. In the model, an option value computed with a dividend-adjusted stock price is compared to the estimated call value obtained by assuming the option is exercised just prior to the stock's ex-dividend date. The larger of the two values is used to price the option.

Pure Expectations Theory Term structure theory in which the term structure of interest rates is based on the impact of investors' and borrowers' expectations about future interest rates.

Pure discount bond A bond that pays no coupon interest. The bond sells at a price below its face value. It is also called a zero-coupon bond.

Put An option that gives the holder the right to sell an asset or security at a specified price on or possibly before a specific date.

Put and Call Brokers and Dealers Association An early association of investment firms who acted as brokers and dealers on option contracts. An investor who wanted to buy an option could do so through a member of the association who either would find a seller through other members or would sell (write) the option himself.

Put-call-futures parity The equilibrium relationship between the prices on put, call, and futures contracts on the same asset. If the equilibrium condition for put-call-futures parity does not hold, then an arbitrage opportunity will exist by taking a position in the put and futures contract and an opposite position in the call and a riskless bond with a face value equal to the difference in the exercise price and futures price.

Put-call parity The equilibrium relationship governing the prices on put and call contracts. If the equilibrium condition for put-call parity does not hold, then an arbitrage opportunity will exist by taking a position in the put and the underlying security and an opposite position in the call and a riskless bond with face value equal to the exercise price.

Put spread A strategy in which one simultaneously buys a put and sells another put on the same stock but with different terms.

Putable bond A bond that gives the bondholder the right to sell the bond back to the issuer at a specified price.

Quality risk A hedging risk that precludes one from obtaining zero risk because the commodity or asset being hedged is not identical to the one underlying the futures contract.

Quality swap A strategy of moving from one quality group to another in anticipation of a change in economic conditions.

Quantity risk A hedging risk that precludes one from obtaining zero risk because the size of the standard futures contract differs from the number of units of the underlying asset to be hedged.

Rainbow option An option that involves two or more assets. For example, a contract that allows one to choose between several assets.

Rate-anticipation strategies   Active strategies of selecting bonds or bond derivatives with specific durations based on interest rate expectations.

Range-forward contract   A combination of a long position in a currency put and a short position in a currency call. It is equivalent to a short position in a currency forward contract.

Ratio call write   An option strategy formed by selling calls against more shares of stock than one owns.

Ratio money spread   A vertical spread formed by taking long and short positions in options that have different exercise prices, with the option positions being combined in a ratio different than 1-to-1.

Ratio put write   A strategy formed by selling puts against shares of stock shorted at a ratio different than 1-to-1.

Real options   The applications of options methodology to capital budgeting and other corporate finance decisions.

Rebundling   Term used to refer to the buying of zero coupon bonds and stripped securities and then forming coupon bonds to sell. This process is also known as *reconstruction*.

Receiver swaption   Swaption that gives the holder the right to receive a specific fixed rate and pay the floating rate; that is, the right to take a floating payer's position.

Redundant security   A security whose possible cash flows can be replicated by another security or portfolio.

Registered option trader   A members of an exchange who can both buy and sell securities for herself and act as a broker.

Regression hedging model   A hedging model in which the estimated slope coefficient from a regression equation is used to determine the hedge ratio. The coefficient, in turn, is found by regressing the spot price on the security to be hedged against its futures price.

Replicating call portfolio   A portfolio consisting of the purchase of H units of a security and borrowing B dollars where the H and B are determined so that the cash flows of the portfolio are equal to the cash flows of a call on the underlying security.

Replicating put portfolio   A portfolio consisting of the shorting of H units of a security and investing I dollars in a risk free security where H and I are determined so that the cash flows of the portfolio are equal to the cash flows of a put on the underlying security.

Repo rate   The rate on a repurchase agreement.

Repurchase agreement, Repo   A transaction in which one party sells a security to another party with the obligation of repurchasing it at a later date. To the seller, the repurchase agreement represents a secured loan in which he receives funds from the sale of the security, with the responsibility of purchasing the security later at a higher price that reflects the shorter time remaining to maturity.

Reversal   An arbitrage portfolio formed by going short in an underlying security, long in a European call, and short in a European put. A reversal generates a credit for the investor at the initiation of the strategy and requires a fixed payment equal to the exercise price at expiration. A reversal is the negative of a conversion.

Reverse collar Combination of a long position in a floor and a short position in a cap with different exercise rates. The sale of the cap is used to defray the cost of the floor.

Reverse corridor Long position in a floor and a short position in a similar floor with a lower exercise rate.

Reverse hedge A strategy formed by purchasing puts and shares of stock in a ratio different than 1-to-1.

Rho The change in an option's price with respect to a small change in interest rates.

Right A security issued by a corporation to an existing shareholder giving him the right to buy new issues of stock at a specified price, known as the subscription price. Rights are issued as part of a new stock issue and are used to ensure that the preemptive rights of existing shareholder are maintained.

Risk-averse market Market in which investors require compensation in the form of a positive risk premium over a risk-free investment to pay them for the risk they are assuming.

Risk-loving market Market in which investors enjoy the excitement of the gamble and are willing to pay for it by accepting an expected return from a risky investment that is less than the risk-free rate. The market has a negative risk premium.

Risk-neutral market A market in which investors accept the same expected rate of return from a risky investment as a risk-free one.

Risk-neutral pricing An approach for pricing securities in which it is assumed that the value of a security is determined as though it and other securities are trading in a risk-neutral market. This approach can be used to price options and other derivative securities.

Risk premium The difference in the yield on a risky bond and the yield on less risky or risk-free bond. The risk premium indicates how much additional return investors must earn to induce them to buy the riskier bond

Roll-down strategy A follow-up strategy in which you move your position to a lower exercise price.

Roll-up strategy A follow-up strategy in which you move your option position to a higher exercise price.

Rolling-credit strategy A defensive follow-up strategy for a naked call (put) write position in which the naked writer sells calls (puts) with a higher (lower) exercise price if the price of the underlying security increases (decreases) and then uses the proceeds to close his initial short position by buying the calls (put) back.

Rolling the hedge forward A hedging strategy that involves taking a futures position, then at expiration closing the position and taking a new one.

Running a dynamic book Term used to describe how swap banks hedged their positions through a portfolio of alternative positions–opposite swap positions, spot positions in T-notes and FRNs, or futures positions.

Scalper A floor trader who buys and sells securities on her own account, holding them for a short period.

SCORE A security that pays the difference between a stock price and an exercise price if the stock price exceeds the exercise price. A score is sold in conjunction with a prime.

Securitization   Process in which the assets of a corporation or financial institution are pooled into a package of securities backed by the assets. The most common types of asset-backed securities are those secured by mortgages, automobile loans, credit card receivables, and home equity loans.

Securitized assets   Claim on cash flows from portfolio loans or assets.

Self-financing requirement   A requirement governing a multiple-period arbitrage strategy that prohibits any outside funds from being added to or removed from an arbitrage position when it is being readjusted.

Sequential-pay collateralized mortgage obligation   A collateralized mortgage obligation that is divided into classes with different priority claims on the collateral's principal. The tranche with the first priority claim has its principal paid entirely before the next priority class, which has its principal paid before the third class, and so on.

Short futures hedge   A short position in a futures contract that is taken to protect against a decrease in the price of the underlying asset.

Short futures position   A position in which an investor agrees to sell the underlying asset on a futures contract.

Short sale   The sale of a security now, then purchasing it later. To implement this strategy the investor must borrow the security, sell it in the market, then repay his debt obligation by later buying the security and returning it to the share lender.

Shout option   A European option giving the holder the right to "shout" or declare one time during the option's life a price that the underlying asset hits. At the option's expiration, the holder receives the maximum of the intrinsic value defined by the shout price or the intrinsic value based on the terminal asset price.

Side-by-side trading   Term used to describe the listing of both American and European options available on the same security.

Simulated long position   A strategy formed by buying a call and selling a put with the same terms.

Simulated put   A position formed by purchasing a call and selling the underlying security short on a 1-to-1 basis. This position yields a profit and security price relationship similar to a put purchase.

Simulated short position   A strategy formed by selling a call and buying a put with the same terms.

Simulated straddle   A position formed by purchasing two calls and shorting one unit of the underlying security (or a multiple of this). This position yields a strategy equivalent to a straddle.

Single monthly mortality rate   Term used to define the monthly prepayment rate.

Sinking fund   Provision in the indenture requiring that the issuer make scheduled payments into a fund. Many sinking fund agreements require an orderly retirement of the issue, commonly handled by the issuer being required to buy up a certain portion of bonds each year either at a stipulated call price or in the secondary market at its market price.

Specialist   A dealer on the exchange who specializes in the trading of a specific security and who is responsible for maintaining the order book.

Speculative-grade bonds   Bonds with relatively high chance of default; they have quality rating below Baa.

Splitting the strike A strategy formed by purchasing a call with a high exercise price and selling a put on the same security with a lower exercise price but with the same expiration date.

Spot market A market in which there is an immediate sale and delivery of the asset or commodity.

Spot option (also called options on actuals) Term used to refer to option contracts on stocks, debt securities, foreign currency, and indexes. The term is used to distinguish them from options on futures contracts.

Spot rates The rate on a zero-coupon bond.

Spot price The price an asset or commodity trades for in the spot market.

Spread An option or futures position consisting of a long position in one contract and a short position in a similar, but not identical, contract.

Stochastic error The estimating error that results from the exclusion of an important explanatory variable and/or an incorrect mathematical specification of the model being tested.

Stock Price Relative A ratio of the stock price in one period to its price in the preceding period.

Straddle purchase A strategy formed by buying a put and a call with the same underlying security, exercise price, and expiration date.

Straddle write A strategy formed by selling a put and a call with the same underlying security, exercise price, and expiration date.

Straight debt value A convertible bond's value as a nonconvertible bond. It is found by discounting the convertible bond's cash flows by the yield to maturity on an identical, but nonconvertible, bond.

Strangle A combination of a long put and long call with different exercise prices.

Strap purchase A strategy formed by purchasing more calls than puts, with the calls and puts having the same terms.

Strap write A strategy formed by selling more calls than puts, with the calls and puts having the same terms.

Strike price *See* Exercise price.

Strip A series of futures contracts with different maturities. Also, a term used to describe a combination of long or short call and put positions in which the number of puts exceeds the number of calls.

Stripped mortgage-backed securities Stripped mortgage-backed securities consisting of principal-only class and an interest-only class.

Strip Purchase A strategy formed by purchasing more puts than calls, with the calls and puts having the same terms.

Strip Write A strategy formed by selling more puts than calls, with the calls and puts having the same terms.

Student Loan Marketing Association (Sallie Mae) Association that provides funds and guarantees for lenders who provide college students loans through the Federal Guaranteed Student Loan Program and college loans to parents of undergraduates through the PLUS loan program (Parents Loans of Undergraduate Students program).

Subscription warrant   *See* Rights.

Surplus management   The management of the surplus value of assets over liabilities.

Supershare   A financial claim that provides the holder a proportion on an underlying portfolio if the value of the underlying portfolio is between a specified upper and lower portfolio values at some specified future date; if the portfolio value lies outside the bound, then the claim is worthless.

Swap   *See* Financial Swap.

Swap banks   Group of brokers and dealers who intermediate swap agreements between swap users. As brokers, swap banks try to match parties with opposite needs; as dealers, swap banks take positions as counterparties.

Swap rate   The average of the bid and ask rates offered by a swap bank on an interest rate swap.

Swaptions   Option on a swap. The purchaser of a swaption buys the right to start an interest rate swap with a specific fixed rate or exercise rate, and with a maturity at or during a specific times period in the future. If the holder exercises, she takes the swap position, with the swap seller obligated to take the opposite counterparty position.

Support class (also called the support bond or the companion bond)   Tranche formed with a PAC bond that receives principal equal to the collateral's principal minus the PAC's principal.

Synthetic call   Portfolio consisting of long positions in the put and the underlying security and a short position in the bond. The portfolio yields the same profit and security price relation as a comparable call.

Synthetic put   Portfolio consisting of long positions in the call and bond and a short position in the underlying security. The portfolio yields the same profit and security price relation as a comparable put.

Systematic risk   The risk of a security that is attributed to market factors (i.e., factors that affect all securities).

Targeted amortization class (TAC) bonds   A PAC-structured collateralized mortgage obligation with PACs with just one PSA rate.

TED spread   A spread formed with Treasury bill and Eurodollar contracts.

Term structure of interest rates   The relationship between the yields on financial assets and their maturities.

Theta   The change in an option's price with respect to a small change in the time to expiration.

Time spread   *See* Horizontal spread.

Time value decay   Term used to describe the decrease in an option's time value as the time to expiration decreases.

Time value premium (TVP)   The difference between the price of an option and its intrinsic value.

Timing risk   A hedging risk that precludes one from obtaining zero risk because the delivery date on the futures contract does not coincide with the date the hedged assets or liabilities need to be purchased or sold.

Total return swap   Swap in which the return from one asset or portfolio of assets is swapped for the return on another asset or portfolio.

Tracking errors The difference between the returns on the index and the index fund.

Trade date Day that counterparties agree to commit to the swap.

Tranches Term used to define the different classes making up a collateralized mortgage obligation. There are two general types of tranches–sequential-pay tranches and planned amortization class tranches.

Treasury bills Short-term Treasury instruments sold on a pure discount basis.

Treasury-bill futures A futures contract that calls for the delivery or purchase of a Treasury bill.

Treasury-bill option An option that gives the holder the right to buy (call) or sell (put) a Treasury bill.

Treasury bonds and notes The Treasury's coupon issues. Both are identical except for maturity: T-notes have original maturities up to 10 years (currently, original notes are offered with maturities of 2, 5, and 10 years), whereas T-bonds have maturities ranging between 10 and 30 years.

Treasury-bond futures contract A futures contract that calls for the delivery or purchase of a Treasury bond.

Treasury-bond option An option on a Treasury bond.

Treasury-note futures contract A futures contract that calls for the delivery or purchase of a Treasury note.

Treasury strips Zero-discount bond that pays a principal received from the interest or principal from a T-bond or T-note.

Triangular arbitrage Arbitrage strategy formed by taking positions in several currencies. It is used when the cross exchange rate relation does not hold.

Triple witching hour The last hour of trading on the day when index futures, stock index options, and options on stock index futures all expire. During this period an abnormally large volume of trading has often occurred on the exchanges as program traders, arbitrageurs, and hedgers close their futures and option positions and liquidate or purchase large blocks of stock.

TURTLE spread A spread formed with a combination of two positions on Treasury bond futures with different expirations and one position in a Treasury bill futures contract.

Uncovered call write *See* Naked call write.

Uncovered put write *See* Naked put write.

Unsystematic risk The risk of a security that is attributed to factors other than market factors.

Variation margin *See* Maintenance margin.

Vega The change in an option's price with respect to a small change in the underlying security's variability.

Vertical spread A spread formed with options that have the same expiration dates but different exercise prices.

Volatility skew Term used to define a negatively-sloped smile.

Volatility smile plot of implied volatilities given different exercise prices.

Volatility term structure   refers to the relation between an option's implied volatility and its time to expiration.

Warehousing   Practice of swap banks in which they enter a swap agreement without another counterparty. Swap banks often will hedge their swap positions with opposite positions in T-notes and FRNs or using Eurodollar futures contracts.

Warrant   A security or a provision in a security that gives the holder the right to buy a specified number of shares of stock or another designated security at a specified price.

Weiner stock process   A process in which the proportional change in stock prices grows along the path of its logarithmic return, known as a drift component, with the actual price being above or below the path at any time, with the extent of the deviation determined by the stock's variability.

Wild-card option   The right on a Chicago Board of Trade's Treasury bond futures contract to deliver the bond after the close of trading on the exchange.

YTM approach   The valuation of off-market swaps by discounting the net cash flows at the current YTM.

Yield curve   A graph showing the relationship between the yields to maturity on comparable bonds and their maturities.

Zero-coupon approach   The valuation of off-market swaps by discounting the net cash flows using spot rates.

Zero-coupon bond   See pure discount bond.

Zero-coupon swaps   Swap in which one or both parties do not exchange payments until the maturity on the swap.

GLOSSARY OF SYMBOLS

- A = Average High and Low Temperature
- B_0 = Dollars Borrowed to form Replicating Call Portfolio
- B_0 = Bond Price
- B^C = Callable Bond Value
- B^{CB} = Convertible Bond Value
- B^M = Market Price of a Bond
- B^{NC} = Noncallable Bond Value
- B^{NSF} = Value of Bond with no Sinking Fund
- B^{SF} = Value of Bond with Sinking Fund
- B_t = Basis at Time t
- BOPM = Binomial Option Pricing Model
- BP = Basis Points
- B-S OPM = Black-Scholes Option Pricing Model
- C = Call Price
- C = Coupon Paid on Bond
- $\{+C\}$ = Long Call Position
- $\{-C\}$ = Short Call Position
- C^a = American Call Price
- C^e = European Call Price
- C^{ex} = Early Exercise Call Price
- C^m = Market Call Price
- C^X = Call Price on Ex-Dividend Date
- C^X = Swaption's Exercise Rate
- C^* = Break-Even Swap Rate (Market Rate)
- C_f^* = Break-Even Forward Swap Rate
- CF_{ex} = Cash Flow on Ex-Dividend Date
- CARDS = Certificates for Amortizing Revolving Debt
- CARS = Certificates for Automobile Receivables
- CDD = Cooling Degree Days
- CDS = Credit Default Swap
- CF = Cash Flow
- CFA = Futures Contract's Conversion Factor on a T-Bond or T-Note
- CH = Clearinghouse
- CP = Call Price
- CMO = Collateralized Mortgage Obligation
- CP = Conversion Price

- CPR = Conditional Prepayment Rate
- CR = Conversion Ratio
- CV = Conversion Value
- D = Value of Dividend
- d = Downward Parameter
- d^f = Downward Parameter of a Futures Price
- D_T = Value of Dividends Expected to Accrue on Proxy Portfolio During the Period
- D_T = Value of Benefits at Time T
- Div = Dividend
- Dur_S = Duration of a Bond
- Dur_f = Duration of the Bond Underlying a Futures Contract
- Dur_{option} = Duration of the Bond Underlying an Option Contract
- E_0 = Exchange Rate = Dollar Price of Foreign Currency
- E^D = Foreign Interest Rate Adjusted Exchange Rate
- $E(E^c)$ = Expected Cutoff Exchange Rate
- $E(R)$ = Expected Rate of Return
- $E(R_C)$ = Expected Rate of Return of a Call
- $E(R_P)$ = Expected Rate of Return of a Put
- $E(R_S)$ = Expected Rate of Return of a Stock
- $E(k)$ = Expected Return from a Risky Investment
- $E(Z_C)$ = Expected Rate of Return on a Replicating Call Portfolio
- $E(Z_P)$ = Expected Rate of Return on a Replicating Put Portfolio
- f = Futures Price
- F = Principal Paid on a Bond
- F = Forward Price
- F^J = Face Value of Bond with Subordinate Claim on Assets
- f^M = Market Price of Futures Contract
- F^S = Face Value of Bond with Senior Claim on Assets
- FC = Foreign Currency
- FRA = Forward Rate Agreement
- FSC = Value of Forward Start Call
- FSP = Value of Forward Start Put
- h = Length of Period in a Binomial Process
- h = Length of Period in Years
- H_0 = Shares of Stock of Replicating Portfolio; Hedge Ratio
- HDD = Heating Degree Days
- HELS = Home Equity Loan-Backed Securities
- I = Quoted Index price of Futures Contract On T-Bill or Eurodollar Futures Contract
- I_0 = Dollars Invested to Form Replicating Put Portfolio
- IO = Interest-Only Security
- IV = Intrinsic Value
- IV_R = Intrinsic Value of a Right
- IV_W = Intrinsic Value of a Warrant
- K = Storage Cost
- K^P = Fixed Rate on Current Par Value Swap
- K^S = Fixed Rate on Existing Swap
- LIBOR = London Interbank Offer Rate
- M = Millions
- M = Market

- M = Number of Payments on a Swap in a Year
- M_0 = Initial Margin Requirement
- Max C = Maximum Call Price
- Min C = Minimum Call Price
- Min B^{CB} = Minimum Convertible Bond Value
- Max P = Maximum Put Price
- MBS = Mortgage-Backed Securities
- Min P = Minimum Put Price
- N = Number of Options or Futures Contracts
- n = Number of Periods to Expiration
- N_C = Number of Call Options
- n_f = Number of Periods to Expiration on a Futures Contract
- n_f = Number of Futures Contracts
- n_0 = Number of Shares
- N_n = Number of New Shares
- N_p = Number of Put Options
- N_R = Number of Rights Needed to Buy One New Share
- n_W = Number of Shares from Exercising a Warrant
- N(d) = Cumulative Normal Probability
- NP = Notional Principal
- NPV = Net Present Value
- P = Put Price
- p = Risk-Neutral Probability = $(r_f\text{-}d)/(u\text{-}d)$
- p = Monthly Mortgage Payment
- {+P} = Long Put Position
- {−P} = Short Put Position
- P^a = American Put Price
- P^e = European Put Price
- P^{ex} = Early Exercise Put Price
- p^f = Risk-Neutral Probability Defined in Terms of Up and Down Parameters for Futures Prices
- P^m = Market Put Price
- P^S = Stock Price
- P^X = Put Price on Ex-Dividend Date
- p_{nj} = Binomial Probability of Security Increasing j times in n periods
- p_t = Probability of Default in Period t; Default Intensity
- $\bar{p}$ = Average Conditional Default Probability
- PAC = Planned Amortization Class
- pf = Pool Factor
- PO = Principal-Only Security
- PP = Put Price on Putable Bond
- PSA = Public Securities Association
- PT = Pass-Through Rate on Mortgage-Backed Security
- PV = Present Value
- $PVIF_a$ = Present Value Interest Factor of an Annuity
- PV(X) = Present Value of Exercise Price
- q = Probability of Security Increasing in One Period
- R = Rate of Return
- R = Continuously Compounded Risk-Free Rate
- R^A = Annualized Risk-Free Rate
- R^{ref} = Refinancing Rate

- R^P = Periodic Rate
- R_D = Annual Discount Yield
- R_F = Risk-Free Rate Earned or Paid on Foreign Currency; Foreign Risk-Free Rate
- $r_F = 1 + R_F$
- R_f = Rate on Risk-Free Security
- R_f = Repo Rate
- $r_f = 1 + R_f$
- R_{fi} = Risk-Free Rate for Swap Period
- R_{Mt} = Implied Forward Rate on M-Year Bond, for t Years from the Present
- R_{US} = Risk-Free Rate Earned or Paid on U.S. Dollars; Domestic (US) Risk-Free Rate
- $r_{US} = 1 + R_{US}$
- R_X = Exercise Rate on Interest Rate Call or Put
- RP = Replicating Portfolio
- RP = Risk Premium
- RR = Recovery Rate
- S = Underlying Stock, Security, or Index Price
- S = Spot Price
- S = Spot Rate
- {+S} = Long Stock Position
- {−S} = Short Stock Position
- S^D = Dividend-Adjusted Stock Price
- SDV = Straight Debt Value
- SMM = Single Monthly Mortality Rate
- SV^{Fl} = Swap Value of Floating-Payer's Position
- SV^{Fix} = Swap Value of Fixed-Payer's Position
- T = Expiration
- t = Time
- t = Time to Expiration on derivative Contract
- T* = Time to Expiration on Interest Rate Option Plus Time Period Applied to Interest Rate Option Payoff Period
- t_i = Payment Dates in years on a Swap
- t* = Time to Ex-Dividend Date
- TRC = Transportation Cost
- TVP = Time Value Premium
- u = Upward Parameter
- u^f = Upward Parameter of a Futures Price
- V = Volatility
- V^A = Annualize Variance
- V^A = Value of the Assets of the Firm
- V^C = Value of Callable Bond's Call Option
- V^{BS} = Value of Bond with Senior Claim on Assets
- V^{BJ} = Value of Bond with Subordinate Claim on Assets
- V^E = Total Equity Value of the Firm
- V^F = Value of Forward Contract
- V^f = Value of Futures Contract
- $V^{Fut\ Ins}$ = Value of Futures-Insured Portfolio
- V^{Ins} = Value of Put-Insured Portfolio
- V^P = Value of Putable Bond's Put Option

- V^{SF} = Value of Sinking Fund Call Option
- V_e = Estimated Variance of the Security's Logarithmic Return
- V_H = Value of Holding a Callable or Putable Bond
- V_0 = Current Value of Replicating Portfolio
- V_0 = Current Portfolio Value
- WAC = Weighted Average Coupon Rate
- X = Exercise Price
- X_S = Subscription Stock Price on a Rights Offering
- YTM = Yield to Maturity
- YTM_f = Yield to Maturity Implied on Futures Contract
- Z = Credit Default Swap Spread
- $Z(t)$ = t-Year Zero Coupon Rate
- ß = Beta of an Investment or Security
- $ß_{TR}$ = Target Beta
- Γ = Change in Delta per Change in Security Price
- Γ_p = Position Gamma
- Δ = Change in Option Price per Change in Security Price
- Δ_p = Position Delta
- Δt = Length of the Binomial Period Expressed as a proportion of a Year
- θ = Change in Option Price per Change in Time
- θ_p = Position Theta
- μ_e = Estimated Mean of the Security's Logarithmic Return
- μ^A = Annualize Mean
- Λ = Change in Option Price per Change in Variability
- π = Profit
- σ = Annualized Standard Deviation of a Security's Logarithmic Return (Black-Scholes Formula)
- σ^A = Standard Deviation of a Futures' Logarithmic Return
- σ_f = Annualized Standard Deviation of a Security's Logarithmic Return
- Θ = Time Period Applied to Interest Rate Option Payoff Period
- ψ = Annual Dividend Yield
- 0 = Current Period
- * = Equilibrium

INDEX